The Bibliography of
Marketing Research
Methods

About MSI

Since its founding in 1961, the Marketing Science Institute (MSI) has brought together the interests of business and academia to identify and study issues of greatest importance to the marketing community. Supported by approximately 50 major corporations, the goal of the nonprofit Institute is to develop marketing knowledge, theory, tools, and insights for practitioners and scholars in the constantly changing marketing environment. Specific subject areas are designated research priorities and targeted for funding by MSI's Board of Trustees, representing member companies and the academic community.

MSI's members reflect the marketing activities and research interests of a wide variety of consumer and industrial product and service businesses. The Institute's academic relationships are also broadly based, involving researchers from approximately 100 universities.

MSI sponsors research and disseminates research findings to the business and academic communities through its conferences, workshops, and steering group meetings as well as through its publication series. The Institute also issues a newsletter that reports on research projects and developments of interest to the field.

The books published jointly by MSI and Lexington Books include:

The Bibliography of Marketing Research Methods, by John R. Dickinson

Effective Television Advertising: A Study of 1000 Commercials,
by David W. Stewart and David H. Furse

Knowledge Development in Marketing: The MSI Experience,
by Paul N. Bloom

Meta-Analysis in Marketing: Empirical Generalizations of Response Models,
by John U. Farley and Donald R. Lehmann

The Bibliography of Marketing Research Methods

Third Edition

John R. Dickinson
University of Windsor

Lexington Books
D.C. Heath and Company/Lexington, Massachusetts/Toronto

Library of Congress Cataloging-in-Publication Data

Dickinson, John R.
　The bibliography of marketing research methods / John R. Dickinson.—
　Third edition.
　p.　　cm.

Includes indexes.
　1.　Marketing research—Bibliography.　I.　Title.
Z7164.M18D52　　1990　　　　　016.6588'3—dc20
[HF5415.2]
ISBN 0-669-21697-6 (alk. paper)　　　　90-33680
　　　　　　　　　　　　　　　　　　　　CIP

Published simultaneously in Canada
Printed in the United States of America
Casebound International Standard Book Number: 0-669-21697-6
Library of Congress Catalog Card Number: 90-33680

The paper used in this publication meets the minimum requirements of
American National Standard for Information Sciences—Permanence of
Paper for Printed Materials, ANSI Z39.48-1984. ∞™

Year and number of this printing:

90　　91　　92　　93　　6　　5　　4　　3　　2　　1

*To my ultimate source,
Margaret Elizabeth Szucs*

Preface

The aim of the third edition of *The Bibliography of Marketing Research Methods* is the same as that of the original version of 1982—to provide a comprehensive directory to research on how to do research in marketing. The near doubling of entries in this edition over the first one reflects more a keeping up with than a catching up with published works addressing all aspects of the marketing-research process.

The Bibliography of Marketing Research Methods is just that—a bibliography of research on how to do research in marketing. It is a compilation of references of publications either appearing in or cited in popular marketing and marketing-research periodicals, handbooks, conference proceedings, and the like. The bulk of the references, therefore, are directly within a marketing context. Marketing researchers frequently make use of methods common to other social sciences, particularly psychology and sociology, and thus many references in *The Bibliography* have been drawn from a larger body of social-sciences literature as well as the literature of technical disciplines dealing with analytical methods. All references, however, have at some time appeared in or been cited in the marketing literature.

The Bibliography consists of a table of contents, the bibliography entries themselves, an author index, and a subject index. It contains over 14,000 entries classified under some 214 headings plus 1,114 subheadings. The data bank comprises 54,240 compressed lines and I hereby lay claim to being able to type "Research" faster than any other mortal.

Within each (sub)heading entries are listed alphabetically in reverse chronological order.

As reflected in its title, *The Bibliography* is of the research process exclusively. In many instances, however, "Applications" (sub)headings have been included for the purpose of illustrating where and how the research methods have been applied.

Organization

The Bibliography of Marketing Research Methods is organized into three broad categories: the marketing-research function, data-collection methods, and data-analysis techniques. The bibliography entries are classified under a great many headings and subheadings for the purpose of indicating quite specifically to the user the nature or content of the associated entries. The resulting table of contents, made up of the headings and subheadings, is therefore extensive.

Several devices, then, have been incorporated to direct the user to the topic of interest.

The schematic on the facing page provides an overview of the sequence of major topic areas. The table of contents comprises all of the headings and subheadings. These are numbered there and throughout *The Bibliography*. The current heading and its number are printed at the top of each even-numbered page.

Many headings and subheadings are followed by cross-references to other (sub)headings. And, of course, specific topics may be found in the subject index.

A Theory of Marketing Research

Amassing this bibliography has been an enriching, if tedious, experience. Though in the course of doing so I have not systematically documented phases or trends, it is clear that the discipline of marketing research is poised for a significant thrust toward formalization.

Marketing research is growing—in numbers, in intellect, and in sophistication. Marketers have adapted and themselves developed research methods at an impressive rate, especially considering the comparatively short period that marketing research has been an identifiable discipline. At the same time, very few specific aspects of the marketing-research process, philosophical or administrative, have been sufficiently tested and systematized as to be accepted as principles.

The formation of new company marketing-research departments is increasing at a geometric rate, and the activities and levels of professionalism of marketing and marketing-research associations have heightened. The supposed gap between theory and practice is continually being obviated. Marketing-research texts are in the maturity stage of their life cycle and a core of marketing-research fundamentals is evolving.

As this bibliography attests, literally thousands of studies of research processes and methods, within marketing and elsewhere, have been conducted. More, and more eclectic, marketing-related journals have been created, and more rigorous criteria for publication are being applied. State-of-the-art

The Bibliography of Marketing Research Methods

Marketing Research Function

(1–3)	The State of Marketing Research
(4)	Management of the Mktg Res Function
(5–8)	Marketing Research and Marketing Management, Marketing Information Systems
(9–10)	Marketing Research and Society, Ethical Issues
(11–14)	Bibliographies, Glossaries, Writing and Publication, Funding
(15)	Philosophy of Science
(17–29)	Topical Area Research Methods

Data Collection Methods

(32–33)	Survey Research, Polls
(34)	Questionnaire Design
(35–61)	Scaling
(62–65)	Multidimensional Scaling
(66–72)	Mail Surveys
(73)	Electronic Surveys
(74–86)	Interviewing, Qualitative and Interpretive Research
(87–89)	Telephone Surveys
(90)	Panels and Longitudinal Studies
(92–97)	Experimentation, Concept Testing, IDBs, Computer-Controlled Exp
(98–100)	Observation Methods, Response Latency, Physiological Measurement
(101–106)	Secondary Research, Data Bases, Content Analysis, Simulation
(107–115)	Sampling
(116–128)	Bias, Reliability, Validity

Data Analysis Techniques

(132–138)	Data Editing, Incomplete Data, Outliers, Graphing, Exploratory Analysis, Transformations
(139–143)	Hypothesis Testing
(146–147)	Nonparametric Statistics
(148–154)	Chi Square, Multinomial Analyses
(155–157)	Correspondence Analysis, Optimal Scaling
(159–170)	Regression Analysis
(171–174)	Logit, Probit, Tobit Analysis
(175–176)	Automatic Interaction Detection, Multiple Classification Analysis
(177–178)	Discriminant Analysis
(179–184)	Analysis of Variance, Covariance
(185–187)	Conjoint Analysis
(190)	Canonical Analysis
(191)	MANOVA
(192–195)	Cluster Analysis
(196–203)	Latent Structure, Factor Analysis
(204–208)	Causal Analysis, Path Analysis, Partial Least Squares
(210–213)	Computer Software
(214)	Meta-Analysis

review articles and meta-analyses summarizing our current knowledge of particular aspects of marketing research methods now appear regularly.

Perhaps these conditions signal the imminent formulation of a comprehensive theory of marketing research founded on a philosophy of the research process and integrating our knowledge of methodology. The potential benefits of such a comprehensive theory are great. For starters, such a theory would suggest a more-or-less universal conceptualization and operationalization of the marketing-research process. By synthesizing and attempting to integrate extant studies, this framework would, in effect, provide an organized statement of what we do and do not now know about the theory and practice of marketing research. It follows that the theory would serve to help standardize concepts, procedures, terms, and operational definitions.

Such a theoretical framework would focus future research, foster comparisons across studies, and aid validity assessment. Contradictory (or nonexistent) beliefs and empirical findings regarding properties of various research methods would become apparent. The presence of numerous exploratory studies might stimulate more conclusive research. Or, in a similar vein, replication of what are taken to be cornerstone studies might be encouraged.

We marketing researches have not been neglectful nor chauvinistic in developing and examining our philosopy and methodology. To this point, however, our scrutiny has not been well-coordinated. The basis for a theory of marketing research, possibly as referenced in this bibliography, exists. The discipline awaits.

Acknowledgments

The genesis of *The Bibliography* lies in an advanced seminar on marketing-research methods I developed several years ago at the encouragement of a respected and admired colleague, the late Bent Stidsen. Several other colleagues have graciously given of their time and knowledge in shaping *The Bibliography*.

Most recently, Gilbert A. Churchill, Jr. of the University of Wisconsin, Madison, provided thoughtful and constructive direction. He melds philosophy and application with a facility reflecting insight over invention. Richard P. Bagozzi of the University of Michigan, Ann Arbor, sustained a faith in providing a model on a plane above structural analysis.

Earlier on, Ralph L. Day (Indiana University, Bloomington), James W. Gentry (University of Nebraska, Lincoln), John O. Summers (Indiana University, Bloomington), and Roger M. Heeler (York University, Toronto) provided substantial definition. This one's for you, Ralph.

There is a certain irony in those whose knowledge is so highly prized giving of it so generously. That they do so partially explains the greater value

I place on their friendship. These gentlemen epitomize scholarship and both *The Bibliography* and I are the better for their influence.

The Bibliography is maintained on a computer-based system that I designed. The University of Windsor provided computer time and the Computer Centre staff willingly lent their expertise.

I am appreciative of the support given by Lexington Books and the Marketing Science Institute. And, of course, a debt of gratitude is owed the authors, named herein, who originated the works of which *The Bibliography* is comprised.

No bibliography is ever complete, especially one in as burgeoning a field as marketing research. Your suggestions for improvement are welcome. I hope you find *The Bibliography of Marketing Research Methods* to be a valuable resource.

John R. Dickinson

The Bibliography of
Marketing Research
Methods

```
*************************
*                       *
*   TABLE OF CONTENTS    *
*                       *
*************************
```

Heading or Subheading   Page

THE BIBLIOGRAPHY OF MARKETING RESEARCH METHODS

TABLE OF CONTENTS

THE BIBLIOGRAPHY OF MARKETING RESEARCH METHODS

TABLE OF CONTENTS

THE BIBLIOGRAPHY OF MARKETING RESEARCH METHODS

TABLE OF CONTENTS

THE BIBLIOGRAPHY OF MARKETING RESEARCH METHODS

TABLE OF CONTENTS

THE BIBLIOGRAPHY OF MARKETING RESEARCH METHODS

TABLE OF CONTENTS

THE BIBLIOGRAPHY OF MARKETING RESEARCH METHODS
TABLE OF CONTENTS

Heading or Subheading   Page

THE BIBLIOGRAPHY OF MARKETING RESEARCH METHODS

TABLE OF CONTENTS

THE BIBLIOGRAPHY OF MARKETING RESEARCH METHODS

TABLE OF CONTENTS

THE BIBLIOGRAPHY OF MARKETING RESEARCH METHODS

TABLE OF CONTENTS

THE BIBLIOGRAPHY OF MARKETING RESEARCH METHODS
TABLE OF CONTENTS

Heading or Subheading   Page

THE BIBLIOGRAPHY OF MARKETING RESEARCH METHODS

TABLE OF CONTENTS

THE BIBLIOGRAPHY OF MARKETING RESEARCH METHODS
TABLE OF CONTENTS

THE BIBLIOGRAPHY OF MARKETING RESEARCH METHODS
TABLE OF CONTENTS

THE BIBLIOGRAPHY OF MARKETING RESEARCH METHODS
TABLE OF CONTENTS

THE BIBLIOGRAPHY OF MARKETING RESEARCH METHODS

TABLE OF CONTENTS

THE BIBLIOGRAPHY OF MARKETING RESEARCH METHODS

TABLE OF CONTENTS

THE BIBLIOGRAPHY OF MARKETING RESEARCH METHODS

TABLE OF CONTENTS

THE BIBLIOGRAPHY OF MARKETING RESEARCH METHODS

TABLE OF CONTENTS

THE BIBLIOGRAPHY OF MARKETING RESEARCH METHODS

TABLE OF CONTENTS

THE BIBLIOGRAPHY OF MARKETING RESEARCH METHODS

TABLE OF CONTENTS

1 ------------------ THE STATE OF MARKETING RESEARCH ------------------
        See also (sub)heading(s) 2.

1.01 ---------- Books Re: The State of Marketing Research

Myers, John G., Massy, William F., and Greyser, Stephen A.
  Marketing Research and Knowledge Development
  (Englewood Cliffs, NJ: Prentice-Hall, Inc., 1980), 306 pp.

1.02 ---------- State of the Marketing Research Discipline

Achenbaum, Alvin A.
  "The Future Challenge to Market Research"
  Journal of Advertising Research, Vol. 27 (June/July 1987), pp. RC3-6.

Advertising Age
  "Researchers Tell Cures for Industry's Problems"
  (June 9, 1975), p. 4.

American Marketing Association Task Force
  "Developing, Disseminating, and Utilizing Marketing Knowledge"
  Journal of Marketing, Vol. 52 (October 1988), pp. 1-25.

Barnard, Philip
  "Research in the U.S.A."
  Journal of the Market Research Society, Vol. 26 (October 1984), pp.
  273-93.

Bogart, Leo (editor)
  Current Controversies in Marketing Research
  (Chicago: Markham Publishing Company, 1969), 164 pp.

Bogart, Leo
  "Inside Marketing Research"
  Public Opinion Quarterly, Vol. 2 (Winter 1963), pp. 562-77.

Churchill, Gilbert A., Jr.
  "Comments on the AMA Task Force Study"
  Journal of Marketing, Vol. 52 (October 1988), pp. 26-31.

Danbury, Thomas
  "An Original In-Depth Segmentation Study of the Market Research
  Industry"
  Journal of Advertising Research, Vol. 25 (August/September 1985), pp.
  52-5.

Day, George S.
  "The Threats to Marketing Research"
  Journal of Marketing Research, Vol. XII (November 1975), pp. 462-7.

Ehrenberg, A. S. C.
  "Where Were You in the Revolution?: Marketing Research in the Future"
  Admap, Vol. 3 (June 1967), pp. 247-50.

Ferber, Robert
  "Editorial: Looking Back to 1967"
  Journal of Marketing Research, Vol. IV (May 1967), pp. 210,1.

Foxall, Gordon R.
  "Academic Consumer Research: Problems and Potential"
  European Research, Vol. 8 (January 1980), pp. 20-3.

Garda, Robert A.
  "Comment by Robert A. Garda (on the AMA Task Force Study)"
  Journal of Marketing, Vol. 52 (October 1988), pp. 32-41.

Goldman, Arieh
  "Publishing Activity in Marketing as an Indicator of Its Structure
  and Disciplinary Boundaries"
  Journal of Marketing Research, Vol. XVI (November 1979), pp. 485-94.

Goldstein, Frederick A.
  "A Practical Guide to Gathering USA Marketing Information and the
  Current Status of Marketing Research in the US"
  Journal of the Market Research Society, Vol. 27 (October 1985), pp.
  243-59.

Haque, Paul
  "Market Research 1976-1986--Swings and Roundabouts"
  Industrial Marketing Digest, Vol. 11 (First Quarter 1986), pp. 85-91.

Haller, Terry
  Danger: Marketing Researcher at Work
  (Westport, CT: Quorum Books, 1983), 200 pp.

Halpern, Richard S.
  "Advice to Researchers: Strategic Planning for the Future"
  European Research, Vol. 12 (April 1984), pp. 60-7.

Hardin, David K.
  "Editorial: Marketing Research--Is It Used or Abused?"
  Journal of Marketing Research, Vol. VI (May 1969), p. 239.

Hinkle, Charles L. and Wolf, Jack S.
  "Academic Research and the Data Drought Dilemma"
  Journal of Marketing Research, Vol. III (May 1966), pp. 196-8.

Honomichl, Jack
  "US Research Industry Structure"
  Journal of the Market Research Society, Vol. 31 (October 1989), pp.
  438-46.

Horne, Annette, Morgan, Judith, and Page, Joanna
  "Where do We Go From Here"
  Journal of the Market Research Society, Vol. 16 (July 1974), pp.
  157-82.

Hunt, Shelby D.
  "Comment by Shelby D. Hunt (on AMA Task Force Study)"
  Journal of Marketing, Vol. 52 (October 1988), pp. 42-7.

Jeuck, John E.
  "Marketing Research: Milestone or Millstone?"
  Journal of Marketing, Vol. 17 (April 1953), pp. 381-7.

Kover, Arthur J.
  "Careers and Noncommunication--A Reply"
  Journal of Marketing Research, Vol. XIV (November 1977), p. 580.

Kover, Arthur J.
  "Careers and Noncommunication: The Case of Academic and Applied
  Marketing Research"
  Journal of Marketing Research, Vol. XIII (November 1976), pp. 339-44.

Lazer, W.
  "Marketing Research: Past Accomplishments and Potential Future
  Developments"
  Journal of the Market Research Society, Vol. 16 (July 1974), pp.
  183-202.

Leet, Don R. and Shaw, John A.
  "The Consequences of Public and Private Research and Development"
  Journal of the Academy of Marketing Science, Vol. 1 (Fall 1973), pp.
  138-47.

Lillis, Charles M.
  "Careers and Noncommunication: The Case of Academic and Applied
  Marketing Research--A Comment"
  Journal of Marketing Research, Vol. XIV (November 1977), p. 579.

Malhotra, Naresh K.
  "Some Observations on the State of the Art in Marketing Research"
  Journal of the Academy of Marketing Science, Vol. 16 (Spring 1988),
  pp. 4-24.

Marshak, Seymour
  "Marketing Researchers Face Extinction Without Action Against Threats
  From Inside and Outside the Industry"
  Marketing News (March 14, 1975), p. 4.

McDaniel, Stephen W., Verille, Perry, and Madden, Charles S.
  "The Threats to Marketing Research: An Empirical Reappraisal"
  Journal of Marketing Research, Vol. XXII (February 1985), pp. 74-80.

Methven, Sir John
  "The Use, Mis-Use and Non-Use of Market Research in Business and
  Industry"
  Journal of the Market Research Society, Vol. 20 (July 1978), pp.
  127-34.

Michiels, Baudoin
  "The Changing Needs of Users: A Source of New Perspectives for Our
  Profession"
  European Research, Vol. 7 (November 1979), pp. 240-5.

Morello, Gabriele
  "Marketing Research: Quo Vadis?"
  European Research, Vol. 4 (January 1976), pp. 3-9.

Nighswonger, Nancy J. and Martin, Claude R.
  "A Study of Marketing Research Commitment by Major Retailers"
  Working Paper No. 207
  Graduate School of Business Administration, University of Michigan
  (February 1980).

O'Connor, Thomas
  "Some Notes on the Existence of a Classic Body of Literature in
  Marketing"
  Proceedings, Southwestern Marketing Association (1982).

Schlossberg, Howard
  "Marketing Research is Merely Evolving, Not Dying"
  Marketing News, Vol. 24 (January 8, 1990), pp. 1-2;13.

Webster, Frederick E., Jr.
  "Comment by Frederick E. Webster, Jr. (on AMA Task Force Study)"
  Journal of Marketing, Vol. 52 (October 1988), pp. 48-51.

Weld, L. D. H.
  "The Progress of Commercial Research"
  Harvard Business Review, Vol. 1 (January 1923), p. 179.

1.03 ---------- Empirical Descriptions of the Mktg Res Discipline

Crisp, Richard D.
  Company Practices in Marketing Research
  Research Report No. 22
  (New York: American Management Association, 1958).

Danbury, Thomas
  "An Original In-Depth Segmentation Study of the Market Research
  Industry"
  Journal of Advertising Research, Vol. 25 (August/September 1985), pp.
  52-5.

Honomichl, Jack J.
  "Top 50 Researchers' 'Real Growth' Tops 13 Percent"
  Advertising Age, Vol. 59 (May 23, 1988), pp. S2-20.

Honomichl, Jack J.
  "Research Business Review: The Nation's Top Marketing Advertising
  Research Companies"
  Advertising Age, Vol. 58 (May 11, 1987), pp. S1-S26.

Honomichl, Jack J.
  "Top Research Companies' Revenues Rise 13.7 Percent/Research Business
  Review: The Nation's Top 40 Marketing/Advertising/Research Companies"
  Advertising Age, Vol. 56 (May 23, 1985), pp. 16-38.

Kinnear, Thomas C. and Root, Ann R. (editors)
  1988 Survey of Marketing Research
  (Chicago: American Marketing Association, 1989), 79 pp.

Krum, James R.
  "Survey of Marketing Research Directors of Fortune 500 Firms"
  Journal of Marketing Research, Vol. III (August 1966), pp. 313-7.

Moulten, E. S.
  Marketing Research Activities of Manufacturers
  Marketing Research Series No. 21
  (Bureau of Foreign and Domestic Commerce, U.S. Department of
  Commerce, April 1939).

Twedt, Dik Warren (editor)
  1983 Survey of Marketing Research
  (Chicago: American Marketing Association, 1983), 70 pp.

Twedt, Dik Warren (editor)
  1978 Survey of Marketing Research
  (Chicago: American Marketing Association).

Twedt, Dik Warren (editor)
  1973 Survey of Marketing Research
  (Chicago: American Marketing Association, 1973).

Twedt, Dik Warren (editor)
  A Survey of Marketing Research
  (Chicago: American Marketing Association, 1963).

1.04 ---------- State of the Mktg Res Process: Philosophical

    See also (sub)heading(s) 2.03, 15.04.

Bowles, Tim and Blyth, Bill
  "How do You Like Your Data: Raw, al Dente or Stewed?"
  European Research, Vol. 13 (October 1985), pp. 170-8.

Calder, Bobby J. and Tybout, Alice M.
  "What Consumer Research Is..."
  Journal of Consumer Research, Vol. 14 (June 1987), pp. 136-40.

Dichter, Ernest
  "Seven Tenets of Creative Research"
  Journal of Marketing, Vol. 25 (April 1961), pp. 1-4.

Duncan, Calvin P. and Lillis, Charles M.
    "Knowledge Development: Opinions of Marketing Research Managers"
    Journal of the Academy of Marketing Science, Vol. 10 (Winter 1982),
    pp. 20-36.

Foxall, Gordon R.
    "Academic Consumer Research: Problems and Potential"
    European Research, Vol. 8 (January 1980), pp. 20-3.

Haller, Terry
    Danger: Marketing Researcher at Work
    (Westport, CT: Quorum Books), 200 pp.

Halpern, Richard S.
    "Advice to Researchers: Strategic Planning for the Future!"
    European Research, Vol. 12 (April 1984), pp. 60-7.

Holbert, Neil
    Research in the Twilight Zone
    Monograph Series No. 7
    (Chicago: American Marketing Association, 1977), 27 pp.

Holbert, Neil Bruce
    "Underground Testing"
    Journal of Marketing Research, Vol. VI (August 1969), p. 374.

Holbrook, Morris B.
    "What is Consumer Research?"
    Journal of Consumer Research, Vol. 14 (June 1987), pp. 128-32.

Holbrook, Morris B.
    "What is Consumer Research? Toward a Definition of Consumology"
    Graduate School of Business, Columbia University (1986), working
    paper.

Holbrook, Morris B. and O'Shaughnessy, John
    "On the Scientific Status of Consumer Research and the Need for an
    Interpretive Approach to Studying Consumption Behavior"
    Journal of Consumer Research, Vol. 15 (December 1988), pp. 398-402.

Jacoby, Jacob
    "Consumer Research: A State of the Art Review"
    Journal of Marketing, Vol. 42 (April 1978), pp. 87-96.

Kernan, Jerome B.
    "Chasing the Holy Grail: Reflections on 'What is Consumer Research?'"
    Journal of Consumer Research, Vol. 14 (June 1987), pp. 133-5.

Klass, Bertrand
    "A Credo to Replace Dichter's 'Tenets'"
    Journal of Marketing, Vol. 25 (July 1961), pp. 61-4.

Leonhard, Dietz
    The Human Equation in Marketing Research
    (New York: American Management Association, 1967), 176 pp.

Martin, Joanne
    "A Garbage Can Model of the Research Process"
    in McGrath, Joseph E., Martin, Joanne, and Kulka, Richard A. (editors)
    Judgment Calls in Research
    (Beverly Hills, CA: Sage Publications, 1982), pp. 17-40.

Miller, J. I.
    "The Real Challenge of Research"
    Business Horizons, Vol. 1 (Winter 1958), pp. 58-64.

Peter, J. Paul
    "Some Philosophical and Methodological Issues in Consumer Research"
    in Hunt, Shelby D. (editor)
    Marketing Theory: The Philosophy of Marketing Science
    (Homewood, IL: Richard D. Irwin, 1983).

Portis, Bernard
    "The Behavioral Sciences and Marketing Research"
    Business Quarterly, Vol. 29 (Fall 1964), pp. 32-9.

Ruczinski, Erich M.
    "Basic Problems in Marketing and Market Research From the Aspect of
    the Theory of Science"
    European Research, Vol. 2 (September 1974), pp. 196-200.

Simon, Hermann
    "Challenges and New Research Avenues in Marketing Science"
    International Journal of Research in Marketing, Vol. 1, No. 4 (1984),
    pp. 249-61.

Weinberger, Martin
    "Seven Perspectives on Consumer Research"
    Marketing Research, Vol. 1 (December 1989), pp. 9-17.

1.05 ---------- State of the Mktg Res Process: Methodological

Andreasen, Alan R.
"Cost-Conscious Marketing Research"
Harvard Business Review, Vol. 61 (July-August 1983), pp. 74-9.

Gentry, Dwight L. and Pressley, Milton M.
"Let's Release Proprietary Research"
Journal of Advertising Research, Vol. 16 (August 1976), pp. 15-9.

Goldstein, Frederick A.
"A Practical Guide to Gathering U.S.A. Marketing Information and the
Current Status of Marketing Research in the U.S."
Journal of the Market Research Society, Vol. 27 (October 1985), pp.
243-59.

Grazer, William F. and Stiff, M. Ronald
"Statistical Analysis and Design in Marketing Journal Articles"
Journal of the Academy of Marketing Science, Vol. 15 (Spring 1987),
pp. 70-3.

Greenberg, Barnett A., Goldstucker, Jac L., and Bellenger, Danny N.
"What Techniques are Used by Marketing Researchers in Business?"
Journal of Marketing, Vol. 41 (April 1977), pp. 62-8.

Hinkle, C. L. and Wolf, J. S.
"Academic Research and the Data Drought Dilemma"
Journal of Marketing Research, Vol. III (May 1966), pp. 196-8.

Keiser, Stephen K., Krum, James R., and Rau, Pradeep A.
"Changing Patterns in Marketing Research"
Marketing Intelligence and Planning, Vol. 5, No. 1 (1987), pp. 10-8.

Lefcowitz, Myron J. and O'Shea, Robert M.
"A Proposal to Establish a National Archives for Social Science
Survey Data"
American Behavioral Scientist, Vol. 6 (March 1963), pp. 27-31.

Lysaker, Richard L.
"Data Collection Methods in the US"
Journal of the Market Research Society, Vol. 31 (October 1989), pp.
477-88.

Market Facts, Inc.
"Consumer Market Research Technique Usage Patterns and Attitudes in
1981"
Market Facts, Inc. (1981).

Morris, Alan
"Computing Now: Computing in Market Research--The Case for a Broader
Perspective"
Journal of the Market Research Society, Vol. 24 (January 1982), pp.
68-74.

Parasuraman, A.
"A Study of Techniques Used and Clients Served by Marketing Research
Firms"
European Research, Vol. 10 (October 1982), pp. 177-85.

Roe, Michael M. and Morgan, Rory
"Research in the '90s: Back to the Individual"
Proceedings, ESOMAR Congress, Lisbon (1988), pp. 625-41.

Webber, John C.
"Six Challenges Facing Marketing Research of Manufacturers"
Journal of Advertising Research, Vol. 28 (December 1988/January
1989), pp. RC7-9.

Yuspeh, Sonia
"Point of View: Dracula and Frankenstein Revisted"
Journal of Advertising Research, Vol. 29 (February/March 1989), pp.
53-9.

1.06 ---------- State of the Marketing Research Profession

Barnard, Philip
"Professionalism, Barriers to Progress, Innovation"
Congress Report, 37th Congress, Rome (September 1984), pp. 4-7 in
European Research, Vol. 12 (October 1984).

Bogart, Leo
"The Researcher's Dilemma"
Journal of Marketing, Vol. 26 (January 1962), pp. 6-11.

Bowey, Stephen
"Editorial: Advancing the Profession"
Marketing and Research Today, Vol. 17 (May 1989), pp. 62,3.

Coe, Ted L. and Coe, Barbara
    "Marketing Research: The Search for Professionalism"
    in Bernhardt, Kenneth L. (editor)
    Marketing: 1776-1976 and Beyond
    (Chicago: American Marketing Association, 1976), pp. 257-9.

Crimp, Margaret
    "The MRS Diploma"
    Journal of the Market Research Society, Vol. 21 (April 1979), pp.
    125-32.

De Gasparis, P.
    "Professionalism: Some of Its Implications for Market Research"
    Proceedings, S.A.M.R.A. Convention (1983), p. 17.

Demby, Emanuel H.
    "Market Researchers Suffer From an Identity Crisis"
    Marketing and Research Today, Vol. 17 (February 1989), pp. 26-9.

Demby, Emanuel H.
    "American Letter: Profiles of Success"
    European Research, Vol. 4 (March 1976), pp. 57-60.

Demby, Emanuel H.
    "American Letter: Differences in Position and Salaries of American
    and European Research Managers"
    European Research, Vol. 4 (January 1976), pp. 21-4.

Gerhold, Paul E. J.
    "Why We Need a Profession, and How to Get One"
    Journal of Advertising Research, Vol. 14 (October 1974), pp. 9-14.

Gerhold, Paul E. J.
    "Point of View: Sixty Years in Search of a Profession"
    Journal of Advertising Research, Vol. 11 (February 1971), p. 47.

Harper, Marion, Jr.
    "A New Profession to Aid Management"
    Journal of Marketing, Vol. 25 (January 1961), pp. 1-6.

Hermet, Gerard
    "Is Marketing Research Going Another Way?"
    Proceedings, ESOMAR Congress, Lisbon (1988), pp. 437-69.

Naples, Michael J.
    "Public Relations for Market Research: The Situation in the United
    States"
    Journal of the Market Research Society, Vol. 31 (October 1989), pp.
    597-610.

Neal, William D.
    "The Profession of Marketing Research: A Strategic Assessment and a
    Prescription for Improvement"
    Marketing Research, Vol. 1 (September 1989), pp. 13-23.

Ramond, Charles
    "Editorial: Toward Professionalism"
    Journal of Advertising Research, Vol. 14 (October 1974), p. 91.

Samuels, John
    "Professionalism in Market Research in the United Kingdom 1978-1983"
    European Research, Vol. 13 (April 1985), pp. 66-74.

Stern, Bruce L. and Crawford, Terry
    "It's Time to Consider Certification of Researchers"
    Marketing News, Vol. 20 (September 12, 1986), pp. 20,1.

Wyss, Werner
    "The Evolution of the Market Researcher--Past, Present and Future of
    a Young Profession"
    ESOMAR Congress, Montreux (August-September 1975).

1.07 ---------- History of Marketing Research

Bottomley, David T.
    "The Origins of Marketing Research"
    Commentary (JMRS), Vol. 13 (Spring 1964).

Bulmer, Martin (editor)
    Essays on the History of British Sociological Research
    (Cambridge University Press, 1985), 250 pp.

Honomichl, Jack J.
    Marketing/Research People: Their Behind-the-Scenes Stories
    (Chicago: Crain Books, 1984), 190 pp.

Lockley, Lawrence C.
    "Notes on the History of Marketing Research"
    Journal of Marketing, Vol. 14 (1950), pp. 733-6.

Poole, Hal, Blankenship, A. B., and Chakrapani, C.
    The History of Marketing Research in Canada
    (Toronto: Professional Marketing Research Society).

1.08 ---------- Directories of Marketing Research Houses

Allen, Marcia (editor)
    1989 Greenbook, 27th Edition
    International Directory of Marketing Research Companies and Services
    (New York: New York Chapter, American Marketing Association, 1989),
    538 pp.

Bradford's Directory of Marketing Research Agencies and Management
    Consultants, Thirteenth Edition
    (Fairfax, VA: 1975).

ESOMAR
    Handbook of Marketing Research 1981-82
    (Amsterdam, The Netherlands: ESOMAR).

Financial Sourcebooks
    Financial Sourcebook's Sources: The Directory of Financial Research,
    Marketing Surveys and Services
    (Naperville, IL: Financial Sourcebooks, 1987), 454 pages.

Findex
    Findex: The Directory of Market Research Reports, Studies and Surveys.

Gale Research Company
    Research Services Directory, First Edition, Issue Number One
    (Detroit, MI: Gale Research Company, 1981), 88 pp.

Gale Research Company
    Statistical Services Directory, Second Edition
    (Detroit, MI: Gale Research Company), 461 pp.

Gill, Kay and Kruzas, Anthony T. (editors)
    International Research Centers Directory 1984, Second Edition
    (Detroit, MI: Gale Research Co.), 739 pp.

Kline, Charles H. and Company
    Directory of U.S. and Canadian Marketing Surveys and Services, Third
    Edition
    (Fairfield, NJ: Charles H. Kline and Company).

Kruzas, Anthony T. and Gill, Kay (editors)
    International Research Centers Directory, First Edition, Issue Number
    1, January 1982
    (Detroit: Gale Research Company, 1981), 115 pp.

Market Research Society
    International Directory of Market Research Organisations, Seventh
    Edition
    (London: Market Research Society and British Overseas Trade Board),
    561 pp.

Marketing Research Association
    MRA Research Service Directory 1986-87
    (Chicago: Marketing Research Association, Inc.).

Thomas, Robert C. and Ruffner, James A. (editors)
    Research Centers Directory, Seventh Edition
    (Detroit, MI: Gale Research Co., 1982), 1139 pp.

Watkins, Mary Michelle and Ruffner, James A. (editors)
    Research Centers Directory, Tenth Edition, 1986
    (Detroit, MI: Gale Research Co.), 1,561 pp.

1.09 ---------- Unclassified (The State of Marketing Research)

American Management Association, Inc.
    Guidelist for Marketing Research and Economic Forecasting
    (New York: American Management Association, 1966).

Carpenter, Robert N.
    Guidelist for Marketing Research
    (New York: American Management Association), 112 pp.

Cooper, Sanford L.
    "Marketing Research's Other Responsibility"
    American Marketing Association, Chicago Chapter, Annual Research
    Conference (1974), address.

May, John
    "Marketing Research: Illuminating Neglected Areas"
    Journal of the Market Research Society, Vol. 23 (July 1981), pp.
    127-36.

Peters, Matthias U. and Zeugin, Peter G.
  "Opinion Research, Official Statistics and Social Indicators"
  European Research, Vol. 6 (July 1978), pp. 145-53.

Rewoldt, Stewart
  Economic Effects of Marketing Research
  (Ann Arbor, MI: University of Michigan Press, 1953).

Walker, Frank D.
  "Their Opinion Counts"
  Twentieth Annual Advertising Research Foundation Conference (November
  1974), address.

2 ---------- THE STATE OF MARKETING RESEARCH - INTERNATIONAL ---------
    See also (sub)heading(s) 1.

2.01 ---------- State of the Mktg Res Discipline--International

Albaum, Gerald and Peterson, Robert A.
    "Empirical Research in International Marketing: 1976-1982"
    Journal of International Business Studies, Vol. 15 (Spring-Summer
    1984), pp. 161-73.

Barnard, Philip
    "Marketing, Advertising and Research: Are There East and West?"
    European Research, Vol. 14, No. 4 (1986), pp. 168-73.

Blauvelt, E. C.
    "Market Research in Asia Pacific: The State of the Industry"
    MICC/ESOMAR Symposium (November 1984), paper presentation.

Bodur, Muzaffer and Cavusgil, S. Tamer
    "Export Market Research Orientations of Turkish Firms"
    European Journal of Marketing, Vol. 19, No. 2 (1985), pp. 5-16.

Bowey, Stephen
    "Editorial: Advancing the Profession"
    Marketing and Research Today, Vol. 17 (May 1989), pp. 62,3.

Bulmer, Martin (editor)
    Essays on the History of British Sociological Research
    (Cambridge University Press, 1985), 250 pp.

Calvi, Gabriel
    "Five Years of Psychographic Research in Italy: Social and Political
    Results"
    European Research, Vol. 10 (July 1982), pp. 113-9.

Cole, Eileen
    "Taking Stock: Our Progress and Our Future"
    European Research, Vol. 13 (October 1985), pp. 151-60.

Cole, Eileen
    "Where are We Starting From: Where are We Going?"
    ESOMAR Congress, Monte Carlo (1980).

Davies, R. W. B., Minter, Chris J. W., Moll, Michael, and Bottomley,
    David T.
    "Hong Kong--The Continuing Miracle"
    European Research, Vol. 15 (May 1987), pp. 114-20.

Delors, Jacques
    "Towards a Market Without Frontiers"
    European Research, Vol. 14, No. 4 (1986), pp. 160-5.

ESOMAR/ICC
    "International Code of Practice: Marketing and Social Research"
    Amsterdam (1977).

Goodyear, John R.
    "The Structure of the British Market Research Industry"
    Journal of the Market Research Society, Vol. 31 (October 1989), pp.
    427-37.

Goodyear, John R.
    "The U.K. Market Research Industry: Past, Present and Future"
    European Research, Vol. 13 (July 1985), pp. 116-23.

Grabowsky, Alan
    The Abaco Guide to Marketing Research in Brazil
    (Sao Paulo: Abco, 1987), mimeograph.

Hansen, Flemming
    "Contemporary Research in Marketing in Denmark"
    Journal of Marketing, Vol. 45 (Summer 1981), pp. 214-8.

Hayes, P. J.
    "The Cost Comparison of Market Research in Western Europe"
    ICC/ESOMAR Symposium on International Marketing Research, Paris
    (November 1984).

Hooley, Graham J. and West, Christopher J.
    "The Untapped Markets for Marketing Research"
    Journal of the Market Research Society, Vol. 26 (October 1984), pp.
    335-52.

Japan Marketing/Advertising
    "Marketing Research"
    Japan Marketing/Advertising (1988), pp. 207-30.

Johansson, Johny K. and Nonaka, Ikujiro
    "Market Research the Japanese Way"
    Harvard Business Review, Vol. 65 (May/June 1987), pp. 16-22.

Kelly, Eileen A.
    "A United States Perspective on the Status and Future of
    International Marketing Research"
    ESOMAR Seminar on International Marketing Research, Paris (November
    1984).

Mattsson, Lars-Gunnar and Naert, Philippe A.
    "Research in Marketing in Europe: Some Reflections on Its Setting,
    Accomplishments and Challenges"
    International Journal of Research in Marketing, Vol. 2, No. 1 (1985),
    pp. 3-25.

Mills, Diana
    "Industrial Marketing Research: Progress and Prospects"
    European Research, Vol. 10 (April 1982), pp. 72-9.

Permut, S.
    "The European View of Marketing Research"
    Columbia Journal of World Business (Fall 1977), pp. 94-104.

Pinheiro de Andrade, Paulo
    "Market Research in Brazil"
    European Research, Vol. 15 (August 1987), pp. 188-96.

Poole, Hal, Blankenship, A. B., and Chakrapani, C.
    The History of Marketing Research in Canada
    (Toronto: Professional Marketing Research Society).

Queiros, Luis and Lima, J. L. Santos
    "Marketing Research in Portugal"
    European Research, Vol. 16 (August 1988), pp. 185-91.

Ramos, Emilio Martinez
    "Marketing Research en Espana. Situacion y Perspectivas"
    IPMARK Magazine, No. 279 (November 1986), pp. 39-44.

Riley, S.
    "The Marketing of Market Research"
    in Proceedings of the 12th Marketing Theory Seminar (1973).

Rugman, A. M.
    "Research and Development by Multinational and Domestic Firms in
    Canada"
    Canadian Public Policy, Vol. 7 (Autumn 1981), pp. 604-16.

Samuels, John A.
    "The Impact of the Recession: Professionalism in Market Research in
    the United Kingdom 1978-83"
    European Research, Vol. 13 (April 1985), pp. 66-74.

Samuels, J. A. and Menneer, P. J.
    "Market Research Executives in Britain--Looking at the Present and
    Providing for the Future"
    Journal of the Marketing Research Society, Vol. 17 (January 1975),
    pp. 2-20.

Schwartz, D.
    "How Public Relations are Improving the Status of Market Research in
    Switzerland"
    European Research, Vol. 2 (September 1974), pp. 206,7.

Shalofsky, I.
    "ESOMAR Study on International Research Prices"
    European Research, Vol. 11, No. 1 (1983).

Simmons, M.
    "The U.K. Market Research Scene"
    Survey (June 1983).

Simmons, M.
    "The Image of the British Market Research Industry in the Business
    World"
    Market Research Society (1982).

Simmons, M.
    "The British Market Research Industry"
    Market Research Society Conference (April 1978), conference paper.

Simmons, M. and Gordon, L.
    "Pattern of Market Research in the 1980s"
    Market Research Society Conference (March 1980), conference paper.

Treasure, John
    "Ten Years Later..."
    Journal of the Market Research Society, Vol. 18 (April 1976), pp.
    54-63.

Wyss, Werner
  "The Evolution of the Market Researcher--Past, Present and Future of
  a Young Profession"
  ESOMAR Congress, Montreux (August-September 1975).

2.02 ---------- Empirical Descriptions of the Discipline--Intern'l

Adler, Max K.
  Market Research and British Industry
  (London, EN: Hallam Press, 1965).

Barnard, Philip
  "Keeping the Customer Satisfied? The ESOMAR Research Client Study"
  Marketing and Research Today, Vol. 17 (August 1989), pp. 140-6.

Barnard, Philip
  "The ESOMAR Annual Market Study: The State of Marketing Research"
  Marketing and Research Today, Vol. 17 (February 1989), pp. 18-22.

Binetti, Giovanni
  "Industrial Marketing Research Usage: A Survey of 103 Italian Firms"
  European Research, Vol. 8 (January 1980), pp. 27-36.

Bolla, Maria Cristina and Trentini, Giancarlo
  "Research in the Field of Marketing: A Follow-Up on Its Use"
  European Research, Vol. 10 (October 1982), pp. 165-70.

Bonvini Furlanetto, Vanna
  "The 1987 ESOMAR Membership Survey"
  European Research, Vol. 16 (February 1988).

Canada Council
  Survey Research: Report of the Consultative Group on Survey Research
  (Ottawa: The Canada Council, 1976), 171 pp.

Cole, Eileen
  "Taking Stock: Our Progress and Our Future"
  European Research, Vol. 13 (October 1985), pp. 151-60.

Demby, Emanuel H.
  "American Letter: Differences in Position and Salaries of American
  and European Research Managers"
  European Research, Vol. 4 (January 1976), pp. 21-4.

Downham, J. S.
  "The E.S.O.M.A.R. Membership Survey: Part 2"
  European Research, Vol. 2 (November 1974), pp. 251-57.

Downham, J. S.
  "The E.S.O.M.A.R. Membership Survey: Part 1"
  European Research, Vol. 2 (September 1974), pp. 194,5;207.

Bonvini Furlanetto, Vanna
  "The 1987 ESOMAR Membership Survey"
  European Research, Vol. 16 (February 1988), 50-63.

Gobbi, Cecilia
  "Does Recession Open New Fields to Marketing Research? Opportunities
  of Expanding Non-Marketing Management Areas Within Companies"
  ESOMAR Congress, rome (1984), pp. 73-84.

Jobber, D. and Rainbow, C.
  "A Study of the Development and Implementation of Marketing
  Information Systems in British Industry"
  Journal of the Market Research Society, Vol. 19 (July 1977), pp.
  104-11.

Kurtulus, Kemal
  "Development of Marketing Research in Turkey"
  European Research, Vol. 8 (January 1980), pp. 42-8.

Kurtulus, Kemal
  "Present Status of Marketing Research in Turkey"
  European Journal of Marketing, Vol. 12, No. 8 (1978), pp. 529-40.

Oostveen, Jan C. J.
  "Industry Study: The State of Marketing Research in Europe"
  European Research, Vol. 14, No. 3 (1986), pp. 100-35.

Piercy, Nigel and Alexander, Nicholas
  "Retailer Marketing Information Systems"
  Journal of the Market Research Society, Vol. 30 (January 1988), pp.
  87-93.

Ruping, Gunter
  "The Organisation of Market Research Within Manufacturing and
  Marketing Companies"
  European Research, Vol. 2 (July 1974), pp. 159-68.

Saddik, S.
   "An Analysis of the Status of Marketing Research in Egypt"
   European Journal of Marketing, Vol. 7, No. 2 (1973), pp. 77-81.

Samuels, J. A. and Menneer, P. J.
   "Market Research Executives in Britain--Looking at the Present and
   Providing for the Future"
   Journal of the Market Research Society, Vol. 17 (January 1975), pp.
   2-20.

Schaefer, Wolfgang
   "On the Relationship Between Awareness and Use: The ESOMAR Membership
   Survey"
   Marketing and Research Today, Vol. 17 (May 1989), pp. 123-6.

Shalofsky, Ivor
   "What Price Market Research?"
   Marketing and Research Today, Vol. 17 (May 1989), pp. 67-80.

Shalofsky, Ivor
   "E.S.O.M.A.R. Study on International Research Prices"
   European Research, Vol. 11 (January 1983), pp. 2-9.

Simmons, Martin
   "The British Market Research Industry"
   Journal of the Market Research Society, Vol. 20 (July 1978), pp.
   135-65.

Southgate, Peter
   "The 1985 MRS Membership Survey"
   Journal of the Market Research Society, Vol. 28 (January 1986), pp.
   67-92.

Stenboek, Tom
   "The Market Research Industry: Norway"
   Journal of the Market Research Society, Vol. 20 (October 1978), p.
   250.

Treasure, J. A. P.
   "A Second Survey of Market Research in Great Britain"
   Market Research Society (1966).

Wells, R. Douglas
   "The Market Research Industry: France"
   Journal of the Market Research Society, Vol. 20 (October 1978), pp.
   248,9.

Wills, Gordon et al.
   "Marketing Research in British Industry: A Survey of Current Practise
   in 553 Companies"
   Market Research Society Annual Conference (1971).

Wilson, Aubrey
   "Industrial Marketing Research in Britain"
   Journal of Marketing Research, Vol. VI (February 1969), pp. 15-27.

Wong, Kenneth B. and Chapman, Randall G.
   Market Research in Canada: A Status Report
   (Ottawa: Conference Board in Canada, 1978).

2.03 ---------- Mktg Res Environment, Practices in Specific Countries

       See also (sub)heading(s) 1.04, 15.04.

Baker, Malcolm
   "Qualitative Research in the US and the UK: A Contrast in Styles and
   Practices"
   ESOMAR Congress, Montreux (1987), pp. 847-58.

Barnard, Philip
   "Research in the U.S.A."
   Journal of the Market Research Society, Vol. 26 (October 1984), pp.
   273-93.

Bigant, Jean and Rickebusch, Yves
   "Marketing Research in France"
   European Research, Vol. 13 (January 1985), pp. 4-11.

Bowers, Diane K.
   "Bundesdatenschutzgesetz"
   Marketing Research, Vol. 1 (September 1989), pp. 73-6.

Brock, Sabra E.
   "Marketing Research in Asia: Problems, Opportunities, and Lessons"
   Marketing Research, Vol. 1 (September 1989), pp. 44-51.

Byrne, Des
   "Small Research Explosion in Ireland: No Casualties"
   Admap (July-August 1986), pp. 100-35.

De Andrade, Paulo Pinheiro
"Marketing Research in Brazil"
European Research, Vol. 15 (August 1987), pp. 188-96.

Denny, David L.
"Now You can do Market Research in China"
China Business Review, Vol. 16 (May-June 1989).

Dietl, Jerzy
"Marketing Research in a Centrally Planned Economy: The Polish
Experience"
European Research, Vol. 5 (September 1977), pp. 235-46.

Fleury, Pascal
"Market Research in France"
European Research, Vol. 13 (April 1985), pp. 80,1.

Freese, Jan
"The Swedish Data Act"
European Research, Vol. 4 (September 1976), pp. 201-4.

Garrido, Gines
"Marketing Research in Spain: A Promising Future"
European Research, Vol. 15 (May 1987), pp. 99-113.

Hamblin, Christopher
"What is Involved in European Market Research for Pharmaceutical
Clients"
European Research, Vol. 1 (November 1973), pp. 248-55.

Hansen, Flemming
"Contemporary Research in Marketing in Denmark"
Journal of Marketing, Vol. 45 (Summer 1981), pp. 214-8.

Hill, M. R., Shenfield, S., and Park, J. D.
"Market Research in the Soviet Union"
Journal of the Market Research Society, Vol. 24 (April 1982), pp.
152-69.

Hirata, Junji, Fukushima, Akira, Omuro, Tsukuru, Shiosaki, Masao, and
Takeda, Katsuaki
"Marketing Research Practices and Problems in Japan"
Journal of Marketing, Vol. 25 (April 1961), pp. 34-7.

Hooley, Graham J.
"The Untapped Markets for Marketing Research"
Journal of the Market Research Society, Vol. 26 (October 1984), pp.
335-52.

Kaiser, Bo P.
"Marketing Research in Sweden"
European Research, Vol. 16 (February 1988), pp. 64-70.

Kurtulus, Kemal
"Development of Marketing Research in Turkey"
European Research, Vol. 8 (January 1980), pp. 42-8.

Kurtulus, Kemal
"Present Status of Marketing Research in Turkey"
European Journal of Marketing, Vol. 12, No. 8 (1978), pp. 529-40.

Kushner, J. M.
"Market Research in a Non-Western Context: The Asian Example"
Journal of the Market Research Society, Vol. 24 (April 1982), pp.
116-22.

Marcotty, Thomas
"Mysterious Germany"
European Research, Vol. 13 (October 1985), pp. 148-50.

Monk, Donald
"Marketing Research in Canada"
European Research, Vol. 15 (November 1987), pp. 271-4.

Ortengren, John
"Pharmaceutical Marketing Research in Sweden"
European Research, Vol. 10 (April 1982), pp. 58-63.

Prusova, Felicia
"Market Research in Czechoslovakia"
Journal of Marketing Research, Vol. II (November 1965), pp. 398-400.

Ramond, Charles K.
"Operations Research in European Marketing"
Journal of Marketing Research, Vol. I (February 1964), pp. 17-24.

Rusby, Peter
"Europe--One Market for Market Research"
European Research, Vol. 2 (January 1974), pp. 22,23;36.

Sarin, Sharad
    "Industrial Market Research in India"
    Industrial Marketing Management, Vol. 16 (November 1987), pp. 257-64.

Stanton, John L., Chandran, Rajan, and Hernandez, Sigfredo A.
    "Marketing Research Problems in Latin America"
    Journal of the Market Research Society, Vol. 24 (April 1982), pp.
    124-39.

Szabo, Laszlo
    "Market Research in Hungary"
    European Research, Vol. 7 (March 1979), pp. 71-7;79.

Vahelainen, Tarmo
    "Marketing Research in Finland"
    European Research, Vol. 15, No. 1 (1987), pp. 62-6.

Vahelainen, Tarmo
    "Marketing Research in the Nordic Countries"
    European Research, Vol. 13 (April 1985), pp. 76-9.

2.04 ---------- State of the Process--International: Methodological

        See also (sub)heading(s) 16.06, 28.

Benazeth, Claude
    "Legal Lessons From the Delicare Affair--2: Europe"
    Marketing and Research Today, Vol. 17 (August 1989), pp. 156-60.

Blanc, H.
    "Multilingual Interviewing in Israel"
    American Journal of Sociology, Vol. 62 (September 1956), pp. 205-9.

Bowles, Tim
    "Data Collection in the United Kingdom"
    Journal of the Market Research Society, Vol. 31 (October 1989), pp.
    467-76.

Brusati, Elio
    "Electoral Polls in Italy"
    European Research, Vol. 15 (August 1987), pp. 152-7.

Carr, Richard P., Jr.
    "Identifying Trade Areas for Consumer Goods in Foreign Markets"
    Journal of Marketing, Vol. 42 (October 1978), pp. 76-80.

Crosby, R. W.
    "Attitude Measurement in a Bilingual Culture"
    Journal of Marketing Research, Vol. VI (November 1969), pp. 421-6.

Johansson, Johny K. and Nonaka, Ikujiro
    "Market Research the Japanese Way"
    Harvard Business Review, Vol. 87 (May-June 1987), pp. 16-22.

Laurent, C. K. and Parra A., A.
    "Use of Mail Questionnaires in Columbia"
    Journal of Marketing Research, Vol. V (February 1968), pp. 101-3.

Mavros, Dimitri
    "The Dawning of Election Polls in Greece"
    European Research, Vol. 15 (August 1987), pp. 166-70

Nisihira, Sigeki
    "Japan: Recent Polling Problems"
    European Research, Vol. 15 (August 1987), pp. 171-3.

Noelle-Neumann, Elisabeth
    "Federal Republic of Germany: Election Forecasts and the Public"
    European Research, Vol. 15 (August 1987), pp. 162-5.

Permut, Steven E.
    "Marketing Research: The European View"
    European Research, Vol. 6 (March 1978), pp. 49-56.

Radvanyi, L.
    "Ten Years of Sample Surveying in Mexico"
    International Journal of Opinion and Attitude Research, Vol. 5
    (Winter 1951-52), pp. 491-510.

Ralis, Max, Suchman, E., and Goldsen, R. L.
    "Applicability of Survey Techniques in Northern India"
    Public Opinion Quarterly, Vol. 22 (Fall 1958), pp. 245-50.

Rohme, Nils
    "A Worldwide Overview of National Restrictions on the Conduct and
    Release of Public Opinion Polls"
    European Research, Vol. 13 (January 1985), pp. 30-7.

Samli, A. Coskun and Lange, Irene
    "Marketing Research Techniques for Assessing Markets of East European
    Economies"
    Journal of the Academy of Marketing Science, Vol. 5 (Special
    Proceedings Issue 1977), pp. 111-4.

Sampson, Peter
    "Qualitative Research in Europe: The State of the Art and the Art of
    the State"
    European Research, Vol. 13 (October 1985), pp. 163-9.

Schweizer, Robert
    "Federal Republic of Germany: Tight Restrictions on Telemarketing"
    European Research, Vol. 15 (May 1987), pp. 82-4.

Shamir, Jacob
    "Preelection Polls in Israel: Structural Constraints on Accuracy"
    Public Opinion Quarterly, Vol. 50 (Spring 1986), pp. 62-75.

Sopariwala, Dorab
    "India: Election Polling in the World's Largest Democracy"
    European Research, Vol. 15 (August 1987), pp. 174-6.

Van Westendorp, Peter H.
    "Political Opinion Polling in the Netherlands: Defeats and Victories"
    European Research, Vol. 15 (August 1987), pp. 158-60.

Worcester, Robert M.
    "Political Opinion Polling in Great Britain: Past, Present and Future"
    European Research, Vol. 15 (August 1987), pp. 143-50.

Worcester, Robert M. (editor)
    Political Opinion Polling--An International Review
    (London: Macmillan, 1983).

Worcester, Robert M.
    "History of Political Polls in Great Britain"
    Silver Jubilee Market Research Society Conference (1982), paper
    presentation.

Yavas, Ugur
    "Marketing Research in an Arabian Gulf Country"
    Journal of the Market Research Society, Vol. 29 (October 1987), pp.
    458-61.

Yavas, Ugur and Kaynak, Erdener
    "Current Status of Marketing Research in Developing Countries:
    Problems and Opportunities"
    Journal of International Marketing and Marketing Research, Vol. 5,
    No. 2 (1980), pp. 78-89.

3 ----------------- PRINCIPALS IN MARKETING RESEARCH -----------------

Abrams, Mark
  "Social Research and Market Research: The Case of Paul Lazarsfeld"
  Journal of the Market Research Society, Vol. 19 (January 1977), pp.
  12-7.

Andreasen, Alan R. and Gardner, David M. (editors)
  Diffusing Marketing Theory and Research: The Contributions of Bauer,
  Green, Kotler and Levitt
  (Chicago: American Marketing Association, 1979), 148 pp.

Bartos, Rena
  "Founding Fathers of Advertising Research" (Ernest Dichter, George
  Gallup, Alfred Politz, Henry Brenner, A. C. Nielsen, Sr., Hans
  Ziesal, Frank Stanton, Archibald Crossley, Daniel Starch)
  Journal of Advertising Research, Vol. 26 (February/March 1986), pp.
  13-53.

Bartos, Rena and Pearson, Arthur S.
  "Daniel Starch: The Founding-Est Father"
  Journal of Advertising Research, Vol. 17 (October 1977), pp. 63-7.

Bartos, Rena and Pearson, Arthur S.
  "The Founding Fathers of Advertising Research"
  Journal of Advertising Research, Vol. 17 (June 1977), pp. 1-32.

Hirschman, Elizabeth C.
  "Scientific Style and the Conduct of Consumer Research"
  Journal of Consumer Research, Vol. 12 (September 1985), pp. 225-39.

Webb, Norman and Wybrow, Bob
  "Henry Durant--Trailblazer"
  Journal of the Market Research Society, Vol. 29 (October 1987), pp.
  385-90.

Wind, Yoram
  "Marketing Research and Management: A Retrospective View of the
  Contributions of Paul E. Green"
  in Andreasen, Alan (editor)
  Proceedings of the Tenth Paul D. Converse Awards Symposium
  (Urbana, IL: University of Illinois Press, 1978).

4 ----------- MANAGEMENT OF THE MARKETING RESEARCH FUNCTION ----------

4.01 ---------- Books Re: Management of the Mktg Res Function

Adler, Lee and Mayer, Charles S. (editors)
Readings in Managing the Marketing Research Function
(Chicago: American Marketing Association, 1980), 200 pp.

Adler, L. and Mayer, C. S.
Managing the Market Research Function
AMA Monograph No. 5
(Chicago: American Marketing Association, 1977), 174 pp.

Balachandra, R.
Early Warning Signals for R and D Projects
(Lexington, MA: Lexington Books, 1989), 240 pp.

Blankenship, A. B. and Doyle, J. B.
Marketing Research Management
(New York: American Management Association, 1965), 370 pp.

Crisp, Richard D.
Marketing Research Organization and Operation
Research Report No. 35
(New York: American Management Association, 1958).

Forman, Lewis W. and Bailey, Earl L.
The Role and Organization of Marketing Research
(New York: National Industrial Conference Board, 1969), 65 pp.

Myers, James H. and Mead, Richard R.
The Management of Marketing Research
(Scranton, PA: International Textbook Co., 1969), 153 pp.

Piercy, Nigel and Evans, M.
Managing Marketing Information
(Beckenham: Croom Helm, 1983).

Thompson, G. Clark
Organization for Market Research (Part 1, Industry Experience),
Studies in Business Policy, No. 12
(New York, NY: National Industrial Conference Board, Inc., 1945).

4.02 ---------- General Discussions Re: Mngt of the Mktg Res Function

Adler, Lee and Mayer, Charles S.
"Managing the Corporate Research Department"
European Research, Vol. 4 (January 1976), pp. 12-20.

Bernstein, D.
"Advertising as a Means of Cutting Research Costs"
Admap (1975).

Boyd, Harper W., Jr. and Britt, Steuart H.
"Making Marketing Research More Effective by Using the Administrative Process"
Journal of Marketing Research, Vol. II (February 1965), pp. 13-9.

Callingham, Martin
"Will the MR Department Disappear?"
Marketing and Research Today, Vol. 17 (August 1989), pp. 148,9.

Cowan, David
"A New Deal for Market Research"
Admap (July-August 1984), pp. 346-50,75.

Dreisbach, Bruce R.
"Marketing: The Key to Successful Research Management"
Marketing News, Vol. 19 (January 4, 1985), p. 3.

ESOMAR
Seminar on "Managing Market Research as a Business"
(Amsterdam, The Netherlands: European Society for Opinion and
Marketing Research, May 1974), 147 pp.

Finn, Adam
"In-House Research Becomes a Factor"
Public Relations Journal, Vol. 40 (July 1984), pp. 18-20.

Gombeski, William R., Jr. and Koscic, Dorothy J.
"Improving Managerial Effectiveness"
Marketing Research, Vol. 1 (September 1989), pp. 68-72.

Grainge, N. J. and Pearson, A. J.
"Managing an In-House R and D Service Department"
R and D Management, Vol. 19 (January 1989).

Haldane, I. R.
"The Selection of Market Research Executives"
Proceedings, E.S.O.M.A.R. Conference (1966).

Hansen, Flemming
  "Managing Marketing Research--Or Not?"
  Marketing and Research Today, Vol. 17 (May 1989), pp. 81,2.

Kelley, Scott W., Skinner, Steven J., and Ferrell, O. C.
  "Opportunistic Behavior in Marketing Research Organizations"
  Journal of Business Research, Vol. 18 (June 1989).

Kiel, Geoffrey
  "Maximising Marketing Research Effectiveness Through Data Analysis"
  Market Intelligence and Planning, Vol. 2, No. 2 (1984), pp. 40-50.

Krum, James R.
  "Role of the Director of Marketing Research Position in Large
  Industrial Corporations: 1975 Survey Results"
  Bureau of Economic and Business Research, University of Delaware
  (1976).

Krum, James R.
  "Perceptions and Evaluation of the Role of the Corporate Marketing
  Research Department"
  Journal of Marketing Research, Vol. VI (November 1969), pp. 459-64.

Lachmann, Ulrich
  "789 Out: Could This be the Future of Market Research in Companies?"
  Proceedings, ESOMAR Congress, Lisbon (1988), pp. 811-22.

Lewis, Jonathan F.
  "Computer Expertise and Manipulation of Knowledge in the Market
  Research Industry"
  Journal of the Market Research Society, Vol. 30 (October 1988), pp.
  467-75.

Locander, W. B. and Scamell, R. W.
  "A Team Approach to Managing the Market Research Process"
  MSU Business Topics (Winter 1977), pp. 15-26.

Ossip, Al
  "Likely Improvements in Data Collection Methods--What do They Mean
  for Day-to-Day Research Management"
  Journal of Advertising Research, Vol. 26 (October/November 1986), pp.
  RC9-12.

Roberts, Edward
  "What do We Know About Managing R and D"
  Research Management, Vol. 21 (November 1978), pp. 6-11.

Saxberg, Borje and Slocum, John W., Jr.
  "The Management of Scientific Manpower"
  Management Science, Vol. 14, No. 8 (1968), pp. B473-89.

Varble, Dale
  "That's an Excellent Idea but... Planning for Cooperation in Research
  and Other Projects"
  Journal of the Market Research Society, Vol. 15 (April 1973), pp.
  136-9.

Wright, David
  "Organising for Innovation"
  Admap (July-August 1984), pp. 340-6.

Young, H. C.
  "Effective Management of Research--Marketing Teams"
  Research Management, Vol. 22 (March 1979), pp. 7-12.

Zaltman, Gerald and Moorman, Christine
  "The Management and Use of Advertising Research"
  Journal of Advertising Research, Vol. 28 (December 1988/January
  1989), pp. 11-8.

4.03 ---------- Budgeting the Marketing Research Function

Bass, Frank M.
  "Marketing Research Expenditures: A Decision Model"
  Journal of Business, Vol. 39 (January 1963), pp. 77-90.

Day, Ralph L.
  "Optimizing Market Research Through Cost-Benefit Analysis"
  Business Horizons, Vol. 9 (Fall 1966), pp. 45-54.

Schlossberg, Howard
  "Cost Allocation can Show True Value of Research"
  Marketing News, Vol. 24 (January 8, 1990), p. 2.

Tomasino, Richard F.
  "Integrate Market Research With Strategic Plan to Get Budget Okay"
  Marketing News, Vol. 19 (January 4, 1985), p. 8.

4.04 ---------- Costing and Pricing Research Projects

Bowers, Diane K.
   "Plus Applicable Sales Tax?"
   Marketing Research, Vol. 1 (June 1989), pp. 60,1.

Collins, M. and Goodhardt, G.
   "Value for Money in Research Design"
   Papers, 21st Annual Conference, Market Research Society (1978), pp.
   93-102.

Gane, Roger and Spackman, Nigel A. G.
   "A Survey of Agency Costing"
   Journal of the Market Research Society, Vol. 14, No. 4 (1972), pp.
   197-212.

Gates, Roger and Solomon, Paul
   "Cost Estimation for Marketing Research Fieldwork"
   College of Business, The University of Texas at Arlington (1980),
   working paper.

Goodyear, John R.
   "A Specialist Agency View (on Costing)"
   Journal of the Market Research Society, Vol. 14, No. 4 (1972), pp.
   223-32.

Haque, Paul
   "Pricing Market Research Projects"
   Industrial Marketing, Vol. 10, Fourth Quarter (1985), pp. 121-6.

Monk, Donald
   "A Research Agency View (on Costing)"
   Journal of the Market Research Society, Vol. 14, No. 4 (1972), pp.
   213-22.

Roberts-Miller, Richard A. and Teer, Frank
   "(Agency) Costs and Pricing--Conclusions"
   Journal of the Market Research Society, Vol. 14, No. 4 (1972), pp.
   239-41.

4.05 ---------- Evaluation and Control of the Mktg Res Function

Assmus, Gert
   "Bayesian Analysis for Evaluation of Marketing Research Expenditures:
   A Reassessment"
   Journal of Marketing Research, Vol. XIV (November 1977), pp. 562-8.

Boyd, Harper W., Jr. and Britt, Steuart Henderson
   "Making Marketing Research More Effective by Using the Administrative
   Process"
   Journal of Marketing Research, Vol. II (February 1965), pp. 13-9.

Crisp, Richard
   "Auditing the Functional Elements of a Marketing Operation"
   Analyzing and Improving Marketing Performance, AMA Management Report
   No. 32
   (New York: American Management Association, 1959), pp. 37-46.

Demby, Emanuel H.
   "Market Researchers Suffer From an Identity Crisis"
   Marketing and Research Today, Vol. 17 (February 1989), pp. 26-9.

Demby, Emanuel H.
   "American Letter: Nitty Gritty"
   European Research, Vol. 4 (May 1976), pp. 112-6.

Gandz, Jeffrey and Whipple, Thomas W.
   "Making Marketing Research Accountable"
   Journal of Marketing Research, Vol. XIV (May 1977), pp. 202-8.

Gombeski, William R., Jr.
   "Client Satisfaction Questionnaires: Why Research Managers Should Use
   Them"
   Marketing Research, Vol. 1 (December 1989), pp. 45-7.

Gombeski, William R., Jr.
   "Success Factors You Can Use in Conducting Marketing Research
   Performance Reviews"
   Marketing Research, Vol. 1 (June 1989), pp. 56-9.

Mayer, Charles S.
   "Quality Control in Research"
   Journal of Advertising Research, Vol. 11 (June 1971), pp. 9-14.

Mayer, Charles S.
   "Assessing the Accuracy of Marketing Research"
   Journal of Marketing Research, Vol. VII (August 1970), pp. 285-91.

Mayer, C. S.
    "Evaluating the Quality of Marketing Research Contractors"
    Journal of Marketing Research, Vol. IV (May 1967), pp. 134-41.

Myers, James H. and Samli, A. Coskun
    "Management Control of Marketing Research"
    Journal of Marketing Research, Vol. VI (August 1969), pp. 267-77.

Randle, C. Wilson
    "Problems of R and D Management"
    Harvard Business Review, Vol. 37 (January-February 1959), pp. 128-36.

Samli, Coskun and Myers, James H.
    "Management Control of Marketing Research"
    Journal of Marketing Research, Vol. VI (August 1969), pp. 267-77.

Schnee, Robert K.
    "Quality Research: Going Beyond the Obvious"
    Journal of Advertising Research, Vol. 28 (February/March 1988), pp.
    RC9-12.

Sessions, Richard E.
    "A Management Audit of Marketing Research"
    Journal of Marketing, Vol. 14 (Summer 1950), pp. 111-9.

Shalofsky, Ivor
    "What Price Market Research?"
    Marketing and Research Today, Vol. 17 (May 1989), pp. 67-80.

Soistman, E. C.
    "Research and Development Can be Controlled"
    Research Management, Vol. 9 (January 1966), pp. 15-27.

Twedt, Dik
    "Authorization, Control, and Evaluation of Marketing Research
    Projects"
    Journal of Marketing Research, Vol. XII (February 1975), pp. 86-92.

Twedt, Dik Warren
    "What is the 'Return on Investment' in Marketing Research?"
    Journal of Marketing, Vol. 30 (January 1966), pp. 62,3.

4.06 ---------- Research Agency-Client Relationships

Abrams, Mark
    "Value for Money in Social Research"
    Journal of the Market Research Society, Vol. 21 (January 1979), pp.
    17-24.

Bailey, Lawrence F. and Scott-Jones, Gill
    "Rational, Irrational, and Other Reasons for Commissioning Research"
    Market Intelligence and Planning, Vol. 2, No. 3 (1984), pp. 36-50.

Bailey, Lawrence F. and Scott-Jones, Gill
    "Rational, Irrational, and Other Reasons for Commissioning Research"
    Market Research Society Conference (March 1984), pp. 111-27.

Beadle, Penny and Smith, Paul
    "How Clients and Planners Use Qualitative Research to Develop
    Advertising: Where do We Go From Here?"
    Proceedings, Market Research Society Conference (March 1987), pp.
    339-60.

Berry, Tina and Fisher, Susie
    "Researcher: Get Back in Your Box"
    Proceedings, Market Research Society Conference (March 1987), pp.
    361-85.

Blankenship, A. B. and Barker, R. F.
    "Selecting Research Firms From Which to Get Proposals"
    Journal of the Academy of Marketing Science, Vol. 1 (Fall 1973), pp.
    81-9.

Cowley, Don
    "Advertising Research Looks Different From the Agency Side"
    Admap (February 1986), pp. 82-5.

Guss, Leonard M.
    "The Care and Feeding of Marketing Consultants"
    Journal of Marketing, Vol. 30 (July 1966), pp. 6-8.

Haynes, Joel B. and Rothe, James T.
    "Competitive Bidding for Marketing Research Services"
    Journal of Marketing, Vol. 38 (July 1974), pp. 69-71.

Hughes, Brian
    "A Research Buyer's View (on Costing)"
    Journal of the Market Research Society, Vol. 14, No. 4 (1972), pp.
    233-8.

ICC/ESOMAR
  Contract Checklist "Reaching Agreement on a Marketing Research
  Project"
  (Amsterdam).

Jarvis, J. and Fisher, C.
  "A Client's View of Fieldwork Standards"
  Marketing Research Society Seminar: "Fieldwork--A Briefing for
  Tomorrow" (1974).

Lazer, William and Warner, Arthur E.
  The Knowledge Industry: Research Consultants in Perspective
  (East Lansing, MI: Michigan State University, Bureau of Business and
  Economic Research, 1965), 34 pp.

Martyn, John
  "Fieldwork Quality--A Client's View"
  Journal of the Market Research Society, Vol. 19 (April 1977), pp.
  46-58.

Myers, James H.
  "Competitive Bidding for Marketing Research Services"
  Journal of Marketing, Vol. 33 (July 1969), pp. 40-5.

National Industrial Conference Board, Inc.
  Using Marketing Consultants and Research Agencies
  (New York: NICB, Inc., 1966), 64 pp.

Potsch, Luis Eduardo and Limeira, Tania Maria
  "The Implications of the Strategic Organisational Dynamics of
  Companies (Market Research Users) for the Patterns of Action of
  Market Research Agencies (Suppliers)"
  Proceedings, ESOMAR Congress, Monte Carlo (1986), pp. 559-75.

Reidesel, Paul L.
  "Avoid Suppliers That Don't Practice What They Preach"
  Marketing News, Vol. 19 (January 4, 1985), p. 43.

Roth, Julius A.
  "Hired Hand Research"
  American Sociologist, Vol. 1 (August 1966), pp. 190-6.

Rothman, James
  "Acceptance Checks for Ensuring Quality in Research"
  Journal of the Market Research Society, Vol. 22 (July 1980), pp.
  192-204.

Tofts, Robert
  "Do We Users Take Fieldwork Quality Too Much for Granted?"
  Marketing and Research Today, Vol. 17 (February 1989), pp. 24,5.

Townsend, Bickley
  "How to Choose a Consumer Research Company"
  American Demographics, Vol. 8 (October 1986), pp. 28-35.

4.07 ---------- Account Planning

Barry, Thomas E., Peterson, Ron L., and Todd, W. Bradford
  "The Role of Account Planning in the Future of Advertising Agency
  Research"
  Journal of Advertising Research, Vol. 27 (February/March 1987), pp.
  15-21.

Butterfield, Leslie
  "Planning: The Great Fear"
  Campaign (February 19, 1982).

Doyle, Peter
  "Broadening the Concept of Account Planning"
  Admap (March 1986), pp. 164-8.

Feuer, Jack
  "Account Planers Put Human Face on Statistics"
  Adweek (April 15, 1985).

Guirl, Gabrielle
  "Account Planning at Chiat/Day Pushes Advertising's Creative
  Boundaries"
  Ad Forum (May 1985).

Hedges, Martin
  "Chiat Expects 'Account Planning' to Hone Strategy"
  Adweek (August 2, 1982).

Meyers, Bruce
  "To Plan or Not to Plan"
  Journal of Advertising Research, Vol. 26, No. 5 (1986), pp. 25,6.

Moran, John P.
  "Account Planning: A Client View"
  Journal of the Market Research Society, Vol. 30 (July 1988), pp.
  361-69.

Moran, John P.
  "Account Planning: A Client View"
  Proceedings, Market Research Society (March 1988), pp. 89-97.

Pollitt, Stanley
  "How I Started Account Planning in Agencies"
  Account Planning
  (London: Institute of Practitioners of Advertising, 1981).

Rayner, Jane
  "The Secret Weapon has Made a Fortune for Chiat/Day"
  Campaign (December 7, 1984).

Sargent, Mike
  "Clients Need Planners as Much as Agencies do"
  Admap (January 1986), pp. 18-21.

Sharfman, William
  "Account Planners Have Arrived"
  Advertising Age (April 7, 1986).

Sharkey, Betsy
  "Do British-Style Account Planners Have a Future in the US?"
  Adweek, Eastern Edition (August 10, 1987).

Stewart, Jennifer
  "The Role and Evolution of the Agency Planner"
  Journal of Advertising Research, Vol. 26, No. 5 (1986), pp. 22-4.

4.08 ---------- Marketing Researcher Training

Blankenship, A. B.
  "What Marketing Research Managers Want in Trainees"
  Journal of Advertising Research, Vol. 15 (February 1975), pp. 7-14.

Blankertz, Donald et al.
  "The Teaching of Marketing Research in Relation to Industry Needs"
  Journal of Marketing, Vol. 21 (April 1957), pp. 401-12.

Capella, L. M. and Jain, S. C.
  "Quantitative Techniques in Marketing: An Assessment of Teaching and
  Usage Patterns"
  Decision Sciences, Vol. 9 (1978), pp. 346-61.

Dandurand, Lawrence
  "Linking Decision Support Systems and Marketing Research Software in
  Marketing Education"
  in Schaffer, Robert W. and Stanble, Vernon R. (editors)
  Marketing Applications in the Computer Age
  (Chicago: American Marketing Association, 1986), pp. 19-32.

Demby, Emanuel H.
  "New Requirement for Researchers: Interactivity With the PC"
  Marketing News, Vol. 19 (May 24, 1985), pp, 7,10.

Demby, Emanuel H.
  "The New Requirement for the Researcher: Interactivity With the
  Personal Computer"
  European Research, Vol. 13 (January 1985), pp. 26-8.

Dyer, Robert F.
  "An Integrated Design for Personal Computers in the Marketing
  Curriculum"
  Journal of the Academy of Marketing Science, Vol. 15 (Summer 1987),
  pp. 16-24.

Gardner, Burleigh B.
  "What Kind of Academic Training Makes the Most Useful Commercial
  Researcher?"
  Printers' Ink, Vol. 264 (July 1958), pp. 61,2.

Goslar, Martin D.
  "MKIS Course Trains Students for Business World"
  Marketing News, Vol. 19 (July 19, 1985), p. 11.

Green, Paul E.
  "A Reply--To Wortzel"
  Journal of Marketing Research, Vol. VI (November 1969), p. 499.

Green, Paul E.
  "Editorial: Where is the Research Generalist?"
  Journal of Marketing Research, Vol. V (November 1968), p. 446.

Holmes, Cliff
"The Values and Practices of Consumer and In-House Research Workshops
in New Product Development"
Proceedings, Market Research Society Conference (March 1986), pp.
43-56.

Jobber, David and Horgan, Ian G.
"Marketing Research Education: Perspectives From Practitioners"
Journal of Marketing Management, Vol. 3 (Summer 1987), pp. 39-49.

Kurtz, David L. and Boone, Louis E.
"The Current Status of Microcomputer Usage in the Marketing Programs
of AACSB-Accredited Colleges and Universities"
Journal of the Academy of Marketing Science, Vol. 15 (Summer 1987),
pp. 10-5.

Liefeld, John and Tanguay, J.
"Computer Usage and Application Software for Teaching Research
Methods Courses in Business and Behavioral Science Programs"
Department of Consumer Studies, University of Guelph, Ontario.

Marketing News
"1989 Marketing News Directory of Professional Development Courses
for Marketing"
Marketing News, Vol. 23 (June 19, 1989), pp. 14-20.

McKinnon, Gary F., Smith, Scott M., and Smith, Milton E.
"The Diffusion of Personal Computers Among Business School Faculty: A
Longitudinal Study of Attitudes, Expectations, and Users"
Journal of Marketing Education, Vol. 7 (Fall 1985), pp. 1-6.

Miller, Fred
"Integrating the Personal Computer Into the Marketing Curriculum: A
Programmatic Outline"
Journal of Marketing Education, Vol. 7 (Fall 1985), pp. 7-11.

Miller, J. Robert
"Preparation of Students for Marketing Research"
Journal of Marketing Research, Vol. IV (February 1967), pp. 82-4.

Morris, Linda J. and Morris, J. S.
"Using a Decision Support System in the Marketing Classroom"
in Dolich, Ira (editor)
Proceedings, Winter Marketing Educators' Conference
(Chicago: American Marketing Association, 1986).

Parasuraman, A.
"Commercial Marketing Researchers' Evaluations of Academic Journals
and Marketing Research Education"
Journal of Marketing Education, Vol. 3 (Fall 1981), pp. 52-8.

Parasuraman, A. and Wright, D. C.
"A Study of Marketing Research Jobs for College Graduates:
Implications for Educators"
Proceedings, American Marketing Association Educators' Conference
(1983), pp. 181-5.

Reynolds, Fred D.
"How to Make a Marketing-Research Professional"
Journal of Advertising Research, Vol. 21 (April 1981), pp. 19-21.

Segal, Madhav
"Graduate Program of Instruction in Marketing Research: A Need
Assessment"
Journal of Marketing Education, Vol. 9 (Spring 1987), pp. 3-11.

Shawver, Donald L.
"The Supply and Demand for New Marketing Doctorates"
Journal of Marketing, Vol. 37 (April 1973), pp. 63-7.

Sherwood, Charles S. and Nordstrom, Richard D.
"Computer Competencies for Marketing: Are Universities Doing Their
Job?"
Journal of Marketing Education, Vol. 8 (Spring 1986), pp. 55-60.

Watkins, T.
"Teaching Marketing Research Using 'Live' Case Studies"
Business Education, Vol. 6, No. 3 (1985), pp. 29-36.

Wortzel, Lawrence H.
"Finding the Research Generalist: The Solution May Not be Black or
White, but It isn't Green Either"
Journal of Marketing Research, Vol. VI (November 1969), pp. 498,9.

Wukitsch, Michael R.
"How can I Begin My Professional Development? Some Help From the AMA"
Marketing Research, Vol. 1 (December 1989), pp. 51-4.

Wukitsch, Michael R.
  "Professional Development--What's the Personal Bottom Line?...Will it
  Help You Keep Your Job?"
  Marketing Research, Vol. 1 (September 1989), pp. 77,8.

4.09 ---------- Profiles of Specific Companies' Research Programs

Ackoff, Russell L. and Emshoff, James R.
  "Advertising Research at Anheusser-Busch, Inc."
  Sloan Management Review (Winter 1975), pp. 1-15.

Azhari, Abdul G. and Kamen, Joseph M.
  "Marketing Research at Amoco Oil: The Culture, the Principles, and
  the Contributions"
  Marketing Research, Vol. 1 (June 1989), pp. 3-10.

Boundy, William B., Jr.
  "High Tech Test Marketing at Campbell Soup Company"
  European Research, Vol. 15, No. 1 (1987), pp. 52-60.

Brinkhoff, Hein G. M.
  "How Does Unilever Work With Its MIS? A Case History"
  European Research, Vol. 12 (April 1984), pp. 88-95.

Brock, Sabra, Lipson, Sara, and Levitt, Ron
  "Trends in Marketing Research and Development at Citicorp/Citibank"
  Marketing Research, Vol. 1 (December 1989), pp. 3-8.

Fountain, Eric
  "The Contribution of Research to General Motors' Corporate
  Communications Strategy in the UK"
  Journal of the Market Research Society, Vol. 28 (January 1986), pp.
  25-42.

Haselhurst, Laurence
  "How Pedigree Petfoods Evaluate Their Advertising Spend"
  Admap (June 1988), pp. 29-31.

Russell, Ed, Jr., Adams, Anthony J., and Boundy, Bill
  "High-Tech Test Marketing at Campbell Soup Company"
  Journal of Consumer Marketing, Vol. 3 (Winter 1986), pp. 71-80.

Von Arx, Dolph W.
  "The Many Faces of Market Research: A Company Study" (Lipton)
  Journal of Consumer Research, Vol. 3 (Spring 1986), pp. 87-90.

Wilkinson, George W.
  "Getting and Using Information, the United Way"
  Marketing Research, Vol. 1 (September 1989), pp. 5-12.

4.10 ---------- Unclassified (Management of the Mktg Res Function)

Blamires, Chris and Tinn, Ian
  "Market Research Allocations, Needs and Priorities of the CWS in a
  Changing Economic Climate"
  Journal of the Market Research Society, Vol. 20 (April 1978), pp.
  86-98.

Kelly, J. Steven
  "Practicing Advertising Researchers and Their Views of Academic
  Researchers"
  Journal of Business Research, Vol. 15 (June 1987), pp. 257-68.

5 ----------- MARKETING RESEARCH AND MARKETING MANAGEMENT ------------
        See also (sub)heading(s) 6, 7.

5.01 ---------- Books Re: Marketing Research and Marketing Management

Alderson, Wroe and Shapiro, Stanley J. (editors)
  Marketing and the Computer
  (Englewood Cliffs, NJ: Prentice-Hall, Inc., 1963).

Broadbent, Simon (editor)
  Market Researchers Look at Advertising
  (Sigmatext, 1980), 368 pp.

Brown, Rex V.
  Research and the Credibility of Estimates: An Appraisal Tool for
  Executives and Researchers
  (Boston: Harvard Business School, Division of Research, 1969).

Gelb, Gabriel M. and Gelb, Betsy D.
  Research at the Top: Better Data for Organizational Policy Making
  American Marketing Association Monograph Series No. 2
  (Chicago: The American Marketing Association), 29 pp.

Glaser, Edward M., Abelson, H. H., and Garrison, K. N.
  Putting Knowledge to Use
  (San Francisco: Josey-Bass Publishers, 1983).

Greyser, Stephen A.
  Improving Business and Academic Collaboration on Research in Marketing
  (Cambridge, MA: Marketing Science Institute, 1977).

Lothrop, Warren C.
  Management Uses of Research and Development
  (New York, NY: Harper and Row, Publishers, 1964), 148 pp.

National Industrial Conference Board, Inc.
  Using Marketing Consultants and Research Agencies
  (New York: NICB, Inc., 1966), 64 pp.

Orlans, Harold
  Contracting for Knowledge
  (San Francisco: Jossey-Bass, 1973).

Rothman, J.
  Using Research in Organizations
  (Beverly Hills, CA: Sage Publications, 1979).

Zaltman, G.
  "Constructing Knowledge Use"
  in Knorr, K., Strasser, H., and Holzner, B. (editors)
  The Political Realization of Social Science Knowledge and Research:
  Toward New Scenarios
  (Frankfurt: Physica Verlag, 1982).

5.02 ---------- Articles etc. Re: Mktg Res and Marketing Management

Abrahamsen, Egil
  "Research for Decision Making"
  European Research, Vol. 5 (November 1977), pp. 249-58.

Adler, Lee
  "Working With Researchers"
  Sales and Marketing Management (November 8, 1976), pp. 116-20.

Adler, Lee
  "Phasing Research Into the Marketing Plan"
  Harvard Business Review, Vol. 38 (May-June 1960), pp. 113-22.

Advertising Age
  "Research Seeks Better Strategic Uses and Higher Survey Response"
  (July 12, 1976), p. 1.

Albaum, G., Tull, D. S., Hanson, J., and Lineweaver, M.
  "The Use by Business of Expected Value Information in Marketing
  Research Decisions"
  Proceedings, Western AIDS Conference
  (Chicago: American Institute for Decision Sciences, 1978).

Alexander, Ralph
  "The Marketing Manager's Dilemma"
  Journal of Marketing, Vol. 30 (January 1966), pp. 62,3.

Assael, Henry and Wilson, C. E.
  "Integrating Consumer and In-Store Research to Evaluate Sales Results"
  Journal of Marketing, Vol. 36 (April 1972), pp. 40-5.

Bailey, Lawrence F. and Scott-Jones, Gill
  "What is the Research Buyer Buying?"
  Management Decision, Vol. 26, No. 1 (1988), pp. 16-9.

Bartram, Peter
    "The Communication of Results: The Neglected Art in Market Research"
    Market Research Society Conference (March 1984), pp. 99-109.

Bellenger, D. N.
    "The Marketing Manager's View of Marketing Research"
    Business Horizons, Vol. 22 (June 1979), pp. 59-65.

Belson, William A.
    "Increasing the Power of Research to Guide Advertising Decisions"
    Journal of Marketing, Vol. 29 (April 1965), pp. 35-42.

Bogart, Leo
    "The Researcher's Dilemma"
    Journal of Marketing, Vol. 26 (January 1962), pp. 6-11.

Brown, L. Dave
    "Research Action, Organizational Feedback, Understanding, and Change"
    Journal of Applied Behavioral Science, Vol. 8 (November-December
    1972), pp. 697-711.

Calder, Bobby J., Phillips, Lynn W., and Tybout, Alice M.
    "Designing Research for Application"
    Journal of Consumer Research, Vol. 8 (September 1981), pp. 197-207.

Cardwell, Jack
    "Management Science and Marketing--Marriage on the Rocks?"
    California Management Review, Vol. 10 (Summer 1968), pp. 3-12.

Channon, Charles
    "Research Modes and Management Styles"
    International Journal of Advertising, Vol. 5, No. 2 (1986), pp.
    161-74.

Channon, Charles
    "Research Modes and Management Styles"
    Journal of Advertising Research, Vol. 25 (October/November 1985), pp.
    RC4-9.

Channon, C.
    "The Role of Advertising Research in Management Decision-Making"
    Market Research Society Conference (1968).

Charnes, A., Cooper, W. W., Learner, D. B., and Phillips, F. Y.
    "Management Science and Marketing Management"
    Journal of Marketing, Vol. 49 (Spring 1985), pp. 93-105.

Christopher, Martin
    "Marketing Research and the Real World"
    European Research, Vol. 6 (May 1978), pp. 93-8.

Crawford, C. Merle
    "Marketing Research and the New Product Failure Rate"
    Journal of Marketing, Vol. 41 (April 1977), pp. 51-61.

Crespi, Irving
    "The Application of Survey Research Methods to 'Model Line' Decisions"
    Journal of Marketing Research, Vol. I (February 1964), pp. 30-4.

Crosier, Keith
    "How Effective is the Contribution of Market Research to Social
    Marketing?"
    Journal of the Market Research Society, Vol. 21 (January 1979), pp.
    3-16.

Deshpande, Rohit
    "The Organizational Context of Market Research Use"
    Journal of Marketing, Vol. 46 (Fall 1982), pp. 91-101.

Deshpande, Rohit
    "Action and Enlightenment Functions of Research: Comparing Private-
    and Public-Sector Perspectives"
    Knowledge: Creation, Diffusion, Utilization, Vol. 2 (March 1981), pp.
    317-30.

Deshpande, Rohit and Zaltman, Gerald
    "A Comparison of Factors Affecting Use of Marketing Information in
    Consumer and Industrial Firms"
    Journal of Marketing Research, Vol. XXIV (February 1987), pp. 114-8.

Deshpande, Rohit and Zaltman, Gerald
    "The Use of Market Research in Industrial Organizations"
    in Spekman, R. and Wilson, D. (editors)
    Strategic Business Marketing
    (Chicago: American Marketing Association, 1985), pp. 58-66.

Deshpande, Rohit and Zaltman, Gerald
   "The Characteristics of Knowledge Use: Corporate and Public Policy
   Insights"
   in Mokwa, M. and Permut, S. (editors)
   Government Marketing: Theory and Practice
   (New York: Praeger Publishers, 1981), pp. 270-8.

Eder, Peter F.
   "Merchandise All Research Results Within Corporation"
   Marketing News, Vol. 19 (January 4, 1985), pp. 40,1.

Eighmey, John
   "The Main Effects of Science on Advertising: The Good, the Bad, and
   the Ugly"
   Journal of Advertising Research, Vol. 28 (February/March 1988), pp.
   RC3-6.

Ernst, L. A.
   "703 Reasons Why Creative People Don't Trust Research"
   Advertising Age (February 10, 1976), pp. 35,6.

Fram, Eugene H.
   "The Swingman in Communicating With Management"
   Journal of Marketing Research, Vol. VIII (February 1971), pp. 128-9.

Fram, Eugene H.
   "Middle Managers Meet the Computer"
   Sales Management, Vol. 102 (April 15, 1969), pp. 41-6; (May 1, 1969),
   41-4; (May 15, 1969), pp. 41-6.

Gagnard, Alice L. and Swartz, James E.
   "Top American Advertising Managers View Agencies and Research"
   Journal of Advertising Research, Vol. 28 (December 1988/January
   1989), pp. 35-40.

Gagnard, Alice L. and Swartz, James E.
   "An Evaluation of Advertising Research and Research Publications by
   Leading American Advertising Managers"
   Proceedings, American Academy of Advertising (1986).

Gerhold, Paul E. J.
   "Point of View: What the User Owes the Researcher"
   Journal of Advertising Research, Vol. 10 (February 1970), p. 41.

Geurts, Michael D. and Wheeler, Gloria E.
   "Converging Conflicting Research Findings: The Oregon Bottle Bill
   Case"
   Journal of Marketing Research, Vol. XVII (November 1980), pp. 552-7.

Gloor, Max
   "The Contribution of Market Research to Marketing Strategy"
   European Research, Vol. 4 (May 1976), pp. 93-100.

Gordon, Howard L.
   "Yes, Virginia, Research Helps Make Better Advertisements"
   Journal of Marketing, Vol. 31 (January 1967), pp. 64-6.

Gordon, Howard L.
   "What is the Next Breakthough in Research?"
   Journal of Marketing, Vol. 29 (January 1965), pp. 25-7.

Greyser, Stephen A.
   "Academic Research Marketing Managers Can Use"
   Journal of Advertising Research, Vol. 18 (April 1978), pp. 9-14.

Halpern, Richard S.
   "Advice to Researchers: Strategic Planning for the Future!"
   European Research, Vol. 12 (April 1984), pp. 60-7.

Hardin, D. K.
   "Marketing Research and Productivity"
   in Greer, T. V. (editor)
   Proceedings of the AMA Educators' Conference
   (Chicago: American Marketing Association, 1973), pp. 169-71.

Holbert, Neil Bruce
   "Research: The Ways of Academic and Business"
   Business Horizons (February 1976).

Holbert, Neil
   "How Managers See Marketing Research"
   Journal of Advertising Research, Vol. 14 (December 1974), pp. 41-6.

Jones, Sue
   "Problem-Definition in Marketing Research: Facilitating Dialog
   Between Clients and Researchers"
   Psychology and Marketing, Vol. 2 (Summer 1985), pp. 83-92.

Keane, John G.
  "Some Observations on Marketing Research in Top Management Decision
  Making"
  Journal of Marketing, Vol. 33 (October 1969), pp. 10-5.

King, Stephen
  "Applying Research to Decision Making"
  London Business School Review (Winter 1983).

King, Stephen
  "Advertising Research for New Brands"
  Journal of the Market Research Society, Vol. 10 (July 1968), pp.
  145-56.

Krum, James R.
  "B for Marketing Research Departments"
  Journal of Marketing, Vol. 42 (October 1978), pp. 8-12.

Krum, James R., Rau, Pradeep A., and Keiser, Stephen K.
  "The Marketing Research Process: Role Perceptions of Researchers and
  Users"
  Journal of Advertising Research, Vol. 27 (December 1987/January
  1988), pp. 9-21.

Larsen, Judith K.
  "The Nature of Information Utilization in Large Organizations"
  in Knorr, K. Strasser, H., and Holzner, B. (editors)
  The Political Realization of Social Science Knowledge and Research:
  Toward New Scenarios
  (Frankfurt: Phssica Verlag, 1982).

Larsen, Judith K.
  "Knowledge Utilization: What is It"
  Knowledge: Creation, Diffusion, Utilization, Vol. 1, No. 3 (1980),
  pp. 421-42.

Lehman, Charles C.
  "The Ambiguities of Actionable Research"
  Journal of Marketing, Vol. 41 (October 1977), pp. 21-3.

Lingwood, D. A.
  "Producing Usable Research"
  American Behavioral Scientist, Vol. 22 (January-February 1979), pp.
  339-62.

Luck, David J. and Krum, James R.
  "Conditions Conducive to the Effective Use of Marketing Research in
  the Corporation"
  (Cambridge, MA: Marketing Science Institute, 1981), working paper.

McCall, David B.
  "What Agency Managers Want From Research"
  Journal of Advertising Research, Vol. 14 (August 1974), pp. 7-10.

McDaniel, Stephen W. and Parasuraman, A.
  "Small Business Experience With and Attitudes Toward Formal Marketing
  Research"
  American Journal of Small Business, Vol. 9 (Spring 1985), pp. 1-6.

Moss, M. G.
  "What the Marketing Men Require From Research"
  Marketing Research Society Annual Conference (1967).

Myers, John G., Greyser, Stephen A., and Massy, William F.
  "The Effectiveness of Marketing's 'R and D' for Marketing Management:
  An Assessment"
  Journal of Marketing, Vol. 43 (January 1979), pp. 17-29.

Newman, Joseph W.
  "Putting Research Into Marketing Decisions"
  in Barksdale, H. and Weilbacker, W. (editors)
  Marketing Research
  (New York, NY: Ronald Press, 1966), pp. 48-73.

Newman, Joseph W.
  "Put Research Into Marketing Decisions"
  Harvard Business Review, Vol. 40 (March-April 1962), pp. 105-12.

O'Dell, William F.
  "Theory or Research for the Marketing Decision-Maker?"
  Journal of Marketing, Vol. 30 (April 1966), pp. 52-5.

Overholser, Charles E. and Kline, John M.
  "Advertising Strategy From Consumer Research"
  Journal of Advertising Research, Vol. 11 (October 1971), pp. 3-9.

Parent, Michael
  "Marketing Research: A Strategic/Competitor Focus"
  European Marketing, Vol. 14, No. 1 (1986), pp. 17-28.

Percy, Larry
    "How Market Segmentation Guides Advertising Strategy"
    Journal of Advertising Research, Vol. 16 (October 1976), pp. 11-22.

Posner, F. I.
    "Research Needs to Move to the Board Room"
    Advertising Age (May 17, 1984).

Prince, Melvin
    "Market Research: Adaptive or Creative"
    Marketing Review, Vol. 22 (October 1966), pp. 11-27.

Radnor, M., Rubenstein, A., and Bean, A.
    "Integration and Utilization of Management Science Activities in
    Organizations"
    Operational Research Quarterly, Vol. 19 (June 1968), pp. 117-41.

Ramond, Charles
    "Editorial: On Getting Research Used"
    Journal of Advertising Research, Vol. 14 (April 1974), pp. 47,8.

Reynolds, Thomas J. and Gutman, Jonathan
    "Advertising is Image Management"
    Journal of Advertising Research, Vol. 24 (February/March 1984), pp.
    27-37.

Ritchie, J. R. Brent
    "Roles of Research in the Management Process"
    Business Topics (Summer 1976), pp. 13-22.

Roberts, Edward
    "Strategies for Improving Research Utilization"
    Technology Review, Vol. 80 (March-April 1978), pp. 33-9.

Roberts, Harry V.
    "The Role of Research in Marketing Management"
    Journal of Marketing, Vol. 21 (July 1957), pp. 21-32.

Rosch, J. Thomas
    "Marketing Research and the Legal Requirements of Advertising"
    Journal of Marketing, Vol. 39 (July 1975), pp. 69-72.

Rosenberg, Richard D.
    "Integrating Strategy, Industrial Product Innovation and Marketing
    Research"
    International Journal of Research in Marketing, Vol. 5, No. 3 (1989),
    pp. 199-211.

Rotfeld, Herbert J., Tinkham, Spencer F., and Reid, Leonard N.
    "What Research Managers Think of Advertising Research by Academics"
    Proceedings, American Academy of Advertising (1983).

Ruch, D. M.
    "Getting the Lowdown...On the Role of Market Research in the
    Corporation"
    Advertising Age (October 1982).

Schultz, Don E.
    "Media Research Users Want"
    Journal of Advertising Research, Vol. 19 (December 1979), pp. 13-7.

Siegel, Henry J.
    "Advertising Research--A Key Tool in Selling"
    Business Perspectives, Vol. 2 (Fall 1965), pp. 31-3.

Simmons, Martin
    "Market Research as an Aid to the Corporate Marketing Decisions for
    Retailers"
    Journal of the Market Research Society, Vol. 14 (July 1972), pp.
    152-70.

Small, Robert and Rosenberg, Larry
    "The Researcher as a Decision Maker: Myth or Reality?"
    Journal of Marketing, Vol. 39 (January 1975), pp. 2-7.

Smith, Stewart A.
    "Research and Pseudo-Research in Marketing"
    Harvard Business Review, Vol. 52 (March-April 1974), pp. 73-6.

Spencer, William J. and Triant, Deborah D.
    "Strengthening the Link Between R and D and Corporate Strategy"
    Journal of Business Strategy, Vol. 10 (January/February 1989).

Tauber, Edward M.
    "Point of View: How to Get Advertising Strategy From Research"
    Journal of Advertising Research, Vol. 20 (October 1980), pp. 67-72.

Tauber, Edward M.
    "How Market Research Discourages Major Innovation"
    Business Horizons (June 1974), pp. 22-6.

Treasure, J.
  "Market Research and Business Efficiency"
  Advertising Quarterly (Summer 1965), pp. 44-50.

Tuvee, Louis
  "A New Challenge: Strategic Research"
  European Research, Vol. 13 (October 1985), pp. 24-8.

Twyman, W. A.
  "Designing Advertising Research for Marketing Decisions"
  Journal of the Market Research Society, Vol. 15, No. 2 (1973).

Van Der Linden, L. A.
  "Untying Knots"
  European Research, Vol. 7 (September 1979), pp. 222-7.

Wottawa, H.
  "Some Suggestions for the More Efficient Use of Experience in
  Marketing and Marketing Research"
  European Research, Vol. 10 (July 1982), pp. 131-42.

Zaltman, Gerald
  "Knowledge Utilization as Planned Social Change"
  Knowledge: Creation, Diffusion, Utilization, Vol. 1 (September 1979),
  pp. 82-105.

Zaltman, Gerald and Moorman, Christine
  "The Importance of Personal Trust in the Use of Research"
  Journal of Advertising Research, Vol. 28 (October/November 1988), pp.
  16-24.

5.03 ---------- Interface Between Mktg Res and Other Functions

Berenson, Conrad
  "The R and D--Marketing Interface: A General Analogue Model for
  Technology Diffusion"
  Journal of Marketing, Vol. 32 (April 1968), pp. 8-15.

Biller, Allan D. and Shanley, Edward S.
  "Understanding the Conflict Between R and D and Other Groups"
  Research Management, Vol. 18 (September 1975), pp. 16-21.

Bush, Alan J. and Lucas, George H., Jr.
  "Personality Profiles of Marketing vs. R and D Managers"
  Psychology and Marketing, Vol. 5 (Spring 1988), pp. 17-32.

Carroad, Paul A. and Carroad, Connie A.
  "Strategic Interfacing of R and D and Marketing"
  Research Management, Vol. 25 (January 1982), pp. 28-33.

Dunn, M. James and Harnden, Boyd M.
  "Interface of Marketing and R and D Personnel in the Product
  Innovation Stream"
  Journal of the Academy of Marketing Science, Vol. 3 (Winter 1975),
  pp. 20-33.

Gruber, W. H., Poensgen, Otto, and Prakke, Frits
  "Isolation of R and D From Corporate Management"
  Research Management, Vol. 16 (November 1973).

Gupta, Ashok K., Raj, S. P., and Wilemon, David
  "A Model for Studying R and D--Marketing Interface in the Product
  Innovation Process"
  Journal of Marketing, Vol. 50 (April 1986), pp. 7-17.

Gupta, Ashok K., Raj, S. P., and Wilemon, David
  "The R and D--Marketing Interface in High-Technology Firms"
  Journal of Product Innovation Management, Vol. 2 (1985), pp. 12-24.

Hammond, J. S.
  "The Roles of the Manager and the Management Scientist in Successful
  Implementation"
  Sloan Management Review, Vol. 16 (1974), pp. 1-24.

Millman, A. F.
  "Understanding Barriers to Product Innovation at the R and D /
  Marketing Interface"
  European Journal of Marketing, Vol. 16, No. 5 (1982), pp. 22-34.

Monteleone, J. P.
  "How R and D and Marketing Can Work Together"
  Research Management, Vol. 19 (March 1976), pp. 19-21.

Plummer, Joseph T.
  "The Dialogue That Needs to Happen"
  Psychology and Marketing, Vol. 1 (Spring 1984), pp. 5-16.

Schlackman, W.
  "The Interface Between Marketing Research, Management and Marketing
  Management in User Organizations"
  Market Research Society Conference (1979).

Souder, W. E.
  "Disharmony Between R and D and Marketing"
  Industrial Marketing Management, Vol. 10 (February 1981), pp. 67-73.

Souder, W. E.
  "Promoting an Effective R and D/Marketing Interface"
  Research Management, Vol. 23 (July 1980), pp. 10-5.

Souder, W. E.
  An Exploratory Study of the Coordinating Mechanisms Between R and D
  and Marketing as an Influence on the Innovation Process
  Final Report to the National Science Foundation
  (Pittsburgh: University of Pittsburgh, School of Engineering, 1977).

Souder, W. E. and Chakrabarti, Alok K.
  "The R and D/Marketing Interface: Results From an Empirical Study of
  Innovation Projects"
  IEEE Transactions on Engineering Management, EM-25 (November 1978),
  pp. 88-93.

Vaughn, Richard L.
  "Point of View: Creatives Versus Researchers: Must They be
  Adversaries?"
  Journal of Advertising Research, Vol. 22 (December 1982/January
  1983), pp. 45-8.

Wells, William D.
  "Point of View: How to End the Never Ending"
  Journal of Advertising Research, Vol. 23 (April/May 1983), pp. 67,8.

Young, H. C.
  Product Development Setting, Information Exchange, and Marketing--R
  and D Coupling
  Northwestern University (1973), Ph.D. dissertation.

5.04 ---------- Studies of Evaluation/Use of Mktg Res by Managers

Alpander, G.
  "Use of Quantitative Methods in International Operations by US
  Overseas Executives"
  Management International Review, Vol. 16 (1976), pp. 71-7.

Borgida, Eugene and Nisbett, Richard
  "The Differential Impact of Abstract vs. Concrete Information on
  Decision"
  Journal of Applied Social Psychology, Vol. 7 (July-September 1977),
  pp. 258-71.

DeSanctis, Geraldine
  "An Examination of an Expectancy Theory Model of Decision Support
  System Use"
  Proceedings, Third International Conference on Information Systems
  (December 1985), pp. 121-35.

Deshpande, Rohit
  "The Organizational Context of Market Research Use"
  Journal of Marketing, Vol. 46 (Fall 1982), pp. 91-101.

Deshpande, Rohit
  "Toward a Theoretical Model of the Utilization of Marketing Research
  Information for Consumer Product Strategy Decisions"
  University of Pittsburgh (1976), unpublished Ph.D. dissertation.

Deshpande, Rohit and Jeffries, Scott
  "Attributes Affecting the Use of Marketing Research in Decision
  Making: An Empirical Investigation"
  in Bernhardt, Kenneth L. et al. (editors)
  Educators' Conference Proceedings, Series #47
  (Chicago: American Marketing Association, 1981), pp. 1-4.

Deshpande, Rohit and Zaltman, Gerald
  "A Comparison of Factors Affecting Researcher and Manager Perceptions
  of Market Research Use"
  Journal of Marketing Research, Vol. XXI (February 1984), pp. 32-8.

Deshpande, Rohit and Zaltman, Gerald
  "Patterns of Research Use in Private and Public Sectors"
  Knowledge: Creation, Diffusion, Utilization, Vol. 4 (June 1983), pp.
  561-75.

Deshpande, Rohit and Zaltman, Gerald
  "Factors Affecting the Use of Market Research Information: A Path
  Analysis"
  Journal of Marketing Research, Vol. XIX (February 1982), pp. 14-31.

Elliott, Richard and Jobber, David
"Expanding the Market for Marketing Research: Factors Discriminating Users From Nonusers of Research"
Proceedings, Market Research Society Conference (March 1988), pp. 155-79.

Hamill, Ruth, Wilson, Timothy D., and Nisbett, Richard E.
"Insensitivity to Sample Bias: Generalizing From Atypical Cases"
Journal of Personality and Social Psychology, Vol. 39 (October 1980), pp. 578-89.

Hooley, Graham J.
"The Untapped Markets for Marketing Research"
Journal of the Market Research Society, Vol. 26 (October 1984), pp. 335-52.

Hu, Michael Y.
"An Experimental Study of Managers' and Researchers' Use of Consumer Marketing Research"
Journal of the Academy of Marketing Science, Vol. 14 (Fall 1986), pp. 44-51.

Kahneman, Daniel and Tversky, Amos
"On the Psychology of Prediction"
Psychological Review, Vol. 80 (July 1973), pp. 237-51.

Kahneman, Daniel and Tversky, Amos
"Subjective Probability: A Judgment of Representativeness"
Cognitive Psychology, Vol. 3 (July 1972), pp. 430-54.

Lee, Hanjoon, Acito, Frank, and Day, Ralph L.
"Evaluation and Use of Marketing Research by Decision Makers: A Behavioral Simulation"
Journal of Marketing Research, Vol. XXIV (May 1987), pp. 187-96.

Piercy, Nigel
"The Power and Politics of Marketing Information"
Journal of the Market Research Society, Vol. 28 (October 1986), pp. 379,80.

Tversky, Amos and Kahneman, Daniel
"Belief in the Law of Small Numbers"
Psychological Bulletin, Vol. 76 (August 1971), pp. 105-10.

Zaltman, Gerald and Deshpande, Rohit
"The Use of Market Research: An Exploratory Study of Manager and Researcher Perspectives"
(Cambridge, MA: Marketing Science Institute, 1982), working paper.

Zinkhan, George M., Joachimsthaler, Erich A., and Kinnear, Thomas C.
"Individual Differences and Marketing Decision Support System Usage and Satisfaction"
Journal of Marketing Research, Vol. XXIV (May 1987), pp. 208-14.

5.05 ---------- Applications of Mktg Res to Marketing Strategy

Aldridge, David N. and Jacobs, Antone
"Overseas Research: A Television Program"
Proceedings, ESOMAR Congress, Special Sessions, Monte Carlo (1986), pp. 53-67.

Berger, David
"Theory Into Practice: The FCB Grid"
European Research, Vol. 14, No. 1 (1986), pp. 35-46.

Bhaduri, Monika
"Developing an International Advertising Strategy for Johnnie Walker Red Label: Looking Back Into the Future"
Proceedings, ESOMAR Congress, Monte Carlo (1986), pp. 441-65.

Black, T. R. L. and Farley, J. U.
"The Application of Market Research in Contraceptive Social Marketing in a Rural Area of Kenya"
Journal of the Market Research Society, Vol. 21, No. 1 (1979), pp. 30-43.

Bonvini, Vanna and Colacicco, Lia
"Diamonds for Men: The Contribution of Research in Identifying Their Trend Setters"
Proceedings, ESOMAR Congress, Monte Carlo (1986), pp. 217-45.

Broadbent, Kay and Cooper, Peter
"Research is Good for You: The Contribution of Research to Guinness Advertising"
Proceedings, Market Research Society Conference (March 1986), pp. 265-79.

Conway, Steffen and Welch, Helen
    "The Use of Research for Petrol Promotions"
    Proceedings, Market Research Society Conference (March 1986), pp.
    235-43.

Dallin, Ray, Hagen, Dan, and Van Westerhoven, Emile
    "The Computerised Automatic Ironing Machine--A Case Study in North
    America and Europe of Research in Support of an Innovative New
    Domestic Appliance"
    Proceedings, ESOMAR Congress, Monte Carlo (1986), pp. 199-215.

Dove, C. J. and Eborall, Christine
    "Out of the Darkroom into the Daylight: From Quantitative Research to
    New Strategies in the European Graphic Arts Market"
    ESOMAR Congress, Montreux (1987), pp. 793-811.

Drake, Nick J. and Winton, David S.
    "The Contribution Made by a Marketing Research Programme Towards the
    Development of a New Major Insurance Product"
    European Research, Vol. 5 (January 1977), pp. 34-44.

Fountain, Eric, Parker, Ian, and Samuels, John
    "The Contribution of Research to General Motors' Corporate
    Communications Strategy in the UK"
    Journal of the Market Research Society, Vol. 28 (January 1986), pp.
    25-42.

Fountain, Eric, Parker, Ian, and Samuels, John
    "The Contribution of Research to GM's Corporate Communications
    Strategy in the UK"
    Award-Winning Papers, 38th ESOMAR Congress, Wiesbaden (September
    1985), pp. 3-9. and European Research, Vol. 13 (October 1985).

Handley, Paul and Macey, Frank
    "'Poundsaver': The Application of Research Techniques to New Product
    Development"
    European Research, Vol. 6 (May 1978), pp. 110-8.

Hartnell, Katherine and Hayes, Peter
    "The Commercial Rejuvenation of Docklands"
    Proceedings, Market Research Society Conference (March 1988), pp.
    333-49.

Higgs, Alan and Shaddick, Colin
    "The Independent--How Research was Used to Help Launch the First New
    Quality Newspaper in Britain in 131 Years"
    Proceedings, Market Research Society Conference (March 1987), pp.
    555-71.

Maiani, Daniela, Van Schijndel, Chris, and Van der Vegt, Joop
    "From Clay Model to Consumer Satisfaction: The Development of a
    Modern Passenger Car and the Role of Market Research"
    ESOMAR Congress, Montreux (1987), pp. 165-86.

Marles, Vivien and Nohr, Nadine
    "EastEnders: The Role of Research in the Launch of a New Brand Into a
    Difficult Market"
    Proceedings, Market Research Society Conference (March 1986), pp.
    295-317.

Licietis, Ivars and Walshe, Peter
    "Come into the Garden Centre, Maude"
    Proceedings, Market Research Society Conference (March 1986), pp.
    123-47.

Lovatt, D. Jerry
    "The Contribution of Consumer Research to the Development of an
    International Advertising Campaign: 'The Man From Del Monte'"
    Proceedings, ESOMAR Congress, Lisbon (1988), pp. 567-85.

Naeve, Donna
    "Integrating Multi-Country Research Into Marketing Strategy
    Decisions: A Case History"
    Award-Winning Papers, 39th ESOMAR Congress, Monte Carlo (September
    1986), pp. 4-9 and European Research, Vol. 14, No. 4 (1986).

Naylor, Geoffrey and Bowen, Jennifer
    "Market Research and the 15 Billion Pound Merger"
    Proceedings, Market Research Society Conference (March 1986), pp.
    185-203.

Oliver, Rodney A.
    "An Evaluation of the Use Made of Evaluation Research in a National
    Tourist Board"
    Journal of the Market Research Society, Vol. 19 (October 1977), pp.
    151-66.

Phillips, Hugh
   "Corporate Logo Research--A Case Study"
   Journal of the Market Research Society, Vol. 20 (October 1978), pp.
   219-27.

Taylor, Fenella and Twyman, W. A. Tony
   "The Effects of Publicity Against Heroin Abuse: A Case History of
   Research for Decision Making"
   ESOMAR Congress, Montreux (1987), pp. 242-400.

Taylor, Fenella, Irving, Andrew, and Twyman, W. A. Tony
   "Developing and Evaluating a Campaign Against Heroin Abuse: Research
   in Action"
   Proceedings, Market Research Society Conference (March 1987), pp.
   1-35.

Tee, Lorna
   "London Theatre: Next Stage"
   European Research, Vol. 14, No. 1 (1986), pp. 12-4.

Termini, Deanne and Harper, Jim
   "Marketing a Regional Newspaper: 'Positioning Research' for the
   Nottingham Evening Post"
   Admap (January 1987), pp. 40-4.

Wolfsie, Budd G.
   "Market Research in the Development of a New Typewriter"
   Journal of Marketing Research, Vol. I (February 1964), pp. 35-7.

Zanner, Rene D.
   "Applications of Survey Research in Corporate Decision-Making"
   in Olshavsky, Richard W. (editor)
   Attitude Research Enters the 80s
   (Chicago: American Marketing Association, 1980).

6 ------------ MARKETING DECISION SUPPORT SYSTEMS (MDSSs) ------------
        See also (sub)heading(s) 5, 7.

6.01 ---------- Books Re: Marketing Decision Support Systems (MDSSs)

Goffman, William and Warren, Kenneth S.
    Scientific Information Systems and the Principle of Selectivity
    (New York: Praeger Publications, 1980), 189 pp.

Keen, Peter G. W. and Morton, Michael S. Scott
    Decision Support Systems: An Organizational Perspective
    (Reading, MA: Addison-Wesley, 1978).

Konrad, Evelyn et al.
    Computer Innovations in Marketing
    (New York: American Management Association, 1970), 387 pp.

Lucas, Henry C., Jr.
    The Implementation of Computer-Based Models
    (New York: National Association of Accountants, 1976).

Mayros, Van and Werner, D. Michael
    Marketing Information Systems: Design and Applications for Marketers
    (Radner, PA: Chilton Book Company, 1982), 330 pp.

Michie, D. (editor)
    Expert Systems in the Microelectronic Age
    (New York: Columbia University Press, 1980).

Miller, David W. and Starr, Martin K.
    Executive Decisions and Operations Research, Second Edition
    (Englewood Cliffs, NJ: Prentice-Hall, Inc., 1969), 607 pp.

Shaffir, Kurt H. and Trentin, George H.
    Marketing Information Systems
    (New York: American Management Association, 1973), 325 pp.

Smith, S. V., Brien, R. H., and Stafford, J. E.
    Readings in Marketing Information Systems: A New Era in Marketing
    Research
    (Boston: Houghton Mifflin Company, 1968), 399 pp.

Sprague, R. H. and Watson, J. J. (editors)
    Decision Support Systems: Putting Theory Into Practice
    (Englewood Cliffs, NJ: Prentice-Hall 1986).

Stern, M. E.
    Marketing Planning
    (New York: McGraw-Hill, 1966), 160 pp.

Tomeski, Edward
    The Executive Use of Computers
    (New York, NY: Collier Books, 1969), 146 pp.

6.02 ---------- State of Marketing Decision Support Systems

Boone, L. E. and Kurtz, David L.
    "Marketing Information Systems: Current Status in American Industry"
    in Alvine, F. C. (editor)
    Proceedings, National Conference of the American Marketing
    Association (1971), pp. 163-7.

Fletcher, K. P.
    "Marketing Information Systems in British Industry"
    Management Decision, Vol. 21, No. 2 (1983), pp. 25-36.

Jobber, David
    "Marketing Information Systems in US and British Industry"
    Management Decision, Vol. 15, No. 2 (1977), pp. 297-304.

Jobber, David and Rainbow, C.
    "A Study of the Development and Implementation of Marketing
    Information Systems in British Industry"
    Journal of the Market Research Society, Vol. 19 (July 1977), pp.
    104-11.

McLeod, Raymond, Jr.
    "Marketing Information Systems--A Review"
    Quarterly Review of Marketing (Spring 1985), pp. 7-18.

McLeod, Raymond, Jr. and Rogers, John C.
    "Marketing Information Systems: Their Current Status in Fortune 1000
    Companies"
    Journal of Management Information Systems, Vol. 1 (Spring 1985), pp.
    57-75.

McLeod, Raymond, Jr. and Rogers, John C.
    "Marketing Information Systems: Uses in the Fortune 500"
    California Management Review, Vol. 25 (Fall 1982), pp. 106-18.

6.03 ---------- Articles etc. Re: MDSSs

Absatzwirtchaft
  "Management Information Systems and Marketing Mix Optimisation"
  European Research, Vol. 11 (April 1983), pp. 79-84.

Ackoff, Russell L.
  "Management Misinformation Systems"
  Management Science, Vol. 14 (December 1967), pp. 147-56.

Adler, L.
  "Systems Approach to Marketing"
  Harvard Business Review, Vol. 45 (May-June 1967), pp. 105-18.

Amstutz, Arnold E.
  "Market-Oriented Management Systems: The Current Status"
  Journal of Marketing Research, Vol. VI (November 1969), pp. 481-96.

Amstutz, A. E.
  "Shaping the Management Environment--First Step in Designing a
  Management-Decision System"
  Computer Operations--The Management Forum on Data Processing
  (March-April 1969), pp. 44-50.

Amstutz, A. E.
  "The Evolution of Management Information Systems"
  European Business (April 1968), pp. 24-33.

Amstutz, A. E.
  "The Marketing Executive and Management Systems"
  in Britt, S. H. and Boyd, H. (editors)
  Marketing Management and Administrative Action
  (New York: McGraw-Hill Book Co., 1968), pp. 730-46.

Amstutz, Arnold E.
  "A Basic Market Oriented Information System"
  Working Paper No. 307-68
  Sloan School of Management, M.I.T. (1968).

Amstutz, Arnold E.
  "The Marketing Executive and Management Information Systems"
  in Haas, Raymond M. (editor)
  Science, Technology, and Marketing
  (Chicago: American Marketing Association, 1966), pp. 69-86.

Amstutz, A. E.
  "A Basic Management Information System"
  The Marketing Concept in Action
  (Chicago: American Marketing Association, June 1964).

Assmus, Gert
  "Evaluating Changes in the Marketing Information System"
  European Journal of Marketing, Vol. 11, No. 4 (1977), pp. 272-80.

Axelrod, Joel N.
  "14 Rules for Building an MIS"
  Journal of Advertising Research, Vol. 10 (June 1970), pp. 3-11.

Barnard, Stuart
  "Setting Up an In-House Marketing Database"
  Industrial Marketing Digest, Vol. 12, First Quarter, (1987), pp.
  51-60.

Berenson, Conrad
  "Marketing Information Systems"
  Journal of Marketing, Vol. 33 (October 1969), pp. 16-23.

Beyer, Robert
  "A Positive Look at Management Information Systems"
  Financial Executive (June 1968), pp. 50-7.

Brien, Richard H.
  "Marketing Information Systems: The State of the Art"
  in Becker, Boris and Becker, Helmut (editors)
  Dynamic Marketing in a Changing World
  (Chicago: American Marketing Association, 1972), pp. 19-27.

Brien, R. H. and Stafford, J. E.
  "Marketing Information Systems: A New Dimension for Marketing
  Research"
  Journal of Marketing, Vol. 32 (July 1968), pp. 19-23.

Brinkhoff, Hein G. M.
  "How Does Unilever Work With Its MIS? A Case History"
  European Research, Vol. 12 (April 1984), pp. 88-95.

Brown, Stephen W. and Goslar, Martin D.
  "New Information Systems for Marketing Decision Making"
  Business, Vol. 38, No. 3 (July-August-September 1988).

Cheney, Paul H. and Dickson, Gary W.
    "Organizational Characteristics and and Information Systems: An
    Exploratory Investigation"
    Academy of Management Journal, Vol. 25, No. 1 (1982), pp. 170-84.

Christian, Richard C.
    "Keeping Pace With the Computer Age"
    Journal of Marketing, Vol. 30 (July 1966), pp. 59-62.

Cohen, Henry M.
    "A MIS That Scores as a Decision-Maker"
    Business Automation (November 1967), pp. 44-8.

Comer, Robert L.
    "Marketing Information Systems: Problems and Issues--A Systems
    Director's Perspective"
    in Alvine, F. C. (editor)
    Marketing in Motion: Relevance in Marketing
    Proceedings, American Marketing Association Conference (1971), pp.
    168-71.

Cox, D. F. and Good, R. E.
    "How to Build a Marketing Information System"
    Harvard Business Review, Vol. 45 (May-June 1967), pp. 145-54.

Dickson, G. W. and Simmons, J. K.
    "The Behavioral Side of MIS"
    Business Horizons, Vol. 13 (1970), pp. 59-71.

Dun's Review and Modern Industry
    "The Office: The Great Information Revolution"
    Vol. 82 (September 1963), p. 94.

Edstrom, Anders
    "User Influence and the Success of the MIS Projects"
    Human Relations, Vol. 30 (1977), pp. 589-607.

Farley, John U., Howard, John A., and Hulbert, James
    "Organizational Approach to an Industrial Marketing Information
    System"
    Sloan Management Review, Vol. XIII (Fall 1971), pp. 35-54.

Fletcher, K. P.
    "Marketing Information Systems: A Lost Opportunity"
    in Thomas, M. J. (editor)
    Bridging the Gap Between Theory and Practice
    Proceedings, Marketing Education Group Conference, Lancaster (1982).

Gibson, Lawrence D., Mayer, Charles S., Nugent, Christopher E., and
    Vollmann, Thomas E.
    "An Evolutionary Approach to Marketing Information Systems"
    Journal of Marketing, Vol. 37 (April 1973), pp. 2-6.

Goslar, Martin D.
    "MKIS Course Trains Students for Business World"
    Marketing News, Vol. 19 (July 19, 1985), p. 11.

Goslar, Martin D. and Brown, Stephen W.
    "Decision Support Systems: Advantages in Consumer Marketing Settings"
    Journal of Consumer Marketing, Vol. 3 (Summer 1986), pp. 43-50.

Goslar, Martin D., Green, Gary I., and Hughes, Terry H.
    "Decision Support Systems: An Empirical Assessment for Decision
    Making"
    Decision Sciences (February 1986).

Graf, F.
    Information Systems for Marketing"
    Marketing Trends, Vol. 2 (1979).

Hackett, D. W.
    "A Conceptual Management Information System for the
    Marketing-Oriented Firm"
    Oklahoma Business Bulletin, Vol. 40 (July 1972), pp. 20-6.

Hulbert, James, Farley, John U., and Howard, John A.
    "Information Processing and Decision Making in Marketing
    Organizations"
    Journal of Marketing Research, Vol. IX (February 1972), pp. 75-7.

Jobber, David and Watts, Martin
    "Organisational Dimensions of Information Systems"
    European Journal of Marketing, Vol. 21, No. 3 (1987), pp. 39-51.

Jobber, David and Watts, Martin
    "Behavioural Aspects of Marketing Information Systems"
    OMEGA International Journal of Management Science, Vol. 14, No. 1
    (1986), pp. 69-79.

Kegerris, Robert J.
  "Marketing Management and the Computer: An Overview of Conflict and
  Contrast"
  Journal of Marketing, Vol. 35 (January 1971), pp. 3-12.

King, William R. and Rodriguez, Jamie I.
  "Participative Design of Strategic Decision Support Systems: An
  Empirical Assessment"
  Management Science, Vol. 27 (June 1981), pp. 717-26.

Knuckles, Barbara M.
  "New Techniques and Changes in Research Design--Their Impact on the
  Brand and Advertising Development Decision Process"
  Journal of Advertising Research, Vol. 26 (October/November 1986), pp.
  RC6-8.

Kotler, Philip
  "The Future of the Computer in Marketing"
  Journal of Marketing, Vol. 34 (January 1970), pp. 11-4.

Kotler, Philip
  "A Design for the Firm's Marketing Nerve Center"
  Business Horizons (Fall 1968), pp. 63-74.

Leslie, Gavin T.
  "Decision Support Systems: Learning to Apply Computers"
  European Research, Vol. 15 (November 1987), pp. 265-70.

Little, John D.
  "Decision Support Systems for Marketing Managers"
  Journal of Marketing, Vol. 43 (Summer 1979), pp. 9-26.

Little, John D., Mohan, L., and Hatoun, A.
  "How Marketing Decision Support Systems can Work for You"
  Industrial Marketing (1982), pp. 46-56.

Losty, P. A.
  "Management Information Systems"
  Cranfield School of Management, paper presentation.

Madansky, Albert
  "Models, Games and Data Banks: Implications for Data Collection"
  Proceedings, Annual Meeting, American Marketing Association (June
  1968), pp. 236-8.

Maish, A. M.
  "A User's Behavior Towards His MIS"
  Management Information Systems Quarterly, Vol. 3, No. 1 (1979), pp.
  39-52.

Malhotra, Naresh K., Tashchian, Armen, and Mahmoud, Essam
  "The Integration of Microcomputers in Marketing Research and Decision
  Making"
  Journal of the Academy of Marketing Science, Vol. 15 (Summer 1987),
  pp. 69-82.

Martell, Deborah
  "Marketing and Information Technology"
  European Journal of Marketing, Vol. 22, No. 9 (1988), pp. 16-24.

Mayer, Charles S., Nugent, Christopher E., and Vollmann, Thomas E.
  "On-Line Data Retrieval and Analysis"
  Proceedings, Annual Meeting American Marketing Association (June
  1969).

McNiven, Malcolm and Hilton, Bob D.
  "Reassessing Marketing Information Systems"
  Journal of Advertising Research, Vol. 10 (February 1970), pp. 3-12.

Mitroff, I. I., Kilmann, R. H., and Barabba, V. P.
  "Management Information Versus Misinformation Systems"
  in Zaltman, G. (editor)
  Management Principles for Nonprofit Agencies
  (New York: AMACOM, 1979), pp. 401-29.

Montgomery, David B.
  "The Outlook for MIS"
  Journal of Advertising Research, Vol. 13 (June 1973), pp. 5-11.

Montgomery, David B. and Urban, Glen L.
  "Marketing Decision-Information Systems: An Emerging View"
  Journal of Marketing Research, Vol. VII (May 1970), pp. 226-34.

Morton, Michael S. Scott
  "Strategic Planning and Management Information Systems--Some
  Implications of Present Research"
  Working Paper No. 168
  Sloan School of Management, M.I.T. (September 27, 1968).

Morton, Michael S. S.
   "Interactive Visual Display Systems and Management Problem Solving"
   Industrial Management Review (Fall 1967), pp. 69-81.

Nijburg, Danny A.
   "Marketing Management Information Systems: How to get Rid of My
   Information?"
   European Research, Vol. 12 (April 1984), pp. 57-9.

Palumbo, Frederick A.
   "Are Bank Marketing Information Systems Relevant?"
   Journal of the Academy of Marketing Science, Vol. 1 (Spring 1973),
   pp. 52-8.

Piercy, Nigel
   "A Social Psychology of Marketing Information--Learning to Cope With
   the Corporate Battleground"
   Journal of the Market Research Society, Vol. 25, No. 2 (1983).

Piercy, Nigel
   "Marketing Information: Bridge the Quicksand Between Technology and
   Decision-Making"
   Quarterly Review of Marketing (Autumn 1981).

Piercy, Nigel
   "Marketing Information Systems: Theory vs. Practice"
   Quarterly Review of Marketing, Vol. 6, No. 1 (1980), pp. 16-24.

Porter, E. H.
   "The Parable of the Spindle"
   Harvard Business Review, Vol. 40 (May-June 1962), pp. 58-66.

Roy, H. S. H.
   "Using Computer-Based Control Systems for Decision Making"
   Advanced Management Journal, Vol. 36 (January 1971), pp. 57-62.

Schewe, Charles D.
   "Marketing Information Systems--The Problem of System Usage"
   Journal of the Academy of Marketing Science, Vol. 2 (Winter 1974),
   pp. 290-8.

Schewe, Charles D.
   "Marketing Information Systems--A Promise Not Yet Realized"
   University of Massachusetts, Amherst, MA (June 1973), working paper.

Schewe, Charles D.
   "The Impact of Marketing Information Systems on System Users'
   Attitudes and System Usage"
   Northwestern University, Evanston, IL (June 1972), unpublished
   doctoral dissertation.

Schewe, Charles D. and Dillon, William R.
   "Marketing Information System Utilization: An Application of
   Self-Concept Theory"
   Journal of Business Research, Vol. 6 (January 1978), pp. 67-79.

Schultz, D. E. and Dewar, R. D.
   "Technology's Challenge to Marketing Management"
   Business Marketing (March 1984).

Seaman, Robert L.
   "A Simulation Approach to the Analytical Aspects of Business
   Acquisition Evaluation"
   Sloan School of Management, M.I.T. (1967), unpublished M.S. thesis.

Smith, Samuel V., Brien, Richard H., and Stafford, James E.
   "Marketing Information Systems: An Introductory Overview"
   in Smith, Samuel V., Brien, Richard H., and Stafford, James E.
   (editors)
   Readings in Marketing information Systems
   (Boston: Houghton Mifflin, 1968), pp. 1-14.

Sparks, Jack D.
   "Taming the 'Paper Elephant' in Marketing Information Systems"
   Journal of Marketing, Vol. 40 (July 1976), pp. 83-6.

Sprague, Ralph H., Jr.
   "A Framework for the Development of Decision Support Systems"
   MIS Quarterly, Vol. 4 (December 1980), pp. 1-26.

Thomas, Daniel T.
   "A Practical Approach to Corporate-Level Computer Based MIS"
   Data Management (October 1968), pp. 22-7.

Trotter, W. R.
   "Organizing a Management Information System"
   Advanced Management Journal, Vol. 34 (April 1969), pp. 40-6.

Uhl, Kenneth P.
  "Better Management of Market Information"
  Business Horizons, Vol. 9 (Spring 1966), pp. 75-82.

Van Nievelt, M. C. Augustus
  "Decision Support Systems Contribute to Better Marketing"
  European Research, Vol. 12 (April 1984), pp. 74-83.

Watkins, E. P. and Vandemark, V. A.
  "Customer Information Strengthens Market Information Systems"
  Journal of Retailing, Vol. 47 (Spring 1971), pp. 50-4.

Weber, Sue
  "Cognitive Processes Involved in Solving Information Systems (IS)
  Design Problems"
  Proceedings, Third International Conference on Information Systems
  (December 1985), pp. 305-12.

Westwood, R. A., Palmer, J. B., Zeitlin, D. M., Levine, D. M., Thio,
  K., and Charney, R.
  "Integrated Information Systems"
  Journal of the Market Research Society, Vol. 17 (July 1975), pp.
  127-80.

Will, H. J.
  "Computerized Marketing Information Systems"
  British Journal of Marketing, Vol. 4 (Autumn 1970), pp. 146-59.

Zani, W. M.
  "Blueprint for Management Information Systems"
  Harvard Business Review, Vol. 48 (November-December 1970), pp. 95-100.

Zannetos, Zenon
  "Toward Intelligent Management Information Systems"
  Industrial Management Review, Vol. 9 (Spring 1968), pp. 21-38.

6.04 ---------- Computer Simulation in MDSSs

        See also (sub)heading(s) 105.

Dolich, Ira
  "Integrating Mainframe Marketing Computer Simulations and
  Microcomputer Information Systems"
  in Belk, Russell et al. (editors)
  Proceedings, AMA Educators' Conference
  (Chicago: American Marketing Association, 1984), pp. 122-6.

Fuerst, William L. and Martin, Merle P.
  "Effective Design and Use of Computer Decision Models"
  MIS Quarterly, Vol. 8 (March 1984), pp. 17-26.

Kotler, Philip and Schultz, Randall L.
  "Marketing Simulations: Review and Prospects"
  Journal of Business, Vol. 43 (July 1970), pp. 237-95.

6.05 ---------- Books Re: Artificial Intelligence, Expert Systems

Alty, J. L. and Coombs, M. J.
  Expert Systems
  (NCC Publications, 1984).

Buchanan, Bruce G. and Shortliffe, Edward H.
  Rule-Based Expert Programs: The MYCIN Experiments of the Stanford
  Heuristic Programming Project
  (Reading, MA: Addison-Wesley Publishing Company, 1984).

Charniak, Eugene and McDermott, Drew
  Introduction to Artificial Intelligence
  (Reading, MA: Addison-Wesley Publishing Company, 1985).

Dreyfus, Hubert L.
  What Computers Can't do: The Limits of Artificial Intelligence
  (New York: Harper and Row, 1972).

Harmon, Paul and King, David
  Expert Systems
  (New York: John Wiley and Sons, Inc., 1985).

Hayes-Roth, Frederick, Waterman, Donald A., and Lenat, Douglas B.
  (editors)
  Building Expert Systems
  (Reading, MA: Addison-Wesley Publishing Co., 1983).

6.06 ---------- Articles Re: Artificial Intelligence, Expert Systems

Bauer, Richard J., Jr. and Griffiths, Mark D.
"Evaluating Expert System Investment: An Introduction to the
Economics of Knowledge"
Journal of Business Research, Vol. 17 (September 1988).

Bayer, Judy and Keon, John W.
"Expert Systems in Marketing: Developmental Issues"
in Lusch, Robert F. et al. (editors)
1985 AMA Educators' Conference Proceedings
(Chicago: American Marketing Association, 1985), pp. 251-5.

Booker, J., Kick, R., and Gardner, J.
"Expert Systems in Accounting: The Next Generation of Computer
Technology"
Journal of Accountancy, Vol. 161 (March 1986), pp. 101-4.

Brachman, Ronald J. et al.
"What are Expert Systems?"
in Hayes-Roth, Waterman, and Lenat (editors)
Building Expert Systems
(Reading, MA: Addison-Wesley, 1983), pp. 31-57.

Buchanan, Bruce G., Barstow, David, Bechtal, Robert, Bennet, William
Clancy, Kulikowski, Casimir, Mitchell, Tom, and Waterman, Donald A.
"Constructing an Expert System"
in Hayes-Roth, Frederick, Waterman, Donald A., and Lenat, Douglas B.
(editors)
Building Expert Systems
(Reading, MA: Addison-Wesley Publishing Company, 1983).

Clifford, James, Jarke, M., and Vassilious, Y.
"Short Introduction to Expert Systems"
IEEE Database Engineering Bulletin, Vol. 8 (December 1983).

Davis, E. John
"The Use of Expert Systems in Marketing"
Proceedings, ESOMAR Congress, Monte Carlo (1986), pp. 281-99.

Davis, Randall
"Expert Systems: Where are We and Where do We go From Here?"
A. I. Memo No. 665
Massachusetts Institute of Technology, Artifical Intelligence
Laboratory (1982).

Fersko-Weiss, Henry
"Expert Systems Decision-Making Power"
Personal Computing (November 1985), pp. 97-105.

Fleck, J.
"Development and Establishment in Artificial Intelligence"
in Bloomfield, B (editor)
A Question of Artificial Intelligence
(London: Croom Helm, 1987), pp. 106-64.

Ford, F. Nelson
"Decision Support Systems and Expert Systems: A Comparison"
Information and Management, Vol. 8 (1985), pp. 21-6.

Gashnig, John, Klahr, P., Pople, H., Shortliffe, E., and Terry, A.
"Evaluation of Expert Systems: Issues and Case Studies"
in Hayes-Roth, Waterman, and Lenat (editors)
Building Expert Systems
(Reading, MA: Addison-Wesley, 1983), pp. 241-80.

Harmon, Paul and King, David
Expert Systems
(New York: John Wiley and Sons, Inc., 1985).

Hayes-Roth, Frederick, Waterman, D. A., and Lenat, D. B.
"An Overview of Expert Systems"
in Hayes-Roth, Waterman, and Lenat (editors)
Building Expert Systems
(Reading, MA: Addison-Wesley, 1983), pp. 3-29.

Holsapple, Clyde and Whinston, Andrew
Manager's Guide to Expert Systems
(Dow Jones-Irwin, 1986).

Keon, John W. and Bayer, Judy
"An Expert Approach to Promotion Management"
New York University (1984).

Kinnucan, Paul
"Software Tools Speed Expert System Development"
High Technology, Vol. 5 (March 1985), pp. 16-20.

Leonard-Barton, Dorothy and Sviokla, John J.
    "Putting Expert Systems to Work"
    Harvard Business Review, Vol. 66 (March-April 1988), pp. 91-8.

Luconi, Fred L., Malone, Thomas W., and Morton, Michael S. Scott
    "Expert Systems: The Next Challenge for Managers"
    Sloan Management Review, Vol. 27 (Summer 1986), pp. 3-14.

Michie, D.
    "Practical Applications of Artificial Intelligence"
    Infotech Conference, London, 1979.

Mingers, J.
    "Inducing Rules for Expert Systems--Statistical Aspects"
    Professional Statistician, Vol. 5 (1988).

Mitchell, Andrew, Sathi, A., Spaulding, C., and Sitole, A.
    "Prospects of Expert Systems in Marketing"
    1984 TIMS College of Marketing Conference, Chicago (1984),
    presentation.

O'Leary, Daniel E.
    "Validation of Expert Systems--With Applications to Auditing and
    Accounting Expert Systems"
    Decision Sciences, Vol. 18 (Summer 1987), pp. 468-86.

Rangaswamy, Arvind, Burke, Raymond R., Wind, Yoram, and Eliashberg,
    Jehoshua
    "Expert Systems for Marketing"
    Report No.87-107
    Marketing Science Institute (November 1987), 50 pp.

Schwoerer, Juergen and Frappa, Jean-Paul
    "Artificial Intelligence and Expert Systems: Any Applications for
    Marketing and Marketing Research?"
    European Research, Vol. 14 (1986), pp. S10-24.

Sheil, Bean
    "Thinking About Artificial Intelligence"
    Harvard Business Review, Vol. 65 (July-August 1987), pp. 91-7.

Stefik, Mark et al.
    "The Architecture of Expert Systems"
    in Hayes-Roth, Waterman, and Lenat (editors)
    Building Expert Systems
    (Reading, MA: Addison-Wesley, 1983), pp. 89-126.

Steinberg, Margery and Plank, Richard E.
    "Expert Systems: The Integrative Sales Management Tool of the Futures"
    Journal of the Academy of Marketing Science, Vol. 15 (Summer 1987),
    pp. 55-62.

Waterman, Donald A.
    A Guide to Expert Systems
    (Addison-Wesley, 1986).

Waterman, Donald A. and Hayes-Roth, Frederick
    "An Investigation of Tools for Building Expert Systems"
    in Hayes-Roth, Frederick, Waterman, Donald A., and Lenat, Douglas B.
    (editors)
    Building Expert Systems
    (Reading, MA: Addison-Wesley Publishing Co., 1983).

Wright, George and Ayton, Peter
    "Eliciting and Modeling Expert Knowledge"
    Decision Support Systems, Vol. 3, No. 1 (1987), pp. 13-26.

Yarnell, Steven M.
    "Artificial Intelligence's 'Frame' Concept: A New Tool for Marketing
    Research"
    Marketing News (May 25, 1984).

6.07 ---------- Theory Re: Artificial Intelligence in Mktg Research

Morgan, Rory P. and Bond, Julian R.
    "Methods of Artificial Intelligence--Some Applications for Market
    Research"
    Journal of the Market Research Society, Vol. 31 (July 1989), pp.
    375-97.

6.08 ---------- Applications of Artif. Intelligence, Expert Systems

Bruce, Margaret
    "New Product Development Strategies of Suppliers of Emerging
    Technologies--A Case Study of Expert Systems"
    Journal of Marketing Management, Vol. 3 (Spring 1988), pp. 313-327.

Cook, Robert Lorin and Schleede, John M.
   "Application of Expert Systems to Advertising"
   Journal of Advertising Research, Vol. 28 (June/July 1988), pp. 47-56.

Entemann, Carl W. and Cannon, Hugh
   "A Rule-Based Expert System for Sales Promotion Mangement"
   Proceedings, 1987 Conference of the American Academy of Advertising
   (Las Vegas, NV: American Academy of Advertising, 1987).

McCann, John M. and Reibstein, David J.
   "Developing a Promotion Expert System"
   ORSA/TIMS Marketing Science Conference (1987), paper presentation.

Rangaswamy, Arvind, Eliashberg, Jehoshua, Burke, Raymond R., and Wind,
   Yoram
   "Developing Marketing Expert Systems: An Application to International
   Negotiations"
   Journal of Marketing, Vol. 53 (October 1989), pp. 24-39.

Schon, Stephen and Helferich, Omar Keith
   "Expert System Applications in Customer Service"
   Dialog Systems Inc. (1986), unpublished report.

6.09 ---------- Theory Re: Marketing Audits

Kotler, Philip, Gregor, William T., and Rodgers, William H., III
   "The Marketing Audit Comes of Age"
   Sloan Management Review, Vol. 10 (Winter 1989).

Naylor, John and Wood, Alan
   Practical Marketing Audits: A Guide to Increased Profitability
   (ABP, 1978), 207 pp.

Tybout, Alice M. and Hauser, John R.
   "A Marketing Audit Using a Conceptual Model of Consumer Behavior:
   Application and Evaluation"
   Journal of Marketing, Vol. 45 (Summer 1981), pp. 82-101.

6.10 ---------- User - System Interface

Bailey, James E. and Pearson, Sammy W.
   "Development of a Tool for Measuring and Analyzing Computer User
   Satisfaction"
   Management Science, Vol. 29 (May 1983), pp. 530-45.

Howells, Robert
   "Consumer Techniques to Build a Business Database"
   Industrial Marketing Digest, Vol. 13 (Third Quarter 1988), pp. 101-8.

Ives, Blake, Olson, Margrethe H., and Baroudi, Jack J.
   "The Measurement of User Information Satisfaction"
   Communications to the ACM, Vol. 26 (October 1983), pp. 785-93.

Jobber, David and Watts, Martin
   "User Attitudes Towards Marketing Information Systems--A UK Survey of
   Manufacturing Companies"
   Marketing Ingelligence and Planning, Vol. 6, No. 2 (1988), pp. 30-5.

6.11 ---------- Studies of Use of MDSSs by Managers

Benbasat, Izak and Dexter, Albert S.
   "Individual Differences in the Use of Decision Support Aids"
   Journal of Accounting Research, Vol. 20 (Spring 1982), pp. 1-11.

DeSanctis, Geraldine
   "An Examination of an Expectancy Theory Model of Decision Support
   System Use"
   Proceedings, Third International Conference on Information Systems
   (December 1985), pp. 121-35.

Dickson, Gary W., Senn, James A., and Chervany, Norman L.
   "Research in Management Information Systems: The Minnesota
   Experiments"
   Management Science, Vol. 23, No. 9 (1977), pp. 913-23.

Fuerst, William L. and Cheney, Paul H.
   "Factors Affecting Perceived Utilization of Computer Based Decision
   Support Systems in the Oil Industry"
   Decision Sciences, Vol. 26 (September 1982), pp. 910-34.

Ives, Blake, Hamilton, Scott, and Davis, Gordon B.
   "A Framework for Research in Computer-Based Management Information
   Systems"
   Management Science, Vol. 26 (October 1980), pp. 982,3.

Jenkins, A. Milton
  "A Program of Research for Investigating Management Information
  Systems (PRIMIS)"
  (1982), working paper.

Lucas, Henry C., Jr.
  "Behavioral Factors in System Implementation"
  in Schultz, R. L. and Slevin, D. P. (editors)
  Implementing Operations Research/Management Science
  (New York: American Elsevier, 1975).

Mason, Richard O. and Mitroff, Ian I.
  "A Program for Research on Management Information Systems"
  Management Science, Vol. 19 (January 1973), pp. 475-87.

Mock, Theodore J.
  "A Longitudinal Study of Some Information Structure Alternatives"
  Data Base, Vol. 5 (1973), pp. 40-6.

Schewe, Charles D.
  "The Management Information System User: An Exploratory Behavioral
  Analysis"
  Academy of Management Journal, Vol. 19 (December 1976), pp. 577-89.

Swanson, E. Burton
  "Management Information Systems: Appreciation and Involvement"
  Management Science, Vol. 21, No. 2 (1974), pp. 74-81.

Taylor, Ronald N.
  "Age and Experience as Determinants of Managerial Information
  Processing and Decision Making Performance"
  Academy of Management Journal, Vol. 19, No. 1 (1975), pp. 74-81.

Taylor, Ronald N. and Dunnette, Marvin D.
  "Influence of Dogmatism, Risk-Taking Propensity, and Intelligence on
  Decision-Making Strategies for a Sample of Industrial Managers"
  Journal of Applied Psychology, Vol. 59, No. 4 (1974), pp. 420-23.

Taylor, Ronald N. and Dunnette, Marvin D.
  "Relative Contribution of Decision-Maker Attributes to Decision
  Process"
  Organizational Behavior and Human Behavior, Vol. 12, No. 4 (1974),
  pp. 286-98.

Vasarhelyi, Miklos A.
  "Man-Machine Planning Systems: A Cognitive Style Examination of
  Interactive Decision Making"
  Journal of Accounting Research, Vol. 15 (Spring 1977), pp. 138-53.

Zinkhan, George M., Joachimsthaler, Erich A., and Kinnear, Thomas C.
  "Individual Differences and Marketing Decision Support System Usage
  and Satisfaction"
  Journal of Marketing Research, Vol. XXIV (May 1987), pp. 208-14.

Zmud, Robert W.
  "Individual Differences and MIS Success: A Review of the Empirical
  Literature"
  Management Science, Vol. 25 (October 1979), pp. 966-79.

6.12 ---------- Sales Forecasting Administration and Implementation

Armstrong, J. Scott
  "The Forecasting Audit"
  in Madridakis, Spyros and Wheelwright, Steven C. (editors)
  The Handbook of Forecasting: A Manager's Guide, Second Edition
  (New York: John Wiley and Sons, Inc., 1987).

Armstrong, J. Scott, Brodie, Roderick J., and McIntyre, Shelby H.
  "Forecasting Methods for Marketing: Review of Empirical Research"
  International Journal of Forecasting, Vol. 3 (1987), pp. 355-76.

Assmus, Gert
  "New Product Forecasting"
  Journal of Forecasting, Vol. 3 (1984), pp. 441-4.

Barron, Michael and Targett, David
  "Sales Forecasting, Market Research and the Value of Information"
  Marketing Intelligence and Planning, Vol. 4, No. 3 (1986), pp. 12-31.

Davidson, Timothy A. and Prusak, Laurence
  "Selecting and Using External Data Sources and Forecasting Services
  to Support a Forecasting Strategy"
  in Makridakis, Spyros and Wheelwright, Steven C. (editors)
  The Handbook of Forecasting: A Manager's Guide, Second Edition
  (New York: John Wiley and Sons, Inc., 1987).

Fildes, Robert
  "Forecasting: The Issues"
  in Makridakis, Spyros and Wheelwright, Steven C. (editors)
  The Handbook of Forecasting: A Manager's Guide, Second Edition
  (New York: John Wiley and Sons, 1987).

Hogarth, Robin M. and Makridakis, Spyros
  "Forecasting and Planning: An Evaluation"
  Management Science, Vol. 27 (1981), pp. 115-38.

Hughes, David G.
  "Sales Forecasting Requirements"
  in Makridakis, Spyros and Wheelwright, Steven C. (editors)
  The Handbook of Forecasting: A Manager's Guide, Second Edition
  (New York: John Wiley and Sons, Inc., 1987).

Lawrence, M. J.
  "An Exploration of Some Practical Issues in the Use of Quantitative
  Forecasting Models"
  Journal of Forecasting, Vol. 2 (1983), pp. 169-79.

Mabert, Vincent A. and Showalter, Michael J.
  "Forecasting for Service Products: Concepts and Systems"
  in Makridakis, Spyros and Wheelwright, Steven C. (editors)
  The Handbook of Forecasting: A Manager's Guide, Second Edition
  (New York: John Wiley and Sons, Inc., 1987).

Mahmoud, Essam
  "Accuracy in Forecasting: A Survey"
  Journal of Forecasting, Vol. 3, No. 2 (1984), pp. 139-59.

Mahmoud, Essam, Rice, Gillian, and Malhotra, Naresh K.
  "Emerging Issues in Sales Forecasting and Decision Support Systems"
  Journal of the Academy of Marketing Science, Vol. 16 (Fall 1988), pp.
  47-61.

Makridakis, Spyros and Hibon, M.
  "Accuracy of Forecasting: An Empirical Investigation"
  Journal of the Royal Statistical Society, Vol. 142, No. 2, pp. 97-145.

Miller, Don M.
  "The Anatomy of a Successful Forecasting Implementation"
  International Journal of Forecasting, Vol. 1 (1985), pp. 69-78.

Moriarty, Mark M.
  "Design Features of Forecasting Systems Involving Management
  Judgments"
  Journal of Marketing Research, Vol. XXII (November 1985), pp. 353-64.

Rice, Gillian and Mahmoud, Essam
  "Forecasting and Data Bases in International Business"
  Management International Review, Vol. 24, No. 4 (1984), pp. 59-71.

Schultz, Randall L.
  "The Implementation of Forecasting Models"
  Journal of Forecasting, Vol. 3 (1984), pp. 43-55.

Tyebjee, Tyzoon T.
  "Behavioral Biases in New Product Forecasting"
  International Journal of Forecasting, Vol. 3 (1987), pp. 393-404.

Weinstein, David
  "Forecasting for Industrial Products"
  in Makridakis, Spyros and Wheelwright, Steven C. (editors)
  The Handbook of Forecasting: A Manager's Guide, Second Edition
  (New York: John Wiley and Sons, Inc., 1987).

Wright, David J.
  "Decision Support Oriented Sales Forecasting Methods"
  Journal of the Academy of Marketing Science, Vol. 16 (Fall 1988), pp.
  71-8.

Wright, David J., Capon, G., Page, R., Quiroga, J., Taseen, A. A., and
  Tomasini, F.
  "Evaluation of Forecasting Methods for Decision Support"
  International Journal of Forecasting, Vol. 2 (1986), pp. 139-52.

6.13 ---------- State of Sales Forecasting MDSSs

Dalrymple, Douglas J.
  "Sales Forecasting Practices Results From a United States Survey"
  International Journal of Forecasting, Vol. 3 (1987), pp. 379-91.

Pan, J. D., Nicholas, R., and Joy, O. M.
  "Sales Forecasting Practice of Large U.S. Industrial Firms"
  Financial Management, Vol. 6, No. 3 (1977), pp. 72-7.

Sparkes, J. R. and McHugh, A. K.
  "Awareness and Use of Forecasting Techniques in British Industry"
  Journal of Forecasting, Vol. 3 (January-March 1984), pp. 37-42.

6.14 ---------- MDSSs in Retailing

Allaway, Arthur, Mason, J. Barry, and Brown, Gene
  "An Optimal Decision Support Model for Department-Level Promotion Mix
  Planning"
  Journal of Retailing, Vol. 63 (Fall 1987), pp. 215-42.

Beaumont, John R.
  "Towards an Integrated Retail Management Information System"
  Environment and Planning (1988).

Beaumont, John R.
  "An Overview of Decision Support Systems for Retail Management"
  Journal of Retailing, Vol. 64 (Winter 1988), pp. 361-73.

6.15 ---------- Other Specific Topical Application Areas of MDSSs

Abraham, Magid M. and Lodish, Leonard M.
  "PROMOTER: An Automated Promotion Evaluation System"
  Marketing Science, Vol. 6 (Spring 1987), pp. 101-23.

Bayer, Judy and Lawrence, Stephen
  "PEP: A Consulting System for Promotion Marketing"
  Carnegie Mellon University (March 1986), working paper.

Chen, Kuang-Chian
  "Developing Decision Support Systems for Small Business Management: A
  Case Study"
  Journal of Small Business Management (July 1989).

Choffray, Jean Marie and Lilien, Gary L.
  "A Decision-Support System for Evaluating Sales Prospects and Launch
  Strategies for New Products"
  Industrial Marketing Management, Vol. 15 (1986), pp. 75-85.

Green, Paul E., Mahajan, Vijay, Goldberg, Stephen M., and Kedia,
  Pradeep K.
  "A Decision-Support System for Developing Retail Promotional Strategy"
  Journal of Retailing, Vol. 59 (Fall 1983), pp. 116-143.

Lodish, Leonard M.
  "A Marketing Decision Support System for Retailers"
  Marketing Science, Vol. 1 (Winter 1982), pp. 31-56.

Mazanec, Josef A.
  "A Decision Support System for Optimizing Advertising Policy of a
  National Tourist Office: Model Outline and Case Study"
  International Journal of Research in Marketing, Vol. 3, No. 2 (1986),
  pp. 63-77.

Mitchell, James W. and Sparks, Leigh
  "Technology and Bank Marketing Information Systems"
  Journal of Marketing Management, Vol. 4 (Summer 1988), pp. 50-61.

Piercy, Nigel and Alexander, Nicholas
  "Retailer Information Strategies"
  Journal of the Market Research Society, Vol. 30 (January 1988), pp.
  87-93.

Zinkhan, George M. and Taylor, James R.
  "RESTSIM: A Simulation Model That Highlights Decision Making Under
  Conditions of Uncertainty"
  Simulation and Games, Vol. 14, No. 4 (1983), pp. 401-16.

Zinkhan, George M. and Taylor, James R.
  "RESTSIM: A Simulation Program for Modeling Restaurant Operations"
  Journal of Marketing Research, Vol. XIX (November 1982), pp. 609,10.

6.16 ---------- Software for Marketing Decision Support Systems

De Nooij, Gert-Jan
  "PcEXPRESS: A Software Tool for Marketing Management Information
  Systems"
  European Research, Vol. 14, No. 2 (1986), pp. 52-8.

7 ------------------ COMPETITOR INTELLIGENCE METHODS ------------------
        See also (sub)heading(s) 5, 6.

7.01 ---------- Books Re: Competitor Intelligence Methods

Fuld, Leonard M.
  Monitoring the Competition
  (John Wiley and Sons, 1988), 204 pp.

Fuld, Leonard M.
  Competitor Intelligence: How to Get It--How to Use It
  (New York: John Wiley and Sons, Inc., 1985), 470 pp.

Greene, Richard M., Jr. (editor)
  Business Intelligence and Espionage
  (Homewood, IL: Dow Jones-Irwin, Inc., 1966), 312 pp.

Hamilton, Peter
  Espionage and Subversion in an Industrial Society
  (London, EN: Hutchinson and Company, Ltd., 1967), 230 pp.

Kelly, John M.
  How to Check Out Your Competition
  (New York: John Wiley and Sons, Inc., 1987).

Kelley, William T.
  Marketing Intelligence
  (London, EN: Staples Press, 1968), 248 pp.

Rothschild, William E.
  How to Gain (and Maintain) the Competitive Advantage in Business
  (New York: McGraw-Hill Book Company, 1984).

Sammon, William L., Kurland, Mark A., and Spitalnic, Robert
  Business Competitor Intelligence: Methods for Collecting, Organizing,
  and Using Information
  (New York: Ronald Press, 1984), 357 pp.

Tyson, Kirk W. M.
  Business Intelligence: Putting It All Together
  (Lombard, IL: Leading Edge Publications, 1986), 270 pp.

7.02 ---------- Articles etc. Re: Competitor Intelligence Methods

Englade, Kenneth F.
  "Competitor Intelligence Comes in From the Cold"
  Across the Board, Vol. XXVI (April 1989).

Evans, Martin
  "Marketing Intelligence: Scanning the Marketing Environment"
  Marketing Intelligence and Planning, Vol. 6, No. 3 (1988), pp. 21-9.

Fahey, Liam
  "Mis-Intelligence"
  Across the Board, Vol. XXVI (April 1989).

Fuld, Leonard M.
  "Study: Many Firms Foolish With Intelligence Funds"
  Marketing News (January 3, 1986), p. 44.

Kelley, William T.
  "Marketing Intelligence for Top Management"
  Journal of Marketing, Vol. 29 (October 1965), pp. 19-24.

McLeod, Raymond, Jr. and Rogers, John
  "Marketing Information Systems: Uses in the Fortune 500"
  California Management Review, Vol. 25 (Fall 1982), pp. 106-18.

Montgomery, David B. and Weinberg, Charles B.
  "Toward Strategic Intelligence Systems"
  Journal of Marketing, Vol. 43 (Fall 1979), pp. 41-52.

Rothschild, William E.
  "Toward Strategic Intelligence Systems--Comment"
  Journal of Marketing, Vol. 43 (Fall 1979), pp. 53,4.

Zinkhan, George M. and Gelb, Betsy D.
  "Competitive Intelligence Practices of Industrial Marketers"
  Industrial Marketing Management, Vol. 14 (1985), pp. 269-75.

8 ---------   MICROCOMPUTERS IN THE RESEARCH PROCESS - GENERAL   ---------

Berry, Dick
   "How Marketers Use Microcomputers--Now and in the Future"
   Business Marketing, Vol. 68 (December 1983), pp. 47-51.

Demby, Emanuel H.
   "New Requirement for Researchers: Interactivity With the PC"
   Marketing News, Vol. 19 (May 24, 1985), pp. 7,10.

Demby, Emanuel H.
   "The New Requirement for the Researcher: Interactivity With the
   Personal Computer"
   European Research, Vol. 13 (January 1985), pp. 26-8.

Hendrickson, Alan
   "Fads, Fashions and Really Truly Useful (DP) Stuff"
   Journal of the Market Research Society, Vol. 31 (October 1989), pp.
   577-80.

Higgins, J. C. and Opdebeeck, E. J.
   "The Microcomputer as a Tool in Marketing Decision Aids: Some Survey
   Results"
   Journal of the Market Research Society, Vol. 26 (July 1984), pp.
   243-54.

Kurtz, David L. and Boone, Louis E.
   "The Current Status of Microcomputer Usage in the Marketing Programs
   of AACSB-Accredited Colleges and Universities"
   Journal of the Academy of Marketing Science, Vol. 15 (Summer 1987),
   pp. 10-5.

Madron, Thomas W., Tate, C. Neal, and Brookshire, Robert G.
   Using Microcomputers in Research
   (Beverly Hills, CA: Sage Publications, Inc., 1985), 87 pp.

Mahon, J. Michael
   "Using Microcomputers for Research: Start-Up Steps"
   Marketing News, Vol. 19 (January 4, 1985), p. 55.

Malhotra, Naresh K., Tashchian, Armen, and Mahmoud, Essam
   "The Integration of Microcomputers in Marketing Research and Decision
   Making"
   Journal of the Academy of Marketing Science, Vol. 15 (Summer 1987),
   pp. 69-82.

McKinnon, Gary F., Smith, Scott M., and Smith, Milton E.
   "The Diffusion of Personal Computers Among Business School Faculty: A
   Longitudinal Study of Attitudes, Expectations, and Users"
   Journal of Marketing Education, Vol. 7 (Fall 1985), pp. 1-6.

Mentzer, John T., Schuster, Camille P., and Roberts, David J.
   "Microcomputers Versus Mainframe Usage by Marketing Professionals"
   Journal of the Academy of Marketing Science, Vol. 15 (Summer 1987),
   pp. 1-9.

Neal, William D.
   "Computering and Software in Marketing Research: The US Perspective"
   Journal of the Market Research Society, Vol. 31 (October 1989), pp.
   567-76.

Pfaffenberger, Bryan
   Microcomputer Applications in Qualitative Research
   (Newbury Park, CA: Sage Publications, 1988), 88 pp.

Schrodt, Philip A.
   Microcomputer Methods for Social Scientists
   (Beverly Hills, CA: Sage Publications, Inc., 1987), 96 pp.

9 ------------------ MARKETING RESEARCH AND SOCIETY ------------------
        See also (sub)heading(s) 10, 29.01, 29.02.

9.01 ---------- (Informed) Consent Issues

Singer, Eleanor
    "The Effect of Informed Consent Procedures on Respondents' Reactions
    to Surveys"
    Journal of Consumer Research, Vol. 5 (June 1978), pp. 49-57.

Singer, E.
    "Informed Consent: Consequences for Response Rate and Response
    Quality in Social Surveys"
    American Sociological Review, Vol. 43, No. 2 (1978), pp. 144-62.

Snyder, Marshall and Lapovsky, D.
    "Enhancing Survey Response from Initial Non-Consenters"
    Journal of Advertising Research, Vol. 24 (June/July 1984), pp. 17-9.

Sobal, Jeffery
    "The Content of Survey Introductions and the Provision of Informed
    Consent"
    Public Opinion Quarterly, Vol. 48 (Winter 1984), pp. 788-93.

Thompson, Teresa L.
    "A Comparison of Methods of Increasing Parental Consent Rates in
    Social Research"
    Public Opinion Quarterly, Vol. 48 (Winter 1984), pp. 779-87.

9.02 ---------- Privacy

Baker, R. C., Dickinson, Roger, and Hollander, Stanley
    "Survey: IRS Shouldn't be Allowed Access to Private Consumer Data"
    Marketing News, Vol. 19 (June 7, 1985), p. 8.

Carlson, Robert O.
    "The Issue of Privacy in Public Opinion Research"
    Public Opinion Quarterly, Vol. 31 (Spring 1967), pp. 1-8.

Goldfield, Edwin D., Turner, Anthony, Cowan, Charles, and Scott, John
    "Privacy and Confidentiality as Factors in Survey Response"
    Proceedings, Social Statistics Section
    (Washington: American Statistical Association, 1977), pp. 219-31.

Marketing News
    "Linowes Sees Major Marketing Impact of Privacy Commission's 162
    Proposals"
    Marketing News (September 23, 1977), p. 1.

Marketing News
    "Privacy Protection Study Commission to Hold Hearing on Possible
    Application of the Privacy Act to Researchers"
    Marketing News (September 10, 1976), p. 1.

Mayer, Charles S. and White, Charles H., Jr.
    "The Law of Privacy and Marketing Research"
    Journal of Marketing, Vol. 33 (April 1969), pp. 1-4.

Rule, James B.
    Private Lives and Public Surveillance: Social Control in the Computer
    Age
    (New York: Schocken Books, 1974), 382 pp.

Tebbutt, Ashley
    "The Data Protection Bill: What It Will Mean for Statistical and
    Other Data Users"
    Statistical News, No. 64 (February 1984), pp. 64.4-.9.

9.03 ---------- Legal Implications for Conducting Research
        See also (sub)heading(s) 29.02.

Advertising Age
    "IRS May Pose Threat to Future Field Services"
    (May 26, 1975), p. 6.

Benazeth, Claude
    "Legal Lessons From the Delicare Affair--2: Europe"
    Marketing and Research Today, Vol. 17 (August 1989), pp. 156-60.

Bowers, Diane K.
    "Bundesdatenschutzgesetz"
    Marketing Research, Vol. 1 (September 1989), pp. 73-6.

Freese, Jan
    "The Swedish Data Act"
    European Research, Vol. 4 (September 1976), pp. 201-4.

Frey, Cynthia J. and Kinnear, Thomas C.
    "Legal Constraints and Marketing Research: Review and Call to Action"
    Journal of Marketing Research, Vol. XVI (August 1979), pp. 295-302.

Heilbrunn, Jeffrey
    "Legal Lessons From the Delicare Affair--1: United States"
    Marketing and Research Today, Vol. 17 (August 1989), pp. 151-4.

Rohme, Nils
    "A Worldwide Overview of National Restrictions on the Conduct and
    Release of Public Opinion Polls"
    European Research, Vol. 13 (January 1985), pp. 30-7.

Rosch, J. Thomas
    "Marketing Research and the Legal Requirements of Advertising"
    Journal of Marketing, Vol. 39 (July 1975), pp. 69-72.

Rotfeld, Herbert J. and Preston, Ivan L.
    "The Potential Impact of Research on Advertising Law"
    Journal of Advertising Research, Vol. 21 (April 1981), pp. 9-17.

Rudolf, Walter
    "Polls, the Press and the Law"
    ESOMAR Seminar on Opinion Polls (January 23-26, 1980), paper
    presentation.

Schweizer, Robert
    "Federal Republic of Germany: Tight Restrictions on Telemarketing"
    European Research, Vol. 15 (May 1987), pp. 82-4.

Schweizer, Robert
    "Present and Future Data Flow Legislation"
    European Research, Vol. 14, No. 1 (1986), pp. 29-34.

Smith, Joseph G. (moderator) et al.
    "Legal Standards for Consumer Survey Research"
    Journal of Advertising Research, Vol. 23 (October/November 1983), pp.
    19-35.

United States Department of Health, Education and Welfare
    Records Computers and the Rights of Citizens
    (Washington: DHEW, 1973), 346 pp.

U.S. Federal Trade Commission
    Federal Trade Commission Decisions 61
    (The Pulse Inc., Docket C-291, 1962).

Zoler, Jon N.
    "Research Requirements for Ad Claims Substantiation"
    Journal of Advertising Research, Vol. 23 (April/May 1983), pp. 9-15.

9.04 ---------- Public Perception of/Reaction to Marketing Research

        See also (sub)heading(s) 32, 33.

Advertising Age
    "How Survey Researchers Meet Public Resistance"
    (July 12, 1976), p. 67.

Advertising Age
    "Public Attitudes Toward Research Favorable--Practitioners Doleful"
    (December 2, 1974), p. 2.

Allen, Irving L. and Colfax, J. David
    "Respondents' Attitudes Toward Legitimate Surveys in Four Cities"
    Journal of Marketing Research, Vol. V (November 1968), pp. 431-3.

Arnold, Rome G.
    "The Interview in Jeopardy: A Problem in Public Relations"
    Public Opinion Quarterly, Vol. 28 (Spring 1964), pp. 119-23.

Bartram, Mary and Bartram, Peter
    "Maintaining Public Acceptance of Market Research: The Way Forward"
    Journal of the Market Research Society, Vol. 31 (October 1989), pp.
    611-7.

Baxter, Richard
    "An Inquiry Into the Misuse of the Survey Technique by Sales
    Solicitors"
    Public Opinion Quarterly, Vol. 28 (Spring 1964), pp. 124-34.

Blankenship, Alan B.
    "Point of View: Consumerism and Consumer Research"
    Journal of Advertising Research, Vol. 11 (August 1971), pp. 44-7.

Bowen, J. M.
"A Survey of the General Public's Attitudes to Market
Research--Summary Report"
Journal of the Market Research Society, Vol. 21 (April 1979), pp.
75-102.

Business Week
"Public Clams Up on Survey Takers"
(September 15, 1973), p. 216.

Cole, Eileen
"The Significance to the Society of the Survey on Public Attitudes to
Market Research"
Journal of the Market Research Society, Vol. 21 (April 1979), pp.
103-6.

Goslar, Martin D. and Brown, Stephen W.
"Decision Support Systems: Advantages in Consumer Marketing Settings"
Journal of Consumer Marketing, Vol. 3 (Summer 1986), pp. 43.

Goyder, John
"Surveys on Surveys: Limitations and Potentialities"
Public Opinion Quarterly, Vol. 50 (Spring 1986), pp. 27-41.

Hodgson, P. B.
"An Examination of Market Research's Public Image--Will the Public
Continue to Cooperate?"
ESOMAR Proceedings (1972).

Miaoulis, George and Baiman, Marvin
"Marketing Research: The Respondent's Perception"
Proceedings, Southern Marketing Association (1979), pp. 224-7.

National Academy of Sciences
Privacy and Confidentiality as Factors in Survey Response
(Washington, DC: National Academy of Sciences, 1979), 274 pp.

Schleifer, Stephen
"Trends in Attitudes Toward and Participation in Survey Research"
Public Opinion Quarterly, Vol. 50 (Spring 1986), pp. 17-26.

Schleifer, Stephen
"Survey Participation is Leaving a Sour Taste With Respondents"
Marketing News, Vol. 19 (February 1985), pp. 1,7.

Schwartz, Alvin
"Interviewing and the Public"
Public Opinion Quarterly, Vol. 28 (Spring 1964), pp. 135-42.

Sheets, Thomas, Radlinski, Allen, Kohne, James, and Brunner, Allen G.
"Deceived Respondents: Once Bitten, Twice Shy"
Public Opinion Quarterly, Vol. 38 (Summer 1974), pp. 261-3.

Singer, Eleanor
"Public Reactions to Some Ethical Issues of Social Research:
Attitudes and Behavior"
Journal of Consumer Research, Vol. 11 (June 1984), pp. 501-9.

Sjoberg, Gideon
"A Questionnaire on Questionnaires"
Public Opinion Quarterly, Vol. 18 (Fall 1954), pp. 423-7.

Swan, John E., Trawick, I. Fredrick, and Carroll, Maxwell G.
"Effect of Participation in Marketing Research on Consumer Attitudes
Toward Research and Satisfaction With a Service"
Journal of Marketing Research, Vol. XVIII (August 1981), pp. 356-63.

9.05 ---------- Unclassified (Marketing Research and Society)

Advertising Age
"Greasing the Opinion Poll"
(April 14, 1975), p. 14.

Baxter, R.
"An Inquiry Into the Misuse of the Survey Technique by Sales
Solicitors"
in Bogart, Leo (editor)
Current Controversies in Marketing Research
(Chicago: Markham, 1969).

Baxter, Richard
"An Inquiry Into the Misuse of the Survey Technique by Sales
Solicitors"
Public Opinion Quarterly, Vol. 28 (Spring 1964), pp. 124-34.

Biel, Alexander
"Abuses of the Survey Research Technique: The Phony Interview"
Public Opinion Quarterly, Vol. 3 (Summer 1967), p. 298.

Bogart, Leo
    Silent Politics--Polls and the Awareness of Public Opinion
    (New York: John Wiley and Sons, 1972), 250 pp.

Bogart, Leo
    "The Researcher's Dilemma"
    Journal of Marketing, Vol. 26 (January 1972), pp. 6-11.

Day, George S.
    "On Confidence and Consumerism"
    in Divita, Sal F. (editor)
    Advertising and the Public Interest
    (Chicago: American Marketing Association, 1975), pp. 130-40.

Dodd, Stuart C.
    "Correspondence and Comment"
    Public Opinion Quarterly, Vol. 29 (Spring 1965), pp. 168,9.

Field, Mervin
    "Nonresponse and the Responsibility of Researchers"
    Public Opinion Quarterly, Vol. 38 (Fall 1974), p. 477.

Kover, Arthur J.
    "Marketing Research and Two Kinds of Legitimacy"
    The American Sociologist, Vol. 6 (June 1971), pp. 72-4.

Morello, Gabriele
    "The Interaction of Research With Business and Society"
    Journal of the Market Research Society, Vol. 24 (January 1982), pp.
    1-8.

Sheatsley, Paul B.
    "The Harassed Respondent: Interviewing Practices"
    in Bogart, Leo (editor)
    Current Controversies in Marketing Research
    (Chicago: Markham, 1969).

Westin, Allan F. and Baker, Michael A.
    Databanks in a Free Society: Computers, Record-Keeping and Privacy
    (New York: Quadrangle/New York Times Book, 1974), 522 pp.

10 ----------------------- ETHICAL ISSUES ------------------------
         See also (sub)heading(s) 9.

10.01 ---------- Books Re: Ethical Issues in Marketing Research

Andrews, Kenneth R. (editor)
   Ethics in Practice
   (Harvard Business School Press, 1989), 368 pp.

Baier, Kurt
   Moral Point of View: A Rational Basis of Ethics
   (Ithaca, NY: Cornell University Press, 1958).

Bower, Robert T. and De Gasparis, Priscilla
   Ethics in Social Research
   (New York: Praeger Publishers, 1978), 227 pp.

Bulmer, Martin (editor)
   Census, Surveys and Privacy
   (The Macmillan Press Ltd., 1979), 279 pp.

Kimmel, Allan J.
   Ethics and Values in Social Research
   (Newbury Park, CA: Sage Publications, Inc., 1988), 152 pp.

Kohlberg, Lawrence
   The Meaning and Measurement of Moral Development
   (Worcester, MA: Clark University Press, 1981).

Reynolds, Paul Davidson
   Ethical Dilemmas and Social Science Research
   (San Francisco, CA: Jossey-Bass Publishers, 1980), 505 pp.

Silbes, Joan E. (editor)
   The Ethics of Social Research: Surveys and Experiments
   (New York: Springer-Verlag, 1982).

Taylor, Paul W.
   Principles of Ethics: An Introduction
   (Encino, CA: Dickensen Publishing Company, Inc., 1975).

10.02 ---------- Theories and Models of Marketing Ethics

Bartels, Robert
   "A Model for Ethics in Marketing"
   Journal of Marketing, Vol. 31 (January 1967), pp. 20-6.

Ferrell, O. C. and Gresham, Larry G.
   "A Contingency Framework for Understanding Ethical Decision-Making in
   Marketing"
   Journal of Marketing, Vol. 49 (Summer 1985), pp. 87-96.

Hunt, Shelby D. and Vitell, Scott
   "A General Theory of Marketing Ethics"
   Journal of Macromarketing (Spring 1986), pp. 5-16.

Kroll, Robert J. and Stampfl, Ronald W.
   "Orientations Toward Consumerism: A Test of a Two-Dimensional Theory"
   Journal of Consumer Affairs, Vol. 20 (Winter 1986), pp. 214-30.

Trevino, Linda Klebe
   "Ethical Decision Making in Organizations: A Person-Situation
   Interactionist Model"
   Academy of Management Review, Vol. 11 (1986), pp. 601-17.

10.03 ---------- Articles, etc. Re: Ethical Issues in Mktg Research

Adair, J., Dushenko, T., and Lindsay, R.
   "Ethical Regulations and Their Impact on Research Practices"
   American Psychologist, Vol. 40 (1985), pp. 59-72.

Advertising Research Foundation
   "ARF Position Paper 'Phony or Misleading Polls'"
   Journal of Advertising Research, Vol. 26 (December 1986/January
   1987), pp. RC3-RC8.

American Statistical Association Conference on Surveys of Human
   Populations
   "Report on the ASA Conference on Surveys of Human Populations"
   The American Statistician, Vol. 28 (February 1974), pp. 30-4.

Bartram, Mary and Bartram, Peter
   "The Ethical Dilemmas of the Market Researcher: Where do We Now Draw
   the Line?"
   Proceedings, ESOMAR Congress, Lisbon (1988), pp. 795-809.

Baumhart, Raymond C.
  "How Ethical are Businessmen?"
  Harvard Business Review, Vol. 39 (July-August 1961), pp. 6-19, 156-76.

Baumrind, D.
  "Some Thoughts on Ethics of Research"
  American Psychologist, Vol. 40 (1964), pp. 165-74.

Bezilla, Robert, Haynes, Joel B., and Elliott, Clifford
  "Ethics in Marketing Research"
  Business Horizons, Vol. 19 (April 1976), pp. 83-6.

Blankenship, A. B.
  "Some Questions of Ethics in Marketing Research"
  Journal of Marketing Research, Vol. I (May 1964), pp. 26-31.

Bogart, Leo
  "The Researcher's Dilemma"
  Journal of Marketing, Vol. 26 (January 1962), pp. 6-11.

Bowers, Diane K.
  "Preventing the Spread of UGS"
  Marketing Research, Vol. 1 (December 1989), pp. 48-50.

Bowers, Diane K.
  "Postscript: Telemarketing and Survey Research: Who'll Face the
  Music?"
  Marketing and Research Today, Vol. 17 (August 1989), pp. 183,4.

Brenner, Steven N. and Molander, Earl A.
  "Is the Ethics of Business Changing?"
  Harvard Business Review, Vol. 55 (January-February 1977), pp. 57-71.

Carroll, Archie B.
  "Managerial Ethics: A Post-Watergate View"
  Business Horizons, Vol. 18 (April 1975), pp. 75-80.

Day, Robert L.
  "A Comment on 'Ethics in Marketing Research'"
  Journal of Marketing Research, Vol. XII (May 1975), pp. 232,3.

Dickson, John P., Casey, Michael J., and Wyckoff, Daniel W.
  "The Invisible Ink Caper: Or a Watergate Mentality in Marketing
  Research Ethics"
  in Schneider, Howard C. (editor)
  Proceedings, American Institute for Decision Sciences (1976), p. 274.

Erdos, Paul L. and Regier, James
  "Visible vs. Disguised Keying on Questionnaires"
  Journal of Advertising Research, Vol. 17 (February 1977), pp. 13-8.

Fulmer, Robert M.
  "Ethical Codes of Business"
  Personnel Administration, Vol. 36 (May-June 1969), pp. 49-57.

Hunt, H. Keith
  "The Ethics of Research in the Consumer Interests: Panel Summary"
  in Ackerman, Norleen M. (editor)
  Proceedings, American Council of Consumer Interests (1979).

Laczniak, Gene R.
  "Business Ethics: A Manager's Primer"
  Business, Vol. 33 (January-March 1983), pp. 23-9.

Marketing News
  "A Pledge: A Personal Code for Practicing Market and Opinion Research"
  Marketing News (September 19, 1980), p. 24.

McGown, K. L.
  "Ethical Issues Involving the Protection of Marketing Research
  Practitioners and Respondents"
  in Hair, J. L. (editor)
  Proceedings of the American Institute for Decision Sciences (1979),
  pp. 195-7.

Mirvis, P. H. and Seashore, S. E.
  "Creating Ethical Relationships in Organizational Research"
  in Silbes, Joan E. (editor)
  The Ethics of Social Research: Surveys and Experiments
  (New York: Springer-Verlag, 1982).

Murphy, Patrick E. and Laczniak, Gene R.
  "Marketing Ethics: A Review With Implications for Managers, Educators
  and Researchers"
  in Enis, Ben M. and Roering, Kenneth J. (editors)
  Review of Marketing, 1981
  (Chicago: American Marketing Association, 1981), pp. 251-66.

Parker, Ben G.
   "Through a Glass Darkly"
   Journal of Advertising Research, Vol. 13 (June 1973), pp. 43-5.

Schneider, Kenneth and Holm, Cynthia K.
   "Deceptive Practices in Marketing Research: The Consumer's Viewpoint"
   California Management Review, Vol.24 (Spring 1982), pp. 89-96.

Schwartz, Alvin
   "Interviewing and the Public"
   Public Opinion Quarterly, Vol. 28 (Spring 1964), pp. 135-42.

Schwartz, Alvin
   "The Public Relations of Interviewing"
   Journal of Marketing, Vol. 27 (July 1963), pp. 34-7.

Schweizer, Robert
   "Federal Republic of Germany: Tight Restrictions on Telemarketing"
   European Research, Vol. 15 (May 1987), pp. 82-4.

Shaw, Robert E.
   "Telemarketing: Its Impact on the Research Industry in the United States"
   European Research, Vol. 15 (May 1987), pp. 78-80.

Skinner, Steven J., Ferrell, O. C., and Dubinsky, Alan J.
   "Organizational Dimensions of Marketing Research Ethics"
   Journal of Business Research, Vol. 16, No. 2 (1988), pp. 209-23.

Stephan, Frederick F. (editor)
   "Public Relations and Research Interviewing"
   Public Opinion Quarterly, Vol. 28 (Spring 1964), p. 118.

Tybout, Alice M. and Zaltman, Gerald
   "A Reply to Comments on 'Ethics in Marketing Research: Their Practical Relevance'"
   Journal of Marketing Research, Vol. XII (May 1975), pp. 234-7.

Tybout, Alice M. and Zaltman, Gerald
   "Ethics in Marketing Research: Their Practical Relevance"
   Journal of Marketing Research, Vol. XI (November 1974), pp. 357-68.

Van Westerhoven, Emile
   "Telemarketing: Finding the Needle in the Haystack"
   European Research, Vol. 15 (May 1987), pp. 72-6.

10.04 ---------- Ethics Guidelines and Standards

ESOMAR
   International Code of Practice for the Publication of Public Opinion Poll Results and Guidelines to Its Interpretation
   (Amsterdam).

ESOMAR
   Guidelines on "Distinguishing Marketing Research From Telemarketing"
   (Amsterdam).

ESOMAR/ICC
   "International Code of Practice: Marketing and Social Research"
   Amsterdam (1977).

Ethics Resource Center
   Codes of Ethics in Corporations and Trade Associations and the Teaching of Ethics in Graduate Business Schools
   (Princeton, NJ: Opinion Research Corporation, 1979).

ICC/ESOMAR
   International Code of Marketing and Social Research Practice
   (Amsterdam).

Marketing Research Standards Committee
   Marketing Research Code of Ethics
   (Chicago: American Marketing Association, 1972).

Olander, Folke and Lindhoff, Hakan
   "Respondents' Rights in Marketing Research"
   European Research, Vol. 5 (May 1977), pp. 99-105.

Schaefer, Wolfgang
   "On a Code for Media Research"
   European Research, Vol. 14, No. 2 (1986), pp. 82-4.

Twedt, Dik Warren
   "Why a Marketing Research Code of Ethics?"
   Journal of Marketing, Vol. 27 (1963), pp. 48-50.

10.05 ---------- Theory Re: Debriefing Subjects

Holmes, D.
  "Debriefing After Psychological Experiments, II: Effectiveness of
  Postdeception Desensitizing"
  American Psychologist, Vol. 31 (1976), pp. 868-75.

Holmes, D.
  "Debriefing After Psychological Experiments, I: Effectiveness of
  Postdeception Dehoaxing"
  American Psychologist, Vol. 31 (1976), pp. 858-67.

Mills, J.
  "A Procedure for Explaining Experiments Involving Deception"
  Personality and Social Psychology Bulletin, Vol. 2 (1976), pp. 3-13.

Perry, L. and Abrahamson, P.
  "Debriefing--A Gratuitous Procedure"
  American Psychologist, Vol. 35 (1980), pp. 298,9.

Ring, K., Wallston, K., and Corey, M.
  "Mode of Debriefing as a Factor Affecting Subjective Reaction to a
  Milgram-Type Obedience Study: An Ethical Inquiry"
  Representative Research in Social Psychology, Vol. 1 (1970), pp. 67,8.

Ross, L., Lepper, M., and Hubbard, M.
  "Perseverance in Self-Perception and Social Perception: Biased
  Attributional Processes in the Debriefing Paradigm"
  Journal of Personality and Social Psychology, Vol. 32 (1975), pp.
  880-92.

Smith, S. and Richardson, D.
  "Amelioration of Deception and Harm in Psychological Research: The
  Important Role of Debriefing"
  Journal of Personality and Social Psychology, Vol. 44 (1983), pp.
  1075-82.

Tesch, F.
  "Debriefing Research Participants: Though This be Method, There is
  Madness to It"
  Journal of Personality and Social Psychology, Vol. 35 (1977), pp.
  217-24.

Toy, Daniel, Olson, Jerry, and Dipboye, R.
  "Effects of Debriefings That Identify a Research Deception"
  in Greenberg, B. and Bellenger, D. (editors)
  Contemporary Marketing Thought
  Proceedings, American Marketing Asso ciation Educators' Conference
  (1977), pp. 395-400.

Toy, Daniel, Olson, Jerry, and Wright, Lauren
  "Effects of Debriefing in Marketing Research Involving 'Mild'
  Deceptions"
  Psychology and Marketing, Vol. 6 (Spring 1989), pp. 69-85.

Wegner, D., Coulton, G., and Wenzlaff, R.
  "The Transparency of Denial: Briefing in the Debriefing Paradigm"
  Journal of Personality and Social Psychology, Vol. 49 (1985), pp.
  338-46.

10.06 ---------- Studies of Ethical Practices and Beliefs in Mktg Res

Akaah, Ishmael P. and Riordan, Edward A.
  "Judgments of Marketing Professionals About Ethical Issues in
  Marketing Research: A Replication and Extension"
  Journal of Marketing Research, Vol. XXVI (February 1989), pp. 112-20.

Beltramini, Richard F., Peterson, Robert A., and Kozmetsky, George
  "Concerns of College Students Regarding Business Ethics"
  Journal of Business Ethics, Vol. 3 (August 1984), pp. 195-200.

Chonko, Lawrence B. and Hunt, Shelby D.
  "Ethics of Marketing Management: An Empirical Examination"
  Journal of Business Research, Vol. 13 (August 1985), pp. 339-59.

Coney, Kenneth A. and Murphy, John H.
  "Attitudes of Marketers Toward Ethical and Professional Marketing
  Research Practices"
  in Naoh, Henry W. and Robin, Donald P. (editors)
  Proceedings, Southern Marketing Association (1976), pp. 172-4.

Crawford, C. Merle
  "Attitudes of Marketing Executives Toward Ethics in Marketing
  Research"
  Journal of Marketing, Vol. 34 (April 1970), pp. 46-52.

Ferrell, O. C. and Skinner, Steven J.
"Ethical Behavior and Bureaucratic Structure in Marketing Research Organizations"
Journal of Marketing Research, Vol. XXV (February 1988), pp. 103-9.

Ferrell, O. C. and Weaver, K. Mark
"Ethical Beliefs of Marketing Managers"
Journal of Marketing, Vol. 42 (July 1978), pp. 69-73.

French, Warren and Ebner, Myra
"A Practical Look at Research Ethics"
Journal of Data Collection, Vol. 26 (Fall 1986), pp. 49-53.

Fritzsche, David J. and Becker, Helmut
"Ethical Behavior of Marketing Managers"
Journal of Business Ethics, Vol. 2 (November 1983), pp. 291-9.

Hunt, Shelby D., Chonko, Lawrence B., and Wilcox, James B.
"Ethical Problems of Marketing Researchers"
Journal of Marketing Research, Vol. XXI (August 1984), pp. 309-24.

Krugman, Dean M. and Ferrell, O. C.
"The Organizational Ethics of Advertising"
Journal of Advertising, Vol. 10 (January 1981), pp. 21-30.

McDaniel, Stephen W., Verille, Perry, and Madden, Charles S.
"The Threats to Marketing Research: An Empirical Appraisal"
Journal of Marketing Research, Vol. XXII (February 1985), pp. 74-80.

Schleifer, S.
"Results of Walker's 1984 Industry Image Study"
Marketing Research (Winter 1985), Walker Research Incorporated.

Weaver, K. Mark and Ferrell, O. C.
"The Impact of Corporate Policy on Reported Ethical Beliefs and Behavior of Marketing Practitioners"
in Greenberg, Barnett and Bellenger, Danny N. (editors)
Contemporary Marketing Thought
(Chicago: American Marketing Association, 1977), pp. 477-80.

Zey-Ferrell, Mary and Ferrell, O. C.
"Role-Set Configuration and Opportunity as Predictors of Unethical Behavior in Organizations"
Human Relations, Vol. 35, No. 7 (1982), pp. 587-604.

11 ------- BIBLIOGRAPHIES, DIRECTORIES, ABSTRACTS, GLOSSARIES --------
          See also (sub)heading(s) 12, 13.

11.01 ---------- Mktg Research Bibliographies/Directories/Abstracts

Belson, William A. and Thompson, Beryl-Anne
     Bibliography on Methods of Social and Business Research
     (New York: John Wiley and Sons, 1973), 300 pp.

British Industrial Market Research Association
     Industrial Marketing Research Abstracts (semiannual)
     (London: British Industrial Market Research Association).

British Institute of Management
     Survey of Marketing Research in Great Britain
     (London: British Institute of Management, 1962).

British Overseas Trade Board
     International Directory of Published Marketing Research, Second
     Edition
     (London: The British Overseas Trade Board, 1977), 520 pp.

Dickinson, John R.
     The Bibliography of Marketing Research Methods, Third Edition
     (Lexington, MA: Lexington Books and Marketing Science Institute,
     1990).

Disch, Wolfgang K. A.
     Bibliography on Marketing Research
     (Hamburg, Ger: Hamburgisches Welt-Wirtschafts-Archiv, 1964).

Ferber, Robert, Cousineau, Alain, Crask, Millard, and Wales, Hugh G.
     A Basic Bibliography on Marketing Research: 1974 Revision
     (Chicago: American Marketing Association, 1974), 299 pp.

Goldstein, Sherry and Vermiero, Joan (editors)
     Findex: The Directory of Market Research Reports, Studies and
     Surveys, 1984 Edition
     (New York: FIND/SVP), 682 pp.

Holloway, Robert J. (editor)
     A Basic Bibliography on Experiments in Marketing
     (Chicago: American Marketing Association, 1967).

Kapferer, Clodwig and Disch, Wolfgang K. A.
     Market Research by Trade Associations
     (Paris: Organization for Economic Co-Operation and Development,
     1964), 92 pp.

Market Research Society, The
     Market Research Abstracts (semiannual)
     (London: The Market Research Society).

Miller, Thomas E. and Sher, Lisa (editors)
     Findex: The Directory of Market Research Reports and Surveys
     (New York: Find/SVP, 1981), 397 pp.

U.S. Bureau of the Census
     Indexes to Survey Methodology Literature
     Technical Paper No. 34
     (Washington, DC: U.S. Government Printing Office, 1974), 225 pp.

Walters, David
     "World Register of Current Research"
     International Journal of Physical Distribution, Vol. 6, No. 15
     (1976), pp. 275-83.

11.02 ---------- Glossaries
          See also (sub)heading(s) 131.07.

Bennett, Peter D.
     Dictionary of Marketing Terms
     (Chicago: American Marketing Association, 1989), 220 pp.

Bodian, Nat G.
     Encyclopedia of Mailing List Terminology and Techniques: A Practical
     Guide for Marketers
     (Winchester, MA: The Bret Scott Press, 1986), 320 pp.

Dutka, Solomon and Roshwalb, Irving
     A Dictionary for Marketing Research
     (New York: Audits and Surveys, Inc., 1975), 61 pp.

ESOMAR
     Glossary of Technical Terms for Market Researchers
     (European Society for Opinion and Market Research, 1974), 81 pp.

Incorporated Society of British Advertisers and Market Research Society
    Dictionary--Marketing Research
    (London, EN: The Market Research Society).

Kruskal, William H. and Tanur, J. M.
    International Encyclopedia of Statistics
    (New York: The Free Press, 1978).

National Association of Broadcasters
    Standard Definitions of Broadcast Research Terms
    (New York: National Association of Broadcasters, 1967), 56 pp.

Newson-Smith, Nigel
    Glossary of Market Research Terminology
    (London: Incorporated Society of British Advertisers, 1972), 24 pp.

O'Muircheartaigh, Colin A. and Francis, David Pitt
    Statistics: A Dictionary of Terms and Ideas
    (Arrow Books, 1981), 295 pp.

Statistics Canada
    Dictionary of the 1971 Census Terms
    (Ottawa: Statistics Canada, 1972), Cat. No. 12-540.

Urdang, Laurence (editor)
    Dictionary of Advertising
    (Lincolnwood, IL: NTC Business Books, 1985), 210 pp.

Van De Merwe, Caspar
    Thesaurus of Sociological Research Terminology
    (Rotterdam University Press, 1974).

Van Rees, Jan (editor)
    Glossary of Marketing Research
    (Amsterdam: European Society for Opinion and Marketing Research,
    1989).

12 ----------------   REPORT WRITING AND PRESENTATIONS   ------------------
        See also (sub)heading(s) 11, 13.

Freeman, D. H. et al.
  "Presenting Statistical Papers"
  The American Statistician, Vol. 37 (May 1983).

Hodnett, E. A.
  Effective Presentations: How to Present Facts, Figures and Ideas
  Successfully
  (West Nyack, NY: Parker Publishing, 1967).

Kahn, S.
  Public Speaking for the Professions and Clubs
  (New York: Greenbry, 1952).

Mohn, N. Carroll
  "How to Present Marketing Research Results Effectively"
  Marketing and Research Today, Vol. 17 (May 1989), pp. 115-8.

Mohn, N. Carroll and Land, Thomas H.
  "A Guide to Quality Marketing Research Proposals and Reports"
  Business, Vol. 39 (January-February-March 1989).

13 ---------- WRITING AND PUBLICATION OF MARKETING RESEARCH ----------
See also (sub)heading(s) 11, 12.

13.01 ---------- Books Re: Writing and Publication of Mktg Research

Bowker, R. R.
Ulrich's International Periodicals Directory
(New York: R. R. Bowker, 1986-1987).

Cabell, David W. E.
Directory of Publishing Opportunities in Business Administration and
Economics, Third Edition
(Beaumont: Cabell Publishing Company, 1981).

Oxbridge Communication
The Standard Periodicals Directory
(New York: Oxbridge Communication, 1988).

Shurter, Robert L., Williamson, J. Peter, and Broehl, Wayne G.
Business Research and Report Writing
(New York: McGraw-Hill, 1965), 204 pp.

Statistical News
"1986 Welsh House Condition Survey: A New Approach to the
Presentation of Survey Results"
Statistical News, No. 82 (August 1988), pp. 28,9.

Strunk, William, Jr. and White, E. B.
The Elements of Style
(New York: Macmillan, 1978).

Tichy, H. J.
Effective Writing
(New York, NY: John Wiley and Sons, Inc., 1966), 320 pp.

Turabian, Kate L.
A Manual for Writers, Third Edition, Revised
(Chicago: The University of Chicago Press, 1967), 125 pp.

13.02 ---------- Writing and Publishing Guides

Bartram, Peter
"The Communication of Results: The Neglected Art in Marketing
Research"
Marketing Intelligence and Planning, Vol. 3, No. 1 (1985), pp. 3-13.

Britt, Steuart Henderson
"The Writing of Readable Research Reports"
Journal of Marketing Research, Vol. VIII (May 1971), pp. 262-6.

Bushman, Anthony F.
"What are the Qualities of a Good Marketing Article?"
Journal of the Academy of Marketing Science, Vol. 6 (Summer 1978),
pp. 151-6.

Campbell, William Giles, Ballou, Stephen Vaughan, and Slade, Carole
Form and Style: Theses, Reports, Term Papers, Seventh Edition
(Dallas, TX: Houghton Mifflin Company), 240 pp.

Chandos, Viscount
"Pray, Don't Call It English"
Columbia Journal of World Business, Vol. 1 (Fall 1965), pp. 137-41.

Ciardi, John
"On Writing and Bad Writing"
Saturday Review, Vol. 45 (December 15, 1962), pp. 10-2.

Ferber, Robert
"How Not to Write a Prize-Winning Article"
Journal of Consumer Research, Vol. 5 (March 1979), pp. 303-5.

Fielden, John S.
"For Better Business Writing"
Harvard Business Review, Vol. 43 (January-February 1965), pp. 164-72.

Fielden, John S.
"What do You Mean I Can't Write?"
Harvard Business Review, Vol. 42 (May-June 1964), pp. 144-52.

Klein, Lawrence R.
"The Professional Journal--Writing Without Fun or Profit"
Business and Society, Vol. 2 (Spring 1962), pp. 31-6.

Reiter, Michael J.
"Reports that Communicate"
Management Services, Vol. 4 (January 1967), pp. 27-36.

Steenrod, N. E., Doub, J. L., Carlitz, F. A. Ficken, and Piranian, G.
  "Manual for Authors of Mathematical Papers"
  Bulletin of the American Mathematical Society, Vol. 68 (September
  1962), pp. 429-44.

Thoman, Henry F.
  "Good Morning, Professor, Want to Write a Textbook?"
  College English, Vol. 19 (November 1957), p. 47.

Wheatley, John J.
  "Research Methodology--How Much Emphasis?"
  Journal of Marketing, Vol. 37 (April 1973), pp. 58,9.

Woodford, F. Peter
  "Sounder Thinking Through Clearer Writing"
  Science, Vol. 156 (May 12, 1967), pp. 743-5.

13.03 ---------- Case Writing

     See also (sub)heading(s) 84.

Leenders, Michiel R. and Erskine, James A.
  Case Research: The Case Writing Process, Second Edition
  (London, Ontario: Research and Publications Division, School of
  Business Administration, University of Western Ontario, 1978).

13.04 ---------- Editorial Policies, Issues Re: The Publishing Process

Churchill, Gilbert A., Jr. and Perreault, William D., Jr.
  "JMR Editorial Policies and Philosophy"
  Journal of Marketing Research, Vol. XIX (August 1982), pp. 283-7.

Churchill, Gilbert A., Jr. and Peter, J. Paul
  "Editorial--Measurement Abstracts: Purpose, Policy, and Procedures"
  Journal of Marketing Research, Vol. XVII (November 1980), pp. 537,8.

Coe, Robert K. and Weinstock, Irwin
  "Publication Policies of Major Business Journals"
  Southern Journal of Business (January 1968), p. 3.

Cunningham, William H.
  "From the Editor"
  Journal of Marketing, Vol. 46 (Winter 1982), pp. 8-13.

Davidson, William R.
  "Introducing the Journal of Marketing Research"
  Journal of Marketing Research, Vol. I (February 1964), pp. 9,10.

Ferber, Robert
  "The Role of Response Rates in Evaluating Manuscripts for Publication"
  in Monroe, Kent B. (editor)
  Advances in Consumer Research, Volume Eight
  (Washington, DC: Association for Consumer Research, 1980), pp. 274,5.

Ferber, Robert
  "What is the JCR Editorial Policy on Samples and Sample Requirements"
  Newsletter, Association for Consumer Research, Vol. 7 (December
  1977), p. 16.

Ferber, Robert
  "Statement of Objectives and Future Goals of JCR--Editorial"
  Journal of Consumer Research, Vol. 3 (September 1976), p. vi.

Frank, Ronald E.
  "The Journal of Consumer Research: An Introduction"
  Journal of Consumer Research, Vol. 1 (June 1974), pp. iv,v.

Holbrook, Morris B.
  "A Note on Sadomasochism in the Review Process: I Hate When That
  Happens"
  Journal of Marketing, Vol. 50 (July 1986), pp. 104-8.

Journal of Consumer Research
  "JCR Statement of Review Philosophy"
  Journal of Consumer Research, Vol. 15 (June 1988).

Kurtz, David L. and Spitz, A. Edward
  An Academic Writer's Guide to Publishing in Business and Economic
  Journals
  (Ypsilanti, MI: Bureau of Business Services and Research, Eastern
  Michigan University, 1972), 222 pp.

Moyer, Charles R. and Crockett, John H.
  "Academic Journals: Policies, Trends, and Issues"
  Academy of Management Journal, Vol. 19 (September 1976), pp. 489-95.

Peterson, Robert A.
"On the Preeminence of the Journal of Marketing Research"
Marketing Educator, Vol. 4 (Spring 1985), p. 8.

Podhoretz, Norman
"In Defense of Editing"
Harper's, Vol. 231 (October 1965), pp. 143-7.

Rosenthal, Robert
"The 'File Drawer Problem' and Tolerance for Null Results"
Psychological Bulletin, Vol. 83 (March 1979), pp. 638-41.

Smith, Mary Lee
"Publication Bias and Meta-Analysis"
Evaluation in Education, Vol. 4 (1980), pp. 22-4.

Wind, Yoram
"The Journal of Marketing at a Crossroad"
Journal of Marketig, Vol. 43 (January 1979), pp. 9-12.

Ziman, J.
"Anonymity of Referees"
Nature (January 1976), p. 264.

13.05 ---------- Perceptions and Evaluations of Specific Periodicals

Becker, Boris W. and Browne, William G.
"Perceived Quality of Marketing Journals"
Journal of Marketing Education (November 1979), pp. 6-15.

Benjamin, J. J. and Brenner, V. C.
"Perceptions of Journal Quality"
Accounting Review, Vol. 49 (April 1974), pp. 360-2.

Billings, B. B. and Viksnins, G. J.
"The Relative Quality of Economics Journals: An Alternative Rating
System"
Western Economic Journal, Vol. 10 (December 1972), pp. 467-9.

Black, Mary Kelly and Gunnigle, J. Robert
"Is JMR a Success?"
Journal of Marketing Research, Vol. IV (February 1967), pp. 88-90.

Browne, William G. and Becker, Boris W.
"Perceptions of Marketing Journals: Awareness and Quality Evaluations"
in Lusch, Robert F. et al. (editors)
1985 Educators' Conference Proceedings
(Chicago: American Marketing Association, 1985), pp. 149-154.

Coe, Robert K. and Weinstock, Irwin
"The Perceived Image and Policies of the Business Journals"
Southern Journal of Business, Vol. 4 (July 1969), pp. 91-8.

Danielson, Albert L. and Delorme, Charles D., Jr.
"Some Empirical Evidence on the Variables Associated With the Ranking
of Economics Journals"
Southern Economic Journal, Vol. 43 (October 1976), pp. 1149-60.

Fry, Elaine Hobbs, Walters, C. Glenn, and Scheurermann, Lawrence E.
"Perceived Quality of Fifty Selected Journals: Academicians and
Practitioners"
Journal of the Academy of Marketing Science, Vol. 13 (Spring 1985),
pp. 352-61.

Gagnard, Alice L. and Swartz, James E.
"An Evaluation of Advertising Research and Research Publications by
Leading American Advertising Managers"
Proceedings, American Academy of Advertising (1986).

Hamilton, Jack
"Physician, Heal Thyself!"
European Research, Vol. 13 (October 1985), pp. 179-85.

Hawkins, Robert G., Ritter, Lawrence S., and Walter, Ingo
"What Economists Think of Their Journals"
Journal of Political Economy, Vol. 81 (July-August 1973), pp. 1017-32.

Luke, Robert H. and Doke, E. Reed
"Marketing Journal Hierarchies: Faculty Perceptions, 1986-1987"
Journal of the Academy of Marketing Science, Vol. 15 (Spring 1987),
pp. 74-8.

McDonough, C. C.
"The Relative Quality of Economics Journals Revisited"
Quarterly Review of Economics and Business, Vol. 15 (Spring 1975),
pp. 91-6.

Moore, L. J. and Taylor, B. W., III
  "A Study of Institutional Publications in Business-Related Academic
  Journals, 1972-78"
  Quarterly Review of Economics and Business, Vol. 20 (Spring 1980),
  pp. 87-97.

Parasuraman, A.
  "Commercial Marketing Researchers' Evaluations of Academic Journals
  and Marketing Research Education"
  Journal of Marketing Education (Fall 1981), pp. 52-8.

Skeels, J. W. and Taylor, R. A.
  "The Relative Quality of Economics Journals: An Alternative Rating
  System"
  Western Economic Journal, Vol. 10 (December 1972), pp. 470-3.

Weaver, Charles N.
  "Evaluations of Sixty-Four Journals Which Publish Articles on
  Management"
  Education and Development Division of the Academy of Management
  (Summer 1975), working paper.

Weber, R. P. and Stevenson, W. C.
  "Evaluations of Accounting Journal and Department Quality"
  Accounting Review, Vol. 56 (July 1981), pp. 596-612.

Wooten, Bob E., Steiert, A. F., and Ryan, J. F.
  "Refereed Journals: A Suvey of Deans and Editors"
  Collegiate News and Views (1984), pp. 47-9.

13.06 ---------- Overviews of Subject Matter of Specific Periodicals

Geistfeld, Loren V. and Key, Rosemary
  "A Decade in Perspective 1975-84: Focus and Trends in the Journal of
  Consumer Affairs"
  Journal of Consumer Affairs, Vol. 20 (Summer 1986), pp. 65-76.

Grazer, William F. and Stiff, M. Ronald
  "Statistical Analysis and Design in Marketing Journal Articles"
  Journal of the Academy of Marketing Science, Vol. 15 (Spring 1987),
  pp. 70-3.

Hunt, Shelby D.
  "The Content of the Journal of Marketing Research: 1970-1983"
  Texas Tech University (1984), unpublished working paper.

Malhotra, Naresh K.
  "Some Observations on the State of the Art in Marketing Research"
  Journal of the Academy of Marketing Science, Vol. 16 (Spring 1988),
  pp. 4-24.

Wahlers, Russell G. and Dunn, Mark G.
  "Journal of Marketing: Topics and Selected Authorship Patterns
  1974-85"
  in Guiltinan, Joseph and Achabal, Dale (editors)
  Winter Educators' Conference Proceedings (1986), pp. 41-3.

Williams, Alvin J. and Oumlil, A. Ben
  "A Classification and Analysis of JPMM Articles"
  Journal of Purchasing and Materials Management, Vol. 23 (Fall 1987),
  pp. 24-8.

Yale, Laura and Gilly, Mary
  "Trends in Advertising Research: A Look at the Content of
  Marketing-Oriented Journals From 1976 to 1985"
  Journal of Advertising, Vol. 17, No. 1 (1988), pp. 11-22.

13.07 ---------- Citation Analyses

Broadus, Robert
  "A Citation Study for Sociology"
  American Sociologist, Vol. 32 (February 1967), pp. 19,20.

Broadus, Robert
  "An Analysis of Literature Cited in the American Sociological Review"
  American Sociological Review, Vol. 17 (June 1952), pp. 355-7.

Brown, Charles Harvey
  Scientific Serials
  ACRL Monograph No. 16
  (Chicago, IL: Association of College and Research Libraries, 1956).

Clark, Gary L.
  "Productivity Ratings of Institutions Based on Publication in Eight
  Marketing Journals: 1983-1984"
  Journal of Marketing Education, Vol. 7 (Fall 1985), pp. 12-23.

Clark, Gary L. and Hanna, Nessim
    "An Analysis of the Source of Articles Appearing in the Journal of
    Marketing Education Since Its Founding in 1979"
    Journal of Marketing Education, Vol. 8 (Summer 1986), pp. 71-4.

Eichorn, Philip and Yankauer, A.
    "Do Authors Check Their References? A Survey of References in Three
    Public Health Journals"
    American Journal of Public Health, Vol. 77, No. 8 (1987), pp. 1011-2.

Fields, D. Michael and Swayne, Linda E.
    "Publication in Major Marketing Journals: 1960-1986"
    Journal of Marketing Education, Vol. 10 (Fall 1988), pp. 36-48.

Garfield, Eugene
    Citation Indexing: Its Theory and Application in Science, Technology,
    and Humanities
    (New York: John Wiley and Sons, 1979).

Goldman, Arieh
    "Publishing Activity in Marketing as an Indicator of Its Structure
    and Disciplinary Boundaries"
    Journal of Marketing Research, Vol. XVI (November 1979), pp. 485-94.

Hamelman, Paul W. and Mazze, Edward M.
    "How Business Journals Cite One Another"
    Journal of Advertising Research, Vol. 14 (June 1974), pp. 23-5.

Hamelman, Paul W. and Mazze, Edward M.
    "Cross-Referencing Between AMA Journals and Other Publications"
    Journal of Marketing Research, Vol. X (May 1973), pp. 215-8.

Henry, William R. and Burch, E. Earl
    "Market Shares of Space in Marketing Journals"
    Journal of the Academy of Marketing Science, Vol. 4 (Winter-Spring
    1976), pp. 473-83.

Institute for Scientific Information
    Social Science Citation Index Journal Citation Reports
    (Philadelphia, PA: Institute for Scientific Information, 1986).

Institute for Scientific Information
    Social Science Citation Index Journal Citation Reports
    (Philadelphia, PA: Institute for Scientific Information, 1981).

Jobber, David and Simpson, Paul
    "A Citation Analysis of Selected Marketing Journals"
    International Journal of Research in Marketing, Vol. 5, No. 2 (1988),
    pp. 137-42.

Leong, Siew Meng
    "A Citation Analysis of the Journal of Consumer Research"
    Journal of Consumer Research, Vol. 15 (March 1989), pp. 492-7.

May, Kenneth O.
    "Abuses of Citation Indexing"
    Science, Vol. 156 (May 1967), pp. 890-2.

Meadows, Arthur Jack
    "The Citation Characteristics of Astronomical Research Literature"
    Journal of Documentation, Vol. 23 (March 1967), pp. 28-32.

Michman, Ronald D. and Gross, Walter
    "Sources of Scholarly Publications in Marketing"
    Akron Business and Economic Review, Vol. 17 (Spring 1986), pp. 56-61.

Moore, L. J. and Taylor, B. W., III
    "A Study of Institutional Publications in Business-Related Academic
    Journals"
    Quarterly Review of Economics and Business, Vol. 20 (Spring 1980),
    pp. 87-97.

Niemi, Albert W., Jr.
    "Publication Performance of Marketing Departments, 1975-1985"
    Journal of Marketing Education, Vol. 10 (Summer 1988), pp. 8-12.

Price, D. J. DeSolla
    "Citation Measures of Hard Science, Soft Science, Technology, and
    Nonscience"
    in Nelson, Carnot E. and Pollock, Donald K. (editors)
    Communication Among Scientists and Engineers
    (Lexington, MA: D. C. Heath, 1970), pp. 3-22.

Robinson, Larry M. and Adler, Roy
    "Measuring the Impact of Marketing Scholars and Institutions: An
    Analysis of Citation Frequency"
    Journal of the Academy of Marketing Science, Vol. 9 (Spring 1981),
    pp. 147-61.

Shull, C. A.
  "Erroneous Citations and Titles of Scientific Papers"
  Science, Vol. 73 (1931), pp. 363,4.

Veldkamp, Albert
  "Contributions to Congresses and Seminars"
  European Research, Vol. 4 (January 1976), pp. 38,9.

Wheatley, John J. and Wilson, Lawrence C.
  "The Origins of Published Marketing Research in the 1980's"
  Proceedings, AMA Educators' Conference (1987), pp. 260-5.

White, Howard D. and Griffith, Belver C.
  "Authors as Markers of Intellectual Space: Co-Citation in Studies of
  Science, Technology, and Society"
  Journal of Documentation, Vol. 38 (December 1982), pp. 255-72.

13.08 ---------- Readership Studies and Profiles of Readers

Clark, Gary L. and Kaminski, Peter F.
  "Marketing Journals Readership Study"
  Journal of Consumer Marketing, Vol. 4 (Winter 1987), pp. 61-69.

Fabianic, David A.
  "Perceived Scholarship and Readership of Criminal Justice Journals"
  Journal of Police Science and Administration, Vol. 8, No. 1 (1980),
  pp. 15-20.

Gottsfeld, Mary L.
  "Who are You? A Profile of the Clinical Social Work Journal Reader"
  Clinical Social Work Journal, Vol. 6, No. 4 (1978), pp. 259,60.

Horne, Annette
  "The Journal Readership Survey"
  Long Range Planning, Vol. 13 (November 1980), pp. 40-4.

Moore, James H.
  "Researching the Researchers: Who's Reading the Journal?"
  Journal of Advertising Research, Vol. 24 (June/July 1984), pp. 64-8.

13.09 ---------- Publishing and Academic Career Issues

Beltramini, Richard F., Schlacter, John L., and Kelly, Craig
  "Marketing Faculty Promotion and Tenure Policies and Practices"
  Journal of Marketing Education, Vol. 7 (Summer 1985), pp. 74-80.

Blunt, Peter
  "Publish or Perish or Neither: What is Happening in Academia"
  Vestes, Vol. 19 (November 1976), pp. 62-4.

Bohrer, Paul and Dolphin, Robert, Jr.
  "Expectations and Support for Scholarly Activity in Schools of
  Business"
  Journal of Education for Business, Vol. 61 (December 1985), pp. 101-5.

Coe, Robert K. and Weinstock, Irwin
  "Evaluating Journal Publications of Marketing Professors: A Second
  Look"
  Journal of Marketing Education, Vol. 5 (Spring 1983), pp. 37-42.

Coe, Robert K. and Weinstock, Irwin
  "Evaluating the Business/Economic Professor's Journal Publications:
  Perceptions Versus Reality"
  Annual Meetings of the Western Association of Collegiate Schools of
  Business, Scottsdale, AZ (1982), paper presentation.

Gaston, Jerry, Lantz, Herman R., and Snyder, Charles R.
  "Publication Criteria for Promotion in Ph.D. Graduate Departments"
  American Sociologist, Vol. 10 (November 1975), pp. 239-42.

Hollingshead, A. B.
  "Climbing the Academic Ladder"
  American Sociological Review, Vol. 5 (1940), pp. 384-94.

Jauch, Lawrence R.
  "Faculty Perceptions of Research Evaluation"
  Journal of the Society of Research Administrators (Fall 1975), pp.
  6-14.

Jauch, Lawrence R. and Glueck, William F.
  "Evaluation of University Professors' Research Performance"
  Management Science, (September 1975), pp. 66-75.

Lamb, Charles W., Jr. and McNeal, James U.
  "An Empirical Analysis of the Relationships Among Marketing Journals,
  Professors and Administrators"
  Journal of the Academy of Marketing Science, Vol. 5 (Fall 1977), pp.
  349-60.

McCullough, Charles D., Wooten, Bob, and Ryan, John
    "Research and Publication Programs in Collegiate Schools of Business:
    A Faculty Development Approach"
    Journal of Business Education, Vol. 57 (November 1981), pp. 46-9.

Miller, Thomas R.
    "Factors of Faculty Promotion in Collegiate Schools of Business"
    AACSB Bulletin (January 1976), pp. 13-9.

Moore, Laurence J. and Taylor, Bernard W., III
    "A Study of Institutional Publications in Business-Related Academic
    Journals, 1972-78"
    Quarterly Review of Economics and Business, Vol. 20 (Spring 1980),
    pp. 87-97.

Murray, John F. T.
    "Publish or Perish--By Suffocation"
    Journal of Legal Education, Vol. 27 (No. 4, 1976), p. 567.

Robertson, David E. and Sharplin, A. D.
    "Factors Relating to Publication Performance of Management Faculty"
    Collegiate News and Views (Fall 1983), pp. 11-4.

Roskies, Ethel
    "Publish and Perish"
    American Psychologist (December 1975), p. 1165.

Scully, Malcolm G.
    "Strained Relationships Worry Scholars, Publishers"
    The Chronicle of Higher Education, (January 1976), pp. 1-5.

Seldin, Peter
    Current Practices in Evaluating Business School Faculty
    Monograph Center for Applied Research, Pace University (August 1985).

Seldin, Peter
    "Current Practices in Evaluating the Business Faculty"
    AACSB Bulletin (April 1976), pp. 1-6.

Tuckman, Howard P. and Leakey, Jack
    "What is an Article Worth?"
    Journal of Political Economy (October 1975), p. 941.

Twedt, Dik Warren
    "A Marketing Strategy for Marketing Knowledge--Or How to Publish and
    Prosper"
    Journal of Marketing, Vol. 41 (April 1977), pp. 69-72.

Varble, Dale L. and Riordan, Edward A.
    "The Perception of Journal Publication in Faculty Performance
    Evaluation"
    Proceedings of the 1975 Southern Marketing Association Conference
    (January 1976), pp. 243-5.

13.10 ---------- Unclassified (Writing and Publication of Mktg Res)

Goldman, Arieh
    "Publishing Activity in Marketing as an Indicator of Its Structure
    and Disciplinary Boundaries"
    Journal of Marketing Research, Vol. XVI (November 1979), pp. 485-94.

Hamilton, Jack
    "Physician, Heal Thyself!"
    European Research, Vol. 13 (October 1985), pp. 179-85.

Hartmann, R. R. K. (editor)
    Lexicography: Principles and Practice
    (New York: Academic Press, Inc., 1983), 228 pp.

Livesey, Frank
    "The Market for Academic Manuscripts"
    European Journal of Marketing, Vol. 15, No. 8 (1981), pp. 52-67.

Livesey, Frank
    "Variations in Contracts Between Publishers"
    British Medical Journal (February 1979).

Wolf, William D.
    An Author's Guide to Business Publications
    (Los Angeles, CA: Research Institute for Business and Economics,
    University of Southern California, 1967), 142 pp.

14 ----------------------- RESEARCH FUNDING -------------------------

Lambert, Douglas M. and Sterling, Jay U.
  "Corporate-Sponsored Research: An Opportunity for Educators"
  Journal of Marketing Education, Vol. 10 (Fall 1988), pp. 20-8.

Locke, Lawrence F., Spirduso, Waneen Wyrick, and Silverman, Stephen J.
  Proposals That Work
  (Newbury Park, CA: Sage Publications, Inc., 1987), 272 pp.

Mohn, N. Carroll and Land, Thomas H.
  "A Guide to Quality Marketing Research Proposals and Reports"
  Business, Vol. 39 (January-February-March 1989).

14.01 ---------- Grants and Other Noncommercial Funding of Research

Locke, Lawrence F., Spirduso, Waneen Wyrick, and Silverman, Stephen J.
  Proposals That Work
  (Newbury Park, CA: Sage Publications, 1987), 272 pp.

Stephens, Keith T., Leonard, Myron J., and Manock, John J.
  "Applying Marketing Strategy to Private Source Grantsmanship"
  Journal of the Academy of Marketing Science, Vol. 11 (Fall 1983), pp.
  433-7.

White, Virginia P.
  Grants: How to Find Out About Them and What to do Next
  (New York: Graduate School University Center of the City University
  of New York, Plenum Press), 354 pp.

15 --------------- PHILOSOPHY OF SCIENCE AND RESEARCH ----------------

15.01 ---------- Books Re: Philosophy of Marketing Research

Bloom, Paul N.
  Knowledge Development in Marketing: The MSI Experience
  (Lexington, MA: Lexington Books, 1987), 256 pp.

Bush, Robert and Hunt, Shelby D. (editors)
  Marketing Theory: Philosophy of Science Perspectives
  (Chicago: American Marketing Association, 1982), 315 pp.

Dholakia, Nikhilesh and Arndt, Johan (editors)
  Changing the Course of Marketing: Alternative Paradigms for Widening
  Marketing Theory
  Research in Marketing, Supplement 2
  (Greenwich, CT: JAI Press, Inc., 1985), 311 pp.

Firat, A. Fuat, Dholakia, Nikhilesh, and Bagozzi, Richard P.
  Philosophical and Radical Thought in Marketing
  (Lexington, MA: Lexington Books, 1987), 392 pp.

Halbert, Michael
  The Meaning and Sources of Marketing Theory
  (New York: McGraw-Hill Book Company, 1965).

Hunt, Shelby D.
  Marketing Theory: The Philosophy of Marketing Science
  (Homewood, IL: Richard D. Irwin, Inc., 1983).

Hunt, Shelby D.
  Marketing Theory: Conceptual Foundations of Research in Marketing
  (Homewood, IL: Richard D. Irwin, Inc., 1976).

Locander, William B. and Cocanougher, A. Benton
  Problem Definition in Marketing
  Marketing Research Techniques Series No. 2
  (Chicago: American Marketing Association, 1975), 11 pp.

Zaltman, Gerald, LeMasters, K., and Heffring, M.
  Theory Construction in Marketing
  (New York: John Wiley and Sons, Inc., 1982).

Zaltman, Gerald, Pinson, Christian R. A., and Angelmar, Reinhard
  Metatheory and Consumer Research
  (New York: Holt, Rinehart and Winston, 1973), 226 pp.

15.02 ---------- Books Re: Philosophy of Science and Research

Ackoff, R. L.
  The Design of Social Research
  (Chicago: The University of Chicago Press, 1953).

Ackoff, R. L., Gupta, S. K., and Minas, J. S.
  Scientific Method: Optimizing Applied Research Decisions
  (New York: John Wiley and Sons, 1962).

Barker, Stephen F.
  The Elements of Logic
  (New York: McGraw-Hill, Inc., 1965).

Barnes, Berry
  Scientific Knowledge and Sociological Theory
  (London: Routledge and Kegan Paul, 1974).

Berkeley, Georges
  A Treatise Concerning the Principles of Human Knowledge
  (Maston, England: Scholar Press, 1971).

Beveridge, W. I. B.
  The Art of Scientific Investigation
  (New York: Vintage Books).

Blalock, H. M., Jr.
  Causal Inferences in Nonexperimental Research
  (Chapel Hill, NC: University of North Carolina Press, 1961).

Boring, E. G. et al.
  Psychology: A Behavioral Reinterpretation
  (Philadelphia: American Philosophical Society, 1964).

Braithwaite, R. B.
  Scientific Explanation
  (New York: Harper, 1953).

Braybrooke, David
  Philosophical Problems of the Social Sciences
  (New York: The Macmillan Company, 1965).

Brewer, Marilynn B. and Collins, Barry E. (editors)
  Scientific Inquiry and the Social Sciences
  (San Francisco: Jossey-Bass Inc., 1981), 523 pp.

Bridgman, P. W.
  The Logic of Modern Physics
  (New York: The Macmillan Co., 1927).

Chalmers, Alan F.
  What is This Thing Called Science?, Second Edition
  (St. Lucia, Australia: University of Queensland Press, 1982).

Churchman, C. West
  Prediction and Optimal Decision: Philosophical Issues of a Science of
  Values
  (Englewood Cliffs, NJ: Prentice-Hall, Inc., 1961).

Churchman, C. West
  Theory of Experimental Inference
  (New York: Harcourt, Brace and World, Inc., 1961).

Churchman, C. W. and Ratoosh, P. (editors)
  Measurement: Definitions and Theories
  (New York: John Wiley and Sons, Inc., 1959).

Cohen, Morris R.
  A Preface to Logic
  (New York, NY: Henry Holt and Company, 1944).

Danto, Arthur and Morgenbesser, Sidney
  Philosophy of Science
  (Cleveland, OH: The World Publishing Company, 1960).

Diesing, Paul
  Science and Ideology in the Policy Sciences
  (New York: Aldine, 1982).

Feigl, Herbert and Broadbeck, May
  The Philosophy of Science
  (New York: Appleton-Century-Crofts, 1958).

Francis, R. G.
  The Rhetoric of Science
  (Minneapolis, MN: The University of Minnesota Press, 1961), 183 pp.

Garfinkel, Alan
  Forms of Explanation
  (New Haven, CT: Yale University Press, 1981).

Gilman, William
  The Language of Science
  (New York: Harcourt, Brace and World, Inc., 1961), 248 pp.

Giere, Richard N.
  Understanding Scientific Reasoning, Second Edition
  (New York: Holt, Rinehart, and Winston, 1984).

Hempel, Carl G.
  Aspects of Scientific Explanation
  (New York: Free Press, 1965).

Husserl, Edmund
  Experience and Judgment
  (Evanston, IL: Northwestern University Press, 1973).

Husserl, Edmund
  Cartesian Meditations: An Introduction to Phenomenology
  (Atlantic Highlands, NJ: Humanities Press, 1960).

Huxley, Julian
  What Dare I Think
  (New York, NY: Harper and Bros., 1931).

Kantor, J. R.
  The Logic of Modern Science
  (Bloomington, IN: Principle Press, 1953).

Kaplan, Abraham
  The Conduct of Inquiry
  (San Francisco: Chandler, 1974).

Keat, Russell and Urry, John
  Social Theory as Science
  (London: Routledge and Kegan Paul, 1975).

Kemeny, J. G.
  A Philosopher Looks at Science
  (New York: Van Nostrand, 1959).

Kuhn, Thomas
   The Structure of Scientific Revolutions, Second Edition
   (Chicago: University of Chicago Press, 1970).

Lakatos, Imre and Musgrave, A. (editors)
   Criticism and the Growth of Knowledge
   (Cambridge: Cambridge University Press, 1970).

Lambert, Karel and Brittan, Gordon G., Jr.
   An Introduction to the Philosophy of Science
   (Englewood Cliffs, NJ: Prentice-Hall, Inc., 1970).

Laudan, Larry
   Science and Values
   (Berkeley, CA: University of California Press, 1984).

Lazarsfeld, Paul F.
   Mathematical Thinking in the Social Sciences
   (Glencoe, IL: The Free Press, 1954).

Mayer, Joseph
   Social Science Principles in the Light of Scientific Method
   (Durham, NC: Duke University Press, 1941).

Meehl, Paul E.
   Clinical Versus Statistical Prediction
   (Minneapolis, MN: University of Minnesota Press, 1954).

Morris, Charles
   Signs, Language and Behavior
   (New York: G. Braziller, inc., 1946).

Nagel, Ernest
   The Structure of Science
   (New York: Harcourt, Brace, Jovanovich, Inc., 1961).

Newton-Smith, W. H.
   The Rationality of Science
   (Boston, MA: Routledge and Kegan Paul, 1981).

Oesterle, John A.
   Logic: The Art of Defining and Reasoning
   (Englewood Cliffs, NJ: Prentice-Hall, Inc., 1963).

Pearson, Karl
   The Grammar of Science, Third Edition
   (London, EN: A. and C. Black, 1911).

Popper, Karl R.
   Conjectures and Refutations
   (New York: Harper Torchbooks, 1963).

Popper, Karl R.
   The Logic of Scientific Discovery
   (New York: Basic Books, 1959).

Rapoport, Anatol
   Operational Philosophy
   (New York: Harper Row and Brothers, 1953).

Ratner, Joseph (editor)
   Intelligence in the Modern World
   (New York, NY: The Modern Library, 1939).

Rudner, Richard S.
   Philosophy of Social Science
   (Englewood Cliffs, NJ: Prentice-Hall, Inc., 1966).

Russell, Bertrand
   Mysticism and Logic
   (New York: Anchor Books, 1957).

Sartre, Jean P.
   Critique of Dialectical Reason
   (London: New Left Books, 1976).

Sartre, Jean P.
   Being and Nothingness
   (New York: Washington Square Press, 1966).

Spiegelberg, Herbert
   The Phenomenological Movement
   (The Hague: Martinus Nijhoff, 1969).

Stevens, S. S. (editor)
   Handbook of Experimental Psychology
   (New York: John Wiley and Sons, Inc., 1962).

Suppe, Frederick (editor)
    The Structure of Scientific Theories, Second Edition
    (Urbana, IL: University of Illinois Press, 1977).

Tarski, Alfred
    Introduction to Logic and the Methodology of Deductive Science
    (New York: Oxford University Press, 1965).

Thrall, R. M., Coombs, C. H., and Davis, R. L. (editors)
    Decision Processes
    (New York: John Wiley and Sons, 1954).

Von Hayek, F.
    The Counter-Revolution of Science
    (New York: The Free Press, 1952).

Wallis, Roy
    On the Margins of Science
    (Keele, UK: University of Keele, 1979).

Watzlawick, P.
    How Real is Real?: Confusion, Disinformation, Communication
    (New York: Vintage Books, Random House, 1977).

Willner, Dorothy (editor)
    Decisions, Values and Groups
    (New York: Pergamon Press, 1960).

Wittgenstein, Ludwig
    Philosophical Investigations
    (Oxford, England: Basil Blackwell and Mott, 1953).

Wolf, A.
    Essentials of Scientific Method
    (New York: Macmillan Company, 1926).

Ziman, J.
    Reliable Knowledge: An Exploration of the Grounds for Belief in
    Science
    (Cambridge University Press, 1978).

15.03 ---------- Problem Definition in the Research Process

Chapman, Randall G.
    "Problem-Definition in Marketing Research Studies"
    Journal of Consumer Marketing, Vol. 6 (Spring 1989), pp. 51-9.

Jones, Sue
    "Problem Definition in Marketing Research: Facilitating Dialog
    Between Clients and Researchers"
    Psychology and Marketing, Vol. 2 (Summer 1985), pp. 83-92.

Lawrence, Raymond J.
    "Comments on 'To Hypothesize or Not to Hypothesize'"
    Journal of the Market Research Society, Vol. 25 (January 1983), p. 90.

Van Westendorp, Peter H.
    "To Hypothesize or Not to Hypothesize"
    Journal of the Market Research Society, Vol. 25 (January 1983), p. 89.

15.04 ---------- Articles etc. Re: Philosophy of Marketing Research

        See also (sub)heading(s) 1.04, 2.03.

Anderson, Paul F.
    "Marketing, Scientific Progress, and Scientific Method"
    Journal of Marketing, Vol. 47 (Fall 1983), pp. 18-31.

Arndt, Johan
    "Paradigms in Consumer Research: A Review of Perspectives and
    Approaches"
    European Journal of Marketing, Vol. 20, No. 8 (1986), pp. 23-40.

Arndt, Johan
    "The Tyranny of Paradigms: The Case for Paradigmatic Pluralism in
    Marketing"
    in Dholakia, Nikhilkesh and Arndt, Johan (editors)
    Changing the Course of Marketing: Alternative Paradigms for Widening
    Marketing Theory
    (Greenwich, CT: JAI Press, Inc., 1985), pp. 3-26.

Arndt, Johan
    "On Making Marketing Science More Scientific: Role of Orientations,
    Paradigms, Metaphors, and Puzzle Solving"
    Journal of Marketing, Vol. 49 (Summer 1985), pp. 11-23.

Arndt, Johan
    "The Political Economy Paradigm: Foundation for Theory Building in
    Marketing"
    Journal of Marketing, Vol. 47 (Fall 1983), pp. 44-54.

Arndt, Johan
    "The Political Economy of Marketing Systems: Reviving the
    Institutional Approach"
    Journal of Macromarketing, Vol. 1 (Fall 1981), pp. 36-42.

Arndt, Johan
    "Reflections on Research in Consumer Behavior"
    in Anderson, B. B. (editor)
    Advances in Consumer Research
    (Ann Arbor, MI: Association for Consumer Research, 1976), pp. 213-21.

Andrus, David, Butler, Daylin, and Norvell, Wayne
    "The Comparative Test in Marketing Research and Theory Development"
    Journal of the Academy of Marketing Science, Vol. 15 (Winter 1987),
    pp. 9-14.

Bagozzi, Richard P.
    "A Prospectus for Theory Construction in Marketing"
    Journal of Marketing, Vol. 48 (Winter 1984), pp. 11-29.

Bartels, R.
    "Can Marketing be a Science?"
    Journal of Marketing, Vol. 15 (January 1951), pp. 319-28.

Brodbeck, May
    "Recent Developments in the Philosophy of Science"
    in Busch, R. F. and Hunt, S. D. (editors)
    Marketing Theory: Philosophy of Science Perspective
    (Chicago: American Marketing Association, 1982), pp. 1-6.

Calder, Bobby J., Phillips, Lynn W., and Tybout, Alice M.
    "Designing Research for Application"
    Journal of Consumer Research, Vol. 8 (September 1981), pp. 197-207.

Carman, James M.
    "Paradigms for Marketing Theory"
    in Sheth, Jagdish N. (editor)
    Research in Marketing, Volume 3
    (Greenwich, CT: JAI Press, Inc.), pp. 1-36.

Converse, Paul D.
    "The Development of a Science of Marketing"
    Journal of Marketing, Vol. 10 (July 1945), pp. 14-23.

Cooper, Lee G.
    "Do We Need Critical Relativism? Comments on 'On Method in Consumer
    Research'"
    Journal of Consumer Research, Vol. 14 (June 1987), pp. 126,7.

Deshpande, Rohit
    "'Paradigms Lost': On Theory and Method in Research in Marketing"
    Journal of Marketing, Vol. 47 (Fall 1983), pp. 101-10.

Dixon, D. F. and Wilkinson, I. F.
    "An Alternative Paradigm for Marketing Theory"
    European Journal of Marketing, Vol. 18, No. 3 (1984), pp. 40-50.

Droge, Cornelia and Calantone, R.
    "Assumptions Underlying the Metatheoretical Debates Regarding Methods
    and Scientific Theory Construction"
    in Anderson, P. F. and Ryan, M. J. (editors)
    Scientific Method in Marketing
    Proceedings, AMA Winter Educators' Conference
    (Chicago: American Marketing Association, 1984), pp. 5-9.

Ferber, Robert
    "How Not to do Research"
    Journal of Marketing Research, Vol. V (February 1968), p. 104.

Gaski, John F.
    "Nomic Necessity in Marketing Theory: The Issue of Counterfactual
    Conditions"
    Journal of the Academy of Marketing Science, Vol. 13 (Spring 1985),
    pp. 310-20.

Hastings, Gerard B. and Lethar, Douglas S.
    "The Creative Potential of Research"
    International Journal of Advertising, Vol. 6, No. 2 (1987), pp.
    159-68.

Hauser, J.
    "The Coming Revolution in Marketing Theory"
    75th Anniversary Marketing Colloquium, Harvard Business School (1983).

Hudson, Laurel Anderson and Ozanne, Julie L.
     "Alternative Ways of Seeking Knowledge in Consumer Research"
     Journal of Consumer Research, Vol. 14 (March 1988), pp. 508-21.

Hunt, Shelby D.
     "Does Logical Empiricism Imprison Marketing?"
     in Dholakia, Nikhilkesh and Arndt, Johan (editors)
     Changing the Course of Marketing: Alternative Paradigms for Widening
     Marketing Theory
     (Greenwich, CT: JAI Press, Inc., 1985), pp. 27-35.

Hunt, Shelby D.
     "General Theories and the Fundamental Explananda of Marketing"
     Journal of Marketing, Vol. 47 (Fall 1983), pp. 9-17.

Hunt, Shelby D.
     "In Support of the '3-Dichotomies Model,' Replying to Criticism by
     Gumucio, Robin, Ross, and Etgar"
     Journal of Marketing, Vol. 42 (April 1978), pp. 107-10.

Hunt, Shelby D.
     "Lawlike Generalizations and Marketing Theory"
     Journal of Marketing, Vol. 37 (July 1973), pp. 69,70.

Laudan, Larry
     "Reconstructing Methodology"
     in Anderson, Paul F. and Ryan, Michael J. (editors)
     Scientific Methods in Marketing
     (Chicago: American Marketing Association, 1984), pp. 1-4.

Lazer, William
     "Some Contributions of a Philosophic Approach to Marketing Thought"
     in Kelley, Eugene J. and Lazer, William (editors)
     Managerial Marketing
     (Homewood, IL: Richard D. Irwin, 1958), pp. 414-9.

Lee, Charles E.
     "Measurement and the Development of Science and Marketing"
     Journal of Marketing Research, Vol. II (February 1965), pp. 20-5.

Leong, Siew Meng
     "Metatheory and Metamethodology in Marketing: A Lakatosian
     Reconstruction"
     Journal of Marketing, Vol. 49 (Fall 1985), pp. 23-40.

Olson, Jerry C.
     "Towards a Science of Consumer Behavior"
     in Mitchell, Andrew A. (editor)
     Advances in Consumer Research, Volume Nine
     (Ann Arbor, MI: Association for Consumer Research, 1981), pp. v-x.

Peter, J. Paul
     "Some Philosophical and Methodological Issues in Consumer Research"
     in Hunt, Shelby (editor)
     Marketing Theory
     (Homewood, IL: Irwin, 1983), pp. 382-94.

Peter, J. Paul
     "Current Issues in the Philosophy of Science: Implications for
     Marketing Theory--A Panel Discussion"
     in Bush, R. F. and Hunt, S. D. (editors)
     Marketing Theory: Philosophy of Science Perspective
     (Chicago: American Marketing Association, 1982).

Peter, J. Paul and Olson, Jerry C.
     "Is Science Marketing?"
     Journal of Marketing, Vol. 47 (Fall 1983), pp. 111-25.

Politz, Alfred
     "Science and Truth in Marketing Research"
     Harvard Business Review (January-February 1957).

Roberts, Wayne A.
     "A Kuhnian Perspective on Marketing Science and 'The Scientific
     Method'"
     in Anderson, Paul F. and Ryan, Michael J. (editors)
     1984 Marketing Educators' Conference
     Scientific Method in Marketing
     (Chicago: American Marketing Association, 1984), pp. 14-7.

Sauer, W. J., Nighswonger, N., and Zaltman, G.
     "Current Issues in the Philosophy of Science: Implications for the
     Study of Marketing"
     in Bush, R. F. and Hunt, S. D. (editors)
     Marketing Theory: Philosophy of Science Perspectives
     (Chicago: American Marketing Association, 1982), pp. 17-21.

Skipper, Robert and Hyman, Michael R.
     "Evaluating and Improving Argument-Centered Works in Marketing"
     Journal of Marketing, Vol. 51 (October 1987), pp. 60-75.

Sternthal, Brian, Tybout, Alice M., and Calder, Bobby J.
    "Confirmatory Versus Comparative Approaches to Judging Theory Tests"
    Journal of Consumer Research, Vol. 14 (June 1987), pp. 114-25.

Tybout, Alice M., Sternthal, Brian, and Calder, Bobby J.
    "Theory Testing Procedures: A Falsificationist's View"
    AMA Workshop on Marketing Theory, Virginia Polytechnic Institute
    (1985), paper presentation.

Uusitalo, Liisa and Uusitalo, Jyrki
    "Scientific Progress and Research Traditions in Consumer Research"
    in Monroe, Kent B. (editor)
    Advances in Consumer Research, Volume Eight
    (Ann Arbor, MI: Association for Consumer Research, 1981), pp. 559-63.

Wilson, Terry C.
    "Scientific Marketing Research and Creativity" (abstract)
    in Lusch, Robert F. et al. (editors)
    1985 AMA Educators' Conference Proceedings
    (Chicago: American Marketing Association, 1985), p. 355.

Zeithaml, Valarie A., Varadarajan, P. "Rajan", and Zeithaml, Carl P.
    "The Contingency Approach: Its Foundations and Relevance to Theory
    Building and Research in Marketing"
    European Journal of Marketing, Vol. 22, No. 7 (1988), pp. 37-64.

15.05 ---------- Articles etc. Re: Philosophy of Science and Research

Adler, Franz
    "Operational Definitions in Sociology"
    American Journal of Sociology, Vol. 52 (March 1947), pp. 438-44.

Alt, M. B.
    "Fact and Fiction in Survey Research: Some Philosophical
    Considerations"
    Quantitative Sociology Newsletter, Vol. 25 (1980), pp. 6-20.

Anderson, Paul F.
    "A Review of Some Recent Philosophy and Sociology of Science
    Literature"
    Virginia Polytechnic Institute and State University (1981), working
    paper.

Armstrong, J. Scott
    "Advocacy and Objectivity in Science"
    Management Science, Vol. 25 (May 1979), pp. 423-38.

Armstrong, J. Scott
    "How to Avoid Exploratory Research"
    Journal of Advertising Research, Vol. 10 (August 1970), pp. 27-30.

Berkson, W.
    "Lakatos One and Lakatos Two: An Appreciation"
    in Cohen, R. S., Feyerabend, P., and Wartofsky, M. W. (editors)
    Essays in Memory of Imre Lakatos: Boston Studies in the Philosophy of
    Science, Volume 39
    (Dordrecht: D. Reidel, 1976), pp. 39-54.

Blankenship, L. Vaughn
    "The Social Context of Science"
    in Nicosia, Francesco M. and Wind, Yoram (editors)
    Behavior Models for Market Analysis
    (Hinsdale, IL: The Dryden Press, 1977), pp. 9-24.

Carnap, R.
    "Testability and Meaning, Part IV"
    Philosophy of Science, Vol. 4 (1937), p. 7.

Carnap, Rudolph
    "Testability and Meaning"
    Philosophy of Science, Vol. 3 (1936), pp. 1-40.

Collins, H. M.
    "The Sociology of Scientific Knowledge: Studies of Contemporary
    Science"
    Annual Review of Sociology, Vol. 9 (1983), pp. 265-85.

Costner, Herbert L.
    "Theory, Deduction, and Rules of Correspondence"
    American Journal of Sociology, Vol. 75 (1969), pp. 245-63.

Diesing, Paul
    "Objectivism vs. Subjectivism in the Social Sciences"
    Philosophy of Science, Vol. 33 (March-June 1966), pp. 124-33.

Ebel, Robert L.
    "And Still the Dryads Linger"
    American Psychologist, Vol. 29 (July 1974), pp. 485-92.

Francis, R. G.
"The Relation of Data to Theory"
Rural Sociology, Vol. 22 (1957), pp. 258-66.

Galtung, Johan
"Empiricism, Criticism, Constructivism: Three Approaches to
Scientific Activity"
Third World Future Research Conference, Bucharest (September 1972),
paper presentation.

Geertz, Clifford
"From the Native's Point of View"
in Local Knowledge, Further Essays in Interpretive Anthropology
(New York: Basic Books, 1983), pp. 55-70.

Geertz, Clifford
"Blurred Genres: The Refiguration of Social Thought"
in Local Knowledge, Further Essays in Interpretive Anthropology
(New York: Basic Books, 1983), pp. 19-35.

Geertz, Clifford
"Thick Description: Toward an Interpretive Theory of Culture"
in Geertz. C. (editor)
The Interpretation of Cultures
(New York: Basic Books, 1973).

Gilbert, G. Nigel
"The Transformation of Research Findings Into Scientific Knowledge"
Social Studies of Science, Vol. 6 (September 1976), pp. 281-306.

Kaplan, Abraham
"Philosophy of Science in Anthropology"
Annual Review of Anthropology, Vol. 13 (1984), pp. 25-39.

Lakatos, Imre
"Falsification and the Methodology of Scientific Research Programs"
in Worrall, J. and Currie, G. (editors)
The Methodology of Scientific Programs: Imre Lakatos Philosophical
Papers, Volume One
(Cambridge: Cambridge University Press, 1978), pp. 8-101.

Lakatos, Imre
"Falsification and the Methodology of Science Research Programs"
in Lakatos, Imre and Musgrave, Alan (editors)
Criticism and the Growth of Knowledge
(London: Cambridge University Press, 1970).

Laudan, Larry
"Why Philosophy of Science has Abandoned Falsificationism"
Association for Consumer Research Annual Conference, Honolulu (1988),
paper presentation.

Laudan, Larry, Donovan, Arthur, Laudan, Rachel, Barker, Peter, Brown,
Harold, Leplin, Jarrett, Thagard, Paul, and Wykstra, Steve
"Scientific Change: Philosophical Models and Historical Research"
Synthese, Vol. 69 (November 1986), pp. 141-223.

Lazarsfeld, Paul
"Evidence and Inference"
Daedelus, Vol. 87 (Fall 1968), pp. 99-131.

Levine, M.
"Scientific Method and the Adversary Model"
American Psychologist, Vol. 29 (1974), pp. 661-77.

MacCorquodale, K. and Meehl, P. E.
"On the Distinction Between Hypothetical Constructs and Intervening
Variables"
Psychological Review, Vol. 55 (March 1948), pp. 95-107.

Masterman, M.
"The Nature of a Paradigm"
in Lakatos, I. and Musgrave, A. (editors)
Criticism and the Growth of Knowledge
(Cambridge: Cambridge University Press, 1970), pp. 59-89.

Mitroff, I. and Kilmann, R.
"On Evaluating Scientific Research: The Contributions of the
Philosophy of Science"
Technological Forecasting and Social Change, Vol. 8 (1975), pp.
163-74.

Morgan, Gareth
"Knowledge, Uncertainty, and Choice"
in Morgan, G. (editor)
Beyond Method: Strategies for Social Research
(Beverly Hills, CA: Sage Publications, Inc., 1983), pp. 383-91.

Morgan, Gareth
"The Significance of Assumptions"
in Morgan, G. (editor)
Beyond Method: Strategies for Social Research
(Beverly Hills, CA: Sage Publications, Inc., 1983), pp. 377-82.

Morgan, Gareth
"Toward a More Reflective Social Science"
in Morgan, G. (editor)
Beyond Method: Strategies for Social Research
(Beverly Hills, CA: Sage Publications, Inc., 1983), pp. 368-76.

Outhwaite, William
"Toward a Realist Perspective"
in Morgan, G. (editor)
Beyond Method: Strategies for Social Research
(Beverly Hills, CA: Sage Publications, Inc., 1983), pp. 321-46.

Petrinovich, Lewis
"Probabilistic Functionalism: A Conception of Research Method"
American Psychologist, Vol. 34 (May 1979), pp. 373-90.

Ryan, Michael J. and O'Shaughnessy, John
"Theory Development: The Need to Distinguish Levels of Abstraction"
in Lamb, C. W., Jr. and Dunne, P. M. (editors)
Theoretical Developments in Marketing
(Chicago: American Marketing Association, 1980), pp. 47-50.

Shapere, Dudley
"Scientific Theories and Their Domains"
in Suppe, Frederick (editor)
The Structure of Scientific Theories, Second Edition
(Urbana, IL: University of Illinois Press, 1977).

Siegel, Harvey
"What is the Question Concerning the Rationality of Science?"
Philosophy of Science, Vol. 52 (December 1985), pp. 517-37.

Siegel, Harvey
"Empirical Psychology, Naturalized Epistemology, and First Philosophy"
Philosophy of Science, Vol. 51 (December 1984), pp. 667-76.

Siegel, Harvey
"Justification, Discovery and the Naturalizing of Epistemology"
Philosophy of Science, Vol. 47 (June 1980), pp. 297-321.

Toulmin, S.
"History, Praxis, and the Third World: Ambiguities in Lakatos' Theory
of Methodology"
in Cohen, R. S., Feyerabend, P., and Wartofsky, M. W. (editors)
Essays in Memory of Imre Lakatos: Boston Studies in the Philosophy of
Science
(Dordrecht: D. Reidel, 1976), pp. 655-75.

Weber, Max
"'Objectivity' in Social Science and Social Policy"
in Shils, E. A. and Finch, H. A. (editors)
The Methodology of the Social Sciences
(Glencoe, IL: The Free Press, 1949).

Woolgar, Steve
"Interests and Explanation in the Social Study of Science"
Social Studies of Science, Vol. 11 (1981), pp. 365-94.

Zilsel, Edgar
"The Development of Rationalism and Empiricism"
International Encyclopedia of Unified Science, II, Vol. 8
(University of Chicago Press, 1941).

15.06 ---------- Theory Re: Replication

Brown, Stephen W. and Gaulden, Corbett F., Jr.
"Replication and Theory Development"
in Lamb, C. W., Jr. and Dunne, P. M. (editors)
Theoretical Developments in Marketing
(Chicago: American Marketing Association, 1980), 240-3.

Farley, John U., Lehmann, Donald R., and Ryan, Michael J.
"Generalizing From 'Imperfect' Replication"
Journal of Business, Vol. 54 (October 1981), pp. 597-610.

Leone, Robert P. and Schultz, Randall L.
"A Study of Marketing Generalizations"
Journal of Marketing, Vol. 44 (Winter 1980), pp. 10-8.

Reid, Leonard N., Rotfeld, Herbert J., and Wimmer, Roger D.
"How Researchers Respond to Replication Requests"
Journal of Consumer Research, Vol. 9 (September 1982), pp. 216-8.

Smith, N. C., Jr.
  "Replication Studies: A Neglected Aspect of Psychological Research"
  American Psychologist, Vol. 25 (October 1970), pp. 970-5.

15.07 ---------- Books Re: Relativism

Bernstein, Richard J.
  Beyond Objectivism and Relativism: Science, Hermeneutics, and Praxis
  (Philadelphia, PA: University of Pennsylvania Press, 1983).

Hollis, Martin and Lukes, Steven
  Rationality and Relativism
  (Cambridge, MA: The MIT Press, 1982).

Krausz, Michael and Meiland, Jack W.
  Relativism: Cognitive and Moral
  (Notre Dame, IN: University of Notre Dame Press, 1982).

Meiland, Jack W. and Krausz, Michael (editors)
  Relativism: Cognitive and Moral
  (Notre Dame, IN: University of Notre Dame Press, 1982).

Siegel, Harvey
  Relativsim Refuted: A Critique of Contemporary Epistemological
  Relativsm
  Synthese Library Volume 189
  (Dordrecht, The Netherlands: D. Reidel, 1987).

15.08 ---------- Theory Re: Relativism

Anderson, Paul F.
  "On Relativism and Interpretivism--With a Prolegomenon to the 'Why'
  Question"
  in Hirschman, Elizabeth (editor)
  Interpretive Consumer Research
  (Provo, UT: Association for Consumer Research, 1989), pp. 10-23.

Anderson, Paul F.
  "Relativism Revidivus: In Defense of Critical Relativism"
  Journal of Consumer Research, Vol. 15 (December 1988), pp. 403-6.

Anderson, Paul F.
  "Relative to What--That is the Question: A Reply to Siegel"
  Journal of Consumer Research, Vol. 15 (June 1988), pp. 133-7.

Anderson, Paul F.
  "On Method in Consumer Research: A Critical Relativist Perspective"
  Journal of Consumer Research, Vol. 13 (September 1986), pp. 155-73.

Anderson, Paul F.
  "Marketing, Scientific Progress, and Scientific Method"
  Journal of Marketing, Vol. 47 (Fall 1983), pp. 18-31.

Barnes, Berry and Bloor, David
  "Relativism, Rationalism, and the Sociology of Knowledge"
  in Hollis, Martin and Lukes, Steven (editors)
  Rationality and Relativism
  (Cambridge, MA: The MIT Press, 1982), pp. 21-47.

Cooper, Lee G.
  "Do We Need Critical Relativism? Comments on 'On Method in Consumer
  Research'"
  Journal of Consumer Research, Vol. 14 (June 1987), pp. 126,7.

Elkana, Yehuda
  "Two-Tier Thinking: Philosophical Realism and Historical Relativism"
  Social Studies of Science, Vol. 8 (August 1978), pp. 309-26.

Gieryn, Thomas F.
  "Relativist/Constructivist Programmes in the Sociology of Science:
  Redundance and Retreat"
  Social Studies of Science, Vol. 12 (1982), pp. 279-97.

Hunt, Shelby D.
  "Should Marketing Adopt Relativism?"
  in Anderson, Paul F. and Ryan, Michael J. (editors)
  1984 AMA Winter Educators' Conference
  Scientific Method in Marketing
  (Chicago: American Marketing Association, 1984), pp. 30-4.

Krausz, Michael
  "Relativism and Foundationalism"
  The Monist, Vol. 67 (July 1984), pp. 395-404.

Laudan, Larry
  "Relativism, Naturalism and Reticulation"
  Synthese, Vol. 71 (June 1987), pp. 221-34.

Laudan, Larry
    "A Note on Collin's Blend of Relativism and Empiricism"
    Social Studies of Science, Vol. 12 (1982), pp. 131,2.

Mandelbaum, Maurice
    "Subjective, Objective and Conceptual Relativisms"
    The Monist, Vol. 62 (October 1979), pp. 403-23.

McCullagh, C. Behan
    "The Intelligibility of Cognitive Relativism"
    The Monist, Vol. 67 (July 1984), pp. 327-40.

Muncy, James A. and Fisk, Raymond P.
    "Cognitive Relativism and the Practice of Marketing Science"
    Journal of Marketing, Vol. 51 (January 1987), pp. 20-33.

Murphy, Arthur E.
    "Objective Relativism in Dewey and Whitehead"
    Philosophical Review, Vol. 36 (March 1927), pp. 121-44.

Peter, J. Paul and Olson, Jerry C.
    "Is Science Marketing?"
    Journal of Marketing, Vol. 47 (Fall 1983), pp. 111-25.

Sayers, Brian
    "Wittgenstein, Relativism, and the Strong Thesis in Sociology"
    Philosophy of the Social Sciences, Vol. 17 (June 1987), pp. 133-45.

Siegel, Harvey
    "Relativism for Consumer Research? (Comments on Anderson)"
    Journal of Consumer Research, Vol. 15 (June 1988), pp. 129-32.

Siegel, Harvey
    "Relativsim, Truth and Incoherence"
    Synthese, Vol. 68 (August 1986), pp. 225-59.

Siegel, Harvey
    "Goodmanian Relativism"
    The Monist, Vol. 67 (July 1984), pp. 359-75.

Vallicella, William F.
    "Relativism, Truth, and the Symmetry Thesis"
    The Monist, Vol. 67 (July 1984), pp. 452-66.

15.09 ---------- Grounded Theory

Conrad, Clifton F.
    "A Grounded Theory of Academic Change"
    Sociology of Education, Vol. 51 (April 1978), pp. 101-12.

Glaser, Barney
    Theoretical Sensitivity: Advances in the Methodology of Grounded
    Theory
    (Mill Valley, CA: Sociology Press, 1978).

Glaser, Barney and Strauss, Anselm L.
    The Discovery of Grounded Theory Strategies for Qualitative Research
    (New York: Aldine Publishing Company, 1967).

Swan, John E.
    "Grounded Theory: An Inductive Methodology for Theory Building
    Research in Marketing"
    in Lusch, Robert F. et al. (editors)
    Proceedings, 1985 Educators' Conference
    (Chicago: American Marketing Association, 1985), pp. 348-54.

Wolman, Benjamin
    Dictionary of Behavioral Science
    (New York: Van Nostrand Reinhold, 1973).

15.10 ---------- Qualitative Versus Quantitative Research

    See also (sub)heading(s) 79.

Greenway, Gill and De Groot, Gerald
    "The Qualitative-Quantitative Dilemma: What's the Question?"
    Journal of the Market Research Society, Vol. 23 (April 1983), p. 147.

Jick, T. D.
    "Mixing Qualitative and Quantitative Methods: Triangulation in Action"
    in Van Maanen, J. (editor)
    Qualitative Methodology
    (Beverly Hills, CA: Sage, 1983), pp. 135-47.

Reichardt, C. S. and Cook, T. D.
    "Beyond Qualitative Versus Quantitative Methods"
    in Cook, T. D. and Reichardt, C. S. (editors)
    Qualitative and Quantitative Methods in Evaluation Research
    (Beverly Hills, CA: Sage, 1979), pp. 7-32.

Seymour, Daniel
    "Soft Data-Hard Data: The Painful Art of Fence-Sitting"
    Journal of Consumer Marketing, Vol. 6 (Spring 1989), pp. 25-32.

Smith, John K. and Heshusius, Louis
    "Closing Down the Conversation: The End of the
    Quantitative-Qualitative Debate"
    Educational Researcher, Vol. 15 (January 1986), pp. 4-12.

15.11 ---------- Interface Between Basic and Applied Research

Berkowitz, Leonard and Donnerstein, Edward
    "External Validity is More Than Skin Deep: Some Answers to Criticism
    of Laboratory Experiments"
    American Psychologist, Vol. 37 (1982), pp. 257-75.

Boehm, Virginia E.
    "Research in the 'Real World'--A Conceptual Model"
    Personnel Psychology, Vol. 33 (1980), pp. 495-503.

Brinberg, David and Hirschman, Elizabeth C.
    "Multiple Orientations for the Conduct of Marketing Research: An
    Analysis of the Academic/Practitioner Distinction"
    Journal of Marketing, Vol. 50 (October 1986), pp. 161-73.

Brinberg, David and McGrath, Joseph E.
    "A Network of Validity Concepts Within the Research Process"
    in Brinberg, D. and Kidder, L. (editors)
    New Directions for Methodology of Social and Behavioral Science:
    Forms of Validity in Research, Number 12
    (San Francisco: Jossey-Bass, Inc., 1982).

Butler, David
    "Academics and Pollsters"
    Journal of the Market Research Society, Vol. 29 (October 1987), pp.
    381-4.

Calder, Bobby J., Phillips, Lynn W., and Tybout, Alice M.
    "Designing Research for Application"
    Journal of Consumer Research, Vol. 8, No. 2 (1981), pp. 197-207.

Ellsworth, Phoebe C.
    "From Abstract Ideas to Concrete Instances: Some Guidelines for
    Choosing Natural Research Settings"
    American Psychologist, Vol. 32 (1977), pp. 604-15.

Freeman, Howard E. and Rossi, Peter H.
    "Furthering the Applied Side of Sociology"
    American Sociological Review, Vol. 49 (1984), pp. 571-80.

Holbrook, Morris B.
    "Whither ACR: some Reflections on Beards, Baltimore, Baseball, and
    Resurrecting Consumer Research"
    in Lutz, R. J. (editor)
    Advances in Consumer Research, Volume 13
    (Ann Arbor, MI: Association for Consumer Research, 1986).

Holbrook, Morris B.
    "Why Business is Bad for Consumer Research"
    in Hirschman, E. C. and Holbrook, M. B. (editors)
    Advances in Consumer Research, Volume Twelve
    (Ann Arbor, MI: Association for Consumer Research, 1985), pp. 145-56.

Jacoby, Jacob
    "Serving Two Masters: Perspectives on Consulting"
    in Hirschman, E. C. and Holbrook, M. B. (editors)
    Advances in Consumer Research, Volume 12
    (Ann Arbor, MI: Association for Consumer Research, 1985), pp. 157-63.

Johnson, D. and Field, D. R.
    "Applied and Basic Social Research: A Difference in Social Context"
    Leisure Studies, Vol. 4 (1981), pp. 269-79.

Lutz, Richard J.
    "Rethinking the Domain of Consumer Research"
    in Lutz, R. J. (editor)
    Advances in Consumer Research, Volume 13
    (Ann Arbor, MI: Association for Consumer Research, 1986).

MacKenzie, Kenneth D. and House, Robert
    "Paradigm Development in the Social Sciences: A Proposed Research
    Strategy"
    Academy of Management Review, Vol. 3, No. 1 (1978), pp. 7-23.

McGrath, Joseph E. and Brinberg, David
  "Alternative Paths for Research: Another View of the Basic vs.
  Applied Distinction"
  in Oskamp, S. (editor)
  Applied Social Psychology Annual
  (Beverly Hills, CA: Sage Publications, Inc., 1984).

McGrath, Joseph E., Martin, J., and Kulka, P. A.
  Judgment Calls in Research
  (Beverly Hills, CA: Sage Publications, Inc., 1982).

Weick, Karl E.
  "Organizations in the Laboratory"
  in Vroom, V. T. (editor)
  Methods of Organizational Research
  (Pittsburgh: University of Pittsburgh Press, 1967).

16 --------------------- RESEARCH METHODS TEXTS ----------------------

16.01 ---------- Comprehensive Reviews of Marketing Research Texts

Albaum, Gerald
  "Recent Marketing Research Texts: A Comparative Review"
  Journal of Marketing Research, Vol. XX (February 1983), pp. 103-8.

Goodrich, Jonathan N.
  "Two Recent Marketing Research Texts: A Comparative Review"
  Journal of Marketing Research, Vol. XXI (February 1984), pp. 124-6.

Jones, Wesley H.
  "Review of Two Marketing Research Texts"
  Journal of Marketing Research, Vol. XIIX (February 1981), pp. 127-30.

Tashchian, Armen, Pucely, Marya J., and Crittenden, Vicky L.
  "Marketing Research Texts: A Comparative Review of the Area"
  in Lusch, Robert F. et al. (editors)
  1985 AMA Educators' Conference Proceedings
  (Chicago: American Marketing Association, 1985), pp. 129-35.

16.02 ---------- Academic Marketing Research Texts

Aaker, David A. and Day, George S.
  Marketing Research, Fourth Edition
  (New York: John Wiley and Sons, Inc., 1990), 739 pp.

Aaker, David A. and Day, George S.
  Marketing Research: Private and Public Sector Decisions
  (New York: John Wiley and Sons, Inc., 1980).

Albaum, Gerald and Venkatesan, M.
  Scientific Marketing Research
  (New York: The Free Press, 1971), 415 pp.

Alderson, Wroe and Green, P. E.
  Planning and Problem Solving in Marketing
  (Homewood, IL: Richard D. Irwin, Inc., 1964).

Barker, Raymond
  Marketing Research: Text With Cases
  (Reston, VA: Reston Publishing Co., 1983), 380 pp.

Barksdale, H. C.
  Problems in Marketing Research: In-Basket Simulation
  (New York, NY: Holt, Rinehart and Winston, Inc., 1963), 446 pp.

Barksdale, Hiram C. and Weilbacher, William M.
  Marketing Research: Selected Readings With Analytical Commentaries
  (New York, NY: The Ronald Press Co., 1966), 696 pp.

Bellenger, Danny N. and Greenberg, Barnett A.
  Marketing Research--A Management Information Approach
  (Homewood, IL: Richard D. Irwin, Inc., 1978), 601 pp.

Boyd, Harper W., Jr., Westfall, Ralph, and Stasch, Stanley F.
  Marketing Research: Text and Cases, Sixth Edition
  (Homewood, IL: Richard D. Irwin, Inc., 1985), 836 pp.

Bradley, Ute
  Applied Marketing and Social Research, Second Edition
  (John Wiley and Sons, 1987), 506 pp.

Brinberg, David and Lutz, Richard J. (editors)
  Perspectives on Methodology in Consumer Research
  (Secaucus, NJ: Springer-Verlag New York, Inc., 1986), 301 pp.

Brown, F. E.
  Marketing Research: A Structure for Decision Making
  (Reading, MA: Addison-Wesley Publishing Co., 1980), 602 pp.

Brown, Lyndon O. and Beik, Leland L.
  Marketing Research and Analysis
  (New York: The Ronald Press Company).

Chisnall, P. M.
  Marketing Research: Analysis and Measurement, Third Edition
  (London: McGraw-Hill, 1986), 352 pp.

Churchill, Gilbert A., Jr.
  Basic Marketing Research
  (New York: The Dryden Press, 1988), 738 pp.

Churchill, Gilbert A., Jr.
  Marketing Research: Methodological Foundations, Fourth Edition
  (Hinsdale, IL: The Dryden Press, 1987), 896 pp.

Cox, Eli P., III
    Marketing Research: Information for Decision Making
    (New York: Harper and Row, 1979), 437 pp.

Cox, Keith K. (editor)
    Readings in Market Research
    (New York: Appleton-Century-Crofts, 1967), 386 pp.

Cox, Keith K. and Enis, Ben M.
    The Marketing Research Process
    (Pacific Palisades, CA: Goodyear Publishing Company, 1972).

Cox, Keith K. and Enis, Ben M. (editors)
    Readings in the Marketing Research Process
    (Pacific Palisades, CA: Goodyear Publishing, 1973), 400 pp.

Cox, Keith K. and Smith, Sam V.
    Analytical Marketing Exercises
    (Englewood Cliffs, NJ: Prentice-Hall, Inc., 1983), 238 pp.

Cox, William E., Jr.
    Industrial Marketing Research
    (New York: John Wiley and Sons, Inc., 1979), 250 pp.

Crimp, Margaret
    The Marketing Research Process, Second Edition
    (London: Prentice-Hall International, 1985), 294 pp.

Day, Ralph L. and Ness, Thomas E.
    Marketing Models--Behavioral Science Applications
    (Scranton, PA: International Textbook, 1971), 556 pp.

Day, Ralph L. and Parsons, Leonard J.
    Marketing Models--Quantitative Applications
    (Scranton, PA: International Textbook, 1971), 693 pp.

De Bruicker, Stewart and Reibstein, David J.
    Cases in Marketing Research
    (Prentice-Hall, 1982), 396 pp.

Dillon, William, Madden, Thomas, and Firtle, Neil
    Marketing Research in a Marketing Environment, Second Edition
    (Homewood, IL: Richard D. Irwin, Inc., 1990), 853 pp.

Dodge, H. Robert, Fullerton, Sam D., and Rink, David R.
    Marketing Research
    (Columbus, OH: Charles E. Merrill Publishing Company, 1982), 530 pp.

Douglas, Susan P. and Craig, S.
    International Marketing Research
    (Englewood Cliffs, NJ: Prentice-Hall, Inc., 1983), 337 pp.

Elliot, Ken and Christopher, Martin
    Research Methods in Marketing
    (New York: Holt, Rinehart and Winston, 1973), 248 pp.

Eskin, Gerald and Montgomery, David
    Data Analysis: Cases in Computer and Model Assisted Marketing
    (Palo Alto, CA: The Scientific Press, 1976), 98 pp.

Ferber, R.
    Statistical Techniques in Market Research
    (New York: McGraw-Hill Book Company, 1949).

Ferber, Robert, Blankertz, Donald F., and Hollander, Sidney, Jr.
    Marketing Research
    (New York, NY: The Ronald Press Company, 1964), 679 pp.

Ferber, Robert and Verdoorn, P. J.
    Research Methods in Economics and Business
    (New York: The Macmillan Co., 1962).

Fitzroy, Peter T.
    Analytical Methods for Marketing Management
    (Maidenhead, Berkshire, England: McGraw-Hill Book Company (UK) Ltd.,
    1976), 337 pp.

Frank, Ronald E., Kuehn, Alfred A., and Massy, William F. (editors)
    Quantitative Techniques in Marketing Analysis: Text and Readings
    (Homewood, IL: Richard D. Irwin, Inc., 1962).

Green, Paul E., Tull, Donald S., and Albaum, Gerald
    Research for Marketing Decisions, Fifth Edition
    (Englewood Cliffs, NJ: Prentice-Hall, Inc., 1988), 784 pp.

Hartley, Robert F., Prough, George E., and Flaschner, Alan B.
    Essentials of Marketing Research
    (Tulsa, OK: Pennwell Publishing Co., 1983), 566 pp.

Holmes, Parker M.
  Marketing Research: Principles and Readings
  (Cincinnati, OH: South-Western Publishing Co., 1960), 646 pp.

Jain, Arun K., Pinson, Christian, and Ratchford, Brian T. (editors)
  Marketing Research: Applications and Problems
  (New York: John Wiley and Sons, Inc., 1982), 555 pp.

Kinnear, Thomas C. and Taylor, James R.
  Marketing Research: An Applied Approach, Third Edition
  (New York: McGraw-Hill, 1987), 718 pp.

Kress, George
  Marketing Research, Second Edition
  (Reston, VA: Reston Publishing Company, Inc., 1982), 427 pp.

Lehmann, Donald R.
  Market Research and Analysis, Third Edition
  (Homewood, IL: Richard D. Irwin, Inc., 1989), 879 pp.

Lorie, James H. and Roberts, Harry V.
  Basic Methods of Marketing Research
  (New York: McGraw-Hill Book Company, 1951).

Luck, David J. and Rubin, Ronald S.
  Marketing Research, Seventh Edition
  (Englewood Cliffs, NJ: Prentice-Hall, Inc., 1987), 683 pp.

McGown, K. L.
  Marketing Research--Text and Cases
  (Cambridge, MA: Winthrop Publishers, Inc., 1979), 432 pp.

Montgomery, David B. and Wittink, Dick R. (editors)
  Market Measurement and Analysis
  (Cambridge, MA: Marketing Science Institute, 1980), 573 pp.

Nelson, James E.
  The Practice of Marketing Research
  (Boston: Kent Publishing Company, 1982), 667 pp.

Parasuraman, A.
  Marketing Research
  (Reading, MA: Addison-Wesley Publishing Company, 1986), 831 pp.

Peterson, Robert A.
  Marketing Research, Second Edition
  (Plano, TX: Business Publications, Inc.).

Prince, Melvin
  Consumer Research for Management Decisions
  (New York: John Wiley and Sons, Inc., 1982), 210 pp.

Schoner, Bertram and Uhl, Kenneth P.
  Marketing Research: A Short Course for Professionals
  (New York: John Wiley and Sons, Inc., 1976), 346 pp.

Schoner, Bertram and Uhl, Kenneth P.
  Marketing Research: Information Systems and Decision Making, Second
  Edition
  (New York: John Wiley and Sons, 1975), 588 pp.

Schreier, Fred T.
  Modern Marketing Research--A Behavioral Science Approach
  (Belmont, CA: Wadsworth Publishing Company, 1963).

Schultz, Randall L., Zaltman, Gerald, and Burger, Philip C.
  Cases in Marketing Research
  (New York: The Dryden Press, 1977), 270 pp.

Sheth, Jagdish N. (editor)
  Research in Marketing: A Research Annual, Volume 2
  (Greenwich, CT: JAI Press, Inc., 1979), 357 pp.

Sheth, Jagdish N. (editor)
  Research in Marketing: A Research Annual, Volume One
  (Greenwich, CT: JAI Press, Inc., 1978), 333 pp.

Stone, M. A. and Proctor, T.
  Marketing Research
  (MacDonald and Evans, 1978).

Sudman, Seymour and Spaeth, Mary A. (editors)
  The Collection and Analysis of Economic and Consumer Behavior Data:
  In Memory of Robert Ferber
  (Champaign, IL: Bureau of Economic and Business Research and Survey
  Research Laboratory, University of Illinois at Urbana-Champaign,
  1984), 406 pp.

Theil, Henri
  System-Wide Explorations in International Economics, Input-Output
  Analysis, and Marketing Research
  (Amsterdam: North Holland Publishing Company, 1980), 143 pp.

Tull, Donald S. and Albaum, Gerald S.
  Survey Research--A Decisional Approach
  (New York: Intext Educational Publishers, 1973), 244 pp.

Tull, Donald S. and Hawkins, Del I.
  Marketing Research: Meaning, Measurement, and Method, Fifth Edition
  (New York: Macmillan Publishing Co., Inc., 1990).

Wasson, Chester R.
  The Strategy of Marketing Research
  (New York, NY: Appleton-Century-Crofts, 1964), 661 pp.

Weiers, Ronald
  Marketing Research, Second Edition
  (Englewood Cliffs, NJ: Prentice-Hall, Inc., 1988).

Wentz, Walter B.
  Marketing Research: Management, Methods and Cases, Second Edition
  (New York: Harper and Row, 1979), 770 pp.

Zaltman, Gerald and Burger, Philip C.
  Marketing Research: Fundamentals and Dynamics
  (New York, NY: The Dryden Press, 1977), 744 pp.

Zikmund, William G.
  Exploring Marketing Research, Third Edition
  (Chicago: The Dryden Press, 1989), 800 pp.

16.03 ---------- Computer Assisted Exercises in Marketing Research

Burns, Alvin C.
  Mail Survey Response Rates
  unpublished.

Lilien, Gary L.
  Marketing Mix Analysis With Lotus 1-2-3
  (Palo Alto, CA: The Scientific Press, 1986), 206 pp.

Schellinck, D. A. and Maddox, R. Neil
  Marketing Research--A Computer Assisted Approach
  (Chicago: The Dryden Press, 1987), 224 pp.

16.04 ---------- Experiential Exercises in Marketing Research

Luck, David J., Rubin, Ronald S., and Taylor, Donald A.
  Experiential Exercises in Marketing Research
  (Englewood Cliffs, NJ: Prentice-Hall, Inc., 1980), 181 pp.

16.05 ---------- Professional Marketing Research Texts

Andreasen, Alan R.
  Cheap but Good Marketing Research
  (Homewood, IL: Dow Jones-Irwin, 1988).

Bellenger, Danny N., Bernhardt, Kenneth L., and Goldstucker, Jac L.
  Qualitative Research in Marketing
  (Chicago: American Marketing Association, 1976), 76 pp.

Berenson, Conrad and Colton, Raymond
  Research and Report Writing for Business and Economics
  (New York, NY: Random House, 1971), 182 pp.

Blankenship, A. B. and Doyle, J. B.
  Marketing Research Management
  (New York, NY: The American Management Association, 1965), 370 pp.

Bradley, Ute (editor)
  Applied Marketing and Social Research
  (Chichester, England: John Wiley and Sons, Inc., 1987).

Breen, George E. and Blankenship, A. B.
  Do-It-Yourself Marketing Research, Second Edition
  (New York: McGraw-Hill Book Company, 1982), 303 pp.

Crisp, Richard D.
  Marketing Research
  (New York, NY: McGraw-Hill Book Company, 1957).

Crouch, Sunny
  Marketing Research for Managers
  (North Pornfret, VT: William Heinemann, 1984), 345 pp.

Davis, Anthony
  The Practice of Marketing Research, Second Edition
  (London: William Heinemann Ltd., 1984), 253 pp.

Drew, Clifford J.
  Introduction to Designing Research and Evaluation
  (London: Henry Kimpton, 1976).

Elliott, C. K. and Christopher, M. G.
  Research Methods in Marketing
  (Holt, Rinehart and Winston).

Emory, C. William
  Business Research Methods
  (Homewood, IL: Richard D. Irwin, Inc., 1976), 483 pp.

Gorton, Keith and Carr, Isobel
  Low-Cost Marketing Research: A Guide for Small Business
  (John Wiley and Sons), 110 pp.

Govani, Norman A. P.
  Contemporary Marketing Research--Perspectives and Applications
  (Morristown, NJ: General Learning Corp., 1972), 538 pp.

Green, Paul E. and Frank, Ronald E.
  A Manager's Guide to Marketing Research: Survey of Recent Developments
  (New York, NY: John Wiley and Sons, Inc., 1967), 185 pp.

Hague, Paul N. and Jackson, Peter
  Do Your Own Market Research
  (Kogan Page, 1987), 249 pp.

Haller, Terry
  Danger: Marketing Researcher at Work
  (Westport, CT: Quorum Books, 1983), 200 pp.

Heidingsfield, Myron S. and Eby, Frank H., Jr.
  Marketing and Business Research
  (New York, NY: Holt, Rinehart and Winston, 1962).

Holmes, Parker M.
  Marketing Research Principles and Readings
  (Cincinnati, OH: Southwestern Publishing Co., 1960), 641 pp.

Honomichl, Jack J.
  Honomichl on Marketing Research
  (Lincolnwood, IL: NTC Business Books, 1986), 330 pp.

Hough, Louis
  Modern Research for Administrative Decisions
  (Englewood Cliffs, NJ: Prentice-Hall, 1970), 609 pp.

Joselyn, Robert W.
  Designing the Marketing Research Project
  (New York: Petrocelli/Charter, 1977), 264 pp.

Kapferer, Clodwig and Disch, Wolfgang K. A.
  Market Research by Trade Associations
  (Paris: Organisation for Economic Co-Operation and Development, 1964), 92 pp.

Konrad, Evelyn and Erickson, Rod (editors)
  Marketing Research: A Management Overview
  (New York, NY: American Management Association, 1966), 224 pp.

Kress, George
  Marketing Research: A Basic Approach, Second Edition
  (Reston, VA: Reston Publishing Co., 1982), 384 pp.

Kurtz, Ronald
  Strategies in Marketing Research, Revised Edition
  (New York: American Management Association, 1970), 231 pp.

Leedy, Paul D.
  Practical Research: Planning and Design, Third Edition
  (New York: Macmillan Publishing Company), 313 pp.

Livingstone, James M.
  Management Guide to Market Research
  (Macmillan), 173 pp.

National Industrial Conference Board
  Marketing Research in Action
  (New York: National Industrial Conference Board, 1964), 128 pp.

Proctor, Tony and Stone, Marilyn A.
  Marketing Research
  (M and E Handbook Series, 1978), 184 pp.

Ramond, Charles
The Art of Using Science in Marketing
(New York: Harper and Row, Publishers, 1974), 298 pp.

Rummell, J. Francis and Ballaine, Wesley C.
Research Methodology in Business
(New York: Harper and Row, 1963), 359 pp.

Sciglimpaglia, Donald
Applied Marketing Research
(Hinsdale, IL: The Dryden Press, 1983), 335 pp.

Seibert, Joseph and Wills, Gordon (editors)
Marketing Research
(Middlesex, EN: Penguin Books Ltd., 1970).

Sekaran, Uma
Research Methods for Managers: A Skill-Building Approach
(New York: John Wiley and Sons, Inc., 1984), 336 pp.

16.06 ---------- Marketing Research Methods Texts--International

See also (sub)heading(s) 2, 28.

Douglas, Susan P. and Craig, C. Samuel
International Marketing Research
(Englewood Cliffs, NJ: Prentice-Hall, Inc., 1983), 337 pp.

Lonner, W. J. and Berry, J. W. (editors)
Field Methods in Cross-Cultural Research
(Beverly Hills, CA: Sage Publications, Inc., 1986).

Sethna, Beheruz N. and Groeneveld, Leonard
Research Methods in Marketing and Management
(New Delhi, India: Tata McGraw-Hill Publishing Company Limited, 1984), 332 pp.

Zheng, Z. C. and Yu, J. W.
Marketing Research Methods (in Chinese)
Zhongshan University Press, 1988), 240 pp.

16.07 ---------- Marketing Research Handbooks

European Society for Opinion and Marketing Research
Marketing Research in Europe: Annual Handbook
(Amsterdam: European Society for Opinion and Marketing Research, 1972), 465 pp.

Ferber, Robert (editor)
Handbook of Marketing Research
(New York: McGraw-Hill Book Company, 1974).

Ruddick, Morris E., Sherwood, Philip K., and Stevens, Robert E.
The Marketing Research Handbook
(Englewood Cliffs, NJ: Prentice-Hall, Inc., 1983), 210 pp.

Vichas, Robert P.
Complete Handbook of Profitable Marketing Research Techniques
(Englewood Cliffs, NJ: Prentice-Hall, Inc., 1982), 432 pp.

Worcester, Robert M. and Downham, John (editors)
Consumer Market Research Handbook, Third Revised Edition
(New York: Elsevier Science Publishing Co., 1986), 840 pp.

16.08 ---------- Nonmarketing Social Sciences Research Methods Books

Ackoff, Russell
The Design of Social Research
(Chicago: The University of Chicago Press, 1953).

Ackoff, Russell L.
Scientific Methods
(New York, NY: John Wiley and Sons, Inc., 1962).

Babbie, Earl R.
The Practice of Social Research, Fourth Edition
(Belmont, CA: Wadsworth Publishing Company, 1986), 577 pp.

Babbie, Earl R. and Huitt, Robert E.
Practicing Social Research
(Belmont, CA: Wadsworth, 1975), 232 pp.

Bailey, Kenneth
Methods of Social Research, Second Edition
(New York: Macmillan, 1982), 544 pp.

Balsley, Howard L. and Clover, Vernon T.
   Business Research Methods, Second Edition
   (Columbus, OH: Grid Publishing, Inc., 1979), 385 pp.

Beals, Ralph L.
   Politics of Social Research
   (Chicago, IL: Aldine Publishing Co., 1969), 228 pp.

Berg, David N. and Smith, Kenwyn K. (editors)
   Exploring Clinical Methods for Social Research
   (Beverly Hills, CA: Sage Publications, 1985), 400 pp.

Berry, William D. and Lewis-Beck, Michael S. (editors)
   New Tools for Social Scientists: Advances and Applications in
   Research Methods
   (Beverly Hills, CA: Sage Publications, Inc., 1986), 288 pp.

Blank, Steven C.
   Practical Business Research Methods
   (Westport, CT: AVI Publishing Co.), 368 pp.

Bogdan, R. and Taylor, S. J.
   Introduction to Qualitative Research Methods
   (New York: John Wiley and Sons, Inc., 1975).

Brewer, John and Hunter, Albert
   Multimethod Research
   (Newbury Park, CA: Sage Publications, Inc., 1989), 224 pp.

Brewer, M. B. and Crano, W. D.
   Principles of Research in Social Work
   (New York: McGraw-Hill Book Co., 1973).

Brislin, Richard W., Lonner, Walter J., and Thorndike, Robert M.
   Cross-Cultural Research Methods
   (New York: John Wiley and Sons, 1973), 352 pp.

Brown, Roy Chamberlain (editor)
   Quantity and Quality in Economic Research, Volume One
   (Lanham, MD: University Press of America Inc.), 423 pp.

Bynner, John and Stribley, Keith M. (editors)
   Social Research: Principles and Procedures
   (New York: Longman, Inc., 1978), 354 pp.

Caplovitz, David
   The Stages of Social Research
   (New York: John Wiley and Sons, Inc., 1983), 434 pp.

Carlsmith, J. Merrill, Ellsworth, Phoebe C., and Aronson, Elliot
   Methods of Research in Social Psychology
   (Reading, MA: Addison-Wesley, 1976).

Cicourel, Aaron V.
   Method and Measurement in Sociology
   (New York, NY: The Free Press of Glencoe, Macmillan Co., 1964), 246
   pp.

Cook, Thomas D. and Reichardt, Charles S. (editors)
   Qualitative and Quantitative Methods in Evaluation Research
   (Beverly Hills, CA: Sage Publications, Inc., 1979).

Cooley, W. W. and Lohnes, P. R.
   Evaluation Research in Education
   (New York: John Wiley and Sons, Inc., 1976).

Crano, William D. and Brewer, Marilynn B.
   Principles of Research in Social Psychology
   (New York: McGraw-Hill, 1973).

Crowl, Thomas K.
   Fundamentals of Research: A Practical Guide for Educators and Special
   Educators
   (Columbus, OH: Publishing Horizons, Inc., 1986), 241 pp.

Davis, Duane and Cosenza, Robert M.
   Business Research for Decision Making
   (Boston, MA: Kent Publishing Company, 1985), 552 pp.

Denzin, Norman K.
   The Research Act: A Theoretical Introduction to Sociological Methods,
   Third Edition
   (Englewood Cliffs, NJ: Prentice-Hall, Inc., 1989).

Dominowski, Roger L.
   Research Methods
   (Englewood Cliffs, NJ: Prentice-Hall, Inc., 1980), 390 pp.

Donahue, Mary and Spates, James L.
    Action Research Handbook for Social Change in Urban America
    (New York: Harper and Row, 1973), 90 pp.

Emory, C. William
    Business Research Methods
    (Homewood, IL: Richard D. Irwin, Inc., 1976), 483 pp.

Fay, Charles H. and Wallace, Marc J., Jr.
    Research-Based Decisions
    (New ork: Random House, Inc., 1987), 399 pp.

Feldman, Elliot J.
    A Practical Guide to the Conduct of Field Research in the Social
    Sciences
    (Boulder, CO: Westview Press, 1981), 122 pp.

Ferber, Robert and Verdoorn, P. J.
    Research Methods in Economics and Business
    (New York: Macmillan, 1962).

Gage, N.
    Handbook of Research on Teaching
    (Skokie, IL: Rand McNally, 1963).

Galtung, Johan
    Theory and Methods of Social Research
    (New York: Columbia University Press, 1969).

Grady, Kathleen E. and Wallston, Barbara Strudler
    Research in Health Care Settings
    (Newbury Park, CA: Sage Publications, 1988).

Grosof, Miriam S. and Sardy, Hyman
    A Research Primer for the Social and Behavioral Sciences
    (Orlando, FL: Academic Press, Inc., 1985), 433 pp.

Haynes, Stephen N.
    Principles of Behavioral Assessment
    (New York: Gardner Press, Inc., 1978).

Helmer, Olaf
    Looking Forward: A Guide to Futures Research
    (London: Sage Publications, 1983).

Hippler, Hans J., Schwartz, Norbert, and Sudman, Seymour (editors)
    Social Information Processing and Survey Methodology
    Recent Research in Psychology Series
    (New York: Springer-Verlag, 1987), 223 pp.

Hyman, Herbert H.
    Secondary Analysis of Sample Surveys: Principles, Procedures and
    Potentialities
    (New York: John Wiley and Sons, 1972), 347 pp.

Isaac, S.
    Handbook of Research and Evaluation
    (San Diego, CA: Edits Publishers, 1971).

Jahoda, Marie, Deutsch, Morton, and Cook, Stuart W.
    Research Methods in Social Relations, Vols. I and II
    (New York: Dryden Press, 1951).

Jessen, Raymond J.
    Statistical Survey Techniques
    (New York: John Wiley and Sons, Inc., 1978), 520 pp.

Johnson, John M.
    Doing Field Research
    (New York: Macmillan, 1978), 224 pp.

Keppel, Geoffrey
    Design and Analysis: A Researcher's Handbook, Second Edition
    (Englewood Cliffs, NJ: Prentice-Hall, Inc., 1982).

Kerlinger, Fred N.
    Behavioral Research: A Conceptual Approach
    (Hinsdale,IL: Holt, Rinehart and Winston, 1979).

Kerlinger, Fred
    Foundations of Behavioral Research, Second Edition
    (New York: Holt Rinehart and Winston, 1973).

Kight, Leila K.
    The Business Researcher's Handbook
    (Washington, DC: Washington Researchers), 153 pp.

Krathwohl, David R.
    Social and Behavioral Science Research: A New Framework for
    Conceptualizing, Implementing, and Evaluating Research
    (San Francisco: Jossey-Bass Publishers, 1985), 324 pp.

Labovitz, Sanford and Hagedorn, Robert
    Introduction to Social Research, 2nd Edition
    (New York: McGraw-Hill Book Company, 1976), 147 pp.

Lansing, John B. and Morgan, James N.
    Economic Survey Methods
    (Ann Arbor, MI: Institute for Social Research, 1971).

Lathrop, Richard G.
    Introduction to Psychological Research
    (New York: Harper and Row, 1969), 295 pp.

Lazarsfeld, Paul F.
    Qualitative Analysis: Historical and Critical Essays
    (Boston: Allyn and Bacon, 1972), 457 pp.

Lazarsfeld, P. F. and Rosenberg, M. (editors)
    The Language of Social Research
    (Glencoe, IL: Free Press, 1955), 590 pp.

Levy, Clifford V. A.
    Primer for Community Research
    (San Francisco: Far West Research, 1972), 98 pp.

Lin, Nan, Burt, Ronald S., and Vaughn, John C.
    Conducting Social Research
    (New York: McGraw-Hill Book Company, 1976), 203 pp.

Long, J. Scott
    Common Problems/Proper Solutions
    (Newbury Park, CA: Sage Publications, Inc., 1988), 360 pp.

Meister, David
    Behavioral Analysis and Measurement Methods
    (New York: John Wiley and Sons, Inc., 1985), 509 pp.

Merton, Robert K., Coleman, James S., and Rossi, Peter H. (editors)
    Qualitative and Quantitative Social Research
    (New York: Macmillan, 1979), 480 pp.

Miller, Brent C.
    Family Research Methods
    (Beverly Hills, CA: Sage Publications, Inc., 1986), 128 pp.

Miller, Delbert C.
    Handbook of Research Design and Social Measurement, Second Edition
    (New York: Longman, Inc., 1977), 518 pp.

Morgan, Gareth
    "Research as Engagement"
    in Morgan, G. (editor)
    Beyond Method: Strategies for Social Research
    (Beverly Hills, CA: Sage Publications, Inc., 1983), pp. 1-19.

Moser, Claus and Kalton, G.
    Survey Methods in Social Investigation, Second Edition
    (New York: Basic Books, 1972), 549 pp.

Mostyn, B.
    A Handbook of Attitude and Motivation Research Techniques
    (Bradford: MCB, 1978).

Murdick, Robert G.
    Business Research: Concept and Practice
    (Scranton, PA: International Textbook Co., 1969), 226 pp.

Murdick, Robert G. and Cooper, Donald R.
    Business Research
    (Columbus, OH: Grid Publishing Inc., 1982), 207 pp.

Noltingk, B. E.
    The Art of Research: A Guide for the Graduate
    (Amsterdam, The Netherlands: Elsevier Publishing Company, 1965), 142
    pp.

Osgood, Charles E.
    Method and Theory in Experimental Psychology
    (New York: Oxford University Press, 1953).

Phillips, Bernard S.
    Social Research: Strategy and Tactics, Third Edition
    (New York: Macmillan, 1976), 365 pp.

Reason, Peter
  Human Inquiry in Action
  (Newbury Park, CA: Sage Publications, 1989), 256 pp.

Reinharz, Shulamit
  On Becoming a Social Scientist: From Survey Research and Participant
  Observation to Experiential Analysis
  (San Francisco, CA: Jossey-Bass, 1979), 422 pp.

Reynolds, Paul Davidson
  Ethical Dilemmas and Social Science Research
  (San Francisco, CA: Jossey-Bass Publishers, 1980), 505 pp.

Rigby, Paul H.
  Conceptual Foundations of Business Research
  (New York, NY: John Wiley and Sons, Inc., 1965), 215 pp.

Riley, Matilda White
  Sociological Research
  (New York: Harcourt, Brace and World, Inc., 1963).

Rosenthal, Robert and Rosnow, Ralph L.
  Essentials of Behavioral Research: Methods and Data Analysis
  (New York: McGraw-Hill Book Company), 500 pp.

Rosenthal, Robert and Rosnow, Ralph L.
  Primer of Methods for the Behavioral Sciences
  (New York: John Wiley and Sons, 1975), 117 pp.

Rossi, Peter H., Wright, James D., and Anderson, Andy B. (editors)
  Handbook of Survey Research
  (New York: Academic Press, Inc., 1983), 755 pp.

Rummell, J. Francis and Ballaine, Wesley C.
  Research Methodology in Business
  (New York: Harper and Row, 1963), 359 pp.

Runkel, P. and McGrath, J. E.
  Research on Human Behavior: A Systematic Guide to Method
  (New York: Holt, Rinehart and Winston, 1972).

Saks, Michael J. and Baron, Charles H. (editors)
  The Use/Nonuse/Misuse of Applied Social Research in the Courts
  (Cambridge, MA: Abt Books, 1980), 189 pp.

Schuessler, Karl F. (editor)
  Sociological Methodology 1980
  (San Francisco, CA: Jossey-Bass Publishers, 1980), 576 pp.

Schwartz, Howard and Jacobs, Jerry
  Qualitative Sociology: A Method to the Madness
  (New York: Macmillan, 1979), 480 pp.

Sellitz, Claire, Jahoda, Marie, Deutsch, Morton, and Cook, Stuart W.
  Research Methods in Social Relations
  (New York: Holt, Rinehart and Winston, 1976).

Shils, E. A. and Finch, H. A. (editors)
  The Methodology of the Social Sciences
  (Glencoe, IL: The Free Press, 1949).

Simon, Julian L.
  Basic Research Methods in Social Science: The Art of Empirical
  Investigation, Second Edition
  (New York: Random House, 1978).

Smith, Charles B.
  A Guide to Business Research
  (Chicago: Nelson-Hall Inc., Publishers, 1981), 190 pp.

Sociological Methodology, Volumes 1-10
  (San Francisco: Jossey-Bass).

Spector, Paul E.
  Research Designs
  (Beverly Hills, CA: Sage Publications, Inc.).

Stevens, S. S.
  Handbook of Experimental Psychology
  (New York, NY: John Wiley and Sons, Inc., 1951).

Stouffer, Samuel A.
  Social Research to Test Ideas
  (New York: The Free Press of Glencoe, 1962), 314 pp.

Struening, E. I. and Guttentag, M. (editors)
  Handbook of Evaluation Research
  (Beverly Hills, CA: Sage Publishing Company, 1975).

Triandis, Harry C. and Berry, John W. (editors)
  Handbook of Cross-Cultural Psychology, Volume 2: Methodology
  (Boston: Allyn and Bacon, Inc., 1980), 546 pp.

U.S. Bureau of Labor Statistics
  BLS Handbook of Methods for Surveys and Studies. Bulletin 1910.
  (Washington, DC: U.S. Government Printing Office, 1976), 283 pp.

U.S. National Center for Health Services Research
  Advances in Health Survey Research Methods: Proceedings of a National
  Invitational Conference
  (DHEW Publication No. (HRA) 77-3154. Rockville, MD: Health Resources
  Administration, 1977), 58 pp.

Warwick, Donald P. and Lininger, Charles
  The Sample Survey: Theory and Practice
  (New York: McGraw-Hill Book Co., 1975), 344 pp.

Weisberg, Herbert F. and Bowen, Bruce D.
  An Introduction to Survey Research and Data Analysis
  (San Francisco: W. H. Freeman and Company, 1977), 243 pp.

Weiss, C. H. and Bucuvalas, M. J.
  Social Science Research and Decision Making
  (New York: Columbia University Press, 1980).

17 ---------------- RESEARCH METHODS IN COMMUNICATION ----------------
        See also (sub)heading(s) 18, 19, 20, 21, 22, 23.

17.01 ---------- Books Re: Research Methods in Communication

Advertising Research Foundation
  Copy Research: A Historical Perspective
  (New York: Advertising Research Foundation).

Advertising Research Foundation
  A Study of Printed Advertising Rating Methods
  (New York: Advertising Research Foundation, 1956).

Buzzell, R. D. and Kolin, Marshall
  Competitive Preference and Sales Effectiveness
  (New York: The Schwerin Research Corporation, September 1964).

Campbell, Roy H.
  Measuring the Sales and Profit Results of Advertising

Colley, Russell (editor)
  Evaluating Advertising Effectiveness, Volume Seven
  (New York: Association of National Advertisers, 1959).

Consterdine, Guy
  Readership Research and the Planning of Press Schedules
  (Aldershot, England: Gower Publishing Company Limited, 1988), 178 pp.

Corkindale, David R. and Kennedy, Sherril H.
  Measuring the Effects of Advertising
  (Saxon House-D. C. Heath, Ltd., 1977), 241 pp.

Corlett, T.
  An Introduction to the Use and Interpretation of Reading Frequency
  Data
  (London: Institute of Practitioners in Advertising, 1967).

Corlett, T. and Osborne, D. W.
  The Development of Reading Frequency Scales
  (London: Institute of Practitioners in Advertising, 1966), 32 pp.

Dewolf, John D.
  Advertising Research
  (New York: Association of Industrial Advertisers, 1968), 78 pp.

ESOMAR
  Broadcasting and Research
  Proceedings, European Society for Opinion and Marketing Research (May
  1985), 301 pp.

Fletcher, Alan D. and Bowers, Thomas A.
  Fundamentals of Advertising Research
  (Columbus, OH: Grid Publishing , Inc., 1979), 340 pp.

Fletcher, Alan D. and Jugenheimer, Donald W.
  Problems and Practices in Advertising Research: Readings Workbook
  (Columbus, OH: Grid Publishing, Inc., 1982), 210 pp.

Handel, Leo A.
  Hollywood Looks at its Audience: A Report of Film Audience Research
  (New York: Arno Press, 1976), 240 pp.

Hansen, Donald A. and Parsons, J. Herschel (editors)
  Mass Communications: A Research Bibliography
  (Berkeley, CA: The Glendessary Press, 1968), 144 pp.

Henry, Harry (editor)
  Readership Research: Theory and Practice--Salzburg 1985
  (Elsevier Science Publishers, 1987), 576 pp.

Henry, Harry (editor)
  Readership Research: Montreal 1983
  Proceedings, Second International Symposium
  (North Holland: 1984), 560 pp.

Holbert, Neil
  Advertising Research
  American Marketing Association Monograph Series
  (Chicago: American Marketing Association, 1975), 17 pp.

Hovland, Carl I.
  Experiments on Mass Communications
  (Princeton, NJ: Princeton University Press, 1949).

Kline, F. Gerald and Tichenor, Phillip J. (editors)
  Current Prospectives in Mass Communications Research
  (Beverly Hills, CA: Sage Publications, 1972), 320 pp.

Leigh, J. H. and Martin, C. R. (editors)
  Current Issues and Research in Advertising 1980
  (University of Michigan, 1980), 232 pp.

Lucas, Darrell Blaine and Britt, Steuart Henderson
  Measuring Advertising Effectiveness
  (New York: McGraw-Hill, 1963), 399 pp.

Lucas, Darrell B. and Britt, Steuart H.
  Advertising Psychology and Research
  (New York: McGraw-Hill, 1950)

Madow, W. G., Hyman, H. H., and Jessen, R. J.
  Evaluation of Statistical Methods in Obtaining Broadcast Ratings:
  Report of the Committee on Interstate and Foreign Commerce
  (Washington, DC: U.S. Government Printing Office, 1961), 163 pp.

Naples, Michael J.
  Effective Frequency: The Relationship Between Frequency and
  Advertising Effectiveness
  (New York: Association of National Advertisers, Inc., 1979).

National Association of Broadcasters
  A Broadcast Research Primer
  (New York: National Association of Broadcasters), 62 pp.

Peerbhoy, Ayaz S.
  Advertising and Research
  (Bombay: Progressive Corporation Private Ltd.), 145 pp.

Ramond, Charles
  Advertising Research: The State of the Art
  (Association of National Advertisers, 1976), 148 pp.

Ramond, Charles K.
  Measurement of Advertising Effectiveness
  (Menlo Park, CA: Stanford Research Institute Long-Range Planning
  Service, 1966), 24 pp.

Schyberger, Bo W:son
  Methods of Readership Research
  (Lund, Sweden: Lund Business Studies, University of Lund, 1963), 266
  pp.

Starch, Daniel
  Measuring Advertising Readership and Results
  (New York: McGraw-Hill Book Company, 1966), 270 pp.

Starch, Daniel
  Factors in Readership Measurement
  (New York: Daniel Starch and Staff, 1946).

Tolley, B. Stuart
  Advertising and Marketing Research: A New Methodology
  (Chicago: Nelson-Hall, Inc., 1977), 312 pp.

Wolfe, Harry Deane, Brown, James K., Greenberg, Stephen H., and
  Thompson, G. Clark
  Pretesting Advertising
  (New York: National Industrial Conference Board, 1963), 214 pp.

Wolfe, Harry D., Brown, James K., and Thompson, G. Clark
  Measuring Advertising Results
  (New York: National Industrial Conference Board, Inc., 1962), 177 pp.

Wolfe, Harry Deane, Brown, James K., Thompson, G. Clark, and Greenberg,
  Stephen H.
  Evaluating Media
  (New York: National Industrial Conference Board, 1966), 185 pp.

17.02 ---------- State of Communication Research

Adler, Eric
  "The Use and Lack of Use of Market Research in Promotional Marketing"
  European Research, Vol. 5 (March 1977), pp. 85-90.

Bogart, Leo
  "Progress in Advertising Research?"
  Journal of Advertising Research, Vol. 26 (June/July 1986), pp. 11-5.

Bogart, Leo
  "What Forces Shape the Future of Advertising Research"
  Journal of Advertising Research, Vol. 26 (February/March 1986), pp.
  99-104.

Bogart, Leo
  "Where Does Advertising Research Go From Here?"
  Journal of Advertising Research, Vol. 9 (March 1969), pp. 3-12.

Grundy, Jean
    "Advertising Research--Is it Time for a Re-Think?"
    European Research, Vol. 15 (November 1987), pp. 214-20.

Katz, Elihu
    "Communications Research Since Lazarsfeld"
    Public Opinion Quarterly, Vol. 51 (Winter 1987), pp. S25-45.

Naples, Michael J.
    "Electronic Media Research: An Update and a Look at the Future"
    Journal of Advertising Research, Vol. 24 (August/September 1984), pp.
    39-46.

Pollitt, S.
    "Has Anything Gone Wrong With Advertising Research?"
    Admap (January 1970).

Pollitt, S.
    "Learning From Research in the Sixties"
    Admap (December 1969).

Prue, Terry
    "Where is the 'Scientific Method' in the Measurement of Advertising
    Effect?"
    Admap (December 1987), pp. 58-62.

Ramond, Charles
    "Advertising Research: The State of the Art"
    ANA (1976).

Spielman, Harold M.
    "Two Views of Advertising Research: US vs. UK"
    Journal of the Market Research Society, Vol. 31 (October 1989), pp.
    537-43.

Twyman, W. A. Tony
    "Progress in Advertising Research: A Critical Review of Some Issues"
    Second AMA/ESOMAR Conference, Paris (April 1981).

Twyman, Tony
    "The State of Media Research"
    Journal of the Market Research Society, Vol. 21 (October 1979), pp.
    221-7.

Wicks, Anne
    "Advertising Research--An Eclectic View From the UK"
    Journal of the Market Research Society, Vol. 31 (October 1989), pp.
    527-35.

17.03 ---------- General Discussions Re: Res Methods in Communication

Arndt, Johan
    "What's Wrong With Advertising Research"
    Journal of Advertising Research, Vol. 16 (June 1976), pp. 9-18.

Axelrod, Joel N.
    "Minnie, Minnie Tickled the Parson"
    Journal of Advertising Research, Vol. 26 (February/March 1986), pp.
    89-95.

Baldinger, Allan L.
    "Synopsis of an ARF-Sponsored Symposium on Marketplace Measurement:
    What are the Critical Testing Needs?"
    Journal of Advertising Research, Vol. 27 (October/November 1987), pp.
    RC3-7.

Blyth, Bill
    "Monitoring Advertising Performance: Innovation in Analytical
    Techniques?"
    Admap (March 1986), pp. 158,9;163.

Broadbent, Simon
    "Measuring Advertising Effects: American Practice and Lessons for
    Brits"
    Admap (June 1988), pp. 25-8.

Broadbent, Simon
    "Is More Media Research the Best Research for Media?"
    ADMAP (April 1984), pp. 184-91.

Campbell, Roy H.
    Measuring the Sales and Profit Results of Advertising: A Managerial
    Approach
    (Association of National Advertisers, 1969).

Channon, C.
    "What do We Know About How Research Works?"
    Market Research Society Conference (June 1983).

Chase, Lawrence J. and Baran, Stanley J.
    "An Assessment of Quantitative Research in Mass Communication"
    Journalism Quarterly, Vol. 53 (Summer 1976), pp. 308-11.

Chase, Lawrence J. and Tucker, Raymond K.
    "A Power-Analytic Examination of Contemporary Communication Research"
    Speech Monographs, Vol. 42 (March 1975), pp. 29-41.

Clancy, Kevin J. and Ostlund, Lyman E.
    "Commercial Effectiveness Measures"
    Journal of Advertising Research, Vol. 16 (February 1976), pp. 29-34.

Corkindale, David R.
    "A Manager's Guide to Measuring the Effects of Advertising"
    Market Intelligence and Planning, Vol. 1, No. 2 (1983), pp. 3-30.

Corkindale, David
    "Are Advertising Tests Useful?"
    European Research, Vol. 3 (March 1975), pp. 66-71.

Coulson, John S.
    "Point of View: How to Reduce Research Waste"
    Journal of Advertising Research, Vol. 17 (October 1977), p. 85.

Cowan, David
    "Advertising Research--Qualitative or Quantitative?"
    Admap (November 1984), pp. 516-20.

Cowley, Don
    "Advertising Research Looks Different From the Agency Side"
    Admap (February 1986), pp. 82-5.

Driver, John C. and Foxall, Gordon R.
    "How Scientific is Advertising Research?"
    International Journal of Advertising, Vol. 5, No. 2 (1986), pp.
    147-60.

East, Robert
    "Methods of Pre-Testing Advertising: A Review and a New Approach"
    International Journal of Advertising, Vol. 3, No. 4 (1984), pp.
    347-60.

Eldridge, C. E.
    "Advertising Effectiveness--How Can It be Measured?"
    Journal of Marketing, Vol. 22, No. 3 (1958), pp. 241-51.

Elliott, Jeremy
    "Monitoring Advertising Performance: Never Mind the Data--What We
    Want is Information"
    Admap (March 1986), pp. 160-3.

Emmett, Brian
    "Never Mind the Why and Wherefore--Some Reflections on Theory in
    Practice"
    Journal of the Market Research Society, Vol. 23 (April 1981), pp.
    63-71.

ESOMAR
    "Effective Advertising: Can Research Help?"
    ESOMAR Seminar, Monte Carlo (1983).

Feldwick, Paul
    "The Dangerous Magic of Numbers"
    European Research, Vol. 15 (November 1987), pp. 209-12.

Festinger, Leon
    "Some Theoretical Foundations for Advertising Research"
    in Proceedings, Sixth Annual Conference
    (New York: Advertising Research Foundation, 1960).

Frankel, Lester
    "How Can We Measure the Influence of Advertising?"
    in Colley, Russell (editor)
    Evaluating Advertising Effectiveness, Volume Seven
    (New York: Association of National Advertisers, 1959), pp. 331-7.

Garbett, Thomas F.
    "Researching Corporate Advertising"
    Journal of Advertising Research, Vol. 23 (February/March 1983), pp.
    33-7.

Green, Andrew
    "Media Research: What the Agencies Want"
    Admap (June 1986), pp. 316-9.

Greenberg, Allan
    "Is Communications Research Really Worthwhile?"
    Journal of Marketing, Vol. 31 (January 1967), pp. 48-50.

Hart, Norman A.
"Industrial Media Research"
Admap (March 1984), pp. 158-60.

Hastings, Gerard B. and Leathar, Douglas S.
"The Creative Potential of Research"
International Journal of Advertising, Vol. 6, No. 2 (1987), pp.
159-68.

Hayes, Matthew J.
"Marketing Research: The Industry's Most Effective Tool in All
Promotional Campaigns"
American Salesman, Vol. 33 (December 1988), pp. 3-6.

Henry, Harry
"Wheels--And Their Re-Invention"
European Research, Vol. 8 (July 1980), pp. 155-63.

Hodgson, Peter
"Sales Promotion Research: A Plea for More Research Involvement"
Journal of the Market Research Society, Vol. 19 (January 1977), pp.
18-21.

Holbert, Neil
"Key Articles in Advertising Research"
Journal of Advertising Research, Vol. 12 (October 1972), pp. 5-13.

Holbrook, Morris B.
"Two Ways to Evaluate an Advertising Campaign"
Journal of Advertising Research, Vol. 16 (August 1976), pp. 45-8.

IARI Research Forum
Advertising Research on a Limited Budget
(Princeton, NJ: Industrial Advertising Research Institute, 1965), 40
pp.

Johnson, Roger M.
"Measuring Advertising Effectiveness"
in Handbook of Marketing Research, pp. 4-151.

Jones, David
"Media Measurement in Australia: Print"
Admap (December 1988), pp. 31-4.

Kimball, Penn T.
"Research: Tool and Weapon"
Columbia Journalism Review, Vol. 1 (Winter 1963), pp. 41-3.

Lannon, Judie
"New Techniques for Understanding Consumer Reactions to Advertising"
Journal of Advertising Research, Vol. 26 (August/September 1986), pp.
RC6-9.

Lannon, Judie
"The Contributions of Qualitative Methodology to Creative Advertising"
ESOMAR Seminar on Qualitative Methods of Research, Amsterdam
(February 1986).

Leckenby, John D. and Plummer, Joseph T.
"Advertising Stimulus Measurement and Assessment Research: A Review
of Advertising Testing Methods"
Current Issues and Research in Advertising, Vol. 2 (1983), pp. 135-65.

Lewis, Ian M.
"Do Concept Scores Measure the Message or the Method?"
Journal of Advertising Research, Vol. 24 (February/March 1984), pp.
54-6.

Lucas, Darrell B.
"The ABC's of ARF's PARM"
Journal of Marketing, Vol. 25, No. 1 (1960), pp. 9-20.

May, J. P.
"Advertising Pre-Testing Research--An Historical Perspective"
The Quarterly Review of Marketing (1978).

McDonald, Colin
"Pretesting and Evaluating Advertising"
Admap (July/August 1987), pp. 54-9.

McKenna, William J.
"The Future of Electronic Measurement Technology in U.S. Media
Research"
Journal of Advertising Research, Vol. 28 (June/July 1988), pp. RC3-7.

Moore, William L.
"Testing Advertising Concepts: Current Practices and Opinions"
Journal of Advertising, Vol. 14, No. 3 (1985), pp. 45-50.

Moran, William T.
   "Coming to Power: The Market Structure of Advertising Research"
   Journal of Advertising Research, Vol. 24 (December 1984/January
   1985), pp. RC12-4.

Phillips, Alan
   "Lord of the Replies: Lessons From Direct-Response Advertising"
   Admap (April 1986), pp. 204-7.

Rehorn, Jorg
   "Abbreviated Simulated Test Markets as Advertising Pretesting Tools"
   ESOMAR Congress, Montreux (1987), pp. 739-56.

Roberts, Harry V.
   "The Measurement of Advertising Results"
   Journal of Business, Vol. 20 (July 1947), pp. 131-45.

Rubens, William
   "We Don't Care About Research Quality Anymore"
   Journal of Advertising Research, Vol. 29 (February/March 1989), pp.
   RC3-6.

Sasieni, Maurice W.
   "What can We Measure in Marketing?"
   Journal of Advertising Research, Vol. 4 (June 1964), pp. 8-11.

Schmalensee, Diane H.
   "Today's Top Priority Advertising Research Questions"
   Journal of Advertising Research, Vol. 23 (April/May 1983), pp. 49-60.

Semon, Thomas T.
   "Assumptions in Measuring Advertising Effectiveness"
   Journal of Marketing, Vol. 28 (July 1964), pp. 43,4.

Starch, Daniel
   "Testing the Effectiveness of Advertisements"
   Harvard Business Review, Vol. 1, No. 4 (1923), pp. 464-74.

Stewart-Hunter, David
   "Effective Advertising--Can Research Help?"
   European Research, Vol. 11 (April 1983), pp. 68-71.

Terris, John
   "The Need for Better Use of Media Researchers"
   Admap (July/August 1988), pp. 42-5.

Thomson, Lord of Fleet
   "The Future of Advertising Research"
   Journal of Advertising Research, Vol. 4 (December 1964), pp. 2,3.

Twyman, W. A. Tony
   "Monitoring Advertising Performance: A Canter 'Round the Field"
   Admap (March 1986), pp. 134,5.

Twyman, W. A. Tony
   "Assessing the Validity of Pre-Testing"
   Admap (February and March 1984).

Twyman, W. A.
   "Designing Advertising Research for Marketing Decisions"
   Journal of the Market Research Society, Vol. 15 (April 1973), pp.
   77-100.

Van Vliet, J.
   "Media Measurement and Media Choice: Progress or Stagnation?"
   European Research, Vol. 8 (July 1980), pp. 147-54.

Whitley, Edward
   "Are Magazines Getting the Right Sort of Research?"
   Admap (February 1984), pp. 102-6.

Winters, Lewis C.
   "Comparing Pretesting and Posttesting of Corporate Advertising"
   Journal of Advertising Research, Vol. 23 (February/March 1983), pp.
   25-32.

17.04 ---------- Guidelines and Standards for Communications Research

Advertising Research Foundation
   ARF Criteria for Marketing and Advertising Research
   (New York: Advertising Research Foundation).

National Association of Broadcasters
   Standard Definitions of Broadcast Research Terms
   (New York: National Association of Broadcasters, 1967), 56 pp.

Schaefer, Wolfgang
   "On a Code for Media Research"
   European Research, Vol. 14, No. 2 (1986), pp. 82-4.

Schwoerer, Juergen
"Measuring Advertising Effectiveness: Emergence of an International Standard"
European Research, Vol. 15, No. 1 (1987), pp. 40-51.

Twyman, W. A. Tony
"How European Research Standards Would be Achieved"
Admap (December 1988), pp. 44-6.

17.05 ---------- Theory Re: Experimentation in Advertising Research

Becknell, James C., Jr.
"Use of Experimental Design in the Study of Media Effectiveness"
Media/Scope, Vol. 6 (August 1962), pp. 46-9.

Blattberg, Robert C.
"The Design of Advertising Experiments Using Statistical Decision Theory"
Journal of Marketing Research, Vol. XVI (May 1979), pp. 191-202.

Coffin, Thomas E.
"A Pioneering Experiment in Assessing Advertising Effectiveness"
Journal of Marketing, Vol. 27 (July 1963), pp. 1-10.

Farris, Paul W. and Reibstein, David J.
"Overcontrol in Advertising Experiments"
Journal of Advertising Research, Vol. 24 (June/July 1984), pp. 37-42.

Fenwick, Ian
"Advertising Experiments by Retailers"
Journal of Advertising Research, Vol. 18 (August 1978), pp. 35-40.

Gibson, Lawrence D.
"Seven Questions for Advertising Researchers: A Client View"
General Mills.

Ginter, James L., Cooper, Martha C., Obermiller, Carl, and Page, Thomas J., Jr.
"The Design of Advertising Experiments: An Extension"
Journal of Marketing Research, Vol. XVIII (February 1981), pp. 120-3.

Hovland, Carl I., Lumsdaine, Arthur A., and Sheffield, Fred D.
"Comparison of the Before-After and the After-Only Design of Experiments"
in Experiments in Mass Communication Studies in Social Psychology in World War II, Volume Three
(Princeton, NJ: Princeton University Press, 1949).

Jessen, Raymond J.
"A Switch-Over Experimental Design to Measure Advertising Effect"
Journal of Advertising Research, Vol. 1 (March 1961), pp. 15-22.

Lancaster, Geoffrey A. and Lomas, Robert A.
"Experimental Error in T-Scope Investigations"
Journal of Advertising Research, Vol. 17 (December 1977), pp. 51-6.

Meissner, Frank
"The Experimental Approach to Measuring the Impact of Advertising"
Commentary (JMRS), No. 9 (Winter 1962-63), pp. 6-9.

Oherlihy, Callaghan
"Why Ad Experiments Fail"
Journal of Advertising Research, Vol. 20 (February 1980), pp. 53-8.

17.06 ---------- Theory Re: Advertising Copy Research

Abeele, P. Vanden and Luysterman, P.
"The Evaluation of Pretests by Advertising People: Results of a Survey in Belgium"
European Journal of Marketing, Vol. 15, No. 1 (1981), pp. 48-57.

Abruzzini, Pompeo
"Measuring Language Difficulty in Advertising Copy"
Journal of Marketing, Vol. 31 (April 1967), pp. 22-6.

Adler, Lee, Greenberg, Allan, and Lucas, Darrell B.
"What Big Agency Men Think of Copy Testing Methods"
Journal of Marketing Research, Vol. II (November 1965), pp. 339-45.

Caffyn, John M.
"On Methods: Psychological Laboratory Techniques in Copy Research"
Journal of Advertising Research, Vol. 4 (December 1964), pp. 45-50.

Downham, J. and Twyman, W. A. Tony
"Can Pre-Testing be Validated? A Critical Review of Possibilities and Evidence"
Can Research Help?
ESOMAR Seminar on Effective Advertising, Monte Carlo (January 1983).

Dunn, Theodore F. and Ziff, Ruth
    "PREP: A New Copy Testing System"
    Journal of Advertising Research, Vol. 14 (October 1974), pp. 53-9.

Gibson, Lawrence D.
    "If the Question is Copy Testing, the Answer is Not Recall"
    Journal of Advertising Research, Vol. 23 (February/March 1983), pp.
    39-46.

Keon, John W.
    "Copy Testing Ads for Imagery Products"
    Journal of Advertising Research, Vol. 23 (December 1983/January
    1984), pp. 41-8.

Lipstein, Benjamin
    "An Historical Retrospective of Copy Research"
    Journal of Advertising Research, Vol. 24 (December 1984/January
    1985), p. 11.

Ostlund, Lyman E.
    "Advertising Copy Testing: A Review of Current Practices"
    Current Issues and Research in Advertising (1978), pp. 87-106.

Ostlund, Lyman E. and Clancy, Kevin J.
    "Copy Testing Methods and Measures Favored by Top Ad Agency and
    Advertising Executives"
    Journal of the Academy of Marketing Science, Vol. 10 (Winter 1982),
    pp. 72-89.

Ostlund, Lyman E., Clancy, Kevin J., and Sapra, Rakesh
    "Inertia in Copy Research"
    Journal of Advertising Research, Vol. 20 (February 1980), pp. 17-23.

Plummer, Joseph T.
    "The Role of Copy Research in Multinational Advertising"
    Journal of Advertising Research, Vol. 26 (October/November 1986), pp.
    11-5.

Roberts, Andrew
    "Improving Advertising Content: Tracking Studies in Pretesting"
    Admap (April 1987), pp. 44-6.

Spielman, Harold M.
    "Copy Research: Facts and Fiction"
    European Research, Vol. 15 (November 1987), pp. 226-31.

Stewart, David W., Furse, David H., and Kozak, R. P.
    "A Guide to Commercial Copy-Testing Services"
    Current Issues and Research in Advertising, Vol. 1 (1983), pp. 1-44.

Stewart, David W., Peckmann, Connie, Ratneshwar, Srinivasan, Stroud,
    Jon, and Bryant, Beverly
    "Methodological and Theoretical Foundations of Advertising Copy
    Testing: A Review"
    Current Issues and Research in Advertising, Vol. 2 (1985), pp. 1-74.

Von Gonten, Michael F.
    "Validity in Copy Testing"
    Proceedings, 22nd Annual Conference
    (New York: Advertising Research Foundation, 1976).

Young, Shirley
    "Copy Testing Without Magic Numbers"
    Journal of Advertising Research, Vol. 12 (February 1972), pp. 3-12.

17.07 ---------- Applications of Copy Testing Research

Sewall, Murphy A. and Sarel, Dan
    "Characteristics of Radio Commercials and Their Recall Effectiveness"
    Journal of Marketing, Vol. 50 (January 1986), pp. 52-60.

17.08 ---------- Theory Re: Audience Measurement (Size)

Agostini, J. M.
    "Analysis of Magazine Accumulative Audience"
    Journal of Advertising Research, Vol. 2 (December 1962), pp. 24-7.

Agostini, Jean-Michel
    "How to Estimate Unduplicated Audiences"
    Journal of Advertising Research, Vol. 1 (March 1961), pp. 11-4.

American Research Bureau
    The Influence of Non-Cooperation in the Diary Method of Television
    Audience Measurement
    (Beltsville, MD: American Research Bureau, 1963), 116 pp.

Appel, V.
"Telescoping: The Skeleton in the Recent Reading Closet"
in Henry, H. (editor)
Readership Research: Theory and Practice
Proceedings of the First International Symposium, New Orleans (1981).

Assael, Henry and Day, George S.
"Attitudes and Awareness as Predictors of Market Share"
Journal of Advertising Research, Vol. 8 (December 1968), pp. 3-10.

Bennike, Sigurd
"Prompt Aids in Readership Research"
European Research, Vol. 1 (November 1973), pp. 259-62.

Benson, Purnell H.
"Bivariate Normal Distribution to Calculate Media Exposure"
Journal of Advertising Research, Vol. 9 (September 1969), pp. 41-7.

Bower, John
"Net Audiences of U.S. and Canadian Magazines: Seven Tests of
Agostini's Formula"
Journal of Advertising Research, Vol. 3 (March 1963), pp. 13-20.

Britt, Steuart Henderson, O'Leary, John C., and Sturges, Ralph R.
"The Accuracy of Claimed Subscribership"
Journal of Advertising Research, Vol. 13 (December 1973), pp. 29-32.

Brown, Michael
"Readership Diary Panels: A JICNARS Review of Selected Aspects"
Admap (April 1984), pp. 215-20.

Caffyn, J. M. and Sagovsky, M.
"Net Audiences of British Newspapers: A Comparison of the Agostini
and Sainsbury Methods"
Journal of Advertising Research, Vol. 3 (March 1963), pp. 21-6.

Cannon, Hugh M.
"Reach and Frequency Estimates for Specialized Target Markets"
Journal of Advertising Research, Vol. 23 (June/July 1983), pp. 45-50.

Clancy, Kevin J., Ostlund, Lyman E., and Wyner, Gordon A.
"False Reporting of Magazine Readership"
Journal of Advertising Research, Vol. 19 (October 1979), pp. 23-30.

Claycamp, H. J. and McClelland, C. W.
"Estimating Reach and the Magic of K"
Journal of Advertising Research, Vol. 8 (June 1968), pp. 44-51.

Clemens, J.
"Page and Advertisement Readership Studies: The Problem of Validation"
Commentary (JMRS), Vol. 7 (July 1965).

Copland, Brian D.
Some Fundamentals of Poster Audience Measurement"
Journal of Advertising Research, Vol. 2 (June 1962), pp. 20-7.

Cornish, Pym
"Geodemographic Sampling in Readership Surveys"
Journal of the Market Research Society, Vol. 31 (January 1989), pp.
45-51.

Cornish, Pym
"Developments in International Readership Research"
Admap (February 1988), pp. 38-43.

Cornish, P.
"Replicated and Parallel Readership"
in Henry, H. (editor)
Readership Research: Theory and Practice
Proceedings, of the First International Symposium, New Orleans (1981).

Davenport, John Scott, Parker, Edwin B., and Smith, Stewart A.
"Measuring Readership of Newspaper Advertisements"
Journal of Advertising Research, Vol. 2 (December 1962), pp. 2-9.

De Bock, Harold
"Readership Research: Explosion From Holland"
Admap (April 1987), pp. 19-21.

De Hond, M. and Huzen, W.
"New Approach to Readership Surveys"
in Henry, H. (editor)
Readership Research: Montreal
Proceedings of the Second International Symposium 1983
(Amsterdam: Elsevier Science Publishers, 1983).

Dodson, Dick
"Readership Diary Panels: The State of the Art"
Admap (March 1988), pp. 28-34.

Ehrenberg, A. S. C.
  "Communicating Market Data"
  Journal of Advertising Research, Vol. 16 (June 1976), pp. 27-32.

Ellerin, Susan
  "Lies, Damn Lies and (Some) Readership Research"
  Business Marketing (April 1989).

Engelman, Fred L.
  "An Empirical Formula for Audience Accumulation"
  Journal of Advertising Research, Vol. 5 (June 1965), pp. 21-8.

Ferber, Robert and Wales, Hugh G.
  "A New Way to Measure Journal Readership"
  Journal of Advertising Research, Vol. 3 (September 1963), pp. 9-16.

Forman, Stan
  "A Theory of Audience Accumulation"
  Journal of Advertising Research, Vol. 16 (February 1976), pp. 21-5.

Fry, Christopher
  "Audience Accumulation: Single Interview Versus Reinterview"
  European Research, Vol. 1 (July 1973), pp. 166-70.

Goodhardt, G. J.
  "The Constant in Duplicated Viewing"
  Nature, Vol. 212 (December 1966), p. 1616.

Greene, Jerome D.
  "Reliability of Cumulative Magazine Audiences"
  Journal of Advertising Research, Vol. 19 (October 1979), pp. 75-9.

Greene, Jerome D.
  "Personal Media Probabilities"
  Journal of Advertising Research, Vol. 10 (October 1970), pp. 12-8.

Gullen, Phil
  "Is Press Research Merely a Currency?"
  Admap (May 1988), pp. 28-30.

Henry, Harry
  "Belson's Studies in Readership"
  Journal of Advertising Research, Vol. 2 (June 1962), pp. 9-14.

Hofmans, Pierre
  "Coverage and Frequency in Urban Outdoor Advertising"
  European Research, Vol. 10 (January 1982), pp. 21-36.

Hofmans, Pierre
  "Measuring the Cumulative Net Coverage of Any Combination of Media"
  Journal of Marketing Research, Vol. III (August 1966), pp. 269-78.

Jones, Robert L. and Beldo, Leslie A.
  "Methodological Improvements in Readership Data Gathering"
  Journalism Quarterly, Vol. 30 (1953), pp. 345-53.

Joyce, Timothy
  "Magazine Readers per Copy"
  Journal of Advertising Research, Vol. 14 (December 1974), pp. 21-4.

Kaatz, Ronald B.
  "Improving Agostini's Formula for Net Audience"
  Journal of Advertising Research, Vol. 3 (September 1963), pp. 43,4.

Kuhn, Walther
  "Net Audiences of German Magazines: A New Formula"
  Journal of Advertising Research, Vol. 3 (March 1963), pp. 30-3.

Kwerel, Seymour M.
  "Estimating Unduplicated Audience and Exposure Distribution"
  Journal of Advertising Research, Vol. 9 (June 1969), pp. 46-53.

Landis, Jack B.
  "Exposure Probabilities as Measures of Media Audiences"
  Journal of Advertising Research, Vol. 5 (September 1965), pp. 24-9.

Langschmidt, Wally
  Reliability of Response in Readership Research
  (Sandton City, South Africa: SA Advertising Research Foundation).

Langschmidt, Wally and Brown, Michael
  "Aspects of Reliability of Response in Readership Research"
  Journal of the Market Research Society, Vol. 21 (October 1979), pp. 228-49.

Liebman, Leon and Lee, Edward
  "Reach and Frequency Estimating Services"
  Journal of Advertising Research, Vol. 14 (August 1974), pp. 23-5.

Mansfield, Terry
  "Researching Magazine Readership"
  Admap (October 1988), pp. 51-3.

Marberg, Stig
  "A Visual Aid to Estimating Net Audiences"
  Journal of Advertising Research, Vol. 6 (September 1966), pp. 21-8.

Marc, Marcel
  "Net Audiences of French Business Papers: Agostini's Formula Applied
  to Special Markets"
  Journal of Advertising Research, Vol. 3 (March 1963), pp. 26-9.

Marder, Eric
  "How Good is the Editorial-Interest Method of Measuring Magazine
  Audiences?"
  Journal of Advertising Research, Vol. 7 (March 1967), pp. 2-6.

Mattison, Mark
  "Techniques for Developing Newspaper Audiences"
  Journal of Advertising Research, Vol. 22 (April/May 1982), pp. 11-4.

McGlathery, Donald G.
  "Claimed Frequency vs. Editorial-Interest Measures of Repeat Magazine
  Audiences"
  Journal of Advertising Research, Vol. 7 (March 1967), pp. 7-15.

Metheringham, Richard A.
  "Measuring the Net Cumulative Coverage of a Print Campaign"
  Journal of Advertising Research, Vol. 4 (December 1964), pp. 23-8.

Mitchell, Dawn
  "Press Readership Research--Present and Future"
  Admap (December 1983), pp. 650-4.

Moore, James H.
  "Researching the Researchers: Who's Reading the Journal"
  Journal of Advertising Research, Vol. 24 (June/July 1984), pp. 64-8.

Moran, William T.
  "Measuring Exposure to Advertisements"
  Journal of Applied Psychology, Vol. 35 (February 1951), pp. 72-7.

Nichols, Al and Powers, Dennis
  "The Probability of Advertising Exposure (1)--Comment to Sherrill"
  Journal of Advertising Research, Vol. 6 (September 1966), pp. 44,5.

Ochs, Malcolm B.
  "Audience Measurement Concepts for Industrial Publications"
  Journal of Marketing, Vol. 30 (January 1966), pp. 59-61.

Patterson, Bill
  "Women's Magazines: The Value of the 14th Reader per Copy"
  Admap (October 1987), pp. 52-4.

Puliyel, Thomas
  "High Readers-per-Copy: An Attempt at Validation"
  Journal of the Market Research Society, Vol. 28 (April 1986), pp.
  115-23.

Ryan, Michael
  "Measuring the Readership of Inflight Magazines"
  Admap (December 1987), pp. 62-5.

Ryan, Michael
  "The Reality in International Readership Research"
  Admap (July/August 1987), pp. 48,9;76.

Ryan, Michael
  "How Many Days Does a Reader Read?"
  Admap (February 1986), pp. 102,3.

Schaefer, Wolfgang
  "Readers per Copy of Trade Publications"
  European Research, Vol. 14, No. 4 (1986), pp. 198-201.

Schaefer, Wolfgang
  "Scale Measures of Magazine Readership"
  Journal of Advertising Research, Vol. 5 (December 1965), pp. 21-6.

Schreiber, Robert J.
  "The Metheringham Method for Media Mix: An Evaluation"
  Journal of Advertising Research, Vol. 9 (June 1969), pp. 54-6.

Schreiber, Robert J.
  "Probability Assignments for the Simulation of Media Reach and
  Frequency"
  Journal of Advertising Research, Vol. 8 (June 1968), pp. 3-8.

Schreiber, Robert J.
    "The Probability of Advertising Exposure (2)--Comment to Sherrill"
    Journal of Advertising Research, Vol. 6 (September 1966), pp. 47-9.

Schyberger, Bo W:son
    "The Accumulative and Repeat Audiences of Swedish Weekly Magazines"
    Journal of Advertising Research, Vol. 3 (December 1963), pp. 25-33.

Sherrill, Peter N.
    "Rejoinder--To Schreiber"
    Journal of Advertising Research, Vol. 6 (September 1966), pp. 49,50.

Sherrill, Peter N.
    "Rejoinder--To Nichols and Powers"
    Journal of Advertising Research, Vol. 6 (September 1966), pp. 45-7.

Sherrill, Peter N.
    "The Probability of Advertising Exposure"
    Journal of Advertising Research, Vol. 6 (March 1966), pp. 24-8.

Simmons, W. R. and Associates
    An Examination of Alternative Methods of Estimating Media Reach and
    Frequency
    (New York: W. R. Simmons and Associates Research, Inc., 1967).

Smith, H. A.
    "The Relationship Between Replicate and Parallel Reading, the Average
    Issue Readership and Multiple Page Exposure"
    Admap (January 1987), pp. 28-30;72.

Smith, H. A.
    "Measuring the Probability That an Advertisement has Been Seen"
    European Research, Vol. 3 (January 1975), pp. 36,7.

Soley, Lawrence C.
    "Can Newspaper Audiences be Simulated?"
    Journal of Advertising Research, Vol. 23 (October/November 1983), pp.
    67-71.

Stock, J. Stevens
    "A Comparison of Eight Audience Estimates"
    Journal of Advertising Research, Vol. 1 (September 1961), pp. 9-15.

Sumner, Paul
    Readership Research and Computers
    (New York: Newsweek Inc.), 199 pp.

Tennstadt, Friedrich and Noelle-Neumann, Elisabeth
    "Experiments in the Measurement of Readership"
    Journal of the Market Research Society, Vol. 21 (October 1979), pp.
    251-67.

Troldahl, Verling C. and Jones, Robert L.
    "Predictors of Newspaper Advertisement Readership"
    Journal of Advertising Research, Vol. 5 (March 1965), pp. 23-7.

Twyman, W. A. Tony
    "Readership Research in Barcelona"
    Marketing and Research Today, Vol. 17 (February 1989), pp. 52,3.

Walsh, Peter
    "Magazine Sourcing"
    Journal of the Market Research Society, Vol. 28 (April 1986), pp.
    105-13.

Walstra, Bouke
    "Validating the First-Time-Read-Yesterday Method"
    Journal of the Market Research Society, Vol. 28 (April 1986), pp.
    157-73.

Wenzel, W. and Speetzen, R.
    "Debugging Random Errors From Media Analysis Data--A New Type of
    Validation"
    in Henry, H. (editor)
    Readership Research
    (Amsterdam: North-Holland, 1985).

Wiegand, Jurgen
    "Combining Different Media Surveys: The German Partnership Model and
    Fusion Experiments"
    Journal of the Market Research Society, Vol. 28 (April 1986), pp.
    189-208.

Yamanaka, Jiro
    "The Prediction of Ad Readership Scores"
    Journal of Advertising Research, Vol. 2 (March 1962), pp. 18-23.

Young, Lawrence F.
    "Estimating Radio Reach"
    Journal of Advertising Research, Vol. 12 (October 1972), pp. 37-41.

17.09 ---------- Applications of Audience Measurement (Size)

Westrup, Sylvia
   "Business Readership: Some Evidence From Yorkshire"
   Admap (July/August 1987), pp. 62,3.

17.10 ---------- Theory Re: Communications Effects Measurement

Appel, Valentine and Blum, Milton L.
   "Ad Recognition and Response Set"
   Journal of Advertising Research, Vol. 1 (June 1961), pp. 13-21.

Appel, Valentine and Jackson, Babette
   "Copy Testing in a Competitive Environment"
   Journal of Marketing, Vol. 39 (January 1975), pp. 84-6.

Axelrod, Joel N.
   "Attitude Measures That Predict Purchase"
   Journal of Advertising Research, Vol. 8 (March 1968), pp. 3-17.

Baker, Chris
   "The Evaluation of Advertising Effects: Philosophy, Planning and
   Practice"
   Admap (April 1984), pp. 192-9.

Barclay, William D.
   "Why Aren't Portfolio Tests Here to Stay?"
   Journal of Marketing, Vol. 26 (July 1962), pp. 73-5.

Baur, Detlef
   "Experiences With Advertising Post-Testing by Panel-Research"
   European Research, Vol. 9 (April 1981), pp. 75-83.

Becknell, James C., Jr.
   "Comment on Webb's Case for the Effectiveness Index"
   Journal of Advertising Research, Vol. 2 (December 1962), pp. 42,3.

Biggs, Howard
   "Assessing Press Advertising Campaigns: A Contribution From Ambridge"
   Proceedings, Market Research Society (March 1988), pp. 399-417.

Brown, Gordon H. A.
   "Findings From Ad Tracking--Ad Awareness, Persuasion and Sales"
   ESOMAR Congress, Montreux (1987), pp. 1-20.

Buzzell, R. D.
   "Predicting Short-Term Changes in Market Share as a Function of
   Advertising Strategy"
   Journal of Marketing Research, Vol. I (August 1964), pp. 27-31.

Chandler, Jon
   "The Buy (C) Test"
   Admap (April 1987), pp. 42,3.

Corey, Lawrence G. and Doub, Richard M.
   "Awareness of Radio Commercials"
   Journal of Advertising Research, Vol. 3 (September 1963), pp. 17-20.

Finn, Adam
   "Print Ad Recognition Readership Scores: An Information Processing
   Perspective"
   Journal of Marketing Research, Vol. XXV (May 1988), pp. 168-77.

Godwin, R. D.
   "Some Problems in the Definition and Measurement of Advertising
   Penetration and an Inquiry Into Two Alternative Methods for Measuring
   One Component"
   Commentary (JMRS), No. 11 (Summer 1963), pp. 3-19.

Grass, Robert C., Wallace, Wallace H., and Robertshaw, Wayne G.
   "The 'NOLAD' Concept"
   Journal of Advertising Research, Vol. 23 (February/March 1983), pp.
   47-55.

Green, Paul E. and Schaffer, Catherine M.
   "Ad Copy Testing"
   Journal of Advertising Research, Vol. 23 (October/November 1983), pp.
   73-80.

Greene, Jerome D. and Stock, J. Stevens
   "Brand Attitudes as Measures of Advertising Effects"
   Journal of Advertising Research, Vol. 6 (June 1966), pp. 14-22.

Hansen, Flemming
   Studies of Communication Effects: Methodological and Theoretical
   Papers on Left/Right Brain Specialization
   (Copenhagen: Civilokonomernes forlag 9/5, 1985).

Joyce, Timothy
   "The Measurement of Magazine Page Exposures"
   Journal of the Market Research Society, Vol. 28 (April 1986), pp.
   145-55.

Krugman, Herbert E.
   "The Measurement of Advertising Involvement"
   Public Opinion Quarterly, Vol. 30 (Winter 1966-67), pp. 583-96.

Leckenby, John D. and Plummer, Joseph T.
   "Advertising Stimulus Measurement and Assessment Research: A Review
   of Advertising Methods"
   in Current Issues and Research in Advertising
   (Ann Arbor, MI: University of Michigan Press, 1983).

Lorimor, E. S. and Dunn, S. Watson
   "Four Measures of Cross-Cultural Advertising Effectiveness"
   Journal of Advertising Research, Vol. 7 (December 1967), pp. 11-3.

Lucas, Darrell B.
   "A Rigid Technique for Measuring the Impression Values of Specific
   Magazine Advertisements"
   Journal of Applied Psychology, Vol. 24 (December 1940), pp. 778-90.

Maloney, John C.
   "More 'Why' About Portfolio Tests"
   Journal of Marketing, Vol. 26 (July 1962), p. 76.

Maloney, John C.
   "Portfolio Tests--Are They Here to Stay?"
   Journal of Marketing, Vol. 25 (July 1961), pp. 32-7.

Marton, Katherin and Rohloff, Albert C.
   "Use One-Interview Studies With Care"
   Journal of Advertising Research, Vol. 14 (April 1974), pp. 35-8.

Matricon, Claude-Pierre
   "A New Index of Advertising Effectiveness"
   Journal of Advertising Research, Vol. 7 (December 1967), pp. 33-40.

Mendelsohn, Harold
   "Measuring the Process of Communications Effect"
   Public Opinion Quarterly, Vol. 26 (Fall 1962), pp. 411-6.

Murphy, M. P. and Buzzell, R. D.
   "How Advertising Creative Strategies Influence Sales Results"
   A.N.A. Workshop on Advertising and Planning Evaluation, New York
   (December 1963), paper presentation.

Murphy, M. P. and Buzzell, R. D.
   "The Multiple Correlation Model and Its Application in Seven Product
   Fields"
   Operations Research Workshop of the Advertising Research Foundation,
   New York (November 1963), paper presentation.

Neu, D. Morgan
   "Measuring Advertisement Recognition"
   Journal of Advertising Research, Vol. 1 (December 1961), pp. 17-22.

O'Neill, Harry W.
   "Pretesting Advertising With the Differential Attitude Technique"
   Journal of Marketing, Vol. 27 (January 1963), pp. 20-4.

Parker, Edwin B., Smith, Stewart A., and Davenport, John Scott
   "Advertising Theory and Measures of Perception"
   Journal of Advertising Research, Vol. 3 (December 1963), pp. 40-3.

Pavasars, John and Derr, Ed
   "Pre-Alerting On-Air Test Respondents"
   Journal of Advertising Research, Vol. 12 (December 1972), pp. 23-8.

Ross, Harold L., Jr.
   "Recall Versus Persuasion: An Answer"
   Journal of Advertising Research, Vol. 22 (February/March 1982), pp.
   13-6.

Schwartz, David A.
   "Measuring the Effectiveness of Your Company's Advertising"
   Journal of Marketing, Vol. 33 (April 1969), pp. 20-5.

Soley, Lawrence C. and James, William L.
   "Estimating the Readership of Retail Newpaper Advertising"
   Journal of Retailing, Vol. 58 (Fall 1982), pp. 59-75.

Staveley, Nicholas
   "Monitoring Advertising Performance: Inherent Limitations in
   Measuring Effects--The Qualitative Dimension"
   Admap (March 1986), pp. 154-7.

Webb, Eugene J.
"Rejoinder to Becknell"
Journal of Advertising Research, Vol. 2 (December 1962), p. 43.

Webb, Eugene J.
"The Case for the Effectiveness Index"
Journal of Advertising Research, Vol. 2 (June 1962), pp. 15-9.

Wells, William D.
"Recognition, Recall, and Rating Scales"
Journal of Advertising Research, Vol. 4 (September 1964), pp. 2-8.

Winick, Charles
"Three Measures of the Advertising Value of Media Context"
Journal of Advertising Research, Vol. 2 (June 1962), pp. 28-33.

Winn, Paul R. and Neville, Thomas
"The Search for a Good Measure of Magazine Readership: The
TGI-Simmons Controversy"
Journal of Advertising, Vol. 5 (Winter 1976), pp. 10-6.

Young, S.
"Copy Testing Without Magic Numbers"
Journal of Advertising Research, Vol. 12 (1972), pp. 3-12.

Zielske, Hubert A.
"Does Day-After Recall Penalize 'Feeling' Ads?"
Journal of Advertising Research, Vol. 22 (February/March 1982), pp.
19-22.

Zinkhan, George M. and Fornell, Claes
"A Test of Two Consumer Response Scales in Advertising"
Journal of Marketing Research, Vol. XXII (November 1985), pp. 447-52.

Zinkhan, George M., Gelb, Betsy D., and Martin, Claude R.
"The Cloze Procedure"
Journal of Advertising Research, Vol. 23 (June/July 1983), pp. 15-20.

Zinkhan, George M. and Martin, Claude R., Jr.
"Two Copy Testing Techniques: The Cloze Procedure and the Cognitive
Complexity Test"
Journal of Business Research, Vol. 11 (June 1983), pp. 217-27.

17.11 ---------- Operant Effects Measurement

Becknell, James C.
"Utilizing Pre-Testing Devices to Reduce Variance in Advertising
Experiments"
Proceedings, Eleventh Annual Conference
(New York: Advertising Research Foundation, Inc., 1965).

Lindsley, Ogden R.
"Rejoinder to Sicher: Evaluation or Procrastination?"
Journal of Advertising Research, Vol. 3 (March 1963), pp. 47-9.

Lindsley, Ogden R.
"A Behavioral Measure of Television Viewing"
Journal of Advertising Research, Vol. 2 (September 1962), pp. 2-12.

Nathan, Peter E. and Wallace, Wallace H.
"An Operant Behavioral Measure of TV Commercial Effectiveness"
Journal of Advertising Research, Vol. 5 (December 1965), pp. 13-20.

Sicher, Frederic
"An Evaluation of Lindsley's New Measure of TV Viewing Behavior"
Journal of Advertising Research, Vol. 3 (March 1963), pp. 44-7.

Winters, Lewis C. and Wallace, Wallace H.
"On Operant Conditioning Techniques"
Journal of Advertising Research, Vol. 10 (October 1970), pp. 39-45.

Wolf, Abraham, Newman, Dianne Z., and Winters, Lewis C.
"Operant Measures of Interest as Related to Ad Lib Readership"
Journal of Advertising Research, Vol. 9 (June 1969), pp. 40-5.

Zielske, H.
"The Remembering and Forgetting of Advertising"
Journal of Marketing, Vol. 23 (January 1959), pp. 239-43.

17.12 ---------- Theory Re: Sales Effects Measurement

Adler, Lee
"Sales Promotion Effectiveness Can be Measured"
Journal of Marketing, Vol. 27 (October 1963), pp. 69,70.

Assmus, Gert, Farley, John U., and Lehmann, Donald R.
"How Advertising Affects Sales: Meta Analysis of Econometric Results"
Journal of Marketing Research, Vol. XXI (February 1984), pp. 65-74.

Brown, Gordon
    "Monitoring Advertising Performance: The Link Between Ad Content and
    Sales Effects"
    Admap (March 1986), pp. 151-3.

Carefoot, John L.
    "Copy Testing With Scanners"
    Journal of Advertising Research, Vol. 22 (February/March 1982), pp.
    25-7.

Clarke, Darral G.
    "Econometric Measurement of the Duration of Advertising Effect on
    Sales"
    Journal of Marketing Research, Vol. 13 (November 1976), pp. 345-57.

Colman, Stephan and Brown, Gordon
    "Advertising Tracking Studies and Sales Effects"
    Journal of the Market Research Society, Vol. 25 (April 1983), p. 165.

Colman, Stephan and Brown, Gordon
    "Advertising Tracking Studies and Sales Effects"
    Conference Papers, Market Research Society, Brighton (March 10-18,
    1983).

Cornish, Pym
    "Precision Marketing: Linking Shopping Behavior to Media Exposure"
    Admap (March 1986), pp. 169-71.

Helmer, Richard M. and Johansson, Johny K.
    "An Exposition of the Box-Jenkins Transfer Function Analysis With an
    Application to the Advertising-Sales Relationship"
    Journal of Marketing Research, Vol. XIV (May 1977), pp. 227-39.

Jenssen, Ward J.
    "Sales Effects of TV, Radio, and Print Advertising"
    Journal of Advertising Research, Vol. 6 (June 1966), pp. 2-7.

Kyle, P. W.
    "Lydia Pinkham Revisited: A Box-Jenkins Approach"
    Journal of Advertising Research, Vol. 18 (April 1978), pp. 31-9.

Leone, Robert P.
    "Modeling Sales-Advertising Relationships: An Integrated Time
    Series-Econometric Approach"
    Journal of Marketing Research, Vol. XX (August 1983), pp. 291-5.

Little, John D. C.
    "Aggregate Advertising Models: The State of the Art"
    Operations Research, Vol. 27 (July-August 1979), pp. 629-67.

Marantz, Marcel
    "Evaluating Department Store Advertising"
    Journal of Advertising Research, Vol. 7 (March 1977), pp. 16-21.

Mayer, Martin
    The Intelligent Man's Guide to Sales Measures of Advertising
    (New York: Advertising Research Foundation, 1965), 72 pp.

Murray, Hugh
    "Advertising's Effect on Sales--Proven or Just Assumed?"
    International Journal of Advertising, Vol. 5, No. 1 (1986), pp. 15-36.

Palda, Kristian S.
    "Sales Effects of Advertising: A Review of the Literature"
    Journal of Advertising Research, Vol. 4 (September 1964), pp. 12-6.

Palda, Kristian S.
    The Measurement of Cumulative Advertising Effects
    (Englewood Cliffs, NJ: Prentice-Hall, 1964).

Prasad, V. Kanti and Ring, L. Winston
    "Measuring Sales Effects of Some Marketing Mix Variables and Their
    Interactions"
    Journal of Marketing Research, Vol. XIII (November 1976), pp. 391-6.

Stapel, Jan
    "Sales Effects of Print Ads"
    Journal of Advertising Research, Vol. 11 (June 1971), pp. 32-6.

Taylor, James W.
    "Two Requirements for Measuring the Effectiveness of Promotion"
    Journal of Marketing, Vol. 29 (April 1965), pp. 43-5.

Twedt, Dik Warren
    "A Cash Register Test of Sales Effectiveness"
    Journal of Marketing, Vol. 26 (April 1962), pp. 41-3.

17.13 ---------- Applications of Sales Effects Measurement

Aaker, David A., Carman, James M., and Jacobson, Robert
   "Modeling Advertising-Sales Relationships Involving Feedback: A Time
   Series Analysis of Six Cereal Brands"
   Journal of Marketing Research, Vol. XIX (February 1982), pp. 116-25.

Bass, Frank
   "A Simultaneous Equation Regression Study of Advertising and Sales of
   Cigarettes"
   Journal of Marketing Research, Vol. VI (August 1969), pp. 291-300.

Demirdjian, Z. S.
   "Sales Effectiveness of Comparative Advertising: An Experimental
   Field Investigation"
   Journal of Consumer Research, Vol. 10 (December 1983), pp. 362-4.

Gatignon, Hubert
   "Competition as a Moderator of the Effect of Advertising on Sales"
   Journal of Marketing Research, Vol. XXI (November 1984), pp. 387-98.

Hanssens, Dominique M.
   "Bivariate Time Series Analysis of the Relationships Between Sales
   and Advertising"
   Applied Economics, Vol. 12 (September 1980), pp. 329-39.

McDonald, Colin
   "What is the Short-Term Effect of Advertising"
   Special Report No. 71-142
   Marketing Science Insititute (1971).

17.14 ---------- Unclassified Measures of Advertising Effectiveness

Keswick, Gordon M. and Corey, Lawrence G.
   "A Sensitive Measure of Ad Exposure"
   Journal of Advertising Research, Vol. 1 (December 1961), pp. 12-6.

17.15 ---------- Radio Advertising Research Methods

Wilkins, Carole, Clemons, John, and Deacon, Ruth
   "Beyond Presence: The Measurement of Advertising Communication"
   Proceedings, ESOMAR Congress, Lisbon (1988), pp. 525-46.

17.16 ---------- Outdoor Advertising Research Methods

Bloom, Derek
   "Poster Coverage and Frequency as Part of the OSCAR System"
   Admap (November 1988), pp. 36-9.

17.17 ---------- Descriptions, Evaluations of Adver Research Services

Blair, William S.
   "The Case Against Magazine Audience Measures"
   Journal of Advertising Research, Vol. 14 (April 1974), pp. 7-10.

Bowman, Peter
   "Readership Data: Is Speed Compatible With Accuracy and Reasonable
   Cost?"
   Admap (October 1986), pp. 40-6.

Copage, Alan
   "The Readership Research System: Is the EML Working?"
   Admap (October 1986), pp. 26-31.

Cordell, Warren N. and Rahmel, Henry A.
   "Are Nielsen Ratings Affected by Non-Cooperation, Conditioning or
   Response Error?"
   Journal of Advertising Research, Vol. 2 (September 1962), pp. 45-9.

Corlett, Thomas
   "The IPA National Readership Survey: Some Problems and Possible
   Solutions"
   Journal of Advertising Research, Vol. 4 (December 1964), pp. 4-10.

Friedman, Lawrence
   "How Good is the Seven-Day TV Diary Now?"
   Journal of Advertising Research, Vol. 29 (August/September 1989), pp.
   RC3-5.

Gruber, Alin
   "Position Effects and the Starch Viewer Impression Studies"
   Journal of Advertising Research, Vol. 6 (September 1966), pp. 14-7.

Holbrook, Morris B. and Lehmann, Donald R.
  "Form Versus Content in Predicting Starch Scores"
  Journal of Advertising Research, Vol. 20 (August 1980), pp. 53-62.

Kruegel, Dave
  "Television Advertising Effectiveness and Research Innovation"
  Journal of Consumer Marketing, Vol. 5 (Summer 1988), pp. 43-51.

Mayer, Martin
  "A Writer Looks at TV Ratings"
  Journal of Advertising Research, Vol. 12 (August 1972), pp. 3-10.

Monk, Donald
  "Understanding What Exists in Readership: A Pre-Condition for Change"
  Admap (December 1986), pp. 22,3.

Nielsen, A. C., Company
  An Appraisal of Nielsen Station Index Samples in Metro Areas of 52
  Major U.S. Markets
  (New York: A. C. Nielsen Company, 1962).

Nielsen, A. C., Company
  Comparative Quality Appraisal of the Nielsen Station Index
  (New York: A. C. Nielsen Company, 1960).

Nielsen, A. C., Company
  Pittsburgh Validation Study
  (New York: A. C. Nielsen Company, 1956).

Rossiter, John R.
  "Predicting Starch Scores"
  Journal of Advertising Research, Vol. 21, No. 5 (1981), pp. 63-8.

Rotzoll, Kim B.
  "The Starch and Ted Bates Correlative Measures of Advertising
  Effectiveness"
  Journal of Advertising Research, Vol. 4 (March 1964), pp. 22-4.

Rubens, William S.
  "A Guide to TV Ratings"
  Journal of Advertising Research, Vol. 18 (February 1978), pp. 11-8.

Russell, J. Thomas and Martin, Charles H.
  "How Ad Agencies View Research"
  Journal of Advertising Research, Vol. 20 (April 1980), pp. 27-31.

Ryan, Michael
  "The BMRC Mysteries"
  Admap (September 1986), pp. 28-31.

Smith, Alan
  "Advertising Rating Research: Lessons From a Classic Study"
  Admap (November 1987), pp. 50-3.

Smith, Alan and Hodson, Mark
  "Evaluating Magazine Advertisements: Findings From the IPC Magazines
  Appraisal Service"
  Admpa (October 1987), pp. 48-51;68.

Spackman, Nigel
  "Regional Research Data for Target Marketing"
  Admap (July-August 1986), pp. 24-6.

Starch, Daniel
  Brief Outline of the Scope, Method, and Technique of the Starch
  Magazine Advertisement Readership Service
  (Chicago: Daniel Starch and Staff, 1955).

Starch, Daniel
  Factors in Readership Measurements
  (New York: Daniel Starch and Staff, 1946).

Thomson, Lynn
  "Comparing Nielsen's and AGB's People-Meter Ratings: A Natural
  Experiment in Sampling"
  Journal of Advertising Research, Vol. 29 (August/September 1989), pp.
  RC8-12.

Whitley, Edward
  "MPX (Magazine Page Exposure) Comes to Britain"
  Admap (September 1986), pp. 20-4.

Zinkhan, George M. and Gelb, Betsy D.
  "What Starch Scores Predict"
  Journal of Advertising Research, Vol. 26 (August 1986), pp. 45-50.

17.18 ---------- Unclassified (Research Methods in Communication)

Agostini, J.-M.
"The Case for Direct Questions on Reading Habits"
Journal of Advertising Research, Vol. 4 (June 1964), pp. 28-33.

Agostini, J.-M.
"Direct Questions on Reading Habits--Are They So Unreliable?"
ESOMAR Conference, Evian (September 1962), mimeograph.

Bloom, Derek, Jay, Andrea, and Twyman, Tony
"The Validity of Advertising Pretests"
Journal of Advertising Research, Vol. 17 (April 1977), pp. 7-16.

Chardin, Clare and McCallum, David
"Enhancing the Contribution of Research to Central Government
Advertising--A Practical Approach to Evaluating a Crime Prevention
Campaign"
ESOMAR Congress, Barcelona (1983), pp. 355-72.

Corkindale, David
"Considerations for Conducting Successful Advertising Expenditure
Tests"
Journal of the Market Research Society, Vol. 18 (January 1976), pp.
2-16.

Cowan, D. and Cowpe, C.
"The Use of Qualitative Research in the Development of Effective
Advertising"
E.S.O.M.A.R. Congress, Venice (1976).

Gordon, Howard L.
"Yes, Virginia, Research Helps Make Better Advertisements"
Journal of Marketing, Vol. 31 (January 1967), pp. 64-6.

Gormley, Richard
"How Drop-Outs Affect On-Air Testing"
Journal of Advertising Research, Vol. 14 (October 1974), pp. 71-4.

Hodock, Calvin L.
"Predicting On-Air Recall From Theater Tests"
Journal of Advertising Research, Vol. 16 (December 1976), pp. 25-32.

James, Meril and Wilkins, Carole
"Research Techniques for Evaluating Radio Campaigns or Getting
Beneath the Wallpaper"
Proceedings, Market Research Society Conference (March 1988), pp.
367-98.

Jones, Robin, Godfrey, Simon, and Twyman, Tony
"Evaluating the Effectiveness of Anti-Drinking and Driving
Advertising: Increasing the Cost Efficiency of Research"
ESOMAR Congress, Rome (1984), pp. 491-514.

King, Stephen
"Advertising Research for New Brands"
Journal of the Market Research Society, Vol. 10 (July 1968), pp.
145-56.

Maloney, John C.
"Portfolio Tests--Are They Here to Stay?"
Journal of Marketing, Vol. 25 (July 1961), pp. 32-7.

May, J. P.
"Qualitative Advertising Research--A Review of the Role of the
Researcher"
Journal of the Market Research Society, Vol. 20 (October 1978), pp.
203-18.

Plasman, Stephen K.
"Single Sample Commercial Testing"
Journal of Advertising Research, Vol. 13 (December 1973), pp. 39-42.

Rosch, J. Thomas
"Marketing Research and the Legal Requirements of Advertising"
Journal of Marketing, Vol. 39 (July 1975), pp. 69-72.

Roshwalb, Irving
"How Much is an Ad Test Worth?"
Journal of Advertising Research, Vol. 15 (February 1975), pp. 17-23.

Schyberger, Bo W:son
"A Case Against Direct Questions on Reading Habits"
Journal of Advertising Research, Vol. 6 (December 1966), pp. 25-9.

Stevens, Bill and Axelrod, Joel
"Three Ways to Improve Ad Pre-Tests"
Journal of Advertising Research, Vol. 1 (December 1961), pp. 33-6.

Treistman, Joan and Gregg, John P.
   "Visual, Verbal, and Sales Responses to Print Ads"
   Journal of Advertising Research, Vol. 19 (August 1979), pp. 41-6.

Van De Sandt, Udolpho
   "Pretesting With Competition"
   Journal of Advertising Research, Vol. 9 (September 1969), pp. 17-9.

18 --------------- RECOGNITION AND RECALL MEASUREMENT ----------------
        See also (sub)heading(s) 17.

18.01 ---------- Books Re: Recognition and Recall

Brown, John (editor)
    Recall and Recognition
    (New York and London: John Wiley and Sons, 1976).

Kintsch, W.
    The Representation of Meaning in Memory
    (Potomac, MD: Lawrence Erlbaum Associates, 1974).

Klatzky, R. L.
    Human Memory: Structures and Processes
    (San Francisco: W. H. Freeman and Company, 1980).

18.02 ---------- Psychological Theories of Recognition and Recall

Anderson, John R. and Bower, Gordon H.
    "A Propositional Theory of Recognition Memory"
    Memory and Cognition, Vol. 3, No. 2 (1974), pp. 406-12.

Anderson, John R. and Bower, Gordon H.
    "Recognition and Retrieval Processes in Free Recall"
    Psychological Review, Vol. 79 (March 1972), pp. 97-123.

Bagozzi, Richard P. and Silk, Alvin J.
    "Recall, Recognition, and the Measurement of Memory for Print
    Advertisements"
    Marketing Science, Vol. 2 (Spring 1983), pp. 95-134.

Bahrick, Harry P.
    "Retention Curves: Facts or Artifacts?"
    Psychological Bulletin, Vol. 61 (March 1964), pp. 188-94.

Gillund, G. and Shiffrin, R. M.
    "A Retrieval Model for Both Recognition and Recall"
    Psychological Review, Vol. 91 (January 1984), pp. 1-67.

Kintsch, Walter
    "Models for Free Recall and Recognition"
    in Norman, D. A. (editor)
    Models of Human Memory
    (New York: Academic Press, Inc., 1970).

Lockhart, R. S., Craik, F. I. M., and Jacoby, J.
    "Depth of Processing, Recognition and Recall"
    in Brown, J. (editor)
    Recall and Recognition
    (New York: John Wiley and Sons, 1976).

Mandler, George
    "Recognizing: The Judgement of Previous Occurrence"
    Psychological Review, Vol 87, No. 3 (1980), pp. 252-71.

Paivio, A.
    "Imagery in Recall and Recognition"
    in Brown, J. (editor)
    Recall and Recognition
    (New York: John Wiley and Sons, 1976).

Tulving, Endel
    "Ecphoric Processes in Recall and Recognition"
    in Brown, J. (editor)
    Recall and Recognition
    (New York: John Wiley and Sons, 1976).

18.03 ---------- Theory Re: Recognition Measurement

Appel, V. and Blum, M. L.
    "Ad Recognition and Respondent Set"
    Journal of Advertising Research, Vol. 1 (June 1961), pp. 13-21.

Atkinson, R. C. and Juola, J. F.
    "Factors Influencing Speed and Accuracy of Word Recognition"
    in Kornblum, S. (editor)
    Attention and Performance, Volume 4
    (New York: Academic Press, 1973).

Bettman, J. R.
    "Memory Factors in Consumer Choice: A Review"
    Journal of Marketing, Vol. 43, No. 2 (1979), pp. 37-53.

Bower, G. H. and Glass, A. L.
    "Structural Limits and the Reintegrative Power of Picture Fragments"
    Journal of Experimental Psychology: Human Learning and Memory, Vol. 2
    (July 1976), pp. 456-66.

Brown, John
  "Recognition Assessed by Ratings and Ranking"
  British Journal of Psychology, Vol. 65, No. 1 (1974), pp. 13-22.

Clancy, K. J., Ostlund, L. E., and Wyner, G. A.
  "False Reporting of Magazine Readership"
  Journal of Advertising Research, Vol. 19 (October 1979), pp. 23-30.

Craik, F. I. M.
  "Age Differences in Recognition Memory"
  Quarterly Journal of Experimental Psychology, Vol. 23 (1971), pp.
  316-23.

Dallett, K., Wilcox, S. G., and D'Andrea, L.
  "Picture Memory Experiments"
  Journal of Experimental Psychology, Vol. 76, No. 2 (1968), pp. 312-20.

Davis, R., Sutherland, N. S., and Judd, B. R.
  "Information Content in Recognition and Recall"
  Journal of Experimental Psychology, Vol. 61 (1961), pp. 422-9.

Eagle, M. and Leiter, E.
  "Recall and Recognition in Intentional and Incidental Learning"
  Journal of Experimental Psychology, Vol. 68, No. 1 (1964), pp. 58-63.

Frazen, R.
  "Inequalities Which Affect Scores on Advertisements"
  Journal of Marketing, Vol. 6 (April 1942), pp. 128-32.

Glass, A. L., Holyoak, K. J., and Santa, J. L.
  Cognition
  (Reading, MA: Addison-Wesley Publishing Company, 1979).

Goldstein, A. G. and Chance, J. E.
  "Visual Recognition Memory for Complex Configurations"
  Perceptions and Psychophysics, Vol. 9 (1970), pp. 237-41.

Haber, R. N.
  "How We Remember What We See"
  Scientific American, Vol. 222 (May 1970), pp. 104-12.

Hansen, Flemming
  "Hemispheral Lateralization: Implications for Understanding Consumer
  Behavior"
  Journal of Consumer Research, Vol. 8 (June 1981), pp. 23-36.

Kintsch, W.
  "Models for Free Recall and Recognition"
  in Norman, D. A. (editor)
  Models of Human Memory
  (New York: Academic Press, 1970).

Krugman, Herbert E.
  "Low Recall and High Recognition of Advertising"
  Journal of Advertising Research, Vol. 26 (February/March 1986), pp.
  79-86.

Krugman, Herbert E.
  "Low Involvement Theory in the Light of New Brain Research"
  in Maloney, J. C. and Silverman, B. S. (editors)
  Attitude Research Plays for High Stakes
  (Chicago: American Marketing Association, 1979).

Krugman, Herbert E.
  "Memory Without Recall, Exposure Without Perception"
  Journal of Advertising Research, Vol. 17, No. 4 (1977), pp. 7-12.

Krugman, Herbert E.
  "Brain Wave Measures of Media Involvement"
  Journal of Advertising Research, Vol. 11 (February 1971), pp. 3-10.

Lockhart, Robert S.
  "The Facilitation of Recognition by Recall"
  Journal of Verbal Learning and Verbal Behavior, Vol. 14 (1975), pp.
  253-8.

Lucas, Darrell B.
  "A Controlled Recognition Technique for Measuring Magazine
  Advertising Audiences"
  Journal of Marketing, Vol. 6 (October 1942), pp. 133-6.

Mandler, G.
  "Organizing and Recognition"
  in Tulving, E. and Donaldson, W. (editors)
  Organization of Memory
  (New York: Academic Press, 1972).

Mandler, G., Pearlstone, Z., and Koopmans, H. S.
"Effects of Organization and Semantic Similarity on Recall and
Recognition"
Journal of Verbal Learning and Verbal Behavior, Vol. 8 (1969), pp.
410-23.

Marder, Eric and David, M.
"Recognition of Ad Elements: Recall or Projection?"
Journal of Advertising Research, Vol. 1 (December 1961), pp. 23-5.

Martin, E.
"Generation-Recognition Theory and the Encoding Specificity Principle"
Psychological Review, Vol. 82 (1975), pp. 150-3.

Moran, W. T.
"A Reply to Heller's Note"
Journal of Applied Psychology, Vol. 35 (February 1951), pp. 78,9.

Moran, W. T.
"Measuring Exposure to Advertisements"
Journal of Applied Psychology, Vol. 35 (February 1951), pp. 72-7.

Neu, D. M.
"Measuring Advertisement Recognition"
Journal of Advertising Research, Vol. 1 (December 1961), pp. 17-22.

Reder, L. M., Anderson, J. R., and Bjork, R. A.
"A Semantic Interpretation of Encoding Specificity"
Journal of Experimental Psychology, Vol. 102 (1974), pp. 648-56.

Santa, J. L. and Lamwers, L. L.
"Where Does the Confusion Lie? Comments on the Wiseman and Tulving
Paper"
Journal of Verbal Learning and Verbal Behavior, Vol. 15 (1976), pp.
53-7.

Santa, J. L. and Lamwers, L. L.
"Encoding Specificity: Fact or Artifact?"
Journal of Verbal Learning and Verbal Behavior, Vol. 13 (1974), pp.
412-23.

Schweiker, Anja
"Advertising Testing Measuring Recall and Persuasion"
European Research, Vol. 15 (November 1987), pp. S14-6.

Shepard, R. N.
"Recognition Memory for Words, Sentences and Pictures"
Journal of Verbal Learning and Verbal Behavior, Vol. 6 (1967), pp.
156-63.

Shepard, R. N. and Chang, J. J.
"Forced Choice Tests of Recognition Memory Under Steady State
Conditions"
Journal of Verbal Learning and Verbal Behavior, Vol. 2 (1963), pp.
93-101.

Simmons, W. R.
"Controlled Recognition in the Measurement of Advertising Perception"
(abstract)
Public Opinion Quarterly, Vol. 25 (Fall 1961), pp. 470,1.

Singh, Surendra N.
Recognition as a Measure of Learning From Television Commercials
(Ann Arbor, MI: University Microfilms International, 1982),
unpublished doctoral dissertation.

Singh, Surendra N. and Cole, Catherine A.
"Forced-Choice Recognition Tests: A Critical Review"
Journal of Advertising, Vol. 14, No. 3 (1985), pp. 52-8.

Singh, Surendra N. and Rothschild, Michael L.
"The Effect of Recall on Recognition: An Empirical Investigation of
Consecutive Learning Measures"
in Bagozzi, Richard P. and Tybout, Alice M. (editors)
Advances in Consumer Research, Volume 10
(Ann Arbor, MI: Association for Consumer Research, 1983), pp. 271-6.

Singh, Surendra N. and Rothschild, Michael L.
"Recognition as a Measure of Learning From Television Commercials"
Journal of Marketing Research, Vol. XX (August 1983), pp. 235-48.

Standing, Lionel
"Learning 10,000 Pictures"
Quarterly Journal of Experimental Psychology, Vol. 25 (1973), pp.
207-22.

Standing, L., Conezio, J., and Haber, R. N.
"Perception and Memory for Pictures: Single Trial Learning of 2500
Visual Stimuli"
Psychological Science, Vol. 19, No. 2 (1970).

Strong, E. K.
  "The Effect of Length of Series Upon Recognition Memory"
  Psychological Review, Vol. 19 (1912), pp. 447-62.

Tulving, Endel
  "Similarity Relations in Recognition"
  Journal of Verbal Learning and Verbal Behavior, Vol. 20 (October
  1981), pp. 479-96.

Tulving, E. and Thomson, D. M.
  "Encoding Specificity and Retrieval Processes in Episodic Memory"
  Psychological Review, Vol. 80 (1973), pp. 352-73.

Tversky, B.
  "Encoding Processes in Recognition and Recall"
  Cognitive Psychology, Vol. 5 (1973), pp. 275-87.

Underwood, B. J.
  "False Recognition Produced by Impact Verbal Responses"
  Journal of Experimental Psychology, Vol. 70, No. 1 (1965), pp. 122-9.

Underwood, B. J. and Freund, J. S.
  "Errors in Recognition, Learning and Retention"
  Journal of Experimental Psychology, Vol. 78, No. 1 (1968), pp. 55-63.

Wallace, W. P.
  "False Recognition Produced by Implicit Verbal Responses"
  Psychological Bulletin, Vol. 88 (November 1980), pp. 686-704.

Weaver, G. E. and Stanny, C. J.
  "Short Term Retention of Pictorial Stimuli as Accessed by a Probe
  Recognition Technique"
  Journal of Experimental Psychology: Human Learning and Memory, Vol. 4
  (January 1978), pp. 55-65.

Wiseman, S. and Tulving, E.
  "Encoding Specificity: Relation Between Recall Superiority and
  Recognition Failure"
  Journal of Experimental Psychology: Human Learning and Memory, Vol. 2
  (1976), pp. 349-61.

18.04 ---------- Theory Re: Recall Measurement

        See also (sub)heading(s) 116.05.

Bucci, Richard P.
  "Erroneous Recall of Media"
  Journal of Advertising Research, Vol. 13 (August 1973), pp. 23-7.

Docker, John
  "Memorability in Advertising"
  Admap (February 1987).

Ehrenberg, A. S. C.
  "Review of 7-Day Aided Recall"
  Commentary (JMRS), No. 12 (Winter 1963), pp. 3-18.

Ehrenberg, A. S. C.
  "How Reliable is Aided Recall of TV Viewing?"
  Journal of Advertising Research, Vol. 1 (June 1961), pp. 29-31.

Gibson, Lawrence D.
  "If the Question is Copy Testing, the Answer is Not Recall"
  Journal of Advertising Research, Vol. 23 (February/March 1983), pp.
  39-46.

Glassman, Myron and Ford, John B.
  "An Empirical Investigation of Bogus Recall"
  Journal of the Academy of Marketing Science, Vol. 16 (Fall 1988), pp.
  38-41.

Haber, Ralph N.
  "How We Remember What We See"
  Scientific American, Vol. 222 (May 1970), pp. 104-12.

Haller, T. P.
  "Predicting Recall of TV Commercials"
  Journal of Advertising Research, Vol. 12 (October 1972), pp. 43-6.

Haskins, Jack B.
  "Factual Recall as a Measure of Advertising Effectiveness"
  Journal of Advertising Research, Vol. 4 (March 1964), pp. 2-8.

Hodock, C. L.
  "Predicting On-Air Recall From Theater Tests"
  Journal of Advertising Research, Vol. 16 (1976), pp. 25-31.

Krugman, Herbert E.
"Low Recall and High Recognition of Advertising"
Journal of Advertising Research, Vol. 26 (February/March 1986), pp. 79-86.

Krugman, Herbert E.
"Measuring Memory--An Industry Dilemma"
Journal of Advertising Research, Vol. 25, No. 4 (1985), pp. 49-51.

Krugman, Herbert E.
"Low Involvement Theory in the Light of New Brain Research"
in Maloney, J. C. and Silverman, B. S. (editors)
Attitude Research Plays for High Stakes
(Chicago: American Marketing Association, 1979).

Krugman, Herbert E.
"Memory Without Recall, Exposure Without Perception"
Journal of Advertising Research, Vol. 17 (August 1977), pp. 7-12.

Krugman, Herbert E.
"Why Three Exposures May be Enough"
Journal of Advertising Research, Vol. 12 (December 1972), pp. 11-14.

Leavitt, Clark
"Response Structure: A Determinant of Recall"
Journal of Advertising Research, Vol. 8 (1968), pp. 3-6.

Leavitt, Clark, Waddell, Charles, and Wells, William
"Improving Day-After Recall Techniques"
Journal of Advertising Research, Vol. 10 (June 1970), pp. 13-7.

Lovell, M. R. C.
"Difficulties With Recall"
Journal of the Market Research Society, Vol. 10 (July 1968), pp. 172-85.

Marder, Eric and David, Mort
"Recognition of Ad Elements: Recall or Projection?"
Journal of Advertising Research, Vol. 1 (December 1961), pp. 23-5.

Percy, L.
"Some Questions on the Validity of Recall Testing as a Measure of Advertising Effectiveness"
Current Issues in Advertising Research, Vol. 16 (June 1978), pp. 21-5.

Perry, Michael and Perry, Arnon
"Ad Recall: Biased Measure of Media?"
Journal of Advertising Research, Vol. 16 (June 1976), pp. 21-5.

Ross, Harold L., Jr.
"Recall Versus Persuasion: An Answer"
Journal of Advertising Research, Vol. 22 (February/March 1982).

Schweiker, Anja
"Advertising Testing Measuring Recall and Persuasion"
European Research, Vol. 15 (November 1987), ESOMAR Supplement, pp. 14-6.

Schweiker, Anja
"Advertising Testing Measuring Recall and Persuasion"
ESOMAR Congress, Montreux (1987), pp. 701-11.

Schwerin Research Corporation
"When Should the Effects of Television Advertising be Measured? Part 1: Recall"
Technical and Analytical Review (Spring 1960), pp. 1-16.

Stapel, Jan
"Viva Recall! Viva Persuasion!"
European Research, Vol. 15 (November 1987), pp. 222-5.

Tele-Research, Incorporated
"More About the Use and Limitations of Recall Scores"
Tele/Scope, Vol. 3 (September 1970), pp. 1-8.

Thorson, Esther and Rothschild, M. L.
"Recognition and Recall of Commercials: Prediction From a Text Comprehension Analysis of Commercial Scripts"
in Percy, L. and Woodside, A. G. (editors)
Advertising and Consumer Psychology
(Lexington, MA: Lexington Books, 1983).

Thorson, Esther and Snyder, Rita
"Viewer Recall of Television Commercials: Prediction From the Propositional Structure of Commercial Scripts"
Journal of Marketing Research, Vol. XXI (May 1984), pp. 127-36.

Walker, David and Von Gonten, Michael F.
"Explaining Related Recall Outcomes: New Answers From a Better Model"
Journal of Advertising Research, Vol. 29 (June/July 1989), pp. 11-21.

Zielske, Hubert A.
  "Does Day-After Recall Penalize 'Feeling' Ads?"
  Journal of Advertising Research, Vol. 22 (February/March 1982), pp.
  19-22.

Zielske, Hubert A. and Henry, Walter A.
  "Remembering and Forgetting Television Ads"
  Journal of Advertising Research, Vol. 20 (April 1980), pp. 7-13.

18.05 ---------- Comparative Studies of Recognition Versus Recall

Bagozzi, Richard P. and Silk, Alvin J.
  "Reply" (to Howard and Sawyer)
  Marketing Science, Vol. 7 (Winter 1988), pp. 99-102.

Bagozzi, Richard P. and Silk, Alvin J.
  "Recall, Recognition and the Measurement of Memory for Print
  Advertisements"
  Marketing Science, Vol. 2 (1983), pp. 95-134.

Darley, C. F. and Murdock, B. B., Jr.
  "Effects of Prior Free Recall Testing on Final Recall and Recognition"
  Journal of Experimental Psychology, Vol. 91 (1971), pp. 66-73.

Howard, Daniel J. and Sawyer, Alan G.
  "Recall, Recognition and the Dimensionality of Memory for Print
  Advertisements: An Interpretative Reappraisal"
  Marketing Science, Vol. 7 (Winter 1988), pp. 94-8.

Postman, Leo, Jenkins, William O., and Postman, Dorothy L.
  "An Experimental Comparison of Active Recall and Recognition"
  American Journal of Psychology, Vol. 61 (1948), pp. 511-9.

Schaefer, Wolfgang
  "Aided Recall and Recognition in Belson's Studies in Readership"
  Marketing and Research Today, Vol. 17 (February 1989), pp. 41-51.

Singh, Surendra N., Rothschild, Michael L., and Churchill, Gilbert A.,
  Jr.
  "Recognition Versus Recall as Measures of Television Commercial
  Forgetting"
  Journal of Marketing Research, Vol. XXV (February 1988), pp. 72-80.

Tulving, Endel and Thomson, Donald M.
  "Encoding Specificity and Retrieval Process in Episodic Memory"
  Psychological Review, Vol. 80 (September 1973), pp. 352-73.

Tulving, Endel and Watkins, M. J.
  "Continuity Between Recall and Recognition"
  American Journal of Psychology, Vol. 86 (1973), pp. 739-48.

Wells, William D.
  "Recognition, Recall and Rating Scales"
  Journal of Advertising Research, Vol. 4, No. 3 (1964), pp. 2-8.

Zinkhan, George M., Locander, William B., and Lee, James H.
  "Dimensional Relationship of Aided Recall and Recognition"
  Journal of Advertising Research, Vol. 15 (March 1986), pp. 38-46.

19 ----------------------- SIGNAL DETECTION ------------------------

See also (sub)heading(s) 17.

19.01 ---------- Books Re: Theory of Signal Detection and Recognition

Coombs, Clyde H., Dawes, Robyn M., and Tversky, Amos
Mathematical Psychology
(Englewood Cliffs, NJ: Prentice-Hall, Inc., 1970).

Corso, J. F.
The Experimental Psychology of Sensory Behavior
(New York: Holt, Rinehart and Winston, Inc., 1967).

Egan, James P.
Signal Detection Theory and ROC Analysis
(New York: Academic Press, Inc., 1975).

Green, D. M. and Swets, J. A.
Signal Detection Theory and Psychophysics
(New York: John Wiley and Sons, Inc., 1966).

Klatzky, R. L.
Human Memory: Structures and Processes
(San Francisco: W. H. Freeman and Company, 1980).

McNicol, D.
A Primer of Signal Detection Theory
(London: Allen and Unwin, 1972).

Swets, J. A. (editor)
Signal Detection and Recognition by Human Observers
(New York: John Wiley and Sons, Inc., 1964).

Swets, John A. and Pickett, Ronald M.
Evaluation of Diagnostic Systems: Methods From Signal Detection Theory
(New York: Academic Press, Inc., 1982).

19.02 ---------- Theory Re: Signal Detection (TSD) and Recognition

Banks, W. P.
"Signal Detection Theory and Human Memory"
Psychological Bulletin, Vol. 74 (August 1970), pp. 81-99.

Egan, J. P. and Clarke, F. R.
"Psychophysics and Signal Detection"
in Sidowski, J. B. (editor)
Experimental Methods and Instrumentation in Psychology
(New York: McGraw-Hill Book Company, 1966).

Elliott, P. B.
"Tables of d'"
in Swets, J. A. (editor)
Signal Detection and Recognition by Human Observers
(New York: John Wiley and Sons, Inc., 1964).

Green, David M.
"General Prediction Relating Yes-No and Forced-Choice Results"
Journal of the Acoustical Society of America, Vol. 36A (May 1964), p. 1042.

Green, David M. and Moses, Franklin L.
"On the Equivalence of Two Recognition Measures of Short-Term Memory"
Psychological Bulletin, Vol. 66 (September 1966), pp. 228-34.

Hodos, W.
"A Nonparametric Index of Response Bias for Use in Detection and Recognition Experiments"
Psychological Bulletin, Vol. 74 (November 1970), pp. 351-4.

MacMillan, Neil A. and Kaplan, Howard L.
"Detection Theory Analysis of Group Data: Estimating Sensitivity From Average Hit and False-Alarm Rates"
Psychological Bulletin, Vol. 98 (July 1985), pp. 185-99.

Norman, Donald A.
"A Comparison of Data Obtained With Different False-Alarm Rates"
Psychological Review, Vol. 71 (May 1964), pp. 243-6.

Pastore, R. E. and Scheirer, C. J.
"Signal Detection Theory: Considerations for General Application"
Psychological Bulletin, Vol. 81 (December 1974), pp. 945-58.

Peterson, W. W., Birdsall, T. G., and Fox, W. C.
"The Theory of Signal Detectability"
Transactions IRE Professional Group on Information Theory, Vol. 4 (September 1954), pp. 171-212.

Pollack, I. and Norman, D. A.
  "A Nonparametric Analysis of Recognition Experiments"
  Psychonomic Science, Vol. 1 (May 1964), pp. 125,6.

Pollack, Irwin, Norman, Donald A., and Galanter, Eugene
  "An Efficient Nonparametric Analysis of Recognition Memory"
  Psychonomic Science, Vol. 1 (May 1964), pp. 327,8.

Rilling, M. and McDiarmid, C.
  "Signal Detection in Fixed-Ratio Schedules"
  Science, Vol. 148, 3669 (1965), pp. 526,7.

Singh, Surendra N. and Churchill, Gilbert A., Jr.
  "Response-Bias-Free Recognition Tests to Measure Advertising Effects"
  Journal of Advertising Research, Vol. 27 (June/July 1987), pp. 23-36.

Singh, Surendra N. and Churchill, Gilbert A., Jr.
  "Using the Theory of Signal Detection to Improve Ad Recognition
  Testing"
  Journal of Marketing Research, Vol. XXIII (November 1986), pp. 327-36.

Sorkin, R. D., Pastore, R. E., and Pohlmann, L. D.
  "Simultaneous Two-Channel Signal Detection II: Correlated and
  Uncorrelated Signals"
  Journal of the Acoustical Society of America, Vol. 51, No. 6 (1972),
  pp. 1960-65.

Subonski, M. D.
  "Signal Detection Methods in the Analysis of Classical and
  Instrumental Discrimination Conditioning Experiments"
  Proceedings, 75th Annual Convention of the American Psychological
  Association (1967).

Swets, John A.
  "Form of Empirical ROCs in Discrimination and Diagnostic Tasks:
  Implications for Theory and Measurement Performance"
  Psychological Bulletin, Vol. 99 (1986), pp. 181-98.

Swets, John A.
  "Indices of Discrimination or Diagnostic Accuracy: Their ROCs and
  Implied Models"
  Psychological Bulletin, Vol. 99 (January 1986) , pp. 100-17.

Swets, J. A., Tanner, W. P., Jr., and Birdsall, T. G.
  "Decision Processes in Perception"
  in Swets, J. A. (editor)
  Signal Detection and Recognition by Human Observers
  (New York: John Wiley and Sons, Inc., 1964).

Tashchian, Armen, White, J. Dennis, and Pak, Sukgoo
  "Signal Detection Analysis and Advertising Recognition: An
  Introduction to Measurement and Interpretation Issues"
  Journal of Marketing Research, Vol. XXV (November 1988), pp. 397-404.

Van Meter, D. and Middleton, D.
  "Modern Statistical Approaches to Reception in Communication Theory"
  Transactions IRE Professional Group on Information Theory, Vol. 4
  (September 1954), pp. 119-41.

19.03 ---------- Theory Re: Estimation Methods for Signal Detection

Dorfman, Donald D. and Alf, Edward, Jr.
  "Maximum-Likelihood Estimation of Parameters of Signal Detection
  Theory and Determination of Confidence Intervals--Rating Method Data"
  Journal of Mathematical Psychology, Vol. 6 (October 1969), pp. 487-96.

Dorfman, Donald D., Beavers, Lynn L., and Saslow, Carl C.
  "Estimation of Signal Detection Theory Parameters from Rating-Method
  Data: A Comparison of the Method of Scoring and Direct Search"
  Bulletin of the Psychonomic Society, Vol. 1 (May 1973), pp. 207,8.

Grier, J. Brown
  "Nonparametric Indexes for Sensitivity and Bias: Computing Formulas"
  Psychological Bulletin, Vol. 75 (June 1971), pp. 424-9.

Ogilvie, John C. and Creelman, C. Douglas
  "Maximum Likelihood Estimation of Receiver Operating Characteristic
  Curve Parameters"
  Journal of Mathematical Psychology, Vol. 5 (October 1968), pp. 377-91.

19.04 ---------- Applications of Signal Detection Theory

Coates, G. D., Loeb, M., and Alluisi, E. A.
  "Influence of Observing Strategies and Stimulus Variables on
  Watchkeeping Performances"
  Ergonomics, Vol. 15 (July 1972), pp. 379-86.

Hutchinson, J. Wesley and Zenor, Mike
  "Product Familiarity and the Strengths of Brand-Attribute
  Associations: A Signal Detection Theory Approach"
  in Lutz, Richard L. (editor)
  Advances in Consumer Research, Volume 13
  (Prove, UT: Association for Consumer Research, 1985), pp. 450-3.

Sheehan, J. J. and Drury, C. G.
  "The Analysis of Industrial Inspection"
  Applied Ergonomics, Vol. 2 (June 1971), pp. 74-8.

Singh, Surendra N. and Churchill, Gilbert A., Jr.
  "Response-Bias-Free Recognition Tests to Measure Advertising Effects"
  Journal of Advertising Research (June/July 1987), pp. 23-36.

Swets, John A.
  "ROC Analysis Applied to the Evaluation of Medical Imaging Techniques"
  Investigative Radiology, Vol. 14 (January 1979), pp. 109-21.

Swets, John A.
  "Effectiveness of Information Retrieval Methods"
  American Documentation, Vol. 20 (January 1969), pp. 72-89.

Synodinos, Nicolaos E.
  "Review and Appraisal of Subliminal Perception Within the Context of
  Signal Detection Theory"
  Psychology and Marketing, Vol. 5 (Winter 1988), pp. 317-36.

20 ---------------- RESEARCH METHODS FOR TELEVISION ------------------
        See also (sub)heading(s) 17.

20.01 ---------- General Discussions Re: Research Methods for TV

Elliott, Jeremy
    "Long-Term Branding: How can Monitoring Research Contribute"
    Admap (January 1986), pp. 33-8.

Jobber, David and Kilbride, Anthony
    "How Major Agencies Evaluate TV Advertising in Britain"
    International Journal of Advertising, Vol. 5, No. 1 (1986), pp.
    187-95.

Lloyd, Simon
    "Television Research: An International Agency's View"
    Admap (December 1987), pp. 32,3.

Philips, Nick
    "Research for Long-Term Branding: The Television Contribution"
    Admap (January 1986), pp. 24-7.

Philips, Nick and Read, Sue
    "Old Sources--New Resources"
    Admap (June 1987), pp. 43-9.

20.02 ---------- Television--Audience Measurement (Size)

Bol, Jan Willem and Lin, Lynn Y. S.
    "Strategies for Utilising Single Source Consumer Panel Records
    (Product Bar Codes) to Determine Effective Media Frequency"
    ESOMAR Congress, Rome (1984), pp. 421-34.

Broeders, Tom
    "Measuring the Changing TV Audience"
    International Journal of Advertising, Vol. 2 (July-September 1983),
    pp. 275-280.

Buck, Stephan
    "Television Audience Measurement Research--Yesterday, Today and
    Tomorrow"
    Journal of the Market Research Society, Vol. 29 (July 1987), pp.
    265-78.

Buck, Stephan F.
    "Television Audience Research--Yesterday, Today and Tomorrow"
    Proceedings, Market Research Society Conference (March 1987), pp.
    405-16.

Buck, S. F.
    "TV Audience Research--Present and Future"
    Admap (December 1983), pp. 636-40.

Buck, Stephan F.
    "The Future of Television Audience Measurement in Europe"
    Admap (April 1982).

Buck, Stephan F., Sherwood, R., and Twyman, W. A. Tony
    "Panels and the Measurement of Changes"
    Proceedings, ESOMAR Conference (1975).

Buck, Stephan F., Sherwood, R., and Twyman, W. A. Tony
    "Operating Effective Panels for Television Audience Measurement"
    Proceedings, ESOMAR Conference (1973).

Dawson, Charles C.
    "Television Audience Research in Europe: The Lessons of
    De-Massification"
    ESOMAR Congress, Rome (1984), pp. 303-49.

Dixon-Ware, Karen
    "Pan-European TV Research: An Advertiser's View"
    Admap (December 1988), pp. 41-3.

Dudek, Frank J.
    "Relations Among Television Rating Indices"
    Journal of Advertising Research, Vol. 4 (September 1964), pp. 24-8.

Ehrenberg, A. S. C.
    "A Comparison of TV Audience Measures"
    Journal of Advertising Research, Vol. 4 (December 1964), pp. 11-6.

Ehrenberg, A. S. C. and Twyman, W. A.
    "On Measuring Television Audiences"
    Journal of the Royal Statistical Society, Vol. 130, Part 1 (1967),
    pp. 1-59.

Friedman, Lawrence
"Calculating TV Reach and Frequency"
Journal of Advertising Research, Vol. 11 (August 1971), pp. 21-5.

Harvey, Bill
"Nonresponse in TV Meter Panels"
Journal of Advertising Research, Vol. 8 (June 1968), pp. 24-7.

Headen, Robert S., Klompmaker, Jay E., and Teel, Jesse E., Jr.
"Predicting Audience Exposure to Spot TV Advertising Schedules"
Journal of Marketing Research, Vol. XIV (February 1977), pp. 1-9.

Headen, Robert S., Klompmaker, Jay E., and Teel, Jesse E., Jr.
"TV Audience Exposure"
Journal of Advertising Research, Vol. 16 (December 1976), pp. 49-52.

Henry, Michael D. and Rinne, Heikki J.
"Predicting Program Shares in New Time Slots"
Journal of Advertising Research, Vol. 24 (April/May 1984), pp. 9-17.

Kitchen, Philip J. and Yorke, David A.
"Commercial Television Breaks, Consumer Behavior, and New Technology:
An Initial Analysis"
European Journal of Marketing, Vol. 20, No. 2 (1986), pp. 40-53.

Logie, Tony
"What TV Research is Needed"
Admap (December 1983), pp. 641-4.

Mayer, Martin
How Good are Television Ratings?
(New York: Television Information Office, 1965), 26 pp.

Phillips, Nick
"Strategy for Television Audience Measurement in the Nineties"
Admap (December 1987), pp. 34-40.

Roberts, Bruce and Higgs, Alan
"Pan European Audience Measurement in Cable Television Homes"
Proceedings, ESOMAR Congress, Monte Carlo (1986), pp. 367-83.

Sargent, Mike
"Where Should TV Audience Measurement be in 1991? An Advertiser's
View"
Admap (May 1988), pp. 24-7.

Shaw, Jim
"Audience Research: The Imperatives of Change"
Admap (December 1983), pp. 631-6.

Spackman, Nigel and Higgs, Alan
"How Will Cable Television Audiences be Measured?"
Admap (January 1984), pp. 57-60.

Svennevig, Michael and Wynberg, Rebecca
"Viewing is Viewing...Or is It?"
Proceedings, Marketing Research Society Conference (March 1986), pp.
281-93.

20.03 ---------- Theory Re: Television--People Meters

Advertising Research Foundation
People Meter Fact Sheet, Number 1
People Meter Committee of ARF's Video Electronic Media Council (June
1987), 8 pp.

Beville, Mal
"Industry is Only Dimly Aware of People Meter Differences"
Television/Radio Age (November 10, 1986), pp. 76-81.

Cook, Barry
"Peoplemeters in the USA: An Historical and Methodological
Perspective"
Admap (January 1988), pp. 32-5.

Friedman, Lawrence
"How Good is the Seven-Day TV Diary Now?"
Journal of Advertising Research, Vol. 29 (August/September 1989), pp.
RC3-5.

Honomichl, Jack
"Collision Course: Stakes High in People-Meter War"
Advertising Age (July 27, 1987), p. 1.

Kasari, Keikki J.
"Metered TV Audience Measurement: How Finland Went it Alone"
Admap (October 1987), pp. 58-63.

Killion, Kevin C.
   "Using Peoplemeter Information"
   Journal of Media Planning, Vol. 2, No. 1 (1987), pp. 47-52.

McKenna, William J.
   "People Meters: The Search for Tomorrow"
   Journal of Advertising Research, Vol. 29 (August/September 1989), pp.
   RC6,7.

Newmann, Thomas
   "International Television Research: Why PETAR"
   Admap (December 1989), pp. 48,9.

Poltrack, David F.
   "Living With People Meters"
   Journal of Advertising Research, Vol. 28 (June/July 1988), pp. RC8-10.

Reitman, Judith
   "Taking Measure of the People Meter"
   Marketing and Media Decisions, Vol. 20 (August 1985), pp. 62,3.

Soong, Roland
   "The Statistical Reliability of People Meter Ratings"
   Journal of Advertising Research, Vol. 28 (February/March 1988), pp.
   50-6.

Spaeth, Jim
   "Single Source Data When Peoplemeters Aren't Enough"
   Admap (January 1988), pp. 36-41.

Stoddard, Laurence R., Jr.
   "The History of People Meters: How We Got to Where We Are (And Why)"
   Journal of Advertising Research, Vol. 27 (October/November 1987), pp.
   RC10-12.

Thomson, Lynn
   "Comparing Nielsen's and AGB's People-Meter Ratings: A Natural
   Experiment in Sampling"
   Journal of Advertising Research, Vol. 29 (August/September 1989), pp.
   RC8-12.

Warrens, Bob
   "People Meters: The Next Logical Step"
   Marketing and Media Decisions, Vol. 22 (June 1987), pp. 107-12.

20.04 ---------- Television--Passive People Meters

Allen, C. L.
   "Photographing the TV Audience"
   Journal of Advertising Research, Vol. 5, No. 1 (1965), pp. 2-8.

Collett, Peter
   "Real-Life Responses to TV Commercials"
   ESOMAR Congress, Montreux (1987), pp. 713-21.

Collett, Peter
   "Video-Recording the Viewers in Their Natural Habitat"
   EOMAR Seminar, Helsinki (April 1986), paper presentation.

Lu, Daozheng and Kiewit, David A.
   "Passive People Meters: A First Step"
   Journal of Advertising Research, Vol. 27 (June/July 1987), pp. 9-14.

20.05 ---------- Applications Using People Meters

Ehrenberg, Andrew S. C. and Wakshlag, Jacob
   "Repeat-Viewing With People Meters"
   Journal of Advertising Research, Vol. 27 (February/March 1987), pp.
   9-13.

20.06 ---------- Television--Audience Measurement (Characteristics)

Allen, Charles L.
   "Photographing the TV Audience"
   Journal of Advertising Research, Vol. 5 (March 1965), pp. 2-8.

Parrish, John
   "Photochronographic Measurement of the Audience for Television News
   Shows"
   Oklahoma State University (1964), unpublished M.S. thesis.

Read, Susan
   "Making BARB Deliver More"
   Admap (September 1986), pp. 36-9;58.

Roslow, Laurence and Roslow, Sydney
  "A Low-Cost Method for Identifying TV Audiences"
  Journal of Marketing, Vol. 27 (April 1963), pp. 13-6.

Whitehead, John
  "BARB--The Last Geodemographic Hurdle?"
  Admap (June 1988), pp. 46-7.

20.07 ---------- Television--Communications Effects Measurement

Achenbaum, Alvin A., Haley, Russell I., and Gatty, Ronald
  "On-Air vs. In-Home Testing of TV Commercials"
  Journal of Advertising Research, Vol. 7 (December 1967), pp. 15-9.

Barwise, T. P., Ehrenberg, Andrew S. C., and Goodhardt, G. J.
  "Audience Appreciation and Audience Size"
  Journal of the Market Research Society, Vol. 21, No. 4 (1979).

Brennan, D.
  "A Programme Maker's Use of Audience Research"
  Media Research Group Conference (1985).

Brown, Gordon
  "Facts From Tracking Studies--and Old Advertising Chestnuts"
  Admap (June 1988), pp. 20-5.

Burke Marketing Research, Incorporated
  Day-After Recall Television Commercial Testing
  (Cincinnati, OH: Burke Marketing Research, Inc., 1980).

Buzzell, Robert D., Kolin, Marshall, and Murphy, Malcolm P.
  "Television Commercial Test Scores and Short-Term Changes in Market
  Shares"
  Journal of Marketing Research, Vol. II (August 1965), pp. 307-13.

Ehrenberg, A. S. C.
  "How Reliable is Aided Recall of TV Viewing?"
  Journal of Advertising Research, Vol. 1 (June 1961), pp. 29-31.

Fothergill, J. E. and Ehrenberg, A. S. C.
  "On the Schwerin Analyses of Advertising Effectiveness"
  Journal of Marketing Research, Vol. II (August 1965), pp. 298-306.

Haley, Russell I. and Gatty, Ronald
  "Measuring Effectiveness of Television Exposure by Computer"
  Journal of Advertising Research, Vol. 9 (September 1969), pp. 9-12.

Haller, T. P.
  "Predicting Recall of TV Commercials"
  Journal of Advertising Research, Vol. 12 (October 1972), pp. 43-6.

Hoyes, Peter
  "Advertising Effectiveness: Let Us Stop Hunting Needles and Start
  Making Hay"
  Admap (September 1987), pp. 49-53.

Leavitt, Clark
  "A Multidimensional Set of Rating Scales for Television Commercials"
  Journal of Applied Psychology, Vol. 54 (1970), pp. 427-9.

March, Robert M. and Swinbourne, Donald W.
  "What is 'Interest' in TV Commercials?"
  Journal of Advertising Research, Vol. 14 (August 1974), pp. 17-22.

Menneer, Peter
  "Audience Appreciation--A Different Story From Audience Numbers"
  Journal of the Market Research Society, Vol. 29 (July 1987), pp.
  241-64.

Menneer, Peter
  "AIs and Audiences: How the BBC Uses AIs"
  BARB Conference (1984).

Menneer, Peter
  "Audience Appreciation--A Different Story From Audience Numbers"
  Proceedings, Market Research Society (March 1987), pp. 417-38.

Murphy, M. P. and Buzzell, R. D.
  "The Conceptual Basis of the Schwerin Advertising Effectiveness Model"
  Operations Workshop of the Advertising Research Foundation, New York
  (November 1963), paper presentation.

Rohloff, Albert C.
  "Quantitative Analyses of the Effectiveness of TV Commercials"
  Journal of Marketing Research, Vol. III (August 1966), pp. 239-45.

Rossiter, John R.
    "Reliability of a Short Test Measuring Children's Attitudes Toward TV
    Commercials"
    Journal of Consumer Research, Vol. 3 (March 1977), pp. 179-84.

Schlinger, Mary Jane Rawlins
    "Respondent Characteristics That Affect Copy-Test Attitude Scales"
    Journal of Advertising Research, Vol. 22 (February/March 1982), pp.
    29-35.

Schmittlein, D. C. and Morrison, D. G.
    "Measuring Miscomprehension for Televised Communication Using
    True-False Questions"
    Journal of Consumer Research, Vol. 10 (September 1983), pp. 147-56.

Schwerin Research Corporation
    "When Should the Effects of Television Advertising be Measured? Part
    2: Changes in Attitude and Behavior"
    Technical and Analytical Review (Summer 1960), pp. 1-14.

Schwerin Research Corporation
    "When Should the Effects of Television Advertising be Measured? Part
    1: Recall"
    Technical and Analytical Review (Spring 1960), pp. 1-16.

Thorson, Esther and Snyder, Rita
    "Viewer Recall of Television Commercials: Prediction From the
    Propositional Structure of Commercial Scripts"
    Journal of Marketing Research, Vol. XXI (May 1984), pp. 127-36.

20.08 ---------- Television--Sales Effects Measurement

Brown, Gordon
    "The Link Between Sales Effects and Advertising Content"
    Admap (April 1987), pp. 33-7.

Dodd, A. R. and Kelly, P. J.
    "New Study Tells TV Advertisers How Advertising Builds Sales and
    Share of Market"
    Printers' Ink (May 1964), pp. 27-38.

Gold, Laurence N.
    "The Evolution of Television Advertising-Sales Measurement"
    Journal of Advertising Research, Vol. 28 (June/July 1988), pp. 19-24.

20.09 ---------- Television--Copy Research Methods

Adams, Arthur, Mehrotra, Sunil, and Van Auken, Stuart
    "Reliability of Forced-Exposure Television Copytesting"
    Journal of Advertising Research, Vol. 23 (June/July 1983), pp. 29-32.

Bowring, Colin
    "Conversations About Advertisements"
    Proceedings, ESOMAR Congress, Lisbon (1988), pp. 587-605.

Brown, Nigel A. and Gatty, Ronald
    "Rough vs. Finished TV Commercials in Telpex Tests"
    Journal of Advertising Research, Vol. 7 (December 1967), pp. 21-4.

Caffyn, John M.
    "Telpex Testing of TV Commercials"
    Journal of Advertising Research, Vol. 5 (June 1965), pp. 29-37.

Coe, Barbara J. and MacLachlan, James
    "How Major TV Advertisers Evaluate Commercials"
    Journal of Advertising Research, Vol. 20 (December 1980), pp. 51-4.

Dunn, Theodore F.
    "ARF's Copy Research Validity Project"
    Journal of Advertising Research, Vol. 24 (December 1984/January
    1985), pp. 40-2.

Eastlack, Joseph O., Jr.
    "How to Take the Controversy Out of TV Copy Testing"
    Journal of Advertising Research, Vol. 24 (December 1984/January
    1985), pp. 37-9.

Green, Paul E. and Schaffer, Catherine M.
    "Ad Copy Testing"
    Journal of Advertising Research, Vol. 23 (October/November 1983), pp.
    73-80.

Klein, Peter R. and Tainiter, Melvin
    "Copy Research Validation: The Advertiser's Perspective"
    Journal of Advertising Research, Vol. 23 (October/November 1983), pp.
    9-17.

Lipstein, Benjamin and Neelankavil, James P.
"Television Advertising Copy Research"
Journal of Advertising Research, Vol. 24 (April/May 1984), pp. 19-25.

Mehrotra, Sunil, Van Auken, Stuart, and Lonial, Subhash C.
"Adjective Profiles in Television Copy Testing"
Journal of Advertising Research, Vol. 21 (August 1981), pp. 21-5.

Plummer, Joseph T.
"Evaluating TV Commercial Tests"
Journal of Advertising Research, Vol. 12 (October 1972), pp. 21-7.

Silk, Alvin J.
"Test-Retest Correlations and the Reliability of Copy Testing"
Journal of Marketing Research, Vol. XIV (1977), pp. 476-86.

Spielman, Harold M.
"Pretesting With Rough Prototype Commercials: Creative and Economic Benefits"
ESOMAR Seminar on Advertising Research, Monte Carlo (1983).

Stocks, J. M. B.
"Validating Television Advertisement Tests"
Commentary (JMRS), Vol. 7 (July 1965).

Weiss, T. and Appel, Valentine
"Sense and Nonsense in Attitude-Change Copy Testing"
Proceedings, Advertising Research Foundation Conference (1973), pp. 54-9.

Wheatley, John J.
"Assessing TV Pretest Audiences"
Journal of Advertising Research, Vol. 11 (February 1971), pp. 21-5.

Williams, Susan
"The Use of Narrative Tapes in Quantitative Ad Testing"
Journal of the Market Research Society, Vol. 29 (October 1987), pp. 451-7.

20.10 ---------- Theory Re: Cable Television Research Methods

Mayer, Charles S.
"CATV Test Laboratory Panels"
Journal of Advertising Research, Vol. 10 (June 1970), pp. 37-43.

Carefoot, John L.
"Media Weight Tests: Tips on Split Cable, Matched Markets"
Marketing News, Vol. 19 (January 4, 1985), p. 5.

Corkindale, David
"Measuring the Sales Effectiveness of Advertising: The Role for an ADLAB in the UK"
Journal of the Market Research Society, Vol. 26 (January 1984), pp. 29-49.

Litzenroth, Heinrich A.
"New Market Research Instruments Through the Application of High Technologies"
ESOMAR Congress, Montreux (1987), pp. 67-92.

Robertson, J. D.
"Measuring Effects of TV Advertising on Sales Revenue Using an Adlab"
Annual Conference, Marketing Research Society, Brighton (1971).

Teer, F.
"ADLABS--Can Controlled Tests of Advertising Effectiveness be Made to Work?"
Admap, Vol. 10 (1974), p. 2.

Ule, G. M.
"Two Years of the Milwaukee Adlab: First Report"
Proceedings, Twelfth Annual Conference of the Advertising Research Foundation, New York (1966).

Wallerstein, Edward
"Measuring Commercials on CATV"
Journal of Advertising Research, Vol. 7 (June 1967), pp. 15-9.

20.11 ---------- Applications of Cable Television Research

Blair, Margaret Henderson
"An Empirical Investigation of Advertising Wearin and Wearout"
Journal of Advertising Research, Vol. 27 (December 1987/January 1988), pp. 45-50.

Krishnamurthi, Lakshman, Narayan, Jack, and Raj, S. P.
  "Intervention Analysis of a Field Experiment to Assess the Buildup
  Effect of Advertising"
  Journal of Marketing Research, Vol. XXIII (November 1986), pp. 337-45.

Krishnamurthi, Lakshman and Raj, S. P.
  "The Effect of Advertising on Consumer Price Sensitivity"
  Journal of Marketing Research, Vol. XXII (May 1985), pp. 119-29.

Zufryden, Fred S.
  "Predicting Trial, Repeat, and Sales Response From Alternative Media
  Plans"
  Journal of Advertising Research, Vol. 22 (June/July 1982), pp. 45-52.

Zufryden, Fred S.
  "A Tested Model of Purchase Response to Advertising Exposure"
  Journal of Advertising Research, Vol. 21 (February 1981), pp. 7-16.

21 ----------- SINGLE-SOURCE METHODOLOGY AND SCANNER DATA ------------
        See also (sub)heading(s) 17.

21.01 ---------- State of Single Source Methodology and Usage

Buck, Stephan
   "Single Source Data--The Theory and the Practice"
   Journal of the Market Research Society, Vol. 31 (October 1989), pp.
   489-500.

Eskin, Gerald J.
   "Single Source Data: The US Experience"
   Journal of the Market Research Society, Vol. 31 (October 1989), pp.
   501-507.

Winters, Lewis C.
   "Home Scan vs. Store Scan Panels: Single-Source Options for the 1990s"
   Marketing Research, Vol. 1 (December 1989), pp. 61-5.

21.02 ---------- Theory Re: Single-Source Research

Antoine, Jacques and Santini, Gilles
   "Fusion Techniques: Alternative to Single-Source Methods"
   European Research, Vol. 15 (August 1987), pp. 178-87.

Audience Concepts Committee
   "Toward Better Media Comparisons"
   Advertising Research Foundation (1961), report.

Basu, Debi and Parfitt, John
   "The Experience of Creating and Running a Single Source Panel in
   India"
   Proceedings, ESOMAR Congress, Lisbon (1988), pp. 485-504.

Bowles, Tim
   "Monitoring Advertising Performance: Measuring Effects--A New
   Perspective"
   Admap (March 1986), pp. 145-7.

Buck, Stephan and Yates, Alan
   "Television Viewing, Consumer Purchasing and Single-Source Research"
   European Research, Vol. 15, No. 1 (1987), pp. 34-9.

Chouvou, Ph.
   "Une Premiere Utilisation du Scanning en France: SCAN 5000"
   Vijfde Vlaams Marketingkongres van de Stichting Marketing, Brussels
   (November 1986).

Chouvou, Ph., Gold, L. N., Schmitt, P. M., Suffolk, G. C., and Zepp, R.
   H.
   "The Single-Source Concept: Past, Present and Future"
   European Research, Vol. 15, No. 1 (1987), pp. 4-11.

Curry, David J.
   "Single-Source Systems: Retail Management Present and Future"
   Journal of Retailing, Vol. 65 (Spring 1989), pp. 1-20.

Eilander, Goos
   "The Use of High Quality Software and Inexpensive Apparatus for High
   Tech Research Service"
   ESOMAR Congress, Montreux (1987), pp. 93-107.

Kiley, D.
   "The Trouble With Single Source"
   Adweek's Marketing Week (June 4, 1989).

Lodish, Leonard M. and Reibstein, David J.
   "New Gold Mines and Minefields in Market Research"
   Harvard Business Review (January-February 1986), pp. 168-82.

McDonald, Colin
   "Advertising Effectiveness Revisited"
   Admap (April 1986), pp. 191-5;203.

McKenna, W. J.
   "In Home Electronic Measurement of Consumer Behavior--The New
   Research Frontier"
   ESOMAR Conference, Tokyo (June 1986).

Naples, M. J.
   "Media Research: Going Beyond Audience Ratings and Demographics to
   Single-Source Data"
   European Research, Vol. 14, No. 4 (1986), pp. 186-96.

Schmitt, P. M.
   "The Comprehensive Research System of the Future--An Integrated
   Approach"
   ARF Workshop, New York (July 1986).

Spaeth, Jim
    "Single Source Data When Peoplemeters Aren't Enough"
    Admap (January 1988), pp. 36-41.

Ward, John
    "Lifestyles and Geodemographics: Why Advertising Agencies Shun a
    Single-Source Approach"
    Admap (June 1987), pp. 53-6.

21.03 ---------- Administration Issues and General Discussions

Bol, Jan Willem and Lin, Lynn Y. S.
    "Strategies for Utilizing Single Source Consumer Panel Records
    (Product Bar Codes) to Determine Effective Media Frequency"
    ESOMAR Congress, Rome (September 1984).

Buck, Stephan and Yates, Alan
    "Television Viewing, Consumer Purchasing and Single Source Research"
    Journal of the Market Research Society, Vol. 28 (July 1986), pp.
    225-33.

Carefoot, John L.
    "Copy Testing With Scanners"
    Journal of Advertising Research, Vol. 22 (February/March 1982), pp.
    25-7.

Gullen, Phil and Johnson, Hugh
    "Relating Product Purchasing and TV Viewing"
    Journal of Advertising Research (December 1986/January 1987), pp.
    9-19.

Kandathil, Jacob
    "The Advantages of Electronic Test Markets: An Advertiser View Based
    on Experience"
    Journal of Advertising Research (December 1985/January 1986), pp.
    RC11,2.

Naples, Michael J.
    "Media Research: Going Beyond Audience Ratings and Demographics to
    Single-Source Data"
    European Research, Vol. 14, No. 4 (1986), pp. 186-96.

Marketing News
    "The Search for Single-Source Data: Testing of TV Commercials Enters
    New Phase"
    Marketing News, Vol. 19 (May 24, 1985), pp. 16,7.

Prince, Melvin
    "Some Uses and Abuses of Single-Source Data for Promotional Decision
    Making"
    Marketing Research, Vol. 1 (December 1989), pp. 18-22.

21.04 ---------- Applications of Single-Source Research

Bolton, Ruth N.
    "The Relationship Between Market Characteristics and Promotional
    Price Elasticities"
    Marketing Science, Vol. 8 (Spring 1989), pp. 153-89.

Broadbent, Simon
    "Two OTS in a Purchase Interval--Some Questions"
    Admap (November 1986), pp. 12-6.

Eskin, Gerald J.
    "Applications of Electronic Single-Source Measurement Systems"
    European Research, Vol. 15, No. 1 (1987), pp. 12-20.

Sunoo, D. H. and Lin, Lynn Y. S.
    "A Search for Optimal Advertising Spending Level"
    Journal of Advertising (1979).

Sunoo, D. H. and Lin, Lynn Y. S.
    "Sales Effects of Promotion and Advertising"
    Journal of Advertising Research (1978).

21.05 ---------- Descriptions of Specific Commercial Services

Eskin, Gerald J.
    "The BehaviorScan System: An Application of New Technologies"
    ESOMAR Congress, Rome (September 1984).

Eskin, Gerald J. and Malec, J.
    "BehaviorScan"
    Proceedings, Fourth Annual Mid-Year Conference of the Advertising
    Research Foundation (October 1979).

Escot, Bryn
    "Monitoring Advertising Performance: ERIM--A New Scanning Service"
    Admap (March 1986), pp. 141-4.

Fulgoni, Gian M.
    "Monitoring Advertising Performance: The BehaviourScan Experience"
    Admap (March 1986), pp. 140;144.

Gold, L. N.
    "New Technology Contributions to New Product and Advertising Strategy
    Testing: The ERIM TESTSIGHT System"
    Proceedings, ESOMAR Congress, Monte Carlo (September 1986), pp.
    345-65.

Harrison, Steve
    "Single-Source Data as Targeting Tools"
    Admap (July-August 1986), pp. 27-9.

Information Resources, Incorporated
    Measuring Advertising Effectiveness With BehaviorScan: Capabilites
    and Case Examples
    (Chicago: Information Resources, Inc., 1986), 21 pp.

Information Resources, Incorporated
    New Product Testing With BehaviorScan: Capabilities and Case Examples
    (Chicago: Information Resources, Inc., 1986), 21 pp.

Jacobs, Brian
    "Stats Scan"
    Admap (October 1988), pp. 48-50.

Jephcott, Jonathan
    "A Breakthough in Household Panels" (BrandScan)
    Admap (September 1986), pp. 52-4.

Kruegel, Dave
    "Television Advertising Effectiveness and Research Innovation"
    (BehaviorScan, AdTel, ERIM)
    Journal of Consumer Marketing, Vol. 5 (Summer 1988), pp. 43-51.

Levin, Gary
    "IRI Tests Show Sales, Ads Related to a Point"
    Advertising Age (September 28, 1987), p. 48.

Lin, Lynn Y. S. and Kim, C. Jay
    "AdTel: Its History and Application"
    European Research, Vol. 15, No. 1 (1987), pp. 22-7.

Litzenroth, Heinrich A.
    "New Market Research Instruments Through the Application of High
    Technologies"
    ESOMAR Congress, Montreux (1987), pp. 67-92.

McKenna, William J.
    "ScanAmerica BuyerGraphic Ratings"
    European Research, Vol. 15, No. 1 (1987), pp. 28-33.

Milde, Heide
    "Using Scanning Data to Measure Price and Promotion Effects"
    Admap (April 1987), pp. 51-3.

Moseley, Susan and Parfitt, John
    "Measuring Advertising Effect From Single Source Data: The Experience
    From the First Year of the AdLab Panel"
    Proceedings, Market Research Society Conference (March 1987), pp.
    439-66.

Pioche, Alain and Gauguier, Marc
    "Scan 5000: The Total Relationship Between the Store Environment and
    the Consumer"
    Proceedings, ESOMAR Congress, Lisbon (1988), pp. 365-80.

Staples, Norman
    "Scanning-Based Services and the Nielsen Contribution"
    Admap (April 1987), pp. 47-50;68.

Winters, Lewis C.
    "Marketing Research's Survey in a Box: VIEWTEL"
    Marketing Research, Vol. 1 (September 1989), pp. 82,3.

Zepp, R. H.
    "TELERIM--Hartetest fur Marketing im Realen Umfeld"
    Werbewirkungsforschung, Band 1, Hamburg (1986).

Zepp, R. H.
    TELERIM--Die Neue Dimension in Testmarketing
    (Frankfurt: A. C. Nielsen, 1986).

21.06 ---------- Theory Re: Scanner Data

Adams, James R.
"UPC: Can We Afford to Miss this Research Opportunity?"
European Research, Vol. 3 (July 1975), pp. 136-9.

Bloom, Derek
"Point of Sale Scanners and Their Implications for Market Research"
Journal of the Market Research Society, Vol. 22 (October 1980), pp. 221-38.

Bogart, Leo
"What the Scanners Show"
Advertising Age (June 8, 1987), p. 18.

Bol, Jan Willem and Lin, Lynn Y. S."Strategies for Utilising Single Sou rce Consumer Panel Records (Product Bar Codes) to Determine Effective M edia Frequency"
ESOMAR Congress, Rome (1984), pp. 421-34.

Business Week
"Market Research by Scanner"
Business Week (May 5, 1980), pp. 113,6.

Carefoot, John L.
"Copy Testing With Scanners"
Journal of Advertising Research, Vol. 22 (February/March 1982), pp. 25-7.

Conlon, Grace
"Closing in on Consumer Behavior"
Marketing Communications, Vol. 11 (November 1986), pp. 53-9.

Corr, Fitzhugh L.
"Scanners in Marketing Research: Paradise (Almost)"
Marketing News, Vol. 19 (January 4, 1985), pp. 1,15.

Fishbein, Martin
"In Defence of Attitudes or Your Tool May be Bigger Than My Tool but It Still Takes Two to Tango"
Singapore Marketing Review, Vol. III (1988), pp. 16-27.

Gorn, Gerald J. and Fraser, Scott D.
"Electronic Data: Marketing Answers Through Behavioural Research"
Singapore Marketing Review, Vol. III (1988), pp. 7-15.

Gullen, Phil and Johnson, Hugh
"Relating Product Purchasing and TV Viewing"
Journal of Advertising Research (December 1986/January 1987), pp. 9-19.

Hall, Carol
"UPC: Super Spy"
Marketing and Media Decisions, Vol. 21 (May 1986), pp. 96-105.

Hawkes, W. J. and Porter, J. C.
"Statistical Issues Associated With the Utilization of Scanner Data"
in Zufryden, Fred S. (editor)
Advances and Practices of Marketing Science
(ORSA/TIMS, 1983), pp. 129-43.

Huppert, Egon
"Scanning: A New Tool for the MMIS"
European Research, Vol. 12 (April 1984), pp. 68-71.

Johnson, M.
"UPC Update: Shaping Up the Symbol"
Progressive Grocer (March 1985), pp. 93-5.

Keon, John
"Profiling Brands' Customer Franchises on Price Sensitivity and Brand Switching Tendencies Using Scanner Panel Data"
Graduate School of Business Administration, New York University (1983), working paper.

Klokis, Holly
"UPC Scanning Scores OK in Bullock's Test"
Chain Store Age Executive (December 1985), pp. 61-4.

Leeflang, Peter S. H. and Plat, Frans W.
"Scanning Scanning Opportunities"
Proceedings, ESOMAR Congress, Lisbon (1988), pp. 471-84.

Levy, Robert
"Scanning for Dollars"
Dun's Business Month, Vol. 128 (September 1986), pp. 63,4.

Lodish, Leonard M. and Reibstein, David J.
"New Gold Mines and Minefields in Market Research"
Harvard Business Review, Vol. 64 (January/February 1986), pp. 168-82.

Marketing News
"Advances in Scanner-Based Research System Yield Fast, Accurate New
Product Test Results"
Marketing News, Vol. 14 (September 18, 1981), p. 20.

Muller, Thomas E.
"Analysing Information Display Effectiveness With Electronic Scanning
Systems"
European Research, Vol. 11 (October 1983), pp. 136-43.

Nielsen Researcher
"The Realization of Scanner-Based Research"
Nielsen Researcher (November 1985).

Prasad, V. Kanti, Casper, Wayne R., and Schieffer, Robert J.
"Alternatives to the Traditional Retail Store Audit: A Field Study"
Journal of Marketing, Vol. 48 (Winter 1984), pp. 54-61.

Rogers, David
"Scan-Based Research Data can Give Sharp Competitive Edge"
Supermarket Business, Vol. 36 (February 1981), pp. 39,40.

Schulz, David
"Is UPC in Your Future?"
Stores (September 1986), pp. 36-42.

Shugan, Steven M.
"Estimating Brand Positioning Maps Using Supermarket Scanning Data"
Journal of Marketing Research, Vol. XXIV (February 1987), pp. 1-18.

Sinkula, James M.
"Status of Company Usage of Scanner Based Research"
Journal of the Academy of Marketing Science, Vol. 14 (Spring 1986),
pp. 63-71.

Suffolk, G. C.
"The Latest Developments in Bar-Code Scanning in Food Stores"
ESOMAR Seminar, Nice (November 1984).

Sugarman, Aaron
"Scanners: The Promotion Appeal"
Incentive Marketing, Vol. 160 (November 1986), pp. 27-30.

Supermarket Business
"Scanning and Market Research: Long Promise, Now a Reality"
Supermarket Business, Vol. 36 (February 1981), pp. 14,15.

Vanhonacker, Wilfried R.
"Structuring and Analyzing Brand Competition Using Scanner Data"
Columbia University (1984), working paper.

Wolfe, Alan
"EPOS Data" A User's View"
Admap (April 1987), pp. 58-60.

Wolfe, Alan
"The Effects of Scanning on the Manufacturer/Retailer Relationship"
Admap (October 1986), pp. 56-9.

Zufryden, Fred S.
"Modeling Purchase Patterns on the Basis of Incomplete and Biased
Consumer Purchase Diary and UPC Panel Data"
International Journal of Research in Marketing, Vol. 1, No. 3 (1984),
pp. 199-213.

21.07 ---------- Applications of Scanner Panels

     See also (sub)heading(s) 90.

Bawa, Kapil and Shoemaker, Robert W.
"The Effects of a Direct Mail Coupon on Brand Choice Behavior"
Journal of Marketing Research, Vol. XXIV (November 1987), pp. 370-6.

Grover, Rajiv and Srinivasan, V.
"An Approach for Tracking Within-Segment Shifts in Market Shares"
Journal of Marketing Research, Vol. XXVI (May 1989), pp. 230-6.

Gupta, Sunil
"Impact of Sales Promotions on When, What, and How Much to Buy"
Journal of Marketing Research, Vol. XXV (November 1988), pp. 342-55.

Klein, Robert L.
"Using Supermarket Scanner Panels to Measure the Effectiveness of
Coupon Promotions"
in Keon, John W. (editor)
Proceedings, Third ORSA/TIMS Special Interest Conference on Market
Measurement and Analysis
(Providence, RI: The Institute of Management Sciences, 1981), pp.
118-24.

Lattin, James M. and Bucklin, Randolph E.
"Reference Effects of Price and Promotion on Brand Choice Behavior"
Journal of Advertising Research, Vol. XXVI (August 1989), pp. 299-310.

Winer, Russell S. and Moore, William L.
"Evaluating the Effects of Marketing-Mix Variables on Brand
Positioning"
Journal of Advertising Research, Vol. 29 (February/March 1989), pp.
39-45.

Zufryden, Fred S.
"Modelling Purchase Patterns on the Basis of Incomplete and Biased
Consumer Purchase Diary and UPC Panel Data"
International Journal of Research in Marketing, Vol. 1, No. 3 (1984),
pp. 199-213.

Zufryden, Fred S.
"An Empirical Evaluation of Alternative Composite Brand
Choice-Purchase Incidence Models"
in Sheth, J. (editor)
Research in Marketing
(JAI Press, 1982).

Zufryden, Fred S.
"An Empirical Evaluation of a Composite Heterogeneous Model of Brand
Choice and Purchase Timing Behavior"
Management Science, Vol. 24 (1978), pp. 761-73.

21.08 ---------- Applications Using Scanner Data

Allenby, Greg M.
"A Unified Approach to Identifying, Estimating and Testing Demand
Structures With Aggregate Scanner Data"
Marketing Science, Vol. 8 (Summer 1989), pp. 265-80.

Blattberg, Robert C. and Levin, Alan
"Modelling the Effectiveness and Profitability of Trade Promotions"
Marketing Science, Vol. 6 (Spring 1987), pp. 124-46.

Blattberg, Robert C. and Wisniewski, Kenneth J.
"Analyzing Intra-Category, Inter-Brand Price Competition: A Theory of
Price Tier Competition"
University of Chicago (January 1986), working paper.

Bolton, Ruth N.
"The Robustness of Retail-Level Price Elasticity Estimates"
Journal of Retailing, Vol. 65 (Summer 1989), pp. 193-219.

Guadagni, Peter M. and Little, John D. C.
"A Logit Model of Brand Choice Calibrated on Scanner Data"
Marketing Science, Vol. 2 (Summer 1983), pp. 203-38.

Kumar, V. and Leone, Robert P.
"Measuring the Effect of Retail Store Promotions on Brand and Store
Substitution"
Journal of Marketing Research, Vol. XXV (May 1988), pp. 178-85.

Peckham, James O., Jr.
"Using Scanner Data to Analyze the Effects of Manufacturer's Coupons"
Nielson Research, A. C. Nielson Company, No. 1 (1985), pp. 6-11.

Russell, Gary J. and Bolton, Ruth N.
"Implications of Market Structure for Elasticity Structure"
Journal of Marketing Research, Vol. XXV (August 1988), pp. 229-41.

Tellis, Gerard J.
"Advertising Exposure, Loyalty, and Brand Purchase: A Two-Stage Model
of Choice"
Journal of Marketing Research, Vol. XXV (May 1988), pp. 134-44.

Wheat, Rita and Morrision, Donald G.
"Exploratory Data Analysis Applied to Scanner Data: How Regularly Do
Consumers Purchase--and Does it Matter"
ORSA/TIMS Conference, Dallas, TX (1986), paper presentation.

21.09 ---------- Unclassified (Single-Source and Scanner Data)

Strand, Patricia
  "K-Mart Moving to Scanners"
  Advertising Age (June 8, 1986), p. 36.

22 ------------ DATA IMPUTATION OR ASCRIPTION TECHNIQUES -------------
        See also (sub)heading(s) 17, 117, 132.04, 133.

22.01 ---------- Books Re: Data Imputation or Ascription

Rubin, D. B.
  Multiple Imputation for Nonresponse Surveys
  (New York: John Wiley and Sons, 1987).

22.02 ---------- Theory Re: Fusion Techniques

Antoine, Jacques
  "A Case Study Illustrating the Objectives and Perspectives of Fusion
  Techniques"
  Proceedings, Salzburg Readership Symposium (1985).

Antoine, Jacques and Santini, Gilles
  "Fusion Techniques: Alternative to Single-Source Methods"
  European Research, Vol. 15 (August 1987), pp. 178-87.

Antoine, Jacques and Santini, Gilles
  "An Experiment to Validate Fusioned Files Obtained by the Referential
  Factorial Method"
  ESOMAR Seminar on New Developments in Media Research, Helsinki (April
  1986).

Antoine, Jacques et al.
  "Fusion Techniques: Objectives, a Case Study, Perspectives"
  Salzburg Media Research Symposium (1985).

Baker, Ken, Harris, Paul N., and O'Brien, John
  "Data Fusion: An Appraisal and Experimental Evaluation"
  Journal of the Market Research Society, Vol. 31 (April 1989), pp.
  153-212.

Barry, J. T.
  "An Investigation of Statistical Matching"
  Journal of Applied Statistics, Vol. 15 (1988).

Benguigui, Alexis and Santini, Gilles
  "Rapprochement de Donnees ou Fusions d'Enquetes"
  IREP Seminaire Media (1984).

Bennike, S.
  "Fusion--An Overview by an Outside Observer"
  Proceedings, Salzburg Readership Symposium (1985).

Bergonier, Henri, Boucharenc, Lucien, and Irrmann, Philippe
  "Fusion d'Enquetes Application a l'Evaluation de Projets de Plans
  Media"
  Revue Francaise du Marketing, Vol. 22, No. 1 (1967).

Boisson, G.
  "Les Fusions d'Enquetes--Le Point de Vue d'un Utilisateur"
  New York Television Research Symposium (1986).

Boucharenc, Lucien
  "Les Techniques de Fusion Appliquees aux Etudes CESP"
  (November 1981), memorandum.

Fellegi, I. P. and Holt, D.
  "A Systematic Approach to Automatic Editing and Imputation"
  Journal of the American Statistical Association, Vol. 71 (1976).

Frankel, M. R.
  "Ascription in Magazine Audience Research"
  Proceedings, New Orleans Readership Symposium (1981).

Holt, D.
  "Correcing for Nonresponse"
  SCPR, Survey Methods Newsletter (1981).

Kalton, Graham
  Compensating for Missing Survey Data
  (Ann Arbor, MI: Institute for Social Research, 1983).

Kalton, Graham
  "Imputing for Missing Survey Responses"
  Proceedings, Section on Survey Methods, American Statistical
  Association, Washington (1982).

Roberts, A.
  "Data Fusion: Effective and Cost Effective?"
  Admap Conference (1989).

Rothman, James
  "Data Fusion and Single Source Surveys"
  Admap (July/August 1988), pp. 37-41.

Rothman, J.
  "Testing Data Fusion"
  ESOMAR Seminar on Media and Media Research, Madrid (1988).

Ruhomon, Brian
  "Data Fusion: Its Role in Media Research and Media Planning"
  Admap (June 1987), pp. 57-61.

Santini, Gilles
  "Validation of Data Fusion Techniques: What can Statistical Theory do
  for Us?"
  Proceedings, Barcelona Readership Symposium (1988).

Santini, Gilles
  "Fusion Processes: A Conceptual and Practical Approach"
  South African Media Research Association (1986).

Santini, Gilles
  "La Methode de Fusion sur Referentiel Factoriel"
  IREP (1984).

Santini, Gilles
  "Methodes de Fusion: Nouvelles Reflexions, Nouvelles Experiences,
  Nouveaus Enseignements"
  IREP (December 1986).

Wendt, Friedrich
  "The AG.MA Model"
  Media Research Symposium, Montreal (1983).

Wendt, Friedrich
  "Beschreibung Eine Fusion"
  Schriftenreihe Band 21
  (Hamburg: Gruner and Jahr AG and Co., 1976).

Wiegand, Jurgen
  "Combining Different Media Surveys: The German Partnership Model and
  Fusion Experiments"
  Journal of the Market Research Society, Vol. 28, No. 2, pp. 189-208.

Wiegand, Jurgen
  "The Combining of Two Separately Derived Datasets Into an Integrated
  Intermedia Planning System: The German Model of Partnership"
  ESOMAR Seminar on New Developments in Media Research, Helsinki (April
  1986).

23 ----------- RESEARCH METHODS IN INFORMAL COMMUNICATION ------------
         See also (sub)heading(s) 17.

23.01 ---------- Books Re: Research Methods in Informal Communication

Burt, Ronald S. and Minor, Michael J. (editors)
   Applied Network Analysis
   (Beverly Hills, CA: Sage Publications, Inc., 1983).

Foster, Brian L. and Seidman, Stephen B.
   Sonet-I: Social Network Analysis and Modeling System, Volume 1
   (Binghamton, NY: Center for Social Analysis, State University of New
   York, 1978).

Hage, Per and Harary, Frank
   Structural Models in Anthropology
   (New York: Cambridge University Press, 1983).

Knoke, David and Kuklinski, James H.
   Network Analysis
   (Beverly Hills, CA: Sage Publications, Inc., 1982).

Rogers, Everett M. and Kincaid, D. Lawrence
   Communication Networks
   (New York: The Free Press, 1983).

23.02 ---------- Research Methods in Referral Networks

Alba, Richard D.
   "A Graph-Theoretic Definition of a Sociometric Clique"
   Journal of Mathematical Sociology, Vol. 3 (1973), pp. 113-26.

Breiger, Ronald L., Boorman, Scott A., and Arabie, P.
   "An Algorithm for Clustering Relational Data With Applications to
   Social Network Analysis and Comparison With Multidimensional Scaling"
   Journal of Mathematical Psychology, Vol. 12 (August 1975), pp. 328-83.

Burt, Ronald S.
   "Cohesion Versus Structural Equivalence as a Basis for Network
   Subgroups"
   in Burt, Ronald S. and Minor, Michael J. (editors)
   Applied Network Analysis
   (Beverly Hills, CA: Sage Publications, Inc., 1983), pp. 262-82.

Burt, Ronald S.
   "Models of Network Structure"
   in Annual Review of Sociology, Volume Six
   (Palo Alto, CA: Annual Reviews, Inc., 1980), pp. 79-141.

Erickson, Bonnie H.
   "Some Problems of Inference From Chain Data"
   in Schuesler, Karl F. (editor)
   Sociological Methodology
   (San Francisco, CA: Jossey-Bass, 1979), pp. 276-302.

Frank, Ove
   "A Survey of Statistical Methods for Graph Analysis"
   in Leinhardt, Samuel (editor)
   Sociological Methodology
   (San Francisco, CA: Jossey-Bass, 1981), pp. 110-55.

Frank, Ove
   "Estimating a Graph From Triad Counts"
   Journal of Statistical Computation and Simulation, Vol. 9 (1979), pp.
   31-49.

Frank, Ove
   "Sampling and Estimation in Large Social Networks"
   Social Networks, Vol. 1 (August 1978), pp. 91-101.

Granovetter, Mark S.
   "The Strength of Weak Ties"
   American Journal of Sociology, Vol. 78 (May 1973), pp. 1360-80.

Reingen, Peter H. and Kernan, Jerome B.
   "Analysis of Referral Networks in Marketing: Methods and Illustration"
   Journal of Marketing Research, Vol. XXIII (November 1986), pp. 370-8.

Seidman, Stephen B. and Foster, Brian L.
   "Sonet-I: Social Network and Modeling System"
   Social Networks, Vol. 2 (November 1979), pp. 85-90.

Seidman, Stephen B. and Foster, Brian L.
   "A Graph-Theoretic Generalization of the Clique Concept"
   Journal of Mathematical Sociology, Vol. 6 (1978), pp. 139-54.

Wasserman, Stanley S.
  "A Stochastic Model for Directed Graphs With Transition Rates
  Determined by Reciprocity"
  in Schuessler, Karl F. (editor)
  Sociological Methodology
  (San Francisco, CA: Jossey-Bass, 1980), pp. 392-412.

Weimann, Gabriel
  "The Strength of Weak Conversational Ties in the Flow of Information
  and Influence"
  Social Networks, Vol. 5 (September 1983), pp. 245-67.

Wellman, Barry
  "Network Analysis: Some Basic Principles"
  in Collins, Randall (editor)
  Sociological Theory
  (San Francisco, CA: Jossey-BAss, 1983), pp. 155-200.

White, Harrison C., Boorman, Scott A., and Breiger, Ronald L.
  "Social Structure From Multiple Networks I: Blockmodels of Roles and
  Position"
  American Journal of Sociology, Vol. 81 (January 1976), pp. 730-80.

23.03 ---------- Unclassified (Res Methods in Informal Communication)

Richards, William D., Jr.
  A Manual for Network Analysis (Using the NEGOPY Analysis Program)
  (Stanford, CA: Institute for Communication Research, Stanford
  University, 1975).

24 -------------- INDUSTRIAL MARKETING RESEARCH METHODS --------------

24.01 ---------- Books Re: Industrial Marketing Research Methods

Cox, William E., Jr.
    Industrial Marketing Research
    (New York: John Wiley and Sons, Inc., 1979), 250 pp.

Haque, Paul N.
    The Industrial Market Research Handbook, Second Edition
    (Kogan Page, 1987), 366 pp.

Healey, M. (editor)
    Urban and Regional Industrial Research: The Changing UK Data Base
    (Norwich: Geo Books, 1983).

Krigman, Alan
    Researching Industrial Markets: How to Identify, Reach and Sell to
    Your Customers
    (Instrument Society of America, 1983), 80 pp.

Lee, Donald D.
    Industrial Marketing Research: Techniques and Practices, Second
    Edition
    (New York: Van Nostrand Reinhold Co., Inc.), 221 pp.

MacLean, Ian (editor) et al.
    Handbook of Industrial Marketing and Research
    (Brentford, Middlesex, EN: Kluwer-Harrap Handbooks, 1975).

Mills, John D.
    Research Your Own Industrial Market, Fifth Edition
    (Tulsa, OK: Marketing Guidelines, Inc.), 300 pp.

National Industrial Conference Board, Inc.
    Using Marketing Consultants and Research Agencies
    (New York: NICB, Inc., 1966), 64 pp.

Rawnsley, Allan (editor)
    A Manual of Industrial Marketing Research
    (John Wiley and Sons, Inc., 1978), 192 pp.

Stacey, A. H. and Wilson, Aubrey
    Industrial Marketing Research: Management and Technique
    (London, EN: W. I. Hutchinson and Co., 1963), 284 pp.

Wilson, Aubrey
    The Assessment of Industrial Markets
    (London, EN: Hutchinson of London, 1968).

24.02 ---------- Articles etc. Re: Industrial Mktg Research Methods

Acito, Franklin and Hustad, Thomas P.
    "Industrial Product Concept Testing"
    Industrial Marketing Management, Vol. 10 (1981), pp. 67-73.

Aucamp, Johan
    "Whither Business-to-Business Research?"
    ESOMAR Congress, Montreux (1987), pp. 757-73.

Aucamp, Johan
    "Changes in Industrial Marketing Research"
    European Research, Vol. 1 (September 1973), pp. 197-201.

Backhaus, Klaus and Koch, Franz-Karl
    "Behavioral Industrial Marketing Research in Germany and the United
    States--A Comparison"
    Journal of Business Research, Vol. 13 (October 1985), pp. 375-82.

Backhaus, Klaus, Meyer, Margit, and Stockert, Andreas
    "Using Voice Analysis for Analyzing Bargaining Processes in
    Industrial Marketing"
    Journal of Business Research, Vol. 13 (October 1985), pp. 435-46.

Binetti, Giovanni
    "Industrial Marketing Research Usage: A Survey of 103 Italian Firms"
    European Research, Vol. 8 (January 1980), pp. 27-36.

Birn, Robin
    "Putting Market Research Into Action"
    Management Decision, Vol. 24, No. 5 (1986), pp. 8-11.

British Industrial Market Research Association
    Industrial Marketing Research Abstracts (Semiannual)
    (London: British Industrial Market Research Association).

Cox, William E., Jr. and Dominguez, Luis V.
    "The Key Issues and Procedures of Industrial Marketing Research"
    Industrial Marketing Management, Vol. 8, No. 1 (1979), pp. 81-93.

De Koning, Co
  "Effective Techniques in Industrial Marketing Research"
  Journal of Marketing, Vol. 28 (April 1964), pp. 57-61.

Domin, William M. and Freymuller, Jack
  "Can Industrial Product Publicity be Measured?"
  Journal of Marketing, Vol. 29 (July 1965), pp. 54-7.

Gross, Irwin
  "The Need for Research in Business Marketing"
  Journal of Advertising Research, Vol. 27 (June/July 1987), pp. RC7-9.

Gross, Irwin
  "Why All of Industry Needs Research"
  Business Marketing, Vol. 72 (April 1987), pp. 112-5.

Hart, Susan
  "The Use of the Survey in Industrial Market Research"
  Journal of Marketing Management, Vol. 3 (Summer 1987), pp. 25-38.

Industrial Marketing Research Association
  Research in Industrial Marketing--First Annual Conference
  (Leeds, EN: Knight and Forster, Ltd., 1965), 111 pp.

Inglis, Robert C.
  "In-Depth Data: Using Focus Groups to Study Industrial Markets"
  Business Marketing, Vol. 72 (November 1987), pp. 78-82.

Jobber, David
  "Improving Response Rates in Industrial Mail Surveys"
  Industrial Marketing Management, Vol. 15 (August 1986), pp. 183-95.

Jobber, David and Bleasdale, Marcus J. R.
  "Interviewing in Industrial Marketing Research: The State-of-the-Art"
  Quarterly Review of Marketing, Vol. 12 (January 1987), pp. 7-11.

Klinger, Walter H.
  "Measuring Market Potential for Industrial Products: An Eight-Step
  Approach"
  Industrial Marketing Management, Vol. 6, No. 1 (1977), pp. 39-42.

Krum, James R.
  "Role of the Director of Marketing Research Position in Large
  Industrial Corporations: 1975 Survey Results"
  Bureau of Economic and Business Research, University of Delaware
  (1976).

McIntosh, Andrew R.
  "Improving the Efficiency of Sample Surveys in Industrial Markets"
  Journal of the Market Research Society, Vol. 17 (October 1975), pp.
  219-31.

Mills, Diana
  "Industrial Marketing Research: Progress and Prospects"
  European Research, Vol. 10 (April 1982), pp. 72-9.

Moller, K. E. Kristian
  "Research Strategies in Analyzing the Organizatioal Buying Process"
  Journal of Business Research, Vol. 13 (February 1985), pp. 3-17.

More, Roger A.
  "Timing of Market Research in New Industrial Product Situations"
  Journal of Marketing, Vol. 48 (Fall 1984), pp. 84-94.

Ochs, Malcolm B.
  "Audience Measurement Concepts for Industrial Publications"
  Journal of Marketing, Vol. 30 (January 1966), pp. 59-61.

Sarin, Sharad
  "Industrial Market Research in India"
  Industrial Marketing Management, Vol. 16 (November 1987), pp. 257-64.

Sommers, Donald E.
  "Industrial Marketing Research Helps Develop Product/Market
  Strategies"
  High Technology Marketing Management, Vol. 12 (February 1986), pp.
  1-6.

Spekman, Robert E. and Gronhaug, Kjell
  "Conceptual and Methodological Issues in Buying Centre Research"
  European Journal of Marketing, Vol. 20, No. 7 (1986), pp. 50-63.

Thomas, G. and Wind, Yoram
  "Conceptual and Methodological Issues in Organization Buying
  Behaviour"
  European Journal of Marketing, Vol. 14 (1980), pp. 239-63.

Van Der Most, Ger
  "Industrial Research Should Go Where the Product Goes"
  European Research, Vol. 12 (July 1984), pp. 104-17.

Walker, Bruce J., Kirchmann, Wayne, and Conant, Jeffrey S.
  "A Method to Improve Response to Industrial Mail Surveys"
  Industrial Marketing Management, Vol. 16 (November 1987), pp. 305-14.

Weinstein, David
  "Forecasting for Industrial Products"
  in Makridakis, Spyros and Wheelwright, Steven C. (editors)
  The Handbook of Forecasting: A Manager's Guide, Second Edition
  (New York: John Wiley and Sons, Inc., 1987).

Wilson, Aubrey
  "Industrial Marketing Research in Britain"
  Journal of Marketing Research, Vol. VI (February 1969), pp. 15-27.

24.03 ---------- Methods for Researching Small Business

Curran, J.
  Bolton Fifteen Years on: A Review and Analysis of Small Business
  Research in Britain 1971-1976
  (London: Small Business Research Trust, 1986).

Ganguly, P.
  "Small Firm Survey: The International Scene"
  British Business (November 1982).

Turner, W. John
  "Small Business Data Collection by Area Censusing: A Field Test of
  'Saturation Surveying' Methodology"
  Journal of the Market Research Society, Vol. 31 (April 1988), pp.
  257-72.

25 ------------- RESEARCH METHODS IN PRODUCT DEVELOPMENT ------------
        See also (sub)heading(s) 58.04, 58.05.

25.01 ---------- Books Re: Research Methods in Product Development

Market Facts, Incorporated
    Product Evaluation: An Evaluation of Research Procedures
    (Chicago: Market Facts, Inc., 1962).

Wind, Yoram, Mahajan, Vijay, and Cardozo, Richard N.
    New Product Forecasting
    (Lexington, MA: D. C. Heath and Company, 1981), 564 pp.

25.02 ---------- Articles, etc. Re: Res Methods in Product Development

Alford, Charles L. and Mason, Joseph Barry
    "Generating New Product Ideas"
    Journal of Advertising Research, Vol. 15 (December 1975), pp. 27-32.

Batsell, Richard R. and Wind, Yoram
    "Product Testing: Current Methods and Needed Developments"
    Journal of the Market Research Society, Vol. 22 (April 1980), pp.
    115-39.

Bengston, R. and Brenner, H.
    "Product Test Results Using Three Different Methodologies"
    Journal of Marketing Research, Vol. I, No. 4 (1964), pp. 49-52.

Brown, G., Copeland, T., and Millward, M.
    "Monadic Testing of New Products--An Old Problem and Some Partial
    Solutions"
    Journal of the Market Research Society, Vol. 15, No. 2 (1973), pp.
    112-31.

Buchanan, Bruce S. and Morrison, Donald G.
    Measuring Simple Preferences: An Approach to Blind, Forced-Choice
    Product Testing
    Report No. 85-103
    (Cambridge, MA: Marketing Science Institute), 28 pp.

Callingham, Martin
    "The Psychology of Product Testing and Its Relationship to Objective
    Scientific Measures"
    Journal of the Market Research Society, Vol. 30 (July 1988), pp.
    247-66.

Chisnall, Peter M.
    "Research for New Consumer Products"
    European Research, Vol. 7 (November 1979), pp. 248-56.

Crawford, C. M.
    "Marketing Research and the New Product Failure Rate"
    Journal of Marketing, Vol. 41 (April 1977), pp. 51-61.

Day, Ralph L.
    "Preference Tests and the Management of Product Features"
    Journal of Marketing, Vol. 32 (July 1968), pp. 24-9.

DeSarbo, Wayne S., Green, Paul E., and Carroll, J. Douglas
    "An Alternating Least-Squares Procedure for Estimating Missing
    Preference Data in Product-Concept Testing"
    Decision Sciences, Vol. 17 (Spring 1986), pp. 163-85.

Douglas, G.
    "Can Market Research be Too Much of a Good Thing for New Products?"
    Marketing Week (1980).

Fourt, Louis A. and Woodlock, Joseph W.
    "Early Prediction of Market Success for New Grocery Products"
    Journal of Marketing, Vol. 25 (April 1960), pp. 31-8.

Foxall, Gordon R.
    "Consumers' Intentions and Behaviour: A Note on Research and a
    Challenge to Researchers"
    Journal of the Market Research Society, Vol. 26 (July 1984), pp.
    231-41.

Goldsmith, R.
    "Methodological Approaches to New Product Development"
    Proceedings, Annual Conference of the Market Research Society (1981),
    pp. 53-68.

Green, Paul E., Carroll, J. Douglas, Goldberg, Stephen M., and Kedia,
    Pradeep K.
    "Product Design Optimization--A Technical Description of the POSSE
    Methodology"
    Wharton School, University of Pennsylvania (1981), working paper.

Hill, Philip
   "The Market Research Contribution to New Product Failure and Success"
   Journal of Marketing Management, Vol. 3 (Spring 1988), pp. 269-77.

Holbrook, Morris B. and Havlena, William J.
   "Assessing the Real-to-Artificial Generalizability of Multiattribute
   Attitude Models in Tests of New Product Designs"
   Journal of Marketing Research, Vol. XXV (February 1988), pp. 25-35.

Kohli, Rajeev and Krishnamurti, Ramesh
   "A Heuristic Approach to Product Design"
   Management Science, Vol. 33 (December 1987), pp. 1123-34.

Manfield, M. N.
   "Bias in Product Tests"
   New York Chapter Newsletter, American Marketing Association, Vol. 18
   (May 1963), pp. 8,9.

Myers, James H.
   "Benefit Structure Analysis: A New Tool for Product Planning"
   Journal of Marketing, Vol. 40 (October 1976), pp. 23-32.

Normile, M. R. E.
   "The State of New Product Market Research in the USA Compared With
   Europe"
   European Research, Vol. 7 (November 1979), pp. 270-3.

Penny, J. C., Hunt, I. M., and Twyman, W. A.
   "Product Testing Methodology in Relation to Marketing Problems--A
   Review"
   Journal of the Market Research Society, Vol. 14 (January 1972), pp.
   1-29.

Peterson, Robert A. and Ross, Ivan
   "How to Name New Brands"
   Journal of Advertising Research, Vol. 12 (December 1972), pp. 29-34.

Pymont, B. C.
   "The State of New Product Research in Europe"
   European Research, Vol. 7 (November 1979), pp. 257-63.

Rehorn, Jorg
   "Product Tested--What Then?: Five Decision Aids for Assessing Test
   Results"
   European Research, Vol. 2 (May 1974), pp. 108-10.

Schlund, Wulf
   "A New Way of Predicting Design Acceptance"
   ESOMAR Congress, Montreux (1987), pp. 137-64.

Seaton, Richard
   "Why Ratings are Better Than Comparisons"
   Journal of Advertising Research, Vol. 14 (February 1974), pp. 45-8.

Seitz, R. M.
   "State of New Product Market Research Around the World"
   European Research, Vol. 7 (September 1979), pp. 264-9.

Silk, Alvin
   "Preference and Perception Measures in New Product Development: An
   Exposition and Review"
   Sloan Management Review, Vol. 11 (1969), pp. 42-55.

Smith, R. P.
   "Research and Other Data in the Monitoring of Product Quality"
   Journal of the Market Research Society, Vol. 21 (July 1979), pp.
   189-205.

Taylor, James W., Houlahan, John J., and Gabriel, Alan C.
   "The Purchase Intention Question in New Product Development: A Field
   Test"
   Journal of Marketing, Vol. 39 (January 1975), pp. 90-2.

Tyebjee, Tyzoon T.
   "Behavioral Biases in New Product Forecasting"
   International Journal of Forecasting, Vol. 3 (1987), pp. 393-404.

Ushikubo, Kazuaki
   "A Method of Structure Analysis for Developing Product Concepts and
   Its Applications"
   European Research, Vol. 14, No. 4 (1986), pp. 174-84.

Watkins, Trevor
   "The Practice of Product Testing in the New Product Development
   Process: The Role of Model-Based Approaches"
   European Journal of Marketing, Vol. 18, No. 6/7 (1984), pp. 14-29.

Webber, John C.
   "Packaged Goods Marketing Research--Where's It All Going?"
   Journal of Advertising Research, Vol. 26 (October/November 1986), pp.
   RC3-5.

Wind, Y., Denny, J., and Cunningham, A.
   "A Comparison of Three Brand Evaluation Procedures"
   Public Opinion Quarterly (Summer 1979).

25.03 ---------- Product Use Testing

Kramer, B. J.
   "Low-Cost Product Use Testing for R and D Guidance and Early Market
   Evaluation"
   Journal of Consumer Marketing, Vol. 3 (Summer 1986), pp. 63-70.

25.04 ---------- Research Methods in Package Design

Schwartz, David
   "Evaluating Packaging"
   Journal of Advertising Research, Vol. 11 (October 1971), pp. 29-32.

Stern, Walter (editor)
   Handbook of Package Design Research
   (New York: John Wiley and Sons, Inc., 1981), 576 pp.

26 --------------- RESEARCH METHODS FOR TASTE TESTING ----------------
        See also (sub)heading(s) 41.

26.01 ---------- Books Re: Research Methods for Taste Testing

Moskowitz, Howard R.
    New Directions for Product Testing and Sensory Analysis of Foods
    (Westport, CT: Food and Nutrition Press, Inc., 1985).

Moskowitz, Howard R.
    Product Testing and Sensory Evaluation of Foods
    (Westport, CT: Food and Nutrition Press, Inc., 1983).

26.02 ---------- Theory Re: Research Methods for Taste Testing

Brown, Clifford E., Zatkalik, Nancy E., Treumann, Alice M., Buehner,
    Timothy M., and Schmidt, Lisa A.
    "The Effect of Experimenter Bias in a Cola Taste Test"
    Psychology and Marketing, Vol. 1 (Summer 1984), pp. 21-6.

Buchanan, Bruce
    "A Model for Repeat Trial Product Tests"
    Psychometrika, forthcoming.

Buchanan, Bruce
    "A Model for Repeat Paired Comparison Preference Tests"
    New York University (1986), working paper.

Buchanan, Bruce S.
    Design Issues in Discrimination and Preference Testing
    Columbia University (1983), unpublished Ph.D. dissertation.

Buchanan, Bruce S. and Morrison, Donald G.
    "Measuring Simple Preferences: An Approach to Blind, Forced Choice
    Product Testing"
    Marketing Science, Vol. 4 (Winter 1985), pp. 93-109.

Buchanan, Bruce S. and Morrison, Donald G.
    "Taste Tests"
    Psychology and Marketing, Vol. 1 (Spring 1984), pp. 69-91.

Buchanan, Bruce S. and Morrison, Donald G.
    "Comparing Two Product Test Designs: Statistical Properties, Validity
    and Decision Making Implications"
    Working Paper Number 83-119
    Graduate School of Business, New York University (1983).

Conner, M. T., Booth, D. A., Clifton, V. J., and Griffiths, R. P.
    "Do Comparisons of a Food Characteristic With Ideal Necessarily
    Involve Learning?"
    British Journal of Psychology, Vol. 79 (February 1988), pp. 121-8.

Conner, M. T., Land, D. G., and Booth, D. A.
    "Effect of Stimulus Range on Judgements of Sweetness Intensity in a
    Lime Drink"
    British Journal of Psychology, Vol. 78 (August 1987), pp. 357-64.

Ferris, George E.
    "The k-Visit Method of Consumer Testing"
    Biometrics, Vol. 14 (March 1958), pp. 39-49.

Givon, Moshe
    "Taste Tests: Changing the Rules to Improve the Game"
    Marketing Science, Vol. 8 (Summer 1989), pp. 281-90.

Givon, Moshe M. and Goldman, Arieh
    "Perceptual and Preferential Discrimination Abilities in Taste Tests"
    Journal of Applied Psychology, Vol. 72 (May 1987), pp. 301-6.

Greenberg, Allan and Collins, Sy
    "Paired Comparison Taste Tests: Some Food for Thought"
    Journal of Marketing Research, Vol. III (February 1966), pp. 76-80.

Gruber, Alin and Lindberg, Barbara
    "Sensitivity, Reliability, and Consumer Taste Testing"
    Journal of Marketing Research, Vol. III (August 1966), pp. 235-8.

Horsnell, Gareth
    "Paired Comparison Product Testing When Individual Preferences are
    Stochastic: An Alternative Model"
    Applied Statistics, Vol. 26, No. 2 (1977), pp. 162-72.

Horsnell, Gareth
    "A Theory of Consumer Preference Derived From Repeat Paired
    Preference Testing"
    Journal of the Royal Statistical Society, Series A, Vol. 132 (1969),
    pp. 164-93.

Hyett, G. P. and McKenzie, J. R.
"Discrimination Tests and Repeat Paired Comparisons Tests"
Journal of the Market Research Society, Vol. 18 (January 1976), pp.
24-31.

Irwin, Francis W.
"An Analysis of the Concepts of Discrimination and Preference"
American Journal of Psychology, Vol. 71 (1958), pp. 152-63.

Morrison, Donald G.
"Triangle Taste Tests: Are the Subjects Who Respond Correctly Lucky
or Good?"
Journal of Marketing, Vol. 45 (Summer 1981), pp. 111-9.

Morrison, Donald G. and Brockway, George
"A Modified Beta Binomial Model With Applications to Multiple Choice
and Taste Tests"
Psychometrika, Vol. 44 (December 1979), pp. 427-42.

Moskowitz, Howard R., Jacobs, Barry, and Firtle, Neil
"Discrimination Testing and Product Decisions"
Journal of Marketing Research, Vol. XVII (February 1980), pp. 84-90.

Penny, J. C., Hunt, I. M., and Twyman, W. A.
"Product Testing Methodology in Relation to Marketing Problems: A
Review"
Journal of the Market Research Society, Vol. 14 (January 1972), pp.
1-29.

Roper, Burns
"Sensitivity, Reliability, and Consumer Taste Testing: Some 'Rights'
and 'Wrongs'"
Journal of Marketing Research, Vol. VI (February 1969), pp. 102-5.

Williams, A. A. and Martin, D. C.
"The Uses of Modern Sensory Analysis in Market Research"
Proceedings, Market Research Society (March 1988), pp. 289-305.

26.03 ---------- Administration Issues in Taste Testing

Buchanan, Bruce and Morrison, Donald G.
"Measuring Simple Preferences: An Approach to Blind, Forced Choice
Product Testing"
Marketing Science, Vol. 4 (Spring 1985), pp. 93-109.

Buchanan, Bruce and Morrison, Donald G.
"Optimal Design of Parity Tests "
Journal of Mathematical Psychology, Vol. 28 (December 1984), pp.
453-66.

Greenhalgh, C.
"Some Techniques and Interesting Results in Discrimination Testing"
Journal of the Market Research Society, Vol. 8 (October 1966), pp.
215-35.

26.04 ---------- Evaluations of Research Methods for Taste Testing

Buchanan, Bruce, Givon, Moshe, and Goldman, Arieh
"Measurement of Discrimination Ability in Taste Tests: An Empirical
Investigation"
Journal of Marketing Research, Vol. XXIV (May 1987), pp. 154-63.

Hopkins, J. W. and Gridgeman, N. T.
"Comparative Sensitivity of Pair and Triad Flavor Difference Tests"
Biometrics, Vol. 11 (March 1955), pp. 63-8.

27 ------------------------ TEST MARKETING ------------------------

27.01 ---------- Books Re: Test Marketing

Forecast Market Research, Ltd.
    The Mini-Test Market
    (London: 1976).

National Industrial Conference Board
    Market Testing Consumer Products
    (New York: National Industrial Conference Board, Experiences in
    Marketing Management, No. 12, 1967).

27.02 ---------- Theory Re: Test Marketing

Brennan, Leslie
    "Special Supplement--Test Marketing"
    Sales and Marketing Management Magazine, Vol. 140 (March 1988), pp.
    50-62.

Chatterjee, Rabikar, Eliashberg, Jehoshua, Gatignon, Hubert, and
    Lodish, Leonard M.
    "A Practical Bayesian Approach to Selection of Optimal Market Testing
    Strategies"
    Journal of Marketing Research, Vol. XXV (November 1988), pp. 363-75.

Chatterjee, Rabikar, Eliashberg, Jehoshua, Gatignon, Hubert, and
    Lodish, Leonard M.
    "A Bayesian Approach to Selection of Optimal Market Testing
    Strategies"
    Working Paper No. 86:040
    The Wharton School, University of Pennsylvania (December 1986).

Marketing Communications
    "Test Marketing in the 80s"
    Marketing Communications, Vol. 9 (June 1984), pp. 79-85.

Paskowski, Marianne
    "New Tools Revolutionize New Product Testing"
    Marketing and Media Decisions, Vol. 19 (November 1984), pp. 76,7,
    128-32.

27.03 ---------- Administration Issues in Test Marketing

Achenbaum, Alvin A.
    "Market Testing: Using the Marketplace as a Laboratory"
    in Ferber, Robert (editor)
    Handbook of Marketing Research
    (New York: McGraw-Hill Book Company, 1974), pp. 4.31-54.

Berdy, Edwin M.
    "Testing Test Market Predictions--Comments"
    Journal of Marketing Research, Vol. II (May 1965), p. 196.

Cadbury, N. D.
    "When, Where, and How to Test Market"
    Harvard Business Review, Vol. 53 (May-June 1975), pp. 96-105.

Cavusgil, S. Tamer and Yavas, Ugur
    "Test Marketing: An Exposition"
    Marketing Intelligence and Planning, Vol. 5, No. 3 (1987), pp. 16-9.

Cole, Victor L.
    "Testing Test Market Predictions--Comments"
    Journal of Marketing Research, Vol. II (May 1965), pp. 197,8.

Davis, E. J.
    "The Validity of Test Marketing"
    Commentary (JMRS), Vol. 7 (1965), pp. 166-75.

Eskin, G. J.
    "A Case for Test Market Experiments"
    Journal of Advertising Research, Vol. 15 (April 1975), pp. 27-33.

Eskin, Gerald J. and Baron, Penny H.
    "Effects of Price and Advertising in Test-Market Experiments"
    Journal of Marketing Research, Vol. XIV (November 1977), pp. 499-508.

Fox, Harold W.
    "Financial ABCs of Test Marketing"
    Business Horizons, Vol. 29 (September/October 1986), pp. 63-70.

Gold, Jack A.
    "Testing Test Market Predictions--Comments"
    Journal of Marketing Research, Vol. II (May 1965), pp. 198-200.

Gold, Jack A.
    "Testing Test Market Predictions"
    Journal of Marketing Research, Vol. I (August 1964), pp. 8-16.

Hardin, D. K.
"Changing Test Market Technology in the U.S."
in Marketing in a Changing World: The Role of Market Research
ESOMAR Proceedings, 1972 Congress, Cannes, France
(Amsterdam, The Netherlands: European Society for Opinion and
Marketing Research), pp. 315-39.

Hardin, D. K.
"A New Approach to Test Marketing"
Journal of Marketing, Vol. 30 (October 1966), pp. 28-31.

Hardin, David K. and Marquardt, Raymond
"Increasing Precision of Market Testing"
Journal of Marketing Research, Vol. IV (November 1967), pp. 396-9.

Johnson, Scott N.
"Test Marketing--The Next Generation"
Nielsen Researcher, No. 3 (1984), pp. 21-3.

Kandathil, Jacob
"The Advantages of Electronic Test Markets: An Advertiser View Based
on Experience"
Journal of Advertising Research, Vol. 25 (December 1985/January
1986), pp. RC11,2.

Karger, Ted
"Test Marketing as Dress Rehearsals: Bundle Tests and Test Market
Diagnostics"
Journal of Consumer Marketing, Vol. 2 (Fall 1985), pp. 49-56.

Ladki, F., Kent, L., and Nahl, P. C.
"Test Marketing of New Consumer Products"
Journal of Marketing, Vol. 24 (1960), pp. 29-34.

Lipstein, Benjamin
"Test Marketing: A Perturbation in the Market Place"
Management Science, Vol. 14 (April 1968), pp. B437-48.

Lipstein, Benjamin
"The Design of Test Marketing Experiments"
Journal of Advertising Research, Vol. 5 (December 1965), pp. 2-7.

Lipstein, Benjamin
"Tests for Test Marketing"
Harvard Business Review, Vol. 39 (March-April 1961), pp. 74-7.

Nielsen Marketing Service
"To Test or Not to Test"
The Nielsen Researcher, Vol. 30, No. 4 (1972), pp. 3-8.

Park, Irene
"Taking Sides on Test Marketing"
Marketing Communications, Vol. 10 (June 1985), pp. 72-8.

Rao, V. R. and Winter, F. W.
"A Bayesian Approach to Test Market Selection"
Management Science, Vol. 12 (December 1981), pp. 1351-68.

Stanton, Frank
"What is Wrong With Test Marketing?"
Journal of Marketing, Vol. 31 (April 1967), pp. 43-7.

Stern, Aimee L.
"Test Marketing Enters a New Era"
Dun's Business Month, Vol. 126 (October 1985), pp. 86-90.

27.04 ---------- Selection, Descriptions of Test Markets

Walsh, Doris J.
"Rating the Test Markets"
American Demographics, Vol. 7 (May 1985), pp. 38-43.

27.05 ---------- Models Related to Test Marketing

Blattberg, Robert C. and Golanty, John
"TRACKER: An Early Test Market Forecasting and Diagnostic Model for
New Product Planning"
Journal of Marketing Research, Vol. XV (May 1978), pp. 192-202.

Charnes, Abraham, Cooper, William W., Devoe, James K., and Learner,
David B.
"DEMON: Decision Mapping via Optimum GO-NO Networks--A Model for
Marketing New Products"
Management Science, Vol. 12 (July 1966), pp. 865-88.

Elton, Geoffrey
"The ASSESSOR Laboratory Test Market Model"
Admap (January 1084), pp. 50-5.

Narasimhan, Chakravarthi and Sen, Subrata K.
"New Product Models for Test Market Data"
Journal of Marketing, Vol. 47 (Winter 1983), pp. 11-24.

Pringle, Lewis G., Wilson, R. Dale, and Brody, Edward I.
"NEWS: A Decision Oriented Model for New Product Analysis and
Forecasting"
Marketing Science, Vol. 1 (Winter 1982), pp. 1-30.

Sampson, Peter and Factor, S.
"Pretest Market Models: Take 'em or Leave 'em?"
Proceedings, Market Research Society Conference, Brighton (1985), pp.
289-306.

Silk, Alvin J. and Urban, Glen L.
"Pre-Test Market Evaluation of New Packaged Goods: A Model and
Measurement Methodology"
Journal of Marketing Research, Vol. XV (May 1978), pp. 171-91.

Urban, Glen
"Sprinter Mod III: A Model for the Analysis of New Frequently
Purchased Consumer Products"
Operations Research, Vol. 18 (September-October 1970), pp. 805-54.

Urban, Glen and Katz, Gerald M.
"Pre-Test Market Models: Validation and Managerial Implications"
Journal of Marketing Research, Vol. XX (August 1983), pp. 221-34.

27.06 ---------- Simulated Test Marketing

Baldinger, Allan L.
"Trends and Issues in STMs: Results of an ARF Pilot Project"
Journal of Advertising Research, Vol. 28 (October/Novembr 1988), pp.
RC3-7.

Godfrey, Simon
"The Sensor Simulated Test Market System"
Admap (October 1983), pp. 534-40.

Harding, Carlos and Nacher, Bernard
"Simulated Test Markets: Can We go One Step Further in Their Use?"
Proceedings, ESOMAR Congress, Lisbon (1988), pp. 695-727.

Higgins, Kevin
"Simulated Test Marketing Winning Acceptance"
Marketing News, Vol. 19 (March 1, 1985), pp. 15,19.

Sampson, Peter
"Comment" (on Watkins)
Journal of the Market Research Society, Vol. 26 (July 1984), pp.
256-8.

Schwoerer, Juergen
"A Critical Comparison of Simulated Test Market Models"
ESOMAR Congress, Rome (1984), pp. 247-65.

Urban, Glen L. and Katz, Gerald M.
"Pre-Test Market Models: Validation and Managerial Implications"
Journal of Marketing Research, Vol. XX (August 1983), pp. 221-34.

Urban, Glen and Katz, G. M.
"How Accurate are Simulated Test Markets and How Should Managers Use
Them?"
in Srivastava, A. K. and Shocker, A. D. (editors)
Analytical Approaches to Product and Marketing Planning
(Cambridge: Marketing Science Institute, 1982).

Watkins, Trevor
"A Consumer-Based Model for Researching New Products"
European Journal of Marketing, Vol. 20, No. 10 (1986), pp. 66-79.

Watkins, Trevor
"Do STM Models Work?"
Journal of the Market Research Society, Vol. 26 (July 1984), pp.
255,6.

27.07 ---------- Applications of Test Marketing

Becknell, James C., Jr. and McIsaac, Robert W.
"Test Marketing Cookware Coated With 'Teflon'"
Journal of Advertising Research, Vol. 3 (September 1963), pp. 2-8.

28 ----   RESEARCH METHODS IN CROSS-CULTURAL/INTERNATIONAL RESEARCH   ----

   See also (sub)heading(s) 2.04, 16.06.

28.01 ---------- Books Re: Methods in Cross-Cultural/Int'l Research

Brislin, Richard W., Lonner, W. J., and Thorndike, R. M.
   Cross-Cultural Research Methods
   (New York: John Wiley and Sons, Inc., 1973).

Douglas, Susan P. and Craig, C. Samuel
   International Marketing Research
   (Englewood Cliffs, NJ: Prentice-Hall, Inc., 1983), 337 pp.

ESOMAR
   International Marketing Research
   Proceedings, European Society for Opinion and Marketing Research
   (November 1984), 282 pp.

Lonner, Walter J. and Berry, John W. (editors)
   Field Methods in Cross-Cultural Research
   (Beverly Hills, CA: Sage Publications, Inc., 1986).

Werner, Oswald and Schoepfle, G. Mark
   Systematic Fieldwork, Volume I: Ethnographic Analysis and Data
   Management
   (Newbury Park, CA: Sage Publications, Inc., 1987).

Werner, Oswald and Schoepfle, G. Mark
   Systematic Fieldwork, Volume II: Foundations of Ethnography and
   Interviewing
   (Newbury Park, CA: Sage Publications, Inc., 1987).

Worcester, Robert M. (editor)
   Political Opinion Polling--A Transnational Look
   (London: Macmillan, 1983), 246 pp.

28.02 ---------- Articles etc. Re: Cross-Cultural/International Res

Adler, Lee
   "Special Wrinkles in International Marketing Research"
   Sales and Marketing Management, Vol. 117 (July 12, 1976), pp. 62-6.

Adler, Lee and Mayer, C. S.
   "Meeting the Challenge of Multinational Marketing Research"
   in Keegan, W. J. and Mayer, C. S. (editors)
   Multinational Product Management
   (Chicago: American Marketing Association, 1977), pp. 147-64.

Albaum, Gerald and Peterson, Robert A.
   "Empirical Research in International Marketing: 1976-1982"
   Journal of International Business Studies, Vol. 15 (Spring-Summer
   1984), pp. 161-73.

Alsegg, Robert J.
   Researching the European Markets
   (New York: American Management Association, 1969).

Ayal, Igal and Zif, J.
   "A Proposal for International Marketing Research"
   Israel Institute of Business Research, Tel Aviv University (1978).

Barker, T. A.
   "The Effect of Economic Development on the Status of Marketing
   Research"
   in Kothari, V. (editor)
   Developments in Marketing Science, Volume V
   (Las Vegas: Academy of Marketing Science, 1982).

Barnard, Philip
   "Conducting and Co-Ordinating Multi-Country Quantitative Studies
   Across Europe"
   Journal of the Market Research Society, Vol. 24 (January 1982), pp.
   46-64.

Berent, Paul H.
   "International Research is Different: The Case for Centralised
   Control"
   in Proceedings, ESOMAR Seminar, Brussels (April 1976).

Berry, J. W.
   "On Cross-Cultural Comparability"
   International Journal of Psychology, Vol. 4 (1979), pp. 119-28.

Boddewyn, J.
   "A Construct for Comparative Marketing Research"
   Journal of Marketing Research, Vol. III (May 1966), pp. 149-53.

Cavusgil, S. Tamer
  "Factor Congruency Analysis: A Methodology for Cross-Cultural
  Research"
  Journal of the Market Research Society, Vol. 27 (April 1985), pp.
  147-55.

Cavusgil, S. Tamer and Kaynak, Erdener
  "Sources of Consumer Dissatisfaction and Difficulties in
  Cross-Cultural Measurement"
  in Baker, M. J. and Saren, M. A. (editors)
  Marketing Into the Eighties
  (Edinburgh: March 1980)

Choudhry, Yusuf A.
  "Pitfalls in International Marketing Research: Are You Speaking
  French Like a Spanish Cow?"
  Akron Business and Economic Review, Vol. 17 (Winter 1986), pp. 18-28.

Cornish, Pym
  "Developments in International Readership Research"
  Admap (February 1988), pp. 38-43.

Czinkota, M. R.
  "The State of Export Research: An Assessment"
  AIB/EIBA Joint International Conference, Barcelona (December 1981),
  paper presentation.

Daina, Luciano
  "Public Data Banks in Europe"
  European Research, Vol. 12 (April 1984), pp. 84-7.

De Camprieu, R.
  "A Paradigm for the Cross-Cultural Investigation of Consumer Behavior"
  Working Paper 80-8
  University of Ottawa, Canada (1980).

Dunn, S. Watson
  "Problems of Cross-Cultural Research"
  in Ferber, Robert (editor)
  Handbook of Marketing Research
  (New York: McGraw-Hill, 1974), pp. 4.360-71.

ESOMAR
  International Research Guidelines
  (Amsterdam).

ESOMAR Working Party
  "A Step Forward in International Research: Harmonisation of
  Demographics for Easier International Comparisons"
  European Research, Vol. 12 (October 1984), pp. 182-9.

Goldstein, Frederick A.
  "International Marketing Research--Myth or Reality?"
  European Research, Vol. 15 (May 1987), pp. 94-8.

Goodyear, Mary
  "Qualitative Research in Developing Countries"
  Journal of the Market Research Society, Vol. 23, No. 1 (1982).

Green, Robert T. and White, P.
  "Methodological Considerations in Cross-National Consumer Research"
  Journal of International Business Studies, Vol. 7 (Fall-Winter 1976).

Grunert, Klaus G., Grunert, Susanne C., and Beatty, Sharon E.
  "Cross-Cultural Research on Consumer Values"
  Marketing and Research Today, Vol. 17 (February 1989), pp. 30-9.

Grunert, Susanne C. and Grunert, Klaus G.
  "Product Testing Organizations as a Source of Information on Consumer
  Values and Needs: A Three-Country Example"
  Journal of International Consumer Marketing.

Hornik, Jacob and Rubinow, Steven C.
  "Expert-Respondents' Synthesis for International Advertising Research"
  Journal of Advertising Research, Vol. 21 (June 1981), pp. 9-17.

Hui, C. H. and Triandis, H. C.
  "Multistrategy Approach to Cross-Cultural Research: The Case of Locus
  of Control"
  Journal of Cross-Cultural Psychology, Vol. 14 (1983), pp. 65-83.

Jaffe, E. D.
  "Multinational Marketing Intelligence: An Information Requirements
  Model"
  Management International Review, Vol. 19, No. 2 (1979), pp. 53-60.

Jaffe, Eugene D.
  "Multinational Marketing Research: The Headquarters Role"
  Akron Business and Economic Review, Vol. 6 (Winter 1975), pp. 9-16.

Kaynak, Erdener and Wikstrom, Solveig
"Methodological Framework for a Cross-National Comparison of
Consumerism Issues in Multiple Environments"
European Journal of Marketing, Vol. 16, No. 1 (1985), pp. 31-46.

Kothari, Vinay R.
"An Empirical Exploration of International Marketing Research
Problems and Solutions"
Journal of the Academy of Marketing Science, Vol. 5, Special
Proceedings Issue (1977), pp. 65-8.

Kushner, J. M.
"Market Research in a Non-Western Context: The Asian Example"
Journal of the Market Research Society, Vol. 23, No. 1 (1982).

Lovell, Enid Baird
Researching Foreign Markets
(New York: National Industrial Conference Board, 1955).

Mayer, C. S.
"The Lessons of Multinational Marketing Research"
Business Horizons, Vol. 21 (December 1978), pp. 7-13.

Mayer, Charles S.
"Multinational Marketing Research: The Magnifying Glass of
Methodological Problems"
European Research, Vol. 6 (March 1978), pp. 77-84.

Mitchell, Robert Edward
"Survey Materials Collected in the Developing Countries: Sampling,
Measurement, and Interviewing Obstacles to Intra- and International
Comparisons"
International Social Science Journal, Vol. 17, No. 4 (1965).

Moyer, R.
"International Market Analysis"
Journal of Marketing Research, Vol. V (November 1968), pp. 353-60.

Newmann, Thomas
"International Television Research: Why PETAR"
Admap (December 1989), pp. 48,9.

Olivier, Lex
"International Marketing Research: Will 1992 Arrive Before 2005?"
Marketing and Research Today, Vol. 17 (May 1989), pp. 127,8.

Plasschaert, Jetty
"Voting for the European Parliament: A Blueprint for International
Qualitative Research"
European Research, Vol. 12 (October 1984), pp. 153-62.

Rao, C. P.
"A Multi-Level Approach to Researching Overseas Markets"
in Jain, S. C. and Tucker, L. R., Jr. (editors)
International Marketing: Managerial Perspectives (1979), pp. 154-65.

Rice, Gillian and Mahmoud, Essam
"Forecasting and Data Bases in International Business"
Management International Review, Vol. 24, No. 4 (1984), pp. 59-71.

Rimberg, John
"Soviet Research on Audience Reaction to Motion Pictures"
Journal of Marketing Research, Vol. II (February 1965), pp. 56,7.

Ryan, Michael
"The Reality in International Readership Research"
Admap (July/August 1987), pp. 48,9;76.

Ryans, J. K., Jr. and Ryans, C. C.
"Northeast Ohio 'International Firms' Evaluation of Selected Foreign
Market Information Sources"
Akron Business and Economic Review, Vol. 11 (Winter 1980), pp. 19-22.

Samli, A. C.
"An Approach for Estimating Market Potential in East Europe"
Journal of International Business Studies, Vol. IX (Winter 1978), pp.
49-53.

Schollhammer, H.
"Strategies and Methodologies in International Business and
Comparative Management Research"
Management International Review, Vol. 6 (1973), pp. 17-32.

Schweizer, Robert
"Federal Republic of Germany: Tight Restrictions on Telemarketing"
European Research, Vol. 15 (May 1987), pp. 82-4.

Schweizer, Robert
"Present and Future Data Flow Legislation"
European Research, Vol. 14, No. 1 (1986), pp. 29-34.

Schwoerer, Juergen
    "Measuring Advertising Effectiveness: Emergence of an International
    Standard"
    European Research, Vol. 15, No. 1 (1987), pp. 40-51.

Sentell, Gerald D.
    "Recognizing and Overcoming Environmentally-Induced Obstacles to
    Marketing Research in Less Developed Countries of the Asia-Pacific
    Region"
    Asia-Pacific Dimensions of International Business
    (Academy of International Business, 1979), pp. 628-37.

Sentell, Gerald D. and Philpot, John W.
    "A Note on Evaluating the Representivity of Samples Taken in Less
    Developed Countries"
    International Journal of Research in Marketing, Vol. 1, No. 1 (1984),
    pp. 81-4.

Sethna, Beheruz N. and Groeneveld, Leonard
    Research Methods in Marketing and Management
    (New Delhi, India: Tata McGraw-Hill Publishing Company Limited,
    1984), 332 pp.

Stanton, John L., Chandran, Rajan, and Hernandez, Sigfredo A.
    "Marketing Research Problems in Latin America"
    Journal of the Market Research Society, Vol. 24 (April 1982), pp.
    124-39.

Stout, Roy G. and Dalvi, Nitin
    "Improving the Effectiveness of Multi-Country Consumer Tracking"
    Journal of the Market Research Society, Vol. 31 (October 1989), pp.
    545-50.

Triandis, H. C.
    "Major Theoretical and Methodological Issues in Cross-Cultural
    Psychology"
    in Dawson, J. L. and Lonner, W. L. (editors)
    Readings in Cross-Cultural Psychology
    (Hong Kong: Hong Kong University Press, 1972), pp. 26-38.

Trip, Johan F. Laman
    "International Research Needs Downstream Pioneering"
    European Research, Vol. 13 (July 1985), pp. 96-108.

UNCTAD/GATT
    Export Marketing Research
    (Geneva: ITC, 1978).

Van de Vijier, F. J. R. and Poortinga, Y. H.
    "Cross-Cultural Generalization and Universality"
    Journal of Cross-Cultural Psychology, Vol. 13 (1982), pp. 387-408.

Van Hamersveld, Mario
    "Marketing Research--Local, Multidomestic or International?"
    Marketing and Research Today, Vol. 17 (August 1989), pp. 132-8.

Van Raaij, W. F.
    "Cross-Cultural Research Methodology as a Case of Construct Validity"
    in Hunt, H. K. (editor)
    Advances in Consumer Research, Volume Five
    (Ann Arbor, MI: Association for Consumer Research, 1978).

Webster, Lucy L.
    "Comparability of Multi-Country Surveys"
    Journal of Advertising Research, Vol. 6 (December 1966), pp. 14-8.

Wilsdon, Michael
    "Productivity in International Research"
    Proceedings, ESOMAR Congress, Lisbon (1988), pp. 793,4.

Wind, Yoram and Douglas, Susan P.
    "Some Issues in International Consumer Research"
    European Journal of Marketing, Vol. 8, No. 3 (1974)

Wind, Y. and Douglas, S.
    "Comparative Consumer Research: The Next Frontier?"
    Working Paper No. 80-012 (June 1980).

Worcester, Robert M.
    "The Internationalisation of Public Opinion Research"
    Public Opinion Quarterly, Vol. 51 (Winter 1987), pp. S79-85.

Zeldenrust-Noordanus, M.
    "Why, When and How Cross-Cultural Behaviour Studies"
    in Proceedings, ESOMAR Seminar, Brussels (April 1976).

28.03 ---------- Cross-Cultural Measurement and Scaling Issues

    See also (sub)heading(s) 37.

Angelmar, Reinhard and Pras, Bernard
  "Verbal Rating Scales for Multinational Research"
  European Research, Vol. 6 (March 1978), pp. 62-7.

Bhalla, Gaurav and Lin, Lynn Y. S.
  "Cross-Cultural Marketing Research: A Discussion of Equivalence
  Issues and Measurement Strategies"
  Psychology and Marketing, Vol. 4 (Winter 1987), pp. 275-85.

Davis, Harry L., Douglas, Susan P., and Silk, Alvin J.
  "Measure Unreliability: A Hidden Threat to Cross-National Marketing
  Research"
  Journal of Marketing, Vol. 45 (Spring 1981), pp. 98-109.

Hui, C. H.
  "Measurement in Cross-Cultural Psychology: A Review and Comparison of
  Strategies for Empirical Research"
  University of Illinois (1982), unpublished paper.

Malhotra, Naresh K.
  "A Methodology for Measuring Consumer Preferences in Developing
  Countries"
  International Marketing Review, Vol. 8 (Autumn 1988), pp. 52-66.

Mayberry, P. W.
  "Analysis of Cross-Cultural Attitudinal Scale Translation Using
  Maximum Likelihood Factor Analysis"
  Meeting of the American Educational Research Association, New Orleans
  (1984), paper presentation.

Miller, D. C.
  "Measuring Cross-Cultural Norms"
  International Journal of Comparative Sociology, Vol. XII, No. 3,4
  (September-December 1972), pp. 201-16.

Munson, J. Michael and McIntyre, Shelby H.
  "Developing Practical Procedures for the Measurement of Personal
  Values in Cross-Cultural Marketing"
  Journal of Marketing Research, Vol. XVI (February 1979), pp. 6-17.

Parameswaran, Ravi and Yaprak, Attila
  "A Cross-National Comparison of Consumer Research Measures"
  Journal of International Business Studies, Vol. 18 (Spring 1987), pp.
  35-49.

Sebald, H.
  "Studying National Character Through Comparative Content Analysis"
  Social Forces, Vol. 40 (May 1962), pp. 318-22.

Sicinski, Anorzej
  "'Don't Know' Answers in Cross-National Surveys"
  Public Opinion Quarterly, Vol. 34 (Spring 1970), pp. 126-9.

Straus, M. A.
  "Phenomenal Identity and Conceptual Equivalence of Measurement in
  Cross-National Comparative Research"
  Journal of Marriage and the Family, Vol. 31 (1969), pp. 233-41.

Wheeler, David R.
  "Content Analysis: An Analytical Technique for International
  Marketing Research"
  International Marketing Review, Vol. 8 (Winter 1988), pp. 34-40.

Yavas, Ugur, Riecken, G., and Haahti, A.
  "Further Evidence on the Cross-National Reliability of King and
  Summers' Opinion Leadership Scale: An Extension to Saudi Arabia"
  in Raaij, W. F. V. and Schelbergen, F. J. C. M. (editors)
  Proceedings, XIIIth Annual Conference of the European Marketing
  Academy, Breukelen, The Netherlands (1984), pp. 633-48.

28.04 ---------- Translation and Wording

    See also (sub)heading(s) 34.03, 34.07.

Brislin, R.
  Translation: Application and Research
  (New York: John Wiley and Sons, 1976).

Brislin, Richard W.
  "Back-Translation for Cross-Cultural Research"
  Journal of Cross Cultural Psychology, Vol. 1 (1970), pp. 185-216.

ESOMAR Committee Report
   "Harmonization of Demographics"
   European Research, Vol. 14, No. 3 (1986), pp. 152-5.

ESOMAR Working Group
   "A Step Forward in International Research: Harmonization of
   Demographics for Easier Comparisons"
   European Research, Vol. 12 (October 1984), pp. 182-9.

Mayberry, P. W.
   "Analysis of Cross-Cultural Attitudinal Scale Translation Using
   Maximum Likelihood Factor Analysis"
   Meeting of the American Educational Research Association, New Orleans
   (1984), paper presentation.

Noelle-Neumann, Elisabeth and Worcester, Bob
   "International Opinion Research: How to Phrase Your Questions on
   Controversial Topics"
   European Research, Vol. 12 (July 1984), pp. 124-31.

Sechrest, Lee, Fay, T. L., and Zaidi, S. M. H.
   "Problems of Translation in Cross-Cultural Research"
   Journal of Cross-Cultural Psychology, Vol. 3 (1972), pp. 41-56.

Werner, O. and Campbell, D. R.
   "Translating Working Through Interpreters and the Problem of
   Decentering"
   in Narroll, R. and Cohen, R. (editors)
   A Handbook of Method in Cross-Cultural Anthropology
   (New York: Natural History Press, 1970), pp. 398-420.

28.05 ---------- International Mail Surveys

   See also (sub)heading(s) 67.

Ayal, Igal and Hornik, Jacob
   "Foreign Source Effects on Response Behavior in Cross-National Mail
   Surveys"
   International Journal of Research in Marketing, Vol. 3, No. 3 (1986),
   pp. 157-67.

Dawson, Scott and Dickinson, Dave
   "Conducting International Mail Surveys: The Effect of Incentives on
   Response Rates With an Industry Population"
   Journal of International Business Studies, Vol. 19 (Fall 1988), pp.
   491-6.

Douglas, Susan P. and Shoemaker, Robert W.
   "Item Non-Response in Cross-National Attitude Surveys"
   European Research, Vol. 9 (July 1981), pp. 124-32.

Eichner, K. and Habermehl, W.
   "Predicting Response Rates to Mailed Questionnaires"
   American Sociological Review, Vol. 46 (1981), pp. 361-3.

Eisenger, Richard A., Janicki, Peter W., Stevenson, Robert L., and
   Thompson, W. L.
   "Increasing Returns in International Mail Surveys"
   Public Opinion Quarterly, Vol. 38 (Spring 1974), pp. 297-301.

Glaser, W. A.
   "International Mail Surveys of Informants"
   Human Organization, Vol. 25 (1966), pp. 78-86.

Heberlein, T. A. and Baumgartner, R.
   "The Effectiveness of the Herberlein-Baumgartner Motives for
   Predicting Response Rates to Mailed Questionnaires: European and U.S.
   Examples"
   American Sociological Review, Vol. 46 (1981), pp. 363-7.

Jaffe, Eugene D.
   "The Efficacy of Mail Surveys in Developing Countries: The Case of
   Israel"
   European Research, Vol. 10 (1982), pp. 102-4.

Jobber, David and Saunders, John
   "An Experimental Investigation Into Cross-National Mail Survey
   Response Rates"
   Journal of International Business Studies, Vol. 19 (Fall 1988), pp.
   483-9.

Keown, Charles F.
   "Foreign Mail Surveys: Response Rates Using Monetary Incentives"
   Journal of International Business Studies, Vol. 16 (Fall 1985), pp.
   151-3.

Nederhof, Anton J.
"A Comparison of European and North American Response Patterns in Mail Surveys"
Journal of the Market Research Society, Vol. 27 (January 1985), pp. 55-63.

Stone, L. and Campbell, J. G.
"The Use and Misuse of Surveys in International Development"
Human Organization, Vol. 43 (1984), pp. 27-37.

28.06 ---------- Research Methods in Specific Countries

Andrus, Roman R.
"Marketing Research in a Developing Nation--Taiwan: A Case Example"
University of Washington Business Review, Vol. 28 (1969).

Backhaus, Klaus and Koch, Franz-Karl
"Behavioral Industrial Marketing Research in Germany and the United States--A Comparison"
Journal of Business Research, Vol. 13 (October 1985), pp. 375-82.

Barker, Raymond F.
"Interviewing Consumers in New Zealand and the United States"
Singapore Marketing Review, Vol. II (March 1987), pp. 77-90.

Black, T. R. L. and Farley, J. U.
"The Application of Market Research in Contraceptive Social Marketing in a Rural Area of Kenya"
Journal of the Market Research Society, Vol. 21, No. 1 (1979), pp. 30-43.

Blanc, H.
"Multilingual Interviewing in Israel"
American Journal of Sociology, Vol. 62 (September 1956), pp. 205-9.

Blauvelt, Euan
"The Chinese Puzzle"
Industrial Marketing Digest, Vol. 11, Fourth Quarter (1986), pp. 95-102.

Corder, C. K.
"Problems and Pitfalls in Conducting Marketing Research in Africa"
Business Proceedings, Series 42
(Chicago: American Marketing Association, 1978).

Denny, David L.
"Now You can do Market Research in China"
China Business Review, Vol. 16 (May-June 1989).

Gronhaug, Kjell and Gripsrud, Geir
"Marketing Research in Norway"
Developments in Marketing Science, Volume 8
(Academy of Marketing Science, 1985).

Jaffe, Eugene D.
"The Efficacy of Mail Surveys in Developing Countries--The Case of Israel"
European Research, Vol. 10 (April 1982), pp. 102-4.

Jones, David
"Media Measurement in Australia: Print"
Admap (December 1988), pp. 31-4.

Korobeinikov, Valery
"Opinion Polls in the Soviet Union: Perestroika and the Public"
European Research, Vol. 16 (August 1988), pp. 160-2.

Laurent, Charles K. and Parra A., Aquileo
"Use of Mail Questionnaires in Columbia"
Journal of Marketing Research, Vol. V (February 1968), pp. 101-3.

Loudon, D. L.
"A Note on Marketing Research in Mexico"
Journal of Business Research, Vol. 4, No. 1 (1976), pp. 69-73.

Minter, Chris
"The People's Republic of China: Researching the Top End of the Market"
Admap (October 1986), pp. 60-3.

Quah, Siam Tee
"Sampling Frames in Marketing Research in Singapore"
Singapore Marketing Review, Vol. II (1987), pp. 91-4.

Radvanyi, L.
"Ten Years of Sample Surveying in Mexico"
International Journal of Opinion and Attitude Research, Vol. 5 (Winter 1951-52), pp. 491-510.

Ralis, Max, Suchman, Edward A., and Goldsen, R. L.
    "Applicability of Survey Techniques in Northern India"
    Public Opinion Quarterly, Vol. 22 (Fall 1958), pp. 245-50.

Samli, A. Coskun and Lange, Irene
    "Marketing Research Techniques for Assessing Markets of East European
    Economies"
    Journal of the Academy of Marketing Science, Vol. 5, Special
    Proceedings Issue (1977), pp. 111-4.

Stanton, John L., Chandran, Rajan, and Hernandez, Sigfredo A.
    "Marketing Research Problems in Latin America"
    Journal of the Market Research Society, Vol. 23, No. 1 (1982).

Tuncalp, Secil
    "The Marketing Research Scene in Saudi Arabia"
    European Journal of Marketing, Vol. 22, No. 5 (1988), pp. 15-22.

Tee, Quah Siam
    "Random Digit Dialing as a Sampling Method in Telephone Surveys in
    Singapore"
    Singapore Marketing Review, Vol. IV (1989), pp. 86-92.

Twyman, W. A. Tony
    "Readership Research in Barcelona"
    Marketing and Research Today, Vol. 17 (February 1989), pp. 52,3.

Van Roo, Mark
    "Researching the Taiwan Market"
    Marketing and Research Today, Vol. 17 (February 1989), pp. 54-7.

28.07 ---------- Research Methods in Developing Countries

Amine, L. S. and Cavusgil, S. T.
    "Demand Estimation in a Developing Country Environment: Difficulties,
    Techniques and Examples"
    Journal of the Market Research Society, Vol. 28 (January 1986), pp.
    43-65.

Andrus, Roman R.
    "Marketing Research in a Developing Nation"
    University of Washington Business Review, Vol. 28, No. 3, pp. 40-4.

Boyd, Harper W., Jr., Frank, Ronald E., Massy, William F., and Zoheir,
    Mostafa
    "On the Use of Marketing Research in the Emerging Economies"
    Journal of Marketing Research, Vol. I (November 1964), pp. 20-3.

Casley, D. J. and Lury, D. A.
    Data Collection in Developing Countries
    (Oxford University Press, 1981), 244 pp.

Goodyear, Mary
    "Qualitative Research in Developing Countries"
    Journal of the Market Research Society, Vol. 24 (April 1982), pp.
    86-96.

Jaffe, Eugene D.
    "The Efficacy of Mail Surveys in Developing Countries--The Case of
    Israel"
    European Research, Vol. 10 (April 1982), pp. 102-4.

Kaynak, Erdener
    "Difficulties of Undertaking Marketing Research in Developing
    Countries"
    European Research, Vol. 6 (November 1978), pp. 251-9.

Kracmar, John Z.
    Marketing Research in the Developing Countries: A Handbook
    (New York: Praeger Publishers, 1971), 323 pp.

Malhotra, Naresh K.
    "A Methodology for Measuring Consumer Preferences in Developing
    Countries"
    International Marketing Review, Vol. 8 (Autumn 1988), pp. 52-66.

Mitchell, R. E.
    "Survey Materials Collected in the Developing Countries: Sampling,
    Measurement, and Interviewing Obstacles to Intra- and International
    Comparisons"
    International Science Journal, Vol. 17 (1965), pp. 665-85.

Yavas, Ugur and Kaynak, Erdener
    "Current Status of Marketing Research in Developing Countries:
    Problems and Opportunities"
    Journal of International Marketing and Marketing Research, Vol. 5,
    No. 2 (1980), pp. 78-89.

29 -------- RESEARCH METHODS IN MISCELLANEOUS TOPICAL AREAS ----------
29.01 ---------- Public Policy Formulation Research Methods

See also (sub)heading(s) 9.

Brobeck, Stephen
"Academics and Advocates: The Role of Consumer Researchers in Public Policy-Making"
Journal of Consumer Affairs, Vol. 22 (Winter 1988).

Bulmer, Martin (editor)
Social Research and Royal Commissions
(London: George Allan and Unwin, 1980), 188 pp.

Caplan, N., Morrison, A., and Stambaugh, R. J.
The Use of Social Science Knowledge in Public Policy Decisions at the National Level
(Ann Arbor, MI: Institute for Social Research, 1975).

Cohen, David K. and Garet, Michael S.
"Reforming Educational Policy and Applied Social Research"
Harvard Educational Review, Vol. 45 (February 1975), pp. 17-43.

Cowell, Donald
"The Role of Market Research in the Development of Public Policy in the Field of Recreation and Leisure"
Journal of the Market Research Society, Vol. 23 (April 1981), pp. 72-83.

Dyer, R. F. and Shimp, T. A.
"Enhancing the Role of Marketing Research in Public Policy Decision Making"
Journal of Marketing, Vol. 41 (January 1977), pp. 63-7.

Field, Mervin D.
"Polls and Public Policy"
Journal of Advertising Research, Vol. 19 (October 1979), pp. 11-7.

Grunewald, Armin
"Opinion Polls and Public Policy"
European Research, Vol. 8 (March 1980), pp. 51-6.

Koschnick, Wolfgang J.
"Opinion Polls, the Mass Media and the Political Environment"
European Research, Vol. 8 (March 1980), pp. 57-63.

Laplaca, Peter J. and Laric, Michael V.
"Community Attitude Measurement: A Methodology for Social Applications of Marketing Research"
European Research, Vol. 7 (May 1979), pp. 122-9.

Maynes, E. Scott (editor)
The Frontier of Research in the Consumer Interest
(Columbia, MO: American Council on Consumer Interests, 1988), 889 pp.

Merton, Robert K.
"The Role of Applied Social Science in the Formation of Policy"
Philosophy of Science, Vol. 16, No. 3 (July 1949).

Patton, Michael Q., Grimes, P., Guthrie, K., Brennan, N., Dickey, B., and Blyth, D.
"In Search of Impact: An Analysis of the Utilization of Federal Health Evaluation Research"
in Weiss, Carol H. (editor)
Using Social Research in Public Policy Making
(Lexington, MA: Lexington-Heath, 1977), pp. 141-63.

Rein, M.
Social Science and Public Policy
(New York: Penguin Books, 1976).

Rich, R.
The Power of Social Science Information and Public Policy Making
(San Francisco: Jossey-Bass, 1979).

Rich, R.
"Uses of Social Science Information by Federal Bureaucrats: Knowledge for Action vs. Knowledge for Understanding"
in Weiss, C. (editor)
Using Social Research in Public Policy Making
(Lexington, MA: D. C. Heath, 1977).

Rich, Robert F.
"Selective Utilization of Social Science Related Information by Federal Policy Makers"
Inquiry, Vol. 8 (1975), pp. 239-45.

Ritchie, J. R. Brent and Labreque, Roger J.
"Marketing Research and Public Policy: A Functional Perspective"
Journal of Marketing, Vol. 39 (July 1975), pp. 12-9.

Weiss, C. (editor)
  Using Social Research in Public Policy Making
  (Lexington, MA: D. C. Heath, 1977).

Weiss, Carol H. and Bucuvalas, Michael J.
  Social Science Research and Decision-Making
  (Lexington, MA: Lexington-Heath, 1980).

Weiss, Carol H. and Bucuvalas, Michael J.
  "Challenge of Social Research to Decision-Making"
  in Weiss, Carol H. (editor)
  Using Social Research in Public Policy Making
  (Lexington, MA: Lexington-Heath, 1977), pp. 213-30.

Wilkie, William L. and Gardner, David M.
  "The Role of Marketing Research in Public Policy Decision Making"
  Journal of Marketing, Vol. 38 (January 1974), pp. 38-47.

Wilson, Sir Harold
  "Market Research in the Private and Public Sectors"
  Journal of the Market Research Society, Vol. 20 (July 1978), pp.
  111-26.

29.02 ---------- Use of Marketing Research as Evidence

       See also (sub)heading(s) 9.03.

Barksdale, Hiram C.
  "The Use of Marketing Data in Courts of Law"
  Journal of Marketing, Vol. 23 (1959), p. 376.

Barksdale, Hiram C.
  The Use of Survey Research Findings as Legal Evidence
  (New London, CO: Printers' Ink Books, 1957), pp. 48,9.

Barter, John
  "The Legal Criteria for Survey Data"
  Journal of the Market Research Society, Vol. 27 (July 1985), pp.
  191-8.

Caughey, Reginald E.
  "The Use of Public Polls, Surveys and Sampling as Evidence in
  Litigation, and Particularly Trademark and Unfair Competition Cases"
  California Law Review, Vol. 44 (1956), p. 539.

Chadwick, Simon and Bartram, Mary
  "Designing a Survey for Court"
  Journal of the Market Research Society, Vol. 27 (July 1985), pp.
  185-90.

Cooke, Mike
  "The Admissibility of Survey Data as Evidence in Courts of Law"
  Journal of the Market Research Society, Vol. 27 (July 1985), pp.
  167-73.

Crespi, Irving
  "Surveys as Legal Evidence"
  Public Opinion Quarterly, Vol. 51 (Spring 1987), pp. 84-91.

England, Len
  "The Expert Witness in Court"
  Journal of the Market Research Society, Vol. 27 (July 1985), pp.
  199-202.

Harvard Law Review
  "Public Opinion Surveys as Evidence: The Pollsters Go to Court"
  Harvard Law Review, Vol. 56 (1953), pp. 505,6.

Menneer, P.
  "Survey Data in Courts of Law"
  Journal of the Market Research Society, Vol. 13, No. 2 (1971).

Miller, Ian
  "The Legal Position of the Expert Witness"
  Journal of the Market Research Society, Vol. 27 (July 1985), pp.
  175-83.

Minnesota Law Review
  "Evidence-Hearsay--Admissibility of Public Opinion Polls"
  Minnesota Law Review, Vol. 37 (1953), p. 386.

Morcom, C.
  "Survey Evidence in Trade Mark Proceedings"
  European Intellectual Property Review (1984).

Morgan, Fred W.
  "The Admissibility of Consumer Surveys as Legal Evidence in Courts"
  Journal of Marketing, Vol. 43 (Fall 1979), pp. 33-40.

Newell, D.
    "The Role of the Statistician as Expert Witness"
    Journal of the Royal Statistical Society, Vol. 145, Part 4 (1982), p.
    403.

Ross, I.
    "Legal Standards for Consumer Survey Research" (panel session)
    Journal of Advertising Research, Vol. 23, No. 5 (October/November
    1983), p. 31.

Saks, Michael J. and Baron, Charles H. (editors)
    The Use/Nonuse/Misuse of Applied Social Research in the Courts
    (Cambridge, MA: Abt Books, 1980), 189 pp.

Smith, Joseph G. (moderator) et al.
    "My Day in Court"
    Journal of Advertising Research, Vol. 9 (December 1973), pp. 9-22.

Snyder, J.
    "Legal Standards for Consumer Survey Research" (panel session)
    Journal of Advertising Research, Vol. 23, No. 5 (October/November
    1983), p. 19.

Sorensen, R. C. and Sorensen, T. C.
    "The Admissibility and Use of Opinion Research Evidence"
    New York University Law Review, Vol. 28 (1953), p. 1214.

Sylvester, Eugene P.
    "Consumer Polls as Evidence in Unfair Trade Cases"
    George Washington Law Review, Vol. 20 (1951), p. 211.

Thompson, Donald L.
    "Survey Data as Evidence in Trademark Infringement Cases"
    Journal of Marketing Research, Vol. II (February 1965), pp. 64-73.

Zeisel, H.
    "The Uniqueness of Survey Evidence"
    Connell Law Quarterly (1960).

Zissman, Lorin
    "Survey Research Can Play Critical Role in Courtroom"
    Marketing News, Vol. 19 (January 4, 1985), p. 44.

Zoler, Jon N.
    "Research Requirements for Ad Claims Substantiation"
    Journal of Advertising Research, Vol. 23 (April/May 1983), pp. 9-15.

29.03 ---------- Pricing Strategy Research Methods

Baker, Paul
    "Econometrics for Pricing Research"
    Journal of the Market Research Society, Vol. 29 (April 1987), pp.
    123-31.

Blamires, Chris
    "'Trade-Off' Pricing Research: A Discussion of Historical and
    Innovatory Applications"
    Journal of the Market Research Society, Vol. 29 (April 1987), pp.
    133-52.

Blamires, Chris
    "Pricing Research Techniques: A Review and a New Approach"
    Journal of the Market Research Society, Vol. 23 (July 1981), pp.
    103-26.

Clarke, Julia
    "What Price Research?"
    Management Decision, Vol. 26, No. 3 (1988), pp. 47-52.

Curry, David
    "Measuring Price and Quality Competition"
    Journal of Marketing, Vol. 49 (Spring 1985), pp. 106-17.

Devinney, Timothy M. (editor)
    Issued in Pricing: Theory and Research
    (Lexington, MA: Lexington Books, 1988), 432 pp.

England, L. R. and Ehrenberg, Andrew S. C.
    "Pricing Research at the London Business School: A Progress Note"
    Journal of the Market Research Society, Vol. 29 (April 1987), pp.
    209,10.

England, L. R. and Ehrenberg, Andrew S. C.
    "Pricing Experiments 1984
    CMaC Working Paper
    London Business School (1985).

Marbeau, Yves
    "What Value Pricing Research Today?"
    Journal of the Market Research Society, Vol. 29 (April 1987), pp.
    153-82.

Moran, W.
    "Insights From Pricing Research"
    in Pricing Practices and Strategies
    Elsevier Business Intelligence Series, Volume Two
    Conference Board Report No. 751
    (Amsterdam: Elsevier Science Publishers BV, 1983), pp. 7-13.

Morgan, Rory P.
    "Ad Hoc Pricing Research--Some Key Issues"
    Journal of the Market Research Society, Vol. 29 (April 1987), pp.
    109-21.

Rao, Vithala R.
    "Pricing Research in Marketing: The State of the Art"
    Cornell University (1982), working paper.

RBL
    Pricing Research: A Problem?
    (London: RBL, 1979), 16 pp.

Van Westendorp, P.
    "NSS-Price Sensitivity Meter: A New Approach to Study Consumer
    Perception of Prices"
    Proceedings, ESOMAR Congress, Venice (1976), pp. 139-67.

29.04 ---------- Channels Research Methods

Rosenberg, L. T. and Stern, L. W.
    "Conflict Measurement in the Distribution Channel"
    Journal of Marketing Research, Vol. VIII (November 1971), pp. 437-2.

Urban, David J.
    "Organisational Development: A New Direction for Marketing Channel
    Research"
    European Journal of Marketing, Vol. 23, No. 6 (1989), pp. 38-54.

29.05 ---------- Image Research Methods

        See also (sub)heading(s) 37.

Beckwith, N. E. and Kubilius, U. V.
    "Empirical Evidence of Halo Effects in Store Image Research"
    Proceedings, Association for Consumer Research (1977).

Brown, Stephen W., Smith, Richard L., III, and Zurowski, George J.
    "The Appropriateness and Applicability of Image Research to Banking"
    Journal of Bank Research, Vol. 8 (Summer 1977), pp. 94-100.

Clevenger, Theodore, Lazier, Gilbert A., and Clark, Margaret
    "Measurement of Corporate Images by Semantic Differential"
    Journal of Marketing Research, Vol. II (February 1965), pp. 80-2.

Cohen, Louis
    "Rejoinder to Rothman"
    Journal of Advertising Research, Vol. 8 (March 1968), pp. 66,7.

Cohen, Louis
    "The Differentiation Ratio in Corporate Image Research"
    Journal of Advertising Research, Vol. 7 (September 1967), pp. 32-6.

Dowling, Grahame R.
    "Measuring Corporate Images: A Review of Alternative Approaches"
    Journal of Business Research, Vol. 17 (August 1988), pp. 27-34.

Gatty, Ronald and Hamje, K. H. L.
    The Error-Choice Technique in Image Research
    Technical Bulletin No. 4
    (New Brunswick, NJ: Department of Agricultural Economics, Rutgers
    University, June 1961), 14 pp.

Golden, Linda L. and Albaum, Gerald
    "An Analysis of Alternative Semantic Differential Formats for
    Measuring Retail Store Image"
    Annual Meeting, Western Region American Institute for Decision
    Sciences (1984), paper presentation.

Golden, Linda L., Albaum, Gerald, and Zimmer, Mary
    "The Numerical Comparative Scale: An Economical Format for Retail
    Image Measurement"
    Journal of Retailing, Vol. 63 (Winter 1987), pp. 393-410.

Hawkins, Del I., Albaum, Gerald, and Best, Roger
"Reliability of Retail Store Images as Measured by the Stapel Scale"
Journal of Retailing, Vol. 52 (Winter 1976-77), pp. 31-8.

Hooley, Graham J. and Cork, David E.
"SIMS: A Store Image Monitoring System"
International Journal of Advertising, Vol. 3, No. 2 (1984), pp.
129-38.

Jain, Arun K. and Etgar, M.
"Measuring Store Image Through Multidimensional Scaling of Free
Response Data"
Journal of Retailing, Vol. 52, No. 4 (1976-77), pp. 61-70.

Jaoui, Hubert
"The Stimulation of the Right Side of the Brain in Market and Brand
Image Research"
ESOMAR Congress, Montreux (1987), pp. 859-72.

Jenkins, R. L. and Forsythe, S. M.
"Retail Image Research: State of the Art Review With Implications for
Retailing Strategy"
in Bellur, V. (editor)
Developments in Marketing Science
(Marquette, MI: Academy of Marketing Science, 1980).

McDougall, Gordon H. G. and Fry, Joseph N.
"Combining Two Methods of Image Measurement"
Journal of Retailing, Vol. 50 (Winter 1974-75), pp. 53-6.

Menezes, Dennis and Elbert, Norbert F.
"Alternative Semantic Scaling Formats for Measuring Store Image: An
Evaluation"
Journal of Marketing Research, Vol. XVI (February 1979), pp. 80-7.

Neidell, Lester A. and Teach, Richard D.
"Measuring Bank Images: A Comparison of Two Approaches"
Journal of the Academy of Marketing Science, Vol. 2 (Spring 1974),
pp. 374-90.

Rothman, L. J.
"The Differentiation Ratio in Corporate Image Research--Comment"
Journal of Advertising Research, Vol. 8 (March 1968), p. 65.

Sims, J. Taylor
"Measuring the Industrial Firm's Image"
Industrial Marketing Management, Vol. 8 (November 1979), pp. 341-7.

Van Westendorp, Peter and Van Der Herberg, L.
"More Value From Image Research for Less Money: The KS Technique"
ESOMAR Congress, Rome (1984), pp. 457-89.

29.06 ---------- Sales Promotions Research Methods

Abraham, Magid M., Little, John D. C., and Lodish, Leonard M.
"Combining Store and Panel Data for Measuring Promotion Effectiveness"
in Measuring and Evaluating Sale Promotion From the Manufacturer and
Retailer Perspectives
Conference Summary 89-102
(Cambridge, MA: Marketing Science Institute, 1989), pp. 12,3.

Allenby, Greg M., Blattberg, Robert C., and Hawkes, William
"Modeling Promotional Competition"
in Measuring and Evaluating Sales Promotion From the Manufacturer and
Retailer Perspectives
Conference Summary 89-102
(Cambridge, MA: Marketing Science Institute, 1989), pp. 31,2.

Bawa, Kapil and Shoemaker, Robert W.
"Analyzing Incremental Sales From a Coupon Promotion"
Journal of Marketing, Vol. 53 (July 1989), pp. 66-78.

Bender, J. Dennis and Harris, T. L.
"Modeling Coupon and Advertising Response Using 'Single-Source' Data"
ORSA/TIMS Joint National Meeting, Denver (October 1988), paper
presentation.

Kumar, V. and Leone, Robert P.
"Measuring the Effect of Retail Store Promotions on Brand and Store
Substitutions"
Journal of Marketing Research, Vol. XXV (May 1988), pp. 178-85.

Lattin, James M. and Bucklin, Randolph E.
The Dynamics of Consumer Response to Price Discounts
Report 88-111
(Cambridge, MA: Marketing Science Institute, 1988).

Ruch, Dudley M.
   "An Agenda for Future Research"
   in Measuring and Evaluating Sales Promotions From the Manufacturer
   and Retailer Perspectives
   Conference Summary 89-102
   (Cambridge, MA: Marketing Science Institute, 1989).

Schmalensee, Diane H.
   "Exciting Breakthroughs in Sales Promotion Research"
   Marketing Research, Vol. 1 (September 1989), pp. 34-43.

Temple, Ron
   "Direct Response Advertising: Eliminating the Guesswork"
   Admap (December 1988), pp. 28-30.

29.07 ---------- Store Location Research Methods

Achabal, Dale D., Gorr, Wilpen L., and Mahajan, Vijay
   "MULTILOC: A Multiple Store Location Decision Model"
   Journal of Retailing, Vol. 58 (Summer 1982), pp. 5-25.

Brehany, Michael J.
   "Modelling Store Location and Performance: A Review"
   European Research, Vol. 11 (July 1983), pp. 111-21.

Brown, Lawrence A., Brown, Marilyn A., and Craig, C. Samuel
   "Innovation Diffusion and Entrepreneurial Activity in a Spatial
   Context: Conceptual Models and Related Case Studies"
   in Sheth, Jagdish N. (editor)
   Research in Marketing
   (Greenwich, CT: JAI Press, Inc., 1981), pp. 69-115.

Burnett, Patricia K.
   "The Application of Conjoint Measurement to Recent Urban Travel"
   in Golledge, Reginald and Rayner, John (editors)
   Data Analysis in Multidimensional Scaling
   (Columbus, OH: Ohio State University Press, 1982), pp. 169-90.

Church, Richard L. and ReVelle, Charles
   "The Maximal Covering Location Problem"
   Papers of the Regional Science Association, Volume 30 (1974), pp.
   101-18.

Cottrell, James L.
   "An Environmental Model of Performance Measurement in a Chain of
   Supermarkets"
   Journal of Retailing, Vol. 49 (Fall 1973), pp. 51-63.

Craig, C. Samuel and Ghosh, Avijit
   "Covering Approaches to Retail Facility Location"
   in Belk, Russell W. et al. (editors)
   AMA Educators' Proceedings, Series 50
   (Chicago: American Marketing Association, 1984), pp. 195-9.

Craig, C. Samuel, Ghosh, Avijit, and McLafferty, Sara
   "Models of the Retail Location Process: A Review"
   Journal of Retailing, Vol. 60 (Spring 1984), pp. 5-36.

Davies, R. L. and Rogers, D. S. (editors)
   Store Location and Store Assessment Research
   (New York: John Wiley and Sons, Inc., 1984), 375 pp.

Davies, R. L.
   "Store Location and Store Assessment Research: The Integration of
   Some New and Traditional Techniques"
   Transactions of the Institute of British Geographers, New Series 2
   (1977), pp. 141-57.

Eagle, Thomas C.
   "Parameter Stability in Disaggregate Retail Choice Models:
   Experimental Evidence"
   Journal of Retailing, Vol. 60 (Spring 1984), pp. 101-23.

Eaton, David, Church, Richard L., and ReVelle, Charles
   "Locational Analysis: A New Tool for Health Planners"
   Methodological Working Document #53
   Sector Analysis Division, Agency for International Development (1984).

Fotheringham, A. Stewart
   "Spatial Structure and Distance Decay Parameters"
   Annals, Association of American Geographers, Vol. 71 (1981), pp.
   425-36.

Ghosh, Avijit
   "Parameter Nonstationarity in Retail Choice Models"
   Journal of Business Research, Vol. 12, No. 5 (1984), pp. 375-82.

Ghosh, Avijit and Craig, C. Samuel
"An Approach to Determining Optimal Locations for a New Service"
Journal of Marketing Research, Vol. XXIII (November 1986), pp. 354-62.

Ghosh, Avijit and Craig, C. Samuel
"Formulating Retail Location Strategy in a Changing Environment"
Journal of Marketing, Vol. 47 (Summer 1983), pp. 56-68.

Ghosh, Avijit and McLafferty, Sara
"Locating Stores in Uncertain Environments: A Scenario Planning
Approach"
Journal of Retailing, Vol. 58 (Winter 1982), pp. 5-22.

Heald, G. I.
"Application of AID Programme and Multiple Regression Techniques to
Assessment of Store Performance and Site Selection"
Operational Research Quarterly, Vol. 23 (1972), pp. 445-57.

Huff, David L.
"Defining and Estimating a Trade Area"
Journal of Marketing, Vol. 28 (July 1964), pp. 34-8.

Jain, Arun K. and Mahajan, Vijay
"Evaluating the Competitive Environment in Retailing Using
Multiplicative Competitive Interactive Models"
in Sheth, Jagdish N. (editor)
Research in Marketing
(Greenwich, CT: JAI Press, Inc., 1979).

Kornblau, Curt (editor)
Guide to Store Location Research With Emphasis on Supermarkets
(Reading, MA: Addison-Wesley Publishing, Inc., 1968), 259 pp.

Lord, J. Dennis and Lynds, Charles
"The Use of Regression Models in Store Location Research: A Review
and Case Study"
Akron Business and Economic Review, Vol. 12 (Summer 1981), pp. 13-19.

Louviere, Jordan and Woodworth, George
"Design and Analysis of Simulated Choice or Allocation Experiments:
An Approach Based on Aggregate Data"
Journal of Marketing Research, Vol. XX (November 1983), pp. 350-67.

Love, Douglas O. and Deichert, Jerome A.
Site Evaluation and Location System
(Lincoln, NE: Bureau of Business Research, University of Nebraska,
1983).

MacKay, D. B.
"A Microanalytic Approach to Store Location Analysis"
Journal of Marketing Research, Vol. IX (1972), pp. 134-41.

Meyer, Robert J. and Eagle, Thomas C.
"Context-Induced Parameter Instability in a Disaggregate Stochastic
Model of Store Choice"
Journal of Marketing Research, Vol. XIX (February 1982), pp. 62-71.

Nakanishi, Masao and Cooper, Lee G.
"Parameter Estimate for Multiplicative Interactive Choice Model:
Least Squares Approach"
Journal of Marketing Research, Vol. XI (August 1974), pp. 303-11.

Nelson, Richard L.
The Selection of Retail Locations
(New York: F. W. Dodge Corporation, 1958).

Olsen, Lola M. and Lord, J. Dennis
"Market Area Characteristics and Branch Bank Performance"
Journal of Bank Research, Vol. 10 (Summer 1979), pp. 102-10.

Parker, Barnett R. and Srinivasan, V.
"A Consumer Preference Approach to the Planning of Rural Primary
Health-Care Facilities"
Operations Research, Vol. 24 (November-December 1976), pp. 991-1029.

Recker, Wilfred W. and Schuler, Harry J.
"Destination Choice and Processing Spatial Information: Some
Empirical Tests With Alternative Constructs"
Economic Geography, Vol. 57 (October 1981), pp. 373-83.

Simkin, L. P., Doyle, P., and Saunders, J.
"UK Retail Store Location Assessment"
Journal of the Market Research Society, Vol. 27 (April 1985), pp.
95-108.

Stanley, Thomas J. and Sewall, Murphy A.
"Image Inputs to a Probabilistic Model: Predicting Retail Potential"
Journal of Marketing, Vol. 40 (July 1976), pp. 48-53.

Simkin, L. P., Doyle, P., and Saunders, J.
  "U.K. Retail Store Location Assessment"
  Journal of the Market Research Society, Vol. 27 (April 1985), pp.
  95-108.

Wrigley, Neil (editor)
  Store Choice, Store Location and Market Analysis
  (Routledge), 358 pp.

Zeller, Richard A., Achabal, Dale D., and Brown, Lawrence A.
  "Market Penetration and Locational Conflict in Channel Systems"
  Decision Sciences, Vol. 11 (January 1980), pp. 58-80.

29.08 ---------- Health Care Services Research Methods

Cooper, Philip and Hisrich, Robert D.
  "Marketing Research for Health Services: Understanding and Applying
  Various Techniques"
  Journal of Health Care Marketing, Vol. 7 (March 1987), pp. 54-60.

Elsesser, Jan
  "Conducting Marketing Research in Health Care: The Changing Roles of
  Physician and Patient"
  Journal of Advertising Research, Vol. 28 (October/November 1988), pp.
  RC15-20.

Grady, Kathleen E. and Wallston, Barbara Strudler
  Research in Health Care Settings
  (Newbury Park, CA: Sage Publications, Inc., 1988), 176 pp.

McMillan, Norman H. and Rosenbaum, George
  Managing Smart: Market Research for Hospital Decision Makers
  (Chicago: American Hospital Association Services, Inc.), 154 pp.

Ortengren, John
  "Pharmaceutical Marketing Research in Sweden"
  European Research, Vol. 10 (April 1982), pp. 58-63.

29.09 ---------- Research Methods Related to Children

Neelankavil, James P., O'Brien, John V., and Tashjian, Richard
  "Techniques to Obtain Market-Related Information From Very Young
  Children"
  Journal of Advertising Research, Vol. 25 (June/July 1985), pp. 41-7.

Roper, Gar
  "Research With Marketing's Paradoxical Subjects: Children"
  Marketing Research, Vol. 1 (June 1989), pp. 16-23.

Taylor, Judy and Browning, Jane
  "The Chameleon Child: Questioning the Ten Commandments of Qualitative
  Research Among Pre-Teenagers"
  Proceedings, Market Research Society Conference (March 1987), pp.
  483-99.

29.10 ---------- Research Methods Related to the Elderly

Abrams, Mark
  "Introduction to 'Researching the Elderly'"
  Journal of the Market Research Society, Vol. 25 (July 1983), p. 215.

Barker, Jonathan
  "Evaluating Provision for the Elderly"
  Journal of the Market Research Society, Vol. 25 (July 1983), p. 275.

Freitag, C. B. and Barry, J. R.
  "Interaction and Interviewer Bias in a Survey of the Aged"
  Psychological Reports, Vol. 34, Part 1 (June 1974), pp. 771-4.

Herzog, A. Regula and Rodgers, Willard L.
  "Interviewing Older Adults"
  Public Opinion Quarterly, Vol. 52 (Spring 1988), pp. 84-99.

Herzog, A. Regula, Rodgers, Willard L., and Kulka, Richard A.
  "Interviewing Older Adults: A Comparison of Telephone and
  Face-to-Face Modalities"
  Public Opinion Quarterly, Vol. 47 (Fall 1983), pp. 405-18.

Hoinville, Gerald W.
  "Carrying Out Surveys Among the Elderly: Some Problems of Sampling
  and Interviewing"
  Journal of the Market Research Society, Vol. 23 (July 1983), p. 223.

Irelan, L. N.
  "The Older Person as a Survey Respondent"
  Proceedings of the Social Sciences Section of the American
  Statistical Association (1969), pp. 347-50.

Klippel, R. Eugene
"Marketing Research and the Aged Consumer: The Need for a New
Perspective"
Journal of the Academy of Marketing Science, Vol. 2 (Winter 1974),
pp. 242-8.

Zelan, J.
"Interviewing the Aged"
Public Opinion Quarterly, Vol. 33 (Fall 1969), pp. 420-4.

29.11 ---------- Res Methods Related to Affluent, Elite Populations

Godwin, R. Kenneth
"The Consequences of Large Monetary Incentives in Mail Surveys of
Elites"
Public Opinion Quarterly, Vol. 43 (1979), pp. 378-87.

Stanley, Thomas J. and Sewall, Murphy A.
"The Response of Affluent Consumers to Mail Surveys"
Journal of Advertising Research, Vol. 26 (June/July 1986), pp. 55-8.

29.12 ---------- Unclassified (Research Methods in Topical Areas)

Acito, Paul L. and Clouthier, Margaret M.
"Research in Performing Arts: Eight Tips"
Marketing News, Vol. 19 (January 4, 1985), p. 4.

Adler, L. and Crespi, Irving (editors)
Attitude Research at Sea
(New York: American Marketing Association, 1966), 189 pp.

Blackett, Tom
"Brand Name Research--Getting It Right"
Marketing and Research Today, Vol. 17 (May 1989), pp. 89-93.

Blankenship, A. B.
"Point of View: Consumerism and Consumer Research"
Journal of Advertising Research, Vol. 11 (August 1971), pp. 44-7.

Blankenship, A. B.
"Creativity in Consumer Research"
Journal of Marketing, Vol. 25 (October 1961), pp. 34-8.

Crespi, Irving
Attitude Research
Marketing Research Techniques Series, No. 7
(Chicago: American Marketing Association, 1965), 44 pp.

Ernst, Otmar
"Marginal Remarks on the Situation of Editorial Research in 1974"
European Research, Vol. 3 (May 1975), pp. 98-104.

Giragosian, N. H. (editor)
Chemical Marketing Research
(New York: Reinhold Publishing Corporation, 1967), 375 pp.

Gronneberg, Jorgen M.
"The Relation Between Human Resource Accounting and Market Research: A
Challenge to Market Researchers"
European Research, Vol. 4 (March 1976), pp. 45-50.

Haley, Russell I. (editor)
Attitude Research in Transition
(Chicago: American Marketing Association, 1972), 309 pp.

Hoefnagels, Cosmas
"Marketing Research in the Aircraft Industry"
European Research, Vol. 12 (July 1984), pp. 144-8.

House, Peter W. and Jones, David W.
Getting It Off the Shelf: A Methodology for Implementing Federal
Research
(Boulder, CO: Westview Press, 1978).

Houseman, Earl E. and Lipstein, Benjamin
"Observation and Audit Techniques for Measuring Retail Sales"
Agricultural Economics, Vol. 12 (July 1960), pp. 61-72.

Hyett, G. P. and Farr, D. J.
"A Technique for the Eighties: Identifying Marketing Areas by Market
Research Methods and a Mathematical Technique"
European Research, Vol. 8 (March 1980), pp. 66-77.

Jacoby, Jacob
"Consumer Research: A State of the Art Review"
Journal of Marketing, Vol. 42 (April 1978), pp. 87-96.

Kapferer, Clodwig and Disch, W. K. A.
  Market Research by Trade Associations
  (New York: OECD Unit, McGraw-Hill Publishing Company, 1964), 92 pp.

King, Charles W. and Tigert, Douglas J. (editors)
  Attitude Research Reaches New Heights
  (Chicago: American Marketing Association), 339 pp.

Kollat, David T., Blackwell, Roger D., and Engel, James F.
  "The Current Status of Consumer Behavior Research: Development During
  the 1968-1972 Period"
  in Venkatesan, M. (editor)
  Proceedings of the Third Annual Conference of the Association for
  Consumer Research (1972), pp. 576-85.

Kramer, Walter
  "How Marketing Research Can Help Railroads"
  Journal of Marketing, Vol. 25 (October 1961), pp. 39-46.

Lantos, Geoffrey P.
  "An Improved Research Methodology for Studying Consumer Information
  Processing Behaviour"
  Journal of the Market Research Society, Vol. 24 (January 1982), pp.
  29-45.

Levy, Ronald (editor)
  Guide to Construction Marketing Research
  (Washington, DC: Producers' Council, Inc., 1975), 91 pp.

Ligthart, Jan
  "Function Research Within the Framework of Editorial Research for
  Regional Newspapers"
  European Research, Vol. 6 (May 1978), pp. 119-27.

Litten, Larry H., Sullivan, Daniel, and Brodigan, David L.
  Applying Market Research in College Admissions
  (New York: College Entrance Examination Board, 1983), 303 pp.

Marchant, Len
  "Investigating Consumer Attitudes and Behaviour"
  European Research, Vol. 7 (July 1979), pp. 146-56.

Oliver, R. A.
  "Small Businesses, Big Decisions: Opportunities for Research"
  Proceedings, Market Research Society Conference (March 1986), pp.
  149-61.

Peterson, Robert A.
  Trends in Consumer Behavior Research
  American Marketing Association Monograph Series No. 6
  (Chicago: American Marketing Association, 1977), 40 pp.

Rao, Vithala R.
  "Books on Quantitative Methods for Consumer Research"
  Journal of Consumer Research, Vol. 7 (September 1980), pp. 198-210.

Roberts-Miller, R. A. and Spackman, N. A. G.
  "Research for Publishers"
  European Research, Vol. 1 (March 1973), pp. 69-72.

Rothenberg, Marvin J. and Blankenship, A. B.
  "How to Survey Trading Areas"
  Journal of Advertising Research, Vol. 20 (February 1980), pp. 41-5.

Sheth, Jagdish N.
  "The Surpluses and Shortages in Consumer Behavior Theory and Research"
  Journal of the Academy of Marketing Science, Vol. 7 (Fall 1979), pp.
  414-27.

Smith, Wendy
  "Market Research and Family Planning"
  Journal of the Market Research Society, Vol. 21 (January 1979), pp.
  25-9.

Van Den Heuvel, Rob R., Feringa, Wytze J., and Striekwold, Rene
  "Research for More Effective Product Assortment Decisions"
  ESOMAR Congress, Rome (1984), pp. 435-56.

Venkatesh, Alladi and Dholakia, Nikhilesh
  "Methodological Issues in Macromarketing"
  Journal of Macromarketing, Vol. 6 (Fall 1986), pp. 36-52.

Walker, Michael C.
  An Introduction to Bank Marketing Research
  (Chicago: Bank Public Relations and Marketing Association Research
  Department, 1968), 157 pp.

Webber, John C.
  "Packaged Goods Marketing Research--Where's It All Going"
  Journal of Advertising Research, Vol. 26 (October/November 1986), pp.
  RC3-5.

Weston, J. Fred (editor)
  Defense-Space Market Research
  (Cambridge, MA: M.I.T. Press, 1964), 186 pp.

Wilson, P.
  "Improving the Methodology of Drinking Surveys"
  The Statistician, Vol. 30 (1981), pp. 159-67.

Wind, Yoram
  "Issues and Advances in Segmentation Research"
  Journal of Marketing Research, Vol. XV (August 1978), pp. 317-37.

30 ----------------- CONTINGENT VALUATION TECHNIQUES -----------------

30.01 ---------- Books Re: Contingent Valuation Techniques

Cummings, Ronald G., Brookshire, David S., and Schulze, William D.
(editors)
Valuing Environmental Goods: An Assessment of the Contingent
Valuation Method
(Totowa, NJ: Rowman and Allanheld, 1986).

Mitchell, Robert C. and Carson, Richard T.
Using Surveys to Value Public Goods: The Contingent Valuation Method
(Washington, DC: Resources for the Future, 1987).

30.02 ---------- Theory Re: Contingent Valuation Techniques

Bishop, Richard C., Heberlein, Thomas A., and Kealy, Mary Jo
"Contingent Valuation of Environmental Assets: Comparisons With a
Simulated Market"
Natural Resources Journal, Vol. 23 (July 1983), pp. 619-33.

Randall, Alan
"The Possibility of Satisfactory Benefit Estimation With Contingent
Markets"
in Cummings, R. G., Brookshire, D. S., and Shulze, W. D. (editors)
Valuing Environmental Goods: An Assessment of the Contingent
Valuation Method
(Totowa, NJ: Rowman and Allanheld, 1986), pp. 114-22.

Sellar, Christine, Stoll, John, and Chavas, Jean-Paul
"Validation of Empirical Measures of Welfare Change: A Comparison of
Nonmarket Techniques"
Land Economics, Vol. 61 (May 1985), pp. 156-75.

30.03 ---------- Estimation Methods for Contingent Valuation

Cameron, Trudy Ann
"A New Paradigm for Valuing Non-Market Goods Using Referendum Data:
Maximum Likelihood Estimation by Censored Logistic Regression"
Journal of Environmental Economics and Management, forthcoming.

Cameron, Trudy Ann and James, Michelle D.
"Estimating Willingness to Pay From Survey Data: An Alternative
Pre-Test-Market Evaluation Procedure"
Journal of Marketing Research, Vol. XXIV (November 1987), pp. 389-95.

Cameron, Trudy Ann and James, Michelle D.
"Efficient Estimation Methods for Use With 'Closed-Ended' Contingent
Valuation Survey Data"
Review of Economics and Statistics, Vol. 69 (May 1987), pp. 269-76.

30.04 ---------- Applications of Contingent Valuation Techniques

Bishop, Richard C. and Heberlein, Thomas A.
"Measuring Values of Extramarket Goods: Are Indirect Measures Biased?"
American Journal of Agricultural Economics, Vol. 61 (December 1979),
pp. 926-30.

Cameron, Trudy Ann and James, Michelle D.
"The Determinants of Value for a Recreational Fishing Day: Estimates
From a Contingent Valuation Survey"
Discussion Paper No. 405
Department of Economics, University of California, Los Angeles (1986).

Sellar, Christine, Chavas, Jean-Paul, and Stoll, John
"Specification of the Logit Model: The Case of Valuation of Nonmarket
Goods"
Journal of Environmental Economics and Management, Vol. 13 (December
1986), pp. 382-90.

31 ------------------- HISTORICAL RESEARCH METHODS ------------------
        See also (sub)heading(s) 79, 84.

31.01 ---------- Theory Re: Historical Research Methods

Fullerton, Ronald A.
    "The Poverty of Ahistorical Analysis: Present Weakness and Future
    Cure in U.S. Marketing Thought"
    in Firat, A. Fuat, Dholakia, Nikhilesh, and Bagozzi, Richard P.
    (editors)
    Philosophical and Radical Thought in Marketing
    (Lexington, MA: Lexington Books, 1987), pp. 97-116.

Hollander, Stanley C.
    "Where is Consumption History Going?"
    Thirteenth Annual Macromarketing Conference, San Jose, CA (1988),
    paper presentation.

Iggers, George C. and Parker, Harold T. (editors)
    International Handbook of Historical Studies
    (Westport, CT: Greenwood Press, 1979).

Laudan, Larry, Donovan, Arthur, Laudan, Rachel, Barker, Peter, Brown,
    Harold, Leplin, Jarrett, Thagard, Paul, and Wykstra, Steve
    "Scientific Change: Philosophical Models and Historical Research"
    Synthese, Vol. 69 (November 1986), pp. 141-223.

McCracken, Grant
    Culture and Consumption: New Approaches to the Symbolic Character of
    Consumer Goods and Activities
    (Bloomington, IN: Indiana University Press, 1988).

McCullagh, C. Behan
    Justifying Historical Descriptions
    (Cambridge, UK: Cambridge University Press, 1984).

Savitt, Ronald
    "Historical Research in Marketing"
    Journal of Marketing, Vol. 44 (Fall 1980), pp. 52-8.

Tan, Chin Tiong and Sheth, Jagdish N. (editors)
    Historical Perspective in Consumer Research: National and
    International Perspectives
    (Singapore: National University of Singapore and Association for
    Consumer Research, 1985).

31.02 ---------- Applications of Historical Research Methods

Fullerton, Ronald A.
    "How Modern is Modern Marketing? Marketing's Evolution and the Myth
    of the 'Production Era'"
    Journal of Marketing, Vol. 52 (January 1988), pp. 108-25.

Savitt, Ronald
    "The 'Wheel of Retailing' and Retail Product Management"
    European Journal of Marketing, Vol. 18, no. 6/7 (1984), pp. 43-54.

Savitt, Ronald
    "An Historical Approach to Comparative Retailing"
    Management Decision, Special Issue: Comparative Marketing Systems,
    Vol. 20 (1982), pp. 16-23.

Witkowski, Terrence H.
    "Colonial Consumers in Revolt: Buyer Values and Behavior During the
    Nonimportation Movement, 1764-1776"
    Journal of Consumer Research, Vol. 16 (September 1989), pp. 216-26.

32 -------------------- SURVEY RESEARCH - GENERAL --------------------

See also (sub)heading(s) 9.04, 33.

32.01 ---------- Books Re: Survey Research - General

Alreck, Pamela L. and Settle, Robert B.
The Survey Research Handbook
(Homewood, IL: Richard D. Irwin, Inc., 1985), 429 pp.

Alwin, D. F. (editor)
Survey Design and Analysis: Current Issues
(Beverly Hills, CA: Sage Publications, 1978).

Andersen, Ronald, Kasper, Judith, Frankel, Martin R., and Associates
Total Survey Error
(San Fransico: Jossey-Bass Publishers, 1979), 296 pp.

Backstrom, Charles H. and Hursch, G. D.
Survey Research
(Evanston, IL: Northwestern University Press, 1963).

Bailar, Barbara A. and Lanphier, C. Michael
Development of Survey Methods to Assess Survey Practices
(Washington: American Statistical Association, 1978).

Bateson, Nicholas
Data Construction in Social Surveys
(Winchester, MA: Allen and Unwin, Inc., 1984), 150 pp.

Belson, William A.
Validity in Survey Research
(Brookfield, VT: Gower Publishing Co., 1986), 584 pp.

Belson, W. A. and Bell, C. R.
A Bibliography of Papers Bearing on the Adequacy of Techniques Used
in Survey Research
(London: The Market Research Society, 1960), 52 pp.

Bradburn, Norman M., Sudman, Seymour, and Associates
Improving Interview Method and Questionnaire Design
(San Francisco: Jossey-Bass Publishers, 1975), 214 pp.

Davis, James A.
Elementary Survey Analysis
(Englewood Cliffs, NJ: Prentice-Hall, 1971).

Dillman, Don
Mail and Telephone Survey: The Total Design Method
(New York: John Wiley and Sons, Inc., 1978).

Dutka, Solomon, Frankel, Lester R., and Roshwalb, Irving
How to Conduct Surveys
(New York: Audits and Surveys, 1982).

Ferber, Robert (editor)
Readings in Survey Research
(Chicago: American Marketing Association, 1978), 604 pp.

Fiedler, Judith
Field Research: A Manual for Logistics and Management of Scientific
Studies in Natural Settings
(San Francisco, CA: Jossey-Bass, Inc., 1978), 188 pp.

Fink, Arlene and Kosecoff, Jacqueline
How to Conduct Surveys
(Beverly Hills, CA: Sage Publications, Inc., 1985), 120 pp.

Fowler, Floyd J., Jr.
Survey Research Methods, Revised Edition
(Newbury Park, CA: Sage Publications, Inc., 1988), 160 pp.

Frey, James H.
Survey Research by Telephone
(Beverly Hills, CA: Sage Publications, 1983).

Glock, Charles Y. (editor)
Survey Research in the Social Sciences
(New York, NY: Russell Sage Foundation, 1967), 543 pp.

Groves, Robert M. and Kahn, Robert L.
Surveys by Telephone: A National Comparison With Personal Interviews
(New York: Academic Press, 1979).

Hochhauser, Richard
"Market Survey, Database or a Combination of Both?"
Direct Marketing, Vol. 49 (October 1986), pp. 136-43.

Hoinville, Gerald, Jowell, Roger, and Associates
Survey Research Practice
(Heinemann Educational Books, 1978), 228 pp.

Hutton, Peter F.
  Survey Research for Managers
  (Macmillan, 1988), 263 pp.

Hyman, Herbert H.
  Secondary Analysis of Sample Surveys: Principles, Procedures and
  Potentialities
  (New York: John Wiley and Sons, 1972), 245 pp.

Jabine, Thomas B., Straf, Miron L., Tanur, Judith M., and Tourangeau,
  Roger
  Cognitive Aspects of Survey Methodology: Building a Bridge Between
  Disciplines
  (Washington, DC: National Academy Press, 1984).

Jolliffe, F. R.
  Survey Design and Analysis
  (New York: Halsted Press Division of John Wiley and Sons, Inc., 1986
  and Chichester, West Sussex, EN: Ellis Horwood Limited, 1986), 178 pp.

Kalton, Thomas and Moser, Claus A.
  Survey Methods in Social Investigation
  (London: Heinemann, 1971).

Lansing, John B. and Morgan, James N.
  Economic Survey Methods
  (Ann Arbor: Survey Research Center, Institute for Social Research,
  University of Michigan, 1971), 448 pp.

Lee, Eun Sul, Forthofer, Ronald N., and Lorimer, Ronald J.
  Analyzing Complex Survey Data
  (Newbury Park, CA: Sage Publications, Inc., 1989), 80 pp.

Long, J. Scott
  Common Problems/Proper Solutions: Avoiding Error in Quantitative
  Research
  (Newbury Park, CA: Sage Publications, Inc., 1988).

MacLean, Mavis and Genn, Hazel
  Methodological Issues in Social Surveys
  (McMillan-SSRC, 1979), 118 pp.

Marsh, Catherine
  The Survey Method: The Contribution of Surveys to Sociological
  Explanation
  (George Allen and Unwin Ltd., 1982), 180 pp.

McKennell, Aubrey C.
  Surveying Attitude Structures: A Discussion of Principles and
  Procedures
  (Amsterdam, The Netherlands: Elsevier Scientific Publishing Company,
  1974), 94 pp.

McKeown, Bruce and Thomas, Dan
  Q Methodology
  (Newbury Park, CA: Sage Publications, Inc., 1988).

Moser, C. A. and Kalton, G.
  Survey Methods in Social Investigation
  (London: Heinemann, 1971).

Moss, Louis and Goldstein, Harvey (editors)
  The Recall Method in Social Surveys
  (London: University of London Insitution of Education, 1979), 176 pp.

Orlich, D. C.
  Designing Sensible Surveys
  (Pleasantville, NY: Redgrave Publishing Co., 1978).

Parten, M. B.
  Surveys, Polls, and Samples
  (New York: Harper and Brothers, 1950), 624 pp.

Pearl, Robert V.
  Methodology of Consumer Expenditures Surveys, (Working Paper No. 27)
  (Washington, DC: U.S. Bureau of the Census, Department of Commerce,
  1968), 78 pp.

Pearson, R. W. and Boruch, R. F. (editors)
  Survey Research Designs: Towards a Better Understanding of Their
  Costs and Benefits
  Lecture Notes in Volume 38
  (New York: Spring-Verlag, 1986), 129 pp.

Rosenberg, Morris
  The Logic of Survey Analysis
  (New York: Basic Books, 1968), 288 pp.

Rosenthal, R.
  Experimental Effects in Behavioral Research
  (New York: Irvington Publishers, Inc., 1976).

Rosenthal, R.
  The Volunteer Subject
  (New York: John Wiley and Sons, Inc., 1975).

Rosenthal, R.
  Experimenter Effects in Behavioral Research
  (New York: Appleton-Century-Crofts, 1966).

Rosenthal, R. and Rosenow, R. (editors)
  Artifact in Behavioral Research
  (New York: Academic Research, 1969).

Rossi, Peter H., Wright, James D., and Anderson, Andy B. (editors)
  Handbook of Survey Research
  (New York: Academic Press, Inc., 1983), 755 pp.

Sonquist, John and Dunkelberg, William
  Survey and Opinion Research: Procedures for Processing and Analysis
  (New York: Prentice-Hall, 1977).

Statistics Canada
  Survey Research for the 1980's: Survey Methodology
  (Statistics Canada, 1980), 242 pp.

Stephan, Frederick F. and McCarthy, Philip J.
  Sampling Opinions
  (New York: John Wiley and Sons, 1958).

Sudman, Seymour
  Reducing the Cost of Surveys
  (Chicago, IL: Aldine Publishing Co., 1967), 246 pp.

Sudman, S. and Bradburn, N. M.
  Response Effects in Surveys: A Review and Synthesis
  (Chicago: Aldine Publishing Co., 1974).

Turner, Charles and Martin, Elizabeth (editors)
  Surveying Subjective Phenomena, Volumes 1 and 2
  (New York: Russell Sage Foundation, 1985), 1120 pp.

Warwick, Donald P. and Lininger, Charles
  The Sample Survey: Theory and Practice
  (New York: McGraw-Hill Book Company, 1975).

Weinberg, Eve
  Community Survey With Local Talent: A Handbook
  (Chicago: National Opinion Research Center, 1971), 294 pp.

Wiseman, Frederick (editor)
  Improving Data Quality in Sample Surveys
  (Cambridge, MA: Marketing Science Institute), 69 pp.

32.02 ---------- Articles, etc. Re: Survey Research - General

Alt, M. B.
  "Fact and Fiction in Survey Research: Some Philosophical
  Considerations"
  Quantitative Sociology Newsletter, Vol. 25 (1980), pp. 6-20.

Baker, Ken
  "Using Geodemographics in Market Research Surveys"
  Journal of the Market Research Society, Vol. 31 (January 1989), pp.
  37-44.

Bloom, Nick
  "The Limitations of Unqualitative Research"
  Industrial Marketing Digest, Vol. 13 (First Quarter 1988), pp. 49-56.

Bowles, Tim and Blyth, Bill
  "How do You Like Your Data: Raw, al Dente or Stewed?"
  European Research, Vol. 13 (October 1985), pp. 170-78.

Dalenius, Tore
  "Time and Survey Design"
  Journal of Advertising Research, Vol. 5 (September 1965), pp. 2-5.

Dalenius, Tore
  "Recent Advances in Sample Survey Theory and Methods"
  Annals of Mathematical Statistics, Vol. 23 (June 1962), pp. 325-49.

Flueck, J. A., Waksberg, J., and Kaitz, H. B.
  "An Overview of Consumer Expenditure Survey Methodology"
  Proceedings of the Social Sciences Section of the American
  Statistical Association (1971), pp. 238-46.

Frankel, Martin R. and Frankel, Lester R.
"Fifty Years of Survey Sampling in the United States"
Public Opinion Quarterly, Vol. 51 (Winter 1987), pp. S127-38.

Frankel, Martin R. and Frankel, Lester R.
"Some Recent Developments in Sample Survey Design"
Journal of Marketing Research, Vol. XIV (August 1977), pp. 280-93.

Gallup, George, Jr.
"Survey Research: Current Problems and Future Opportunities"
Journal of Consumer Marketing, Vol. 5 (Winter 1988), pp. 27-30.

Goyder, John
"Survey on Surveys: Limitations and Potentialities"
Public Opinion Quarterly, Vol. 50 (Spring 1986), pp. 27-41.

Groves, Robert M.
"Survey Data Quality"
Public Opinion Quarterly, Vol. 51 (Winter 1987), pp. S156-72.

Hoinville, Gerald W.
"Developing Survey Methods"
Journal of the Market Research Society, Vol. 28 (January 1986), pp.
3-14.

Johnson, F. J.
"The Price and Relevance of Accuracy of Market Research Survey Data"
Journal of the Market Research Society, Vol. 25 (April 1983), p. 121.

Kiecolt, K. Jill and Nathan, Laura E.
Secondary Analysis of Survey Data
Beverly Hills, CA: Sage Publications, Inc.).

Kohr, R. L. and Suydam, M. N.
"An Instrument for Evaluating Survey Research"
Journal of Educational Research, Vol. 64 (October 1970), pp. 78-81.

Market Research Society Research and Development Committee
"Report of the Second Working Party on Respondent Co-Operation:
1977-80"
Journal of the Market Research Society, Vol. 23 (January 1981), pp.
3-25.

Menneer, Peter
"Retrospective Data in Survey Research"
Journal of the Market Research Society, Vol. 20 (July 1978), pp.
182-95.

Miller, Marvin L.
"Survey Fatigue: It's Killing Your Market Research"
Medical Marketing, Vol. 21 (April 1962), pp. 3-8.

Moss, Louis and Goldstein, Harvey (editors)
The Recall Method in Social Surveys
(University of London Institute of Education, 1979), 176 pp.

Nichols, Don
"Consumer Surveys"
Incentive, Vol. 162 (July 1988), pp. 22-5.

O'Keefe, Terrence and Homer, Pamela
"Selecting Cost-Effective Survey Methods"
Journal of Business Research (August 1987), pp. 365-76.

Payne, Stanley L.
"Combination of Survey Methods"
Journal of Marketing Research, Vol. I (May 1964), pp. 61,2.

Smith, T. M. F.
"Present Position and Potential Developments--Some Personal Views:
Sample Surveys"
Journal of the Royal Statistical Society, Series A, Part II (1984),
pp. 208-21.

Stephan, F. F.
"Advances in Survey Methods and Measurement Techniques"
Public Opinion Quarterly, Vol. 21, No. 1 (1957), pp. 79-90.

Stock, J. S. and Auerbach, B. K.
"How Not to do Consumer Research"
Journal of Marketing, Vol. 27 (July 1963), pp. 20-5.

Sudman, Seymour
"Sample Surveys"
Annual Review of Sociology, Vol. 2 (1976), pp. 107-20.

Swanick, Robert V.
"Shopper Surveys--A Credible Source of Service Quality"
Bank Marketing, Vol. 20 (July 1988), pp. 24-7.

Williams, T. R.
  "A Critique of Some Assumptions of Social Survey Research"
  Public Opinion Quarterly, Vol. 23 (Spring 1959), pp. 55-62.

Wilson, E. C.
  "Problems of Survey Research in Modernizing Areas"
  Public Opinion Quarterly, Vol. 22 (Fall 1958), pp. 230-4.

32.03 ---------- Theory Re: Subject Response Strategies

Ursic, Michael and Helgeson, James G.
  "Variability in Survey Questionnaire Completion Strategies: A
  Protocol Analysis"
  Journal of the Market Research Society, Vol. 31 (April 1989), pp.
  225-40.

32.04 ---------- Dual Frame Survey Design

Lepkowski, James M. and Groves, Robert M.
  "A Mean Squared Error Model for Dual Frame, Mixed Mode Survey Design"
  Journal of the American Statistical Association, Vol. 81 (December
  1986), pp. 930-7.

Traugott, Michael W., Groves, Robert M., and Lepkowski, James M.
  "Using Dual Frame Designs to Reduce Nonresponse in Telephone Surveys"
  Public Opinion Quarterly, Vol. 51 (Winter 1987), pp. 523-39.

32.05 ---------- Total Survey Error

Anderson, Ronald, Kasper, Judith, and Frankel, Martin R.
  "Total Survey Error: Bias and Random Error in Health Survey Estimates"
  The University of Chicago (1977), prepublication manuscript.

Assael, Henry and Keon, John
  "Nonsampling vs. Sampling Errors in Survey Research"
  Journal of Marketing, Vol. 46 (Spring 1982), pp. 114-23.

Brown, Rex V.
  "Evaluation of Total Survey Error"
  Journal of Marketing Research, Vol. IV (May 1967), pp. 117-27.

Brown, R. V.
  "Post Credence Analysis of a Sample Survey of British Officers"
  Harvard Business School (1966), unpublished paper.

Brown, R. V.
  "The Strategy of Market Research: A Formal Approach"
  Journal of Advertising Research, Vol. 4 (December 1964), pp. 34-9.

Brown, R. V.
  "Measuring Uncertainty in Business Investigation"
  Journal of Management Studies, Vol. 1 (September 1964), pp. 143-63.

Brown, R. V.
  "Credence Analysis, Part B--Some Market Research Applications"
  Cambridge University (1963), unpublished paper.

Brown, R. V.
  "Credence Analysis"
  Metra 2 (September 1963), pp. 361-83.

Brown, R. V. and Mayer, C. S.
  "Towards a Rationale of Non-Probability Sampling"
  Proceedings, Fall Conference, American Marketing Association (1965).

Keon, John
  "Measuring Total Survey Error: An Unbiased Estimate"
  Frontiers in Marketing Series
  New York University (1980), working paper.

32.06 ---------- Miscellaneous Errors in Survey Research

Artingstall, R. W.
  "Random Thoughts on Non-Sampling Error"
  European Research, Vol. 6 (November 1978), pp. 229-37.

Barrett, Francis D., Jr.
  "The CANIS Method of Reducing Bias in Survey Research"
  Journal of Marketing Research, Vol. IX (August 1972), pp. 329,30.

Benson, Purnell H.
  "Eliminating Consumer Biases in Survey Data by Balanced Tabulation"
  Journal of Marketing Research, Vol. I (November 1964), pp. 66-71.

Deming, W. E.
"On Errors in Surveys"
American Sociological Review, Vol. 9 (August 1944), pp. 359-69.

Sigelman, Lee and Presser, Stanley
"Measuring Public Support for the New Christian Right: The Perils of
Point Estimation"
Public Opinion Quarterly, Vol. 52 (Fall 1988), pp. 325-37.

Suchman, Edward A.
"An Analysis of Bias in Survey Research"
Public Opinion Quarterly, Vol. 26 (Spring 1962), pp. 102-11.

Tortolani, Ray
"Introducing Bias Intentionally Into Survey Techniques"
Journal of Marketing Research, Vol. II (February 1965), pp. 51-5.

Wiseman, Frederick
"Methodological Bias in Public Opinion Surveys"
Public Opinion Quarterly, Vol. 36 (Spring 1972), pp. 105-8.

32.07 ---------- Pretesting and Pilot Studies

Hunt, Shelby D., Sparkman, Richard M., Jr., and Wilcox, James B.
"The Pretest in Survey Research: Issues and Preliminary Findings"
Journal of Marketing Research, Vol. XIX (May 1982), pp. 269-73.

Sletto, Raymond F.
"Pretesting of Questionnaires"
American Sociological Review, Vol. 5 (April 1940), pp. 193-200.

Stubbs, Roger J.
"The Value of a Large Scale Pilot: A Case History"
European Research, Vol. 4 (July 1976), pp. 170-6.

32.08 ---------- Identification of Survey Respondents

Erdos, Paul L. and Regier, James
"Visible vs. Disguised Keying on Questionnaires"
Journal of Advertising Research, Vol. 17 (February 1977), pp. 13-8.

Kearney, Kathleen A., Hopkins, Ronald H., Mauss, Armand L., and
Weisheit, Ralph A.
"Self Generated Identification Codes for Anonymous Collection of
Longitudinal Questionnaire Data"
Public Opinion Quarterly, Vol. 48 (Spring 1984), pp. 370-8.

Ridgway, N. M. and Price, L. L.
"The Effects of Respondent Identification in a Mail Survey"
Proceedings, American Marketing Association Educators' Conference
(1982), pp. 410-3.

Stevens, R. E.
"Does Precoding Mail Questionnaires Affect Response Rates?"
Public Opinion Quarterly, Vol. 38, No. 4 (1974), pp. 621,2.

32.09 ---------- Unclassified (Survey Research - General)

Jones, D. Frank
"A Survey Technique to Measure Demand Under Various Pricing
Strategies"
Journal of Marketing, Vol. 39 (July 1975), pp. 75-7.

Kemsley, W. F. F.
"Designing a Budget Survey"
Applied Statistics, Vol. 8 (June 1959), pp. 114-23.

Mandell, Lewis, Katona, George, Morgan, James N., and Schmiedeskamp, Jay
Surveys of Consumers 1971-72
(Ann Arbor: Institute for Social Research, 1973), 335 pp.

Pearl, Robert
"Methodology of Consumer Expenditure Surveys"
Working Paper No. 27
(Washington, DC: U.S. Bureau of the Census, 1968).

33 ----------------------- POLLS AND POLLING -----------------------
      See also (sub)heading(s) 9.04, 32, 101.03.

33.01 ---------- Books Re: Polls and Polling

Asher, Herbert
    Polling and the Public: What Every Citizen Should Know
    (Washington, DC: CQ Press, 1988), 168 pp.

Bradburn, Norman M. and Sudman, Seymour
    Polls and Surveys: Understanding What They Tell Us
    (San Francisco: Jossey-Bass, Inc., 1988), 269 pp.

Roll, Charles W., Jr. and Cantril, Albert H.
    Polls: Their Use and Misuse in Politics
    (New York: Basic Books, Inc., 1972).

Watkins, Leslie and Worcester, Robert M.
    Private Opinions, Public Polls
    (London: Thames and Hudson, 1986), 207 pp.

Worcester, Robert M. (editor)
    Political Opinion Polling--A Transnational Look
    (London: Macmillan, 1983), 246 pp.

33.02 ---------- Theory Re: Polls and Polling

Advertising Research Foundation
    "ARF Position Paper 'Phony or Misleading Polls'"
    Journal of Advertising Research, Vol. 26 (December 1986/January
    1987), pp. RC3-RC8.

Altschuler, Bruce E.
    "Lyndon Johnson and the Public Polls"
    Public Opinion Quarterly, Vol. 50 (Fall 1986), pp. 285-99.

Brusati, Elio
    "Electoral Polls in Italy"
    European Research, Vol. 15 (August 1987), pp. 152-7.

Butler, David
    "Academics and Pollsters"
    Journal of the Market Research Society, Vol. 29 (October 1987), pp.
    381-4.

Collins, Martin
    "Lessons From the Polls"
    Proceedings, Market Research Society Conference (March 1988), pp.
    1-13.

Dowling, G. R. and Walsh, P. K.
    "Estimating and Reporting Confidence Intervals for Market and Opinion
    Research"
    European Research, Vol. 13 (July 1985), pp. 130-3.

England, Len
    "The Market Research Society Initiative"
    Journal of the Market Research Society, Vol. 29 (October 1987), pp.
    391-404.

ESOMAR
    International Code of Practice for the Publication of Public Opinion
    Poll Results and Guidelines to Its Interpretation
    (Amsterdam).

Grunewald, Armin
    "Opinion Polls and Public Policy"
    European Research, Vol. 8 (March 1980), pp. 51-6.

Hall, Dale, Dobson, Alan, Blackaby, David, Manning, Robert and
    Worcester, Robert M.
    "Robert Worcester and Marginal Reliability--A Note: The BBC's
    Election Polls"
    Journal of the Market Research Society, Vol. 30 (April 1988), pp.
    235-8.

Harvard Law Review
    "Public Opinion Surveys as Evidence: The Pollsters Go to Court"
    Vol. 56 (1953), pp. 505,6.

Hess, Theo A. and Weijtlandt, Arnold J.
    "Gallup: The Whole World is Our Market"
    European Research, Vol. 12 (October 1984), pp. 172-81.

Katz, D.
    "Survey Techniques and Polling Procedures as Methods in Social
    Science"
    Journal of Social Issues (1946).

Korobeinikov, Valery
    "Opinion Polls in the Soviet Union: Perestroika and the Public"
    European Research, Vol. 16 (August 1988), pp. 160-2.

Koschnick, Wolfgang J.
    "Opinion Polls, the Mass Media and the Political Environment"
    European Research, Vol. 8 (March 1980), pp. 57-63.

Marsh, C.
    "Back on the Bandwagon: The Effect of Opinion Polls on Public Opinion"
    British Journal of Political Science, Vol. 15, No. 1 (1984).

Marsh, Catherine and O'Brien, John
    "Opinion Bandwagons in Attitudes Towards the Common Market"
    Journal of the Market Research Society, Vol. 31 (July 1989), pp.
    295-305.

Mavros, Dimitri
    "The Dawning of Election Polls in Greece"
    European Research, Vol. 15 (August 1987), pp. 166-70

Nisihira, Sigeki
    "Japan: Recent Polling Problems"
    European Research, Vol. 15 (August 1987), pp. 171-3.

Noelle-Neumann, Elisabeth
    "Federal Republic of Germany: Election Forecasts and the Public"
    European Research, Vol. 15 (August 1987), pp. 162-5.

Rohme, Nils
    "A Worldwide Overview of National Restrictions on the Conduct and
    Release of Public Opinion Polls"
    European Research, Vol. 13 (January 1985), pp. 30-7.

Rudolf, Walter
    "Polls, the Press and the Law"
    ESOMAR Seminar on Opinion Polls (January 23-26, 1980), paper
    presentation.

Schaefer, Wolfgang
    "On a Code for Media Research"
    European Research, Vol. 14, No. 2 (1986), pp. 82-4.

Smith, Tom W.
    "The Art of Asking Questions 1936-1985"
    Public Opinion Quarterly, Vol. 51 (Winter 1987), pp. S95-108.

Sopariwala, Dorab
    "India: Election Polling in the World's Largest Democracy"
    European Research, Vol. 15 (August 1987), pp. 174-6.

Sudman, Seymour and Bradburn, Thomas M.
    "The Organisational Growth of Public Opinion Research in the United
    States"
    Public Opinion Quarterly, Vol. 51 (Winter 1987), pp. S67-78.

Taylor, Humphrey
    "The Influences and Effects of Opinion Polls"
    Journal of the Market Research Society, Vol. 16 (October 1974), pp.
    287-90.

Van Westendorp, Peter H.
    "Political Opinion Polling in the Netherlands: Defeats and Victories"
    European Research, Vol. 15 (August 1987), pp. 158-60.

Wilson, R.
    "The Uncertainty of Opinion Polls"
    New Scientist (April 26, 1979), pp. 251-3.

Worcester, Robert M.
    "The BBC's Election Polls"
    Journal of the Market Research Society, Vol. 30 (April 1988), pp.
    237,8.

Worcester, Robert M.
    "The Internationalisation of Public Opinion Research"
    Public Opinion Quarterly, Vol. 51 (Winter 1987), pp. S79-85.

Worcester, Robert M.
    "Political Opinion Polling in Great Britain: Past, Present and Future"
    European Research, Vol. 15 (August 1987), pp. 143-50.

Worcester, Robert M.
    "The History of Public Opinion Polls"
    ESOMAR Congress, Montreux (1987), pp. 419-30.

Worcester, Robert M.
    "History of Political Polls in Great Britain"
    Silver Jubilee Market Research Society Conference (1982), paper
    presentation.

33.03 ---------- Sampling Methods Related to Polling

    See also (sub)heading(s) 89, 107.

Bowden, Roger J.
  "Repeated Sampling in the Presence of Publication Effects"
  Journal of the American Statistical Association, Vol. 82 (June 1987),
  pp. 476-84.

Traugott, Michael W.
  "The Importance of Persistence in Respondent Selection for
  Pre-Election Surveys"
  Public Opinion Quarterly, Vol. 51 (Spring 1987), pp. 48-57.

33.04 ---------- Descriptions of Specific Polls

Adler, Kenneth P.
  "Voting for an American President II"
  European Research, Vol. 13 (April 1985), pp. 60-5.

Clemens, J.
  "The Telephone Poll Bogeyman: A Case Study in Election Paranoia"
  in Crewe, I. and Harrop, M. (editors)
  Political Communications: The General Election Campaign of 1983
  (Cambridge University Press, 1987).

Ellis, Katrina
  "The Range of 1987 Polling"
  Journal of the Market Research Society, Vol. 29 (October 1987), pp.
  429-34.

Hess, Theo A. and Weijtlandt, Arnold J.
  "Gallup: The Whole World is Our Market"
  European Research, Vol. 12 (October 1984), pp. 172-81.

Husbands, Christopher T.
  "The Telephone Study of Voting Intentions in the June 1987 General
  Election"
  Journal of the Market Research Society, Vol 29 (October 1987), pp.
  405-11.

Lipset, Seymour Martin
  "Voting for an American President I"
  European Research, Vol. 13 (April 1985), pp. 48-58.

Sudman, Seymour
  "The Network Polls: A Critical Review"
  Public Opinion Quarterly, Vol. 47 (Winter 1983), pp. 490-6.

Waller, Robert
  "The Harris/ITN Exit Poll--11 June 1987"
  Journal of the Market Research Society, Vol. 29 (October 1987), pp.
  419-28.

Walter, Debbie
  "Telephone Polls and the General Election"
  Journal of the Market Research Society, Vol. 29 (October 1987), pp.
  413-8.

33.05 ---------- Evaluations and Comparisons of Polls

Adler, Kenneth P.
  "Voting for an American President II: Differing Polling Methods Yield
  Varied Results"
  European Research, Vol. 13 (April 1985), pp. 60-5.

Borrelli, Stephen, Lockerbie, Brad, and Niemi, Richard G.
  "Why the Democrat-Republican Partisanship Gap Varies From Poll to
  Poll"
  Public Opinion Quarterly, Vol. 51 (Spring 1987), pp. 115-9.

Buchanan, William
  "Election Predictions: An Empirical Assessment"
  Public Opinion Quarterly, Vol. 50 (Summer 1986), pp. 222-7.

Crewe, I.
  "Improving but You Could do Better: A Report on the Media and the
  Polls in the 1979 General Election"
  in Harrop, M. and Worcester, R. (editors)
  Political Communication and the General Election of 1979
  (London: Macmillan, 1981).

Kohut, Andrew
  "Rating the Polls: The Views of Media Elites and the General Public"
  Public Opinion Quarterly, Vol. 50 (Spring 1986), pp. 1-10.

Lemert, James B.
  "Picking the Winners: Politicians vs. Voter Predictions of Two
  Controversial Ballot Measures"
  Public Opinion Quarterly, Vol. 50 (Summer 1986), pp. 208-21.

Roper, Burns W.
  "Evaluating Polls With Poll Data"
  Public Opinion Quarterly, Vol. 50 (Spring 1986), pp. 10-6.

Shamir, Jacob
  "Preelection Polls in Israel: Structural Constraints on Accuracy"
  Public Opinion Quarterly, Vol. 50 (Spring 1986), pp. 62-75.

34 --------------------- QUESTIONNAIRE DESIGN ----------------------
          See also (sub)heading(s) 37, 116, 117.

34.01 ---------- Books Re: Questionnaire Design

Belson, William A.
    The Design and Understanding of Survey Questions
    (Aldershot, EN: Gower Publishing Company, Ltd., 1981), 399 pp.

Berdie, Douglas R., Anderson, John F., and Niebuhr, Marsha A.
    Questionnaires: Design and Use, Second Edition
    (Metuchen, NJ: Scarecrow Press, 1987), 330 pp.

Bradburn, Norman M., Sudman, Seymour, and Associates
    Improving Interview Method and Questionnaire Design: Response Effects
    to Threatening Questions in Survey Research
    (San Francisco: Jossey-Bass, 1979).

Converse, Jean M. and Presser, Stanley
    Survey Questions: Handcrafting the Standardized Questionnaire
    (Beverly Hills, CA: Sage Publications, Inc., 1986).

Hogarth, Robin M. (editor)
    Question Framing and Response Consistency
    (San Francisco, CA: Jossey-Bass Inc., Publishers, 1982), 109 pp.

Labaw, Patricia
    Advanced Questionnaire Design
    (Cambridge, MA: Abt Books, 1981), 183 pp.

Lessler, Judith, Mitzel, H., Salter, William, and Tourangeau, Roger
    Cognitive Aspects of Questionnaire Design: Part A Report
    (Chicago: NORC, 1985).

Marketing Guidelines, Inc.
    Questionnaire Reference Manuals
    (Tulsa, OK: Marketing Guidelines, Inc.).

Oppenheim, A. N.
    Questionnaire Design and Attitude Measurement
    (New York: Basic Books, Inc., 1966), 298 pp.

Payne, Stanley L.
    The Art of Asking Questions
    (Princeton, NJ: Princeton University Press, 1951).

Platek, R., Pierre-Pierre, F. K., and Stevens, P.
    Development and Design of Survey Questionnaires
    (Ottawa: Statistics Canada), 117 pp.

Potter, Dale R., Sharpe, Kathryn M., Hindee, John C., and Clark, Roger
    N.
    Questionnaires for Research: An Annotated Bibliography on Design,
    Construction, and Use
    (Portland, OR: U.S. Department of Agriculture Forest Service, 1973),
    80 pp.

Schuman, H. and Presser, S.
    Questions and Answers in Attitude Surveys. Experiments on Question
    Form, Wording, and Context
    (New York: Academic Press, 1981), 370 pp.

Sheatsley, Paul B.
    Questionnaire Design and Wording
    (Chicago: National Opinion Research Center, 1969).

Sudman, Seymour and Bradburn, Norman M.
    Asking Questions
    (San Francisco: Jossey-Bass Publishers, 1982), 413 pp.

Tourangeau, Roger, Lessler, Judith, and Salter, William
    Cognitive Aspects of Questionnaire Design: Part B Report
    (Chicago: NORC, 1985).

34.02 ---------- Questionnaire Construction

Bishop, George F., Oldendick, Robert W., and Tuchfarber, Alfred J.
    "Effects of Filter Questions in Public Opinion Surveys"
    Public Opinion Quarterly, Vol. 47 (Winter 1983), pp. 528-46.

Borus, M. E.
    "Response Error and Questioning Technique in Earnings Surveys"
    Journal of the American Statistical Association, Vol. 65 (June 1970),
    pp. 566-75.

Brierly, P. W.
    "Ask a Silly Question"
    Statistical News, Vol. 30 (August 1975), pp. 20-4.

Clogg, Clifford C.
"Some Statistical Models for Analyzing Why Surveys Disagree"
in Turner, C. F. and Martin, E. (editors)
Surveying Subjective Phenomena, Volume 2
(New York: Russell Sage Foundation, 1984).

Converse, Jean M. and Schuman, Howard
"The Manner of Enquiry: An Analysis of Survey Question Form Across
Organisations and Over Time"
Panel on Survey Measurement of Subjective Phenomena
National Research Council (1981).

Crespi, I.
"Use of Scaling Techniques in Surveys"
Journal of Marketing, Vol. 25 (July 1961), pp. 69-72.

Elias, G.
"Self-Evaluation Questionnaires as Projective Measures of Personality"
Journal of Consulting Psychology, Vol. 15 (December 1951), pp.
496-500.

Gadel, M. S.
"The Relationship of Item Validity Shrinkage to Curvilinearity of
Response Distributions"
Educational and Psychological Measurement, Vol. 18 (Spring 1958), pp.
145-52.

Gallup, G.
"The Quintamensional Plan of Question Design"
Public Opinion Quarterly, Vol. 11 (Fall 1947), pp. 385-93.

Giles, W. F. and Field, H. S.
"Effects of Amount, Format, and Location of Demographic Information
on Questionnaire Return Rate and Response Bias of Sensitive and
Nonsensitive Items"
Personnel Psychology, Vol. 31 (August 1978), pp. 549-59.

Haque, Paul
"Good and Bad in Questionnaire Design"
Industrial Marketing, Vol. 12, Third Quarter (1987), pp. 161-70.

Hall, D. M.
"Built-In Reliability Checks for Questionnaires"
Journal of Farm Economics, Vol. 40 (February 1958), pp. 136-9.

Hartley, J., Davies, L., and Burnhill, P.
"Alternatives in the Typographic Design of Questionnaires"
Journal of Occupational Psychology, Vol. 50 (December 1977), pp.
299-304.

Herzog, A. R. and Bachman, J. G.
"Effective Questionnaire Length and Response Quality"
Public Opinion Quarterly, Vol. 45 (Winter 1981), pp. 549-59.

Jaffe, Eugene D.
"How to Improve Questionnaire Design"
European Research, Vol. 11 (January 1983), pp. 31-4.

Jaffe, Eugene D. and Nebenzahl, Israel D.
"Alternative Questionnaire Formats for Country Image Studies"
Journal of Marketing Research, Vol. XXI (November 1984), pp. 463-71.

Kinard, A. J.
"Randomizing Error in Multiple-Choice Questions"
Journal of Marketing, Vol. 19 (January 1955), pp. 260-3.

Kornhauser, Arthur and Sheatsley, Paul B.
"Questionnaire Construction and Interview Procedure"
in Sellitz, M., Jahoda, M. Deutsch, and Cook, S. W. (editors)
Research Methods in Social Relations
(New York: Henry Holt and Co., 1959), pp. 546-87.

Laurent, A.
"Effects of Question Length on Reporting Behaviour in the Survey
Interview"
Journal of the American Statistical Association, Vol. 67 (June 1972),
pp. 298-305.

Levine, Daniel B. and Miller, Herman P.
Response Variation Encountered With Different Questionnaire Forms
(U.S. Department of Agriculture, Marketing Research Report No. 163,
1957).

Litwak, E.
"A Classification of Biased Questions"
American Journal of Sociology, Vol. 62 (September 1956), pp. 182-6.

Major, Brenda N., Jacoby, Jacob, and Sheluga, David A.
   "Questionnaire Research on Questionnaire Construction: The Type and
   Positioning of Response Blanks"
   Purdue Papers in Consumer Psychology, No. 166 (1976).

Mandell, Lewis and Lundsten, Norman L.
   "Some Insight Into the Underreporting of Financial Data by Sample
   Survey Respondents"
   Journal of Marketing Research, Vol. XV (May 1978), pp. 294-9.

Mayer, Charles S. and Piper, Cindy
   "A Note on the Importance of Layout in Self-Administered
   Questionnaires"
   Journal of Marketing Research, Vol. XIX (August 1982), pp. 390,1.

Metzner, C. A.
   "An Application of Scaling to Questionnaire Construction"
   Journal of the American Statistical Association, Vol. 45 (March
   1950), pp. 112-8.

Miniard, Paul W., Obermiller, Carl, and Page, Thomas J., Jr.
   "A Further Assessment of Measurement Influences on the
   Intention-Behavior Relationship"
   Journal of Marketing Research, Vol. XX (May 1983), pp. 206-12.

Morton-Williams, J.
   "The Use of Verbal Interaction Coding for Evaluating a Questionnaire"
   Quality and Quantity, Vol. 13 (1979), pp. 59-75.

Morton-Williams, J.
   "Questionnaire Design"
   in Worcester, R. M. (editor)
   Consumer Market Research Handbook
   (McGraw-Hill, 1972).

Nixon, J. E.
   "The Mechanics of Questionnaire Construction"
   Journal of Educational Research, Vol. 47 (March 1954), pp. 481-7.

O'Brien, John
   "How Do Market Researchers Ask Questions?"
   Journal of the Market Research Society, Vol. 26 (April 1984), pp.
   93-107.

Payne, S. L.
   "Thoughts About Meaningless Questions"
   Public Opinion Quarterly, Vol. 14 (Winter 1950-51), pp. 687-96.

Petty, Richard E., Rennier, Greg A., and Cacioppo, John T.
   "Assertion Versus Interrogation Format in Opinion Surveys: Questions
   Enhance Thoughtful Responding"
   Public Opinion Quarterly, Vol. 51 (Winter 1987), pp. 481-94.

Poe, Gail S., Seeman, Isadore, McLaughlin, Joseph, Mehl, Eric, and
   Dietz, Michael
   "'Don't Know' Boxes in Factual Questions in a Mail Questionnaire:
   Effects on Level and Quality of Response"
   Public Opinion Quarterly, Vol. 52 (Summer 1988), pp. 212-22.

Politz, A.
   "Questionnaire Validity Through the Opinion-Forming Question"
   Journal of Psychology, Vol. 36 (July 1953), pp. 11-6.

Reagan, Barbara B.
   Condensed vs. Detailed Schedule for Collection of Family Expenditure
   Data
   (U.S. Department of Agriculture, Agricural Research Service, 1954).

Rothwell, N. D.
   "Results of Comparisons Made in 1962 SORAR Between Two Questionnaires"
   U.S. Bureau of the Census (1963), unpublished memorandum.

Rothwell, Naomi D. and Rustmeyer, Anitra M.
   "Studies of Census Mail Questionnaires"
   Journal of Marketing Research, Vol. XVI (August 1979), pp. 401-9.

Schuman, Howard and Duncan, Otis Dudley
   "Questions About Attitude Survey Questions"
   in Costner, Herbert L. (editor)
   Sociological Methodology 1973-1974
   (San Francisco: Jossey-Bass, 1974), pp. 232-51.

Spagna, Gregory J.
   "Questionnaires: Which Approach Do You Use?"
   Journal of Advertising Research, Vol. 24 (February/March 1984), pp.
   67-70.

Stem, Donald E., Jr., Lamb, Charles W., Jr., and MacLachlan, Douglas L.
"Remote Versus Adjacent Scale Questionnaire Designs"
Journal of the Market Research Society, Vol. 20 (January 1978), pp.
3-13.

Stember, H. and Hyman, H.
"How Interviewer Effects Operate Through Question Form"
International Journal of Opinion and Attitude Research, Vol. 3
(Winter 1949-50), pp. 493-512.

Sykes, Wendy and Collins, Martin
"A Classification of Questions by Form and Function"
SCPR Working Paper (November 1981).

U.S. National Center for Health Statistics
Measurement of Personal Health Expenditures
Series 2, No. 2, U.S. Department of Health, Education, and Welfare
(1963).

Voas, R. B.
"A Procedure for Reducing the Effects of Slanting Questionnaire
Responses Toward Social Acceptability"
Educational and Psychological Measurement, Vol. 18 (Summer 1958), pp.
337-45.

Westfall, R. L., Boyd, H. W., and Campbell, D. T.
"The Use of Structured Techniques in Motivation Research"
Journal of Marketing, Vol. 22 (October 1957), pp. 134-9.

Wolfe, D. F.
"A New Questionnaire Design"
Journal of Marketing, Vol. 21 (October 1956), pp. 186-90.

34.03 ---------- Wording of Questions

See also (sub)heading(s) 28.04, 34.07.

Barnes, James H., Jr. and Dotson, Michael J.
"The Effect of Mixed Grammar Chains on Response to Survey Questions"
Journal of Marketing Research, Vol. XXVI (November 1989), pp. 468-72.

Belson, William A.
"Respondent Understanding of Survey Questions"
Polls, Vol. 3, No. 4 (1968), pp. 1-13.

Buchanan, Bruce and Morrison, Donald G.
"Asking Recency Questions"
New York University (1985), working paper.

Drayton, Leslie E.
"Bias Arising in Wording Consumer Questionnaires"
Journal of Marketing, Vol. 19 (1954), pp. 140-5.

Duncan, Otis D. and Schuman, Howard
"Effects of Question Wording and Context: An Experiment With
Religious Indicators"
Journal of the American Statistical Association, Vol. 75 (June 1980),
pp. 269-75.

Hippler, Hans J. and Schwartz, Norbert
"Not Forbidding Isn't Allowing: The Cognitive Basis of the
Forbid-Allow Asymmetry"
Public Opinion Quarterly, Vol. 50 (Spring 1986), pp. 87-96.

Hitlin, Robert
"A Research Note on Question Wording and Stability of Response"
Social Science Research, Vol. 5 (March 1976), pp. 39-41.

Hubbard, A. W.
"Phrasing Questions"
Journal of Marketing, Vol. 15 (July 1950), pp. 48-56.

Kalton, Graham, Collins, Martin A., and Brook, Lindsay L.
"Experiments in Wording Opinion Questions"
Applied Statistics, Vol. 27 (1978), pp. 149-61.

Molenaar, N. J.
"Response Effects of Formal Characteristics of Questions"
in Dijkstra, W. and Van der Zouwen, J. (editors)
Response Behavior in the Survey Interview
(Academic Press, 1982).

Noelle-Neumann, Elisabeth
"Wanted: Rules for Wording Structured Questionnaires"
Public Opinion Quarterly, Vol. 34 (Summer 1970), pp. 191-201.

Noelle-Neumann, Elisabeth and Worcester, Bob
    "International Opinion Research: How to Phrase Your Questions on
    Controversial Topics"
    European Research, Vol. 12 (July 1984), pp. 124-31.

O'Brien, John
    "Two Answers are Better Than One"
    Journal of the Market Research Society, Vol. 29 (July 1987), pp.
    223-40.

O'Brien, John
    "How do Market Researchers Ask Questions?"
    Journal of the Market Research Society, Vol. 26, No. 2 (1984), pp.
    93-107.

Petty, Richard E., Rennier, Greg A., and Cacioppo, John T.
    "Assertion Versus Interrogation Format in Opinion Surveys"
    Public Opinion Quarterly, Vol. 51 (Winter 1987), pp. 481-94.

Presser, Stanley and Schuman, Howard
    "Question Wording as an Independent Variable in Survey Analysis: A
    First Report"
    Proceedings, Social Statistics Section, American Statistical
    Association (1975), pp. 16-25.

Roper, Elmo
    "Wording Questions for the Polls"
    Public Opinion Quarterly, Vol. 4 (March 1940), p. 129.

Rosenstone, Steven J., Hansen, John Mark, and Kinder, Donald R.
    "Measuring Change in Personal Economic Well-Being"
    Public Opinion Quarterly, Vol. 50 (Summer 1986), pp. 176-92.

Rugg, W. Donald
    "Experiments in Wording Questions: II"
    Public Opinion Quarterly (March 1941), pp. 91,2.

Rugg, W. Donald and Cantril, Hadley
    "The Wording of Questions"
    in Cantril, H. et al. (editors)
    Gauging Public Opinion
    (Princeton, NJ: Princton University Press, 1947).

Rugg, W. Donald and Cantril, Hadley
    "The Wording of Questions in Public Opinion Polls"
    Journal of Abnormal and Social Psychology, Vol. 37 (October 1942),
    pp. 469-95.

Smith, Tom W.
    "That Which We Call Welfare by any Other Name Would Smell Sweeter: An
    Analysis of the Impact of Question Wording on Response Patt erns"
    Public Opinion Quarterly, Vol. 51 (Spring 1987), pp. 77-83.

Sorensen, Aage B.
    "Estimating Rates From Retrospective Questions"
    in Heise, David (editor)
    Sociological Methodology 1977
    (San Francisco: Jossey-Bass, 1977).

34.04 ---------- Instructions

Kamen, Joseph M. and Eindhoven, Jan
    "Instructions Affecting Food Preferences"
    Journal of Advertising Research, Vol. 3 (June 1963), pp. 35-8.

Smith, Edward M. and Mason, Joseph Barry
    "The Influence of Instructions on Respondent Error"
    Journal of Marketing Research, Vol. VII (May 1970), pp. 254,5.

34.05 ---------- Theory Re: Open-Ended Questions

        See also (sub)heading(s) 46.01, 86.05, 132.02.

Belson, William and Duncan, Judith A.
    "A Comparison of the Check List and Open Response Questioning System,
    Part 2"
    Applied Statistics, Vol. 11 (June 1962), pp. 120-32.

Clanton, Earl S., III
    "Effects of Alternative Positioning of Open-Ended Questions in
    Multiple-Choice Questionnaires"
    Journal of Applied Psychology, Vol. 59 (1974), pp. 776-8.

Collins, Martin
    "A Comparative Study of Field and Office Coding"
    Proceedings, Section on Survey Research Methods, American Statistical
    Association (1983).

Collins, Martin and Countenay, G.
    "The Effect of Question Form on Survey Data"
    Market Research Society Conference, Brighton (1983).

Converse, Jean M.
    "Strong Arguments and Weak Evidence: The Open/Closed Questioning
    Controversy of the 1940's"
    Public Opinion Quarterly, Vol. 48 (Spring 1984), pp. 267-82.

Dohrenwend, Barbara S.
    "Some Effects of Open and Closed Questions on Respondents' Answers"
    Human Organization, Vol. 24 (Summer 1965), pp. 175-84.

Falthzik, A. M. and Carroll, S. J.
    "Rate of Return for Close vs. Open-Ended Questions in a Mail Survey
    of Industrial Organizations"
    Psychological Reports, Vol. 29 (1971), pp. 1121,2.

Geer, John G.
    "What do Open-Ended Questions Measure?"
    Public Opinion Quarterly, Vol. 52 (Fall 1988), pp. 365-71.

Hodges, Bob S. and Cosse, Thomas J.
    "Computer Code, Edit Open-Ended Questions to Improve Survey Accuracy
    and Efficiency"
    Marketing News (January 21, 1983), p. 10.

Payne, S. L.
    "Are Open-Ended Questions Worth the Effort?"
    Journal of Marketing Research, Vol. II (November 1965), pp. 417,8.

Schuman, H. and Presser, S.
    "The Open and Closed Question"
    American Sociological Review, Vol. 44 (1979), pp. 692-712.

34.06 ---------- Evaluations and Comparisons of Question Types

    See also (sub)heading(s) 60.

Agostini, Jean-Michel
    "The Case for Direct Questions on Reading Habits"
    Journal of Advertising Research, Vol. 4 (June 1964), pp. 27-33.

Belkin, Marvin and Lieberman, Seymour
    "Effect of Question Wording on Response Distribution"
    Journal of Marketing Research, Vol. IV (August 1967), pp. 312,3.

Belson, William and Duncan, Judith A.
    "A Comparison of the Check List and Open Response Questioning System,
    Part 2"
    Applied Statistics, Vol. 11 (June 1962), pp. 120-32.

Blankenship, A. B.
    "The Influence of the Question Form Upon the Response in a Public
    Opinion Poll"
    Psychological Record, Vol. 3 (1940), pp. 345-422.

Buchanan, Bruce and Morrison, Donald G.
    "Sampling Properties of Rate Questions With Implications for Survey
    Research"
    Marketing Science, Vol. 6 (Summer 1987), pp. 286-98.

Converse, Jean M.
    "Strong Arguments and Weak Evidence: The Open/Closed Questioning
    Controversy of the 1940's"
    Public Opinion Quarterly, Vol. 48 (Spring 1984), pp. 267-82.

Dohrenwend, Barbara S.
    "Some Effects of Open and Closed Questions on Respondents' Answers"
    Human Organization, Vol. 24 (Summer 1965), pp. 175-84.

Ghiselli, E. E.
    "All or None Versus Graded Response Questionnaires"
    Journal of Applied Psychology, Vol. 23 (June 1939), pp. 405-13.

NOP Market Research Limited
    "The Effect of Alternative Wording on the Outcome of the EEC
    Referendum"
    NOP/8349 (1975).

Peterson, Robert A.
    "Asking the Age Question: A Research Note"
    Public Opinion Quarterly, Vol. 48 (Spring 1984), pp. 379-83.

Schuman, H.
    "The Random Probe: A Technique for Evaluating the Validity of Closed
    Questions"
    American Sociological Review, Vol. 31 (April 1966), pp. 218-22.

Sudman, Seymour, Finn, Adam, and Lannon, Linda
"The Use of Bounded Recall Procedures in Single Interviews"
Public Opinion Quarterly, Vol. 48 (Summer 1984), pp. 520-4.

U.S. Department of Agriculture
"Response Variations Encountered With Different Questionnaire Forms"
Marketing Research Report No. 163 (1957).

34.07 ---------- Language and Literacy Issues

        See also (sub)heading(s) 28.04.

Billins, Peter
"Research or R'search"
Journal of the Market Research Society, Vol. 26 (April 1984), pp.
379-83.

Robinson, Peter
"Language in Data Collection: Difficulties With Diversity"
Journal of the Market Research Society, Vol. 26 (April 1984), pp.
159-69.

Shephard, Peter
"Literacy and Numeracy and Their Implications for Survey
Research--Evidence From the National Child Development Study"
Journal of the Market Research Society, Vol. 26 (April 1984), pp.
147-58.

Webb, Norman
"Levels of Adult Numeracy"
Journal of the Market Research Society, Vol. 26 (April 1984), pp.
129-39.

34.08 ---------- Question Order or Sequential Position Effects

        See also (sub)heading(s) 61.02, 61.05, 116.

Becker, S. L.
"Why an Order Effect"
Public Opinion Quarterly, Vol. 18 (Fall 1954), pp. 271-8.

Bishop, George F., Oldendick, Robert W., and Tuchfarber, Alfred
"What Must My Interest in Politics be if I Just Told You 'I Don't
Know'?"
Public Opinion Quarterly, Vol. 48 (Summer 1984), pp. 510-9.

Blunch, Niels J.
"Position Bias in Multiple-Choice Questions"
Journal of Marketing Research, Vol. XXI (May 1984), pp. 216-20.

Bradburn, Norman M. and Mason, William M.
"The Effect of Question Order on Responses"
Journal of Marketing Research, Vol. I (November 1964), pp. 57-61.

Carp, Frances M.
"Position Effects on Interview Responses"
Journal of Gerontology, Vol. 29, No. 5 (1974), pp. 581-7.

Clancy, K. J. and Wachsler, R. A.
"Positional Effects in Shared-Cost Surveys"
Public Opinion Quarterly, Vol. 35 (Summer 1972), pp. 258-65.

Clanton, Earl S., III
"Effects of Alternative Positioning of Open-Ended Questions in
Multiple-Choice Questionnaires"
Journal of Applied Psychology, Vol. 59 (1974), pp. 776-8.

Crespi, Irving and Morris, Dwight
"Question Order Effect and the Measurement of Candidate Preference in
the 1982 Connecticut Elections"
Public Opinion Quarterly, Vol. 48 (Fall 1984), pp. 578-91.

Dickinson, John R. and Kirzner, Eric
"A Secondary Order Effect on Questionnaire Item Omissions"
in Laroche, Michel (editor)
Proceedings, Administrative Sciences Association of Canada (1982),
pp. 49-54.

Duncan, Otis Dudley and Schuman, Howard
"Effects of Question Wording and Context: An Experiment With
Religious Indicators"
Journal of the American Statistical Association, Vol. 75 (June 1980),
pp. 269-75.

Ferber, R.
"Order Bias in a Mail Survey"
Journal of Marketing, Vol. 17 (October 1952), pp. 171-8.

Gross, Edwin J.
  "The Effect of Question Sequence on Measures of Buying Interest"
  Journal of Advertising Research, Vol. 4 (September 1964), pp. 40,1.

Hyman, H. H. and Sheatsley, P. B.
  "The Current Status of American Public Opinion"
  in Payne, John C. (editor)
  The Teaching of Contemporary Affairs: Twenty-First Yearbook of the
  National Council for the Social Studies
  (Washington: National Council for the Social Studies, 1950).

Jain, A. K. and Pinson, C.
  "The Effect of Order of Presentation of Similarity Judgements on
  Multidimensional Scaling Results: An Empirical Examination"
  Journal of Marketing Research, Vol. XIII (November 1976), pp. 435-9.

Johnson, W. Russell, Sieveking, Nicholas A., and Clanton, Earl S., III
  "Effects of Alternative Positioning of Open-Ended Questions in
  Multiple-Choice Questionnaires"
  Journal of Applied Psychology, Vol. 59 (December 1974), pp. 776-8.

Kelley, Jonathan and McAllister, Ian
  "Ballot Paper Cues and the Vote in Australia and Britain: Alphabetic
  Voting, Sex and Title"
  Public Opinion Quarterly, Vol. 48 (Summer 1984), pp. 452-66.

Kraut, Allen I., Wolfson, Alan D., and Rothenberg, Alan
  "Some Effects of Position on Opinion Survey Items"
  Journal of Applied Psychology, Vol. 60 (December 1975) pp. 774-6.

Krosnick, Jon A. and Alwin, Duane F.
  "An Evaluation of a Cognitive Theory of Response-Order Effects in
  Survey Measurement"
  Public Opinion Quarterly, Vol. 51 (Summer 1987), pp. 201-19.

Major, Brenda N., Jacoby, Jacob, and Sheluga, David A.
  "Questionnaire Research on Questionnaire Construction: The Type and
  Positioning of Response Blanks"
  Purdue Papers in Consumer Psychology, No. 166 (1976).

Mathews, C. O.
  "The Effect of Position of Printed Response Words Upon Children's
  Answers to Two-Response Types of Tests"
  Journal of Educational Psychology, Vol. 18 (1927), pp. 445-57.

McClendon, McKee J. and O'Brien, David J.
  "Question-Order Effects on the Determinants of Subjective Well-Being"
  Public Opinion Quarterly, Vol. 52 (Fall 1988), pp. 351-64.

Metzner, H. and Mann, F.
  "Effects of Grouping Related Questions in Questionnaires"
  Public Opinion Quarterly, Vol. 17 (Spring 1953), pp. 136-41.

Nakamura, C. Y.
  "Salience of Norms and Order of Questionnaire Items: Their Effect on
  Responses to the Items"
  Journal of Abnormal and Social Psychology, Vol. 59 (July 1959), pp.
  139-42.

National Opinion Research Center
  "Nation-Wide Attitudes on Occupations: Preliminary Report, The Social
  Status of Ninety Occupations"
  (Denver, Co: University of Denver, March 1947), mimeographed.

National Opinion Research Center
  "Placement of Questions on the Ballot"
  (Denver, CO: University of Denver, May 1946), unpublished memorandum.

O'Brien, John
  "Two Answers are Better Than One"
  Journal of the Market Research Society, Vol. 29 (July 1987), pp.
  223-40.

Perreault, William D., Jr.
  "Controlling Order-Effect Bias"
  Public Opinion Quarterly, Vol. XXXIX (Winter 1975-76), pp. 544-51.

Sayre, Jeanette
  "A Comparison of Three Indices of Attitude Toward Radio Advertising"
  Journal of Applied Psychology, Vol. 23 (1939).

Schroder, Susanne
  "Towards a Theory of How People Answer Questions"
  European Research, Vol. 13 (April 1985), pp. 82-90.

Schuman, Howard and Presser, Stanley
  "Question Order and Response Order"
  in Questions and Answers in Attitude Surveys
  (New York: 1981), pp. 23-77.

Schuman, Howard, Presser, Stanley, and Ludwig, Jacob
  "Context Effects on Survey Responses to Questions About Abortion"
  Public Opinion Quarterly, Vol. 45 (1981), pp. 216-23.

Sigelman, Lee
  "Question Order Effects on Presidential Popularity"
  Public Opinion Quarterly, Vol. 45 (1981), pp. 199-207.

Smith, Tom W.
  "Conditional Order Effects"
  GSS Technical Report Number 33
  (Chicago: NORC, 1982).

Sudman, Seymour and Bradburn, Norman M.
  "Position of Question and Deliberate Bias or Deception"
  in Sudman, Seymour and Bradburn, Norman M.
  Response Effects in Surveys: A Review and Synthesis
  (Chicago: Aldine Publishing, 1974), pp. 33-5.

Trussell, R. E. and Elinson, Jack
  Chronic Illness in a Rural Area: The Hunterdon Study
  (Cambridge, MA: Harvard University Press, 1959).

Willick, D. H. and Ashley, R. K.
  "Survey Question Order and the Political Party Preferences of College
  Students and Their Parents"
  Public Opinion Quarterly, Vol. 35 (1971), pp. 189-99.

34.09 ---------- Standardized Coding Guidelines

        See also (sub)heading(s) 132.02.

Adler, Franz
  "Operational Definitions in Sociology"
  American Journal of Sociology, Vol. 52 (March 1947), pp. 438-44.

Brewer, Richard I.
  "A Note on the Changing Status of the Registrar General's
  Classification of Occupations"
  British Journal of Sociology, Vol. XXXVII (March 1986), pp. 131-40.

Demby, Emanuel H.
  "ESOMAR Urges Changes in Reporting Demographics, Issues Worldwide
  Report"
  Marketing News, Vol. 24 (January 8, 1990), pp.24,5.

Eckhardt, Kenneth W. and Wenger, Dennis E.
  "Respondent Coding of Occupation"
  Public Opinion Quarterly, Vol. 39 (Summer 1975), pp. 246-54.

Elkins, David J. and Hall, Jacqueline
  "The Standardization of Socio-Demographic Data in Canadian Social
  Surveys"
  in The Canada Council
  Survey Research: Report of the Consultative Group on Survey Research
  (Ottawa: The Canada Council, 1976), 110 pp.

ESOMAR Committee Report
  "Harmonization of Demographics"
  European Research, Vol. 14, No. 3 (1986), pp. 152-5.

ESOMAR Working Party
  "A Step Forward in International Research: Harmonisation of
  Demographics for Easier International Comparisons"
  European Research, Vol. 12 (October 1984), pp. 182-9.

Green, Lawrence W.
  "Manual for Scoring Socioeconomic Status for Research on Health
  Behavior"
  Public Health Reports, Vol. 85 (September 1970), pp. 815-27.

Gross, E.
  "The Occupational Variable as a Research Category"
  American Sociological Review, Vol. 24 (October 1959), pp. 640-9.

Market Research Society
  Guide to Good Coding Practice
  (London: Market Research Society, 1983), 23 pp.

Market Research Society
  Standardised Questions
  (London: Market Research Society, 1972).

Morrisey, Elizabeth R.
  "Sources of Error in the Coding of Questionnaire Data"
  Sociological Methods and Research, Vol. 3 (November 1974), pp. 209-32.

Nemanich, Dorothy and O'Rourke, Diane
  A Manual for the Coding of Survey Data
  (Dubuque, IA: Kendall/Hunt Publishing Co., 1975), 50 pp.

Social Sciences Research Council
  Basic Background Items for U.S. Household Surveys
  (New York: Social Sciences Research Council, 1975).

Statistics Canada
  Social Concepts Directory for Statistical Surveys, First Edition
  (Ottawa: Statistics Canada, 1977).

Statistics Canada
  Dictionary of the 1971 Census Terms
  (Ottawa: Statistics Canada, 1972), Cat. No. 12-540.

Szreter, Simon R. S.
  "The Genesis of the Registrar-General's Social Classification of
  Occupations"
  British Journal of Sociology, Vol. XXXV (December 1984), pp. 522-46.

Taylor, D. Garth
  "The Accuracy of Respondent Coded Occupation"
  Public Opinion Quarterly, Vol. 40 (Summer 1976), pp. 245-55.

U.S. Department of Commerce
  Standard Occupational Classification Manual
  (Washington, DC: U.S. Government Printing Office, 1977).

Van Dusen, Roxann A. and Zill, Nicholas
  Basic Items for U.S. Household Surveys
  (Washington, DC: Center for Coordination of Research on Social
  Indicators, Social Science Research Council, 1975), 63 pp.

Weilbacher, William M.
  "Standard Classification of Consumer Characteristics"
  Journal of Marketing, Vol. 31 (January 1967), pp. 27-31.

34.10 ---------- Computer Assisted Questionnaire Construction

        See also (sub)heading(s) 38.05, 73, 76.06, 76.07, 88.

East, Robert
  Behavior Prediction Software
  (Kingston, England: Kingston Polytechnic, 1985).

Green, Paul E., Kedia, Pradeep K., and Nikhil, Rishiyur S.
  Electronic Questionnaire Design and Analysis With CAPPA
  (Palo Alto, CA: The Scientific Press, 1985), 206 pp.

Jackling, P.
  "Computer Assisted Questionnaire Design: The Real Breakthrough"
  in Are Interviewers Obsolete? Drastic Changes in Data Collection and
  Data Presentation
  (Amsterdam: ESOMAR, 1984).

Johnson, Richard M.
  Ci2 System
  (Ketchum, ID: Sawtooth Software, Inc., 1985), 253 pp.

Sawtooth Software, Incorporated
  ACA System for Adaptive Conjoint Analysis
  (Ketchum, ID: Sawtooth Software, Inc., 1986).

34.11 ---------- Unclassified (Questionnaire Design)

Alderfer, C. P. and Brown, L. D.
  "Designing an Emphatic Questionnaire for Organizational Research"
  Journal of Applied Psychology, Vol. 56 (December 1972), pp. 456-60.

Barker, R. F. and Blankenship, A. B.
  "The Manager's Guide to Survey Questionnaire Evaluation"
  Journal of the Market Research Society, Vol. 17 (October 1975), pp.
  233-41.

Brown, R. V.
  "Just How Credible are Your Research Estimates?"
  Journal of Marketing, Vol. 33 (July 1969), pp. 46-50.

Herriot, Roger A.
  "Collecting Income Data on Sample Surveys: Evidence From Split-Panel
  Studies"
  Journal of Marketing Research, Vol. XIV (August 1977), pp. 322-9.

Keane, John G.
  "Low Cost, High Return Mail Surveys"
  Journal of Advertising Research, Vol. 3 (September 1963), pp. 28-30.

Marketing Guidelines, Inc.
  The Solution Prober
  (Tulsa, OK: Marketing Guidelines, Inc.).

Petry, Glenn H. and Quackenbush, Stanley F.
  "The Conservation of the Questionnaire as a Research Resource"
  Business Horizons, Vol. 17 (August 1974), pp.43-7.

U.S. Department of Commerce, Office of Business Economics
  "Development of National Income Measures"
  Supplement to Survey of Current Business
  (Washington, DC: 1954).

35 -------------- COLLECTION OF SENSITIVE INFORMATION ----------------
        See also (sub)heading(s) 36, 116, 116.14, 117.

35.01 ---------- Topical Areas of Sensitive Information

Blair, Ed, Sudman, Seymour, Bradburn, Norman M., and Stocking, Carol
    "How to Ask Questions About Drinking and Sex: Response Effects in
    Measuring Consumer Behavior"
    Journal of Marketing Research, Vol. XIV (August 1977), pp. 316-21.

Boruch, Robert F.
    "Maintaining Confidentiality in Educational Research: A Systematic
    Analysis"
    American Psychologist, Vol. 26 (1971), pp. 413-30.

Clark, Alexander L. and Wallin, Paul
    "The Accuracy of Husbands' and Wives' Reports of Frequency of Martial
    Coitus"
    Population Studies, Vol. 18 (November 1964), pp. 165-73.

Clark, John P. and Tifft, Larry L.
    "Polygraph and Interview Validation of Self-Reported Deviant
    Behaviour"
    American Sociological Review, Vol. 31 (August 1966), pp. 516-23.

David, Martin
    "The Validity of Income Reported by a Sample of Families Who Received
    Welfare Assistance During 1959"
    Journal of the American Statistical Association, Vol. 57 (September
    1962), pp. 680-5.

Delamater, John and MacCorquodale, Patricia
    "The Effects of Interview Schedule Variations on Reported Sexual
    Behaviour"
    Sociological Methods and Research, Vol. 4 (November 1975), pp. 215-36.

Ellis, Albert
    "Questionnaire Versus Interview Methods in the Study of Human Love
    Relationships"
    American Sociological Review, Vol. 12 (August 1947), pp. 541-53.

Johnson, T. P., Houghland, J. G., Jr., and Clayton, R. R.
    "Obtaining Reports of Sensitive Behavior: A Comparison of Substance
    Use Reports From Telephone and Face to Face Interviews"
    Social Science Quarterly, Vol. 70 (March 1989).

Johnson, Weldon T. and Delamater, John D.
    "Response Effects in Sex Surveys"
    Public Opinion Quarterly, Vol. 40 (Summer 1976), pp. 165-81.

Knudson, Dean O., Pope, Hallowell, and Irish, Donald P.
    "Response Differences to Questions on Sexual Standards: An Interview
    Questionnaire Comparison"
    Public Opinion Quarterly, Vol. 31 (Summer 1967), pp. 290-7.

Levinger, George
    "Systematic Distortion in Spouses' Reports of Preferred and Actual
    Sexual Behavior"
    Sociometry, Vol. 29 (September 1966), pp. 291-9.

Malvin, Janet H. and Moskowitz, Joel M.
    "Anonymous Versus Identifiable Self-Reports of Adolescent Drug
    Attitudes, Intentions and Use"
    Public Opinion Quarterly, Vol. 47 (Winter 1983), pp. 557-66.

Mandell, Lewis and Lundsten, Norman L.
    "Some Insight Into the Underreporting of Financial Data by Sample
    Survey Respondents"
    Journal of Marketing Research, Vol. XV (May 1978), pp. 294-9.

McCourt, Kathleen and Taylor, D. Garth
    "Determining Religious Affiliation Through Survey Research: A
    Methodological Note"
    Public Opinion Quarterly, Vol. 4 (Spring 1975), pp. 124-7.

Mensch, Barbara S. and Kandel, Denise B.
    "Under-Reporting of Substances Use in a National Longitudinal Youth
    Cohort"
    Public Opinion Quarterly, Vol. 52 (Spring 1988), pp. 100-24.

Mudd, Emily H., Stein, Marvin, and Mitchell, Howard E.
    "Paired Reports of Sexual Behavior of Husbands and Wives in
    Conflicted Marriages"
    Comprehensive Psychiatry, Vol. 2 (June 1961), pp. 149-56.

Mulholland, Heather
    "Advertising Home Pregnancy Tests: A Case for Sensitive Research"
    European Research, Vol. 15 (November 1987), pp. 242-7.

Peterson, Robert A.
    "Asking the Age Question: A Research Note"
    Public Opinion Quarterly, Vol. 48 (Spring 1984), pp. 379-83.

Poti, S. J., Chakraborti, B., and Malaker, C. R.
    "Reliability of Data Relating Contraceptive Practices"
    in Kiser, Clyde V. (editor)
    Research in Family Planning
    (Princeton, NJ: Princeton University Press, 1962), pp. 51-65.

Wallin, Paul and Clark, Alexander
    "Cultural Norms and Husbands' and Wives' Reports of Their Marital
    Partners' Preferred Frequency of Coitus Relative to Their Own"
    Sociometry, Vol. 21 (September 1958), pp. 247-54.

Weigel, Russell H., Hessing, Dick J., and Elffers, Henk
    "Tax Evasion Research: A Critical Appraisal and Theoretical Model"
    Journal of Economic Psychology, Vol. 8 (June 1987), pp. 215-35.

Yaukey, David, Roberts, Beryl J., and Griffiths, William
    "Husbands' vs. Wives' Responses to a Fertility Survey"
    Population Studies, Vol. 19 (July 1965), pp. 29-43.

35.02 ---------- Unclassified (Collection of Sensitive Information)

Barton, A. J.
    "Asking the Embarassing Question"
    Public Opinion Quarterly, Vol. 22 (Spring 1958), pp. 67,8.

Bradburn, Norman M., Sudman, Seymour, and Associates
    Improving Interview Method and Questionnaire Design: Response Effects
    to Threatening Questions in Survey Research
    (San Francisco: Jossey-Bass, 1979).

Butler, Richard P.
    "Effects of Signed and Unsigned Questionnaires for Both Sensitive and
    Nonsensitive Items"
    Journal of Applied Psychology, Vol. 57 (1973), pp. 348,9.

Engel, James F. and Wales, Hugh G.
    "Rejoinder to Wenderoth"
    Journal of Advertising Research, Vol. 3 (March 1963), pp. 43,4.

Engel, J. F. and Wales, H. G.
    "Spoken Versus Pictured Questions on Taboo Topics"
    Journal of Advertising Research, Vol. 2 (March 1962), pp. 11-7.

Johnson, B. and Sturtevant, V.
    "A Comparison of Computer Interviewing With Traditional Paper and
    Pencil Format: Soliciting Sensitive Information"
    Southern Oregon State College, unpublished paper.

Kearney, Kathleen A., Hopkins, Ronald H., Mauss, Armand L., and
    Weisheit, Ralph A.
    "Self Generated Identification Codes for Anonymous Collection of
    Longitudinal Questionnaire Data"
    Public Opinion Quarterly, Vol. 48 (Spring 1984), pp. 370-8.

Marquis, Kent H., Marquis, Susan M., and Polich, J. Michael
    "Response Bias and Reliability in Sensitive Topic Surveys"
    Journal of the American Statistical Association, Vol. 81 (June 1986),
    pp. 381-9.

Nederhof, Anton J.
    "Methods of Coping With Social Desireability Bias: A Review"
    European Journal of Social Psychology, Vol. 15 (July/September 1985),
    pp. 263-80.

Noelle-Neumann, Elisabeth and Worcester, Bob
    "International Opinion Research: How to Phrase Your Questions on
    Controversial Topics"
    European Research, Vol. 12 (July 1984), pp. 124-31.

Wenderoth, Peter M.
    "Comment on 'Spoken Versus Pictured Questions on Taboo Topics'"
    Journal of Advertising Research, Vol. 3 (March 1963), pp. 42,3.

36 -------------------- RANDOMIZED RESPONSE MODEL --------------------
        See also (sub)heading(s) 35, 116.14.

36.01 ---------- Books Re: Randomized Response Model

Chaudhuri, Arijit and Mukerjee, Rahul
  Randomized Response: Theory and Techniques
  (New York: Marcel Dekker, Inc., 1988), 162 pp.

Fox, James Alan and Tracy, Paul E.
  Randomized Response: A Method for Sensitive Surveys
  (Beverly Hills, CA: Sage Publications, Inc., 1986), 80 pp.

36.02 ---------- General Discussions of Randomized Response Techniques

Campbell, Cathy and Joiner, Brian L.
  "How to Get the Answer You Want Without Being Sure You've Asked the
  Question"
  The American Statistician, Vol. 26 (December 1973), pp. 229-31.

Fox, J. A. and Tracy, P. E.
  "Indeterminate Response: A Simplified Alternative to Randomized
  Response"
  Northeastern University (1986), mimeograph.

Fox, J. A. and Tracy, P. E.
  "The Randomized Response Approach: Applicability to Criminal Justice
  Research Evaluation"
  Evaluation Review, Vol. 4 (1980), pp. 601-22.

Frankel, Martin R. and Frankel, Lester R.
  "Some Recent Developments in Sample Survey Design"
  Journal of Marketing Research, Vol. XIV (August 1977), pp. 280-93.

Greenberg, Bernard G., Abernathy, James R., and Horvitz, Daniel G.
  "A New Survey Technique and Its Application in the Field of Public
  Health"
  Milibank Memorial Fund Quarterly, Vol. 68 (1970), pp. 39-55.

Greenberg, Bernard G., Abernathy, James R., and Horvitz, Daniel G.
  "Application of Randomized Response Technique in Obtaining
  Quantitative Data"
  Proceedings, Social Statistics Section, American Statistical
  Association (August 1969), pp. 40-3.

Greenberg, Bernard G., Kuebler, Roy T., Jr., Abernathy, James R., and
  Horvitz, D. G.
  "Application of the Randomized Response Technique in Obtaining
  Quantitative Data"
  Journal of the American Statistical Association, Vol. 66 (June 1971),
  pp. 243-50.

Himmelfarb, S. and Licksteig, C.
  "Social Desireability and the Randomized Response Technique"
  Journal of Personality and Social Psychology, Vol. 43 (1982), pp.
  710-7.

Horvitz, Daniel G., Greenberg, Bernard G., and Abernathy, James R.
  "Randomized Response: A Data Gathering Device for Sensitive Questions"
  International Statistical Review, Vol. 44 (August 1976), pp. 181-96.

Raghavarao, D. and Federer, W. T.
  "Block Total Response as an Alternative to the Randomized Response
  Method in Surveys"
  Journal of the Royal Statistical Society, Series B, Vol. 41 (1979),
  pp. 40-5.

Warner, Stanley L.
  "Randomized Response: A Survey Technique for Eliminating Evasive
  Answer Bias"
  Journal of the American Statistical Association, Vol. 60 (March
  1965), pp. 63-9.

Wiseman, Frederick
  "Estimating Public Opinion With the Randomized Response Model"
  Public Opinion Quarterly, Vol. XXXIX (Winter 1975-76).

36.03 ---------- Theory Re: Randomized Response Model

Abdul-Ela, Abdel-Latif A., Greenberg, Bernard G., and Horvitz, Daniel G.
  "A Multi-Proportions Randomized Response Model"
  Journal of the American Statistical Association, Vol.62 (September
  1967), pp. 990-1008.

Dowling, T. A. and Shachtman, Richard
  "On the Relative Efficiency of Randomized Response Models"
  Journal of the American Statistical Association, Vol. 70 (March
  1975), pp. 84-8.

Drane, W.
  "On the Theory of Randomized Response to Two Sensitive Questions"
  Communications in Statistics: Theory and Methods, Vol. 5 (1976), pp.
  565-74.

Edgell, Stephen E., Himmelfarb, Samuel and Cira, Darrell J.
  "Statistical Efficiency of Using Two Quantitative Randomised Response
  Techniques to Estimate Correlation"
  Psychological Bulletin, Vol. 100 (September 1986), pp. 251-6.

Greenberg, Bernard G., Abdul-Ela, Abdel-Latif A., Simmons, Walt R., and
  Horvitz, D. G.
  "The Unrelated Question Randomized Response Model Theoretical
  Framework"
  Journal of the American Statistical Association, Vol. 64 (June 1969),
  pp. 520-39.

Himmelfarb, S. and Edgell, S. E.
  "Additive Constants Model: A Randomized Response Technique for
  Eliminating Evasiveness to Quantitative Response Questions"
  Psychological Bulletin, Vol. 87 (1980), pp. 525-30.

Liu, P. T. and Chow, L. P.
  "A New Discrete Quantitative Randomized Response Model"
  Journal of the American Statistical Association, Vol. 71 (March
  1976), pp. 72,3.

Scheers, N. J. and Dayton, C. Mitchell
  "Covariate Randomised Response Models"
  Journal of the American Statistical Association, Vol. 83 (December
  1988), pp. 969-74.

Shah, B. V. and Simmons, Walt R.
  "The Unrelated Question Randomized Response Model"
  Proceedings, Social Statistics Section, American Statistical
  Association (1967), pp. 65-72.

Simmons, R. and Horvitz, D. G.
  "The Unrelated Question Randomized Response Model, Theoretical
  Framework"
  Journal of the American Statistical Association, Vol. 64 (June 1969),
  pp. 520-39.

36.04 ---------- Theory Re: Randomized Response Data Collection

Begin, G. and Boivin, M.
  "Comparison of Data Gathered on Sensitive Questions via Direct
  Questionnaire, Randomized Response Technique, and a Projective Method"
  Psychological Reports, Vol. 47 (December 1980), pp. 743-50.

Brown, G. H.
  "Randomized Inquiry vs. Conventional Questionnaire Methods in
  Estimating Drug Usage Rates Through Mail Surveys"
  HUMRO Technical Report 75-14
  (Alexandria, VA: Human Resources Research Organization, 1975).

Durham, A. M. and Lichtenstein, M. J.
  "Response Bias in Self-Report Surveys: Evaluation of Randomized
  Responses"
  in Waldo, G. P. (editor)
  Measurement Issues in Criminal Justice
  (Beverly Hills, CA: Sage Publishing Co., 1983).

Edgell, S. E., Himmelfarb, S., and Duchan, K. L.
  "The Validity of Forced Responses in a Randomized Response Model"
  Sociological Methods and Research, Vol. 11 (1982), pp. 89-100.

Folsom, R. E.
  "A Randomized Response Validation Study: Comparison of Direct and
  Randomized Reporting of DUI Arrests"
  Final Report 2550-807
  Research Triangle Institute, Chapel Hill, NC (1974).

Folsom, R. E., Greenberg, B. G., Horvitz, D. G., and Abernathy, J. R.
  "The Two Alternative Questions Randomized Response Model for Human
  Surveys"
  Journal of the American Statistical Association, Vol. 68 (September
  1973), pp. 525-31.

Fox, J. A. and Tracy, P. E.
  "A Comparative Validation of the Randomized Response and Direct
  Question Methods"
  Final report to the National Institute of Law Enforcement and
  Criminal Justice, Washington, DC (1980).

Goodstadt, Michael S. and Gruson, Valerie
  "The Randomized Response Technique: A Test on Drug Use"
  Journal of the American Statistical Association, Vol. 70 (December
  1975), pp. 814-18.

Greenberg, Bernard G., Keubler, R. T., Abernathy, James R., and
   Horvitz, Daniel G.
   "Respondent Hazards in the Unrelated Question Randomized Response
   Model"
   Journal of Statistical Planning and Inference, Vol. 1 (1977), pp.
   53-60.

Horvitz, Daniel G., Shah, B. V., and Simmons, Walt R.
   "The Unrelated Question Randomized Response Model"
   Proceedings, Social Statistics Section, American Statistical
   Association (1969), pp. 65-72.

Lamb, Charles W., Jr. and Stem, Donald E., Jr.
   "An Empirical Validation of the Randomized Response Technique"
   Journal of Marketing Research, Vol XV (November 1978), pp. 616-21.

Lanke, J.
   "On the Choice of the Unrelated Question in Simmons' Version of
   Randomized Response"
   Journal of the American Statistical Association, Vol. 70 (1975), pp.
   80-3.

Leysieffer, Frederick W.
   "Respondent Jeopardy in Randomized Response Procedures"
   Statistics Report M338
   Florida State University (1975).

Leysieffer, Frederick W. and Warner, Stanley L.
   "Respondent Jeopardy and Optimal Designs in Randomized Response
   Models"
   Journal of the American Statistical Association, Vol. 71 (September
   1976), pp. 649-55.

Liu, P. T. and Chow, L. P.
   "The Efficiency of the Multiple Trial Randomized Response Technique"
   Biometrics, Vol. 32 (1976), pp. 607-18.

Liu, P. T., Chow, L. P., and Mosley, W. Henry
   "Use of Randomized Response Technique With a New Randomizing Device"
   Journal of the American Statistical Association, Vol. 70 (June 1975),
   pp. 329-32.

Moriarty, Mark and Wiseman, Frederick
   "On the Choice of a Randomization Technique With the Randomized
   Response Model"
   Proceedings, Social Statistics Section, American Statistical
   Association (1976).

Reaser, J. M., Hartsock, S., and Hoehn, A. J.
   "A Test of the Forced-Alternative Randomized Response Questionnaire
   Technique"
   HUMRO Technical Report 75-9
   Human Resources Research Organization, Alexandria, VA (1975).

Reinmuth, James E. and Geurts, Michael D.
   "The Collection of Sensitive Information Using Two-Stage, Randomized
   Response Model"
   Journal of Marketing Research, Vol. XII (November 1975), pp. 402-7.

Stem, Donald E., Jr. and Steinhorst, R. Kirk
   "Telephone Interview and Mail Questionnaire Applications of the
   Randomized Response Model"
   Journal of the American Statistical Association, Vol. 79 (September
   1984), pp. 555-64.

Tracy, P. E. and Fox, J. A.
   "The Validity of Randomized Response for Sensitive Measurements"
   American Sociological Review, Vol. 46 (1981), pp. 187-200.

Zdep, S. M. and Rhodes, Isabelle N.
   "Making the Randomized Response Technique Work"
   Public Opinion Quarterly, Vol. 40 (Winter 1976-77), pp. 531-7.

36.05 ---------- Theory Re: Analysis of Randomized Response Data

Bourke, Patrick D.
   "Estimation of Proportions Using Symmetric Randomised Response
   Designs"
   Psychological Bulletin, Vol. 96 (July 1984), pp. 166-72.

Bourke, Patrick D.
   "Symmetry of Response in Randomized Response Designs"
   Errors in Surveys, Report No. 76
   (Stockholm: University of Stockholm, Istitute of Statistics, 1974).

Bourke, Patrick D. and Dalenius, Tore
   "Some New Ideas in the Realm of Randomized Inquiries"
   Confidentiality in Surveys, Report No. 5
   (Stockholm: University of Stockholm, Institute of Statistics, 1975).

Bourke, Patrick D. and Dalenius, Tore
  "Multi-Proportions Randomized Response Using a Single Sample"
  Errors in Surveys, Report No. 68
  (Stockholm: University of Stockholm, Institute of Statistics, 1973).

Bourke, Patrick D. and Moran, Michael A.
  "Estimating Proportions From Randomised Response Data Using the EM
  Algorithm"
  Journal of the American Statistical Association, Vol. 83 (December
  1988), pp. 964-8.

Chen, T. T.
  "Analysis of Randomized Response as Purposively Misclassified Data"
  Proceedings, Survey Research Methods Section, American Statistical
  Association (1979).

Chen, T. T.
  "Log-Linear Models for the Categorical Data Obtained From Randomized
  Response Techniques"
  Proceedings, Social Statistics Section, American Statistical
  Association (1978).

Dawes, R. M.
  "Guttman Scaling Randomized Responses: A Technique for Evaluating the
  Underlying Structures of Behaviors to Which People may not Wish to
  Admit"
  Oregon Research Institute, University of Oregon (1974), mimeograph.

Moors, J. J. A.
  "Optimization of the Unrelated Question Randomized Response Model"
  Journal of the American Statistical Association, Vol. 66 (1971), pp.
  627-9.

O'Hagan, A.
  "Bayes Linear Estimators for Randomised Response Models"
  Journal of the American Statistical Association, Vol. 82 (June 1987),
  pp. 580-5.

Rosenberg, M. J.
  "Categorical Data Analysis by a Randomized Response Technique for
  Statistical Disclosure Control"
  Proceedings, Survey Research Section, American Statistical
  Association (1980).

Rosenberg, M. J.
  Multivariable Analysis by a Randomized Response Technique for
  Statistical Disclosure Control
  University of Michigan (1979), Ph.D. dissertation.

36.06 ---------- Applications of Randomized Response Models

Locander, William, Sudman, S., and Bradburn, N.
  "An Investigation of Interview Method, Threat and Response Distortion"
  Journal of the American Statistical Association, Vol. 71 (June 1976),
  pp. 269-75.

37 -------------------------- SCALING -----------------------------
       See also (sub)heading(s) 28.03, 29.05, 34, 36, 38, 39, 40,
    41, 43, 44, 45, 46, 47, 48, 49, 50, 51, 52, 53, 54, 55, 56,
    59, 60, 61, 62, 63, 64, 65, 122.

37.01 ---------- Books Re: Scaling

American Psychological Association
   Standards for Educational and Psychological Tests
   (Washington, DC: American Psychological Association, 1974).

Anastasi, Anne
   Psychological Testing
   (New York: Macmillan Publishing Co., Inc., 1976).

Andrich, David
   Rasch Models for Measurement
   (Newbury Park, CA: Sage Publications, Inc., 1988).

Attneave, Fred
   Applications of Information Theory to Psychology
   (New York: Holt, Rinehart and Winston, 1959).

Audits and Surveys Company, Inc.
   A Modern Marketing Approach in Measuring Consumer Preference
   Modern Marketing Series Number 4
   (New York: Audits and Surveys Company, Inc., 1966), 16 pp.

Blalock, Hubert M., Jr.
   Conceptualization and Measurement in the Social Sciences
   (Beverly Hills, CA: Sage Publications, Inc., 1982).

Blalock, Hubert M., Jr. (editor)
   Measurement in the Social Sciences
   (Chicago: Aldine, 1971).

Bock, R. D. and Jones, L. V.
   The Measurement and Prediction of Judgement and Choice
   (San Francisco, CA: Holden-Day, Inc., 1968).

Churchman, C. W. (editor)
   Measurement, Definitions, and Theories
   (New York, NY: John Wiley and Sons, Inc., 1959).

Coombs, C. H.
   A Theory of Data
   (New York: John Wiley and Sons, Inc., 1964).

Cronbach, L. J.
   Essentials of Psychological Testing, Second Edition
   (New York: Harper and Row, 1960).

Cronbach, Lee J., Gleser, Goldine C., Nanda, Harinder, and Rajaratnam,
   Nageswari
   The Dependability of Behavioral Measurements: Theory of
   Generalizability for Scores and Profiles
   (New York: John Wiley and Sons, 1972), 410 pp.

Dawes, R. M.
   Fundamentals of Attitude Measurement
   (New York: John Wiley and Sons, Inc., 1972).

Dick, Walter and Hagerty, Nancy
   Topics in Measurement: Reliability and Validity
   (New York: McGraw-Hill Book Company, 1971), 190 pp.

Doeblin, Ernest O.
   Measurement Systems
   (New York: McGraw-Hill Book Company, 1975).

Edwards, Allen L.
   Techniques of Attitude Scale Construction
   (New York: Century Crofts, 1957).

Fiske, Donald W.
   Measuring the Concepts of Personality
   (Chicago: Aldine-Atherton, 1971).

Ghiselli, Edwin E.
   Theory of Psychological Measurement
   (New York: McGraw-Hill Book Company, 1964).

Ghiselli, Edwin E., Campbell, John P., and Zedeck, Sheldon
   Measurement Theory for the Behavioral Sciences
   (San Francisco: W. H. Freeman and Company, 1981).

Gorden, Raymond L.
   Unidimensional Scaling of Social Variables--Concepts and Procedures
   (New York: The Free Press, 1977), 175 pp.

Guilford, J. P.
  Psychometric Methods
  (New York: McGraw-Hill Book Company, 1954).

Gulliksen, Harold
  Theory of Mental Tests
  (New York: John Wiley and Sons, Inc., 1950).

Gulliksen, Harold and Messick, Samuel (editors)
  Psychological Scaling
  (New York: John Wiley and Sons, Inc., 1960), 211 pp.

Henerson, Marlene E., Morris, Lynn Lyons, and Fitz-Gibbon, Carol Taylor
  How to Measure Attitudes
  (Beverly Hills, CA: Sage Publications, 1978), 184 pp.

Horst, Paul
  Psychological Measurement and Prediction
  (Belmont, CA: Wadsworth, 1966).

Hughes, G. David
  Attitude Measurement for Marketing Strategies
  (Glenview, IL: Scott, Foresman and Company, 1971).

Johnson, Donald
  The Psychology of Thought and Judgment
  (New York: Harper, 1955).

Krantz, David H., Luce, R. Duncan, Suppes, Patrick, and Tversky, Amos
  Foundations of Measurement
  (New York: Academic Press, 1971).

Lemon, Nigel
  Attitudes and Their Measurement
  (New York: Halsted Press, 1974), 294 pp.

Ley, Philip
  Quantitative Aspects of Psychological Assessment
  (London: Gerald Duckworth and Co., Ltd., 1972).

Lodge, Milton
  Magnitude Scaling
  (Beverly Hills, CA: Sage Publications, Inc.).

Lord, Frederic M. and Novick, Melvin R.
  Statistical Theories of Mental Test Scores
  (Reading, MA: Addison-Wesley, 1968).

Maranell, G. M. (editor)
  Scaling--A Source Book for Behavioral Scientists
  (Chicago: Aldine Publishing Company, 1974).

McIver, John P. and Carmines, Edward G.
  Unidimensional Scaling
  (Beverly Hills, CA: Sage Publications, Inc.).

Nunnally, J. C.
  Psychometric Theory, Second Edition
  (New York: McGraw-Hill Book Company, 1978).

Oppenheim, A. N.
  Questionnaire Design and Attitude Measurement
  (New York: Basic Books, Inc., 1966).

Osgood, C. E., Suci, G. J., and Tannenbaum, P. H.
  The Measurement of Meaning
  (Urbana, IL: University of Illinois Press, 1957).

Peter, J. Paul and Ray, Michael L.
  Measurement Readings for Marketing Research
  (Chicago: American Marketing Association, 1984).

Robinson, J. P. and Shaver, P. R. (editors)
  Measures of Social Psychological Attitudes
  (Ann Arbor: Institute for Social Research, 1971), 463 pp.

Robinson, J. P. and Shaver, P. R. (editors)
  Measures of Social Psychological Attitudes
  (Ann Arbor, MI: Institute for Social Research, University of
  Michigan, 1969), 662 pp.

Shannon, Claude and Weaver, Warren
  The Mathematical Theory of Communication
  (Urbana, IL: University of Illinois Press, 1949).

Shaw, Martin and Wright, Jack M.
  Scales for the Measurement of Attitude
  (New York: McGraw-Hill Book Company, 1967).

Sherif, Muzafer, Sherif, Carolyn, and Nebergall, R.
  Attitude and Attitude Change
  (Philadelphia: W. B. Saunders, 1965).

Smith, Patricia, Kendall, L., and Hulin, C.
  The Measurement of Satisfaction in Work and Retirement: A Strategy
  for the Study of Attitudes
  (Chicago, IL: Rand McNally, 1969).

Stouffer, S. A. et al.
  Measurement and Prediction
  (Princeton, NJ: Princeton University Press, Studies in Social
  Psychology in World War II, 1950), 756 pp.

Thorndike, Robert Ladd
  Applied Psychometrics
  (Boston: Houghton-Mifflin Company, 1982).

Thorndike, R. L. and Hagen, E.
  Measurement and Evaluation in Psychology and Education, Fourth Edition
  (New York: John Wiley and Sons, Inc., 1977).

Thurstone, L. L.
  The Measurement of Values
  (Chicago: University of Chicago Press, 1959).

Thurstone, Louis Leon and Chave, E. J.
  The Measurement of Attitude
  (Chicago: University of Chicago Press, 1929).

Torgerson, W. S.
  Theory and Methods of Scaling
  (New York: John Wiley and Sons, 1958).

Van Der Ven, Andrew H. G. S.
  Introduction to Scaling
  (New York: John Wiley and Sons, Inc., 1980), 301 pp.

Zeller, Richard A. and Carmines, Edward G.
  Measurement in the Social Sciences
  (Cambridge, MA: Cambridge University Press, 1980), 198 pp.

37.02 ---------- Theory Re: Scaling

Blalock, Hubert M., Jr.
  "The Measurement Problem: A Gap Between the Languages of Theory and
  Research"
  in Blalock, H. M., Jr. and Blalock, Ann B. (editors)
  Methodology in Social Research
  (New York: McGraw-Hill Book Company, 1968), pp. 5-27.

Churchill, Gilbert A., Jr.
  "A Paradigm for Developing Better Measures of Marketing Constructs"
  Journal of Marketing Research, Vol. XVI (February 1979), pp. 64-73.

Churchill, Gilbert A., Jr. and Peter, J. Paul
  "Research Design Effects on the Reliability of Rating Scales: A
  Meta-Analysis"
  Journal of Marketing Research, Vol. XXI (November 1984), pp. 360-75.

Collins, Gwyn
  "On Methods: Measures of Attitude Change"
  Journal of Advertising Research, Vol. 1 (March 1961), pp. 28-33.

Comrey, Andrew L.
  "An Operational Approach to Some Problems in Psychological
  Measurement"
  Psychological Review, Vol. LVII (1950).

Cronbach, Lee J. and Furby, Lita
  "How We Should Measure 'Change'--Or Should We?"
  Psychological Bulletin, Vol. 74 (July 1970), pp. 68-80.

Davis, J. A.
  "On Criteria for Scale Relationships"
  American Journal of Sociology, Vol. 63 (January 1958), pp. 371-80.

Dawes, R. M.
  "Suppose We Measured Height With Rating Scales Instead of Rulers"
  Oregon Research Institute Technical Report, II, I (1971).

Day, D. D.
  "Methodological Problems in Attitude Research"
  Journal of Social Psychology, Vol. 14 (August 1941), pp. 164-79.

Day, R. L.
"Measuring Preferences"
in Ferber, R. (editor)
Handbook of Marketing Research
(New York: McGraw-Hill, 1974).

Furth, R.
"The Limits of Measurement"
Scientific American, Vol. 183 (July 1950).

Garner, W. R. and Hake, H. W.
"The Amount of Information in Absolute Judgments"
Psychological Review, Vol. 58 (November 1951), pp. 446-59.

Gerbing, David W. and Anderson, James C.
"An Updated Paradigm for Scale Development Incorporating
Unidimensionality and Its Assessment"
Journal of Marketing Research, Vol. XXV (May 1988), pp. 186-92.

Goldberger, Arthur S.
"Econometrics and Psychometrics: A Survey of Communalities"
Psychometrika, Vol. 36 (June 1971), pp. 83-107.

Guttman, Louis
"The Problem of Attitude and Opinion Measurement"
in Stouffer, S. A. (editor)
Measurement and Prediction
(Princeton: Princeton University Press, 1950), pp. 46-59.

Hustad, Thomas P. and Pessemier, Edgar A.
A Review of Current Developments in the Use of "Attitude and
Activity" Measures
in Consumer Market Research, Preliminary Research Report P-42-D
(Cambridge: Marketing Science Institute, 1971).

Jones, L. V.
"The Nature of Measurement"
in Thorndike, R. L. (editor)
Educational Measurement, Second Edition
(Washington: American Council on Education, 1971), pp. 335-55.

Keats, J. A. and Lord, F. M.
"A Theoretical Distribution for Mental Health Scores"
Psychometrika, Vol. 27 (March 1962), pp. 59-72.

Kim, Jae-On and Rabjohn, James
"Binary Variables and Index Construction"
in Schuessler, Karl F. (editor)
Sociological Methodology
(San Francisco: Jossey-Bass Publishers, 1980), pp. 120-59.

Lord, F. M.
"A Strong True-Score Theory With Applications"
Psychometrika, Vol. 30 (September 1965), pp. 239-70.

Lord, F. M.
"An Approach to Mental Test Theory"
Psychometrika, Vol. 24 (December 1959), pp. 283-302.

McGill, William J.
"Multivariate Information Transmission"
Psychometrika, Vol. 19 (June 1954), pp. 97-116.

McKelvey, W.
"An Approach for Developing Shorter and Better Measuring Instruments"
Working Paper 76-6
Human Systems Development Study Center, Graduate School of
Management, UCLA (1967).

Miller, George A.
"A Note on the Bias of Information Estimates"
in Quastler, Henry (editor)
Information Theory in Psychology: Problems and Methods
(Glencoe, IL: The Free Press, 1955), pp. 95-100.

Miller, George A. and Frick, Frederick C.
"Statistical Behavioristics and Sequences of Responses"
Psychological Review, Vol. 56 (November 1949), pp. 311-24.

Mills, Fred C.
"On Measurement in Economics"
in Tugwell, R. G. (editor)
Chapter II, the Trend of Economics
(New York: F. S. Crofts and Company, 1935).

Moscovici, Serge
"Attitudes and Opinions"
in Farnsworth, Paul R. (editor)
Annual Review of Psychology, Vol. 14 (1963), pp. 231-60.

Peter, J. Paul and Churchill, Gilbert A., Jr.
"Relationships Among Research Design Choices and Psychometric
Properties of Rating Scales: A Meta-Analysis"
Journal of Marketing Research, Vol. XXIII (February 1986), pp. 1-10.

Ray, Michael L.
"Introduction to the Special Section: Measurement and Marketing
Research--Is the Flirtation Going to Lead to a Romance?"
Journal of Marketing Research, Vol. XVI (February 1979), pp. 1-5.

Robinson, John P., Rush, Jerrold G., and Head, Kendra B.
"Criteria for An Attitude Scale"
in Maranell, G. M. (editor)
Scaling--A Source Book for Behavioural Scientists
(Chicago: Aldine Publishing Company, 1974).

Seaton, Richard
"Why Ratings are Better Than Comparisons"
Journal of Advertising Research, Vol. 14 (February 1974), pp. 45-8.

Stevens, S. S.
"On the Theory of Scales of Measurement"
Science, Vol. 103 (1946), pp. 677-80.

Stevens, S. S.
"On the Problem of Scales for Measurement of Psychological Magnitudes"
Journal of Unified Science, Vol. 9 (1939), pp. 94-9.

Thurstone, L.
"The Measurement of Social Attitudes"
Journal of Abnormal and Social Psychology, Vol. 26 (1931), pp. 249-69.

Thurstone, L. L. and Jones, Lyle V.
"The Rational Origin for Measuring Subjective Values"
Journal of American Statistical Association, Vol. 52 (December 1957),
pp. 458-71.

Volkmann, John
"Scales of Judgment and Their Implications for Sociology"
in Rohrer, J. H. and Sheriff, M. (editors)
Social Psychology at the Crossroads
(New York: Harper and Brothers, 1951), pp. 272-94.

Wilks, S. S.
"Some Aspects of Quantification in Science"
in Woolf, H. (editor)
Quantification
(New York: Bobbs-Merrill Co., Inc., 1961).

Weitzenhoffer, Andre M.
"Mathematical Structures and Psychological Measurement"
Psychometrika, Vol. 16 (December 1951).

37.03 ---------- Theory Re: Spatial Versus Nonspatial Scaling

Carroll, J. Douglas
"Spatial, Non-Spatial and Hybrid Models for Scaling"
Psychometrika, Vol. 41, No. 4 (1976), pp. 439-63.

Shepard, Roger N.
"Representation of Structure in Similarity Data: Problems and
Prospects"
Psychometrika, Vol. 39, No. 4 (1974), pp. 373-421.

Tversky, Amos
"Preference Trees"
Psychological Review, Vol. 86 (November 1979), pp. 542-93.

38 -------------- ITEM RESPONSE OR LATENT TRAIT THEORY ---------------

38.01 ---------- Books Re: Item Response or Latent Trait Theory

Hambleton, Ronald K. and Swaminathan, Hariharan
  Item Response Theory: Principles and Applications
  (Boston, MA: Kluwer-Nijhoff Publishing, 1985).

Hulin, Charles L., Drasgow, Fritz, and Parsons, Charles K.
  Item Response Theory: Application to Psychological Measurement
  (Homewood, IL: Dow-Jones Irwin, 1983).

Kolakowski, D. and Bock, R. Darrell
  Maximum Likelihood Item Analysis and Test Scoring: Logistic Model for
  Multiple Item Responses
  (Ann Arbor, MI: National Educational Resources, Inc., 1973).

Lord, Frederic M.
  Applications of Item Response Theory to Practical Testing Problems
  (Hillsdale, NJ: Lawrence Erlbaum Associates, 1980).

38.02 ---------- Theory Re: Item Response or Latent Trait Theory

Andersen, Erling B.
  "Sufficient Statistics and Latent Trait Models"
  Psychometrika, Vol. 42 (1977), pp. 69-81.

Andersen, Erling B.
  "The Logistic Model for m Answer Categories"
  in Kempf, Wilhelm F. and Repp, Bruno H. (editors)
  Mathematical Models for Social Psychology
  (New York: John Wiley and Sons, Inc., 1977), pp. 59-80.

Andrich, David
  "An Index of Person Separation in Latent Trait Theory, the
  Traditional KR-20 Index, and the Guttman Scale Response Pattern"
  Educational Research and Perspectives, Vol. 9 (1982), pp. 95-104.

Andrich, David
  "Application of a Psychometric Rating Model to Ordered Categories
  Which are Scored With Successive Integers"
  Applied Psychological Measurement, Vol. 2 (Fall 1978), pp. 581-94.

Bechtel, Gordon G. and Wiley, James B.
  "Probabilistic Measurement of Attributes: A Logit Analysis by
  Generalized Least Squares"
  Marketing Science, Vol. 2 (Fall 1983), pp. 389-405.

Birnbaum, Allan
  "Some Latent Trait Models and Their Use in Inferring an Examinee's
  Ability"
  in Lord, Frederic M. and Novick, Melvin R. (editors)
  Statistical Theories of Mental Test Scores
  (Reading, MA: Addision-Wesley Publishing Company, 1968).

Bock, R. Darrell
  "Estimating Item Parameters and Latent Ability When Responses are
  Scored in Two or More Nominal Categories"
  Psychometrika, Vol. 37 (March 1972), pp. 29-51.

Drasgow, Fritz and Parsons, Charles K.
  "Application of Unidimensional Item Response Theory Models to
  Multidimensional Data"
  Applied Psychological Measurement, Vol. 7 (Spring 1983), pp. 189-99.

Hambleton, Ronald K., Swaminathan, Hariharan, Cook, Linda L., Eignor,
  Daniel R., and Gifford, Janice A.
  "Developments in Latent Trait Theory: Models, Technical Issues and
  Applications"
  Review of Educational Research, Vol. 48 (Fall 1985), pp. 467-510.

Kamakura, Wagner A. and Srivastava, Rajendra K.
  "Adapting Latent Trait Theory for Attitude Scaling"
  in Darden, William R., Monroe, Kent B., and Dillon, William R.
  (editors)
  Proceedings, AMA Winter Educators' Conference
  (Chicago: American Marketing Association, 1983), pp. 263-7.

Lord, Frederic M.
  "Estimation of Latent Ability and Item Parameters When There are
  Omitted Responses"
  Psychometrika, Vol. 39 (June 1974), pp. 247-64.

Reckase, Mark D.
  "Unifactor Latent Trait Models Applied to Multifactor Tests: Results
  and Implications"
  Journal of Educational Statistics, Vol. 4 (Fall 1979), pp. 207-30.

Reckase, Mark D. and McKinley, Robert L.
    "Some Latent Trait Theory in a Multidimensional Latent Space"
    in Weiss, David J. (editor)
    Proceedings, 1982 Item Response Theory and Computerized Adaptive
    Testing Conference
    (Minneapolis, MN: Department of Psychology, Computerized Adaptive
    Testing Laboratory, University of Minnesota, April 1985), pp. 151-77.

Reckase, Mark D. and McKinley, Robert L.
    "Multidimensional Latent Trait Models"
    Annual Meeting, National Council of Measurement in Education, New
    York (1982), paper presentation.

Samejima, Fumiko
    "Normal Ogive Model on the Continuous Response Level in
    Multidimensional Latent Space"
    Psychometrika, Vol. 39 (1974), pp. 111-21.

Samejima, Fumiko
    "Homogeneous Case of the Continuous Response Model"
    Psychometrika, Vol. 38 (1973), pp. 203-19.

Samejima, Fumiko
    "Estimation of Latent Ability Using a Response Pattern of Graded
    Scores"
    Psychometrika Monograph, Number 17 (1969).

Wright, Benjamin D. and Douglas, Graham A.
    "Conditional Versus Unconditional Procedures for Sample Free Item
    Analysis"
    Educational and Psychological Measurement, Vol. 37 (Autumn 1977), pp.
    573-86.

Wright, Benjamin D. and Panchapakesan, Nargis
    "A Procedure for Sample-Free Item Analysis"
    Educational and Psychological Measurement, Vol. 29 (Spring 1969), pp.
    23-48.

38.03 ---------- Books Re: Rasch Model

Andrich, David
    Rasch Models for Measurement
    (Newbury Park, CA: Sage Publications, 1988), 95 pp.

Rasch, Georg
    Probabilistic Models for Some Intelligence and Attainment Tests
    (Chicago: The University of Chicago Press, 1980).

Wright, Benjamin D. and Stone, M. H.
    Best Test Design: Rasch Measurement
    (Chicago: MESA Press, 1979).

38.04 ---------- Theory Re: Rasch Model

Andrich, David
    "Relationships Between the Thurstone and Rasch Approaches to Item
    Scaling"
    Applied Psychological Measurement, Vol. 3 (1978), pp. 446-60.

Bechtel, Gordon G.
    "Generalizing the Rasch Model for Consumer Rating Scales"
    Marketing Science, Vol. 4 (Winter 1985), pp. 62-73.

Choppin, B.
    "A Fully Conditional Estimation Procedure for Rasch Model Parameters"
    Report No. 196
    Graduate School of Education, Center for the Study of Evaluation,
    University of California (1983).

Fischer, G.
    "On the Existence and Uniqueness of Maximum-Likelihood Estimates in
    the Rasch Model"
    Psychometrika, Vol. 46 (1981), pp. 59-77.

Gustafsson, J.-E.
    "Testing and Obtaining Fit of Data to the Rasch Model"
    British Journal of Mathematics and Statistical Psychology, Vol. 33
    (1980), pp. 205-33.

Gustafsson, J.-E.
    "A Solution of the Conditional Estimation Problem for Long Tests in
    the Rasch Model for Dichotomous Items"
    Educational and Psychological Measurement, Vol. 40 (1980), pp. 377-85.

Gustafsson, J.-E.
"The Rasch Model for Dichotomous Items: Theory, Applications and a Computer Program"
Report No. 63
(Goteborg: University of Goteborg, Institute of Education, 1977).

Kelderman, H.
"Loglinear Rasch Model Tests"
Psychometrika, Vol. 49 (1984), pp. 222-45.

Masters, Geoff N.
"A Rasch Model for Partial Credit Scoring"
Psychometrika, Vol. 47 (June 1982), pp. 149-74.

Mead, R. J.
The Assessment of Fit of Data to the Rasch Model Through Analysis of Residuals
University of Chicago (1976), Ph.D. dissertation.

Molenaar, I. W.
"Some Improved Diagnostics for Failure of the Rasch Model"
Psychometrika, Vol. 48 (1983), pp. 49-72.

Perline, R., Wright, B. D., and Wainer, H.
"The Rasch Model as Additive Conjoint Measurement"
Applied Psychological Measurement, Vol. 3 (1979), pp. 237-56.

Rasch, Georg
"On Specific Objectivity: An Attempt at Formalising the Request for Generality and Validity of Scientific Statements"
Danish Yearbook of Philosophy, Vol. 14 (1977), pp. 58-94.

Rasch, Georg
"A Mathematical Theory of Objectivity and Its Consequences for Model Contribution"
European Meeting on Statistics, Econometrics, and Management Science, Amsterdam (1968).

Rasch, Georg
"An Item Analysis Which Takes Individual Differences Into Account"
British Journal of Mathematical and Statistical Psychology, Vol. 19 (1966), pp. 49-57.

Rasch, Georg
"On General Laws and the Meaning of Measurement in Psychology"
in Proceedings, Fourth Berkeley Symposium on Mathematical Statistics and Probability, IV
(Berkeley, CA: University of California Press, 1961), pp. 321-34.

Rasch, Georg
Probabilistic Models for Some Intelligence and Attainment Tests
(Copenhagen: Danish Institute for Educational Research, 1960).

Roskam, E. E. and Jansen, P. G. W.
"A New Derivation of the Rasch Model"
in Degreef, E. and Van Buggenhaut, J. (editors)
Trends in Mathematical Psychology
(New York: Elsevier, 1984), pp. 293-307.

Van Den Wollenberg, A. L.
"Two New Statistics for the Rasch Model"
Psychometrika, Vol. 47 (1982), pp. 123-40.

Wright, B. D.
"Misunderstanding the Rasch Model"
Journal of Educational Measurement, Vol. 14 (1977), pp. 219-25.

Wright, B. D. and Mead, R. J.
"BICAL: Calibrating Items With the Rasch Model"
Research Memorandum No. 23
Department of Education, Statistical Laboratory (1976).

38.05 ---------- Theory Re: Tailored Tests

See also (sub)heading(s) 34.10, 73, 76.06, 88.

Balasubramanian, Siva K. and Kamakura, Wagner A.
"Measuring Consumer Attitudes Toward the Marketplace With Tailored Interviews"
Journal of Marketing Research, Vol. XXVI (August 1989), pp. 311-26.

Green, Bert F.
"The Promise of Tailored Tests"
in Wainer, Howard and Messick, Samuel (editors)
Principles of Modern Psychological Measurement
(Hillsdale, NJ: Lawrence Erlbaum Associates, 1983), pp. 69-80.

Green, Bert F., Bock, R. Darrell, Humphreys, Lloyd G., Linn, Robert L.,
and Reckase, Mark D.
"Technical Guidelines for Assessing Computerized Adaptive Tests"
Journal of Educational Measurement, Vol. 21 (Winter 1984), pp. 347-60.

Jensema, Carl J.
"The Validity of Bayesian Tailored Testing"
Educational and Psychological Measurement, Vol. 34 (Winter 1974), pp.
757-66.

Owen, Roger J.
"A Bayesian Sequential Procedure for Quantal Response in the Context
of Adaptive Mental Testing"
Journal of the American Statistical Association, Vol. 70 (June 1975),
pp. 351-6.

Owen, Roger J.
"A Bayesian Approach to Tailored Testing"
Research Bulletin 69-92
(Princeton, NJ: Educational Testing Service, 1969).

Sympson, James B.
"A Model for Testing With Multidimensional Items"
in Weiss, David J. (editor)
Proceedings, 1977 Computerized Adaptive Testing Conference
(Minneapolis, MN: Department of Psychology, University of Minnesota,
July 1978), pp. 82-98.

Urry, Vern W.
"Tailored Testing: A Successful Application of Latent Trait Theory"
Journal of Educational Measurement, Vol. 14 (Summer 1977), pp. 181-96.

Weiss, David J.
"Improving Measurement Quality and Efficiency With Adaptive Testing"
Applied Psychological Measurement, Vol. 6 (Fall 1982), pp. 473-92.

Weiss, David J. and Kingsbury, G. Gage
"Application of Computerized Adaptive Testing to Educational Problems"
Journal of Educational Measurement, Vol. 21 (Winter 1984), pp. 473-92.

38.06 ---------- Applications of Item Response or Latent Trait Theory

Singh, Jagdip
"Modeling Consumer Responses to Negative Disconfirmation of
Expectations: An Empirical Investigation Using Item Response Theory
Based Measures"
Texas Tech University (1985), unpublished D.B.A. thesis.

38.07 ---------- Software for IRT or Tailored Testing

McKinley, Robert L. and Reckase, Mark D.
"A Comparison of the ANCILLES and LOGIST Parameter Estimation
Procedures for the Three-Parameter Logistic Model Using
Goodness-of-Fit as a Criterion"
Research Report 80-2
Educational Psychology Department, University of Missouri (1980).

Mislevy, Robert J. and Bock, R. Darrell
BILOG: Maximum Likelihood Item Analysis and Test Scoring With
Logistic Models for Binary Items
(Chicago: International Educational Services, 1982).

Urry, Vern W.
ANCILLES: Item Parameter Estimation Program With Normal Ogive and
Logistic Three-Parameter Model Options
(Washington, DC: U.S. Civil Service Commission, Personnel Research
and Development Center, 1978).

Wingersky, Marilyn S., Barton, Mark A., and Lord, Frederic M.
LOGIST User's Guide
(Princeton, NJ: Educational Testing Service, 1982).

Wood, R. L., Wingersky, Marilyn S., and Lord, Frederic M.
LOGIST--A Computer Program for Estimating Examinee Ability and Item
Characteristic Curve Parameters
Research Memorandum 76-6
(Princeton, NJ: Educational Testing Service, 1976).

Wright, Benjamin D. and Mead, Ronald J.
BICAL: Calibrating Items and Scales With the Rasch Model
Research Memorandum Number 23
Department of Education, University of Chicago (1977).

39 ------------------- SEMANTIC DIFFERENTIAL SCALE -------------------
      See also (sub)heading(s) 37.

39.01 ---------- Books Re: Semantic Differential Scale

Nordenstreng, Kaarle
    Toward Quantification of Meaning--An Evaluation of the Semantic
    Differential Technique
    (Helsinki: The Finnish Academy of Science and Letters, 1969), 35 pp.

Osgood, C. E., Suci, G. J., and Tannenbaum, P. H.
    The Measurement of Meaning
    (Urbana, IL: University of Illinois Press, 1957).

Snider, James G. and Osgood, Charles E. (editors)
    Semantic Differential Technique: A Sourcebook
    (Chicago: Aldine, 1969), 681 pp.

39.02 ---------- Theory Re: Semantic Differential Scale

Albaum, Gerald, Best, Roger, and Hawkins, Del
    "The Measurement Properties of Semantic Scale Data"
    Journal of the Market Research Society, Vol. 19 (January 1977), pp.
    21-6.

Albaum, Gerald S. and Dickson, J.
    "A Method for Developing Tailormade Semantic Differentials for
    Specific Marketing Content Areas"
    Journal of Marketing Research, Vol. XIV (February 1977), pp. 87-91.

Albaum, Gerald and Munsinger, G.
    "Methodological Questions Concerning the Use of the Semantic
    Differential"
    Southern Marketing Association (Spring 1973).

Allison, R. B., Jr.
    "Using Adverbs as Multipliers in Semantic Differentials"
    Journal of Psychology, Vol. 56 (July 1963), pp. 115-7.

Bentler, P. M.
    "Semantic Space is (Approximately) Bipolar"
    Journal of Psychology, Vol. 71 (January 1969), pp. 33-40.

Best, Roger J., Albaum, Gerald S., Hawkins, Del I., and Kenyon, Georgia
    "Number of Response Intervals and Reliability of Factor Analyzed
    Semantic Scale Data"
    Southwestern Marketing Association (1978).

Brinton, James E.
    "Deriving an Attitude Scale From Semantic Differential Data"
    Public Opinion Quarterly, Vol. 25 (Summer 1961), pp. 289-95.

Brown, R. W.
    "Is a Boulder Sweet or Sour?"
    Contemporary Psychology, Vol. III (May 1958), pp. 113-9.

Bunder, P., Vincent, F., and Ursic, M.
    "Graphic Versus Semantic Differential Scales: An Empirical Comparison"
    Annual Conference, Southeast American Institute for Decision Sciences
    (1984), paper presentation.

Clark, V. A. and Kerrick, J. S.
    "A Method of Obtaining Summary Scores From Semantic Differential Data"
    Journal of Psychology, Vol. 66 (May 1967), pp. 77-85.

Clevenger, T., Jr., Lazier, G. A., and Clark, M. L.
    "Measurement of Corporate Images by the Semantic Differential"
    Journal of Marketing Research, Vol. II (February 1965), pp. 80-2.

Crockett, W. H. and Nidorf, L. J.
    "Individual Differences in Response to the Semantic Differential"
    Journal of Social Psychology, Vol. 73 (December 1967), pp. 211-8.

Denmark, F. L. and Shirk, E. J.
    "The Effect of Ethnic and Social Class Variables on Semantic
    Differential Performance"
    Journal of Social Psychology, Vol. 86 (February 1972), pp. 3-9.

Dickson, J. and Albaum, G.
    "Effects of Polarity of Semantic Differential Scales in Consumer
    Research"
    Advances in Consumer Research, Vol. 2 (Fall 1974), pp. 507-14.

Downs, Phillip E.
    "Testing the Upgraded Semantic Differential"
    Journal of the Market Research Society, Vol. 20 (April 1978), pp.
    99-103.

Evans, R. H.
    "The Upgraded Semantic Differential: A Further Test"
    Journal of the Market Research Society, Vol. 22 (April 1980), pp.
    143-7.

Fry, Joseph N. and Claxton, John D.
    "Semantic Differential and Nonmetric Multidimensional Scaling
    Descriptions of Brand Images"
    Journal of Marketing Research, Vol. VIII (May 1971), pp. 238-40.

Gatty, Ronald
    "Multivariate Analysis for Marketing Research: An Evaluation"
    Journal of the Royal Statistical Society (Applied Statistics), Vol.
    15 (November 1966), pp. 157-72.

Golden, Linda L. and Albaum, Gerald
    "An Analysis of Alternative Semantic Differential Formats for
    Measuring Retail Store Image"
    Annual Meeting, Western Region American Institute for Decision
    Sciences (1984), paper presentation.

Heaps, R. A.
    "Use of the Semantic Differential Technique in Research: Some
    Precautions"
    Journal of Psychology, (January 1972), pp. 121-5.

Heise, D. R.
    "Some Methodological Issues in Semantic Differential Research"
    Psychological Bulletin, Vol. 72 (1969), pp. 406-22.

Hofman, J. E.
    "An Analysis of Concept-Clusters in Semantic Inter-Concept Space"
    American Journal of Psychology, Vol. 80 (September 1967), pp. 345-54.

Hughes, G. David
    "Upgrading the Semantic Differential"
    Journal of the Market Research Society, Vol. 17 (January 1975), pp.
    41-4.

Kerby, J. K.
    "Semantic Generalization in the Formation of Consumer Attitudes"
    Journal of Marketing Research, Vol. IV (August 1967), pp. 314-7.

Landon, E. Laird
    "Order Bias, the Ideal Rating, and the Semantic Differential"
    Journal of Marketing Research, Vol. VIII (August 1971), pp. 375-8.

Lusk, Edward J.
    "A Bipolar Adjective Screening Methodology"
    Journal of Marketing Research, Vol. X (May 1973), pp. 202,3.

Lyle, Jack
    "Semantic Differential Scales for Newspaper Research"
    Journalism Quarterly, Vol. 37 (Autumn 1960), pp. 559-646.

McCraskey, J., Prichard, S., and Arnold, W.
    "Attitude Intensity and the Neutral Point on Semantic Differential
    Scales"
    Public Opinion Quarterly, Vol. 31 (Winter 1967), pp. 642-5.

Menezes, Dennis and Elbert, Norbert F.
    "Alternative Semantic Scaling Formats for Measuring Store Image: An
    Evaluation"
    Journal of Marketing Research, Vol. XVI (February 1979), pp. 80-7.

Mindak, W. A.
    "Fitting the Semantic Differential to the Marketing Problem"
    Journal of Marketing, Vol. 25 (April 1961), pp. 28-33.

Mindak, William A.
    "A New Technique for Measuring Advertising Effectiveness"
    Journal of Marketing Vol. 20 (April 1956), pp. 367-9.

Mordkoff, A. M.
    "An Empirical Test of the Functional Autonomy of Semantic
    Differential Scales"
    Journal of Verbal Learning and Verbal Behavior, Vol. 2 (1963), pp.
    504-8.

Norman, W. T.
    "Stability-Characteristics of the Semantic Differential"
    American Journal of Psychology, Vol. 72 (December 1959), pp. 581-4.

Oetting, E. R.
    "The Effect of Forcing Response on the Semantic Differential"
    Educational and Psychological Measurement, Vol. 27 (Autumn 1967), pp.
    699-702.

Oliver, B. L.
    "The Semantic Differential: A Device for Measuring Interprofessional
    Communication of Selected Accounting Concepts"
    National Meeting, American Accounting Association (1972), paper
    presentation.

Osgood, C. E.
    "The Nature and Meaning and Measurement of Meaning"
    Psychological Bulletin, Vol. 49 (August 1952), pp. 197-213.

Priest, P. N.
    "The Influence of Psychiatric Status and Sex on Semantic Differential
    Response Style"
    Personality: An International Journal, Vol. 2 (1971), pp. 9-14.

Scott, William E., Jr.
    "The Development of Semantic Differential Scales as Measures of
    'Morale'"
    Personnel Psychology, Vol. 20 (Summer 1967), pp. 179-97.

Sharpe, L. K. and Anderson, W. T., Jr.
    "Concept-Scale Interaction in the Semantic Differential"
    Journal of Marketing Research, Vol. 9 (November 1972), pp. 432-4.

Szalay, L. B., Windle, C., and Lysne, D. A.
    "Attitude Measurement by Free Verbal Associations"
    Journal of Social Psychology, Vol. 82 (October 1970), pp. 43-55.

Thomas, R. E., Smith, Joan MacFarlane, and Spence, P. A.
    "Wheeling and Dealing--A New Approach to the Collection of Attitude
    and Motivational Data by the Use of Semantic Differential Scales"
    Journal of the Market Research Society, Vol. 10 (April 1968), pp.
    78-86.

Vidali, J. J., Jr.
    "Single-Anchor Stapel Scales Versus Double-Anchor Semantic
    Differential Scales"
    Psychological Reports, Vol. 33 (1973), pp. 373,4.

Vidali, J. J., Jr. and Holeway, R. E.
    "Stapel Scales Versus Semantic Differential Scales"
    Psychological Reports, Vol. 35 (1975), pp. 165,6.

39.03 ---------- Applications of the Semantic Differential

Barban, Arnold M. and Cundiff, Edward W.
    "Negro and White Response to Advertising"
    Journal of Marketing Research, Vol. I (November 1964), pp. 53-6.

Barclay, William D.
    "The Semantic Differential as an Index of Brand Attitude"
    Journal of Advertising Research, Vol. 4 (March 1964), pp. 30-3.

Bloom, Paul E.
    "Match the Concept and the Product"
    Journal of Advertising Research, Vol. 17 (October 1977), pp. 25-7.

Brown, Jacqueline J., Light, C. David, and Gazda, Gregory M.
    "Attitudes Towards European, Japanese, and US Cars"
    European Journal of Marketing, Vol. 21, No. 5 (1987), pp. 90-100.

Burdick, H. A., Green, E. J., and Lovelace, J. W.
    "Predicting Trademark Effectiveness"
    Journal of Applied Psychology, Vol. 43 (October 1959), pp. 285-6.

Cagley, James W. and Cardozo, Richard N.
    "White Response to Integrated Advertising"
    Journal of Advertising Research, Vol. 10 (April 1970), pp. 35-9.

Clevenger, Theodore, Jr., Clark, M. L., and Lazier, G. A.
    "Measurement of Corporate Images by the Semantic Differential"
    Journal of Marketing Research, Vol. II (February 1965), pp. 80-2.

Cohen, Joel B. and Goldberg, Marvin E.
    "The Dissonance Model in Post-Decision Product Evaluation"
    Journal of Marketing Research, Vol. VII (August 1970), pp. 315-21.

Cotham, James C., III
    "Job Attitudes and Sales Performance of Major Appliance Salesmen"
    Journal of Marketing Research, Vol. V (November 1968), pp. 370-75.

Dolich, Ira J.
    "Congruence Relationships Between Self Images and Product Brands"
    Journal of Marketing Research, Vol. VI (February 1969), pp. 80-4.

Eastlack, J. O., Jr.
    "Consumer Flavor Preference Factors in Food Product Design"
    Journal of Marketing Research, Vol. I (February 1964), pp. 38-42.

Fritz, Nancy K.
"Claim Recall and Irritation in Television Commercials: An
Advertising Effectiveness Study"
Journal of the Academy of Marketing Science, Vol. 7 (Winter-Spring
1979), pp. 1-13.

Gatty, R. and Allais, C.
The Semantic Differential Applied to Image Research
(New Brunswick, NJ: Department of Agricultural Economics, Rutgers
University, Technical Bulletin Number 2).

Hoar, J. R. and Meek, E. E.
"The Semantic Differential as a Measure of Subliminal Message Effects"
Journal of Psychology, Vol. 60 (July 1965), pp. 165-9.

Holbrook, Morris B. and Huber, Joel
"Separating Perceptual Dimensions From Affective Overtones: An
Application to Consumer Aesthetics"
Journal of Consumer Research, Vol. 5 (March 1979), pp. 272-83.

Holstius, Karin
"Exploring Copywriters' Ability to Perceive Target Group Attitudes
Towards Advertising Copy"
European Journal of Marketing, Vol. 17, No. 5 (1983), pp. 55-71.

Kelley, R. F. and Stephenson, R.
"The Semantic Differential: An Information Source for Designing
Retail Patronage Appeals"
Journal of Marketing, Vol. 31 (October 1967), pp. 43-7.

Kerrick, J. S.
"The Effect of Relevant and Non-Relevant Sources on Attitude Change"
Journal of Social Psychology, Vol. 47 (February 1958), pp. 15-20.

Landon, James A.
"Attitudes Toward Commercial and Educational Television"
Journal of Advertising Research, Vol. 2 (September 1962), pp. 33-6.

Mehling, R.
"A Single Test for Measuring Intensity of Attitudes"
Public Opinion Quarterly, Vol. 23 (Winter 1959-60), pp. 576-8.

Meisels, M. and Leroy, H. F., Jr.
"Social Desireability Response Set and Semantic Differential
Evaluative Judgements"
Journal of Social Psychology, Vol. 78 (June 1969), pp. 45-54.

Reitter, Robert N.
"Product Testing in Segmented Markets"
Journal of Marketing Research, Vol. VI (May 1969), pp. 179-84.

Robertson, Dan H. and Hackett, Donald W.
"Saleswomen: Perceptions, Problems and Prospects"
Journal of Marketing, Vol. 41 (July 1977), pp. 66-71.

Roman, Hope S.
"Semantic Generalization in Formation of Consumer Attitudes"
Journal of Marketing Research, Vol. VI (August 1969), pp. 369-73.

Settle, R. B. and Gibby, L. B.
"The Measurement of Attributed Image"
California Management Review, Vol. 14 (Summer 1972), pp. 70-4.

Spector, A. J.
"Basic Dimensions of Corporate Image"
Journal of Marketing, Vol. 25 (October 1961), pp. 47-51.

Sternthal, Brian, Dholakia, Ruby, and Leavitt, Clark
"The Persuasive Effect of Source Credibility: Tests of Cognitive
Response"
Journal of Consumer Research, Vol. 4 (March 1978), pp. 252-60.

Thumin, Fred J., Craddick, Ray A., and Barclay, Allen G.
"A Study of the Meaning and Compatibility of a Proposed Corporate
Name and Symbol"
Journal of the Academy of Marketing Science, Vol. 2 (Spring 1974),
pp. 406-12.

Tobolski, Francis P.
"Direct Mail: Image, Return and Effectiveness"
Journal of Advertising Research, Vol. 10 (August 1970), pp. 19-25.

40 ------------------------ LIKERT SCALES ------------------------
        See also (sub)heading(s) 37, 54.03.

40.01 ---------- Theory Re: Likert Scales

Dixon, Paul, Bobo, Mackie, and Stevick, Richard A.
    "Response Differences and Preferences for All: Category-Defined and
    End-Defined Likert Format"
    Educational and Psychological Measurement, Vol. 44 (Spring 1984), pp.
    61-6.

Falthzik, Alfred M. and Jolson, Marvin A.
    "Statement Polarity in Attitude Studies"
    Journal of Marketing Research, Vol. XI (February 1974), pp. 102-5.

Ferguson, L. W.
    "A Study of the Likert Technique of Attitude Scale Construction"
    Journal of Social Psychology, Vol. 13 (February 1941), pp. 51-7.

Guest, Lester
    "A Comparison of Two-Choice and Four-Choice Questions"
    Journal of Advertising Research, Vol. 2 (March 1962), pp. 32-4.

Jacoby, Jacob and Matell, Michael S.
    "Three-Point Likert Scales are Good Enough"
    Journal of Marketing Research, Vol. VIII (November 1971), pp. 495-500.

Johnson, William L. and Dixon, Paul M.
    "Response Alternatives in Likert Scaling"
    Educational and Psychological Measurement, Vol. 44 (Autumn 1984), pp.
    563-7.

Komorita, S. S.
    "Attitude Content, Intensity and the Neutral Point on a Likert Scale"
    Journal of Social Psychology, Vol. 61 (December 1963), pp. 327-34.

Lehmann, Donald R. and Hulbert, James
    "Are Three-Point Scales Always Good Enough?"
    Journal of Marketing Research, Vol. IX (November 1972), pp. 444-6.

Likert, Rensis
    "The Method of Constructing an Attitude Scale"
    in Fishbein (editor)
    Readings in Attitude Theory and Measurement
    (New York: John Wiley and Sons, 1967).

Likert, R.
    "A Technique for the Measurement of Attitudes"
    Archives of Psychology, Vol. 22 (June 1932), 55 pp.

Masters, J. R.
    "Number of Categories of a Summated Rating Scale"
    University of Pittsburgh (1972), unpublished dissertation.

Matell, M. S. and Jacoby, J.
    "Is There an Optimal Number of Alternatives for Likert-Scale Items"
    Journal of Applied Psychology, Vol. 56 (December 1972), pp. 506-9.

Murphy, Gardner and Likert, Rensis
    Public Opinion and the Individual
    (New York: Harper and Brothers Publishers, 1938).

Rotter, G. S.
    "Attitudinal Points of Agreement and Disagreement"
    Journal of Social Psychology, Vol. 86 (April 1972), pp. 211-8.

Sternthal, Brian, Dholakia, Ruby, and Leavitt, Clark
    "The Persuasive Effect of Source Credibility: Tests of Cognitive
    Response"
    Journal of Consumer Research, Vol. 4 (March 1978), pp. 252-60.

Ward, C. D.
    "Ego Involvement and the Absolute Judgement of Attitude Statements"
    Journal of Personality and Social Psychology, Vol. 2 (August 1965),
    pp. 202-8.

Worcester, Robert M. and Burus, Timothy R.
    "A Statistical Examination of the Relative Precision of Verbal Scales"
    Journal of the Market Research Society, Vol. 17 (July 1975), pp.
    181-97.

Wyatt, Randall C. and Meyers, Lawrence S.
    "Psychometric Properties of Four 5-Point Likert-Type Response Scales"
    Educational and Psychological Measurement, Vol. 47 (Spring 1987), pp.
    27-35.

Zavalloni, M. and Cook, S. W.
"Influence of Judges' Attitudes on Ratings of Favorableness of
Statements About a Social Group"
Journal of Personality and Social Psychology, Vol. 1 (January 1965),
pp. 43-54.

40.02 ---------- Applications of Likert Scales

Ahkter, Syed H. and Laczniak, Gene R.
"The Future US Business Environment With Strategic Marketing
Implications for European Exporters"
European Journal of Marketing, Vol. 23, No. 5 (1989), pp. 58-74.

Albonetti, Joseph G. and Dominguez, Luis V.
"Major Influences on Consumer-Goods Marketers' Decision to Target
U.S. Hispanics"
Journal of Advertising Research, Vol. 29 (February/March 1989), pp.
9-21.

Allen, Bruce H. and Lambert, David R.
"Searching for the Best Price: An Experimental Look at Consumer
Search Effort"
Journal of the Academy of Marketing Science, Vol. 6 (Fall 1978), pp.
245-57.

Barker, A. Tansu
"Consumerism in New Zealand"
International Marketing Review, Vol. 4 (Autumn 1987), pp. 63-74.

Howard, Donald G.
"Will American Export Trading Companies Replace Traditional Export
Management Companies?"
International Marketing Review, Vol. 8 (Winter 1988), pp. 41-50.

Jensen, Thomas D. and Rao, C. P.
"Inflation, Customer Adaptations, and Retailing"
Journal of Retailing, Vol. 64 (Winter 1988), pp. 453-70.

John, George and Martin, John
"Effects of Organizational Structure of Marketing Planning on
Credibility and Utilization of Plan Output"
Journal of Marketing Research, Vol. XXI (May 1984), pp. 170-83.

Kelly, J. Patrick, Gable, Myron, and Hise, Richard T.
"Conflict, Clarity, Tension, and Satisfaction in Chain Store Manager
Roles"
Journal of Retailing, Vol. 57 (Spring 1981), pp. 27-42.

Tyagi, Pradeep K.
"Relative Importance of Key Job Dimensions and Leadership Behaviors
in Motivating Salesperson Work Performance"
Journal of Marketing, Vol. 49 (Summer 1985), pp. 75-86.

41 ---------------------- PAIRED COMPARISONS ------------------------
        See also (sub)heading(s) 26, 37.

Davidson, R. R. and Farquhar, P. H.
    "A Bibliography on the Method of Paired Comparisons"
    Biometrics, Vol. 32 (1976), pp. 241-52.

41.01 ---------- Theory Re: Paired Comparisons

Arthur, David
    "On Not Understanding Round Robin Product Testing--Comment"
    Journal of the Market Research Society, Vol. 17 (January 1975), p. 49.

Benson, P. H.
    "A Paired Comparison Approach to Evaluating Interviewer Performance"
    Journal of Marketing Research, Vol. VI (February 1969), pp. 66-70.

Berdy, David
    "Order Effects and How Not to Solve Them--Comment"
    Journal of the Market Research Society, Vol. 17 (January 1975), pp.
    45-7.

Blankenship, A. B.
    "Let's Bury Paired Comparisons"
    Journal of Advertising Research, Vol. 6 (March 1966), pp. 13-7.

Boyd, K. T.
    "On Understanding Round Robin Product Testing--Comment"
    Journal of the Market Research Society, Vol. 16 (April 1974), pp.
    138-40.

Bradley, R. A.
    "Another Interpretation of a Model for Paired Comparisons"
    Psychometrika, Vol. 30 (1965), pp. 315-18.

Bradley, R. A.
    "Some Statistical Methods in Taste Testing and Evaluation"
    Biometrics, Vo. 9 (1953), pp. 22-38.

Byer, Albert J. and Abrams, Dorothy
    "A Comparison of the Triangular and Two-Sample Taste Test Methods"
    Food Technology, Vol. 7 (April 1953), pp. 185-7.

Calder, B. and Rowland, K.
    "STIMULI: A FORTRAN IV Program for Presenting Optimally Ordered
    Paired Comparison Stimuli"
    Journal of Marketing Research, Vol. XIV (August 1977), p. 410.

Clarke, T. J.
    "Product Testing in New Product Development"
    Commentary (JMRS), Vol. 9 (July 1967), pp. 135-46.

Clunies-Ross, Charles
    "Round Robins Explained--Comment"
    Journal of the Market Research Society, Vol. 16 (April 1974), pp.
    140-2.

Daniels, Peter and Lawford, John
    "Order Effects and How Not to Solve Them--Reply to Berdy"
    Journal of the Market Research Society, Vol. 17 (January 1975), pp.
    47,8.

Daniels, Peter and Lawford, John
    "The Effect of Order in the Presentation of Samples in Paired
    Comparison Product Tests"
    Journal of the Market Research Society, Vol. 16 (April 1974), pp.
    127-33.

David, H. A.
    The Method of Paired Comparisons
    (New York: Hafner Publishing Company, 1963).

Day, Ralph L.
    "Position Bias in Paired Product Tests"
    Journal of Marketing Research, Vol. VI (February 1969), pp. 98-100.

Day, R. L.
    "Preference Distribution Analysis: A Rejoinder"
    Journal of Marketing Research, Vol. V (November 1968), pp. 438-41.

Day, R. L.
    "Systematic Paired Comparisons in Preference Analysis"
    Journal of Marketing Research, Vol. II (November 1965), pp. 406-12.

Day, R. L.
    "Simulation of Consumer Preference"
    Journal of Advertising Research, Vol. 5 (September 1965), pp. 6-10.

Draper, N. R., Hunter, W. G., and Tierney, D. E.
"Which Product is Better?"
Technometrics, Vol. 11 (May 1969), pp. 309-20.

Greenberg, Allan
"Paired Comparisons vs. Monadic Tests"
Journal of Advertising Research, Vol. 3 (December 1963), pp. 44-7.

Greenberg, A.
"Paired Comparisons in Consumer Product Tests"
Journal of Marketing, Vol. 22 (April 1958), pp. 411-4.

Greenberg, Allan and Collins, Sy
"Paired Comparison Taste Tests: Some Food for Thought"
Journal of Marketing Research, Vol. III (February 1966), 76-80.

Greenhalgh, C.
"Discrimination Tests and Repeated Paired Comparison Tests--Comment"
Journal of the Market Research Society, Vol. 18 (October 1976), pp.
214,5.

Greenhalgh, C.
"Discrimination Testing: Further Results and Developments"
ESOMAR Congress (1970).

Greenhalgh, C.
"Some Techniques and Interesting Results in Discrimination Testing"
Commentary (JMRS), Vol. 8, No. 4 (1966), pp. 215-36.

Gridgeman, N. T.
"Paired Comparison, With and Without Ties"
Biometrics (September 1959), pp. 382-8.

Gruber, Alin and Lindberg, Barbara
"Reaffirmation and a Reply"
Journal of Marketing Research, Vol. VI (February 1969), pp. 105,6.

Gruber, Alin and Lindberg, Barbara
"Sensitivity, Reliability and Consumer Taste Testing"
Journal of Marketing Research, Vol. III (August 1966), pp. 235,6.

Haller, Terry P.
"Let's Not Bury Paired Comparisons"
Journal of Advertising Research, Vol. 6 (September 1966), pp. 29,30.

Hammond, R.
"On Not Understanding Round Robin Product Testing--Reply to Arthur"
Journal of the Market Research Society, Vol. 17 (January 1975), p. 49.

Hammond, R.
"On Not Understanding Round Robin Product Testing--Comment"
Journal of the Market Research Society, Vol. 16 (July 1974), pp.250,1.

Hay, E. N.
"A Simple Method of Recording Paired Comparisons"
Journal of Applied Psychology, Vol. 42 (April 1958), pp. 130-40.

Hill, R. J.
"A Note on Inconsistency in Paired Comparison Judgments"
American Sociological Review, Vol. 18 (October 1953), pp. 564-6.

Hopkins, J. W. and Gridgeman, N. T.
"Comparative Sensitivity of Pair and Triad Flavor Difference Tests"
Biometrics (March 1955).

Horsnell, G.
"Paired Comparison Product Testing When Individual Preferences are
Stochastic: An Alternative Model"
Applied Statistics, Vol. 26 (June 1977), pp. 162-72.

Horsnell, G.
"A Theory of Consumer Preferences Derived From Repeat Paired
Preference Testing"
Journal of the Royal Statistical Society, A, Vol. 132 (1969), pp.
164-93.

Hyett, G. P. and McKenzie, J. R.
"Discrimination Tests and Repeated Paired Comparison Tests--Reply to
Greenhalgh"
Journal of the Market Research Society, Vol. 18 (October 1976), pp.
216,7.

Hyett, G. P. and McKenzie, J. R.
"Discrimination Tests and Repeated Paired Comparison Tests"
Journal of the Market Research Society, Vol. 18 (January 1976), pp.
24-31.

Kaiser, Henry F. and Serlin, Ronald C.
"Contributions to the Method of Paired Comparisons"
Applied Psychological Measurement, Vol. 2 (Summer 1978), pp. 421-30.

Kephart, N. C. and Oliver, J. E.
"A Punched Card Procedure for Use With the Method of Paired
Comparisons"
Journal of Applied Psychology, Vol. 36 (February 1952), pp. 47,8.

Marchant, L. J.
"Non-Additivity in Round Robin Product Tests"
European Research, Vol. 6 (May 1978), pp. 128-31.

Marchant, L. J.
"On Not Understanding Round Robin Product Testing--Reply to Hammond"
Journal of the Marketing Research Society, Vol. 16 (July 1974), p.
251.

Marchant, Len
"On Understanding Round Robin Product Testing--Replies to Willson,
Boyd, and Clunies-Ross"
Journal of the Market Research Society, Vol. 16 (April 1974), pp.
142,3.

Marchant, Len
"On Not Understanding Round Robin Product Testing"
Journal of the Market Research Society, Vol. 16 (January 1974), pp.
46-9.

McCormick, E. J. and Bachus, J. A.
"Paired Comparison Ratings: I. The Effect on Ratings of Reductions in
the Number of Pairs"
Journal of Applied Psychology, Vol. 36 (April 1952), pp. 123-7.

McCormick, E. J. and Roberts, W. K.
"Paired Comparisons: II. The Reliability of Ratings Based on Partial
Pairings"
Journal of Applied Psychology, Vol. 36 (June 1952), pp. 188-92.

Morrison, Henry W., Jr.
"Intransitivity of Paired Comparison Choices"
University of Michigan (1962), unpublished Ph.D. dissertation, 97 pp.

Mosteller, F.
"Remarks on the Method of Paired Comparisons"
Psychometrika, Vol. 16 (1951), pp. 3-11.

Neslin, Scott A.
"Linking Product Features to Perceptions: Application and Analysis of
Graded Paired Comparisons"
in Jain, Subhash C. (editor)
Research Frontiers in Marketing: Dialogues and Directions
(Chicago: American Marketing Association, 1978), pp. 6-11.

Odesky, S. H.
"Handling the Neutral Vote in Paired Comparison Product Testing"
Journal of Marketing Research, Vol. IV (May 1967), pp. 199-201.

Oliver, J. E.
"A Punched Card Procedure for Use With Partial Pairing"
Journal of Applied Psychology, Vol. 37 (April 1953), pp. 129-30.

Pilgrim, Francis J. and Woods, Kenneth R.
"Comparative Sensitivity of Rating Scale and Paired Comparison
Methods for Measuring Consumer Preference"
Food Technology, Vol. 9 (August 1955), pp. 385-7.

Roper, Burns W.
"Sensitivity, Reliability, and Consumer Taste Testing: Some 'Rights'
and 'Wrongs'"
Journal of Marketing Research, Vol. VI (February 1969), pp. 102-6.

Ross, Ivan
"Handling the Neutral Vote in Product Testing"
Journal of Marketing Research, Vol. VI (May 1969), pp. 221,2.

Ross, R. T.
"Optimum Orders for the Presentation of Pairs in the Method of Paired
Comparisons"
Journal of Educational Psychology, Vol. 25 (March 1934), pp. 375-82.

Slater, Patrick
"Inconsistencies in a Schedule of Paired Comparisons"
Biometrika, Vol. 48 (1961), pp. 303-12.

Taylor, J. R.
"Reevaluation of Preference Distribution Analysis"
Journal of Marketing Research, Vol. V (November 1968), pp. 434-8.

Wierenga, B.
"Paired Comparison Product Testing When Individual Preferences are
Stochastic"
Applied Statistics, Vol. 23 (September 1974), pp. 284-96.

Willson, Eric
"On Understanding Round Robin Product Testing--Comment"
Journal of the Market Research Society, Vol. 16 (April 1974), pp.
136-8.

Winick, C.
"Art Work Versus Photography: An Experimental Study"
Journal of Applied Psychology, Vol. 43 (June 1959), pp. 180-2.

41.02 ---------- Theory Re: Analysis of Paired Comparisons

Balinsky, B., Blum, M. L., and Dutka, S.
"The Coefficient of Agreement in Determining Product Preferences"
Journal of Applied Psychology, Vol. 35 (October 1951), pp. 348-51.

Bennett, Sidney C.
"PAIRED: A Program to Analyze Paired Comparisons or Ordinal Data"
Journal of Marketing Research, Vol. XVI (November 1979), pp. 561,2.

Bockenholt, I. and Gaul, W.
"Probabilistic Multidimensional Scaling of Paired Comparisons"
in Bock, H. H. (editor)
Proceedings, First Conference of the International Federation of
Classification Societies
(Aachen: North-Holland, 1987).

Bradley, R. A. and Terry, M. E.
"Rank Analysis of Incomplete Block Designs, I: The Method of Paired
Comparisons"
Biometrika, Vol. 39 (1952), pp. 324-45.

Cohen, Louis
"Use of Paired-Comparison Analysis to Increase Statistical Power of
Ranked Data"
Journal of Marketing Research, Vol. IV (August 1967), pp. 309.

Draper, N. R., Hunter, W. G., and Tierney, D. E.
"Analyzing Paired Comparison Tests"
Journal of Marketing Research, Vol. VI (November 1969), pp. 477-80.

Greenberg, M. G.
"A Method of Successive Cumulations for the Scaling of
Pair-Comparison Preference Judgments"
Psychometrika, Vol. 30 (December 1965), pp. 441-8.

Guttman, L.
"An Approach for Quantifying Paired Comparisons and Rank Orders"
Annals of Mathematical Statistics, Vol. 17 (1946), pp. 144-63.

Huber, Joel and Sheluga, David A.
"The Analysis of Graded Paired Comparisons in Marketing Research"
Graduate School of Business, Columbia University, working paper.

Kernan, J. B.
"Paired Comparisons and Graph Theory"
Journal of Marketing Research, Vol. IV (February 1967), pp. 67-72.

Moore, William L. and Lehmann, Donald R.
"A Paired Comparison Nested Logit Model of Individual Preference
Structures"
Journal of Marketing Research, Vol. XXVI (November 1989), pp. 420-8.

Mosteller, F.
"A Test of Significance for Paired Comparisons When Equal Standard
Deviations and Equal Correlations are Assumed"
Psychometrika, Vol. 16 (1951), pp. 207,8.

Nishisato, Shizuhiko
"Optimal Scaling of Paired Comparisons and Rank Order Data: An
Alternative to Guttman's Formulation"
Psychometrika, Vol. 43 (1978), pp. 263-71.

Pessemier, E. A. and Teach, R. D.
"Disaggregation of Analysis Variance for Paired Comparisons: An
Application to Marketing Experiments"
Paper No. 282
Krannert Graduate School of Industrial Administration, Purdue
University (1970).

Reitter, Robert
"Statistical Regression--Comment to Reynolds"
Journal of Advertising Research, Vol. 6 (June 1966), pp. 54,5.

Reynolds, William H.
"Rejoinder--To Reitter"
Journal of Advertising Research, Vol. 6 (June 1966), p. 55.

Reynolds, William H.
  "Statistical Regression in Before-And-After Paired Comparison Studies"
  Journal of Advertising Research, Vol. 6 (March 1966), pp. 18-20.

Scheffe, H.
  "The Analysis of Variance for Paired Comparisons"
  Journal of the American Statistical Association, Vol. 47 (1952), pp.
  381-400.

Sirotnik, Barbara W. and Beaver, Robert J.
  "Paired Comparison Experiments Involving All Possible Pairs"
  British Journal of Mathematical and Statistical Psychology, Vol. 37
  (May 1984), pp. 22-33.

Van De Sandt, Udolpho
  "Incomplete Paired Comparisons Using Balanced Lattice Designs"
  Journal of Marketing Research, Vol. VII (May 1970), pp. 246-8.

Weingarden, P. and Nishisato, Shizuhiko
  "Can a Method of Rank Ordering Reproduce Paired Comparisons? An
  Analysis by Dual Scaling (Correspondence Analysis)"
  Canadian Journal of Marketing Research, Vol. 5 (1986), pp. 11-8.

Wong, George Y.
  "Rank-One Round Robin Designs"
  Journal of the American Statistical Association, Vol. 79 (March
  1984), pp. 136-44.

42 ------------------ PICK K OF N OR PICK-ANY DATA -------------------
42.01 ---------- Theory Re: Pick K of N or Pick-Any Data

Dempster, Arthur P., Laird, Nan M., and Rubin, Donald B.
"Maximum Likelihood Estimation From Incomplete Data via the E. M.
Algorithm"
Journal of the Royal Statistical Society, Vol. B39 (1977), pp. 1-38.

Green, Paul E. and DeSarbo, Wayne
"Two Models for Representing Unrestricted Choice Data"
in Monroe, Kent B. (editor)
Advances in Consumer Research, Volume Eight
(Ann Arbor, MI: Association for Consumer Research, 1981), pp. 309-12.

Green, Paul E. and DeSarbo, Wayne
"Two Models for Representing Unrestricted Choice Data"
University of Pennsylvania (September 1979), working paper.

Green, Paul E. and Schaffer, Catherine M.
"A Simple Method for Analysing Consumer Preferences for Product
Benefits"
Journal of the Market Research Society, Vol 26 (January 1984),
pp.51-61.

Holbrook, Morris B., Moore, William L., and Winer, Russell S.
"Constructing Joint Spaces From 'Pick-Any' Data: A New Tool for
Consumer Analysis"
Journal of Consumer Research, Vol. 9 (June 1982), pp. 99-105.

Holbrook, Morris B., Moore, William L., and Winer, Russell S.
"Using 'Pick Any' Data to Represent Competitive Positions"
in Leone, Robert P. (editor)
Proceedings, Second ORSA/TIMS Special Interest Conference on Market
Measurement and Analysis
(Austin, TX: Institute of Management Science, 1980), pp. 129-34.

Levine, Joel H.
"Joint-Space Analysis of 'Pick-Any' Data: Analysis of Choices From an
Unconstrained Set of Alternatives"
Psychometrika, Vol. 44 (1979), pp. 85-92.

Schmittlein, David C.
"Assessing Validity and Test-Retest Reliability for 'Pick K of N'
Data"
Marketing Science, Vol. 3 (Winter 1984), pp. 23-40.

Takane, Yoshio
"Choice Model Analysis of the 'Pick Any/n' Type of Binary Data"
European Psychometric and Classification Meetings (July 1983),
handout.

43 ------------------------ REPERTORY GRID -------------------------

See also (sub)heading(s) 37.

43.01 ---------- Theory Re: The Repertory Grid

Bannister, Donald
  "A New Theory of Personality"
  in Foss, B. M. (editor)
  New Horizons in Psychology
  (London: Penguin Books, 1966), pp. 361-80.

Bannister, Donald and Mair, J. M. M.
  The Evaluation of Personal Constructs
  (London: Academic Press, 1968).

Bannister, Donald
  "Personal Construct Theory: A Summary and Experimental Paradigm"
  Acta Psychologica, Vol. 20 (March 1962), pp. 104-20.

Eden, Colin and Jones, Sue
  "Using Repertory Grids for Problem Construction"
  Journal of the Operational Research Society, Vol. 35 (September
  1984), pp. 779-90.

Fransella, Fay and Bannister, Don
  A Manual for Repertory Grid Techniques
  (Academic Press).

Gutman, Jonathan and Reynolds, Thomas J.
  "An Improved Format for Reporting Repertory Grid Results"
  Proceedings, 1983 AMA Fall Educators' Conference
  (Chicago: American Marketing Association, 1983).

Kelly, George A.
  The Psychology of Personal Constructs, Volumes I and II
  (New York: Norton, 1955).

Lunn, J. A.
  Perspectives in Attitude Research: Methods and Applications"
  Journal of the Market Research Society, Vol. 11 (July 1969), pp.
  201-13.

Reynolds, Thomas J. and Gutman, J.
  "Laddering: Extending the Repertory Grid Methodology to Construct
  Attribute-Consequence-Value Hierarchies"
  in Pitts, R. and Woodside, A. G. (editors)
  Personal Values and Consumer Psychology
  (Lexington, MA: Lexington Books, 1984).

Sampson, Peter
  "Using the Repertory Grid Test"
  Journal of Marketing Research, Vol. IX (February 1972), pp. 78-81.

Stewart, Valerie, Stewart, Andrew, and Fonda, Nickie
  Business Applications of Repertory Grid
  (McGraw-Hill Book Company (UK) Ltd., 1981), 271 pp.

43.02 ---------- Applications of the Repertory Grid

Clemens, John and Thornton, Crossley
  "Evaluating Nonexistent Products"
  Admap, Vol. IV (April 1968), p. 5.

Frost, W. A. K.
  "The Development of a Technique for TV Program Assessment"
  Journal of the Market Research Society, Vol. 11 (January 1969), pp.
  25-44.

Frost, W. A. K. and Braine, R. L.
  "The Application of the Repertory Grid to Problems in Market Research"
  Commentary, Vol. 9 (October 1967), pp. 161-75.

Riley, Stuart and Palmer, John
  "Of Attitudes and Latitudes: A Repertory Grid Study of Perceptions of
  Seaside Resorts"
  Journal of the Market Research Society, Vol. 17 (April 1975), pp.
  74-89.

Sampson, Peter
  "An Examination of Exploratory Research Techniques"
  Proceedings, ESOMAR Congress (1969), pp. 1-18.

Sampson, Peter
  "The Repertory Grid and Its Application to Market Research"
  Proceedings, Conference on Attitude and Motivation Research, American
  Marketing Association.

44 ------------------------ GRAPH THEORY ------------------------
        See also (sub)heading(s) 37.

44.01 ---------- Graph Theory

Berge, Claude
    The Theory of Graphs and Its Applications
    (New York, NY: John Wiley and Sons, Inc., 1962).

Bettman, James R.
    "A Graph Theory Approach to Comparing Consumer Information Processing
    Models"
    Management Science, Vol. 19, Part II (December 1971), pp. 114-29.

Kernan, Jerome B.
    "Paired Comparisons and Graph Theory"
    Journal of Marketing Research, Vol. IV (February 1967), pp. 67-72.

Kernan, Jerome B.
    "Graph Theoretic Models in Marketing"
    Scientific Business, Vol. 3 (Spring 1966), pp. 331-43.

Spier, Leo
    "Graph Theory as a Method for Exploring Business Behavior"
    in McGuire, J. W. (editor)
    Interdisciplinary Studies in Business Behavior
    (Cincinnati, OH: South-Western Publishing Company, 1962), pp. 70-98.

44.02 ---------- Applications of Graph Theory

Flament, Claude
    Applications of Graph Theory to Group Structure
    (Englewood Cliffs, NJ: Prentice-Hall, Inc., 1963).

Harary, Frank and Lipstein, Benjamin
    "The Dynamics of Brand Loyalty: A Markovian Approach"
    Operations Research, Vol. 10 (January-February 1962), pp. 19-40.

Shannon, C. E. and Weaver, Warren
    The Mathematical Theory of Communication
    (Urbana, IL: University of Illinois Press, 1962).

45 ------------ WORD, PHRASE, AND STATEMENT SCALE VALUES -------------
          See also (sub)heading(s) 37.

Angelmar, Reinhard and Pras, Bernard
  "Verbal Rating Scales for Multinational Research"
  European Research, Vol. 6 (March 1978), pp. 62-7.

Bartram, Peter and Yelding, David
  "Adverbial Qualifiers for Adjectival Scales--Reply to Schofield"
  Journal of the Market Research Society, Vol. 17 (July 1975), pp.
  207,8.

Bartram, Peter and Yelding, David
  "The Development of an Empirical Method of Selecting Phrases Used in
  Verbal Rating Scales: A Report on a Recent Experiment"
  Journal of the Market Research Society, Vol. 15 (July 1973), pp.
  151-6.

Cliff, Norman
  "Adverbs as Multipliers"
  Psychological Review, Vol. 66 (January 1959), pp. 27-44.

Copper, G.
  "Semantic Properties of Selected Evaluative Adjectives--Replication"
  University of Lancaster (1973), masters thesis.

Dodd, S. C. and Gerbrick, T. R.
  "Word Scales for Degrees of Opinion"
  Language and Speech, Vol. 3 (1960), pp. 18-31.

Ferber, R.
  "Gradational Adjectives in Market Surveys"
  Journal of Applied Psychology, Vol. 39 (June 1955), pp. 173-7.

Fine, B. J. and Haggard, D. F.
  "Contextual Effects in Scaling"
  Journal of Applied Psychology, Vol. 42 (1958), pp. 247-51.

Friedman, H. H., Wilamowsky, Y., and Friedman, W.
  "A Comparison of Balanced and Unbalanced Rating Scales"
  Mid-Atlantic Journal of Business, Vol. 19 (1981), pp. 1-7.

Holmes, C.
  "A Statistical Evaluation of Rating Scales"
  Journal of the Market Research Society, Vol. 16 (1974), pp. 87-107.

Jones, Lyle V. and Thurstone, L. L.
  "The Psychophysics of Semantics: An Experimental Investigation"
  Journal of Applied Psychology, Vol. 39 (February 1955), pp. 31-6.

Lusk, Edward J.
  "A Bipolar Adjective Screening Methodology"
  Journal of Marketing Research, Vol. X (May 1973), pp. 202,3.

Mittelstaedt, Robert A.
  "Semantic Properties of Selected Evaluation Adjectives: Other
  Evidence"
  Journal of Marketing Research, Vol. VIII (May 1971), pp. 236,7.

Myers, James H. and Warner, W. Gregory
  "Semantic Properties of Selected Evaluation Adjectives"
  Journal of Marketing Research, Vol. V (November 1968), pp. 409-13.

Schertzer, Clinton B. and Kernan, Jerome B.
  "More on the Robustness of Response Scales"
  Journal of the Market Research Society, Vol. 27 (October 1985), pp.
  261-82.

Schofield, A.
  "Adverbial Qualifiers for Adjectival Scales--Comment"
  Journal of the Market Research Society, Vol. 17 (July 1975), pp.
  204-7.

Vidali, Joseph J.
  "Context Effects on Scaled Evaluatory Adjective Meaning"
  Journal of the Market Research Society, Vol. 17 (January 1975), pp.
  21-5.

Wells, W. D., Andriuli, F. J., Goi, F. J., and Seader, S.
  "An Adjective Check List for the Study of Product Personality"
  Journal of Applied Psychology, Vol. 41 (1957), pp. 317-9.

Wildt, A. R. and Mazis, M. B.
  "Determinants of Scale Response: Label Versus Position"
  Journal of Marketing Research, Vol. XV (1978), pp. 261-7.

Worcester, R. M. and Burns, T. R.
  "A Statistical Examination of the Relative Precision of Verbal Scales"
  Journal of the Market Research Society, Vol. 17 (1975), pp. 181-97.

46 --------------- SCALING - MISCELLANEOUS TECHNIQUES ----------------
            See also (sub)heading(s) 37.

46.01 ---------- Free Response
            See also (sub)heading(s) 34.05, 79, 86.05, 131.04, 132.02.

Boivin, Yvan
    "A Free Response Approach to the Measurement of Brand Perceptions"
    International Journal of Research in Marketing, Vol. 3, No. 1 (1986),
    pp. 11-7.

Canter, R. R., Jr.
    "A Rating-Scoring Method for Free-Response Data"
    Journal of Applied Psychology, Vol. 37 (December 1953), pp. 455-7.

Jain, Arun K. and Etgar, M.
    "Measuring Store Image Through Multidimensional Scaling of Free
    Response Data"
    Journal of Retailing, Vol. 52, No. 4 (1976-77), pp. 61-70.

Green, Paul E., Wind, Yoram, and Jain, Arun K.
    "Analyzing Free-Response Data in Marketing Research"
    Journal of Marketing Research, Vol. X (1973), pp. 45-52.

Olson, J. C. and Muderrisoglu, A.
    "The Stability of Response Obtained by Free Elicitation: Implications
    for Measuring Attribute Salience and Memory Structure"
    Advances in Consumer Research, Volume 6 (1978), pp. 269-75.

46.02 ---------- Stapel Scales

Crespi, I.
    "Use of a Scaling Technique in Surveys"
    Journal of Marketing, Vol. 25 (July 1961), pp. 69-72.

Hawkins, Del I.
    "Utilization of the Stapel Scale in Attitude Measurement"
    Southwestern Social Science Association (1973).

Vidali, J. J., Jr.
    "Single-Anchor Stapel Scales Versus Double-Anchor Semantic
    Differential Scales"
    Psychological Reports, Vol. 33 (1973), pp. 373,4.

Vidali, J. J., Jr. and Holeway, R. E.
    "Stapel Scales Versus Semantic Differential Scales"
    Psychological Reports, Vol. 35 (1975), pp. 165,6.

46.03 ---------- Thurstone's Equal-Appearing Interval Scales

Thurstone, Louis Leon
    "Attitudes can be Measured"
    American Journal of Sociology, Vol. 33 (January 1928), pp. 529-54.

46.04 ---------- Anchoring Issues

Bendig, A. W.
    "The Reliability of Self-Rating as a Function of the Amount of Verbal
    Anchoring and of the Number of Categories on the Scale"
    Journal of Applied Psychology, Vol. 37 (1953), pp. 38-41.

Boote, Alfred S.
    "Reliability Testing of Psychographic Scales"
    Journal of Advertising Research, Vol. 21 (October 1981), pp. 53-60.

Dickinson, John R.
    "Impact of Scale Anchor Points on Response Variance"Proceedings,
    Administrative Sciences Association of Canada (May 1985).

Haley, Russell I. and Case, Peter B.
    "Testing Thirteen Attitude Scales for Agreement and Brand
    Discrimination"
    Journal of Marketing, Vol. 43 (Fall 1979), pp. 20-32.

Smith, P. C. and Kendall, L. M.
    "Retranslation of Expectations: An Approach to the Construction of
    Unambiguous Anchors for Rating Scales"
    Journal of Applied Psychology, Vol. 47 (1963), pp. 149-55.

46.05 ---------- Graphic or Continuous Scales

See also (sub)heading(s) 54.04.

Altuner, H. J., Altuner, D., and Chappell, V. G.
"The Effect of Traditional Versus Graphic Positioning Scales on Response Rate and Accuracy in Mail Surveys" unpublished paper.

Bunder, P., Vincent, F., and Ursic, M.
"Graphic Versus Semantic Differential Scales: An Empirical Comparison" Annual Conference, Southeast Association for Decision Sciences (1984), paper presentation.

Champney, Horace and Marshall, Helen
"Optimal Refinement of the Rating Scale"
Journal of Applied Psychology, Vol. 23 (June 1939), pp. 323-31.

Friedman, Linda Weiser and Friedman, Hershey H.
"Comparison of Itemised vs. Graphic Rating Scales: A Validity Approach"
Journal of the Market Research Society, Vol. 28 (July 1986), pp. 285-9.

Golden, Linda L., Albaum, Gerald, and Zimmer, Mary
"The Numerical Comparative Scale: An Economical Format for Retail Image Measurement"
Journal of Retailing, Vol. 63 (Winter 1987), pp. 393-410.

Grigg, A. O.
"Some Problems Concerning the Use of Rating Scales for Visual Assessment"
Journal of the Market Research Society, Vol. 22, No. 1 (1980), pp. 29-43.

Katz, Daniel
"The Measurement of Intensity"
in Cantril, Hadley (editor)
Gauging Public Opinion
(Princeton, NJ: Princeton University Press, 1944), pp. 51-65.

Keaveny, Timothy J. and McGann, Anthony F.
"A Comparison of Behavioral Expectation Scales and Graphic Rating Scales"
Journal of Applied Psychology, Vol. 60 (1975), pp. 695-703.

Narayana, Chem L.
"Graphic Positioning Scale: An Economical Instrument for Surveys"
Journal of Marketing Research, Vol. XIV (February 1977), pp. 118-22.

Ramsey, J. O. and Case, P.
"Attitude Measurement and the Linear Model"
Psychological Bulletin, Vol. 74 (1970), pp. 185-92.

Rizzo, William A. and Frank, Fredric D.
"Influence of Irrelevant Cues and Alternate Forms of Graphic Rating Scales on the Halo Effect"
Personnel Psychology, Vol. 30 (1977), pp. 405-17.

Smith, P. C. and Kendall, L. M.
"Retranslation of Expectations: An Approach to the Construction of Unambiguous Anchors for Rating Scales"
Journal of Applied Psychology, Vol. 47 (1963), pp. 149-55.

Stem, D. E., Jr. and Noazin, S.
"The Effects of Number of Objects and Scale Positions on Graphic Position Scale Reliability"
American Marketing Association Educators' Conference (1985), paper presentation.

Taylor, Erwin K. and Hastman, Roy
"Relation of Format and Administration to the Characteristics of Graphic Rating Scales"
Personnel Psychology, Vol. 9 (1956), pp. 181-206.

Taylor, J. R. and Parker, H. A.
"Graphic Ratings and Attitude Measurement: A Comparison of Research Tactics"
Journal of Applied Psychology, Vol. 48 (February 1964), pp. 37-42.

Van Doorn, L., Saris, Willem E., and Lodge, M. M.
"Discrete or Continuous Measurement: What Difference Does it Make?"
Kwantitatieve Methoden, Vol. 10 (1983), pp. 104-21.

Wildt, Albert R. and Mazis, Michael B.
"Determinants of Scale Response: Label Versus Position"
Journal of Marketing Research, Vol. XV (May 1978), pp. 261-7.

46.06 ---------- Pollimeter Scale

Lampert, Shlomo I.
"A New Scale for Consumer Research"
Journal of Advertising Research, Vol. 21 (April 1981), pp. 23-29.

Lampert, Shlomo I.
"The Attitude Pollimeter--A New Attitude Scaling Device"
Journal of Marketing Research, Vol. XVI (November 1979), pp. 578-82.

Lampert, Shlomo I.
"A New Approach to Pre-Election Polling"
Public Opinion Quarterly, Vol. 42 (1978), pp. 259-64.

46.07 ---------- Theory Re: Laddering

Reynolds, Thomas J. and Gutman, Jonathan
"Laddering Theory, Method, Analysis, and Interpretation"
Journal of Advertising Research, Vol. 28 (February/March 1988), pp. 11-31.

Reynolds, Thomas J. and Gutman, Jonathan
"Laddering: Extending the Repertory Grid Methodology to Construct Attribute-Consequence-Value Hierarchies"
in Pitts, R. and Woodside, A. (editors)
Personal Values and Consumer Psychology, Volume II
(Lexington, MA: Lexington Books, 1984).

46.08 ---------- Applications of Laddering

Gutman, Jonathan
"Analyzing Consumer Orientations Toward Beverages Through Means-Ends Chain Analysis"
Psychology and Marketing, Vol. 1, No. 3/4 (1984), pp. 23-43.

Gutman, Jonathan and Alden, Scott
"Adolescents' Cognitive Structures of Retail Stores and Fashion Consumption: A Means-End Analysis"
in Jacoby, J. and Olson, J. (editors)
Perceive Quality of Products, Services and Stores
(Lexington, MA: Lexington Books, 1984).

Gutman, Jonathan and Reynolds, Thomas J.
"An Investigation at the Levels of Cognitive Abstraction Utilized by the Consumers in Product Differentiation"
in Eighmey, John (editor)
Attitude Research Under the Sun
(Chicago: American Marketing Association, 1979).

Gutman, Jonathan, Reynolds, Thomas J., and Fiedler, John
"The Value Structure Map: A New Analytic Framework for Family Decision-Making"
in Roberts, M. L. and Woertzel, L. (editors)
(Ballinger Publishing, 1984).

Olson, Jerry C. and Reynolds, Thomas J.
"Understanding Consumers' Cognitive Structures: Implications for Advertising Strategy"
in Percy, L. and Woodside, A. (editors)
Advertising and Consumer Psychology, Volume I
Lexington, MA: Lexington Books, 1983).

Reynolds, Thomas J. and Craddock, Alice Byrd
"The Application of the MECCAS Model to the Development and Assessment of Advertising Strategy"
Journal of Advertising Research, Vol. 28 (April/May 1988), pp. 43-54.

Reynolds, Thomas J. and Gutman, Jonathan
"Advertising is Image Management"
Journal of Advertising Research, Vol. 24, No. 1 (1984), pp. 27-36.

Reynolds, Thomas J., Gutman, Jonathan, and Fiedler, John
"Understanding Consumers' Cognitive Structures: The Relationship of Levels of Abstraction to Judgments of Psychological Distance and Preference"
in Mitchell, A. and Alwitt, L. (editors)
Psychological Processes of Advertising Effects: Theory, Research and Application
(Erlbaum, 1984).

Reynolds, Thomas J. and Jamieson, Linda
"Image Representations: An Analytical Framework"
in Jacoby, J. and Olson, J. (editors)
Perceived Quality of Products, Services and Stores
(Lexington, MA: Lexington Books, 1984).

Steward, Jeanne
"Image Management: The Use of the Laddering Technique in
Understanding and Developing Product Images"
Proceedings, ESOMAR Congress, Lisbon (1988), pp. 775-92.

46.09 ---------- Theory Re: Balanced Incomplete Block Designs

Bose, R. C.
"On the Construction of Balanced Incomplete Block Designs"
Annals of Eugenics, Vol. 9 (June 1939), pp. 353-99.

Bradley, Ralph and Terry, Milton
"Rank Analysis of Incomplete Block Designs"
Biometrika, Vol. 39 (January 1952), pp. 324-45.

Clatworthy, Willard
"Partially Balanced Incomplete Block Designs With Two Associate
Classes and Two Treatments per Block"
Journal of Research of the National Bureau of Standards, Vol. 54
(April 1955), pp. 177-90.

Durbin, J.
"Incomplete Blocks in Ranking Experiments"
British Journal of Psychology, Statistical Section 4 (November 1951),
pp. 85-90.

Rink, David R.
"An Improved Preference Data Collection Method: Balanced Incomplete
Block Designs"
Journal of the Academy of Marketing Science, Vol. 15 (Spring 1987),
pp. 54-61.

Yates, F.
"A New Method of Arranging Variety Trials Involving a Large Number of
Varieties"
Journal of Agricultural Science, Vol. 26 (June 1936), pp. 424-55.

Yates, F.
"Incomplete Randomized Blocks"
Annals of Eugenics, Vol. 7 (March 1936), pp. 121-40.

Wiley, James B.
"BIBD: A Data Management Program for 'BIBD' Choice Data"
Journal of Marketing Research, Vol. XV (August 1978), pp. 472-4.

46.10 ---------- Applications of Balanced Incomplete Block Designs

Youden, W. J.
"Use of Incomplete Block Replications in Estimating Tobacco-Mosaic
Virus"
Contributions From Boyce Thompson Institute, Vol. 9 (November 1937),
pp. 41-8.

46.11 ---------- Unclassified (Scaling - Miscellaneous Techniques)

Allaire, Yvan
"The Measurement of Heterogeneous Semantic, Perceptual, and
Preference Structures"
Massachusetts Institute of Technology (1973), unpublished Ph.D.
thesis.

Attneave, Fred
"A Method of Graded Dichotomies for the Scaling of Judgments"
Psychological Review, Vol. 56 (November 1949), pp. 334-40.

Bennett, E. M., Kemler, D., and Levin, B. T.
"Emotional Associations With Air and Rail Transportation"
Journal of Psychology, Vol. 43 (January 1957), pp. 65-75.

Benson, P. H.
"A Short Method for Estimating a Distribution of Consumer Preferences"
Journal of Applied Psychology, Vol. 46 (October 1962), pp. 307-13.

Bernardin, H. John and Walter, C. S.
"Effects of Rater Training and Diary-Keeping on Psychometric Error in
Ratings"
Journal of Applied Psychology, Vol. 62 (1977), pp. 64-9.

Bernberg, R. E.
"The Direction of Perception Technique of Attitude Measurement"
International Journal of Opinion and Attitude Research, Vol. 5 (Fall
1951), pp. 397-406.

Borman, Walter C.
"Consistency of Rating Accuracy and Rating Errors in the Judgment of
Human Performance"
Organizational Behavior and Human Performance, Vol. 20 (1977), pp.
238-52.

Borman, Walter C.
"Effects of Instructions to Avoid Halo Error on Reliability and
Validity of Performance Evaluation Ratings"
Journal of Applied Psychology, Vol. 60 (1975), pp. 556-60.

Borman, Walter C. and Vallon, W. Robert
"A View of What can Happen When Behavioral Expectations Scales are
Developed in One Setting and Used in Another"
Journal of Applied Psychology, Vol. 59 (1974), pp. 197-201.

Brabb, G. J. and Morrison, D.
"The Evaluation of Subjective Information"
Journal of Marketing Research, Vol. I (November 1964), pp. 40-4.

Brown, George H.
"Measuring Consumer Attitudes Towards Products"
Journal of Marketing, Vol. 14 (April 1950), pp. 691-8.

Comrey, Andrew L.
"A Proposed Method for Absolute Ratio Scaling"
Psychometrika, Vol. 15 (September 1950), pp. 317-25.

Davis, John Marcell
"The Transitivity of Preferences"
Behavioural Science, Vol. III (January 1958), pp. 26-33.

Dodd, Robert W. and Whipple, Thomas W.
"Item Selection: A Practical Tool in Attitude Research"
Journal of Marketing, Vol. 40 (July 1976), pp. 87-9.

Duncan, G. T.
"An Empirical Bayes Approach to Scoring Multiple Choice Tests in the
Misinformation Model"
Journal of the American Statistical Association, Vol. 69 (March
1974), pp. 50-7.

Edwards, Allen L.
"The Scaling of Stimuli by the Method of Successive Intervals"
Journal of Applied Psychology, Vol. 36 (April 1952), pp. 118-22.

Eiser, J. R.
"Enhancement of Contrast in the Absolute Judgement of Attitude
Statements"
Journal of Personality and Social Psychology, Vol. 17 (January 1971),
pp. 1-10.

Friedman, Barry A. and Cornelius, Edwin T., III
"Effect of Rater Participation in Scale Construction on the
Psychometric Characteristics of Two Rating Scale Formats"
Journal of Applied Psychology, Vol. 61 (1976), pp. 210-6.

Grigg, A. O.
"Some Problems Concerning the Use of Rating Scales for Visual
Assessment"
Journal of the Market Research Society, Vol. 22 (January 1980).

Hamblin, Robert L.
"Reducing Error in Question and Scale Design: A Conceptual Framework"
Decision Sciences

Hamilton, C. H.
"Bias and Error in Multiple Choice Tests"
Psychometrika, Vol. 15 (June 1950), pp. 151-68.

Hauser, John R. and Shugan, Steven M.
"Efficient Measurement of Consumer Preference Functions: A General
Theory for Intensity of Preference"
Working Paper 602-001
Graduate School of Management, Northwestern University (1980).

Hughes, G. D.
"Some Confounding Effects of Forced Choice Scales"
Journal of Marketing Research, Vol. VI (May 1969), pp. 223-6.

Hughes, G. D.
"A New Tool for Sales Managers"
Journal of Marketing Research, Vol. I (May 1964), pp. 32-8.

Keats, J. A. and Lord, F. M.
"A Theoretical Distribution for Mental Test Scores"
Psychometrika, Vol. 27 (March 1962), pp. 59-72.

Kilpatrick, F. P. and Cantril, Hadley
"Self-Anchoring Scaling--A Measure of Individuals' Unique Reality
Worlds"
Journal of Individual Psychology, Vol. 16 (November 1960).

Lord, F. M. and Stocking, M. L.
"An Interval Estimate for Making Statistical Inferences About True
Scores"
Psychometrika, Vol. 41 (March 1976), pp. 79-87.

Lyerly, S. B.
"A Note for Correcting for Chance Success in Objective Tests"
Psychometrika, Vol. 16 (March 1951), pp. 21-30.

Moskowitz, H. R. and Jacobs, B.
"Ratio Scaling of Perception vs. Image: Its Use in Evaluating
Advertising Promise vs. Product Delivery"
in Leigh, J. H. and Martin, C. R., Jr. (editors)
Current Issues and Research in Advertising
(Ann Arbor, MI: Division of Research, Graduate School of Business
Administration, University of Michigan, 1980).

Pessemier, Edgar A., Burger, Philip, Teach, Richard, and Tigert, Douglas
"Using Laboratory Brand Preference Scales to Predict Consumer Brand
Purchases"
Management Science, Vol. 17 (1971), pp. B371-85.

Reynolds, W. H.
"Some Empirical Observations on a Ten-Point Poor-To-Excellent Scale"
Journal of Marketing Research, Vol. III (November 1966), pp. 388-90.

Stapel, J.
"Two Dimensional 'Trade Offs'"
European Research, pp. 145-50.

Symonds, Percival M.
"Notes on Rating"
Journal of Applied Psychology, Vol. 9 (1925), pp. 189-95.

Thorndike, Edward L.
"A Consistent Error in Psychological Ratings"
Journal of Applied Psychology, Vol. 4 (1920), pp. 25-9.

Tisdale, J. R.
"Assessing Qualitative Difference Between Sets of Data"
Journal of Psychology, Vol. 66 (July 1967), pp. 175-9.

Tversky, Amos
"Intransitivity of Preferences"
Psychological Review, Vol. 76 (January 1969), pp. 31-48.

Upah, Gregory D. and Cosmas, Stephen C.
"The Use of Telephone Dials as Attitude Scales: A Laboratory
Experiment"
Journal of the Academy of Marketing Science, Vol. 8 (Fall 1980), pp.
416-26.

Wells, William D.
"EQ, Son of EQ, and the Reaction Profile"
Journal of Marketing, Vol. 28 (October 1964), pp. 45-52.

Wells, William D.
"Recognition, Recall, and Rating Scales"
Journal of Advertising Research, Vol. IV (September 1964), pp. 2-8.

Willis, R. H.
"Manipulation of Item Marginal Frequencies by Means of
Multiple-Response Items"
Psychological Review, Vol. 67 (January 1960), pp. 32-50.

Worcester, Robert M. and Burns, Timothy R.
"A Statistical Examination of the Relative Precision of Verbal Scales"
Journal of the Market Research Society, Vol. 17 (July 1975), pp.
181-97.

Zedeck, Sheldon, Kafry, Ditsa, and Jacobs, Rick
"Format and Scoring Variations in Behavioral Expectation Evaluations"
Organizational Behavior and Human Performance, Vol. 17 (1976), pp.
171-84.

47 ------------- THURSTONE'S LAW OF COMPARATIVE JUDGMENT ------------
        See also (sub)heading(s) 37.

47.01 ---------- Books Re: Thurstone's Law

Thurstone, L. L.
  The Measurement of Values
  (Chicago: University of Chicago Press, 1959).

Thurstone, L. L. and Chave, E. J.
  The Measurement of Attitude
  (Chicago: University of Chicago Press, 1929), 97 pp.

47.02 ---------- Theory Re: Thurstone's Law

Ager, J. W. and Dawes, R. M.
  "The Effect of Judges' Attitudes on Judgment"
  Journal of Personality and Social Psychology, Vol. 1 (May 1965), pp.
  533-8.

Ayad, J. M. and Farnsworth, P. R.
  "Shifts in the Values of Opinion Items: Further Data"
  Journal of Psychology, Vol. 36 (October 1953), pp. 295-8.

Benson, P. H. and Platten, J. H., Jr.
  "Preference Measurement by the Methods of Successive Intervals and
  Monetary Estimates"
  Journal of Applied Psychology, Vol. 40 (December 1956), pp. 412-4.

Greenberg, Marshall G.
  "A Modification of Thurstone's Law of Comparative Judgment to
  Accommodate a Judgment Category of 'Equal' or 'No Difference'"
  Psychological Bulletin, Vol. 64 (August 1965), pp. 108-12.

Hefner, R. A.
  "Extensions of the Law of Comparative Judgment to Discriminable and
  Multidimensional Stimuli"
  University of Michigan (1958), doctoral dissertation.

Himmelfarb, S.
  "The Stability of Attitude Item Scale Values"
  Journal of Social Psychology, Vol. 77 (February 1969), pp. 107-11.

Hovland, Carl I. and Sherif, Muzafer
  "Judgmental Phenomena and Scales of Attitude Measurement: Item
  Displacement in Thurstone Scales"
  Journal of Abnormal and Social Psychology, Vol. 47 (October 1952),
  pp. 822-32.

Huber, Joel and Sewall, Murphy A.
  "Covariance Bias of Thurstone Case V Scaling as Applied to Consumer
  Preferences and Purchase Intentions"
  in Wilkie, William L. (editor)
  Advances in Consumer Research, Volume Six
  (Ann Arbor, MI: Association for Consumer Research, 1979), pp. 578-81.

Mosteller, F.
  "A Test of Significance for Paired Comparisons When Equal Standard
  Deviations and Equal Correlations are Assumed"
  Psychometrika, Vol. 16 (1951), pp. 207,8.

Rambo, W. W.
  "Own-Attitude and the Aberrant Placement of Socially Relevant Items
  on an Equal Appearing Interval Scale"
  Journal of Social Psychology, Vol. 79 (December 1969), pp. 163-70.

Rambo, W. W.
  "The Distribution of Successive Interval Judgments of Attitude
  Statements: A Note"
  Journal of Social Psychology, Vol. 60 (August 1963), pp. 251-4.

Schulman, G. I. and Tittle, C. R.
  "Assimilation-Contrast Effects and Item Selection in Thurstone
  Scaling"
  Social Forces, Vol. 46 (June 1968), pp. 484-91.

Sewall, Murphy A.
  "Nonmetric Unidimensional Scaling of Consumer Preferences for
  Proposed Product Designs"
  in Hunt, H. Keith (editor)
  Advances in Consumer Research, Volume Five
  (Ann Arbor, MI: Association for Consumer Research, 1978), pp. 22-5.

Sims, J. Taylor and Hammack, Terry
  "TS-V: Thurstone's Law of Comparative Judgment (Case V)" (computer
  abstract)
  Journal of Marketing Research, Vol. XIII (May 1976), pp. 161,2.

Stouffer, S. A., and Others
"Measurement and Prediction"
Studies in Social Psychology in World War II, Vol. IV
(Princeton: Princeton University Press, 1950).

Thurstone, L. L.
"A Law of Comparative Judgment"
Psychological Review, Vol. 4 (July 1927), pp. 273-86.

Thurstone, L. L.
"Psychophysical Analysis"
American Journal of Psychology, Vol. 38 (1927), pp. 368-89.

Walker, Orville C., Jr. and Sauter, Richard F.
"Consumer Preferences for Alternative Retail Credit Terms: A Concept
Test of the Effects of Consumer Legislation"
Journal of Marketing Research, Vol. XI (February 1974), pp. 70-8.

47.03 ----------   Applications of Thurstone's Law

Albaum, Gerald, Best, Roger, and Hawkins, Del
"The Measurement Properties of Semantic Scale Data"
Journal of the Market Research Society, Vol. 19 (January 1977), pp.
21-6.

Bennett, Sidney C.
"PAIRED: A Program to Analyze Paired Comparisons or Ordinal Data"
Journal of Marketing Research, Vol. XVI (November 1979), pp. 561,2.

Brown, F. E.
"Price Image vs. Price Reality"
Journal of Marketing Research, Vol. VI (May 1969), pp. 185-91.

Etgar, Michael and Malhotra, Naresh K.
"Determinants of Price Dependency: Personal and Perceptual Factors"
Journal of Consumer Research, Vol. 8 (September 1981), pp. 217-22.

Moriarty, Mark M. and Venkatesan, M.
"Concept Evaluation and Market Segmentation"
Journal of Marketing, Vol. 42 (July 1978), pp. 82-6.

Scheibe, M., Skutsch, M., and Schofer, J.
"Experiments in Delphi Methodology"
in Linstone, Harold A. and Turoff, Murray (editors)
The Delphi Method
(Reading, MA: Addison-Wesley Publishing Company, 1975), pp. 262-87.

Sewall, Murphy A.
"Market Segmentation Based on Consumer Ratings of Proposed Product
Designs"
Journal of Marketing Research, Vol. XV (November 1978), pp. 547-64.

Walker, Orville C., Jr. and Sauter, Richard F.
"Consumer Preferences for Alternative Retail Credit Terms: A Concept
Test of the Effects of Consumer Legislation"
Journal of Marketing Research, Vol. XI (February 1974), pp. 70-8.

Wind, Yoram
"A New Procedure for Concept Evaluation"
Journal of Marketing, Vol. 37 (October 1973), pp. 2-11.

Wind, Yoram and Silver, Stephen E.
"Segmenting Media Buyers"
Journal of Advertising Research, Vol. 13 (December 1973), pp. 33-8.

48 ------------------ GUTTMAN SCALOGRAM ANALYSIS --------------------
        See also (sub)heading(s) 37.

48.01 ---------- Theory Re: Guttman Scalogram Analysis

Borgatta, E. F. and Hays, D. G.
   "Some Limitations on the Arbitrary Classification of Non-Scale
   Response Patterns in a Guttman Scale"
   Public Opinion Quarterly, Vol. 16 (Fall 1952), pp. 410-6.

Chevan, A.
   "Minimum-Error Scalogram Analysis"
   Public Opinion Quarterly, Vol. 36 (Fall 1972), pp. 379-87.

Chilton, R. J.
   "A Review and Comparison of Simple Statistical Tests for Scalogram
   Analysis"
   American Sociological Review, Vol. 34 (April 1969), pp. 237-45.

Green, B. F.
   "A Method of Scalogram Analysis Using Summary Statistics"
   Psychometrika, Vol. 21 (March 1956), pp. 79-88.

Guttman, Louis
   "A Cornell Technique for Scale and Intensity Analysis"
   in Summers, Gene F. (editor)
   Attitude Measurement
   (Chicago: Rand McNally, 1971), pp. 187-202.

Guttman, L.
   "Measuring the True State of Opinion"
   in Ferber, R. and Wales, H. (editors)
   Motivation and Market Behavior
   (Homewood, IL: Richard D. Irwin, Inc., 1958).

Guttman, Louis
   "The Basis for Scalogram Analysis"
   in Stouffer, S. A. et al. (editors)
   Measurement and Prediction: Studies in Social Psychology in World War
   II, Volume Four
   (Princeton, NJ: Princeton University Press, 1950).

Guttman, L.
   "The Cornell Technique for Scale and Intensity Analysis"
   Educational and Psychological Measurement, Vol. 7 (Summer 1947), pp.
   247-79.

Guttman, L.
   "A Basis for Scaling Qualitative Data"
   American Journal of Sociology, Vol. 9 (April 1944), pp. 139-50.

Hayes, D. P.
   "Item Order and Guttman Scales"
   American Journal of Sociology, Vol. 70 (July 1964), pp. 51-8.

Henry, A. F. and Borgatta, E. F.
   "A Consideration of Some Problems of Content Identification in
   Scaling"
   Public Opinion Quarterly, Vol. 20 (Summer 1956), pp. 457-69.

Macrae, D., Jr.
   "An Experimental Model for Assessing Fourfold Tables"
   Sociometry, Vol. 19 (June 1956), pp. 84-94.

Maxwell, A. E.
   "A Statistical Approach to Scalogram Analysis"
   Educational and Psychological Measurement, Vol. 19 (Autumn 1959), pp.
   337-49.

McGinnis, R.
   "Scaling Interview Data"
   American Sociological Review, Vol. 18 (October 1953), pp. 514-21.

Menzel, Herbert
   "A New Coefficient for Scalogram Analysis"
   Public Opinion Quarterly, Vol. 17 (Summer 1953), pp. 268-80.

Niven, J. R.
   "A Comparison of Two Attitude Scaling Techniques"
   Educational and Psychological Measurement, Vol. 13 (Spring 1953), pp.
   65-76.

Proctor, C. H.
   "A Probabilistic Formulation and Statistical Analysis of Guttman
   Scaling"
   Psychometrika, Vol. 35 (March 1970), pp. 73-8.

Riland, L. H.
    "Relationship of the Guttman Components of Attitude Intensity and
    Personal Involvement"
    Journal of Applied Psychology, Vol. 43 (August 1959), pp. 279-84.

Steiner, I. D.
    "Scalogram Analysis as a Tool for Selecting Poll Questions"
    Public Opinion Quarterly, Vol. 19 (Winter 1955-6), pp. 415-24.

Stover, R. V.
    "The Measurement of a Change in a Unidimensional Attitude by Guttman
    Scale Analysis Techniques"
    Public Opinion Quarterly, Vol. 22 (Summer 1958), pp. 116-22.

Suchman, E. A.
    "The Scalogram Board Technique for Scale Analysis"
    in Stouffer et al. (editors)
    Measurement and Prediction
    (New Jersey: Princeton University Press, 1950).

Suchman, E. A.
    "The Utility of Scalogram Analysis"
    in Stouffer et al. (editors)
    Measurement and Prediction
    (New Jersey: Princeton University Press, 1950).

48.02 ---------- Applications of Guttman Scalogram Analysis

Brown, D. A., Buck, S. F., and Pyatt, F. G.
    "Improving the Forecast for Consumer Durables"
    Journal of Marketing Research, Vol. II (August 1965), pp. 229-34.

Clarke, Yvonne and Soutar, Geoffrey N.
    "Consumer Acquisition Patterns for Durable Goods: Australian Evidence"
    Journal of Consumer Research, Vol. 8 (March 1982), pp. 456-60.

Dickinson, John R. and Kirzner, Eric
    "Priority Patterns of Acquisitions of Financial Assets"
    Journal of the Academy of Marketing Science, Vol. 14 (Summer 1986),
    pp. 43-9.

Dickson, Peter R., Lusch, Robert F., and Wilkie, William L.
    "Consumer Acquisition Priorities for Home Appliances: A Replication
    and Re-Evaluation"
    Journal of Consumer Research, Vol. 9 (March 1983), pp. 432-5.

Guest, Lester
    "A Comparison of Two-Choice and Four-Choice Questions"
    Journal of Advertising Research, Vol. 2 (March 1962), pp. 32-4.

Hays, D. G. and Borgatta, E. F.
    "An Empirical Comparison of Restricted and General Latent Distance
    Analysis"
    Psychometrika, Vol. 19 (December 1954), pp. 271-9.

Hebden, J. J. and Pickering, J. F.
    "Patterns of Acquisition of Consumer Durables"
    Oxford Bulletin of Economics and Statistics, Vol. 36 (May 1974), pp.
    67-94.

Kasulis, Jack J., Lusch, Robert F., and Stafford, Edward F., Jr.
    "Consumer Acquisition Patterns for Durable Goods"
    Journal of Consumer Research, Vol. 6 (June 1979), pp. 47-57.

Landis, Jack B.
    "Exposure Probabilities as Measures of Media Audiences"
    Journal of Advertising Research, Vol. 5 (September 1965), pp. 24-9.

McFall, John
    "Priority Patterns and Consumer Behavior"
    Journal of Marketing, Vol. 33 (October 1969), pp. 50-5.

Paroush, Jacob
    "The Order of Acquisition of Consumer Durables
    "Econometrica, Vol. 33 (January 1965), pp. 225-35.

Pessemier, Edgar A., Bemmaor, Albert C., and Hanssens, Dominique M.
    "Willingness to Supply Human Body Parts: Some Empirical Results"
    Journal of Consumer Research, Vol. 4 (December 1977), pp. 131-40.

Pickering, J. F.
    The Acquisition of Consumer Durables
    (New York: John Wiley and Sons, Inc., 1977).

Pyatt, F. Graham (editor)
    Priority Patterns and the Demand for Household Durables Goods
    (London: Cambridge University Press, 1964).

Richards, E. A.
  "A Commercial Application of Guttman Attitude Scaling Techniques"
  Journal of Marketing, Vol. 22 (October 1957), pp. 166-73.

Stafford, Edward F., Jr., Kasulis, Jack J., and Lusch, Robert F.
  "Consumer Behavior in Accumulating Household Financial Assets"
  Journal of Business Research, Vol. 10 (December 1982), pp. 397-417.

Steiner, Ivan D.
  "Scalogram Analysis as a Tool for Selecting Poll Questions"
  Public Opinion Quarterly, Vol. 19 (Winter 1955-56), pp. 279-84.

49 ----------------------- UNFOLDING THEORY ------------------------
       See also (sub)heading(s) 37, 64.

49.01 ---------- Books Re: Unfolding Theory

Coombs, C.
  Theory of Data
  (New York: John Wiley and Sons, Inc., 1964).

49.02 ---------- Theory Re: Unfolding Theory

DeSarbo, Wayne S., DeSoete, Geert, Carroll, J. Douglas, and Ramaswamy,
  Venkatram
  "A New Stochastic Ultrametric Tree Unfolding Methodology for
  Assessing Competitive Market Structure and Deriving Market Segments"
  Applied Stochastic Models and Data Analysis.

DeSarbo, Wayne S. and Rao, Vithala R.
  "A Constrained Unfolding Model for Product Positioning and Market
  Segmentation"
  First Annual Marketing Science Conference, University of Southern
  California (March 1983), paper presentation.

Taylor, James R.
  "An Empirical Evaluation of Coombs' Unfolding Theory"
  University of Minnesota (1967), Ph.D. thesis.

49.03 ---------- Applications of Unfolding Theory

Moore, William L., Pessemier, Edgar A., and Little, Taylor E.
  "Predicting Brand Purchase Behavior: Marketing Application of the
  Schonemann and Wang Unfolding Model"
  Journal of Marketing Research, Vol. XVI (May 1979), pp. 203-10.

Taylor, James R.
  "Unfolding Theory Applied to Market Segmentation"
  Journal of Advertising Research, Vol. 9 (December 1969), pp. 39-46.

50 ------------------------ Q METHODOLOGY -------------------------
        See also (sub)heading(s) 37, 197.

50.01 ---------- Books Re: Q Methodology

Brown, Steven R.
  Political Subjectivity: Applications of Q Methodology in Political
  Science
  (New Haven, CT: Yale University Press, 1980), 355 pp.

Stephenson, William
  The Study of Behavior: Q-Technique and Its Methodology
  (Chicago: University of Chicago Press, 1953).

50.02 ---------- Theory Re: Q Methodology

Brown, S. R.
  "Q Technique and Method"
  in Berry, W. D. and Lewis-Beck, M. S. (editors)
  New Tools for Social Scientists
  (Beverly Hills, CA: Sage Publications, Inc., 1986).

Hilden, Arnold
  "Manual for Q-Sort and Random Sets of Personal Concepts"
  Washington University (1954), working paper.

Martin, Warren S. and Reynolds, Fred D.
  "On the Usefulness of Q-Methodology for Consumer Segmentation"
  Journal of the Academy of Marketing Science, Vol. 4 (Winter-Spring
  1976), pp. 440-6.

McKeown, Bruce and Thomas, Dan
  Q Methodology
  Sage University Paper Series on Quantitative Applications in the
  Social Sciences
  (Beverly Hills, CA: Sage Publications, Inc., 1988), 83 pp.

Schlinger, Mary J.
  "Cues on Q-Technique"
  Journal of Advertising Research, Vol. 9 (June 1969), pp. 53-60.

50.03 ---------- Theory Re: Q Factor Analysis

Block, Jack
  "The Difference Between Q and R"
  Psychological Review, Vol. 62 (1955), pp. 356-8.

Cattell, Raymond B.
  "On the Disuse and Misuse of R, P, Q, and O Techniques in Clinical
  Psychology"
  Journal of Clinical Psychology, Vol. 7 (1951), pp. 203-14.

Johnson, Richard M.
  "Q Analysis of Large Samples"
  Journal of Marketing Research, Vol. VII (February 1970), pp. 104,5.

Stephen, T. D.
  "Technique of Factor Analysis"
  Nature, Vol. 136 (1935), p. 297.

Stephenson, William
  "Some Observations on Q Technique"
  Psychological Bulletin, Vol. 49 (September 1952), pp. 483-98.

50.04 ---------- Applications of Q Methodology

Akaah, Ishmael P.
  "Cluster Analysis Versus Q-Type Factor Analysis as a Disaggregation
  Method in Hybrid Conjoint Modeling: An Empirical Investigation"
  Journal of the Academy of Marketing Science, Vol. 16 (Summer 1988),
  pp. 11-8.

Boote, Alfred S.
  "Psychographic Segmentation in Europe"
  Journal of Advertising Research, Vol. 22 (December 1982/January
  1983), pp. 19-25.

Cocanougher, A. Benton and Bruce, Grady D.
  "Socially Distant Reference Groups and Consumer Aspirations"
  Journal of Marketing Research, Vol. VIII (August 1971), pp. 379-81.

Dawson, Scott
  "An Exploration of the Store Prestige Hierarchy: Reification, Power,
  and Perceptions"
  Journal of Retailing, Vol. 64 (Summer 1988), pp. 133-52.

Greeno, Daniel, Sommers, Montrose, and Kernan, Jerome B.
    "Personality and Implicit Behavior Patterns"
    Journal of Marketing Research, Vol. X (February 1973), pp. 63-9.

Hamm, B. Curtis
    "A Study of the Differences Between Self-Actualizing Sources and
    Product Perceptions Among Female Consumers"
    Proceedings, Winter Conference, American Marketing Association,
    (1967), pp. 275,6.

Hamm, B. Curtis and Cundiff, Edward W.
    "Self-Actualization and Product Perceptions"
    Journal of Marketing Research, Vol. VI (November 1969), pp. 470-2.

Lesser, Jack A. and Hughes, Marie Adele
    "The Generalizability of Psychographic Market Segments Across
    Geographic Locations"
    Journal of Marketing, Vol. 50 (January 1986), pp. 18-27.

Morrison, Bruce John and Sherman, Richard C.
    "Who Responds to Sex in Advertising?"
    Journal of Advertising Research, Vol. 12 (April 1972), pp. 15-9.

Sommers, Montrose S.
    "The Use of Product Symbolism to Differentiate Social Strata"
    University of Houston Business Review, Vol. XI (Fall 1964).

Sommers, Montrose S.
    "Product Symbolism and the Perception of Social Strata"
    Proceedings, Winter Conference, American Marketing Association,
    (1963), pp. 200-16.

Stephenson, William
    "Public Images of Public Utilities"
    Journal of Advertising Research, Vol. III (December 1963), pp. 34-9.

51 ----------------- PSYCHOPHYSICAL LAWS AND SCALES ------------------
        See also (sub)heading(s) 37, 52.

51.01 ---------- Books Re: Psychophysical Laws and Scales

Baird, J. C. and Noma, E.
    Fundamentals of Scaling and Psychophysics
    (New York: John Wiley and Sons, Inc., 1978).

Lodge, M.
    Magnitude Scaling: Quantitative Measurement of Opinions
    (Beverly Hills, CA: Sage Publications, 1981).

Marks, L. E.
    Sensory Processes: The New Psychophysics
    (New York and London: Academic Press, 1974).

Stevens, S. S.
    Psychophysics: Introduction to Its Perceptual, Neural, and Social
    Prospects
    (New York: John Wiley and Sons, Inc., 1975).

Wegener, B. (editor)
    Social Attitudes and Psychophysical Measurement
    (Hillsdale, NJ: Erlbaum, 1982).

51.02 ---------- Theory Re: Psychophysical Laws and Scales

Anderson, Norman H.
    "How Functional Measurement can Yield Validated Interval Scales of
    Mental Quantities"
    Journal of Applied Psychology, Vol. 61 (December 1976), pp. 677-92.

Anderson, Norman H.
    "Functional Measurement and Psychophysical Judgment"
    Psychological Review, Vol. 77 (May 1970), pp. 153-70.

Birnbaum, Michael H.
    "Differences and Ratios in Psychological Measurement"
    in Castellan, N. J. and Restle, F. (editors)
    Cognitive Theory, Volume 3
    (Hillsdale, NJ: Lawrence Erlbaum Associates, 1978).

Birnbaum, Michael H.
    "Using Context Effects to Derive Psychophysical Scales"
    Perception and Psychophysics, Vol. 15 (January 1974), pp. 89-96.

Birnbaum, Michael H. and Veit, Clairice T.
    "Scale Convergence as a Criterion for Rescaling: Information
    Integration With Difference, Ratio, and Averaging Tasks"
    Perception and Psychophysics, Vol. 15 (January 1974), pp. 7-15.

Cross, D. V.
    "Some Technical Notes on Psychophysical Scaling"
    in Moskowitz et al. (editors)
    Sensation and Measurement: Papers in Honor of S. S. Stevens
    (Dordrecht, The Netherlands: Reidel, 1974).

Hamblin, R. L.
    "Social Attitudes: Magnitude Measurement and Theory"
    in Blalock, H. M., Jr. (editor)
    Measurement in the Social Sciences
    (Chicago: Aldine, 1974).

Hensel, P. J. and Lavenka, N. M.
    "On the Extension of Psychophysical Scaling and Cross-Modality
    Triangulation to the Measurement of Product Quality"
    in Belk, R. W. et al. (editors)
    Proceedings, American Marketing Association
    (Chicago: American Marketing Association, 1984).

Hovland, Carl I. and Sherif, Muzafer
    "Judgmental Phenomena and Scales of Attitude Measurement: Item
    Displacement in Thurstone Scales"
    Journal of Abnormal and Social Psychology, Vol. 47 (October 1952),
    pp. 822-32.

Jones, L. V. and Thurstone, Louis Leon
    "The Psychophysics of Semantics: An Experimental Investigation"
    Journal of Applied Psychology, Vol. 39, No. 1 (1955), pp. 31-6.

Miller, R. L.
    "Dr. Weber and the Consumer"
    Journal of Marketing, Vol. 26 (January 1962), pp. 57-61.

Monroe, K. B.
    "Measuring Price Thresholds by Psychophysics and Latitudes of
    Acceptance"
    Journal of Marketing Research, Vol. VIII (November 1971), pp. 460-4.

Monroe, Kent B. and Venkatesan, M.
    "The Concept of Price Limits and Psychophysical Measurement: A
    Laboratory Experiment"
    Proceedings, Fall Conference, American Marketing Association (1969),
    pp. 345-51.

Neibecker, Bruno
    "The Validity of Computer-Controlled Magnitude Scaling to Measure
    Emotional Impact of Stimuli"
    Journal of Marketing Research, Vol. XXI (August 1984), pp. 325-31.

Pollack, Irwin
    "The Information of Elementary Auditory Displays"
    Journal of the Acoustical Society of America, Vol. 24 (November
    1952), pp. 745-9.

Saffir, Milton
    "A Comparative Study of Scales Constructed by Three Psychophysical
    Methods"
    Psychometrika, Vol. 2 (September 1937), pp. 179-98.

Sherif, Carolyn W.
    "Social Categorization as a Function of Latitude of Acceptance and
    Series Range"
    Journal of Abnormal Psychology, Vol. 67 (August 1963), pp. 148-56.

Sherif, Muzafer and Hovland, Carl I.
    "Judgmental Phenomena and Scales of Attitude Measurement: Placement
    of Items With Individual Choice of Number of Categories"
    Journal of Abnormal and Social Psychology, Vol. 48 (January 1953),
    pp. 135-41.

Stevens, S. S.
    "Issues in Psychophysical Measurement"
    Psychological Review, Vol. 78 (September 1971), pp. 426-50.

Stevens, S. S.
    "On the Psychophysical Law"
    Psychological Review, Vol. 64 (1957), pp. 153-81.

Thurstone, L. L.
    "Psychological Analysis"
    Journal of American Psychology, Vol. 38 (July 1927), pp. 368-89.

Torgerson, W. S.
    "Quantitative Judgment Scales"
    in Gulliksen, H. and Messick, S. (editors)
    Psychological Scaling: Theory and Applications
    (New York: John Wiley and Sons, Inc., 1960), pp. 21-31.

Tursky, B., Lodge, M., and Reeder, R.
    "Psychophysical and Psychophysiological Evaluation of the Direction,
    Intensity, and Meaning of Race-Related Stimuli"
    Psychophysiology, Vol. 16 (1979), pp. 452-62.

Wegener, B.
    "Fitting Category to Magnitude Scales for a Dozen Survey-Assessed
    Attitudes"
    in Wegener, B. (editor)
    Social Attitudes and Psychophysical Measurement
    (Hillsdale, NJ: Erlbaum, 1982), pp. 379-99.

51.03 ---------- Applications of Psychophysical Laws and Scales

Gabor, A. and Granger, C. W. J.
    "Price Sensitivity of the Consumer"
    Journal of Advertising Research, Vol. 4 (December 1964), pp. 40-4.

Gabor, Andre, Granger, Clive W. J., and Sowter, Anthony P.
    "Comments on 'Psychophysics of Prices'"
    Journal of Marketing Research, Vol. VIII (May 1971), pp. 251,2.

Kamen, Joseph M. and Toman, Robert J.
    "'Psychophysics of Prices': A Reaffirmation"
    Journal of Marketing Research, Vol. VIII (May 1971), pp. 252-7.

Kamen, Joseph M. and Toman, Robert J.
    "Psychophysics of Prices"
    Journal of Marketing Research, Vol. VII (February 1970), pp. 27-35.

Lodge, M., Cross, D., Tursky, Bernard, and Tanenhaus, J.
    "The Psychophysical Scaling and Validation of a Political Support
    Scale"
    American Journal of Political Science, Vol. 19 (1975), pp. 611-49.

Monroe, Kent B.
    "'Psychophysics of Prices': A Reappraisal"
    Journal of Marketing Research, Vol. VIII (May 1971), pp. 248-51.

Shinn, A., Jr.
  "An Application of Psychophysical Scaling Techniques to the
  Measurement of National Power"
  Journal of Politics, Vol. 31 (1969), pp. 932-51.

Webb, Eugene
  "Weber's Law and Consumer Prices"
  American Psychologist, Vol. 16 (July 1961), p. 450.

52 ----------------------- MAGNITUDE SCALING -----------------------
          See also (sub)heading(s) 37, 51.

52.01 ---------- Books Re: Magnitude Scaling

Lodge, Milton
  Magnitude Scaling: Quantitative Measurement of Opinions
  (Beverly Hills, CA: Sage Publications, Inc., 1981).

Stevens, S. S.
  Psychophysics and Social Scaling
  (Morristown: General Learning Press, 1972).

52.02 ---------- Theory Re: Magnitude Scaling

Dawson, William E.
  "On the Parallel Between Direct Ratio Scaling of Social Opinion and
  of Sensory Magnitude"
  in Wegener, Bernd (editor)
  Social Attitudes and Psychophysical Measurement
  (Hillsdale: Lawrence Erlbaum Associates, 1982).

Finnie, B. and Luce, R. D.
  Magnitude Estimation, Pair Comparison and Successive Interval Scales
  of Attitude Items
  Department of Psychology, University of Pennsylvania (1960),
  monograph.

Lavenka, Noel M.
  "The Measurement of Intrinsic and Extrinsic Product Quality: A
  Magnitude Estimation Approach"
  Journal of the Market Research Society, Vol. 31 (April 1989), pp.
  213-24.

Neibecker, Bruno
  "The Validity of Computer-Controlled Magnitude Scaling to Measure
  Emotional Impact of Stimuli"
  Journal of Marketing Research, Vol. XXI (August 1984), pp. 325-31.

Teas, R. Kenneth
  "Magnitude Scaling of the Dependent Variable in Decompositional
  Multiattribute Preference Models"
  Journal of the Academy of Marketing Science, Vol. 15 (Fall 1987), pp.
  64-73.

52.03 ---------- Applications of Magnitude Scaling

Corson, W. H.
  Conflict and Cooperation in East-West Crises: Dynamics of Crisis
  Intervention
  Harvard University (1970), Ph.D. dissertation.

Dawson, William E. and Brinker, R. P.
  "Validation of Ratio Scales of Opinion by Multimodality Matching"
  Perception and Psychophysics, Vol. 9 (1971), pp. 413-7.

Ekman, G.
  "Measurement of Moral Judgment: A Comparison of Scaling Methods"
  Perceptual and Motor Skills, Vol. 15 (1962), pp. 3-9.

Hamblin, R. L.
  "Mathematical Experimentation and Sociological Theory: A Critical
  Analysis"
  Sociometry, Vol. 34 (1971), pp. 423-52.

Hamblin, R. L., Bridger, D., Day, R., and Yancey, W.
  "The Interference-Agression Law?"
  Sociometry, Vol. 26 (1963), pp. 190-216.

Hensel, P. J. and Lavenka, N. M.
  "On the Extension of Psychophysical Scaling and Cross-Modality
  Triangulation to the Measurement of Product Quality"
  in Belk, R. W. et al. (editors)
  Proceedings, 1984 American Marketing Association
  (Chicago: American Marketing Association, 1984).

Kuennapas, T. and Sillen, M.
  Measurement of "Political Preferences: A Comparison of Scaling Methods
  Report No. 172
  Psychological Laboratory of Stockholm (1964).

Kuennapas, T. and Wikstroem, I.
  "Measurement of Occupational Preferences: A Comparison of Scaling
  Methods"
  Perceptual and Motor Skills, Vol. 17 (1963), pp. 611-24.

Lodge, Milton, Cross, D., Tursky, B., and Tanenhaus, J.
"The Development and Validation of Political Attitude Scales: A
Psychophysical Approach"
in Leege, D. (editor)
The Shaping of Scientific Research on Politics, Epistema Series
(Holland: D. Reidel, 1974).

Moskowitz, H. R. and Jacobs, J.
"Ratio Scaling of Perception vs. Image: Its Use in Evaluating
Advertising Promises vs. Product Delivery"
in Leigh, J. H. and Martin, C. J., Jr. (editors)
Current Issues and Research in Advertising
(Ann Arbor, MI: Graduate School of Business Administration,
University of Michigan, 1980).

Rainwater, L.
The Measurement of Social Status
Department of Sociology, Harvard University (1971), Ph.D. thesis.

Sellin, J. T. and Wolfgang, M. E.
The Measurement of Delinquency
(New York: John Wiley and Sons, 1964).

Shinn, A., Jr.
The Application of Psychophysical Scaling Techniques to Measurement
of Political Variables
Institute for Research in Social Science, University of North Carolina
(Chapel-Hill Press, 1969).

Stevens, S. S.
"Operations of Words"
Psychological Monographs, Vol. 80 (1966), pp. 33-8.

Welch, R.
"The Use of Magnitude Scaling Estimation in Attitude Scaling:
Constructing a Measure of Political Dissatisfaction"
in Nimmo, D. and Bonjean, C. (editors)
Political Attitudes and Public Opinion
(New York: David McKay Co., 1974).

Wyler, A. R., Masuda, M., and Holmes, T.
"Magnitude of Life Events and Seriousness of Illness"
Psychosomatic Medicine, Vol. 33 (1971), pp. 115-22.

53 -------- PREFERENCE MEASUREMENT USING LIMITED INFORMATION ---------
        See also (sub)heading(s) 37.

53.01 ---------- Theory Re: Measurement and Preference Thresholds

Malhotra, Naresh K.
  "An Approach to the Measurement of Consumer Preferences Using Limited
  Information"
  Journal of Marketing Research, Vol. XXIII (February 1986), pp. 33-40.

53.02 ---------- Theory Re: Analysis of Preferences Using Ltd Info

Amemiya, Takeshi
  "Regression Analysis When the Dependent Variable is Truncated Normal"
  Econometrica, Vol. 41, November 1973), pp. 997-1016.

Greene, William H.
  "Estimation of Limited Dependent Variable Models by Ordinary Least
  Squares and the Method of Moments"
  Journal of Econometrics, Vol. 21 (February 1983), pp. 195-212.

Maddala, G. S.
  Limited-Dependent and Qualitative Variables in Econometrics
  (Cambridge: Cambridge University Press, 1983).

Maddala, G. S.
  "Identification and Estimation Problems in Limited Dependent Variable
  Models"
  in Blinders, A. S. and Friedman, P. (editors)
  Natural Resources, Uncertainty and General Equilibrium Systems:
  Essays in Memory of Rafael Lusky
  (New York: Academic Press, Inc., 1977), pp. 219-39.

Nelson, Forrest D.
  "Censored Regression Models With Unobserved, Stochastic, Censoring
  Thresholds"
  Journal of Econometrics, Vol. 6 (November 1977), pp. 309-27.

Olsen, Randall J.
  "Approximating a Truncated Normal Regression With the Method of
  Moments"
  Econometrica, Vol. 48 (July 1980), pp. 1099-1105.

Robinson, P. M.
  "On the Asymptotic Properties of Estimators of Models Containing
  Limited Dependent Variables"
  Econometrica, Vol. 50 (January 1982), pp. 27-42.

Schmee, Joseph and Hahn, Gerald J.
  "A Simple Method for Regression Analysis With Censored Data"
  Technometrics, Vol. 21 (November 1979), pp. 417-32.

54 ---------------- NUMBER OF RESPONSE ALTERNATIVES ----------------
        See also (sub)heading(s) 37, 55.

54.01 ---------- General Discussions Re: Number of Resp Alternatives

Cox, Eli P., III
   "The Optimal Number of Response Alternatives for a Scale: A Review"
   Journal of Marketing Research, Vol. XVII (November 1980), pp. 407-22.

54.02 ---------- Rating Scales

Behar, Isaac
   "On the Relation Between Response Uncertainty and Prediction Time in
   Category Judgments"
   Perceptual and Motor Skills, Vol. 16 (April 1963), pp. 595,6.

Bendig, A. W.
   "Transmitted Information and the Length of Rating Scales"
   Journal of Experimental Psychology, Vol. 47 (May 1954), pp. 303-8.

Bendig, A. W.
   "Reliability and the Number of Rating Categories"
   Journal of Applied Psychology, Vol. 38 (February 1954), pp. 38-40.

Bendig, A. W.
   "The Reliability of Self-Ratings as a Function of the Amount of
   Verbal Anchoring and of the Number of Categories on a Scale"
   Journal of Applied Psychology, Vol. 37 (February 1953), pp. 38-41.

Bendig, A. W. and Hughes, J. B.
   "Effect of Amount of Verbal Anchoring and Number of Rating-Scale
   Categories Upon Transmitted Information"
   Journal of Experimental Psychology, Vol. 46 (August 1953), pp. 87-90.

Benson, Purnell H.
   "How Many Scales and How Many Categories Shall We Use in Consumer
   Research?--A Comment"
   Journal of Marketing, Vol. 35 (October 1971), pp. 59-61.

Best, Roger J., Albaum, Gerald S., Hawkins, Del I., and Kenyon, Georgia
   "Number of Response Intervals and Reliability of Factor Analyzed
   Semantic Scale Data"
   Southwestern Marketing Association (1978).

Bevan, William and Avant, Lloyd L.
   "Response Latency, Response Uncertainty, Information Transmitted and
   the Number of Available Judgmental Categories"
   Journal of Experimental Psychology, Vol. 76 (March 1968), pp. 394-7.

Boote, Alfred S.
   "Reliability Testing of Psychographic Scales"
   Journal of Advertising Research, Vol. 21 (October 1981), pp. 53-60.

Friedman, Hershey H. and Friedman, Linda Weiser
   "On the Danger of Using Too Few Points in a Rating Scale: A Test of
   Validity"
   Journal of Data Collection, Vol. 26 (1986), pp. 60-3.

Garner, W. R.
   "Rating Scales, Discriminability, and Information Transmission"
   Psychological Review, Vol. 67 (November 1960), pp. 343-52.

Givon, Moshe M. and Shapira, Zur
   "Response to Rating Scales: A Theoretical Model and Its Application
   to the Number of Categories Problem"
   Journal of Marketing Research, Vol. XXI (November 1984), pp. 410-9.

Green, Paul E. and Rao, Vithala R.
   "A Rejoinder to 'How Many Scales and How Many Categories Shall We Use
   in Consumer Research?--A Comment'"
   Journal of Marketing, Vol. 35 (October 1971), pp. 61,2.

Green, Paul E. and Rao, Vithala R.
   "Rating Scales and Information Recovery--How Many Scales and Response
   Categories to Use?"
   Journal of Marketing, Vol. 34 (July 1970), pp. 33-9.

Hulbert, James
   "Information Processing Capacity and Attitude Measurement"
   Journal of Marketing Research, Vol. XII (February 1975), pp. 104-6.

Jenkins, G. Douglas, Jr. and Taber, Thomas D.
   "A Monte Carlo Study of Factors Affecting Three Indices of Composite
   Scale Reliability"
   Journal of Applied Psychology, Vol. 62 (August 1977), pp. 392-8.

Lawrence, Raymond J.
    "How Many Categories for Respondent Classification?"
    Journal of the Market Research Society, Vol. 23 (October 1981), pp.
    220-38.

Lissitz, Robert W. and Green, Samuel B.
    "Effect of the Number of Scale Points on Reliability: A Monte Carlo
    Approach"
    Journal of Applied Psychology, Vol. 60 (February 1975), pp. 10-3.

Martin, Warren S.
    "Effects of Scaling on the Correlation Coefficient: Additional
    Considerations"
    Journal of Marketing Research, Vol. XV (May 1978), pp. 304-8.

Martin, Warren S.
    "The Effects of Scaling on the Correlation Coefficient: A Test of
    Validity"
    Journal of Marketing Research, Vol. X (August 1973), pp. 316-8.

Martin, Warren S., Fruchter, Benjamin, and Mathis, William J.
    "An Investigation of the Effects of the Number of Scale Intervals on
    Principal Components Factor Analysis"
    Educational and Psychological Measurement, Vol. 34 (Autumn 1974), pp.
    537-45.

Morrison, Donald G.
    "Regression With Discrete Dependent Variables: The Effect on R-Square"
    Journal of Marketing Research, Vol. IX (August 1972), pp. 38-40.

Nishisato, Shizuhiko and Torii, Yukhiko
    "Effects of Categorizing Continuous Normal Variables"
    Japanese Psychological Review, Vol. 13 (May 1971), pp. 45-9.

Peabody, Dean
    "Two Components in Bipolar Scales: Direction and Extremeness"
    Psychological Review, Vol. 69 (March 1962), pp. 65-73.

Pemberton, H. Earl
    "A Technique for Determining the Optimal Rating Scale for Opinion
    Measures"
    Sociology and Social Research, Vol. 17 (May-June 1933), pp. 470-2.

Peterson, Robert A. and Sharma, Subhash
    "A Note on the Information Content of Rating Scales"
    Proceedings of the American Marketing Association (1977), pp. 324-6.

Peterson, Robert A. and Sharma, Subhash
    "Adjusting Correlation Coefficients for the Effects of Scaling"
    Proceedings of the American Statistical Association (1977).

Ramsey, J. O.
    "The Effect of Number of Categories in Rating Scales on Precision of
    Estimation of Scale Values"
    Psychometrika, Vol. 38 (December 1973), pp. 513-32.

Sheppard, W. W.
    "On the Calculation of the Most Probable Values of Frequency
    Constants for Data Arranged According to Equi-Distant Divisions of a
    Scale"
    Proceedings of the London Mathematical Society, Vol. 29 (March 1898),
    pp. 353-80.

Spagna, Gregory J.
    "Questionnaires: Which Approach do You Use?"
    Journal of Advertising Research, Vol. 24 (February/March 1984), pp.
    67-70.

Symonds, Percival M.
    "On the Loss of Reliability in Ratings Due to Coarseness of the Scale"
    Journal of Experimental Psychology, Vol. 7 (December 1924), pp.
    456-61.

54.03 ---------- Likert Scales

        See also (sub)heading(s) 40.

Ghiselli, Edwin E.
    "All or None Versus Graded Response Questionnaires"
    Journal of Applied Psychology, Vol. 23 (June 1939), pp. 405-15.

Guest, Lester
    "A Comparison of Two-Choice and Four-Choice Questions"
    Journal of Advertising Research, Vol. 2 (March 1962), pp. 32-4.

Jacoby, Jacob and Matell, Michael S.
    "Three-Point Likert Scales are Good Enough"
    Journal of Marketing Research, Vol. VIII (November 1971), pp. 495-500.

Komorita, S. S.
    "Attitude Content, Intensity, and the Neutral Point on A Likert Scale"
    Journal of Social Psychology, Vol. 61 (December 1963), pp. 327-34.

Komorita, S. S. and Graham, William K.
    "Number of Scale Points and the Reliability of Scales"
    Educational and Psychological Measurement, Vol. 25 (November 1965),
    pp. 987-95.

Lehmann, Donald R. and Hulbert, James
    "Are Three-Point Scales Always Good Enough?"
    Journal of Marketing Research, Vol. IX (November 1972), pp. 444-6.

Matell, Michael S. and Jacoby, Jacob
    "Is There an Optimal Number of Alternatives for Likert Scale Items?
    Journal of Applied Psychology, Vol. 56 (December 1972), pp. 506-9.

Matell, Michael S. and Jacoby, Jacob
    "Is There an Optimal Number of Alternatives for Likert Scale Items?
    Study I: Reliability and Validity"
    Educational and Psychological Measurement, Vol. 31 (Autumn 1971), pp.
    657-74.

54.04 ---------- Graphic Scales

See also (sub)heading(s) 46.05.

Champney, Horace and Marshall, Helen
    "Optimal Refinement of the Rating Scale"
    Journal of Applied Psychology, Vol. 23 (June 1939), pp. 323-31.

McKelvie, S. J.
    "Graphic Rating Scales--How Many Categories?"
    British Journal of Psychology, Vol. 69 (May 1978), pp. 185-202.

54.05 ---------- Balanced (Symmetric) Versus Unbalanced Categories

See also (sub)heading(s) 61.07.

Friedman, Hershey H., Wilamowsky, Y., and Friedman, Linda Weiser
    "A Comparison of Balanced and Unbalanced Rating Scales"
    Mid-Atlantic Journal of Business, Vol. 19 (Summer 1981), pp. 1-7.

54.06 ---------- Unclassified (Number of Response Alternatives)

Boyce, Arthur C.
    "Methods for Measuring Teachers' Efficiency"
    in Parker, S. Chester (editor)
    The Fourteenth Yearbook of the National Society for the Study of
    Education
    (Chicago: University of Chicago Press, 1915).

Bricker, P. D.
    "The Identification of Redundant Stimulus Patterns"
    Journal of Experimental Psychology, Vol. 49 (February 1955), pp.
    73-81.

Conklin, Edmund S.
    "The Scale Values Method for Studies in Genetic Psychology"
    University of Oregon Publication, Vol. 2 (1923), pp. 3-36.

Connor, Robert J.
    "Grouping for Tests of Trend in Categorical Data"
    Journal of the American Statistical Association, Vol. 67 (September
    1972), pp. 601-4.

Cox, D. R.
    "Note on Grouping"
    Journal of the American Statistical Association, Vol. 52 (December
    1957), pp. 543-7.

Cronbach, Lee J.
    "Further Evidence on Response Sets and Test Design"
    Educational and Psychological Measurement, Vol. 10 (Spring 1950), pp.
    3-31.

Garner, W. R. and Hake, H. W.
    "The Amount of Information in Absolute Judgments"
    Psychological Review, Vol. 58 (November 1951), pp. 446-59.

Guest, Lester
    "A Comparison of Two-Choice and Four-Choice Questions"
    Journal of Advertising Research, Vol. 2 (March 1962), pp. 32-4.

Jones, Richard R.
  "Differences in Response Consistency and Subjects' Preferences for
  Three Personality Inventory Response Formats"
  Proceedings, 76th Annual Conference of the American Psychological
  Association (1968), pp. 247,8.

Lazarsfeld, P. F. and Barton, A. J.
  "Some General Principles of Questionnaire Classification"
  in Lazarsfeld, P. F. and Rosenberg, M. (editors)
  The Language of Social Research
  (Glencoe: The Free Press, 1955), pp. 83-93.

Miller, George A.
  "The Magical Number Seven, Plus or Minus Two: Some Limits on Our
  Capacity for Processing Information"
  Psychological Review, Vol. 63 (March 1956), pp. 81-97.

Reynolds, F. D. and Neter, J.
  "Toward a Method for Assessing Adequacy of Classifications of
  Consumer Characteristics"
  Journal of the Market Research Society, Vol. 22, No. 1 (1980), pp.
  3-27.

55 -------------- NUMBER OF ITEMS IN MULTI-ITEM SCALES ---------------
        See also (sub)heading(s) 37, 54.

Benson, Purnell H.
  "How Many Scales and How Many Categories Shall We Use in Consumer
  Research?--A Comment"
  Journal of Marketing, Vol. 35 (October 1971), pp. 59-61.

Best, Roger J., Albaum, Gerald S., Hawkins, Del I., and Kenyon, Georgia
  "Number of Response Intervals and Reliability of Factor Analyzed
  Semantic Scale Data"
  Southwestern Marketing Association (1978).

Ghiselli, Edwin E.
  "All or None Versus Graded Response Questionnaires"
  Journal of Applied Psychology, Vol. 23 (June 1939), pp. 405-15.

Givon, Moshe M. and Shapira, Zur
  "Response to Rating Scales: A Theoretical Model and Its Application
  to the Number of Categories Problem"
  Journal of Marketing Research, Vol. XXI (November 1984), pp. 410-9.

Green, Paul E. and Rao, Vithala R.
  "A Rejoinder to 'How Many Scales and How Many Categories Shall We Use
  in Consumer Research?--A Comment'"
  Journal of Marketing, Vol. 35 (October 1971), pp. 61,2.

Green, Paul E. and Rao, Vithala R.
  "Rating Scales and Information Recovery--How Many Scales and Response
  Categories to Use?"
  Journal of Marketing, Vol. 34 (July 1970), pp. 33-9.

Jenkins, G. Douglas, Jr. and Taber, Thomas D.
  "A Monte Carlo Study of Factors Affecting Three Indices of Composite
  Scale Reliability"
  Journal of Applied Psychology, Vol. 62 (August 1977), pp. 392-8.

Komorita, S. S. and Graham, William K.
  "Number of Scale Points and the Reliability of Scales"
  Educational and Psychological Measurement, Vol. 25 (November 1965),
  pp. 987-95.

Lehmann, Donald R. and Hulbert, James
  "Are Three-Point Scales Always Good Enough?"
  Journal of Marketing Research, Vol. IX (November 1972), pp. 444-6.

Lissitz, Robert W. and Green, Samuel B.
  "Effect of the Number of Scale Points on Reliability: A Monte Carlo
  Approach"
  Journal of Applied Psychology, Vol. 60 (February 1975), pp. 10-3.

Murphy, Gardner and Likert, Rensis
  Public Opinion and the Individual
  (New York: Harper and Brothers Publishers, 1938).

56 ----- ORDINAL, INTERVAL, RATIO PROPERTIES OF SCALING DEVICES   ------
        See also (sub)heading(s) 37, 137.

Borgatta, E. F. and Bohrnstedt, G. W.
    "Levels of Measurement: Once Over Again"
    in Bohrnstedt, G. W. and Borgatta, G. F. (editors)
    Social Measurement: Current Issues
    (Beverly Hills, CA: Sage Publications, 1981).

Collins, Martin
    "Scale Data"
    Journal of the Market Research Society, Vol. 26 (January 1984), p. 77.

Cox, D. R.
    "Note on Grouping"
    Journal of the American Statistical Association, Vol. 52 (December
    1957), pp. 543-7.

Crask, Melvin R. and Fox, Richard J.
    "An Exploration of the Interval Properties of Three Commonly Used
    Marketing Research Scales: A Magnitude Estimation Approach"
    Journal of the Market Research Society, Vol. 29 (July 1987), pp.
    317-39.

Dawes, R. M.
    "Suppose We Measured Height With Rating Scales Instead of Rulers"
    Applied Psychological Measurement, Vol. 1 (Spring 1977), pp. 267-73.

Dawson, W. E. and Brinker, R. P.
    "Validation of Ratio Scales of Opinion by Multimodality Matching"
    Perception and Psychophysics, Vol. 9, No. 4 (1971), pp. 413-7.

Lawrence, Ray
    "Scale Data Points"
    Journal of the Market Research Society, Vol. 26 (April 1984), pp.
    171-3.

Rothman, James and Buck, Stephan
    "Reply" (to Collins)
    Journal of the Market Research Society, Vol. 26 (January 1984), pp.
    77,8.

Srinivasan, V. and Basu, Amiya K.
    "The Metric Quality of Ordered Categorical Data"
    Marketing Science, Vol. 8 (Summer 1989), pp. 205-30.

Traylor, Mark B.
    "Ordinal and Interval Scaling"
    Journal of the Market Research Society, Vol. 25, No. 4 (1983), p. 297.

57 --------------------- MEASUREMENT OF VALUES ---------------------

See also (sub)heading(s) 37.

57.01 ---------- Discussions and Overviews

Munson, J. Michael
"Personal Values: Considerations on Their Measurement and Application
to Five Areas of Research Inquiry"
in Pitts, R. E. and Woodside, A. G. (editors)
Personal Values and Consumer Psychology
(Lexington, MA: D. C. Heath, 1984), pp. 13-34.

Reynolds, Thomas J.
"Implications for Value Research: A Macro vs. Micro Perspective"
Psychology and Marketing, Vol. 2 (Winter 1985), pp. 297-305.

Reynolds, Thomas J. and Jolly, James P.
"Measuring Personal Values: An Evaluation of Alternative Methods"
Journal of Marketing Research, Vol. XVII, No. 4 (1980), pp. 531-6.

Veltri, John J. and Schiffman, Leon G.
"Fifteen Years of Consumer Life Style and Value Research at A T and T"
in Pitts, Robert E. and Woodside, Arch G.
Personal Values and Consumer Psychology
(Lexington, MA: Lexington Books, 1984).

57.02 ---------- Theory Re: Values and Lifestyle Segmentation (VALS)

See also (sub)heading(s) 58.02.

Holman, Rebecca
"A Value and Life Styles Perspective on Human Behavior"
in Pitts, Robert E., Jr. and Woodside, Arch G. (editors)
Personal Values and Consumer Psychology
(Lexington, MA: Lexington Books, 1984).

Kahle, Lynn R., Beatty, Sharon E., and Homer, Pamela M.
"Alternative Measurement Approaches to Consumer Values: The List of
Values (LOV) and Values and Lifestyle Segmentation (VALS)"
Journal of Consumer Research, Vol. 13 (December 1986), pp. 405-9.

Kahle, L. R., Beatty, S. E., and Homer, P. M.
"Alternative Measurement Approaches to Consumer Values: The List of
Values (LOV) and Values and Lifestyle Segmentation (VALS)"
University of Oregon (1985), working paper.

Mitchell, A.
Consumer Values: A Typology
(Menlo Park, CA: SRI International, 1978).

Winters, Lewis C.
"SRI Announces VALS 2"
Marketing Research, Vol. 1 (June 1989), pp. 67-9.

Yuspeh, Sonia
"Syndicated Values/Life Styles Segmentation Schemes: Use Them as
Descriptive Tools, Not to Select Targets"
Marketing News, Vol. 18 (May 25, 1984), pp. 1;12.

57.03 ---------- Applications of VALS

Winters, Lewis C.
"Does it Pay to Advertise to Hostile Audiences With Corporate
Advertising?"
Journal of Advertising Research, Vol. 28 (April/May 1988), pp. 11-8.

57.04 ---------- Theory Re: Rokeach Value Survey

Austin, J. J. and Garwood, B. A.
"The Relationship of the Hartman Value Profile (HVP), Rokeach Value
Survey (RVS), Allport-Vernon-Lindzey Study of Values (AVL) and
Kohlberg's Theory of Moral Development (KMD): A Series of Axiometric
Studies"
National Association of School Psychologists Convention, Cincinnati
(1970), paper presentation.

Beatty, Sharon E., Kahle, Lynn R., Homer, Pamela, and Misra, Shekhar
"Alternative Measurement Approaches to Consumer Values: The List of
Values and the Rokeach Value Survey"
Psychology and Marketing, Vol. 2 (Fall 1985), pp. 181-200.

Kelly, K., Silverman, B. I., and Cochrane, R.
"Social Desireability and the Rokeach Value Survey"
Journal of Experimental Research in Personality, Vol. 6 (1972), pp.
84-7.

Munson, J. Michael and McIntyre, S. H.
   "Developing Practical Procedures for the Measurement of Personal
   Values in Cross-Cultural Marketing"
   Journal of Marketing Research, Vol. XVI (1979), pp. 48-52.

Rokeach, M.
   The Nature of Human Values
   (New York: The Free Press, 1973).

Vinson, D. E., Munson, J. Michael, and Nakanishi, M.
   "An Investigation of the Rokeach Value Survey for Consumer
   Application"
   in Perreault, W. D. (editor)
   Advances in Consumer Research, Volume Four
   (Ann Arbor, MI: Association for Consumer Research, 1976).

57.05 ---------- Applications of the Rokeach Value Survey

Apasu, Yao
   "The Importance of Value Structures in the Perception of Rewards by
   Industrial Salespersons"
   Journal of the Academy of Marketing Science, Vol. 15 (Spring 1987),
   pp. 1-10.

Goldsmith, Ronald E., White, J. Dennis, and Stith, Melvin T.
   "Values of Middle-Class Blacks and Whites: A Replication and
   Extension"
   Psychology and Marketing, Vol. 4 (Summer 1987), pp. 135-44.

Henry, Walter A.
   "Cultural Values do Correlate With Consumer Discontent"
   Journal of Marketing Research, Vol. XIII, No. 3 (1976), pp. 121-7.

McQuarrie, Edward F., and Langmeyer, Daniel
   "Using Values to Measure Attitudes Toward Discontinuous Innovation"
   Psychology and Marketing, Vol. 2 (Winter 1985), pp. 239-52.

Pitts, Robert E., Canty, Ann L., and Tsalikis, John
   "Exploring the Impact of Personal Values on Socially Oriented
   Communications"
   Psychology and Marketing, Vol. 2 (Winter 1985), pp. 267-78.

Prakash, Ved and Munson, J. Michael
   "Values, Expectations From the Marketing System and Product
   Expectations"
   Psychology and Marketing, Vol. 2 (Winter 1985), pp. 279-96.

Scott, Jerome E. and Lamont, Lawrence M.
   "Relating Consumer Values to Consumer Behavior: A Model and Method
   for Investigation"
   in Greer, Thomas V. (editor)
   Increasing Market Productivity
   (Chicago: American Marketing Association, 1980).

Vinson, Donald E. and Munson, J. Michael
   "Personal Values: An Approach to Market Segmentation"
   in Bernhardt, Kenneth L (editor)
   Marketing: 1776-1976 and Beyond
   (Chicago: American Marketing Association, 1976), pp. 313-7.

Vinson, Donald E., Scott, Jerome E., and Lamont, Lawrence M.
   "The Role of Personal Values in Marketing and Consumer Behavior"
   Journal of Marketing, Vol. 41, No. 2 (1977), pp. 44-50.

57.06 ---------- Theory Re: The List of Values (LOV)

Beatty, Sharon E., Kahle, Lynn R., Homer, Pamela, and Misra, Shekhar
   "Alternative Measurement Approaches to Consumer Values: The List of
   Values and the Rokeach Value Survey"
   Psychology and Marketing, Vol. 2 (Fall 1985), pp. 181-200.

Kahle, Lynn R. (editor)
   Social Values and Social Change: Adaptation to Life in America
   (New York: Praeger, 1983).

Kahle, Lynn R., Beatty, Sharon E., and Homer, Pamela M.
   "Alternative Measurement Approaches to Consumer Values: The List of
   Values (LOV) and Values and Lifestyle Segmentation (VALS)"
   Journal of Consumer Research, Vol. 13 (December 1986), pp. 405-9.

57.07 ---------- Applications of the LOV

Kahle, Lynn R., Poulos, Basil, and Sukhdial, Ajay
   "Changes in Social Values in the United States During the Past Decade"
   Journal of Advertising Research, Vol. 28 (February/March 1988), pp.
   35-41.

57.08 ---------- Theory Re: Hartman Value Profile (HVP)

Austin, J. J. and Garwood, B. A.
   "The Relationship of the Hartman Value Profile (HVP), Rokeach Value
   Survey (RVS), Allport-Vernon-Lindzey Study of Values (AVL) and
   Kohlberg's Theory of Moral Development (KMD): A Series of Axiometric
   Studies"
   National Association of School Psychologists Convention, Cincinnati
   (1970), paper presentation.

Bystam, E. and Freund, D.
   "A Testing of the HVP-Test's Reliability"
   University of Stockholm (1977), unpublished exam paper.

Elliott, B. C.
   "Item Homogeneity and Factorial Invariance for Normative and Ipsative
   Responses to the Hartman Value Inventory"
   University of Tennessee (1969), Ph.D. dissertation.

Hartman, R. S.
   The Hartman Value Profile (HVP): Manual of Interpretation
   (Muskegon, MI: Research Concepts, 1973).

Schildt, E.
   "A Comparison Between the Results at Self-Estimation and at
   HVP-Measuring of Six Abilities to Value"
   Stockholm (1975), unpublished abstract.

57.09 ---------- Other Value Scales

Allport, G. W., Vernon, P. E., and Lindzey, G.
   Manual for Study of Values: A Scale for Measuring the Dominant
   Interests in Personality
   (Boston: Houghton Mifflin, 1970).

Kahle, L. R. (editor)
   Social Values and Social Change: Adaptation to Life in America
   (New York: Praeger, 1983).

Kluckhohn, F. and Strodtbeck, F.
   Variations in Value Orientations
   (Evanston: Row, Peterson, 1961).

Mattsson, Jan
   "Developing an Axiological Method to Measure Company Values"
   European Journal of Marketing, Vol. 22, No. 6 (1988), pp. 21-35.

Moorcroft, Sheila
   "Lifestyle and Values: The European Dimension"
   Admap (April 1987), pp. 27-31.

58 ------------ MEASUREMENT OF OTHER SPECIFIC CONSTRUCTS ------------
       See also (sub)heading(s) 37.

58.01 ---------- Consumer Satisfaction

Aiello, Albert, Czepiel, John A., and Rosenberg, Larry J.
    "Scaling the Heights of Consumer Satisfaction: An Evaluation of
    Alternative Measures"
    in Day, Ralph (editor)
    Consumer Satisfaction, Dissatisfaction and Complaining Behavior
    (Bloomington, IN: Indiana University, April 1977), pp. 43-50.

Day, Ralph L.
    "Alternative Definitions and Designs for Measuring Coonsumr
    Satisfaction"
    in Hunt, H. Keith (editor)
    The Conceptualization and Measurment of Consumer Satisfaction and
    Dissatisfaction
    (Cambridge, MA: Marketing Science Institute, 1977).

Hunt, H. Keith (editor)
    The Conceptualization and Measurement of Consumer Satisfaction and
    Dissatisfaction
    (Cambridge, MA: Marketing Science Institute, 1977).

LaTour, Stephen A. and Peat, Nancy C.
    "Conceptual and Methodological Issues in Consumer Satisfaction
    Research"
    in Wilkie, William L. (editor)
    "Advances in Consumer Research
    (Association for Consumer Research, 1979), pp. 432-7.

Leavitt, Clark
    "Consumer Satisfaction and Dissatisfaction: Bipolar or Independent"
    in Hunt, H. Keith (editor)
    Conceptualization and Measurement of Consumer Satisfaction and
    Dissatisfaction
    (Cambridge, MA: Marketing Science Institute, May 1977), pp. 132-52.

Oliver, Richard L.
    "Measurement and Evaluation of the Satisfaction Process in Retail
    Settings"
    Journal of Retailing, Vol. 57 (Fall 1981), pp. 25-48.

Oliver, Richard L.
    "Conceptualization and Measurement of Disconfirmation Perceptions in
    the Prediction of Consumer Satisfaction"
    in Hunt, H. Keith and Day, Ralph L. (editors)
    Proceedings, Fourth Annual Conference on Consumer Satisfaction,
    Dissatisfaction, and Complaining Behavior
    (Bloomington, IN: School of Business, Indiana University, 1980).

Pfaff, Anita B.
    "An Index of Consumer Satisfaction"
    Proceedings of the Third Annual Conference
    (Association for Consumer Research, November 1972), pp. 713-37.

Pfaff, Martin
    "The Index of Consumer Satisfaction: Measurement Properties and
    Opportunities"
    in Hunt, H. Keith (editor)
    Conceptualization and Measurement of Consumer Satisfaction and
    Dissatisfaction
    (Cambridge, MA: Marketing Science Institute, May 1977), pp. 36-71.

Westbrook, Robert A. and Oliver, Richard L.
    "Developing Better Measures of Consumer Satisfaction: Some
    Preliminary Results"
    in Monroe, K. B. (editor)
    Advances in Consumer Research
    (Ann Arbor, MI: Association for Consumer Research, 1980), pp. 94-9.

58.02 ---------- Lifestyle

       See also (sub)heading(s) 57.02, 57.03.

Baker, Ken and Fletcher, Robert
    "Outlook--A Generalised Lifestyle System"
    Admap (March 1987), pp. 23-8.

Moorcroft, Sheila
    "Lifestyle and Values: The European Dimension"
    Admap (April 1987), pp. 27-31.

58.03 ---------- Involvement

Arora, Raj
"Involvement: Its Measurement for Retail Store Research"
Journal of the Academy of Marketing Science, Vol. 13 (Spring 1985),
pp. 229-41.

Arora, Rajinder and Baer, Robert
"Measuring Consumer Involvement in Products: Comment on Traylor and
Joseph"
Psychology and Marketing, Vol. 2 (Spring 1985), pp. 57-62.

Bloch, Peter H.
"An Exploration Into the Scaling of Consumers' Involvement With a
Product Class"
Advances in Consumer Research, Volume Eight (1981), pp. 61-5.

Chokan, E. J.
"A Validity Test of Product Involvement Measures"
Cleveland State University (1985), unpublished paper.

Houston, M. J. and Rothschild, M. L.
"A Paradigm for Research on Consumer Involvement"
Working Paper No. 11-77-46
University of Wisconsin-Madison (1977).

Kapferer, Jean-Noel and Laurent, Gilles
"Marketing Analysis on the Basis of Consumers' Degree of Involvement"
ESOMAR Congress, Rome (1984), pp. 223-45.

Laurent, Gilles and Kapferer, Jean-Noel
"Measuring Consumer Involvement Profiles"
Journal of Marketing Research, Vol. XXII (February 1985), pp. 41-53.

Mahajan, Jayashree
The Involvement Construct: A Multivariate Approach
Faculty of Business Administration, University of Windsor, Ontario
(1981), M.B.A. major paper.

Mittal, Banwari
"Measuring Purchase-Decision Involvement"
Psychology and Marketing, Vol. 6 (Summer 1989), pp. 147-62.

Ratchford, Brian T.
"Operationalizing Involvement and Thinking/Feeling Dimensionality in
the FCB Grid"
(1985), working paper.

Shimp, T. A. and Sharma, S.
"The Dimensionality of Involvement: A Test of the Automobile
Involvement Scale"
in Darden, W. R., Monroe, K. B., and Dillon, W. R. (editors)
Research Methods and Causal Modeling in Marketing
(Chicago: American Marketing Association, 1983), pp. 58-61.

Slama, Mark E. and Tashchian, Armen
"Validating the S-O-R Paradigm for Consumer Involvement With a
Convenience Good"
Journal of the Academy of Marketing Science, Vol. 15 (Spring 1987),
pp. 36-45.

Slama, Mark E. and Tashchian, Armen
"Selected Socioeconomic and Demographic Characteristics Associated
With Purchasing Involvement"
Journal of Marketing, Vol. 49 (Winter 1985), pp. 72-82.

Slama, Mark E. and Tashchian, A.
"Comparing Methods of Measuring Involvement With Product Classes: A
Structural Equation Approach"
in Darden, W. R., Monroe, K. B., and Dillon, W. R. (editors)
Research Methods and Causal Modeling in Marketing
(Chicago: American Marketing Association, 1983), pp. 66-9.

Traylor, Mark B. and Joseph, W. Benoy
"Reply to Arora and Baer's Comment on Measuring Consumer Involvement
in Products"
Psychology and Marketing, Vol. 2 (Summer 1985), pp. 127-32.

Traylor, Mark B. and Joseph, W. Benoy
"Measuring Consumer Involvement in Products"
Psychology and Marketing, Vol. 1 (Summer 1984), pp. 65-77.

Zaichkowsky, Judith Lynne
"Measuring the Involvement Construct"
Journal of Consumer Research, Vol. 12 (December 1985), pp. 341-52.

58.04 ---------- Product Quality

> See also (sub)heading(s) 25.

Curry, David J. and Faulds, David J.
  "Indexing Product Quality: Issues, Theory, and Results"
  Journal of Consumer Research, Vol. 13 (June 1986), pp. 134-45.

Hjorth-Andersen, Chr.
  "More on Multidimensional Quality: A Reply"
  Journal of Consumer Research, Vol. 13 (June 1986), pp. 149-54.

Juster, F. Thomas
  "Comments on 'The Concept and Measurement of Product Quality'"
  in Terleckyj, Nestor E. (editor)
  Household Production and Consumption
  (New York: Columbia University Press, 1975).

Maynes, E. Scott
  "The Concept and Measurement of Product Quality"
  in Terleckyj, Nestor E. (editor)
  Household Production and Consumption
  (New York: Columbia University Press, 1975).

Morris, Ruby T.
  Consumers Unions Methods, Implications, Weaknesses, and Strengths
  (New London, CT: Litfield, 1971).

58.05 ---------- Service Quality

Gronroos, Christian
  "A Service Quality Model and Its Marketing Implications"
  European Journal of Marketing, Vol. 18, No. 4 (1984), pp. 36-44.

Parasuraman, A., Zeithaml, Valarie A., and Berry, Leonard L.
  "SERVQUAL: A Multiple-Item Scale for Measuring Consumer Perceptions
  of Service Quality"
  Journal of Retailing, Vol. 64 (Spring 1988), pp. 12-40.

Parasuraman, A., Zeithaml, Valarie A., and Berry, Leonard L.
  "A Conceptual Model of Service Quality and Its Implications for
  Future Research"
  Journal of Marketing (Fall 1985), pp. 41-50.

58.06 ---------- Perceived Risk

Bettman, James R.
  "Perceived Risk and Its Components: A Model and Empirical Test"
  Journal of Marketing Research, Vol. X (1975), pp. 184-90.

Bettman, James R.
  "Perceived Risk: A Measurement Methodology and Preliminary Findings"
  in Venkatesan, M. (editor)
  Proceedings, Third Annual Conference for Consumer Research
  (Chicago: Association for Consumer Research, 1972), pp. 394-403.

Dowling, G. R.
  "Perceived Risk: The Concept and Its Measurement"
  Psychology and Marketing, Vol. 3 (Fall 1986), pp. 193-210.

Evans, R. H.
  "Measuring Perceived Risk: A Replication and an Application of Equity
  Theory"
  in Mitchell, A. (editor)
  Advances in Consumer Behavior
  (Chicago: Association for Consumer Research, 1981), pp. 550-5.

Stem, D. E., Lamb, Charles W., and MacLachlan, D.
  "Perceived Risk: A Synthesis"
  European Journal of Marketing, Vol. 11, No. 4 (1977), pp. 312-9.

58.07 ---------- Opinion Leadership

Childers, Terry L.
  "Assessment of the Psychometric Properties of an Opinion Leadership
  Scale"
  Journal of Marketing Research, Vol. XXIII (May 1986), pp. 184-8.

King, Charles W. and Summers, John O.
  "Overlap of Opinion Leadership Across Consumer Product Categories"
  Journal of Marketing Research, Vol. VII (February 1970), pp. 43-50.

Riecken, Glen and Yavas, Ugur
  "Internal Consistency Reliability of King and Summers' Opinion
  Leadership Scale: Further Evidence"
  Journal of Marketing Research, Vol. XX (August 1983), pp. 325,6.

Rogers, Everett and Cartano, David G.
"Methods of Measuring Opinion Leadership"
Public Opinion Quarterly, Vol. 26 (Fall 1962), pp. 435-41.

Summers, John O.
"The Identity of Women's Clothing Fashion Opinion Leaders"
Journal of Marketing Research, Vol. VII (May 1970), pp. 178-85.

Yavas, Ugur and Riecken, Glen
"Extensions of King and Summers' Opinion Leadership Scale: A
Reliability Study"
Journal of Marketing Research, Vol. XIX (February 1982), pp. 154,5.

58.08 ---------- Social Class or Social Status

Abbott, Pamela and Sapsford, Roger
"Class Identification of Married Working Women: A Critical
Replication of Ritter and Hargens"
British Journal of Sociology, Vol. XXXII (December 1986), pp. 534-49.

Duke, Vic and Edgell, Stephen
"The Operationalisation of Class in British Sociology: Theoretical
and Empirical Considerations"
British Journal of Sociology, Vol. XXXVIII (December 1987), pp.
445-63.

O'Brien, Sarah and Ford, Rosemary
"Can We at Last Say Goodbye to Social Class?"
Proceedings, Market Research Society Conference (March 1988), pp.
249-88.

Rainwater, L.
The Measurement of Social Status
Department of Sociology, Harvard University (1971), Ph.D. thesis.

Rothman, James
"Different Measures of Social Grade"
Journal of the Market Research Society, Vol. 31 (January 1989), pp.
139,40.

58.09 ---------- MMPI

Barnes, E. H.
"Response Bias in the MMPI"
Journal of Consulting Psychology, Vol. 20 (1956), pp. 371-4.

Bock, R. Darrell, Dicken, Charles, and Van Pelt, John
"Methodological Implications of Content-Acquiescence Correlations in
the MMPI"
Psychological Bulletin, Vol. 71 (January 1969), pp. 127-39.

Edwards, Allen L.
"Social Desireability and Performance on the MMPI"
Psychometrika (1964), pp. 295-308.

Kassebaum, G. G., Couch, Arthur S., and Slater, Patrick E.
"The Factorial Dimensions of the MMPI"
Journal of Consulting Psychology, Vol. 23 (1959), pp. 226-36.

Welsh, G. S.
"Factor Dimensions A and R"
in Welsh, G. S. and Dahlstrom, W. G. (editors)
Basic Readings on the MMPI in Psychology and Medicine
(Minneapolis, MN: University of Minnesota Press, 1956).

58.10 ---------- Probability Estimates Provided by Respondents

Becker, Boris W. and Greenberg, Marshall G.
"Probability Estimates by Respondents: Does Weighting Improve
Accuracy?"
Journal of Marketing Research, Vol. XV (August 1978), pp. 482-6.

Roshwalb, Irving
"Probability Estimates by Respondents: Adjustments May Improve
Accuracy"
Journal of Marketing Research, Vol. XV (August 1978), pp. 487,8.

Roshwalb, Irving
"A Consideration of Probability Estimates Provided by Respondents"
Journal of Marketing Research, Vol. XII (February 1975), pp. 100-3.

58.11 ---------- Intent and Other Measures Related to Purchase
        See also (sub)heading(s) 116.15.

Adams, F. Gerard
    "Commentary on McNeil, 'Federal Programs to Measure Consumer Purchase
    Expectations'"
    Journal of Consumer Research, Vol. 1 (December 1974), pp. 11,2.

Armstrong, J. Scott and Overton, Terry S.
    "Brief vs. Comprehensive Descriptions in Measuring Intentions to
    Purchase"
    Journal of Marketing Research, Vol. VIII (February 1971), pp. 114-7.

Axelrod, J. N.
    "Attitude Measures That Predict Purchase"
    Journal of Advertising Research, Vol. 8 (March 1968), pp. 3-17.

Blightman, Tim
    "Market Researchers do It With Questions--But are They Doing It
    Right?"
    Proceedings, Market Research Society Conference (March 1987), pp.
    75-85.

Gormley, Richard
    "A Note on Seven Brand Rating Scales and Subsequent Purchase"
    Journal of the Market Research Society, Vol. 16 (July 1974), pp.
    242-4.

Granbois, Donald H. and Summers, John O.
    "Primary and Secondary Validity of Consumer Purchase Probabilities"
    Journal of Consumer Research, Vol. 1 (March 1975), pp. 31-8.

Jamieson, Linda F. and Bass, Frank M.
    "Adjusting Stated Intention Measures to Predict Trial Purchase of New
    Products: A Comparison of Models and Methods"
    Journal of Marketing Research, Vol. XXVI (August 1989), pp. 336-45.

Johnson, Jeffrey S.
    "A Study of the Accuracy and Validity of Purchase Intention Scales"
    Armour-Dial Company, Phoenix, AZ (1979), privately circulated working
    paper.

Juster, F. Thomas
    "Consumer Buying Intentions and Purchase Probability: An Experiment
    in Survey Design"
    Journal of the American Statistical Association, Vol. 61 (September
    1966), pp. 658-96.

Kalwani, Manohar U. and Silk, Alvin J.
    "On the Reliability and Predictive Validity of Purchase Intention
    Measures"
    Marketing Science, Vol. 1 (Summer 1982), pp. 243-86.

McNeil, John M.
    "Federal Programs to Measure Consumer Purchase Expectations, 1946-73:
    A Post-Mortem"
    Journal of Consumer Research, Vol. 1 (December 1974), pp. 1-10.

Morrison, Donald G.
    "Purchase Intentions and Purchase Behavior"
    Journal of Marketing, Vol. 43 (Spring 1979), pp. 65-74.

Penny, J. C., Hunt, I. M., and Twyman, W. A. Tony
    "Product Testing Methodology in Relation to Marketing Problems"
    Journal of the Market Research Society, Vol. 14 (January 1972), pp.
    1-29.

Rothman, J.
    "Formulation of an Index of Propensity to Buy"
    Journal of Marketing Research, Vol. 1 (May 1964), pp. 21-5.

Tauber, Edward M.
    "Predictive Validity in Consumer Research"
    Journal of Advertising Research, Vol. 15 (October 1975), pp. 59-64.

Taylor, J. W., Houlahan, J. J., and Gabriel, A. C.
    "The Purchase Intention Question in New Product Development: A Field
    Test"
    Journal of Marketing (January 1975), pp. 90-2.

Warshaw, Paul R.
    "Predicting Purchase and Other Behaviors From General and
    Contextually Specific Intentions"
    Journal of Marketing Research, Vol. XVII (February 1980), pp. 26-33.

Wells, William D.
    "Measuring Readiness to Buy"
    Harvard Business Review, Vol. 39 (July-August 1961), pp. 81-7.

58.12 ---------- Attribute Importance

Heeler, Roger M., Okechuku, Chike, and Reid, Stan
    "Attribute Importance: Contrasting Measurements"
    Journal of Marketing Research, Vol. XVI (1979), pp. 60-3.

Jaccard, James, Brinberg, David, and Ackerman, Lee J.
    "Assessing Attribute Importance: A Comparison of Six Methods"
    Journal of Consumer Research, Vol. 12 (March 1986), pp. 463-8.

Neslin, Scott A.
    "Linking Product Features to Perceptions: Self-Stated Versus
    Statistically Revealed Importance Weights"
    Journal of Marketing Research, Vol. XVIII (1981), pp. 80-6.

Wiley, James B., MacLachlan, Douglas L., and Moinpour, Reza
    "Comparison of Stated and Inferred Parameter Values in Additive
    Models"
    in Perreault, William A., Jr. (editor)
    Advances in Consumer Research, Volume Four
    (Atlanta, GA: Association for Consumer Research, 1977), pp. 106-10.

58.13 ---------- Sex-Role Self-Concept

Bem, S. L.
    "Bem Sex-Role Inventory"
    Consulting Psychology Press (1981).

Bem, S. L.
    "Theory and Measurement of Androgyny: A Reply to the
    Pedhazur-Tetenbaum and Locksley-Colten Critiques"
    Journal of Personality and Social Psychology, Vol. 37 (1979), pp.
    1047-54.

Bem, S. L.
    "The Measurement of Psychological Androgyny"
    Journal of Consulting and Clinical Psychology, Vol. 42 (1974), pp.
    155-62.

Gough, H. G.
    "Identifying Psychological Femininity"
    Educational and Psychological Measurement, Vol. 22 (1952), pp. 433-55.

Kelly, J., Furman, W., and Young, V.
    "Problems Associated With the Typological Measurement of Sex Roles
    and Androgyny"
    Journal of Consulting and Clinical Psychology, Vol. 46 (1978), pp.
    1574-6.

Lubinski, D., Tellegen, A., and Butcher, J. N.
    "Masculinity, Femininity, and Androgyny Viewed and Assessed as
    Distinct Concepts"
    Journal of Personality and Social Psychology, Vol. 44 (1983), pp.
    428-39.

Spence, J. T.
    "Comment on Lubinski, Tellegen and Butcher's Masculinity, Femininity,
    and Androgyny Viewed and Assessed as Distinct Concepts"
    Journal of Personality and Social Psychology, Vol. 44 (1983), pp.
    440-6.

Spence, J. T. and Helmreich, A. L.
    "The Many Faces of Androgyny: A Reply to Locksley and Colten"
    Journal of Personality and Social Psychology, Vol. 37 (1979), pp.
    1032-46.

Spence, J. T., Helmreich, R., and Stapp, J.
    "The Personal Attributes Questionnaire: A Measure of Sex Role
    Stereotypes and Masculinity-Femininity"
    Journal of Supplement Abstract Service Catalog of Selected Documents
    in Psychology, Vol. 4 (1974), p. 43.

Stern, Barbara B.
    "Sex-Role Self-Concept Measures and Marketing: A Research Note"
    Psychology and Marketing, Vol. 5 (Spring 1988), pp. 85-99.

Taylor, M. C. and Hall, J. A.
    "Psychological Androgyny: Theories, Methods, and Conclusions"
    Psychological Bulletin, Vol. 92 (1982), pp. 347-466.

58.14 ---------- Job Satisfaction

Comer, James M., Machleit, Karen A., and Lagace, Rosemary R.
    "Psychometric Assessment of a Reduced Version of INDSALES"
    Journal of Business Research, Vol. 18 (June 1989).

Futrell, Charles M.
"Measurement of Salespeople's Job Satisfaction: Convergent and
Discriminant Validity of Corresponding INDSALES and Job Descriptive
Index Scales"
Journal of Marketing Research, Vol. XVI (November 1979), pp. 594-7.

58.15 ---------- Scaling of Miscellaneous Specific Constructs

Bachelet, Daniel and Lion, Joseph
"A Method for Evaluating the Importance of Perceived Attributes
Applied to the Development and Positioning of New Products"
Proceedings, ESOMAR Congress, Lisbon (1988), pp. 669-94.

Belk, Russell
"Three Scales to Measure Constructs Related to Materialism:
Reliability, Validity, and Relationships to Measures of Happiness"
in Kinnear, Thomas (editor)
Advances in Consumer Research, Volume Eleven
(Ann Arbor, MI: Association for Consumer Research, 1984), pp. 291-7.

Childers, Terry L., Churchill, Gilbert A., Jr., Ford, Neil M., and
Walker, Orville C.
"Towards a More Parsimonious Measure of Job Satisfaction in the
Industrial Salesforce"
in Bagozzi, Richard P. et al. (editors)
Proceedings, Educators' Conference (Chicago: American Marketing
Association, 1980), pp. 344-9.

Dudek, F. J. and Thoman, E.
"Scaling Preferences for Television Shows"
Journal of Applied Psychology, Vol. 48 (August 1964), pp. 237-40.

Ekman, G.
"Measurement of Moral Judgement: A Comparison of Scaling Methods"
Perceptual and Motor Skills, Vol. 15 (1962), pp. 3-9.

Fiske, Donald W.
Measuring the Concepts of Personality
(Chicago: Aldine-Atherton, 1971).

Gaski, John F. and Etzel, Michael J.
"The Index of Consumer Sentiment Toward Marketing"
Journal of Marketing, Vol. 50 (July 1986), pp. 71-81.

Golden, Linda L., Albaum, Gerald, and Zimmer, Mary
"The Numerical Comparative Scale: An Economical Format for Retail
Image Measurement"
Journal of Retailing, Vol. 63 (Winter 1987), pp. 393-410.

Holmes, T. H. and Rahe, R. H.
"The Social Readjustment Rating Scale"
Journal of Pyschosomatic Research, Vol. 2 (1967), pp. 213-8.

Hopkins, H. Donald
"Firm Size: The Interchangeability of Measures"
Human Relations, Vol. 41 (February 1988), pp. 91-102.

Horton, Raymond L.
"The Edwards Personal Preference Schedule and Consumer Personality
Research"
Journal of Marketing Research, Vol. XI (August 1974), pp. 335-7.

Kohn, Carol A. and Jacoby, Jacob
"Operationally Defining the Consumer Innovator"
Proceedings, 81st Annual Convention of the American Psychological
Association, Vol. 8, Issue 2 (1973), pp. 837,8.

Landy, Frank J., Farr, James L., Saal, Frank E., and Freytag, Walter R.
"Behaviorally Anchored Scales for Rating the Performance of Police
Officers"
Journal of Applied Psychology, Vol. 61 (1976), pp. 750-8.

Mukherjee, Ramkrishna
The Quality of Life: Valuation in Social Research
(Newbury Park, CA: Sage Publications, 1989), 248 pp.

Peryam, D. R., Polemis, B. W., Kamen, J. M., Eindhoven, J., and
Pilgrim, F. J.
Food Preferences of Men in the U.S. Armed Forces
(U.S. Department of the Army, Quartermaster Research and Engineering
Command, 1960), 160 pp.

Peterson, Robert A. and Sauber, Matthew
"A Mood Scale for Survey Research"
in Murphy, Patrick E., et al. (editors)
AMA Educators' Proceedings, Series 49
(Chicago: American Marketing Association, 1983), pp. 409-14.

Reece, Bonnie B. and Kinnear, Thomas C.
"Indices of Consumer Socialization for Retailing Research"
Journal of Retailing, Vol. 62 (Fall 1986), pp. 267-80.

Richards, Ruth, Kinney, Dennis K., Benet, Maria, and Merzel, Ann P. C.
"Assessing Everyday Creativity: Characteristics of the Lifetime
Creativity Scales and Validation With Three Large Samples"
Journal of Personality and Social Psychology, Vol. 54 (March 1988),
pp. 476-85.

Robinson, J. P. and Shaver, P. R.
Measures of Social Psychology Attitudes, Revised Edition
(Ann Arbor, MI: Survey Research Center, Institute for Social
Research, 1973).

Shimp, Terence A. and Sharma, Subhash
"Consumer Ethnocentrism: Construction and Validation of the CETSCALE"
Journal of Marketing Research, Vol. XXIV (August 1987), pp. 280-9.

Simpson, Edward K. and Kahler, Ruel C.
"A Scale for Source Credibility Validated in the Selling Context"
Journal of Personal Selling and Sales Management, Vol. 1 (Fall-Winter
1981), pp. 17-25.

Smith, Patricia, Kendall, L., and Hulin, C.
The Measurement of Satisfaction in Work and Retirement: A Strategy
for the Study of Attitudes
(Chicago, IL: Rand McNally, 1969).

Zelkowitz, Robin S.
"The Construction and Validation of a Measure of Vocational Maturity
for Adult Males"
Columbia University (1975), Ph.D. dissertation.

Zuckerman, Marvin and Link, Kathryn
"Construct Validity for the S.S.S."
Journal of Consulting and Clinical Psychology, Vol. 32 (1968), pp.
420-6.

59 ----------------- DEVELOPMENTS OF SCALING DEVICES -----------------
          See also (sub)heading(s) 37.

Ahmed, Sadrudin A. and Jackson, Douglas N.
   "Psychographics for Social Policy Decisions: Welfare Assistance"
   Journal of Consumer Research, Vol. 5 (March 1979), pp. 229-39.

Allison, Neil K.
   "A Psychometric Development of a Test for Consumer Alienation From
   the Marketplace"
   Journal of Marketing Research, Vol. XV (November 1978), pp. 565-75.

Bass, B. M.
   "Development and Evaluation of a Scale for Measuring Social
   Acquiescence"
   Journal of Abnormal and Social Psychology, Vol. 53 (1956), pp. 296-9.

Bearden, William O., Netemeyer, Richard G., and Teel, Jesse E.
   "Measurement of Consumer Susceptibility to Interpersonal Influence"
   Journal of Consumer Research, Vol. 15 (March 1989), pp. 473-81.

Belcher, John C. and Sharp, Emmit F.
   "A Short Scale for Measuring Farm Family Living: A Modification of
   Sewell's Socio-Economic Scale"
   Oklahoma Agricultural Experiment Station, Technical Bulletin T-46
   (Stillwater, OK: 1952).

Bendig, A. W.
   "The Development of a Short Form of the Manifest Anxiety Scale"
   Journal of Consulting Psychology, Vol. 20 (1956), p. 384.

Bendig, A. W., Vaughn, C. L., Ray, O., and Klions, H. L.
   "Attitudes Toward Man-into-Space: Development and Validation of an
   Attitude Scale"
   Journal of Social Psychology, Vol. 52 (1960), pp. 67-75.

Block, Peter H.
   "An Exploration Into the Scaling of Consumers' Involvement With a
   Product Class"
   in Mitchell, Andrew A.
   Advances in Consumer Research, Volume 9
   (Ann Arbor, MI: Association for Consumer Research, 1981), pp. 61-5.

Brinton, James E.
   "Deriving an Attitude Scale From Semantic Differential Data"
   Public Opinion Quarterly, Vol. 25 (1961), pp. 289-95.

Brooker, George
   "An Instrument to Measure Consumer Self-Actualization"
   in Schlinger, Mary Jane (editor)
   Advances in Consumer Research, Vol. 2
   (Chicago: Association for Consumer Research, Inc., 1975), pp. 563-75.

Buggie, Stephen and Makubals, Elizabeth L.
   "A Guttman Quasi-Scale on Intention Towards Rural Resettlement"
   Educational and Psychological Measurement, Vol. 47 (Spring 1987), pp.
   69-85.

Carr, Richard P., Jr.
   "Identifying Trade Areas for Consumer Goods in Foreign Markets"
   Journal of Marketing, Vol. 42 (October 1978), pp. 76-80.

Chapin, F. Stuart
   Measurement of Social Status by the Use of the Social Status Scale,
   1933
   (Minneapolis: University of Minnesota Press).

Childers, Terry L., Houston, Michael J., and Heckler, Susan E.
   "Measurement of Individual Differences in Visual Versus Verbal
   Information Processing"
   Journal of Consumer Research, Vol. 12 (September 1985), pp. 125-34.

Churchill, Gilbert A., Jr., Ford, Neil M., and Walker, Orville C., Jr.
   "Measuring the Job Satisfaction of Industrial Salesmen"
   Journal of Marketing Research, Vol. XI (August 1974), pp. 254-60.

Cleland, Charles L.
   "Level of Living Scales"
   in Cleland C. L. (editor)
   Scaling Social Data
   Tennessee Agricultural Experiment Station, Southern Cooperative
   Series Bulletin 108.
   (Knoxville, TN: 1965), pp. 17-29.

Cocanougher, A. Benton and Ivancevich, John M.
   "Bars Performance Rating for Sales Force Personnel"
   Journal of Marketing, Vol. 42 (July 1978), pp. 87-95.

Comer, James M.
"A Psychometric Assessment of a Measure of Sales Representatives'
Power Perceptions"
Journal of Marketing Research, Vol. XXI (May 1984), pp. 221-5.

Dickson, John and Albaum, Gerald
"A Method for Developing Tailormade Semantic Differentials for
Specific Marketing Content Areas"
Journal of Marketing Research, Vol. XIV (February 1977), pp. 87-91.

Feick, Lawrence F. and Price, Linda L.
"The Market Maven: A Diffuser of Marketplace Information"
Journal of Marketing, Vol. 51 (January 1987), pp. 83-97.

Frazier, Gary L.
"On the Measurement of Interfirm Power in Channels of Distribution"
Journal of Marketing Research, Vol. XX (May 1983), pp. 158-66.

Gaski, John F. and Etzel, Michael J.
"The Index of Consumer Sentiment Toward Marketing"
Journal of Marketing, Vol. 50 (July 1986), pp. 71-81.

Goldberg, Marvin E.
"Identifying Relevant Psychographic Segments: How Specifying Product
Functions Can Help"
Journal of Consumer Research, Vol.3 (December 1976), pp. 163-9.

Harari, Oren and Zedeck, Sheldon
"Development of Behaviourally Anchored Scales for the Evaluation of
Faculty Teaching"
Journal of Applied Psychology, Vol. 58 (March 1973), pp. 261-5.

Hogan, Robert
"Development of an Empathy Scale"
Journal of Consulting and Clinical Psychology, Vol. 33 (1969), p. 308.

Holmes, T. H.
"Development and Application of a Quantitative Measure of Life Change
Magnitude"
in Barrett, J. E. (editor)
Stress and Mental Disorder
(New York: Raven Press, 1979).

Holzbach, Robert L., Jr.
"An Investigation of a Model for Managerial Effectiveness: The
Effects of Leadership Style and Leader Attributed Social Power on
Subordinate Job Performance"
Carnegie-Mellon University (1974), doctoral dissertation.

Kunin, T.
"The Development of a New Type of Attitude Measure"
Personnel Psychology, Vol. 8 (1955), pp. 65-78.

Landy, Frank J. and Guion, Robert M.
"Development of Scales for the Measurement of Work Motivation"
Organizational Behaviour and Human Performance, Vol. V (1970), pp.
93-103.

Laurent, Gilles and Kapferer, Jean-Noel
"Measuring Consumer Involvement Profiles"
Journal of Marketing Research, Vol. XXII (February 1985), pp. 41-53.

Leavitt, Clark
"A Multidimensional Set of Rating Scales for Television Commercials"
Journal of Applied Psychology, Vol. 54 (1970), pp. 427-9.

Leavitt, Clark and Walton, John
"Development of a Scale for Innovativeness"
in Schlinger, M. J. (editor)
Advances in Consumer Research, Vol. 2
(Chicago: Association for Consumer Research, 1975), pp. 545-54.

Leonard-Barton, Dorothy
"Voluntary Simplicity Lifestyles and Energy Conservation"
Journal of Consumer Research, Vol. 8 (December 1981), pp. 243-52.

Lill, David J.
"The Development of a Standardized Student Evaluation Form"
Journal of the Academy of Marketing Science, Vol. 7 (Summer 1979),
pp. 252-4.

Locander, William B. and Spivey, W. Austin
"A Functional Approach to Attitude Measurement"
Journal of Marketing Research, Vol. XV (November 1978), pp. 576-87.

Lundstrom, William J. and Lamont, Lawrence M.
"The Development of a Scale to Measure Consumer Discontent"
Journal of Marketing Research, Vol. XIII (November 1976), pp. 373-81.

Magrabi, Frances M., Pennock, Jean L., Poole, W. Kenneth, and Rachal,
   J. Valley
   "An Index of the Economic Welfare of Rural Families"
   Journal of Consumer Research, Vol. 2 (December 1975), pp. 178-87.

Malhotra, Naresh K.
   "A Scale to Measure Self-Concepts, Person Concepts, and Product
   Concepts"
   Journal of Marketing Research, Vol. XVIII (November 1981), pp. 456-64.

Michaels, Ronald E. and Day, Ralph L.
   "Measuring Customer Orientation of Salespeople: A Replication With
   Industrial Buyers"
   Journal of Marketing Research, Vol. XXII (November 1985), pp. 443-6.

Monroe, Kent B.
   "Measuring Price Thresholds by Psychophysics and Latitudes of
   Acceptance"
   Journal of Marketing Research, Vol. VIII (November 1971), pp. 460-4.

Morrison, Donald G.
   "Purchase Intentions and Purchase Behavior"
   Journal of Marketing, Vol. 43 (Spring 1979), pp. 65-74.

Newman, John E.
   "Development of a Measure of Perceived Work Environment"
   Academy of Management Journal, Vol. 20, No. 4 (1977), pp. 520-34.

Parasuraman, A., Zeithaml, Valarie A., and Berry, Leonard L.
   "SERVQUAL: A Multiple-Item Scale for Measuring Consumer Perceptions
   of Service Quality"
   Journal of Retailing, Vol. 64 (Spring 1988), pp. 12-40.

Penney, Ronald K. and Reinehr, Robert C.
   "Development of a Stimulus Variation Seeking Scale for Adults"
   Psychological Reports, Vol. 18 (1966), pp. 631-38.

Poresky, Robert H., Hendrix, Charles, Mosier, Jacob E., and Samuelson,
   Marvin L.
   "The Companion Animal Semantic Differential: Long and Short Form
   Reliability and Validity"
   Educational and Psychological Measurement, Vol. 48 (Spring 1988), pp.
   255-60.

Price, Linda L. and Ridgway, Nancy M.
   "Development of a Scale to Measure Use Innovativeness"
   in Bagozzi, Richard P. and Tybout, Alice M. (editors)
   Advances in Consumer Research, Volume 10
   (Ann Arbor, MI: Association for Consumer Research, 1983), pp. 679-84.

Pruden, Henry O., Shuptrine, F. Kelly, and Longman, Douglas S.
   "A Measure of Alienation From the Marketplace"
   Journal of the Academy of Marketing Science, Vol. 2 (Fall 1974), pp.
   610-9.

Rachal, J. Valley, Bates, J. D., and Gould, W. Lawrence
   "An Index of Economic Status of Individual Rural Families"
   Research Triangle Institute, Final Report: RTI Project Su346 (1971).

Rachal, J. Valley, Bates, J. D., Poole, W. Kenneth, and Moore, R. Paul
   "An Operational Consumption Measure of Economic Status: With
   Applicability to United States Rural Families"
   Research Triangle Institute, Final Report: RTI Project 23U669 (1972).

Rosen, Ned
   "Anonymity and Attitude Measurement"
   Public Opinion Quarterly, Vol. 24 (Winter 1960), pp. 675-80.

Ruekert, Robert W. and Churchill, Gilbert A., Jr.
   "Reliability and Validity of Alternative Measures of Channel Member
   Satisfaction"
   Journal of Marketing Research, Vol. XXI (May 1984), pp. 226-33.

Saxe, Robert and Weitz, Barton A.
   "The SOCO Scale: A Measure of Customer Orientation of Salespeople"
   Journal of Marketing Research, Vol. XIX (August 1982), pp. 343-51.

Schuessler, Karl F.
   Measuring Social Life Feelings
   (San Francisco: Jossey-Bass Publishers, 1982), 183 pp.

Seaton, Richard
   "Why Ratings are Better Than Comparisons"
   Journal of Advertising Research, Vol. 14 (February 1974), pp. 45-8.

Sewell, William H.
   "The Construction and Standardization of a Scale for the Measurement
   of the Socio-Economic Status of Oklahoma Farm Families"
   Oklahoma Agricultural Experiment Station, Technical Bulletin 9
   (Stillwater, OK: 1940).

Seymour, Daniel and Lessne, Greg
"Spousal Conflict Arousal: Scale Development"
Journal of Consumer Research, Vol. 11 (December 1984), pp. 810-21.

Shimp, Terence A. and Sharma, Subhash
"Consumer Ethnocentrism: Construction and Validation of the CETSCALE"
Journal of Marketing Research, Vol. XXIV (August 1987), pp. 280-9.

Simpson, Edward K. and Kahler, Ruel C.
"A Scale for Source Credibility Validated in the Selling Context"
Journal of Personal Selling and Sales Management, Vol. 1 (Fall-Winter
1981), pp. 17-25.

Sproles, George B. and Kendall, Elizabeth L.
"A Methodology for Profiling Consumers' Decision-Making Styles"
Journal of Consumer Affairs, Vol. 20 (Winter 1986), pp. 267-79.

Stevens, S. S.
"Ratio Scales of Opinion"
in Whitla, D. K. (editor)
Handbook of Measurement and Assessment in Behavioral Sciences
(Addison-Wesley Publishing Co., 1968).

Stevens, S. S.
"Mathematics, Measurement, and Psychophysics"
in Stevens, S. S. (editor)
Handbook of Mathematical Psychology
(New York: John Wiley and Sons, Inc., 1962).

Sullivan, Gary and O'Connor, P. J.
"A Structural Assessment of the Original and a Modified Version of
the CAD Scale"
Journal of the Academy of Marketing Science, Vol. 12 (Fall 1984), pp.
41-51.

Swasy, J. L.
"Measuring the Bases of Social Power"
Proceedings, Association for Consumer Research (1978), pp. 340-6.

Templer, Donald I.
"The Construction and Validation of a Death Anxiety Scale"
Journal of General Psychology, Vol. 82 (April 1970), pp. 165-77.

Vaughn, C. L.
"A Scale for Assessing Socio-Economic Status in Survey Research"
Public Opinion Quarterly, Vol. 22 (Spring 1958), pp. 18-34.

Wells, William D., Leavitt, Clark, and McConville, Maureen
"A Reaction Profile for TV Commercials"
Journal of Advertising Research, Vol. 11 (December 1971), pp. 11-7.

Westbrook, Robert A.
"A Rating Scale for Measuring Product/Service Satisfaction"
Journal of Marketing, Vol. 44 (Fall 1980), pp. 68-72.

Williams, Faith M.
"Scales for Family Measurement"
Proceedings of the American Statistical Association (March 1930), pp.
135-9.

Wu, Bob T. W. and Petroshius, Susan M.
"The Halo Effect in Store Image Measurement"
Journal of the Academy of Marketing Science, Vol. 15 (Fall 1987), pp.
44-51.

Zaichkowsky, Judith Lynne
"Measuring the Involvement Construct"
Journal of Consumer Research, Vol. 12 (December 1985), pp. 341-52.

Zelkowitz, Robin S.
"The Construction and Validation of a Measure of Vocational Maturity
for Adult Males"
Columbia University (1975), Ph.D. dissertation.

Zelnio, Robert N. and Gagnon, Jean P.
"The Construction and Testing of an Image Questionnaire"
Journal of the Academy of Marketing Science, Vol. 9 (Summer 1981),
pp. 288-99.

Zuckerman, Marvin
"Development of a Sensation-Seeking Scale"
Journal of Consulting Psychology, Vol. 28 (1964), pp. 477-82.

60 -------------- COMPARATIVE STUDIES OF SCALING DEVICES --------------
          See also (sub)heading(s) 34.06, 37.

Abrams, Jack
   "Reducing the Risk of New Product Marketing Strategies Testing"
   Journal of Marketing Research, Vol. VI (May 1969), pp. 216-20.

Abrams, Jack
   "Evaluation of Alternative Rating Devices for Consumer Research"
   Journal of Marketing Research, Vol. III (May 1966), pp. 189-93.

Acker, Mary and McReynolds, Paul
   "The Need for Novelty: A Comparison of Six Instruments"
   Psychological Record, Vol. 17 (1967), pp. 177-82.

Alwin, Duane F. and Krosnick, Jon A.
   "The Measurement of Values in Surveys: A Comparison of Ratings and
   Rankings"
   Public Opinion Quarterly, Vol. 49 (Winter 1985), pp. 535-52.

Bartlett, C. J., Heerman, E., and Retis, S.
   "A Comparison of Six Different Scaling Techniques"
   Journal of Social Psychology, Vol. 51 (May 1960), pp. 343-8.

Bernardin, H. John
   "Behavioral Expectation Scales Versus Summated Scales: A Fairer
   Comparison"
   Journal of Applied Psychology, Vol. 62 (1977), pp. 422-7.

Blair, Ed, Sudman, Seymour, Bradburn, Norman M., and Stocking, Carol
   "How to Ask Questions About Drinking and Sex: Response Effects in
   Measuring Consumer Behavior"
   Journal of Marketing Research, Vol. XIV (August 1977), pp. 316-21.

Blumberg, Herbert H., De Soto, Clinton B., and Kuethe, James L.
   "Evaluation of Rating Scale Formats"
   Personnel Psychology, Vol. 19 (1966), pp. 243-59.

Brown, John
   "Recognition Assessed by Ratings and Ranking"
   British Journal of Psychology, Vol. 65, No. 1 (1974), pp. 13-22.

Burnaska, Robert F. and Hollmann, Thomas D.
   "An Empirical Comparison of Rater Response Biases on Three Rating
   Scale Formats"
   Journal of Applied Psychology, Vol. 59 (1974), pp. 307-12.

Carr, Richard P., Jr.
   "Identifying Trade Areas for Consumer Goods in Foreign Markets"
   Journal of Marketing, Vol. 42 (October 1978), pp. 76-80.

Clancy, Kevin J. and Garsen, Robert
   "Why Some Scales Predict Better"
   Journal of Advertising Research, Vol. 10 (October 1970), pp. 33-5.

Cook, Richard L. and Stewart, Thomas R.
   "A Comparison of Seven Methods for Obtaining Subjective Descriptions
   of Judgment Policy"
   Organizational Behavior and Human Performance, Vol. 13 (February
   1975), pp. 31-45.

Crespi, Irving
   "What Kind of Attitude Measures are Predictive of Behavior"
   Public Opinion Quarterly, Vol. 35 (Fall 1971), pp. 327-34.

Crosby, Richard W.
   "Attitude Measurement in a Bilingual Culture"
   Journal of Marketing Research, Vol. VI (November 1969), pp. 421-6.

Curry, D. J., Levin, I. P., and Gray, M. J.
   "A Comparison of Additive Conjoint Measurement and Functional
   Measurement in a Study of Apartment Preferences"
   Technical Report 98
   Institute of Regional Research, University of Iowa (1978).

Davenport, John Scott, Parker, Edwin B., and Smith, Stewart A.
   "Measuring Readership of Newspaper Advertisements"
   Journal of Advertising Research, Vol. 2 (December 1962), pp. 2-9.

Dickinson, John R.
   "A Comparison of Alternative Means of Collecting Unidimensional
   Proportions Data"
   Southwestern Marketing Association Conference, Houston, TX (March
   1979), paper presentation.

Dickinson, John R.
"Test-Retest Reliability of Alternative Means of Collecting Unidimensional Proportions Data"
in Gitlow, Howard S. and Wheatley, Edward W. (editors)
Developments in Marketing Science, Volume II
(Miami, FL: Academy of Marketing Science, 1979), pp. 212-6.

Ferguson, L. W.
"A Study of the Likert Technique of Attitude Scale Construction"
Journal of Social Psychology, Vol. 13 (February 1941), pp. 51-7.

Friedman, Linda Weiser and Friedman, Hershey H.
"Comparison of Itemized vs. Graphic Rating Scales"
Journal of the Market Research Society, Vol. 28, (July 1986), pp. 285-9.

Fry, Joseph N. and Claxton, John D.
"Semantic Differential and Nonmetric Multidimensional Scaling Descriptions of Brand Images"
Journal of Marketing Research, Vol. VIII (May 1971), pp. 238-40.

Golden, Linda L., Albaum, Gerald, and Zimmer, Mary
"The Numerical Comparative Scale: An Economical Format for Retail Image Measurement"
Journal of Retailing, Vol. 63 (Winter 1987), pp. 393-410.

Gormley, Richard
"A Note on Seven Brand Rating Scales and Subsequent Purchase"
Journal of the Market Research Society, Vol. 16 (July 1974), pp. 242-4.

Grigg, A. O.
"Some Problems Concerning the Use of Rating Scales for Visual Assessment"
Journal of the Market Research Society, Vol. 22, No. 1 (1980), pp. 29-43.

Guest, L.
"A Comparison of Two-Choice and Four-Choice Questions"
Journal of Advertising Research, Vol. 2 (March 1962), pp. 32-4.

Haley, Russell I. and Case, Peter B.
"Testing Thirteen Attitude Scales for Agreement and Brand Discrimination"
Journal of Marketing, Vol. 43 (Fall 1979), pp. 20-32.

Hawkins, Del I., Albaum, Gerald, and Best, Roger
"Stapel Scale or Semantic Differential in Marketing Research"
Journal of the Market Research Society, Vol. 11 (August 1974), pp. 318-22.

Henry, Walter A. and Stumpf, Robert V.
"Time and Accuracy Measures for Alternative Multidimensional Scaling Data Collection Methods"
Journal of Marketing Research, Vol. XII (May 1975), pp. 165-70.

Holbrook, Morris B. and Williams, Rebecca S.
"A Test of the Correspondence Between Perceptual Spaces Based on Pairwise Similarity Judgments Collected With and Without the Inclusion of Explicit Ideal Objects"
Journal of Applied Psychology, Vol. 63 (1978), pp. 373-6.

Holmes, Cliff
"A Statistical Evaluation of Rating Scales"
Journal of the Market Research Society, Vol. 16 (April 1974), pp. 87-107.

Hughes, G. D.
"Selecting Scales to Measure Attitude Change"
Journal of Marketing Research, Vol. IV (February 1967), pp. 85-7.

Jacobson, Alvin L. and Lalu, N. M.
"An Empirical and Algebraic Analysis of Alternative Techniques for Measuring Unobserved Variables"
in Blalock, Hubert M. (editor)
Measurement in the Social Sciences
(Chicago: Aldine, 1974), pp. 215-42.

Jaffe, Eugene D. and Nebenzahl, Israel D.
"Alternative Questionnaire Formats for Country Image Studies"
Journal of Marketing Research, Vol. XXI (November 1984), pp. 463-71.

Kassarjian, Harold H. and Nakanishi, Masao
"A Study of Selected Opinion Measurement Techniques"
Journal of Marketing Research, Vol. IV (May 1967), pp. 148-53.

Keaveny, Timothy J. and McGann, Anthony F.
"A Comparison of Behavioral Expectation Scales and Graphic Rating Scales"
Journal of Applied Psychology, Vol. 60 (1975), pp. 695-703.

Kohan, Stephanie, Demille, Richard, and Myers, James H.
"Two Comparisons of Attitude Measures"
Journal of Advertising Research, Vol. 13 (August 1972), pp. 695-703.

Krosnick, Jon A. and Alwin, Duane F.
"A Test of the Form-Resistant Correlation Hypothesis"
Public Opinion Quarterly, Vol. 52 (Winter 1988), pp. 526-38.

Lampert, Shlomo I.
"The Attitude Pollimeter: A New Attitude Scaling Device"
Journal of Marketing Research, Vol. XVI (November 1979), pp. 578-82.

Lindzey, G. E. and Guest, L.
"To Repeat: Check Lists Can be Dangerous"
Public Opinion Quarterly, Vol. 15 (Summer 1951), pp. 355-8.

Looft, William R. and Baranowski, Marc D.
"An Analysis of Five Measures of Sensation-Seeking and Preferences
for Complexity"
Journal of General Psychology, Vol. 85 (1971), pp. 307-13.

Martin, Warren S. and French, Warren A.
"Inter-Instrument Consistency"
Journal of the Market Research Society, Vol. 19 (October 1977), pp.
177-86.

McCarroll, James E., Mitchell, Kevin M., Carpenter, Ronda J., and
Anderson, J. P.
"Analysis of Three Stimulation-Seeking Scales"
Psychological Reports, Vol. 21 (1967), pp. 853-56.

McIntyre, Shelby H. and Ryans, Adrian
"Time and Accuracy Measures for Alternative Multidimensional Scaling
Data Collection Methods: Some Additional Results"
Journal of Marketing Research, Vol. XIV (November 1977), pp. 607-10.

Menezes, Dennis and Elbert, Norbert F.
"Alternative Semantic Scaling Formats for Measuring Store Image: An
Evaluation"
Journal of Marketing Research, Vol. XVI (February 1979), pp. 80-7.

Metzner, C. A.
"An Application of Scaling to Questionnaire Construction"
Journal of the American Statistical Association, Vol. 45 (March
1950), pp. 112-8.

Michie, Donald A. and Roering, Kenneth J.
"Alternative Measures of Channel Member Satisfaction"
in Meredith, Jack and Swanson, Paul (editors)
Proceedings, Ninth Annual Conference, Midwest American Institute for
Decision Sciences (1978), pp. 41-3.

Mohn, N. Carroll
"Comparing the Statistical Quality of Two Methods for Collecting
Brand Image Data: Coca-Cola's Experience"
Marketing and Research Today, Vol. 17 (August 1989), pp. 167-71.

Munson, J. Michael and McIntyre, Shelby H.
"Developing Practical Procedures for the Measurement of Personal
Values in Cross-Cultural Marketing"
Journal of Marketing Research, Vol. XVI (February 1979), pp. 48-52.

Neidell, Lester A.
"Procedures for Obtaining Similarities Data"
Journal of Marketing Research, Vol. IX (August 1972), pp. 335-7.

Newman, Joseph W. and Lockeman, Bradley D.
"Measuring Prepurchase Information Seeking"
Journal of Consumer Research, Vol. 2 (December 1975), pp. 216-22.

Pessemier, Edgar A. and Bruno, Albert
"An Empirical Investigation of the Reliability and Stability of
Selected Activity and Attitude Measures"
Proceedings, Second Annual Conference, Association for Consumer
Research (1971), pp. 389-403.

Ptacek, Charles H. and Ross, Ivan
"Propensity-to-Buy Ratings"
Journal of Advertising Research, Vol. 19 (December 1979), pp. 43-7.

Reynolds, Thomas J. and Jolly, James P.
"Measuring Personal Values: An Evaluation of Alternative Methods"
Journal of Marketing Research, Vol. XVII (November 1980), pp. 531-6.

Ricker, B. L.
"A Comparison of Methods Used in Attitude Research"
Journal of Abnormal and Social Psychology, Vol. 39 (January 1944),
pp. 24-42.

Rogers, Everett M. and Cartano, David G.
    "Methods of Measuring Opinion Leadership"
    Public Opinion Quarterly, Vol. 26 (Fall 1962), pp. 431-41.

Rothman, James
    "Formulation of an Index of Propensity to Buy"
    Journal of Marketing Research, Vol. I (May 1964), pp. 21-5.

Spagna, Gregory J.
    "Questionnaires: Which Approach Do You Use?"
    Journal of Advertising Research, Vol. 24 (February/March 1984), pp.
    67-70.

Szalay, L. B., Windle, C., and Lysne, D. A.
    "Attitude Measurement by Free Verbal Associations"
    Journal of Social Psychology, Vol. 82 (October 1970), pp. 43-55.

Tittle, C. R. and Hill, R. J.
    "Attitude Measurement and Prediction of Behavior: An Evaluation of
    Conditions and Measurement Techniques"
    Sociometry, Vol. 30 (June 1967), pp. 199-214.

Van Doorn, L., Saris, Willem E., and Lodge, M. M.
    "Discrete or Continuous Measurement: What Difference Does it Make?"
    Kwantitatieve Methoden, Vol. 10 (1983), pp. 104-21.

Vidali, J. J., Jr.
    "Single Anchor Stapel Scales Versus Double Anchor Semantic
    Differential Scales"
    Psychological Reports, Vol. 33 (October 1973), pp. 373,4.

Vidali, J. J., Jr. and Holeway, R. E.
    "Stapel Scales Versus Semantic Differential Scales"
    Psychological Reports, Vol. 35 (1975), pp. 165,6.

Villani, Kathryn E. and Wind, Yoram
    "On the Usage of Modified Personality Trait Measures in Consumer
    Research"
    Journal of Consumer Research, Vol. 2 (December 1975), pp. 223-8.

Waters, Carrie and Waters, L. K.
    "Relationships Between a Measure of Sensation-Seeking and Personal
    Preference Schedule Need Scales"
    Educational and Psychological Measurement, Vol. 29 (1969), pp. 983-5.

Whipple, Thomas W.
    "Variation Among Multidimensional Scaling Solutions: An Examination
    of the Effect of Data Collection Differences"
    Journal of Marketing Research, Vol. XIII (February 1976), pp. 98-103.

Young, F. W.
    "Nonmetric Scaling of Line Lengths Using Latencies, Similarity, and
    Same-Different Judgements"
    Perception and Psychophysics, Vol. 8 (1970), pp. 363-9.

Zinkhan, George M. and Fornell, Claes
    "A Test of Two Consumer Response Scales in Advertising"
    Journal of Marketing Research, Vol. XXII (November 1985), pp. 447-52.

61 --------------- SOURCES OF BIAS IN SCALING METHODS ----------------
       See also (sub)heading(s) 34.08, 37, 77, 87.07, 116, 118,
    123.

61.01 ---------- Books Re: Sources of Bias in Scaling Methods

Schuman, H. and Presser, S.
    Questions and Answers in Attitude Surveys. Experiments on Question
    Form, Wording, and Context
    (New York: Academic Press, 1981).

61.02 ---------- Sequence Effects

       See also (sub)heading(s) 34.08.

Campbell, D. T. and Mohr, P. J.
    "The Effect of Ordinal Position Upon Responses to Items in a Check
    List"
    Journal of Applied Psychology, Vol. 34 (February 1950), pp. 62-7.

Dickinson, John R.
    "Order Related Biases in Perception Ratings"
    in Wyckham, Robert (editor)
    Proceedings, Administrative Sciences Association of Canada (1981),
    pp. 65-72.

Dickinson, John R.
    "Sequence, Pole, and Context Effects in Similarities Ratings"
    in Bellur, Venkatakrishna V. (editor)
    Developments in Marketing Science, Volume IV
    (Academy of Marketing Science, 1981), pp. 214-7.

Dickinson, John R. and Kirzner, Eric
    "Questionnaire Item Omission as a Function of Within-Group Question
    Position"
    Journal of Business Research, Vol. 13 (February 1985), pp. 71-5.

Dickinson, John R. and Mahajan, Jayashree
    "An Absence of Order-Related Effects in Self-Report Ratings"
    Proceedings, American Institute for Decision Sciences (November 1983).

Dickinson, John R. and Kirzner, Eric
    "Split-Sample Reliability of a Secondary Sequence Effect on
    Questionnaire Item Omission"
    Proceedings, Academy of Marketing Science (May 1983).

Kelley, Jonathan and McAllister, Ian
    "Ballot Paper Cues and the Vote in Australia and Britain: Alphabetic
    Voting, Sex and Title"
    Public Opinion Quarterly, Vol. 48 (Summer 1984), pp. 452-66.

Krosnick, Jon A. and Alwin, Duane F.
    "An Evaluation of a Cognitive Theory of Response-Order Effects in
    Survey Measurement"
    Public Opinion Quarterly, Vol. 51 (Summer 1987), pp. 201-19.

Payne, J. D.
    "The Effects of Reversing the Order of Verbal Rating Scales in a
    Postal Survey"
    Journal of the Market Research Society, Vol. 14 (January 1972), pp.
    30-44.

Ring, Erp
    "Asymmetrical Rotation"
    European Research, Vol. 3 (May 1975), pp. 111-4,119.

61.03 ---------- Contextual Contamination Effects

       See also (sub)heading(s) 34.08.

Bishop, George F., Oldendick, Robert W., and Tuchfarber, Alfred
    "What Must My Interest in Politics be if I Just Told You 'I Don't
    Know'?"
    Public Opinion Quarterly, Vol. 48 (Summer 1984), pp. 510-9.

Clanton, Earl S., III
    "Effects of Alternative Positioning of Open-Ended Questions in
    Multiple-Choice Questionnaires"
    Journal of Applied Psychology, Vol. 59 (1974), pp. 776-8.

Dickinson, John R.
    "Order Related Biases in Perception Ratings"
    in Wyckham, Robert (editor)
    Proceedings, Administrative Sciences Association of Canada (1981),
    pp. 65-72.

Dickinson, John R.
"Sequence, Pole, and Context Effects in Similarities Ratings"
in Bellur, Venkatakrishna V. (editor)
Developments in Marketing Science, Volume IV
(Academy of Marketing Science, 1981), pp. 214-7.

Dickinson, John R. and Mahajan, Jayashree
"An Absence of Order-Related Effects in Self-Report Ratings"
Proceedings, American Institute for Decision Sciences (November 1983).

Duncan, Otis Dudley and Schuman, Howard
"Effects of Question Wording and Context: An Experiment With
Religious Indicators"
Journal of the American Statistical Association, Vol. 75 (June 1980),
pp. 269-75.

Feldman, Jack M. and Lynch, John G., Jr.
"Self-Generated Validity and Other Effects of Measurement on Belief,
Attitude, Intention and Behavior"
Journal of Applied Psychology, Vol. 73 (August 1988), pp. 421-35.

Fine, B. J. and Haggard, D. F.
"Contextual Effects in Scaling"
Journal of Applied Psychology, Vol. 61 (1976), pp. 247-51.

Landon, E. Laird, Jr.
"Order Bias, the Ideal Rating, and the Semantic Differential"
Journal of Marketing Research, Vol. VIII (August 1971), pp. 375-8.

Schroder, Susanne
"Towards a Theory of How People Answer Questions"
European Research, Vol. 13 (April 1985), pp. 82-90.

Schuman, Howard, Presser, Stanley, and Ludwig, Jacob
"Context Effects on Survey Responses to Questions About Abortion"
Public Opinion Quarterly, Vol. 45 (1981), pp. 216-23.

Sigelman, Lee
"Question Order Effects on Presidential Popularity"
Public Opinion Quarterly, Vol. 45 (1981), pp. 199-207.

Smith, Tom W.
"Conditional Order Effects"
GSS Technical Report Number 33
(Chicago: NORC, 1982).

Vidali, Joseph J.
"Context Effects on Scaled Evaluatory Adjective Meaning"
Journal of the Market Research Society, Vol. 17 (January 1975), pp.
21-5.

61.04 ---------- Pole Orientation Effects

Dickinson, John R.
"Order Related Biases in Perception Ratings"
in Wyckham, Robert (editor)
Proceedings, Administrative Sciences Association of Canada (1981),
pp. 65-72.

Dickinson, John R.
"Sequence, Pole, and Context Effects in Similarities Ratings"
in Bellur, Venkatakrishna V. (editor)
Developments in Marketing Science, Volume IV
(Academy of Marketing Science, 1981), pp. 214-7.

Dickinson, John R. and Mahajan, Jayashree
"An Absence of Order-Related Effects in Self-Report Ratings"
Proceedings, American Institute for Decision Sciences (November 1983).

Friedman, Hershey H., Friedman, Linda Weiser, and Gluck, Beth
"The Effects of Scale-Checking Styles on Responses to a Semantic
Differential Scale"
Journal of the Market Research Society, Vol. 30 (October 1988), pp.
477-81.

Holmes, C.
"A Statistical Evaluation of Rating Scales"
Journal of the Market Research Society, Vol. 16, No. 2 (1974), pp.
87-107.

61.05 ---------- Position Bias, Order-of-Answer-Alternatives Effects

        See also (sub)heading(s) 34.08.

Belson, William A.
"The Effects of Reversing the Presentation Order of Verbal Rating
Scales"
Journal of Advertising Research, Vol. 30 (December 1966), pp. 30-7.

Belson, W. A.
  A Study of the Effects of Reversing the Order of Presentation of
  Verbal Rating Scales
  (Survey Research Centre, 1965).

Berg, I. and Rapaport, G. M.
  "Response Bias in an Unstructured Questionnaire"
  Journal of Psychology, Vol. 38 (1954), pp. 475-81.

Blunch, Niels J.
  "Position Bias in Multiple-Choice Questions"
  Journal of Marketing Research, Vol. XXI (May 1984), pp. 216-20.

Carp, Frances M.
  "Position Effects on Interview Responses"
  Journal of Gerontology, Vol. 29, No. 5 (1974), pp. 581-7.

Coney, Kenneth A.
  "Order Bias: The Special Case of Letter Preference"
  Public Opinion Quarterly, Vol. 41 (1977), pp. 385-8.

Day, Ralph L.
  "Position Bias in Paired Product Tests"
  Journal of Marketing Research, Vol. VI (February 1969), pp. 98-100.

Friedman, Hershey H. and Leefer, Joanna R.
  "Label Versus Position in Rating Scales"
  Journal of the Academy of Marketing Science, Vol. 9 (Spring 1981),
  pp. 88-92.

Jain, A. K. and Pinson, C.
  "The Effect of Order of Presentation of Similarity Judgements on
  Multidimensional Scaling Results: An Empirical Examination"
  Journal of Marketing Research, Vol. XIII (November 1976), pp. 435-9.

Landon, E. Laird, Jr.
  "Order Bias, the Ideal Rating, and the Semantic Differential"
  Journal of Marketing Research, Vol. VIII (August 1971), pp. 375-8.

Mathews, C. O.
  "The Effect of Position of Printed Response Words Upon Children's
  Answers to Two-Response Types of Tests"
  Journal of Educational Psychology, Vol. 18 (1927), pp. 445-57.

Quinn, Susan B. and Belson, William A.
  The Effects of Reversing the Order of Presentation of Verbal Rating
  Scales in Survey Interviews
  (Survey Research Centre of the London School of Economics, 1969).

Ring, E.
  "Asymmetrical Rotation"
  European Research, Vol. 3 (May 1975), pp. 111-14,9.

Rugg, D. and Cantril, H.
  "The Wording of Questions in Public Opinion Polls"
  Journal of Abnormal and Social Psychology, Vol. 37 (1942), pp. 469-95.

61.06 ---------- Statement Polarity

Falthzik, Alfred M. and Jolson, Marvin A.
  "Statement Polarity in Attitude Studies"
  Journal of Marketing Research, Vol. XI (February 1974), pp. 102-5.

61.07 ---------- Inclusion of a Neutral Position

        See also (sub)heading(s) 54.05.

Bartram, Peter and Yielding, David J.
  "The Development of an Empirical Method of Selecting Phrases Used in
  Verbal Rating Scales: A Report on a Recent Experiment"
  Journal of the Market Research Society, Vol. 15 (July 1973), pp.
  151-6.

Bishop, George F.
  "Experiments With the Middle Response Alternative in Survey Questions"
  Public Opinion Quarterly, Vol. 51 (Summer 1987), pp. 220-32.

Schertzer, Clinton B. and Kernan, Jerome B.
  "More on the Robustness of Response Scales"
  Journal of the Market Research Society, Vol. 27 (October 1985), pp.
  261-82.

Worcester, R. M. and Burns, T. R.
  "A Statistical Examination of the Relative Precision of Verbal Scales"
  Journal of the Market Research Society, Vol. 17, No. 3 (1975), pp.
  181-97.

61.08 ---------- Halo Effects and Affective Overtones

Beckwith, N. E. and Lehmann, D. R.
  "The Importance of Halo Effects in Muti-Attribute Attitude Models"
  Journal of Marketing Research, Vol. XII (August 1975), pp. 265-75.

Cooper, W. H.
  "Ubiquitous Halo"
  Psychological Bulletin, Vol. 90, No. 2 (1981), pp. 218-44.

Dillon, William R., Mulani, Narendra, and Frederick, Donald G.
  "Removing Perceptual Distortions in Product Space Analysis"
  Journal of Marketing Research, Vol. XXI (May 1984), pp. 184-93.

Gilinsky, A. S.
  "The Influence of the Procedure of Judging on the Halo Effect"
  American Psychologist, Vol. 2 (1947), pp. 309,10.

Holbrook, M. B. and Huber, J.
  "Separating Perceptual Dimensions From Affective Overtones: An
  Application to Consumer Aesthetics"
  Journal of Consumer Research, Vol. 5 (March 1979), pp. 272-83.

Huber, J. and Holbrook, M. B.
  "Using Attribute Ratings for Product Positioning: Some Distinctions
  Among Compositional Approaches"
  Journal of Marketing Research, Vol. XVI (November 1979), pp. 507-16.

Myers, J. H.
  "Removing Halo From Job Evaluation Factor Structure"
  Journal of Applied Psychology, Vol. 49 (1965), pp. 217-21.

Spagna, Gregory J.
  "Questionnaires: Which Approach do You Use?"
  Journal of Advertising Research, Vol. 24 (February/March 1984), pp.
  67-70.

Symonds, P. M.
  "Notes on Rating"
  Journal of Applied Psychology, Vol. 9 (1925), pp. 188-95.

Thorndike, E. L.
  "A Consistent Error in Psychological Rating"
  Journal of Applied Psychology, Vol. 4 (1920), pp. 25-9.

62 ------------------- MULTIDIMENSIONAL SCALING ---------------------
         See also (sub)heading(s) 37, 42, 63, 64, 65, 133.15, 185.04.

62.01 ---------- Books Re: Multidimensional Scaling

Arabie, Phipps, Carroll, J. Douglas, and DeSarbo, Wayne S.
  Three-Way Scaling and Clustering
  (Beverly Hills, CA: Sage Publications, Inc.), 92 pp.

Bechtel, Gordon G.
  Multidimensional Preference Scaling
  (Berlin: Walter De Gruyter and Co., 1976). 170 pp.

Coxon, A. P. M.
  The User's Guide to Multidimensional Scaling
  (London: Heinemann Educational Books, 1982).

Davison, Mark L.
  Multidimensional Scaling
  (New York: John Wiley and Sons, Inc., 1983), 241 pp.

Golledge, Reginald G.
  Multidimensional Scaling: Review and Geographical Applications
  (Washington, DC: Association of American Geographers, 1972).

Golledge, R. G. and Rayner, J. N. (editors)
  Proximity and Preference: Problems in Multidimensional Analysis of
  Large Data Sets
  (Minneapolis: University of Minnesota Press, 1982).

Green, P. E. and Carmone, F. J.
  Multidimensional Scaling and Related Techniques in Marketing Analysis
  (Boston: Allyn and Bacon, 1970).

Green, Paul E., Carmone, Frank J., Jr., and Smith, Scott M.
  Multidimensional Scaling: Concepts and Applications
  (Needham Heights, MA: Allyn and Bacon, Inc., 1989).

Green, Paul E. and Rao, Vithala R.
  Applied Multidimensional Scaling
  (New York: Holt, Rinehart and Winston, 1972), 292 pp.

Green, Paul E. and Wind, Yoram
  Multiattribute Decisions in Marketing
  (Hinsdale, IL: The Dryden Press, 1973).

Kruskal, Joseph B. and Wish, Myron
  Multidimensional Scaling
  (Beverly Hills, CA: Sage Publications, Inc., 1978).

Lingoes, James C.
  Geometric Representation of Relational Data
  (Ann Arbor, MI: Mathesis, 1977).

Noma, Elliot and Johnson, J.
  Constraining Nonmetric Multidimensional Scaling Configurations
  Technical Report 60
  (Human Performance Center, University of Michigan, 1977).

Romney, A. K., Shepard, R. N., and Nerlove, S. B. (editors)
  Multidimensional Scaling: Theory and Applications in the Behavioral
  Sciences
  (New York and London: Seminar Press, 1972).

Sawtooth Software, Incorporated
  Proceedings of the Sawtooth Software Conference on Perceptual
  Mapping, Conjoint Analysis, and Computer Interviewing
  (Ketchum, ID: Sawtooth Software, Inc., 1987).

Schiffman, Susan S., Reynolds, M. Lance, and Young, Forrest W.
  Introduction to Multidimensional Scaling
  (New York: Academic Press, 1981), 412 pp.

Shepard, Roger N., Romney, A. Kimbal, and Nerlove, Sara Beth (editors)
  Multidimensional Scaling: Theory and Applications in the Behavioral
  Sciences, Volumes One and Two: New York: Seminar Press, 1972).

62.02 ---------- Theory Re: Multidimensional Scaling

Abelson, R. P.
  "A Technique and a Model for Multi-Dimensional Attitude Scaling"
  Public Opinion Quarterly, Vol. 18 (Winter 1954-55), pp. 405-18.

Abelson, Robert P. and Tukey, John W.
  "Efficient Utilization of Non-Numerical Information in Quantitative
  Analysis: General Theory and the Case of Simple Order"
  Annals of Mathematical Statistics, Vol. 34 (August 1963), pp. 1347-69.

Beals, R., Krantz, D. H., and Tversky, A.
  "Foundations of Multidimensional Scaling"
  Psychological Review, Vol. 75 (March 1968), pp. 127-42.

Bechtel, Gordon G.
  "Nonlinear Submodels of Orthogonal Linear Models"
  Psychometrika, Vol. 38 (September 1973), pp. 379-92.

Bechtel, Gordon G., Tucker, Ledyard R., and Chang, Wei-Ching
  "A Scaler Product Model for the Multidimensional Scaling of Choice"
  Psychometrika, Vol. 36 (December 1971), pp. 369-88.

Bentler, Peter M. and Weeks, David G.
  "Restricted Multidimensional Scaling Models"
  Journal of Mathematical Psychology, Vol. 17 (April 1978), pp. 138-51.

Bloxom, Bruce
  "Constrained Multidimensional Scaling in n Spaces"
  Psychometrika, Vol. 43 (September 1978), pp. 397-408.

Bloxom, B.
  "Individual Differences in Multidimensional Scaling"
  (Princeton, NJ: Educational Testing Services, ETS Research Bulletin,
  1968).

Carroll, J. Douglas
  "Models and Methods for Multidimensional Analysis of Preferential
  Choice (or Other Dominance) Data"
  in Lautermann, E. D. and Feger, H. (editors)
  Similarity and Choice
  (Bern: Huber, 1980).

Carroll, J. Douglas
  "Impact Scaling: Theory, Mathematical Model, and Estimation
  Procedures"
  Proceedings, Human Factors Society, Vol. 21 (1977), pp. 513-7.

Carroll, J. Douglas
  "Spatial, Non-Spatial, and Hybrid Models for Scaling"
  Psychometrika, Vol. 41 (1976), pp. 439-63.

Carroll, J. Douglas
  "Parametric Mapping of Similarities Data"
  Bell Laboratories (1967), unpublished paper.

Carroll, J. D. and Arabie, P.
  "Multidimensional Scaling"
  in Rosenzweig, M. R. and Porter, L. W. (editors)
  Annual Review of Psychology
  (Palo Alto, CA: Annual Reviews, 1980).

Carroll, J. Douglas and Chang, Jih-Jie
  "A General Index of Non-Linear or Linear Correlation and Its
  Application to the Interpretation of Multidimensional Scaling
  Solutions"
  American Psychologist, Vol. 19 (July 1964), p. 540.

Carroll, J. Douglas, Pruzansky, Sandra, and Kruskal, Joseph B.
  "CANDELINC: A General Approach to Multidimensional Analysis of
  Many-Way Arrays With Linear Constraints on Parameters"
  Psychometrika, Vol. 45 (March 1980), pp. 3-24.

Christopher, Martin
  "Non-Metric Scaling: The Principles and Marketing Possibilities"
  European Research, Vol. 1 (May 1973), pp. 108-14.

Clarke, Darral G.
  "Strategic Advertising Planning: Merging Multidimensional Scaling and
  Econometric Analysis"
  Management Science, Vol. 24 (December 1978), pp. 1687-99.

Cliff, Norman and Young, Forrest W.
  "On the Relation Between Unidimensional Judgments and
  Multidimensional Scaling"
  Organizational Behavior and Human Performance, Vol. 3 (August 1968),
  pp. 207,8.

Coleman, J. S.
  "Multidimensional Scale Analysis"
  American Journal of Sociology, Vol. 63 (November 1957), pp. 253-63.

Coombs, Clyde H.
  "Psychological Scaling Without a Unit of Measurement"
  Psychological Review, Vol. 57 (May 1950), pp. 148-58.

Cooper, Lee
  "A Review of Multidimensional Scaling in Marketing Research"
  Applied Psychological Measurement, Vol. 7 (Fall 1983), pp. 427-50.

Cooper, Lee G.
"A New Solution to the Additive Constant Problem in Metric
Multidimensional Scaling"
Psychometrika, Vol. 37 (September 1972), pp. 311-22.

Cooper, Lee G.
"Metric Multidimensional Scaling and the Concept of Preference"
University of Illinois (1970), unpublished doctoral dissertation.

Day, George S.
"Evaluating Models of Attitude Structure"
Journal of Marketing Research, Vol. IX (August 1972), pp. 279-86.

Day, George S., Deutscher, Terry, and Ryans, Adrian B.
"Data Quality, Level of Aggregation and Nonmetric Multidimensional
Scaling Solutions"
Journal of Marketing Research, Vol. XIII (February 1976), pp. 92-7.

De Leeuw, Jan and Heiser, Willem
"Multidimensional Scaling With Restrictions on the Configuration"
in Krishnaiah, P. R. (editor)
Multivariate Analysis, Volume Five
(New York: North Holland Publishing Company, 1980), pp. 501-22.

DeSarbo, Wayne S., Oliver, Richard L., and DeSoete, Geert
"A New Probabilistic MDS Vector Model"
Applied Psychological Measurement, Vol. 10 (March 1986), pp. 79-98.

Dillon, William R., Frederick, Donald G., and Tangpanichdee, Vanchai
"Decision Issues in Building Perceptual Product Spaces With
Multi-Attribute Rating Data"
Journal of Consumer Research, Vol. 12 (June 1985), pp. 47-63.

Dillon, William R., Frederick, Donald G., and Tangpanichdee, Vanchai
"A Note on Accounting for Sources of Variation in Perceptual Maps"
Journal of Marketing Research, Vol. XIX (August 1982), pp. 302-11.

Dillon, William R., Frederick, Donald G., and Tangpanichdee, Vanchai
"Issues in Perceptual Mapping Applications: Relations Between
Alternative Techniques"
University of Massachusetts (1981), working paper.

Doyle, Peter
"Nonmetric Multidimensional Scaling: A User's Guide"
European Journal of Marketing, Vol. 7 (1973), pp. 82-8.

Eckart, C. and Young, G.
"The Approximation of One Matrix by Another of Lower Rank"
Psychometrika, Vol. 1 (1936), pp. 211-8.

Farley, John U. and Leavitt, Harold J.
"A Model of the Distribution of Branded Personal Products in Jamaica"
Journal of Marketing Research, Vol. V (November 1968), pp. 362-8.

Gold, E. M.
"Metric Unfolding: Data Requirements for Unique Solutions and
Solutions and Clarification of Schonemann's Algorithm"
Psychometrika, Vol. 38 (December 1973), pp. 555-69.

Green, Paul E.
"Marketing Applications of MDS: Assessment and Outlook"
Journal of Marketing, Vol. 39 (January 1975), pp. 24-31.

Green, Paul E. and Carmone, Frank J.
"Design Considerations in Attitude Measurement"
in Wind, Y. and Greenberg, M. G. (editors)
Moving Ahead With Attitude Research
(Chicago: American Marketing Association, 1977), pp. 9-18.

Green, Paul E., Carmone, Frank J., and Robinson, Patrick J.
"Nonmetric Scaling Methods: An Exposition and Overview"
Wharton Quarterly, Vol. 2 (Winter-Spring 1968), pp. 27-41.

Green, Paul E. and Claycamp, Henry J.
"Brand-Features Congruence Mapping"
Journal of Marketing Research, Vol. XII (August 1975), pp. 306-13.

Green, Paul E. and DeSarbo, Wayne S.
"Componential Segmenting in the Analysis of Consumer Trade-Offs"
Journal of Marketing, Vol. 43 (Fall 1979), pp. 83-91.

Green, Paul E., Krieger, Abba M., and Carroll, J. Douglas
"Conjoint Analysis and Multidimensional Scaling: A Complementary
Approach"
Journal of Advertising Research, Vol. 27 (October/November 1987), pp.
21-7.

Green, Paul E. and Maheshwari, Arun
"A Note on the Multidimensional Scaling of Conditional Proximity Data"
Journal of Marketing Research, Vol. VII (February 1970), pp. 106-10.

Green, Paul E., Maheshwari, Arun, and Rao, Vithala R.
"Dimensional Interpretation and Configuration Invariance in
Multidimensional Scaling: An Empirical Study"
Multivariate Behavioral Research, Vol. 6 (April 1969), pp. 159-80.

Green, Paul E. and Rao, Vithala R.
"Multidimensional Scaling and Individual Differences"
Journal of Marketing Research, Vol. VIII (February 1971), pp. 71-7.

Green, Paul E. and Vallieres, Raymond
"A Note on the Spaeth-Guthery Multidimensional Scaling Analysis of
Synthetic Data"
Marketing Science Institute (1970), unpublished paper.

Green, Paul E., Wind, Yoram, and Claycamp, Henry J.
"Brand-Features Congruence Mapping"
Journal of Marketing Research, Vol. XII (August 1975), pp. 306-13.

Green, Paul E., Wind, Yoram, and Jain, Arun K.
"A Note on Measurement of Social-Psychological Belief Systems"
Journal of Marketing Research, Vol. IX (May 1972), pp. 204-8.

Guttman, L.
"A General Non-Metric Technique for Finding the Smallest Co-ordinate
Space for a Configuration of Points"
Psychometrika, Vol. 33 (1968), pp. 469-506.

Hauser, J. R. and Koppelman, F. S.
"Alternate Perceptual Mapping Techniques: Relative Accuracy and
Usefulness"
Journal of Marketing Research, Vol. XVI (November 1979), pp. 495-506.

Hooley, G. J.
"Perceptual Mapping for Product Positioning: A Comparison of Two
Approaches"
European Research, Vol. 7 (January 1979), pp. 17-23,40.

Horton, Raymond L.
"The Effects of Incorrect Specification of the Minkowski Metric: Some
Analytical Results"
Journal of the Academy of Marketing Science, Vol. 2 (Summer 1974),
pp. 478-87.

Isaac, Paul D. and Poor, David D. S.
"On the Determination of Appropriate Dimensionality in Data With
Error"
Psychometrika, Vol. 39 (March 1974), pp. 91-109.

Johnson, Richard M.
"Pairwise Nonmetric Multidimensional Scaling"
Psychometrika, Vol. 38 (March 1973), pp. 11-8.

Johnson, Richard M.
"Market Segmentation: A Strategic Management Tool"
Journal of Marketing Research, Vol. VIII (February 1971), pp. 13-8.

Keon, John W.
"Product Positioning: TRINODAL Mapping of Brand Images, Ad Images,
and Consumer Preference"
Journal of Marketing Research, Vol. XX (November 1983), pp. 380-92.

Krantz, D. H.
"Rational Distance Functions for Multidimensional Scaling"
Journal of Mathematical Psychology, Vol. 4 (1967), pp. 226-45.

Kruskal, Joseph B.
"Analysis of Factorial Experiments by Estimating Monotone
Transformations of the Data"
Journal of the Royal Statistical Society, Vol. B27 (March 1965), pp.
251-63.

Kruskal, J. B.
"Nonmetric Multidimensional Scaling: A Numerical Method"
Psychometrika, Vol. 29 (June 1964), pp. 115-29.

Kruskal, J. B.
"Multidimensional Scaling by Optimizing Goodness of Fit to a
Nonmetric Hypothesis"
Psychometrika, Vol. 29 (March 1964), pp. 1-27.

Lehmann, Donald R.
"Judged Similarity and Brand-Switching Data as Similarity Measures"
Journal of Marketing Research, Vol. IX (August 1972), pp. 331-4.

Lingoes, J. C. and Guttman, Louis
"Nonmetric Factor Analysis: A Rank Reducing Alternative to Linear
Factor Analysis"
Multivariate Behavioral Research, Vol. 2 (1967), pp 485-505.

Luce, R. D.
   "A Choice Theory Analysis of Similarity Judgements"
   Psychometrika, Vol. 26 (1961), pp. 151-63.

McCallum, R. C.
   "Effects on INDSCAL of Nonorthogonal Perceptions of Object Space
   Dimensions"
   Psychometrika, Vol. 41 (1976), pp. 177-88.

McGee, V. E.
   "Multidimensional Scaling of N Sets of Similarity Measures: A
   Nonmetric Individual Differences Approach"
   Multivariate Behavioural Research, Vol. III (1968), pp. 233-48.

McQuitty, L. L.
   "Isolation Predictor Patterns Associated With Major Criterion
   Patterns"
   Educational and Psychological Measurement, Vol. 17 (Spring 1957), pp.
   3-42.

Meidan, A.
   "When to Use Nonmetric Multidimensional Techniques in Marketing
   Research"
   European Research, Vol. 3 (March 1975), pp. 58-65.

Messick, S. J.
   "Some Recent Theoretical Developments in Multidimensional Scaling"
   Educational and Psychological Measurement, Vol. 16 (Spring 1956), pp.
   82-100.

Miller, J. E., Shepard, R. N., and Chang, J. J.
   "An Analytical Approach to the Interpretation of Multidimensional
   Scaling Solutions"
   American Psychologist, Vol. 19 (September 1964), pp. 579,80.

Moore, William L. and Lehmann, Donald R.
   "Effects of Usage and Name on Perceptions of New Products"
   Marketing Science, Vol. 1 (Fall 1982), pp. 351-70.

Moore, William L., Pessemier, Edgar A., and Little, Taylor E.
   "Predicting Brand Purchase Behavior: Marketing Application of the
   Schonemann and Wang Unfolding Model"
   Journal of Marketing Research, Vol. XVI (May 1979), pp. 203-10.

Moskowitz, Howard R.
   "Profile Attributes as Similarities"
   Fall Conference, Association for Consumer Research, Boston (1973),
   paper presentation.

Napior, David
   "Nonmetric Multidimensional Techniques for Summated Ratings"
   in Shepard, Roger N., Romney, A. Kimball, and Nerlove, Sara Beth
   (editors)
   Multidimensional Scaling: Theory and Applications in the Behavioral
   Sciences, Volume I, Theory
   (New York: Seminar Press, 1972), pp. 157-78.

Neidell, Lester A.
   "The Use of Nonmetric Multidimensional Scaling in Marketing Analysis"
   Journal of Marketing, Vol. 33 (October 1969), pp. 37-43.

Nishisato, Shizuhiko
   "Multidimensional Scaling: A Historical Sketch and Bibliography"
   Department of MECA, OISE (1978), technical report.

Phillips, J. P. N.
   "A Procedure for Determining Slater's I and All Nearest Adjoining
   Orders"
   The British Journal of Mathematical and Statistical Psychology, Vol.
   20 (November 1967), pp. 217-25.

Pipkin, John S.
   "Some Remarks on Multidimensional Scaling in Geography"
   in Golledge, R. G. and Rayner, J. N. (editors)
   Proximity and Preference: Problems in Multidimensional Analysis of
   Large Data Sets
   (Minneapolis: University of Minnesota Press, 1982), pp. 47-79.

Ramsey, J. O.
   "Some Statistical Approaches to Multidimensional Scaling Data"
   Journal of the Royal Statistical Society, Series A (1982).

Rao, Vithala R.
   "Changes in Explicit Information and Brand Perceptions"
   Journal of Marketing Research, Vol. IX (May 1972), pp. 209-13.

Roberts, Mary Lou and Taylor, James R.
   "Analyzing Proximity Judgments in an Experimental Design"
   Journal of Marketing Research, Vol. XII (February 1975), pp. 68-78.

Ross, John and Cliff, Norman
"A Generalization of the Interpoint Distance Model"
Psychometrika, Vol. 29 (June 1964), pp. 167-76.

Schonemann, Peter H. and Wang, Ming Mei
"An Individual Difference Model for Multidimensional Analysis of
Preference Data"
Psychometrika, Vol. 37 (1972), pp. 275-309.

Shepard, Roger N.
"Representation of Structure in Similarity Data: Problems and
Prospects"
Psychometrika, Vol. 39 (December 1974), pp. 373-421.

Shepard, Roger N.
"A Taxonomy of Some Principal Types of Data and of Multidimensional
Methods for Their Analysis"
in Shepard, R. N. et al. (editors)
Multidimensional Scaling: Theory and Applications in the Behavioral
Sciences: Volume 1
(New York: Seminar Press, 1972), pp. 23-51.

Shepard, Roger N.
"Metric Structures in Ordinal Data"
Journal of Mathematical Psychology, Vol. 3 (May 1966), pp. 287-315.

Shepard, R. N.
"The Analysis of Proximities: Multidimensional Scaling With an
Unknown Distance Function: I and II"
Psychometrika, Vol. 27 (June 1962, September 1962), pp. 125-40,
219-46.

Shepard, Roger N. and Carroll, J. Douglas
"Parametric Representation of Non-Linear Data Structures"
in Krishnaiah, P. R. (editor)
Multivariate Analysis
(New York: Academic Press, 1966), pp. 561-92.

Sibson, Robin
"Studies in the Robustness of Multidimensional Scaling:
Perturbational Analysis of Classical Scaling"
Journal of the Royal Statistical Society, Series B, Vol. 41 (1979),
pp. 217-29.

Slater, Patrick
"Inconsistencies in a Schedule of Paired Comparisons"
Biometrika, Vol. 48 (November 1961), pp. 303-12.

Spaeth, Harold J. and Guthery, Scott B.
"The Use and Utility of the Monotone Criterion on Multidimensional
Scaling"
Multivariate Behavioral Research, Vol. 4 (October 1969), pp. 501-15.

Spence, Ian
"On Random Ranking Studies in Nonmetric Scaling"
Psychometrika, Vol. 39 (June 1974), pp. 267,8.

Stefflre, Volney
"Multidimensional Scaling as a Model for Individual and Aggregate
Perception and Cognition"
in Jain, Subhash C. (editor)
Research Frontiers in Marketing: Dialogues and Directions
(Chicago: American Marketing Association, 1978).

Takane, Yoshio
"Analysis of Categorizing Behavior by a Quantification Method"
Behaviormetrika, Vol. 8 (1980), pp. 75-86.

Takane, Yoshio, Young, Forrest W., and De Leeuw, Jan
"Nonmetric Individual Differences Multidimensional Scaling: An
Alternating Least Squares Method With Optimal Scaling Features"
Psychometrika, Vol. 42 (March 1977), pp. 7-67.

Taylor, James R.
"Management Experience With Applications of Multidimensional Scaling
Methods"
Marketing Science Institute (1970), preliminary research report.

Torgerson, Warren S.
"Multidimensional Scaling of Similarity"
Psychometrika, Vol. 30 (December 1965), pp. 379-93.

Torgerson, W. S.
"Multidimensional Scaling: I. Theory and Method"
Psychometrika, Vol. XVII (December 1952), pp. 401-19.

Tucker, L. R.
"Relations Between Multidimensional Scaling and Three-Mode Factor
Analysis"
Psychometrika, Vol. 37 (1972), pp. 3-27.

Tucker, L. R. and Messick, S.
"An Individual Differences Model for Multidimensional Scaling"
Psychometrika, Vol. 28 (December 1963), pp. 333-67.

Tversky, Amos and Hutchinson, J. Wesley
"Nearest Neighbor Analysis of Psychological Spaces"
Psychological Review, Vol. 93 (January 1986), pp. 3-22.

Tversky, Amos and Krantz, David
"The Dimensional Representation and the Metric Structure of
Similarity Data"
Working Paper MMPP 69-70
Mathematical Psychology Program, University of Michigan (1969).

Weksel, W. and Ware, E. E.
"The Reliability and Consistency of Complex Personality Judgments"
Multivariate Behavioral Research, Vol. 2 (October 1967), pp. 537-41.

Young, F. W.
"Scaling Conditional Rank-Order Data"
Sociological Methodology (1975), pp. 129-70.

Young, F. W.
"An Asymmetric Euclidean Model for Multi-Process Asymmetric Data"
U.S.-Japan Seminar on Multidimensional Scaling (1975).

Young, Forrest W.
"A Model for Polynomial Conjoint Analysis Algorithms"
in Shepard, R. N. et al. (editors)
Multidimensional Scaling: Theory and Applications in Behavioral
Sciences: Volume 1
(New York: Seminar Press, 1972), pp. 69-104.

Young, F. W.
"Nonmetric Multidimensional Scaling: Recovery of Metric Information"
Psychometrika, Vol. 35 (December 1970), pp. 455-73.

Young, G. and Householder, A. S.
"Discussion of a Set of Points in Terms of Their Mutual Distances"
Psychometrika, Vol. 3 (1938), pp. 19-22.

62.03 ---------- Multidimensional Scaling by Linear Programming

Dakin, R. J.
"A Tree Search Algorithm for Mixed Integer Programming Problems"
Computer Journal, Vol. 8 (1965), pp. 250-5.

Srinivasan, Seenu and Shocker, Allan D.
"Linear Programming Techniques for Multidimensional Analysis of
Preferences"
Psychometrika, Vol. 38 (September 1973), pp. 337-69.

62.04 ---------- Multidimensional Scaling of Binary Data

Bockenholt, I. and Gaul, W.
"Probabilistic Multidimensional Scaling of Paired Comparisons"
in Bock, H. H. (editor)
Proceedings, First Conference of the International Federation of
Classification Societies
(Aachen: North-Holland, 1987).

DeSarbo, Wayne S. and Hoffman, Donna L.
"Constructing MDS Joint Spaces From Binary Choice Data: A
Multidimensional Unfolding Threshold Model for Marketing Research"
Journal of Marketing Research, Vol. XXIV (February 1987), pp. 40-54.

DeSarbo, Wayne S. and Hoffman, Donna L.
"A New Unfolding Threshold Model for the Spatial Representation of
Binary Choice Data"
Applied Psychological Measurement

DeSarbo, Wayne S., Keramidas, Elaine M., and Clark, Linda A.
"A New Multidimensional Scaling Methodology for the Spatial
Representation of Binary Choice Data"
University of Pennsylvania (1985), unpublished paper.

DeSarbo, Wayne S., Lehmann, Donald, Gupta, Sunil, Holbrook, Morris, and
Havlena, William
"A Three-Way Unfolding Methodology for Asymmetric Binary Proximity
Data"
University of Pennsylvania (1985), working paper.

Jedidi, Kamel
"A Three-Way Stochastic MDS Choice Methodology"
University of Pennsylvania, Philadelphia (1987), dissertation
proposal.

Kruskal, Joseph B.
"Multidimensional Scaling by Optimizing Goodness-of-Fit to a
Nonmetric Hypothesis"
Psychometrika, Vol. 29 (March 1964), pp. 1-28.

62.05 ---------- Theory Re: MDS of Asymmetric Data

Chino, Naohito
"A Graphical Technique in Representing the Asymmetric Relationships
Between n Objects"
Behaviormetrika, Vol. 5 (1978), pp. 23-40.

Constantine, A. G. and Gower, John C.
"Graphical Representation of Asymmetric Matrices"
Applied Statistics, Vol. 27 (1978), pp. 294-304.

Gower, John C.
"The Analysis of Asymmetry and Orthogonality"
in Barra, J. R. et al. (editors)
Recent Developments in Statistics
(The Netherlands: North Holland Publishing Co., 1977).

Harshman, Richard A.
"Scaling and Rotation of DEDICOM Solutions"
University of Western Ontario (1982), unpublished manuscript.

Harshman, Richard A.
"DEDICOM: A Family of Models Generalizing Factor Analysis and
Multidimensional Scaling for Decomposition of Asymmetric
Relationships"
University of Western Ontario (1982), unpublished manuscript.

Harshman, Richard A.
"DEDICOM Multidimensional Analysis of Skew Symmetric Data. Part 1:
Theory"
Bell Laboratories, Murray Hill, NJ (1981), unpublished technical
paper.

Harshman, Richard A.
"Models for Analysis of Asymmetrical Relationships Among N Objects or
Stimuli"
First Joint Meeting, Psychometric Society and the Society for
Mathematical Psychology, Hamilton, Ontario (1978), paper presentation.

Harshman, Richard A., Green, Paul E., Wind, Yoram, and Lundy, Margaret
E.
"A Model for the Analysis of Asymmetric Data in Marketing Research"
Marketing Science, Vol. 1 (Spring 1982), pp. 205-42.

Harshman, Richard A. and Lundy, Margaret E.
"DEDICOM Multidimensional Analysis of Skew Symmetric Data. Part 2:
Applications"
University of Western Ontario (1982), unpublished manuscript.

Levin, Joseph and Brown, Morton
"Scaling a Conditional Proximity Matrix to Symmetry"
Psychometrika, Vol. 44 (June 1979), pp. 239-44.

Young, Forrest W.
"An Asymmetric Euclidean Model for Multiprocess Asymmetric Data"
in Theory, Methods and Applications of Multidimensional Scaling and
Related Techniques
Proceedings, U.S.-Japan Joint Seminar, University of San Diego
(August 1974).

62.06 ---------- Theory Re: Statistical Inference in MDS

Klahr, David A.
"A Monte Carlo Investigation of the Statistical Significance of
Kruskal's Nonmetric Scaling Procedure"
Psychometrika, Vol. 34 (September 1969), pp. 319-30.

Schonemann, Peter H., James, W. L., and Carter, F. S.
"Statistical Inference in Multidimensional Scaling: A Method for
Fitting and Testing Horan's Model"
in Lingoes, J. C., Roskam, E. E., and Borg, I. (editors)
Geometric Representations of Relational Data--Readings in
Multidimensional Scaling
(Ann Arbor,MI: Mathesis Press, 1979).

62.07 ---------- Data Collection Issues for Multidimensional Scaling

Deutscher, Terry
"Issues in Data Collection and Reliability in Marketing
Multidimensional Scaling Studies--Implications for Large Stimulus
Sets"
in Golledge, Reginald G. and Rayner, John N. (editors)
Proximity and Preference: Problems in the Multidimensional Analysis
of Large Data Sets
(Minneapolis: University of Minnesota Press, 1982).

Dickinson, John R.
"Sequence, Pole, and Context Effects in Similarities Ratings"
Proceedings, Academy of Marketing Science, Miami (April 1981).

Dong, Hei-Ki
"Method of Complete Triads: An Investigation of Unreliability in
Multidimensional Perception of Nations"
Multivariate Behavioral Research, Vol. 18 (January 1983), pp. 85-96.

Green, Paul E. and Carmone, Frank
"The Effect of Task on Intra-Individual Differences in Similarities
Judgments"
Multivariate Behavioral Research, Vol. 6 (October 1971), pp. 433-50.

Green, Paul E. and Carmone, Frank J.
"Stimulus Context and Task Effects on Individuals' Similarity
Judgements"
in King, Charles W. and Tigert, Douglas J. (editors)
Attitude Research Reaches New Heights
(Chicago: American Marketing Association, 1971), pp. 263-99.

Henry, Walter A. and Stumpf, Robert V.
"Time and Accuracy Measures for Alternative Multidimensional Scaling
Data Collection Methods"
Journal of Marketing Research, Vol. XII (May 1975), pp. 165-70.

Humphreys, Marie Adele
"Data Collection Effects on Nonmetric Multidimensional Scaling
Solutions"
Educational and Psychological Measurement (1982), pp. 1005-22.

Jain, Arun K. and Pinson, Christian
"The Effect of Order of Presentation of Similarity Judgements of
Multidimensional Scaling Results: An Empirical Examination"
Journal of Marketing Research, Vol. XIII (November 1976), pp. 435-9.

Lehmann, D. R.
"Judged Similarity and Brand-Switching Data as Similarity Measures"
Journal of Marketing Research, Vol. IX (August 1972), pp. 331-4.

McIntyre, Shelby H. and Ryans, Adrian B.
"Time and Accuracy Measures for Alternative Multidimensional Scaling
Data Collection Methods: Some Additional Results"
Journal of Marketing Research, Vol. XIV (November 1977), pp. 607-10.

Neidell, Lester A.
"Procedures for Obtaining Similarities Data"
Journal of Marketing Research, Vol. IX (August 1972), pp. 335-7.

Rao, Vithala R. and Katz, Ralph
"Alternative Multidimensional Scaling Methods for Large Stimulus Sets"
Journal of Marketing Research, Vol. VIII (November 1971), pp. 488-94.

Taylor, James R.
"Alternative Methods for Collecting Similarities Data"
Proceedings, Fall Conference, American Marketing Association (1969),
pp. 150-2.

Taylor, James R. and Kinnear, Thomas C.
"Empirical Comparison of Alternative Methods for Collecting Proximity
Judgments"
Proceedings, Fall Conference, American Marketing Association, pp.
547-50.

Whipple, Thomas W.
"Variation Among Multidimensional Scaling Solutions: An Examination
of the Effect of Data Collection Differences"
Journal of Marketing Research, Vol. XIII (February 1976), pp. 98-103.

Wish, Myron
"Comparison Among Multidimensional Structures of Nations Based on
Different Measures of Subjective Similarity"
General Systems, Vol. 15 (1970), pp. 55-65.

62.08 ---------- Large Data Sets and Incomplete Data Collection

   See also (sub)heading(s) 117, 132.04, 133.

Graef, Jed and Spence, Ian
   "Using Distance Information in the Design of Large Multidimensional
   Scaling Experiments"
   Psychological Bulletin, Vol. 86 (January 1979), pp. 60-6.

Issac, Paul D.
   "Considerations in the Selection of Stimulus Pairs for Data
   Collection in Multidimension Scaling"
   in Golledge, R. G. and Raynor, J. N. (editors)
   Proximity and Preference: Problems in the Multidimensional Analysis
   of Large Data Sets
   (Minneapolis: University of Minnesota Press, 1982), pp. 80-9.

Issac, Paul D. and Poor, David S.
   "On the Determinants of Appropriate Dimensionality in Data With Error"
   Psychometrika, Vol. 39 (March 1974), pp. 91-109.

Malhotra, Naresh K., Jain, Arun K., and Pinson, Christian
   "The Robustness of MDS Configurations in the Case of Incomplete Data"
   Journal of Marketing Research, Vol. XXV (February 1988), pp. 95-102.

Spector, Aron N. and Rivizzigno, Victoria L.
   "Sampling Designs and Recovering Cognitive Representations of an
   Urban Area"
   in Golledge, R. G. and Raynor, J. N. (editors)
   Proximity and Preference: Problems in the Multidimensional Analysis
   of Large Data Sets
   (Minneapolis: University of Minnesota Press, 1982), pp. 47-79.

Spence, Ian
   "Monte Carlo Simulation Studies"
   Applied Psychological Measurement, Vol. 7 (Fall 1983), pp. 405-26.

Spence, Ian
   "Incomplete Experimental Designs for Multidimensional Scaling"
   in Golledge, R. G. and Rayner, J. N. (editors)
   Proximity and Preference: Problems in the Multidimensional Analysis
   of Large Data Sets
   (Minneapolis: University of Minnesota Press, 1982), pp. 29-46.

Spence, Ian and Domoney, Dennis W.
   "Single Subject Incomplete Designs for Nonmetric Multidimensional
   Scaling"
   Psychometrika, Vol. 39 (December 1974), pp. 469-90.

Young, Forrest W. and Cliff, Norman
   "Interactive Scaling With Individual Subjects"
   Psychometrika, Vol. 37 (December 1972), pp. 385-415.

62.09 ---------- Longitudinal Multidimensional Scaling

   See also (sub)heading(s) 90.

Elrod, Terry
   "Choice Map: A Product-Market Map From Panel Data"
   Marketing Science, Vol. 7 (Winter 1988), pp. 21-40.

Houston, Franklin S.
   "An Econometric Analysis of Positioning"
   Journal of Business Administration, Vol. 9 (Fall 1977), pp. 1-11.

King, Charles W.
   "Local Retail Market Monitoring: Strategic Implications"
   in Hunt, Keith (editor)
   Advances in Consumer Research, Volume Five (1978), pp. 688-92.

McCullough, James M., MacLachlan, Douglas L., and Moinpour, Reza
   "Temporal Links Between Preference and Perceptions"
   in Monroe, Kent B. (editor)
   Advances in Consumer Research, Volume Eight (1981), pp. 178-81.

Moinpour, Reza, McCullough, James M., and MacLachlan, Douglas L.
   "Time Changes in Perception: A Longitudinal Application of
   Multidimensional Scaling"
   Journal of Marketing Research, Vol. XII (1976), pp. 245-53.

Moinpour, Reza and MacLachlan, Douglas L.
   "Longitudinal Image Measurement With Multidimensional Scaling"
   Proceedings, Fall Conference of the American Marketing Association
   (1973), pp. 333-9.

Moore, William L. and Winer, Russell S.
"A Panel-Data Based Method for Merging Joint Space and Market
Response Function Estimation"
Marketing Science, Vol. 6 (Winter 1987), pp. 25-42.

62.10 ---------- Theory Re: Measures of Fit in MDS

Klahr, David
"A Monte Carlo Investigation of the Statistical Significance of
Kruskal's Nonmetric Scaling Procedure"
Psychometrika, Vol. 34 (September 1969), pp. 319-30.

Kruskal, Joseph B. and Carroll, J. Douglas
"Geometrical Models and Badness-of-Fit Functions"
in Krishnaiah, P. R. (editor)
Multivariate Analysis II
(New York: Academic Press, 1969), pp. 639-70.

Langeheine, R.
"Statistical Evaluation of Measures of Fit in the Lingoes-Borg
Procrustean Individual Differences Scaling"
Psychometrika, Vol. 47 (1982), pp. 427-42.

Levine, D. M.
"A Monte Carlo Study of Kruskal's Variance Based Measure of Stress"
Psychometrika, Vol. 43 (1978), pp. 307-15.

Lingoes, James C. and Schonemann, Peter H.
"Alternative Measures of Fit for the Schonemann-Carroll Matrix
Fitting Algorithm"
Psychometrika, Vol. 39 (1974), pp. 423-7.

Spence, Ian and Graef, Jed
"The Determination of Underlying Dimensionality of an Empiricially
Obtained Matrix of Proximities"
Multivariate Behavioral Research, Vol. 9 (July 1974), pp. 331-42.

Spence, Ian and Ogilvie, John C.
"A Table of Expected Stress Values for Random Rankings in Nonmetric
Multidimensional Scaling"
Multivariate Behavioral Research, Vol. 8 (October 1973), pp. 511-8.

Stenson, H. H. and Knoll, R. L.
"Goodness of Fit for Random Ranking in Kruskal's Nonmetric Scaling
Procedure"
Psychological Bulletin, Vol. 71 (August 1969), pp. 122-6.

Wagenaar, W. A. and Padmos, P.
"Quantitative Interpretation of Stress in Kruskal's Multidimensional
Scaling Technique"
British Journal of Mathematical and Statistical Psychology, Vol. 24
(May 1971), pp. 101-10.

62.11 ---------- Comparing, Combining MDS Solutions

Carroll, J. Douglas
"Generalization of Canonical Correlation Analysis in Three or More
Sets of Variables"
Proceedings, American Psychological Association (1968), pp. 227,8.

Cliff, Norman
"Orthogonal Rotation to Congruence"
Psychometrika, Vol. 31 (1966), pp. 33-42.

Green, Paul E. and Carroll, J. Douglas
"A Simple Procedure for Finding a Composite of Several
Multidimensional Scaling Solutions"
Journal of the Academy of Marketing Science, Vol. 16 (Spring 1988),
pp. 25-35.

Green, Paul E. and Rao, Vithala R.
"Configural Synthesis in Multidimensional Scaling"
Journal of Marketing Research, Vol. IX (February 1972), pp. 65-8.

Horan, C. B.
"Multidimensional Scaling: Combining Observations When Individuals
Have Different Perceptual Structures"
Psychometrika, Vol. 34 (1969), pp. 139-65.

Kristof, W. and Vingersky, B.
"Generalization of the Orthogonal Procrustes Rotation Procedure to
Two or More Matrices"
Proceedings, 79th Annual Convention of the American Psychological
Association (1971), pp. 81-90.

Schonemann, Peter H. and Carroll, Robert M.
    "Fitting One Matrix to Another Under Choice of a Central Dilation and
    Rigid Motion"
    Psychometrika, Vol. 35 (1970), pp. 245-56.

62.12 ---------- Evaluations and Comparisons of MDS Algorithms

Arabie, Phipps
    "Concerning Monte Carlo Evaluations of Nonmetric Multidimensional
    Scaling: Recovery of Metric Information"
    Psychometrika, Vol. 35 (December 1970), pp. 455-73.

Brockhoff, Klaus and Waldeck, Bernd
    "The Robustness of PREFMAP-2"
    International Journal of Research in Marketing, Vol. 1, No. 3 (1984),
    pp. 215-33.

Cohen, Harvey S. and Jones, Lawrence E.
    "The Effects of Random Error and Subsampling of Dimensions on
    Recovery of Configurations by Nonmetric Multidimensional Scaling"
    Psychometrika, Vol. 39 (March 1974), pp. 69-90.

Green, Paul E.
    "On the Robustness of Multidimensional Scaling Techniques"
    Journal of Marketing Research, Vol. XII (February 1975), pp. 73-81.

Green, Paul E. and Jain, Arun K.
    "A Note on the 'Robustness' of INDSCAL Individual Differences Scaling
    to Departure From Linearity"
    Proceedings, Fall Conference, American Marketing Association (1972).

Green, Paul E. and Rao, Vithala R.
    "Alternative Approaches to the Multidimensional Scaling of
    Similarities Data"
    Fall Conference, American Marketing Association (1970), paper
    presentation.

Green, Paul E. and Rao, Vithala R.
    "Configuration Invariance in Multidimensional Scaling: An Empirical
    Study"
    Proceedings, Fall Conference, American Marketing Association (1969),
    pp. 182-7.

Lingoes, James C. and Roskam, Edward E.
    A Mathematical and Empirical Analysis of Two Multidimensional Scaling
    Algorithms
    Psychometrika Monograph Supplements, Vol. 38 (December 1973).

MacCallum, Robert C. and Cornelius, Edwin T.
    "A Monte Carlo Investigation of Recovery of Structure by ALSCAL"
    Psychometrika, Vol. 42 (September 977), pp. 401-28.

Sherman, C. R.
    "Nonmetric Multidimensional Scaling: A Monte Carlo Study of the Basic
    Parameters"
    Psychometrika, Vol. 37 (September 1972), pp. 323-55.

Spence, Ian
    "A Monte Carlo Investigation of Three Nonmetric Multidimensional
    Scaling Algorithms"
    Psychometrika, Vol. 37 (1972), pp. 461-86.

62.13 ---------- Structural Reliability and Stimulus Domain Effects

Green, Paul E., Maheshwari, Arun, and Rao, Vithala R.
    "Dimensional Interpretation and Configuration Invariance in
    Multidimensional Scaling: An Empirical Study"
    Multivariate Behavioral Research, Vol. 4 (April 1969), pp. 159-80.

Malhotra, Naresh K.
    "Validity and Structural Reliability of Multidimensional Scaling"
    Journal of Marketing Research, Vol. XXIV (May 1987), pp. 164-73.

Malhotra, Naresh K.
    "Structural Reliability and Stability of Nonmetric Conjoint Analysis"
    Journal of Marketing Research, Vol. XIX (May 1982), pp. 199-207.

62.14 ---------- Computer Programs for MDS - Mainframe Computer

Carmone, Frank J., Green, Paul E., and Robinson, Patrick J.
    "TRICON-An IBM 360/65 FORTRAN IV Program for the Triangularization of
    Conjoint Data"
    Journal of Marketing Research, Vol. V (May 1968), pp. 219,20.

Carroll, J. Douglas and Chang, Jih-Jie
    "How to Use INDSCAL: A Computer Program for Canonical Decomposition
    of N-Way Tables and Individual Differences in Multidimensional
    Scaling"
    (Murray Hill, NJ: Bell Telephone Laboratories, 1969).

Chang, J. J. and Carroll, J. D.
    "How to Use PREFMAP and PREFMAP 2: Programs Which Relate Preference
    Data to Multidimensional Scaling Solution"
    Bell Telephone Laboratories, Murray Hill, NJ (1971).

Cooper, Lee G.
    "COSCAL: Program for Multidimensional Scaling"
    Journal of Marketing Research, Vol. IX (May 1972), pp. 201,2.

Jolly, Stuart M. and Green, Paul E.
    "TRICON II: An IBM 360/65 FORTRAN Program for Computing Slater's I in
    the Triangularization of Conjoint Similarities Data"
    Journal of Marketing Research, Vol. VI (May 1969), p. 215.

Keon, John W.
    "CONFSCAL: A Joint Space Mapping Routine of Brands and Their
    Advertisements"
    Graduate School of Business, New York University (1981), working
    paper.

Kruskal, J. B.
    "How to Use M-D-SCAL: A Program to do Multidimensional Scaling and
    Multidimensional Unfolding" (Version 4 and 4M of MDSCAL)
    (Murray Hill, NJ: Bell Telephone Laboratories, March 1968),
    mimeographed.

Kruskal, Joseph B. and Carmone, Frank J.
    How to Use M-D-SCAL (Version 5-M) and Other Useful Information
    (Murray Hill, NJ: Bell Laboratories, 1967).

Kruskal, J. B., Young, F. W., and Seery, J. B.
    "How to Use KYST: A Very Flexible Program to do Multidimensional
    Scaling and Unfolding"
    Bell Telephone Laboratories (1973), unpublished manuscript.

McGee, Victor E.
    "EMD: A FORTRAN IV Program for Nonmetric (Elastic) Multidimensional
    Data Reduction"
    Journal of Marketing Research, Vol. V (August 1968), p. 331.

McGee, Victor E.
    "CEMD/DEMD: Nonmetric Individual Differences for (Elastic)
    Multidimensional Data Reduction-To Handle N Sets of Multivariate Data"
    Journal of Marketing Research, Vol. V (August 1968), p. 322.

Pennell, R. J. and Young, F. W.
    "An IBM System/360 Program for Orthogonal Least-Squares Matrix
    Fitting"
    Behavioral Science, Vol. 12 (March 1967), p. 165.

Rice, Sandra (editor)
    "MDS(X): A Multi-Dimensional Scaling Package"
    Journal of Marketing Research, Vol. XV (August 1978), pp. 468-71.

Roberts, C. Richard
    "SIMDATA: A Computer Program to Produce Matrices of Similarity
    Measures for Subsequent Input to Cluster or Multidimensional Scaling
    Algorithms"
    Journal of Marketing Research, Vol. XVI (November 1979), pp. 566,7.

Stefflre, Volney
    "Some Applications of Multidimensional Scaling to Social Science
    Problems"
    in Romney, A. K., Shepard, R. N., and Nerlove, S. B. (editors)
    Multidimensional Scaling: Theory and Applications in the Behavioral
    Sciences, Volume II
    (New York: Academic Press, Inc., 1972), pp. 2211-43.

Takane, Yoshio
    "IDSORT: An Individual Differences Multidimensional Scaling Program
    for Sorting Data"
    Journal of Marketing Research, Vol. XX (November 1983), pp. 447,8.

Takane, Yoshio
    "How to Use IDSORT: An Individual Differences Multidimensional
    Scaling Program for Sorting Data"
    McGill University (1982), unpublished users' manual.

Takane, Yoshio
    "MDSORT: A Special Purpose Multidimensional Scaling Program for
    Sorting Data"
    Journal of Marketing Research, Vol. XVIII (November 1981), pp. 480,1.

Takane, Yoshio
  "How to Use MDSORT: A Special Purpose Multidimensional Scaling
  Program for Sorting Data"
  McGill University (1981), unpublished users manual.

Wang, Ming Mei, Schonemann, Peter, and Rudk, Jerrold G.
  "A Conjugate Gradient Algorithm for the Multidimensional Analysis of
  Preference Data"
  Multivariate Behavioral Research, Vol. 10 (1975), pp. 45-80.

Wilkes, Robert E.
  "Product Positioning by Multidimensional Scaling"
  Journal of Advertising Research, Vol. 17 (August 1977), pp. 15-9.

Young, F.
  "POLYCON: A Program for Multidimensional Scaling One-, Two-, or
  Three-Way Data in Additive Difference or Multiplicative Spaces"
  Behavioral Science, Vol. 18 (August 1973), pp. 152-5.

Young, F. W.
  TORSCA: An IBM Program for Nonmetric Multidimensional Scaling"
  Journal of Marketing Research, Vol. V (August 1968), pp. 319-21.

Young, F. W. and Pennell, R. J.
  "An IBM System/360 Program for Points of View Analysis"
  Behavioral Science, Vol. 12 (March 1967), p. 166.

Young, Forrest W., Takane, Yoshio, and Lewyckyj, Rostyslaw
  "ALSCAL: A Nonmetric Multidimensional Scaling Program With Several
  Individual-Differences Options"
  Journal of Marketing Research, Vol. XV (November 1978), pp. 612-5.

Young, Forrest W. and Torgerson, Warren S.
  "TORSCA: A FORTRAN IV Program for Shepard-Kruskal Multidimensional
  Scaling Analysis"
  Behavioral Science, Vol. 12 (November 1967), p. 498.

62.15 ---------- Multidimensional Scaling Software - Personal Computer

Johnson, Richard M.
  APM System for Adaptive Perceptual Mapping"
  (Ketchum, ID: Sawtooth Software, Inc., 1987).

63 -------- MAXIMUM LIKELIHOOD/PROBABILISTIC/CONFIRMATORY MDS --------
        See also (sub)heading(s) 37, 62.

63.01 ---------- Theory Re: Max Likelihood/Probabilistic/Conf MDS

Fornell, Claes and Denison, Daniel R.
"A New Approach to Nonlinear Structural Modeling by Use of
Confirmatory Multidimensional Scaling"
in Fornell, Claes (editor)
A Second Generation of Multivariate Analysis
(New York: Praeger Publishers, 1982), pp. 367-92.

Hefner, R. A.
"Extensions of the Law of Comparative Judgment to Discriminable and
Multidimensional Stimuli"
University of Michigan (1958), doctoral dissertation.

MacKay, David B.
"Alternate Probabilistic Scaling Models for Spatial Data"
Geographical Analysis, Vol. 15 (July 1983), pp. 173-86.

MacKay, David B. and Zinnes, Joseph L.
"A Probabilistic Model for the Mutidimensional Scaling of Proximity
and Preference Data"
Marketing Science, Vol. 5 (Fall 1986), pp. 325-44.

MacKay, David B. and Zinnes, Joseph L.
"Probabilistic Scaling of Spatial Judgements"
Geographical Analysis, Vol. 13 (January 1984), pp. 21-37.

Ramsey, James O.
"Some Statistical Approaches to Multidimensional Scaling Data"
Journal of the Royal Statistical Society, Series A, Vol. 145, Part 3
(presented in February 1982), pp. 285-312.

Ramsey, James O.
"Some Small Sample Results for Maximum Likelihood Estimation in
Multidimensional Scaling"
Psychometrika, Vol. 45 (March 1980), pp. 139-44.

Ramsey, James O.
"Maximum Likelihood Estimation in Multidimensional Scaling"
Psychometrika, Vol. 42 (June 1977), pp. 241-65.

Takane, Yoshio
"Multidimensional Successive Categories Scaling: A Maximum Likelihood
Method"
Psychometrika, Vol. 46 (March 1981), pp. 9-28.

Young, Forrest W.
"Scaling"
in Rosenzweig, Mark R. and Porter, Lyman W. (editors)
Annual Review of Psychology, Vol. 35
(Palo Alto, CA: Annual Reviews, Inc., 1984), pp. 55-81.

Zinnes, Joseph L. and MacKay, David B.
"Probabilistic Multidimensional Analysis of Preference Ratio
Judgments"
Communication and Cognition, Vol. 20 (January 1987).

Zinnes, Joseph L. and MacKay, David B.
"Probabilistic Multidimensional Scaling: Complete and Incomplete Data"
Psychometrika, Vol. 48 (March 1983), pp. 47,8.

63.02 ---------- Applications of Max Likelihood/Probabilistic/Conf MDS

Droge, Cornelia and Darmon, Rene Y.
"Associative Positioning Strategies Through Comparative Advertising:
Attribute Versus Overall Similarity Approaches"
Journal of Marketing Research, Vol. XXIV (November 1987), pp. 377-88.

63.03 ---------- Computer Programs for Max Likelihood/Prob/Conf MDS

MacKay, David B. and Zinnes, Joseph L.
"PROSCAL: A Program for Probabilistic Scaling"
Discussion Paper 218
Indiana University (1984).

Ramsey, James O.
"MULTISCALE: Four Programs of Multidimensional Scaling by the Method
of Maximum Likelihood"
(Chicago: International Educationa l Services, 1978).

64 ------------------- MULTIDIMENSIONAL UNFOLDING ---------------------
        See also (sub)heading(s) 37, 49.

64.01 ---------- Theory Re: Multidimensional Unfolding

Bennett, Joesph F. and Hays, William L.
    "Multidimensional Unfolding: Determining the Dimensionality of Ranked
    Preference Data"
    Psychometrika, Vol. 25 (March 1960), pp. 27-43.

Bloxom, B.
    "Constrained Multidimensional Scaling in N Spaces"
    Psychometrika, Vol. 43 (1978), pp. 138-51.

Carroll, J. Douglas
    "Models and Methods for Multidimensional Analysis of Preferential
    Choice (or Other Dominance Data)"
    in Lantermann, E. D. and Feger, H. (editors)
    Similarity and Choice
    (Vienna: Hans Huber Publishers, 1980), pp. 234-89.

Carroll, J. Douglas
    "Individual Differences and Multidimensional Scaling"
    in Shepard, R. N., Romney, A. K., and Nerlove, S. B. (editors)
    Multidimensional Scaling: Theory and Applications in the Behavioral
    Sciences, Volume 1, Theory
    (New York: Seminar Press, 1972), pp. 105-55.

Carroll, J. Douglas and Chang, Jih-Jie
    "Analysis of Individual Differences in Multidimensional Scaling via
    an N-Way Generalization of 'Eckart-Young' Decomposition"
    Psychometrika, Vol. 35 (1970), pp. 238-319.

Carroll, J. Douglas and Chang, Jih-Jie
    "Relating Preferences Data to Multidimensional Scaling Solutions via
    a Generalization of Coombs' Unfolding Model"
    (Murray Hill, NJ: Bell Telephone Laboratories, 1967), mimeograph.

Davison, Mark L.
    "Fitting and Testing Carroll's Weighted Unfolding Model for
    Preferences"
    Psychometrika, Vol. 41 (June 1976), pp. 233-47.

DeSarbo, Wayne S. and Carroll, J. Douglas
    "Three-Way Metric Unfolding via Weighted Alternating Least Squares"
    Psychometrika, Vol. 50 (December 1985), pp. 275-300.

DeSarbo, Wayne S. and Carroll, J. Douglas
    "Three Way Metric Unfolding"
    in Keon, J. W. (editor)
    Market Measurement and Analysis
    (Providence, RI: TIMS College on Marketing, 1980).

DeSarbo, Wayne S. and Eliashberg, J.
    "A New Stochastic Multidimensional Unfolding Model for the
    Investigation of Paired Comparison Consumer Preference Choice Data"
    University of Pennsylvania (December 1985), working paper.

DeSarbo, Wayne S. and Hoffman, Donna L.
    "Constructing MDS Joint Spaces From Binary Choice Data: A
    Multidimensional Unfolding Threshold Model for Marketing Research"
    Journal of Marketing Research, Vol. XXIV (February 1987), pp. 40-54.

DeSarbo, Wayne S. and Hoffman, Donna L.
    "A New Unfolding Threshold Model for the Spatial Representation of
    Binary Choice Data"
    Applied Psychological Measurement (1986).

DeSarbo, Wayne S. and Hoffman, Donna L.
    "A New Multidimensional Scaling Methodology for Spatial
    Representation of Binary Choice Data"
    University of Pennsylvania (October 1984), working paper.

DeSarbo, Wayne S. and Rao, Vithala R.
    "A Constrained Unfolding Model for Product Positioning Analysis"
    Marketing Science, Vol. 5 (Winter 1986), pp. 1-19.

DeSoete, G., Carroll, J. Douglas, and DeSarbo, Wayne S.
    "The Wandering Ideal Point Model: A Probabilistic Multidimensional
    Unfolding Model for Paired Comparisons Data"
    Journal of Mathematical Psychology (1986).

Gold, E. M.
    "Metric Unfolding: Data Requirements for Unique Solutions and
    Clarification of Schonemann's Algorithm"
    Psychometrika, Vol. 38 (December 1973), pp. 555-69.

Green, Paul E. and Carmone, Frank J.
  "Multidimensional Scaling: An Introduction and Comparison of
  Nonmetric Unfolding Techniques"
  Journal of Marketing Research, Vol. VI (August 1969), pp. 330-41.

Greenacre, M. J. and Brown, M. W.
  "An Alternating Least-Squares Algorithm for Multidimensional
  Unfolding"
  Joint Meeting, Psychometric and Classification Societies, Montreal
  (1982), paper presentation.

Heiser, W. J.
  Unfolding Analysis of Proximity Data
  University of Leiden, The Netherlands (1981).

Percy, Larry H.
  "Multidimensional Unfolding of Profile Data: A Discussion and
  Illustration With Attention to Badness-of-Fit"
  Journal of Marketing Research, Vol. XII (February 1975), pp. 93-9.

Schonemann, Peter H.
  "On Metric Multidimensional Unfolding"
  Psychometrika, Vol. 35 (September 1970), pp. 349-65.

Spence, I.
  "A General Metric Unfolding Model"
  Psychometric Society Conference, San Diego (1980), paper presentation.

Waldeck, B.
  The Sensitivity of a Multidimensional Unfolding Technique. A
  Simulation Study of PREFMAP-2 (Phase 2)
  University of Kiel, Germany, doctoral dissertation.

Zinnes, Joseph L. and Griggs, Richard A.
  "Probabilistic, Multidimensional Unfolding Analysis"
  Psychometrika, Vol. 39 (September 1974), pp. 327-50.

64.02 ---------- Computer Programs for Multidimensional Unfolding

DeSarbo, Wayne S. and Rao, Vithala R.
  "GENFOLD2: A Set of Models and Algorithms for the GENeral unFOLDing
  Analysis of Preference/Dominance Data"
  Journal of Classification, Vol. 1 (Winter 1984), pp. 147-86.

Kruskal, Joseph B.
  "How to Use M-D-SCAL: A Program to do Multidimensional Scaling and
  Multidimensional Unfolding" (Version 4 and 4M of MDSCAL)
  (Murray Hill, NJ: Bell Telephone Laboratories, March 1968).

Kruskal, Joseph B., Young, Forrest W., and Seery, J. B.
  "How to Use KYST2: A Very Flexible Program to do Multidimensional
  Scaling and Unfolding"
  Bell Laboratories, Murray Hill, NJ (1977), unpublished memorandum.

Kruskal, Joseph B., Young, Forrest W., and Seery, J. B.
  "How to Use KYST: A Very Flexible Program to do Multidimensional
  Scaling and Unfolding"
  (Murray Hill, NJ: Bell Telephone Laboratories, 1973), unpublished
  manuscript.

Young, Forrest W.
  "TORSCA: An IBM Program for Nonmetric Multidimensional Scaling"
  Journal of Marketing Research, Vol. V (August 1968), pp. 319-21.

Young, Forrest W. and Torgerson, Warren S.
  "TORSCA: A FORTRAN IV Program for Shepard-Kruskal Multidimensional
  Scaling Analysis"
  Behavioral Science, Vol. 12 (November 1967), p. 498.

65 -------------- MULTIDIMENSIONAL SCALING APPLICATIONS --------------

See also (sub)heading(s) 37, 62, 63, 64.

Agostini, J. M. and Boss, J. F.
"Classifying Informants in Consumer Surveys According to Their Areas
of Interest"
European Research, Vol. 1 (January 1973), pp. 20-5,42.

Arabie, Phipps and Boorman, S. A.
"Multidimensional Scaling of Measures of Distance Between Partitions"
Journal of Mathematical Psychology, Vol. 10 (1973), pp. 148-203.

Arora, Raj
"Consumer Involvement in Retail Store Positioning"
Journal of the Academy of Marketing Science, Vol. 10 (Spring 1982),
pp. 109-24.

Brinberg, David and Wood, Ronald
"A Resource Exchange Theory Analysis of Consumer Behavior"
Journal of Consumer Research, Vol. 10 (December 1983), pp. 330-8.

Brummel, A. C. and Harman, E. J.
"Behavioral Geography and Multidimensional Scaling"
McMaster University, Hamilton, Ontario (1974), unpublished working
paper.

Carter, Steve
"Is This the Stuff That Marketers are Made of?"
European Journal of Marketing, Vol. 19, No. 6 (1985), pp. 53-64.

Day, G. S.
"Evaluating Models of Attitude Structure"
Journal of Marketing Research, Vol. IX (August 1972), pp. 279-86.

Day, George S., Shocker, Allan D., and Srivastava, Rajendra K.
"Consumer-Oriented Approaches to Identifying Product Markets"
Journal of Marketing, Vol. 43 (Fall 1979), pp. 8-20.

Doyle, Peter and Hutchinson, Peter
"Individual Differences in Family Decision Making"
Journal of the Market Research Society, Vol. 15 (October 1973), pp.
193-206.

Doyle, Peter and McGee, John
"Perceptions of and Preferences for Alternative Convenience Foods"
Journal of the Market Research Society, Vol. 15 (January 1973), pp.
24-34.

Fornell, Claes and Denison, Daniel R.
"Evaluating Convergent, Discriminant, and Nomological Validity via
Confirmatory Multidimensional Scaling"
The Graduate School of Business Administration, The University of
Michigan (1981), working paper.

Green, Paul E.
"A Multidimensional Model of Product-Features Association"
Journal of Business Research, Vol. 2 (April 1974), pp. 107-18.

Green, Paul E. and Carmone, Frank J.
"Marketing Research Applications of Nonmetric Scaling Methods"
in Rommey, Kimball, Shepard, Roger, and Nerlove, Sara (editors)
Multidimensional Scaling, Volume II
(New York: Seminar Press, 1972).

Green, Paul E., Maheshwari, Arun, and Rao, Vithala R.
"Self-Concept and Brand Preference: An Empirical Application of
Multidimensional Scaling"
Journal of the Market Research Society, Vol. 11 (October 1969), pp.
343-60.

Green, Paul E., Wind, Yoram, and Jain, Arun K.
"A Note on Measurement of Social-Psychological Belief Systems"
Journal of Marketing Research, Vol. IX (May 1972), pp. 204-8.

Greenberg, M. G.
"Some Applications of Nonmetric Multidimensional Scaling"
Proceedings of the Business and Economic Statistics Section of the
American Statistical Association (1969), pp. 104-9.

Havlena, William J., Holbrook, Morris B., and Lehmann, Donald R.
"Assessing the Validity of Emotional Typologies"
Psychology and Marketing, Vol. 6 (Summer 1989), pp. 97-112.

Holbrook, Morris B. and Holloway, Douglas V.
"Marketing Strategy and the Structure of Aggregate Segment-Specific,
and Differential Preferences"
Journal of Marketing, Vol. 48 (Winter 1984), pp. 62-7.

Holbrook, Morris B. and Lehmann, Donald R.
    "Allocating Discretionary Time: Complementarity Among Activities"
    Journal of Consumer Research, Vol. 7 (March 1981), pp. 395-406.

Holbrook, Morris B., Lehmann, Donald R., and O'Shaughnessy, John
    "Using Versus Choosing: The Relationship of the Consumption
    Experience to Reasons for Purchasing"
    European Journal of Marketing, Vol. 20, No. 8 (1986), pp. 49-62.

Horne, David A. and Johnson, Michael D.
    "Subject/Referent Position in Comparative Advertising"
    Working Paper No. 461
    University of Michigan (June 1986).

Hustad, Thomas P., Mayer, Charles S., and Whipple, Thomas W.
    "Consideration of Context Differences in Product Evaluation and
    Market Segmentation"
    Journal of the Academy of Marketing Science, Vol. 3 (Winter 1975),
    pp. 34-47.

Jain, Arun K.
    "A Prediction Study in Perceptual and Evaluative Mapping"
    Journal of the Academy of Marketing Science, Vol. 6 (Fall 1978), pp.
    300-13.

Johnson, Richard M.
    "Market Segmentation: A Strategic Management Tool"
    Journal of Marketing Research, Vol. VIII (February 1971), pp. 13-8.

Karni, E. S. and Levin, J.
    "The Use of Small Space Analysis in Studying Scale Structure: An
    Application to the California Psychological Inventory"
    Journal of Applied Psychology, Vol. 56 (August 1972), pp. 341-6.

Kehoe, Jerard and Reynolds, Thomas J.
    "Interactive Multidimensional Scaling of Cognitive Structure
    Underlying Person Perception"
    Applied Psychological Measurement, Vol. 1 (Spring 1977), pp. 155-69.

Kinnear, Thomas C. and Taylor, James R.
    "The Effect of Ecological Concern on Brand Perceptions"
    Journal of Marketing Research, Vol. X (May 1973), pp. 191-7.

Lautman, Martin R., Percy, Larry H., and Kordish, Gail R.
    "Campaigns From Multidimensional Scaling"
    Journal of Advertising Research, Vol. 18 (June 1978), pp. 35-9.

Leavitt, C.
    "A Multidimensional Set of Rating Scales for Television Commercials"
    Journal of Applied Psychology, Vol. 54 (October 1970), pp. 427-9.

Little, T. and Moore, W.
    "An Application of the Schonemann and Wang Individual Difference
    Model for Preference"
    Paper No. 516
    Krannert Graduate School of Industrial Administration, Purdue
    University (1975).

MacKay, David B. and Olshavsky, Richard W.
    "Cognitive Maps of Retail Locations: An Investigation of Some Basic
    Issues"
    Journal of Consumer Research, Vol. 2 (December 1975), pp. 197-205.

Malhotra, Naresh K.
    "Consumer Information Seeking and Information Processing: An
    Alternative Theoretical Framework and Some Empirical Investigations"
    State University of New York at Buffalo (1979), unpublished
    dissertation.

Mazanec, Josef A. and Schwieger, Gunter C.
    "Improved Marketing Efficiency Through Multi-Product Brand Names?"
    European Research, Vol. 9 (January 1981), pp. 32-44.

Morris, Michael H., Stanton, Wilbur W. and Calantone, Roger J.
    "Measuring Coalitions in the Industrial Buying Center"
    Journal of the Academy of Marketing Science, Vol. 13 (Fall 1985), pp.
    18-39.

Narayana, Chem L.
    "Market Behavior Towards Brand Choice--Multidimensional Scaling
    Approach"
    Journal of Academy of Marketing Science, Vol. 5 (Summer 1977), pp.
    221-8.

Narayana, Chem L.
    "The Stability of Perceptions"
    Journal of Advertising Research, Vol. 16 (April 1976), pp. 45-9.

Perry, Michael, Izraeli, Dov, and Perry, Arnon
"Image Change as a Result of Advertising"
Journal of Advertising Research, Vol. 16 (February 1976), pp. 45-50.

Perry, M. and Perry, A.
"The Case of Avocado: Using Consumer Research to Plan the Launching
of an Unfamiliar and New Product in the Market"
European Research, Vol. 2 (January 1974), pp. 10-6.

Rao, Vithala R.
"Changes in Explicit Information and Brand Perceptions"
Journal of Marketing Research, Vol. IX (May 1972), pp. 209-13.

Rao, Vithala R.
"Salience of Price in the Perception of Product Quality"
Proceedings, Fall Conference, American Marketing Association (1971),
pp. 571-7.

Richardson, M. W.
"Multidimensional Psychophysics"
Psychological Bulletin, Vol. 35 (November 1938), pp. 659,60.

Ritchie, J. R. Brent
"An Exploratory Analysis of the Nature and Extent of Individual
Differences in Perception"
Journal of Marketing Research, Vol. XI (February 1974), pp. 41-9.

Roberts, Mary Lou and Taylor, James R.
"Analyzing Proximity Judgments in an Experimental Design"
Journal of Marketing Research, Vol. XII (February 1975), pp. 68-72.

Shocker, Allan D. and Steward, David W.
"Strategic Marketing Decision Making and Perceptual Mapping"
in Zufryden, F. S. (editor)
Advances and Practices of Marketing Science--1983 Proceedings
(Providence, RI: Institute of Management Science, 1983), pp. 224-39.

Singston, Ricardo
"Multidimensional Scaling Analysis of Store Image and Shopping
Behavior"
Journal of Retailing, Vol. 51 (1975), p. 2.

Smith, Robert E. and Lusch, Robert F.
"How Advertising Can Position a Brand"
Journal of Advertising Research, Vol. 16 (February 1976), pp. 37-43.

Srivastava, Rajendra K., Alpert, Mark I., and Shocker, Allan D.
"A Customer Oriented Approach for Determining Market Structures"
Journal of Marketing, Vol. 48 (Spring 1984), pp. 32-45.

Stefflre, Volney
"Some Applications of Multidimensional Scaling to Social Science
Problems"
in Romney, A. K., Shepard, R. N., and Nerlove, S. B. (editors)
Multidimensional Scaling: Theory and Applications in the Behavioral
Sciences, Vol. II--Applications
(New York: Seminar Press, 1972), pp. 211-48.

Teas, R. Kenneth and Deliva, W. L.
"Conjoint Measurement of Consumers' Preference for Multiattribute
Financial Services"
Journal of Marketing, Vol. 16 (Summer 1985), pp. 99-112.

Turner, Ronald E.
"Market Measures From Salesmen: A Multidimensional Scaling Approach"
Journal of Marketing Research, Vol. VIII (May 1971), pp. 165-72.

Wierenga, Berend
"Empirical Test of the Lancaster Characteristics Model"
International Journal of Research in Marketing, Vol. 1, No. 4 (1984),
pp. 263-93.

Wilkes, Robert E.
"Product Positioning by Multidimensional Scaling"
Journal of Advertising Research, Vol. 17 (August 1977), pp. 15-9.

Wilson, M. Keith
A Multidimensional Scaling Analysis of Customer Service: An
Evaluation of Manufacturers by Their Distributors
Indiana University (1974), unpublished doctoral dissertation.

Wind, Y. and Robinson, P. J.
"Product Positioning: An Application of Multidimensional Scaling"
in Haley, R. I. (editor)
Attitude Research in Transition
(Chicago: American Marketing Association, 1972).

Wish, Myron
    "Individual Differences in Perceptions and Preferences Among Nations"
    in King, C. W. and Tigert, D. (editors)
    Attitude Research Reaches New Heights
    (Chicago: American Marketing Association, 1971), pp. 312-28.

Wish, M., Deutsch, M., and Biener, L.
    "Differences in Perceived Similarity of Nations"
    in Shepard, R. N., Romney, A. K., and Nerlove, S. (editors)
    Multidimensional Scaling: Theory and Applications in the Behavioral
    Sciences
    (New York: Seminar Press, 1972).

66 ------------ COMPLIANCE OR MULTIPLE REQUEST TECHNIQUES ------------
       See also (sub)heading(s) 68.

66.01 ---------- Books Re: Compliance Techniques

Cialdini, Robert B.
    Influence: Science and Practice
    (Glenview, IL: Scott, Foresman and Company, 1985), 264 pp.

Zimbardo, Philip and Ebbesen, Ebbe B.
    Influencing Attitudes and Changing Behavior
    (Reading, MA: Addison-Wesley Publishing Co., 1970).

66.02 ---------- Theory Re: Foot-in-the-Door Technique

Allen, Chris T., Schewe, Charles D., and Wijk, Gosta
    "More on Self-Perception Theory's Foot Technique in the Pre-Call/Mail
    Survey Setting"
    Journal of Marketing Research, Vol. XVII (November 1980), pp. 498-502.

Baer, Robert and Goldman, Morton
    "Compliance as a Function of Prior Compliance, Familiarization,
    Effort and Benefits: The Foot-in-the-Door Technique Extended"
    Psychological Reports, Vol. 43 (December 1978), pp. 887-93.

Baron, R. A.
    "The Foot-in-the-Door Phenomenon: Mediating Effects of Size of First
    Request and Sex of Requester"
    Bulletin of the Psychonomic Society, Vol. 2 (August 1973), pp. 113,4.

Beaman, Arthur L., Cole, C. Maureen, Preston, Marilyn, Klentz, Bonnel,
    and Steblay, Nancy M.
    "Fifteen Years of Foot-in-the-Door Research: A Meta Analysis"
    Personality and Social Psychology Bulletin, Vol. 9 (June 1983), pp.
    181-96.

Burger, Jerry M. and Petty, Richard E.
    "The Low-Ball Compliance Technique: Task or Person Commitment?"
    Journal of Personality and Social Psychology, Vol. 40 (March 1981),
    pp. 492-500.

Cann, A., Sherman, S. J., and Elkes, R.
    "Effects of Initial Request Size and Timing of a Second Request on
    Compliance: The Foot-in-the-Door and the Door-in-the-Face"
    Journal of Personality and Social Psychology, Vol. 32 (1975), pp.
    774-82.

Cialdini, R. B. and Ascani, K.
    "Test of a Concession Procedure for Inducing Verbal, Behavioral, and
    Further Compliance With a Request to Give Blood"
    Journal of Applied Psychology, Vol. 61 (1976), pp. 295-300.

Cialdini, R. B., Cacioppo, John R., Bassett, Rodney, and Miller, John A.
    "The Low-Ball Procedure for Producing Compliance: Commitment Then
    Cost"
    Journal of Personality and Social Psychology, Vol. 36 (May 1978), pp.
    463-76.

DeJong, W.
    "An Examination of Self-Perception Mediation of the Foot-in-the-Door
    Effect"
    Journal of Personality and Social Psychology, Vol. 37 (1979), pp.
    2221-39.

DeJong, William and Funder, David
    "Effect of Payment for Initial Compliance: Unanswered Questions About
    the Foot-in-the-Door Phenomenon"
    Personality and Social Psychology Bulletin, Vol. 3 (Fall 1977), pp.
    662-5.

Dillard, James P., Hunter, John E., and Burgoon, Michael
    "A Meta-Analysis of Two Sequential-Request Strategies for Gaining
    Compliance: Foot-in-the-Door and Door-in-the-Face"
    Annual Convention of the International Communication Association,
    Dallas, TX (May 1983), paper presentation.

Fern, Edward F., Monroe, Kent B., and Avila, Ramon A.
    "Effectiveness of Multiple Request Strategies: A Synthesis of
    Research Results"
    Journal of Marketing Research, Vol. XXIII (May 1986), pp. 144-52.

Fish, Barry and Kaplan, Kalman J.
    "Does a 'Foot-in-the-Door' Get You in or Out?"
    Psychological Reports, Vol. 34 (February 1974), pp. 34-42.

Foss, R. D. and Dempsey, C. B.
    "Blood Donation and the Foot-in-the-Door Technique: A Limiting Case"
    Journal of Personality and Social Psychology, Vol. 37, No. 4 (1979),
    pp. 580-90.

Freedman, Jonathan L. and Fraser, Scott D.
"Compliance Without Pressure: The Foot-in-the-Door Technique"
Journal of Personality and Social Psychology, Vol. 4 (October 1966),
pp. 195-202.

Furse, D. H. and Stewart, D. W.
"Toward a Cognitive Dissonance Theory of Mail Questionnaire Response"
Working Paper 81-102
Owen Graduate School of Management, Vanderbilt University (1981).

Furse, David H., Stewart, David W., and Rados, David L.
"Effects of Foot-in-the-Door, Cash Incentives, and Followups on
Survey Response"
Journal of Marketing Research, Vol. XVIII (November 1981), pp. 473-8.

Goldman, Morton, Creason, Christopher, and McCall, Cynthia G.
"Compliance Employing a Two-Feet-in-the-Door Procedure"
Journal of Social Psychology, Vol. 114 (August 1981), pp. 259-65.

Groves, Robert M. and Magilavy, Lou J.
"Increasing Response Rates to Telephone Surveys: A Door in the Face
or Foot in the Door?"
Public Opinion Quarterly, Vol. 45 (1981), pp. 346-58.

Hansen, R. A. and Robinson, L. M.
"Testing the Effectiveness of Alternative Foot-in-the-Door
Manipulations"
Journal of Marketing Research, Vol. XVII (August 1980), pp. 359-64.

Harris, M. B.
"The Effects of Performing One Altruistic Act on the Likelihood of
Performing Another"
Journal of Social Psychology, Vol. 88 (1972), pp. 65-73.

Hornik, Jacob
"Cognitive Thoughts Mediating Compliance in Multiple Request
Situations"
Journal of Economic Psychology, Vol. 9 (March 1988), pp. 69-79.

Kamins, Michael A.
"The Enhancement of Response Rates to a Mail Survey Through a
Labelled Probe Foot-in-the-Door Approach"
Journal of the Market Research Society, Vol. 31 (April 1989), pp.
273-83.

O'Keefe, Terrence B. and Homer, Pamela M.
"Selecting Cost-Effective Survey Methods: Foot-in-Door and Prepaid
Monetary Incentives"
Journal of Business Research, Vol. 15 (August 1987), pp. 365-76.

Pliner, Patricia, Hart, H., Kohl, J., and Saari, D.
"Compliance Without Pressure: Some Further Data on the
Foot-in-the-Door Technique"
Journal of Experimental Social Psychology, Vol. 10 (January 1974),
pp. 17-22.

Reingen, Peter H.
"On Inducing Compliance With Requests"
Journal of Consumer Research, Vol. 5 (September 1978), pp. 365-9.

Reingen, P. H. and Kernan, J. B.
"More Evidence on Interpersonal Yielding"
Journal of Marketing Research, Vol. XVI (November 1979), pp. 588-93.

Reingen, Peter H. and Kernan, Jerome B.
"Compliance With an Interview Request: A Foot-in-the-Door,
Self-Perception Interpretation"
Journal of Marketing Research, Vol. XIV (August 1977), pp. 365-9.

Scott, Carol A.
"Modifying Socially-Conscious Behavior: The Foot-in-the-door
Technique"
Journal of Consumer Research, Vol. 4 (December 1977), pp. 156-64.

Seligman, Clive, Bush, M., and Kirsch, K.
"Relationship Between Compliance in the Foot-in-the-Door Paradigm and
Size of First Request"
Journal of Personality and Social Psychology, Vol. 33 (May 1976), pp.
517-20.

Snyder, Mark and Cunningham, Michael R.
"To Comply or Not to Comply: Testing the Self-Perception Explanation
of the 'Foot-in-the-Door' Phenomenon"
Journal of Personality and Social Psychology, Vol. 31 (January 1975),
pp. 64-7.

Sternthal, Brian, Scott, C., and Dholakia, Ruby
    "Self-Perception Explanations as a Means of Personal Influence: The
    Foot-in-the-Door Technique"
    in Anderson, B. (editor)
    Advances in Consumer Research
    (Cincinnati: Association for Consumer Research, 1976).

Swan, John E. and Martin, Warren S.
    "Foot-in-the-Door for Increasing Mail Questionnaire Returns: A
    Critical Review"
    in Walker, B. J. et al. (editors)
    AMA Educators' Conference Proceedings
    (Chicago: American Marketing Association, 1982), pp. 414-7.

Tybout, Alice M.
    "Relative Effectiveness of Three Behavioral Influence Strategies as
    Supplements to Persuasion in a Marketing Context"
    Journal of Marketing Research, Vol. XV (May 1978), pp. 229-42.

Tybout, Alice M., Sternthal, Brian, and Calder, Bobby J.
    "Information Availability as a Determinant of Multiple Request
    Effectiveness"
    Journal of Marketing Research, Vol. XX (August 1983), pp. 280-90.

Uranowitz, S. W.
    "Helping and Self-Attributions: A Field Experiment"
    Journal of Personality and Social Psychology, Vol. 31 (1975), pp.
    852-4.

Vredenburg, Harrie
    "On the Theoretical Interpretation of a Multiple Request Influence
    Strategy in an Industrial Marketing Setting"
    in Malhotra, Naresh K. and Hawes, Jon M. (editors)
    Developments in Marketing Science, Volume Nine
    (Anaheim, CA: Academy of Marketing Science, 1986), pp. 436-41.

Vredenburg, Harrie and Marshall, Judith J.
    "Extending the External Validity of the FITD Effect to the Industrial
    Marketplace"
    Journal of the Academy of Marketing Science, Vol. 16 (Summer 1988),
    pp. 49-56.

Wynn, George W. and McDaniel, Stephen W.
    "The Effect of Alternative Foot-in-the-Door Manipulations on Mailed
    Questionnaire Response Rate and Quality"
    Journal of the Market Research Society, Vol. 27 (January 1985), pp.
    15-26.

Wynn, George W. and McDaniel, Stephen W.
    "The Effect of Alternative Foot-in-the-Door Manipulations on Mailed
    Questionnaire Response Quality"
    Proceedings, American Institute for Decision Sciences (November
    1983), pp. 32-5.

66.03 ---------- Theory Re: Door-in-the-Face Technique

Cann, A., Sherman, S. J., and Elkes, R.
    "Effects of Initial Request Size and Timing of a Second Request: The
    Foot-in-the-Door and the Door-in-the-Face"
    Journal of Personality and Social Psychology, Vol. XXXII (1975), pp.
    774-82.

Cialdini, R. B. and Ascani, K.
    "Test of a Concession Procedure for Inducing Verbal, Behavioral, and
    Further Compliance With a Request to Give Blood"
    Journal of Applied Psychology, Vol. 61 (1976), pp. 295-300.

Cialdini, R. B., Vincent, J. E., Lewis, S. Y., Catalan, J., Wheeler,
    D., and Darby, B. L.
    "A Reciprocal Concessions Procedure for Inducing Compliance"
    Journal of Personality and Social Psychology, Vol. XXXI (1975), pp.
    206-15.

Dillard, James P., Hunter, John E., and Burgoon, Michael
    "A Meta-Analysis of Two Sequential-Request Strategies for Gaining
    Compliance: Foot-in-the-Door and Door-in-the-Face"
    Annual Convention of the International Communication Association,
    Dallas, TX (May 1983), paper presentation.

Fern, Edward F., Monroe, Kent B., and Avila, Ramon A.
    "Effectiveness of Multiple Request Strategies: A Synthesis of
    Research Results"
    Journal of Marketing Research, Vol. XXIII (May 1986), pp. 144-52.

Goldman, Morton, McVeigh, James F., and Richterkessing, Joy L.
    "Door-in-the-Face Procedure: Reciprocal Concession, Perceptual
    Contrast, or Worthy Person"
    Journal of Social Psychology, Vol. 123 (August 1984), pp. 245-51.

Groves, Robert M. and Magilavy, Lou J.
    "Increasing Response Rates to Telephone Surveys: A Door in the Face
    or Foot in the Door?"
    Public Opinion Quarterly, Vol. 45 (1981), pp. 346-58.

Mowen, John C., and Cialdini, Robert B.
    "On Implementing the Door-in-the-Face Compliance Technique in a
    Business Context"
    Journal of Marketing Research, Vol. XVII (May 1980), pp. 253-8.

Mowen, J. C. and Cialdini, R.
    "Recent Research on the Door-in-the-Face Compliance Technique"
    American Psychology Association, Toronto (1978), paper presentation.

Tybout, A.
    "Relative Effectiveness of Three Behavioral Strategies as Supplements
    to Persuasion in a Marketing Context"
    Journal of Marketing Research, Vol. XV (May 1978), pp. 229-42.

Tybout, Alice M., Sternthal, Brian, and Calder, Bobby J.
    "Information Availability as a Determinant of Multiple Request
    Effectiveness"
    Journal of Marketing Research, Vol. XX (August 1983), pp. 280-90.

66.04 ---------- Labeling Effect on Compliance

   See also (sub)heading(s) 68.05.

Goldman, Morton, Seever, M., and Seever, M.
    "Social Labeling and the Foot in the Door Effect"
    Journal of Social Psychology, Vol. 117 (January 1982), pp. 19-23.

Gurwitz, S. B. and Topol, B.
    "Determinants of Confirming and Disconfirming Response to Negative
    Social Labels"
    Journal of Experimental Social Psychology, Vol. 88 (January 1978),
    pp. 31-42.

Kraut, Robert E.
    "Effects of Social Labeling on Giving to Charity"
    Journal of Experimental Social Psychology, Vol. 9 (November 1973),
    pp. 551-62.

Moore, Ellen M., Bearden, William O., and Teel, Jesse E.
    "Use of Labeling and Assertions of Dependency in Appeals for Consumer
    Support"
    Journal of Consumer Research, Vol. 12 (June 1985), pp. 90-6.

Reingen, P. H. and Bearden, William O.
    "Salience of Behavior and the Effects of Labeling"
    in Bagozzi, Richard and Tybout, Alice (editors)
    Advances in Consumer Research, Volume Eight
    (Ann Arbor, MI: Association for Consumer Research, 1983), pp. 51-4.

Steele, C. M.
    "Name Calling and Compliance"
    Journal of Personality and Social Psychology, Vol. 31 (February
    1975), pp. 361-9.

Wechasara, Guntalee, Motes, William H., and Boya, Unal O.
    "Examining the Effects of Positive Social Labeling, Time, and Request
    Sizes on Compliance in a Multistage Marketing Survey Context"
    Journal of the Academy of Marketing Science, Vol. 15 (Winter 1987),
    pp. 15-21.

66.05 ---------- Guilt

Carlsmith, J. Merrill and Gross, Alan E.
    "Some Effects of Guilt on Compliance"
    Journal of Personality and Social Psychology, Vol. 11 (March 1969),
    pp. 232-9.

Freedman, Jonathan L., Wallington, Sue Ann, and Bless, Evelyn
    "Compliance Without Pressure: The Effect of Guilt"
    Journal of Personality and Social Psychology, Vol. 7 (October 1967),
    pp. 117-24.

66.06 ---------- Unclassified (Compliance Techniques)

Cialdini, R. B. and Schroeder, D. A.
    "Increasing Compliance by Legitimizing Paltry Contributions: When
    Even a Penny Helps"
    Journal of Personality and Social Psychology, Vol. 34 (1976), pp.
    599-604.

Wagner, C. and Wheeler, L.
    "Model, Need, and Cost Effects in Helping Behavior"
    Journal of Personality and Social Psychology, Vol. 12 (1969), pp.
    111-6.

67 -------------- MAIL SURVEYS - ADMINISTRATION ISSUES ---------------
       See also (sub)heading(s) 28.05, 68, 69, 70, 71, 72.

67.01 ---------- Books Re: Mail Survey Administration

Dillman, Don A.
  Mail and Telephone Surveys
  (New York: John Wiley and Sons, Inc., 1978), 325 pp.

Erdos, Paul
  Professional Mail Surveys, Revised Edition
  (Malabar, FL: Robert E. Krieger Publishing Company, 1983), 286 pp.

Lockhart, Daniel C. (editor)
  Making Effective Use of Mailed Questionnaires
  (San Francisco, CA: Jossey-Bass, Inc.), 98 pp.

Marshall, Brian G. and Gee, Carol Ann
  Mail Questionnaire Research: A Selected Bibliography With Selected
  Annotations
  (Monticello, IL: Council of Planning Librarians, March 1976), 17 pp.

67.02 ---------- Articles etc. Re: Mail Survey Administration

Alutto, J.
  "A Note on Determining Questionnaire Destination in Survey Research"
  Social Forces, Vol. 48 (December 1969), p. 251.

Benson, L. E.
  "Mail Surveys can be Valuable"
  Public Opinion Quarterly, Vol. 10 (Summer 1946), pp. 234-41.

Berdie, Douglas R.
  "Reassessing the Value of High Response Rates to Mail Surveys"
  Marketing Research, Vol. 1 (September 1989), pp. 52-64.

Bruvold, Norman T. and Comer, James M.
  "A Model for Estimating the Response Rate to a Mailed Survey"
  Journal of Business Research, Vol. 16 (March 1988), pp. 101-16.

Comer, J. M. and Bryner, R. E.
  "Planning Mail Surveys: A Managerial Model"
  Decision Sciences, Vol. 13 (1982), pp. 654-67.

Dillman, Don A.
  "Mail and Other Self-Administered Questionnaires"
  in Rossi, P. H., Wright, J. D., and Anderson, A. B. (editors)
  Handbook of Survey Research
  (New York: Academic Press, 1983), pp. 359-77.

Dolde, Walter, Staelin, Richard, and Yao, Tsu
  "Estimating Response Rates for Different Market Segments From
  Questionnaire Data"
  Journal of Marketing Research, Vol. XVII (May 1980), pp. 245-52.

El-Badry, M. A.
  "A Sampling Procedure for Mailed Questionnaires"
  Journal of the American Statistical Association, Vol. 51 (June 1956),
  pp. 209-27.

Erdos, P. L.
  "Data Collection Methods: Mail Surveys"
  in Ferber, R. (editor)
  Handbook of Marketing Research
  (New York: McGraw-Hill Book Company, 1974), pp. 2-90-104.

Erdos, P. L.
  "Mail Surveys are Valid and Inexpensive"
  Advertising Agency, Vol. 44 (1951), pp. 68,9.

Franzen, Raymond and Lazarsfeld, Paul
  "Mail Questionnaire as a Research Problem"
  Journal of Psychology, Vol. 20 (1945), pp. 293-320.

Guffey, Hugh J., Jr., Harris, James R., and Guffey, Mary M.
  "Stamps Versus Postal Permits: A Decisional Guide for Return Postage
  in Mail Questionnaires"
  Journal of the Academy of Marketing Science, Vol. 8 (Summer 1980),
  pp. 234-42.

Hansell, Stephen, Sparacino, Jack, Ronchi, Don, and Strodtbeck, Fred L.
  "Ego Development Responses in Written Questionnaires and Telephone
  Interviews"
  Journal of Personality and Social Psychology, Vol. 47 (November
  1984), pp. 1118,9.

Highman, A.
  "The Audited Self-Administered Questionnaire"
  Journal of Marketing, Vol. 20 (October 1955), pp. 155-9.

Houston, Michael J. and Ford, Neil M.
  "Broadening the Scope of Methodological Research on Mail Surveys"
  Journal of Marketing Research, Vol. XIII (November 1976), pp. 397-403.

Keane, John G.
  "Low Cost, High Return Mail Surveys"
  Journal of Advertising Research, Vol. 3 (September 1963), pp. 28-30.

Kerin, R. A. and Harvey, M. G.
  "Methodological Considerations in Corporate Mail Surveys: A Research
  Note"
  Journal of Marketing Research, Vol. XV (August 1976), pp. 276-82.

Leslie, Larry
  "Are High Response Rates Essential to Valid Surveys?"
  Social Science Research, Vol. 1 (September 1972), pp. 323-334.

McCrohan, Kevin F. and Lowe, Larry S.
  "A Cost/Benefit Approach to Postage Used on Mail Questionnaires"
  Journal of Marketing, Vol. 45 (Winter 1981), pp. 130-3.

McIntyre, Shelby H. and Bender, Sherry D. F. G.
  "The Purchase Intercept Technique (PIT) in Comparison to Telephone
  and Mail Surveys"
  Journal of Retailing, Vol. 62 (Winter 1986), pp. 364-83.

Neuhauser, Walter
  "Experiences With Postal Multiple Purpose Surveys"
  European Research, Vol. 4 (July 1976), pp. 177-83.

Robinson, R. A.
  "How to Design a Mail Survey"
  Printers' Ink, Vol. 239 (May 30, 1952), pp. 27-9.

Rollins, Malcolm
  "The Practical Use of Repeated Questionnaire Waves"
  Journal of Applied Psychology, Vol. 24 (December 1940), pp. 770-2.

Scott, Christopher
  "Research on Mail Surveys"
  Journal of the Royal Statistical Society, 124, Series A, Part 2
  (1961), pp. 143-205.

Wallace, David
  "A Case For-and-Against Mail Questionnaires"
  Public Opinion Quarterly, Vol. 18 (1954), pp. 40-52.

Watson, Richmond
  "Investigations by Mail"
  Market Research, Vol. 5 (1937), pp. 11-6.

Whitley, Edward W.
  "The Case for Postal Research"
  Journal of the Market Research Society, Vol. 27 (January 1985), pp.
  5-13.

67.03 ---------- Postcard Technique in Mail Surveys

Boek, Walter E. and Lade, James H.
  "A Test of the Usefulness of the Postcard Technique in a Mail
  Questionnaire Study"
  Public Opinion Quarterly, Vol. 27 (Summer 1963), pp. 303-6.

Bradt, Kenneth
  "The Usefulness of a Postcard Technique in a Mail Questionnaire Study"
  Public Opinion Quarterly, Vol. 19 (Summer 1955), pp. 218-22.

Brown, Morton B.
  "Use of a Postcard Query in Mail Surveys"
  Public Opinion Quarterly, Vol. 29 (Winter 1965), pp. 635-7.

Goldstein, Larry and Friedman, Hershey H.
  "A Case for Double Postcards in Surveys"
  Journal of Advertising Research, Vol. 15 (April 1975), pp. 43-7.

67.04 ---------- Drop-Off Questionnaire Delivery

Brown, Stephen
  "Drop and Collect Surveys: A Neglected Research Technique"
  Marketing Intelligence and Planning, Vol. 5, No. 1 (1987), pp. 19-23.

Lovelock, Christopher H., Stiff, Ronald, Culliwick, David, and Kaufman,
  Ira M.
  "An Evaluation of the Effectiveness of Drop-Off Questionnaire
  Delivery"
  Journal of Marketing Research, Vol. XIII (November 1977), pp. 358-64.

Stover, Robert V. and Stone, Walter J.
  "Hand Delivery of Self-Administered Questionnaires"
  Public Opinion Quarterly, Vol. 37 (Summer 1974), pp. 284-7.

67.05 ---------- Means of Identifying Respondents
        See also (sub)heading(s) 68.07, 68.08.

Childers, Terry L. and Skinner, Steven J.
  "Theoretical and Empirical Issues in the Identification of Survey
  Respondents"
  Journal of the Market Research Society, Vol. 27 (January 1985), pp.
  39-53.

Erdos, Paul L. and Regier, J.
  "Visible vs. Disguised Keying on Questionnaires"
  Journal of Advertising Research, Vol. 17 (February 1977), pp. 13-8.

Skinner, Steven J. and Childers, Terry L.
  "Respondent Identification in Mail Surveys"
  Journal of Advertising Research, Vol. 20 (December 1980), pp. 57-61.

67.06 ---------- Predicting Response Rates
        See also (sub)heading(s) 68, 69.

Eichner, K. and Habermehl, W.
  "Predicting Response Rates to Mailed Questionnaires"
  American Sociological Review, Vol. 46 (1981), pp. 361-3.

Heberlein, T. A. and Baumgartner, R.
  "The Effectiveness of the Herberlein-Baumgartner Motives for
  Predicting Response Rates to Mailed Questionnaires: European and U.S.
  Examples"
  American Sociological Review, Vol. 46 (1981), pp. 363-7.

Hill, Richard W.
  "Using S-Shaped Curves to Predict Response Rates"
  Journal of Marketing Research, Vol. XVIII (May 1981), pp. 240-2.

Huxley, Stephen J.
  "Predicting Response Speed in Mail Surveys"
  Journal of Marketing Research, Vol. XVII (February 1980), pp. 63-8.

Parasuraman, A.
  "More on the Prediction of Mail Survey Response Rates"
  Journal of Marketing Research, Vol. XIX (May 1982), pp. 261-8.

67.07 ---------- Mailing Lists

Burns, Karen L.
  Mailing Lists: A Practical Guide
  (New York: Direct Marketing Association), 450 pp.

68 ------------ MAIL SURVEYS - INCREASING RESPONSE RATES ------------
See also (sub)heading(s) 28.05, 66, 67, 69, 70, 71, 72, 117.

68.01 ---------- Behavioral Theories of Mail Survey Response

Albaum, Gerald S. and Venkatesan, M.
"Explaining Survey Response Behavior"
in Moller, K. and Paltschik, M. (editors)
Contemporary Research in Marketing, Volume 1
Proceedings, Annual Conference of the European Marketing Academy
(June 1986).

Allen, C.
"Perspectives on Mail Survey Response Rates: The Self-Perception
Paradigm and Beyond"
Conference on Marketing Theory, American Marketing Association
(1982), paper presentation.

Becker, H. S.
"Notes on the Concept of Commitment"
American Journal of Sociology, Vol. 66 (July 1960), pp. 32-40.

Childers, Terry L.
"Conceptualising Mail Survey Response Behavior"
Graduate School of Management, University of Minnesota (1984),
working paper.

Furse, David H.
"Toward a Theory of Mail Questionnaire Response"
Advances in Advertising Research and Management
Proceedings, American Academy of Advertising (1979), pp. 161-6.

Furse, David H. and Stewart, David W.
"Manipulating Dissonance to Improve Mail Survey Response"
Psychology and Marketing, Vol. 1 (Summer 1984), pp. 79-94.

Furse, David H. and Stewart, David W.
"Cognitive Dissonance and Response to Mail Surveys"
Working Paper No. 81-119
Owen Graduate School of Management, Vanderbilt University (September
1981).

Furse, David H. and Stewart, David W.
"Toward a Cognitive Dissonance Theory of Mail Questionnaire Response"
Working Paper No. 81-102
Owen Graduate School of Management, Vanderbilt University (January
1981).

Tullar, William, Pressley, Milton M., and Gentry, Dwight L.
"Toward a Theoretical Framework for Mail Survey Response"
Developments in Marketing Science, Vol. II (1979), pp. 243-7.

68.02 ---------- Definitions of Response Rate

CASRO
"On the Definition of Response Rates"
Special Report
(Port Jefferson, NY: Council of American Survey Research
Organizations, 1982).

Kviz, F. J.
"Toward a Standard Definition of Response Rate"
Public Opinion Quarterly, Vol. 41 (1977), pp. 265-7.

Williams-Jones, Joy
"Lack of Agreement on the Standardization of Response Rate
Terminology in the Survey Research Industry"
Proceedings, pp. 281-6.

Wiseman, Frederick and Billington, Maryann
"Comment on a Standard Definition of Response Rates"
Journal of Marketing Research, Vol. XXI (August 1984), pp. 336-8.

Wiseman, Frederick and McDonald, Philip
"Toward the Development of Industry Standards for Response and
Nonresponse Rates"
Report No. 80-101
(Cambridge, MA: Marketing Science Institute, 1980).

68.03 ---------- General Discussions, Studies Re: Increasing Resp Rate

Bachrach, Stanley D. and Scoble, Harry M.
"Mail Questionnaire Efficiency: Controlled Reduction of Non-Response"
Public Opinion Quarterly, Vol. 3 (Summer 1967), pp. 265-71.

Berdie, Douglas R. and Anderson, John F.
"Mail Questionnaire Response Rates--Updating Outmoded Thinking"
Journal of Marketing, Vol. 40 (January 1976), pp. 71-3.

Cox, Eli P., III, Anderson, W. Thomas, Jr., and Fulcher, David G.
"Reappraising Mail Survey Response Rates"
Journal of Marketing Research, Vol. XI (November 1974), pp. 413-7.

Duncan, J.
"Mail Questionnaires in Survey Research: A Review of Response
Inducement Techniques"
Journal of Management, Vol. 5 (1979), pp. 39-55.

Erdos, P. L.
"Successful Mail Surveys: High Returns and How to Get Them"
Printers' Ink, Vol. 258 (March 1957), pp. 56-60.

Fox, Richard J., Crask, Melvin R., and Kim, Jonghoon
"Mail Survey Response Rate: A Meta-Analysis of Selected Techniques
for Inducing Response"
Public Opinion Quarterly, Vol. 52 (Winter 1988), pp. 467-91.

Goyder, John
"Face-to-Face Interviews and Mailed Questionnaires: The Net
Difference in Response Rate"
Public Opinion Quarterly, Vol. 49 (Summer 1985), pp. 234-52.

Harvey, Lee
"Factors Affecting Response Rates to Mailed Questionnaires: A
Comprehensive Literature Review"
Journal of the Market Research Society, Vol. 29 (July 1987), pp.
341-53.

Heberlein, Thomas A. and Baumgartner, Robert
"Factors Affecting Response Rates to Mailed Questionnaires: A
Quantitative Analysis of the Published Literature"
American Sociological Review, Vol. 43 (August 1978), pp. 447-62.

Hodgson, Peter
"Factors Affecting Response Rates to Mailed Surveys" (comment on
Harvey)
Journal of the Market Research Society, Vol. 29 (October 1987), p.
435.

Horowitz, Joseph L. and Sedlacek, William F.
"Initial Returns on Mail Questionnaires: A Literature Review and
Research Note"
Research in Higher Education, Vol. 2, No. 4 (1974), pp. 361-7.

Janssens, Daniel and Pessemier, Edgar A.
"Response Rates in Mail Surveys: A Review and Survey"
Paper No. 714
Krannert Graduate School of Management, Purdue University (1980).

Jobber, David
"Improving Response Rates in Industrial Mail Surveys"
Industrial Marketing Management, Vol. 15 (August 1986), pp. 183-95.

Kanuck, Leslie and Berenson, Conrad
"Mail Surveys and Response Rates: A Literature Review"
Journal of Marketing Research, Vol. XII (November 1975), pp. 440-53.

Leslie, Larry
"Are High Response Rates Essential to Valid Surveys?"
Social Science Research, Vol. 1 (June 1972), pp. 323-34.

Linsky, Arnold S.
"Stimulating Responses to Mailed Questionnaires: A Review"
Public Opinion Quarterly, Vol. 39 (Spring 1975), pp. 82-101.

MRS Research and Development Committee
"Response Rates in Sample Surveys"
Journal of the Market Research Society, Vol. 18 (July 1976), pp.
113-42.

Pressley, Milton M.
Mail Survey Response: A Critically Annotated Bibliography
(Greensboro, NC: Faber and Company, 1976), 49 pp.

Schillmoeller, Edward A.
"Tackling Declining Response Rates"
Journal of Advertising Research, Vol. 27 (December 1987/January
1988), pp. RC10,11.

Sosdian, Carol P. and Sharp, Laure M.
"Nonresponse in Mail Surveys: Access Failure or Respondent Resistance"
Public Opinion Quarterly, Vol. 44 (1980), pp. 396-401.

Sosdian, C. P. and Sharp, L. M.
"Response Rates and Respondent Resistance: The Case of Mail Surveys"
AAPOR Conference, Buck Hills Falls, PA (May-June 1979), paper
presentation.

Steele, C. M.
   "Trends in Response and Non-Response Rates, 1952-1979"
   unpublished manuscript.

Whitley, Edward W.
   "The Case for Postal Research"
   Journal of the Market Research Society, Vol. 27 (January 1985), pp.
   5-13.

Yu, Julie and Cooper, Harris
   "A Quantitative Review of Research Design Effects on Response Rates
   to Questionnaires"
   Journal of Marketing Research, Vol. XX (February 1983), pp. 36-44.

68.04 ---------- Prior Notification

Allen, Chris T., Schewe, Charles D., and Wijk, Gosta
   "More on Self-Perception Theory's Foot Technique in the Pre-Call/Mail
   Survey Setting"
   Journal of Marketing Research, Vol. XVII (November 1980), pp. 498-502.

Bellizzi, Joseph A. and Hite, Robert E.
   "Face-to-Face Advance Contact and Monetary Incentives Effects on Mail
   Survey Return Rates, Response Differences, and Survey Costs"
   Journal of Business Research, Vol. 14 (February 1986), pp. 33-40.

Brunner, Allen G. and Carroll, Stephen J., Jr.
   "The Effect of Prior Notification on the Refusal Rate in Fixed
   Address Surveys"
   Journal of Advertising Research, Vol. 9 (March 1969), pp. 42-4.

Brunner, Allen G. and Carroll, Stephen J., Jr.
   "The Effect of Prior Telephone Appointments on the Completion Rates
   and Response Content Patterns in Two Fixed Address Surveys"
   Public Opinion Quarterly, Vol. 31 (Winter 1967-68), pp. 652-4.

Chebat, Jean-Charles and Picard, Jacques
   "The Prenotification of Respondents in Mailed Questionnaire Surveys
   as a Source of Sample Bias"
   International Journal of Research in Marketing, Vol. 1, No. 3 (1984),
   pp. 235-9.

Filipic, Timothy V., Faria, A. J., and Dickinson, John R.
   "The Effect of Prenotification on Mail Survey Response Rate, Speed,
   Quality and Cost"
   Proceedings, Academy of Marketing Science (Montreal: 1988).

Ford, Neil M.
   "Advance Letter in Mail Surveys"
   Journal of Marketing Research, Vol. IV (May 1967), pp. 202-4.

Freedman, Jonathan L. and Fraser, Scott D.
   "Compliance Without Pressure: the Foot-in-the-Door Technique"
   Journal of Personality and Social Psychology, Vol. 4 (October 1966),
   pp. 195-202.

Hansen, Robert A. and Robinson, Larry M.
   "Testing the Effectiveness of Alternative Foot-in-the-Door
   Manipulations"
   Journal of Marketing Research, Vol. XVII (August 1980), pp. 359-64.

Heaton, Eugene E., Jr.
   "Increasing Mail Questionnaire Returns With a Preliminary Letter"
   Journal of Advertising Research, Vol. 5 (December 1965), pp. 36-9.

Hornik, Jacob
   "Impact of Pre-Call Request Form and Gender Interaction on Response
   to a Mail Survey"
   Journal of Marketing Research, Vol. XIX (February 1982), pp. 144-51.

Hornik, Jacob
   "Comparative Effectiveness of Four Models of Telephone
   Prenotification on Refusals to a Mail Questionnaire"
   in Larson, Hanne and Heede, Syren (editors)
   Proceedings of the European Academy for Advanced Research in
   Marketing, Copenhagen (March 1981), pp. 77-96.

Jobber, David, Allen, Neal, and Oakland, John
   "The Impact of Telephone Notification Strategies on Response to an
   Industrial Mail Survey"
   International Journal of Research in Marketing, Vol. 2, No. 4 (1985),
   pp. 291-6.

Jobber, David and Sanderson, Stuart
   "The Effects of a Prior Letter and Coloured Questionnaire Paper on
   Mail Survey Response Rates"
   Journal of the Market Research Society, Vol. 25 (October 1983), pp.
   339-49.

Jolson, Marvin A.
  "How to Double or Triple Mail-Survey Response Rates"
  Journal of Marketing, Vol. 41 (October 1977), pp. 78-81.

Kephart, W. M. and Bressler, M.
  "Increasing the Responses to Mail Questionnaires: A Research Study"
  Public Opinion Quarterly, Vol. 22 (1958), pp32.

Myers, James H. and Haug, Arne F.
  "How a Preliminary Letter Affects Mail Survey Returns and Costs"
  Journal of Advertising Research, Vol. 9 (September 1969), pp. 37-9.

Parsons, Robert J. and Medford, Thomas S.
  "The Effect of Advance Notice in Mail Surveys of Homogeneous Groups"
  Public Opinion Quarterly, Vol. 36 (Summer 1972), pp. 258,9.

Peterson, Robert A., Albaum, Gerald, and Kerin, Roger A.
  "A Note on Alternative Contact Strategies in Mail Surveys"
  Journal of the Market Research Society, Vol. 31 (July 1981), pp.
  409-18.

Pucel, D. J. et al.
  "Questionnaire Follow-Up Returns as a Function of Incentives and
  Respondent Characteristics"
  Vocational Guidance Quarterly, Vol. 19 (1971), pp. 188-93.

Robin, S. S.
  "Procedure for Securing Returns to Mail Questionnaires"
  Sociology and Social Research, Vol. 50 (October 1965), pp. 24-35.

Smith, Edward M. and Hewett, Wendall
  "The Value of a Preliminary Letter in Postal Survey Response"
  Journal of the Market Research Society, Vol. 14, No. 3 (1972), pp.
  145-51.

Snyder, Marshall and Lapovsky, David
  "Enhancing Survey Response from Initial Non-Consenters"
  Journal of Advertising Research, Vol. 24 (June/July 1984), pp. 17-20.

Stafford, James E.
  "Influence of Preliminary Contact on Mail Returns"
  Journal of Marketing Research, Vol. III (November 1966), pp. 410,1.

Waisanen, F. B.
  "A Note on the Response to a Mailed Questionnaire"
  Public Opinion Quarterly, Vol. 18 (Summer 1954), pp. 210-2.

Walker, Bruce J. and Burdick, Richard K.
  "Advance Correspondence and Error in Mail Surveys"
  Journal of Marketing Research, Vol. XIV (August 1977), pp. 379-82.

68.05 ---------- Labeling of Subject

See also (sub)heading(s) 66.04.

Goldman, Morton, Creason, Christopher, and McCall, Cynthia G.
  "Compliance Employing a Two-Feet-in-the-Door Procedure"
  Journal of Social Psychology, Vol. 114 (August 1981), pp. 259-65.

Kraut, Robert E.
  "Effects of Social Labeling on Giving to Charity"
  Journal of Experimental Social Psychology, Vol. 9 (November 1973),
  pp. 551-62.

Miller, Richard L., Brickman, Philip, and Bolen, Diana
  "Attribution Versus Persuasion as a Means for Modifying Behavior"
  Journal of Personality and Social Psychology, Vol. 31 (March 1975),
  pp. 430-42.

Moore, E. M., Bearden, William O., and Teel, Jesse E.
  "Use of Labeling and Assertions of Dependency in Appeals for Consumer
  Support"
  Journal of Consumer Research, Vol. 12 (June 1985), pp. 90-6.

Reingen, P. H. and Bearden, William O.
  "Salience of Behavior and the Effects of Labeling"
  in Bagozzi, R. P. and Tybout, A. M. (editors)
  Advances in Consumer Behavior, Volume Ten
  (Ann Arbor, MI: Association for Consumer Research, 1983), pp. 51-5.

Resnik, Alan J. and Harmon, Robert R.
  "The Impact of Sponsorship, Labeling and Incentives on Mail Survey
  Response Rates: A Foot-in-the-Door Perspective"
  in Lusch, Robert F. et al. (editors)
  1985 AMA Educators' Conference Proceedings
  (Chicago: American Marketing Association, 1985), pp. 59-64.

Steele, Claude M.
    "Name-Calling and Compliance"
    Journal of Personality and Social Psychology, Vol. 31 (February
    1975), pp. 361-9.

Swinyard, William R. and Ray, Michael L.
    "Effect of Praise and Small Requests on Receptivity to Direct Mail
    Appeals"
    Journal of Social Psychology, Vol. 108 (August 1979), pp. 177-84.

68.06 ---------- Signed Versus Unsigned Questionnaires

Butler, Richard P.
    "Effects of Signed and Unsigned Questionnaires for Both Sensitive and
    Nonsensitive Items"
    Journal of Applied Psychology, Vol. 57 (1973), pp. 348,9.

Corey, Stephen M.
    "Signed Versus Unsigned Attitude Questionnaires"
    Journal of Educational Psychology, Vol. 28 (January 1937), pp. 144-8.

Fischer, Robert P.
    "Signed Versus Unsigned Personal Questionnaires"
    Journal of Applied Psychology, Vol. 30 (April 1946), pp. 220-5.

Futrell, Charles M.
    "Effects of Signed Versus Unsigned Attitude Questionnaires"
    Journal of the Academy of Marketing Science, Vol. 9 (Spring 1981),
    pp. 93-8.

Futrell, Charles, Stem, Donald E., Jr., and Fortune, Bill D.
    "Effects of Signed vs. Unsigned Internally Administered
    Questionnaires for Managers"
    Journal of Business Research, Vol. 6 (May 1978), pp. 1-8.

Gerberich, J. B. and Mason, J. M.
    "Signed Versus Unsigned Questionnaires"
    Journal of Educational Research, Vol. 42 (September 1948), pp. 122-6.

Hamel, LaVerne and Reil, Hans G.
    "Should Attitude Questionnaires be Signed?"
    Personnel Psychology, Vol. 5 (Summer 1952), pp. 87-91.

Kawash, Mary B. and Aleamoni, Lawrence M.
    "Effect of Personal Signature on the Initial Rate of Return of a
    Mailed Questionnaire"
    Journal of Applied Psychology, Vol. 55 (December 1971), pp. 589-92.

68.07 ---------- Personalization

Andreasen, Alan
    "Personalizing Mail Questionnaire Correspondence"
    Public Opinion Quarterly, Vol. 34 (Summer 1970), pp. 273-7.

Carpenter, Edwin H.
    "Personalizing Mail Surveys: A Replication and Reassessment"
    Public Opinion Quarterly, Vol. 38 (Winter 1974-75), pp. 614-20.

Clark, Gary L. and Kaminski, Peter F.
    "How to Get More for Your Money in Mail Surveys"
    Journal of Consumer Marketing (Summer 1989).

Colombotos, John and Frey, James H.
    "Contribution of Personalization to Mail Questionnaire Response as an
    Element of a Previously Tested Method"
    Journal of Applied Psychology, Vol. 59 (1974), pp. 297-301.

Cosse, T. J. and Hodges, B. S., III
    "The Mail Survey: More to It Than Counting the Returns"
    Bank Marketing, Vol. 15 (April 1983), pp. 10-3.

Dillman, Don A. and Frey, James H.
    "Contribution of Personalization to Mail Questionnaire Response as an
    Element of a Previously Tested Method"
    Journal of Applied Psychology, Vol. 59 (June 1974), pp. 297-301.

Eastman, J. F.
    "How to Boost the Rate of Return on Direct Mail Surveys"
    Bank Marketing, Vol. 15 (September 1983), pp. 16-20.

Hawes, Jon M., Crittenden, Vicky L., and Crittenden, William F.
    "The Effects of Personalization, Source, and Offer on Mail Survey
    Response Rate and Speed"
    Akron Business and Economic Review, Vol. 18 (Summer 1987), pp. 54-63.

Houston, Michael J. and Jefferson, Robert W.
"On the Personalization-Anonymity Relationship in Mail Surveys--A Reply"
Journal of Marketing Research, Vol. XIII (February 1976), pp. 112,3.

Houston, Michael J. and Jefferson, Robert W.
"The Negative Effects of Personalization on Response Patterns in Mail Surveys"
Journal of Marketing Research, Vol. XII (February 1975), pp. 114-7.

Kahle, Lynn R. and Sales, Bruce D.
"Personalization of the Outside Envelope in Mail Surveys"
Public Opinion Quarterly, Vol. 42 (Winter 1978), pp. 547-50.

Kerin, Roger A.
"Personalization Strategies, Response Rate and Response Quality in a Mail Survey"
Social Science Quarterly, Vol. 55 (June 1974), pp. 175-81.

Kerin, Roger A. and Peterson, Robert A.
"Personalization, Respondent Anonymity and Response Distortion in a Mail Survey"
Journal of Applied Psychology, Vol. 62 (February 1977), pp. 86-9.

King, J. O. and Wilson, D. D.
"The Influence of Personalization on Mail Survey Response Rates"
Arkansas Business and Economic Review, Vol. 14 (1978), pp. 15-8.

Linsky, A.
"A Factorial Experiment to Inducing Responses to a Mail Questionnaire"
Sociology and Social Research, Vol. 49 (1965), pp. 183-9.

Moore, C. C.
"Increasing the Returns From Questionnaires"
Journal of Educational Research, Vol. 35 (1941), pp. 138-41.

Nederhof, Anton J.
"The Effects of Repetition and Consistency of Personalization Treatments on Response Rate in Mail Surveys"
Social Science Research, Vol. 12 (1983), pp. 1-9.

Pearlin, Leonard I.
"The Appeals of Anonymity in Questionnaire Response"
Public Opinion Quarterly, Vol. 25 (Winter 1961), pp. 640-7.

Rucker, M., Hughes, R., Thompson, R., Harrison, A., and Vanderlip, N.
"Personalisation of Mail Surveys: Too Much of a Good Thing?"
Educational and Psychological Measurement, Vol. 44 (Winter 1984), pp. 893-905.

Simon, Raymond
"Response to Personal and Form Letters in Mail Surveys"
Journal of Advertising Research, Vol. 7 (March 1967), pp. 28-30.

Snelling, W. Rodman
"The Impact of a Personalized Questionnaire"
Journal of Educational Research, Vol. 63 (November 1969), pp. 126-9.

Weilbacher, William and Walsh, H. Robert
"Mail Questionnaires and the Personalized Letter of Transmittal"
Journal of Marketing, Vol. 16 (January 1952), pp. 331-6.

Wiseman, Frederick
"A Reassessment of the Effects of Personalization on Response Patterns in Mail Surveys"
Journal of Marketing Research, Vol. XIII (February 1976), pp. 110,1.

Wunder, Gene C. and Wynn, George W.
"The Effects of Address Personalization on Mailed Questionnaires' Response Rate, Time and Quality"
Journal of the Market Research Society, Vol. 30 (January 1988), pp. 95-101.

68.08 ---------- Anonymity

See also (sub)heading(s) 67.05.

Albaum, Gerald
"Do Source and Anonymity Affect Mail Survey Results?"
Journal of the Academy of Marketing Science, Vol. 15 (Fall 1987), pp. 74-81.

Ash, Philip and Abromson, Edward
"The Effect of Anonymity on Attitude-Questionnaire Response"
Journal of Abnormal and Social Psychology, Vol. 47 (1952), pp. 722,3.

Butler, R.
"Effects of Signed and Unsigned Questionnaires for Both Sensitive and
Nonsensitive Items"
Journal of Applied Psychology, Vol. 57 (1973), pp. 348,9.

Childers, Terry L. and Skinner, Steven J.
"Theoretical and Empirical Issues in the Identification of Survey
Respondents"
Journal of the Market Research Society, Vol. 27 (January 1985), pp.
39-53.

Dickson, John P., Casey, Michael J., and Wyckoff, Daniel W.
"The Invisible Ink Caper: Or a Watergate Mentality in Marketing
Research Ethics"
in Schneider, Howard C. (editor)
Proceedings, American Institute for Decision Sciences (1976), p. 274.

Downs, Phillip E. and Kerr, John R.
"Recent Evidence on the Relationship Between Anonymity and Response
Variables for Mail Surveys"
Journal of the Academy of Marketing Science, Vol. 14 (Spring 1986),
pp. 72-82.

Elinson, Jack and Haines, Valerie T.
"Role of Anonymity in Attitude Surveys"
American Psychologist, Vol. 5 (1950), p. 315.

Erdos, P. and Regier, J.
"Visible vs. Disguised Keying on Questionnaires"
Journal of Advertising Research, Vol. 17 (1977), pp. 13-8.

Faria, A. J. and Dickinson, John R.
"The Effect of Survey Sponsor, Questionnaire Length, and Anonymity on
Mail Survey Response Rate and Response Speed"
World Marketing Congress, Academy of Marketing Science, Singapore
(July 1989), paper presentation.

Fuller, Carol
"Effect of Anonymity on Return Rate and Response Bias in a Mail
Survey"
Journal of Applied Psychology, Vol. 59 (June 1974), pp. 292-6.

Futrell, Charles M., Stem, D., Jr., and Fortune, B.
"Effects of Signed Versus Unsigned Internally Administered
Questionnaires for Managers"
Journal of Business Research, Vol. 6 (1978), pp. 91-8.

Futrell, Charles M. and Swan, John E.
"Anonymity and Response by Salespeople to a Mail Questionnaire"
Journal of Marketing Research, Vol. XIV (November 1977), pp. 611-6.

Haines, Valerie T. and Elinson, Jack
"Role of Anonymity in Attitude Surveys"
American Psychologist, Vol. 5 (1950), p. 315.

Hise, R. T. and McGinnis, M. A.
"Evaluating the Effects of Anonymous Respondents on Mail Survey
Results"
Journal of the Academy of Marketing Science, Vol. 4 (Summer 1976),
pp. 592-8.

Jones, Wesley H.
"Generalizing Mail Survey Inducement Methods: Population Interactions
With Anonymity and Sponsorship"
Public Opinion Quarterly, Vol. 43 (Spring 1979), pp. 102-11.

Kerin, Roger A. and Peterson, Robert A.
"Personalization, Respondent Anonymity and Response Distortion in a
Mail Survey"
Journal of Applied Psychology, Vol. 62 (February 1977), pp. 86-9.

King, Francis W.
"Anonymous Versus Identifiable Questionnaires in Drug Usage Surveys"
American Psychologist, Vol. 25 (October 1970), pp. 982-5.

Mason, Ward S., Dressel, Robert J., and Bain, Robert K.
"An Experimental Study of Factors Affecting Response to a Mail Survey
of Beginning Teachers"
Public Opinion Quarterly, Vol. 25 (Summer 1961), pp. 296-309.

Matteson, Michael T. and Smith, Samuel V.
"Effects of Voluntary Anonymity on Questionnaire Responses"
in Day, Ralph L. (editor)
Consumer Satisfaction, Dissatisfaction and Complaining Behavior
(Bloomington, IN: School of Business, Indiana University, 1977), pp.
176,7.

McDaniel, Stephen W. and Rao, C. P.
    "An Investigation of Respondent Anonymity's Effect on Mailed
    Questionnaire Response Rate and Quality"
    Journal of the Market Research Society, Vol. 23 (July 1981), pp.
    150-60.

Mitchell, W.
    "Factors Affecting the Rates of Return on Mailed Questionnaires"
    Journal of the American Statistical Association (December 1939), pp.
    683-92.

Olson, Willard C.
    "The Waiver of Signature in Personal Reports"
    Journal of Applied Psychology, Vol. 20 (1936), pp. 442-50.

Pearlin, Leonard I.
    "The Appeals of Anonymity in Questionnaire Response"
    Public Opinion Quarterly, Vol. 25 (Winter 1961), pp. 640-7.

Ridgway, N. M. and Price, L. L.
    "The Effects of Respondent Identification in a Mail Survey"
    Proceedings, American Marketing Association Educators' Conference
    (1982), pp. 410-3.

Rosen, Ned A.
    "Anonymity and Attitude Measurement"
    Public Opinion Quarterly, Vol. 24 (Winter 1960), pp. 675-80.

Skinner, Steven J. and Childers, Terry L.
    "Respondent Identification in Mail Surveys"
    Journal of Advertising Research, Vol. 20 (December 1980), pp. 57-61.

Stevens, R. E.
    "Does Precoding Mail Questionnaires Affect Response Rates?"
    Public Opinion Quarterly, Vol. 38, No. 4 (1974), pp. 621,2.

Tyagi, Pradeep K.
    "The Effects of Appeals, Anonymity, and Feedback on Mail Survey
    Response Patterns From Salespeople"
    Journal of the Academy of Marketing Science, Vol. 17 (Summer 1989),
    pp. 235-41.

Wildman, Richard C.
    "Effects of Anonymity and Social Setting on Survey Responses"
    Public Opinion Quarterly, Vol. 41 (Spring 1977), pp. 74-9.

68.09 ----------   Inducements and Incentives

Armstrong, J. Scott
    "Monetary Incentives in Mail Surveys"
    Public Opinion Quarterly, Vol. 39 (Spring 1975), pp. 111-6.

Bellizzi, Joseph A. and Hite, Robert E.
    "Face-to-Face Advance Contact and Monetary Incentives Effects on Mail
    Survey Return Rates, Response Differences, and Survey Costs"
    Journal of Business Research, Vol. 14 (February 1986), pp. 33-40.

Bevis, Joseph C.
    "Economic Incentives Used for Mail Questionnaires"
    Public Opinion Quarterly, Vol. 12 (Fall 1948), pp. 492,3.

Blumberg, Herbert H., Fuller, Carolyn, and Hare, A. Paul
    "Response Rates in Postal Surveys"
    Public Opinion Quarterly, Vol. 38 (Spring 1974), pp. 113-23.

Brennan, Robert
    "Trading Stamps as an Incentive"
    Journal of Marketing, Vol. 22 (January 1958), pp. 306,7.

Brown, Stephen W. and Coney, Kenneth A.
    "Comments on 'Mail Survey Premiums and Response Bias'"
    Journal of Marketing Research, Vol. XIV (August 1977), pp. 385-7.

Cannell, C. F. and Henson, R.
    "Incentives, Motives and Response Bias"
    Annals of Economic and Social Measurement, Vol. 3 (1974), pp. 307-17.

Chromy, James R. and Horvitz, Daniel G.
    "The Use of Monetary Incentives in National Assessment Household
    Surveys"
    Journal of the American Statistical Association, Vol. 73(363) (1978),
    pp. 473-8.

Dohrenwend, B.
    "An Experimental Study of Payments to Respondents"
    Public Opinion Quarterly, Vol. 34 (Winter 1970-71), pp. 621-4.

Dommeyer, Curt J.
"How Form of the Monetary Incentive Affects Mail Survey Response"
Journal of the Market Research Society, Vol. 30 (July 1988), pp.
379-84.

Doob, Anthony N., Freedman, Jonathan L., and Carlsmith, J. Merrill
"Effects of Sponsor and Prepayment on Compliance With a Mailed
Request"
Journal of Applied Psychology, Vol. 57 (1973), pp. 346,7.

Doob, Anthony N. and Zabrack, M.
"The Effect of Freedom-Threatening Instructions and Monetary
Inducement on Compliance"
Canadian Journal of Behavioural Science, Vol. 3 (October 1971), pp.
408-12.

Dotson, Floyd
"Intensive Interviewing in Community Research"
Journal of Educational Sociology, Vol. 27 (1954), pp. 225-30.

Ferber, Robert and Sudman, Seymour
"Effects of Compensation in Consumer Expenditure Surveys"
Annals of Economic and Social Measurement, Vol. 3 (1974), pp. 319-31.

Frankel, Lester R.
"How Incentives and Subsamples Affect the Precision of Mail
Surveys--Rejoinder to Haskins"
Journal of Advertising Research, Vol. 1 (December 1960), pp. 23,4.

Frankel, L. R.
"How Incentives and Subsamples Affect the Precision of Mail Surveys"
Journal of Advertising Research, Vol. 1 (September 1960), pp. 1-5.

Friedman, Hershey H. and San Augustine, Andre J.
"The Effects of a Monetary Incentive and the Ethnicity of the
Sponsor's Signature on the Rate and Quality of Response to a Mail
Survey"
Journal of the Academy of Marketing Science, Vol. 7, No. 2 (1979),
pp. 95-101.

Furse, David H. and Stewart, David W.
"Monetary Incentives Versus Promised Contribution to Charity: New
Evidence on Mail Survey Response"
Journal of Marketing Research, Vol. XIX (August 1982), pp. 375-80.

Furse, David H., Stewart, David W., and Rados, David L.
"Effects of Foot-in-the-Door, Cash Incentives, and Follow-Ups on
Survey Response"
Journal of Marketing Research, Vol. XVIII (November 1981), pp. 473-8.

Gajraj, Ananda M., Dickinson, John R., and Faria, A. J.
"A Comparison of the Effect of Promised and Provided Lotteries,
Monetary, and Gift Incentives on Mail Survey Response Rate, Speed,
and Cost"
Journal of the Market Research Society, Vol. 32 (1990).

Gajraj, Ananda M., Dickinson, John R., and Faria, A. J.
"A Comparison of the Effect of Promised and Provided Lotteries,
Monetary, and Gift Incentives on Mail Survey Response Rate, Speed,
and Cost" (Abstract)
Proceedings, American Marketing Association (August 1989).

Gelb, Betsy
"Incentives to Increase Survey Returns: Social Class Considerations"
Journal of Marketing Research, Vol. XII (February 1975), pp. 107-9.

Godwin, R. Kenneth
"The Consequences of Large Monetary Incentives in Mail Surveys of
Elites"
Public Opinion Quarterly, Vol. 43 (1979), pp. 378-87.

Golden, Linda L., Anderson, W. T., and Sharpe, L. K.
"The Effects of Salutation, Monetary Incentive, and Degree of
Urbanization on Mail Questionnaire Response Rate, Speed, and Quality"
in Monroe, K. S. (editor)
Advances in Consumer Research (1980), pp. 292-8.

Goodstadt, Michael S., Chung, Linda, Kronitz, Reena, and Cook, Gaynoll
"Mail Survey Response Rates: Their Manipulation and Impact"
Journal of Marketing Research, Vol. XIV (August 1977), pp. 391-5.

Hackler, James C. and Bourgette, Patricia
"Dollars, Dissonance, and Survey Returns"
Public Opinion Quarterly, Vol. 37 (Summer 1973), pp. 276-81.

Hancock, John W.
"An Experimental Study of Four Methods of Measuring Unit Costs of
Obtaining Attitude Toward the Retail Store"
Journal of Applied Psychology, Vol. 24 (April 1940), pp. 213-30.

Hansen, Robert A.
   "A Self-Perception Interpretation of the Effect of Monetary and
   Nonmonetary Incentives on Mail Survey Respondent Behavior"
   Journal of Marketing Research, Vol. XVII (February 1980), pp. 77-83.

Haskins, Jack B.
   "Comment on 'How Incentives and Subsamples Affect the Precision of
   Mail Surveys'"
   Journal of Advertising Research, Vol. 1 (December 1960), pp. 22,3.

Heads, J. and Thrift, H. J.
   "Notes on a Study in Postal Response Rates"
   Journal of the Market Research Society (April 1966), p. 257.

Hopkins, K. D. and Podolak, J.
   "Class of Mail and the Effects of Monetary Gratuity on the Response
   Rate of Mail Questionnaires"
   Journal of Experimental Education, Vol. 51 (1983), pp. 69,70.

Hubbard, Raymond and Little, Eldon L.
   "Promised Contributions to Charity and Mail Survey Responses:
   Replication With Extension"
   Public Opinion Quarterly, Vol. 52 (Summer 1988), pp. 223-30.

Huck, Schuyler W. and Gleason, Edwin M.
   "Using Monetary Inducements to Increase Response Rates From Mail
   Surveys"
   Journal of Applied Psychology, Vol. 59 (April 1974), pp. 222-5.

Isaacson, H. L., Koenigsberg, A., and Smith, H.
   "Mail Survey Research in Britain: An Experiment With Incentives"
   Journal of the Market Research Society (November 1967), p. 213.

Jobber, David and Saunders, John
   "Modelling the Effects of Prepaid Monetary Incentives on Mail Survey
   Response"
   Journal of the Operational Research Society, Vol. 39 (April 1988),
   pp. 365-72.

Jones, Wesley H.
   "Generalizing Mail Survey Inducement Methods: Population Interactions
   With Anonymity and Sponsorship"
   Public Opinion Quarterly, Vol. 43 (April 1979), pp. 102-11.

Jones, Wesley H. and Lang, James R.
   "Sample Composition Bias and Response Bias in a Mail Survey: A
   Comparison of Inducement Methods"
   Journal of Marketing Research, Vol. XVII (February 1980), pp. 69-76.

Keown, Charles F.
   "Foreign Mail Surveys: Response Rates Using Monetary Incentives"
   Journal of International Business Studies, Vol. 16 (Fall 1985), pp.
   151-3.

Kephart, W. M. and Bressler, M.
   "Increasing the Response to Mail Questionnaires"
   Public Opinion Quarterly, Vol. 22 (Summer 1958), pp. 123-32.

Kimball, Andrew E.
   "Increasing the Rate of Return in Mail Surveys"
   Journal of Marketing, Vol. 25 (October 1961), pp. 63,4.

Laurent, C. K. and Parra A., A.
   "Use of Mail Questionnaires in Columbia"
   Journal of Marketing Research, Vol. V (February 1968), pp. 101-3.

Lorenzi, Peter, Friedman, Roberto, and Paolillo, Joseph G. P.
   "Consumer Mail Survey Responses: More (Unbiased) Bang for the Buck"
   Journal of Consumer Marketing, Vol. 5 (Fall 1988), pp. 31-40.

Maloney, Paul W.
   "Comparabilty of Personal Attitude Scale Adminstration With and
   Without Incentive"
   Journal of Applied Psychology, Vol. 38 (August 1954), pp. 238,9.

Mizes, J. Scott, Flecce, E. Louis, and Roos, Cindy
   "Incentives for Increasing Return Rates: Magnitude Levels, Response
   Bias, and Format"
   Public Opinion Quarterly, Vol. 48 (Winter 1984), pp. 794-800.

Nederhof, Anton J.
   "The Effects of Material Incentives in Mail Surveys: Two Studies"
   Public Opinion Quarterly, Vol. 47 (1983), pp. 103-11.

Newman, Sheldon W.
   "Differences Between Early and Late Respondents to a Mailed Survey"
   Journal of Advertising Research, Vol. 2 (June 1962), pp. 37-9.

O'Keefe, Terrence B. and Homer, Pamela M.
"Selecting Cost-Effective Survey Methods: Foot-in-Door and Prepaid Monetary Incentives"
Journal of Business Research, Vol. 15 (August 1987), pp. 365-76.

Paolillo, Joseph G. P. and Lorenzi, Peter
"Monetary Incentives and Mail Questionnaire Response Rates"
Journal of Advertising, Vol. 13 (1984), pp. 46-8.

Peck, John K., Dresch, Stephen P., and Cole, Candace P.
"Financial Incentives, Survey Response, and Sample Representativeness: Does Money Matter?"
Institute for Demographic and Economic Studies, Inc., New Haven, CT, (1977).

Pressley, Milton M.
"Care Needed When Selecting Response Inducements in Mail Surveys of Commercial Populations"
Journal of the Academy of Marketing Science, Vol. 6 (Fall 1978), pp. 336-43.

Pressley, Milton M. and Tullar, William L.
"A Factor Interactive Investigation of Mail Survey Response Rates From a Commercial Population"
Journal of Marketing Research, Vol. XIV (February 1977), pp. 108-11.

Pucel, D. J., Nelson, H. F., and Wheeler, D. N.
"Questionnaire Follow-Up Returns as a Function of Incentives and Responder Characteristics"
Vocational Guidance Quarterly, Vol. 19 (March 1971), pp. 188-93.

Resnik, Alan J. and Harmon, Robert R.
"The Impact of Sponsorship, Labeling and Incentives on Mail Survey Response Rates: A Foot-in-the-Door Perspective"
in Lusch, Robert F. et al. (editors)
1985 AMA Educators' Conference Proceedings
(Chicago: American Marketing Association, 1985), pp. 59-64.

Response Analysis Corporation
"The Sampler"
No. 25 (1982).

Robertson, Dan H. and Bellenger, Danny N.
"A New Method of Increasing Mail Survey Responses: Contributions to Charity"
Journal of Marketing Research, Vol. XV (November 1978), pp. 632,3.

Robin, Donald P. and Nash, H. W.
"An Analysis of Monetary Incentives in Mail Questionnaire Studies"
Journal of Business Communication, Vol. 11 (1973), pp. 38-42.

Robin, Donald P. and Walters, C. Glenn
"The Effect on Return Rate of Messages Explaining Monetary Incentives in Mail Questionnaire Studies"
Journal of Business Communication, Vol. 13, No. 3 (1976), pp. 49-54.

Shackleton, V. J. and Wild, J. M.
"Effect of Incentives and Personal Contact on Response Rate to a Mail Questionnaire"
Psychological Reports, Vol. 50 (1982), pp. 365,6.

Skinner, Steven J., Ferrell, O. C., and Pride, William M.
"Personal and Nonpersonal Incentives in Mail Surveys: Immediate Versus Delayed Inducements"
Journal of the Academy of Marketing Science, Vol. 12 (Winter/Spring 1984), pp. 106-14.

Stanley, Thomas J. and Sewall, Murphy A.
"The Response of Affluent Consumers to Mail Surveys"
Journal of Advertising Research, Vol. 26 (June/July 1986), pp. 55-8.

Watson, John J.
"Improving the Response Rate in Mail Research"
Journal of Advertising Research, Vol. 5 (June 1977), pp. 48-50.

Weiss, Carol H.
"Interviewing in Evaluation Research"
in Struening, E. I. and Guttentag, M. (editors)
Handbook of Evaluation Research
(Beverly Hills, CA: Sage Publishing Company, 1975), pp. 355-95.

Whitmore, William J.
"A Reply on 'Mail Survey Premiums and Response Bias'"
Journal of Marketing Research, Vol. XIV (August 1977), pp. 388-90.

Whitmore, William J.
"Mail Survey Premiums and Response Bias"
Journal of Marketing Research, Vol. XIII (February 1976), pp. 46-50.

Wiseman, Frederick
    "Factor Interaction Effects in Mail Survey Response Rates"
    Journal of Marketing Research, Vol. X (August 1973), pp. 330-3.

Wotruba, Thomas R.
    "Monetary Inducements and Mail Questionnaire Response"
    Journal of Marketing Research, Vol. III (November 1966), pp. 393-400.

68.10 ---------- Prepaid Versus Promised Inducements and Incentives

Blumberg, Herbert H., Fuller, Carolyn, and Hare, A. Paul
    "Response Rates in Postal Surveys"
    Public Opinion Quarterly, Vol. 38 (Spring 1974), pp. 113-23.

Cox, Eli P., III
    "A Cost/Benefit View of Prepaid Monetary Incentives in Mail
    Questionnaires"
    Public Opinion Quarterly, Vol. 40 (Spring 1976), pp. 101-4.

Gajraj, Ananda M., Dickinson, John R., and Faria, A. J.
    "A Comparison of the Effect of Promised and Provided Lotteries,
    Monetary, and Gift Incentives on Mail Survey Response Rate, Speed,
    and Cost" (Abstract)
    Proceedings, American Marketing Association (August 1989).

Gelb, Betsy D.
    "Incentives to Increase Survey Returns: Social Class Considerations"
    Journal of Marketing Research, Vol. XII (February 1975), pp. 107-9.

Goodstadt, Michael S., Chung, Linda, Kronitz, Reena, and Cook, Gaynoll
    "Mail Survey Response Rates: Their Manipulation and Impact"
    Journal of Marketing Research, Vol. XIV (August 1977), pp. 391-5.

Hancock, John W.
    "An Experimental Study of Four Methods of Measuring Unit Costs of
    Obtaining Attitude Toward the Retail Store"
    Journal of Applied Psychology, Vol. 24 (April 1940), pp. 213-30.

Paolillo, Joseph G. P. and Lorenzi, Peter
    "Monetary Incentives and Mail Questionnaire Response Rates"
    Journal of Advertising, Vol. 13 (1984), pp. 46-8.

Schewe, Charles D. and Cournoyer, Norman G.
    "Prepaid vs. Promised Monetary Incentives to Questionnaire Response:
    Further Evidence"
    Public Opinion Quarterly, Vol. 40 (Spring 1976), pp. 105-7.

Skinner, Steven J., Ferrell, O. C., and Pride, William M.
    "Personal and Nonpersonal Incentives in Mail Surveys: Immediate
    Versus Delayed Inducements"
    Journal of the Academy of Marketing Science, Vol. 12 (Winter 1984),
    pp. 106-14.

Weiss, Louis I., Friedman, Debra, and Shoemaker, Carlisle L.
    "Prepaid Incentives Yield Higher Response Rates to Mail Surveys"
    Marketing News, Vol. 19 (January 4, 1985), pp. 30,1.

Wotruba, Thomas R.
    "Monetary Inducements and Mail Questionnaire Response"
    Journal of Marketing Research, Vol. III (November 1966), pp. 393-400.

68.11 ---------- Offer of Survey Results

Dommeyer, Curt J.
    "Offering Mail Survey Results in a Lift Letter"
    Journal of the Market Research Society, Vol. 31 (July 1989), pp.
    399-408.

Dommeyer, Curt J.
    "Does Response to an Offer of Mail Survey Results Interact With
    Questionnaire Interest?"
    Journal of the Market Research Society, Vol. 27 (January 1985), pp.
    27-38.

Erdos, P. L.
    "How to Get Higher Returns From Your Mail Surveys"
    Printers' Ink, Vol. 22 (1957), pp. 30,1.

Jobber, D. and Sanderson, S.
    "The Effect of Two Variables on Industrial Mail Survey Returns"
    Industrial Marketing Management, Vol. 14 (1985), pp. 119-21.

Kerin, Roger A., Barry, T. E., Dubinsky, A. J., and Harvey, M. G.
    "Offer of Results and Mail Survey Response From a Commercial
    Population: A Test of Gouldner's Norm of Reciprocity"
    Proceedings, American Institute for Decision Science (1981), pp.
    283-5.

May, R. C.
   "What Approach Gets the Best Return in Mail Surveys?"
   Industrial Marketing, Vol. 45 (1960), pp. 50,1.

Powers, D. E. and Alderman, D. L.
   "Feedback as an Incentive for Responding to a Mail Questionnaire"
   Research in Higher Education, Vol. 17 (1982), pp. 207-11.

Wiseman, F.
   "Factor Interaction Effects in Mail Survey Response Rates"
   Journal of Marketing Research, Vol. X (1973), pp. 330-3.

68.12 ---------- Probabilistic Incentives

Chebat, Jean-Charles and Picard, Jacques
   "The Prenotification of Respondents in Mailed Questionnaire Surveys
   as a Source of Sample Bias"
   International Journal of Research in Marketing, Vol. 1, No. 3 (1984),
   pp. 235-9.

Gajraj, Ananda M., Dickinson, John R., and Faria, A. J.
   "A Comparison of the Effect of Promised and Provided Lotteries,
   Monetary, and Gift Incentives on Mail Survey Response Rate, Speed,
   and Cost"
   Journal of the Market Research Society, Vol. 32 (1990).

Gajraj, Ananda M., Dickinson, John R., and Faria, A. J.
   "A Comparison of the Effect of Promised and Provided Lotteries,
   Monetary, and Gift Incentives on Mail Survey Response Rate, Speed,
   and Cost" (Abstract)
   Proceedings, American Marketing Association (August 1989).

Hubbard, Raymond and Little, Eldon L.
   "Cash Prizes and Mail Survey Response Rates: A Threshold Analysis"
   Journal of the Academy of Marketing Science, Vol. 16 (Fall 1988), pp.
   42-4.

McDaniel, Stephen W. and Jackson, R. W.
   "Exploring the Probabilistic Incentive in Mail Surveys"
   Proceedings, AMA Educators' Conference (1984), pp. 372-4.

McEnally, Martha R.
   "The Differential Effectiveness of Contests and Monetary Incentives
   on Response to Mail Surveys"
   in Rees, L. P. (editor)
   Proceedings, S.E. Transactions of the Institute of Management (1984),
   pp. 252-4.

68.13 ---------- Questionnaire Appearance

Bender, Donald H.
   "Colored Stationery in Direct-Mail Advertising"
   Journal of Applied Psychology, Vol. 41 (1957), pp. 161-4.

Blumenfeld, Warrent S.
   "Effect of Appearance of Correspondence on Response Rate to a Mail
   Questionnaire"
   Psychological Reports, Vol. 32 (February 1973), p. 178.

Crittenden, William F., Crittenden, Vicky L., and Hawes, Jon M.
   "Examining the Effects of Questionnaire Color and Print Font on Mail
   Survey Response Rates"
   Akron Business and Economic Review, Vol. 16 (Winter 1985), pp. 51-6.

Dunlap, William J.
   "The Effect of Color in Direct Mail Advertising"
   Journal of Applied Psychology, Vol. 34 (August 1950), pp. 280,1.

Erdos, P. L.
   "How to Get Higher Returns From Your Mail Surveys"
   Printers' Ink (February 22, 1957), pp. 30,1.

Etcheverry, B. E.
   "Want Confidential Purchase Data? It's All in How You Ask"
   Sales Management (March 1, 1954), p. 48.

Ford, Neil M.
   "Questionnaire Appearance and Response Rates in Mail Surveys"
   Journal of Advertising Research, Vol. 8 (September 1968), pp. 43-5.

Hyett, G. P. and Farr, D. J.
   "Postal Questionnaires: Double-Sided Printing Compared With
   Single-Sided Printing"
   European Research, Vol. 5 (May 1977), pp. 136,7.

Jobber, David
   "Questionnaire Factors and Mail Survey Response Rates"
   European Research, Vol. 13 (July 1985), pp. 124-9.

Jobber, David and Sanderson, Stuart
  "The Effects of a Prior Letter and Coloured Questionnaire Paper on
  Mail Survey Response Rates"
  Journal of the Market Research Society, Vol. 25 (October 1983), pp.
  339-49.

Levine, S. and Gordon, G.
  "Maximizing Returns on Mail Questionnaires"
  Public Opinion Quarterly, Vol. 22 (1958-59), pp. 568-75.

Matteson, Michael T.
  "Type of Transmittal Letter and Questionnaire Color as Two Variables
  Influencing Response Rates in a Mail Survey"
  Journal of Applied Psychology, Vol. 59 (August 1974), pp. 535,6.

Robinson, R. A.
  "How to Boost Returns From Mail Questionnaires"
  Printers' Ink (June 6, 1952), pp. 35-7.

Seitz, R. M.
  "How Mail Surveys May be Made to Pay"
  Printers' Ink (December 1, 1944), pp. 17-9.

Smith, K.
  "Signing Off in the Right Color can Boost Mail Survey Response"
  Industrial Marketing, Vol. 62 (1977), pp. 59-62.

68.14 ---------- (Perceived) Size/Length/Completion Time

Berdie, Douglas R.
  "Questionnaire Length and Response Rate"
  Journal of Applied Psychology, Vol. 58 (1973), pp. 278-80.

Cartwright, A. and Ward, A. W. M.
  "Variations in General Practitioners' Response to a Postal
  Questionnaire"
  British Journal of Preventive and Social Medicine, Vol. 22 (1968),
  pp. 199-205.

Champion, Dean and Sear, Alan M.
  "Questionnaire Response Rate: A Methodological Analysis"
  Social Forces, Vol. 47 (1969), pp. 335-9.

Childers, Terry L. and Ferrell, O. C.
  "Response Rate and Perceived Questionnaire Length in Mail Surveys"
  Journal of Marketing Research, Vol. XVI (August 1979), pp. 429-31.

Faria, A. J. and Dickinson, John R.
  "The Effect of Survey Sponsor, Questionnaire Length, and Anonymity on
  Mail Survey Response Rate and Response Speed"
  World Marketing Congress, Academy of Marketing Science, Singapore
  (July 1989), paper presentation.

Goyder, J.
  "Further Evidence on Factors Affecting Response Rates to Mailed
  Questionnaires"
  American Sociological Review, Vol. 47 (1982), pp. 550-3.

Groves, Robert M.
  "On the Mode of Administering a Questionnaire and Responses to
  Open-Ended Items"
  Social Science Research, Vol. 7 (1978), pp. 257-71.

Hornik, Jacob
  "Time Cue and Time Perception Effect on Response to Mail Surveys"
  Journal of Marketing Research, Vol. XVIII (May 1981), pp. 243-8.

Mason, W. S. et al.
  "An Experimental Study of Factors Affecting Response Rate to a Mail
  Survey of Beginning Teachers"
  Public Opinion Quarterly, Vol. 25 (1961), pp. 296-9.

Powers, D. E. and Alderman, D. L.
  "Feedback as an Incentive for Responding to a Mail Questionnaire"
  Research in Higher Education, Vol. 17 (1982), pp. 207-11.

Roscoe, A. Marvin, Lang, Dorothy, and Sheth, Jagdish N.
  "Follow-Up Methods, Questionnaire Length, and Market Differences in
  Mail Surveys"
  Journal of Marketing, Vol. 39 (April 1975), pp. 20-7.

Sheth, Jagdish N. and Roscoe, A. Marvin
  "Impact of Questionnaire Length, Follow-Up Methods, and Geographical
  Location on Response Rate to a Mail Survey"
  Journal of Applied Psychology, Vol. 60 (1975), pp. 252-4.

Stanley, Thomas J. and Sewall, Murphy A.
  "The Response of Affluent Consumers to Mail Surveys"
  Journal of Advertising Research, Vol. 26 (June/July 1986), pp. 55-8.

68.15 ---------- Follow-Up Methods

Anderson, John F. and Berdie, Douglas R.
"Effects on Response Rates of Formal and Informal Questionnaire
Follow-Up Techniques"
Journal of Applied Psychology, Vol. 60 (April 1975), pp. 255-7.

Comer, J. M. and Kelly, J. S.
"Follow-Up Techniques: The Effect of Method and Source Appeal"
Proceedings, AMA Educators' Conference (1982), pp. 430-4.

Eckland, Bruce
"Effects of Prodding to Increase Mail Back Returns"
Journal of Applied Psychology, Vol. 49 (June 1965), pp. 165-9.

Etzel, Michael J. and Walker, Bruce J.
"Effects of Alternative Follow-Up Procedures on Mail Survey Response
Rates"
Journal of Applied Psychology, Vol. 59 (April 1974), pp. 219-21.

Ferrell, O. C. and Krugman, Dean
"Response Patterns and the Importance of the Follow-Up Duplicate
Questionnaire in a Mail Survey of Advertising Managers"
European Research, Vol. 11 (October 1983), pp. 157-63.

Futrell, Charles M. and Lamb, Charles W.
"Effect on Mail Survey Return Rates of Including Questionnaires With
Follow-Up Letters"
Perceptual and Motor Skills, Vol. 52 (1981), pp. 11-5.

Goulet, Waldemar M.
"Efficacy of a Third Request Letter in Mail Surveys of Professionals"
Journal of Marketing Research, Vol. XIV (February 1977), pp. 112-4.

Gullahorn, J. T. and Gullahorn, J. E.
"Increasing Returns From Non-Respondents"
Public Opinion Quarterly, Vol. 23 (Spring 1959), pp. 119-21.

Heberlein, Thomas A. and Baumgartner, Robert
"Is a Questionnaire Necessary in a Second Mailing"
Public Opinion Quarterly, Vol. 45 (1981), pp. 102-8.

Hinrichs, J. R.
"Effects of Sampling, Follow-Up Letters, and Commitment to
Participation on Mail Attitude Survey Response"
Journal of Applied Psychology, Vol. 60 (April 1975), pp. 249-51.

Hise, Richard T. and McGinnis, Michael A.
"Evaluating the Effect of a Follow-Up Request on Mail Survey Results"
Akron Business and Economic Review, Vol. 5 (Winter 1974), pp. 19-21.

Hochstim, Joseph R. and Athanasopoulos, Demetrious A.
"Personal Follow-Up in a Mail Survey: Its Contribution and Its Cost"
Public Opinion Quarterly, Vol. 34 (Spring 1970), pp. 69-81.

Kephart, W. M. and Bressler, M.
"Increasing the Responses to Mail Questionnaires"
Public Opinion Quarterly, Vol. 22 (Summer 1958), pp. 123-32.

Levine, S. and Gordon, G.
"Maximizing Returns on Mail Questionnaires"
Public Opinion Quarterly, Vol. 22 (Winter 1958), pp. 568-75.

Lindsay, E. E.
"Questionnaires and Follow-Up Letters"
Pedagogical Seminary, Vol. 28 (September 1921), pp. 303-7.

Nichols, Robert C. and Meyer, Mary Alice
"Timing Post-Card Follow-Ups in Mail Surveys"
Public Opinion Quarterly, Vol. 30 (Summer 1966), pp. 306,7.

Paliwoda, S. J.
"Using a Mail Questionnaire as a Research Tool"
Quarterly Review of Marketing, Vol. 6 (1981), pp. 9-14.

Peterson, Robert A.
"An Experimental Investigation of Mail-Survey Responses"
Journal of Business Research, Vol. 3 (July 1975), pp. 199-209.

Pucel, D. J., Nelson, H. F., and Wheeler, D. N.
"Questionnaire Follow-Up Returns as a Function of Incentives and
Responder Characteristics"
Vocational Guidance Quarterly, Vol. 19 (March 1971), pp. 188-93.

Robin, S. S.
"A Procedure for Securing Returns to Mail Questionnaires"
Sociology and Social Research, Vol. 50 (1965), pp. 24-36.

Roscoe, A. Marvin, Lang, Dorothy, and Sheth, Jagdish N.
    "Follow-Up Methods, Questionnaire Length, and Market Differences in
    Mail Surveys"
    Journal of Marketing, Vol. 39 (April 1975), pp. 20-7.

Sheth, Jagdish N. and Roscoe, A. Marvin, Jr.
    "Impact of Questionnaire Length, Follow-Up Methods, and Geographical
    Location on Response to a Mail Survey"
    Journal of Applied Psychology, Vol. 60 (April 1975), p. 254.

Sirken, M. G. and Brown, M. L.
    "Quality of Data Elicited by Successive Mailings in Mail Surveys"
    Proceedings, Social Statistics Section, American Statistical
    Association (1962), pp. 118-25.

Sletto, R. F.
    "Pretesting of Questionnaires"
    American Sociological Review, Vol. 5 (1940), pp. 193-200.

Suchman, E. A. and McCandless, B.
    "Who Answers Questionnaires?"
    Journal of Applied Psychology, Vol. 24 (1940), pp. 758-69.

Sudman, Seymour
    "Estimating Response to Follow-Ups in Mail Surveys"
    Public Opinion Quarterly, Vol. 46 (1982), pp. 582-4.

Tallent, Norman and Reiss, William J.
    "A Note on an Unusually High Rate of Returns for a Mail Questionnaire"
    Public Opinion Quarterly, Vol. 23 (Winter 1959), pp. 579-81.

Tedin, Kent L. and Hofstetter, Richard
    "The Effect of Cost and Importance Factors on the Return Rate for
    Single and Multiple Mailings"
    Public Opinion Quarterly, Vol. 46 (1982), pp. 122-8.

Von Reisen, R. D.
    "Postcard Reminders Versus Questionnaires and Mail Survey Response
    Rates From a Professional Population"
    Journal of Business Research, Vol. 7 (1979), pp. 1-7.

68.16 ---------- Postage

Armstrong, J. Scott and Lusk, Edward J.
    "Return Postage in Mail Surveys: A Meta-Analysis"
    Public Opinion Quarterly, Vol. 51 (Summer 1987), pp. 233-48.

Bridge, R. G.
    "Alternative Postage Methods in Mail Surveys"
    Survey Research Center Occasional Paper No. 7101
    University of California at Los Angeles (1971).

Brook, Lindsay L.
    "The Effect of Different Postage Combinations on Response Levels and
    Speed of Reply"
    Journal of the Market Research Society, Vol. 20 (October 1978), pp.
    238-44.

Champion, Dean J. and Sear, Alan M.
    "Questionnaire Response Rates: A Methodological Analysis"
    Social Forces, Vol. 47 (March 1969), pp. 335-9.

Clark, Gary L. and Kaminski, Peter F.
    "How to Get More for Your Money in Mail Surveys"
    Journal of Consumer Marketing (Summer 1989).

Clausen, J. A. and Ford, R. N.
    "Controlling Bias in Mail Questionnaires"
    Journal of the American Statistical Association, Vol. 42 (1947), pp.
    497-511.

Gullahorn, Jeanne E. and Gullahorn, John T.
    "Increasing Returns From Non-Respondents"
    Public Opinion Quarterly, Vol. 23 (1959), pp. 118-21.

Hammond, E. C.
    "Isolation in Relation to Type and Amount of Smoking"
    Journal of the American Statistical Association, Vol. 54 (1959), pp.
    35-51.

Harris, James R. and Guffey, Hugh J., Jr.
    "Questionnaire Returns: Stamps Versus Business Reply Envelopes
    Revisited"
    Journal of Marketing Research, Vol. XV (May 1978), pp. 290-3.

Harvey, Lee
"A Research Note on the Impact of Class-of-Mail on Response Rates to
Mailed Questionnaires"
Journal of the Market Research Society, Vol. 28 (July 1986), pp.
299,300.

Hensley, Wayne E.
"Increasing Response Rate by Choice of Postage Stamps"
Public Opinion Quarterly, Vol. 38 (1974), pp. 280-3.

Hewett, W. C.
"How Different Combinations of Postage on Outgoing and Return
Envelopes Affect Questionnaire Returns"
Journal of the Market Research Society, Vol. 16 (January 1974), pp.
49,50.

Hopkins, K. D. and Podolak, J.
"Class of Mail and the Effects of Monetary Gratuity on the Response
Rate of Mail Questionnaires"
Journal of Experimental Education, Vol. 51 (1983), pp. 69,70.

Kephart, W. M. and Bressler, M.
"Increasing the Response Rate of Mail Questionnaires"
Journal of Experimental Education, Vol. 51 (1958), pp. 123-32.

Kernan, Jerome B.
"Are 'Bulk-Rate Occupants' Really Unresponsive?"
Public Opinion Quarterly, Vol. 35 (1971), pp. 420-2.

Kimball, Andrew E.
"Increasing the Rate of Return in Mail Surveys"
Journal of Marketing, Vol. 25 (October 1961), pp. 63-5.

Longworth, D. S.
"Use of a Mailed Questionnaire"
American Sociological Review, Vol. 18 (June 1953), pp. 310-3.

Mayer, Edward N., Jr.
"Postage Stamps do Affect Your Mailing"
Printers' Ink, Vol. 217 (October 4, 1946), pp. 91-3.

McCrohan, Kevin F. and Lowe, Larry S.
"A Cost/Benefit Approach to Postage Used on Mail Questionnaires"
Journal of Marketing, Vol. 45 (Winter 1981), pp. 130-3.

Newland, C. A., Waters, W. E., Standford, A. P., and Batchelor, B. G.
"A Study of Mail Survey Method"
International Journal of Epidemiology, Vol. 6, No. 1 (1977), pp. 65-7.

Perry, Norman
"Postage Combinations in Postal Questionnaire Surveys--Another View"
Journal of the Market Research Society, Vol. 16 (July 1974), pp.
245,6.

Peterson, Robert A.
"An Experimental Investigation of Mail-Survey Responses"
Journal of Business Research, Vol. 3 (July 1975), pp. 199-209.

Price, D. O.
"The Use of Stamped Return Envelopes With Mailed Questionnaires"
American Sociological Review, Vol. 15 (1950), pp. 672,3.

Robertson, Dan H. and Hackett, Donald W.
"Saleswomen: Perceptions, Problems and Prospects"
Journal of Marketing, Vol. 41 (July 1977), pp. 66-71.

Robinson, R. A. and Agasim, Philip
"Making Mail Surveys More Reliable"
Journal of Marketing, Vol. 15 (April 1951), pp. 415-24.

Shaffer, J. D.
"Differences in Costs and Returns of Stamped and Business Reply
Envelopes in a Mail Survey"
Journal of Farm Economics, Vol. 41 (May 1959), pp. 268-71.

Wallace, D.
"A Case For and Against Mail Questionnaires"
Public Opinion Quarterly, Vol. 18 (1954), pp. 40-52.

Watson, J. J.
"Improving the Response Rate in Mail Research"
Journal of Advertising Research, Vol. 5 (1965), pp. 48-50.

Wolfe, Arthur C. and Treiman, Beatrice R.
"Postage Types and Response Rates to Mail Surveys"
Journal of Advertising Research, Vol. 19 (February 1979), pp. 43-8.

68.17 ---------- Appeal

Bachmann, Duane P.
"Cover Letter Appeals and Sponsorship Effects on Mail Survey Response Rates"
Journal of Marketing Education, Vol. 9 (Fall 1987), pp. 45-51.

Champion, D. J. and Sear, A. M.
"Questionnaire Response Rates: A Methodological Analysis"
Social Forces, Vol. 47 (March 1969), pp. 335-9.

Childers, Terry L., Pride, William M., and Ferrell, O. C.
"A Reassessment of the Effects of Appeals on Response to Mail Surveys"
Journal of Marketing Research, Vol. XVII (August 1980), pp. 365-70.

Dommeyer, Curt J.
"The Effects of Negative Cover Letter Appeals on Mail Survey Response"
Journal of the Market Research Society, Vol. 29 (October 1987), pp. 445-51.

Doob, A. N. and Zabrack, M.
"The Effect of Freedom-Threatening Instructions and Monetary Inducement on Compliance"
Canadian Journal of Behavioral Science, Vol. 3 (1971), pp. 408-12.

Hendrick, Clyde, Borden, Richard, Giesen, Martin, Murray, Edward J., and Seyfried, B. A.
"Effectiveness of Ingratiation Tactics in a Cover Letter on Mail Questionnaires"
Psychonomic Science, Vol. 26 (1972), pp. 349-5.

Houston, Michael J. and Nevin, John R.
"The Effect of Source and Appeal on Mail Survey Response Patterns"
Journal of Marketing Research, Vol. XIV (August 1977), pp. 374-8.

Linsky, A.
"A Factorial Experiment in Inducing Responses to a Mail Questionnaire"
Sociology and Social Research, Vol. 49 (January 1965), pp. 183-9.

May, R. C.
"What Approach Gets the Best Return in Mail Surveys?"
Industrial Marketing, Vol. 45 (1960), pp. 50,1.

Tyagi, Pradeep K.
"The Effects of Appeals, Anonymity, and Feedback on Mail Survey Response Patterns From Salespeople"
Journal of the Academy of Marketing Science, Vol. 17 (Summer 1989), pp. 235-41.

68.18 ---------- Deadlines

Futrell, Charles M. and Hise, Richard T.
"The Effects of Anonymity and a Deadline on the Response Rate to Mail Surveys"
European Research, Vol. 10 (October 1982), pp. 171-5.

Henley, James R., Jr.
"Response Rate to Mail Questionnaires With a Return Deadline"
Public Opinion Quarterly, Vol. 40 (Fall 1976), pp. 374,5.

Nevin, John R. and Ford, Neil M.
"Effects of a Deadline and a Veiled Threat on Mail Survey Responses"
Journal of Applied Psychology, Vol. 61 (February 1976), pp. 116-8.

Roberts, Robert F., McCrory, Owen F., and Forthofer, Ronald N.
"Further Evidence on Using a Deadline to Stimulate Responses to a Mail Survey"
Public Opinion Quarterly (1978), pp. 407-10.

Vocino, T.
"Three Variables in Stimulating Responses to Mailed Questionnaires"
Journal of Marketing, Vol. 41 (1977), pp. 76,7.

68.19 ---------- Source or Sponsor

Albaum, Gerald
"Do Source and Anonymity Affect Mail Survey Results?"
Journal of the Academy of Marketing Science, Vol. 15 (Fall 1987), pp. 74-81.

Ayal, Igal and Hornik, Jacob
"Foreign Source Effects on Response Behavior in Cross-National Mail Surveys"
International Journal of Research in Marketing, Vol. 3, No. 3 (1986), pp. 157-67.

Bachmann, Duane P.
"Cover Letter Appeals and Sponsorship Effects on Mail Survey Response Rates"
Journal of Marketing Education, Vol. 9 (Fall 1987), pp. 45-51.

Doob, Anthony N., Freedman, Jonathan L., and Carlsmith, J. Merrill
"Effects of Sponsor and Prepayment Compliance With a Mailed Request"
Journal of Applied Psychology, Vol. 57 (June 1973), pp. 346,7.

Erdos, P. and Regier, J.
"Visible vs. Disguised Keying on Questionnaires"
Journal of Advertising Research, Vol. 17 (1977), pp. 13-8.

Faria, A. J. and Dickinson, John R.
"The Effect of Survey Sponsor, Questionnaire Length, and Anonymity on Mail Survey Response Rate and Response Speed"
World Marketing Congress, Academy of Marketing Science, Singapore (July 1989), paper presentation.

Futrell, Charles M.
"Effects of Signed Versus Unsigned Attitude Questionnaires"
Journal of the Academy of Marketing Science, Vol. 9 (Spring 1981), pp. 93-8.

Hawes, Jon M., Crittenden, Vicky L., and Crittenden, William F.
"The Effects of Personalization, Source, and Offer on Mail Survey Response Rate and Speed"
Akron Business and Economic Review, Vol. 18 (Summer 1987), pp. 54-63.

Hawkins, Del I.
"The Impact of Sponsor Identification and Direct Disclosure of Respondent Rights on the Quantity and Quality of Mail Survey Data"
Journal of Business, Vol. 52 (October 1979), pp. 577-90.

Houston, Michael J. and Nevin, John R.
"The Effects of Source and Appeal on Mail Survey Response Patterns"
Journal of Marketing Research, Vol. XIV (August 1977), pp. 374-8.

Jones, Wesley H.
"Generalizing Mail Survey Inducement Methods: Population Interactions With Anonymity and Sponsorship"
Public Opinion Quarterly, Vol. 43 (Spring 1979), pp. 102-11.

Jones, Wesley H. and Lang, J.
"Sample Composition Bias and Response Bias in a Mail Survey: A Comparison of Inducement Methods"
Journal of Marketing Research, Vol. XVII (February 1980), pp. 69-76.

Jones, Wesley H. and Linda, Gerald
"Multiple Criteria Effects in a Mail Survey Experiment"
Journal of Marketing Research, Vol. XV (May 1978), pp. 280-4.

Nitecki, D.
"Effects of Sponsorship and Nonmonetary Incentive on Response Rate"
Journalism Quarterly, Vol. 55 (1975), pp. 581-3.

Peterson, Robert A.
"An Experimental Investigation of Mail Survey Responses"
Journal of Business Research, Vol. 3 (July 1975), pp. 199-210.

Resnik, Alan J. and Harmon, Robert R.
"The Impact of Sponsorship, Labeling and Incentives on Mail Survey Response Rates: A Foot-in-the-Door Perspective"
in Lusch, Robert F. et al. (editors)
1985 AMA Educators' Conference Proceedings
(Chicago: American Marketing Association, 1985), pp. 59-64.

68.20 ---------- Topic or Subject Matter

Blair, William S.
"How Subject Matter Can Bias a Mail Survey"
Media/Scope, Vol. 8 (February 1964), pp. 70-2.

Dommeyer, Curt J.
"Does Response to an Offer of Mail Survey Results Interact With Questionnaire Interest?"
Journal of the Market Research Society, Vol. 27 (January 1985), pp. 27-38.

68.21 ---------- Miscellaneous Factors Affecting Response Rates

Brown, Morton B.
"Use of a Postcard Query in Mail Surveys"
Public Opinion Quarterly, Vol. 29 (1965-66), pp. 635-7.

Eisenger, Richard A., Janicki, Peter W., Stevenson, Robert L., and
Thompson, W. L.
"Increasing Returns in International Mail Surveys"
Public Opinion Quarterly, Vol. 38 (Spring 1974), pp. 297-301.

Erdos, Paul L. and Regier, James
"Visible vs. Disguised Keying on Questionnaires"
Journal of Advertising Research, Vol. 17 (February 1977), pp. 13-8.

Falthzik, A. M. and Carroll, S. J.
"Rate of Return for Close vs. Open-Ended Questions in a Mail Survey
of Industrial Organizations"
Psychological Reports, Vol. 29 (1971), pp. 1121,2.

Ferris, Abbot L.
"A Note on Stimulating Response to Questionnaires"
American Sociological Review, Vol. 16 (April 1951), pp. 247-9.

Field, Hubert S.
"Effects of Sex of Investigator on Mail Survey Response Rates and
Response Bias"
Journal of Applied Psychology, Vol. 60 (December 1975), pp. 772,3.

Forsythe, John B.
"Obtaining Cooperation in a Survey of Business Executives"
Journal of Marketing Research, Vol. XIV (August 1977), pp. 370-3.

Francel, E. G.
"Mail-Administered Questionnaires: A Success Story"
Journal of Marketing Research, Vol. III (February 1966), pp. 89-92.

Frazier, George and Bird, Kermit
"Increasing the Response of a Mail Questionnaire"
Journal of Marketing, Vol. 22 (October 1958), pp. 186,7.

Friedman, Hershey H. and Goldstein, Larry
"Effect of Ethnicity of Signature on the Rate of Return and Content
of a Mail Questionnaire"
Journal of Applied Psychology, Vol. 60 (December 1975), pp. 770,1.

Friedman, Hershey H. and San Augustine, Andre J.
"The Effects of a Monetary Incentive and the Ethnicity of the
Sponsor's Signature on the Rate and Quality of Response to a Mail
Survey"
Journal of the Academy of Marketing Science, Vol. 7 (Winter-Spring
1979), pp. 95-101.

Giles, W. F. and Field, H. S.
"Effects of Amount, Format, and Location of Demographic Information
on Questionnaire Return Rate and Response Bias of Sensitive and
Nonsensitive Items"
Personnel Psychology, Vol. 31 (August 1978), pp. 549-59.

Goldstein, Hyman and Kroll, Bernard H.
"Methods of Increasing Mail Response"
Journal of Marketing, Vol. 21 (July 1957), pp. 55-7.

Goldstein, Larry and Friedman, Hershey H.
"A Case for Double Postcards in Surveys"
Journal of Advertising Research, Vol. 15 (April 1975), pp. 43-7.

Gullahorn, Jeanne E. and Gullahorn, John T.
"An Investigation of the Effects of Three Factors on Response to Mail
Questionnaires"
Public Opinion Quarterly, Vol. 27 (Summer 1963), pp. 294-6.

Heads, J. and Thrift, H. J.
"Notes on a Study in Postal Response Rates"
Commentary (JMRS), Vol. VIII (1966), pp. 257-62.

Hoppe, A. D.
"Certain Factors Found to Improve Mail Survey Returns"
Proceedings, Iowa Academy of Science, Vol. 59 (1952), pp. 374-6.

Hornik, Jacob
"Time Cue and Time Perception Effect on Response to Mail Surveys"
Journal of Marketing Research, Vol. XVIII (May 1981), pp. 243-8.

Jobber, David and Sanderson, Stuart
"The Effect of Two Variables on Industrial Mail Survey Returns"
Industrial Marketing Management, Vol. 14 (May 1985), pp. 119-21.

Kindra, G. S., McGown, K. L., and Bougie, M.
"Stimulating Responses to Mailed Questionnaires: An Experimental
Study"
International Journal of Research in Marketing, Vol. 2, No. 3 (1985),
pp. 219-35.

Labrecque, David P.
    "A Response Rate Experiment Using Mail Questionnaires"
    Journal of Marketing, Vol. 42 (October 1978), pp. 82,3.

Laurent, A.
    "Effects of Question Length on Reporting Behavior in the Survey
    Interview"
    Journal of the American Statistical Association, Vol. 67 (1972), pp.
    298-305.

Little, Taylor E., Jr. and Pressley, Milton M.
    "A Multifactor Experiment on the Generalizability of Direct Mail
    Advertising Response Techniques to Mail Survey Design"
    Journal of the Academy of Marketing Science, Vol. 8 (Fall 1980), pp.
    390-404.

Martin, J. David and McConnell, Jon P.
    "Mail Questionnaire Response Induction: The Effect of Four Variables
    on the Response of a Random Sample to a Difficult Questionnaire"
    Social Science Quarterly, Vol. 51 (September 1973), pp. 409-14.

Martin, Warren S., Duncan, W. J., and Sawyer, J. C.
    "The Interactive Effects of Four Response Rate Inducements in Mail
    Questionnaires"
    University of Alabama, College Student Journal, Vol. 18 (1984), pp.
    143-9.

Mason, Ward S., Dressel, Robert J., and Bain, Robert K.
    "An Experimental Study of Factors Affecting Response to a Mail Survey
    of Beginning Teachers"
    Public Opinion Quarterly, Vol. 25 (Summer 1961), pp. 296-9.

McGinnis, Michael A. and Hollon, Charles J.
    "Mail Survey Response Rate and Bias: The Effect of Home Versus Work
    Address"
    Journal of Marketing Research, Vol. XIV (August 1977), pp. 383,4.

Neider, Linda L. and Sugrue, Paul K.
    "Addressing Procedures as a Mail Survey Inducement Technique"
    Journal of the Academy of Marketing Science, Vol. 11 (Fall 1983), pp.
    455-60.

Orr, D. B. and Neyman, C. A., Jr.
    "Considerations, Costs and Returns in a Large-Scale Follow-Up Study"
    Journal of Educational Research, Vol. 58 (April 1965), pp. 373-8.

Pace, C. Robert
    "Factors Influencing Questionnaire Returns From Former University
    Students"
    Journal of Applied Psychology, Vol. 23 (June 1939), pp. 388-97.

Pressley, Milton M. and Tullar, William L.
    "A Factor Interactive Investigation of Mail Survey Response Rates
    From a Commercial Population"
    Journal of Marketing Research, Vol. XIV (February 1977), pp. 108-11.

Price, D. O.
    "On the Use of Stamped Return Envelopes With Mail Questionnaires"
    American Sociological Review, Vol. 15 (October, 1950), pp. 672,3.

Roeher, G. Allan
    "Effective Techniques in Increasing Response to Mailed Questionnaires"
    Public Opinion Quarterly, Vol. 27 (Summer 1963), pp. 299-302.

Sheth, Jagdish N., Leclaire, Arthur, Jr., and Wachspress, David
    "Impact of Asking Race Information in Mail Surveys"
    Journal of Marketing, Vol. 44 (Winter 1980), pp. 67-70.

Singer, E.
    "Informed Consent: Consequences for Response Rate and Response
    Quality in Social Surveys"
    American Sociological Review, Vol. 43, No. 2 (1978), pp. 144-62.

Slocum, W. L., Empey, L. T., and Swanson, H. S.
    "Increasing Response to Questionnaires and Structured Interviews"
    American Sociological Review, Vol. XXI (April 1956), pp. 221-5.

Stevins, Robert E.
    "Does Precoding Mail Questionnaires Affect Response Rates"
    Public Opinion Quarterly, Vol. 38 (Winter 1974-75), pp. 621,2.

Tallent, Norman and Reiss, William J.
    "A Note on an Unusually High Rate of Returns for a Mail Questionnaire"
    Public Opinion Quarterly, Vol. 23 (Winter 1959), pp. 579-81.

Vocino, Thomas
    "Three Variables in Stimulating Responses to Mailed Questionnaires"
    Journal of Marketing, Vol. 41 (October 1977), pp. 76,7.

68.22 ---------- Unclassified (Mail Surveys - Increasing Resp Rates)

Backrack, Stanley D. and Scoble, Harry M.
"Mail Questionnaire Efficiency: Controlled Reduction of Nonresponse"
Public Opinion Quarterly, Vol. 31 (1967), pp. 265-71.

Ballweg, J. A.
"Husband-Wife Response Similarities on Evaluative and Non-Evaluative Survey Questions"
Public Opinion Quarterly, Vol. 33 (Summer 1969), pp. 249-54.

Cahalan, Don
"Effectiveness of a Mail Questionnaire Technique in the Army"
Public Opinion Quarterly, Vol. 15 (Fall 1951), pp. 575-8.

Childers, Terry L. and Skinner, Steven J.
"Gaining Respondent Cooperation in Mail Surveys Through Prior Commitment"
Public Opinion Quarterly, Vol. 16 (Winter 1979), pp. 558-61.

De Jonge, Leendert and Oppedijk Van Veen, Walle M.
"The Response Pattern in a Longitudinal Mail Survey and Some Cost Considerations"
European Research, Vol. 6 (July 1978), pp. 136-44.

Deutscher, Irwin
"Physicians' Reaction to a Mailed Questionnaire: A Study in Resistentialism"
Public Opinion Quarterly, Vol. 20 (Fall 1956), pp. 599-604.

Dillman, Don A.
"Increasing Mail Questionnaire Response in Large Samples of the General Public"
Public Opinion Quarterly, Vol. 36 (Summer 1972), pp. 254-7.

Dillman, Don A., Christenson, James A., Carpenter, Edwin H., and Brooks, Ralph M.
"Increasing Mail Questionnaire Response: A Four State Comparison"
American Sociological Review, Vol. 39 (October 1974), pp. 744-56.

Dimling, John A., Jr.
"Rates of Response in Local Television Research"
Proceedings, Business and Economic Statistics Section, American Statistical Association (1975), pp. 86-9.

Goyder, John C.
"Further Evidence on Factors Affecting Response Rates to Mailed Questionnaires"
American Sociological Review, Vol. 47 (August 1982), pp. 550-3.

Hinrichs, J. R.
"Factors Related to Survey Response Rates"
Journal of Applied Psychology, Vol. 60, No. 2 (1975), pp. 249-51.

Hochstim, Joseph R.
"A Critical Comparison of Three Strategies of Collecting Data From Households"
Journal of the American Statistical Society, Vol. 62 (September 1967), pp. 976-89.

House, James S., Gerber, Wayne, and McMichael, Anthony J.
"Increasing Mail Questionnaire Response: A Controlled Replication and Extension"
Public Opinion Quarterly, Vol. 41 (1977), pp. 95-9.

Keane, John G.
"Low Cost, High Return Mail Surveys"
Journal of Advertising Research, Vol. 3 (September 1963), pp. 28-30.

Knox, John B.
"Maximizing Responses to Mail Questionnaires"
Public Opinion Quarterly, Vol. 15 (Summer 1951), pp. 366,7.

Knudson, Dean O., Pope, Hallowell, and Irish, Donald P.
"Response Differences to Questions on Sexual Standards: An Interview Questionnaire Comparison"
Public Opinion Quarterly, Vol. 31 (Summer 1967), pp. 290-7.

Leslie, L. L.
"Increasing Response Rates to Long Questionnaires"
Journal of Educational Research, Vol. 63 (April 1970), pp. 347-50.

Levine, Sol and Gordon, Gerald
"Maximizing Returns on Mail Questionnaires"
Public Opinion Quarterly, Vol. 22 (Winter 1958), pp. 568-75.

Linsky, Arnold S.
"A Factorial Experiment in Inducing Responses to a Mail Questionnaire"
Sociology and Social Research, Vol. 49 (January 1965), pp. 183-9.

McDonagh, Edward C. and Rosenblum, A. Leon
    "A Comparison of Mailed Questionnaires and Subsequent Structured
    Interviews"
    Public Opinion Quarterly, Vol. 29 (Spring 1965), pp. 131-6.

Nuckols, Robert C.
    "The Validity and Comparability of Mail and Personal Interview
    Surveys"
    Journal of Marketing Research, Vol. I (February 1964), pp. 11-6.

O'Dell, William F.
    "Personal Interviews or Mail Panels"
    Journal of Marketing, Vol. 26 (October 1962), pp. 34-9.

Petry, Glenn H. and Quackenbush, Stanley F.
    "The Conservation of the Questionnaire as a Research Resource"
    Business Horizons, Vol. 17 (August 1974), pp. 43-50.

Power, A. P. and Beaumont, J. A.
    "Anatomy of a Postal Survey"
    Statistical News, Vol. 30 (August 1975), pp. 7-11.

Scott, Christopher
    "Research on Mail Surveys"
    Journal of the Royal Statistical Society, Vol. 124 (February 15,
    1961), pp. 143-205.

Shosteck, H. and Fairweather, W. R.
    "Physician Response Rates to Mail and Personal Interview Surveys"
    Public Opinion Quarterly, Vol. 43 (Summer 1979), pp. 206-16.

Shuttleworth, Frank K.
    "A Study of Questionnaire Technique"
    The Journal of Educational Psychology, Vol. 22 (December 1931), pp.
    652-8.

Stevens, R. E.
    "Does Precoding Mail Questionnaires Affect Response Rates?"
    Public Opinion Quarterly, Vol. 38 (1974), pp. 621,2.

Veiga, John F.
    "Getting the Mail Questionnaire Returned: Some Practical Research
    Considerations"
    Journal of Applied Psychology, Vol. 59 (April 1974), pp. 217,8.

Walker, Bruce J., Kirchmann, Wayne, and Conant, Jeffrey S.
    "A Method to Improve Response to Industrial Mail Surveys"
    Industrial Marketing Management, Vol. 16 (November 1987), pp. 305-14.

Wind, Yoram and Learner, David
    "A Note on the Measurement of Purchase Data Surveys vs. Purchase
    Diaries"
    Wharton School (1977), working paper.

Wiseman, Frederick
    "Methodological Bias in Public Opinion Surveys"
    Public Opinion Quarterly, Vol. 36 (Spring 1972), pp. 105-8.

69 ------------------ MAIL SURVEYS - RESPONSE SPEED ------------------
        See also (sub)heading(s) 67, 67.06, 68, 70, 71, 72.

69.01 ---------- Speed of Response Patterns in Mail Surveys

Cox, William E.
"Response Patterns to Mail Surveys"
Journal of Marketing Research, Vol. III (November 1966), pp. 392-7.

De Jonge, Leen, Oppedijk Van Veen, Walle M., and Pooters, Cor
"Accounting for the Speed of Response in Mail-Panel Surveys"
European Research (July 1977), pp. 172-80.

Gray, P. G.
"A Sample Survey With Both a Postal and an Interview Stage"
Applied Statistics, Vol. 6 (June 1957), pp. 139-53.

Hill, Richard W.
"Using S-Shaped Curves to Predict Response Rates"
Journal of Marketing Research, Vol. XVIII (May 1981), pp. 240-2.

Huxley, Stephen J.
"Predicting Response Speed in Mail Surveys"
Journal of Marketing Research, Vol. XVII (February 1980), pp. 63-8.

Lawson, Faith
"Varying Group Responses to Postal Questionnaires"
Public Opinion Quarterly, Vol. 13 (Spring 1949), pp. 114-6.

Lindsay, E. E.
"Questionnaires and Follow-Up Letters"
Pedagogical Seinary, Vol. 28 (September 1921), pp. 303-7.

Manfield, M. N.
"Similarity Between American and British Experience With Mail Returns"
Public Opinion Quarterly, Vol. 13 (Fall 1949), pp. 563,4.

Manfield, M. N.
"A Pattern of Response to Mail Surveys"
Public Opinion Quarterly, Vol. 12 (Fall 1948), pp. 493-5.

Nederhof, Anton J.
"A Comparison of European and North American Response Patterns in Mail Surveys"
Journal of the Market Research Society, Vol. 27 (January 1985), pp. 55-63.

Parasuraman, A.
"More on the Prediction of Mail Survey Response Rates"
Journal of Marketing Research, Vol. XIX (May 1982), pp. 261-8.

Robinson, R. A. and Agasim, Philip
"Making Mail Surveys More Reliable"
Journal of Marketing, Vol. 15 (April 1951), pp. 415-24.

Scott, Christopher
"Research on Mail Surveys"
Journal of the Royal Statistical Society, Series A, Vol. 124 (Part 2, 1961), pp. 143-205.

Stanton, F.
"Notes on the Validity of Mail Questionnaire Returns"
Journal of Applied Psychology, Vol. 23 (1939), pp. 95-104.

Tallent, Norman and Reiss, William J.
"A Note on an Unusually High Rate of Returns for a Mail Questionnaire"
Public Opinion Quarterly, Vol. 23 (Winter 1959), pp. 579-81.

69.02 ---------- Factors Affecting Speed of Response in Mail Surveys

Brook, Lindsay L.
"The Effect of Different Postage Combinations on Response Levels and Speed of Reply"
Journal of the Market Research Society, Vol. 20 (October 1978), pp. 238-44.

Cox, Eli P., III, Anderson, W. Thomas, Jr., and Fulcher, David G.
"Reappraising Mail Survey Response Rates"
Journal of Marketing Research, Vol. XI (November 1974), pp. 413-7.

Cox, William E., Jr.
"Response Patterns to Mail Surveys"
Journal of Marketing Research, Vol. III (November 1966), pp. 392-7.

Dommeyer, Curt J.
"How Form of the Monetary Incentive Affects Mail Survey Response"
Journal of the Market Research Society, Vol. 30 (July 1988), pp. 379-84.

Dommeyer, Curt J.
"Questionnaire Interest?"
Journal of the Market Research Society, Vol. 27 (January 1985), pp.
27-38.

Faria, A. J. and Dickinson, John R.
"The Effect of Survey Sponsor, Questionnaire Length, and Anonymity on
Mail Survey Response Rate and Response Speed"
World Marketing Congress, Academy of Marketing Science, Singapore
(July 1989), paper presentation.

Ford, Neil M.
"The Advance Letter in Mail Surveys"
Journal of Marketing Research, Vol. IV (May 1967), pp. 202-4.

Gajraj, Ananda M., Dickinson, John R., and Faria, A. J.
"A Comparison of the Effect of Promised and Provided Lotteries,
Monetary, and Gift Incentives on Mail Survey Response Rate, Speed,
and Cost"
Journal of the Market Research Society, Vol. 32 (1990).

Gajraj, Ananda M., Dickinson, John R., and Faria, A. J.
"A Comparison of the Effect of Promised and Provided Lotteries,
Monetary, and Gift Incentives on Mail Survey Response Rate, Speed,
and Cost" (Abstract)
Proceedings, American Marketing Association (August 1989).

Hawes, Jon M., Crittenden, Vicky L., and Crittenden, William F.
"The Effects of Personalization, Source, and Offer on Mail Survey
Response Rate and Speed"
Akron Business and Economic Review, Vol. 18 (Summer 1987), pp. 54-63.

Hornik, Jacob
"Time Cue and Time Perception Effect on Response to Mail Surveys"
Journal of Marketing Research, Vol. XVIII (May 1981), pp. 243-8.

Houston, Michael J. and Jefferson, Robert W.
"The Negative Effects of Personalization on Response Patterns in Mail
Surveys"
Journal of Marketing Research, Vol. XII (February 1975), pp. 114-7.

Little, Taylor E., Jr. and Pressley, Milton M.
"A Multifactor Experiment on the Generalizability of Direct Mail
Advertising Response Techniques to Mail Survey Design"
Journal of the Academy of Marketing Science, Vol. 8 (Fall 1980), pp.
390-404.

Nevin, John R. and Ford, Neil M.
"Effects of a Deadline and a Veiled Threat on Mail Survey Responses"
Journal of Applied Psychology, Vol. 61 (February 1976), pp. 116-8.

Robinson, R. A. and Agasim, P.
"Making Mail Surveys More Reliable"
Journal of Marketing, Vol. XV (April 1951), pp. 415-24.

70 ---------- EARLY VERSUS LATE RESPONDENTS TO MAIL SURVEYS ----------
          See also (sub)heading(s) 67, 68, 69, 71, 72, 117.04.

Anastasiow, N. J.
  "A Methodological Framework for Analyzing Non-Response to
  Questionnaires"
  California Journal of Educational Research, Vol. 15, No. 4 (1964),
  pp. 205-8.

Ball, R. J.
  "The Correspondence Method in Follow-Up Studies of Delinquent Boys"
  Journal of Juvenile Research, Vol. 14 (1930), pp. 107-13.

Baur, E. J.
  "Response Bias in a Mail Survey"
  Public Opinion Quarterly, Vol. 11 (Winter 1947), pp. 394-600.

Berdie, Douglas R.
  "Reassessing the Value of High Response Rates to Mail Surveys"
  Marketing Research, Vol. 1 (September 1989), pp. 52-64.

Bobren, Howard M.
  "The Time Order of Response and Nonresponse Bias in Mail Surveys"
  University of Illinois (1962), unpublished Ph.D. dissertation, 74 pp.

Borton, W. M.
  A Comparison of Attitudes of University Seniors and Sales Executives
  Toward Outside Selling as Revealed by Clinical Interview and
  Questionnaire Method"
  University of Southern California (1956), doctoral dissertation.

Byrnes, A. F.
  A Study of Job Satisfactions and Dissatisfactions of Teachers in
  Selected Schools of Indiana"
  New York University (1951), doctoral dissertation.

De Jonge, Leen, Oppedijk Van Veen, Walle M., and Pooters, Cor
  "Accounting for the Speed of Response in Mail-Panel Surveys"
  European Research (July 1977), pp. 172-80.

Dickinson, John R. and Kirzner, Eric
  "Early Survey Respondents May be Sufficient"
  Proceedings, Administrative Sciences Association of Canada (May 1983).

Dickinson, John R. and Kirzner, Eric
  "An Absence of Bias in Attribute Preferences Between Early and Total
  Sample Survey Respondents"
  Proceedings, American Institute for Decision Sciences (November 1982).

Dickinson, John R. and Kirzner, Eric
  "An Absence of Bias in Attribute Preferences Between Early and Total
  Sample Survey Respondents"
  in White, Greg (editor)
  Proceedings, American Institute for Decision Sciences (1982).

Dickinson, John R. and Kirzner, Eric
  "Are Late Survey Respondents Worth Waiting For? An Analysis of
  Demographics"
  in Kothari, Vinay (editor)
  Developments in Marketing Science, Volume Five
  (Academy of Marketing Science, 1982), pp. 370-3.

Dickinson, John R. and Kirzner, Eric
  "Planned Purchases of Early, Late, and Total Sample Survey
  Respondents"
  in Corrigan, Daniel R., Kraft, Frederic B., and Ross, Robert H.
  (editors)
  Proceedings, Southwestern Marketing Association Conference (1982),
  pp. 47-50.

Donald, M. N.
  "Implications of Nonresponse for the Interpretation of Mail
  Questionnaire Data"
  Public Opinion Quarterly, Vol. 24 (Spring 1960), pp. 90-114.

Ferber, R.
  "The Problem of Bias in Mail Returns: A Solution"
  Public Opinion Quarterly, Vol. 12 (Winter 1948), pp. 669-76.

Ford, R. N. and Zeisel, H.
  "Bias in Mail Surveys Cannot be Controlled by One Mailing"
  Public Opinion Quarterly, Vol. 13 (Fall 1949), pp. 495-501.

Goodstadt, Michael, Chung, Linda, Kronitz, Reena, and Cook, Gaynoll
  "Mail Survey Response Rates: Their Manipulation and Impact"
  Journal of Marketing Research, Vol. XIV (August 1977), pp. 391-5.

Leslie, Larry
  "Are High Response Rates Essential to Valid Surveys?"
  Social Science Research, Vol. 1 (September 1972), pp. 323-34.

McDaniel, Stephen W. and Rao, C. P.
"An Investigation of Response Quality and Demographic Characteristics of Initial vs. Post-Followup Respondents"
Proceedings, American Marketing Association Educators' Conference (1981), pp. 401-4.

Newman, Sheldon W.
"Differences Between Early and Late Respondents to a Mailed Survey"
Journal of Advertising Research, Vol. 2 (June 1962), pp. 37-9.

Pace, C. R.
"Factors Influencing Questionnaire Returns From Former University Students"
Journal of Applied Psychology, Vol. 23, No. 3 (1939), pp. 388-97.

Parasuraman, A.
"A Comparison of 'Early' vs. 'Late' Respondents in Mail Surveys of Commercial Populations"
in Ross, Robert H., Kraft, Frederic B., and Davis, Charles H. (editors)
1981 Proceedings, Southwestern Marketing Association Conference, New Orleans, pp. 239-42.

Pucel, D. J., Nelson, H. F., and Wheeler, D. N.
"Questionnaire Follow-Up Returns as a Function of Incentives and Responder Characteristics"
Vocational Guidance Quarterly, Vol. 19, No. 3 (1971), pp. 188-93.

Robinson, R. A. and Agasim, Philip
"Making Mail Surveys More Reliable"
Journal of Marketing, Vol. 15, No. 4 (1951), pp. 415-24.

Rollins, M.
"The Practical Use of Repeated Questionnaire Waves"
Journal of Applied Psychology, Vol. 24, No. 6 (1940), pp. 770-2.

Rothney, J. W. M. and Mooren, R. L.
"Sampling Problems in Follow-Up Research"
Occupations, Vol. 30, No. 8 (1952), pp. 573-8.

Shuttleworth, F. K.
"Sampling Errors Involved in Incomplete Returns to Mail Questionnaires"
Journal of Applied Psychology, Vol. 25, No. 4 (1941), pp. 588-91.

Stanton, F.
"Notes on the Validity of Mail Questionnaire Returns"
Journal of Applied Psychology, Vol. 23 (1939), pp. 95-104.

Suchman, Edward and McCandless, Boyd
"Who Answers Questionnaires?"
Journal of Applied Psychology, Vol. 24, No. 6 (1940), pp. 758-69.

71 ----------------- MAIL SURVEYS - RESPONSE QUALITY -----------------
        See also (sub)heading(s) 67, 68, 69, 70, 72, 116.

71.01 ---------- Response Quality: Item Omission

Craig, C. Samuel and McCann, John M.
    "Item Nonresponse in Mail Surveys: Extent and Correlates"
    Journal of Marketing Research, Vol. XV (May 1978), pp. 285-9.

Dickinson, John R. and Kirzner, Eric
    "Questionnaire Item Omission as a Function of Within-Group Question
    Position"
    Journal of Business Research, Vol. 13 (February 1985), pp. 71-5.

Dickinson, John R. and Kirzner, Eric
    "Split-Sample Reliability of a Secondary Sequence Effect on
    Questionnaire Item Omission"
    Proceedings, Academy of Marketing Science (May 1983).

Dickinson, John R. and Kirzner, Eric
    "A Secondary Order Effect on Questionnaire Item Omissions"
    in Laroche, Michel (editor)
    Proceedings, Administrative Sciences Association of Canada (1982),
    pp. 49-54.

Dickinson, John R. and Kirzner, Eric
    "Questionnaire Item Omission Rates by Question Content and Form"
    in Corrigan, Daniel R., Kraft, Frederic B., and Ross, Robert H.
    (editors)
    Proceedings, Southwestern Marketing Association (1982), pp. 54-7.

Dommeyer, Curt J.
    "Questionnaire Interest?"
    Journal of the Market Research Society, Vol. 27 (January 1985), pp.
    27-38.

Douglas, Susan and Shoemaker, Robert
    "Item Non-Response in Cross-National Attitude Surveys"
    European Research, Vol. 9 (July 1981), pp. 124-32.

Downs, Phillip E. and Kerr, John R.
    "Recent Evidence on the Relationship Between Anonymity and Response
    Variables for Mail Surveys"
    Journal of the Academy of Marketing Science, Vol. 14 (Spring 1986),
    pp. 72-82.

Durand, Richard M., Guffey, Hugh J., Jr., and Planchon, John M.
    "An Examination of the Random Versus Nonrandom Nature of Item
    Omissions"
    Journal of Marketing Research, Vol. XX (August 1983), pp. 305-13.

Ferber, Robert
    "Item Nonresponse in a Consumer Survey"
    Public Opinion Quarterly, Vol. 30 (Fall 1966), pp. 399-415.

Ford, Neil M.
    "The Advance Letter in Mail Surveys"
    Journal of Marketing Research, Vol. IV (May 1967), pp. 202-4.

Hansen, Robert A. and Scott, Carol A.
    "Alternative Approaches to Assessing the Quality of Self Report Data"
    in Hunt, H. Keith (editor)
    Advances in Consumer Research, Volume 5
    (Ann Arbor, MI: Association for Consumer Research, 1978), pp. 99-102.

Hansen, Robert A. and Scott, Carol A.
    "Improving the Representativeness of Survey Research: Some Issues and
    Unanswered Questions"
    in Greenberg, Barnett A. and Bellenger, Danny N. (editors)
    Contemporary Marketing Thought
    (Chicago: American Marketing Association, 1977), pp. 401-4.

Hattie, John
    "The Tendency to Omit Items: Another Deviant Response Characteristic"
    Educational and Psychological Measurement, Vol. 43 (Winter 1983), pp.
    1041-5.

Hornik, Jacob
    "Time Cue and Time Perception Effect on Response to Mail Surveys"
    Journal of Marketing Research, Vol. XVIII (May 1981), pp. 243-8.

Jones, Wesley H. and Linda, Gerald
    "Multiple Criteria Effects in a Mail Survey Experiment"
    Journal of Marketing Research, Vol. XV (May 1978), pp. 280-4.

Little, Taylor E., Jr. and Pressley, Milton M.
    "A Multifactor Experiment on the Generalizability of Direct Mail
    Advertising Response Techniques to Mail Survey Design"
    Journal of the Academy of Marketing Science, Vol. 8 (Fall 1980), pp.
    390-404.

Matteson, M. T. and Smith, S. V.
  "Effects of Voluntary Anonymity on Questionnaire Responses"
  in Day, Ralph (editor)
  Consumer Satisfaction, Dissatisfaction and Complaining Behavior
  (Bloomington, IN: School of Business, Indiana University 1977).

McDaniel, Stephen W. and Rao, C. P.
  "An Investigation of Response Quality and Demographic Characteristics
  of Initial vs. Post-Followup Respondents"
  Proceedings, American Marketing Association Educators' Conference
  (1981), pp. 401-4.

McDaniel, Stephen W. and Rao, C. P.
  "An Investigation of Respondent Anonymity's Effect on Mailed
  Questionnaire Response Rate and Quality"
  Journal of the Market Research Society, Vol. 23 (July 1981), pp.
  150-60.

McDaniel, Stephen W. and Rao, C. P.
  "The Effect of Monetary Inducement on Mailed Questionnaire Response
  Quality"
  Journal of Marketing Research, Vol. XVII (May 1980), pp. 265-8.

Hawkins, Del I., Coney, Kenneth A., and Jackson, Donald W., Jr.
  "The Impact of Monetary Inducement on Uninformed Response Error"
  Journal of the Academy of Marketing Science, Vol. 16 (Summer 1988),
  pp. 30-5.

71.02 ---------- Response Quality: Completeness of Answers

McDaniel, Stephen W. and Rao, C. P.
  "An Investigation of Respondent Anonymity's Effect on Mailed
  Questionnaire Response Rate and Quality"
  Journal of the Market Research Society, Vol. 23 (July 1981), pp.
  150-60.

McDaniel, Stephen W. and Rao, C. P.
  "The Effect of Monetary Inducement on Mailed Questionnaire Response
  Quality"
  Journal of Marketing Research, Vol. XVII (May 1980), pp. 265-8.

71.03 ---------- Mail Surveys - Income Nonresponse

      See also (sub)heading(s) 117.

Gronhaug, Kjell, Gilly, Mary C., and Enis, Ben M.
  "Exploring Income Non-Response: A Logit Model Analysis"
  Journal of the Market Research Society, Vol. 30 (July 1988), pp.
  371-7.

Ono, M. and Miller, Herman P.
  "Income Nonresponse in the Current Population Survey"
  Proceedings, Social Statistics Section of the American Statistical
  Association (1969), pp. 227-88.

72 ---------- MAIL SURVEYS - SOURCES AND ASSESSMENT OF BIAS ----------
          See also (sub)heading(s) 67, 68, 69, 70, 71.

72.01 ---------- Articles, etc. Re: Nonresponse bias
          See also (sub)heading(s) 117.

Armstrong, J. Scott and Overton, Terry S.
    "Estimating Nonresponse Bias in Mail Surveys"
    Journal of Marketing Research, Vol. XIV (August 1977), pp. 396-402.

Barnette, W. L., Jr.
    "The Non-Respondent Problem in Questionnaire Research"
    Journal of Applied Psychology, Vol. 34 (December 1950), pp. 397,8.

Craig, C. Samuel and McCann, John M.
    "Item Nonresponse in Mail Surveys: Extent and Correlates"
    Journal of Marketing Research, Vol. XV (May 1978), pp. 285-9.

Daniel, Wayne W.
    "Nonresponse in Sociological Surveys: A Review of Some Methods for
    Handling the Problem"
    Sociological Methods and Research, Vol. 3 (February 1975), pp.
    291-307.

Dickinson, John R. and Kirzner, Eric
    "The Validity of Estimating Nonresponse Bias by Extrapolation"
    Proceedings, American Institute for Decision Sciences (November 1985).

Donald, Marjorie N.
    "Implications of Non-Response for the Interpretation of Mail
    Questionnaire Data"
    Public Opinion Quarterly, Vol. 24 (Spring 1960), pp. 99-114.

Dunkelberg, William C. and Day, George S.
    "Nonresponse Bias and Call Backs in Sample Surveys"
    Journal of Marketing Research, Vol. X (May 1973), pp. 160-8.

Ellis, Robert A., Endo, Calvin M., and Armer, Michael J.
    "The Use of Potential Nonrespondents for Studying Nonresponse Bias"
    Pacific Sociological Review, Vol. 13 (Spring 1970), pp. 103-9.

Ferber, Robert
    "Item Nonresponse in a Consumer Survey"
    Public Opinion Quarterly, Vol. 30 (Fall 1966), pp. 399-415.

Ferber, Robert
    "More on Bias in Mail Surveys"
    Public Opinion Quarterly, Vol. 13 (Winter 1949), pp. 193-7.

Filion, F. L.
    "Exploring and Correcting for Nonresponse Bias Using Follow-Ups of
    Nonrespondents"
    Pacific Sociological Review, Vol. 19 (July 1976), pp. 401-8.

Filion, F. L.
    "Estimating Bias Due to Nonresponse in Mail Surveys"
    Public Opinion Quarterly, Vol. 40 (Winter 1975-76), pp. 482-92.

Finkner, A. L.
    "Adjustment for Non-Response Bias in a Rural Mail Survey"
    Agricultural Economics Research, Vol. 4 (July 1952), pp. 77-82.

Franzen, R. and Lazarsfeld, P. F.
    "Mail Questionnaires as a Research Problem"
    Journal of Psychology, Vol. 20 (1945), pp. 293-320.

Hansen, Morris H. and Hurwitz, W. N.
    "The Problem of Non-Response in Mail Surveys"
    Journal of the American Statistical Association, Vol. 41 (December
    1946), pp. 517-29.

Hendricks, W. A.
    "Adjustment for Bias by Non-Response in Mail Surveys"
    Agricultural Economics Research, Vol. 1 (1949), pp. 52-6.

Lehman, Edward C., Jr.
    "Tests of Significance and Partial Returns to Mail Questionnaires"
    Rural Sociology, Vol. 28 (September 1963), pp. 284-9.

Mayer, Charles S. and Pratt, Robert W., Jr.
    "A Note on Nonresponse in a Mail Survey"
    Public Opinion Quarterly, Vol. 30 (Winter 1966), pp. 667-76.

McMillan, James R.
    "Cutting Nonresponse Bias: Are Benefits Worth the Extra Cost?"
    Marketing News, Vol. 19 (January 4, 1985), pp. 37,8.

Ognibene, P.
  "Correcting Non-Response Bias in Mail Questionnaires"
  Journal of Marketing Research, Vol. VIII (May 1971), pp. 233-5.

Peters, W. S.
  "Selective Response Factors in Tourist Surveys"
  Journal of Marketing, Vol. 25 (January 1961), pp. 68-71.

Schwirian, Kent P. and Blaine, Harry R.
  "Questionnaire-Return Bias in the Study of Blue-Collar Workers"
  Public Opinion Quarterly, Vol. 30 (Winter 1966), pp. 656-63.

Shaffer, J. D.
  "Estimating Population Characteristics by Mail Survey"
  Journal of Farm Economics, Vol. 41 (November 1959), pp. 833-7.

Zimmer, H.
  "Validity of Extrapolating Non-Response Bias From Mail Questionnaire
  Follow-Ups"
  Journal of Applied Psychology, Vol. 40 (1956), pp. 117-21.

72.02 ---------- Studies of Nonrespondents

       See also (sub)heading(s) 70.

Barton, Judith, Bain, C., Henneken, C., Rosner, B., Belanger, C., Roth,
  A., and Speizer, F.
  "Characteristics of Respondents and Non-Respondents to a Mail
  Questionnaire"
  American Journal of Public Health, Vol. 70, No. 8 (1980), pp. 823-5.

Benson, L. E.
  "Mail Surveys can be Valuable"
  Public Opinion Quarterly, Vol. 10 (1946), pp. 234-41.

Britton, Joseph J. and Oppenheimer, Jean
  "Factors in the Return of Questionnaires Mailed to Older Persons"
  Journal of Applied Psychology, Vol. 35, No. 1 (1951), pp. 57-60.

Crawford, Alex
  "A Comparison of Participants and Non-Participants From a British
  General Population Survey of Alcohol Drinking Practices"
  Journal of the Market Research Society, Vol. 28 (July 1986), pp.
  291-7.

DeMaio, Theresa
  "Refusals: Who, Where and Why"
  Public Opinion Quarterly, Vol. 44 (1980), pp. 223-3.

Donald, Marjorie N.
  "Implications of Nonresponse for the Interpretation of Mail
  Questionnaire Data"
  Public Opinion Quarterly, Vol. 24 (Spring 1960), pp. 99-114.

Edgerton, Harold A., Britt, Steuart Henderson, and Norman, Ralph D.
  "Objective Differences Among Various Types of Respondents to a Mailed
  Questionnaire"
  American Sociological Review, Vol. 12, No. 4 (1947), pp. 435-49.

El-Badry, M. A.
  "A Sampling Procedure for Mailed Questionnaires"
  Journal of the American Statistical Association, Vol. 51, No. 274,
  pp. 209-27.

Finn, David W., Wang, Chih-Kang, and Lamb, Charles W.
  "An Examination of the Effects of a Sample Composition Bias in a Mail
  Survey"
  Journal of the Market Research Society, Vol. 25 (October 1983), pp.
  331-8.

Futrell, Charles M.
  "Salesmen's Personality Characteristics and Sample Bias"
  Journal of the Academy of Marketing Science, Vol. 5 (Summer 1977),
  pp. 180-4.

Gannon, Martin, Nothern, Joseph, and Carroll, Stephen J., Jr.
  "Characteristics of Non-Respondents Among Workers"
  Journal of Applied Psychology, Vol. 55 (December 1971), pp. 586-8.

Gough, Harrison and Hall, Wallace
  "A Comparison of Physicians Who Did or Did Not Respond to a Postal
  Questionnaire"
  Journal of Applied Psychology, Vol. 62, No. 6 (1977), pp. 777-80.

Guggenheim, Bernard
  "All Research is Not Created Equal"
  Journal of Advertising Research, Vol. 29 (February/March 1989), pp.
  RC7-11.

Kemsley, W. F. and Nicholson, J. L.
    "Some Experiments in Methods of Conducting Family Expenditure Surveys"
    Journal of the Royal Statistical Society, Series A, Vol. 123, Part 3,
    pp. 307-28.

Kernan, Jerome B.
    "Are Bulk-Rate Occupants Really Unresponsive?"
    Public Opinion Quarterly, Vol. 35 (Fall 1971), pp. 420-4.

Kirchner, Wayne K. and Mousley, Nancy B.
    "A Note on Job Performance: Differences Between Respondent and
    Nonrespondent Salesmen to an Attitude Survey"
    Journal of Applied Psychology, Vol. 47 (Summer 1963), pp. 223-44.

Lubin, Bernard, Levitt, Eugene E., and Zuckerman, Marvin
    "Some Personality Differences Between Respondents and Nonrespondents
    to a Survey Questionnaire"
    Journal of Consulting Psychology, Vol. 26 (April 1962), pp. 192-7.

Macek, Albert and Miles, Guy
    "IQ Score and Mailed Questionnaire Response"
    Journal of Applied Psychology, Vol. 60, No. 2 (1975), pp. 258,9.

Malek, Albert J. and Miles, Guy H.
    "IQ Score and Mailed Questionnaire Response"
    Journal of Applied Psychology, Vol. 60 (April 1975), pp. 258-9.

Mayer, C. S. and Pratt, R. W., Jr.
    "A Note on Nonresponse in a Mail Survey"
    Public Opinion Quarterly, Vol. 30, No. 4, pp. 637-46.

Ognibene, Peter
    "Traits Affecting Questionnaire Response"
    Journal of Advertising Research, Vol. 10 (June 1970), pp. 18-20.

Pavalko, Ronald M. and Lutterman, Kenneth G.
    "Characteristics of Willing and Reluctant Respondents"
    Pacific Sociological Review, Vol. 16 (1973), pp. 463-76.

Redpath, Bob
    "National Food Survey: A Second Study of Differential Response,
    Comparing Census Characteristics of NFS Respondents and
    Nonrespondents: Also a Comparison of NFS and FES Response Bias"
    Statistical News, No. 80 (February 1988), pp. 6-10.

Reid, Seerley
    "Respondents and Non-Respondents to Mail Questionnaires"
    Educational Research Bulletin, Vol. 21 (April 1942), pp. 87-96.

Reuss, Carl F.
    "Differences Between Persons Responding and Not Responding to a
    Mailed Questionnaire"
    American Sociological Review, Vol. 8 (August 1943), pp. 433-8.

Rosenau, James N.
    "Meticulousness as a Factor in the Response to Mail Questionnaires"
    Public Opinion Quarterly, Vol. 28 (Summer 1964), pp. 312-4.

Schwirian, Kent P. and Blaine, Harry R.
    "Questionnaire-Return Bias in the Study of Blue-Collar Workers"
    Public Opinion Quarterly, Vol. 30, No. 4, pp. 656-63.

Speer, David and Zold, Anthony
    "An Example of Self-Selection Bias in Follow-Up Research"
    Journal of Clinical Psychology, Vol. 27, No. 1 (1971), pp. 64-8.

Suchman, Edward A. and McCandless, Boyd
    "Who Answers Questionnaires?"
    Journal of Applied Psychology, Vol. 24 (December 1940), pp. 758-69.

Toops, H. A.
    "The Factors of Mechanical Arrangement and Topography in
    Questionnaires"
    Journal of Applied Psychology, Vol. 21 (1937), pp. 225-9.

Vincent, Clark E.
    "Socioeconomic Status and Familial Variables in Mail Questionnaire
    Responses"
    American Journal of Sociology, Vol. 69 (May 1964), pp. 647-53.

Wallace, D.
    "A Case For and Against Mail Questionnaires"
    Public Opinion Quarterly, Vol. 18 (1954), pp. 40-52.

72.03 ---------- Articles, etc. Re: Response Bias

    See also (sub)heading(s) 116.

Adams, J. S.
  "An Experiment on Question and Response Bias"
  Public Opinion Quarterly, Vol. 20 (Fall 1960), pp. 593-8.

Baur, E. Jackson
  "Response Bias in a Mail Survey"
  Public Opinion Quarterly, Vol. 11 (Winter 1947), pp. 594-600.

Bennett, E. M., Blomquist, R. L., and Goldstein, A. G.
  "Response Stability in Limited-Response Questioning"
  Public Opinion Quarterly, Vol. 18 (Summer 1954), pp. 218-23.

Clausen, A. R.
  "Response Validity: Vote Report"
  Public Opinion Quarterly, Vol. 32 (1968), pp. 588-606.

Cohen, S. E. and Lipstein, B.
  "Response Errors in the Collection of Wage Statistics by Mail
  Questionnaires"
  Journal of the American Statistical Association, Vol. 49 (June 1954),
  pp. 240-50.

Ford, Neil M.
  "Consistency of Responses in a Mail Survey"
  Journal of Advertising Research, Vol. 9 (December 1969), pp. 31-3.

Giles, W. F. and Field, H. S.
  "Effects of Amount, Format, and Location of Demographic Information
  on Questionnaire Return Rate and Response Bias of Sensitive and
  Nonsensitive Items"
  Personnel Psychology, Vol. 31 (August 1978), pp. 549-59.

Houston, Michael J. and Nevin, John R.
  "The Effects of Source and Appeal on Mail Survey Response Patterns"
  Journal of Marketing Research, Vol. XIV (August 1977), pp. 374-8.

Jones, Wesley H. and Linda, Gerald
  "Multiple Criteria Effects in a Mail Survey Experiment"
  Journal of Marketing Research, Vol. XV (May 1978), pp. 280-4.

Leroux, A. A.
  "A Method of Detecting Errors of Classification by Respondents to
  Postal Inquiries"
  Applied Statistics, Vol. 17 (No. 1, 1968), pp. 64-9.

Mandell, Lewis and Lundsten, Norman L.
  "Some Insight Into the Underreporting of Financial Data by Sample
  Survey Respondents"
  Journal of Marketing Research, Vol. XV (May 1978), pp. 292-9.

Mizes, J. Scott, Flecce, E. Louis, and Roos, Cindy
  "Incentives for Increasing Return Rates: Magnitude Levels, Response
  Bias, and Format"
  Public Opinion Quarterly, Vol. 48 (Winter 1984), pp. 794-800.

Stanton, Frank
  "Notes on Validity of Mail Questionnaire Returns"
  Journal of Applied Psychology, Vol. 23 (February 1939), pp. 95-104.

Suchman, E. A.
  "An Analysis of 'Bias' in Survey Research"
  Public Opinion Quarterly, Vol. 26 (1962), pp. 102-11.

72.04 ---------- Other Sources and Assessment of Bias

Allen, I. L.
  "Detecting Respondents Who Fake and Confuse Information About
  Question Areas on Surveys"
  Journal of Applied Psychology, Vol. 50 (December 1966), pp. 523-8.

Belkin, M. and Lieberman, S.
  "Effect of Question Wording on Response Distribution"
  Journal of Marketing Research, Vol. IV (August 1967), pp. 312,3.

Blair, William S.
  "How Subject Matter Can Bias a Mail Survey"
  Mediascope (February 1964), pp. 70-2.

Brown, R. V.
  "Evaluation of Total Survey Error"
  Journal of Marketing Research, Vol. IV (May 1967), pp. 117-27.

Campbell, Donald T.
  "Bias in Mail Surveys"
  Public Opinion Quarterly, Vol. 13 (Fall 1949), p. 562.

Chebat, Jean-Charles and Picard, Jacques
  "The Prenotification of Respondents in Mailed Questionnaire Surveys
  as a Source of Sample Bias"
  International Journal of Research in Marketing, Vol. 1, No. 3 (1984),
  pp. 235-9.

Clausen, John A. and Ford, Robert N.
  "Controlling Bias in Mail Questionnaires"
  Journal of the American Statistical Association, Vol. 42 (September
  1947), pp. 497-511.

Cotton, B. C. and Wonder, D. D.
  "Mail Survey Response Rate and Corporate Size"
  Psychological Reports, Vol. 51 (1982), pp. 12-8.

Deming, W. Edwards
  "On a Probability Mechanism to Attain an Economic Balance Between the
  Resultant Error of Response and the Bias of Non-Response"
  Journal of the American Statistical Association, Vol. 48 (December
  1953), pp. 363-70.

Drayton, L. E.
  "Bias Arising in Wording Consumer Questionnaires"
  Journal of Marketing, Vol. 19 (October 1954), pp. 140-5.

Dunnette, M. D., Ophoff, W. H., and Aylward, M.
  "The Effect of Lack of Information on the Undecided Response in
  Attitude Surveys"
  Journal of Applied Psychology, Vol. 40 (June 1956), pp. 150-3.

Edgerton, Harold A., Britt, Steuart H., and Norman, Ralph D.
  "Objective Differences to a Mailed Questionnaire"
  American Sociological Review, Vol. 12 (Summer 1947), pp. 435-44.

Ferber, Robert
  "The Problem of Bias in Mail Returns: A Solution"
  Public Opinion Quarterly, Vol. 12 (Winter 1948), pp. 669-76.

Ford, Robert N. and Zeisel, Hans
  "Bias in Mail Surveys Cannot be Controlled by One Mailing"
  Public Opinion Quarterly, Vol. 13 (Fall 1949), pp. 495-501.

Frankel, Lester R.
  "How Incentives and Subsamples Affect the Precision of Mail Surveys"
  Journal of Advertising Research, Vol. 1 (September 1960), pp. 1-5.

Friedman, Hershey H. and San Augustine, Andre J.
  "The Effects of a Monetary Incentive and the Ethnicity of the
  Sponsor's Signature on the Rate and Quality of Response to a Mail
  Survey"
  Journal of the Academy of Marketing Science, Vol. 7 (Winter-Spring
  1979), pp. 95-101.

Kivlin, Joseph E.
  "Contributions to the Study of Mail-Back Bias"
  Rural Sociology, Vol. 30 (Fall 1965), pp. 332-369

Larson, Richard F. and Catton, William R., Jr.
  "Can the Mail-Back Bias Contribute to a Study's Validity?"
  American Sociological Review, Vol. 24 (April 1959), pp. 243-5.

Nuckols, Robert C.
  "The Validity and Comparability of Mail and Personal Interview
  Surveys"
  Journal of Marketing Research, Vol. I (February 1964), pp. 11-6.

Nuckols, Robert C. and Mayer, Charles S.
  "Can Independent Responses be Obtained From Various Members in a Mail
  Panel Household"
  Journal of Marketing Research, Vol. VII (February 1970), pp. 90-4.

O'Connor, P. J., Sullivan, Gary L., and Jones, Wesley H.
  "An Evaluation of the Characteristics of Response Quality Induced by
  Follow-Up Survey Methods"
  in Mitchell, Andrew (editor)
  Advances in Consumer Research, Volume 9
  (Ann Arbor, MI: Association for Consumer Research, 1981), pp. 257-60.

Omura, Glenn S.
  "Correlates of Item Non-Response"
  Journal of the Market Research Society, Vol. 25 (October 1983), pp.
  321-30.

Robinson, R. A. and Agasim, Philip
  "Making Mail Surveys More Reliable"
  Journal of Marketing, Vol. 15 (April 1951), pp. 415-24.

Rosen, H. and Rosen, R. A. H.
  "The Validity of Undecided Answers in Questionnaire Responses"
  Journal of Applied Psychology, Vol. 39 (June 1955), pp. 178-81.

Schwirian, Kent P. and Blaine, Harry R.
  "Questionnaire Return Bias in the Study of Blue Collar Workers"
  Public Opinion Quarterly, Vol. 30 (Winter 1966), pp. 656-63.

Shuttleworth, Frank K.
  "Sampling Errors Involved in Incomplete Returns to Mailed
  Questionnaires"
  Psychological Bulletin, Vol. 37 (September 1940), p. 437.

Singer, Eleanor
  "Informed Consent: Consequences for Response Rate and Response
  Quality in Social Surveys"
  American Sociological Review, Vol. 43 (April 1978), pp. 144-61.

Skelton, V. C.
  "Patterns Behind Income Refusals"
  Journal of Marketing, Vol. 27 (July 1963), pp. 38-41.

Stanton, Frank
  "Notes on the Validity of Mail Questionnaire Returns"
  Journal of Applied Psychology, Vol. 23 (February 1939), pp. 95-104.

Suchman, Edward A.
  "An Analysis of Bias in Survey Research"
  Public Opinion Quarterly, Vol. 26 (Spring 1962), pp. 102-11.

Suchman, E. A. and Guttman, L.
  "A Solution to the Problem of Question Bias"
  Public Opinion Quarterly, Vol. 11 (Fall 1947), pp. 445-55.

Sudman, S. and Bradburn, M.
  Response Effects in Surveys
  (Chicago: Aldine Publishing Co., 1974).

Tortolani, Ray
  "Introducing Bias Intentionally Into Survey Techniques"
  Journal of Marketing Research, Vol. II (February 1965), pp. 51-5.

Vincent, Clark E.
  "Socioeconomic Status and Familial Variables in Mail Questionnaire
  Responses"
  American Journal of Sociology, Vol. 69 (May 1964), pp. 647-53.

Wells, W. D.
  "The Influence of Yeasaying Response Style"
  Journal of Advertising Research, Vol. 1 (June 1961), pp. 1-12.

Whitmore, William J.
  "Mail Survey Premiums and Response Bias"
  Journal of Marketing Research, Vol. XIII (February 1976), pp. 46-50.

Wiseman, Frederick
  "Methodological Bias in Public Opinion Surveys"
  Public Opinion Quarterly, Vol. 36 (Spring 1972), pp. 105-8.

Wiseman, Frederick and Schafer, Marianne
  "If Respondents Won't Respond, Ask Nonrespondents Why"
  Marketing News, Vol. IX (September 1977), pp. 8,9.

73 ---------------------- ELECTRONIC SURVEYS ------------------------

See also (sub)heading(s) 38.05, 76.06, 88, 97, 100.07.

73.01 ---------- Theory Re: Interactive Computerized Interviewing

Bartram, D. and Bayliss, R.
  "Automated Testing: Past, Present and Future"
  Journal of Occupational Psychology, Vol. 57 (1984), pp. 221-37.

Bemelmans-Stork, M. and Sikkel, D.
  "Data Collection With Handheld Computers"
  Proceedings, 45th ISI Conference, Amsterdam (1985).

Bronner, Alfred E. and De Hoog, Robert
  "Computer Assisted Decision Making: A New Tool for Market Research"
  ESOMAR Congress, Rome (1984), pp. 171-92.

Bronner, Alfred E. and De Hoog, Robert
  "Non-Expert Use of a Computerized Decision Aid"
  in Humphreys, P., Svenson, O., and Vari, A. (editors)
  Analysing and Aiding Decision Processes
  (Budapest: Hungarian Academy of Sciences, 1983), pp. 281-99.

Church, Nancy J.
  "Computer Interactive Data Collection Methodology: A Review and
  Preliminary Observations"
  in Chebat, J. (editor)
  Marketing, Volume 6, Part 3
  Proceedings of the Administrative Sciences Association of Canada
  (Quebec: University of Montreal, 1985), pp. 73-82.

Clemens, J.
  "The Use of Viewdata Panels for Data Collection"
  in Are Interviewers Obsolete? Drastic Changes in Data Collection and
  Data Presentation
  (Amsterdam: ESOMAR, 1984), pp. 47-65.

Clopton, Stephen W. and Barksdale, Hiram C., Jr.
  "Microcomputer Based Methods for Dyadic Interaction Research in
  Marketing"
  Journal of the Academy of Marketing Science, Vol. 15 (Summer 1987),
  pp. 63-8.

Denner, S.
  "Automated Psychological Testing: A Review"
  British Journal of Social and Clinical Psychology, Vol. 16 (1977),
  pp. 175-9.

Franzkowials, Michel and Korber, Pierre
  "Video Questionnaire: Telematics and Marketing"
  ESOMAR Congress, Rome (1984), pp. 155-169.

Gaines, B. R. and Hill, D. R. (editors)
  "Special Issue on Automated Psychological Testing"
  International Journal of Man-Machine Studies, Vol. 17 (1982).

Groves, Robert M. and Mathiowetz, Nancy A.
  "Computer Assisted Telephone Interviewing: Effects on Interviewers
  and Respondents"
  Public Opinion Quarterly, Vol. 48 (Spring 1984), pp. 356-69.

Higgins, C. A., Dimnik, T. P., and Greenwood, H. P.
  "The DISCQ Survey Method"
  Journal of the Market Research Society, Vol. 29 (October 1987), pp.
  437-45.

Holder, Matthew and Johnson, Douglas
  "Recent Developments in Computer Applications for Market Research"
  ESOMAR Congress, Rome (1984), pp. 193-212.

Karweit, N. and Meyers, E. D., Jr.
  "Computers in Survey Research"
  in Rossi, P. H., Wright, J. D., and Anderson, A. B. (editors)
  Handbook of Survey Research
  (Orlando, FL: Academic Press, 1983), pp. 379-414.

Kiesler, Sara and Sproull, Lee S.
  "Response Effects in the Electronic Survey"
  Public Opinion Quarterly, Vol. 50 (Fall 1986), pp. 402-13.

Larson, J. D.
  "Considerations for the Design of Computer Aided Interviewing Systems"
  in Lusch, R. F., et al. (editors)
  1985 AMA Educators' Proceedings
  (Chicago: American Marketing Association, 1985), p. 362.

Liefeld, John P.
"Field Experience in Computer Interviewing With Consumer Samples"
in Synodinos, N. E. (editor)
Proceedings, AMA Microcomputers in Marketing Workshop
(Honolulu: University of Hawaii at Manoa, 1987), pp. 129-40.

Madron, Thomas W., Tate, C. Neal, and Brookshire, Robert G.
Using Microcomputers in Research
(Beverly Hills, CA: Sage Publications, 1985).

Market Research Society
The Computer as Interviewer
Proceedings
(London: The Market Research Society, 1982).

O'Brien, Terry and Dugdale, Valerie
"Questionnaire Administration by Computer"
Journal of the Market Research Society, Vol. 20 (October 1978), pp.
228-37.

Palit, C. D.
"A Microcomputer Based Computer Assisted Interviewing System"
Proceedings, Section on Survey Research Methods
(Washington, DC: American Statistical Association, 1980), pp. 516-8.

Rafael, Joseph E.
"Self-Administered CRT Interviews: Benefits Far Outweigh the Problems"
Marketing News, Vol. 23 (November 9, 1984), p. 16.

Rowley, G., Barker, K., and Callaghan, V.
"The Market Research Terminal and Developments in Survey Research"
European Journal of Marketing, Vol. 20, No. 2 (1986), pp. 35-9.

Saris, Willem E., De Pijper, W. Marius, and Neijens, P.
"Some Notes on the Computer Steered Interview"
in Middendorp, C. P., Niemoller, B., and Saris, W. E. (editors)
Proceedings, Sociometry Meeting
(Amsterdam: SRF, 1980), pp. 306-10.

Sawtooth Software, Incorporated
Proceedings of the Sawtooth Software Conference on Perceptual
Mapping, Conjoint Analysis, and Computer Interviewing
(Ketchum, ID: Sawtooth Software, Inc., 1987).

Skinner, H. A. and Pakula, A.
"Challenge of Computers in Psychological Assessment"
Professional Psychology: Research and Practice, Vol. 17 (1986), pp.
44-50.

Stout, R. L.
"New Approaches to the Design of Computerized Interviewing and
Testing Systems"
Behavior Research Methods and Instrumentation, Vol. 13 (1981), pp.
436-42.

Sudman, Seymour
"Survey Research and Technological Change"
Sociological Methods and Research, Vol. 12 (1983), pp. 217-230.

Suneson, Paul A. and Cadotte, Ernest R.
"Research Suggests Automated Polling Machines Yield Reliable and
Valid Data"
Marketing News, Vol. 18 (January 6, 1984), pp. 8,9.

Synodinos, Nicolaos E. and Brennan, Jerry M.
"Computer Interactive Interviewing in Survey Research"
Psychology and Marketing, Vol. 5 (Summer 1988), pp. 117-37.

Whalen, Bernie
"On-Site Computer Interviewing Yields Research Data Instantly"
Marketing News, Vol. 18 (November 9, 1984), pp. 1,17.

73.02 ---------- Empirical Studies of Computer Interactive Interviewing

Erdman, Harold, Klein, Marjorie H., and Greist, John H.
"The Reliability of a Computer Interview for Drug Use/Abuse
Information"
Behaviour Research Methods and Instrumentation, Vol. 15 (February
1983), pp. 66-8.

Greist, John H., Klein, Marjorie H., and Van Cura, Lawrence J.
"A Computer Interview for Psychiatric Patient Target Symptoms"
Archives of General Psychiatry, Vol. 29 (August 1973), pp. 247-53.

Greist, John H., Van Cura, Lawrence J., and Kneppreth, Norwood P.
"A Computer Interview for Emergency Room Patients"
Computers and Biomedical Research, Vol. 6 (June 1973), pp. 257-65.

Hedl, J. J., O'Neil, H. F., and Hansen, D. N.
  "Affective Reactions Towards Computer-Based Intelligence Testing"
  Journal of Consulting and Clinical Psychology, Vol. 40 (1973), pp.
  217-22.

Johnson, B. and Sturtevant, V.
  "A Comparison of Computer Interviewing With Traditional Paper and
  Pencil Format: Soliciting Sensitive Information"
  Southern Oregon State College, unpublished paper.

Kiesler, Sara and Sproull, Lee S.
  "Response Effects in the Electronic Survey"
  Public Opinion Quarterly, Vol. 50 (Fall 1986), pp. 402-13.

Koson, D., Kitchen, C., Kochen, M., and Stodolsky, D.
  "Psychological Testing by Computer: Effect on Response Bias"
  Educational and Psychological Measurement, Vol. 30 (Winter 1970), pp.
  803-10.

Liefeld, John P.
  "Response Effects in Computer-Administered Questioning"
  Journal of Marketing Research, Vol. XXV (November 1988), pp. 405-9.

Lucas, R. W., Mullin, P. J., Luna, C. B. X., and McInroy, D. C.
  "Psychiatrists and a Computer as Interrogators of Patients With
  Alcohol-Related Illnesses: A Comparison"
  British Journal of Psychiatry, Vol. 131 (1977), pp. 160-7.

Newsted, Peter R.
  "Paper Versus Online Presentations of Subjective Questionnaires"
  International Journal of Man-Machine Studies, Vol. 23 (September
  1985), pp. 231-47.

O'Brian, Terry O. and Dugdale, Valerie
  "Questionnaire Administration by Computer"
  Journal of the Market Research Society, Vol. 20 (October 1978), pp.
  228-37.

Saris, Willem E.
  "Een Eerste Evaluatie van de Tele-Interviewing Procedure"
  Research Memorandum Number 1025
  (Amsterdam: SSO, 1985).

Saris, Willem E.
  "Different Questions, Different Variables"
  in Fornell, C. (editor)
  Second Generation of Multivariate Analysis
  (New York: Praeger, 1982), pp. 78-96.

Slack, Warner V. and Van Cura, Lawrence J.
  "Patient Reaction to Computer Based Medical Interviewing"
  Computers and Biomedical Research, Vol. 1 (December 1968), pp. 527-31.

Waterton, J. J. and Duffy, J. C.
  "A Comparison of Computer Interviewing Techniques and Traditional
  Methods in the Collection of Self-Report Alcohol Consumption Data in
  a Field Survey"
  International Statistical Review, Vol. 52 (1984), pp. 173-82.

73.03 ---------- Applications of Interactive Computerized Interviewing

Bronner, Alfred E. and De Hoog, Robert
  "A Recipe for Mixing Decision Ingredients"
  European Research, Vol. 13 (July 1985), pp. 109-15.

Robins, L. N., Helzer, J. E., Croughan, J., and Ratliff, K. S.
  "National Institute of Mental Health Diagnostic Interview Schedule"
  Archives of General Psychiatry, Vol. 38 (1981), pp. 381-9.

73.04 ---------- Mailing of Diskettes for PC Data Elicitation

Higgins, C. A., Dimnik, T. P., and Greenwood, H. P.
  "The DISKQ Survey Method"
  Journal of the Market Research Society, Vol. 29 (1987), pp. 437-45.

Marketing News
  "Survey Method Uses Computer"
  Marketing News (September 13, 1985), p. 44.

Quirk's Marketing Research Review
  "Conjoint Analysis Enhances Computer-Based Interviews"
  Quirk's Marketing Research Review, Vol. 1, No. 4 (March 1987), p. 22.

73.05 ---------- Administration of Electronic Mail Surveys

Perlman, G.
"Electronic Surveys"
Behavior Research Methods, Instruments, and Computers, Vol. 17
(1985), pp. 203-5.

Saris, Willem E. and De Pijper, W. Marius
"Computer Assisted Interviewing Using Home Computers"
European Research, Vol. 14, No. 3 (1986), pp. 144-50.

Sawtooth Software, Incorporated
"Ci2 Dialup"
News from Sawtooth Software (February 1986), p. 2.

73.06 ---------- Evaluations of Electronic Mail Surveys

Helgeson, J. G. and Ursic, M. L.
"The Electronic Versus the Paper Survey: A Preliminary Examination of
Equivalency"
in Synodinos, N. E. (editor)
Proceedings, AMA Microcomputers in Marketing Workshop
(Honolulu: University of Hawaii at Manoa, 1987), pp. 141-9.

Kiesler, S. and Sproull, L. S.
"Response Effects in the Electronic Survey"
Public Opinion Quarterly, Vol. 50 (1986), pp. 402-13.

Kiesler, S., Zubrow, D., Moses, A. M., and Geller, V.
"Affect in Computer-Mediated Communication: An Experiment in
Synchronous Terminal-to-Terminal Discussion"
Human-Computer Interaction, Vol. 1 (1985), pp. 77-104.

McBrien, B. D.
"The Role of the Personal Computer in Data Collection, Data Analysis,
and Data Presentation: A Case Study"
82nd ESOMAR Seminar, Nice, France (March 1984), paper presentation.

O'Brien, T. and Dugdale, V.
"Questionnaire Administration by Computer"
Journal of the Market Research Society, Vol. 20 (1978), pp. 228-37.

Sproull, L. S.
"Using Electronic Mail for Data Collection in Organizational Research"
Academy of Management Journal, Vol. 29 (1986), pp. 159-69.

73.07 ---------- Surveying by Television

Baker, David and Holmes, Cliff
"Does Research Through the Television Screen Produce Valid Results?"
Proceedings, Market Research Society Conference (March 1987), pp.
233-58.

Baker, David and Holmes, Cliff
"The Validity and Efficiency of Data Collection Using Screen
Interviews Compared With Telephone Research"
ESOMAR Congress, Montreux (1987), pp. 813-27.

73.08 ---------- Computer Programs for Computer Interactive Interviewin

Green, Paul E., Kedia, Pradeep K., and Hikhil, Rishiyur S.
Electronic Questionnaire Design and Analysis With CAPPA
(Palo Alto, CA: Scientific Press, 1985).

Humphreys, P. C. and Wisudha, A.
"MAUD--An Interactive Computer Program for the Structuring,
Decomposition and Recomposition of Preferences Between
Multiattributed Alternatives"
Technical Report 79-2
Decision Analysis Unit, Brunel University, Uxbridge (1979).

Johnson, Robert
Ci2 System
(Ketchum, ID: Sawtooth Software, 1985).

Sawtooth Software, Incorporated
ACA System for Adaptive Conjoint Analysis
(Ketchum, ID: Sawtooth Software, Inc., 1986).

Smith, Scott
"Review of CAPPA and Ci2 System"
Journal of Marketing Research, Vol. XXIII (February 1986), pp. 83-5.

74 ----------------- PERSONAL INTERVIEWING - GENERAL -----------------
         See also (sub)heading(s) 75, 76, 77, 78, 79, 108.

74.01 ---------- Books Re: Personal Interviewing - General

Bradburn, Norman M., Sudman, Seymour, and Associates
   Improving Interview Method and Questionnaire Design
   (San Francisco: Jossey-Bass, 1979), 214 pp.

Brenner, Michael, Brown, Jennifer, and Canter, David
   The Research Interview: Uses and Approaches
   (London: Academic Press, Inc., 1985), 276 pp.

ESOMAR
   Are Interviewers Obsolete? Drastic Changes in Data Collection and
   Data Presentation
   Proceedings, European Society for Opinion and Marketing Research, 154
   pp.

Fowler, Floyd J., Jr. and Mangione, Thomas W.
   Standardized Survey Interviewing
   (Newbury Park, CA: Sage Publications, 1989), 160 pp.

Hyman, H. H., Cobb, W. J., Feldman, J. J., Hart, C. W., and Stember, C.
   H.
   Interviewing in Social Research
   (Chicago: University of Chicago Press, 1954).

Kahn, R. L. and Cannell, C. F.
   The Dynamics of Interviewing
   (New York: John Wiley and Sons, 1957).

McCracken, Grant
   The Long Interview
   (Newbury Park, CA: Sage Publications, Inc., 1988).

Richardson, Stephen A., Dohrenwend, Barbara Snell, and Klein, David
   Interviewing: Its Form and Functions
   (New York: Basic Books, Inc., 1965), 380 pp.

Smith, Joan MacFarlane
   Interviewing in Market and Social Research
   (London and Boston:Routledge and Kegan Paul, 1972), 169 pp.

Stewart, Charles J. and Cash, William B., Jr.
   Interviewing: Principles nd Practices, Fourth Edition
   (Dubuque, IA: William C. Brown Publishers, 1985), 371 pp.

Werner, O. and Schoepfle, G. M.
   Systematic Fieldwork, Volume 1: Foundations of Ethnography and
   Interviewing
   (Newbury Park, CA: Sage Publications, Inc., 1987).

74.02 ---------- Articles etc. Re: Personal Interviewing - General

Bancroft, G.
   "Consistency of Information From Records and Interviews"
   Journal of the American Statistical Association, Vol. 35 (1940), pp.
   377-81.

Cobb, Sidney and Cannell, Charles F.
   "Some Thoughts About Interview Data"
   International Epidemiological Bulletin, Vol. 13 (June 1966), pp.
   43-54.

Dexter, L. A.
   "Role Relationships and Conceptions of Neutrality in Interviewing"
   American Journal of Sociology, Vol. 62 (September 1956), pp. 153-7.

Fouss, James H. and Solomon, Elaine
   "Salespeople as Researchers: Help or Hazard?"
   Journal of Marketing, Vol. 44 (Summer 1980), pp. 36-9.

Herzog, A. Regula, Rodgers, Willard L., and Kulka, Richard A.
   "Interviewing Older Adults: A Comparison of Telephone and
   Face-to-Face Modalities"
   Public Opinion Quarterly, Vol. 47 (Fall 1983), pp. 405-18.

Jaffe, Eugene D., Paternak, Hanoch, and Grifel, Avi
   "Response Results of Lottery Buyer Behavior Surveys: In-Home vs.
   Point-of-Purchase Interviews"
   Public Opinion Quarterly, Vol. 47 (Fall 1983), pp. 419-26.

Jobber, David and Bleasdale, Marcus J. R.
   "Interviewing in Industrial Marketing Research: The State-of-the-Art"
   Quarterly Review of Marketing, Vol. 12 (January 1987), pp. 7-11.

MacCoby, E. E. and MacCoby, Nathan
"The Interview: A Tool of Social Science"
in Lindzey, Gardner (editor)
Handbook of Social Psychology, Volume One
(Cambridge, MA: Addison-Wesley, 1954), pp. 467-70.

Mayer, C. S.
"Data Collection Methods: Personal Interviews"
in Ferber, R. (editor)
Handbook of Marketing Research
(New York: McGraw-Hill, 1974), pp. 2-82-9.

Mayer, Charles S.
"Pretesting Field Interviewing Costs Through Simulation"
Journal of Marketing, Vol. 28 (April 1964), pp. 47-50.

Morton-Williams, Jean
"How Much do You Care Whether Your Survey Results are Accurate?"
Admap (June 1986), pp. 293-6.

Neter, John and Waksberg, Joseph
"Conditioning Effects from Repeated Household Interviews"
Journal of Marketing, Vol. 28 (April 1964), pp. 51-6.

Nuckols, Robert C.
"The Validity and Comparability of Mail and Personal Interview
Surveys"
Journal of Marketing Research, Vol. I (February 1964), pp. 11-6.

O'Dell, William F.
"Personal Interviews or Mail Panels"
Journal of Marketing, Vol. 26 (October 1962), pp. 34-9.

Ruch, F. L.
"Effects of Repeated Interviewing on the Respondent's Answers"
Journal of Consulting Psychology, Vol. 5 (July-August 1941), pp.
179-82.

Scheler, Hans-Erdmann and Wendt, Friedrich
"A New Fieldwork Model: Development, Experiences and Non-Response
Problems"
European Research, Vol. 4 (May 1976), pp. 101-11.

Schwartz, Alvin
"The Public Relations of Interviewing"
Journal of Marketing, Vol. 27 (July 1963), pp. 34-7.

Sjoberg, G.
"The Interviewer as a Marginal Man"
The Southwestern Social Science Quarterly, Vol. 38 (September 1957),
pp. 125-32.

Sternlieb, George
"Household Research in the Urban Core"
Journal of Marketing, Vol. 32 (January 1968), pp. 25-8.

74.03 ---------- Response Rates and Refusals

See also (sub)heading(s) 66, 117.01.

Bowen, J. M.
"Refusals and Non-Contacts"
Market Research Society Newsletter (July 1979).

Dohrenwend, Barbara Snell and Dorhenwend, Bruce P.
"Sources of Refusals in Surveys"
Public Opinion Quarterly, Vol. 32 (Spring 1968), pp. 74-83.

Dommermuth, William P. and Cateora, Philip R.
"Can Refusals by Respondents be Decreased?"
Journal of Marketing, Vol. 27 (July 1963), pp. 74-6.

Goyder, John
"Face-to-Face Interviews and Mailed Questionnaires: The Net
Difference in Response Rate"
Public Opinion Quarterly, Vol. 49 (Summer 1985), pp. 234-52.

Hodgson, Peter B.
"Factors Affecting Response Rates in Market Research Surveys--A
Critical Evaluation"
ESOMAR Congress, Hamburg (1974).

Hughes, Charles J.
"Why Bother to Decrease Interview Refusals?"
Journal of Marketing, Vol. 28 (April 1964), p. 67.

Lievesley, D.
   "Reducing Unit Nonresponse in Interview Surveys"
   Proceedings, 1983 ASA Conference, Survey Research Methods Section
   (1983).

Shosteck, Herschel and Fairweather, William R.
   "Physician Response Rates to Mail and Personal Interview Surveys"
   Public Opinion Quarterly, Vol. 43 (Summer 1979), pp. 206-16.

Singer, Eleanor
   "Informed Consent: Consequences for Response Rate and Response
   Quality in Social Surveys"
   American Sociological Review, Vol. 43 (1978), pp. 144-62.

Singer, Eleanor
   "The Effect of Informed Consent Procedures on Respondent's Reactions
   to Surveys"
   Journal of Consumer Research, Vol. 5 (June 1978), pp. 49-57.

Smith, Joan MacFarlane et al.
   "Response Rates in Sample Surveys"
   Report of a Working Party of the Market Research Society's Research
   and Development Committee
   Journal of the Market Research Society, Vol. 18 (July 1976), pp.
   113-42.

Van Westerhoven, E. M. C.
   "Covering Non-Response: Does It Pay? A Study of Refusers and
   Absentees"
   Journal of the Market Research Society, Vol. 20 (October 1978), pp.
   245-7.

Wiseman, Frederick and Billington, Maryann
   "Comment on a Standard Definition of Response Rates"
   Journal of Marketing Research, Vol. XXI (August 1984), pp. 336-8.

Wiseman, Frederick and McDonald, Philip
   "Toward the Development of Industry Standards for Response and
   Nonresponse Rates"
   Report No. 80-101
   (Cambridge, MA: Marketing Science Institute, 1980).

74.04 ---------- Point-of-Sale Interviewing

Atkinson, P. L. and Ogden, A. J.
   "Sample Surveys at the Point-of-Sale: A Case History From the Petrol
   Market"
   Journal of the Market Research Society, Vol. 16 (April 1974), pp.
   69-86.

Ogden, A. J. and Atkinson, P. L.
   "Sample Surveys at the Point of Sale: A Case History From the Petrol
   Market--Reply to Watson"
   Journal of the Market Research Society, Vol. 16 (October 1974), pp.
   302,3.

Watson, D. Lowe
   "Sample Surveys at the Point of Sale: A Case History From the Petrol
   Market--Comment"
   Journal of the Market Research Society, Vol. 16 (October 1974), p.
   302.

74.05 ---------- Unclassified (Personal Interviewing - General)

Adler, Lee
   "Confessions of an Interview Reader"
   Journal of Marketing Research, Vol. III (May 1966), pp. 194,5.

Allen, Irving L. and Colfax, J. David
   "Respondents' Attitudes Toward Legitimate Surveys in Four Cities"
   Journal of Marketing Research, Vol. V (November 1968), pp. 431-3.

Blanc, H.
   "Multilingual Interviewing in Israel"
   American Journal of Sociology, Vol. 62 (September 1956), pp. 205-9.

Cannell, C. F. and Axelrod, M.
   "The Respondent Reports on the Interview"
   American Journal of Sociology, Vol. 62 (September 1956), pp. 177-81.

U.S. Bureau of the Census
   Evaluation and Research Program of the United States Censuses of
   Population and Housing, 1960: Accuracy of Data on Population
   Characteristics as Measured by CPS-Census Match
   (Washington, DC: U.S. Bureau of the Census, Series Er60, No. 5,
   1964), 58 pp.

75 -------------- MANAGEMENT OF PERSONAL INTERVIEWERS ---------------
          See also (sub)heading(s) 74.

75.01 ---------- Books Re: Management of the Interview Process

Clark, Ronald E.
    The Complete Guide to Interviewing Cost Estimation
    (Los Angeles, CA: Drossler Research Corp., 1970), 94 pp.

Clark, Ronald E.
    Interviewing Cost Management: A Cost Control Handbook
    (1970), 158 pp.

Mayer, C. S.
    Interviewing Costs in Survey Research
    (Ann Arbor, MI: Bureau of Business Research, University of Michigan,
    1964), 114 pp.

Sudman, Seymour
    Reducing the Cost of Surveys
    (Chicago: Aldine Publishing Company, 1967).

75.02 ---------- Books Re: Interviewer Selection, Training, Evaluation

Cannell, Charles F., Lawson, Sally A., and Hausser, Doris L.
    A Technique for Evaluating Interviewer Performance
    (Ann Arbor, MI: The Institute for Social Research, 1975), 138 pp.

Hauck, Mathew and Steinkamp, Stanley
    Survey Reliability and Interviewer Competence
    Studies in Consumer Savings, No. 4
    (Urbana: Bureau of Economic and Business Research, University of
    Illinois, 1964), 112 pp.

75.03 ---------- Empirical Descriptions of Personal Interviewers

Barker, Raymond F.
    "A Demographic Profile of Marketing Research Interviewers"
    Journal of the Market Research Society, Vol. 29 (July 1987), pp.
    279-92.

Barker, Raymond F.
    "Interviewing Consumers in New Zealand and the United States"
    Singapore Marketing Review, Vol. II (March 1987), pp. 77-90.

NOP Market Research Limited
    Interviewers Survey
    (London: NOP Market Research Limited, 1978).

75.04 ---------- Interviewer Selection and Training

Andrews, L.
    "That Dreadful Interviewer Problem Again"
    International Journal of Opinion and Attitude Research, Vol. 3
    (Winter 1949-50), pp. 587-90.

Axelrod, M. and Cannell, C. F.
    "A Research Note on an Attempt to Predict Interviewer Effectiveness"
    Public Opinion Quarterly, Vol. 23 (Winter 1959-60), pp. 571-6.

Barioux, M.
    "A Method for the Selection, Training, and Evaluation of Interviewers"
    Public Opinion Quarterly, Vol. 16 (Spring 1952), pp. 128-30.

Barker, Raymond F.
    "A Demographic Profile of Marketing Research Interviewers"
    Journal of the Market Research Society, Vol. 29 (July 1987), pp.
    279-92.

Benson, Purnell H.
    Eliminating Consumer Biases in Product Evaluation
    (Madison, NJ: Consumer and Personnel Studies, 1965), monograph.

Benson, Purnell H.
    "Eliminating Consumer Biases in Survey Data by Balanced Tabulation"
    Journal of Marketing Research, Vol. I (November 1964), pp. 66-71.

Billiet, Jacques and Loosveldt, Geert
    "Improvement of the Quality of Responses to Factual Survey Questions
    by Interviewer Training"
    Public Opinion Quarterly, Vol. 52 (Summer 1988), pp. 190-211.

Dvorak, B. J. and Meigh, C.
    "Tests for Field Survey Interviewers"
    Journal of Marketing, Vol. 16 (January 1952), pp. 301-6.

Fellegi, I. P.
  "An Improved Method of Estimating the Correlated Response Variance"
  Journal of the American Statistical Association, Vol. 69 (1974), pp.
  496-501.

Fellegi, I. P.
  "Response Variance and Its Estimation"
  Journal of the American Statistical Association, Vol. 59 (1964), pp.
  1016-41.

Guest, L.
  "A New Training Method for Opinion Interviewing"
  Public Opinion Quarterly, Vol. 18 (Fall 1954), pp. 287-99.

Guest, L.
  "A Study of Interviewer Competence"
  International Journal of Opinion and Attitude Research, Vol. 1
  (December 1947), pp. 17-30.

Guest, Lester and Nuckols, R.
  "A Laboratory Experiment in Recording in Public Interviewing"
  International Journal of Opinion and Attitude Research, Vol. 4 (Fall
  1950), pp. 346-52.

Hall, Dale, Dobson, Alan, Blackaby, David, and Manning, Neil
  "Standing to be Counted: Robert Worcester and Universities"
  Journal of the Market Research Society, Vol. 30 (July 1988), pp.
  397,8.

Hall, Dale, Dobson, Alan, Blackaby, David, and Manning, Neil
  "Robert Worcester and Marginal Reliability--A Note"
  Journal of the Market Research Society, Vol. 30 (April 1988), pp.
  235-7.

Mayer, C. S.
  "A Computer System for Controlling Interviewer Costs"
  Journal of Marketing Research, Vol. V (August 1968), pp. 312-8.

Morgan, Elizabeth G.
  "The Right Interviewer for the Job"
  Journal of Marketing, Vol. 16 (October 1951), pp. 201,2.

Peterson, Robin T.
  "How Efficient are Salespeople in Surveys of Buyer Intentions?"
  Journal of Business Forecasting, Vol. 7 (Spring 1988), pp. 11,2.

Schyberger, Bo W:son
  "A Study of Interviewer Behavior"
  Journal of Marketing Research, Vol. IV (February 1967), pp. 32-5.

Smith, J. M.
  "Selection and Training of Interviewers"
  Journal of the Marketing Research Society, Vol. 12 (April 1970), pp.
  99-111.

Steinkamp, S. W.
  "The Identification of Effective Interviewers"
  Journal of the American Statistical Association, Vol. 59 (December
  1964), pp. 1165-74.

Steinkamp, Stanley W.
  "Some Characteristics of Effective Interviewers"
  Journal of Applied Psychology, Vol. 50 (December 1960), pp. 487-92.

Stuart, Elnora W.
  "Hiring and Training: In-House Interviewers"
  Public Relations Journal, Vol. 40 (July 1984), pp. 24-7.

Sudman, Seymour
  "New Approaches to Control of Interviewing Costs"
  Journal of Marketing Research, Vol. III (February 1966), pp. 56-61.

Sudman, Seymour
  "What Makes a Good Interviewer"
  in Webster, Frederick (editor)
  New Directions in Marketing, Proceedings of the 48th National
  Conference
  American Marketing Association (1965), pp. 369-89.

Summers, G. F. and Beck, E. M.
  "Social Status and Personality Factors in Predicting Interviewer
  Performance"
  Sociological Method and Research, Vol. 2 (1973), pp. 111-22.

Twedt, Dik Warren
  "Is an 'Audit Bureau of Interviews' Needed Now?"
  Journal of Marketing, Vol. 30 (April 1966), pp. 59,60.

Womer, S. and Boyd, H. W., Jr.
"The Use of a Voice Recorder in the Selection and Training of Field Workers"
Public Opinion Quarterly, Vol. 15 (Summer 1951), pp. 358-63.

75.05 ---------- Interviewer Evaluation and Control

Benson, Purnell H.
"CAVEIN: A Program for Computer Aided Validation and Evaluation of Interviewing"
Journal of Marketing Research, Vol. XIII (August 1976), pp. 273-5.

Benson, P. H.
"A Paired Comparison Approach to Evaluating Interviewer Performance"
Journal of Marketing Research, Vol. VI (February 1969), pp. 66-70.

Case, Peter
"How to Catch Interviewer Errors"
Journal of Advertising Research, Vol. 11 (April 1971), pp. 39-43.

Dutka, S.
"The Application of Statistical Quality Control to the Field Work of Audits and Surveys"
in Clewett, R. L. (editor)
Marketings Role in Scientific Management
(Chicago, IL: American Marketing Association, 1957), pp. 483-91.

Glasser, G. J., Metzger, G. D., and Miaoulis, G., Jr.
"Measurement and Control of Interviewer Variability"
Proceedings of the Business and Economic Statistics Section of the American Statistical Association, (1970), pp. 314-9.

Hansen, Morris H. and Stemberg, Joseph
"Control of Errors in Surveys"
Biometrics (December 1956), pp. 463-74.

Hauck, M.
"Is Survey Postcard Verification Effective?"
Public Opinion Quarterly, Vol. 33 (Spring 1969), pp. 117-20.

Heneman, G. H. and Paterson, D. G.
"Refusal Rates and Interviewer Quality"
International Journal of Opinion and Attitude Research (1949), pp. 392-8.

Juster, F. Thomas
"Validity Procedures at the Survey Research Center"
in Schlinger, Mary Jane (editor)
Advances in Consumer Research, Volume Two
(Association for Consumer Research, 1975), pp. 725-40.

Martyn, John
"Fieldwork Quality Control in the UK"
European Research, Vol. 7 (January 1979), pp. 11-6.

Namias, Jean
"Measuring Variation in Interviewer Performance"
Journal of Advertising Research, Vol. 6 (March 1966), pp. 8-12.

Namias, J.
"A Rapid Method to Detect Differences in Interviewer Performance"
Journal of Marketing, Vol. 26 (April 1962), pp. 68-72.

Potter, Jack
"Interviewer Reaction to a Difficult Interviewing Situtation"
Proceedings, Market Research Society Conference (March 1987), pp. 57-74.

Sheatsley, Paul B.
"An Analysis of Interviewer Characteristics and Their Relationship to Performance, Part III"
International Journal of Opinion and Attitude Research, Vol. 5 (1951), pp. 193-7.

Stock, J. S. and Hochstim, J. R.
"A Method of Measuring Interviewer Variability"
Public Opinion Quarterly, Vol. 15 (Summer 1951), pp. 322-34.

Sudman, Seymour
"Quantifying Interviewer Quality"
Public Opinion Quarterly, Vol. 30 (Winter 1966), pp. 664-7.

75.06 ---------- Behavior or Interaction Coding

See also (sub)heading(s) 77.05.

Bales, R. F.
Interaction: A Method for the Study of Small Groups
(Massachusetts: Addison-Wesley, 1950_.

Brenner, M.
"Response Effects of 'Role-Restricted' Characteristics of the
Interviewer"
in Dijkstra, W. and Vand Der Zouwen, J. (editors)
Response Behavior in the Survey Interview
(London: Academic Press, 1982).

Brenner, M.
"Assessing Social Skills in the Survey Interview"
in Singleton, W. T., Spurgeon, P. and Stammers, R. (editors)
The Analysis of Social Skills
(New York: Plenum, 1980).

Cannell, C. F.
Some Experiments in Dyadic Interactions and Response Accuracy in
Survey Interviews
ISR, University of Michigan (1973).

Morton-Williams, Jean
"The Use of Verbal Interaction Coding for Evaluating a Questionnaire"
Quality and Quantity, Vol. 13 (1979), pp. 59-75.

Morton-Williams, Jean and Sykes, Wendy
"The Use of Interaction Coding and Follow-Up Interviews to
Investigate Comprehension of Survey Questions"
Journal of the Market Research Society, Vol. 26 (April 1984), pp.
109-27.

Morton-Williams, Jean and Sykes, Wendy
"Interaction Coding: The Use of a Detailed Observation Technique for
the Improvement of Interviewer Performance"
Proceedings, The Market Research Society Conference (1983).

75.07 ---------- Interviewer Cheating

Andrews, L.
"Court Decree on the 'Cheater Problem'"
Journal of Marketing, Vol. 18 (October 1953), pp. 167-9.

Bennett, Archibald S.
"Observations on the So-Called Cheater Problem Among Field
Interviewers"
International Journal of Opinion and Attitude Research, Vol. 2
(Spring 1948), p. 89.

Crespi, L. P.
"The Cheater Problem in Polling"
Public Opinion Quarterly, Vol. 9 (Winter 1945-46), pp. 431-45.

Elinson, J. and Cisin, I. H.
"Detection of Interviewer Cheating Through Scale Technique"
Public Opinion Quarterly, Vol. 12 (Summer 1948), p. 325.

75.08 ---------- Interviewer Compensation

Ferber, Robert and Sudman, Seymour
"Effects of Compensation in Consumer Expenditure Studies"
Annals of Economic and Social Measurement, Vol. 3 (1974), p. 319.

Sudman, Seymour
"New Pay Methods for Interviewers"

75.09 ---------- Interview Scheduling and Timing

Brunner, A. G. and Carroll, S. J., Jr.
"Weekday Evening Interviews of Employed Persons are Better"
Public Opinion Quarterly, Vol. 33 (Summer 1969), pp. 265-8.

Gross, N. and Mason, W. S.
"Some Methodological Problems of Eight-Hour Interviews"
American Journal of Sociology, Vol. 59 (November 1953), pp. 197-204.

Mayer, Charles S.
"The Interviewer and His Environment"
Journal of Marketing Research, Vol. I (November 1964), pp. 225-36.

Sudman, Seymour
   "Time Allocation for Interviewers"
   Public Opinion Quarterly, Vol. 29 (Winter 1965), pp. 638-48.

Sudman, Seymour
   "Time Allocation of Survey Interviewers and Other Field Occupations"
   Proceedings, Social Statistics Section of the American Statistical
   Association (1964), pp. 41-51.

75.10 ---------- Sampling Issues in Interviewing

      See also (sub)heading(s) 107.

Carter, R. E., Jr., Troldahl, V. C., and Schuneman, R. S.
   "Interviewer Bias in Selecting Households"
   Journal of Marketing, Vol. 27 (April 1963), pp. 27-34.

Delamater, John and MacCorquodale, Patricia
   "The Effects of Interview Schedule Variations on Reported Sexual
   Behavior"
   Sociological Methods and Research, Vol. 4 (November 1975), pp. 215-36.

Manheimer, Dean and Hyman, Herbert
   "Interviewer Performance in Area Sampling"
   Public Opinion Quarterly (Spring 1949), pp. 87,8.

75.11 ---------- Unclassified (Management of Interviewers)

Bailar, B. A.
   "Recent Research in Reinterview Procedures"
   Journal of the American Statistical Association, Vol. 63 (March
   1968), pp. 41-63.

Bauman, Karl E. and Chase, Charles L.
   "Interviewers as Coders of Occupation"
   Public Opinion Quarterly, Vol. 38 (Spring 1974), pp. 107-12.

Cialdini, Robert B., Cacioppo, John R., and Bassett, Rodney
   "Throwing the Low-Ball for Charity: A Field Study"
   Meeting of the Midwestern Psychological Association, Chicago (1974),
   paper presentation.

Colombotos, John
   "The Effects of Personal vs. Telephone Interviews on Socially
   Acceptable Responses"
   Annual Meeting of the American Association for Public Opinion
   Research, Groton, CT (May 1965), paper presentation.

Crutchfield, R. S. and Gordon, D. A.
   "Variations in Respondents' Interpretations of an Opinion Poll
   Question"
   International Journal of Opinion and Attitude Research, Vol. 1
   (September 1947), pp. 1-12.

Dalenius, Tore
   "Treatment of the Non-Response Problem"
   Journal of Advertising Research, Vol. 2 (September 1961), pp. 3-5.

Dining, W. Edwards
   "On a Probability Mechanism to Attain an Economic Balance Between the
   Resultant Error of Response and the Bias of Non-Response"
   Journal of the American Statistical Association, Vol. 48 (December
   1953), pp. 743-72.

Dohrenwend, B. S.
   "An Experimental Study of Directive Interviewing"
   Public Opinion Quarterly, Vol. 34 (Spring 1970), pp. 621-5.

Dohrenwend, B. S. and Richardson, S. A.
   "Analysis of the Interviewer's Behavior"
   Human Organization, Vol. 15 (Summer 1956), pp. 29-32.

Durbin, J. and Stuart, A.
   "Differences in Response Rates of Experienced Interviewers"
   Journal of the Royal Statistical Society, Vol. 114, Part II (1951),
   p. 173.

Edsall, R. L.
   "Getting 'Not-at-Homes' to Interview Themselves"
   Journal of Marketing, Vol. 23 (October 1958), pp. 184,5.

Ferber, Robert and Hauck, Mathew
   "A Framework for Dealing With Response Errors in Consumer Surveys"
   Proceedings, National Conference, American Marketing Association
   (June 1964), pp. 533-40.

Garber, C. W., Jr.
  "Play Techniques for Interviewing on Durable Goods"
  Public Opinion Quarterly, Vol. 15 (Spring 1951), pp. 139-40.

Gaudet, H. and Wilson, E. C.
  "Who Escapes the Personal Investigator?"
  Journal of Applied Psychology, Vol. 24 (December 1940), pp. 773-7.

Gerson, E. J.
  "Methodological and Interviewing Problems in Household Surveys of
  Employment Problems in Urban Poverty Neighborhoods"
  Proceedings of the Social Statistics Section of the American
  Statistical Association (1969), pp. 19-23.

Hauck, M.
  "Planning Field Operations"
  in Ferber, R. (editor)
  Handbook of Marketing Research
  (New York: McGraw-Hill, 1974).

Hauck, Mathew and Steinkamp, Stanley
  Survey Reliability and Interviewer Competence
  (Urbana, IL: Bureau of Economic and Business Research, 1964), 112 pp.

Kensley, Patricia
  "Fieldwork From an Interviewer's Point of View"
  Market Research Society Fieldwork Supplement (March 1975).

Kincaid, H. V. and Bright, M.
  "The Tandem Interview: A Trial of the Two-Interviewer Team"
  Public Opinion Quarterly, Vol. 21 (Summer 1957), pp. 304-12.

Kiser, Clyde V.
  "Pitfalls in Sampling for Population Study"
  Journal of the American Statistical Association, Vol. 59 (September
  1964), p. 251.

Locander, William B., Sudman, Seymour, and Bradburn, Norman
  "An Investigation of Interview Method, Threat and Response Distortion"
  Journal of the American Statistical Association, Vol. 71 (June 1976),
  pp. 269-75.

Love, Lawrence T. and Turner, Anthony G.
  "The Census Bureau's Experience: Response Rates"
  Proceedings, Business and Economic Statistics Section, American
  Statistical Association (1975), pp. 76-85.

Manniche, E. and Hayes, D. P.
  "Respondent Anonymity and Data-Matching"
  Public Opinion Quarterly, Vol. 21 (Fall 1957), pp. 384-8.

Marquis, K. H.
  "Effects of Social Reinforcement on Health Reporting in the Household
  Interview"
  Sociometry, Vol. 33 (June 1970), pp. 203-15.

Marton, Katherin and Rohloff, Albert C.
  "Use One-Interview Studies With Care"
  Journal of Advertising Research, Vol. 14 (April 1974), pp. 35-8.

Mayer, C. S.
  "The Overlooked Ingredient in Survey Research"
  Business Horizons, Vol. 9 (Fall 1966), pp. 75-82.

Phillips, D. L. and Clancy, K. J.
  "Some Effects of Social Desirability in Survey Studies"
  American Journal of Sociology, Vol. 77 (March 1972), pp. 921-40.

Powell, B. A.
  "Recent Research in Reinterview Procedures"
  Proceedings of the Social Statistics Section of the American
  Statistical Association (1966), pp. 420-33.

Reingen, Peter H.
  "On Inducing Compliance With Requests"
  Journal of Consumer Research, Vol. 5 (September 1978), pp. 96-102.

Ross, H. L.
  "The Inaccessible Respondent: A Note on Privacy in City and Country"
  Public Opinion Quarterly, Vol. 27 (Summer 1963), pp. 269-75.

Sammis, F.
  "Are the Field Mice Getting Foxy?"
  in Dolva, W. K. (editor)
  Marketing Keys to Profits in the 1960's
  (Chicago: American Marketing Association, 42nd National Conference,
  1960), pp. 304-8.

Schwarzenauer, Wilhelm
"An Experiment on the Effect Internal Circular Letters Have on
Interviewers"
European Research, Vol. 2 (November 1974), pp. 243-7.

Sheatsley, P. B.
"Some Uses of Interviewer Report-Forms"
Public Opinion Quarterly, Vol. 11 (Winter 1947), pp. 601-22.

Sheets, Thomas, Radlinski, Allen, Kohne, James, and Brunner, Allen G.
"Deceived Respondents: Once Bitten, Twice Shy"
Public Opinion Quarterly, Vol. 38 (Summer 1974), pp. 261-3.

Singer, Eleanor
"The Effect of Informed Consent Procedures on Respondents' Reactions
to Surveys"
Journal of Consumer Research, Vol. 5 (June 1978), pp. 49-57.

Snead, R. P.
"Problems of Field Interviewers"
Journal of Marketing, Vol. 7 (October 1942), pp. 139-45.

Star, S. A.
"Obtaining Household Opinions From a Single Respondent"
Public Opinion Quarterly, Vol. 17 (Fall 1953), pp. 386-91.

Sternlieb, George
"Household Research in the Urban Core"
Journal of Marketing, Vol. 32 (January 1968), pp. 25-8.

U.S. Bureau of the Census
Response Errors in Collection of Expenditures Data by Household
Interviews: An Experimental Study
Technical Paper No. 11
(Washington, DC: U.S. Government Printing Office, 1965).

Weiss, Carol H.
"Research Organizations Interview the Poor"
Social Problems, Vol. 22 (December 1974), pp. 246-59.

Weitz, J.
"Verbal and Pictorial Questionnaires in Market Research"
Journal of Applied Psychology, Vol. 34 (October 1950), pp. 363-6.

Willingale, D. K.
"Fieldwork Quality--The Life and Death of the Industry"
ESOMAR Congress, Montreux (1975).

Wispe, L. G.
"Some Methodological Problems in the Analysis of the Unstructured
Interview"
Public Opinion Quarterly, Vol. 18 (Summer 1954), pp. 223-7.

Wolfe, D. F.
"A New Questionnaire Design"
Journal of Marketing, Vol. 21 (October 1956), pp. 186-90.

76 ---------------- PERSONAL INTERVIEWING TECHNIQUES ------------------
        See also (sub)heading(s) 74.

76.01 ---------- Books Re: Personal Interviewing Techniques

Adams, J. S.
    Interviewing Procedures: A Manual for Survey Interviewers
    (Chapel Hill, NC: University of North Carolina Press, 1958), 56 pp.

Bingham, W. V. D., Moore, B. V., and Gustad, J. W.
    How to Interview, Fourth Edition
    (New York: Harper and Bros., 1959), 277 pp.

Briggs, Charles
    Learning How to Ask
    (Cambridge, England: Cambridge University Press, 1986).

Cannell, Charles F., Oksenberg, Lois, and Converse, Jean M.
    Experiments in Interviewing Techniques
    (Ann Arbor, MI: The Institute for Social Research, 1979), 444 pp.

Douglas, J. D.
    Creative Interviewing
    (Beverly Hills, CA: Sage Publications, 1985).

Gorden, Raymond L.
    Interviewing: Strategy, Techniques, and Tactics, Revised Edition
    (Dorsey Press, 1975), 587 pp.

Kahn, R. L. and Cannell, C. F.
    The Dynamics of Interviewing: Theory, Techniques and Cases
    (New York: John Wiley and Sons, 1957), 351 pp.

McCrossan, Liz
    A Handbook for Interviewers: A Manual of Social Survey Practice and
    Procedures on Structured Interviewing
    (HMSO, 1984), 96 pp.

Sharma, Prakash C.
    Interview and Techniques of Interviewing: A Selected Research
    Bibliography (1930-66)
    (Monticello, IL: Council of Planning Librarians, December 1974), 29
    pp.

Survey Research Center
    Interviewer's Manual, Revised Edition
    (Ann Arbor, MI: The Institute for Social Research, 1976), 143 pp.

76.02 ---------- Interviewing Specific Populations

Becker, Theodore M. and Meyers, Peter R.
    "Empathy and Bravado: Interviewing Reluctant Bureaucrats"
    Public Opinion Quarterly, Vol. 38 (Winter 1974-1975), pp. 605-13.

Herzog, A. Regula, Rodgers, Willard L., and Kulka, Richard A.
    "Interviewing Older Adults: A Comparison of Telephone and
    Face-to-Face Modalities"
    Public Opinion Quarterly, Vol. 47 (Fall 1983), pp. 405-18.

Hunt, William H., Crane, Wilder W., and Wahlke, John C.
    "Interviewing Political Elites in Cross-Cultural Comparative Research"
    The American Journal of Sociology, Vol. 70 (July 1964), pp. 59-68.

Jones, Charles O.
    "Notes on Interviewing Members of the House of Representatives"
    Public Opinion Quarterly, Vol. 23 (Fall 1959), pp. 404-6.

Kincaid, Harry V. and Bright, Margaret
    "Interviewing the Business Elite"
    The American Journal of Sociology, Vol. 63 (November 1957), pp.
    304-11.

Menzel, H. and Katz, E.
    "Social Relations and Innovation in the Medical Profession: The
    Epidemiology of a New Drug"
    Public Opinion Quarterly, Vol. 19 (1956), pp. 337-52.

Smigel, E. O.
    "Interviewing a Legal Elite: The Wall Street Lawyer"
    American Journal of Sociology, Vol. 64 (September 1974), pp. 159-64.

Weiss, Carol H.
    "Interviewing Low-Income Respondents"
    Welfare in Review, Vol. 4 (October 1966), p. 3.

Zelan, J.
    "Interviewing the Aged"
    Public Opinion Quarterly, Vol. 33 (Fall 1969), pp. 420-4.

Zuckerman, Harriet
   "Interviewing an Ultra-Elite"
   Public Opinion Quarterly, Vol. 36 (Summer 1972), pp. 159-75.

76.03 ---------- Interview Questionnaire Design

Dichter, Ernest
   "Ask the Right Question and You'll Get the Right Answer"
   Journal of Consumer Marketing, Vol. 1, No. 2 (1984), pp. 91,2.

Kornhauser, Arthur and Sheatsley, Paul B.
   "Questionnaire Construction and Interview Procedure"
   in Sellitz, M., Jahoda, M. Deutsch, and Cook, S. W. (editors)
   Research Methods in Social Relations
   (New York: Henry Holt and Co., 1959), pp. 546-87.

Riesman, David and Benney, Mark
   "Asking and Answering"
   Journal of Business, Vol. 29 (October 1956), pp. 225-36.

Suchman, Edward A. and Guttman, Louis
   "A Solution to the Problem of Question 'Bias'"
   Public Opinion Quarterly, Vol. 11 (Fall 1947), pp. 445-55.

76.04 ---------- Personal Interview Introductions

Morton-Williams, Jean and Young, Penny
   "Obtaining the Survey Interview--An Analysis of Tape Recorded
   Doorstep Introductions"
   Journal of the Market Research Society, Vol. 29 (January 1987), pp.
   35-54.

Morton-Williams, Jean and Young, Penny
   "Interviewer Strategies on the Doorstep"
   Proceedings, Market Research Society Conference (March 1986), pp.
   1-11.

76.05 ---------- Use of the Tape Recorder in Interviewing

Belson, W. A.
   "Tape Recording: Its Effect on Accuracy of Response in Survey
   Interviews"
   Journal of Marketing Research, Vol. IV (August 1967), pp. 253-60.

Bevis, J. C.
   "Interviewing With Tape Recorder"
   Public Opinion Quarterly, Vol. 16 (Winter 1949), pp. 629-34.

Brody, E. E., Newman, Richard, and Redlich, F. C.
   "Sound Recording and the Problem of Evidence in Psychiatry"
   Science, Vol. 113 (April 1951), pp. 379,80.

Bucher, Rue, Fritz, C. E., and Quarantelli, E. L.
   "Tape Recorded Interviews in Social Research"
   American Sociological Review, Vol. 21, No. 3 (1956), pp. 359-64.

Bucher, R., Fritz, C. E., and Quarantelli, E. L.
   "Tape Recorded Research: Some Field and Data Processing Problems"
   Public Opinion Quarterly, Vol. 20 (Summer 1956), pp. 427-40.

Covner, B. J.
   "Studies in Phonographic Recordings of Verbal Material: IV. Written
   Reports of Interviews"
   Journal of Applied Psychology, Vol. 28 (April 1944), pp. 89-98.

Covner, B. J.
   "Studies of Phonographic Recording of Verbal Material: III. The
   Completeness and Accuracy of Counseling Interview Reports"
   Journal of General Psychology, Vol. 30 (April 1944), pp. 181-203.

Eitzen, D. D.
   "Objective Recording Procedures in Counseling and Research"
   Marriage and Family Living, Vol. 14 (August 1952), pp. 225-8.

Engel, J. F.
   "Tape Recorders in Consumer Research"
   Journal of Marketing, Vol. 26 (April 1962), pp. 73,4.

Harper, R. A. and Hudson, J. W.
   "The Use of Recordings in Marriage Counseling: A Preliminary
   Empirical Investigation"
   Marriage and Family Living, Vol. 14 (November 1952), pp. 332-4.

Ives, Edward D.
   The Tape-Recorded Interview
   (Knoxville, TN: University of Tennessee Press, 1974).

Morton-Williams, Jean and Young, Penny
    "Obtaining the Survey Interview--An Analysis of Tape Recorded
    Doorstep Introductions"
    Journal of the Market Research Society, Vol. 29 (January 1987), pp.
    35-54.

Raimy, V. C.
    "Functional Specifications for a Sound Recorder for the Psychological
    Clinic"
    American Psychologist, Vol. 3 (November 1948), pp. 513-8.

76.06 ---------- Theory Re: Computer Assisted Personal Interviewing

        See also (sub)heading(s) 34.10, 38.05, 73, 88, 97, 100.07.

Baden, Robert W., Boerema, Elso M., and Bon, Emiel P. M.
    "Computer Assisted Interviewing in a Face-to-Face Situation"
    ESOMAR Congress, Montreux (1987), pp. 829-45.

Bemelmans-Stork, M. and Sikkel, D.
    "Data Collection With Handheld Computers"
    Proceedings, 45th ISI Conference, Amsterdam (1985).

Freeman, H. E. and Shanks, J. M. (editors)
    "Special Issue on the Emergence of Computer-Assisted Research"
    Sociological Methods and Research, Vol. 12 (November 1983).

Rowley, Gwyn, Barker, Keith, and Callaghan, Victor
    "The Ferranti Market Research Terminal"
    European Research, Vol. 14, No. 2 (1986), pp. 74-6.

Rowley, Gwyn, Barker, Keith, and Callaghan, Victor
    "The Market Research Terminal and Developments in Survey Research"
    European Journal of Marketing, Vol. 20, No. 2 (1986), pp. 35-39.

Saris, Willem E., De Pijper, W. Marius, and Neijens, P.
    "Some Notes on the Computer Steered Interview"
    in Middendorp, C. P., Niemoller, B., and Saris, W. E. (editors)
    Proceedings, Sociometry Meeting
    (Amsterdam: SRF, 1980), pp. 306-10.

Van Doorn, Leo and Hess, Theo
    "New Research Possibilities by Computerized Personal Interviewing"
    Proceedings, ESOMAR Congress, Lisbon (1988), pp. 505-24.

Whalen, B.
    "On-Site Computer Interviewing Yields Research Data Instantly"
    Marketing News (November 1, 1984), p. 17.

76.07 ---------- Applications of CAPI

Mount, J. W.
    "A Personal Computer in Research"
    Proceedings, Business and Economics Section, American Statistical
    Association
    (Washington: American Statistical Association, 1981), pp. 67-72.

76.08 ---------- Software for Interviewing

Computers for Marketing Corporation
    SURVENT: CRT Interviewing (Central Facility)
    (San Francisco, CA: Computers for Marketing Corporation).

76.09 ---------- Unclassified (Interviewing Techniques)

Biggs, Howard
    "The Choice Optimisation Board"
    European Research, Vol. 1 (May 1973), pp. 124-7.

Birt, E. M. and Brogren, R. H.
    "Minimizing Interviews Through Sequential Sampling"
    Journal of Marketing Research, Vol. I (February 1964), pp. 65-7.

Cannell, Charles F., Oksenberg, Lois, and Converse, Jean M.
    "Striving for Response Accuracy: Experiments in New Interviewing
    Techniques"
    Journal of Marketing Research, Vol. XIV (August 1977), pp. 306-15.

Caplow, T.
    "The Dynamics of Information Interviewing"
    American Journal of Sociology, Vol. 62 (September 1956), pp. 153-7.

Gill, Rafael E.
    "Round Hand-Out Cards"
    European Research, Vol. 4 (May 1976), p. 128.

Hodgson, P. B.
"Do We Represent Racial Minorities Adequately in Survey Research?"
Market Research Society Annual Conference, Bournemouth (1975).

Oksenberg, Lois, Vinokur, Arminian, and Cannell, Charles F.
"The Effects of Commitment to Being a Good Respondent on Interview Performance"
Survey Research Center, The University of Michigan (1975).

Sudman, Seymour, Greeley, Andrew, and Pinto, Leonard
"The Effectiveness of Self-Administered Questionnaires"
Journal of Marketing Research, Vol. II (August 1965), pp. 293-7.

Trull, S. G.
"Strategies of Effective Interviewing"
Harvard Business Review, Vol. 4 (January-February 1964), pp. 89-94.

Vinokur, Arminian, Oksenberg, Lois, and Cannell, Charles F.
"The Effects of Feedback and Reinforcement on the Report of Health Information in Household Interviews"
(Ann Arbor, MI: The Institute for Social Research, 1975), research report.

Walters, J. H., Jr.
"Structured or Unstructured Techniques"
Journal of Marketing, Vol. 25 (April 1961), pp. 58-62.

Westfall, R. L., Boyd, H. W., and Campbell, D. T.
"The Use of Structured Techniques in Motivation Research"
Journal of Marketing, Vol. 22 (October 1957), pp. 134-9.

Zehner, Robert B. and McCalla, Mary Ellen
"Response Rates and Prior Letters"
Journal of Advertising Research, Vol. 17 (February 1977), pp. 31-5.

77 ------------------ BIAS IN PERSONAL INTERVIEWING ------------------
        See also (sub)heading(s) 74.

77.01 ---------- General Discussions Re: Bias in Personal Interviewing

Boyd, Harper W., Jr. and Westfall, Ralph
    "Interviewer Bias Once More Revisited"
    Journal of Marketing Research, Vol. VII (May 1970), pp. 249-53.

Boyd, Harper W., Jr. and Westfall, Ralph
    "Interviewer Bias Revisited"
    Journal of Marketing Research, Vol. II (February 1965), pp. 58-63.

Boyd, Harper W., Jr. and Westfall, Ralph
    "Interviewers as a Source of Error in Surveys"
    Journal of Marketing, Vol. 19 (April 1955), pp. 311-24.

Collins, Martin
    "Interviewer Variability: A Review of the Problem"
    Journal of the Market Research Society, Vol. 22 (April 1980), pp. 77-94.

77.02 ---------- Effects of Interviewer's Physical Characteristics

Anderson, Barbara A., Silver, Brian D., and Abramson, Paul R.
    "The Effects of Race of the Interviewer on Race-Related Attitudes of Black Respondents in SRC/CPS National Election Studies"
    Public Opinion Quarterly, Vol. 52 (Fall 1988), pp. 289-34.

Anderson, Barbara A., Silver, Brian D., and Abramson, Paul R.
    "The Effects of Race of the Interviewer on Measures of Electoral Participation by Blacks in SRC National Election Studies"
    Public Opinion Quarterly, Vol. 52 (Spring 1988), pp. 53-83.

Athey, E. R., Coleman, John E., Reitmans, Audrey P., and Long, Jenny
    "Two Experiments Showing the Effect of the Interviewer's Racial Background in Responses to Questionnaires Concerning Racial Issues"
    Journal of Applied Psychology, Vol. 44 (December 1960), pp. 381-5.

Benney, Mark, Reesman, David, and Star, Shirley A.
    "Age and Sex in the Interview"
    American Journal of Sociology, Vol. 62 (September 1956), pp. 143-52.

Colombotos, John, Elinson, Jack, and Loewenstein, Regina
    "Effect of Interviewer Sex on Interview Responses"
    Public Health Report, Vol. 83 (1968), pp. 685-90.

Ehrlich, June Sachar and Riesman, David
    "Age and Authority in the Interview"
    Public Opinion Quarterly, Vol. 25 (Spring 1961), pp. 39-56.

Hatchett, Shirley and Schuman, Howard
    "White Respondents and Race-of-Interviewer Effects"
    Public Opinion Quarterly, Vol. XXXIX (Winter 1975-76).

Kindel, W. I.
    "Sex of Observer and Spousal Roles in Decision-Making"
    Marriage and Family Living (May 1961), p. 186.

Klugman, S. F.
    "The Effect of Age Upon Estimation of Age"
    Journal of Social Psychology, Vol. 26 (August 1947), pp. 29-33.

McClelland, Lou
    "Effects of Interviewer-Respondent Race Interactions on Household Interview Measures of Motivation and Intelligence"
    Journal of Personality and Social Psychology, Vol. 29 (March 1974), pp. 392-7.

Reese, Stephen D., Danielson, Wayne A., Shoemaker, Pamela J., Chang, Tsan-Kuo, and Hus, Huei-Ling
    "Ethnicity-of-Interviewer Effects Among Mexican-Americans and Anglos"
    Public Opinion Quarterly, Vol. 50 (Winter 1986), pp. 563-72.

Schneider, D. E. and Bayroff, A. G.
    "The Relationship Between Rater Characteristics and Validity of Ratings"
    Journal of Applied Psychology (August 1953), pp. 278-80.

Schuman, H. and Converse, J. M.
    "The Effects of Black and White Interviewers on Black Responses in 1968"
    Public Opinion Quarterly, Vol. 35 (1971), pp. 44-68.

Singer, Eleanor, Frankel, M. R., and Glassman, M. B.
    "The Effects of Interviewer Characteristics and Expectations on Response"
    Public Opinion Quarterly, Vol. 47 (Spring 1983), pp. 68-83.

77.03 ---------- Voice and Verbal Related Biasing Effects

Barath, Arpad and Cannell, Charles F.
"Effect of Interviewer's Voice Intonation"
Public Opinion Quarterly, Vol. 40 (Fall 1976), pp. 370-3.

Collins, W. Andrew
"Interviewers' Verbal Idiosyncracies as a Source of Bias"
Public Opinion Quarterly, Vol. 34 (Fall 1970), pp. 416-23.

Collins, W. Andrew
"Idiosyncratic Verbal Behavior of Interviewers"
Institute for Communication Research, Stanford University (1968),
unpublished paper.

Henson, Ramon
"Effects of Instructions and Verbal Modeling in a Survey Interviewing
Setting"
Social Science Research, Vol. 3 (December 1974), pp. 323-42.

Hildum, D. C. and Brown, R. W.
"Verbal Reinforcement and Interviewer Bias"
Journal of Abnormal and Social Psychology (July 1956), pp. 100-11.

Rosenthal, Robert et al.
"Instruction-Reading Behavior of the Experimentor as an Unintended
Determinant of Experimental Results"
Journal of Experimental Research in Personality, Vol. 1 (May 1966),
pp. 221-6.

77.04 ---------- Effects of Interviewer Expectations

Rice, S.
"Contagious Bias in the Interview"
American Journal of Sociology, Vol. 35 (1929), pp. 420-3.

Rosenthal, Robert
"Experimenter Outcome-Orientation and the Results of the
Psychological Experiment"
Psychological Bulletin, Vol. 61 (June 1964), pp. 405-12.

Singer, Eleanor, Frankel, M. R., and Glassman, M. B.
"The Effects of Interviewer Characteristics and Expectations on
Response"
Public Opinion Quarterly, Vol. 47 (Spring 1983), pp. 68-83.

Singer, Eleanor and Kolinke-Aguirre, Luane
"Interviewer Expectation Effects: A Replication and Extension"
Annual Meeting of AAPOR, Roanoke, VA (1978), paper presentation.

Smith, Harry L. and Hyman, Herbert
"The Biasing Effect of Interviewer Expectations on Survey Results"
Public Opinion Quarterly, Vol. 14 (Fall 1950), pp. 491-506.

Sudman, Seymour, Bradburn, Norman M., Blair, Ed, and Stocking, Carol
"Modest Expectations: The Effects of Interviewers' Prior Expectations
on Responses"
Sociological Methods and Research, Vol. 6 (1977), pp. 177-82.

Wyatt, Dale F. and Campbell, Donald T.
"A Study of Interviewer Bias as Related to Interviewers' Expectations
and Own Opinions"
International Journal of Opinion and Attitude Research, Vol. 4
(Spring 1950), pp. 77-83.

77.05 ---------- Interviewer Coding and Recording Error

See also (sub)heading(s) 75.06.

Fisher, H.
"Interviewer Bias in the Recording Operation"
International Journal of Opinion and Attitude Research, Vol. 4 (Fall
1950), pp. 391-411.

Guest, L. and Nuckols, R.
"A Laboratory Experiment in Recording in Public Opinion Interviewing"
International Journal of Opinion and Attitude Research, Vol. 4 (Fall
1950), pp. 336-52.

Stember, H. and Hyman, H.
"Interviewer Effects in the Classification of Responses"
Public Opinion Quarterly, Vol. 13 (Winter 1949), pp. 669-82.

77.06 ---------- Unclassified (Bias in Personal Interviewing)

Atkin, C. K. and Chaffee, S. H.
    "Instrumental Response Strategies in Opinion Interviews"
    Public Opinion Quarterly, Vol. 36 (Spring 1972), pp. 69-79.

Back, Kurt W. and Gergen, Kenneth J.
    "Idea Orientation and Ingratiation in the Interview"
    Proceedings of the Social Statistics Section, American Statistical
    Association (1963), pp. 284-8.

Bailar, Barbara A.
    "Some Sources of Error and Their Effect on Census Statistics"
    Demography, Vol. 13 (1976), pp. 273-86.

Bailar, Barbara, Bailey, Leroy, and Stevens, Joyce
    "Measures of Interviewer Bias and Variance"
    Journal of Marketing Research, Vol. XIV (August 1977), pp. 337-43.

Bailey, Leroy, Moore, Thomas, and Bailar, Barbara
    "An Interviewer Variance Study for the Eight Impact Cities of the
    National Crime Survey Cities Sample"
    Presentation at the American Statistical Association Meetings,
    Boston, MA (1976).

Barr, A.
    "Differences Between Experienced Interviewers"
    Applied Statistics, Vol. 6 (1957), pp. 180-8.

Belden, J. et al.
    "Interviewer Bias and What to do About It"
    Public Opinion Quarterly, Vol. 15 (Winter 1951-52), pp. 774-8.

Berg, I. A. and Rapaport, G. M.
    "Response Bias in an Unstructured Questionnaire"
    Journal of Psychology, Vol. 38 (October 1954), pp. 475-81.

Booker, H. S. and David, S. T.
    "Differences in Results Obtained by Experienced and Inexperienced
    Interviewers"
    Journal of the Royal Statistical Society, Vol. 155, Part 2 (1952),
    pp. 232-57.

Bradburn, N. M. and Mason, W. M.
    "The Effect of Question Order on Responses"
    Journal of Marketing Research, Vol. I (November 1964), pp. 57-61.

Bridge, R. Gary, Reeder, Leo G., Kanouse, David, Kinder, Donald R.,
    Nagy, Vivian Tong, and Judd, Charles M.
    "Interviewing Changes Attitudes--Sometimes"
    Public Opinion Quarterly, Vol. 41 (Spring 1977), pp. 56-64.

Cahalan, D., Tamulonis, V., and Verner, H. W.
    "Interviewer Bias Involved in Certain Types of Opinion Survey
    Questions"
    International Journal of Opinion and Attitude Research, Vol. 1 (March
    1947), pp. 63-77.

Cannell, Charles F. and Fowler, Floyd J., Jr.
    "A Note on Interviewer Effect in Self Enumeration Procedure"
    American Sociological Review, Vol. 29 (April 1964), p. 270.

Cannell, C. F., Fowler, F. J., and Marquis, K. H.
    The Influence of Interviewer and Respondent Psychological and
    Behavioural Variables on the Reporting in Household Interviews
    (Washington, DC: U.S. Government Printing Office, 1968).

Carter, Roy E., Jr., Troldahl, Verling C., and Schuneman, R. Smith
    "Interviewer Bias in Selecting Households"
    Journal of Marketing, Vol. 27 (April 1963), pp. 27-34.

Clancy, K. J. and Wachsler, R. A.
    "Positional Effects in Shared-Cost Surveys"
    Public Opinion Quarterly, Vol. 35 (Summer 1971), pp. 258-65.

Cole, Dorothy E.
    "Field Work in Sample Surveys of Household Income"
    Applied Statistics (March 1956), pp. 49-61.

Collins, M.
    "Interviewer Variability: Milton Keynes Household Survey"
    Methodological Working Paper No. 16
    (London: SCPR, 1979).

Collins, Martin
    "Interviewer Variability: The North Yorkshire Experiment"
    Journal of the Market Research Society, Vol. 20 (April 1978).

Crespi, L. P.
   "The Interview Effect in Polling"
   Public Opinion Quarterly, Vol. 12 (Spring 1948), pp. 99-111.

Dohrenwend, B. S., Colombotos, J., and Dohrenwend, B. P.
   "Social Distance and Interviewer Effects"
   Public Opinion Quarterly, Vol. 32 (Fall 1968), pp. 410-22.

Dohrenwend, B. S. and Dohrenwend, B. P.
   "Sources of Refusals in Surveys"
   Public Opinion Quarterly, Vol. 32 (Spring 1968), pp. 74-83.

Duncan, S., Jr., Rosenberg, M. J., and Finkelstein, J.
   "The Paralanguage of Experimenter Bias"
   Sociometry, Vol. 32 (June 1969), pp. 207-19.

Durbin, J. and Stuart, A.
   "Callbacks and Clustering in Sample Surveys"
   Journal of the Royal Statistical Society, Vol. IV (1954), pp. 387-428.

Durbin, J. and Stuart, A.
   "Differences in Response Rates of Experienced Interviewers"
   Journal of the Royal Statistical Society, Vol. 114, Part II (1951),
   p. 173.

Farber, B.
   "Response Falsification and Spurious Correlation in Survey Research"
   American Sociological Review, Vol. 28 (February 1963), pp. 123-30.

Feldman, J. J., Hyman, H., and Hart, C. W.
   "A Field Study of Interviewer Effects on the Quality of Survey Data"
   Public Opinion Quarterly, Vol. 15 (Winter 1951-52), pp. 734-61.

Ferber, R.
   "On the Reliability of Responses Secured in Sample Surveys"
   Journal of the American Statistical Association, Vol. 50 (September
   1955), pp. 788-811.

Ferber, R. and Wales, H. G.
   "Detection and Correction of Interviewer Bias"
   Public Opinion Quarterly, Vol. 16 (Spring 1952), pp. 107-27.

Fleiss, J. L.
   "Estimating the Reliability of Interview Data"
   Psychometrika, Vol. 35 (June 1970), pp. 143-62.

Flinn, Nancy
   "One Effect of Interviewer Bias"
   Viewpoints--The Journal of Data Collection, Vol. 16 (May 1976), pp.
   2-5.

Freeman, John and Butler, Edgar W.
   "Some Sources of Interviewer Variance in Surveys"
   Public Opinion Quarterly, Vol. 40 (Spring 1976), pp. 79-91.

Freitag, C. B. and Barry, J. R.
   "Interaction and Interviewer Bias in a Survey of the Aged"
   Psychological Reports, Vol. 34, Part 1 (June 1974), pp. 771-4.

Friedman, Neil, Kurland, Daniel, and Rosenthal, Robert
   "Experimenter Behavior as an Unintended Determinant of Experimental
   Results"
   Journal of Projective Techniques and Personality Assessment, Vol. 29
   (December 1965), pp. 479-90.

Gales, K. and Kendall, M. G.
   "An Inquiry Concerning Interviewer Variability"
   Journal of the Royal Statistical Society, Series A, Vol. 120 (1957),
   pp. 121-47.

Getzels, T. W.
   "The Question-Answer Process: A Conceptualization and Some Derived
   Hypotheses for Empirical Examination"
   Public Opinion Quarterly, Vol. 18 (Spring 1954), pp. 80-91.

Goudy, Willis J. and Potter, Harry R.
   "Interviewer Rapport: Demise of a Concept"
   Public Opinion Quarterly, Vol. XXXIX (Winter 1975-76).

Gray, P. G.
   "Examples of Interviewer Variability Taken From Two Sample Surveys"
   Applied Statistics, Vol. V (June 1956), pp. 73-85.

Gray, P. G.
   "The Memory Factor in Social Surveys"
   Journal of the American Statistical Association, Vol. 50 (June 1955),
   pp. 344-63.

Hansen, M. H., Hurwitz, W. N., and Bershad, M. A.
    "Measurement Errors in Census and Surveys"
    Bulletin of the International Statistical Institute, Vol. 38 (1961),
    pp. 359-74.

Hanson, R. H. and Marks, E. S.
    "Influence of the Interviewer on the Accuracy of Survey Results"
    Journal of the American Statistical Association, Vol. 53 (September
    1958), pp. 635-55.

Hauck, M. and Steinkamp, S.
    "Survey Reliability and Interviewer Competence"
    Studies in Consumer Savings, No. 4
    Bureau of Economics and Business Research, University of Illinois
    (1964).

Heller, K., Davis, J. D., and Myers, R. A.
    "The Effect of Interviewer Style in a Standardized Interview"
    Journal of Consulting Psychology, Vol. 30 (December 1966), pp. 501-8.

Johnson, T. P., Houghland, J. G., Jr., and Clayton, R. R.
    "Obtaining Reports of Sensitive Behavior: A Comparison of Substance
    Use Reports From Telephone and Face to Face Interviews"
    Social Science Quarterly, Vol. 70 (March 1989).

Katz, D.
    "Do Interviewers Bias Poll Results?"
    Public Opinion Quarterly, Vol. 6 (Summer 1942), pp. 248-68.

Kemsley, W. F. F.
    "Interviewer Variability in Expenditure Surveys"
    Journal of the Royal Statistical Society, Vol. A128 (Part 1, 1965),
    pp. 118-39.

Kemsley, W. F. F.
    "Interviewer Variability and a Budget Survey"
    Applied Statistics, Vol. 9 (June 1960), pp. 122-8.

Kish, L.
    "Studies of Interviewer Variance for Attitudinal Variables"
    Journal of the American Statistical Association, Vol. 57 (1962), pp.
    92-115.

Kish, Leslie and Hess, Irene
    "On Non-Coverage of Sample Dwellings"
    Journal of the American Statistical Association, Vol. 53 (June 1958),
    pp. 509-24.

Kish, L. and Lansing, J. B.
    "Response Errors in Estimating Value of Homes"
    Journal of the American Statistical Association, Vol. 49 (September
    1954), pp. 520-38.

Lansing, J. B., Ginsberg, G. P., and Braaten, K.
    "An Investigation of Response Error"
    Studies in Consumer Savings, No. 2
    Bureau of Economics and Business Research, University of Illinois
    (1961).

Lenski, Gerhard E. and Leggett, John C.
    "Caste, Class and Deference in the Research Interview"
    The American Journal of Sociology, Vol. 65 (March 1960), pp. 463-7.

Lindzey, G.
    "A Note on Interviewer Bias"
    Journal of Applied Psychology, Vol. 35 (June 1951), pp. 182-4.

Mahalanobis, P. C.
    "Recent Experiments in Statistical Sampling in the Indian Statistical
    Institute"
    Journal of the Royal Statistical Society, Part 4 (1946), pp. 326-78.

Marquis, Kent H. and Cannell, Charles F.
    "A Study of Interviewer-Respondent Interaction in the Urban
    Employment Survey"
    Survey Research Center, The University of Michigan (1969).

Marquis, Kent H., Cannell, Charles F., and Laurent, Andre
    "Reporting of Health Events in Household Interviews: Effects of
    Reinforcement, Question Length, and Reinterviews"
    Vital and Health Statistics
    (Washington, DC: U.S. Public Health Service, Series 2, No. 45, March
    1972).

Manheimer, D. and Hyman, H.
    "Interviewer Performance in Area Sampling"
    Public Opinion Quarterly, Vol. 13 (Spring 1949), pp. 83-92.

McGuigan, F. J.
  "The Experimenter: A Neglected Stimulus Object"
  Psychological Bulletin, Vol. 60 (July 1963), pp. 421-8.

McKenzie, J. R.
  "An Investigation Into Interviewer Effects in Market Research"
  Journal of Marketing Research, Vol. XIV (August 1977), pp. 330-6.

Neter, John and Waksberg, Joseph
  "Response Errors in Collection of Expenditures by Household
  Interviews: An Experimental Study"
  Technical Paper No. 11
  U.S. Bureau of the Census (1965).

Neter, John and Waksberg, Joseph
  "A Study of Response Errors in Expenditures Data From Household
  Interviews"
  Journal of the American Statistical Association, Vol. 59 (March
  1964), pp. 18-55.

Nuckols, Robert C.
  "The Validity and Comparability of Mail and Personal Interview
  Surveys"
  Journal of Marketing Research, Vol. I (February 1964), pp. 11-6.

O'Muircheartaigh, C. A.
  "Response Errors in an Attitudinal Sample Survey"
  Qualtity and Quantity, Vol. 10 (1976), pp. 97-115.

Parker, C. A., Wright, E. W., and Clark, S. G.
  "Questions Concerning the Interview as a Research Technique"
  Journal of Educational Research, Vol. 51 (November 1957), pp. 215-21.

Parfitt, J. H.
  "How Accurately Can Product Purchasing Behaviour be Measured by
  Recall at a Single Interview?"
  ESOMAR/WAPOR Congress, Vienna (1967).

Rosenthal, Robert
  "Letter to the Editor"
  Behavioral Science, Vol. 9 (July 1964), pp. 256,7.

Rosenthal, Robert
  "Experimenter Modeling Effects as Determinants of Subjects' Responses"
  Journal of Projective Techniques and Personality Assessment, Vol. 27
  (December 1963), pp. 467-71.

Rosenthal, Robert
  "On the Social Psychology of the Psychological Experiment: The
  Experimenter's Hypothesis as Unintended Determinant of Experimental
  Results"
  American Scientist, Vol. 51 (June 1963), pp. 268-83.

Rosenthal, Robert
  "Note on the Fallible E"
  Psychological Reports, Vol. 4 (December 1958), p. 662.

Rosenthal, Robert and Fode, K. L.
  "Psychology of the Scientist: V. Three Experiments in Experimenter
  Bias"
  Psychological Reports, Vol. 12 (April 1963), pp. 491-511.

Rosenthal, Robert et al.
  "Variables Affecting E Bias in a Group Situation"
  Genetic Psychology Monographs, Vol. 70 (June 1964), pp. 271-96.

Rosenthal, Robert et al.
  "The Effect of Early Data Returns on Data Subsequently Obtained by
  Outcome-Biased Experimenters"
  Sociometry, Vol. 26 (December 1963), pp. 487-98.

Rosenthal, Robert et al.
  "The Role of the Research Assistant in the Mediation of Experimenter
  Bias"
  Journal of Personality, Vol. 31 (September 1963), pp. 313-35.

Schyberger, B. W.
  "A Study of Interviewer Behavior"
  Journal of Marketing Research, Vol. IV (February 1967), pp. 32-5.

Shapiro, M. J.
  "Discovering Interviewer Bias in Open-Ended Survey Responses"
  Public Opinion Quarterly, Vol. 34 (1970), pp. 412-5.

Shapiro, Sam and Eberhardt, John C.
  "Interviewer Differences in an Intensive Interview Situation"
  International Journal of Opinion and Attitude Research, Vol. 1 (June
  1947), pp. 1-17.

Sheatsley, P. B.
  "An Analysis of Interviewer Characteristics and Their Relationship to
  Performance"
  International Journal of Opinion and Attitude Research, Vol. 4
  (Winter 1950-51), pp. 473-98; Vol. 5 (Spring 1951), pp. 79-94; Vol. 5
  (Summer 1951), pp. 191-220.

Skelly, F.
  "Interviewer Appearance Stereotypes as a Possible Source of Bias"
  Journal of Marketing, Vol. 19 (July 1954), pp. 74,5.

Stember, H.
  "Which Respondents are Reliable"
  International Journal of Opinion and Attitude Research, Vol. 5
  (Winter 1951-52), pp. 475-9.

Stember, H. and Hyman, H.
  "How Interviewer Effects Operate Through Question Form"
  International Journal of Opinion and Attitude Research, Vol. 23
  (Winter 1949-50), pp. 405-13.

Stevens, Joyce A. and Bailar, Barbara A.
  "The Relationship Between Various Interviewer Characteristics and the
  Collection of Income Data"
  American Statistical Association Meetings, Boston (1976), paper
  presentation.

Suchman, E., Phillips, B. S., and Streib, G. F.
  "An Analysis of the Validity of Health Questionnaires"
  Social Forces, Vol. 36 (March 1958), pp. 223-32.

Thumin, F. J.
  "Watch for Those Unseen Variables"
  Journal of Marketing, Vol. 26 (July 1962), pp. 58-60.

U.S. Department of HEW
  The Influence of Interviewer and Respondent Psychological and
  Behavioral Variables on Reporting in Household Interviews
  Public Health Service Publication No. 1000, Series 2, No. 26
  (Washington, DC: U.S. Department of Health, Education and Welfare,
  1968), 65 pp.

Vaughn, C. L. and Reynolds, W. A.
  "Reliability of Personal Interview Data"
  Journal of Applied Psychology, Vol. 35 (February 1951), pp. 61-3.

Weiss, D. J. and Davis, R. V.
  "An Objective Validation of Factual Interview Data"
  Journal of Applied Psychology, Vol. 44 (December 1960), pp. 381-5.

Williams, J. A., Jr.
  "Interviewer Role Performance: A Further Note on Bias in the
  Information Interview"
  Public Opinion Quarterly, Vol. 32 (Summer 1968), pp. 287-94.

Williams, J. A., Jr.
  "Interviewer-Respondent Interaction: A Study of Bias in the
  Information Interview"
  Sociometry, Vol. 27 (September 1964), pp. 338-52.

78 ---------------------- GROUP INTERVIEWING ------------------------
      See also (sub)heading(s) 74, 79.

78.01 ---------- Books Re: Focus Group and Group Depth Interviewing

Advertising Research Foundation
    Focus Groups: Issues and Approaches
    (New York: Advertising Research Foundation, 1985).

Cox, Keith K. and Higginbotham, James B.
    Focus Group Interviews
    (Chicago: American Marketing Association, 1979).

Goldman, Alfred E. and McDonald, Susan Schwartz
    The Group Depth Interview: Principles and Practice
    (Englewood Cliffs, NJ: Prentice-Hall, Inc., 1987).

Greenbaum, Thomas L.
    The Practical Handbook and Guide to Focus Group Research
    (Lexington, MA: D. C. Heath and Company, 1988), 208 pp.

Krueger, Richard A.
    Focus Groups: A Practical Guide for Applied Research
    (Newbury Park, CA: Sage Publications, Inc., 1988), 200 pp.

Merton, Robert K., Fiske, Marjorie, and Kendall, Patricia L.
    The Focused Interview
    (New York: The Free Press, 1956).

Moore, Carl M.
    Group Techniques for Idea Building
    (Newbury Park, CA: Sage Publications, Inc., 1987).

Morgan, David L.
    Focus Groups as Qualitative Research
    Quantitative Research Methods, Volume 16
    (Newbury Park, CA: Sage Publications, Inc., 1988), 88 pp.

Templeton, Jane Farley
    Focus Groups: A Guide for Marketing and Advertising Professionals
    (Chicago: Probus Publishing Company, 1987).

78.02 ---------- Theory Re: Focus Group Interviewing

Anastas, Michael
    "For Sensitive Research Subjects, One to One Interviews Work Best"
    Bank Marketing, Vol. 20 (July 1988), pp. 18-22.

Axelrod, Myril D.
    "The Dynamics of the Group Interview"
    Proceedings
    (Association for Consumer Research, 1976), pp. 437-41.

Axelrod, Myril D.
    "The Dynamics of the Group Interview"
    in Anderson, Beverlee B. (editor)
    Advances in Consumer Research, Volume Three
    (Association for Consumer Research, 1976), pp. 437-41.

Axelrod, M. D.
    "Marketers Get an Eyeful When Focus Groups Expose Products, Ideas,
    Images, Ad Copy, Etc. to Consumers"
    Marketing News (February 28, 1975), pp. 6,7.

Calder, Bobby J.
    "Focus Groups and the Nature of Qualitative Marketing Research"
    Journal of Marketing Research, Vol. XIV (August 1977), pp. 353-64.

Cook, William A.
    "Turning Focus Groups Inside Out"
    Advances in Consumer Research, Vol. IX (October 1981), pp. 62-4.

Cox, K. K., Higginbotham, J. B., and Burton, J.
    "Applications of Focus Group Interviews in Marketing"
    Journal of Marketing, Vol. 40 (January 1976), pp. 77-80.

De Almeida, Pergentino Mendes
    "A Review of Group Discussion Methodology"
    European Research, Vol. 8 (March 1980), pp. 114-20.

DeNicola, Nino
    "Debriefing Sessions: The Missing Link in Focus Groups"
    Marketing News, Vol. 24 (January 8, 1990), p. 20.

Dunnette, Marvin D., Campbell, John, and Jaastad, Kay
    "The Effect of Group Participation on Brainstorming Effectiveness for
    Two Industrial Samples"
    Journal of Applied Psychology, Vol. 47 (January 1963), pp. 30-7.

Dupont, Thomas D.
"Exploratory Group Interview in Consumer Research: A Case Example"
in Anderson, Beverlee B. (editor)
Advances in Consumer Research, Volume Three
(Association for Consumer Research, 1976), pp. 431-3.

Durgee, Jeffrey F.
"New Product Ideas From Focus Groups"
Journal of Consumer Marketing, Vol. 4 (Fall 1987), pp. 57-65.

Durgee, Jeffrey F.
"Point of View: Using Creative Writing Techniques in Focus Groups"
Journal of Advertising Research, Vol. 26 (December 1986/January
1987), pp. 57-65.

Egbert, Harry A.
"Focus Groups: A Basic Tool to Probe Buyers' Attitudes"
Industrial Marketing (March 1983), pp. 82,3.

Fahad, G. A.
"Group Discussions: A Misunderstood Technique"
Journal of Marketing Management, Vol. 1 (Spring 1986), pp. 315-27.

Fern, Edward F.
"Why do Focus Groups Work: A Review and Integration of Small Group
Process Theories"
in Mitchell, Andrew (editor)
Advances in Consumer Research
(Ann Arbor, MI: University of Michigan).

Hammond, Meryl
"Creative Focus Groups: Uses and Misuses"
Marketing and Media Decisions, Vol. 21 (July 1986), pp. 154,56.

Hess, John M.
"Group Interviewing"
in King, Robert L. (editor)
1968 ACR Fall Conference Proceedings
(Chicago: American Marketing Association, 1968), pp. 193-6.

Inglis, Robert C.
"In-Depth Data: Using Focus Groups to Study Industrial Markets"
Business Marketing, Vol. 72 (November 1987), pp. 78-82.

Karger, Ted
"Focus Groups are for Focusing and for Little Else"
Marketing News (August 28, 1987), pp. 52-4.

Keown, Charles
"Focus Group Research: Tool for the Retailers"
Journal of Small Business Management (April 1983), pp. 59-65.

Langmaid, Roy and Ross, Barry
"Games Respondents Play"
Journal of the Market Research Society, Vol. 26 (July 1984), pp.
221-9.

Lautman, Martin R.
"Focus Groups: Theory and Method"
in Mitchell, Andrew (editor)
Advances in Consumer Research, Volume Nine
(Ann Arbor, MI: Association for Consumer Research, 1981), pp. 52-6.

Lazarsfeld, Paul
"The Controversy Over Detailed Interviews--An Offer for Negotiation"
Public Opinion Quarterly, Vol. 8 (1944), pp. 38-80.

McQuarrie, Edward F. and McIntyre, Shelby H.
"Conceptual Underpinnings for the Use of Group Interviews in Consumer
Research"
in Houston, Michael J. (editor)
Advances in Consumer Research, Volume Fifteen
(Provo, UT: Association for Consumer Research, 1988), pp. 580-6.

McQuarrie, Edward F. and McIntyre, Shelby H.
"What Focus Groups Can and Cannot Do: A Reply to Seymour"
Journal of Product Innovation Management, Vol. 4 (March 1987), pp.
55-60.

Merton, Robert K.
"The Focused Interview and Focus Groups: Continuities and
Discontinuities"
Public Opinion Quarterly, Vol. 51 (1987), pp. 550-66.

Merton, Robert K. and Kendall, P. L.
"The Focused Interview"
American Journal of Sociology, Vol. 51 (1946), pp. 541-57.

Nasser, David L.
"How to Run a Focus Group"
Public Relations Journal, Vol. 44 (March 1988), pp. 33,4.

Nelson, James E. and Frontczak, Nancy
"How Acquaintanceship and Analyst can Influence Focus Group Results"
Journal of Advertising, Vol. 17, No. 1 (1988), pp. 41-8.

Payne, Melanie S.
"Preparing for Group Interviews"
in Anderson, Beverlee B. (editor)
Advances in Consumer Research, Volume Three
(Association for Consumer Research, 1976), pp. 434-6.

Percy, L.
"Using Qualitative Focus Groups in Generating Hypotheses for
Subsequent Quantitative Validation and Strategy Development"
Advances in Consumer Research, Vol. IX (October 1981), pp. 57-61.

Reynolds, Fred D. and Johnson, Deborah K.
"Validity of Focus-Group Findings"
Journal of Advertising Research, Vol. 18 (June 1978), pp. 21-4.

Roe, Michael M.
"The Group Discussion Under the Microscope"
Proceedings, Market Research Society Conference (March 1988), pp.
235-48.

Ruback, R. Barry, Dabbs, James M., Jr., and Hopper, Charles H.
"The Process of Brainstorming: An Analysis With Individual and Group
Vocal Parameters"
Journal of Personality and Social Psychology, Vol. 47 (September
1984), pp. 558-67.

Sampson, Peter
"Qualitative Research and Motivation Research"
in Worchester, Robert M. (editor)
Consumer Market Research Handbook
(Maidenhead, EN: McGraw-Hill Book Co. (U.K.), Ltd., 1972), pp. 7-27.

Schlackman, W.
"A Discussion of the Use of Sensitivity Panels in Market Research:
The Use of Trained Respondents in Qualitative Studies"
Market Research Society Conference (March 1984), pp. 279-94.

Schwartz, M. S. and Schwartz, C. G.
"Problems in Participant Observation"
American Journal of Sociology, Vol. 60 (January 1955), pp. 343-53.

Seymour, Daniel T., McQuarrie, Edward F., and McIntyre, Shelby H.
"Focus Groups and the Development of New Products by Technologically
Driven Companies: A Comment/What Focus Groups Can and Cannot Do: A
Reply to Seymour"
Journal of Product Innovation Management, Vol. 4 (March 1987), pp.
50-60.

Shapiro, E. P.
"The Group Interview as a Tool of Research"
Journal of Marketing, Vol. 16 (April 1952), pp. 452-4.

Smith, Joan MacFarlane
"Group Discussions"
in Interviewing in Market and Social Research
(London and Boston: Routledge and Kegan Paul, 1972).

Stanton, H., Back, K. W., and Litwak, E.
"Role-Playing in Survey Research"
American Journal of Sociology, Vol. 62 (September 1956), pp. 172-6.

Szybillo, George J.
"What Administrators Should Know About the Group Interview"
in Anderson, Beverlee B. (editor)
Advances in Consumer Research, Vol. 3, Association for Consumer
Research (1976), pp. 447,8.

Szybillo, George J. and Berger, Robert
"What Advertising Agencies Think of Focus Groups"
Journal of Advertising Research, Vol. 19 (June 1979), pp. 29-33.

Taylor, Donald W., Berry, Paul C., and Block, Clifford H.
"Does Group Participation, When Using Brainstorming, Facilitate or
Inhibit Creative Thinking?"
Administrative Science Quarterly, Vol. 3 (June 1958), pp. 23-47.

Tynan, A. Caroline and Drayton, Jennifer L.
"Conducting Focus Groups--A Guide for First-Time Users"
Marketing Intelligence and Planning, Vol. 6, No. 1 (1988), pp. 5-9.

Vidich, A. J.
    "Participant Observation and the Collection and Interpretation of
    Data"
    American Journal of Sociology, Vol. 60 (January 1955), pp. 354-60.

Wells, W. D.
    "Group Interviewing"
    in Ferber, R. (editor)
    Handbook of Marketing Research
    (New York: McGraw-Hill Book Co., Inc., 1974).

78.03 ---------- Theory Re: Focus Group Size and Composition

Bean, Glynis J.
    "Don't let a Dominator Spoil the Session for Everyone"
    Marketing News (January 4, 1988), p. 6.

Bouchard, Thomas J., Jr., Barsaloux, Jean, and Drauden, Gail
    "Brainstorming Procedure, Group Size, and Sex as Determinants of the
    Problem-Solving Effectiveness of Groups and Individuals"
    Journal of Applied Psychology, Vol. 59 (April 1974), pp. 135-8.

Bouchard, Thomas J., Jr. and Hare, Melana
    "Size, Performance, and Potential in Brainstorming Groups"
    Journal of Applied Psychology, Vol. 54 (February 1970), pp. 51-5.

Fern, Edward F.
    "The Use of Focus Groups for Idea Generation: The Effects of Group
    Size, Acquaintanceship, and Moderator on Response Quantity and
    Quality"
    Journal of Marketing Research, Vol. XIX (February 1982), pp. 1-13.

Slater, P. E.
    "Contrasting Correlates of Group Size"
    Sociometry, Vol. 21 (March 1958), pp. 129-39.

78.04 ---------- Depth Interviewing

Berent, Paul H.
    "The Depth Interview"
    Journal of Advertising Research, Vol. 6 (June 1966), pp. 32-9.

Berg, David and Smith, Kenwyn K.
    Exploring Clinical Methods for Social Research
    (Beverly Hills, CA: Sage Publications, Inc., 1985), 400 pp.

Durgee, Jeffrey F.
    "Depth Interview Techniques for Creative Advertising"
    Journal of Advertising Research, Vol. 25, No. 6 (1986), pp. 29-37.

Goldman, Alfred E.
    "The Group Depth Interview"
    Journal of Marketing, Vol. 26 (July 1962), pp. 61-8.

Gorden, R. L.
    "Dimensions of the Depth Interview"
    American Journal of Sociology, Vol. 62 (September 1956), pp. 158-64.

Paradise, L. M. and Blankenship, A. B.
    "Depth Questioning"
    Journal of Marketing, Vol. 15 (January 1951), pp. 274-88.

Scates, D. E. and Scates, A. Y.
    "Developing a Depth Questionnaire to Explore Motivation and
    Likelihood of Action"
    Educational and Psychological Measurement, Vol. 12 (Winter 1952), pp.
    620-31.

78.05 ---------- Group Testing

Belson, William A.
    "Group Testing in Market Research"
    Journal of Advertising Research, Vol. 3 (June 1963), pp. 39-43.

Belson, W. A.
    "Volunteer Bias in Test-Room Groups"
    Public Opinion Quarterly, Vol. 24 (Spring 1960), pp. 115-26.

De Almeida, Pergentino Mendes
    "A Review of Group Discussion Methodology"
    European Research, Vol. 8 (March 1980), pp. 114-20.

78.06 ---------- Theory Re: Nominal Group Technique

Claxton, John D., Ritchie, J. R. Brent, and Zaichkowsky, Judy
"The Nominal Group Technique: Its Potential for Consumer Research"
Journal of Consumer Research, Vol. 7 (December 1980), pp. 308-13.

Delbecq, Andre L. and Van De Ven, Andrew H.
"A Group Process Model for Problem Identification and Program
Planning"
Journal of Applied Behavioral Science, Vol. 7 (1974), p. 4.

Delbecq, Andre L., Van De Ven, Andrew H., and Gustafson, David H.
Group Techniques for Program Planning
(Glenview, IL: Scott, Foresman and Co., 1975).

Gustafson, David H., Shukla, Ramesh K., Delbecq, Andre L., and Walster,
G. William
"A Comparative Study of Differences in Subjective Likelihood
Estimates Made by Individuals, Interacting Groups, Delphi Groups and
Nominal Groups"
Organizational Behavior and Hyuman Performance, Vol. 9 (April 1973),
pp. 280-91.

78.07 ---------- Respondent Incentives

Jones, Linda and Essex, Paul
"Respondent Incentives--Thank You or Bait?"
Market Research Society Conference (March 1984), pp. 129-39.

78.08 ---------- Observer, Moderator Effects

Checkman, David
"Focus Group Research as Theater: How it Affects the Players and
Their Audience"
Marketing Research, Vol. 1 (December 1989), pp. 33-40.

Guerin, B.
"Mere Presence Effects in Humans: A Review"
Journal of Experimental Psychology, Vol. 22 (1986), pp. 38-77.

Nelson, James E. and Frontczak, Nancy
"How Acquaintanceship and Analyst can Influence Focus Group Results"
Journal of Advertising, Vol. 17, No. 1 (1988), pp. 41-8.

Robson, Sue and Wardle, Judith
"Who's Watching Whom? A Study of the Effects of Observers on Group
Discussions"
Journal of the Market Research Society, Vol. 30 (July 1988), pp.
333-59.

Robson, Sue and Wardle, Judith
"Who's Watching Whom?"
Proceedings, Market Research Society Conference (March 1988), pp.
191-233.

78.09 ---------- Software for Focus Group Management

Sophisticated Data Research, Inc.
GEMS: Group Experience Management System
(Atlanta, GA: Sophisticated Data Research, Inc.).

79 --------------------- QUALITATIVE RESEARCH ----------------------
        See also (sub)heading(s) 15.10, 31, 74, 78, 83, 85.

79.01 ---------- Books Re: Qualitative Research Methods

Adler, Patricia A. and Adler, Peter
  Membership Roles in Field Research
  (Beverly Hills, CA: Sage Publications, Inc., 1987), 96 pp.

Bellenger, Danny N., Bernhardt, Kenneth L., and Goldstucker, Jac L.
  Qualitative Research in Marketing
  (Chicago: American Marketing Association, 1976).

Bogdan, R. and Taylor, S. J.
  Introduction to Qualitative Research Methods
  (New York: John Wiley and Sons, Inc., 1975).

Cook, Thomas D. and Reichardt, Charles S. (editors)
  Qualitative and Quantitative Methods in Evaluation Research
  (Beverly Hills, CA: Sage Publications, Inc., 1979).

ESOMAR
  Qualitative Methods of Research: A Matter of Interpretation
  (Amsterdam: European Society for Opinion and Marketing Research,
  1986), 264 pp.

Filstead, W. J.
  Qualitative Methodology: Firsthand Involvement With the Social World
  (Chicago: Markham, 1970).

Glaser, Barney G. and Strauss, Anselm L.
  The Discovery of Grounded Theory: Strategies for Qualitative Research
  (Chicago: Aldin, 1967).

Gordon, Wendy and Langmaid, Roy
  Qualitative Market Research--A Practitioner's and Buyer's Guide
  (Brookfield, VT: Gower Publising Co., 1988).

Henry, Harry
  Motivation Research
  MCB Special Classic Reprint With a 1986 Forward
  (MCB University Press, 1986), 240 pp.

Higginbotham, James B. and Cox, Keith K.
  Focus Group Interviews: A Reader
  (Chicago: American Marketing Association, 1979).

Kirk, Jerome and Miller, Marc L.
  Reliability and Validity in Qualitative Research
  (Beverly Hills, CA: Sage Publications, Inc., 1986), 87 pp.

Manning, Peter K.
  Semiotics and Fieldwork
  (Beverly Hills, CA: Sage Publications, Inc., 1987), 96 pp.

Marshall, Catherine and Rossman, Gretchen B.
  Designing Qualitative Research
  (Newbury Park, CA: Sage Publications, Inc., 1989), 172 pp.

Miles, Matthew B. and Huberman, A. Michael
  Qualitative Data Analysis: A Sourcebook of New Methods
  (Beverly Hills, CA: Sage Publications, 1984).

Mitroff, Ian I.
  The Subjective Side of Science
  (New York: Elsevier, 1974).

Morgan, Gareth
  "Research as Engagement"
  in Morgan, G. (editor)
  Beyond Method: Strategies for Social Research
  (Beverly Hills, CA: Sage Publications, Inc., 1983), pp. 1-19.

Patton, Michael Quinn
  Qualitative Evaluation Methods
  (Beverly Hills, CA: Sage Publications, Inc., 1980).

Pfaffenberger, Bryan
  Microcomputer Applications in Qualitative Research
  (Newbury Park, CA: Sage Publications, Inc., 1988), 88 pp.

Schein, Edgar H.
  The Clinical Perspective in Fieldwork
  (Beverly Hills, CA: Sage Publications, Inc., 1987), 96 pp.

Taylor, Steven and Bogdan, Robert
  Introduction to Qualitative Research Methods: The Search for Meanings
  (New York: John Wiley, 1984).

Van Maanen, John, Dabbs, James M. Jr., and Faulkner, Robert R. (editors)
  Varieties of Qualitative Research
  (Beverly Hills, CA: Sage Publications, 1982).

Walker, Robert (editor)
  Applied Qualitative Research
  (Brookfield, VT: Gower Publishing Company, 1985), 194 pp.

79.02 ---------- General Discussions Re: Qualitative Research Methods

  See also (sub)heading(s) 46.01.

Abbott, D.
  "Group Discussions"
  Admap (October 1975).

Baker, Malcolm
  "Qualitative Research in the US and the UK: A Contrast in Styles and
  Practices"
  ESOMAR Congress, Montreux (1987), pp. 847-58.

Bartos, Rena
  "Qualitative Research: What It Is and Where It Came From"
  Journal of Advertising Research, Vol. 26 (June/July 1986), pp. RC3-6.

Bryman, Alan
  "The Debate About Quantitative and Qualitative Research: A Question
  of Method or Epistemology"
  British Journal of Sociology, Vol. XXXV (March 1984), pp. 75-92.

Bryman, Alan, Bresnen, Michael, Beardsworth, Alan, and Keil, Teresa
  "Qualitative Research and the Study of Leadership"
  Human Relations, Vol. 41 (January 1988), pp. 13-30.

Cohen, Ronald Jay
  "Computer-Enhanced Qualitative Research"
  Journal of Advertising Research, Vol. 25 (June/July 1985), pp. 48-52.

Cooper, Peter
  "Comparison Between the UK and the US: The Qualitative Dimension"
  Journal of the Market Research Society, Vol. 31 (October 1989), pp.
  509-20.

Cooper, Peter
  "Differing Roles of Qualitative Research: Europe and the USA"
  Advertising Research Foundation Conference, New York (1987).

Cooper, Peter
  "The New Qualitative Technology"
  in Sampson, P. (editor)
  ESOMAR Monographs, Volume Two (1987).

Cooper, P. and Branthwaite, A.
  "Qualitative Technology: New Perspectives on Measurement and Meaning
  Through Qualitative Research"
  The Market Research Society Conference, Brighton (1977).

Cowan, David
  "Advertising Research--Qualitative or Quantitative?"Admap (November
  1984), pp. 516-20.

Cowan, D. and Cowpe, C.
  "The Use of Qualitative Research in the Development of Effective
  Advertising"
  E.S.O.M.A.R. Congress, Venice (1976).

De Groot, Gerald
  "New, Noxious or Nebulous?"
  Proceedings, Market Research Society Conference (March 1987), pp.
  123-47.

De Groot, Gerald
  "Qualitative Research: Deep, Dangerous, or Just Plain Dotty?"
  European Research, Vol. 14, No. 3 (1986), pp. 136-41.

De Groot, Gerald
  "Qualitative Research: Some Reflections on Current Approaches"
  Admap (February 1986), pp. 72-6.

Deslandes, Jean and Motte, Sylvie
  "The Qualitative Approaches and Their Anticipatory Function"
  Proceedings, ESOMAR Congress, Monte Carlo (1986), pp. 431-9.

Duncan, Robert B.
  "Qualitative Research Methods in Strategic Management"
  in Schendel, Dan E. and Hofer, Charles W. (editors)
  Strategic Management: A New View of Business Policy and Planning
  (Boston, MA: Little, Brown, and Company, Inc., 1979), pp. 424-7.

Durgee, Jeffrey F.
    "Richer Findings From Qualitative Research"
    Journal of Advertising Research, Vol. 26 (August/September 1986), pp.
    36-44.

Falconer, R.
    "Group Discussion Research"
    Marketing (1976).

Fedder, Curtis J.
    "Listening to Qualitative Research"
    Journal of Advertising Research, Vol. 25 (December 1985/January
    1986), pp. 57-9.

Feldwick, Paul and Winstanley, Lorna
    "Qualitative Recruitment: Policy and Practice"
    Proceedings, Market Research Society Conference (March 1986), pp.
    57-72.

Fleury, Pascal
    "Market Research in France"
    European Research, Vol. 13 (April 1985), pp. 80-1.

Fleury, Pascal
    "New Qualitative Studies"
    ESOMAR Congress, Rome (1984), pp. 629-47.

Frankel, Nina
    "Team Approach is Essential in Qualitative Research
    Marketing News, Vol. 20 (September 12, 1986), pp. 12-4.

Fuller, Linda
    "Use of Panels for Qualitative Research"
    Journal of the Market Research Society, Vol. 26, No. 3 (July 1984),
    pp. 209-20.

Fuller, Linda
    "Use of Panels for Qualitative Research"
    Market Research Society Conference (March 1984), pp. 267-78.

Goodyear, J. R.
    "Qualitative Research Studies"
    in Aucamp, J. (editor)
    The Effective Use of Market Research
    (London: Staple Press, 1971), pp. 47-65.

Goodyear, Mary
    "Qualitative Research in Developing Countries"
    Journal of the Market Research Society, Vol. 24 (April 1982), pp.
    86-96.

Harvey, M.
    "The Group Discussion in Action"
    The Market Research Society Course on Qualitative Research (November
    1971), paper presentation.

Kover, Arthur J.
    "Point of View: The Legitimacy of Qualitative Research"
    Journal of Advertising Research, Vol. 22 (December 1982/January
    1983), pp. 49,50.

Mariampolski, Hy
    "The Resurgence of Qualitative Research"
    Public Relations Journal, Vol. 40 (July 1984), pp. 21-3.

Market Research Society Research and Development Sub-Committee on
    Qualitative Research
    "Qualitative Research--A Summary of the Concepts Involved"
    Journal of the Market Research Society, Vol. 21 (April 1979), pp.
    107-24.

May, John P.
    "A Buyer's Guide to Qualitative Research"
    Market Intelligence and Planning, Vol. 2 (1984), pp. 67-76.

May, J. P.
    "Qualitative Advertising Research--A Review of the Role of the
    Researcher"
    Journal of the Market Research Society, Vol. 20 (October 1978), pp.
    203-18.

Moran, William T.
    "The Science of Qualitative Research"
    Journal of Advertising Research, Vol. 26 (June/July 1986), pp. RC16-9.

Morgan, Gareth and Smircich, Linda
    "The Case of Qualitative Research"
    Academy of Management Review, Vol. 5, No. 4 (1980), pp. 491-500.

Overholser, Charles
  "Quality, Quantity, and Thinking Real Hard"
  Journal of Advertising Research, Vol. 26 (June/July 1986), pp. RC7-12.

Peshkin, Allen
  "Virtuous Subjectivity"
  in Berg, David N. and Smith, Kenwyn K. (editors)
  Exploring Clinical Methods for Social Research
  (Beverly Hills, CA: Sage Publications, Inc., 1985), pp. 267-81.

Plasschaert, Jetty
  "Voting for the European Parliament: A Blueprint for International
  Qualitative Research"
  European Research, Vol. 12 (October 1984), pp. 153-62.

Reichardt, Charles S. and Cook, Thomas D.
  "Beyond Qualitative Versus Quantitative Methods"
  in Cook, Thomas D. and Reichardt, Charles S. (editors)
  Qualitative and Quantitative Methods in Evaluation Research
  (Beverly Hills, CA: Sage Publications, Inc., 1979), pp. 7-33.

Robson, Sue
  "The Qualitative Story"
  Survey (Spring 1986), pp. 13,4.

Sampson, Peter
  "Qualitative Research and Motivation Research"
  in Worcester, Robert M. and Downham, John (editors)
  Consumer Marketing Research Handbook, Third Edition
  (New York: North Holland, 1986), pp. 29-55.

Sampson, Peter
  "Qualitative Research in Europe: The State of the Art and the Art of
  the State"
  European Research, Vol. 13 (October 1985), pp. 163-9.

Sampson, Peter and Bhaduri, M.
  "Qualitative Research Techniques in the Context of Different Time
  Frames"
  Burke Marketing Research, U.K. (1985), technical paper.

Satow, Kay
  "The Changing State of Qualitative Research in the United States"
  Journal of the Market Research Society, Vol. 31 (October 1989), pp.
  521-5.

Schlackman, W.
  "A Discussion of the Use of Sensitivity Panels in Market Research"
  Journal of the Market Research Society, Vol. 26, No. 3 (July 1984),
  pp. 191-208.

Tisler, Susana and Alos, Juan S.
  "The Predictive Value of Qualitative Research--The Case of an
  Automatic Cashier Network"
  Proceedings, ESOMAR Congress, Monte Carlo (1986), pp. 403-19.

Van Maanen, John
  "Introduction"
  in Van Maanen, John, Dabbs, J. M., Jr., and Faulkner, Robert R.
  (editors)
  Varieties of Qualitative Research
  (Beverly Hills, CA: Sage Publications, 1982), pp. 11-29.

Van Maanen, John
  "Fieldwork on the Beat"
  in Van Maanen, John, Dabbs, J. M., Jr., and Faulkner, Robert R.
  (editors)
  Varieties in Qualitative Research
  (Beverly Hills, CA: Sage Publications, 1982), pp. 103-51.

Van Maanen, John
  "The Fact of Fiction in Organizational Ethnography"
  Administrative Science Quarterly, Vol. 24 (December 1979), pp. 539-50.

Van Maanen, John
  "Reclaiming Qualitative Methods for Organization Research: A Preface"
  Administrative Science Quarterly, Vol. 24 (December 1979), pp. 520-6.

Wallace, Kathleen M.
  "The Use and Value of Qualitative Research Studies"
  Industrial Marketing Management, Vol. 13 (August 1984), pp. 181-5.

Wells, William D.
  "Truth and Consequences"
  Journal of Advertising Research, Vol. 26 (June/July 1986), pp. RC13-6.

Wolfe, Oliver H.
  "Beyond Old and New: Choosing Qualitative Methods Appropriate to
  Research Objectives"
  Proceedings, ESOMAR Congress, Lisbon (1988), pp. 729-45.

79.03 ---------- Theory Re: Qualitative Research Data Analysis

    See also (sub)heading(s) 46.01, 131.04.

Alt, M. B. and Brighton, M.
    "Analysing Data: Or Telling Stories?"
    Journal of the Market Research Society, Vol. 23, No. 4 (1981), pp.
    209-19.

Chamberlain, G.
    "Analysis of Covariance With Qualitative Data"
    Review of Economic Studies, Vol. 47 (1980), pp. 225-38.

Fielding, Nigel G. and Fielding, Jane L.
    Linking Data
    (Beverly Hills, CA: Sage Publications, 1986), 95 pp.

Griggs, Steve
    "Analysing Qualitative Data"
    Journal of the Market Research Society, Vol. 29 (January 1987), pp.
    15-34.

Jain, Arun K. and Etgar, M.
    "Measuring Store Image Through Multidimensional Scaling of Free
    Response Data"
    Journal of Retailing, Vol. 52, No. 4 (1976-77), pp. 61-70.

Jones, Sue
    "Listening to Complexity--Analysing Qualitative Marketing Research
    Data"
    Journal of the Market Research Society, Vol. 23 (January 1981), pp.
    26-39.

Krieger, Murray
    "Literary Analysis and Evaluation--And the Ambidextrous Critic"
    in Dembo, L. S. (editor)
    Criticism: Speculative and Analytical Essays
    (Madison, WI: University of Wisconsin Press, 1968), pp. 17-36.

Miles, Matthew B.
    "Qualitative Data as an Attractive Nuisance"
    Administrative Science Quarterly, Vol. 24 (December 1979), pp.
    590-601.

Miles, Matthew B. and Huberman, A. Michael
    Qualitative Data Analysis: A Sourcebook of New Methods
    (London, EN: Sage Publications, 1984), 264 pp.

Piore, Michael J.
    "Qualitative Research Techniques in Economics"
    Administrative Science Quarterly, Vol. 24 (December 1979), pp. 560-9.

Siddall, John and Santry, Eamonn
    "Tabloids of Stone"
    Proceedings, Market Research Society Conference (March 1988), pp.
    491-505.

79.04 ---------- Applications of Qualitative Research

Lunn, Tony, Cooper, Peter, and Murphy, Oliver
    "The Fluctuating Fortunes of the U.K. Social Democratic Party: An
    Application of Creative Qualitative Research"
    ESOMAR Congress, Barcelona (1983), pp. 151-79.

79.05 ---------- Unclassified (Qualitative Research)

Goodyear, J. R.
    "The Impact of Economic Growth and Recession on Qualitative Research
    Agencies and on the Use of Qualitative Research"
    Market Research Society Conference, Brighton (1978).

Salancik, Gerald R.
    "Field Simulations for Organizational Behavior Research"
    Administrative Science Quarterly, Vol. 24 (December 1979), pp. 638-48.

80 --------------------- INTERPRETIVE RESEARCH ---------------------
       See also (sub)heading(s) 1.04, 2.03, 15, 81, 83.

80.01 ---------- Books Re: Interpretive Research

Bouchard, Thomas J.
   "Field Research Methods: Interviewing, Questionnaires, Participant
   Observation, Systematic Observation, Unobtrusive Measures"
   in Dunnette, Marvin D. (editor)
   Handbook of Industrial and Organizational Psychology
   (Chicago: Rand-McNally, 1976), pp. 363-413.

Denzin, Norman K.
   Interpretive Interactionism
   (Newbury Park, CA: Sage Publications, 1989), 160 pp.

Denzin, Norman K.
   Interpretive Biography
   (Newbury Park, CA: Sage Publications, 1989), 96 pp.

Hirsch, E. D., Jr.
   Validity in Interpretation
   (New Haven, CT: Yale University Press, 1967).

Hirschman, Elizabeth C. (editor)
   Interpretive Consumer Research
   (Provo, UT: Association for Consumer Research, 1989).

Jorgenson, Danny L.
   Participant Observation
   (Newbury Park, CA: Sage Publications, 1989), 136 pp.

Plummer, Ken
   Documents of Life: An Introduction to the Problems and Literature of
   a Humanistic Method
   (George Allen and Unwin Ltd., 1983), 175 pp.

Ricoeur, Paul
   Interpretation Theory: Discourse and the Surplus of Meaning
   (Fort Worth, TX: The Texas Christian University Press, 1976).

80.02 ---------- Theory Re: Interpretive Research

Anderson, Paul F.
   "On Relativism and Interpretivism--With a Prolegomenon to the 'Why'
   Question"
   in Hirshman, Elizabeth C. (editor)
   Interpretive Consumer Research
   (Provo, UT: Association for Consumer Research, 1989), pp. 10-23.

Buczynska-Garewicz, Hanna
   "The Meaning of 'Interpretant'"
   Semiosis, Vol. 21 (1981), pp. 10-4.

Giorgi, Amedeo
   "The Context of Discovery-Context of Justification: Distinction and
   Descriptive Science"
   Journal of Phenomenological Psychology, Vol. 17 (Fall 1986), pp.
   151-67.

Holbrook, Morris B. and O'Shaughnessy, John
   "On the Scientific Status of Consumer Research and the Need for an
   Interpretive Approach to Studying Consumption Behavior"
   Journal of Consumer Research, Vol. 15 (December 1988), pp. 398-402.

Hudson, Laurel Anderson and Ozanne, Julie L.
   "Alternative Ways of Seeking Knowledge in Consumer Research"
   Journal of Consumer Research, Vol. 14 (March 1988), pp. 508-21.

80.03 ---------- Theory Re: Naturalistic Inquiry

Brinberg, David and Kumar, Ajith
   "Validity Issues in Experimental and Naturalistic Inquiry"
   State University of New York at Albany (1987), working paper.

Knorr-Cetina, Karin D.
   "The Naturalistic/Ethnographic Analysis of Social Life"
   Sociology Department, Virginia Polytechnic Institute and State
   University (1983), working paper.

Lincoln, Yvonna S. and Guba, Egon G.
   Naturalistic Inquiry
   (Beverly Hills, CA: Sage Publications, 1985).

Lutz, Richard J.
   "Positivism, Naturalism, and Pluralism in Consumer Research:
   Paradigms in Paradise"
   in Srull, Thomas K. (editor)
   Advances in Consumer Research, Volume Sixteen
   (Prove, UT: Association for Consumer Research, 1989), pp. 1-7.

80.04 ---------- Applications of Naturalistic Inquiry

Belk, Russell W., Sherry, John F., Jr., and Wallendorf, Melanie
   "A Naturalistic Inquiry Into Buyer and Seller Behavior at a Swap Meet"
   Journal of Consumer Research, Vol. 14 (March 1988), pp. 449-70.

Belk, Russell W., Wallendorf, Melanie, and Sherry, John F., Jr.
   "The Sacred and the Profane in Consumer Behavior: Theodicy on the
   Odyssey"
   Journal of Consumer Research, Vol. 16 (June 1989), pp. 1-38.

O'Guinn, Thomas C. and Belk, Russell W.
   "Heaven on Earth: Consumption at Heritage Village, USA"
   Journal of Consumer Research, Vol. 16 (September 1989), pp. 227-38.

80.05 ---------- Theory Re: Humanistic Inquiry

Belk, Russell and Wallendorf, Melanie
   "Humanistic Inquiry: A Comment"
   University of Utah (1987), working paper.

Denzin, Norman K.
   "Interpretive Interactionism"
   in Morgan, Gareth (editor)
   Beyond Method: Strategies for Social Research
   (Beverly Hills, CA: Sage Publications, 1983), pp. 129-46.

Geertz, Clifford
   "Thick Description: Toward an Interpretive Theory of Culture"
   in Geertz. C. (editor)
   The Interpretation of Cultures
   (New York: Basic Books, 1973).

Hirschman, Elizabeth C.
   "Humanistic Inquiry in Marketing Research: Philosophy, Method, and
   Criteria"
   Journal of Marketing Research, Vol. XXIII (August 1986), pp. 237-49.

Hirschman, Elizabeth C.
   "Scientific Style and the Conduct of Consumer Research"
   Journal of Consumer Research, Vol. 12, No. 2 (1985), pp. 142-54.

Hirschman, Elizabeth C. and Holbrook, Morris B.
   "Philosophies and Methodologies for Research on Experiential Consumer
   Behavior"
   in Brinberg, D. and Lutz, R. (editors)
   Innovations in Consumer Research
   (New York: Springer-Verlag, Inc., 1986).

Lincoln, Yvonna S. and Guba, Egon G.
   Naturalistic Inquiry
   (Beverly Hills, CA: Sage Publications, Inc., 1985).

Morgan, Gareth
   Beyond Method: Strategies for Social Research
   (Beverly Hills, CA: Sage Publications, Inc., 1983).

Morgan, Gareth
   "Research as Engagement"
   in Morgan, G. (editor)
   Beyond Method: Strategies for Social Research
   (Beverly Hills, CA: Sage Publications, Inc., 1983), pp. 1-19.

Polanyi, Michael
   Personal Knowledge: Toward Post-Critical Philosophy
   (Chicago: University of Chicago Press, 1962).

Sherry, John
   "A Comment on Hirschman's Humanistic Inquiry in Marketing Research"
   Northwestern University (1987), working paper.

80.06 ---------- Applications of Humanistic Inquiry

Association for Consumer Research
   "Applying Humanistic Methods to Consumer Research"
   ACR Special Session
   in Lutz, Richard J. (editor)
   Advances in Consumer Research, Volume Thirteen
   (Provo, UT: Association for Consumer Research, 1985), pp. xiv-xv.

Levy, Sidney J.
    "Interpreting Consumer Mythology: A Structural Approach to Consumer
    Behavior"
    Journal of Marketing, Vol. 45 (Summer 1981), pp. 49-62.

80.07 ---------- Theory Re: Phenomenology, Existentialism

Bruyn, Severyn T.
    "The New Empiricists: The Participant Observer and Phenomenologist"
    Sociology and Social Research, Vol. 51, No. 3 (1967), pp. 317-28.

Crosson, Frederick J.
    "Information Theory and Phenomenology"
    in Crosson, Frederick J. and Sayre, Kenneth M. (editors)
    Philosophy and Cybernetics
    (Notre Dame, IN: University of Notre Dame Press, 1967).

Fennell, Geraldine
    "Things of Heaven and Earth: Phenomenology, Marketing and Consumer
    Research"
    in Hirschman, Elizabeth C. and Holbrook, Morris B. (editors)
    Advances in Consumer Research, Volume Twelve
    (Provo, UT: Association for Consumer Research, 1985).

Gier, Nicholas F.
    Wittgenstein and Phenomenology
    (Albany, NY: State University Press, 1981).

Giorgi, Amedeo
    "Concerning the Possibility of Phenomenological Research"
    Journal of Phenomenological Psychology, Vol. 14 (Fall 1983), pp.
    129-70.

Husserl, Edmund
    Cartesian Meditations: An Introduction to Phenomenology
    (Atlantic Highlands, NJ: Humanities Press, 1960).

Kvale, Steinar
    "The Qualitative Research Interview: A Phenomenological and a
    Hermeneutical Mode of Understanding"
    Journal of Phenomenological Psychology, Vol. 14 (Fall 1983), pp.
    171-96.

May, Rollo and Yalom, Irvin
    "Existential Psychotherapy"
    in Corsini, Raymond J. (editor)
    Current Psychotherapies
    (Itasca, IL: F. E. Peacock, 1984), pp. 354-91.

McLeod, Robert B.
    "Phenomenology: A Challenge to Experimental Psychology"
    in Mann, Thomas W. (editor)
    Behaviorism and Phenomenology: Contrasting Bases for Psychology
    (Chicago: University of Chicago press, 1964), pp. 47-73.

Merleau-Ponty, Maurice
    The Phenomenology of Perception
    (London: Routledge and Kegan Paul, 1962).

Oiler, Carolyn
    "The Phenomenological Approach in Nursing Research"
    Nursing Research, Vol. 31, No. 3 (1982), pp. 178-81.

Thompson, Craig J., Locander, William B., and Pollio, Howard R.
    "Putting Consumer Experience Back Into Consumer Research: The
    Philosophy and Method of Existential-Phenomenology"
    Journal of Consumer Research, Vol. 16 (September 1989), pp. 133-46.

Valle, Ronald S. and King, Mark
    "An Introduction to Existential-Phenomenological Thought in
    Psychology"
    in Valle, Ronald S. and King, Mark (editors)
    Existential-Phenomenological Alternatives for Psychology
    (New York: Oxford University Press, 1978), pp. 6-17.

Van Den Berg, Jan H.
    A Different Existence: Principles of a Phenomenological
    Psychopathology
    (Pittsburgh, PA: Dusquesne University Press, 1970).

Zane, Richard M.
    The Way of Phenomenology
    (New York: Pegasus, 1970).

80.08 ---------- Applications of Phenomenology, Existentialism

Colaizzi, Paul F.
  Reflection and Research in Psychology: A Phenomenological Study of
  Learning
  (Dubuque, IA: Kendall/Hunt, 1973).

Dapkus, Marilyn A.
  "A Thematic Analysis of the Experience of Time"
  Journal of Personality and Social Psychology, Vol. 49 (August 1985),
  pp. 408-19.

Fischer, William F.
  "An Empirical-Phenomenological Investigation of Being Anxious: An
  Example of the Meanings of Being Emotional"
  in Valle, Ronald S. and King, Mark (editors)
  Existential-Phenomenological Alternatives for Psychology
  (New York: Oxford University Press, 1978), pp. 166-81.

Giorgi, Amedeo
  "A Phenomenological Approach to the Problem of Meaning and Serial
  Learning"
  in Giorgi, Amedeo et al. (editors)
  Dusquesne Studies in Phenomenology, Volume One
  (Pittsburgh, PA: Dusquesne University Press, 1971), pp. 88-100.

Iser, Wolfgang
  "The Reading Process: A Phenomenological Approach"
  New Literary History, Vol. 3, No. 2 (1972), pp. 279-99.

Myers, Elizabeth
  "Phenomenological Analysis of the Importance of Special Possessions"
  in Hirschman, Elizabeth C. and Holbrook Morris B. (editors)
  Advances in Consumer Research, Volume Twelve
  (Provo, UT: Association for Consumer Research, 1985), pp. 560-5.

O'Guinn, Thomas C. and Faber, Ronald J.
  "Compulsive Buying: A Phenomenological Exploration"
  Journal of Consumer Research, Vol. 16 (September 1989), pp. 147-57.

80.09 ---------- Theory Re: Hermeneutical or Structural Research

Arnold, Stephen J. and Fischer, Eileen
  Hermeneutic Analysis in Marketing
  Queen's University (1989), working paper.

Bernstein, Richard J.
  Beyond Objectivism and Relativism: Science, Hermeneutics, and Praxis
  (Philadelphia, PA: University of Pennsylvania Press, 1983).

Bleicher, Josef
  Contemporary Hermeneutics
  (London: Routledge and Kegan Paul, 1980).

Hekman, Susan J.
  Hermeneutics and the Sociology of Knowledge
  (Notre Dame, IN: University of Notre Dame Press, 1986).

Kvale, Steinar
  "The Qualitative Research Interview: A Phenomenological and a
  Hermeneutical Mode of Understanding"
  Journal of Phenomenological Psychology, Vol. 14 (Fall 1983), pp.
  171-96.

Levy, Sidney J.
  "Interpreting Consumer Mythology: A Structural Approach to Consumer
  Behavior"
  Journal of Marketing, Vol. 45 (Summer 1981), pp. 49-62.

O'Shaughnessy, John
  "A Return to Reason in Consumer Behavior: An Hermeneutical Approach"
  in Hirschman, Elizabeth C. and Holbrook, Morris B. (editors)
  Advances in Consumer Research, Volume Twelve
  (Provo, UT: Association for Consumer Research, 1985), pp. 305-11.

Ricoeur, Paul
  Hermeneutics and the Human Sciences
  (Cambridge, EN: Cambridge University Press, 1981).

Ricoeur, Paul
  The Conflict of Interpretations: Essays on Hermeneutics
  (Evanston, IL: Northwestern University Press, 1974).

Wertz, Frederick J.
  "From Everyday to Psychological Descriptions: Analyzing the Moments
  of a Qualitative Data Analysis"
  Journal of Phenomenological Psychology, Vol. 14 (Fall 1983), pp.
  197-242.

81 -------------------------- SEMIOTICS ----------------------------
        See also (sub)heading(s) 80, 103, 104.

81.01 ---------- Books Re: Semiotics

Barthes, Roland
  The Fashion System
  Ward, Matthew and Howard, Richard (translators)
  (New York: Hill and Wang, 1983).

Barthes, Roland
  Mythologies
  Lovers, Annette (translator)
  (New York: Hill and Wang, 1972).

Barthes, Roland
  Elements of Semiology
  Lovers, Annette and Smith, Colin (translators)
  (New York: Hill and Wang, 1970).

Culler, Jonathan
  The Pursuit of Signs
  (Ithaca, NY: Cornell University Press, 1981).

Deely, John
  Introducing Semiotics
  (Bloomington, IN: Indiana University Press, 1982).

Douglas, Mary
  Natural Symbols
  (New York: Pantheon Books, 1970).

Eco, Umberto
  Semiotics and the Philosophy of Language
  (Bloomington, IN: Indiana University Press, 1984).

Eco, Umberto
  The Role of the Reader
  (Bloomington, IN: Indiana University Press, 1979).

Eco, Umberto
  A Theory of Semiotics
  (Bloomington, IN: Indiana University Press, 1976).

Hawkes, Terence
  Structuralism and Semiotics
  (Berkeley, CA: University of California Press, 1977).

Gallant, Mary J. and Kleinman, Sherryl
  "Symbolic Interactionism vs. Ethnomethodology"
  Symbolic Interaction, Vol. 6, No. 1 (1983), pp. 1-18.

Gopnick, Myrna
  "Language, Cognition, and the Theory of Signs"
  Recherches Semiotiques Semiotic Inquiry, Vol. 1, No. 4 (1981), pp.
  310-27.

Hirschman, Elizabeth C. and Holbrook, Morris B. (editors)
  Symbolic Consumer Behavior
  (Provo, UT: Association for Consumer Research, 1981).

Innis, Robert E.
  Semiotics: An Introductory Anthology
  (Bloomington, IN: Indiana University Press, 1985).

Kristeva, Julia
  Semiotike: Recherches pour une Semanalyse
  (Paris: Sevil, 1969).

Morris, Charles W.
  Image
  (New York: Vantage, 1976).

Morris, Charles W.
  Writings on the General Theory of Signs
  (The Hague: Mouton, 1971).

Morris, Charles W.
  Signification and Significance: A Study of the Relations of Signs and
  Values
  (Cambridge, MA: M.I.T. Press, 1964).

Morris, Charles W.
  Signs, Language, and Behavior
  (New York: Prentice-Hall, 1946).

Morris, Charles W.
  Foundations of the Theory of Signs
  (Chicago: University of Chicago Press, 1938).

Nauta, Doede
   The Meaning of Information
   (The Hague: Mouton, 1972).

Ogden, C. K. and Richards, I. A.
   The Meaning of Meaning
   (New York: Harcourt Brace, 1923).

Peirce, Charles Sanders
   Collected Papers (1931-58)
   Hartshorne, Charles, Weiss, Paul, and Burks, Arthur W. (editors)
   (Cambridge, MA: Harvard Uni versity Press).

Saussure, Ferdinand de
   Cour de Linguistic Generale (Course in General Linguistics)
   Baskin, Wade (translator)
   (New York: McGraw-Hill, 1915/1966).

Scholes, Robert
   Semiotics and Interpretation
   (New Haven, CT: Yale University Press, 1982).

Sebeok, Thomas A.
   The Play of Musement
   (Bloomington, IN: Indiana University Press, 1981).

Sebeok, Thomas A.
   Contributions to the Doctrine of Signs
   (Bloomington, IN: Indiana University Press, 1976).

Sebeok, Thomas A.
   The Sign and Its Masters
   (Austin, TX: University of Texas Press, 1974).

Sebeok, Thomas A.
   Perspectives in Zoosemiotics
   (The Hague: Mouton, 1972).

Shands, Harley C.
   Semiotic Approaches to Psychiatry
   (The Hague: Mouton, 1970).

Sperber, Dan
   Rethinking Symbolism
   (Cambridge, MA: Cambridge University Press, 1974).

Umiker-Sebeok, Jean (editor)
   Marketing and Semiotics: New Directions in the Study of Signs for Sale
   (Berlin: Mouton de Gruyter, 1987).

81.02 ---------- Theory Re: Semiotics

Anderson, Myrdene, Deely, John, Krampen, Martin, Ransdell, Joseph,
   Sebeok, Thomas A., and Von Uexkull, Thure
   "A Semiotic Perspective on the Sciences: Steps Toward a New Paradigm"
   Semiotic, Vol. 52, No. 1/2 (1984), pp. 7-47.

Buczynska-Garewicz, Hanna
   "Sign and Dialogue"
   American Journal of Semiotics, Vol. 2, No. 1-2 (1983), pp. 27-43.

Douglas, Mary
   "The Future of Semiotics"
   Semiotica, Vol. 38, No. 3/4 (1982), pp. 197-203.

Eco, Umberto
   "Semiotics: A Discipline or an Interdisciplinary Method?"
   in Sebeok, Thomas A. (editor)
   Sight, Sound, and Sense
   (Bloomington, IN: Indiana University Press, 1978), pp. 73-83.

Fisch, Max H.
   "Peirce's General Theory of Signs"
   in Sebeok, Thomas A. (editor)
   Sight, Sound, and Sense
   (Bloomington, IN: Indiana University Press, 1978).

Kehret-Ward, Trudy L.
   "A Strategy for Understanding the Semiology of Product Choice"
   1982 Association for Consumer Research Convention, San Francisco
   (1982), paper presentation.

Mike, David Glen
   "Schema-Theoretics and Semiotics: Toward More Wholistic, Programmatic
   Research on Marketing Communication"
   Semiotica (1987).

Mick, David Glen
"Consumer Research and Semiotics: Exploring the Morphology of Signs,
Symbols, and Significance"
Journal of Consumer Research, Vol. 13 (September 1986), pp. 196-213.

Ransdell, Joseph
"Some Leading Ideas of Peirce's Semiotic"
Semiotica, Vol. 19, No. 3/4 (1977), pp. 157-78.

Rochberg-Halton, Eugene and McMurtrey, Kevin
"The Foundations of Modern Semiotic: Charles Peirce and Charles
Morris"
American Journal of Semiotics, Vol. 2, No. 1-2 (1983), pp. 129-56.

Steiner, Wendy
"Modern American Semiotics"
in Bailey, R. W., Matejka, L., and Steiner, P. (editors)
The Sign: Semiotics Around the World
(Ann Arbor, MI: University of Michigan Press, 1978), pp. 99-118.

Thayer, Lee
"Human Nature: Of Communications, of Structuralism, of Semiotics"
Semiotica, Vol. 41, No. 1/4 (1982), pp. 25-40.

Winner, Irene Portis
"Cultural Semiotics and Anthropology"
in Bailey, R. W., Matejka, L., and Steiner, P. (editors)
The Sign: Semiotics Around the World
(Ann Arbor, MI: University of Michigan Press, 1978), pp. 335-63.

81.03 ---------- Applications of Semiotics

Holbrook, Morris B. and Grayson, Mark W.
"The Semiology of Cinematic Consumption: Symbolic Consumer Behavior
in 'Out of Africa'"
Journal of Consumer Research, Vol. 13 (December 1986), pp. 374-81.

Holman, Rebecca H.
Communicational Properties of Women's Clothing: Isolation of
Discriminable Clothing Ensembles and Identification of Attribtutions
Made to One Person Wearing Each Ensemble
University of Texas at Austin (1976), unpublished Ph.D. dissertation.

Kehret-Ward, Trudy L., Johnson, Marcia W., and Louie, Therese A.
"Improving Recall by Manipulating the Syntax of Consumption Rituals"
in Hirschman, Elizabeth C. and Holbrook, Morris B. (editors)
Advances in Consumer Research, Volume Twelve
(Provo, UT: Association for Consumer Research, 1985), pp. 319-24.

Mulholland, Heather and Harrison, Mark
"Defining Female Attractiveness: A Semiotic Approach"
Proceedings, Market Research Society Conference (March 1988), pp.
129-54.

Murray, Trudy L.
Developing the Ability to Relate Scarcity and Communication Value:
How Children Come to Use Products as Linguistic Units
University of Washington (1981), unpublished Ph.D. dissertation.

Shands, Harley C. and Meltzer, James D.
"Unexpected Semiotic Implications of Medical Inquiry"
in Sebeok, Thomas A. (editor)
A Perfusion of Signs
(Bloomington, IN: Indiana University Press, 1977).

Sherry, John F., Jr. and Camargo, Eduardo G.
"May Your Life be Marvelous: English Language Labelling and the
Semiotics of Japanese Promotion"
Journal of Consumer Research, Vol. 14 (September 1987), pp. 174-88.

81.04 ---------- Unclassified (Interpretive Research)

Gruber, Janet
"BC or AC--Before Coca-Cola or After Coca-Cola: The Relevance of
Anthropology to Market Research"
Proceedings, ESOMAR Congress, Lisbon (1988), pp. 79-88.

82 ---------------------- LITERARY CRITICISM ------------------------

82.01 ---------- Books Re: Literary Criticism

Berman, Art
    From the New Criticism to Deconstruction: The Reception of
    Structuralism and Post-Structuralism
    (Urbana, IL: University of Illinois Press, 1988).

Crane, R. S.
    The Languages of Criticism and the Structure of Poetry
    (Toronto, Ontario, Canada: University of Toronto Press, 1953).

Eagleton, Terry
    The Function of Criticism: From the Spectator to Post-Structuralism
    (London: Verso, 1983).

Eagleton, Terry
    Literary Theory: An Introduction
    (Minneapolis: University of Minnesota Press, 1983).

Frye, Northrup
    Anatomy of Criticism: Four Essays
    (Princeton, NJ: Princeton University Press, 1973).

Handy, William J. and Westbrook, Max (editors)
    Twentieth Century Criticism: The Major Statements
    (New York: Free Press, 1974).

Hartman, Geoffrey H.
    Criticism in the Wilderness: The Study of Literature Today
    (New Haven, CT: Yale University Press, 1980).

Staton, Shirley F.
    Literary Theories in Praxis
    (Philadelphia, PA: University of Pennsylvania Press, 1987).

Wellek, Rene
    Concepts of Criticism
    Nichols, Stephen G. (editor)
    (New Haven, CT: Yale University Press, 1963).

82.02 ---------- Theory Re: Literary Criticism

Stern, Barbara B.
    "Literary Criticism and Consumer Research: Overview and Illustrative
    Analysis"
    Journal of Consumer Research, Vol. 16 (December 1989), pp. 322-34.

Stern, Barbara B.
    "Literary Explication: A Methodology for Consumer Research"
    in Hirschman, Elizabeth C. (editor)
    Interpretive Consumer Research
    (Provo, UT: Association for Consumer Research, 1989), pp. 48-59.

Stern, Barbara B.
    "How Does an Ad Mean? Language in Advertising"
    Journal of Advertising, Vol. 17 (Summer 1988), pp. 3-14.

82.03 ---------- Applications of Literary Criticism

Stern, Barbara B.
    "Literary Analysis of the Services Company Persona: A Speaker Schema"
    in Martin, Claude R., Jr. and Leigh, James H. (editors)
    Current Issues and Research in Advertising, Volume Eleven
    (1988).

Stern, Barbara B.
    "Figurative Language in Services Advertising: The Nature and Uses of
    Imagery"
    in Houston, Michael J. (editor)
    Advances in Consumer Research, Volume Fifteen
    (Provo, UT: Association for Consumer Research, 1988), pp. 180-5.

83 ------------------------- ETHNOGRAPHY --------------------------
See also (sub)heading(s) 79.

83.01 ---------- Books Re: Ethnography

Agar, Michael
Speaking of Ethnography
(Beverly Hills, CA: Sage Publications, 1986), 78 pp.

Fetterman, David M.
Ethnography
(Newbury Park, CA: Sage Publications, 1989), 160 pp.

Punch, Maurice
The Politics and Ethics of Fieldwork
(Beverly Hills, CA: Sage Publications, 1986), 91 pp.

Werner, Oswald and Schoepfle, G. Mark
Systematic Fieldwork: Ethnographic Analysis and Data Management,
Volume One
(Beverly Hills, CA: Sage Publications, 1987).

83.02 ---------- Articles, etc. Re: Ethnography

Gallant, Mary J. and Kleinman, Sherryl
"Symbolic Interactionism vs. Ethnomethodology"
Symbolic Interaction, Vol. 6, No. 1 (1983), pp. 1-18.

Greenburg, J. H.
"Linguistics and Ethnology"
in Hymes, Del (editor)
Language in Culture and Society
(New York: Harper and Row, 1964), pp. 27-31.

Knorr-Cetina, Karin D.
"The Naturalistic/Ethnographic Analysis of Social Life"
Sociology Department, Virginia Polytechnic Institute and State
University (1983), working paper.

Sanday, Peggy Reeves
"The Ethnographic Pardigms"
Administrative Science Quarterly, Vol. 24 (December 1979), pp. 527-38.

83.03 ---------- Applications of Ethnography

Sherry, John F., Jr.
"Market Pitching and the Ethnography of Speaking"
in Houston, Michael (editor)
Advances in Consumer Research, Volume Fifteen
(Provo, UT: Association for Consumer Research, 1988), pp. 543-7.

84 ------------------------ CASE RESEARCH -------------------------
        See also (sub)heading(s) 13.03, 31, 79.

84.01 ---------- Books Re: Case Research

Yin, Robert K.
  Case Study Research
  (Newbury Park, CA: Sage Publications, 1989), 160 pp.

84.02 ---------- Theory Re: Case Research

Bonoma, Thomas V.
  "Case Research in Marketing: Opportunities, Problems, and a Process"
  Journal of Marketing Research, Vol. XXII (May 1985), pp. 199-208.

Campbell, Donald T.
  "Degrees of Freedom and the Case Study"
  in Cook, T. D. and Reichardt, C. S. (editors)
  Qualitative and Quantitative Methods in Evaluation Research
  (Beverly Hills, CA: Sage Publications, Inc., 1979).

Fombrun, Charles J.
  "Strategies for Network Research in Organizations"
  Academy of Management Review, Vol. 7, No. 2 (1982), pp. 280-91.

Lin, Lynn Y., Pioche, Alain, and Standen, Patrick
  "Estimating Sales Volume Potential for New Innovative Products With
  Case Histories"
  European Research, Vol. 14 (1986), pp. S25-32.

McClintock, Charles C., Barnard, D., and Maynard-Moody, S.
  "Applying the Logic of Sample Surveys to Qualitative Case Studies:
  The Case Cluster Method"
  Administrative Science Quartely, Vol. 24 (December 1979), pp. 612-29.

McGrath, Joseph E.
  "Dilemmatics: The Study of Choices and Dilemmas"
  in McGrath, Joseph E., Martin, Joanne, and Kulka, Richard A. (editors)
  Judgment Calls in Research
  (Beverly Hills, CA: Sage Publications, 1982), pp. 69-102.

McGrath, Joseph E., Martin, Joanne, and Kulka, Richard A.
  "Some Quasi-Rules for Making Judgment Calls in Research"
  in McGrath, Joseph E., Martin, Joanne, and Kulka, Richard A. (editors)
  Judgment Calls in Research
  (Beverly Hills, CA: Sage Publications, 1982), pp. 103-18.

Piore, Michael J.
  "Qualitative Research Techniques in Economics"
  Administrative Science Quarterly, Vol. 24 (December 1979), pp. 560-9.

84.03 ---------- Applications of Case Research

Woodside, Arch G. and Fleck, Robert A., Jr.
  "The Case Approach to Understanding Brand Choice"
  Journal of Advertising Research, Vol. 19 (April 1979), pp. 23-30.

84.04 ---------- Unclassified (Case Research)

Feinstein, Alvan R.
  "The Haze of Bayes, the Aerial Palaces of Decision Analysis, and the
  Computerized Ouija Board"
  Clinical Pharmacology and Therapeutics, Vol. 21 (April 1977), pp.
  482-96.

Leenders, Michiel R. and Erskine, James A.
  Case Research: The Case Writing Process, Second Edition
  (London, Ontario: Research and Publications Division, School of
  Business Administration, University of Western Ontario, 1978).

85 -------------------- PROJECTIVE TECHNIQUES ----------------------
       See also (sub)heading(s) 79.

85.01 ---------- Books Re: Projective Techniques

Abt, Lawrence E. and Bellack, Leopold (editors)
   Projective Techniques
   (New York: Grove Press, Inc., 1950).

Anderson, H. H. and Anderson, G. L. (editors)
   An Introduction to Projective Techniques
   (New York: Prentice-Hall, 1951), 720 pp.

Bell, John E.
   Projective Techniques
   (New York, NY: Longmans, Green and Company, Inc., 1948).

Henry, W. E.
   The Analysis of Fantasy: The Thematic Apperception Technique in the
   Study of Personality
   (New York: John Wiley and Sons, 1956), 305 pp.

Leonhard, Dietz
   The Human Equation in Marketing Research
   (New York: American Management Association, Inc., 1967), 176 pp.

Newman, Joseph W.
   Motivation Research and Marketing Management
   (Cambridge, MA: Harvard University Graduate School of Business
   Administration, 1957).

Smith, G. H.
   Motivational Research in Advertising and Marketing
   (New York: McGraw-Hill, 1954), 242 pp.

85.02 ---------- Theory Re: Projective Techniques

Anderson, James C.
   "The Validity of Haire's Shopping List Projective Technique"
   Journal of Marketing Research, Vol. XV (November 1978), pp. 644-9.

Begin, G. and Boivin, M.
   "Comparison of Data Gathered on Sensitive Questions via Direct
   Questionnaire, Randomized Response Technique, and a Projective Method"
   Psychological Reports, Vol. 47 (December 1980), pp. 743-50.

Brockbill, G. A.
   "Some Effects of Color on Thematic Fantasy"
   Journal of Consulting Psychology, Vol. 15 (October 1951), pp. 412-8.

Caputo, D. V., Plapp, J. M., Hanf, C., and Angel, A. S.
   "The Validity of the Edwards Personal Preference Schedule Employing
   Projective and Behavioral Criteria"
   Educational and Psychological Measurement, Vol. 25 (Autumn 1965), pp.
   829-48.

Cobliner, W. G.
   "On the Place of Projective Tests in Opinion and Attitude Surveys"
   International Journal of Opinion and Attitude Research, Vol. 5
   (Winter 1951-52), pp. 480-90.

Day, Ellen
   "Share of Heart: What is It and How can It be Measured?"
   Journal of Consumer Marketing, Vol. 6 (Winter 1989), pp. 5-12.

Engel, James F. and Wales, Hugh G.
   "Spoken Versus Pictured Questions on Taboo Topics"
   Journal of Advertising Research, Vol. 2 (March 1962), pp. 11-7.

Getzels, T. W. and Walsh, J. J.
   "The Method of Paired Direct and Projective Questionnaires in the
   Study of Attitude Structure and Socialization"
   Psychological Monographs, Vol. 63 (1959).

Greenberg, A.
   "Pictorial Stereotypes in a Projective Test"
   Journal of Marketing, Vol. 24 (October 1959), pp. 72-4.

Haire, Mason
   "Projective Techniques in Marketing Research"
   Journal of Marketing, Vol. 14 (April 1950), pp. 649-56.

Hill, Conrad R.
   "Another Look at Two Instant Coffee Studies"
   Journal of Advertising Research, Vol. 1 (December 1960), pp. 18-21.

Hollander, Sharon L.
   "Projective Techniques Uncover Real Consumer Attitudes"
   Marketing News (January 4, 1988), p. 4.

Korner, A. F.
"Theoretical Considerations Concerning the Scope and Limitations of Projective Techniques"
Journal of Abnormal and Social Psychology, Vol. 45 (October 1950), pp. 619-27.

Krugman, Herbert E.
"The Draw a Supermarket Technique"
Public Opinion Quarterly, Vol. 24 (Spring 1960), pp. 148,9.

Levy, Sidney J.
"Dreams, Fairy Tales, Animals, and Cars"
Psychology and Marketing, Vol. 2 (Summer 1985), pp. 67-81.

Levy, Sidney J.
"Interpreting Consumer Mythology: A Structural Approach to Consumer Behavior"
Journal of Marketing, Vol. 45 (Summer 1981), pp. 49-61.

Levy, Sidney
"Figure Drawing as a Projective Test"
in Abt, Lawrence E. and Bellak, Leopold (editors)
Projective Techniques
(New York, NY: Grove Press, Inc., 1950), pp. 257-97.

Lysaker, R. and Bradley, J. E.
"What Is a Pictorial Projective Technique"
Journal of Marketing, Vol. 21 (January 1957), pp. 339,40.

McCord, H.
"Discovering the 'Confused' Respondent: A Possible Projective Method"
Public Opinion Quarterly, Vol. 15 (Summer 1951), pp. 363-6.

Napoli, Peter J.
"Finger-Painting and Personality Diagnosis"
Genetic Psychology Monographs, Vol. 34 (July 1946), pp. 133-230.

Politz, Alfred
"Motivation Research From a Research Viewpoint"
The Public Opinion Quarterly, Vol. 20 (Winter 1956-1957), pp. 663-73.

Rapaport, D.
"Principles Underlying Projective Techniques"
Character and Personality, Vol. X (March 1942), pp. 213-9.

Robertson, Dan H. and Joselyn, Robert W.
"Projective Techniques in Research"
Journal of Advertising Research, Vol. 14 (October 1974), pp. 27-31.

Rogers, E. M. and Beal, G. M.
"Projective Techniques: Potential Tools for Agricultural Economists"
Journal of Farm Economics, Vol. 41 (August 1959), pp. 644-8.

Rogers, E. M. and Beal, G. M.
"Projective Techniques in Interviewing Farmers"
Journal of Marketing, Vol. 23 (October 1958), pp. 177-9.

Rothwell, N. D.
"Motivational Research Revisited"
Journal of Marketing, Vol. 20 (October 1955), pp. 150-4.

Sanford, F. H.
"The Use of a Projective Device in Attitude Surveying"
Public Opinion Quarterly, Vol. 14 (Winter 1950-51), pp. 697-709.

Sanford, F. H. and Rosenstock, I. M.
"Projective Techniques on the Doorstep"
Journal of Abnormal and Social Psychology, Vol. 47 (January 1952), pp. 3-16.

Sarason, Irwin G.
"Relationships of Measures of Anxiety and Experimental Instructions to Word Association Test Performance"
Journal of Abnormal and Social Psychology, Vol. 59 (July 1959), pp. 37-42.

Schlackman, William
"The Application of Projective Tests to Psychographic Analysis of Markets"
Proceedings, Market Research Society Conference (March 1986), pp. 27-41.

Steele, Howard L.
"On the Validity of Projective Questions"
Journal of Marketing Research, Vol. I (August 1964), pp. 46-9.

Vicary, J. M.
"Seasonal Psychology"
Journal of Marketing, Vol. 20 (April 1956), pp. 394-7.

Walters, J. H.
"Structured or Unstructured Techniques"
Journal of Marketing, Vol. 25 (April 1961), pp. 58-61.

Weschler, I. R.
"Problems in the Use of Indirect Methods of Attitude Measurement"
Public Opinion Quarterly, Vol. 15 (Spring 1951), pp. 133-8.

Zober, M.
"Some Projective Techniques Applied to Marketing Research"
Journal of Marketing, Vol. 20 (January 1956), pp. 262-8.

85.03 ---------- Theory Re: Thematic Apperception Test (TAT)

Bijou, S. W. and Kenny, D. T.
"The Ambiguity Values of TAT Cards"
Journal of Consulting Psychology, Vol. 15 (June 1951), pp. 203-9.

Davenport, B. F.
"The Semantic Validity of TAT Interpretations"
Journal of Consulting Psychology, Vol. 16 (June 1952), pp. 171-5.

Eron, L. D.
"Responses of Women to the Thematic Apperception Test"
Journal of Consulting Psychology, Vol. 17 (August 1953), pp. 269-82.

Eron, L. D. and Ritter, A. M.
"A Comparison of Two Methods of Administration of the Thematic
Apperception Test"
Journal of Consulting Psychology, Vol. 15 (February 1951), pp. 55-61.

Fry, F. D.
"Manual for Scoring the Thematic Apperception Test"
Journal of Psychology, Vol. 35 (April 1953), pp. 181-95.

Fry, F. D.
"TAT Scoring Blank"
Journal of Psychology, Vol. 35 (April 1953), pp. 197-200.

Garfield, S. L., Bleck, L., and Melker, F.
"The Influence of Method of Administration and Sex Differences on
Selected Aspects of TAT Stories"
Journal of Consulting Psychology, Vol. 16 (April 1952), pp. 140-4.

Weisskopf, E. A. and Dieppa, J. J.
"Experimentally Induced Faking of TAT Responses"
Journal of Consulting Psychology, Vol. 15 (December 1951), pp. 469-74.

85.04 ---------- Applications of Thematic Apperception Tests (TAT)

Batz, Gerhard
"Tell Me a Story. An Application of the TAT-Technique to Anticipate
Effects of Advertising"
Proceedings, ESOMAR Congress, Monte Carlo (1986), pp. 497-525.

Rook, Dennis W.
"The Ritual Dimension of Consumer Behavior"
Journal of Consumer Research, Vol. 12 (December 1985), pp. 251-64.

85.05 ---------- Applications of Projective Techniques

Arndt, Johan
"Haire's Shopping List Revisited"
Journal of Advertising Research, Vol. 13 (October 1973), pp. 57-61.

Hill, Conrad R.
"Haire's Classic Instant Coffee Study--Eighteen Years Later"
Journalism Quarterly, Vol. 45 (August 1968), pp. 466-72.

Lane, George S. and Watson, Gayne L.
"A Canadian Replication of Mason Haire's 'Shopping List' Study"
Journal of the Academy of Marketing Science, Vol. 3 (Winter 1975),
pp. 48-59.

Sheth, Jagdish N.
"Projective Attitudes Toward Instant Coffee in the Late Sixties"
Markedskommunikasjon, Vol. VIII (1971), pp. 73-9.

Webster, F. E. and Von Pechman, F.
"A Replication of the 'Shopping List' Study"
Journal of Marketing, Vol. 34 (April 1970), pp. 61-3.

86 ------------------------- PROTOCOL DATA -------------------------

86.01 ---------- Books Re: Protocol Data

Ericsson, K. Anders and Simon, Herbert A.
    Protocol Analysis: Verbal Reports as Data
    (Cambridge, MA: MIT Press, 1984), 426 pp.

86.02 ---------- Theory Re: Protocol Data

Nisbett, Richard E. and Wilson, Timothy D.
    "Telling More Than We Know: Verbal Reports on Mental Processes"
    Psychological Review, Vol. 54 (1977), pp. 321-59.

Olshavsky, Richard W. and Acito, Frank
    "Conjoint Analysis and Protocol Analysis--A Simultaneous Approach"
    Graduate School of Business, Indiana University (1979), working paper.

Wright, Peter L.
    "Message Evoked Thoughts: Persuasion Research Using Thought
    Verbalizations"
    Journal of Consumer Research, Vol. 7 (1980), pp. 155-75.

86.03 ---------- Empirical Studies of Protocol Data Collection

Biehal, Gabriel and Chakravarti, Dipankar
    "The Effects of Concurrent Verbalization on Choice Processing"
    Journal of Marketing Research, Vol. XXVI (February 1989), pp. 84-96.

Ericsson, K. Anders and Simon, Herbert A.
    "Protocols as Data I: Effects of Verbalization"
    Department of Psychology, Carnegie-Mellon University (1978), working
    paper.

Fidler, Eduard J.
    "The Reliability and Validity of Concurrent, Retrospective and
    Interpretive Verbal Reports"
    in Humphreys, P., Svenson, Ola, and Vari, A. (editors)
    Analyzing and Aiding Decision Processes
    (Amsterdam: North-Holland Publishing Company, 1983), pp. 429-40.

Nisbett, Richard E. and Wilson, Timothy D.
    "Telling More Than We Can Know: Verbal Reports on Mental Processes"
    Psychological Review, Vol. 84 (1977), pp. 231-59.

Russo, Jay Edward, Johnson, Eric J., and Stephens, Debra M.
    "The Validity of Verbal Protocols"
    University of Maryland (1987), working paper.

Smead, Raymond J., Wilcox, James B., and Wilkes, Robert E.
    "How Valid are Product Descriptions and Protocols in Choice
    Experiments?"
    Journal of Consumer Research, Vol. 8 (June 1981), pp. 37-42.

Smith, Eliot R. and Miller, Frederick D.
    "Limits on Perception of Cognitive Processes: A Reply to Nisbett and
    Wilson"
    Psychological Review, Vol. 85 (1978), pp. 355-62.

86.04 ---------- Administration Issues Re: Protocol Data

Ericsson, K. Anders and Simon, Herbert A.
    "Verbal Reports as Data"
    Psychological Review, Vol. 87 (1980), pp. 215-51.

Ericsson, K. Anders and Simon, Herbert A.
    "Thinking Aloud Protocols as Data"
    CIP Working Paper No. 397
    Department of Psychology, Carnegie-Mellon University, Pittsburgh, PA
    (1979).

Ericsson, K. Anders and Simon, Herbert A.
    "Protocols as Data II: Verticality of Verbalized Information"
    Department of Psychology, Carnegie-Mellon University (1978), working
    paper.

Ericsson, K. Anders and Simon, Herbert A.
    "Retrospective Verbal Reports as Data"
    Department of Psychology, Carnegie-Mellon University (1978), working
    paper.

Payne, John W. and Ragsdale, E. K. Easton
    "Verbal Protocols and Direct Observation of Supermarket Shopping
    Behavior: Some Findings and a Discussion of Methods"
    in Hunt, H. Keith (editor)
    Advances in Consumer Research, Volume Five
    (Ann Arbor, MI: Association for Consumer Research, 1978), pp. 571-7.

Smead, Raymond J., Wilcox, James B., and Wilkes, Robert E.
"An Illustration and Evaluation of a Joint Process Tracing
Methodology: Eye Movement and Protocols"
in Olson, Jerry C. (editor)
Advances in Consumer Research, Volume Seven
(Ann Arbor, MI: Association for Consumer Research, 1979), pp. 507-12.

86.05 ---------- Theory Re: Protocol Data Coding Schemes

See also (sub)heading(s) 34.05, 46.01, 131.04, 132.02.

Bettman, James R. and Park, C. Whan
"Effects of Prior Knowledge and Experience and Phase of Choice
Process on Consumers' Decision Processes: A Protocol Analysis"
Journal of Consumer Research, Vol. 7 (December 1980), pp. 234-48.

Bettman, James R. and Park, C. Whan
"Implications of a Constructive View of Choice for Analysis of
Protocol Data: A Coding Scheme for Elements of Choice Processes"
in Olson, Jerry C. (editor)
Advances in Consumer Research, Volume Seven
(Ann Arbor, MI: Association for Consumer Research, 1980), pp. 148-53.

Bettman, James R. and Park, C. Whan
"Descriptions and Examples of a Protocol Coding Scheme for Elements
of Choice Processes"
Working Paper No. 76
UCLA Center for Marketing Studies, Los Angeles, CA (1979).

Biehal, Gabriel and Chakravarti, Dipankar
"Experiences With the Bettman-Park Verbal-Protocol Coding Scheme"
Journal of Consumer Research, Vol. 8 (March 1982), pp. 442-8.

Downham, J.
"The Function of Coding"
in Readings in Market Research
(London, 1956).

Franke, George R. and Didow, Nicholas M.
"Phenomenological Validity in Marketing Research: Self Coding Versus
Independent Judge Coding of Ambiguous Response Measures" (abstract)
Proceedings, AMA Educators' Conference
(Chicago: American Marketing Association, 1987), p. 237.

Lammers, H. Bruce
"A Multitrait-Multimethod Analysis of the Validity of Cognitive
Response Assessment Procedures"
in Hirschman, E. and Holbrook, M. (editors)
Advances in Consumer Research, Volume 12
(Ann Arbor, MI: Association for Consumer Research, 1985), pp. 164-8.

Wright, Peter L.
"The Cognitive Processes Mediating Acceptance of Advertising"
Journal of Marketing Research, Vol. X (February 1973), pp. 53-62.

86.06 ---------- Applications of Protocol Data Collection

Alexis, Marcus, Haines, George, and Simon, Leonard
"Consumer Information Processing: The Case of Women's Clothing"
in King, Robert (editor)
Marketing and the New Science of Planning
(Chicago: American Marketing Association, 1968), pp. 197-205.

Batra, Rajeev and Ray, Michael L.
"Affective Responses Mediating Acceptance of Advertising"
Journal of Consumer Research, Vol. 13 (September 1986), pp. 234-49.

Bettman, James R.
"Information Processing Models of Consumer Behavior"
Journal of Marketing Research, Vol. VII (August 1970), pp. 370-6.

Bettman, James R. and Zins, Michel A.
"Constructive Processes in Consumer Choice"
Journal of Consumer Research, Vol. 4 (September 1977), pp. 75-85.

Biehal, Gabriel J.
"An Exploration of Consumer Search Strategies in Internal and
External Environments"
Working Paper No. 23
Center for Consumer Research, University of Florida, Gainsville, FL
(1980).

Biehal, Gabriel J. and Chakravarti, Dipankar
"Consumers' Use of Memory and External Information in Choice: Macro
and Micro Processing Perspectives"
Journal of Consumer Research, Vol. 12 (March 1986), pp. 382-405.

Biehal, Gabriel and Chakravarti, Dipankar
   "Information-Presentation Format and Learning Goals as Determinants
   of Consumers' Memory Retrieval and Choice Processes"
   Journal of Consumer Research, Vol. 8 (March 1982), pp. 431-41.

Blair, Edward and Burton, Scot
   "Cognitive Processes Used by Survey Respondents to Answer Behavioral
   Frequency Questions"
   Journal of Consumer Research, Vol. 14 (September 1987), pp. 280-8.

Clarkson, G. P. E.
   "A Model of Trust Investment Behavior"
   in Feigenbaum, Edward and Feldman, Julian (editors)
   Computers and Thought
   (New York: McGraw-Hill Book Company, 1963), pp. 347-71.

Clarkson, Geoffrey P. E.
   Portfolio Selection: A Simulation of Trust Investment
   (Englewood Cliffs, NJ: Prentice Hall, 1962).

Cox, Anthony D. and Summers, John O.
   "Heuristics and Biases in the Intuitive Projection of Retail Sales"
   Journal of Marketing Research, Vol. XXIV (August 1987), pp. 290-7.

Crow, Lowell E., Olshavsky, Richard W., and Summers, John O.
   "Industrial Buyers' Choice Strategies: A Protocol Analysis"
   Journal of Marketing Research, Vol. XVII (February 1980), pp. 34-44.

D'Astous, Alain and Rouzies, Dominique
   "Selection and Implementation of Processing Strategies in Consumer
   Evaluative Judgment and Choice"
   International Journal of Research in Marketing, Vol. 4, No. 2 (1987),
   pp. 99-110.

Edell, Julie A. and Staelin, Richard A.
   "The Information Processing of Pictures in Print Advertisements"
   Journal of Consumer Research, Vol. 10 (June 1983), pp. 45-61.

Hulbert, James, Farley, John U., and Howard, John A.
   "Information Processing and Decision Making in Marketing
   Organizations"
   Journal of Marketing Research, Vol. IX (February 1972), pp. 75-7.

John, Deborah Roedder and Whitney, John C., Jr.
   "The Development of Consumer Knowledge in Children: A Cognitive
   Structure Approach"
   Journal of Consumer Research, Vol. 12 (March 1986), pp. 406-17.

Johnson, Eric J. and Russo, J. Edward
   "Product Familiarity and Learning New Information"
   Journal of Consumer Research, Vol. 11 (June 1984), pp. 542-50.

Johnson, Eric J. and Russo, Jay Edward
   "What is Remembered After a Purchase Decision?"
   Center for Decision Research, Unversity of Chicago (1978), working
   paper.

Johnson, Michael D.
   "The Differential Processing of Product Category and Noncomparable
   Choice Alternatives"
   Journal of Consumer Research, Vol. 16 (December 1989), pp. 300-9.

Johnson, Michael D.
   "Comparability and Hierarchical Processing in Multialternative Choice"
   Journal of Consumer Research, Vol. 15 (December 1988), pp. 303-14.

Klein, Noreen M. and Bither, Stewart W.
   "An Investigation of Utility-Directed Cutoff Selection"
   Journal of Consumer Research, Vol. 14 (September 1987), pp. 240-56.

Lussier, Denis A. and Olshavsky, Richard W.
   "Task Complexity and Contingent Processing in Brand Choice"
   Journal of Consumer Research, Vol. 6 (September 1979), pp. 154-65.

MacKenzie, Scott B.
   "The Role of Attention in Mediating the Effect of Advertising on
   Attribute Importance"
   Journal of Consumer Research, Vol. 13 (September 1986), pp. 174-95.

Meyer, Robert J.
   "The Learning of Multiattribute Judgment Policies"
   Journal of Consumer Research, Vol. 14 (September 1987), pp. 155-73.

Olson, Jerry C. and Mudderisoglu, Aydin
   "The Stability of Responses Obtained by Free Elicitation:
   Implications for Measuring Attribute Salience and Memory Structure"
   in Wilkie, William L. (editor)
   Advances in Consumer Research, Volume Six
   (Ann Arbor, MI: Association for Consumer Research, 1979), pp. 269-75.

Park, C. Whan
"A Conflict Resolution Choice Model"
Journal of Consumer Research, Vol. 5 (September 1978), pp. 124-37.

Park, C. Whan, Iyer, Easwar S., and Smith, Daniel C.
"The Effects of Situational Factors on In-Store Grocery Shopping
Behavior: The Role of Store Environment and Time Available for
Shopping"
Journal of Consumer Research, Vol. 15 (March 1989), pp. 422-33.

Park, C. Whan and Lessig, V. Parker
"Familiarity and Its Impact on Consumer Decision Biases and
Heuristics"
Journal of Consumer Research, Vol. 8 (September 1981), pp. 223-30.

Park, C. Whan and Smith, Daniel C.
"Product-Level Choice: A Top-Down or Bottom-Up Process?"
Journal of Consumer Research, Vol. 16 (December 1989), pp. 289-99.

Payne, John
"Task Complexity and Contingent Processing in Decision Making: An
Information Search and Protocol Analysis"
Organization Behavior and Human Performance, Vol. 16 (June 1976), pp.
355-87.

Rip, Peter D.
"The Extent and Basis of Insight in Decision Making: A Study in
Consumer Behavior"
Graduate School of Business, Stanford University (1979), unpublished
doctoral dissertation.

Russo, J. Edward and Johnson, Eric J.
"What do Consumers Know About Familiar Products?"
in Olson, Jerry C. (editor)
Advances in Consumer Research, Volume Seven
(Ann Arbor, MI: Association for Consumer Research, 1980), pp. 417-23.

Simonson, Itamar
"Choice Based on Reasons: The Case of Attraction and Compromise
Effects"
Journal of Consumer Research, Vol. 16 (September 1989), pp. 158-74.

Stiles, Gerald
"An Information Process Model of Industrial Buyer Behavior"
University of Minnesota (1972), unpublished doctoral dissertation.

Svenson, Ola
"Coded Think Aloud Protocols Obtained When Making a Choice to
Purchase One of Seven Hypothetically Offered Houses: Some Examples"
University of Stockholm (1974), working paper.

Thorson, Esther and Snyder, Rita
"Viewer Recall of Television Commercials: Prediction From the
Propositional Structure of Commercial Scripts"
Journal of Marketing Research, Vol. XXI (May 1984), pp. 127-36.

Wind, Yoram
"Applying the Behavioral Theory of the Firm to Industrial Buying
Decisions"
The Economic and Business Bulletin, Vol. 10 (1968), pp. 22-8.

Wright, Peter
"Consumer Choice Strategies: Simplifying Versus Optimizing"
Journal of Marketing Research, Vol. XI (February 1975), pp. 60-7.

Wright, Peter L. and Barbour, R. Frederick
"Phased Decision Strategies: Sequels to an Initial Screening"
in Starr, Martin K. and Zeleny, Milan (editors)
North Holland/TIMS Studies in the Management Sciences, Volume Six:
Multiple Criterion Decision Making
(Amsterdam: North Holland, 1977), pp. 91-109.

Wright, Peter L. and Barbour, R. Frederick
"The Relevance of Decision Process Models in Structuring Persuasive
Messages"
Communications Research, Vol. 2 (1975), pp. 246-9.

Wright, Peter and Rip, Peter D.
"Product Class Advertising Effects on First-Time Buyers' Decision
Strategies"
Journal of Consumer Research, Vol. 7 (September 1980), pp. 176-88.

Wright, Peter L. and Rip, Peter D.
"Retrospective Reports on Consumers' Decision Processes"
in Olson, Jerry C. (editor)
Advances in Consumer Research, Volume Seven
(Ann Arbor, MI: Association for Consumer Research, 1980), pp. 146,7.

87 ----------------------- TELEPHONE SURVEYS -------------------------

87.01 ---------- Books Re: Telephone Surveys

Blankenship, A. B.
  Professional Telephone Surveys
  (New York: McGraw-Hill Book Co., 1977), 244 pp.

Dillman, Don A.
  Mail and Telephone Surveys
  (New York: John Wiley and Sons, Inc., 1978), 325 pp.

Frey, James H.
  Survey Research by Telephone, Second Edition
  (Newbury Park, CA: Sage Publications, 1989), 296 pp.

Groves, Robert M. et al. (editors)
  Telephone Survey Methodology
  (New York: John Wiley and Sons, Inc., 1988).

Groves, Robert M. and Kahn, Robert L.
  Surveys by Telephone: A National Comparison With Personal Interviews
  (New York: Academic Press, 1979), 384 pp.

Lavrakas, Paul J.
  Telephone Survey Methods: Sampling, Selection, and Supervision
  (Newbury Park, CA: Sage Publications, Inc., 1987), 157 pp.

Lucas, William A. and Adams, William C.
  An Assessment of Telephone Survey Methods
  (Santa Monica, CA: 1977).

Wiseman, Frederick and McDonald, Philip
  The Nonresponse Problem in Telephone Surveys
  (Cambridge, MA: Marketing Science Institute, 1979), 78 pp.

87.02 ---------- Administration Issues in Telephone Surveys

Baker, David and Holmes, Cliff
  "The Validity and Efficiency of Data Collection Using Screen
  Interviews Compared With Telephone Research"
  ESOMAR Congress, Montreux (1987), pp. 813-27.

Barker, Raymond F.
  "Interviewing Consumers in New Zealand and the United States"
  Singapore Marketing Review, Vol. II (March 1987), pp. 77-90.

Biemer, Paul P.
  "Measuring Data Quality"
  in Groves, Robert et al. (editors)
  Telephone Survey Methodology
  (New York: 1988), pp. 51-69.

Blankenship, A. B. and Pearson, Michael M.
  "Guidelines for a Telephone Group Interview"
  Journal of the Academy of Marketing Science, Vol. 5 (Winter-Spring
  1977), pp. 1-8.

Bortner, Bruce Z. and Assael, Henry
  "Continuous Tracking Studies via WATS Lines and Personal Inverviewing"
  Annual Conference of the Advertising Research Foundation, New York
  (1967), presentation.

Bush, Alan J. and Parasuraman, A.
  "Mall Intercept Versus Telephone Interviewing Environment"
  Journal of Advertising Research, Vol. 25 (April/May 1985), pp. 36-43.

Cahalan, D.
  "Measuring Newspaper Readership by Telephone: Two Comparisons With
  Face-to-Face Interviews"
  Journal of Advertising Research, Vol. 1 (December 1960), pp. 1-6.

Colombotos, John
  "The Effects of Personal vs. Telephone Interviews on Socially
  Acceptable Responses"
  Annual Meeting of the American Association for Public Opinion
  Research, Groton, CT (May 14, 1965), paper presentation.

Day, Robert L.
  "Some Thoughts About the Telephone as a Mode of Interviewing in
  Consumer Research"
  European Research, Vol. 2 (May 1974), pp. 119-22.

DeVere, Stephen P., Burns, Alvin C., and Bush, Ronald F.
  "Broadening the Scope of Methodological Research on Telephone Surveys"
  Proceedings, AMA Educators' Conference
  (Chicago: American Marketing Association, 1979), pp. 14-8.

Eastlack, J. O., Jr. and Assael, Henry
"Better Telephone Surveys Through Centralized Interviewers"
Journal of Advertising Research, Vol. 6 (March 1966), pp. 2-7.

Frankel, Martin R. and Frankel, Lester R.
"Some Recent Developments in Sample Survey Design"
Journal of Marketing Research, Vol. XIV (August 1977), pp. 280-93.

French, C. E. and Kranz, D. C.
"Telephone Interviews as a Means of Surveying Farmers"
Journal of Farm Economics, Vol. 39 (February 1957), pp. 153-5.

Frey, James H.
"An Experiment With a Confidentiality Reminder in a Telephone Survey"
Public Opinion Quarterly, Vol. 50 (Summer 1986), pp. 267-9.

Groves, Robert M.
"An Empirical Comparison of Two Telephone Designs"
Survey Research Center, The University of Michigan (January 1977),
prepublication manuscript.

Groves, Robert M. and Lepkowski, J.
"Cost and Error Modelling for Large-Scale Telephone Surveys"
Proceedings, Bureau of the Census First Annual Conference, Reston, VA
(1985), pp. 330-57.

Hansell, Stephen, Sparacino, Jack, Ronchi, Don, and Strodtbeck, Fred L.
"Ego Development Responses in Written Questionnaires and Telephone
Interviews"
Journal of Personality and Social Psychology, Vol. 47 (November
1984), pp. 1118,9.

Herzog, A. Regula, Rodgers, Willard L., and Kulka, Richard A.
"Interviewing Older Adults: A Comparison of Telephone and
Face-to-Face Modalities"
Public Opinion Quarterly, Vol. 47 (Fall 1983), pp. 405-18.

Hoinville, Gerald and Sykes, Wendy
"Methodological Research on Telephone Interviews"
Proceedings, The Market Research Society Conference (1984).

Hyett, G. P. and Morgan, J. S.
"Collection of Data by Telephone: Validation of Factual Data"
European Research, Vol. 4 (July 1976), pp. 184-7.

Judd, Robert C.
"Telephone Usage and Survey Research--Comment to Kildegaard"
Journal of Advertising Research, Vol. 6 (December 1966), pp. 38,9.

Kegeles, S. Stephen, Fink, Clinton F., and Kirscht, John P.
"Interviewing a National Sample by Long-Distance Telephone"
Public Opinion Quarterly, Vol. 33 (1969), pp. 412-9.

Kildegaard, Ingrid C.
"Rejoinder--To Judd"
Journal of Advertising Research, Vol. 6 (December 1966), pp. 40,1.

Kildegaard, Ingrid C.
"Telephone Trends"
Journal of Advertising Research, Vol. 6 (June 1966), pp. 56-60.

Kinnear, Thomas C.
"Research Execs Say Phone Interviewing Beats Door-to-Door, Mall
Intercepts"
Marketing News (September 21, 1979), p. 1.

Lyberg, Lars
"Introduction: Administration of Telephone Surveys"
in Groves, Robert M. et al. (editors)
Telephone Survey Methodology
(New York: 1988), pp. 453-6.

Macey, Frank
"Telephone Research: A Progress Report"
Admap (June 1986), pp. 310-5.

McDonald, C. and Bowles, T.
"Telephone Surveys: A Review of Research Findings"
in Telephone Research
(London: Market Research Development Fund, 1981).

McIntyre, Shelby H. and Bender, Sherry D. F. G.
"The Purchase Intercept Technique (PIT) in Comparison to Telephone
and Mail Surveys"
Journal of Retailing, Vol. 62 (Winter 1986), pp. 364-83.

Miln, D., Hunter, Stewart, and Marchant, Len
"The Telephone in Consumer Research"
E.S.O.M.A.R. Conference, Hamburg (1974), Special Groups Volume, pp.
229-64.

Mitchell, G. H. and Rogers, E. M.
  "Telephone Interviewing"
  Journal of Farm Economics, Vol. 40 (August 1958), pp. 743-7.

Nielsen Company
  Total Telephone Frame
  (1976), brochure.

Payne, S. L.
  "Data Collection Methods: Telephone Surveys"
  in Ferber, R. (editor)
  Handbook of Marketing Research
  (New York: McGraw-Hill, 1974).

Payne, S. L.
  "Some Advantages of Telephone Surveys"
  Journal of Marketing, Vol. 20 (January 1956), pp. 278-80.

Rogers, Theresa
  "Interviews by Telephone and in Person: Quality of Responses and
  Field Performance"
  Public Opinion Quarterly, Vol. 40 (Spring 1976), pp. 51-65.

Ruppe, Harald
  "From Where I Sit..."
  European Research, Vol. 15 (May 1987), pp. 85-7.

Schmiedeskamp, J. W.
  "Reinterviews by Telephone"
  Journal of Marketing, Vol. 26 (January 1962), pp. 28-34.

Shaw, Robert E.
  "Telemarketing: Its Impact on the Research Industry in the United
  States"
  European Research, Vol. 15 (May 1987), pp. 78-80.

Smead, Raymond J. and Wilcox, James B.
  "Ring Policy in Telephone Surveys"
  Public Opinion Quarterly, Vol. 44 (Spring 1980), pp. 115,6.

Smith, R. P. and Watson, A. J. K.
  "Product Excellence on a Complex Product Through Telephone
  Interviewing"
  European Research, Vol. 11 (January 1983), pp. 11-9.

Sudman, S.
  "New Uses of Methods in Survey Research"
  Journal of Marketing Research, Vol. III (May 1966), pp. 163-7.

Sykes, Wendy and Hoinville, Gerald
  "Methodological Research on Telephone Interviewing"
  Market Research Society Conference (March 1984), pp. 87-97.

Tyebjee, T.
  "Telephone Survey Methods: The State of the Art"
  Journal of Marketing, Vol. 43 (Summer 1979), pp. 68-78.

Van Westerhoven, Emile
  "Telemarketing: Finding the Needle in the Haystack"
  European Research, Vol. 15 (May 1987), pp. 72-6.

Vere, S., Burns, A., and Bush, R.
  "Broadening the Scope of Methodological Research on Telephone Surveys"
  1979 Educators' Conference Proceedings
  (American Marketing Association), pp. 14-8.

Wilson, Terry C.
  "Collecting Conjoint Data Through Telephone Interviews"
  Journal of the Academy of Marketing Science, Vol. 12 (Fall 1984), pp.
  190-9.

87.03 ---------- Specific Telephone Interviewing Techniques

Frey, James H.
  "An Experiment With a Confidentiality Reminder in a Telephone Survey"
  Public Opinion Quarterly, Vol. 50 (Summer 1986), pp. 267-9.

Locander, William B. and Burton, John P.
  "The Effect of Question Form on Gathering Income Data by Telephone"
  Journal of Marketing Research, Vol. XIII (May 1976), pp. 189-92.

Loken, Barbara, Pirie, Phyllis, Virnig, Karen A., Hinkle, Ronald L.,
  and Salmon, Charles T.
  "The Use of 0-10 Scales in Telephone Surveys"
  Journal of the Market Research Society, Vol. 29 (July 1987), pp.
  353-62.

Miller, Peter V.
"Alternative Question Forms for Attitude Scale Questions in Telephone
Interviews"
Public Opinion Quarterly, Vol. 48 (Winter 1984), pp. 766-8.

Miller, Peter V. and Cannell, Charles F.
"A Study of Experimental Techniques for Telephone Interviewing"
Public Opinion Quarterly, Vol. 46 (1982), pp. 250-69.

Upah, Gregory D. and Cosmas, Stephen C.
"The Use of Telephone Dials as Attitude Scales: A Laboratory
Experiment"
Journal of the Academy of Marketing Science, Vol. 8 (Fall 1980), pp.
416-26.

87.04 ---------- Scheduling and Repeat Calling

Allen, Bruce F., Nieva, Veronica F., Rhodes, Michael D., and Englehart,
Susan M.
"Call Attempts and the Probability of Interview Completion"
Rockville (1988), unpublished paper.

Brosius, Hans-Bernd and Donsbach, Wolfgang
"Resource Optimisation and Sample Quality in Telephone Surveys"
Marketing and Research Today, Vol. 17 (May 1989), pp. 96-106.

Falthzik, Alfred M.
"When to Make Telephone Interviews"
Journal of Marketing Research, Vol. IX (November 1972), pp. 451,2.

Gates, Roger and McDaniel, Carl
"Improving Completion Rates by More Efficient Scheduling of Telephone
Interviews"
Viewpoints--The Journal for Data Collection, Vol. 16 (May 1976), pp.
8-10.

Kerin, Roger A. and Peterson, Robert A.
"Scheduling Telephone Interviews"
Journal of Advertising Research, Vol. 23 (April/May 1983), pp. 41-7.

Traugott, Michael W.
"The Importance of Persistence in Respondent Selection for
Pre-Election Surveys"
Public Opinion Quarterly, Vol. 51 (Spring 1987), pp. 48-57.

Vigderhous, Gideon
"Scheduling Telephone Interviews: A Study of Seasonal Patterns"
Public Opinion Quarterly, Vol. 45 (Summer 1981), pp. 250-9.

Weeks, Michael F., Kulka, Richard A., and Pierson, Stephanie
"Optimal Call Scheduling for a Telephone Survey"
Public Opinion Quarterly, Vol. 51 (Winter 1987), pp. 540-9.

87.05 ---------- Increasing Response Rates in Telephone Surveys

          See also (sub)heading(s) 66.

Goetz, Edward G., Tyler, Tom R., and Cook, Fay Lomax
"Promised Incentives in Media Research: A Look at Data Quality,
Sample Representativeness, and Response Rate"
Journal of Marketing Research, Vol. XXI (May 1984), pp. 148-54.

Groves, Robert M. and Magilavy, Lou J.
"Increasing Response Rates to Telephone Surveys: A Door in the Face
or Foot in the Door?"
Public Opinion Quarterly, Vol. 45 (1981), pp. 346-58.

Gunn, Walter J. and Rhodes, Isabelle N.
"Physician Response Rates to a Telephone Survey: Effects of Monetary
Incentive Level"
Public Opinion Quarterly, Vol. 45 (1981), pp. 109-15.

Michitti, Marjorie A. and Kennedy, Gregg
"On-Line Sample Control: Cost-Efficient Way to Raise Response Rates
in Phone Surveys"
Marketing News, Vol. 19 (January 4, 1985), p. 34.

Traugott, Michael W., Groves, Robert M., and Lepkowski, James M.
"Using Dual Frame Designs to Reduce Nonresponse in Telephone Surveys"
Public Opinion Quarterly, Vol. 51 (Winter 1987), pp. 523-39.

87.06 ---------- Nonresponse and Refusal Issues in Telephone Surveys

See also (sub)heading(s) 117.01.

DeMaio, Theresa J.
"Refusals: Who, Where, and Why"
Public Opinion Quarterly, Vol. 44 (1980), pp. 223-33.

Dillman, Don A., Gallegos, Jean Gorton, and Frey, James H.
"Reducing Refusal Rates for Telephone Interviews"
Public Opinion Quarterly, Vol. 40 (Spring 1976), pp. 66-78.

Groves, Robert M. and Lyberg, Lars E.
"An Overview of Nonresponse Issues in Telephone Surveys"
in Groves, Robert M. et al. (editors)
Telephone Survey Methodology
(New York: 1988), pp. 191-282.

Leigh, James H. and Martin, Claude R., Jr.
"'Don't Know' Item Nonresponse in a Telephone Survey: Effects of
Question Form and Respondent Characteristics"
Journal of Marketing Research, Vol. XXIV (November 1987), pp. 418-24.

McDaniel, Stephen W., Madden, Charles S., and Verille, Perry
"Do Topic Differences Affect Survey Non-Response?"
Journal of the Market Research Society, Vol. 29 (January 1987), pp.
55-66.

Oksenberg, Lois, Coleman, Lerita, and Cannell, Charles F.
"Interviewers' Voices and Refusal Rates in Telephone Surveys"
Public Opinion Quarterly, Vol. 50 (Spring 1986), pp. 97-111.

O'Neil, Michael J.
"Estimating the Nonresponse Bias Due to Refusals in Telephone Surveys"
Public Opinion Quarterly, Vol. 43 (Summer 1979), pp. 218-32.

Peterson, Robert A., Leone, R. P., and Sabertehrani, M. H.
"Investigating 'Income Refusals' in a Telephone Survey by Means of
Logit Analysis"
in Monroe, K. B. (editor)
Advances in Consumer Research, Volume Eight
(Ann Arbor, MI: Association for Consumer Research, 1980), pp. 287-91.

Struebbe, Jolene M., Kernan, Jerome B., and Grogan, Thomas J.
"The Refusal Problem in Telephone Surveys"
Journal of Advertising Research, Vol. 26 (June/July 1986), pp. 29-37.

Traugott, Michael W., Groves, Robert M., and Lepkowski, James M.
"Using Dual Frame Designs to Reduce Nonresponse in Telephone Surveys"
Public Opinion Quarterly, Vol. 51 (Winter 1987), pp. 522-39.

Wiseman, Frederick and McDonald, Philip
"Noncontact and Refusal Rates in Consumer Telephone Surveys"
Journal of Marketing Research, Vol. XVI (November 1979), pp. 478-84.

Wiseman, Frederick and McDonald, Philip
"The Nonresponse Problem in Consumer Telephone Surveys"
(Cambridge, MA: Marketing Science Institute, 1978).

87.07 ---------- Bias Issues in Telephone Surveys

See also (sub)heading(s) 61, 87.08, 116, 117.

Johnson, T. P., Houghland, J. G., Jr., and Clayton, R. R.
"Obtaining Reports of Sensitive Behavior: A Comparison of Substance
Use Reports From Telephone and Face to Face Interviews"
Social Science Quarterly, Vol. 70 (March 1989).

Jordan, Lawrence A., Marcus, Alfred C., and Reeder, Leo G.
"Response Styles in Telephone and Household Interviewing: A Field
Experiment"
Public Opinion Quarterly, Vol. 44 (1980), pp. 210-22.

Leupker, Russell V. et al.
"Validity of Telephone Surveys in Assessing Cigarette Smoking in
Young Adults"
AJPH, Vol. 79 (February 1989).

Schmidley, A. Dianne
"How to Overcome Bias in a Telephone Survey"
American Demographics, Vol. 8 (November 1986), pp. 50,1.

87.08 ---------- Interviewer Effects in Telephone Surveys

Ballou, Janice and Delboca, Frances K.
"Gender Interaction Effects on Survey Measures in Telephone Interviews"
American Association for Public Opinion Research, Mason, OH (May 1980), presentation.

Groves, Robert M. and Fultz, N. H.
"Gender Effects Among Telephone Interviewers in a Survey of Economic Attitudes"
Sociological Methods and Research, Vol. 14, No. 1 (1985), pp. 31-52.

Groves, Robert M. and Magilavy, Lou J.
"Measuring and Explaining Interviewer Effects in Centralized Telephone Surveys"
Public Opinion Quarterly, Vol. 50 (Summer 1986), pp. 251-66.

Lakner, Edward and O'Rourke, Diane
"Gender Bias: Analysis of Factors Causing Male Underrepresentation in Surveys"
Urbana, IL (1988), unpublished.

Oksenberg, Lois, Coleman, Lerita, and Cannell, Charles F.
"Interviewers' Voices and Refusal Rates in Telephone Surveys"
Public Opinion Quarterly, Vol. 50 (Spring 1986), pp. 97-111.

Reese, Stephen D., Danielson, Wayne A., Shoemaker, Pamela J., Chang, Tsan-Kuo, and Hsu, Huei-Ling
"Ethnicity of Interview Effects Among Mexican-Americans and Anglos"
Public Opinion Quarterly, Vol. 50 (Winter 1986), pp. 563-72.

Stokes, Lynne
"Estimation of Interviewer Effects for Categorical Items in a Random Digit Dial Telephone Survey"
Journal of the American Statistical Association, Vol. 83 (September 1988), pp. 623-30.

88 --------- COMPUTER ASSISTED TELEPHONE INTERVIEWING (CATI)   ---------
        See also (sub)heading(s) 38.05, 73, 76.06, 100.07.

88.01 ---------- Administration of Computer Assisted Tele. Int.

Computers for Marketing Corporation
    SURVENT: CRT Interviewing (Central Facility)
    (San Francisco, CA: Computers for Marketing Corporation).

Curry, J.
    "Computer-Assisted Telephone Interviewing: Technology and
    Organizational Management"
    (June 1987), unpublished manuscript.

Dandurand, L.
    "Historical Perspectives and the Future of Computer Interviewing"
    Sawtooth Software Conference on Perceptual Mapping, Conjoint
    Analysis, and Computer Inverviewing
    (Ketchum, ID: Sawtooth Software, 1987), pp. 1-9.

Fink, J. C.
    "CATI's First Decade: The Chilton Experience"
    Sociological Methods and Research, Vol. 12 (1983), pp. 153-68.

Gates, R. H. and Jarboe, G. R.
    "Changing Trends in Data Acquisition for Marketing Research"
    Journal of Data Collection, Vol. 27 (1987), pp. 25-9.

Groves, Robert M.
    "Implications of CATI: Costs, Errors, and Organization of Telephone
    Survey Research"
    Sociological Methods and Research, Vol. 12 (1983), pp. 199-215.

Groves, Robert M., Berry, M., and Mathiowetz, Nancy A.
    "Some Impacts of Computer Assisted Telephone Interviewing on Survey
    Methods"
    Proceedings, Section on Survey Research Methods
    (Washington, DC: American Statistical Association, 1980), pp. 519-24.

Groves, Robert M. and Mathiowetz, Nancy A.
    "Computer Assisted Telephone Interviewing: Effects on Interviewers
    and Respondents"
    Public Opinion Quarterly, Vol. 48 (1984), pp. 356-69.

Honomichl, Jack
    "No End to Growth of CATI Systems"
    Advertising Age (April 13, 1981), pp. 86,8.

Marquis, K. and Blass, R.
    "Nonsampling Error Considerations in the Design and Operation of
    Telephone Surveys"
    Proceedings, Bureau of the Census First Annual Conference, Reston, VA
    (1985), pp. 301-29.

Nicholls, W. L.
    "CATI Research and Development at the Census Bureau"
    Sociological Methods and Research, Vol. 12 (1983), pp. 191-7.

Ossip, Al
    "Likely Improvements in Data Collection Methods: What do They Mean
    for Day-to-Day Research Management?"
    Journal of Advertising Research, Vol. 26 (October/November 1986), pp.
    RC9-12.

Roshwalb, I.
    "CATI and the Dynamics of Research"
    in Are Interviewers Obsolete? Drastic Changes in Data Collection and
    Data Presentation
    (Amsterdam: ESOMAR, 1984).

Shanks, J. M.
    "The Current Status of Computer-Assisted Telephone Interviewing:
    Recent Progress and Future Prospects"
    Sociological Methods and Research, Vol. 12 (1983), pp. 119-42.

Shanks, J. M., Lavender, G., and Nicholls, W.
    "Continuity and Change in Computer-Assisted Surveys: The Development
    of Berkeley SRC CATI"
    Proceedings, Section on Survey Research Methods
    (Washington, DC: American Statistical Association, 1980), pp. 507-12.

Shanks, J. M. and Tortora, R. D.
    "Beyond CATI: Generalized and Distributed Systems for
    Computer-Assisted Surveys"
    Proceedings, Bureau of the Census First Annual Research Conference,
    Reston, VA (March 1985), pp. 358-71.

Shure, G. H. and Meeker, R. J.
"A Minicomputer System for Multiperson Computer-Assisted Telephone Interviewing"
Behavior Research Methods and Instrumentation, Vol. 10 (1978), pp. 196-202.

Tashchian, Armen
"Computer-Assisted Telephone Interviewing (CATI): Potentials and Limitations"
in Klein, David M. and Smith, Allen E. (editors)
Marketing Comes of Age
(Boca Raton, FL: Southern Marketing Association, 1984), pp. 181-3.

88.02 ---------- Evaluations of Computer Assisted Tele. Interviewing

Groves, Robert M. and Mathiowetz, Nancy A.
"Computer Assisted Telephone Interviewing: Effects on Interviewers and Respondents"
Public Opinion Quarterly, Vol. 48 (Spring 1984), pp. 356-69.

Smith, R. and Smith, R.
"Evaluation and Enhancements of Computer Controlled Telephone Interviewing"
Proceedings, Section on Survey Research Methods
(Washington, DC: American Statistical Association, 1980), pp. 513-5.

88.03 ---------- Applications of Computer Assisted Tele. Interviewing

Bowen, A.
"General Foods Faces the Computerization of Personal Interviewing"
Sawtooth Conference on Perceptual Mapping, Conjoint Analysis, and Computer Interviewing
(Ketchum, ID: Sawtooth Software, Inc., 1987), pp. 73-6.

De Bock, Harold
"Readership Research: Explosion From Holland"
Admap (April 1987), pp. 19-21.

Shanks, J. M., Nicholls, W. L., and Freeman, H. E.
"The California Disability Survey: Design and Execution of a Computer-Assisted Telephone Study"
Sociological Methods and Research, Vol. 10 (1981), pp. 123-40.

Toscano, G. A.
"Computer-Aided Telephone Interviewing Used in the Hours at Work Survey"
Monthly Labor Review, Vol. 109, No. 5 (1986), pp. 39-41.

88.04 ---------- Computer Programs for CATI

Sawtooth Software, Incorporated
Ci2 CATI System for Computer-Aided Telephone Interviewing
(Ketchum, ID: Sawtooth Software, Inc., 1986).

89 ---------------- TELEPHONE SURVEY SAMPLING METHODS ----------------
          See also (sub)heading(s) 33.03, 112.

89.01 ---------- General Discussions of Telephone Survey Sampling

Lepkowski, James M.
  "Telephone Sampling Methods in the United States"
  in Groves, Robert M. et al. (editors)
  Telephone Survey Methodology
  (New York: 1988), pp. 73-98.

Market Research Society
  Guide to Sources of Samples for Telephone Research
  (London, EN: The Market Research Society).

Smith, Tom V.
  "Phone Home? An Analysis of Household Telephone Ownership"
  International Conference on Telephone Survey Methodology, Charlotte
  (1987).

89.02 ---------- Sampling by Telephone Directory

Sudman, Seymour
  "The Uses of Telephone Directories for Survey Sampling"
  Journal of Marketing Research, Vol. X (May 1973), pp. 204-7.

89.03 ---------- Random Digit Dialing

Blair, Johnny and Czaja, Ronald
  "Locating a Special Population Using Random Digit Dialing"
  Public Opinion Quarterly, Vol. 46 (Winter 1982), pp. 585-90.

Gates, Roger and Brobst, Robert
  "RANDIAL: A Program for Generating Random Telephone Numbers in
  Interviewer Usable Form"
  Journal of Marketing Research, Vol. XIV (May 1977), pp. 240,1.

Glasser, Gerald J. and Metzger, Gale D.
  "Random-Digit Dialing as a Method of Telephone Sampling"
  Journal of Marketing Research, Vol. IX (February 1972), pp. 59-64.

Hauck, Mathew and Cox, Michael
  "Locating a Sample by Random Digit Dialing"
  Public Opinion Quarterly, Vol. 38 (Summer 1974), pp. 253-60.

Klecka, William R. and Tuchfarber, Alfred J.
  "Random Digit Dialing as an Efficient Method for Political Polling"
  Georgia Political Science Association Journal, Vol. 2 (Spring 1974),
  pp. 135-51.

Lyons, W. and Durant, R.
  "Interviewer Costs Associated With the Use of Random Digit Dialing in
  Large Area Samples"
  Journal of Marketing, Vol. 44 (Summer 1980), pp. 65-9.

Maklan, David and Wakshlag, Joseph
  "Within-Household Coverage in RDD Surveys"
  in Groves, Robert M. et al. (editors)
  Telephone Survey Methodology
  (New York: 1988), pp. 51-9.

Potthoff, Richard F.
  "Some Generalisations of the Mitofsky-Waksberg Technique for Random
  Digit Dialing"
  Journal of the American Statistical Association, Vol. 82 (June 1987),
  pp. 409-18.

Quah, Siam Tee
  "Random Digit Dialing as a Sampling Method in Telephone Surveys in
  Singapore"
  Singapore Marketing Review, Vol. IV (1989), pp. 86-92.

Rich, Clyde L.
  "Is Random Digit Dialing Really Necessary?"
  Journal of Marketing Research, Vol. XIV (August 1977), pp. 300-5.

Segal, Madhav N. and Hekmat, Firooz
  "Random Digit Dialing: A Comparison of Methods"
  Journal of Advertising, Vol. 14, No. 4 (1985), pp. 36-43.

Traugott, Michael W., Groves, Robert M., and Lepkowski, James M.
  "Using Dual Frame Designs to Reduce Nonresponse in Telephone Surveys"
  Public Opinion Quarterly, Vol. 51 (Winter 1987), pp. 523-39.

Trendex, Inc.
  "A Comparison of Phone Book Samples and Random Digit Dialing Samples"
  Annual Conference of the Advertising Research Foundation, New York
  (1976).

Tuchfarber, Alfred J. and Klecka, William R.
  Random Digit Dialing: Lowering the Cost of Victimization Surveys
  (Washington, DC: The Police Foundation, 1976), 177 pp.

Tull, Donald S. and Albaum, Gerald S.
  "Bias in Random Digit Dialed Surveys"
  Public Opinion Quarterly, Vol. 41 (Fall 1977), pp. 389-95.

Waksberg, Joseph
  "Sampling Methods for Random Digit Dialing"
  Journal of the American Statistical Association, Vol. 73 (March
  1978), pp. 40-6.

89.04 ---------- Other Telephone Survey Sampling Techniques

      See also (sub)heading(s) 107.13.

Bryant, Barbara
  "Respondent Selection in a Time of Changing Household Composition"
  Journal of Marketing Research, Vol. XII (May 1975), pp. 129-35.

Chilton Research Services
  A National Probabilty Sample of Telephone Households Using
  Computerized Sampling Techniques
  (Radnor, PA: Chilton Way, 1976).

Cooper, Sanford L.
  "Random Sampling by Telephone--An Improved Method"
  Journal of Marketing Research, Vol. I (November 1964), pp. 45-8.

Czaja, Ronald, Blair, Johnny, and Sebestik, Jutta P.
  "Respondent Selection in a Telephone Survey: A Comparison of Three
  Techniques"
  Journal of Marketing Research, Vol. XIX (August 1982), pp. 381-5.

Eastlack, J. O., Jr.
  "Recall of Advertising by Two Telephone Samples"
  Journal of Advertising Research, Vol. 4 (March 1964), pp. 25-9.

Frankel, Martin R. and Frankel, Lester R.
  "Some Recent Developments in Sample Survey Design"
  Journal of Marketing Research, Vol. XIV (August 1977), pp. 280-93.

Groves, Robert M.
  "An Empirical Comparison of Two Telephone Sample Designs"
  Journal of Marketing Research, Vol. XV (November 1978), pp. 622-31.

Hagen, Dan E. and Collier, Charlotte Meier
  "Must Respondent Selection Procedures for Telephone Surveys be
  Invasive?"
  Public Opinion Quarterly, Vol. 47 (Winter 1983), pp. 547-56.

Hagen, Dan and Collier, Charlotte Meier
  "Respondent Selection Procedures for Telephone Surveys: Must They be
  Invasive"
  Annual Meeting, American Association for Public Opinion Research
  (1982), paper presentation.

Kish, Leslie
  "A Procedure for Objective Respondent Selection Within the Household"
  Journal of the American Statistical Association (September 1949), pp.
  380-7.

Kviz, Frederick J.
  "Bias in a Directory Sample for a Mail Survey of Rural Households"
  Public Opinion Quarterly, Vol. 48 (Winter 1984), pp. 801-6.

Landon, E. Laird, Jr. and Banks, Sharon K.
  "Relative Efficiency and Bias of Plus-One Telephone Sampling"
  Journal of Marketing Research, Vol. XIV (August 1977), pp. 294-9.

Moriarity, Rowland T. and Bateson, John E. G.
  "Exploring Complex Decision Making Units: A New Approach"
  Journal of Marketing Research, Vol. XIX (May 1982), pp. 182-91.

O'Rourke, Diane and Blair, Johnny
  "Improving Random Respondent Selection in Telephone Surveys"
  Journal of Marketing Research, Vol. XX (November 1983), pp. 428-32.

Salmon, Charles T. and Nichols, John Spicer
  "Respondent Selection Techniques for Telephone Surveys"
  Annual Meeting, Midwest Association of Public Opinion Research
  (1980), paper presentation.

Salmon, Charles T. and Spicer, John
  "The Next-Birthday Method of Respondent Selection"
  Public Opinion Quarterly, Vol. 47 (1983), pp. 270-6.

Stock, J. Stevens
    "How to Improve Samples Based on Telephone Listings"
    Journal of Advertising Research, Vol. 2 (September 1962), pp. 50,1.

Swint, Albert G. and Powell, Terry E.
    "CLUSFONE Computer-Generated Telephone Sampling Offers Efficiency and
    Minimal Bias"
    Marketing News, Vol. 17 (May 13, 1983), Section 2, pp. 2,3.

Traugott, Michael W.
    "The Importance of Persistance in Respondent Selection for
    Preelection Surveys"
    Public Opinion Quarterly, Vol. 51 (1987), pp. 48-57.

Traugott, Michael W., Groves, Robert M., and Lepkowski, J. M.
    "Using Dual Frame Designs to Reduce Nonresponse in Telephone Surveys"
    Public Opinion Quarterly, Vol. 51 (1987), pp. 522-39.

Troldahl, V. C. and Carter, R. E., Jr.
    "Random Selection of Respondents Within Households in Phone Surveys"
    Journal of Marketing Research, Vol. I (May 1964), pp. 71-6.

89.05 ---------- Representativeness of Telephone Survey Samples

Blackston, M.
    A Comparison of the Characteristics of the Populations Accessible for
    Telephone and Face-to-Face Surveys
    (London: Market Research Development Fund, 1985).

Blankenship, A. B.
    "Listed Versus Unlisted Numbers in Telephone-Survey Samples"
    Journal of Advertising Research, Vol. 17 (February 1977), pp. 39-42.

Brunner, James A. and Brunner, Allen
    "Are Voluntarily Unlisted Telephone Subscribers Really Different?"
    Journal of Marketing Research, Vol. VIII (February 1971), pp. 121-4.

Bryson, Maurice
    "The Literary Digest Poll: Making of a Statistical Myth"
    The American Statistician, Vol. 30 (November 1976), pp. 184,5.

Collins, Martin and Sykes, Wendy
    "The Problems of Non-Coverage and Unlisted Numbers in Telephone
    Surveys in Britain"
    Journal of the Royal Statistical Society, Series A, Vol. 150, Part 3
    (1987), pp. 241-53.

Glasser, Gerald J. and Metzger, Gale D.
    "National Estimates of Nonlisted Telephone Households and Their
    Characteristics"
    Journal of Marketing Research, Vol. XII (August 1975), pp. 359-61.

Juarez, Nicandro F.
    "Phone Surveys Most Efficient Way to Survey U.S. Hispanics"
    Marketing News, Vol. 24 (January 8, 1990), p. 28.

Kahn, Robert and Groves, Robert M.
    An Empirical Comparison of Two Telephone Sample Designs
    Survey Research Center, University of Michigan (1977).

Kildegaard, Ingrid C.
    "Telephone Trends"
    Journal of Advertising Research, Vol. 6 (June 1966), pp. 56-60.

Leuthold, D. A. and Scheele, R.
    "Patterns of Bias in Samples Based on Telephone Directories"
    Public Opinion Quarterly, Vol. 35 (Summer 1971), pp. 249-57.

Miller, William L.
    "The British Vote and the Telephone at the 1983 Election"
    Journal of the Market Research Society, Vol. 29 (January 1987), pp.
    67-82.

Moberg, Patricia E.
    "Biases in Unlisted Phone Numbers"
    Journal of Advertising Research, Vol. 22 (August/September 1982), pp.
    51-5.

Phillips, D. L. and Clancy, K. J.
    "Modeling Effects in Survey Research"
    Public Opinion Quarterly, Vol. 36 (Summer 1972), pp. 246-58.

Rich, Clyde L.
    "Is Random Digit Dialing Really Necessary?"
    Journal of Marketing Research, Vol. XIV (August 1977), pp. 300-5.

Roslow, Sydney and Roslow, Laurence
    "Unlisted Phone Subscribers are Different"
    Journal of Advertising Research, Vol. 12 (August 1972), pp. 35-8.

U.S. Bureau of the Census
  "Characteristics of Households With Telephones"
  Current Population Reports, Series P-20, No. 146
  (Washington, DC: U.S. Government Printing Office, 1965).

Weaver, Charles N., Holmes, Sandra L., and Glenn, Norval D.
  "Some Characteristics of Inaccessible Respondents in a Telephone
  Survey"
  Journal of Applied Psychology, Vol. 60 (April 1975), pp. 260-2.

Wolfle, Lee M.
  "Characteristics of Persons With and Without Home Telephones"
  Journal of Marketing Research, Vol. XVI (August 1979), pp. 421-5.

90 --------------- PANELS AND/OR LONGITUDINAL STUDIES ----------------
         See also (sub)heading(s) 21.07, 62.09, 169.

90.01 ---------- Books Re: Panels and/or Longitudinal Research

Boyd, Harper W., Jr. and Westfall, Ralph L.
    An Evaluation of Continuous Consumer Panels as a Source of Marketing
    Information
    Marketing Research Techniques, Series "A"
    (Chicago, IL: American Marketing Association, 1960).

Goldfarb, N.
    An Introduction to Longitudinal Statistical Analysis
    (Glencoe, IL: The Free Press, 1960), 220 pp.

Goldstein, Harvey
    The Design and Analysis of Longitudinal Studies--Their Role in the
    Measurement of Change
    (Academic Press, 1979), 199 pp.

Kessler, R. C. and Greenberg, D. F.
    Linear Panel Analysis: Models of Quantitative Change
    (New York: Academic Press, 1981), 203 pp.

Markus, Gregory B.
    Analyzing Panel Data
    (Beverly Hills, CA: Sage Publications, Inc., 1979), 88 pp.

Nicosia, Francesco M.
    Panel Designs and Analysis in Marketing
    Research Program in Marketing, Reprint No. 13
    (Berkeley, CA: University of California, Graduate School of Business
    Administration).

Sudman, S. and Ferber, R.
    Consumer Panels
    (Chicago: American Marketing Association, 1979), 123 pp.

Wiggins, Lee M.
    Panel Analysis: Latent Probability Models for Attitude and Behavior
    Processes
    (Amsterdam: Elsevier, 1973), 248 pp.

90.02 ---------- Theory Re: Panels and/or Longitudinal Studies

Andreasen, Alan R.
    "Potential Marketing Applications of Longitudinal Methods"
    in Bennett, Peter D. (editor)
    1965 Fall Conference Proceedings of the AMA, pp. 261-75.

Baur, Detlef
    "Experiences With Advertising Post-Testing by Panel-Research"
    European Research, Vol. 9 (April 1981), pp. 75-83.

Blyth, W. G.
    "Turning Data Into Information: A New Generation of Integrated
    Consumer Research"
    ESOMAR Congress, Montreux (1987), pp. 21-39.

Buck, S. F.
    "Consumer Panels in the U.K.: Past, Present and Future"
    in Proceedings of the Market Research Society Conference
    (London: The Market Research Society, 1982).

Buck, S. F., Sherwood, R., and Twyman, W. A.
    "Panels and the Measurement of Changes"
    ESOMAR Congress--Special Groups (1975).

Carman, J. M.
    "Consumer Panels"
    in Ferber, R. (editor)
    Handbook of Marketing Research
    (New York: McGraw-Hill, 1974).

Ehrenberg, A. S. C.
    "The Time and the Place for Readership Panels"
    Journal of Advertising Research, Vol. 8 (June 1968), pp. 19-22.

Ferber, Robert
    "Does a Panel Operation Increase the Reliabilty of Survey Data: The
    Case of Consumer Savings"
    Journal of the American Statistical Association, Vol. 50 (1955), pp.
    788-810.

Ferber, R.
    "Observations on a Consumer Panel Operation"
    Journal of Marketing, Vol. 17 (January 1953), pp. 246-59.

Fink, Raymond
   "The Retrospective Question"
   Public Opinion Quarterly, Vol. 24 (Spring 1960), pp. 143-8.

Fleishman, E. A.
   "An Experimental Consumer Panel Technique"
   Journal of Applied Psychology, Vol. 35 (April 1951), pp. 133-5.

Franklin, Crawl
   "The Continuing Panel Technique"
   Journal of Marketing, Vol. 8 (1943), pp. 45-50.

Fuller, Linda
   "Use of Panels for Qualitative Research"
   Market Research Society Conference (March 1984), pp. 267-78.

Goldstein, J.
   "The Relative Advantages and Limitations of Panel and
   Successive-Sample Techniques in the Analysis of Opinion Change"
   Journal of Social Psychology, Vol. 50 (November 1959), pp. 305-20.

Granbois, Donald H. and Engel, James F.
   "The Longitudinal Approach to Studying Marketing Behavior"
   in Bennett, Peter D. (editor)
   Marketing and Economic Development
   Proceedings of Fall Conference of the AMA, 1965
   (Chicago, IL: American Marketing Association, 1966), pp. 205-21.

Grootaert, Christiaan
   "The Use of Multiple Diaries in a Household Expenditure Survey in
   Hong Kong"
   Journal of the American Statistical Association, Vol. 81 (December
   1986), pp. 938-44.

Hardin, David K. and Johnson, Richard M.
   "Patterns of Use of Consumer Purchase Panels"
   Journal of Marketing Research, Vol. VIII (August 1971), pp. 364-7.

Hargens, L. L., Reskin, B., and Allison, P. D.
   "Problems in Estimating Measurement Error From Panel Data: An Example
   Involving the Measure of Scientific Productivity"
   Sociological Methods and Research, Vol. 4 (1978), pp. 439-58.

Herriot, Roger A.
   "Collecting Income Data on Sample Surveys: Evidence from Split-Panel
   Studies"
   Journal of Marketing Research, Vol. XIV (August 1977), pp. 322-9.

Hill, R. W.
   "Some Reflections on Consumer Panels"
   British Journal of Marketing, Vol. 3 (Summer 1969), pp. 63-75.

Kahn, B. and Morrison, D. G.
   "Limitations of Panel Data in the Testing and Estimation of Choice
   Models"
   Graduate School of Management, University of California, Los Angeles
   (1984), working paper.

Kahn, Barbara E., Morrison, Donald G., and Wright, Gordon P.
   "Aggregating Individual Purchases to the Household Level"
   Marketing Science, Vol. 5 (Summer 1986), pp. 260-8.

Kemsley, W. F. F.
   "Collecting Data on Economic Flow Variables Using Interviews and
   Record Keeping"
   in Moss, Ed. L. and Goldstein, H. (editors)
   The Recall Method in Social Surveys
   (London: University of London Institute of Education, Studies in
   Education 9, 1979), pp. 115-41.

Kemsley, W. F. F.
   "Family Expenditure Survey: A Study of Differential Response Based on
   a Comparison of the 1971 Sample With the Census"
   Statisical News, Vol. 31 (November 1975), pp. 16-21.

Lewis, Harrie
   "A Comparison of Consumer Responses to Weekly and Monthly Purchase
   Panels"
   Journal of Marketing, Vol. 12 (1948), pp. 449-54.

Lievesley, D. A. and Waterton, J.
   "Advantages and Limitations of a Panel Approach in an Attitude Survey"
   Proceedings, Market Research Society Conference (March 1986), pp.
   109-21.

McKenzie, John
   "The Accuracy of Telephone Call Data Collected by Diary Methods"
   Journal of Marketing Research, Vol. XX (November 1983), pp. 417-27.

Moore, William L. and Winer, Russell S.
    "A Panel-Data Based Method for Merging Joint Space and Market
    Response Function Estimation"
    Marketing Science, Vol. 6 (Winter 1987), pp. 25-42.

Neter, J.
    "Measurement Errors in Reports of Consumer Expenditures"
    Journal of Marketing Research, Vol. VII (February 1970), pp. 11-25.

Nicosia, Francesco M.
    "Panel Designs and Analyses in Marketing"
    in Bennett, Peter D. (editor)
    1965 Fall Conference of AMA, pp. 222-43.

Nuckols, Robert C. and Mayer, Charles S.
    "Can Independent Responses be Obtained From Various Members in a Mail
    Panel Household?"
    Journal of Marketing Research, Vol. VII (February 1970), pp. 90-4.

Ortengren, J.
    "When Don't Research Panels Wear Out?"
    Journal of Marketing, Vol. 21 (April 1957), pp. 40-2.

Parfitt, J.
    "A General Summary of the Types of Panels in Use, Their Common
    Characteristics and Some of the Technical Considerations Involved in
    Their Operation"
    ESOMAR Seminar on Panels (1972), pp. 1-22.

Parfitt, John H.
    "A Comparison of Purchase Recall With Diary Panel Records"
    Journal of Advertising Research, Vol. 7 (September 1967), pp. 16-31.

Pelz, D. C. and Andrews, F. M.
    "Detecting Causal Priorities in Panel Study Data"
    American Sociological Review, Vol. 29 (December 1964), pp. 836-48.

Ring, L. Winston
    "Towards More Efficient Usage of Consumer Purchase Panels and Test
    Markets
    University of Wisconsin-Milwaukee (1971), unpublished paper.

Rothman, James
    "Handling Change in a Continuous Survey"
    Journal of the Market Research Society, Vol. 28 (April 1986), pp.
    125-44.

Sandage, C. H.
    "Do Research Panels Wear Out?"
    Journal of Marketing, Vol. 20 (April 1956), pp. 397-401.

Sargood, Roger and England, Leonard
    "New Tricks for Old Dogs"
    European Research, Vol. 3 (July 1975), pp. 140-3.

Schlackman, W.
    "A Discussion of the Use of Sensitivity Panels in Market Research"
    Journal of the Market Research Society, Vol. 26, No. 3 (July 1984),
    pp. 191-208.

Sermul, Marilyn J.
    "Comparison of Panel and Comparable Group Sampling Results in a
    Before-After Study"
    Human Organization, Vol. 3 (Fall 1961), pp. 149,50.

Shaffer, J. D.
    "The Reporting Period for a Consumer Purchase Panel"
    Journal of Marketing, Vol. 19 (January 1955), pp. 252-7.

Stanton, J. L. and Tucci, L. A.
    "The Measurement of Consumption: A Comparison of Surveys and Diaries"
    Journal of Marketing Research, Vol. XIX (May 1982), pp. 274-7.

Sudman, S.
    "Maintaining a Consumer Panel"
    in Dolva, W. K. (editor)
    Marketing Keys to Profits in the 1960's
    (Chicago: American Marketing Association, 42nd National Conference,
    1960), pp. 322-6.

Sudman, Seymour and Ferber, Robert
    "Experiments in Obtaining Consumer Expenditures by Diary Methods"
    Journal of the American Statistical Association, Vol. 66 (December
    1971), pp. 725-35.

Webber, Harold H.
    "Point of View: The Panel Numbers Game Recalled"
    Journal of Advertising Research, Vol. 14 (August 1974), pp. 47-9.

Webber, Harold
"The Consumer Panel: A Method of Media Evaluation"
Journal of Marketing, Vol. 9 (1944), pp. 137-40.

Wind, Yoram and Lerner, David
"On the Measurement of Purchase Data: Surveys Versus Purchase Diaries"
Journal of Marketing Research, Vol. XVI (February 1979), pp. 39-47.

Yelding, David J. and Haldane, Ian R.
"An Incentive Test"
Journal of the Market Research Society, Vol. 15 (April 1973), pp. 101-11.

Zufryden, Fred S.
"Modelling Purchase Patterns on the Basis of Incomplete and Biased Consumer Purchase Diary and UPC Panel Data"
International Journal of Research in Marketing, Vol. 1, No. 3 (1984), pp. 199-213.

90.03 ---------- Administration Issues Re: Panels, Longitud'l Studies

Allison, H. E., Zwick, C. J., and Brinser, A.
"Recruiting and Maintaining a Consumer Panel"
Journal of Marketing, Vol. 22 (April 1958), pp. 377-90.

Bailar, Barbara A.
"The Effects of Rotation Group Bias on Estimates from Panel Surveys"
Journal of the American Statistical Association, Vol. 70 (March 1975), pp. 23-30.

Bucklin, Louis P. and Carman, James M.
The Design of Consumer Research Panels: Conception and Administration of the Berkeley Food Panel
(Berkeley, CA: Institute of Business and Economic Research, University of California, 1967).

De Jonge, L. and Oppedijk Van Veen, W. M.
"Some Problems of Collecting Data About Household's Purchasing Behaviour Concerning Durable Goods"
European Research, Vol. 6 (January 1978), pp. 3-19.

Industrial Surveys Company (edited by USDA Bureau of Agricultural Economics)
Problems of Establishing a Consumer Panel in the New York Metropolitan Area
(Washington, DC: U.S. Government Printing Office, May, 1952).

Kemsley, W. F. F.
"Designing a Budget Survey"
Applied Psychology, Vol. 8 (June 1959), pp. 114-23.

Kimberly, J. R.
"Issues in the Design of Longitudinal Organizational Research"
Sociological Methods and Research, Vol. 4 (1976), pp. 321-47.

U.S. Department of Agriculture
Problems of Establishing a Consumer Panel in the New York Metropolitan Area
Marketing Research Report No. 8 (1952).

Walsh, T. C.
"Selected Results From the 1972-73 Diary Surveys"
Journal of Marketing Research, Vol. XIV (August 1977), pp. 344-52.

90.04 ---------- Electronic Panels

Winters, Lewis C.
"Marketing Research's Survey in a Box: VIEWTEL"
Marketing Research, Vol. 1 (September 1989), pp. 82,3.

90.05 ---------- Bias in the Use of Panels and/or Longitudinal Studies

Buck, S. F., Fairclough, E. E., Jephcott, J. St. G., and Ringer, D. W. C.
"Conditioning and Bias in Consumer Panels--Some New Results"
Journal of the Market Research Society, Vol. 19 (April 1977), pp. 59-75.

Crider, D. M., Willits, F. K., and Bealer, R. C.
"Teaching Respondents in Longitudinal Surveys"
Public Opinion Quarterly, Vol. 35 (Winter 1971-72), pp. 613-20.

Ehrenberg, A. S. C.
"A Study of Some Potential Biases in the Operation of a Consumer Panel"
Applied Statistics: A Journal of the Royal Statistical Society, Vol. 9 (March 1960), pp. 20-7.

Ferber, Robert
    The Reliability of Consumer Reports of Financial Asset and Debt
    (Urbana, IL: Bureau of Economic and Business Research, University of
    Illinois, 1966).

Ferber, Robert
    "Observations on a Consumer Panel Operation"
    Journal of Marketing, Vol. 17 (January 1953), pp. 246-59.

Griliches, Zvi, Hall, Bronwyn H., and Hausman, Jerry A.
    "Missing Data and Self-Selection in Large Panels"
    Annales de l'insee, Vols. 30-31 (April-September 1978), pp. 137-76.

Hansen, Jochen
    "How Problematic are Random Responses in Panel Studies?"
    European Research, Vol. 16 (February 1988), pp. 34-41.

Hausman, Jerry A. and Wise, David A.
    "Attrition Bias in Experimental and Panel Data: The Gary Income
    Maintenance Experiment"
    Econometrica, Vol. 47 (March 1979), pp. 455-73.

Hausman, Jerry A. and Wise, David A.
    "Social Experimentation, Truncated Distributions, and Efficient
    Estimation"
    Econometrica, Vol. 45 (May 1977), pp. 919-38.

Hausman, Jerry A. and Wise, David A.
    "The Evaluation of Results From Truncated Samples: The New Jersey
    Income Maintenance Experiment"
    Annals of Economic and Social Measurement, Vol. 5, No. 4 (1976), pp.
    421-45.

Heckman, James J.
    "Sample Selection Bias as a Specification Error"
    Econometrica, Vol. 47 (January 1979), pp. 153-61.

Heckman, James J.
    "The Common Structure of Statistical Models of Truncation, Sample
    Selection and Limited Dependent Variables and a Simple Estimator for
    Such Models"
    Annals of Social and Economic Measurement, Vol. 5, No. 4 (1976), pp.
    475-92.

Hyett, G. P. and McKenzie, J. R.
    "Effect of Underreporting by Consumer Panels on Level of Trial and
    Repeat Purchasing of New Products"
    Journal of Marketing Research, Vol. XIII (February 1976), pp. 80-6.

Kandel, Denise, Raveis, Victoria, and Logan, John
    "Sex Differences in the Characteristics of Members Lost to a
    Longitudinal Panel: A Speculative Research Note"
    Public Opinion Quarterly, Vol. 47 (Winter 1983), pp. 567-75.

Leeflang, Peter S. H. and Olivier, Alex J.
    "Bias in Consumer Panel and Store Audit Data"
    International Journal of Research in Marketing, Vol. 2, No. 1 (1985),
    pp. 27-41.

Leeflang, Peter S. H. and Olivier, Alex J.
    "Facing Panel Nonresponse: Consequences and Solutions"
    Proceedings, 35th ESOMAR Congress (1982), pp. 17-39.

McGloughlin, T. I.
    "Continuous Purchasing Data Can be Collected From Individuals--But Is
    It Valid?"
    ESOMAR-WAPOR Congress, Helsinki (1971).

Morrison, D. G., Frank, R., and Massy, W. F.
    "A Note on Panel Bias"
    Journal of Marketing Research, Vol. III (February 1966), pp. 85-8.

Olsen, Randall J.
    "A Least Squares Correction for Selectivity Bias"
    Econometrica, Vol. 48 (November 1980), pp. 1815-20.

Parfitt, J. H.
    "A Comparison of Purchase Recall With Diary Panel Records"
    Journal of Advertising Research, Vol. 7 (September 1967), pp. 16-31.

Peck, John K.
    "The Problem of Attrition"
    in Watts, H. W. and Rees, A. (editors)
    The New Jersey-Pennsylvania Graduated Work Incentive Final Report
    (Madison, WI: Institute for Research on Poverty, University of
    Wisconsin, 1973).

Prais, S. J.
    "Some Problems in the Measurement of Price Changes With Special
    Reference to the Cost of Living"
    Journal of the Royal Statistical Society, Series A, Vol. 121, Part 3
    (1958).

Schaffer, J. D. and Quackenbush, G. G.
    "Cooperation and Sampling in Four Years of M.S.U. Consumer Panel
    Operation"
    Quarterly Bulletin, Michigan Agricultural Experiment Station,
    Michigan State University of Agriculture and Applied Science, Vol. 38
    (August 1955).

Sheth, J. N.
    "A Report on Conditioning Bias in Fixed Panels"
    University of Illinois (1971).

Shoemaker, Robert and Staelin, Richard
    "The Effects of Sampling Variation on Sales Forecasts for New
    Consumer Products"
    Journal of Marketing Research, Vol. XIII (May 1976), pp. 138-43.

Sobol, M. G.
    "Panel Mortality and Panel Bias"
    Journal of the American Statistical Association, Vol. 54 (March
    1959), pp. 52-68.

Sudman, S.
    "On the Accuracy of Recording of Consumer Panels: Part Two"
    Journal of Marketing Research, Vol. I (August 1964), pp. 69-83.

Sudman, S.
    "On the Accuracy of Recording of Consumer Panels: Part One"
    Journal of Marketing Research, Vol. I (May 1964), pp. 14-20.

Sudman, Seymour and Ferber, Robert
    "Experiments in Obtaining Consumer Expenditures by Diary Methods"
    Journal of the American Statistical Association, Vol. 66 (December
    1971), pp. 725-35.

United States Department of Agriculture
    "Establishing a National Consumer Panel From a Probability Sample"
    Marketing Research Report 40
    (Washington DC: U.S. Government Printing Office, 1953).

U.S. Department of Agriculture
    Response Variations Encountered With Different Questionnaire Forms
    Market Research Report No. 163 (1957).

Wiley, D. E. and Wiley, J. A.
    "The Estimation of Measurement Error in Panel Data"
    in Blalock, H. M., Jr. (editor)
    Causal Models in the Social Sciences
    (Chicago: Aldine-Atherton, 1971).

Williams, W. H. and Mallows, C. L.
    "The Potential Systematic Behavior of Some Panel Survey Estimates"
    Proceedings of the Social Statistics Section of the American
    Statistical Society (1969), pp. 44-54.

Winer, Russell S.
    "Attrition Bias in Econometric Models Estimated With Panel Data"
    Journal of Marketing Research, Vol. XX (May 1983), pp. 177-86.

90.06 ---------- Descriptions of Specific Panels

Emery, Richard
    "Central's AdLab Measurement of Advertising Effectiveness"
    Admap (November 1986), pp. 24-31.

Strom, Leslie
    "The MRCA National Consumer Panel and the National Household Menu
    Census: Operation and Application"
    Proceedings, Ninth National Symposium on Dairy Market Development
    (Chicago: United Dairy Industry Association, 1972).

90.07 ---------- Applications of Panels and/or Longitudinal Studies

Bagozzi, Richard P.
    "Structural Equation Models in Experimental Research"
    Journal of Marketing Research, Vol. XIV (May 1977), pp. 209-26.

Bass, Frank M. and Pilon, Thomas L.
    "A Stochastic Brand Choice Framework for Econometric Modeling of Time
    Series Market Share Behavior"
    Journal of Marketing Research, Vol. XVII (November 1980), pp. 486-97.

Baur, Detlef
   "Experiences With Advertising Post-Testing by Panel-Research"
   European Research, Vol. 9 (April 1981), pp. 75-83.

Bawa, Kapil and Shoemaker, Robert W.
   "The Coupon-Prone Consumer: Some Findings Based on Purchase Behavior
   Across Product Classes"
   Journal of Marketing, Vol. 51 (October 1987), pp. 99-110.

Bearden, William O. and Shimp, Terence A.
   "The Use of Extrinsic Cues to Facilitate Product Adoption"
   Journal of Marketing Research, Vol. XIX (May 1982), pp. 229-39.

Bearden, William O. and Teel, Jesse E.
   "Selected Determinants of Consumer Satisfaction and Complaint Reports"
   Journal of Marketing Research, Vol. XX (February 1983), pp. 21-8.

Charlton, P. and Ehrenberg, A. S. C.
   "An Experiment in Brand Choice"
   Journal of Marketing Research, Vol. XIII (May 1976), pp. 152-60.

Cotton, B. C. and Babb, Emerson M.
   "Consumer Response to Promotional Deals"
   Journal of Marketing, Vol. 42 (July 1978), pp. 109-13.

Currim, Imran S., Meyer, Robert J., and Le, Nhan T.
   "Disaggregate Tree-Structured Modeling of Consumer Choice Data"
   Journal of Marketing Research, Vol. XXV (August 1988), pp. 253-65.

Curry, David J. and Riesz, Peter C.
   "Prices and Price/Quality Relationships: A Longitudinal Analysis"
   Journal of Marketing, Vol. 52 (January 1988), pp. 36-51.

De Jonge, L. and Oppedijk Van Veen, W. M.
   "A Micro Model of Purchasing Behaviour for Consumer Durable Goods,
   Part II"
   European Research, Vol. 4 (May 1976), pp. 129-40.

Dyer, Robert F. and Kuehl, Phillip G.
   "A Longitudinal Study of Corrective Advertising"
   Journal of Marketing Research, Vol. XV (February 1978), pp. 39-48.

Farley, John U., Howard, John A., and Lehmann, Donald R.
   "A 'Working' System Model of Car Buyer Behavior"
   Management Science, Vol. 23 (November 1976), pp. 235-47.

Farley, John U., Lehmann, Donald R., Winer, Russell S., and Katz,
   Jerrold P.
   "Parameter Stability and Carryover Effects in a Consumer Decision
   Process Model"
   Journal of Consumer Research, Vol. 8 (March 1982), pp. 465-70.

Futrell, Charles, and Jenkins, Omer C.
   "Pay Secrecy Versus Pay Disclosure for Salesmen: A Longitudinal Study"
   Journal of Marketing Research, Vol. XV (May 1978), pp. 214-9.

Goldman, Arieh and Johansson, J. K.
   "Determinants of Search for Lower Prices: An Empirical Assessment of
   the Economics of Information Theory"
   Journal of Consumer Research, Vol. 5 (December 1978), pp. 176-86.

Grover, Rajiv and Srinivasan, V.
   "A Simultaneous Approach to Market Segmentation and Market
   Structuring"
   Journal of Marketing Research, Vol. XXIV (May 1987), pp. 139-53.

Gullen, Phil and Johnson, Hugh
   "Relating Product Purchasing and TV Viewing"
   Journal of Advertising Research, Vol. 26 (December 1986/January
   1987), pp. 9-19.

Headey, Bruce
   "Quality of Life Studies: Their Implications for Social and Market
   Researchers"
   European Research, Vol. 11 (July 1983), pp. 124-32.

Hirschman, Elizabeth C.
   "A Longitudinal Analysis of Information Source Utilization"
   Journal of the Academy of Marketing Science, Vol. 6 (Fall 1978), pp.
   314-24.

Hite, Robert E. and Kiser, Edward
   "Consumers' Attitudes Toward Lawyers With Regard to Advertising
   Professional Services"
   Journal of the Academy of Marketing Science, Vol. 13 (Spring 1985),
   pp. 321-39.

Jones, J. Morgan and Zufryden, Fred S.
"An Approach for Assessing Demographic and Price Influences on Brand
Purchase Behavior"
Journal of Marketing, Vol. 46 (Winter 1982), pp. 36-46.

Kahn, Barbara E., Kalwani, Manohar U., and Morrison, Donald G.
"Niching Versus Change-of-Pace Brands: Using Purchase Frequencies and
Penetration Rates to Infer Brand Positionings"
Journal of Marketing Research, Vol. XXV (November 1988), pp. 384-90.

Kahn, Barbara E., Kalwani, Manohar U., and Morrison, Donald G.
"Measuring Variety-Seeking and Reinforcement Behaviors Using Panel
Data"
Journal of Marketing Research, Vol. XXII (May 1986), pp. 89-100.

Keng, Kau Ah and Ehrenberg, A. S. C.
"Patterns of Store Choice"
Journal of Marketing Research, Vol. XXI (November 1984), pp. 399-409.

LaBarbera, Priscilla A. and Mazursky, David
"A Longitudinal Assessment of Consumer Satisfaction/Dissatisfaction:
The Dynamic Aspect of the Cognitive Process"
Journal of Marketing Research, Vol. XX (November 1983), pp. 393-404.

Lawrence, Raymond J.
"Consumer Brand Choice: A Random Walk"
Journal of Marketing Research, Vol. XII (August 1975), pp. 314-24.

Lee, Jinjoo and Kim, Hong-Bumm
"Determinants of New Product Outcome in a Developing Country: A
Longitudinal Analysis"
International Journal of Research in Marketing, Vol. 3, No. 3 (1986),
pp. 143-56.

Llewellyn, Geoff and Stone, Mark
"Understanding Complex Industrial Markets--A Panel Approach"
Proceedings, Market Research Society (March 1987), pp. 149-65.

Lucas, George H., Jr., Parasuraman, A., Davis, Robert A., and Enis, Ben
M.
"An Empirical Study of Salesforce Turnover"
Journal of Marketing, Vol. 51 (July 1987), pp. 34-59.

McEwen, William J.
"Bridging the Information Gap"
Journal of Consumer Research, Vol. 4 (March 1978), pp. 247-51.

Midgley, David F.
"A Simple Mathematical Theory of Innovative Behavior"
Journal of Consumer Research, Vol. 3 (June 1976), pp. 31-41.

Moore, William L. and Winer, Russell S.
"A Panel Data Based Method for Merging Joint Space and Market
Response Function Estimation"
Marketing Science.

Motes, William H. and Castleberry, Stephen B.
"A Longitudinal Field Test of Stockout Effects on Multi-Brand
Inventories"
Journal of the Academy of Marketing Science, Vol. 13 (Fall 1985), pp.
54-68.

Motes, William H., Castleberry, Stephen B., and Motes, Susan G.
"A Longitudinal Test of Price Effects on Brand Choice Behavior"
Journal of Business Research, Vol. 12 (December 1984), pp. 493-503.

Neslin, Scott A. and Shoemaker, Robert W.
"An Alternative Explanation for Lower Repeat Rates After Promotion
Purchases"
Journal of Marketing Research, Vol. XXVI (May 1989), pp. 205-13.

Olson, Jerry C. and Dover, Philip A.
"Cognitive Effects of Deceptive Advertising"
Journal of Marketing Research, Vol. XV (February 1978), pp. 29-38.

Pitts, Robert E., Willenborg, John F., and Sherrell, Daniel L.
"Consumer Adaptation to Gasoline Price Increases"
Journal of Consumer Research, Vol. 8 (December 1981), pp. 322-30.

Prasad, V. Kanti and Ring, L. Winston
"Measuring Sales Effects of Some Marketing Mix Variables and Their
Interactions"
Journal of Marketing Research, Vol. XIII (November 1976), pp. 391-6.

Rao, Vithala R. and Sabavala, Darius Jal
"Inference of Hierarchical Choice Processes From Panel Data"
Journal of Consumer Research, Vol. 8 (June 1981), pp. 85-96.

Ross, Harold L., Jr.
    "Recall Versus Persuasion: An Answer"
    Journal of Advertising Research, Vol. 22 (February/March 1982), pp.
    13-6.

Shoemaker, Robert W. and Shoaf, F. Robert
    "Behavioral Changes in the Trial of New Products"
    Journal of Consumer Research, Vol. 2 (September 1975), pp. 104-9.

Shuchman, Abe and Riesz, Peter C.
    "Correlates of Persuasibility: The Crest Case"
    Journal of Marketing Research, Vol. XII (February 1975), pp. 7-11.

Tankersley, Clint B.
    "Attitude and Brand Loyalty: A Longitudinal Study of Multiattribute
    Attitude Models and Intervening Variables"
    Journal of the Academy of Marketing Science, Vol. 5 (Summer 1977),
    pp. 249-62.

Walsh, T. C.
    "Selected Results From the 1972-73 Diary Surveys"
    Journal of Marketing Research, Vol. XIV (August 1977), pp. 344-52.

Winer, Russell S.
    "Estimation of a Longitudinal Model to Decompose the Effects of an
    Advertising Stimulus on Family Consumption Behavior"
    Management Science, Vol. 26 (May 1980), pp. 471-82.

90.08 ---------- Unclassified (Panels and/or Longitudinal Studies)

Frank, Ronald E. and Massy, William F.
    Computer Programs for the Analysis of Consumer Panel Data
    (Graduate School of Business, Stanford University, 1965).

Pelz, Donald C. and Andrews, Frank M.
    "Detecting Causal Priorities in Panel Study Data"
    American Sociological Review, Vol. 29 (December 1964), pp. 836-48.

Rozelle, Richard M. and Campbell, Donald T.
    "More Plausible Rival Hypotheses in the Cross-Lagged Panel
    Correlation Technique"
    Psychological Bulletin, Vol. 71 (January 1969), pp. 74-80.

91 ------------------------ DELPHI METHOD -------------------------

91.01 ---------- Books Re: The Delphi Process

Brown, Bernice B.
  Delphi Process: A Methodology Used for the Elicitation of Opinions of
  Experts
  (Santa Monica: The Rand Corporation, 1968).

Dalkey, Norman C.
  The Delphi Method: An Experimental Study of Group Opinion
  (Santa Monica: The Rand Corporation, 1969).

Dalkey, Norman C. and Helmer, O.
  An Experimental Application of the Delphi Method to the Use of Experts
  (Santa Monica: The Rand Corporation, 1962).

Delbecq, Andre L., Van De Ven, Andrew H., and Gustafson, David H.
  Group Techniques for Program Planning: A Guide to Nominal Group and
  Delphi Processes
  (Glenview, IL: Scott Foresman and Company, 1975).

Harman, Alvin J. and Press, S. James
  Collecting and Analyzing Expert Group Judgment Data
  (Santa Monica, CA: The Rand Corporation, P-5467, 1975).

Helmer, Olaf
  Analyses of the Future
  (Santa Monica: The Rand Corporation, 1967).

Linstone, Harold A. and Turoff, Murray (editors)
  The Delphi Method
  (Reading, MA: Addison-Wesley Publishing Company, 1975).

Sackman, Harold
  Delphi Critique: Expert Opinion, Forecasting, and Group Process
  (Lexington, MA: Lexington Books, 1975).

91.02 ---------- Theory Re: The Delphi Method

Best, Roger J.
  "An Experiment in Delphi Estimation in Marketing Decision Making"
  Journal of Marketing Research, Vol. XI (November 1974), pp. 448-52.

Campbell, R.
  "A Methodological Study of Utilization of Experts in Business
  Forecasting"
  University of California at Los Angeles (1966), unpublished doctoral
  dissertation.

Dalkey, N. C., Brown, B., and Cochran, S.
  "The Delphi Method III: Use of Self Ratings to Improve Groups
  Estimates"
  (Santa Monica, CA: Rand, November 1969), Rm-6115-Pr.

Dalkey, Norman C. and Helmer, Olaf
  "An Experimental Application of the Delphi Method to the Use of
  Experts"
  Management Science (April 1963), pp. 458-67.

Gordon, T. and Helmer, O.
  Report on a Long-Range Forecasting Study
  The Rand Corporation (September 1962), P-2982.

Gustafson, David H., Shukla, Ramesh K., Delbecq, Andre, and Walster, G.
  William
  "A Comparative Study of Differences in Subjective Likelihood
  Estimates Made by Individuals, Interacting Groups, Delphi Groups and
  Nominal Groups"
  Organizational Behavior and Human Performance, Vol. 9 (April 1973),
  pp. 280-91.

Jain, C. L.
  "Delphi--Forecast With Experts' Opinion"
  Journal of Business Forecasting, Vol. 4 (Winter 1985-1986), pp. 22,3.

Jolson, Marvin A. and Rossow, Gerald L.
  "The Delphi Process in Marketing Decision Making"
  Journal of Marketing Research (November 1971), pp. 443-8.

Larreche, Jean-Claude and Moinpour, Reza
  "Managerial Judgment in Marketing: The Concept of Expertise"
  Journal of Marketing Research, Vol. XX (May 1983), pp. 110-21.

Larreche, Jean-Claude and Montgomery, David B.
  A Framework for the Comparison of Marketing Models: A Delphi Study
  (Cambridge, MA: Marketing Science Institute, 1977), 35 pp.

MacPherson, N. C.
    "Future Research: Using Delphi as a Technique"
    Quarterly Review of Marketing, Vol. 4, No. 1 (1978), pp. 1-8.

Milkovich, George T., Annoni, Anthony J., and Mahoney, Thomas A.
    "The Use of the Delphi Procedures in Manpower Forecasting"
    Management Science (December 1972), pp. 381-8.

91.03 ----------   Applications of the Delphi Method

Adelson, Marvin et al.
    "Planning Education for the Future: Comments on a Pilot Study"
    American Behavioral Scientist, Vol. 10 (March 1967), pp. 1-12; 21-31.

Basu, Shankar and Schroeder, Roger G.
    "Incorporating Judgments in Sales Forecasts: Application of the
    Delphi Method at American Hoist and Derrick"
    Interfaces, Vol. 7 (May 1977), pp. 18-27.

Grunenwald, Joseph P. and Ackerman, Leonard
    "A Modified Delphi Approach for the Development of Student
    Evaluations of Faculty Teaching"
    Journal of Marketing Education, Vol. 8 (Summer 1986), pp. 32-8.

Hampton, Gerald M. and Van Gent, Aart P.
    "International Marketing: 50 Suggested Research Projects for the
    1980's"
    European Research, Vol. 12 (July 1984), pp. 134-42.

Larreche, Jean-Claude and Montgomery, David B.
    "A Framework for the Comparison of Marketing Models: A Delphi Study"
    Journal of Marketing Research, Vol. XIV (November 1977), pp. 487-98.

Milkovich, George T., Annoni, Anthony J., and Mahoney, Thomas A.
    "The Use of the Delphi Procedures in Manpower Forecasting"
    Management Science, Vol. 19 (December 1972), pp. 381-8.

Watt, A. W.
    "The Use of Delphi Forecasting in the U.K. Textile Industry"
    Proceedings, Marketing Education Group Annual Workshops (1978).

Wensley, J. R. C.
    "Short Term Forecasting Using the Delphi Approach"
    European Research, Vol. 5 (March 1977), pp. 57-61.

92 ----------------------- EXPERIMENTATION ------------------------
See also (sub)heading(s) 93, 94, 95, 96, 97, 106, 204.08.

92.01 ---------- Books Re: Experimentation

Anderson, Virgil L. and McLean, Robert A.
  Design of Experiments: A Realistic Approach
  (New York: Marcel Dekkar, 1974).

Banks, Seymour
  Experimentation in Marketing
  (New York: McGraw-Hill Book Co., 1965).

Brunswik, Egon
  Perception and the Representative Design of Psychological
  Experiments, Second Edition
  (Berkeley, CA: University of California Press, 1956).

Campbell, Donald T. and Stanley, Julian C.
  Experimental and Quasi-Experimental Designs in Research
  (Chicago: Rand-McNally, 1963).

Cochran, William G. and Cox, Gertrude M.
  Experimental Designs
  (New York, NY: John Wiley and Sons, Inc., 1957).

Cook, Thomas D. and Campbell, Donald T.
  Quasi-Experimentation: Design and Analysis Issues for Field Settings
  (Boston: Houghton-Mifflin Company, 1979).

Cox, D. R.
  Planning of Experiments
  (New York: John Wiley, 1958).

Cox, Keith K. and Enis, Ben M.
  Experimentation for Marketing Decisions
  (Scranton, PA: International Textbook, 1969), 112 pp.

Das, M. N. and Giri, N. C.
  Design and Analysis of Experiments
  (New York: Halsted Press, 1979), 295 pp.

Davis, E. J.
  Experimental Marketing
  (New York: American Management Association, Inc., 1971), 186 pp.

Edwards, Allen L.
  Experimental Design in Psychological Research, Third Edition
  (New York: Holt, Rinehart and Winston, Inc.).

Evan, William M.
  Organizational Experiments: Laboratory and Field Research
  (New York: Harper and Row, 1971), 274 pp.

Fisher, Ronald A.
  The Design of Experiments
  (Edinburgh: Oliver and Boyd, 1935).

Fleiss, Joseph L.
  The Design and Analysis of Clinical Experiments
  (New York: John Wiley and Sons, Inc., 1986), 432 pp.

Gardner, David M. and Belk, Russell W.
  A Basic Bibliography on Experimental Design in Marketing
  (Chicago: American Marketing Association, 1980), 59 pp.

Heise, David R.
  Causal Analysis
  (New York: John Wiley and Sons, Inc., 1975), 301 pp.

Hicks, Charles R.
  Fundamental Concepts in the Design of Experiments
  (New York: Holt, Rinehart and Winston, 1966).

Holloway, Robert J. (editor)
  A Basic Bibliography on Experiments in Marketing
  (Chicago: American Marketing Association, 1967).

John, A. and Quenouille, M. H.
  Experiments: Design and Analysis
  (New York: Hafner Press, Division of Macmillan, 1977).

Kirk, Roger E.
  Experimental Design: Procedures for the Behavioral Sciences
  (Monteray, CA: Brooks/Cole, 1982).

Kish, Leslie
  Statistical Design for Research
  (New York: John Wiley and Company, 1987), 250 pp.

Lindquist, E. F.
   Design and Analysis of Experiments in Psychology Education
   (Boston: Houghton Mifflin, 1953).

Maxwell, A. E.
   Experimental Design in Psychology and the Medical Sciences
   (London: Methuen and Company, Ltd., 1958).

Montgomery, Douglas C.
   Design and Analysis of Experiments, Second Edition
   (New York: John Wiley and Sons, Inc., 1984), 538 pp.

Pessemier, Edgar A.
   Experimental Methods of Analyzing Demand for Branded Consumer Goods
   With Applications to Problems in Marketing Strategy
   (Pullman, WA: Washington State University Press, 1963), 165 pp.

Plutchik, Robert
   Foundations of Experimental Research
   (New York, NY: Harper and Row, Publishers, 1968), 290 pp.

Rosenthal, Robert
   Experimenter Effects in Behavioral Research
   (New York, NY: Appleton-Century-Crofts, Inc., 1966), 463 pp.

Rosenthal, R. and Rosnow, R. L. (editors)
   Artifact in Behavioral Research
   (New York: Academic Press, 1969), 400 pp.

Venkatesan, M. and Holloway, Robert J.
   An Introduction to Marketing Experimentation: Method, Applications,
   and Problems
   (New York: The Free Press, 1971), 141 pp.

Wood Research Corporation
   The Experimental Method in Marketing Research
   (Philadelphia: Wood Chips, February 1959).

92.02 ---------- Theory Re: Experimentation

Addelman, S.
   "Orthogonal Main Effect Plans for Asymmetrical Factorial Experiments"
   Technometrics, Vol. 4 (1962), pp. 21-46.

Aronson, Elliot and Carlsmith, J. Merrill
   "Experimentation in Social Psychology"
   in Lindzey, Gardner and Aronson, Elliot (editors)
   The Handbook of Social Psychology, Second Edition, Volume 2
   (Reading, MA: Addison-Wesley, 1968, pp. 1-79.

Atkinson, G. F.
   "Design for Sequence of Treatment With Carryover Effects"
   Biometrics, Vol. 22, No. 2 (1966), pp. 292-309.

Banks, Seymour
   "Designing Marketing Research to Increase Validity"
   Journal of Marketing, Vol. 28 (October 1964), pp. 32-40.

Banks, Seymour
   "On Methods: Marketing Experiments"
   Journal of Advertising Research, Vol. 3 (March 1963), pp. 34-41.

Becknell, James C., Jr.
   "Use of Experimental Design in the Study of Media Effectiveness"
   Media/Scope, Vol. 6 (August 1962), pp. 46-9.

Berkowitz, Leonard and Donnerstein, Edward
   "External Validity is More Than Skin Deep: Some Answers to Criticism
   of Laboratory Experiments"
   American Psychologist, Vol. 37 (1982), pp. 257-75.

Blattberg, Robert C.
   "The Design of Advertising Experiments Using Statistical Decision
   Theory"
   Journal of Marketing Research, Vol. XVI (May 1979), pp. 191-202.

Brown, N.
   "Is Anyone Using Experimental Designs?"
   Market Research Society Newsletter, No. 180 (March 1981), p. 3.

Brunk, M. E.
   "Use of Experimental Design in Marketing Research"
   Journal of Farm Economics, Vol. 40 (December 1958), pp. 1237-46.

Brunk, Max E. and Federer, Walter T.
   "Experimental Designs and Probability Sampling in Marketing Research"
   Journal of the American Statistical Association, Vol. 48 (September
   1953), pp. 440-52.

Campbell, D. T.
"Factors Relevant to the Validity of Experiments in Social Settings"
Psychological Bulletin, Vol. 54 (1957), pp. 297-312.

Cook, Thomas D. and Campbell, Donald T.
"The Design and Conduct of Quasi-Experiments and True Experiments in
Field Settings"
in Dunnette, M. D. (editor)
Handbook of Industrial and Organizational Research
(Chicago: Rand McNally, 1976), pp. 223-326.

Day, George S. and Heeler, Roger M.
"Using Cluster Analysis to Improve Marketing Experiments"
Journal of Marketing Research, Vol. VIII (August 1971), pp. 340-7.

Doyle, Peter and Gidengil, B. Zeki
"A Review of In-Store Experiments"
Journal of Retailing, Vol. 53 (Summer 1977), pp. 47-62.

Ellsworth, Phoebe
"From Abstract Ideas to Concrete Instances: Some Guidelines for
Choosing Natural Research Settings"
American Psychologist, Vol. 32 (1977), pp. 604-15.

Enis, Ben M. and Cox, Keith K.
"Ad Experiments for Management Decisions"
Journal of Advertising Research, Vol. 15 (April 1975), pp. 35-41.

Eskin, G. J.
"A Case for Test Marketing Experiments"
Journal of Advertising Research, Vol. 15 (April 1975), pp. 27-33.

Festinger, Leon
"Laboratory Experiments"
in Festinger, Leon and Katz, Daniel (editors)
Research Methods in the Behavioral Sciences
(New York: Holt, Rinehart and Winston), pp. 136-72.

Fromkin, Howard and Streufert, Siegfried
"Laboratory Experimentation"
in Dunnette, Marvin D. (editor)
Handbook of Industrial and Organizational Psychology
(Chicago: Rand McNally and Co., 1976), pp. 415-65.

Gatty, Ronald
"How to Control the Duration of a Sales Test"
Journal of Advertising Research, Vol. 5 (March 1965), pp. 18-22.

Ginter, James, Cooper, Martha, Obermiller, Carl, and Page, Thomas
"The Design of Advertising Experiments Using Statistical Decision
Theory: An Extension"
Journal of Marketing Research, Vol. XVIII (February 1981), pp. 120-3.

Glass, Gene V. and Hakstian, A. Ralph
"Measures of Association in Comparative Experiments: Their
Development and Interpretation"
American Educational Research Journal, Vol. 6 (May 1969), pp. 403-14.

Green, Paul E.
"On the Design of Multiattribute Choice Experiments Involving Large
Numbers of Factors and Factor Levels"
in Ward, Scott and Wright, Peter (editors)
Advances in Consumer Research, Volume One
(Urbana, IL: Association for Consumer Research, 1974), pp. 228-41.

Green, Paul
"The Role of Experimental Research in Marketing: Its Potentials and
Limitations"
in Haas, Raymond (editor)
Science, Technology, and Marketing
(Chicago: American Marketing Association, 1966), pp. 483-94.

Herzberg, A. M. and Cox, D. R.
"Recent Work on the Design of Experiments: A Bibliography and a
Review"
Journal of the Royal Statistical Society, Series A, Vol. 132 (Part 1,
1969), pp. 29-67.

Hinchen, J. D.
"From Opinion to Fact Through Sequential Experimentation"
Industrial Quality Control, Vol. 23 (September 1966), pp. 114-7.

Holloway, Robert J. and White, Tod
"Advancing the Experimental Method in Marketing"
Journal of Marketing Research, Vol. I (February 1964), pp. 25-9.

Hoofnagle, William S.
"Experimental Designs in Measuring the Effectiveness of Promotion"
Journal of Marketing Research, Vol. II (May 1965), pp. 154-62.

Hovland, Carl I., Lumsdaine, Arthur A., and Sheffield, Fred D.
    "Comparison of the Before-After and the After-Only Design of
    Experiments"
    in Experiments in Mass Communication
    Studies in Social Psychology in World War II, Volume Three
    (Princeton, NJ: Princeton University Press, 1949).

Jessen, Raymond J.
    "A Switch-Over Experimental Design to Measure Advertising Effect"
    Journal of Advertising Research, Vol. 1 (March 1961), pp. 15-22.

Levin, I. P., Louviere, J. J., Norman, K. L., and Schepanski, A.
    "External Validity Tests of Laboratory Studies of Information
    Integration"
    Organizational Behavior and Human Performance, Vol. 31 (1983), pp.
    173-93.

Lipstein, Benjamin
    "The Design of Test Marketing Experiments"
    Journal of Advertising Research, Vol. 5 (December 1965), pp. 2-7.

Lodish, Leonard and Pekelman, Dov
    "Increasing Precision of Marketing Experiments by Matching Sales
    Areas"
    Journal of Marketing Research, Vol. XV (August 1978), pp. 449-55.

Lynch, John G., Jr.
    "On the External Validity of Experiments in Consumer Research"
    Journal of Consumer Research, Vol. 9 (December 1982), pp. 225-39.

McGuire, William
    "Theory-Oriented Research in Natural Settings: The Best of Both
    Worlds for Social Psychology"
    in Sherif, M. and Sherif, C. (editors)
    Interdisciplinary Relationships in the Social Sciences
    (Chicago: Aldine Publishing, 1969).

Meissner, Frank
    "The Experimental Approach to Measuring the Impact of Advertising"
    Commentary (JMRS), No. 9 (Winter 1962-63), pp. 6-9.

Milligan, Glenn W. and McFillen, James M.
    "Statistical Conclusion Validity in Experimental Designs Used in
    Business Research"
    Journal of Business Research, Vol. 12 (December 1984), pp. 437-62.

Namboodiri, N. K.
    "A Statistical Exposition of the 'Before-After' and 'After-Only'
    Designs and Their Combinations"
    American Journal of Sociology, Vol. 76 (July 1970), pp. 83-102.

Nevin, John R.
    "Laboratory Experiments for Estimating Consumer Demand: A Validation
    Study"
    Journal of Marketing Research, Vol. XI (August 1974), pp. 261-8.

Oherlihy, Callaghan
    "Why Ad Experiments Fail"
    Journal of Advertising Research, Vol. 20 (February 1980), pp. 53-8.

Opp, Karl-Dieter
    "The Experimental Method in the Social Sciences: Some Problems and
    Proposals for Its More Effective Use"
    Quality and Quantity, Vol. 34 (1970), pp. 39-54.

Paksoy, Christie, Wilkinson, J. B., and Mason, J. Barry
    "Learning and Carryover Effects in Retail Experimentation"
    Journal of the Market Research Society, Vol. 27 (April 1985), pp.
    109-29.

Pessemier, Edgar A.
    "Forecasting Brand Performance Through Simulation Experiments"
    Journal of Marketing, Vol. 28 (April 1964), pp. 41-6.

Pessemier, Edgar A., Burger, Philip, Teach, Richard, and Tigert, Douglas
    "Using Laboratory Brand Preference Scales to Predict Consumer Brand
    Purchases"
    Management Science, Vol. 17 (February 1971), pp. B-371-85.

Purcell, W. R.
    "Group Randomizing"
    Industrial Quality Control, Vol. 20 (October 1963), pp. 20-32.

Riecken, Henry
    "A Program for Research on Experiments in Social Psychology"
    in Washburn, Norman (editor)
    Decisions, Values, and Groups, Volume Two
    (New York: Pergamon Press, 1962), pp. 25-41.

Ross, J. and Smith, P.
"Orthodox Experimental Design"
in Blalock, Hubert and Blalock, Ann (editors)
Methodology in Social Research
(San Francisco: McGraw-Hill Book Co., 1968).

Ross, J. A. and Smith, P.
"Experimental Designs of the Single-Stimulus, All-or-Nothing Type"
American Sociological Review, Vol. 30 (February 1965), pp. 68-80.

Sawyer, A. G.
"The Effects of Repetition: Conclusions and Suggestions About
Experimental Laboratory Research"
in Hughes, G. D. and Ray, M. L. (editors)
Buyer/Consumer Information Processing
(Chapel Hill, NC: University of North Carolina Press, 1974).

Sawyer, Alan G., Worthing, Parker, and Sendak, Paul
"The Role of Laboratory Experiments to Test Marketing Strategies"
Journal of Marketing, Vol. 43 (Summer 1979), pp. 60-7.

Sechrest, Lee and Yeaton, William H.
"Estimating Magnitudes of Experimental Effects"
Institute of Social Research, University of Michigan (1981).

Sirotnik, Barbara W. and Beaver, Robert J.
"Paired Comparison Experiments Involving All Possible Pairs"
British Journal of Mathematical and Statistical Psychology, Vol. 37
(May 1984), pp. 22-33.

Tunnell, Gilbert
"Three Dimensions of Naturalness: An Expanded Definition of Field
Research"
Psychological Bulletin, Vol. 84 (1977), pp. 426-77.

Uhl, Kenneth
"Field Experimentation: Some Problems, Pitfalls, and Perspectives"
in Haas, Raymond (editor)
Science, Technology, and Marketing
(Chicago: American Marketing Association, pp. 561-72.

Uhl, Kenneth P.
"Factorial Design--Aid to Management"
Journal of Marketing, Vol. 26 (January 1962), pp. 62-6.

Webster, Murray and Kervin, John
"Artificiality in Experimental Sociology"
Canadian Review of Sociology and Anthropology, Vol. 8 (1971), pp.
263-72.

Weick, K. E.
"Laboratory Experimentation With Organizations"
in March, J. G. (editor)
Handbook of Organizations
(Chicago: Rand McNally and Company, 1965).

Winer, Russell S.
"Analysis of Advertising Experiments"
Journal of Advertising Research, Vol. 20 (June 1980), pp. 25-31.

92.03 ---------- Experimenter Bias

Barber, T. X. and Silver, M. J.
"Fact, Fiction and the Experimenter Bias Effect"
Psychological Bulletin Monograph, Vol. 70, No. 6, Part 2 (1968).

Brown, Clifford E., Zatkalik, Nancy E., Treumann, Alice M., Buehner,
Timothy M., and Schmidt, Lisa A.
"The Effect of Experimenter Bias in a Cola Taste Test"
Psychology and Marketing, Vol. 1 (Summer 1984), pp. 21-6.

Finkelstein, J. E.
"Experimenter Expectancy Effects"
Journal of Communication, Vol. 26 (1976), pp. 31-8.

Kintz, B. L., Delprato, D. J., Mettee, D. R., Persons, C. E., and
Schappe, R. H.
"The Experimenter Effect"
Psychological Bulletin, Vol. 63 (April 1965), pp. 223-32.

Rosenthal, R.
Experimenter Effects in Behavior Research
(New York: Appleton-Century Crofts, 1966).

Rosenthal, R. and Fode, K. L.
"Psychology of the Scientist, Part V: Three Experiments in
Experimenter Bias"
Psychological Reports, Vol. 12 (1963), pp. 491-511.

92.04 ---------- Subject Effects and Demand Artifacts

Golding, Stephen L. and Lichtenstein, Edward
    "Confession of Awareness and Prior Knowledge of Deception as a
    Function of Interview Set and Approval Motivation"
    Journal of Personality and Social Psychology, Vol. 14 (1970), pp.
    213-23.

Levy, L. H.
    "Awareness, Learning, and the Beneficent Subject as Expert Witness"
    Journal of Personality and Social Psychology, Vol. 6 (1967), pp.
    365-670.

Orne, Martin T.
    "Demand Characteristics and the Concept of Quasi-Controls"
    in Rosenthal, Robert and Rosnow, Ralph L. (editors)
    Artifact in Behavioral Research
    (New York: Academic Press, 1969), pp. 143-79.

Rosnow, R. L. and Aiken, L. S.
    "Mediation of Artifacts in Behavioral Research"
    Journal of Experimental Social Psychology, Vol. 9 (1973), pp. 181-201.

Venkatesan, M.
    "Laboratory Experiments in Marketing: The Experimenter Effect"
    Journal of Marketing Research, Vol. IV (May 1967), pp. 142-6.

Sawyer, Alan G.
    "Demand Artifacts in Laboratory Experiments"
    Journal of Consumer Research, Vol. 1 (March 1975), pp. 20-30.

Sawyer, Alan G.
    "Detecting Demand Characteristics in Laboratory Experiments in
    Consumer Research: The Case of Repetition-Affect Research"
    in Schlinger, Mary Jane (editor)
    Advances in Consumer Research, Volume 2
    (Ann Arbor, MI: Association for Consumer Research, 1974), pp. 713-23.

Sherman, Steven J., Ahlm, Karin, Berman, Leonard, and Lynn, Steven
    "Contrast Effects and Their Relationship to Subsequent Behavior"
    Journal of Experimental Social Psychology, Vol. 14 (July 1978), pp.
    340-50.

Weber, Stephen J. and Cook, Thomas D.
    "Subject Effects in Laboratory Research: An Examination of Subject
    Roles, Demand Characteristics, and Valid Inference"
    Psychology Bulletin, Vol. 77 (1972), pp. 273-95.

92.05 ---------- Order of Presentation Effects

Berdy, David
    "Order Effects in Taste Tests"
    Journal of the Marketing Research Society, Vol. 11 (October 1969),
    pp. 361-71.

Coney, Kenneth A.
    "Order Bias: The Special Case of Letter Preference"
    Public Opinion Quarterly, Vol. 41 (1977), pp. 385-8.

Daniels, Peter and Lawford, John
    "The Effect of Order in the Presentation of Samples in Paired
    Comparison Product Tests"
    Journal of the Market Research Society, Vol. 16 (April 1974), pp.
    127-33.

Jones, Edward E. and Goethals, George R.
    "Order Effects in Impression Formation: Attribution Context and
    Nature of the Entity"
    in Jones, E. E., et al. (editors)
    Attribution: Perceiving the Causes of Behavior
    (Morristown: General Seminar Press, 1972).

Martin, John
    "Sequential Bias: Impact on a Bank Credit Card Concept Test"
    International Journal of Bank Marketing, Vol. 5, No. 3 (1987), pp.
    5-19.

92.06 ---------- Applications of Field Experiments

Banks, Seymour
    "Sales Effects of a New Counter Display: Two Additional Analyses"
    Journal of Advertising Research, Vol. 9 (June 1969), pp. 29-33.

Barclay, William D.
    "Factorial Design in a Pricing Experiment"
    Journal of Marketing Research, Vol. VI (November 1969), pp. 427-9.

Bawa, Kapil and Shoemaker, Robert W.
"The Effects of a Direct Mail Coupon on Brand Choice Behavior"
Journal of Marketing Research, Vol. XXIV (November 1987), pp. 370-6.

Bayus, Barry L., Carroll, Vincent P., Lee, Hau L., and Rao, Ambar G.
"Market Segment Response Through Field Experimentation"
International Journal of Advertising, Vol. 6, No. 2 (1987), pp.
107-20.

Bearden, William O. and Shimp, Terence A.
"The Use of Extrinsic Cues to Facilitate Product Adoption"
Journal of Marketing Research, Vol. XIX (May 1982), pp. 229-39.

Bogart, Leo and Tolley, B. Stuart
"The Impact of Blank Space: An Experiment in Advertising Readership"
Journal of Advertising Research, Vol. 4 (June 1964), pp. 21-7.

Brunk, M. E. and Federer, W. T.
"Experimental Designs and Probability Sampling in Marketing Research"
Journal of the American Statistical Association, Vol. 48 (September
1953), pp. 440-52.

Brunk, M. E. and Federer, W. T.
"How Marketing Problems of the Apple Industry Were Attacked and the
Research Results Applied"
Methods of Research in Marketing, Paper No. 4
(Ithaca, NY: Cornell University, Department of Agricultural
Economics, January 1953), 15 pp.

Burnett, John J. and Oliver, Richard L.
"Fear Appeal Effects in the Field: A Segmentation Approach"
Journal of Marketing Research, Vol. XVI (May 1979), pp. 181-90.

Busch, Paul and Wilson, David T.
"An Experimental Analysis of a Salesman's Expert and Referent Bases
of Social Power in the Buyer-Seller Dyad"
Journal of Marketing Research, Vol. XIII (February 1976), pp. 3-11.

Charlton, P. and Ehrenberg, A. S. C.
"An Experiment in Brand Choice"
Journal of Marketing Research, Vol. XIII (May 1976), pp. 152-60.

Coffin, Thomas E.
"A Pioneering Experiment in Assessing Advertising Effectiveness"
Journal of Marketing, Vol. 27 (July 1963), pp. 1-10.

Cox, Keith K.
"The Effect of Shelf Space Upon Sales of Branded Products"
Journal of Marketing Research, Vol. VII (February 1970), pp. 55-8.

Craig, C. Samuel and McCann, John M.
"Assessing Communication Effects on Energy Conservation"
Journal of Consumer Research, Vol. 5 (September 1978), pp. 82-8.

Donnelly, James H., Jr. and Ivancevich, John M.
"Post-Purchase Reinforcement and Back-Out Behavior"
Journal of Marketing Research, Vol. VII (August 1970), pp. 399,400.

Eastlack, Joseph O., Jr. and Rao, Ambar G.
"Advertising Experiments at the Campbell Soup Company"
Marketing Science, Vol. 8 (Winter 1989), pp. 57-71.

Floyd, Thomas E. and Stout, Roy G.
"Measuring Small Changes in a Market Variable"
Journal of Marketing Research, Vol. VII (February 1970), pp. 114-6.

Hartmann, George W.
"A Field Experiment on the Comparative Effectiveness of 'Emotional'
and 'Rational' Political Leaflets in Determining Election Results"
Journal of Abnormal and Social Psychology, Vol. 31 (1936), pp. 99-114.

Heberlein, Thomas A., Linz, Daniel, and Ortiz, Bonnie P.
"Satisfaction, Commitment, and Knowledge of Customers on a Mandatory
Participation Time-of-Day Electricity Pricing Experiment"
Journal of Consumer Research, Vol. 9 (June 1982), pp. 106-14.

Henion, Karl E.
"The Effect of Ecologically Relevant Information on Detergent Sales"
Journal of Marketing Research, Vol. IX (February 1972), pp. 10-4.

Hutton, R. Bruce, Mauser, Gary A., Filiatrault, Pierre, and Ahtola,
Olli T.
"Effects of Cost-Related Feedback on Consumer Knowledge and
Consumption Behavior: A Field Experimental Approach"
Journal of Consumer Research, Vol. 13 (December 1986), pp. 327-36.

Kasulis, Jack J., Huettner, David A., and Dikeman, Neil J.
"The Feasibility of Changing Electricity Consumption Patterns"
Journal of Consumer Research, Vol. 8 (December 1981), pp. 279-90.

Kennedy, John R.
    "The Effect of Display Location on the Sales and Pilferage of
    Cigarettes"
    Journal of Marketing Research, Vol. VII (May 1970), pp. 210-5.

Kotzan, Jeffrey A. and Evanson, Robert V.
    "Responsiveness of Drug Store Sales to Shelf Space Allocations"
    Journal of Marketing Research, Vol. VI (November 1969), pp. 465-9.

Latour, Stephen A. and Manrai, Ajay K.
    "Interactive Impact of Informational and Normative Influence on
    Donations"
    Journal of Marketing Research, Vol. XXVI (August 1989), pp. 327-35.

Litvack, David S., Calantone, Roger J., and Warshaw, Paul R.
    "An Examination of Short-Term Retail Grocery Price Effects"
    Journal of Retailing, Vol. 61 (Fall 1985), pp. 9-25.

McClure, Peter J. and West, E. James
    "Sales Effects of a New Counter Display"
    Journal of Advertising Research, Vol. 9 (March 1969), pp. 29-34.

McConnell, J. Douglas
    "The Development of Brand Loyalty: An Experimental Study"
    Journal of Marketing Research, Vol. V (February 1968), pp. 13-9.

McKinnon, Gary F., Kelly, J. Patrick, and Robison, E. Doyle
    "Sales Effects of Point-of-Purchase In-Store Signing"
    Journal of Retailing, Vol. 57 (Summer 1981), pp. 49-63.

Middlestadt, Susan E. and Fishbein, Martin
    "Estimating the Effects of a Two Dollar Price Reduction on Customer
    Purchases of Prerecorded Cassettes: A Field Experiment"
    Singapore Marketing Review, Vol. IV (1989), pp. 34-44.

Miller, Bill R. and Strain, Charles E.
    "Determining Promotional Effects by Experimental Design"
    Journal of Marketing Research, Vol. VII (November 1970), pp. 513-6.

Milliman, Ronald E.
    "The Influence of Background Music on the Behavior of Restaurant
    Patrons"
    Journal of Consumer Research, Vol. 13 (September 1986), pp. 286-9.

Muller, Thomas E.
    "Structural Information Factors Which Stimulate the Use of Nutrition
    Information"
    Journal of Marketing Research, Vol. XXII (May 1985), pp. 143-57.

Prasad, V. Kanti and Ring, L. Winston
    "Measuring Scales Effects of Some Marketing Mix Variables and Their
    Interactions"
    Journal of Marketing Research, Vol. XIII (November 1976), pp. 391-6.

Pritchard, Robert D., Deleo, Philip J., and Von Bergan, Clarence W., Jr.
    "A Field Experimental Test of Expectancy-Valence Incentive
    Motivational Techniques"
    Organizational Behavior and Human Performance, Vol. 15 (June 1976),
    pp. 355-406.

Qualls, William J. and Puto, Christopher P.
    "Organizational Climate and Decision Framing: An Integrated Approach
    to Analyzing Industrial Buying Decisions"
    Journal of Marketing Research, Vol. XXVI (May 1989), pp. 179-92.

Rosenthal, Robert, Persinger, Gordon W., Vikan-Kline, Linda, and Fode,
    Kermit L.
    "The Effect of Early Data Returns on Data Subsequently Obtained by
    Outcome-Biased Experimenters"
    Sociometry, Vol. 26 (December 1963), pp. 487-98.

Russo, J. Edward
    "The Value of Unit Price Information"
    Journal of Marketing Research, Vol. XIV (May 1977), pp. 202-8.

Russo, J. Edward, Staelin, Richard, Nolan, Catherine A., Russell, Gary
    J., and Metcalf, Barbara L.
    "Nutrition Information in the Supermarket"
    Journal of Consumer Research, Vol. 13 (June 1986), pp. 48-70.

Scott, Carol A.
    "Modifying Socially-Conscious Behavior: The Foot-in-the-Door
    Technique"
    Journal of Consumer Research, Vol. 4 (December 1977), pp. 156-63.

Sexton, Richard J., Johnson, Nancy Brown, and Konakayama, Akira
    "Consumer Response to Continuous-Display Electricity-Use Monitors in
    a Time-of-Use Pricing Experiment"
    Journal of Consumer Research, Vol. 14 (June 1987), pp. 55-62.

Strong, Edward C.
"The Use of Field Experimental Observations in Estimating Advertising Recall"
Journal of Marketing Research, Vol. XI (November 1974), pp. 369-78.

Swan, John E., Trawick, I. Fredrick, and Carroll, Maxwell G.
"Effect of Participation in Marketing Research on Consumer Attitudes Toward Research and Satisfaction With a Service"
Journal of Marketing Research, Vol. XVIII (August 1981), pp. 356-63.

Swinyard, William R. and Coney, Kenneth A.
"Promotional Effects on a High- Versus Low-Involvement Electorate"
Journal of Consumer Research, Vol. 5 (June 1978), pp. 41-8.

Swinyard, William R. and Ray, Michael L.
"Advertising-Selling Interactions: An Attribution Theory Experiment"
Journal of Marketing Research, Vol. XIV (November 1977), pp. 509-16.

Van Houwelingen, Jeannet H. and Van Raaij, W. Fred
"The Effect of Goal-Setting and Daily Electronic Feedback on In-Home Energy Use"
Journal of Consumer Research, Vol. 16 (June 1989), pp. 98-105.

Vinson, Donald E. and McVandon, Wayne
"Developing a Market for a New E.F.T.S. Bank Service"
Journal of Marketing, Vol. 42 (April 1978), pp. 83-6.

Wilkinson, J. B., Paksoy, Christie H., and Masson, J. Berry
"A Demand Analysis of Newspaper Advertising and Changes in Space Allocation"
Journal of Retailing, Vol. 57 (Summer 1981), pp. 30-48.

Winer, Leon
"The Effect of Product Sales Quotas on Sales Force Productivity"
Journal of Marketing Research, Vol. X (May 1973), pp. 180-3.

Wright, Peter
"Concrete Action Plans in TV Messages to Increase Reading of Drug Warnings"
Journal of Consumer Research, Vol. 6 (December 1979), pp. 256-69.

92.07 ---------- Unclassified (Experimentation)

Barber, T. X., Calverley, D. S., Forgione, A., McPeake, J. D., Chaves, J. F., and Bowen, B.
"Five Attempts to Replicate the Experimental Bias Effect"
Journal of Consulting and Clinical Psychology, Vol. 33 (February 1969), pp. 1-6.

Doll, R. E.
"Item Susceptibility to Attempted Faking as Related to Item Characteristics and Adopted Fake Set"
Journal of Psychology, Vol. 77 (January 1971), pp. 9-16.

Hood, T. C. and Back, K. W.
"Self-Disclosure and the Volunteer: A Source of Bias in Laboratory Experiments"
Journal of Personality and Social Psychology, Vol. 17 (February 1971), pp. 130-6.

Hovland, Carl I. and Mandell, Wallace
"An Experimental Comparison of Conclusion-Drawing by the Communicator and by the Audience"
Journal of Abnormal and Social Psychology, Vol. 47 (1952), pp. 581-8.

Knower, Franklin H.
"Experimental Studies of Changes in Attitudes: 1. A Study of the Effect of Oral Argument on Changes of Attitude"
Journal of Social Psychology, Vol. 6 (1935), pp. 315-57.

Miller, Kenneth E. and Ginter, James L.
"An Investigation of Situational Variation in Brand Choice Behaviour and Attitude"
Journal of Marketing Research, Vol. XVI (February 1979), pp. 111-23.

Rubin, Z. and Moore, J. C., Jr.
"Assessment of Subjects' Suspicions"
Journal of Personality and Social Psychology, Vol. 17 (February 1971), pp. 163-70.

93 --------------- MANIPULATION OR CONFOUNDING CHECKS ----------------

See also (sub)heading(s) 92.

93.01 ---------- Theory Re: Manipulation or Confounding Checks

Bagozzi, Richard P.
"Structural Equation Models in Experimental Research"
Journal of Marketing Research, Vol. XIV (May 1977), pp. 209-26.

Garner, Wendell R., Hake, Harold W., and Eriksen, Charles W.
"Operationism and the Concept of Perception"
Psychological Review, Vol. 63 (May 1956), pp. 149-59.

Kidd, Robert F.
"Manipulation Checks: Advantage or Disadvantage"
Representative Research in Social Psychology, Vol. 7, No. 2 (1976),
pp. 160-5.

Perdue, Barbara C. and Summers, John O.
"Checking the Success of Manipulations in Marketing Experiments"
Journal of Marketing Research, Vol. XXIII (November 1986), pp. 317-26.

Wetzel, Christopher G.
"Manipulation Checks: A Reply to Kidd"
Representative Research in Social Psychology, Vol. 8, No. 2 (1977),
pp. 88-93.

93.02 ---------- Applications of Manipulation or Confounding Checks

Anand, Punam
"Inducing Franchisees to Relinquish Control: An Attribution Analysis"
Journal of Marketing Research, Vol. XXIV (May 1987), pp. 215-21.

Baker, Michael J. and Churchill, Gilbert A., Jr.
"The Impact of Physically Attractive Models on Advertising
Evaluations"
Journal of Marketing Research, Vol. 14 (November 1977), pp. 538-55.

Batra, Rajeev and Ray, Michael L.
"Situational Effects of Advertising Repetition: The Moderating
Influence of Motivation, Ability, and Opportunity to Respond"
Journal of Consumer Research, Vol. 12 (March 1986), pp. 432-45.

Bearden, William O. and Shimp, Terence A.
"The Use of Extrinsic Cues to Facilitate Product Adoption"
Journal of Marketing Research, Vol. XIX (May 1982), pp. 229-39.

Biehal, Gabriel and Chakravarti, Dipankar
"Consumers' Use of Memory and External Information in Choice: Macro
and Micro Perspectives"
Journal of Consumer Research, Vol. 12 (March 1986), pp. 382-405.

Biehal, Gabriel and Chakravarti, Dipankar
"Information Accessibility as a Moderator of Consumer Choice"
Journal of Consumer Research, Vol. 10 (June 1983), pp. 1-14.

Burnkrant, Robert E. and Howard, Daniel J.
"Effects of the Use of Introductory Rhetorical Questions Versus
Statements on Information Processing"
Journal of Personality and Social Psychology, Vol. 47 (December
1984), ppp. 1218-30.

Calder, Bobby J. and Sternthal, Brian
"Television Commercial Wearout: An Information Processing View"
Journal of Marketing Research, Vol. XVII (May 1980), pp. 173-86.

Childers, Terry L. and Houston, Michael J.
"Conditions for a Picture-Superiority Effect on Consumer Memory"
Journal of Consumer Research, Vol. 11 (September 1984), pp. 643-54.

Churchill, Gilbert A., Jr. and Surprenant, Carol
"An Investigation Into the Determinants of Customer Satisfaction"
Journal of Marketing Research, Vol. XIX (November 1982), pp. 491-504.

Clopton, Stephen W.
"Seller and Buying Firm Factors Affecting Industrial Buyers'
Negotiation Behavior and Outcomes"
Journal of Marketing Research, Vol. XXI (February 1984), pp. 39-53.

Cole, Catherine A. and Houston, Michael J.
"Encoding and Media Effects on Consumer Learning Deficiencies in the
Elderly"
Journal of Marketing Research, Vol. XXIV (February 1987), pp. 55-63.

Curry, David J. and Menasco, Michael B.
"On the Separability of Weights and Brand Values: Issues and
Empirical Results"
Journal of Consumer Research, Vol. 10 (June 1983), pp. 83-95.

DeTurck, Mark A. and Goldhaber, Gerald M.
"Effectiveness of Product Warning Labels: Effects of Consumers'
Information Processing Objectives"
Journal of Consumer Affairs, Vol. 23 (Summer 1989), pp. 111-26.

Dholakia, Ruby Roy and Sternthal, Brian
"Highly Credible Sources: Persuasive Facilitators or Persuasive
Liabilities?"
Journal of Consumer Research, Vol. 3 (March 1977), pp. 223-32.

Edell, Julie A. and Staelin, Richard A.
"The Information Processing of Pictures in Print Advertisemenst"
Journal of Consumer Research, Vol. 10 (June 1983), pp. 45-61.

Farnsworth, Paul R. and Misumi, Issei
"Further Data on Suggestion in Pictures"
American Journal of Psychology, Vol. 43 (October 1931), p. 632.

Gardner, Merl Paula
"Advertising Effects on Attributes Recalled and Criteria Used for
Brand Evaluations"
Journal of Consumer Research, Vol. 10 (December 1983), pp. 310-8.

Holbrook, Morris B.
"Beyond Attitude Structure: Toward the Informational Determinants of
Attitude"
Journal of Marketing Research, Vol. XV (November 1978), pp. 545-56.

Kisielius, Jolita and Sternthal, Brian
"Detecting and Explaining Vividness Effects in Attitudinal Judgments"
Journal of Marketing Research, Vol. XXI (February 1984), pp. 54-64.

Krishnamurthi, Lakshman
"The Salience of Relevant Others and Its Effect on Individual and
Joint Preferences: An Experimental Investigation"
Journal of Consumer Research, Vol. 10 (June 1983), pp. 62-72.

Lammers, H. Bruce, Leibowitz, Laura, Seymour, George E., and Hennessey,
Judith
"Humor and Cognitive Responses to Advertising Stimuli: A Trace
Consolation Approach"
Journal of Business Research, Vol. 11 (June 1983), pp. 173-85.

Madden, Thomas J., Allen, Chris T., and Twible, Jacquelyn L.
"Attitude Toward the Ad: An Assessment of Diverse Measurement Indices
Under Different Processing 'Sets'"
Journal of Marketing Research, Vol. XXV (August 1988), pp. 242-52.

Marks, Lawrence J. and Kamins, Michael A.
"The Use of Product Sampling and Advertising: Effects of Sequence of
Exposure and Degree of Advertising Claim Exaggeration on Consumers'
Belief Strength, Belief Confidence, and Attitudes"
Journal of Marketing Research, Vol. XXV (August 1988), pp. 266-81.

Menasco, Michael B. and Curry, David J.
"Utility and Choice: An Empirical Study of Wife/Husband Decision
Making"
Journal of Consumer Research, Vol. 16 (June 1989), pp. 87-97.

Miniard, Paul W. and Cohen, Joel B.
"Isolating Attitudinal and Normative Influences in Behavioral
Intentions Models"
Journal of Marketing Research, Vol. XVI (February 1979), pp. 102-10.

Moore, David J. and Reardon, Richard
"Source Magnification: The Role of Multiple Sources in the Processing
of Advertising Appeals"
Journal of Marketing Research, Vol. XXIV (November 1987), pp. 412-7.

Obermiller, Carl
"Varieties of Mere Exposure: The Effects of Processing Style and
Repetition on Affective Response"
Journal of Consumer Research, Vol. 12 (June 1985), pp. 17-30.

Park, C. Whan and Young, S. Mark
"Consumer Response to Television Commercials: The Impact of
Involvement and Background Music on Brand Attitude Formation"
Journal of Marketing Research, Vol. XXIII (February 1986), pp. 11-24.

Patzer, Gordon L.
"Source Credibility as a Function of Communicator Physical Attraction"
Journal of Business Research, Vol. 11 (June 1983), pp. 229-41.

Saadi, Mitchel and Farnsworth, Paul R.
"The Degrees of Acceptance of Dogmatic Statements and Preferences for
Their Supposed Makers"
Journal of Abnormal and Social Psychology, Vol. 29, No. 2 (1934), pp.
143-50.

Schurr, Paul H. and Ozanne, Julie L.
  "Influences on Exchange Processes: Buyers' Preconceptions of a
  Seller's Trustworthiness and Bargaining Toughness"
  Journal of Consumer Research, Vol. 11 (March 1985), pp. 939-53.

Stanley, Thomas J.
  "Are Highly Credible Sources Persuasive?"
  Journal of Consumer Research, Vol. 5 (June 1978), pp. 66-7.

Sternthal, Brian and Dholakia, Ruby Roy
  "Rejoinder"
  Journal of Consumer Research, Vol. 5 (June 1978), pp. 67-9.

Sujan, Mita, Bettman, James R., and Sujan, Harish
  "Effects of Consumer Expectations on Information Processing in
  Selling Encounters"
  Journal of Marketing Research, Vol. XXIII (November 1986), pp. 346-53.

Surprenant, Carol F. and Solomon, Michael R.
  "Predictability and Personalization in the Service Encounter"
  Journal of Marketing, Vol. 51 (April 1987), pp. 86-96.

Tse, David K. and Wilton, Peter C.
  "Models of Consumer Satisfaction Formation: An Extension"
  Journal of Marketing Research, Vol. XXV (May 1988), pp. 204-12.

Yalch, Richard F. and Elmore-Yalch, Rebecca
  "The Effect of Numbers on the Route to Persuasion"
  Journal of Consumer Research, Vol. 11 (June 1984), pp. 522-7.

94 ------------------------ NON-EXPERIMENTS ------------------------
        See also (sub)heading(s) 92.

94.01 ---------- Theory Re: Non-Experiments

Orne, Martin T.
    "Demand Characteristics and the Concept of Quasi-Controls"
    in Rosenthal, Robert and Rosnow, Ralph L. (editors)
    Artifact in Behavioral Research
    (New York: Academic Press, 1969), pp. 143-79.

Sawyer, Alan G.
    "Demand Artifacts in Laboratory Experiments"
    Journal of Consumer Research, Vol. 1 (March 1975), pp. 20-30.

94.02 ---------- Applications of Non-Experiments

Lim, Jeen-Su and Summers, John O.
    "A Non-Experimental Investigation of Demand Artifacts in a Personal
    Selling Experiment"
    Journal of Marketing Research, Vol. XXI (August 1984), pp. 251-8.

Sawyer, Alan G.
    "Detecting Demand Characteristics in Laboratory Experiments in
    Consumer Research: The Case of Repetition-Affect Research"
    in Schlinger, Mary Jane (editor)
    Advances in Consumer Research, Volume 2
    (Ann Arbor, MI: Association for Consumer Research, 1974), pp. 713-23.

95 ----------------------- CONCEPT TESTING -------------------------
        See also (sub)heading(s) 92, 96.

95.01 ---------- Books Re: Concept Testing

Green, Paul E., Robinson, Patrick J., and Fitzroy, Peter T.
   Experiments on the Value of Information in Simulated Marketing
   Environments
   (Boston: Allyn and Bacon, 1967).

Schwartz, David
   Concept Testing
   (New York: AMACOM, 1987).

95.02 ---------- Theory Re: Concept Testing

Axelrod, Joel N.
   "Reducing Advertising Failures by Concept Testing"
   Journal of Marketing, Vol. 28 (October 1964), pp. 41-4.

Bloom, Harold E.
   "Match the Concept and the Product"
   Journal of Advertising Research, Vol. 17 (October 1977), pp. 25-7.

Frank, Newton
   "Can We Predict New Product Success From Concept Testing"
   AMA New York Chapter 1972 New Products Conference (1972), paper
   presentation.

Gensch, Dennis H. and Golob, Thomas F.
   "Testing the Consistency of Attribute Meaning in Empirical Concept
   Testing"
   Journal of Marketing Research, Vol. XII (August 1975), pp. 348-54.

Golden, Hal
   "Concept Tests--Often Used, but How Well"
   Marketing Review, Vol. 27 (September 1973), pp. 20-4.

Haley, Russell I. and Gatty, Ronald
   "The Trouble With Concept Testing"
   Journal of Marketing Research, Vol. VIII (May 1971), pp. 230-2.

Hecker, Sid
   "A Brain-Hemisphere Orientation Toward Concept Testing"
   Journal of Advertising Research, Vol. 21 (August 1981), pp. 55-60.

Hollingsworth, Kirk
   "The Fragility of Attribute Data"
   Journal of Advertising Research, Vol. 24 (December 1984/January
   1985), pp. 44-9.

Iuso, Bill
   "Concept Testing: An Appropriate Approach"
   Journal of Marketing Research, Vol. XII (May 1975), pp. 228-31.

Lewis, Ian M.
   "Do Concept Scores Measure the Message or the Method?"
   Journal of Advertising Research, Vol. 24 (February/March 1984), pp.
   54-6.

Moore, William L.
   "Testing Advertising Concepts: Current Practices and Opinions"
   Journal of Advertising, Vol. 14 (1985), pp. 45-50.

Moore, William L.
   "Concept Testing"
   Journal of Business Research, Vol. 10 (1982), pp. 279-94.

Moriarty, Mark and Venkatesan, M.
   "Concept Evaluation and Market Segmentation"
   Journal of Marketing, Vol. 42 (July 1978), pp. 82-6.

Peterson, Robert A.
   "Concept Testing: Some Experimental Evidence"
   Mississippi Valley Journal of Business and Economics, Vol. 7 (Spring
   1972), pp. 84-8.

Schocker, Allan D. and Srinivasan, V.
   "Multi-Attribute Approaches for Product Concept Evaluation and
   Generation: A Critical View"
   Journal of Marketing Research, Vol. XVI (May 1979), pp. 159-80.

Smead, Raymond J., Wilcox, James B., and Wilkes, Robert E.
   "How Valid are Product Descriptions and Protocols in Choice
   Experiments?"
   Journal of Consumer Research, Vol. 8 (June 1981), pp. 37-42.

Tauber, Edward M.
The Decision Risks With New Product Concept Testing
(New York: Fitzgerald, Sample Inc., 1979).

Tauber, Edward M.
"What is Measured by Concept Testing?"
Journal of Advertising Research, Vol. 12 (December 1972), pp. 35-7.

Wind, Yoram, Jolly, Stuart M., and O'Connor, Arthur
"Concept Testing as Input to Strategic Marketing Simulations"
in Mazze, E. (editor)
Proceedings of the 58th International AMA Conference (April 1975),
pp. 120-4.

Yuspeh, Sonia
"Diagnosis--The Handmaiden of Prediction"
Journal of Marketing, Vol. 39 (January 1975), pp. 87-9.

95.03 ---------- Administration Issues Re: Concept Testing

Acito, Franklin and Hustad, Thomas P.
"Industrial Product Concept Testing"
Industrial Marketing Management, Vol. 10 (1981), pp. 67-73.

Armstrong, J. Scott and Overton, Terry
"Brief vs. Comprehensive Descriptions in Measuring Purchase
Intentions"
Journal of Marketing Research, Vol. VIII (February 1971), pp. 114-7.

Bettman, James R.
"Issues in Designing Consumer Information Environments"
Journal of Consumer Research, Vol. 2 (December 1975), pp. 169-77.

Bettman, James R. and Kakkar, Pradeep
"Effects of Information Presentation Format on Consumer Information
Acquisition Strategies"
Journal of Consumer Research, Vol. 3 (March 1977), pp. 233-40.

Ehrenberg, A. S. C.
"The Pattern of Consumer Purchases"
Applied Statistics, Vol. 8 (1959), pp. 26-41.

Gaarder, R. O. and Strand, N. V.
"Use of Photographs in Consumer Preference Studies of Pork"
Journal of Farm Economics, Vol. 39 (February 1957), pp. 59-66.

Green, Paul E., Krieger, Abba M., and Schaffer, Catherine M.
"Quick and Simple Benefit Segmentation"
Journal of Advertising Research, Vol. 25 (June/July 1985), pp. 9-17.

Holbrook, Morris B. and Moore, William L.
"Feature Interactions in Consumer Judgments of Verbal Versus
Pictorial Presentations"
Journal of Consumer Research, Vol. 8 (June 1981), pp. 103-13.

Miller, James B., Bruvold, Norman T., and Kernan, Jerome B.
"Does Competitive-Set Information Affect the Results of Concept
Tests?"
Journal of Advertising Research, Vol. 27 (April/May 1987), pp. 16-24.

Moore, William L.
"Testing Advertising Concepts: Current Practices and Opinions"
Journal of Advertising, Vol. 14, No. 3 (1985), pp. 45-50.

Rose, John and Heath, Sue
"Stimulus Material: A Dual Viewpoint"
Market Research Society Conference (March 1984), pp. 47-64.

Trebbi, George C., Jr. and Flesch, Edward J.
"Single Versus Multiple Concept Tests"
Journal of Advertising Research, Vol. 23 (June/July 1983), pp. 21-6.

Ushikubo, Kazuaki
"A Method of Structure Analysis for Developing Product Concepts and
Its Applications"
European Research, Vol. 14, No. 4 (1986), pp. 174-84.

Wind, Yoram
"A New Procedure for Concept Evaluation"
Journal of Marketing, Vol. 37 (October 1973), pp. 2-11.

95.04 ---------- Studies of Artificial-to-Real Generalizability

Dickinson, John R.
"A Test of Concept Testing: Some Empirical Results"
in Stidsen, Bent (editor)
Marketing in the 1970's and Beyond
(Edmonton, Alberta: Canadian Association of Administrative Sciences,
1975).

Green, Paul E., Rao, Vithala R., and DeSarbo, Wayne S.
"Incorporating Group-Level Similarity Judgments in Conjoint Analysis"
Journal of Consumer Research, Vol. 5 (December 1978), pp. 187-93.

Holbrook, Morris B.
"On the Importance of Using Real Products in Research on
Merchandising Strategy"
Journal of Retailing, Vol. 59 (Spring 1983), pp. 4-20.

Holbrook, Morris B., Moore, William L., Dodgen, Gary N., and Havlena,
William J.
"Nonisomorphism, Shadow Features, and Imputed Preferences"
Marketing Science, Vol. 4 (Summer 1985), pp. 215-33.

Levin, Irwin P., Louviere, Jordan J., Schepanski, Albert A., and
Norman, Kent L.
"External Validity Tests of Laboratory Studies of Information
Integration"
Organizational Behavior and Human Performance, Vol. 31, No. 2 (1983),
pp. 173-93.

Moore, William L. and Holbrook, Morris B.
"On the Predictive Validity of Joint-Space Models in Consumer
Evaluations of New Concepts"
Journal of Consumer Research, Vol. 9 (September 1982), pp. 206-10.

Parker, Barnett R. and Srinivasan, V.
"A Consumer Preference Approach to the Planning of Rural Primary
Health Care Facilities"
Operations Research, Vol. 24 (September-October 1976), pp. 991-1025.

Tauber, Edward M.
"New Criteria for Concept Evaluation"
Journal of Consumer Marketing, Vol. 1, No. 3 (1984), pp. 13-5.

Tauber, Edward M.
"Why Concept and Product Tests Fail to Predict New Product Results"
Journal of Marketing, Vol. 39 (October 1975), pp. 69-71.

Wittink, Dick R. and Montgomery, David B.
"Predictive Validity of Trade-Off Analysis for Alternative
Segmentation Schemes"
in Beckwith, Neil et al. (editors)
Educators' Conference Proceedings, Series 44
(Chicago: American Marketing Association, 1979), pp. 69-73.

95.05 ---------- Studies of Real-to-Artificial Generalizability

Holbrook, Morris B. and Havlena, William J.
"Assessing the Real-to-Artificial Generalizability of Multiattribute
Attitude Models in Tests of New Product Designs"
Journal of Marketing Research, Vol. XXV (February 1988), pp. 25-35.

Moore, William L. and Holbrook, Morris B.
"On the Predictive Validity of Joint-Space Models in Consumer
Evaluations of New Concepts"
Journal of Consumer Research, Vol. 9 (September 1982), pp. 206-10.

95.06 ---------- Applications of Concept Testing

Abrams, Jack
"Reducing the Risk of New Product Marketing Strategies Testing"
Journal of Marketing Research, Vol. VI (May 1969), pp. 216-20.

Bloom, Paul E.
"Match the Concept and the Product"
Journal of Advertising Research, Vol. 17 (October 1977), pp. 25-7.

Crespi, Irving
"The Application of Survey Research Methods to Model Line Decisions"
Journal of Marketing Research, Vol. I (February 1964), pp. 30-4.

Currim, Imran S. and Sarin, Rakesh K.
"A Procedure for Measuring and Estimating Consumer Preferences Under
Uncertainty"
Journal of Marketing Research, Vol. XX (August 1983), pp. 249-56.

Ettenson, Richard, Wagner, Janet, and Gaeth, Gary
"Evaluating the Effect of Country of Origin and the 'Made in the USA'
Campaign: A Conjoint Approach"
Journal of Retailing, Vol. 64 (Spring 1988), pp. 85-100.

Faberman, Jay and Tarlow, Allan
"Point-of-View: Price--The Forgotten Marketing Variable"
Journal of Advertising Research, Vol. 22 (October/November 1982), pp.
49-51.

Friedman, Margaret L. and Churchill, Gilbert A., Jr.
"Using Consumer Perceptions and a Contingency Approach to Improve
Health Care Delivery"
Journal of Consumer Research, Vol. 13 (March 1987), pp. 492-510.

Haskins, Jack B.
"Pretesting Interest in Messages"
Journal of Advertising Research, Vol. 15 (October 1975), pp. 31-5.

Holbrook, Morris B.
"Aims, Concepts, and Methods for the Representation of Individual
Differences in Esthetic Responses to Design Features"
Journal of Consumer Research, Vol. 13 (December 1986), pp. 337-47.

Holbrook, Morris B.
"Beyond Attitude Structure: Toward the Informational Determinants of
Attitude"
Journal of Marketing Research, Vol. XV (November 1978), pp. 545-56.

Hong, Sung-Tai and Wyer, Robert S., Jr.
"Effects of Country-of-Origin and Product-Attribute Information on
Product Evaluation: An Information Processing Perspective"
Journal of Consumer Research, Vol. 16 (September 1989), pp. 175-87.

Huber, Joel
"Predicting Preferences on Experimental Bundles of Attributes: A
Comparison of Models"
Journal of Marketing Research (August 1975), pp. 290-7.

Hughes, G. David and Guerrero, Jose L.
"Simultaneous Concept Testing With Computer-Controlled Experiments"
Journal of Marketing, Vol. 35 (January 1971), pp. 28-33.

Lambert, David R.
"Price as a Quality Cue in Industrial Buying"
Journal of the Academy of Marketing Science, Vol. 9 (Summer 1981),
pp. 227-38.

Mauser, Gary A.
"Positioning Political Candidates--An Application of Concept
Evaluation"
Journal of the Market Research Society, Vol. 22 (July 1980), pp.
181-91.

Meyer, Robert J.
"A Model of Multiattribute Judgments Under Attribute Uncertainty and
Informational Constraint"
Journal of Marketing Research, Vol. XVIII (November 1981), pp. 428-41.

Moriarty, Mark M. and Venkatesan, M.
"Concept Evaluation and Market Segmentation"
Journal of Marketing, Vol. 42 (July 1978), pp. 82-6.

Prasad, V. Kanti
"Communications-Effectiveness of Comparative Advertising: A
Laboratory Analysis"
Journal of Marketing Research, Vol. XIII (May 1976), pp. 128-37.

Puto, Christopher P.
"The Framing of Buying Decisions"
Journal of Consumer Behavior, Vol. 14 (December 1987), pp. 301-15.

Rao, Akshay R. and Monroe, Kent B.
"The Moderating Effect of Prior Knowledge on Cue Utilization in
Product Evaluations"
Journal of Consumer Research, Vol. 15 (September 1988), pp. 253-64.

Ratneshwar, Srinivasan, Shocker, Allan D., and Stewart, David W.
"Toward Understanding the Attraction Effect: The Implications of
Product Stimulus Meaningfulness and Familiarity"
Journal of Consumer Research, Vol. 13 (March 1987), pp. 520-33.

Sujan, Mita
"Consumer Knowledge: Effects on Evaluation Strategies Mediating
Consumer Judgments"
Journal of Consumer Research, Vol. 12 (June 1985), pp. 31-46.

Swinyard, William R. and McNeil, Dennis L.
   "The Effects of Comparative Information, Brand Name, and Product
   Class on Consumer Decision Making"
   Singapore Marketing Review, Vol. IV (1989), pp. 21-33.

Tyebjee, Tyzoon T.
   "Response Latency: A New Measure for Scaling Brand Preference"
   Journal of Marketing Research, Vol. XVI (February 1979), pp. 96-101.

Walker, Orville C., Jr. and Sauter, Richard F.
   "Consumer Preferences for Alternative Retail Credit Terms: A Concept
   Test of the Effects of Consumer Legislation"
   Journal of Marketing Research, Vol. XI (February 1974), pp. 70-8.

Will, R. Ted and Hasty, Ronald W.
   "Attitude Measurement Under Conditions of Multiple Stimuli"
   Journal of Marketing, Vol. 35 (January 1971), pp. 66-70.

Wright, Peter and Kriewall, Mary Ann
   "State-of-Mind Effects on the Accuracy With Which Utility Functions
   Predict Marketplace Choice"
   Journal of Marketing Research, Vol. XVII (August 1980), pp. 277-93.

95.07 ---------- Scenario Research

Karger, Ted
   "Marketplace Scenario Research"
   Journal of Consumer Marketing, Vol. 5 (Spring 1988), pp. 17-21.

95.08 ---------- Theory Re: In-Basket Testing

Jaffee, Cabot L.
   Problems in Supervision: An In-Basket Training Exercise
   (Reading, MA: Addison-Wesley Publishing Company, 1968).

Lopez, Felix M.
   Evaluating Executive Decision Making: The In-Basket Technique
   (New York: American Management Association, Inc., 1966).

95.09 ---------- Applications of In-Basket Testing

Lee, Hanjoon, Acito, Frank, and Day, Ralph L.
   "Evaluation and Use of Marketing Research by Decision Makers: A
   Behavioral Simulation"
   Journal of Marketing Research, Vol. XXIV (May 1987), pp. 187-96.

96 -------------- INFORMATION DISPLAY (BOARD) RESEARCH --------------
     See also (sub)heading(s) 92, 95.

96.01 ---------- Books Re: Information Display Research

Quelch, John A.
  The Application of Information Display Research
  (Cambridge, MA: Marketing Science Institute, 1979), 20 pp.

96.02 ---------- Administration Issues Re: Information Display Res

Bettman, James R.
  "Issues in Designing Information Environments"
  Journal of Consumer Research, Vol. 2 (December 1975), pp. 169-77.

Heeler, Roger M., Okechuku, Chike, and Reid, Stan
  "Attribute Importance: Contrasting Measurements"
  Journal of Marketing Research, Vol. XVI (February 1979), pp. 60-3.

Hutton, R. Bruce, McNeil, Dennis L., and Wilkie, William L.
  "Some Issues in Designing Consumer Information Studies in Public
  Policy"
  in Hunt, H. K. (editor)
  Advances in Consumer Research, Volume Five
  (Ann Arbor, MI: Association for Consumer Research, 1978), pp. 131-7.

Jacoby, Jacob, Chestnut, Robert, Hoyer, Wayne D., Sheluga, David A.,
  and Donahue, Michael J.
  "Psychometric Characteristics of Behavioral Process Data: Preliminary
  Findings on Validity and Reliability"
  in Hunt, H. Keith (editor)
  Advances in Consumer Research, Volume Five
  (Ann Arbor, MI: Association for Consumer Research, 1978).

Lehmann, Donald R. and Moore, William L.
  "Validity of Information Display Boards: An Assessment Using
  Longitudinal Data"
  Journal of Marketing Research, Vol. XVII (November 1980), pp. 450-9.

Quelch, John A.
  "Measurement of the Relative Importance of Product Attribute
  Information: A Review of the Information Display Approach"
  Journal of Consumer Policy, Vol. 3 (1979), pp. 232-45.

96.03 ---------- Applications of Information Display Research

Arch, David C., Bettman, James R., and Kakkar, Pradeep
  "Subjects' Information Processing in Information Display Board
  Studies"
  in Hunt, H. Keith (editor)
  Advances in Consumer Research, Volume Five
  (Ann Arbor, MI: Association for Consumer Research, 1978).

Bettman, James R. and Kakkar, Pradeep
  "Effects of Information Presentation Format on Consumer Information
  Acquisition Strategies"
  Journal of Consumer Research, Vol. 3 (March 1977), pp. 233-40.

Capon, Noel and Burke, Marian
  "Individual, Product Class, and Task-Related Factors in Consumer
  Information Processing"
  Journal of Consumer Research, Vol. 7 (December 1980), pp. 314-26.

Chestnut, R. W. and Jacoby, Jacob
  "Consumer Information Processing: Emerging Theory and Findings"
  in Woodside, A., Bennett, P. D., and Sheth, J. N. (editors)
  Foundations of Consumer and Industrial Buying Behavior
  (New York: American Elsevier, 1977).

Green, Richard, Mitchell, Andrew, and Staelin, Richard
  "Longitudinal Decision Studies Using a Process Approach: Some Results
  From a Preliminary Experiment"
  in Greenberg, B. A. and Bellenger, D. A. (editors)
  Contemporary Marketing Thought
  (Chicago: American Marketing Association, 1977).

Holbrook, M. B. and Maier, K. A.
  "A Study of the Interface Between Attitude Structure and Information
  Acquisition Using a Questionnaire-Based Information-Display Sheet"
  in Hunt, H. K. (editor)
  Advances in Consumer Research, Volume Five
  (Ann Arbor, MI: Association for Consumer Research, 1978).

Jacoby, Jacob
  "Consumer Reaction to Information Displays: Packaging and Advertising"
  in Divita, Sal (editor)
  Advertising and the Public Interest
  (Chicago: American Marketing Association, 1974).

Jacoby, Jacob and Chestnut, Robert
    "Amount, Type and Order of Package Information Acquisition in
    Purchasing Decisions"
    Final Report to National Science Foundation, GI-43687 (1977).

Jacoby, Jacob, Chestnut, Robert, and Fisher, William A.
    "A Behavioral Process Approach to Information Acquisition in
    Nondurable Purchasing"
    Journal of Marketing Research, Vol. XV (November 1978), pp. 532-44.

Jacoby, Jacob, Speller, Donald E., and Kohn, Carol A.
    "Brand Choice Behavior as a Function of Information Load"
    Journal of Marketing Research, Vol. XI (February 1974), pp. 63-9.

Jacoby, Jacob, Szybillo, George J., and Busato-Schach, Jacqueline
    "Information Acquisition Behavior in Brand Choice Situations"
    Journal of Consumer Research, Vol. 3 (March 1977), pp. 209-16.

Schaninger, Charles M. and Sciglimpaglia, Donald
    "The Influence of Cognitive Personality Traits and Demographics on
    Consumer Information Acquisition"
    Journal of Consumer Research, Vol. 8 (September 1981), pp. 208-16.

97 --------------- COMPUTER CONTROLLED EXPERIMENTATION ---------------
See also (sub)heading(s) 73, 76.06, 92, 100.07.

97.01 ---------- Theory Re: Computer Controlled Experimentation

Brucks, Merrie
"Search Monitor: An Approach for Computer-Controlled Experiments
Involving Consumer Information Search"
Journal of Consumer Research, Vol. 15 (June 1988), pp. 117-21.

Clopton, Stephen W. and Barksdale, Hiram C., Jr.
"Microcomputer Based Methods for Dyadic Interaction Research in
Marketing"
Journal of the Academy of Marketing Science, Vol. 15 (Summer 1987),
pp. 63-8.

Curry, David
"Evaluating Qualitative Laws of Preference Using Computer-Controlled
Experiments"
Proceedings of the American Marketing Association
(Chicago: American Marketing Association, 1975).

Hughes, G. David and Guerrero, Jose L.
"Testing Cognitive Models Through Computer-Controlled Experiments"
Journal of Marketing Research, Vol. VIII (August 1971), pp. 291-7.

Hughes, G. D. and Guerrero, J. L.
"Simultaneous Concept Testing With Computer-Controlled Experiments"
Journal of Marketing, Vol. 35 (January 1971), pp. 28-33.

Hughes, G. David and Guerrero, Jose L.
"Pretesting Marketing Strategies"
Cornell University (May 20, 1970), working paper.

Hughes, G. David and Naert, Philippe A.
"A Computer-Controlled Experiment in Consumer Behavior"
Journal of Business, Vol. 43 (July 1970), pp. 354-72.

Johnson, Richard M.
"Measurement of Consumer Values Using Computer Interactive Techniques"
in Montgomery, David B. and Wittink, Dick R. (editors)
Market Measurement and Analysis
(Cambridge, MA: Marketing Science Institute, 1980), pp. 271-7.

Johnson, Richard M.
"Measurement of Consumer Values Using Computer Interactive Techniques"
ORSA/TIMS Market Measurement and Analysis Conference, Stanford
University (1979), paper presentation.

MacLachlan, James, Czepiel, John, and LaBarbera, Priscilla
"Implementation of Response Latency Measures"
Journal of Marketing Research, Vol. XVI (November 1979), pp. 573-7.

97.02 ---------- Applications of Computer Controlled Experimentation

Allen, Chris T. and Janiszewski, Chris A.
"Assessing the Role of Contingency Awareness in Attitudinal
Conditioning With Implications for Advertising Research"
Journal of Marketing Research, Vol. XXVI (February 1989), pp. 30-43.

Brucks, Merrie
"The Effects of Product Class Knowledge on Information Search
Behavior"
Journal of Consumer Research, Vol. 12 (June 1985), pp. 1-16.

Burke, Raymond R. and Srull, Thomas K.
"Competitive Interference and Consumer Memory for Advertising"
Journal of Consumer Research, Vol. 15 (June 1988), pp. 55-68.

Cardozo, Richard, Ross, Ivan, and Rudelius, William
"New Product Decisions by Marketing Executives: A Computer-Controlled
Experiment"
Journal of Marketing, Vol. 36 (January 1972), pp. 10-6.

Dickinson, John R.
A Comparison of Subject Behavior Toward Real Products and Toward an
Abstract Product Model
Indiana University (1971), unpublished doctoral dissertation.

Drumwright, Minette E.
The Effects of Prior Beliefs and Time Pressure on Covariation
Assessments of Price-Quality Relationships for a Consumer Service
Graduate School of Business Administration, University of North
Carolina (1986), unpublished dissertation.

Hoyer, Wayne D. and Jacoby, Jacob
    "Three-Dimensional Information Acquisition: An Application to
    Contraceptive Decision Making"
    in Bagozzi, Richard P. and Tybout, Alice M. (editors)
    Advances in Consumer Research, Volume Ten
    (Ann Arbor, MI: Association for Consumer Research, 1983), pp. 618-23.

Johnson, Eric J., Payne, John W., Bettman, James R., and Schkade, David
    A.
    "Monitoring Information Acquisitions in Decision-Making: Experiences
    With MouseLab, A Computer-Based Process Tracing System"
    Association for Consumer Research Annual Conference, Toronto (1986),
    paper presentation.

Meyers-Levy, Joan and Tybout, Alice M.
    "Schema Congruity as a Basis for Product Evaluation"
    Journal of Consumer Research, Vol. 16 (June 1989), pp. 39-54.

Olshavsky, Richard W. and Rosen, Dennis L.
    "Use of Product-Testing Organizations' Recommendations as a Strategy
    for Choice Simplification"
    Journal of Consumer Affairs, Vol. 19 (Summer 1985), pp. 118-39.

Ozanne, Julie L.
    "Keyword Recognition: A New Methodology for the Study of Information
    Seeking Behavior"
    in Houston, Michael (editor)
    Advances in Consumer Research, Volume Fifteen
    (Provo, UT: Association for Consumer Research, 1988).

Painton, Scott and Gentry, James W.
    "Another Look at the Impact of Information Presentation Format"
    Journal of Consumer Research, Vol. 12 (September 1985), pp. 240-4.

Rosen, Dennis L. and Olshavsky, Richard W.
    "A Protocol Analysis of Brand Choice Strategies Involving
    Recommendations"
    Journal of Consumer Research, Vol. 14 (December 1987), pp. 440-4.

Rosen, Dennis L. and Olshavsky, Richard W.
    "The Dual Role of Informational Social Influence: Implications for
    Marketing Management"
    Journal of Business Research, Vol. 15 (April 1987), pp. 257-71.

Simonson, Itamar, Huber, Joel, and Payne, John
    "The Relationship Between Prior Brand Knowledge and Information
    Acquisition Order"
    Journal of Consumer Research, Vol. 14 (March 1988), pp. 566-78.

Tyebjee, Tyzoon T.
    "Response Time, Conflict, and Involvement in Brand Choice"
    Journal of Consumer Research, Vol. 6 (December 1979), pp. 295-304.

Urbany, Joel E.
    "An Experimental Examination of the Economics of Information"
    Journal of Consumer Research, Vol. 13 (September 1986), pp. 257-71.

Urbany, Joel E., Bearden, William O., and Weilbaker, Dan C.
    "The Effect of Plausible and Exaggerated Reference Prices on Consumer
    Perceptions and Price Search"
    Journal of Consumer Research, Vol. 15 (June 1988), pp. 95-110.

98 ------------------- OBSERVATION METHODS -----------------------

See also (sub)heading(s) 99, 100.

98.01 ---------- Books Re: Observation Methods

Cochran, William G.
Planning and Analysis of Observational Studies
(New York: John Wiley and Sons, Inc., 1983), 145 pp.

98.02 ---------- General Discussions Re: Observation Methods

Wagner, L. C.
"The Use of the Observational Method in Marketing Research"
University of Washington Business Review, Vol. 27 (Autumn 1968), pp.
18-24.

98.03 ---------- Graphology

Bunker, M. N.
Handwriting Analysis: The Art and Science of Reading Character by
Grapho-Analysis
(Chicago, IL: Nelson-Hall Co., 1959).

Durant, Henry
"Graphology as a Marketing Aid"
Journal of Marketing Research, Vol. VI (February 1969), p. 108.

Fluckiger, Fritz A., Tripp, Clarence A., and Weinberg, George H.
"A Review of Experimental Research in Graphology, 1933-1960"
Perceptual and Motor Skills, Vol. 12 (January 1961), pp. 67-90.

Frederick, Calvin J.
"Some Phenomena Affecting Handwriting Analysis"
Perceptual and Motor Skills, Vol. 20 (February 1965), pp. 211-8.

Galbraith, Dorothy and Wilson, Warner
"Reliability of the Graphoanalytic Approach to Handwriting Analysis"
Perceptual and Motor Skills, Vol. 19 (September 1964), pp. 615-8.

Green, Paul E., Rao, Vithala R., and Armani, Diana E.
"Graphology and Marketing Research: A Pilot Experiment in Validity
and Inter-Judge Reliability"
Journal of Marketing, Vol. 35 (April 1971), pp. 56-62.

Lewinson, T. Stein
"An Introduction to the Graphology of Ludwig Klages"
Character and Personality, Vol. 6 (June 1938), pp. 163-76.

Linton, Harriet B., Epstein, Laurence, and Hartford, Huntington
"Personality and Perceptual Correlates of Secondary Beginning
Upstrokes in Handwriting"
Perceptual and Motor Skills, Vol. 12 (June 1961), pp. 271-81.

McNeal, James U.
"Graphology: A New Marketing Research Technique"
Journal of Marketing Research, Vol. IV (November 1967), pp. 363-7.

Monroe, Ruth L.
"Three Diagnostic Methods Applied to Sally"
Journal of Abnormal and Social Psychology, Vol. 40 (April 1945), pp.
215-27.

Myers, James H.
"More on Graphology and Marketing: An Empirical Validation of
Marketing Graphology"
Journal of Marketing Research, Vol. VI (February 1969), pp. 107,8.

Plog, Stanley C.
"A Literacy Index for the Mailbag"
Journal of Applied Psychology, Vol. 50 (February 1966), pp. 86-91.

Rast, George H.
"Value of Handwriting Analysis in Bank Work"
Burroughs Clearing House, Vol. 50 (March 1966), pp. 40,1.

Sonnemann, Ulrich and Kernan, John P.
"Handwriting Analysis--A Valid Selection Tool?"
Personnel, Vol. 39 (November-December 1962), pp. 8-14.

Wolfson, Rose
"Graphology"
in Anderson, Harold H. and Anderson, Gladys L. (editors)
An Introduction to Projective Techniques
(Englewood Cliffs, NJ: Prentice-Hall, Inc., 1951), pp. 416-56.

98.04 ---------- Unobtrusive Measures

Ray, Michael L.
    "Neglected Problems (Opportunities) in Research: The Development of
    Multiple and Unobtrusive Measures"
    Proceedings, Fall Conference, American Marketing Association (1968),
    pp. 176-83.

Ray, Michael L. and Sherrill, Peter N.
    "Unobtrusive Marketing Research Techniques"
    in Britt, Stuart H. (editor)
    Marketing Handbook
    (Chicago: Dartnell).

Sechrest, Lee (editor)
    New Directions for Methodology of Behavioral Science: Unobtrusive
    Measurement Today
    (San Francisco, CA: Jossey-Bass Publishers, 1979), 97 pp.

Webb, E., Campbell, D., Schartz, R., and Sechrest, L.
    Unobtrusive Measures: Nonreactive Research in the Social Sciences
    (Chicago: Rand-McNally, 1966), 225 pp.

Webb, Eugene J. and Weick, Karl
    "Unobtrusive Measures in Organization Theory: A Reminder"
    Administrative Science Quarterly, Vol. 24 (1979), pp. 650-9.

98.05 ---------- Theory Re: The Lost-Letter Technique

Forbes, Gordon B. and Gromoll, Henry F.
    "The Lost-Letter Technique as a Measure of Social Variables: Some
    Exploratory Findings"
    Social Forces (September 1971), pp. 113-5.

Georgoff, D. M., Hersker, B. H., and Murdick, R. G.
    "The Lost-Letter Technique: A Scaling Experiment"
    Public Opinion Quarterly (Spring 1972), pp. 114-9.

Himes, Samuel H., Jr. and Mason, Joseph Barry
    "A Note on Unobtrusive Attitude Measurment: The Lost-Letter Technique"
    Journal of the Market Research Society, Vol. 16 (January 1974), pp.
    42-6.

Milgram, Stanley
    "Comment on 'A Failure to Validate the Lost-Letter Technique'"
    Public Opinion Quarterly (Summer 1969), pp. 263,4.

Milgram, Stanley, Mann, Leon, and Harter, Susan
    "The Lost-Letter Technique: A Tool of Social Research"
    Public Opinion Quarterly (Fall 1965), pp. 437,8.

Shotland, R. Lance, Berger, Wallace G., and Forsythe, Robert
    "A Validation of the Lost-Letter Technique"
    Public Opinion Quarterly (Summer 1970), pp. 278-81.

Wicker, Allen
    "A Failure to Validate the Lost-Letter Technique"
    Public Opinion Quarterly (Summer 1969), pp. 260-2.

98.06 ---------- Filming, Videorecording, Photography Methods

Collier, John, Jr. and Collier, Malcolm
    Visual Anthropology: Photography as a Research Tool
    (Albuquerque, NM: University of New Mexico Press, 1986).

Dabbs, James M., Jr.
    "Making Things Visible"
    in Van Maanan, John, Dabbs, J. M., Jr., and Faulkner, Robert R.
    (editors)
    Varieties of Qualitative Research
    (Beverly Hills, CA: Sage Publications, 1982).

Carpenter, Gregory S. and Lehmann, Donald R.
    "Model of Marketing Mix, Brand Switching, and Competition"
    Journal of Marketing Research, Vol. XXII (August 1985), pp. 318-29.

98.07 ---------- Theory Re: Garbology

Cote, Joseph A.
    "Use of Household Refuse Analysis to Measure Usual and
    Period-Specific Food Consumption"
    American Behavioral Scientist, Vol. 28, No. 1 (1984), pp. 129-38.

Hughes, W.
    "The Method to Our Madness"
    American Behavioral Scientist, Vol. 28, No. 1 (1984), pp. 41-9.

Rathje, William L.
"Archeological Ethnography"
in Gould, Richard A. (editor)
Exploration in Ethno-Archeology
(Albuquerque, NM: University of New Mexico Press, 1978), pp. 49-76.

Rathje, William L. and Ritenbaugh, C. K.
"The Household Refuse Analysis"
American Behavioral Scientist, Vol. 28 (September/October 1984), pp. 115-28.

Ritenbaugh, C. K. and Harrison, G. G.
"Reactivity of Garbage Analysis"
American Behavioral Scientist, Vol. 28 (September-October 1984), pp. 51-70.

98.08 ---------- Applications of Garbology

Cote, Joseph A., McCullough, James, and Reilly, Michael
"Effects of Unexpected Situations on Behavior-Intention Differences: A Garbology Analysis"
Journal of Consumer Research, Vol. 12 (September 1985), pp. 188-94.

Reilly, Michael D. and Wallendorf, Melanie
"A Comparison of Group Differences in Food Consumption Using Household Refuse"
Journal of Consumer Research, Vol. 14 (September 1987), pp. 289-94.

Wallendorf, Melanie and Nelson, Daniel
"An Archaeological Examination of Ethnic Differences in Body Care Rituals"
Psychology and Marketing, Vol. 3 (Winter 1986), pp. 273-89.

98.09 ---------- Direct Observation of Purchasing Behavior

Claremont Graduate School Class in Marketing Research
"Note on Direct Observation of Purchasing Behavior"
Journal of Marketing Research, Vol. IV (November 1967), pp. 402-4.

Cobb, Cathy J. and Hoyer, Wayne D.
"Direct Observation of Search Behavior in the Purchase of Two Nondurable Products"
Psychology and Marketing, Vol. 2 (Fall 1985), pp. 161-79.

Kendall, K. W. and Fenwick, Ian
"What do You Learn Standing in a Supermarket Aisle?"
in Wilkie, W. (editor)
Advances in Consumer Research, Volume Six
(Ann Arbor, MI: Association for Consumer Research, 1979), pp. 153-60.

Payne, John W. and Ragsdale, E. K. Easton
"Verbal Protocols and Direct Observation of Supermarket Shopping Behavior: Some Findings and a Discussion of Methods"
in Hunt, H. Keith (editor)
Advances in Consumer Research, Volume Five
(Ann Arbor, MI: Association for Consumer Research, 1978).

Wells, William D. and Losciuto, Leonard A.
"Direct Observation of Purchasing Behavior--A Reply"
Journal of Marketing Research, Vol. IV (November 1967), p. 404.

Wells, William D. and Losciuto, Leonard A.
"Direct Observation of Purchasing Behavior"
Journal of Marketing Research, Vol. III (August 1966), pp. 227-34.

98.10 ---------- Unclassified (Observation Methods)

Allen, Charles L.
"Photographing the TV Audience"
Journal of Advertising Research, Vol. 5 (March 1965), pp. 2-8.

Barker, Roger G.
"Explorations in Ecological Psychology"
American Psychologist, Vol. 20 (January 1965), pp. 1-14.

Crabtree, Larry D. and Paris, James A.
"Survey Car License Plates to Define Retail Trade Area"
Marketing News, Vol. 19 (January 4, 1985), p. 12.

Dutka, S. and Frankel, L. R.
"Observation Techniques in Store Auditing"
Agricultural Economics Research, Vol. 12 (July 1960), pp. 70-2.

Granbois, Donald H.
"Improving the Study of Customer In-Store Behavior"
Journal of Marketing, Vol. 32 (October 1968), pp. 28-33.

Hicks, J. W. and Kohl, R. L.
  "Memomotion Study as a Method of Measuring Consumer Behavior"
  Journal of Marketing, Vol. 20 (October 1955), pp. 168-70.

Houseman, Earl E. and Lipstein, Benjamin
  "Observation and Audit Techniques for Measuring Retail Sales"
  Agricultural Economics, Vol. 12 (July 1960), pp. 61-72.

Lindsley, Ogden R.
  "A Behavioral Measure of Television Viewing"
  Journal of Advertising Research, Vol. 2 (September 1962), pp. 2-12.

Parrish, John
  "Photochronographic Measurement of the Audience for Television News
  Shows"
  Oklahoma State University (1964), unpublished M.S. thesis.

Richer, John
  "Observation, Ethology and Marketing Research"
  European Research, Vol. 9 (January 1981), pp. 22-30.

Rubens, William
  "Camouflage Can be Made to do Double Work"
  Journal of Marketing, Vol. 20 (October 1955), pp. 168-70.

Smith, Joseph G.
  "Should We Measure Involuntary Responses?"
  Journal of Advertising Research, Vol. 19 (October 1979), pp. 35-9.

Waldrop, Judith
  "How to Find and Use Traffic Counts"
  American Demographics, Vol. 10 (April 1988), pp. 42,3.

99 ----------------------- RESPONSE LATENCY ------------------------
      See also (sub)heading(s) 98.

99.01 ---------- Theory Re: Response Latency

Aaker, David A., Bagozzi, Richard P., Carman, James M., and MacLachlan, James M.
  "On Using Response Latency to Measure Preference"
  Journal of Marketing Research, Vol. XVII (May 1980), pp. 237-44.

Bergum, B. O. and Dooley, R. P.
  "Forced Choice Preferences and Response Latency"
  Journal of Applied Psychology, Vol. 53 (1969), pp. 396-8.

Bevan, William and Avant, Lloyd L.
  "Response Latency, Response Uncertainty, Information Transmitted and the Number of Available Judgmental Categories"
  Journal of Experimental Psychology, Vol. 76 (March 1968), pp. 394-7.

Curtis, D. W., Paulos, M. A., and Rule, S. J.
  "Relation Between Disjunctive Reaction Time and Stimulus Difference"
  Journal of Experimental Psychology, Vol. 99 (1973), pp. 167-73.

Dashiell, John F.
  "Affective Value-Distance as a Determinant of Esthetic Judgment-Times"
  American Journal of Psychology, Vol. 50 (1975), pp. 57-67.

Dember, W. N.
  "The Relation of Decision-Time to Stimulus Similarity"
  Journal of Experimental Psychology, Vol. 53 (1957), pp. 68-72.

Festinger, Leon
  "Studies in Decision"
  Journal of Experimental Psychology, Vol. 32 (1943), pp. 411-23.

Grass, Robert C., Wallace, Wallace H., and Zuckerkandel, Samuel
  "Response Latency in Industrial Advertising Research"
  Journal of Advertising Research, Vol. 20 (December 1980), pp. 63-5.

Johnson, Donald M.
  "Confidence and Speed in Two-Category Judgment"
  Archives of Psychology, No. 241.

LaBarbera, Priscilla and MacLachlan, James M.
  "Response Latency in Telephone Interviews"
  Journal of Advertising Research, Vol. 19 (June 1979), pp. 49-55.

LaBarbera, P. A. and MacLachlan, J. M.
  "Response Latency as a Measure of Certainty in Telephone Interview Situations"
  New York University (1977), working paper.

MacLachlan, J. M.
  Response Latency: A New Measure of Advertising
  (New York: Advertising Research Foundation, 1977).

MacLachlan, James, Czepiel, John, and LaBarbera, Priscilla
  "Implementation of Response Latency Measures"
  Journal of Marketing Research, Vol. XVI (November 1979), pp. 573-7.

MacLachlan, James and Myers, John G.
  "Using Response Latency to Identify Commercials That Motivate"
  Journal of Advertising Research, Vol. 25 (October/November 1983), pp. 51-7.

Shipley, W. C., Coffin, J. I., and Hadsell, K. C.
  "Affective Distance and Other Factors Determining Reaction Time in Judgements of Color Preference"
  Journal of Experimental Psychology, Vol. 35 (1945), pp. 206-15.

Shipley, Walter C., Norris, Elizabeth D., and Roberts, Margaret L.
  "The Effect of Changed Polarity of Set on Decision Time of Affective Judgements"
  Journal of Experimental Psychology (1946), pp. 237-43.

Siegel, P. S., Williams, J., and Szabo, S.
  "Speed of Choosing in Relation to the Preference Value of the Incentive"
  Psychonomic Science, Vol. 10 (1968), pp. 405,6.

Snodgrass, J. G. and Kass, R.
  "Time and Consistency as Measures of Psychological Distance"
  Perceptual and Motor Skills, Vol. 35 (1972), pp. 635-45.

Tyebjee, Tyzoon T.
  "Response Latency: A New Measure for Scaling Brand Preference"
  Journal of Marketing Research, Vol. XVI (February 1979), pp. 96-101.

99.02 ---------- Applications of Response Latency

Burroughs, W. Jeffrey and Feinberg, Richard A.
  "Using Response Latency to Assess Spokesperson Effectiveness"
  Journal of Consumer Research, Vol. 14 (September 1987), pp. 295-9.

Curry, David
  "Evaluating Qualitative Laws of Preference Using Computer-Controlled
  Experiments"
  Proceedings of the American Marketing Association
  (Chicago: American Marketing Association, 1975).

Kardes, Frank R.
  "Spontaneous Inference Processes in Advertising: The Effects of
  Conclusion Omission and Involvement on Persuasion"
  Journal of Consumer Research, Vol. 15 (September 1988), pp. 225-33.

Sherrill, P. N. and Ray, Michael L.
  "A Practical Survey Measure of the Strength of Voting Intent"
  Research Paper No. 24
  Graduate School of Business, Stanford University (1971).

100 -------------------- PHYSIOLOGICAL MEASUREMENT --------------------
        See also (sub)heading(s) 98.

100.01 ---------- Books Re: Physiological Measurement

Andreassi, J. L.
  Psychophysiology: Human Behavior and Physiological Response
  (New York: Oxford University Press, 1980).

Cacioppo, John T. and Petty, Richard E.
  Social Psychophysiology: A Sourcebook
  (New York: The Guilford Press, 1983).

Coles, Michael G. H., Donchin, Emanuel, and Porges, Stephen W. (editors)
  Psychophysiology: Systems, Processes, and Applications
  (New York: The Guilford Press, 1986), 761 pp.

Dunbar, Flanders
  Emotions and Bodily Changes, Fourth Edition
  (New York: Columbia University Press, 1954).

Greenfield, Norman S. and Stenbach, Richard A.
  Handbook of Psychophysiology
  (New York: Holt, Rinehart and Winston, 1972).

Grings, William and Dawson, Michael E.
  Emotion and Bodily Responses: A Psychophysiological Approach
  (New York: Academic Press, 1978).

Hassett, James
  A Primer for Psychophysiology
  (San Francisco: W. H. Freeman, 1978).

Martin, Irene and Venables, Peter H.
  Techniques in Psychophysiology
  (New York: John Wiley and Sons, Inc., 1980).

Stern, Robert M., Ray, William J., and Davis, Christopher
  Psychophysiological Recording
  (New York: Oxford University Press, 1980).

Thompson, Richard F.
  Introduction to Physiological Psychology
  (New York: Harper and Row, 1975).

Thompson, Richard F. and Patterson, Michael M.
  Bioelectric Recording Techniques. Part B: Electroencephalography and
  Human Brain Potential
  (New York: Academic Press, 1974).

Venables, Peter H. and Martin, Irene
  A Manual of Psychophysiological Methods
  (Amsterdam: North-Holland Publishing Company, 1967).

100.02 ---------- Articles, etc. Re: Physiological Measurement

Cacioppo, John T. and Petty, Richard E.
  "Physiological Responses and Advertising Effects: Is the Cup Half
  Full or Half Empty?"
  Psychology and Marketing, Vol. 2 (Summer 1985), pp. 115-26.

Caffyn, John M.
  "On Methods: Psychological Laboratory Techniques in Copy Research"
  Journal of Advertising Research, Vol. 4 (December 1964), pp. 45-50.

Kroeber-Riel, Werner
  "Activation Research: Psychobiological Approaches in Consumer
  Research"
  Journal of Consumer Research, Vol. 5 (March 1979), pp. 240-50.

Ray, William J. and Olson, Jerry C.
  "Perspectives on Psychophysiological Assessment of Psychological
  Responses to Advertising"
  in Percy, L. andWoodside, A. G. (editors)
  Advertising and Consumer Psychology
  (Lexington, MA: D. C. Heath, 1983), pp. 253-69.

Stewart, David W.
  "Physiological Measurement of Advertising Effects"
  Psychology and Marketing, Vol. 1 (Spring 1984), pp. 43-8.

Stewart, David W. and Furse, David H.
  "Applying Psychophysiological Measures to Marketing and Advertising
  Research Problems"
  in Leigh, J. and Martin, C. (editors)
  Current Issues and Research in Advertising 1982
  (Ann Arbor, MI: University of Michigan Graduate School of Business
  Administration, 1982), pp. 1-37.

Stewart, David W. and Furse, David H.
  "Applying Psychophysiological Measures to Marketing and Advertising
  Research Problems"
  Owen Graduate School of Management, Vanderbilt University (1981),
  working paper.

Watson, Paul J. and Gatchel, Robert J.
  "Autonomic Measures of Advertising"
  Journal of Advertising Research, Vol. 19 (June 1979), pp. 15-26.

100.03 ---------- Theory Re: Pupil Dilation, Eye Fixation and Movement

Beatty, J. and Kahneman, D.
  "Pupillary Changes in Two Memory Tasks"
  Psychonomic Science, Vol. 5 (1966), pp. 371,2.

Berhard, Ulrich
  "Exposure to Advertising: Eye Movement and Memory"
  University of the Saarland, Germany (1978), Ph.D. dissertation (in
  German).

Bernick, Niles and Oberlander, Mark
  "Effect of Verbalization on Two Different Modes of Experiencing on
  Pupil Size"
  Perception and Psychophysics, Vol. 3 (May 1968), pp. 327-30.

Blackwell, Roger D., Hensel, James S., and Sternthal, Brian
  "Pupil Dilation: What Does It Measure"
  Journal of Advertising Research, Vol. 10 (1970), pp. 15-9.

Gaarder, Kenneth R.
  Eye Movements, Vision, and Behavior
  (Washington, DC: Halsted Press, 1975).

Halpern, R. S.
  "Application of Pupil Response to Before-and-After Experiments"
  Journal of Marketing Research, Vol. IV (August 1967), pp. 320,1.

Hess, E. H.
  "Attitude and Pupil Size"
  Scientific American, Vol. 212 (April 1965), pp. 46-54.

Hess, E. H. and Polt, J. M.
  "Pupil Size as Related to Interest Value of Visual Stimuli"
  Science, Vol. 132 (August 1960), pp. 349,50.

Janisse, Michael P.
  Pupillometry--The Psychology of the Pupillary Response
  (New York: John Wiley and Sons, Inc., 1977).

Kahneman, D. and Beatty, J.
  "Pupil Diameter and Load on Memory"
  Science, Vol. 45 (1966), pp. 1583-5.

King, Albert S.
  "Pupil Size, Eye Direction, and Message Appeal: Some Preliminary
  Findings"
  Journal of Marketing, Vol. 36 (July 1972), pp. 55-8.

Krugman, H. E.
  "A Comparison of Physical and Verbal Responses to Television
  Commercials"
  Public Opinion Quarterly (Summer 1965), pp. 323-5.

Krugman, Herbert E.
  "Pupil Measurement at Marplan"
  Brewers Digest (November 1964).

Loftus, Geoffrey R.
  "Eye Fixations and Recognition Memory for Pictures"
  Cognitive Psychology, Vol. 3 (1972), pp. 525-51.

Lowenfeld, I. E.
  "Pupil Size"
  Ophthalmology, Vol. 11 (1966), pp. 291-4.

Monty, Richard A. and Senders, John W.
  Eye Movements and Psychological Processes
  (Hillsdale, NJ: Lawrence Erlbaum Associates, 1976).

Pavio, A. and Simpson, H. M.
  "The Effect of Word Abstractness and Pleasantness on Pupil Size
  During an Imaginary Test"
  Psychonomic Science, Vol. 5 (1966), pp. 55,6.

Payne, Donald T., Parry, Mary Ellen, and Harasymiw, Stefan J.
  "Percentage of Pupillary Dilation as a Measure of Item Difficulty"
  Perception and Psychophysics, Vol. 4 (September 1968), pp. 139-43.

Peavler, W. S. and McLaughlin, J. P.
"The Question of Stimulus Content and Pupil Size"
Psychonomic Science, Vol. 8 (1967), pp. 505,6.

Polt, J. M. and Hess, E. H.
"Changes in Pupil Size to Visually Presented Words"
Psychonomic Science, Vol. 12, No. 8 (1968), pp. 389,90.

Russo, J. Edward
"Adaptation of Cognitive Processes to the Eye Movement System"
in Senders, John W., Fisher, Dennis F., and Monty, Richard (editors)
Eye Movements and the Higher Psychological Functions
(Hillsdale, NJ: Lawrence Erlbaum Associates, 1978).

Russo, J. Edward
"Eye Fixations Can Save the World: A Critical Evaluation and a
Comparison Between Eye Fixations and Other Information Processing
Methodologies"
in Hunt, H. Keith (editor)
Advances in Consumer Research, Volume Five
(Ann Arbor, MI: Association for Consumer Research, 1978), pp. 561-70.

Senders, John W., Fisher, Dennis F., and Monty, Richard A. (editors)
Eye Movements and the Higher Psychological Functions
(Hillsdale, NJ: Lawrence Associates, 1978).

Smead, Raymond J., Wilcox, James B., and Wilkes, Robert E.
"An Illustration and Evaluation of a Joint Process Tracing
Methodology: Eye Movement and Protocols"
in Olson, Jerry C. (editor)
Advances in Consumer Research, Volume Seven
(Ann Arbor, MI: Association for Consumer Research, 1979), pp. 507-12.

Thoman, E. L.
"Movements of the Eye"
Scientific American, Vol. 219 (August 1968), pp. 88-95.

Tversky, Barbara
"Eye Fixations in Prediction of Recognition and Recall"
Memory and Cognition, Vol. 2 (1974), pp. 275-8.

Van Raaij, W. Fred
"Direct Monitoring of Consumer Information Processing by Eye Movement
Recorder"
Tilburg University (1976), unpublished paper.

Witt, Dieter
"Emotional Advertising: The Relationship Between Eye-Movement Patterns
and Memory--Empirical Study With the Eye-Movement Monitor"
University of Saarland, Germany (1977), Ph.D. dissertation.

Woodmanese, J. J.
"Methodological Problems in Pupillographic Experiments"
American Psychological Association, New York (1986), paper
presentation.

100.04 ---------- Applications of Pupil Dilation, Eye Fixation/Movement

Bogart, Leo and Tolley, B. Stuart
"The Search for Information in Newspaper Advertising"
Journal of Advertising Research, Vol. 28 (April/May 1988), pp. 9-19.

Krugman, Herbert E.
"White and Negro Responses to Package Designs"
Journal of Marketing Research, Vol. III (May 1966), pp. 199,200.

Krugman, Herbert E.
"Some Applications of Pupil Measurement"
Journal of Marketing Research, Vol. I (November 1964), pp. 15-9.

Morrison, Bruce John and Dainoff, Marvin J.
"Advertisement Complexity and Looking Time"
Journal of Marketing Research, Vol. IX (November 1972), pp. 396-400.

Russo, J. Edward and Rosen, Larry D.
"An Eye Fixation Analysis of Multi-Alternative Choice"
Memory and Cognition, Vol. 3 (May 1975), pp. 267-76.

Stafford, James E., Birdwell, Al E., and Van Tassel, Charles E.
"Integrated Advertising--White Backlash?"
Journal of Advertising Research, Vol. 10 (April 1970), pp. 15-20.

100.05 ---------- Theory Re: Voice Pitch Analysis (VOPAN)

Atkinson, James E.
  "Correlational Analysis of Physiological Factors Controlling
  Fundamental Voice Frequency"
  Journal of the Acoustical Society of America, Vol. 63 (January 1978),
  pp. 211-22.

Atkinson, James E.
  "Inter- and Intraspeaker Variability in Fundamental Voice Frequency"
  Journal of the Acoustical Society of America, Vol. 60 (August 1976),
  pp. 440-5.

Brickman, Glen A.
  "Uses of Voice-Pitch Analysis"
  Journal of Advertising Research, Vol. 20 (April 1980), pp. 69-73.

Brickman, Glen A.
  "Voice Analysis"
  Journal of Advertising Research, Vol. 16 (June 1976), pp. 43-8.

Fairbanks, G. and Pronovost, W.
  "An Experimental Study of the Pitch Characteristics of the Voice
  During the Expression of Emotions"
  Speech Monographs, Vol. 6 (1939), pp. 87-104.

Friedhoff, Arnold J., Alpert, Murray, and Kurtzberg, Richard L.
  "An Effect of Emotion on Voice"
  Nature, Vol. 193(4813) (1973), pp. 357,8.

Haas, Charlie
  "Charlie Haas on Advertising"
  New West (November 5, 1979), pp. 31-59.

Hensel, James Stephen
  "Physiological Measures of Advertising Effectiveness: A Theoretical
  and Empirical Investigation"
  The Ohio State University (1971), doctoral dissertation.

Kubis, Joseph F.
  "Comparison of Voice Analysis and Polygraph as Lie Detection
  Procedures"
  Polygraph, Vol. 3 (March 1974), pp. 1-41.

Kubis, Joseph F.
  Comparisons of Voice Analysis and Polygraph as Lie Detection
  Procedures
  Report of Contract DAAD 05-72-C-0217
  (U.S. Army Land Warfare Laboratory, August 1973).

Lieberman, Philip and Michaels, S.
  "Some Aspects of Fundamental Frequency, Envelope Amplitude, and the
  Emotional Content of Speech"
  Journal of the Acoustical Society of America, Vol. 34 (1962), pp.
  922-7.

Nelson, Ronald G. and Schwartz, David
  "Voice-Pitch Analysis"
  Journal of Advertising Research, Vol. 19 (October 1979), pp. 55-9.

Nighswonger, Nancy J. and Martin, Claude R., Jr.
  "On Using Voice Analysis in Marketing Research"
  Journal of Marketing Research, Vol. XVIII (August 1981), pp. 350-5.

Schwartz, D.
  "Listening to Voices: A Tool of Research"
  Advertising Age (October 15, 1979), pp. S28,9,31.

Vopan Marketing Research
  "Vopan Voice Pitch Analysis in Marketing and Advertising Research"
  The Vopan Company, Boston (January 1980), unpublished company
  literature.

Williams, Carl E. and Stevens, Kenneth N.
  "Emotions and Speech: Some Acoustical Correlates"
  Journal of the Acoustical Society of America, Vol. 52(4) (1972), pp.
  1238-50.

100.06 ---------- Applications of Voice Analysis

Backhaus, Klaus, Meyer, Margit, and Stockert, Andreas
  "Using Voice Analysis for Analyzing Bargaining Processes in
  Industrial Marketing"
  Journal of Business Research, Vol. 13 (October 1985), pp. 435-46.

100.07 ---------- Theory Re: Computer-Aided Voice Chronography

See also (sub)heading(s) 73, 76.06, 88, 92, 97.

Dabbs, James M. and Swielder, Thomas C.
"Group AVTA: A Microcomputer System for Group Voice Chronography"
Behavioral Research Methods and Instrumentation, Vol. 15, No. 1
(1983), pp. 79-84.

Feldstein, S. and Welkowitz, J.
"A Chronography of Conversations: In Defense of an Objective Approach"
in Siegman, A. and Feldstein, S. (editors)
Nonverbal Behavior in Communication
(Hillsdale, NJ: Lawrence Erlbaum Associates, 1978).

100.08 ---------- Applications of Computer-Aided Voice Chronography

Clopton, Stephen W. and Barksdale, Hiram C., Jr.
"Microcomputer Based Methods for Dyadic Interaction Research in
Marketing"
Journal of the Academy of Marketing Science, Vol. 15 (Summer 1987),
pp. 63-8.

100.09 ---------- Theory Re: Electrodermal or Skin Response

Burstein, Kenneth R., Frenz, Walter D., Bergeron, James, and Epstein,
Seymour
"A Comparison of Skin Potential and Skin Resistance Responses as
Measures of Emotional Responsivity"
Psychophysiology, Vol. 2 (1965), pp. 14-25.

Grings, W. W.
"Methodological Considerations Underlying Electrodermal Measurement"
Journal of Psychology, Vol. 35 (April 1953), pp. 271-82.

Horvath, F.
"An Experimental Comparison of the Psychological Stress Evaluator and
the Galvanic Skin Response in Detection of Deception"
Journal of Applied Psychology, Vol. 63 (1978), pp. 338-44.

Kubis, Joseph F.
Comparisons of Voice Analysis and Polygraph as Lie Detection
Procedures
Report of Contract DAAD 05-72-C-0217
(U.S. Army Land Warfare Laboratory, August 1973).

Lykken, David T. and Venables, Peter H.
"Direct Measurement of Skin Conductance: A Proposal for
Standardization"
Psychophysiology, Vol. 8 (1971), pp. 656-72.

McCurdy, Harold Grier
"Consciousness and the Galvanometer"
Psychological Review, Vol. 57 (1950), pp. 322-7.

Mundy-Castle, A. C.
"The Psycho-Physiological Significance of the Galvanic Skin Response"
Journal of Experimental Psychology, Vol. 46 (1953), pp. 15-24.

Prokasy, William F. and Raskin, David C.
Electrodermal Activity in Psychological Research
(New York: Academic Press, 1973).

Rankin, R. E. and Campbell, D. T.
"Galvanic Skin Response to Negro and White Experimenters"
Journal of Abnormal and Social Psychology, Vol. 51 (1955), pp. 30-3.

Roessler, Robert, Burch, Neil R., and Childers, Harold E.
"Personality and Arousal Correlates of Specific Galvanic Skin
Responses"
Psychophysiology, Vol. 3 (1966), pp. 115-31.

100.10 ---------- Applications of Electrodermal or Skin Response

Aaker, David A., Stayman, Douglas M., and Hagerty, Michael R.
"Warmth in Advertising: Measurement, Impact, and Sequence Effect"
Journal of Consumer Research, Vol. 12 (March 1986), pp. 365-81.

100.11 ---------- Theory Re: Brain Activity

Alwitt, Linda F.
   "EEG Activity Reflects the Content of Commercials"
   in Alwitt, Linda F. and Mitchell, Andrew A. (editors)
   Psychological Processes and Advertising Effects
   (Hillsdale, NJ: Lawrence Erlbaum Associates, Publishers, 1985), pp.
   201-17.

Appel, V., Weinstein, Sidney, and Weinstein, Curt
   "Brain Activity and Recall of TV Advertising"
   Journal of Advertising Research, Vol. 19 (1979), pp. 7-15.

Beaumont, J. G.
   "The EEG and Task Performance: A Tutorial Review"
   in Gaillard, A. W. K. and Ritter, W. (editors)
   Tutorials in Event Related Potential Research: Endogenous Components
   (New York: North-Holland, 1983), pp. 385-406.

Beaumont, J. G., Mayes, A. R., and Rugg, M. D.
   "Asymmetry in EEG Alpha Coherence and Power: Effects of Task and Sex"
   Electroencephalography and Clinical Neurophysiology, Vol. 45 (1978),
   pp. 393-401.

Donchin, Emanuel, Kutas, Marta, and McCarthy, Gregory
   "Electrocortical Indices of Hemispheric Utilization"
   in Harnard, Steven et al. (editors)
   Lateralization in the Nervous System
   (New York: Academic Press, 1977), pp. 339-84.

Doyle, Joseph C., Ornstein, Robert, and Galin, David
   "Lateral Specialization of Cognitive Mode: II. EEG Frequency Analysis"
   Psychophysiology, Vol. 11, No. 5 (1974), pp. 567,8.

Hansen, Flemming
   Studies of Communication Effects: Methodological and Theoretical
   Papers on Left/Right Brain Specialization
   (Copenhagen: Civilokonomernes forlag 9/5, 1985).

Katz, William A.
   "Point of View: A Critique of Split-Brain Theory"
   Journal of Advertising Research, Vol. 23 (April/May 1983), pp. 63-6.

Krugman, Herbert E.
   "Low Involvement Theory in the Light of New Brain Research"
   in Maloney, J. C. and Silverman, B. S. (editors)
   Attitude Research Plays for High Stakes
   (Chicago: American Marketing Association, 1979).

Krugman, Herbert E.
   "Brainwave Measures of Media Involvement"
   Journal of Advertising Research, Vol. 11 (1971), pp. 3-9.

Lang, R. J., Rice, D. G., and Sternbach, R. A.
   "The Psychophysiology of Emotion"
   in Greenfield, N. and Sternbach, R. (editors)
   Handbook of Psychophysiology
   (New York: Holt, Rinhart and Winston, 1972), pp. 623-43.

Mulholland, Thomas
   "A Program for EEG Study of Attention in Visual Communication"
   in Randhawa, Bikkar S. and Goffman, William F. (editors)
   Visual Learning: Thinking and Communication
   (New York: Academic Press, 1978), pp. 77-91.

Mulholland, Thomas
   "Objective EEG Methods for Studying Covert Shifts of Visual
   Attention"
   in McGuigan, F. J. and Schoonover, R. A. (editors)
   The Psychophysiology of Thinking
   (New York: Academic Press, 1973), pp. 109-51.

Nevid, Jeffrey S.
   "Methodological Considerations in the Use of Electroencephalographic
   Techniques in Advertising Research"
   Psychology and Marketing, Vol. 1 (Summer 1984), pp. 5-19.

Olson, Jerry C. and Ray, William J.
   Using Brain-Wave Measures to Assess Advertising Effects
   Report No. 83-108
   (Cambridge, MA: Marketing Science Institute), 43 pp.

Ray, William J., Olson, Jerry C., Hansen, Flemming, and Lundsgaard,
   Niels Erik
   "Models and Myths of Brain Lateralisation: Are There Right and Left
   Hemispheric People, Stimuli and Contexts?"
   ESOMAR Congress, Rome (1984), pp. 287-302.

Reeves, Byron B., Thorson, Esther, Rothschild, Michael L., McDonald,
    Daniel, Hirsch, Judith E., and Goldstein, Robert
    "Attention to Television: Intrastimulus Effect of Movement and Scene
    Changes on Alpha Variation Over Time"
    International Journal of Neuroscience, Vol. 27, No. 3 and 4 (1985),
    pp. 241-56.

Rothschild, Michael L.
    "Brain Wave Data as an Advertising Diagnostic" (summary)
    in Bagozzi, R. P. and Tybout, A. M. (editors)
    Advances in Consumer Research, Volume Ten
    (Ann Arbor, MI: Association for Consumer Research, 1983).

Rothschild, Michael L., Hyun, Yong J., Reeves, Byron, Thorson, Esther,
    and Goldstein, Robert
    "Hemispherically Lateralized EEG as a Response to Television
    Commercials"
    Journal of Consumer Research, Vol. 15 (September 1988), pp. 185-98.

Rothschild, Michael L. and Thorson, Esther
    "Electroencephalographic Activity as a Response to Complex Stimuli: A
    Review of Relevant Psychophysiology and Advertising Literature"
    in Percy, L. and Woodside, A. G. (editors)
    Advertising and Consumer Psychology
    (Lexington, MA: D. C. Heath, 1983), pp. 239-51.

Rothschild, Michael L., Thorson, Esther, Reeves, Byron B., Hirsch,
    Judith E., and Goldstein, Robert
    "EEG Activity and the Processing of Television Commercials"
    Communication Research, Vol. 13, No. 2 (1986), pp. 102-220.

Rossiter, John R.
    "Point of View: Brain Hemisphere Activity"
    Journal of Advertising Research, Vol. 20 (October 1980), pp. 75,6.

Schafer, Edward W. P.
    "Brain Responses While Viewing Television Reflect Program Interest"
    International Journal of Neuroscience, Vol. 8, No. 2 (1978), pp. 71-7.

Sperry, Roger
    "Some Effects of Disconnecting the Cerebral Hemispheres"
    Science, Vol. 217 (1982), pp. 1223-6.

Stewart, David W.
    "Differences Between Basic Research and the Validation of Specific
    Measures: A Reply to Weinstein et al."
    Psychology and Marketing, Vol. 2 (Spring 1985), pp. 41-9.

Tucker, D. M.
    "Lateralized Brain Function, Emotion, and Conceptualization"
    Psychological Bulletin, Vol. 89 (1981), pp. 19-46.

Walker, James L.
    "Changes in EEG Rhythms During Television Viewing: Preliminary
    Comparisons With Reading and Other Tasks"
    Perceptual and Motor Skills, Vol. 51, No. 1 (1980), pp. 255-61.

Weinstein, Sidney
    "A Review of Brain Hemisphere Research"
    Journal of Advertising Research, Vol. 22 (June/July 1982), pp. 59-63.

Weinstein, Sidney
    "Brain Wave Analysis in Attitude Research: Past, Present, and Future"
    Marketing Review, Vol. 35, No. 9 (1980), pp. 23-36.

Weinstein, Sidney
    "Brain Wave Analyses for Evaluation of TV Commercials and Print Ads
    are No Longer Science Fiction"
    Marketing Review, Vol. 34, No. 6 (1979), pp. 17-20.

Weinstein, Sidney
    "Monday Memo: Probing the Brain for Ad Input"
    Broadcasting (September 17, 1979), p. 22.

Weinstein, Sidney, Appel, Valentine, and Weinstein, Curt
    "Brain-Activity Responses to Magazine and Television Advertising"
    Journal of Advertising Research, Vol. 20 (June 1980), pp. 57-63.

Weinstein, Sidney, Drozdenko, Ronald, and Weinstein, Curt
    "Advertising Evaluation using Brain-Wave Measures: A Response to the
    Question of Validity"
    Journal of Advertising Research, Vol. 24 (April/May 1984), pp. 67-71.

Weinstein, Sidney, Weinstein, Curt, and Drozdenko, Ronald
    "Brain Wave Analysis"
    Psychology and Marketing, Vol. 1 (Spring 1984), pp. 17-42.

100.12 ---------- Applications of Brain Activity Measures

Appel, Valentine, Weinstein, Sidney, and Weinstein, Curt
    "Brain Activity and Recall of TV Advertising"
    Journal of Advertising Research, Vol. 19, No. 4 (1979), pp. 7-15.

Price, Linda, Rust, Roland T., and Kumar, V.
    "Brain Wave Analysis of Consumer Responses to Advertising"
    in Olson, Jerry and Sentis, Keith (editors)
    Advances in Advertising and Consumer Psychology
    (New York: Praeger Publishers, 1985).

Rockey, E. A., Greene, W. F., and Perold, E. A.
    "Attention, Memory and Attitudinal Reactions to Television
    Commercials Under Single and Multiple Exposure Conditions as Measured
    by Brain Research"
    26th Annual Conference, Advertising Research Foundation (1980), paper
    presentation.

Rust, Roland T., Price, Linda L., and Kumar, V.
    "EEG Response to Advertisements in Print and Broadcast Media"
    Working Paper No. 85-111
    Marketing Science Institute (1985).

100.13 ---------- Theory Re: Cardiovascular Measures

Cacioppo, John T. and Petty, Richard E.
    Perspectives in Cardiovascular Psychophysiology
    (New York: The Guilford Press, 1982).

Obrist, Paul A.
    Cardiovascular Psychophysiology: A Perspective
    (New York: Plenum Press, 1981).

Obrist, Paul A., Black, A. H., Brener, Jasper, and DiCara, Leo V.
    Cardiovascular Psychophysiology
    (Chicago: Aldine Publishing Company, 1974).

100.14 ---------- Theory Re: Electrophysiology and Electromyography

Cacioppo, John T. and Petty, Richard E.
    "Electromyograms as Measures of Extent of Affectivity of Information
    Processing"
    American Psychologist, Vol. 36 (1981), pp. 441-56.

Cacioppo, John T. and Petty, Richard E.
    "Attitudes and Cognitive Response: An Electrophysiological Approach"
    Journal of Personality and Social Psychology, Vol. 37 (1979), pp.
    2181-99.

Cacioppo, John T., Petty, Richard E., Losch, M. E., Kim, H. S.
    "Electromyographic Activity Over Facial Muscle Regions can
    Differentiate the Valence and Intensity of Affective Reactions"
    Journal of Personality and Social Psychology, forthcoming.

Cacioppo, John T., Petty, Richard E. and Marshall-Goodell, B.
    "Electromyographic Specificity During Simply Physical and Attitudinal
    Tasks: Location and Topographical Features of Integrated EMG
    Responses"
    Biological Psychology, Vol. 18 (1984), pp. 85-121.

Ekman, P.
    "About Brows: Emotional and Conversational Signals"
    in Von Cranach, M., Foppa, K., Lepenies, W., and Ploog, D. (editors)
    Human Ethology
    (Cambridge: Cambridge University Press, 1979).

Eckman, P. and Friesen, W. V.
    Unmasking the Face
    (Englewood Cliffs, NJ: Prentice-Hall, 1975).

Fridlund, A. J. and Izard, C. E.
    "Electromyographic Studies of Facial Expressions of Emotions and
    Patterns of Emotions"
    in Cacioppo, J. T. and Petty, R. E. (editors)
    Social Psychophysiology: A Sourcebook
    (New York: Guilford Press, 1983).

Izard, C. E.
    The Face of Emotion
    (New York: Appleton-Century-Crofts, 1971).

Petty, Richard E. and Cacioppo, John T.
    "The Role of Bodily Responses in Attitude Measurement and Change"
    in Cacioppo, J. T. and Petty, R. E. (editors)
    Social Psychophysiology: A Sourcebook
    (New York: Guilford Press, 1983).

Rinn, W. E.
    "The Neuropsychology of Facial Expression: A Review of the
    Neurological and Psychological Mechanisms for Producing Facial
    Expression"
    Psychological Bulletin, Vol. 95 (1984), pp. 52-77.

Schwartz, G. E., Fair, P. L., Salt, P., Mandel, M. R., and Klerman, G.
    "Facial Muscle Patterning to Affective Imagery in Depressed and
    Nondepressed Subjects"
    Science, Vol. 192 (1976), pp. 489-91.

100.15 ---------- Unclassified (Physiological Measurement Methods)

Barg, Claus-Dieter
    "Measurement and Effects of Psychological Activation Through
    Advertising"
    University of the Saarland, Germany (1977), Ph.D. dissertation (in
    German).

Clements, Paul R., Hafer, Marilyn D., and Vermillion, Mary E.
    "Psychometric, Diurnal, and Electro-Physiological Correlates of
    Activation"
    Journal of Personality and Social Psychology, Vol. 33 (1976), pp.
    387-95.

Craig, Kenneth D. and Wood, Keith
    "Autonomic Components of Observers' Responses to Pictures of Homicide
    Victims and Nude Females"
    Journal of Experimental Research in Personality, Vol. 5 (1971), pp.
    304-9.

Greene, Jerome D. and Maloney, John F.
    "Fingerprints Can't Test for Validity"
    Journal of Advertising Research, Vol. 16 (June 1976), pp. 49,50.

Kohan, Xavier
    "A Physiological Measure of Commercial Effectiveness"
    Journal of Advertising, Vol. 8 (1968), pp. 46-8.

Perry, John W., Jr.
    "Arousal and Memory: Psycho-Physiological and Personality Factors"
    University of Texas (1971), Ph.D. dissertation.

Russo, J. Edward and Dosher, Barbara A.
    "Dimensional Evaluation: A Heuristic for Binary Choice"
    Department of Psychology, University of California, San Diego (1975),
    unpublished working paper.

Schul, Patrick L. and Lamb, Charles W., Jr.
    "Decoding Nonverbal and Vocal Communications: A Laboratory Study"
    Journal of the Academy of Marketing Science, Vol. 10 (Spring 1982),
    pp. 154-64.

Schwerin, Paul and Murphy, Malcolm P.
    "The Development of Salivation Measurements as a Possible New
    Technique for Objectively Determining Consumer Reactions to Pictorial
    Advertisements"
    Schwerin Research Corporation Technical and Analytical Review (May
    1963), pp. 1-5.

Thayer, Robert E.
    "Activation States as Assessed by Verbal Report and Four
    Psychophysiological Variables"
    Psychophysiology, Vol. 7 (1970), pp. 86-94.

Traxel, Werner
    "The Possibility of an Objective Measurement of the Strength of
    Feelings"
    Psychologische Forschung, Vol. 26 (1960), pp. 75-90.

Venables, P. H. and Christie, M. J.
    "Mechanisms, Instrumentation, Recording Techniques and Quantification
    of Responses"
    in Prokasy, William F. and Raskin, David C. (editors)
    Electrodermal Activity in Psychological Research
    (New York: Academic Press, 1973).

101 ----------------------- SECONDARY RESEARCH -----------------------

101.01 ---------- Books Re: Secondary Research

Hakim, Catherine
    Secondary Analysis in Social Research: A Guide to Data Sources and
    Methods With Examples
    (George Allen and Unwin Ltd., 1982), 202 pp.

Jacob, Herbert
    Using Published Data: Errors and Remedies
    (Beverly Hills, CA: Sage Publications, Inc., 1984).

Stewart, David W.
    Secondary Research: Information Sources and Methods
    (Beverly Hills, CA: Sage Publications, Inc., 1984), 136 pp.

101.02 ---------- Descriptions of Specific Secondary Sources

Davidson, Jeffrey P.
    "Low-Cost Research Sources"
    Journal of Small Business Management, Vol. 23 (April 1985), pp. 73-7.

Deville, J. C. and Malinvaude, E.
    "Data Analysis in Official Socio-Economic Statistics"
    Journal of the Royal Statistical Society, Vol. 146, Series A General
    (1983), pp. 335-61.

Evans, Henry K.
    "A Vast New Storehouse of Transportation and Marketing Data"
    Journal of Marketing, Vol. 30 (January 1966), pp. 33-40.

Goyer, Doreen S. and Domschke, Elaine
    The Handbook of National Population Censuses
    (Westport, CT: Greenwood Press), 711 pp.

Kern, Richard
    "1984 Survey of Buying Power: The Local Numbers Racket"
    Sales and Marketing Management Magazine, Vol. 133 (July 1984), pp.
    A38-44.

Norwood, Janet L. and Early, John F.
    "A Century of Methodological Progress at the U.S. Bureau of Labor
    Statistics"
    Journal of the American Statistical Association, Vol. 79 (December
    1984), pp. 748-61.

Prasad, V. Kanti, Casper, Wayne R., and Schieffer, Robert J.
    "Alternatives to the Traditional Retail Store Audit: A Field Study"
    Journal of Marketing, Vol. 48 (Winter 1984), pp. 54-61.

Sales and Marketing Management Magazine
    "The Survey of Buying Power--55 Years Young and Still Going Strong"
    Sales and Marketing Management Maga zine, Vol. 133 (July 23, 1984),
    pp. A7-34.

101.03 ---------- Census Methodology

        See also (sub)heading(s) 33.

Bailey, Leroy
    "Toward a More Complete Analysis of the Total Mean Square Error of
    Census Sample Survey Statistics"
    Proceedings, Social Statistics Section, American Statistical
    Association (1975), pp. 1-10.

Brandt, J. D. and Chalk, S. M.
    "The Use of Automatic Editing in the 1981 Census"
    Journal of the Royal Statistical Society, Series A, Vol. 148 (1985).

Citro, Constance F. and Cohen, Michael L. (editors)
    The Bicentennial Census: New Directions for Methodology in 1990
    (Washington, DC: National Academy Press, 1985), 404 pp.

Gonzalez, Maria, Ogus, Jack L., Shapiro, Gary, and Tepping, Benjamin J.
    "Standards for Discussion and Presentation of Errors in Survey and
    Census Data"
    Journal of the American Statistical Association, Vol. 70 (September
    1975), Part II, p. 23.

Littman, Mark S.
    "The 1980 Census of Population: Content and Coverage Improvement
    Plans"
    Journal of Consumer Research, Vol. 6 (September 1979), pp. 204-12.

Marks, Eli S., Mauldin, W. P., and Nisselson, H.
"The Post-Enumeration Survey of the 1950 Census: A Case History in
Survey Design"
Journal of the American Statistical Association, Vol. 48 (June 1953),
pp. 220-43.

Mitroff, Ian I., Mason, Richard O., and Barabba, Vincent P.
The 1980 Census: Policymaking Amid Turbulance
(Lexington, MA: Lexington Books), 238 pp.

Rhind, David
"Making Marketing Sense of the Census"
Admap ((July-August 1986), pp. 21-3.

Thatcher, A. R.
"The 1981 Census of Population in England and Wales"
Journal of the Royal Statistical Society, Series A, Part II (1984),
pp. 222-32.

U.S. Bureau of the Census
The Current Population Survey: Design and Methodology
(Washington, DC: U.S. Bureau of the Census, 1977).

U.S. Bureau of the Census
Procedural History
1970 Census of Population and Housing PHC(R)-1
(Washington, DC: U.S. Government Printing Office, 1976), 681 pp.

Wilson, P. R. and Elliot, D. J.
"An Evaluation of the Postcode Address File as a Sampling Frame and
Its Use Within OPCS"
Journal of the Royal Statistical Society, Series A, Vol. 150, Part 3
(1987), pp. 230-40.

101.04 ---------- Electronic Sources of Information

Haque, Paul
"Desk Research--Electronically"
Industrial Marketing Digest, Vol. 10 (First Quarter 1985), pp. 121-32.

Wasik, John F.
The Electronic Business Information Sourcebook
(New York: John Wiley and Sons, Inc., 1987), 208 pp.

101.05 ---------- Guides for Use of Secondary Sources

Buckingham, Bruce, Janes, Michael J., and Reeves, Bernard
"Using the Family Expenditure Survey"
Statistical News (February 1986), pp. 8-12.

Clemens, John
"One Nation--A Paper Demonstrating the Value of Commercial Data in
the Field of Social Research"
European Research, Vol. 1 (November 1973), pp. 242-6.

Deming, W. E. and Stephan, F. F.
"On the Interpretation of Censuses as Samples"
Journal of the American Statistical Association, Vol. 36 (1941), pp.
45-9.

Ehrenberg, A. S. C.
"The Neglected Use of Data"
Journal of Advertising Research, Vol. 7 (June 1967), pp. 2-7.

Gross, Walter
"Research and Other Applications of the Marketing Abstracts"
Journal of Marketing, Vol. 42 (April 1978), pp. 32-7.

Katzer, J., Cook, K. H., and Crouch, W. W.
Evaluating Information--A Guide for Users of Social Science Research
(Addison-Wesley Publishing Company, 1978), 191 pp.

Kiecolt, K. Jill and Nathan, Laura E.
Secondary Analysis of Survey Data
(Beverly Hills, CA: Sage Publications, Inc.).

Kildegaard, Ingrid C.
"Consumer Income Data"
Journal of Advertising Research, Vol. 1 (December 1961), pp. 37-9.

May, Eleanor C.
A Handbook for Business on the Use of Government Statistics
(Charlottsville, NC: University of Virginia), 159 pp.

Murray, Bruce W.
"Marketing's Little-Known Microscope"
Journal of Marketing, Vol. 28 (July 1964), pp. 1-5.

Plotkin, Manuel D.
"Uses of Census Retail Sales Data for More Effective Marketing"
in Mazze, Edward M. (editor)
1975 Combined Proceedings
(Chicago: American Marketing Association, 1976), pp. 411-4.

Rust, Roland T.
"Recategorizing Secondary Data"
1981 Educators' Conference Proceedings
(Chicago: American Marketing Association, 1981), pp. 384-6.

Sales and Marketing Management
"A User's Guide to the Survey of Buying Power--Part II"
Sales and Marketing Management, Vol. 140 (November 7, 1988), pp.
6-133.

Stephens, J. M.
"Making Dependable Use of Published Research: A Proposed Check List"
Journal of Educational Research, Vol. 61 (November 1967), pp. 99-104.

Stern, P. C.
Evaluating Social Science Research
(Oxford University Press, 1979), 240 pp.

U.S. Department of Commerce
Measuring Markets: A Guide to the Use of Federal and State
Statistical Data
(Washington, DC: U.S. Department of Commerce, 1979).

Wetzel, James R.
"Marketing Research Data From the US Census Bureau"
Journal of the Market Research Society, Vol. 31 (October 1989), pp.
590-5.

101.06 ---------- Store Audits

Leeflang, Peter S. H. and Olivier, Alex J.
"Bias in Consumer Panel and Store Audit Data"
International Journal of Research in Marketing, Vol. 2, No. 1 (1985),
pp. 27-41.

Leeflang, Peter S. H. and Olivier, Alex J.
"What is Wrong With the Audit Data We Use for Decision-Making in
Marketing"
Proceedings, 33rd ESOMAR Congress (1980), pp. 219-39.

Mensing, W. C. J. J.
The Representation of Noncooperating Chains in the Nielsen Retail
Index
(Amsterdam: A. C. Nielsen Company, 1981), unpublished.

Shoemaker, R. and Pringle, L. G.
"Possible Biases in Parameter Estimation With Store Audit Data"
Journal of Marketing Research, Vol. XVII (1980), pp. 91-6.

101.07 ---------- Standard Industrial Classification (SIC)

Clarke, Richard N.
"SICs as Delineators of Economic Markets"
Journal of Business, Vol. 62 (January 1989).

Haas, R. W.
"SIC System and Related Data for More Effective Market Research"
Industrial Marketing Management, Vol. 6, No. 6 (1977), pp. 429-35.

Hellborn, Ludwig S.
"Can the SIC Yield Accurate Marketing Data?"
Journal of Marketing, Vol. 20 (October 1956), pp. 157-62.

Kern, Robert
"At Long Last. Changes in the SIC System"
Sales and Marketing Management, Vol. 136 (April 28, 1986), pp.
8-22,24-6.

101.08 ---------- Studies and Evaluations of Secondary Sources

Advertising Age
"Studies Yield Contrasting Data for Magazines"
Vol. 36 (August 16, 1965), p. 66.

Bailar, Barbara A. and Sturdevant, Tyler R.
"How Well do Retailers Report Their Sales"
in Mazze, Edward M. (editor)
1975 Combined Proceedings
(Chicago: American Marketing Association, 1976), pp. 415-21.

Citro, Constance F. and Cohen, Michael L.
    The Bicentennial Census: New Directions for Methodology in 1990
    (Washington, D.C.: National Academy Press), 384 pp.

Cox, William E., Jr.
    "The 'Census' of Business: Some Contrary Evidence"
    Journal of Marketing, Vol. 31 (July 1967), pp. 47-51.

Ferber, Robert, Hawkes, William J., Jr., and Plotkin, Manuel D.
    "How Reliable are Retail Sales Estimates?"
    Journal of Marketing, Vol. 40 (October 1976), pp. 13-22.

Gray, P. G. and Gee, F.
    Quality Check on the 1966 Ten Percent Sample Census of England and
    Wales
    (HMSO, 1972).

Hansen, M. H., Horwitz, W. N., and Bershad, M. A.
    "Measurements of Errors in Censuses and Surveys"
    Bulletin of the International Statistical Institute, Vol. 38, No. 2
    (1961), pp. 359-74.

Hansen, M. H., Hurwitz, W. N., and Pritzker, L.
    "The Accuracy of Census Results"
    American Sociological Review, Vol. 18 (August 1953), pp. 416-23.

Johnson, Frank
    "Census Distortions of Food Broker Sales"
    Journal of Marketing, Vol. 27 (July 1963), pp. 67-9.

Kildegaard, Ingrid C.
    "Checking the Checkers"
    Journal of Advertising Research, Vol. 6 (September 1966), pp. 51-3.

Miller, Ann R.
    "Retrospective Data on Work Status in the 1970 Census of Population:
    An Attempt at Evaluation"
    Journal of the American Statistical Association, Vol. 71 (1976), pp.
    286-92.

Morganstern, Oskar
    On the Accuracy of Economic Observations
    (Princeton, NJ: Princeton University Press, 1963).

North, Max H. and Woodruff, Ralph S.
    "Reconciliation of the 1958 Census of Retail Trade With the Monthly
    Retail Trade Report"
    (Bureau of the Census Technical Paper No. 9, 1963).

Redpath, Bob
    "Family Expenditure Survey: A Second Study of Differential Response,
    Comparing Census Characteristics of FES Respondents and
    Non-Respondents"
    Statistical News (February 1986), pp. 13-6.

Roy, A. D.
    "An Exercise in Errors"
    Journal of the Royal Statistical Society, Vol. 115, Part 4 (1952),
    pp. 507-20.

Shoemaker, Robert, and Pringle, Lewis G.
    "Possible Biases in Parameter Estimation With Store Audit Data"
    Journal of Marketing Research, Vol. XVII (February 1980), pp. 91-6.

Smith, Tom W.
    "The Hidden 25 Percent: An Analysis of Non-Response on the 1980
    General Social Survey"
    Public Opinion Quarterly, Vol. 47 (Fall 1983), pp. 386-404.

U.S. Bureau of the Census
    Accuracy of Data for Selected Population Characteristics as Measured
    by Reinterviews
    1970 Census of Population and Housing Evaluation and Research
    Program, PHC(E)-9
    (Washington, DC: U.S. Government Printing Office, 1970).

Waite, Preston Jay
    "An Evaluation of Nonsampling Errors in the Monthly Retail Trade
    Sales Data"
    Annual Meeting, American Statistical Association, St. Louis, MO
    (August 1974), paper presentation.

Waldo, Charles and Fuller, Dennis
    "Just How Good Is the Survey of Buying Power"
    Journal of Marketing, Vol. 41 (October 1977), pp. 64-6.

Walsh, Thomas C. and Schneider, Paula Bucholdt
    "Accuracy of Retrospectively Reporting Work Status and Occupation
    Five Years Ago"
    U.S. Bureau of the Census (1970), unpublished paper E15,3.

101.09 ---------- Unclassified (Secondary Sources)

Menneer, Peter
   "The Cancellation of the 1976 Census of Population: Filling the Gap"
   Journal of the Market Research Society, Vol. 18 (April 1976), pp.
   93-9.

Menneer, P. J.
   "Whither the Census?"
   Journal of the Market Research Society, Vol. 14, No. 2 (1972), pp.
   126-9.

102 -------------------------- DATA BASES --------------------------

102.01 ---------- Guides to Data Banks and Their Use

Dodson, Dick
"Getting Usable Data Out of Databanks"
Admap (July/August 1988), pp. 46-9.

102.02 ---------- Commercial Data Bases

Hagerty, Michael R., Carman, James M., and Russell, Gary J.
"Estimating Elasticities With PIMS Data: Methodological Issues and
Substantive Implications"
Journal of Marketing Research, Vol. XXV (February 1988), pp. 1-9.

Haggblom, Diane
"States and Metros on Diskette"
American Demographics, Vol. 7 (February 1985), pp. 38-41.

Hochhauser, Richard
"Market Survey, Database or a Combination of Both?"
Direct Marketing, Vol. 49 (October 1986), pp. 136-43.

Howells, Robert
"Hunting Down Prospects for Your Marketing Database"
Industrial Marketing Digest, Vol. 12 (Fourth Quarter 1987), pp.
93-102.

Johnson, Carol Tanzer
"Information Brokers: New Breed With Access to Secondary Research"
Marketing News, Vol. 21 (February 27, 1987), p. 14.

Wiersema, Fred D.
"Hidden Information in Your Database"
Direct Marketing, Vol. 49 (October 1986), pp. 144-9.

102.03 ---------- Public or Shared Bases

Daina, Luciano
"Public Data Banks in Europe"
European Research, Vol. 12 (April 1984), pp. 84-7.

Fienberg, Stephen E. and Straf, Miron L. (editors)
Sharing Research Data
(Washington, DC: National Academy Press, 1985), 225 pp.

Treasure, John
"The Availability and Use of Public Statistics in the UK"
Journal of the Market Research Society, Vol. 31 (October 1989), pp.
581-89.

Vaughn, Ronald L.
"Demographic Data Banks: A New Management Resource"
Business Horizons, Vol. 27 (November/December 1984), pp. 38-42.

Zarozny, Sharon and Horner, Monica
The Federal Data Base Finder, 1984-85 Edition
(Potomac, MD: Information USA), 368 pp.

102.04 ---------- Descriptions, Uses of the PIMS Data Bases

Anderson, Carl R. and Paine, Frank T.
"PIMS: A Re-Examination"
Academy of Management Review, Vol. 3 (July 1978), pp. 602-11.

Buzzell, Robert D. and Gale, Bradley T.
The PIMS Principles: Linking Strategy to Performance
(New York: The Free Press, 1987), 322 pp.

Buzzell, Robert D. and Wiersema, F. D.
"Successful Share-Building Strategies"
Harvard Business Review (January-February 1981).

Lubatkin, Michael and Pitts, Michael
"PIMS: Fact or Folklore"
Journal of Business Strategy, Vol. 3 (Winter 1983), pp. 38-43.

Strategic Planning Institute
"PIMS Data Form"
(1979, 1981).

Strategic Planning Institute
The PIMS Program
(Cambridge: Strategic Planning Institute, 1980).

102.05 ---------- Applications Using the PIMS Data Bases

Carpenter, Gregory S.
"Modelling Competitive Marketing Strategies: The Impact of
Marketing-Mix Relationships and Industry Structure"
Marketing Science, Vol. 6 (Spring 1987), pp. 208-21.

Clarke, Kim B. and Griliches, Zvi
"Productivity Growth and R and D at the Business Level: Results From
the PIMS Data Base"
Working Paper 83-03
Harvard Business School (1983).

Farris, Paul W. and Buzzell, Robert D.
"Why Advertising and Promotional Costs Vary: Some Cross-Sectional
Analyses"
Journal of Marketing, Vol. 43 (Fall 1979), pp. 112-22.

Hambrick, Donald C., MacMillan, Ian, and Day, Diana L.
"Strategic Attributes and Performance in the BCG Matrix--A PIMS-Based
Analysis of Industrial Product Businesses"
Academy of Management Journal, Vol. 25 (1982), pp. 510-31.

Hawkins, Del I., Best, Roger J., and Lillis, Charles M.
"The Nature and Measurement of Marketing Productivity in Consumer
Durables Industries: A Firm Level Analysis"
Journal of the Academy of Marketing Science, Vol. 15 (Winter 1987),
pp. 1-8.

Jacobson, Robert and Aaker, David A.
"The Strategic Role of Product Quality"
Journal of Marketing, Vol. 51 (October 1987), pp. 31-44.

Jacobson, Robert and Aaker, David A.
"Is Market Share All That It's Cracked Up to Be?"
Journal of Marketing, Vol. 49 (Fall 1985), pp. 11-22.

MacMillan, Ian C., Hambrick, Donald C., and Day, Diana L.
"The Product Portfolio and Profitability--A PIMS-Based Analysis of
Industrial Products Businesses"
Academy of Management Journal, Vol. 25 (1982), pp. 733-55.

Quelch, John A., Marshall, Cheri T., and Chang, Dae R.
"Structural Determinants of Ratios of Promotion and Advertising to
Sales"
in Jocz, Katherine E. (editor)
Research on Sales Promotion: Collected Papers
(Cambridge, MA: Marketing Science Institute, 1984), pp. 83-105.

Ramanujam, Vasu and Venkatraman, N.
An Inventory and Critique of Strategy Research Using the PIMS
Database"
Academy of Management Review, Vol. 9 (1984), pp. 138-51.

Wind, Yoram and Mahajan, Vijay
"Market Share: Concepts, Findings, and Directions for Future Research"
The Wharton School, University of Pennsylvania (1981), working paper.

Woo, Carolyn Y. and Cooper, Arnold C.
"The Surprising Case for Low Market Share"
Harvard Business Review (November-December 1982), pp. 106-13.

103 ----------------------- CONTENT ANALYSIS -----------------------

See also (sub)heading(s) 81, 86.05, 104, 132.02.

103.01 ---------- Books Re: Content Analysis

Berelson, B.
Content Analysis in Communications Research
(Glencoe, IL: The Free Press, 1952).

Budd, R. W., Thorp, R. K., and Donohew, L.
Content Analysis of Communications
(New York: Macmillan, 1967), 147 pp.

Cronbach, Lee J.
Essentials of Psychological Testing, Third Edition
(New York: John Wiley and Sons, Inc., 1972).

Cronbach, Lee J., Gleser, Goldine C., Nanda, Harinder, and Rajaratnam,
Nageswari
The Dependability of Behavioral Measurements
(New York: John Wiley and Sons, Inc., 1972).

Ferber, R. and Wales, H. G. (editors)
Motivation and Market Behavior
(Homewood, IL: Irwin, 1958).

Flesch, R.
How to Test Readability
(New York: Harper, 1970).

Gerbner, G., Holsti, O. R., Krippendorff, K., Paisley, W. J., and
Stone, P. J. (editors)
The Analysis of Communications Content: Developments in Scientific
Theories and Computer Techniques
(New York: Wiley, 1969).

Gottschalk, Louis A. and Gleser, Goldine C.
The Measurement of Psychological States Through the Content Analysis
of Verbal Behavior
(Berkeley: University of California Press, 1969).

Holsti, O. R.
Content Analysis for the Social Sciences and Humanities
(Reading, MA: Addison-Wesley, 1969).

Kerlinger, F. N.
Foundations of Behavioral Research: Educational and Psychological
Inquiry
(New York: Holt, Rinehart and Winston, 1964).

Krippendorff, Klaus
Content Analysis: An Introduction to Its Methodology
(Beverly Hills, CA: Sage Publications, Inc., 1980).

Lasswell, H. D., Leites, N., and Associates (editors)
Language of Politics: Studies in Quantitative Semantics
(New York: George Steward, 1949).

Lasswell, H. D., Lerner, D., and Pool, I. DeSola
The Comparative Study of Symbols
(Stanford, CA: Stanford University Press, 1952).

Mead, G. H.
Mind, Self, and Society
(Chicago: University of Chicago Press, 1934).

Morris, C.
Signs, Language, and Behavior
(Englewood Cliffs, NJ: Prentice Hall, Inc., 1946).

North, R. C., Holsti, O. R., Zaninovich, M. G., and Zinnes, D. A.
Content Analysis: A Handbook With Applications for the Study of
International Crisis
(Evanston, IL: Northwestern University Press, 1963).

Pool, I. (editor)
Trends in Content Analysis
(Urbana, IL: University of Illinois Press, 1959).

Stone, P. J., Dunphy, D. C., Smith, M. S., Ogilvie, D. M., and
Associates (editors)
The General Inquirer: A Computer Approach to Content Analysis
(Cambridge, MA: The MIT Press, 1966).

Webb, E. J., Campbell, D. T., Schwartz, R. D., and Sechrest, L.
Unobtrusive Measures: Non-Reactive Research in the Social Sciences
(Chicago: Rand McNally, 1966).

Weber, Robert Philip
    Basic Content Analysis
    Quantitative Applications in the Social Sciences, Paper No. 49
    (Beverly Hills, CA: Sage Publications, Inc., 1985), 93 pp.

103.02 ---------- Theory Re: Content Analysis

Berelson, B.
    "Content Analysis"
    in Lindzey, G. (editor)
    Handbook of Social Psychology: Theory and Method, Vol. 1
    (Cambridge, MA: Addison-Wesley, 1954), pp. 488-522.

Bonoma, Thomas V. and Rosenberg, Helen
    "Theory-Based Content Analysis: A Social Influence Perspective for
    Evaluating Group Process"
    (Chicago: Institute for Juvenile Research, 1975).

Cartwright, D. P.
    "Analysis of Qualitative Material"
    in Festinger, L. and Katz, D. (editors)
    Research Methods in the Behavioral Sciences
    (New York: Holt, Rinehart and Winston, 1953), pp. 421-70.

DeWeese, L. C.
    "Computer Content Analysis of Printed Media: A Feasibility Study"
    Public Opinion Quarterly, Vol. 40 (1976), pp. 91-4.

Dunphy, Dexter C., Stone, Philip J., and Smith, Marshall S.
    "The General Inquirer: Further Developments in a Computer System for
    Content Analysis of Verbal Data in the Social Sciences"
    Behavioral Science, Vol. 10 (October 1965), pp. 468-80.

Fearing, F.
    "Human Communication"
    Department of Psychology, University of California (1954),
    unpublished.

Fearing, F.
    "Towards a Psychological Theory of Human Communication"
    Journal of Personality, Vol. 22 (1953), pp. 71-88.

Ferber, Robert
    "Can Consumer Research be Interdisciplinary"
    Journal of Consumer Research, Vol. 4 (December 1977), pp. 189-92.

Guetzkow, Harold
    "Unitizing and Categorizing Problems in Coding Qualitative Data"
    Journal of Clinical Psychology, Vol. 6 (1960), pp. 47-58.

Hendon, Donald W.
    "Mechano-Content Analysis as an Aid in Predicting Effects of
    Advertising on Microcommunications"
    Journal of Applied Psychology, Vol. 59 (1974), pp. 773-5.

Holbrook, Morris B.
    "More on Content Analysis in Consumer Research"
    Journal of Consumer Research, Vol. 4 (December 1977), pp. 176,7.

Holsti, Ole R.
    "Content Analysis"
    in Lindzey, G. and Aronson, E. (editors)
    The Handbook of Social Psychology, Vol. III
    (Reading, MA: Addison-Wesley, 1968), pp. 596-692.

Janis, I. L.
    "Meaning and the Study of Symbolic Behavior"
    Psychiatry, Vol. 6 (1933), pp. 425-39.

Kassarjian, Harold H.
    "Content Analysis in Consumer Research"
    Journal of Consumer Research, Vol. 4 (June 1977), pp. 8-18.

Kracauer, S.
    "The Challenge of Qualitative Content Analysis"
    Public Opinion Quarterly, Vol. 16 (1952), pp. 631-42.

Kranz, Peter
    "Content Analysis by Word Group"
    Journal of Marketing Research, Vol. VII (August 1970), pp. 377-80.

Kranz, Peter
    "What do People do All Day?"
    Behavioral Science, Vol. 15 (May 1970), pp. 286-91.

Markoff, J. G., Shapiro, G., and Wettman, S. R.
"Toward the Integration of Content Analysis and General Methodology"
in Heise, D. R. (editor)
Sociological Methodology
(San Francisco: Jossey-Bass, 1974), pp. 1-58.

Mitchell, R. E.
"The Use of Content Analysis for Explanatory Studies"
Public Opinion Quarterly, Vol. 26 (Summer 1967), pp. 230-41.

Osgood, Charles E., Saporta, S., and Nunnally, J. C.
"Evaluative Assertions Analysis"
Litera, Vol. 3 (1956).

Paisley, W. J.
"Studying Style as Deviation From Encoding Norms"
in Gerbner, G. et al. (editors)
The Analysis of Communications Content: Developments in Scientific
Theories and Computer Techniques
(New York: Wiley, 1969), pp. 133-46.

Pool, I. DeSola
"Trends in Content Analysis Today: A Summary"
in Pool, I. DeSola (editor)
Trends in Content Analysis
(Urbana, IL: The University of Illinois Press, 1959).

Psychological Bulletin
"Technical Recommendations for Psychological Tests and Diagnostic
Techniques"
Psychological Bulletin Supplement (1954), pp. 201-38.

Rosenberg, Helen and Bonoma, Thomas V.
"A Social Influence Rating Method for Group Interaction and Some
Pilot Results on Group Therapy Process"
Personality and Social Psychology Bulletin, Vol. 1 (1974), pp. 259-62.

Rust, Langbourne W.
"Using Test Scores to Guide the Content Analysis of TV Materials"
Journal of Advertising Research, Vol. 25 (October/November 1985), pp.
17-23.

Schutz, W. C.
"On Categorizing Qualitative Data in Content Analysis"
Public Opinion Quarterly, Vol. 22 (1958), pp. 503-15.

Starkweather, J. A. and Decker, J. B.
"Computer Analysis of Interview Content"
Psychological Reports, Vol. 15 (1964), pp. 875-82.

Stone, P. J., Bales, R. F., Namenwirth, J. Z., and Ogilvie, D. M.
"The General Inquirer: A Computer System for Content Analysis and
Retrieval Based on the Sentence as a Unit of Information"
Behavioral Science, Vol. 7 (October 1962), pp. 484-94.

Stone, P. J., Dunphy, D. C., and Bernstein, A.
"Content Analysis Applications at Simulmatics"
American Behavioral Scientist, Vol. 8 (1965), pp. 23-8.

Stone, Philip J., Smith, Marshall S. et al.
"Improved Quality of Content Analysis Categories, Computerized
Disambiguation Rules for High Frequency English Words"
National Conference on Content Analysis, University of Pennsylvania
(November 1971), paper presentation.

Webb, E. J. and Roberts, K. H.
"Unconventional Uses of Content Analysis in Social Science"
in Gerbner, G. et al. (editors)
The Analysis of Communications Content: Development in Scientific
Theories and Computer Techniques
(New York: Wiley, 1969), pp. 319-32.

Wheeler, David R.
"Content Analysis: An Analytical Technique for International
Marketing Research"
International Marketing Review, Vol. 8 (Winter 1988), pp. 34-40.

Wright, P. and Barbour, F.
"The Relevance of Decision Process Models in Structuring Persuasive
Messages"
Communications Research, Vol. 2 (1975), pp. 246-59.

103.03 ---------- Empirical Evaluations of Content Analysis

Kaplan, Abraham and Goldsen, J. M.
"The Reliability of Content Analysis Categories"
in Lasswell, H. D., Leites, N., and Associates (editors)
Language of Politics: Studies in Quantitative Semantics
(New York: George Steward, 1949), pp. 83-112.

Schutz, W. C.
"Reliability, Ambiguity and Content Analysis"
Psychological Review, Vol. 59 (1959), pp. 119-29.

Scott, William A.
"Reliability of Content Analysis: The Case of Nominal Scale Coding"
Public Opinion Quarterly, Vol. 19 (Fall 1955), pp. 321-5.

103.04 ---------- Theory Re: Language Analysis by Computer

Fleury, Pascal
"Words and Bytes: The Use of Linguistics in Qualitative Studies"
Proceedings, ESOMAR Congress, Lisbon (1988), pp. 59-77.

103.05 ---------- Theory Re: Readability Measurement

Dale, E. and Chall, J. S.
"A Formula for Predicting Readability"
Educational Research Bulletin, Vol. 27 (1948), pp. 11-20.

Flesch, R.
How to Test Readability
(New York: Harper and Row, 1951).

103.06 ---------- Applications of Readability Measurement

Shuptrine, F. Kelly and McVicker, Daniel D.
"Readability Levels of Magazine Ads"
Journal of Advertising Research, Vol. 21 (October 1981), pp. 45-51.

103.07 ---------- Applications of Content Analysis in Advertising

Andren, Gunnar
"The Rhetoric of Advertising"
Journal of Communication, Vol. 30 (August 1980), pp. 74-80.

Armstrong, Gary M.
"An Evaluation of the Children's Advertising Review Unit"
Journal of Public Policy and Marketing, Vol. 3 (1984), pp. 38-55.

Belk, Russell W. and Pollay, Richard W.
"Materialism and Status Appeals in Japanese and U.S. Print
Advertising: An Historical and Cross-Cultural Content Analysis"
International Marketing Review, Vol. 2 (December 1985), pp. 38-47.

Belk, Russell W. and Pollay, Richard W.
"Images of Ourselves: The Good Life in Twentieth Century Advertising"
Journal of Consumer Research, Vol. 11 (March 1985), pp. 887-97.

Belkaoui, A. and Belkaoui, Janice M.
"A Comparative Analysis of the Roles Portrayed by Women in Print
Advertisements: 1958, 1970, 1972"
Journal of Marketing Research, Vol. XIII (May 1976), pp. 168-72.

Beltramini, Richard F. and Blasko, Vincent J.
"An Analysis of Award-Winning Advertising Headlines"
Journal of Advertising Research, Vol. 26 (April/May 1986), pp. 48-52.

Berkman, Dave
"Advertising in 'Ebony' and 'Life': Negro Aspirations vs. Reality"
Journalism Quarterly, Vol. 40 (Winter 1963), pp. 53-64.

Boyenton, W. H.
"The Negro Turns to Advertising"
Journalism Quarterly, Vol. 42 (1965), pp. 227-35.

Bush, R. F., Solomon, P. J., and Hair, J. F., Jr.
"There are More Blacks in TV Commercials"
Journal of Advertising Research, Vol. 17 (1977), pp. 21-5.

Bush, R. F., Solomon, P. J., and Hair, J. F., Jr.
"A Content Analysis of the Portrayal of Black Models in Television
Advertising"
Proceedings, American Marketing Association (1974), pp. 427-30.

Cosse, Thomas J. and Swan, John E.
  "Power and Safety Appeals in Auto Advertising"
  Journal of Advertising Research, Vol. 21 (August 1981), pp. 27-34.

Courtney, A. E. and Lockeretz, S. W.
  "An Analysis of the Roles Portrayed by Women in Magazine
  Advertisements"
  Journal of Marketing Research, Vol. VIII (February 1971), pp. 92-5.

Cox, K. K.
  "An Audit of Integrated Advertisements in Television, Magazines, and
  Newspapers"
  Meeting of the Western Psychological Association, Los Angeles (1970),
  paper presentation.

Cox, K. K.
  "Changes in Stereotyping of Negros and Whites in Magazine
  Advertisements"
  Public Opinion Quarterly, Vol. 33 (1969-70), pp. 603-6.

Dominick, J. R. and Greenberg, B. S.
  "Three Seasons of Blacks on Television"
  Journal of Advertising Research, Vol. 10 (1970), pp. 21-7.

Dornbush, S. M. and Hickman, L. C.
  "Other-Directedness in Consumer-Goods Advertising: A Test of
  Riesman's Historical Theory"
  Social Forces, Vol. 38 (1959), pp. 389-94.

Evans, F. B.
  "Motivation Research and Advertising Readership"
  Journal of Business, Vol. 30 (April 1957), pp. 141-6.

Ferguson, R. D., Jr.
  "The Role of Blacks in Magazine and Television Advertising"
  Boston University (1970), unpublished Master's thesis.

Francher, J. Scott
  "'It's the Pepsi Generation...' Accelerated Aging and the Television
  Commercial"
  International Journal of Aging and Human Development, Vol. 4 (Summer
  1973), pp. 245-55.

Gantz, Walter, Gartenberg, Howard M., and Rainbow, Cindy K.
  "Approaching Invisibility: The Portrayal of the Elderly in Magazine
  Advertisements"
  Journal of Communication, Vol. 30 (Winter 1980), pp. 56-60.

Geizer, R.
  "Advertising in Ebony: 1960 and 1969"
  Journalism Quarterly, Vol. 48 (1971), pp. 131-4.

Gross, Barbera L. and Sheth, Jagdish N.
  "Time-Oriented Advertising: A Content Analysis of United States
  Magazine Advertising, 1890-1988"
  Journal of Marketing, Vol. 53 (October 1989), pp. 76-83.

Hair, J. F., Jr., Solomon, P. J., and Bush, R. F.
  "A Factor Analytic Study of Black Models in Television Commercials"
  Journal of Business, Vol. 5 (1977), pp. 208-15.

Healey, John S., Fisher, Melvyn E., and Healey, Grace F.
  "Advertising Screamers Versus Hummers"
  Journal of Advertising Research, Vol. 26 (December 1986/January
  1987), pp. 43-9.

Healey, John S. and Kassarjian, Harold H.
  "Advertising Substantiation and Advertiser Response: A Content
  Analysis of Magazine Advertisements"
  Journal of Marketing, Vol. 47 (Winter 1983), pp. 107-17.

Hite, Robert E., Schultz, Norman O., and Weaver, Judith A.
  "A Content Analysis of CPA Advertising in National Print Media From
  1979 to 1984"
  Journal of the Academy of Marketing Science, Vol. 16 (Fall 1988), pp.
  1-15.

Jackson, Donald W., Jr., Brown, Stephen W., and Harmon, Robert R.
  "Comparative Magazine Advertisements"
  Journal of Advertising Research, Vol. 19 (December 1979), pp. 21-6.

Jacoby, Jacob, Nelson, Margaret C., and Hoyer, Wayne D.
  "Corrective Advertising and Affirmative Disclosure Statements: Their
  Potential for Confusing and Misleading the Consumer"
  Journal of Marketing, Vol. 46 (Winter 1982), pp. 61-72.

Kassarjian, H. H.
   "Some Evidence on the Changing Image of Black People"
   in Bobo, B. F. and Osborne, A. E. (editors)
   Emerging Issues in Black Economic Development
   (Lexington: Heath-Lexington, 1976), pp. 167-87.

Kassarjian, H. H.
   "The Negro and American Advertising: 1946-1965"
   Journal of Marketing Research, Vol. VI (February 1969), pp. 29-39.

Kassarjian, Harold H. and Kassarjian, Waltraud M.
   "The Impact of Regulation on Advertising: A Content Analysis"
   Journal of Consumer Policy, Vol. 11 (September 1988).

Laczniak, Gene R.
   "Information Content in Print Advertising"
   Journalism Quarterly, Vol. 56 (1979), pp. 324-7,45.

Lucki, Deborah D. and Pollay, Richard W.
   "Content Analysis of Advertising: A Review of the Literature"
   History of Advertising Archives, University of British Columbia
   (1980), working paper.

Lysonski, Steven
   "Role Portrayals in British Magazine Advertisements"
   European Journal of Marketing, Vol. 19, No. 7 (1985), pp. 37-55.

Madden, C. S., Caballero, M. J., and Matsukubo, S.
   "Analysis of Information Content in US and Japanese Magazine
   Advertising"
   Journal of Advertising, Vol. 15, No. 3 (1986), pp. 38-45.

Marlow, Julia, Selnow, Gary, and Blosser, Lois
   "A Content Analysis of Problem-Resolution Appeals in Television
   Commercials"
   Journal of Consumer Affairs, Vol. 23 (Summer 1989), pp. 175-94.

McIntyre, Pat, Hosch, Harmon M., Harris, Richard Jackson, and Novell,
   D. Wayne
   "Effects of Sex and Attitudes Toward Women on the Processing of
   Television Commercials"
   Psychology and Marketing, Vol. 3 (Fall 1986), pp. 181-90.

Merton, R. K.
   Mass Persuasion: The Social Psychology of a War Bond Drive
   (New York: Harper, 1946).

Pollay, Richard W.
   "The Subsiding Sizzle: A Descriptive History of Print Advertising,
   1900-1980"
   Journal of Marketing, Vol. 49 (Summer 1985), pp. 24-37.

Resnik, A. and Stern, B. L.
   "An Analysis of Information Content in Television Advertising"
   Journal of Marketing, Vol. 41 (January 1977), pp. 50-3.

Rice, Marshall D. and Lu, Zaiming
   "A Content Analysis of Chinese Magazine Advertisements"
   Journal of Advertising, Vol. 17, No. 4 (1988).

Shimp, T.
   "Comparison Advertising in National Television Commercials"
   Combined Proceedings, American Marketing Association (1975), pp.
   504-8.

Stern, Bruce L., Krugman, Dean M., and Resnik, Alan
   "Magazine Advertising: An Analysis of Its Information Content"
   Journal of Advertising Research, Vol. 21 (April 1981), pp. 39-44.

Stone, P. J., Dunphy, D. C., and Bernstein, A.
   "The Analysis of Product Image"
   in Stone, P. J. et al. (editors)
   The General Inquirer: A Computer Approach to Content Analysis
   (Cambridge, MA: The MIT Press, 1966).

Taylor, David B.
   "The Information Content of Women's Magazine Advertising in the UK"
   European Journal of Marketing, Vol. 17, No. 5 (1983), pp. 28-32.

Tse, David K., Belk, Russell W., and Zhou, Nan
   "Becoming a Consumer Society: A Longitudinal and Cross-Cultural
   Content Analysis of Print Ads From Hong Kong, the People's Republic
   of China, and Taiwan"
   Journal of Consumer Research, Vol. 15 (March 1989), pp. 457-72.

Venkatesan, M. and Losco, J.
   "Women in Magazine Ads: 1959-1971"
   Journal of Advertising Research, Vol. 5 (1975), pp. 49-54.

Wagner, L. C. and Banos, J. B.
"A Women's Place: A Follow-Up Analysis of the Roles Portrayed by Women
in Magazine Advertisements"
Journal of Marketing Research, Vol. X (May 1973), pp. 213,4.

Wanderer, Aviva
"The Negro in Television Advertising--1970"
Theatre Arts Department, University of California (1970), unpublished
Master's thesis.

Whipple, Thomas W. and Courtney, Alice E.
"How to Portray Women in TV Commercials"
Journal of Advertising Research, Vol. 20 (April 1980), pp. 53-9.

Ybarra, F. M.
"Advertising to the Nontechnical Graduate in a College Newspaper"
Graduate School of Business Administration, University of California,
Berkeley (1970), unpublished Master's thesis.

103.08 ---------- Applications of Content Analysis Outside Advertising

Angelmar, Reinhard and Stern, Louis W.
"Development of a Content Analytic System for Analysis of Bargaining
Communication in Marketing"
Journal of Marketing Research, Vol. XV (February 1978), pp. 93-102.

Arnheim, R.
"The World of the Daytime Serial"
in Lazarsfeld, P. F. and Stanton, F. N. (editors)
Radio Research: 1942-1943
(New York: Duell, Sloan, and Pearce, 1976), pp. 34-85.

Barcus, Francis E.
"A Content Analysis of Trends in Sunday Comics 1900-1959"
Journalism Quarterly, Vol. 38, No. 2 (1961), pp. 171-80.

Belk, Russell W.
"Material Values in the Comics: A Content Analysis of Comic Books
Featuring Themes of Wealth"
Journal of Consumer Research, Vol. 14 (June 1987), pp. 26-42.

Bennett, Edward M., Alpert, R., and Goldstein, A. G.
"Communications Through Limited Response Questioning"
Public Opinion Quarterly, Vol. 18 (1954), pp. 303-6.

Berelson, B. and Salter, P. J.
"Majority and Minority Americans: An Analysis of Magazine Fiction"
Public Opinion Quarterly, Vol. 10 (1946), pp. 168-90.

Bettman, James R. and Weitz, Barton A.
"Attributions in the Board Room: Causal Reasoning in Corporate Annual
Reports"
Administrative Science Quarterly, Vol. 28 (June 1983), pp. 165-83.

Carey, J. T.
"Changing Courtship Patterns in the Popular Song"
American Journal of Sociology, Vol. 74 (1968), pp. 720-31.

DeFleur, M. L.
"Occupational Roles as Portrayed on Television"
Public Opinion Quarterly, Vol. 28 (1964), pp. 57-74.

Farley, John U. and Swinth, R. L.
"Effects of Choice and Sales Messages on Customer-Salesman
Interaction"
Journal of Applied Psychology, Vol. 52 (April 1967), pp. 107-10.

Friedman, Monroe
"Commercial Influences in the Lyrics of Popular American Music of the
Postwar Era"
Journal of Consumer Affairs, Vol. 20 (Winter 1986), pp. 193-213.

Friedman, Monroe and Rees, Jennifer
"A Behavioral Science Assessment of Selected Principles of Consumer
Education"
Journal of Consumer Affairs, Vol. 22 (Winter 1988), pp. 284-302.

Garret, Dennis E.
"The Effectiveness of Marketing Policy Boycotts: Environmental
Opposition to Marketing"
Journal of Marketing, Vol. 51 (April 1987), pp. 46-57.

Greenberg, B. S. and Kahn, S.
"Blacks in Playboy Cartoons"
Journalism Quarterly, Vol. 48 (1971), pp. 557-60.

Harvey, J.
"The Content Characteristics of Best-Selling Novels"
Public Opinion Quarterly, Vol. 17 (1953), pp. 91-114.

Hayes, Radar
   "Determining the Consumer Information Content of Newspapers: A
   Proposed Analytical Framework and Illustrative Application"
   Journal of Consumer Affairs, Vol. 23 (Summer 1989), pp. 127-44.

Helgeson, James G., Kluge, E. Alan, Mager, John, and Taylor, Cheri
   "Trends in Consumer Behavior Literature: A Content Analysis"
   Journal of Consumer Research, Vol. 10 (March 1984), pp. 449-54.

Hite, Robert E., Bellizzi, Joseph A., and Fraser, Cynthia
   "A Content Analysis of Ethical Policy Statements Regarding Marketing
   Activities"
   Journal of Business Ethics, Vol. 7 (October 1988).

Horton, D.
   "The Dialogue of Courtship in Popular Songs"
   American Journal of Sociology Vol. 62 (1957), pp. 569-78.

Janis, I. L. and Fadner, R.
   "The Coefficient of Imbalance"
   in Lasswell, H. D., Leites, N., and Associates (editors)
   Language of Politics: Studies in Quantitative Semantics
   (New York: George Steward, 1949), pp. 153-69.

Johns-Heine, P. and Garth, H. H.
   "Values in Mass Periodical Fiction, 1921-1940"
   Public Opinion Quarterly, Vol. 13 (1949), pp. 105-13.

Kassarjian, Harold H.
   "Males and Females in the Funnies: A Content Analysis"
   in Pitts, Robert E. and Woodside, Arch G. (editors)
   Values and Consumer Psychology
   (Lexington, MA: Lexington Books, 1984), pp. 87-109.

Kassarjian, Harold H.
   "Social Values and the Sunday Comics: A Content Analysis"
   (in Bagozzi, Richard P. and Tybout, Alice M. (editors)
   Advances in Consumer Research, Volume Ten
   (Ann Arbor, MI: Association for Consumer Research, 1983), pp. 434-8.

Kracauer, S.
   From Caligari to Hitler: A Psychological History of the German Film
   (Princeton, NJ: Princeton University Press, 1947).

Lacho, K. J., Stearns, G. K., and Villere, M. F.
   "An Analysis of the Readability of Marketing Journals"
   Combined Proceedings, American Marketing Association (1975), pp.
   489-97.

Leong, Siew Meng, Busch, Paul S., and John, Deborah Roedder
   "Knowledge Bases and Salesperson Effectiveness: A Script-Theoretic
   Analysis"
   Journal of Marketing Research, Vol. XXVI (May 1989), pp. 164-78.

Makinson, J. and Welge, B.
   The Content Analysis of Recruitment Appeals
   Graduate School of Business Administration, University of California,
   Los Angeles (1970), unpublished.

McDonough, J. J.
   "One Day in the Life of Ivan Denisovich: A Study of the Structural
   Requisites of Organization"
   Human Relations, Vol. 28 (1975), pp. 295-328.

Merritt, R. L.
   "Public Opinion in Colonial America: Content Analyzing the Colonial
   Press"
   Public Opinion Quarterly, Vol. 27 (1963), pp. 365-71.

Roberts, C.
   "The Portrayal of Blacks on Network Television"
   Journal of Broadcasting, Vol. 15 (1970-71), pp. 45-53.

Roberts, D. F., Sikorski, L. A., and Paisley, W. J.
   "Letters in Mass Magazines as Outcroppings of Public Concern"
   Journalism Quarterly, Vol. 46 (1969), pp. 743-52.

Rudd, Joel and Buttolph, Vicki L.
   "Consumer Curriculum Materials: The First Content Analysis"
   Journal of Consumer Affairs, Vol. 21 (Summer 1987), pp. 108-21.

Shuey, A. M., King, M., and Griffith, B.
   "Stereo-Typing of Negros and Whites: An Analysis of Magazine Pictures"
   Public Opinion Quarterly, Vol. 17 (1953), pp. 281-7.

Spiegelman, M., Terwilliger, C., and Fearing, F.
   "The Content of Comics: Goals and Means to Goals of Comic Strip
   Characters"
   Journal of Social Psychology, Vol. 37 (1953), pp. 189-203.

Spiegelman, M., Terwilliger, C., and Fearing, F.
  "The Content of Comic Strips: A Study of a Mass Medium of
  Communication"
  Journal of Social Psychology, Vol. 36 (1952), pp. 37-57.

Spiggle, Susan
  "Measuring Social Values: A Content Analysis of Sunday Comics and
  Underground Comix"
  Journal of Consumer Research, Vol. 13 (June 1986), pp. 100-13.

Spranger, E. (translated by Pigors, P. J.)
  Types of Men
  (Halle, East Germany: Max Niemeyer Verlag, 1928).

Wayne, I.
  "American and Soviet Themes and Values: A Content Analysis of
  Pictures in Popular Magazines"
  Public Opinion Quarterly, Vol. 21 (1956), pp. 314-20.

Woodside, A. G.
  "A Shopping List Experiment of Beer Brand Images"
  Journal of Applied Psychology, Vol. 56 (1972), pp. 512,3.

Zimmer, Mary R. and Golden, Linda L.
  "Impressions of Retail Stores: A Content Analysis of Consumer Images"
  Journal of Retailing, Vol. 64 (Fall 1987), pp. 265-293.

104 -------------------- SCRIPT OR FRAME ANALYSIS -------------------
        See also (sub)heading(s) 80, 81, 103.

104.01 ---------- Books Re: Script or Frame Analysis

Mandler, Jean Matter
    Stories, Scripts, and Scenes: Aspects of Schema Theory
    (Hillsdale, NJ: Lawrence Erlbaum Associates, 1984).

Schank, Robert C. and Abelson, Robert P.
    Scripts, Plans, Goals, and Understanding: An Inquiry Into Human
    Knowledge Structures
    (Hillsdale, NJ: Lawrence Erlbaum Associates, 1977).

104.02 ---------- Theory Re: Use of Games for Primary Data Collection

Pruitt, Dean G. and Kimmel, Melvin J.
    "Twenty Years of Experimental Gaming: Critique, Synthesis, and
    Suggestions for Future Research"
    Annual Review of Psychology, Vol. 28 (1977), pp. 363-92.

104.03 ---------- Theory Re: Script/Frame Elicitation and Analysis

Abelson, Robert P.
    "Psychological Status of the Script Concept"
    American Psychologist, Vol. 36 (July 1981), pp. 715-29.

Abelson, Robert P.
    "Script Processing in Attitude Formation"
    in Carroll, John I. and Payne, John W. (editors)
    Cognition and Social Behavior
    (Hillsdale, NJ: Lawrence Erlbaum Associates, 1976), pp. 33-45.

Anderson, Craig A.
    "Imagination and Expectation: The Effect of Imagining Behavioral
    Scripts on Personal Intentions"
    Journal of Personality and Social Psychology, Vol. 45, No. 2 (1983),
    pp. 293-305.

Bower, Gordon H., Black, John B., and Turner, Terrence J.
    "Scripts in Memory for Texts"
    Cognitive Psychology, Vol. 11, No. 2 (1979), pp. 177-220.

Graesser, Arthur C., Gordon, Sallie E., and Sawyer, John D.
    "Recognition Memory for Typical and Atypical Actions in Scripted
    Activities: Tests of a Script Pointer Plus Tag Hypothesis"
    Journal of Verbal Learning and Verbal Behavior, Vol. 18 (June 1979),
    pp. 319-32.

Graesser, Arthur C., Woll, S. B., Kowalski, D. J., and Smith, D. A.
    "Memory for Typical and Atypical Actions in Scripted Activities"
    Journal of Experimental Psychology: Human Learning and Memory, Vol. 6
    (September 1980), pp. 503-15.

John, George and Whitney, John C.
    "An Empirical Investigation of the Serial Structure of Scripts"
    in Walker, Bruce J. et al. (editors)
    AMA Educators' Proceedings
    (Chicago: American Marketing Association, 1982), pp. 75-9.

Lakshmi-Ratan, R. A. and Iyer, Easwar S.
    "Similarity Analysis of Cognitive Scripts"
    Journal of the Academy of Marketing Science, Vol. 16 (Summer 1988),
    pp. 36-42.

Leigh, Thomas W.
    "Cognitive Selling Scripts and Sales Training"
    Journal of Personal Selling and Sales Management, Vol. 7 (August
    1987), pp. 39-48.

Leigh, Thomas W. and Rethans, Arno J.
    "Script-Theoretic Analysis of Industrial Purchasing Behavior"
    Journal of Marketing, Vol. 48 (Fall 1984), pp. 22-32.

Martin, Joanne
    "Stories and Scripts in Organizational Settings"
    in Hastdorf, A. and Izen, A. (editors)
    Cognitive Social Psychology
    (New York: Elsevier North Holland, 1982), pp. 225-305.

Whitney, John C. and John, George
    "An Experimental Investigation of Intrusion Errors in Memory for
    Script Narratives"
    in Tybout, Alice M. and Bagozzi, Richard P. (editors)
    Advances in Consumer Research, Volume 10
    (Ann Arbor, MI: Association for Consumer Research, 1983), pp. 661-6.

Yarnell, Steven M.
"Frame Analysis"
Psychology and Marketing, Vol. 2 (Spring 1985), pp. 31-9.

104.04 ---------- Evaluations of Script/Frame Analysis Methodology

Leigh, Thomas W. and Rethans, Arno J.
"Experiences With Script Elicitation Within Consumer Decision Making
Contexts"
in Bagozzi, R. M. and Tybout, Alice M. (editors)
Advances in Consumer Research, Volume Ten
(Ann Arbor, MI: Association for Consumer Research, 1983).

Rittenburg, Terri L. and Mittelstaedt, Robert A.
"Validation of the Serial Ordering of a Sales Encounter Script"
in Lusch, Robert F., et al. (editors)
1985 AMA Educators' Proceedings
(Chicago: American Marketing Association, 1985), pp. 16-20.

Smith, Ruth Ann and Houston, Michael J.
"A Psychometric Assessment of Measures of Scripts in Consumer Memory"
Journal of Consumer Research, Vol. 12, No. 2 (1985), pp. 214-24.

104.05 ---------- Script/Frame Analysis Applications

Andersen, Kristi and Thorson, S.
"How Ohioans See the Energy Crisis: The Role of 'Frames'"
Meetings of the Western Social Science Association, San Francisco
(1981), paper presentation.

Bozinoff, Lorne
"A Script Theoretic Approach to Information Processing: An Energy
Conservation Application"
in Mitchell, Andrew (editor)
Advances in Consumer Research, Volume Nine
(Ann Arbor, MI: Association for Consumer Research, 1982).

Bozinoff, Lorne and Roth, Victor J.
"Recognition Memory for Script Activities: An Energy Conservation
Application"
in Bagozzi, Richard M. and Tybout, Alice M. (editors)
Advances in Consumer Research, Volume Ten
(Ann Arbor, MI: Association for Consumer Research, 1983).

Gioia, Dennis A. and Manz, Charles C.
"Linking Cognition and Behavior: A Script Processing Interpretation
of Vicarious Learning"
Academy of Management Review, Vol. 10 (1985), pp. 527-39.

Iyer, Easwar S.
"Unplanned Purchasing: Knowledge of Shopping Environment and Time
Pressure"
Journal of Retailing, Vol. 65 (Spring 1989), pp. 40-57.

Iyer, Easwar S.
Impact of Time Pressure and Prior Knowledge of the Store Environment
on In-Store Information Processing and Purchase Patterns
University of Pittsburgh (1984) unpublished doctoral dissertation.

Iyer, Easwar S. and Park, C. Whan
"Effects of Time Pressue and Prior Knowledge of Store Environment on
Grocery Purchasing Behavior"
University of Massachusetts (1986), working paper.

Leigh, Thomas W. and McGraw, Patrick F.
"Mapping the Procedural Knowledge of Industrial Sales Personnel: A
Script-Theoretic Investigation"
Journal of Marketing, Vol. 53 (January 1989), pp. 16-34.

Leigh, Thomas W. and Rethans, Arno J.
"Consumer Scripts for Insurance Salesperson Behavior in Sales
Encounters"
in Jacoby, J. and Craig, C. S. (editors)
Personal Selling: Theory, Research and Practice
(Lexington, MA: D. C. Heath, 1984).

Rethans, Arno J. and Taylor, Jack L., Jr.
"A Script Theoretic Analysis of Consumer Decision Making"
in Walker, Bruce J. et al. (editors)
AMA Educators' Proceedings
(Chicago: American Marketing Association, 1982), pp. 71-4.

105 ---------------------- COMPUTER SIMULATION ----------------------
        See also (sub)heading(s) 6.04, 106.

105.01 ---------- Books Re: Computer Simulation

Alderson, Wroe and Green, P. E.
    Planning and Problem Solving in Marketing
    (Homewood, IL: Richard D. Irwin, Inc., 1964), Chapter 8.

Amstutz, Arnold E.
    Computer Simulation of Competitive Market Response
    (Cambridge, MA: The Massachusetts Institute of Technology Press,
    1970), 457 pp.

Balderston, F. E. and Hoggatt, Austin C.
    Simulation of Market Processes
    (Berkeley, CA: Institute of Business and Economic Research,
    University of California, 1962).

Bonini, Charles P.
    Simulation of Information and Decision Systems in the Firm
    (Englewood Cliffs, NJ: Prentice-Hall, 1963), 160 pp.

Bush, Ronald F. and Brobst, Bob
    Marketing Simulation: Analysis for Decision Making
    (New York: Harper and Row, 1979), 144 pp.

Dutton, John M. and Starbuck, William H.
    Computer Simulation of Human Behavior
    (New York: John Wiley and Sons, 1971), 708 pp.

Forrester, J. W.
    Industrial Dynamics
    (New York: John Wiley and Sons, Inc., 1962).

Hammersley, J. M. and Handscomb, D. C.
    Monte Carlo Methods
    (London, EN: John Wiley and Sons, Inc., 1964), 178 pp.

Kleijnen, J. P. C.
    Statistical Techniques in Simulation, Part II
    (New York: Marcel Dekker, Inc., 1975).

Mize, Joe H. and Cox, J. Grady
    Essentials of Simulation
    (Englewood Cliffs, CA: Prentice-Hall, Inc., 1968), 234 pp.

Naylor, Thomas H. (editor)
    Simulation Models in Corporate Planning
    (New York: Holt, Rinehart and Winston, 1979), 294 pp.

Naylor, Thomas H.
    Computer Simulation Experiments With Models of Economic Systems
    (New York, NY: John Wiley and Sons, 1971), 502 pp.

Pessemier, Edgar A.
    Simulation Methods as an Aid to Designing Market Map Studies: A
    Managerial Review
    (Cambridge, MA: Marketing Science Institute, 1979).

Preston, L. E. and Collins, N. R.
    Studies in a Simulated Market
    (Berkeley: Institute of Business and Economic Research, University of
    California, 1966), 180 pp.

Ripley, B. D.
    Stochastic Simulation
    (New York: John Wiley and Sons, Inc., 1987).

Schmidt, J. W. and Taylor, R. E.
    Simulation and Analysis of Industrial Systems
    (Homewood, IL: Richard D. Irwin, 1970).

105.02 ---------- Theory Re: Monte Carlo Simulation

Acito, Franklin and Anderson, Ronald D.
    "On Simulation Methods for Investigating Structural Modeling"
    Journal of Marketing Research, Vol. XXI (February 1984), pp. 107-12.

Arabie, Phipps
    "Concerning Monte Carlo Evaluations of Nonmetric Multidimensional
    Scaling: Recovery of Metric Information"
    Psychometrika, Vol. 35 (December 1970), pp. 455-73.

Balderston, F. E. and Hoggatt, A. C.
    Simulation of Marketing Processes (Monograph)
    IBER Special Publications Series, Number 1
    (Berkeley: University of California, Institute of Business and
    Economics, 1962).

Box, George E. P. and Muller, M. E.
  "A Note on the Generation of Random Normal Deviates"
  Annals of Mathematical Statistics, Vol. 29 (January 1958), pp. 610,1.

Chapman, Randall G.
  "A Note on Generating Correlated Data"
  Graduate School of Business, University of Chicago (1981).

Fornell, Claes and Larcker, David F.
  "Misapplications of Simulations in Structural Equation Models: Reply
  to Acito and Anderson"
  Journal of Marketing Research, Vol. XXI (February 1984), pp. 113-7.

Friedman, Lawrence
  "Constructing a Media Simulation Model"
  Journal of Advertising Research, Vol. 10 (August 1970), pp. 33-9.

King, William R.
  "Methodological Simulation in Marketing"
  Journal of Marketing, Vol. 34 (April 1970), pp. 8-13.

Kotler, Philip and Schultz, Randall L.
  "Marketing Simulations: Review and Prospects"
  Journal of Business, Vol. 43 (July 1970), pp. 237-95.

Malcolm, D. G.
  "A Bibliography on the Use of Simulation in Management Analysis"
  Operations Research, Vol. 8 (March-April 1960).

Martin, E. W., Jr.
  "Simulation in Organization Research"
  Business Horizons, Vol. 2 (Fall 1959), pp. 68-77.

Morgenroth, W. M. and Sims, J. T.
  "Simulation: Methods and Applications"
  in Ferber, R. (editor)
  Handbook of Marketing Research
  (New York: McGraw-Hill, 1974).

Moshman, J.
  "The Application of Sequential Estimation to Computer Simulation and
  Monte Carlo Procedures"
  Journal of the Association for Computing Machinery, Vol. 5 (1958),
  pp. 343-52.

Shycon, H. N. and Maffei, R.
  "Simulation--Tool for Better Distribution"
  Harvard Business Review, Vol. 38 (November-December 1960), pp. 65-75.

Wegner, Trevor
  "Simulation as a Market Research Tool With Microcomputer Applications"
  Journal of the Market Research Society, Vol. 25 (October 1983), pp.
  305-20.

Weiss, Doyle L.
  "Simulation for Decision Making in Marketing"
  Journal of Marketing, Vol. 28 (July 1964), pp. 45-50.

Weitz, Harold
  "The Promise of Simulation in Marketing"
  Journal of Marketing, Vol. 31 (July 1967), pp. 28-33.

105.03 ---------- Simulating Variates From Specific Distributions

Fleishman, Allen J.
  "A Method for Simulating Non-Normal Distributions"
  Psychometrika, Vol. 43 (1978), pp. 465-71.

Johnson, D. G. and Welch, W. J.
  "The Generation of Pseudo-Random Correlation Matrices"
  Journal of Statistical Computation and Simulation, Vol. 11 (1980),
  pp. 55-69.

Vale, C. David and Maurelli, Vincent A.
  "Simulating Multivariate Nonnormal Distributions"
  Psychometrika, Vol. 48 (1983), pp. 465-71.

105.04 ---------- Applications of Monte Carlo Simulation

Acito, Franklin and Anderson, Ronald D.
  "A Simulation Study of Factor Score Indeterminacy"
  Journal of Marketing Research, Vol. XXIII (May 1986), pp. 111-8.

Acito, Franklin and Anderson, Ronald D.
  "A Monte Carlo Comparison of Factor Analytical Methods"
  Journal of Marketing Research, Vol. XVII (May 1980), pp. 228-36.

Acito, Franklin, Anderson, Ronald D., and Engledow, Jack L.
"A Simulation Study of Methods for Hypothesis Testing in Factor
Analysis"
Journal of Consumer Research, Vol. 7 (September 1980), pp. 141-50.

Barcikowski, Robert S. and Stevens, James P.
"A Monte Carlo Study of the Stability of Canonical Correlations,
Canonical Weights and Canonical Variate-Variable Correlations"
Multivariate Behavioral Research, Vol. 10 (July 1975), pp. 353-64.

Bass, Frank M. and Leone, Robert P.
"Estimating Micro Relationships From Macro Data: A Comparative Study
of Two Approximations of the Brand Loyal Model Under Temporal
Aggregation"
Journal of Marketing Research, Vol. XXIII (August 1986), pp. 291-7.

Carmone, Frank J., Green, Paul E., and Jain, Arun K.
"Robustness of Conjoint Analysis: Some Monte Carlo Results"
Journal of Marketing Research, Vol. XV (May 1978), pp. 330-3.

Cattin, Philippe and Wittink, Dick R.
"A Monte-Carlo Study of Metric and Non-Metric Estimation Methods for
Multiattribute Models"
Research Paper No. 341
Graduate School of Business, Stanford University (1976).

Colberg, Roger T.
"A Monte Carlo Simulation of Metric Recovery of Conjoint Measurement
Algorithms"
in Research Frontiers in Marketing: Dialogues and Directions, Series
43
(Chicago: American Marketing Association, 1978).

Dempster, A. P., Schatzoff, Martin, and Wermuth, Nancy
"A Simulation Study of Alternatives to Ordinary Least Squares"
Journal of the American Statistical Association, Vol. 72 (March
1977), pp. 77-91.

Graef, Jed and Spence, Ian
"Using Distance Information in the Design of Large Multidimensional
Scaling Experiments"
Psychological Bulletin, Vol. 86 (January 1979), pp. 60-6.

Johnson, Eric J., Meyer, Robert J., and Ghose, Sanjoy
"When Choice Models Fail: Compensatory Models in Negatively
Correlated Environments"
Journal of Marketing Research, Vol. XXVI (August 1989), pp. 255-70.

Kanetkar, Vinay, Weinberg, Charles B., and Weiss, Doyle L.
"Esimating Parameters of the Autocorrelated Current Effects Model
From Temporally Aggregated Data"
Journal of Marketing Research, Vol. XXIII (November 1986), pp. 379-86.

Kanetkar, Vinay, Weinberg, Charles B., and Weiss, Doyle L.
"Recovering Micro Parameters From Aggregate Data for the Koyck and
Brand Loyal Models"
Journal of Marketing Research, Vol. XXIII (August 1986), pp. 298-304.

Keller, Kevin Lane and Staelin, Richard
"Assessing Biases in Measuring Decision Effectiveness and Information
Overload"
Journal of Consumer Research, Vol. 15 (March 1989), pp. 504-8.

Klahr, David
"A Monte Carlo Investigation of the Statistical Significance of
Kruskal's Nonmetric Scaling Procedure"
Psychometrika, Vol. 34 (September 1969), pp. 319-30.

Linn, R. L.
"A Monte Carlo Approach to the Number of Factors Problem"
Psychometrika, Vol. 33 (March 1968), pp. 37-71.

Lissitz, Robert W. and Green, Samuel B.
"Effect of the Number of Scale Points on Reliability: A Monte Carlo
Approach"
Journal of Applied Psychology, Vol. 60 (February 1975), pp. 10-3.

MacCallum, Robert C.
"Recovery of Structure in Incomplete Data by ALSCAL"
Psychometrika, Vol. 44 (March 1978), pp. 69-74.

MacCallum, Robert C. and Cornelius, Edwin T.
"A Monte Carlo Investigation of Recovery of Structure by ALSCAL"
Psychometrika, Vol. 42 (September 977), pp. 401-28.

Malhotra, Naresh K.
"An Approach to the Measurement of Consumer Preferences Using Limited
Information"
Journal of Marketing Research, Vol. XXIII (February 1986), pp. 33-40.

Maggard, Michael J.
"Determining Electronic Point-of-Sale Cash Register Requirements"
Journal of Retailing, Vol. 57 (Summer 1981), pp. 64-86.

Mandeville, Garrett Kile
"A Monte Carlo Investigation of the Adequacy of Standard Analysis of
Variance Test Procedures for Dependent Binary Variates"
University of Minnesota (1969), unpublished doctoral dissertation.

McDonald, G. C. and Galarneau, D. I.
"A Monte Carlo Evaluation of Some Ridge-Type Estimators"
Journal of the American Statistical Association, Vol. 70 (1975), pp.
407-16.

Meyer, Robert J. and Johnson, Eric J.
"Information Overload and the Nonrobustness of Linear Models: A
Comment on Keller and Staelin"
Journal of Consumer Research, Vol. 15 (March 1989), pp. 498-503.

Montanelli, R. G. and Humphreys, L. G.
"Latent Roots of Random Data Correlation Matrices With Squared
Multiple Correlation on the Diagonal: A Monte Carlo Study"
Psychometrika, Vol. 41, No. 3 (1976), pp. 341-8.

Mullet, Gary M. and Karson, Marvin J.
"Percentiles of LINMAP Conjoint Indices of Fit for Various Orthogonal
Arrays: A Simulation Study"
Journal of Marketing Research, Vol. XXIII (August 1986), pp. 286-90.

Sherman, C. R.
"Nonmetric Multidimensional Scaling: A Monte Carlo Study of the Basic
Parameters"
Psychometrika, Vol. 37 (September 1972), pp. 323-55.

Spence, Ian
"Monte Carlo Simulation Studies"
Applied Psychological Measurement, Vol. 7 (Fall 1983), pp. 405-26.

Vanhonacker, Wilfried R.
"Estimating an Autoregressive Current Effects Model of Sales Response
When Observations are Aggregated Over Time: Least Squares Versus
Maximum Likelihood"
Journal of Marketing Research, Vol. XXV (August 1988), pp. 301-7.

Wiley, James B. and Low, James T.
"A Monte Carlo Simulation Study of Two Approaches for Aggregating
Conjoint Data"
Journal of Marketing Research, Vol. XX (November 1983), pp. 405-16.

Wittink, Dick R. and Cattin, Philippe
"Alternative Estimation Methods for Conjoint Analysis: A Monte Carlo
Study"
Journal of Marketing Research, Vol. XVIII (February 1981), pp. 101-6.

105.05 ---------- Unclassified Applications of Computer Simulation

Abelson, R. P. and Bernstein, A.
"A Computer Simulation Model of Community Referendum Controversies"
Public Opinion Quarterly, Vol. 27 (1963), p. 93-122.

Babakus, Emin, Ferguson, Carl E., Jr., and Joreskog, Karl G.
"The Sensitivity of Confirmatory Maximum Likelihood Factor Analysis
to Violations of Measurement Scale and Distributional Assumptions"
Journal of Marketing Research, Vol. XXIV (May 1987), pp. 222-8.

Bernstein, Alex
"Computer Simulation of Media Exposure"
A Report of the Sixth Meeting of the ARF Operations Research
Discussion Group
(New York, NY: Advertising Research Foundation, 1961).

Chapman, Randall G. and Staelin, Richard
"Exploiting Rank Ordered Choice Set Data Within the Stochastic
Utility Model"
Journal of Marketing Research, Vol. XIX (August 1982), pp. 288-301.

Claycamp, H. J. and Amstutz, A. E.
"Behavioral Simulation in Evaluating Alternative Marketing Strategies"
Proceedings: Application of the Sciences in Marketing Management
(Lafayette, IN: Purdue University Conference, 1966).

Day, R. L.
"Simulation of Consumer Preference"
Journal of Advertising Research, Vol. 5 (September 1965), pp. 6-10.

Dillon, William R. and Westin, Stuart
"Scoring Frequency Data for Discriminant Analysis: Perhaps Discrete
Procedures Can be Avoided"
Journal of Marketing Research, Vol. XIX (February 1982), pp. 44-56.

Erickson, Gary M.
  "A Model of Advertising Competition"
  Journal of Marketing Research, Vol. XXII (August 1985), pp. 297-304.

Fornell, Claes and Larcker, David F.
  "Evaluating Structural Equation Models With Unobservable Variables
  and Measurement Error"
  Journal of Marketing Research, Vol. XVIII (February 1981), pp. 39-50.

Fromm, Gary and Taubman, Paul
  Policy Simulations With an Econometric Model
  (Washington, DC: The Brookings Institution, 1968), 179 pp.

Gandz, Jeffrey and Whipple, Thomas W.
  "Making Marketing Research Accountable"
  Journal of Marketing Research, Vol. XIV (May 1977), pp. 202-8.

Gensch, Dennis H.
  "A Computer Simulation Model for Selecting Advertising Schedules"
  Journal of Marketing Research, Vol. VI (May 1969), pp. 203-14.

Gensch, Dennis H.
  "Computer Models in Advertising Media Selection"
  Journal of Marketing Research, Vol. V (November 1968), pp. 414-24.

Grashof, John F.
  "Supermarket Chain Product Mix Decision Criteria: A Simulation
  Experiment"
  Journal of Marketing Research, Vol. VII (May 1970), pp. 235-42.

Hoffman, T. R.
  "Programmed Heuristics and the Concept of Par in Business Games"
  Behavioral Science, Vol. 10 (April 1965), pp. 169-72.

Hora, Stephen C. and Wilcox, James B.
  "Estimation of Error Rates in Several-Population Discriminant
  Analysis"
  Journal of Marketing Research, Vol. XIX (February 1982), pp. 57-61.

Horton, Raymond L.
  "The Effects of Incorrect Specification of the Minkowski Metric: A
  Simulation Experiment"
  Journal of the Academy of Marketing Science, Vol. 3 (Summer-Fall
  1975), pp. 244-58.

Huang, Philip Y., Rees, Loren P., and Taylor, Bernard W.
  "A Simulation Analysis of the Japanese Just-in-Time Technique (With
  Kanbans) for a Multiline, Multistage Production System"
  Decision Sciences, Vol. 14 (July 1983), pp. 326-43.

Kuehn, A. A.
  "Simulation of Consumer Behavior"
  Proceedings of the Business and Economics Statistics Section of the
  American Statistical Association (1965), pp. 39-42.

MacKay, David B.
  "A Microanalytic Approach to Store Location Analysis"
  Journal of Marketing Research, Vol. IX (May 1972), pp. 134-40.

Massy, William F. and Frank, Ronald E.
  "The Study of Consumer Purchase Sequences Using Factor Analysis and
  Simulation"
  Proceedings of the Business and Economic Statistics Section, American
  Statistical Association (1964), pp. 421-21.

Mayer, Charles S.
  Interviewing Costs in Survey Research: A Computer Simulation Study
  (Ann Arbor, MI: University of Michigan, Bureau of Business Research),
  114 pp.

McIntyre, Shelby H., Montgomery, David B., Srinivasan, V., and Weitz,
  Barton A.
  "Evaluating the Statistical Significance of Models Developed by
  Stepwise Regression"
  Journal of Marketing Research, Vol. XX (February 1983), pp. 1-11.

Michael, George C.
  "A Computer Simulation Model for Forecasting Catalog Sales"
  Journal of Marketing Research, Vol. VIII (May 1971), pp. 224-9.

Miller, John K.
  "The Sampling Distribution and a Test for the Significance of the
  Bimultivariate Redundancy Statistic: A Monte Carlo Study"
  Multivariate Behavioral Research, Vol. 10 (April 1975), pp. 233-44.

Morgenroth, W. M.
  "A Method for Understanding Price Determinants"
  Journal of Marketing Research, Vol. I (August 1964), pp. 17-26.

Naylor, Thomas H., Wallace, William H., and Sasser, W. Earl
"A Computer Simulation Model of the Textile Industry"
Journal of the American Statistical Association, Vol. 62 (December
1967), pp. 1338-62.

Naylor, Thomas H., Wertz, Kenneth, and Wonnacott, Thomas H.
"Spectral Analysis of Data Generated by Simulation Experiments With
Econometric Models"
Econometrica, Vol. 37 (April 1969), pp. 333-52.

Pekelman, Dov and Sen, Subrata K.
"Measurement and Estimation of Conjoint Utility Functions"
Journal of Consumer Research, Vol. 5 (March 1979), pp. 263-71.

Platt, W. J. and Maines, N. R.
"Pretest Your Long-Range Plans"
Harvard Business Review, Vol. 37 (January-February 1959), pp. 119-27.

Preston, Lee E. and Collins, Norman R.
Studies in a Simulated Market
(Berkeley, CA: University of California, Institute of Business and
Economic Research, 1966).

Preston, Lee E. and Collins, Norman R.
"The Analysis of Market Efficiency"
Journal of Marketing Research, Vol. III (May 1966), pp. 154-62.

Seaman, Robert L.
"A Simulation Approach to the Analytical Aspects of Business
Acquisition Evaluation"
Sloan School of Management, M.I.T. (1967), unpublished M.S. thesis.

Sharma, Subhash, Durand, Richard M., and Gur-Arie, Oded
"Identification and Analysis of Moderator Variables"
Journal of Marketing Research, Vol. XVIII (August 1981), pp. 291-300.

Stokes, Charles J. and Mintz, Philip
"How Many Clerks on a Floor?"
Journal of Marketing Research, Vol. II (November 1965), pp. 388-93.

Weiss, Doyle L., Weinberg, Charles B., and Windal, Pierre M.
"The Effects of Serial Correlation and Data Aggregation on
Advertising Measurement"
Journal of Marketing Research, Vol. XX (August 1983), pp. 268-79.

105.06 ---------- Computer Programs and Languages for Simulation

Schriber, Thomas J.
Simulation Using GPSS
(New York: John Wiley and Sons, Inc., 1974).

106 --------------- GAMING FOR PRIMARY DATA COLLECTION ---------------
    See also (sub)heading(s) 92, 105.

106.01 ---------- Theory Re: Gaming for Primary Data Collection

Chandler, Jon and Owen, Mike
  "The Role of Gaming Techniques in Understanding Decision Processes"
  Proceedings, Market Research Society Conference (March 1986), pp.
  13-25.

106.02 ---------- Applications Using Games for Primary Data Collection

Campbell, Nigel C. G., Graham, John L., Jolibert, Alain, and Meissner,
  Hans Gunther
  "Marketing Negotiations in France, Germany, the United Kingdom, and
  the United States"
  Journal of Marketing, Vol. 52 (April 1988), pp. 49-62.

Clopton, Stephen W.
  "Seller and Buying Firm Factors Affecting Industrial Buyers'
  Negotiation Behavior and Outcomes"
  Journal of Marketing Research, Vol. XXI (February 1984), pp. 39-53.

Graham, John L.
  "Cross-Cultural Marketing Negotiations: A Laboratory Experiment"
  Marketing Science, Vol. 4 (Spring 1985), pp. 130-46.

Graham, John L., Kim, Dong Ki, Lin, Chi-Yuan, and Robinson, Michael
  "Buyer-Seller Negotiations Around the Pacific Rim: Differences in
  Fundamental Exchange Processes"
  Journal of Consumer Research, Vol. 15 (June 1988), pp. 48-54.

Lewis, S. A. and Fry, W. R.
  "Effects of Visual Access and Orientation on the Discovery of
  Integrative Bargaining Alternatives"
  Organizational Behavior and Human Performance, Vol. 20 (1977), pp.
  75-92.

Neu, Joyce, Graham, John L., and Gilly, Mary C.
  "The Influence of Gender on Behaviors and Outcomes in a Retail
  Buyer-Seller Negotiation Simulation"
  Journal of Retailing, Vol. 64 (Winter 1988), pp. 427-51.

Pruitt, Dean G. and Lewis, Steven A.
  "Development of Integrative Solution in Bilateral Negotiation"
  Journal of Personality and Social Psychology, Vol. 31, No. 4 (1975),
  pp. 621-33.

107 -------------------------- SAMPLING ---------------------------
    See also (sub)heading(s) 33.03, 75.10, 108, 109, 110, 111,
    112, 113, 114, 115, 142.

107.01 ---------- Books Re: Sampling

Cochran, William G.
    Sampling Techniques, Third Edition
    (New York: John Wiley and Sons, Inc., 1977).

Dalenius, T.
    Sampling in Sweden: Contributions to the Methods and Theories of
    Sample Survey Practice
    (Stockholm, Sweden: Almqvist and Wiksell, 1957), 247 pp.

Deming, W. E.
    Some Theory of Sampling
    (New York: Dover Publications, Inc., 1966), 602 pp.

Deming, W. Edwards
    Sample Design in Business Research
    (New York: John Wiley and Sons, 1960).

Dommermuth, William P.
    The Use of Sampling in Marketing Research
    Marketing Research Techniques Series, No. 3
    (Chicago: American Marketing Association, 1975), 37 pp.

Hajek, Jaroslav
    Sampling From a Finite Population
    (New York: Marcel Dekker, Inc., 1981), 264 pp.

Hansen, M. H., Hurwitz, W. N., and Madow, W. G.
    Sample Survey Methods and Theory, Vols. I and II
    (New York: John Wiley and Sons, Inc., 1953).

Hyman, H.
    Survey Design and Analysis
    (Glencoe, IL: Free Press, 1965), 424 pp.

Jaeger, Richard M.
    Sampling in Education and the Social Sciences
    (New York: Longman, 1984), 352 pp.

Johnson, Norman and Smith, Harry, Jr. (editors)
    New Developments in Survey Sampling
    (New York: John Wiley and Sons, Inc., 1969).

Kalton, Graham
    Introduction to Survey Sampling
    (Beverly Hills, CA: Sage Publications, Inc.).

Kish, Leslie
    Statistical Design for Research
    (New York: John Wiley and Company, 1987), 250 pp.

Kish, L.
    Survey Sampling
    (New York: John Wiley and Sons, Inc., 1965).

Mendenhall, William, Ott, Lyman, and Schaeffer, Richard L.
    Elementary Survey Sampling
    (Belmont, CA: Wadsworth, 1971), 247 pp.

Namias, Jean
    Handbook of Selected Sample Surveys in the Federal Government
    (New York: St. John's University Press, 1969), 310 pp.

Raj, Des
    Sampling Theory
    (New York: McGraw-Hill Book Co., Inc., 1968).

Rosenthal, Robert and Rosnow, Ralph L.
    The Volunteer Subject
    (New York: Wiley-Interscience, 1975), 266 pp.

Schaeffer, Richard L., Mendenhall, William, and Ott, Lyman
    Elementary Survey Sampling, Second Edition
    (North Scituate, MA: Duxbury Press, 1978), 278 pp.

Slonim, Morris James
    Sampling
    (New York: Simon and Schuster, 1960), 145 pp.

Stephan, F. F. and McCarthy, P. J.
    Sampling Opinions: An Analysis of Survey Procedure
    (New York: John Wiley and Sons, 1965), 451 pp.

Stopher, Peter R. and Meyburg, Arnim H.
    Surveying Sampling and Multivariate Analysis for Social Scientists
    and Engineers
    (Lexington, MA: Lexington Books, 1979), 408 pp.

Sudman, Seymour
    Applied Sampling
    (New York: Academic Press, 1976), 249 pp.

Sukhatme, P. V. and Sukhatme, B. V.
    Sampling Theory of Surveys With Applications
    (Ames: Iowa State University Press, 1970), 452 pp.

Williams, Bill
    A Sampler on Sampling
    (New York: John Wiley and Sons, Inc., 1978), 254 pp.

World Fertility Survey--Manual on Sample Design
    Basic Documentation No. 3
    (The Hague-Voorburg: International Statistical Institute, March
    1975), 72 pp.

Yates, Frank
    Sampling Methods for Censuses and Surveys
    (New York: Macmillan Publishing Co., Inc., 1981), 458 pp.

107.02 ---------- Overviews, Descriptions of Sampling Practices

Frankel, Martin R.
    "Current Research Practices: General Population Sampling Including
    Geodemographics"
    Journal of the Market Research Society, Vol. 31 (October 1989), pp.
    447-55.

Permut, Steven Eli, Michel, Allen J., and Joseph, Monica
    "The Researcher's Sample: A Review of the Choice of Respondents in
    Marketing Research"
    Journal of Marketing Research, Vol. XIII (August 1976), pp. 278-83.

Rothman, James and Mitchell, Dawn
    "Statisticians can be Creative Too"
    Journal of the Market Research Society, Vol. 31 (October 1989), pp.
    456-66.

107.03 ---------- Theory Re: Sampling

Atkinson, P. L. and Ogden, A. J.
    "Sample Surveys at the Point of Sale: A Case History From the Petrol
    Market"
    Journal of the Market Research Society, Vol. 16 (April 1974), pp.
    69-86.

Bauer, Raymond A.
    "Exploring the Exploratory Sample"
    Harvard Business Review, Vol. 41 (March-April 1963), pp. 128-31.

Boyd, K. T.
    "Sampling Large Populations"
    Market Research Society Conference Paper (1975), pp. 29-35.

Cochran, W. G.
    "Two Recent Areas of Sample Survey Research"
    in Srivastava, J. N. (editor)
    A Survey of Sample Design and Linear Models
    (Amsterdam, Netherlands: North-Holland Publishing Co., 1975), pp.
    101-15.

Cochran, W. G., Mosteller, F., and Tukey, J.
    "Principles of Sampling"
    Journal of the American Statistical Association, Vol. 49 (March
    1954), pp. 13-35.

Cornish, Pym and Marchant, Len
    "A Method of Extending the Coverage of Probability Samples"
    Admap (December 1976), pp. 628,9.

Dalenius, Tore
    "Recent Advances in Sample Survey Theory and Methods"
    Annals of Mathematical Statistics, Vol. 33 (June 1962), pp. 325-49.

Deming, W. E.
    On the Possible Types of Sampling Unit in the Last Stage of Selection
    in a Probability Sample
    (New York: Advertising Research Foundation, 1955), 16 pp.

Deming, W. E.
"On the Distinction Between Enumerative and Analytic Surveys"
Journal of the American Statistical Association, Vol. 48 (June 1953),
pp. 244-55.

Deming, W. E.
"Some Criteria for Judging the Quality of Surveys"
Journal of Marketing, Vol. 12 (October 1947), pp. 145-57.

Deming, W. E. and Glasser, G. J.
"On the Problem of Matching Lists by Samples"
Journal of the American Statistical Association, Vol. 54 (June 1959),
pp. 403-15.

Deming, W. E. and Stuart, A.
"Sample Surveys"
in International Encyclopedia of the Social Sciences
(New York: Macmillan Free Press, 1968).

Ericson, W. A.
"Prior Information"
Journal of the American Statistical Association, Vol. 63 (September
1968), pp. 964-83.

Fellegi, I. P. and Gray, G. G.
"Sampling Errors in Periodic Surveys"
Proceedings, Social Statistics Section, American Statistical
Association (1971).

Ferber, Robert
"What Is the JCR Editorial Policy on Samples and Sample Requirements"
Newsletter, Association for Consumer Research, Vol. 7 (December
1977), p. 16.

Ferber, Robert
"Research by Convenience"
Journal of Consumer Research, Vol. 4 (June 1977), pp. 57,8.

Frankel, Martin R. and Frankel, Lester R.
"Some Recent Developments in Sample Survey Design"
Journal of Marketing Research, Vol. XIV (August 1977), pp. 280-93.

Holmes, C.
"Sample Designs and Their Efficiencies"
Marketing Research Society paper (1976).

Hulbert, James and Lehmann, Donald R.
"A Taxonomy of Noise in Survey Sampling"
Columbia University (1971), working paper.

Kiser, Clyde V.
"Pitfalls in Sampling for Population Study"
Journal of the American Statistical Association (September 1934), p.
251.

Koerner, Roy E.
"The Design Factor--An Underutilised Concept?"
European Research, Vol. 8 (November 1980), pp. 266-72.

Lipstein, Benjamin
"In Defense of Small Samples"
Journal of Advertising Research, Vol. 15 (February 1975), pp. 33-40.

Mahalanobis, P. C.
"On Large-Scale Sample Surveys"
Philosophical Transactions Royal Society, B231 (1964), pp. 329-451.

Payne, S. L.
"Combination of Survey Methods"
Journal of Marketing Research, Vol. I (May 1964), pp. 61,2.

Peterson, P. G. and O'Dell, W. F.
"Selected Sampling Methods in Commercial Research"
Journal of Marketing, Vol. 15 (October 1950), pp. 182-9.

Sam, R. K.
"On Sampling Design in Opinion and Marketing Research"
Public Opinion Quarterly, Vol. 22 (Winter 1958-59), pp. 564-6.

Semon, T. T., Cohen, R., Richmond, S. B., and Stock, J. S.
"Sampling in Marketing Research"
Journal of Marketing, Vol. 23 (January 1959), pp. 263-73.

Slonim, M. J.
"Sampling in a Nutshell"
Journal of the American Statistical Association, Vol. 52 (June 1957),
pp. 143-61.

Stephan, F. F.
   "Sampling"
   American Journal of Sociology, Vol. 55 (January 1950), pp. 371-5.

Stephan, Frederick F.
   "Practical Problems of Sampling Procedure"
   American Sociological Review, Vol. 1 (1936), pp. 569-80.

Sudman, Seymour
   "Bayesian Framework for Sample Design"
   in Ferber, Robert (editor)
   Handbook of Marketing Research
   (New York: McGraw-Hill Book Co., 1974), pp. 2-247-61.

Wasson, Chester R.
   "Common Sense in Sampling"
   Harvard Business Review, Vol. 41 (January-February 1963), pp. 109-14.

Yates, Frank
   "A Review of Recent Statistical Developments in Sampling and Sample
   Surveys"
   Journal of the Royal Statistical Society, A, Vol. 109 (1946), pp.
   12-43.

107.04 ---------- History of Sampling

Cassady, R., Jr.
   "Statistical Sampling Techniques and Marketing Research"
   Journal of Marketing, Vol. 9 (April 1945), pp. 317-41.

Frankel, Martin R. and Frankel, Lester R.
   "Fifty Years of Survey Sampling in the United States"
   Public Opinion Quarterly, Vol. 51 (Winter 1987), pp. S127-38.

Seng, Y. P.
   "Historical Survey of the Development of Sampling Theories and
   Practice"
   Journal of the Royal Statistical Society, Vol. 114 (Part 2, 1951),
   pp. 214-31.

Snedecor, G. W.
   "Design of Sampling Experiments in the Social Sciences"
   Journal of Farm Economics, Vol. 21 (November 1939), pp. 846-55.

Stephan, F. F.
   "History of the Uses of Modern Sampling Procedures"
   Journal of the American Statistical Association, Vol. 43 (March
   1948), pp. 12-39.

107.05 ---------- Theory Re: Cluster Sampling

Backman, C. W.
   "Sampling Mass Media Content: The Use of the Cluster Design"
   American Sociological Review, Vol. 21 (December 1956), pp. 729-33.

Chokel, F. J. and Payne, S. L.
   "A Pitfall in Cluster Samples"
   Journal of Marketing, Vol. 15 (January 1951), pp. 329-31.

Harris, Paul
   "The Effect of Clustering on Costs and Sampling Errors of Random
   Samples"
   Journal of the Market Research Society, Vol. 19 (July 1977), pp.
   112-22.

Hochstim, J. R. and Smith, D. M. K.
   "Area Sampling or Quota Control--Three Sampling Experiments"
   Public Opinion Quarterly, Vol. 12 (Spring 1948), pp. 73-80.

Piper, Lanny L. and Chromy, James R.
   "Design Effects for Alphabetic Cluster Samples"
   Proceedings, Social Statistics Section, American Statistical
   Association (1975), pp. 596-600.

Sudman, Seymour
   "Optimum Cluster Designs Within a Primary Unit Using Combined
   Telephone Screening and Face-to-Face Interviewing"
   Journal of the American Statistical Association, Vol. 73 (June 1978),
   pp. 300-4.

107.06 ---------- Theory Re: Stratified Sampling

Dalenius, Tore
   "The Economics of One-Stage Stratified Sampling"
   Sankhya, Vol. 12 (1952), pp. 351-6.

DuMouchel, William H. and Duncan, Greg J.
"Using Sample Survey Weights in Multiple Regression Analysis of
Stratified Samples"
Journal of the American Statistical Association, Vol. 78 (September
1983), pp. 535-43.

Folks, J. L. and Antle, C. E.
"Optimum Allocation of Sampling Units to Strata When There are R
Responses of Interest"
Annals of Mathematical Statistics, Vol. 60 (March 1965), pp. 225-33.

Showel, M.
"How Much Stratification"
International Journal of Opinion and Attitude Research, Vol. 5
(Summer 1951), pp. 229-40.

Swires-Hennessy, Ed and Thomas, Gwyneth W.
"The Good, the Bad and the Ugly: Multiple Stratified Sampling in the
1986 Welsh House Condition Survey"
Statistical News, No. 79 (November 1987), pp. 24-6.

Yeomans, K. A. and Golder, P. A.
"On the Efficiency of Alternative First Stage Stratification Factors
in a National Sample Design"
Journal of the Market Research Society, Vol. 25 (January 1983), p. 73.

107.07 ---------- Theory Re: Quota Sampling

Hochstim, J. R. and Smith, D. M. K.
"Area Sampling or Quota Control--Three Sampling Experiments"
Public Opinion Quarterly, Vol. 12 (Spring 1948), pp. 73-80.

Mitchell, Paul
"Designing an Optimal Quota Assignment Scheme When Using Independent
Controls"
European Research, Vol. 7 (September 1979), pp. 230-6.

Moser, C. A.
"Quota Sampling"
Journal of the Royal Statistical Society, Vol. 115 (Part 3, 1952),
pp. 411-23.

Moser, C. A. and Stuart, A.
"An Experimental Study of Quota Sampling"
Journal of the Royal Statistical Society, Vol. 116 (Part 4, 1953),
pp. 349-405.

Smith, T. M. F.
"On the Validity of Inferences From Non-Random Samples"
Journal of the Royal Statistical Society, Vol. 146, Series A General
(1983), pp. 394-403.

Sudman, S.
"Probability Sampling With Quotas"
Journal of the American Statistical Association, Vol. 61 (September
1966), pp. 749-71.

Weinberger, Martin
"Getting the Quota Sample Right"
European Research, Vol. 2 (May 1974), pp. 123-5.

Weinberger, Martin
"Getting the Quota Sample Right"
Journal of Advertising Research, Vol. 13 (October 1973), pp. 69-72.

107.08 ---------- Unclassified Specific Sampling Methods

Hornik, Jacob
"An Empirical Synthesis of Experts/Small-Sample Estimates for Applied
Research"
European Research, Vol. 11 (October 1983), pp. 145-50.

Landon, E. L. and Banks, S. K.
"Relative Efficiency of Plus-One Telephone Sampling"
Journal of Marketing Research, Vol. XIV (August 1977).

Lazerwitz, Bernard
"A Sample of a Scattered Group"
Journal of Marketing Research, Vol. I (February 1964), pp. 68-71.

Robson, D. S. and King, A. J.
"Multiple Sampling of Attributes"
Journal of the American Statistical Association, Vol. 47 (June 1952),
pp. 203-15.

107.09 ---------- Screening Methods

Sudman, Seymour
 "Efficient Screening Methods for the Sampling of Geographically
 Clustered Special Populations"
 Journal of Marketing Research, Vol. XXII (February 1985), pp. 20-9.

Sudman, Seymour
 "Optimum Cluster Designs Within a Primary Unit Using Combined
 Telephone Screening and Face-to-Face Interviewing"
 Journal of the American Statistical Association, Vol. 73 (June 1978),
 pp. 300-4.

107.10 ---------- Sampling Rare Populations

Czaja, Ronald F., Snowden, Cecelia B., and Casady, Robert J.
 "Reporting Bias and Sampling Errors in a Survey of a Rare Population
 Using Multiplicity Counting Rules"
 Journal of the American Statistical Association, Vol. 81 (June 1986),
 pp. 411-9.

Kalton, Graham and Anderson, Dallas W.
 "Sampling Rare Populations"
 Journal of the Royal Statistical Association, Vol. 149, Part 1
 (1986), pp. 65-82.

107.11 ---------- Sampling Mobile Populations

Bailey, N. T. J.
 "On Estimating the Size of Mobile Populations From Capture-Recapture
 Data"
 Biometrika, Vol. 38 (1951), pp. 293-6.

Chapman, D. G.
 "The Estimation of Biological Populations"
 Annals of Mathematical Statistics, Vol. 25 (1954), pp. 1-15.

Darroch, J. N.
 "The Multiple-Recapture Census: II"
 Biometrika, Vol. 46 (1959), pp. 336-51.

Darroch, J. N.
 "The Multiple-Recapture Census: I"
 Biometrika, Vol. 45 (1958), pp. 343-59.

Deming, W. Edwards and Keyfitz, Nathan
 "Theory of Surveys to Estimate Total Populations"
 United Nations World Population Conference, Belgrade, Yugoslavia
 (August 30 to September 10, 1965).

Frankel, L. R.
 "The Design of Leisure Time Activity Studies"
 Proceedings, ESOMAR Congress, Cannes, France (September 10-14, 1972).

Fuller, W. A. and Goebel, J. J.
 "On the Estimation of Season Total Number of Different Households
 Utilizing a Park"
 Biometrics, Vol. 34 (1978), pp. 139-41.

Hammersley, J. M.
 "Capture-Recapture Analysis"
 Biometrika, Vol. 40 (1953), pp. 265-78.

Jolly, G. M.
 "Explicit Estimates From Capture-Recapture Data With Both Death and
 Immigration-Stochastic Model"
 Biometrika, Vol. 52 (1965), pp. 225-47.

Leslie, P. H.
 "The Estimation of Population Parameters Obtained by Means of the
 Capture-Recapture Method: II"
 Biometrika, Vol. 39 (1953), pp. 363-88.

Leslie, P. H.
 "The Estimation of Population Parameters Obtained by Means of the
 Capture-Recapture Method: I"
 Biometrika, Vol. 38 (1952), pp. 269-92.

Leslie, P. H., Chitty, Dennis, and Chitty, Helen
 "The Estimation of Population Parameters From Data Obtained by Means
 of the Capture-Recapture Method: III"
 Biometrika, Vol. 40 (1953), pp. 265-78.

Robson, D. S. and Wright, V. J.
 "Estimation of Season Total Number of Different Households Utilizing
 a Park"
 Biometrics, Vol. 33 (1977), pp. 421-5.

Serber, G. A. F.
"The Multi-Sample Single Recapture Census"
Biometrika, Vol. 49 (1962), pp. 339-49.

Sudman, Seymour
"Improving the Quality of Shopping Center Sampling"
Journal of Marketing Research, Vol. XVII (November 1980), pp. 423-31.

107.12 ---------- Sampling Specific Populations

Abeles, N., Iscoe, I., and Brown, W. F.
"Some Factors Influencing the Random Sampling of College Students"
Public Opinion Quarterly, Vol. 18 (Winter 1954-55), pp. 419-23.

Cornish, Pym and Yates, Alan
"Sampling Minorities in Changing Television Markets"
Admap (December 1988), pp. 47,8.

Ericksen, Eugene P.
"Sampling a Rare Population: A Case Study"
Journal of the American Statistical Association, Vol. 71 (December 1976), pp. 816-22.

Hodgson, Peter
"Sampling Racial Minority Groups"
Journal of the Market Research Society, Vol. 17 (April 1975), pp. 104-6.

Hoinville, Gerald
"Carrying Out Surveys Among the Elderly"
Journal of the Market Research Society, Vol. 25 (July 1983), pp. 223-37.

Irelan, L. N.
"The Older Person as a Survey Respondent"
Proceedings of the Social Sciences Section of the American Statistical Association (1969), pp. 347-50.

McIntosh, Andrew R.
"Improving the Efficiency of Sample Surveys in Industrial Markets"
Journal of the Market Research Society, Vol. 17 (October 1975), pp. 219-31.

Miles, G.
"A Method of Sampling Small Minorities"
Journal of the Market Research Society, Vol. 12 (July 1970), pp. 181-9.

Sudman, Seymour
"On Sampling of Very Rare Human Populations"
Journal of the American Statistical Association, Vol. 67 (June 1972), pp. 335-9.

Weiss, Carol H.
"Interviewing Low-Income Respondents"
Welfare in Review, Vol. 4 (October 1966), p. 3.

107.13 ---------- Respondent Selection Within the Household

See also (sub)heading(s) 89.04.

Bryant, Barbara E.
"Respondent Selection in a Time of Changing Household Composition"
Journal of Marketing Research, Vol. XII (May 1975), pp. 129-35.

Czaja, Ronald, Blair, Johnny, and Sebestik, Jutta P.
"Respondent Selection in a Telephone Survey: A Comparison of Three Techniques"
Journal of Marketing Research, Vol. XIX (August 1982), pp. 381-5.

Hagen, Dan E. and Collier, Charlotte Meier
"Must Respondent Selection Procedures for Telephone Surveys be Invasive?"
Public Opinion Quarterly, Vol. 47 (Winter 1983), pp. 547-56.

Hagen, Dan and Collier, Charlotte Meier
"Respondent Selection Procedures for Telephone Surveys: Must They be Invasive"
Annual Meeting, American Association for Public Opinion Research (1982), paper presentation.

Kish, Leslie
"A Procedure for Objective Respondent Selection Within the Household"
Journal of the American Statistical Association, Vol. 44 (September 1949), pp. 380-7.

O'Rourke, Diane and Blair, Johnny
    "Improving Random Respondent Selection in Telephone Surveys"
    Journal of Marketing Research, Vol. XX (November 1983), pp. 428-32.

Paisley, William J. and Parker, Edwin B.
    "A Computer-Generated Sampling Table for Selecting Respondents Within
    Households"
    Public Opinion Quarterly, Vol. 29 (Fall 1965), pp. 431-6.

Salmon, Charles T. and Nichols, John Spicer
    "Respondent Selection Techniques for Telephone Surveys"
    Annual Meeting, Midwest Association of Public Opinion Research
    (1980), paper presentation.

Troldahl, Verling and Carter, Roy E., Jr.
    "Random Selection of Respondents Within Households in Phone Surveys"
    Journal of Marketing Research, Vol. I (May 1964), pp. 71-6.

Weber, Dean and Burt, Richard C.
    Who's Home When
    Working Paper No. 37
    (Washington, DC: U.S. Bureau of the Census, 1972).

107.14 ---------- Mini Surveys

Finsterbusch, Kurt
    "Demonstrating the Value of Mini Surveys in Survey Research"
    Sociological Methods and Research, Vol. 5 (August 1976), pp. 117-36.

Finsterbusch, Kurt
    "The Mini Survey: An Underemployed Research Tool"
    Social Science Research, Vol. 5 (March 1976), pp. 81-93.

107.15 ---------- Coverage Error Estimation and Adjustment

Wolter, Kirk M.
    "Some Coverage Error Models for Census Data"
    Journal of the American Statistical Association, Vol. 81 (June 1986),
    pp. 338-46.

107.16 ---------- Use of Students as Subjects

Albert, Bernard
    "Non-Businessmen as Surrogates for Businessmen in Behavioral
    Experiments"
    Journal of Business, Vol. 40 (April 1967), pp. 203-7.

Ashton, Robert H. and Kramer, Sandra S.
    "Students as Surrogates in Behavioral Accounting Research: Some
    Evidence"
    Journal of Accounting Research, Vol. 18 (Spring 1980), pp. 1-15.

Beltramini, Richard F.
    "Student Surrogates in Consumer Research"
    Journal of the Academy of Marketing Science, Vol. 11 (Fall 1983), pp.
    438-43.

Burnett, John J. and Dunne, Patrick M.
    "An Appraisal of the Use of Student Subjects in Marketing Research"
    Journal of Business Research, Vol. 14 (August 1986), pp. 329-43.

Calder, B. J., Phillips, W. L., and Tybout, A. M.
    "Designing Research for Application"
    Journal of Consumer Research, Vol. 8 (1981), pp. 197-201.

Copeland, Ronald M., Francia, Arthur J., and Strawer, Robert H.
    "Students as Subjects in Behavioral Business Research"
    Accounting Review, Vol. 48 (1973), pp. 365-72.

Cunningham, William H., Anderson, W. T., and Murphy, John H.
    "Are Students Real People?"
    Journal of Business, Vol. 47 (July 1974), pp. 399-409.

Enis, Ben M., Cox, Keith K., and Stafford, James E.
    "Students as Subjects in Consumer Behavior Experiments"
    Journal of Marketing Research, Vol. IX (February 1972), pp. 72-4.

Ferber, Robert
    "Editorial--Research by Convenience"
    Journal of Consumer Research, Vol. 4 (June 1977), pp. 57,8.

Fram, Eugene H.
    "Student Participation in Marketing Research"
    Journal of Marketing Research, Vol. III (August 1966), pp. 311,2.

Khera, Inder P. and Benson, James D.
   "Are Students Really Poor Substitutes for Businessmen in Behavioral
   Research?"
   Journal of Marketing Research, Vol. VII (November 1970), pp. 529-32.

Morgan, Fred W., Jr.
   "Students in Marketing Research: Surrogates vs. Role-Players"
   Journal of the Academy of Marketing Science, Vol. 7 (Summer 1979),
   pp. 255-64.

Oaks, W.
   "External Validity and the Use of Real People as Subjects"
   American Psychologist, Vol. 27 (1972), pp. 959-62.

Park, C. Whan and Lessig, V. Parker
   "Students and Housewives: Differences in Susceptibility to Reference
   Group Influence"
   Journal of Consumer Research, Vol. 4 (September 1977), pp. 102-10.

Remus, William
   "Graduate Students as Surrogates for Managers in Experiments on
   Business Decision Making"
   Journal of Business Research, Vol. 14 (February 1986), pp. 19-25.

Sheth, Jagdish N.
   "Are There Differences in Dissonance Reduction Behavior Between
   Students and Housewives?"
   Journal of Marketing Research, Vol. VII (May 1970), pp. 243-5.

Shuptrine, F. Kelly
   "On the Validity of Using Students as Subjects in Consumer Behavior
   Investigations"
   Journal of Business, Vol. 48 (1975), pp. 383-90.

Soley, Lawrence C. and Reid, Leonard N.
   "On the Validity of Students as Subjects in Advertising Experiments"
   Journal of Advertising Research, Vol. 23 (August/September 1983), pp.
   57-9.

Vinson, Donald E. and Lundstrom, William J.
   "The Use of Students as Experimental Subjects in Marketing Research"
   Journal of the Academy of Marketing Science, Vol. 6 (Winter-Spring
   1978), pp. 114-25.

Vinson, Donald E. and Lundstrom, William J.
   "An Examination of the External Validity of Using Students as
   Surrogates in Marketing Research"
   Proceedings, Southern Marketing Association (1976).

107.17 ---------- Unclassified (Sampling)

Althauser, R. P. and Rubin, D.
   "The Computerized Construction of a Matched Sample"
   American Journal of Sociology, Vol. 76 (September 1970), pp. 325-46.

Blair, Edward
   "Sampling Issues in Trade Area Maps Drawn From Shopper Surveys"
   Journal of Marketing, Vol. 47 (Winter 1983), pp. 98-106.

Blyth, W. G. and Marchant, L. J.
   "Random Samples of Individuals--Reply"
   Journal of the Market Research Society, Vol. 15 (October 1973), p.
   235.

Blyth, W. G. and Marchant, L. J.
   "A Self-Weighting Random Sampling Technique"
   Journal of the Market Research Society, Vol. 15 (July 1973), pp.
   157-62.

Brislin, R. and Baumgardner, S.
   "Non-Random Sampling of Individuals in Cross-Cultural Research"
   Journal of Cross-Cultural Psychology, Vol. II (December 1971), pp.
   397-400.

Brown, M. M. and Bermingham, J. P.
   "Some Aspects of the New NRS Self-Weighting Sample Design"
   The Market Research Society Conference, Bournemouth (1975).

Carter, Roy E., Jr., Troldahl, Verling C., and Schuneman, R. Smith
   "Interviewer Bias in Selecting Households"
   Journal of Marketing, Vol. 27 (April 1963), pp. 27-34.

Dalenius, T.
   "The Panel Approach to Continuous Sample Survey Activity"
   Metrika, Vol. 6 (1963), pp. 30-6.

Durant, H.
   "Experiences of Random (Probability) Sampling"
   Public Opinion Quarterly, Vol. 15 (Winter 1951-52), pp. 765,6.

Ericson, W. A.
"Optimal Sample Design With Non-Response"
Journal of the American Statistical Association, Vol. 62 (March 1967), pp. 63-78.

Goodman, R. and Kish, L.
"Controlled Selection--A Technique in Probability Selection"
Journal of the American Statistical Association, Vol. 45 (September 1950), pp. 350-72.

Greenglass, Esther and Stewart, Mary
"The Under-Representation of Women in Social Psychological Research"
The Ontario Psychologist, Vol. 5 (1973), pp. 21-9.

Groves, Robert M.
"An Empirical Comparison of Two Telephone Sample Designs"
Journal of Marketing Research, Vol. XV (November 1978), pp. 622-31.

Hedges, B. M.
"Random Samples of Individuals--Comment"
Journal of the Market Research Society, Vol. 15 (October 1973), pp. 233-5.

Houseman, E. E.
Application of Probability Area Sampling to Farm Surveys
Agricultural Handbook No. 67
(Washington, DC: U.S. Department of Agriculture, 1954), 25 pp.

Jones, H. L.
"The Application of Sampling Procedures to Business Operations"
Journal of the American Statistical Association, Vol. 50 (September 1955), pp. 763-74.

Jones, H. L.
"Sampling Plans for Verifying Clerical Work"
Industrial Quality Control, Vol. 3 (January 1947), pp. 5-11.

Kemsley, W. F. F.
"Sampling Errors in the Family Expenditure Survey"
Applied Statistics, Vol. 15 (No. 1, 1966), pp. 1-14.

Kiser, Clyde V.
"Pitfalls in Sampling for Population Study"
Journal of the American Statistical Association, Vol. 59 (September 1964), p. 251.

Kish, L.
"Sampling Organizations and Groups of Unequal Sizes"
American Sociological Review, Vol. 30 (August 1965), pp. 564-72.

Kish, L.
"Efficient Allocation of a Multi-Purpose Sample"
Econometrica, Vol. 29 (July 1961), pp. 363-85.

Kish, Leslie and Hess, Irene
"On Non-Coverage of Sample Dwellings"
Journal of the American Statistical Association, Vol. 53 (June 1958), pp. 509-24.

Labovitz, S. I.
"Methods for Control With Small Sample Size"
American Sociological Review, Vol. 30 (April 1965), pp. 243-9.

Lazerwitz, Bernard
"A Sample of a Scattered Group"
Journal of Marketing Research, Vol. I (February 1964), pp. 68-71.

Lipstein, Benjamin
"In Defense of Small Samples"
Journal of Advertising Research, Vol. 15 (February 1975), pp. 33-40.

Mahalanobis, P. C.
"Recent Experiments in Statistical Sampling in the Indian Statistical Institute"
Journal of the Royal Statistical Society, Vol. 109 (1946), pp. 326-78.

Manheimer, Dean and Hyman, Herbert
"Interviewer Performance in Area Sampling"
Public Opinion Quarterly, Vol. 13 (Spring 1949), pp. 87,8.

McCarthy, Philip J.
"Pseudo-Replication: Half Samples"
Review of the International Statistical Institute, Vol. 37 (1969), pp. 239-64.

Moser, C. A.
"Recent Developments in the Sampling of Human Populations in Great Britain"
Journal of the American Statistical Association, Vol. 50 (December 1955), pp. 1195-214.

Nathan, Gad
"An Empirical Study of Response and Sampling Errors for Multiplicity
Estimates With Different Counting Rules"
Journal of the American Statistical Association, Vol. 71 (December
1976), pp. 808-15.

Oakes, William
"External Validity and the Use of Real People as Subjects"
American Psychologist, Vol. 27 (October 1972), pp. 959-62.

Pearl, Robert P. and Levine, Daniel B.
"A New Methodology for a Consumer Expenditure Survey"
Proceedings of the Business and Economic Statistics Section
American Statistical Association (August 1971), pp. 254-9.

Peters, William S.
"Selective Response Factors in Tourist Surveys"
Journal of Marketing, Vol. 25 (January 1961), pp. 68-71.

Schultz, Duane P.
"The Human Subject in Psychological Research"
Psychological Bulletin, Vol. 72 (September 1969), pp. 241-58.

Sharp, H. and Feldt, A.
"Some Factors in a Probability Sample Survey of a Metropolitan
Community"
American Sociological Review, Vol. 24 (October 1959), pp. 650-61.

Shoemaker, Robert and Staelin, Richard
"The Effects of Sampling Variation on Sales Forecasts for New
Consumer Products"
Journal of Marketing Research, Vol. XIII (May 1976), pp. 138-43.

Shuttleworth, Frank K.
"Sampling Errors Involved in Incomplete Returns to Mailed
Questionnaires"
Psychological Bulletin, Vol. 37 (September 1940), p. 437.

Simmons, W. R.
"Prelisting in Market or Media Surveys"
Journal of Marketing, Vol. 18 (July 1953), pp. 6-17.

Sirken, Monroe G.
"The Counting Rule Strategy in Sample Surveys"
Proceedings of the Social Statistics Section, American Statistical
Association (1974), pp. 119-23.

Sirken, Monroe G.
"Household Surveys With Multiplicity"
Journal of the American Statistical Association, Vol. 65 (March
1970), pp. 257-66.

Smart, R.
"Subject Selection Bias in Psychological Research"
Canadian Psychologist, Vol. 7A (1966), pp. 115-21.

Twedt, Dik Warren
"What About Other Sources of Sampling Error?"
Journal of Marketing, Vol. 30 (October 1966), pp. 62,3.

Watson, A. N.
Respondent Preselection
Technical Series No. 1
(Philadelphia: Curtis Publishing Company, Research Department, 1946),
15 pp.

Williams, W. H.
"The Seriousness of Selection Biases, Including Nonresponse"
Proceedings, Social Statistics Section, American Statistical
Association (1975), pp. 11-5.

108 ----------------------- MALL INTERCEPT -------------------------
          See also (sub)heading(s) 74, 107.

108.01 ---------- Theory Re: Mall Intercept Data Collection

Advertising Age
   "Field Research Alive and Well in the Malls"
   Advertising Age, Vol. 54 (May 23, 1983), pp. M27-9.

Barker, Raymond F.
   "Interviewing Consumers in New Zealand and the United States"
   Singapore Marketing Review, Vol. II (March 1987), pp. 77-90.

Blair, Edward
   "Sampling Issues in Trade Area Maps Drawn From Shopper Surveys"
   Journal of Marketing, Vol. 47 (Winter 1983), pp. 98-106.

Bush, Alan J. and Hair, Joseph F., Jr.
   "An Assessment of the Mall Intercept as a Data Collection Method"
   Journal of Marketing Research, Vol. XXII (May 1985), pp. 158-67.

Bush, Alan J. and Parasuraman, A.
   "Mall Intercept Versus Telephone Interviewing Environment"
   Journal of Advertising Research, Vol. 25 (April/May 1985), pp. 36-43.

Cowan, C. D.
   "Mall Intercepts and Clinical Trials: The Philosophy of Inference
   From Different Types of Research Design"
   Marketing Research (March 1989), pp. 15-22.

DuPont, Thomas D.
   "Do Frequent Mall Shoppers Distort Mall-Intercept Survey Results?"
   Journal of Advertising Research, Vol. 27 (August/September 1987), pp.
   45-51.

Gates, Roger and Solomon, Paul
   "Research Using the Mall Intercept: State of the Art"
   Journal of Advertising Research, Vol. 22 (August/September 1982), pp.
   43-9.

Hornik, Jacob and Ellis, Shmuel
   "Strategies to Secure Compliance for a Mall Intercept Interview"
   Public Opinion Quarterly, Vol. 52 (Winter 1988), pp. 539-51.

Kinnear, Thomas C.
   "Research Execs Say Phone Interviewing Beats Door-to-Door, Mall
   Intercepts"
   Marketing News (September 21, 1979), p. 1.

McIntyre, Shelby H. and Bender, Sherry D. F. G.
   "The Purchase Intercept Technique (PIT) in Comparison to Telephone
   and Mail Surveys"
   Journal of Retailing, Vol. 62 (Winter 1986), pp. 364-83.

Murry, John P., Jr., Lastovicka, John L., and Bhalla, Gaurav
   "Demographic and Lifestyle Selection Error in Mall-Intercept Data"
   Journal of Advertising Research, Vol. 29 (February/March 1989), pp.
   46-52.

Reid, Patricia
   "Purists May Disagree, but Almost All Types of Surveys can be
   Conducted in Malls"
   Marketing News (January 6, 1984), p. 6.

Sudman, Seymour
   "Improving the Quality of Shopping Center Sampling"
   Journal of Marketing Research, Vol. XVII (November 1980), pp. 423-31.

Wiseman, Frederick, Schafer, Marianne, and Schafer, Richard
   "An Experimental Test of the Effects of a Monetary Incentive on
   Cooperation Rates and Data Collection Costs in Central-Location
   Interviewing"
   Journal of Marketing Research, Vol. XX (November 1983), pp. 439-42.

108.02 ---------- Theory Re: Purchase Intercept Technique (PIT)

McIntyre, Shelby H. and Bender, Sherry D. F. G.
   "The Purchase Intercept Technique (PIT) in Comparison to Telephone
   and Mail Surveys"
   Journal of Retailing, Vol. 62 (Winter 1986), pp. 364-83.

108.03 ---------- Applications of Mall Intercepts

Lautman, Martin R., Edwards, Melanie T., and Farrell, Bryan
   "Predicting Direct-Mail Response From Mall Intercept Data"
   Journal of Advertising Research, Vol. 31 (October 1981), pp. 31-4.

108.04 ---------- Software for Mall Intercept Interviewing
Computers for Marketing Corporation
  MICROSURVENT: Portable CRT Interviewing (Malls)
  (San Francisco, CA: Computers for Marketing Corporation).

109 ----------------------- SNOWBALL SAMPLING -----------------------

         See also (sub)heading(s) 107.

109.01 ---------- Theory Re: Snowball Sampling

Goodman, Leo A.
  "Snowball Sampling"
  Annals of Mathematical Statistics, Vol. 32 (1961), pp. 148-70.

Greeno, D. W. and Sommers, M. S.
  "What Kind of Subjects Can a Referral System Generate"
  European Research, Vol. 2 (July 1974), pp. 170-2.

Greeno, D. W., Sommers, Montrose S., and Haines, George H., Jr.
  "What Kinds of Subjects Can a Referral System Generate? A Case
  Analysis"
  Journal of the Market Research Society, Vol. 18 (October 1976), pp.
  207-10.

Welch, Susan
  "Sampling by Referral in a Dispersed Population"
  Public Opinion Quarterly, Vol. 39 (Summer 1975), pp. 237-45.

109.02 ---------- Applications of Snowball Sampling

Brand, G. T.
  The Industrial Buying Decision
  (New York: John Wiley and Sons, Inc., 1972).

Cooley, J. R., Jackson, D. W., and Ostrom, L. L.
  "Relative Power in Industrial Buying Decisions"
  Journal of Purchasing and Materials Management (Spring 1978).

Gronhaug, K.
  "Exploring a Complex Organizational Buying Decision"
  Industrial Management, Vol. 6 (December 1976), pp. 439-44.

Johnston, W. J. and Bonoma, T. V.
  "The Buying Center: Structure and Interaction Patterns"
  Journal of Marketing, Vol. 45 (Summer 1981), pp. 143-56.

Kelly, J. P.
  "Functions Performed in Industrial Purchasing Decisions With
  Implications for Marketing Strategy"
  Journal of Business Research, Vol. 2 (October 1974), pp. 420-34.

Moriarity, Rowland T. and Bateson, John E. G.
  "Exploring Complex Decision Making Units: A New Approach"
  Journal of Marketing Research, Vol. XIX (May 1982), pp. 182-91.

Moriarity, Rowland T., Jr. and Spekman, Robert E.
  "An Empirical Investigation of the Information Sources Used During
  the Industrial Buying Process"
  Journal of Marketing Research, Vol. XXI (May 1984), pp. 137-47.

Ozanne, U. B. and Churchill, G. A.
  "Five Dimensions of the Industrial Adoption Process"
  Journal of Marketing Research, Vol. VII (August 1971), pp. 322-8.

Patchen, M.
  "The Locus and Basis of Influence on Organizational Decisions"
  Organizational Behavior and Human Performance, Vol. 11 (1974), pp.
  195-221.

Spekman, R. E. and Stern, L. W.
  "Environmental Uncertainty and Buying Group Structure: An Empirical
  Investigation"
  Journal of Marketing, Vol. 43 (Spring 1979), pp. 54-64.

110 ---------------------- INFORMANT SAMPLING ----------------------
See also (sub)heading(s) 107.

110.01 ---------- Theory Re: Key Informant Sampling

Achrol, R. S.
"The Interpretation of Measurement Error in 'Key Informant' Reports:
Instrumental vs. Determinative Criteria"
Proceedings, AMA Summer Educators' Conference (1985), pp. 380-6.

Anderson, James C.
"A Measurement Model to Assess Measure-Specific Factors in
Multiple-Informant Research"
Journal of Marketing Research, Vol. XXII (February 1985), pp. 86-92.

Bagozzi, Richard P. and Phillips, Lynn W.
"Representing and Testing Organizational Theories: A Holistic
Construal"
Administrative Science Quarterly, Vol. 27 (1982), pp. 459-89.

Campbell, Donald T.
"The Informant in Quantitative Research"
American Journal of Sociology, Vol. 60 (January 1955), pp. 339-43.

Houston, Michael J. and Sudman, Seymour
"A Methodological Assessment of the Use of Key Informants"
Social Science Research, Vol. 4 (June 1975), pp. 151-64.

John, George and Reve, Torger
"The Reliability and Validity of Key Informant Data From Dyadic
Relationships in Marketing Channels"
Journal of Marketing Research, Vol. XIX (November 1982), pp. 517-24.

Krishnamurthi, Lakshman
"The Salience of Relevant Others and Its Effect on Individual and
Joint Preferences: An Experimental Investigation"
Journal of Consumer Research, Vol. 10 (June 1983), pp. 62-72.

McGranahan, David
"Correcting for Informant Bias"
American Sociological Review, Vol. 4 (1976), pp. 176-8.

Phillips, Lynn W.
"Assessing Measurement Error in Key Informant Reports: A
Methodological Note on Organizational Analysis in Marketing"
Journal of Marketing Research, Vol. XVIII (November 1981), pp.
395-415.

Phillips, Lynn W.
"On Studying Collective Behavior: Methodological Issues in the Use of
Key Informants"
Northwestern University (1980), unpublished Ph.D. thesis.

Phillips, Lynn W. and Bagozzi, Richard P.
"On Measuring Organizational Properties: Methodological Issues in the
Use of Key Informants"
Graduate School of Business, Stanford University (1982), working
paper.

Phillips, Lynn W. and Bagozzi, Richard P.
"On Measuring Organizational Properties: Methodological Issues in the
Use of Key Informants"
Sloan School of Management, Massachusetts Institute of Technology
(1980), working paper.

Seidler, John
"On Using Informants: A Technique for Collecting Quantitative Data
and Controlling Measurement Error in Organizational Analysis"
American Sociological Review, Vol. 39 (December 1974), pp. 816-31.

110.02 ---------- Applications of Key Informant Sampling

Brandt, William K. and Hulbert, James M.
"Headquarters Guidance in Marketing Strategy in the Multinational
Subsidiary"
Columbia Journal of World Business, Vol. 12 (Winter 1977), pp. 7-14.

Brandt, William K. and Hulbert, James M.
"Patterns of Communication in the Multinational Corporation: An
Empirical Study"
Journal of International Business Studies, Vol. 7 (Spring 1976), pp.
57-64.

Brandt, William K. and Hulbert, James M.
"Organizational Structure and Marketing Strategy in the Multinational
Subsidiary"
Proceedings, American Marketing Association, Vol. 37 (Spring-Fall
1975), pp. 320-5.

Butaney, Gul and Wortzel, Lawrence H.
  "Distributor Power Versus Manufacturer Power: The Customer Role"
  Journal of Marketing, Vol. 52 (January 198), pp. 52-63.

Buzzell, Robert D., Gale, Bradley, and Sultan, Robert
  "Market Share--A Key to Profitability"
  Harvard Business Review, Vol. 53 (January-February 1975), pp. 97-106.

Davis, Harry L.
  "Measurement of Husband-Wife Influence in Consumer Purchase Decisions"
  Journal of Marketing Research, Vol. VIII (August 1971), pp. 305-12.

Davis, Harry L., Douglas, Susan P., and Silk, Alvin J.
  "Measuring Unreliability: A Hidden Threat to Cross-National Consumer
  Research"
  Journal of Marketing, Vol. 45 (Spring 1981), pp. 98-109.

El-Ansary, Adel and Stern, Louis W.
  "Power Measurement in the Distribution Channel"
  Journal of Marketing Research, Vol. IX (February 1972), pp. 47-52.

Etgar, Michael
  "Selection of an Effective Channel Control Mix"
  Journal of Marketing, Vol. 42 (July 1978), pp. 53-8.

Etgar, Michael
  "Channel Environment and Channel Leadership"
  Journal of Marketing Research, Vol. XIV (February 1977), pp. 69-76.

Etgar, Michael
  "The Effect of Administrative Control on the Efficiency of Vertical
  Marketing Systems"
  Journal of Marketing Research, Vol. XIII (February 1976), pp. 12-24.

Etgar, Michael
  "An Empirical Analysis of the Motivations for the Development of
  Centrally Controlled Vertical Marketing Systems: The Case of the
  Property and Casualty Insurance Industry"
  University of California at Berkeley (1974), Ph.D. thesis.

Farris, Paul W. and Buzzell, Robert D.
  "Why Advertising and Promotional Costs Vary: Some Cross Sectional
  Analyses"
  Journal of Marketing, Vol. 43 (Fall 1979), pp. 112-22.

Gaski, John F. and Nevin, John R.
  "The Differential Effects of Exercised and Unexercised Power Sources
  in a Marketing Channel"
  Journal of Marketing Research, Vol. XXII (May 1985), pp. 130-42.

Hunt, Shelby and Nevin, John
  "Power in a Channel of Distribution: Sources and Consequences"
  Journal of Marketing Research, Vol. XI (May 1974), pp. 186-93.

John, George
  "An Empirical Investigation of Some Antecedents of Opportunism in a
  Marketing Channel"
  Journal of Marketing Research, Vol. XXI (August 1984), pp. 278-89.

Lawton, Leigh and Parasuraman, A.
  "The Impact of the Marketing Concept on New Product Planning"
  Journal of Marketing, Vol. 44 (Winter 1980), pp. 19-25.

Lusch, Robert
  "Sources of Power: Their Impact on Intrachannel Conflict"
  Journal of Marketing Research, Vol. XIII (November 1976), pp. 382-90.

McClintock, Charles C., Brannen, Diane, and Maynard-Moody, Steven
  "Applying the Logic of Sample Surveys to Qualitative Case Studies:
  The Case Cluster Method"
  Administrative Science Quarterly, Vol. 24 (1979), pp. 613-29.

Molnar, Joseph J. and Rogers, David I.
  "A Comparative Model of Inter-Organizational Conflict"
  Administrative Science Quarterly, Vol. 24 (1979), pp. 406-25.

Patchen, Marvin
  "Alternative Questionnaire Approaches to the Measurement of Influence
  in Organizations"
  American Journal of Sociology, Vol. 69 (1963), pp. 41-52.

Pennings, Johannes
  "Measures of Organizational Structure: A Methodological Note"
  American Journal of Sociology, Vol. 79 (1973), pp. 686-704.

Phillips, Lynn W.
  "Explaining Control Losses in Corporate Marketing Channels: An
  Organizational Analysis"
  Journal of Marketing Research, Vol. XIX (November 1982), pp. 525-49.

Provan, Keith, Beyer, Janice, and Krytbosch, Carlos
"Environmental Linkages and Power in Resource-Dependence Relations
Between Organizations"
Administrative Science Quarterly, Vol. 25 (1980), pp. 200-25.

Rosenberg, Larry and Stern, Louis W.
"Conflict Measurement in the Distribution Channel"
Journal of Marketing Research, Vol. VIII (November 1971), pp. 437-42.

Schoeffler, Sidney, Buzzell, Robert D., and Heany, Donald F.
"Impact of Strategic Planning on Profit Performance"
Harvard Business Review, Vol. 52 (March-April 1974), pp. 137-45.

Silk, Alvin J. and Kalwani, Manohar U.
"Measuring Influence in Organizational Purchase Decisions"
Journal of Marketing Research, Vol. XIX (May 1982), pp. 165-81.

111 ---------------- SEQUENTIAL SAMPLING AND ANALYSIS ----------------

See also (sub)heading(s) 107.

111.01 ---------- Books Re: Sequential Sampling and Analysis

Armitage, P.
Sequential Medical Trials, Second Edition
(Oxford: Blackwell, 1975).

Columbia University Statistical Research Group
Sequential Analysis of Statistical Data: Applications
(New York: Columbia University Press, 1945), 367 pp.

Ghosh, B. K.
Sequential Tests of Statistical Hypotheses
(Reading, MA: Addison-Wesley, 1970), 454 pp.

Wald, A.
Sequential Analysis
(New York: John Wiley and Sons, 1948), 212 pp.

Wetherill, G. B.
Sequential Methods in Statistics, Second Edition
(London: Methuen, 1975).

111.02 ---------- Theory Re: Sequential Sampling and Analysis

Anderton, E. J., Gorton, K., and Tudor, R.
"The Application of Sequential Analysis in Market Research"
Journal of Marketing Research, Vol. XVII (February 1980), pp. 97-105.

Anderton, E. J., Tudor, R., and Gorton, K.
"Sequential Analysis: A Reappraisal for Market Research"
Journal of the Market Research Society, Vol. 18 (October 1976), pp. 166-79.

Anscombe, F. J.
"Sequential Estimation"
Journal of the Royal Statistical Society, Series B15 (1953), pp. 1-21.

Armitage, P.
"Restricted Sequential Procedures"
Biometrika, Vol. 44 (1957), pp. 9-26.

Birt, E. M. and Brogren, R. H.
"Minimizing Number of Interviews Through Sequential Sampling"
Journal of Marketing Research, Vol. I (February 1964), pp. 65-7.

Bross, I.
"Sequential Medical Plans"
Biometrics, Vol. 8, (1952), pp. 188-205.

Girshick, M. A.
"Contributions to Sequential Analysis: I"
Annals of Mathematical Statistics, Vol. 17 (June 1946), pp. 123-43.

Goodman, Leo A.
"Serial Number Analysis"
Journal of the American Statistical Association, Vol. 47 (December 1952), pp. 622-34.

Moshman, Jack
"Sequential Estimation as a Tool in Marketing Research"
Journal of Marketing Research, Vol. I (November 1964), pp. 62-5.

Moshman, J.
"A Method for Selecting the Size of the Initial Sample in Stein's Two-Sample Procedure"
Annals of Mathematical Statistics, Vol. 29 (1958), pp. 1271-5.

Moshman, J.
"The Application of Sequential Estimation to Computer Simulation and Monte Carlo Procedures"
Journal of the Association for Computing Machinery, Vol. 5 (1958), pp. 343-52.

Peal, J. and Shipworth, G. E.
"Sequential Sampling as a Technique in Sociological Surveys"
Applied Statistics, Vol. 19 (November 1970), pp. 27-33.

Rothfield, R.
"Analysis for Sequential Product Testing Using a Balanced Incomplete Block Design"
Commentary (JMRS), Vol. 7, No. 2 (1965), pp. 82-97.

Stein, C.
"A Two-Sample Test for a Linear Hypothesis Whose Power Is Independent of the Variance"
Annals of Mathematical Statistics, Vol. 16 (1945), pp. 1271-5.

Wald, A.
  "Sequential Method of Sampling Between Two Courses of Action"
  Journal of the American Statistical Association, Vol. 40 (September
  1945), pp. 277-306.

111.03 ---------- Applications of Sequential Sampling and Analysis

Anderton, E. J., Gorton, K., Hammersley, J., and Tudor, R.
  "An Application of Sequential Analysis in Pricing Research"
  European Journal of Marketing, Vol. 12 (1978), pp. 428-35.

Myers, Lawrence, Jr. and Gardner, Eric F.
  "An Inexpensive Method to Determine the Efficiency of a Television
  Program"
  Journal of Applied Psychology, Vol. 44 (February 1960), pp. 39-42.

112 ----------------------- SAMPLING FRAMES -------------------------
        See also (sub)heading(s) 89.02, 107.

112.01 ---------- Evaluations of Common Sampling Frames

Kviz, Frederick J.
  "Bias in a Directory Sample for a Mail Survey of Rural Households"
  Public Opinion Quarterly, Vol. 48 (Winter 1984), pp. 801-6.

Quah, Siam Tee
  "Sampling Frames in Marketing Research in Singapore"
  Singapore Marketing Review, Vol. II (1987), pp. 91-4.

Sudman, Seymour
  "The Uses of Telephone Directories for Survey Sampling"
  Journal of Marketing Research, Vol. X (May 1973), pp. 204-7.

Wilson, P. R. and Elliot, D. J.
  "An Evaluation of the Postcode Address File as a Sampling Frame and
  Its Use Within OPCS"
  Journal of the Royal Statistical Society, Series A, Vol. 150, Part 3
  (1987), pp. 230-40.

113 ------------------ NOT-AT-HOME'S AND CALLBACKS ------------------
        See also (sub)heading(s) 107, 117.

113.01 ---------- Theory Re: Not-at-Home's and Callbacks

Advertising Research Foundation
    "A Comparison of Estimates From the Nights-at-Home Formula With
    Estimates From Six Calls"
    Advertising Research Foundation Report
    (New York: Advertising Research Foundation, Inc., 1961).

Axelrod, Morris
    "An Experimental Attempt to Reduce Field Costs by Limiting Call Backs
    and Increasing Cluster Size"
    Proceedings, American Statistical Association, Business and Economics
    Statistics Section (1964).

Bartholomew, D. J.
    "A Method of Allowing for 'Not-at-Home' Bias in Sample Surveys"
    Applied Statistics, Vol. 10 (March 1961), pp. 52-9.

Durbin, J. and Stuart, A.
    "Callbacks and Clustering in Sample Surveys"
    Journal of the Royal Statistical Society, Vol. 117(A) (1954), pp.
    387-428.

Dunkelberg, William C. and Day, George S.
    "Nonresponse Bias and Callbacks in Sample Surveys"
    Journal of Marketing Research, Vol. X (May 1973), pp. 160-8.

Ehrenberg, A. S. C.
    "A Comparison of Estimates From the Nights-at-Home Formula With
    Estimates From Six Calls"
    Advertising Research Foundation Report No. 6 (1961), pp. 45-9.

Hilgard, E. R. and Payne, S. L.
    "Those Not at Home: Riddle for Pollsters"
    Public Opinion Quarterly (1944), pp. 254-61.

Politz, A. and Simmons, W.
    "An Attempt to Get Not-at-Homes into the Sample Without Callbacks"
    Journal of the American Statistical Association, Vol. 44 (1949), pp.
    9-31.

Ross, H. Laurence
    "The Inaccessible Respondent: A Note on Privacy in City and Country"
    Public Opinion Quarterly, Vol. 27 (Summer 1963), pp. 269-75.

Simmons, W.
    "A Plan to Account for Not-at-Homes by Combining Weighting and
    Callbacks"
    Journal of Marketing, Vol. 19 (1954), pp. 42-53.

Ward, James C., Russick, Bertram, and Rudelius, William
    "A Test of Reducing Callbacks and Not-at-Home Bias in Personal
    Interviews by Weighting At-Home Respondents"
    Journal of Marketing Research, Vol. XXII (February 1985), pp. 66-73.

Wilcox, James B.
    "The Interaction of Refusal and Not-at-Home Sources of Nonresponse
    Bias"
    Journal of Marketing Research, Vol. XIV (November 1977), pp. 592-7.

113.02 ---------- Applications of Not-at-Home Bias Reduction Techniques

Gallup, George H.
    "The 14th Annual Gallup Poll of the Public's Attitudes Toward the
    Public Schools"
    Phi Delta Kappan, Vol. 64 (September 1982).

Smith, Tom
    "The Hidden 25 Percent: An Analysis of Nonresponse on 1980 General
    Social Survey"
    Public Opinion Quarterly, Vol. 47 (Fall 1983), pp. 386-404.

114 ------------------- SAMPLE SIZE DETERMINATION -------------------
          See also (sub)heading(s) 107, 160.06.

114.01 ---------- Books Re: Sample Size Determination

Kraemer, Helena Chmura and Thiemann, Sue
     How Many Subjects? Statistical Power Analysis in Research
     (Beverly Hills, CA: Sage Publications, Inc., 1987), 120 pp.

Mace, Arthur E.
     Sample Size Determination
     (New York: Reinhold Publishing Corporation, 1965), 226 pp.

Portman, Roger H., Mouradian, Robert A., and Bruno, R. Richard
     Tables for Determining Sample Size and Sample Error
     (Mission Viejo, CA: National Research Foundation Press, 1975), 280 pp.

U.S. National Center for Health Statistics
     Distribution and Properties of Variance Estimators for Complex
     Multistage Probability Samples: An Empirical Distribution
     Vital and Health Statistics, Series 2, No. 65
     (Rochville, MD: Health Resources Administration, March 1975), 46 pp.

114.02 ---------- Theory Re: Sample Size Determination

Blattberg, Robert C.
     "The Design of Advertising Experiments Using Statistical Decision
     Theory"
     Journal of Marketing Research, Vol. XVI (May 1979), pp. 191-202.

Bruvold, N. T. and Murphy, R. A.
     "Sample Sizes for Comparison of Proportions"
     Technometrics, Vol. 20 (November 1978), pp. 437-55.

Dalal, Siddhartha R. and Srinivasan, V.
     "Determining Sample Size for Pretesting Comparative Effectiveness of
     Advertising Copies"
     Management Science, Vol. 23 (August 1977), pp. 1284-94.

Feldt, L. S. and Mahmond, M. W.
     "Power Function Charts for Specification of Sample Size"
     Psychometrika, Vol. 23 (September 1958), pp. 201-10.

Ginter, James, Cooper, Martha, Obermiller, Carl, and Page, Thomas
     "The Design of Advertising Experiments Using Statistical Decision
     Theory: An Extension"
     Journal of Marketing Research, Vol. XVIII (February 1981), pp. 120-3.

Givon, Moshe M.
     "Determination of Optimal Sample Sizes in the Beta-Binomial Brand
     Choice Model"
     Journal of Marketing Research, Vol. XVII (May 1980), pp. 258-67.

Guenther, W. C. and Thomas, P. O.
     "Some Graphs Useful for Statistical Inference"
     Journal of the American Statistical Association, Vol. 60 (March
     1965), pp. 334-43.

Harris, M., Horvitz, D. G., and Mood, A. M.
     "On the Determination of Sample Sizes in Designing Experiments"
     Journal of the American Statistical Association, Vol. 43 (September
     1948), pp. 391-402.

Hinkle, Dennis E. and Oliver, J. Dale
     "How Large Should the Sample Be? A Question With No Simple Answer?
     Or...."
     Educational and Psychological Measurement, Vol. 43 (Winter 1983), pp.
     1051-60.

Kalwani, Manohar U. and Morrison, Donald G.
     "Sample Size Requirements for Zero-Order Models"
     Journal of Marketing Research, Vol. XVII (May 1980), pp. 721-7.

Kalwani, Manohar U. and Morrison, Donald G.
     "Estimating the Proportion of 'Always Buy' and 'Never Buy' Consumers:
     A Likelihood Ratio Test With Sample Size Implications"
     Journal of Marketing Research, Vol. XIV (November 1977), pp. 601-6.

McHugh, R. B.
     "Determining Sample Size in Validation Research"
     Educational and Psychological Measurement, Vol. 17 (Spring 1957), pp.
     136-41.

Milton, Sande
     "A Sample Size Formula for Multiple Regression Studies"
     Public Opinion Quarterly, Vol. 50 (Spring 1986), pp. 112-8.

Miner, R. B.
"A Critique of the Cumulative Frequency Method for Testing Adequacy of the Sample Size"
Journal of Marketing, Vol. 21 (July 1956), pp. 76,7.

Overall, John E. and Dalal, Sudhin N.
"Design of Experiments to Maximize Power Relative to Cost"
Psychological Bulletin, Vol. 64 (November 1965), pp. 339-50.

Sprowls, R. Clay
"Sample Sizes in Chi-Square Tests for Measuring Advertising Effectiveness"
Journal of Marketing Research, Vol. I (February 1964), pp. 60-4.

114.03 ---------- Theory Re: Use of Pilot Sample Information

Adams, Arthur J. and Shiffler, Ronald E.
"Commentary on Biasing Effects of Pilot Samples and Gillett's Observations on the Stein Confidence Interval"
Journal of Marketing Research, Vol. XXVI (May 1989), pp. 241-3.

Birnbaum, Allan and Healy, William C.
"Estimates With Prescribed Variance Based on Two-Stage Sampling"
Annals of Mathematical Statistics, Vol. 31 (1960), pp. 662-76.

Gillett, Raphael
"Confidence Interval Construction by Stein's Method: A Practical and Economical Approach to Sample Size Determination"
Journal of Marketing Research, Vol. XXVI (May 1989), pp. 237-40.

Goldman, Aaron S. and Zeigler, R. K.
"Comparisons of Some Two-Stage Sampling Methods"
Annals of Mathematical Statistics, Vol. 37 (1966), pp. 891-7.

Seelbinder, B. M.
"On Stein's Two-Stage Sampling Scheme"
Annals of Mathematical Statistics, Vol. 24 (1953), pp. 640-9.

Shiffler, Ronald E. and Adams, Arthur J.
"A Correction for Biasing Effects of Pilot Sample Size on Sample Size Determination"
Journal of Marketing Research, Vol. XXIV (August 1987), pp. 319-21.

Stein, Charles
"A Two-Sample Test for a Linear Hypothesis Whose Power is Independent of the Variance"
Annals of Mathematical Statistics, Vol. 16 (1945), pp. 243-58.

115 ---------- STATISTICAL IMPLICATIONS OF SAMPLING METHODS ----------
          See also (sub)heading(s) 107, 141.04, 141.05.

Achrol, R. S.
    "The Interpretation of Measurement Error in 'Key Informant' Reports:
    Instrumental vs. Determinative Criteria"
    Proceedings, AMA Summer Educators' Conference (1985), pp. 380-6.

Chambers, J. C.
    "Consideration of a Biased Estimate in an Information-Sampling
    Situation"
    Operations Research, Vol. 6 (September-October 1958), pp. 729-39.

DuMouchel, William H. and Duncan, Greg J.
    "Using Sample Survey Weights in Multiple Regression Analysis of
    Stratified Samples"
    Journal of the American Statistical Association, Vol. 78 (September
    1983), pp. 535-43.

Hansen, Morris H., Madow, William G., and Tepping, Benjamin J.
    "An Evaluation of Model Dependent and Probability Sampling Inferences
    in Sample Surveys"
    Journal of the American Statistical Association, Vol. 78 (December
    1983), pp. 776-93.

Kish, L.
    "Standard Errors for Indexes From Complex Samples"
    Journal of the American Statistical Association, Vol. 63 (June 1968),
    pp. 512-29.

Kish, Leslie
    "Variances for Indexes From Complex Samples"
    Proceedings, Social Statistics Section, American Statistical
    Association (1962), pp. 190-9.

Kish, Leslie
    "On Variances of Ratios and Their Differences in Multi-Stage Samples"
    Journal of the American Statistical Association, Vol. 54 (1959), pp.
    416-46.

Kish, L.
    "Confidence Intervals for Clustered Samples"
    American Sociological Review, Vol. 22 (April 1957), pp. 154-65.

Kish, Leslie and Frankel, Martin R.
    "Balanced Repeated Replication for Standard Errors"
    Journal of the American Statistical Association, Vol. 65 (1970), pp.
    1071-94.

Kish, Leslie and Hess, Irene
    "On Variances of Ratios and Their Differences in Multi-Stage Samples"
    Journal of the American Statistical Association, Vol. 54 (1959), pp.
    416-46.

Koerner, Roy E.
    "The Design Factor--An Underutilised Concept?"
    European Research, Vol. 8 (November 1980), pp. 266-72.

Platten, J. H.
    "Weighting Procedures in Probability-Type Samples"
    Journal of Marketing, Vol. 23 (July 1958), pp. 47-52.

Roshwalb, I.
    "Effect of Weighting by Card-Duplication on Efficiency of Survey
    Results"
    Journal of the American Statistical Association, Vol. 48 (December
    1953), pp. 773-7.

Smith, T. M. F.
    "On the Validity of Inferences From Non-Random Samples"
    Journal of the Royal Statistical Society, Vol. 146, Series A General
    (1983), pp. 394-403.

Tepping, Benjamin J.
    "The Estimation of Variance in Complex Surveys"
    Proceedings of the Social Statistics Section, American Statistical
    Association (1968).

Tukey, John W.
    "Bias and Confidence in Not-Quite Large Samples: Abstract"
    Annals of Mathematical Statistics, Vol. 29 (1958), p. 614.

Woodruff, Ralph S.
    "A Simple Method for Approximating the Variance of a Complicated
    Estimate"
    Journal of the American Statistical Association, Vol. 66 (June 1971),
    pp. 411-4.

Woodruff, Ralph S. and Causey, Beverley D.
"Computerized Method for Approximating the Variance of a Complicated Estimator"
Journal of the American Statistical Association, Vol. 71 (June 1976), pp. 315-21.

116 ----------------------- RESPONSE BIAS -------------------------
        See also (sub)heading(s) 22, 34, 35, 36, 71, 72.03, 87.07.

116.01 ---------- Books Re: Response Bias

Bradburn, Norman M., Sudman, Seymour, and Associates
   Improving Interview Method and Questionnaire Design: Response Effects
   to Threatening Questions in Survey Research
   (San Francisco: Jossey-Bass, 1979).

Dutka, Solomon and Frankel, Lester R.
   Let's Not Forget About Response Error
   Modern Marketing Series No. 12
   (New York: Audits and Surveys, Inc., 1976).

Hogarth, Robin M. (editor)
   Question Framing and Response Consistency
   (San Francisco, CA: Jossey-Bass Inc., Publishers, 1982), 109 pp.

Jaech, John L.
   Statistical Analysis of Measurement Errors
   (New York: John Wiley and Sons, Inc., 1985), 293 pp.

Sudman, Seymour and Bradburn, Norman M.
   Response Effects in Surveys: A Review and Synthesis
   (Chicago: Aldine Publishing, 1974).

116.02 ---------- Theory Re: Response Bias

Andrews, Frank M. and Herzog, Regula
   "The Quality of Survey Data as Related to Age of Respondent"
   Journal of the American Statistical Association, Vol. 81 (June 1986),
   pp. 403-10.

Bradburn, Norman M.
   "Response Effects"
   in Rossi, Peter, Wright, James, and Anderson, Andy (editors)
   Handbook of Survey Research
   (New York: Academic Press, Inc., 1983), pp. 289-32.

Deming, W. Edwards
   "On a Probability Mechanism to Attain an Economic Balance Between the
   Resultant Error of Response and the Bias of Non-Response"
   Journal of the American Statistical Association, Vol. 48 (December
   1953), p. 745.

Ferber, Robert and Hauck, Mathew
   "A Framework for Dealing With Response Errors in Consumer Surveys"
   National Conference of the American Marketing Association (June
   1964), paper presentation.

Neter, John
   "Measurement Errors in Reports of Consumer Expenditures"
   Journal of Marketing Research, Vol. VII (February 1970), pp. 11-25.

Peterson, Robert A. and Kerin, Roger A.
   "The Quality of Self-Report Data: Review and Synthesis"
   in Enis, Ben M. and Roering, Kenneth J. (editors)
   Review of Marketing 1981
   (Chicago: American Marketing Association, 1981), pp. 5-20.

116.03 ---------- General Empirical Studies of Response Bias

Cronbach, Lee J.
   "Further Evidence on Response Sets and Test Design"
   Educational and Psychological Measurements, Vol. 10 (Spring 1950),
   pp. 3-31.

Damarin, F. L. and Messick, S. J.
   "Response Styles as Personality Variables: A Theoretical Integration
   of Multivariate Research"
   Research Bulletin No. 65-10
   (Princeton, NJ: Educational Testing Services, 1965).

Ghosh, A.
   "A Note on the Accuracy of Family Budget Data With Reference to the
   Period of Recall"
   Calcutta Statistical Association Bulletin, Vol. 5 (1953), pp. 16-23.

Hui, C. Harry and Triandis, Harry C.
   "The Instability of Response Sets"
   Public Opinion Quarterly, Vol. 49 (Summer 1985), pp. 253-60.

Kildegaard, Ingrid C.
   "How Consumers Misreport What They Spent"
   Journal of Advertising Research, Vol. 5 (June 1965), pp. 51-5.

Lamale, Helen Humes
Study of Consumer Expenditures, Incomes, and Savings: Methodology of
the Survey of Consumer Expenditures in 1950
(University of Pennsylvania, 1959).

Lansing, John B., Ginsberg, Gerald P., and Braaten, Kaisa
An Investigation of Response Error
(Urbana, IL: University of Illinois Bureau of Economic and Business
Research, 1961).

Metz, Joseph F.
Accuracy of Response Obtained in a Milk Consumption Study
Methods of Research in Marketing, Paper No. 5
(Cornell University, Agricultural Experiment Station, July 1956).

Neter, John and Waksberg, Joseph
Response Errors in Collection of Expenditures Data by Household
Interviews: An Experimental Study"
Technical Paper No. 11
(U.S. Department of Commerce, Bureau of the Census, 1965).

Politz, Alfred
Description of Operational Design and Procedures
Life Magazine Study of Consumer Expenditures--Volume Four
(1958).

Prais, S. J.
"Some Problems in the Measurement of Price Changes With Special
Reference to the Cost of Living"
Journal of the Royal Statistical Society, Series A, Part 3 (1958),
pp. 312-32.

Presser, Stanley
"Is Inaccuracy on Factual Survey Items Item-Specific or
Respondent-Specific?"
Public Opinion Quarterly, Vol. 48 (Spring 1984), pp. 344-55.

Rorer, Leonard G.
"The Great Response-Style Myth"
Psychological Bulletin, Vol. 63 (March 1965), pp. 129-56.

Sudman, Seymour
"On the Accuracy of Recording of Consumer Panels: II"
Journal of Marketing Research, Vol. I (August 1964), pp. 69-83.

Sudman, Seymour
"On the Accuracy of Recording of Consumer Panels: I"
Journal of Marketing Research, Vol. I (May 1964), pp. 14-20.

116.04 ---------- Estimation of and Adjustment for Response Bias

Bye, Barry V. and Schechter, Evan S.
"A Latent Markov Model Approach to the Estimation of Response Errors
in Multiwave Panel Data"
Journal of the American Statistical Association, Vol. 81 (June 1986),
pp. 375-80.

Garfinkel, R. S., Kunnathur, A. S., and Liepins, G. E.
"Optimal Imputation of Erroneous Data: Categorical Data, General
Edits"
Operations Research, Vol. 34 (September-October 1986), pp. 744-51.

Gruber, Robert E. and Lehmann, Donald R.
"The Effect of Omitting Response Tendency Variables From Regression
Models"
in Darden, William R., Monroe, Kent B., and Dillon, William R.
(editors)
Research Methods and Causal Modelling in Marketing
(Chicago: American Marketing Association, 1983), pp. 131-6.

Marquis, Kent H., Marquis, Susan M., and Polich, J. Michael
"Response Bias and Reliability in Sensitive Topic Surveys"
Journal of the American Statistical Association, Vol. 81 (June 1986),
pp. 381-9.

Schaninger, Charles M. and Buss, W. Christian
"Removing Response-Style Effects in Attribute-Determinance Ratings to
Identify Market Segments"
Journal of Business Research, Vol. 14 (June 1986), pp. 237-52.

Selen, Jan
"Adjusting for Errors in Classification and Measurement in the
Analysis of Partly and Purely Categorical Data"
Journal of the American Statistical Association, Vol. 81 (March
1986), pp. 75-81.

Sharot, Trevor
    "Weighting Survey Results"
    Journal of the Market Research Society, Vol. 28 (July 1986), pp.
    269-84.

116.05 ---------- Recall Errors

        See also (sub)heading(s) 18.04.

Byham, William C. and Perloff, Robert
    "Recall of Product Purchase and Use after Six Years"
    Journal of Advertising Research, Vol. 5 (September 1965), pp. 16-9.

Cash, W. S. and Moss, A. J.
    "Methodology Study for Determining the Optimum Recall Period for the
    Reporting of Motor Vehicle Accidental Injury"
    Proceedings of the Social Statistics Section of the American
    Statistical Association (1969), pp. 364-78.

Cole, Dorothy and Utting, J. E. G.
    "Estimating Expenditure, Saving and Income From Household Budgets"
    Journal of the Royal Statistical Society, Series A, Part 4 (1956),
    pp. 371-92.

Cook, William A.
    "Telescoping and Memory's Other Tricks"
    Journal of Advertising Research, Vol. 27 (February-March 1987), pp.
    5-8.

Cornfield, Jerome
    "On Certain Biases in Samples of Human Populations"
    Journal of the American Statistical Association, Vol. 37 (March
    1942), pp. 63-8.

Ehrenberg, A. S. C.
    "How Reliable Is Aided Recall of TV Viewing?"
    Journal of Advertising Research, Vol. 1 (June 1961), pp. 29-31.

Fink, R.
    "The Retrospective Question"
    Public Opinion Quarterly, Vol. 24 (1960), pp. 143-8.

Goldberg, S. A.
    "Nonsampling Error in Household Surveys--A General Review of Some
    Canadian Work"
    Meeting of the International Statistical Institute, Stockholm (1957),
    paper presentation.

Greene, Robert L.
    "Sources of Recency Effects in Free Recall"
    Psychological Bulletin, Vol. 99 (March 1986), pp. 221-8.

Jaeger, Carol M. and Pennock, Jean L.
    "A Note on Accuracy and Consistency of Response in Household Surveys"
    U.S. Department of Agriculture (1962), unpublished memorandum.

Jaeger, Carol M. and Pennock, Jean L.
    "An Analysis of Consistency of Response in Household Surveys"
    Journal of the American Statistical Association, Vol. 56 (June 1961),
    pp. 320-7.

Juster, F. Thomas
    "Response Errors in the Measurement of Time Use"
    Journal of the American Statistical Association, Vol. 81 (June 1986),
    pp. 390-402.

Kemsley, W. F. F.
    "Interviewer Variability in Expenditure Surveys"
    Journal of the Royal Statistical Society, Series A, Part 1 (1965),
    pp. 118-39.

Leavitt, Clark
    "Response Structure: A Determinant of Recall"
    Journal of Advertising Research, Vol. 8 (September 1968), pp. 3-6.

Lewis, Harrie F.
    "A Comparison of Consumer Responses to Weekly and Monthly Purchase
    Panels"
    Journal of Marketing, Vol. XII (April 1948), pp. 449-54.

Mahalanobis, P. C. and Sen, S. B.
    "On Some Aspects of the Indian National Sample Survey"
    Bulletin de l'Institut International de Statistique, Vol. 34, Part 2
    (1953), pp. 5-14.

Menneer, Peter
    "Retrospective Data in Survey Research"
    Journal of the Market Research Society, Vol. 20 (July 1978), pp.
    182-95.

Parfitt, John H.
"A Comparison of Purchase Recall With Diary Panel Records"
Journal of Advertising Research, Vol. 7 (September 1967), pp. 16-31.

Rothwell, N. D.
"Measurements of Bias in SORAR--1963"
U.S. Bureau of the Census (1964), unpublished memorandum.

Sikkel, Dirk
"Models for Memory Effects"
Journal of the American Statistical Association, Vol. 80 (December
1985), pp. 835-41.

Smith, Tom W.
"Recalling Attitudes: An Analysis of Retrospective Questions on the
1982 GSS"
Public Opinion Quarterly, Vol. 48 (Fall 1984), pp. 639-49.

Sudman, Seymour and Bradburn, Norman
"Effects of Time and Memory on Response in Surveys"
Journal of the American Statistical Association, Vol. 68 (December
1973), pp. 805-15.

U.S. Bureau of the Census
Consumer Buying Indicators
Series P-65, No. 19 (September 29, 1967).

Utting, J. E. G. and Cole, Dorothy
"Sampling for Social Accounts--Some Aspects of the Cambridgeshire
Survey"
Bulletin de l'Institut International de Statistique, Vol. 34, Part 2
(1953), pp. 301-28.

Withey, S. B.
"Reliability of Recall of Income"
Public Opinion Quarterly, Vol. 18 (1954), pp. 197-204.

Zarkovich, S. S.
Quality of Statistical Data
(Rome, IT: Food and Agriculture Organization of the United Nations,
1966).

116.06 ---------- Uninformed Responses

       See also (sub)heading(s) 117.02.

Bishop, George F., Oldendick, Robert W., Tuchfarber, Alfred J., and
Bennet, Stephen E.
"Pseudo-Opinions and Public Affairs"
Public Opinion Quarterly, Vol. 44 (Summer 1980), pp. 198-209.

Bishop, George F., Tuchfarber, Alfred J., and Oldendick, Robert W.
"Opinions on Fictitious Issues: The Pressure to Answer Survey
Questions"
Public Opinion Quarterly, Vol. 50 (Summer 1986), pp. 240-50.

Converse, Philip E.
"Attitudes and Non-Attitudes: Continuation of a Dialogue"
in Tufte, E. R. (editor)
The Quantitative Analysis of Social Problems
(Reading, MA: Addison-Wesley, 1970).

Ferber, Robert
"The Effect of Respondent Ignorance on Survey Results"
Journal of the American Statistical Association, Vol. 51 (December
1956), pp. 576-86.

Gill, Sam N.
"How do You Stand on Sin?"
Tide, Vol. 72 (March 14, 1947).

Glassman, Myron and Ford, John B.
"An Empirical Investigation of Bogus Recall"
Journal of the Academy of Marketing Science, Vol. 16 (Fall 1988), pp.
38-41.

Hawkins, Del I. and Coney, Kenneth A.
"Uninformed Response Error in Survey Research"
Journal of Marketing Research, Vol. XVIII (August 1981), pp. 370-4.

Hawkins, Del I., Coney, Kenneth A., and Jackson, Donald W., Jr.
"The Impact of Monetary Inducement on Uninformed Response Error"
Journal of the Academy of Marketing Science, Vol. 16 (Summer 1988),
pp. 30-5.

Presser, Stanley
"Is Inaccuracy on Factual Survey Items Item-Specific or Respondent
Specific?"
Public Opinion Quarterly, Vol. 48 (Spring 1984), pp. 344-55.

Schneider, Kenneth C.
    "Uninformed Response Rates in Survey Research: New Evidence"
    Journal of Business Research, Vol. 13 (April 1985), pp. 153-62.

Schneider, Kenneth C. and Johnson, James C.
    "Respondent Concern, Response Pressure and Uninformed Response: A
    Research Note"
    Working Paper No. 429
    Office of Research and Development, College of Business, St. Cloud
    State University.

Schuman, Howard and Presser, Stanley
    "Public Opinion and Public Ignorance: The Fine Line Between Attitudes
    and Nonattitudes"
    American Journal of Sociology, Vol. 85 (March 1980), pp. 1214-25.

116.07 ---------- Cue Effects

Alba, Joseph W. and Chattopadhyay, Amitava
    "Effects of Context and Part-Category Cues on Recall of Competing
    Brands"
    Journal of Marketing Research, Vol. XXII (August 1985), pp. 340-9.

Basden, David R.
    "Cued and Uncued Recall of Unrelated Words Following Interpolated
    Learning"
    Journal of Experimental Psychology, Vol. 98 (1973), pp. 429-31.

Cagley, James W., Schneider, Kenneth C., and Johnson, James C.
    "A Research Note on Techniques for Controlling Uninformed Responses"
    Journal of the Market Research Society, Vol. 30 (October 1988), pp.
    483-7.

Hudson, Robert L. and Austin, James B.
    "Effect of Context and Category Name on the Recall of Categorized
    Word Lists"
    Journal of Experimental Psychology, Vol. 86 (1970), pp. 43-7.

Lewis, Marion Quinn
    "Categorized Lists and Cued Recall"
    Journal of Experimental Psychology, Vol. 87 (1971), pp. 129-31.

Parker, Richard E. and Warren, Linda
    "Partial Category Cuings: The Accessibility of Categories"
    Journal of Experimental Psychology, Vol. 102 (1974), pp. 1123-5.

Raaijmakers, Jeroen G. W. and Shiffrin, Richard M.
    "Search of Associative Memory"
    Psychological Review, Vol. 88 (1981), pp. 93-134.

Roediger, Henry L., III
    "Recall as a Self-Limiting Process"
    Memory and Cognition, Vol. 6 (1978), pp. 54-63.

Roediger, Henry L., III
    "Inhibiting Effects of Recall"
    Memory and Cognition, Vol. 2 (1974), pp. 261-9.

Roediger, Henry L., III
    "Inhibition in Recall From Cueing With Recall Targets"
    Journal of Verbal Learning and Verbal Behavior, Vol. 12 (1973), pp.
    644-57.

Roediger, Henry L., III and Schmidt, Stephen R.
    "Output Interference in the Recall of Categorized and
    Paired-Associate Lists"
    Journal of Experimental Psychology: Human Learning and Memory, Vol. 6
    (1980), pp. 91-105.

Roediger, Henry L., III, Stellon, Christina C., and Tulving, Endel
    "Inhibition From Part-List Cues and Rate of Recall"
    Journal of Experimental Psychology: Human Learning and Memory, Vol. 3
    (1977), pp. 174-88.

Rundus, Dewey
    "Negative Effects of Using List Items as Recall Cues"
    Journal of Verbal Learning and Verbal Behavior, Vol. 12 (1973), pp.
    43-50.

Slamecka, Norman J.
    "Testing for Associative Storage in Multitrial Free Recall"
    Journal of Experimental Psychology, Vol. 81 (1969), pp. 557-60.

Slamecka, Norman J.
    "An Examination of Trace Storage in Free Recall"
    Journal of Experimental Psychology, Vol. 76 (1968), pp. 504-13.

Tulving, Endel and Pearlstone, Zena
"Availability Versus Accessibility of Information in Memory for Words"
Journal of Verbal Learning and Verbal Behavior, Vol. 5 (1966), pp.
381-91.

Tulving, Endel and Psotka, Joseph
"Retroactive Inhibition in Free Recall: Inaccessibility of
Information Available in the Memory State"
Journal of Experimental Psychology, Vol. 87 (1971), pp. 1-8.

Wood, Gordon
"Retrieval Cues and the Accessibility of Higher-Order Memory Units in
Multitrial Free Recall"
Journal of Verbal Learning and Verbal Behavior, Vol. 9 (1969), pp.
782-9.

116.08 ---------- Conditioning Effects

Ehrenberg, A. S. C.
"A Study of Some Potential Biases in the Operation of a Consumer
Panel"
Applied Statistics, Vol. 9 (March 1960), pp. 20-7.

Ferber, Robert
"Observations in a Consumer Panel Operation"
Journal of Marketing, Vol. XVII (January 1953), pp. 246-59.

Kemsley, W. F. F.
"The Household Expenditure Enquiry of the Ministry of Labour:
Variability in the 1953-54 Enquiry"
Applied Statistics (November 1961), pp. 117-35.

Turner, Robert
"Inter-Week Variations in Expenditure Recorded During a Two-Week
Survey of Family Expenditures"
Applied Statistics, Vol. 10 (November 1961), pp. 117-35.

116.09 ---------- Context Effects

Alba, Joseph W. and Chattopadhyay, Amitava
"Effects of Context and Part-Category Cues on Recall of Competing
Brands"
Journal of Marketing Research, Vol. XXII (August 1985), pp. 340-9.

Barclay, J. R., Bransford, John D., Franks, Jeffrey J., McCarrell,
Nancy S., and Nitsch, Kathy
"Comprehension and Semantic Flexibility"
Journal of Verbal Learning and Verbal Behavior, Vol. 13 (1974), pp.
471-81.

Flexser, Arthur J. and Tulving, Endel
"Retrieval Independence in Recognition and Recall"
Psychological Review, Vol. 85 (1978), pp. 153-71.

Hudson, Robert L. and Austin, James B.
"Effect of Context and Category Name on the Recall of Categorized
Word Lists"
Journal of Experimental Psychology, Vol. 86 (1970), pp. 43-7.

Lewis, Marion Quinn
"Categorized Lists and Cued Recall"
Journal of Experimental Psychology, Vol. 87 (1971), pp. 129-31.

Pellegrino, James W. and Salzberg, Philip M.
"Encoding Specificity in Associative Processing Tasks"
Journal of Experimental Psychology: Human Learning and Memory, Vol. 1
(1975), pp. 538-48.

116.10 ---------- Reporting Load Effects

Reagan, Barbara B. and Grossman, Evelyn
Rural Levels of Living in Lee and Jones Counties, Mississippi, 1945,
and a Comparison of Two Methods of Data Collection
(U.S. Department of Agriculture, Information Bulletin 41, 1951).

116.11 ---------- Yeasaying and Naysaying, Noting Set Bias

Arndt, Johan and Crane, Edgar
"Response Bias, Yea-Saying, and the Double Negative"
Journal of Marketing Research, Vol. XII (May 1975), pp. 218-21.

Asch, M. J.
"Negative Response Bias and Personality Adjustment"
Journal of Counseling Psychology, Vol. 5 (1958), pp. 206-10.

Bachman, Jerald G. and O'Malley, Patrick M.
    "Yea-Saying, Nay-Saying, and Going to Extremes: Black-White
    Differences in Response Styles"
    Public Opinion Quarterly, Vol. 48 (Summer 1984), pp. 491-509.

Becker, Boris W. and Myers, John G.
    "Yeasaying Response Style"
    Journal of Advertising Research, Vol. 10 (December 1970), pp. 31-7.

Berg, I. A. and Rapaport, G. M.
    "Response Bias in an Unstructured Questionnaire"
    Journal of Psychology, Vol. 38 (1954), pp. 475-81.

Block, Jack
    The Challenge of Response Sets
    (New York: Appleton-Century-Crofts, 1965).

Bylund, Bruce and Sanders, David
    "Validity of High Scores on Certain Self-Evaluation Questions"
    Rural Sociology, Vol. 32 (September 1957), pp. 346-51.

Campbell, Donald T., Siegman, Carole R., and Reese, Matilda B.
    "Direction-of-Wording Effects in the Relationship Between Scales"
    Psychological Bulletin, Vol. 68 (November 1967), pp. 293-303.

Clancy, Kevin J. and Garsen, Robert
    "Why Some Scales Predict Better"
    Journal of Advertising Research, Vol. 10 (October 1970), pp. 33-8.

Couch, Arthur and Kenniston, Kenneth
    "Yeasayers and Naysayers: Agreeing Response Set as a Personality
    Variable"
    Journal of Abnormal and Social Psychology, Vol. 60 (March 1960), pp.
    151-74.

Cronbach, L. J.
    "Further Evidence on Response Sets and Test Design"
    Educational and Psychological Measurement, Vol. 10 (Spring 1950), pp.
    3-31.

Cronbach, L. J.
    "Response Sets and Test Validity"
    Educational and Psychological Measurement, Vol. 6 (1946), pp. 475-94.

Dohrenwend, Bruce P.
    "Social Status and Psychiatric Disorder: An Issue of Substance and an
    Issue of Method"
    American Sociological Review, Vol. 31 (February 1966), pp. 14-34.

Guilford, J. P.
    "Response Biases and Response Sets"
    in Fishbein, Martin (editor)
    Readings in Attitude Theory and Measurement
    (New York: John Wiley and Sons, Inc., 1967).

Hare, A. P.
    "Interview Responses: Personality or Conformity?"
    Public Opinion Quarterly, Vol. 24, No. 4 (1960), pp. 679-85.

Hathaway, S. R.
    "Some Considerations Relative to Nondirective Counseling as Therapy"
    Journal of Clinical Psychology, Vol. 4 (1948), pp. 226-31.

Jackson, D. N. and Messick, S.
    "Content and Style in Personality Assessment"
    Psychological Bulletin, Vol. 55 (July 1958), pp. 243-52.

Lenski, G. E. and Leggett, J. C.
    "Caste, Class and Deference in the Research Interview"
    American Journal of Sociology, Vol. 65, pp. 463-7.

Lewis, N. A. and Taylor, J. A.
    "Anxiety and Extreme Response Preferences"
    Educational and Psychological Measurement, Vol. 15 (1955), pp. 111-6.

Lorge, I. Gen-Like
    "Halo or Reality?" (abstract)
    Psychological Bulletin, Vol. 34 (1937), pp. 545,6.

Peabody, Dean
    "Authoritarianism Scales and Response Bias"
    Psychological Bulletin, Vol. 65 (January 1966), pp. 11-23.

Peabody, Dean
    "Models for Estimating Content and Set Components in Attitude and
    Personality Scales"
    Educational and Psychological Measurement, Vol. 24 (Summer 1964), pp.
    255-69.

Peabody, Dean
    "Attitude Content and Agreement Set in Scales of Authoritarianism,
    Dogmatism, Anti-Semitism, and Economic Conservatism"
    Journal of Abnormal and Social Psychology, Vol. 66 (January 1963),
    pp. 1-11.

Rokeach, Milton
    "The Double Agreement Phenomenon: Three Hypotheses"
    Psychological Review, Vol. 70 (July 1963), pp. 304-9.

Rorer, Leonard G.
    "The Great Response-Style Myth"
    Psychological Bulletin, Vol. 63 (March 1965), pp. 129-56.

Rundquist, E. A.
    "Response Sets: A Note on Consistency in Taking Extreme Positions"
    Educational and Psychological Measurement, Vol. 10 (1950), pp. 97-9.

Samelson, Franz
    "Agreement Set and Anticontent Attitudes in the F Scale: A
    Reinterpretation"
    Journal of Abnormal and Social Psychology, Vol. 68 (March 1964), pp.
    338-42.

Sanford, Fillmore H.
    Authoritarianism and Leadership
    (Philadelphia: Stephenson Publishing, 1950).

Singer, W. B. and Young, P. T.
    "Studies in Affective Reaction: III--The Specificity of Affective
    Reactions"
    Journal of General Psychology, Vol. 24 (1941), pp. 327-41.

Smith, J. Walker
    "Dependence as a Research Design Strategy"
    Marketing Research, Vol. 1 (June 1989), pp. 64-6.

Solomon, Leonard and Klein, Edward
    "The Relationship Between Agreeing Response Set and Social
    Desirability"
    Journal of Abnormal and Social Psychology, Vol. 66 (February 1963),
    pp. 176-9.

Webster, H.
    "The Meaning of 'Response Set' in Personality Inventories" (abstract)
    American Psychologist, Vol. 15 (July 1960), p. 431.

Wells, William D.
    "How Chronic Overclaimers Distort Survey Findings"
    Journal of Advertising Research, Vol. 3 (June 1963), pp. 8-18.

Wells, William D.
    "The Influence of Yeasaying Response Style"
    Journal of Advertising Research, Vol. 1 (June 1961), pp. 1-12.

Wells, William D. and Dames, Joel
    "Hidden Errors in Survey Data"
    Journal of Marketing, Vol. 26 (October 1962), pp. 50-4.

116.12 ---------- Acquiescence

Appel, Valentine and Blum, Milton L.
    "Ad Recognition and Response Set"
    Journal of Advertising Research, Vol. 1 (June 1961), pp. 13-21.

Bass, B. M.
    "Development and Evaluation of a Scale for Measuring Social
    Acquiescence"
    Journal of Abnormal and Social Psychology, Vol. 53 (1956), pp. 296-9.

Bock, R. Darrell, Dicken, Charles, and Van Pelt, John
    "Methodological Implications of Content-Acquiescence Correlations in
    the MMPI"
    Psychological Bulletin, Vol. 71 (January 1969), pp. 127-39.

Chapman, L. J. and Campbell, D. T.
    "The Effect of Acquiescence Response-Set Upon Relationships Among the
    F Scale, Ethnocentrism and Intelligence"
    Sociometry, Vol. 22 (1959), pp. 153-61.

Jackson, D. N.
    "Acquiescence Response Styles: Problems of Identification and Control"
    in Berg, I. A. (editor)
    Response Set in Personality Assessmet
    Chicago: Aldine, 1967).

Jackson, Douglas N. and Messick, Samuel
    "A Note on Ethnocentrism and Acquiescent Response Sets"
    Journal of Abnormal Psychology, Vol. 54 (May 1957), pp. 424-6.

Lentz, T. F.
  "Acquiescence as a Factor in the Measurement of Personality"
  (abstract)
  Psychological Bulletin, Vol. 25 (1938), p. 659.

Lichtenstein, E., Quinn, R. P., and Hover, G. L.
  "Dogmatism and Acquiescent Response Set"
  Journal of Abnormal and Social Psychology, Vol. 63 (1961), pp. 636-8.

Ray, John J.
  "Re-Inventing the Wheel: Winkler, Kanouse and Ware on Acquiescent
  Response Set"
  Journal of Applied Psychology, Vol. 69 (May 1984), pp. 353-5.

Winkler, John D., Kanouse, David E., and Ware, John E., Jr.
  "Does Acquiescence Distort Attitude Scale Structure: Round and Round
  With Ray"
  Journal of Applied Psychology, Vol. 69 (May 1984), pp. 356-8.

116.13 ---------- Nondiscrimination

Gold, Bertram and Salkind, William
  "What do 'Top Box' Scores Measure?"
  Journal of Advertising Research, Vol. 14 (April 1974), pp. 19-23.

116.14 ---------- Socially Desireable Response Bias

        See also (sub)heading(s) 35, 36.

Edwards, Allen L.
  "Social Desireability and Performance on the MMPI"
  Psychometrika (1964), pp. 295-308.

Silver, Brian D., Abramson, Paul R., and Anderson, Barbara A.
  "Public Opinion Quarterly, Vol. 50 (Summer 1986), pp. 228-39.

116.15 ---------- Income, Savings, Assets, Expenditures Response Bias

        See also (sub)heading(s) 58.11.

Borus, M. E.
  "Response Error and Questioning Technique in Earnings Surveys"
  Journal of the American Statistical Association, Vol. 65 (June 1970),
  pp. 566-75.

Borus, M. E.
  "Response Error in Survey Reports of Earnings Information"
  Journal of the American Statistical Association, Vol. 61 (September
  1966), pp. 729-38.

Erritt, J. J. and Nicholson, J. L.
  "The 1955 Savings Survey"
  Bulletin of the Oxford University Institute of Statistics (May 1959),
  pp. 111-29.

Ferber, Robert
  The Reliability of Consumer Reports of Financial Assets and Debts
  (Champaign, IL: Bureau of Economic and Business Research, University
  of Illinois, 1966).

Ferber, Robert, Forsythe, John B., Guthrie, Harold W., and Maynes, E.
  Scott
  "Validation of Consumer Financial Characteristics: Common Stock"
  Journal of the American Statistical Association (June 1969), pp.
  415-32.

Friend, Irwin and Schor, Stanley
  "Who Saves?"
  Review of Economics and Statistics, Part II (May 1959).

Haberman, Paul W. and Elinson, Jack
  "Family Income Reported in Surveys: Husbands Versus Wives"
  Journal of Marketing Research, Vol. IV (May 1967), pp. 191-4.

Kish, Leslie and Lansing, John B.
  "Response Errors in Estimating the Value of Homes"
  Journal of the American Statistical Association, Vol. 49 (September
  1954), pp. 520-38.

Lydall, J. F.
  British Incomes and Saving
  (Oxford, EN: Basil Blackwell, 1955).

Maynes, E. Scott
  "Minimizing Response Errors in Financial Data: The Possibilities"
  Journal of the American Statistical Association, Vol. 63 (March
  1968), pp. 214-27.

Maynes, E. Scott
     "The Anatomy of Response Errors: Consumer Saving"
     Journal of Marketing Research, Vol. II (November 1965), pp. 378-87.

Neter, John and Waksberg, Joseph
     "A Study of Response Errors in Expenditures Data From Household
     Interviews"
     Journal of the American Statistical Association, Vol. 59 (March
     1964), pp. 18-55.

U.S. Bureau of the Census
     Response Errors in Collection of Expenditures Data by Household
     Interviews: An Experimental Study
     Technical Paper No. 11
     (Washington, DC: U.S. Government Printing Office, 1965).

Van Arsdol, Maurice D. and Jahn, Julius A.
     "Time and Population Sampling Applied to the Estimation of
     Expenditures of University Students"
     American Sociological Review, Vol. 17 (December 1952), pp. 738-46.

Withey, Stephen B.
     Consistency of Immediate and Delayed Report of Financcial Data
     University of Michigan (1952), unpublished Ph.D. dissertation.

116.16 ---------- Unclassified (Response Bias)

Back, Kurt W. and Gergen, Kenneth J.
     "Idea Orientation and Ingratiation in the Interview"
     Proceedings of the Social Statistics Section, American Statistical
     Association (1963), pp. 284-8.

Barnes, E. H.
     "Response Bias in the MMPI"
     Journal of Consulting Psychology, Vol. 20 (1956), pp. 371-4.

Belkin, Marvin and Lieberman, Seymour
     "Effect of Question Wording on Response Distribution"
     Journal of Marketing Research, Vol. IV (August 1967), pp. 312,3.

Bell, C. R.
     "Psychological Versus Sociological Variables in Studies of Volunteer
     Bias in Surveys"
     Journal of Applied Psychology, Vol. 45 (April 1961), pp. 80-5.

Berg, I. A. and Rapaport, G. M.
     "Response Bias in an Unstructured Questionnaire"
     Journal of Psychology, Vol. 38 (October 1954), pp. 475-81.

Bobren, Howard M.
     The Time Order of Response and Nonresponse Bias in Mail Surveys
     University of Illinois (1962), unpublished Ph.D. dissertation, 74 pp.

Bradburn, Norman M., Sudman, Seymour, Blair, Ed, and Stocking, Carol
     "Question Threat and Response Bias"
     Public Opinion Quarterly.

Bray, James H., Maxwell, Scott E., and Howard, George S.
     "Methods of Analysis With Response-Shift Bias"
     Educational and Psychological Measurement, Vol. 44 (Winter 1984), pp.
     781-804.

Broida, Arthur L.
     "Consumer Surveys as a Source of Information for Social
     Accounting--The Problems"
     in National Bureau of Economic Research
     The Flow-of-Funds Approach to Social Accounting
     (Princeton, NJ: The Princeton University Press, 1963).

Cannell, Charles F. and Henson, Ramon
     "Incentives, Motives and Response Bias"
     Annals of Economic and Social Measurement, Vol. 3 (1974), p. 319.

Drevenstedt, J.
     "Scale-Checking Styles on the Semantic Differential Among Older
     People"
     Journal of Gerontology, Vol. 30 (March 1975), pp. 170-3.

Duncanson, J. P.
     "The Average Telephone Call Is Better Than the Average Telephone Call"
     Public Opinion Quarterly, Vol. 33 (Spring 1969), pp. 112-6.

Federal Reserve Board
     Reports of Federal Reserve Consultant Committees on Economic
     Statistics: The "Smithies Committee"
     The "Goldsmith Committee"
     (Washington, DC: Government Printing Office, 1955).

Ferber, R.
  "The Effect of Respondent Ignorance on Survey Results"
  Journal of the American Statistical Association, Vol. 51 (December
  1956), pp. 576-86.

Frankel, Lester R.
  "The Role of Accuracy and Precision of Response in Sample Surveys"
  in Johnson, Norman and Smith, Harry, Jr. (editors)
  New Developments in Survey Sampling
  (New York: John Wiley and Sons, Inc., 1969).

Hansen, Jochen
  "How Problematic are Random Responses in Panel Studies?"
  European Research, Vol. 16 (February 1988), pp. 34-41.

Hansen, Morris H., Hurwitz, W. N., and Bershad, M. A.
  "Measurement Errors in Censuses and Surveys"
  Bulletin of the International Statistical Institute, Tokyo, Vol. 38,
  Part 2 (1961), pp. 359-74.

Hansen, M. H., Hurwitz, W. N., Marks, E. S., and Mauldin, W. P.
  "Response Errors in Surveys"
  Journal of the American Statistical Association, Vol. 46 (June 1951),
  pp. 147-90.

Hoofnagle, W. S. and Anderson, K. E.
  "Problems of Response Bias in Collecting Milk Consumption Data From
  School Children"
  Journal of Farm Economics, Vol. 42 (August 1960), pp. 699-703.

Horn, W.
  "Non-Response in an Interview Survey"
  Reprint of an article in Het Pit-Bedriff (May 1963).

Horn, W.
  "Reliability Survey: A Survey on the Reliability of Response to an
  Interview Survey"
  Reprint of an article in Het Pit-Bedriff (October 1960).

Ito, R.
  "An Analysis of Reponse Errors: A Case Study"
  Journal of Business, Vol. 36 (October 1963), pp. 440-7.

Jackman, Mary R.
  "Education and Prejudice or Education and Response Set"
  American Sociological Review, Vol. 38 (1973), pp. 327-39.

Jaeger, Carol M. and Pennock, Jean L.
  "An Analysis of Consistency of Response in Household Surveys"
  Journal of the American Statistical Association, Vol. 56 (June 1961),
  pp. 320-7.

Johnson, Weldon T. and Delamater, John D.
  "Response Effects in Sex Surveys"
  Public Opinion Quarterly, Vol. 40 (Summer 1976), pp. 165-81.

Jordan, Lawrence A., Marcus, Alfred C., and Reeder, Leo G.
  "Response Styles in Telephone and Household Interviewing: A Field
  Experiment"
  Public Opinion Quarterly, Vol. 44 (Summer 1980), pp. 210-21.

Krosnick, Jon A. and Schuman, Howard
  "Attitude Intensity, Importance and Certainty and Susceptibility to
  Response Effects"
  Journal of Personality and Social Psychology, Vol. 54 (June 1988),
  pp. 940-52.

Madow, W. G.
  "On Some Aspects of Response Error Measurement"
  Proceedings of the Social Statistics Section of the American
  Statistical Association (1965), pp. 182-92.

McGee, R. K.
  "Response Style as a Personality Variable: By What Criterion"
  Psychological Bulletin, Vol. 59 (1962), pp. 284-95.

Metz, Joseph F.
  Accuracy of Response Obtained in a Milk Consumption Study
  Methods of Research in Marketing, Paper No. 5
  (Cornell University, Agricultural Experiment Station, July 1965).

Nathan, Gad
  "An Empirical Study of Response and Sampling Errors for Multiplicity
  Estimates With Different Counting Rules"
  Journal of the American Statistical Association, Vol. 71 (December
  1976), pp. 808-15.

National Council of Applied Economic Research
  Urban Income and Saving
  (New Delhi, India: 1961).

National Health Survey
    Reporting of Hospitalization in the The Health Interview
    (U.S. Department of Health, Education, and Welfare, Public Health
    Service, 1961).

Neter, John, Maynes, E. Scott, and Ramanathan, R.
    "The Effect of Mis-Matching on the Measurement of Response Errors"
    Journal of the American Statistical Association, Vol. 61 (1966).

Neter, John and Waksberg, Joseph
    "A Study of Response Errors in Expenditures Data From Household
    Interviews"
    Journal of the American Statistical Association, Vol. 59 (March
    1964), pp. 18-55.

O'Muircheartaigh, C.
    "Response Error"
    in O'Muircheartaigh, C. and Payne, C. (editors)
    The Analysis of Survey Data: Model Fitting
    (London: John Wiley and Sons, Ltd., 1977).

Rosenthal, Robert
    "How Often are Our Numbers Wrong?"
    American Psychologist, Vol. 33 (November 1978), pp. 1005-8.

Schreiber, E. M.
    "Dirty Data in Britain and the USA: The Reliability of 'Invariant'
    Characteristics Reported in Surveys"
    Public Opinion Quarterly, Vol. XXXIX (Winter 1975-76).

Sudman, Seymour and Bradburn, Norman M.
    "Effect of Time and Memory Factors on Response in Surveys"
    Journal of the American Statistical Association, Vol. 68 (December
    1973), pp. 805-15.

Tull, Donald S.
    "Intentional Bias in Public Opinion Polls for Decisional Purposes"
    Public Opinion Quarterly, Vol. XXXIX (Winter 1975-76).

Wells, W. D. and Dames, J.
    "Hidden Errors in Survey Data"
    Journal of Marketing, Vol. 26 (October 1962), pp. 50-4.

Whitmore, William J.
    "Mail Survey Premiums and Response Bias"
    Journal of Marketing Research, Vol. XIII (February 1976), pp. 46-50.

Zarkovich, S. S.
    Quality of Statistical Data
    (Rome, Italy: Food and Agriculture Organization of the United
    Nations, 1966).

117 ----------------------- NONRESPONSE BIAS -----------------------
        See also (sub)heading(s) 34, 35, 36, 62.08, 71.03, 72.01,
        87.07, 132.04, 133.

117.01 ---------- Refusals

        See also (sub)heading(s) 74.03, 87.06.

Benson, S. W., Boomen, W. P., and Clark, K.
  "A Study of Interview Refusals"
  Journal of Applied Psychology, Vol. 35 (April 1951), pp. 116-9.

Dohrenwend, Barbara S. and Dohrenwend, Bruce P.
  "Sources of Refusals in Surveys"
  Public Opinion Quarterly, Vol. 32 (Spring 1968), pp. 74-83.

Dommermuth, William P. and Cateora, Philip R.
  "Can Refusals by Respondents be Decreased?"
  Journal of Marketing, Vol. 27 (July 1963), pp. 74-6.

Dunkelberg, W. and Day, G.
  "Nonresponse Bias and Callbacks in Sample Surveys"
  Journal of Marketing Research, Vol. X (May 1973), pp. 160-8.

Fox, F. L.
  "Noncooperation Bias in Television Ratings"
  Public Opinion Quarterly, Vol. 27 (Summer 1963), pp. 312-4.

Harding, John
  "Refusals as a Source of Bias"
  in Cantril, Hadley (editor)
  Gauging Public Opinion
  (Princeton, NJ: Princeton University Press, 1947).

Kruglov, L. P. and Davidson, H. H.
  "The Willingness to be Interviewed: A Selective Factor in Sampling"
  Journal of Social Psychology, Vol. 38 (August 1953), pp. 39-47.

O'Neil, Michael J.
  "Estimating the Nonresponse Bias Due to Refusals in Telephone Surveys"
  Public Opinion Quarterly, Vol. 43 (Summer 1979), pp. 218-32.

Pomeroy, Wardell B.
  "The Reluctant Respondent"
  Public Opinion Quarterly, Vol. 28 (Summer 1963), pp. 287-93.

Robins, Lee N.
  "The Reluctant Respondent"
  Public Opinion Quarterly, Vol. 27 (Summer 1963), pp. 276-86.

Skelton, Vincent C.
  "Patterns Behind 'Income Refusals'"
  Journal of Marketing, Vol. 27 (July 1963), pp. 38-41.

Van Westerhoven, E. M. C.
  "Covering Non-Response: Does It Pay? A Study of Refusers and
  Absentees"
  Journal of the Market Research Society, Vol. 20 (October 1978), pp.
  245-7.

Wilcox, James B.
  "The Interaction of Refusal and Not-at-Home Sources of Nonresponse
  Bias"
  Journal of Marketing Research, Vol. XIV (November 1977), pp. 592-7.

117.02 ---------- No Opinion and I Don't Know (Non)Responses

        See also (sub)heading(s) 116.06.

Bishop, George F., Oldendick, Robert W., and Tuchfarber, Alfred J., Jr.
  "What Must My Interest in Politics be if I Just Told You 'I Don't
  Know'?"
  Public Opinion Quarterly, Vol. 48 (Summer 1984), pp. 510-9.

Bishop, George F., Oldendick, Robert W., and Tuchfarber, Alfred J.
  "Effects of Filter Questions in Public Opinion Surveys"
  Public Opinion Quarterly, Vol. 47 (Winter 1983), pp. 528-46.

Bogart, Leo
  "No Opinion, Don't Know, and Maybe No Answer"
  Public Opinion Quarterly, Vol. 31 (Fall 1967), pp. 331-45.

Converse, Jean M.
  "Predicting No Opinion in the Polls"
  Public Opinion Quarterly, Vol. 40 (Winter 1976-77), pp. 515-30.

Coombs, Clyde H. and Coombs, Lolagene C.
  "Don't Know: Item Ambiguity or Respondent Uncertainty"
  Public Opinion Quarterly, Vol. 40 (Winter 1976-77), pp. 497-514.

Duncan, Otis Dudley and Stenbeck, Magnus
"No Opinion or Not Sure?"
Public Opinion Quarterly, Vol. 52 (Winter 1988), pp. 513-25.

Durand, Richard M. and Lambert, Zarrel V.
"Don't Know Responses in Surveys: Analyses and Interpretational
Consequences"
Journal of Business Research, Vol. 16 (March 1988), pp. 169-88.

Faulkenberry, G. David and Mason, Robert
"Characteristics of Nonopinion and No Opinion Response Groups"
Public Opinion Quarterly, Vol. 42 (Winter 1978), pp. 533-43.

Francis, Joe D. and Busch, Lawrence
"What We Know About 'I Don't Knows'"
Public Opinion Quarterly, Vol. 39 (Summer 1975), pp. 207-18.

Leigh, James H. and Martin, Claude R., Jr.
"'Don't Know' Item Nonresponse in a Telephone Survey: Effects of
Question Form and Respondent Characteristics"
Journal of Marketing Research, Vol. XXIV (November 1987), pp. 418-24.

Poe, Gail S., Seeman, Isadore, McLaughlin, Joseph, Mehl, Eric, and
Dietz, Michael
"'Don't Know' Boxes in Factual Questions in a Mail Questionnaire:
Effects on Level and Quality of Response"
Public Opinion Quarterly, Vol. 52 (Summer 1988), pp. 212-22.

Schuman, Howard and Presser, Stanley
"The Assessment of 'No Opinion' in Attitude Surveys"
in Schuessler, Karl F. (editor)
Sociological Methodology 1979
(San Francisco: Jossey-Bass, 1978), pp. 241-75.

Sicinski, Anorzej
"'I Don't Know' Answers in Cross-National Surveys"
Public Opinion Quarterly, Vol. 34 (Spring 1970), pp. 126-9.

Ziller, R. C. and Long, B. H.
"Some Correlates of the Don't-Know Response in Opinion Questionnaires"
Journal of Social Psychology, Vol. 67 (October 1965), pp. 139-47.

117.03 ---------- Nonresponse Bias Estimation and Adjustment Procedures

See also (sub)heading(s) 132.04, 133.

Armstrong, J. Scott and Overton, Terry S.
"Estimating Nonresponse Bias in Mail Surveys"
Journal of Marketing Research, Vol. XIV (August 1977), pp. 396-402.

Baker, Stuart G. and Laird, Nan M.
"Regression Analysis for Categorical Variables With Outcome Subject
to Non-Ignorable Nonresponse"
Journal of the American Statistical Association, Vol. 83 (March
1988), pp. 62-9.

Bronner, Alfred E.
"A Way to Handle Non-Response: Simulation of Missing Values"
European Research, Vol. 11 (July 1983), pp. 86-92.

Fay, Robert E.
"Causal Models for Patterns of Nonresponse"
Journal of the American Statistical Association, Vol. 81 (June 1986),
pp. 354-65.

Gilley, Otis W. and Leone, Robert P.
"A Two-Stage Imputation Procedure for Item Nonresponse in Surveys"
Marketing Department, The University of Texas at Austin (1985),
working paper.

Hartley, H. O.
"Comments on Paper by F. Yates"
Journal of the Royal Statistical Society, A, Vol. 109 (1946), pp.
37,8.

Hawkins, D.
"Estimation of Nonresponse Bias"
Sociological Methods and Research, Vol. 3 (May 1975), pp. 461-83.

Hendricks, Walter A.
"Adjustment for Bias by Non-Response in Mail Surveys"
Agricultural Economics Research, Vol. 1 (1949), pp. 52-6.

Kish, Leslie and Hess, Irene
"A 'Replacement' Procedure for Reducing the Bias of Nonresponse"
American Statistician, Vol. 13 (1959), pp. 17-9.

Lagay, B.
   "Assessing Bias: A Comparison of Two Methods"
   Public Opinion Quarterly, Vol. 33 (Winter 1969-70), pp. 615-8.

Miller, William L.
   "The British Vote and the Telephone at the 1983 Election"
   Journal of the Market Research Society, Vol. 29 (January 1987), pp.
   67-82.

Ognibene, Peter
   "Correcting Non-Response Bias in Mail Questionnaires"
   Journal of Marketing Research, Vol. VIII (May 1971), pp. 233-5.

Pearl, Dennis K. and Fairley, David
   "Testing for the Potential for Nonresponse Bias in Sample Surveys"
   Public Opinion Quarterly, Vol. 49 (Winter 1985), pp. 553-60.

Politz, A. and Simmons, W.
   "An Attempt to get the 'Not at Homes' Into the Sample Without
   Callbacks. II. Further Theoretical Considerations for Eliminating
   Callbacks"
   Journal of the American Statistical Association, Vol. 44 (1949), pp.
   9-31.

Rubin, Donald B.
   Multiple Imputation for Nonresponse in Surveys
   (New York: John Wiley and Sons, Inc., 1987), 258 pp.

Smith, Tom W.
   "The Hidden 25 Percent: An Analysis of Non-Response on the 1980
   General Social Survey"
   Public Opinion Quarterly, Vol. 47 (Fall 1983), pp. 386-404.

117.04 ---------- Extrapolation Techniques

          See also (sub)heading(s) 70.

Dickinson, John R. and Kirzner, Eric
   "A Comparison of Survey Respondent to Nonrespondent Extrapolation
   Methods" (abstract)
   Proceedings, America n Marketing Association Educators' Conference
   (August 1988).

Dickinson, John R. and Kirzner, Eric
   "The Validity of Estimating Nonresponse Bias by Extrapolation"
   Proceedings, American Institute for Decision Sciences, (November
   1985).

Ellis, Robert A., Endo, Calvin M., and Armer, Michael J.
   "The Use of Potential Nonrespondents for Studying Nonresponse Bias"
   Pacific Sociological Review, Vol. 13 (Spring 1970), pp. 103-9.

Filion, F. L.
   "Exploring and Correcting for Nonresponse Bias Using Follow-Ups of
   Nonrespondents"
   Pacific Sociological Review, Vol. 19 (July 1976), pp. 401-8.

Filion, F. L.
   "Estimating Bias Due to Nonresponse in Mail Surveys"
   Public Opinion Quarterly, Vol. 40 (Winter 1975-76), pp. 482-92.

Zimmer, H.
   "Validity of Extrapolating Non-Response Bias From Mail Questionnaire
   Follow-Ups"
   Journal of Applied Psychology, Vol. 40 (1956), pp. 117-21.

117.05 ---------- Theory Re: Weighting Data

          See also (sub)heading(s) 133, 138.

Collins, M. and Hedges, B.
   "Variable Sampling Fractions and the Effect of Weighting"
   SCPR Methodological Working Paper No. 4
   (October 1977).

Conway, S.
   "The Weighting Game"
   Market Research Society Conference Papers (1982), pp. 193-207.

Deming, W. E. and Stephan, F. F.
   "On a Least Squares Adjustment of a Sampled Frequency Table When the
   Expected Marginal Totals are Known"
   Annals of Mathematical Statistics, Vol. 11 (1940), pp. 427-44.

Kalton, G. and Kasprzyk, D.
   "The Treatment of Missing Survey Data"
   Survey Methodology (Statistics Canada), Vol. 12, No. 1 (1986).

Sharot, Trevor
  "Response" (to Upton)
  Journal of the Market Research Society, Vol. 29 (July 1987), p. 366.

Sharot, Trevor
  "Weighting Survey Results"
  Journal of the Market Research Society, Vol. 28 (July 1986), pp.
  269-84.

Upton, Graham J. G.
  On the Use of Rim Weighting"
  Journal of the Market Research Society, Vol. 29 (July 1987), pp.
  363-6.

117.06 ---------- Applications of Weighting Schemes

Miller, William L.
  "The British Vote and the Telephone at the 1983 Election"
  Journal of the Market Research Society, Vol. 29 (January 1987), pp.
  67-82.

Stephenson, C. Bruce
  "Weighting the General Social Surveys for Bias Related to Household
  Size"
  655 Technical Report Number 3
  (Chicago: 1978).

117.07 ---------- Unclassified (Nonresponse Bias)

Benson, S. W., Boomen, W. P., and Clark, K.
  "A Study of Interview Refusals"
  Journal of Applied Psychology, Vol. 35 (April 1951), pp. 116-9.

Birnbaum, Z. W. and Sirken, M. G.
  "On the Total Error Due to Non-Interview and to Random Sampling"
  International Journal of Opinion and Attitude Research (1950), pp.
  179-91.

Birnbaum, Z. W. and Sirken, M. G.
  "Bias Due to Non-Availability in Sampling Surveys"
  Journal of the American Statistical Association, Vol. 45 (March
  1950), pp. 98-111.

Bobren, Howard M.
  The Time Order of Response and Nonresponse Bias in Mail Surveys
  University of Illinois (1962), unpublished Ph.D. dissertation, 74 pp.

Crossley, H. M. and Fink, R.
  "Response and Non-Response in a Probability Sample"
  International Journal of Opinion and Attitude Research (1951), pp.
  1-19.

Dalenius, T.
  "Treatment of the Non-Response Problem"
  Journal of Advertising Research, Vol. 1 (September 1961), pp. 1-7.

Dalenius, T.
  "The Problem of Not-at-Homes"
  Statistisk Tidskrift (1955), pp. 208-11.

Dalenius, T.
  "The Problem of Non-Response in Statistical Surveys"
  The Swedish Market (1951).

Daniel, W.
  "Nonresponse in Sociological Surveys"
  Sociological Methods and Research, Vol. 3 (February 1975), pp.
  291-305.

Day, R. and Wilcox, J.
  "A Simulation Analysis of Nonresponse Error in Survey Sampling"
  Combined Proceedings, 1971 Spring and Fall Conferences, American
  Marketing Association, pp. 478-83.

Deming, W. E.
  "On a Probability Mechanism to Attain an Economic Balance Between the
  Resultant Error of Response and the Biases of Nonresponses"
  Journal of the American Statistical Association, Vol. 48 (1953), pp.
  743-72.

Donald, Marjorie N.
  "Implications of Nonresponse for the Interpretation of Mail Data"
  Public Opinion Quarterly, Vol. 24 (Spring 1960), pp. 90-114.

Dunkelberg, W. and Day, G.
  "Nonresponse Bias and Callbacks in Sample Surveys"
  Journal of Marketing Research, Vol. X (May 1973), pp. 160-8.

Goudy, Willis J.
    "Nonresponse Effects: Studies of the Failure of Potential Respondents
    to Reply to Survey Instruments"
    Exchange Bibliography No. 1236
    (Monticello, IL: Council of Planning Librarians, 1977), 14 pp.

Goudy, Willis J.
    "Nonresponse Effects on Relationships Between Variables"
    Public Opinion Quarterly, Vol. 40 (Fall 1976), pp. 360-9.

Guggenheim, Bernard
    "All Research is Not Created Equal"
    Journal of Advertising Research, Vol. 29 (February/March 1989), pp.
    RC7-11.

Hansen, M. H. and Hurwitz, W. N.
    "The Problem of Nonresponse in Sample Surveys"
    Journal of the American Statistical Association, Vol. 41 (December
    1946), pp. 517-29.

Hilgard, E. R. and Payne, S. L.
    "Those Not at Home: Riddle for Pollsters"
    Public Opinion Quarterly (1944), pp. 254-61.

Kirchner, Wayne K. and Mousley, Nancy B.
    "A Note on Job Performance: Differences Between Respondent and
    Nonrespondent Salesmen to an Attitude Survey"
    Journal of Applied Psychology, Vol. 47 (June 1963), pp. 223,4.

Leslie, Larry
    "Are High Response Rates Essential to Valid Surveys?"
    Social Science Research, Vol. 1 (September 1972), pp. 323-34.

Maynes, E. Scott and Rolnick, Arthur J.
    "Nonreporting of Savings Accounts in Sample Surveys: Causes and
    Correlates"
    Proceedings of the Business and Economic Statistics Section of the
    American Statistical Association (1975), pp. 160-5.

Rubin, Donald B.
    "Formalizing Subjective Notions About the Effect of Nonrespondents in
    Sample Surveys"
    Journal of American Statistical Association, Vol. 72 (1977), pp.
    538-43.

Wayne, Ivor
    "Nonresponse, Sample Size, and the Allocation of Resources"
    Public Opinion Quarterly, Vol. XXXIX (Winter 1975-76).

Williams, W. H.
    "The Seriousness of Selection Biases, Including Nonresponse"
    Proceedings, Social Statistics Section, American Statistical
    Association (1975), pp. 11-5.

Williams, W. H.
    "The Systematic Bias Effects of Incomplete Responses in Rotation
    Samples"
    Public Opinion Quarterly, Vol. 33 (Winter 1969-70), pp. 593-602.

118 ------------------------- RELIABILITY ------------------------

See also (sub)heading(s) 119, 120, 121, 122, 139.

118.01 ---------- Books Re: Reliability

Bohrnstedt, George W., Mohler, Peter P., and Muller, Walter (editors)
An Empirical Study of the Reliability and Stability of Survey
Research Items
(Beverly Hills, CA: Sage Publications, Inc., 1987), 180 pp.

Carmines, Edward G. and Zeller, Richard A.
Reliability and Validity Assessment
(Beverly Hills, CA: Sage Publications, Inc., 1980), 68 pp.

Kirk, Jerome and Miller, Marc L.
Reliability and Validity in Qualitative Research
(Beverly Hills, CA: Sage Publications, Inc., 1986), 87 pp.

118.02 ---------- Theory Re: Reliability

Alexander, H. W.
"The Estimation of Reliability When Several Trials are Available"
Psychometrika, Vol. 12 (June 1947), pp. 79-99.

Bagozzi, Richard P.
"Reliability Assessment by Analysis of Covariance Structures"
in Jain, S. C. (editor)
Research Frontiers in Marketing: Dialogues and Directions
(Chicago: American Marketing Association, 1978), pp. 71-5.

Bohrnstedt, G. W.
"Reliability and Validity Assessment in Attitude Measurement"
in Summers, G. F. (editor)
Attitude Measurement
(Skokie, IL: Rand McNally, 1970), pp. 81-99.

Cattell, R. B.
"Validity and Reliability: A Proposed More Basic Set of Concepts"
Journal of Educational Psychology, Vol. 55 (February 1964), pp. 1-22.

Cleary, T. Anne, Linn, Robert, and Walster, G. William
"Effect of Reliability and Validity on Power of Statistical Tests"
in Borgatta, Edgar F. and Bohrnstedt, George W. (editors)
Sociology Methodology
(San Francisco: Jossey-Bass, 1970), pp. 130-8.

Cronbach, L. J.
"Test 'Reliability': Its Meaning and Determination"
Psychometrika, Vol. 12 (March 1947), pp. 1-16.

Ebel, Robert L.
"Estimation of the Reliability of Ratings"
Psychometrika, Vol. 16 (December 1951), pp. 407-24.

Epstein, S.
"The Stability of Behavior: I. On Predicting Most of the People Much
of the Time"
Journal of Personality and Social Psychology, Vol. 37 (July 1979),
pp. 1097-1126.

Guttman, Louis
"Problems of Reliability"
in Measurement and Prediction
Studies in Social Psychology in World War II, Volume Four
(Princeton, NJ: Princeton University Press, 1950).

Heise, D. R.
"Validity, Invalidity, and Reliability"
in Borgatta, E. F. and Bohrnstedt, G. W. (editors)
Sociological Methodology
(San Francisco: Jossey-Bass, 1970), pp. 104-29.

John, George and Roedder, Deborah L.
"Reliability Assessments: Coefficients Alpha and Beta"
in Bernhardt, Kenneth et al. (editors)
The Changing Marketing Environment: New Theories and Applications
(Chicago: American Marketing Association, 1981), pp. 354-7.

Morrison, Donald G.
"Reliability of Tests: A Technique Using the 'Regression to the Mean'
Fallacy"
Journal of Marketing Research, Vol. X (February 1973), pp. 91-3.

Mosier, Charles I.
"On the Reliability of a Weighted Composite"
Psychometrika, Vol. 8 (September 1943), pp. 161-8.

Naylor, James C. and Schenck, E. Allen
  "Rho-M as an 'Error-Free' Index of Rater Agreement"
  Educational and Psychological Measurement, Vol. 26 (1966), pp. 815-24.

Peter, J. Paul
  "Reliability: A Review of Psychometric Basics and Recent Marketing
  Practices"
  Journal of Marketing Research, Vol. XVI (February 1979), pp. 6-17.

Ray, Michael L.
  "Introduction to the Special Section: Measurement and Marketing
  Research: Is the Flirtation Going to Lead to a Romance?
  Journal of Marketing Research, Vol. XVI (February 1979), pp. 1-6.

Smith, K. W.
  "On Estimating the Reliability of Composite Indices Through Factor
  Analysis"
  Sociological Methods and Research, Vol. 2 (May 1974), pp. 485-510.

Sutcliffe, J. P.
  "On the Relationship of Reliability to Statistical Power"
  Psychological Bulletin, Vol. 88 (September 1980), pp. 509-15.

Werts, Charles E., Linn, Robert L., and Joreskog, Karl G.
  "A General Method of Estimating the Reliability of a Composite"
  Educational and Psychological Measurement, Vol. 38 (1978), pp. 933-8.

Werts, C. E., Linn, R. L., and Joreskog, K. G.
  "Interclass Reliability Estimates: Testing Structural Assumptions"
  Educational and Psychological Measurement, Vol. 34 (1974), pp. 25-33.

118.03 ---------- Theory Re: Test-Retest Reliability

Heise, David R.
  "Separating Reliability and Stability in Test-Retest Correlation"
  American Sociological Review, Vol. 34 (February 1969), pp. 93-101.

Schmittlein, D. C.
  "Assessing Validity and Test-Retest Reliability for 'Pick K of N'
  Data"
  Marketing Science, Vol. 3 (Winter 1984), pp. 23-40.

118.04 ---------- Applications of Test-Retest Reliability

Bearden, William O., Teel, Jesse E., and Wright, Robert R.
  "Family Income Effects on Measurement of Children's Attitudes Toward
  Televison Commercials"
  Journal of Consumer Research, Vol. 6 (December 1979), pp. 308-11.

Best, Roger, Hawkins, Del I., and Albaum, Gerald
  "Reliability of Measured Beliefs in Consumer Research"
  in Perreault, W. D. (editor)
  Advances in Consumer Research, Vol. 4
  (Atlanta: Association for Consumer Research, 1977), pp. 19-23.

Best, Roger, Hawkins, Del I., and Albaum, Gerald
  "The Role of Random Weights and Reliability in the Assessment of
  Multiattribute Attitude Models"
  in Anderson, B. B. (editor)
  Advances in Consumer Research, Vol. 3
  (Chicago: Association for Consumer Research, 1976).

Blackston, Max and Van Der Zanden, Nico
  "Validity of Conjoint Analysis: Some Real Market Results"
  European Research, Vol. 8 (November 1980), pp. 243-50.

Byham, William C. and Perloff, Robert
  "Recall of Product Purchase and Use after Six Years"
  Journal of Advertising Research, Vol. 5 (September 1965), pp. 16-9.

Dickinson, John R.
  "Test-Retest Reliability of Alternative Means of Collecting
  Unidimensional Proportions Data"
  Proceedings, Academy of Marketing Science, Miami (May 1979).

Kassarjian, Harold H. and Nakanishi, Masao
  "A Study of Selected Opinion Measurement Techniques"
  Journal of Marketing Research, Vol. IV (May 1967), pp. 148-53.

Kirsch, Arthur D., Berger, Philip K., and Belford, R. J., II
  "Are Reports of Brands Bought Last Reliable and Valid?"
  Journal of Advertising Research, Vol. 2 (June 1962), pp. 34-6.

Leavitt, Clark, Waddell, Charles, and Wells, William
  "Improving Day-After Recall Techniques"
  Journal of Advertising Research, Vol. 10 (June 1970), pp. 13-7.

Leigh, Thomas W., MacKay, David B., and Summers, John O.
   "Reliability and Validity of Conjoint Analysis and Self-Explicated
   Weights: A Comparison"
   Journal of Marketing Research, Vol. XXI (November 1984), pp. 456-62.

Lindquist, Jay D.
   "Measuring Children's Attitudes Toward TV Commercials: An Instrument
   Reliability Test"
   Journal of the Academy of Marketing Science, Vol. 9 (Fall 1981), pp.
   409-18.

Malhotra, Naresh K.
   "A Scale to Measure Self-Concepts, Person Concepts, and Product
   Concepts"
   Journal of Marketing Research, Vol. XVIII (November 1981), pp. 456-64.

Reynolds, Thomas J. and Jolly, James P.
   "Measuring Personal Values: An Evaluation of Alternative Methods"
   Journal of Marketing Research, Vol. XVII (November 1980), pp. 531-6.

Riecken, Glen and Samli, A. Coskun
   "Measuring Children's Attitudes Toward Television Commercials:
   Extension and Replication"
   Journal of Consumer Research, Vol. 8 (June 1981), pp. 57-61.

Rossiter, John R.
   "Reliability of a Short Test Measuring Children's Attitudes Toward TV
   Commercials"
   Journal of Consumer Research, Vol. 3 (March 1977), pp. 179-84.

Segal, Madhav N.
   "Reliability of Conjoint Analysis: Contrasting Data Collection
   Procedures"
   Journal of Marketing Research, Vol. XIX (February 1982), pp. 139-43.

Silk, Alvin J.
   "Test-Retest Correlations and the Reliability of Copy Testing"
   Journal of Marketing Research, Vol. XIV (November 1977), pp. 476-86.

Summers, J. O. and MacKay, D. B.
   "On the Validity and Reliability of Direct Similarity Judgments"
   Journal of Marketing Research, Vol. XIII (August 1976), pp. 289-95.

Tigert, D. J.
   "Psychographics: A Test-Retest Reliability Analysis"
   in McDonald, Phillip R. (editor)
   Marketing Involvement in Society and the Economy
   (Chicago: American Marketing Association, 1969).

Villani, Kathryn E. and Lehmann, Donald R.
   "An Examination of the Stability of AIO Measures"
   in Mazze, Edward M. (editor)
   Marketing: The Challenges and Opportunities
   (Chicago: American Marketing Association, 1975), pp. 484-8.

Villani, Kathryn E. and Wind, Yoram
   "On the Usage of 'Modified' Personality Trait Measures in Consumer
   Research"
   Journal of Consumer Research, Vol. 2 (December 1975), pp. 223-8.

Westbrook, Robert A.
   "A Rating Scale for Measuring Product/Service Satisfaction"
   Journal of Marketing, Vol. 44 (Fall 1980), pp. 68-72.

Wilkes, Robert E. and Wilcox, James B.
   "On the Validity and Reliability of Direct Similarity Judgments: A
   Comment"
   Journal of Marketing Research, Vol. XIV (May 1977), pp. 261,2.

118.05 ---------- Unclassified Reliability Studies

Angelmar, Reinhard and Stern, Louis W.
   "Development of a Content Analytic System for Analysis of Bargaining
   Communication in Marketing"
   Journal of Marketing Research, Vol. XV (February 1978), pp. 93-102.

Appel, Valentine
   "The Reliability and Decay of Advertising Measurements"
   Marketing Conference of the National Industrial Conference Board
   (October 1966), paper presentation.

Bagozzi, Richard P.
   "Salesforce Performance and Satisfaction as a Function of Individual
   Difference, Interpersonal, and Situational Factors"
   Journal of Marketing Research, Vol. XV (November 1978), pp. 517-31.

Bain, R.
   "Stability in Questionnaire Response"
   American Journal of Sociology, Vol. 37 (1931), pp. 445-53.

Bancroft, G.
   "Consistency of Information From Records and Interviews"
   Journal of the American Statistical Association, Vol. 35 (1940), pp.
   377-81.

Bendig, A. W.
   "Reliability and the Number of Rating Categories"
   Journal of Applied Psychology, Vol. 38 (February 1954), pp. 38-40.

Bendig, A. W.
   "The Reliability of Self-Ratings as a Function of the Amount of Verbal
   Anchoring and of the Number of Categories on a Scale"
   Journal of Applied Psychology, Vol. 37 (February 1953), pp. 38-41.

Best, Roger J.
   "Validity and Reliability of Criterion-Based Preferences"
   Journal of Marketing Research, Vol. XV (February 1978), pp. 154-60.

Best, Roger J., Albaum, Gerald S., Hawkins, Del I., and Kenyon, Georgia
   "Number of Response Intervals and Reliability of Factor Analyzed
   Semantic Scale Data"
   Southwestern Marketing Association (1978).

Best, Roger J., Hawkins, Del I., and Albaum, Gerald
   "Reliability of Measured Beliefs in Consumer Research"
   in Perreault, William D., Jr. (editor)
   Advances in Consumer Research, Volume 4
   (Ann Arbor, MI: Association for Consumer Research, 1977), pp. 19-23.

Bohrnstedt, George W.
   "Reliability and Validity Assessment in Attitude Measurement"
   in Summers, G. F. (editor)
   Attitude Measurement
   (Chicago: Rand McNally, 1970), pp. 81-99.

Bohrnstedt, G. W.
   "A Quick Method for Determining the Reliability and Validity of
   Multiple-Item Scales"
   American Sociological Review, Vol. 34 (August 1969), pp. 542-8.

Boruch, Robert F. and Wolins, Leroy
   "A Procedure for Estimation of Trait, Method and Error Variance
   Attributable to a Measure"
   Educational and Psychological Measurement, Vol. 30 (November 1970),
   pp. 547-74.

Burns, Alvin C. and Harrison, Mary C.
   "A Test of the Reliability of Psychographics"
   Journal of Marketing Research, Vol. XVI (February 1979), pp.32-8.

Cuber, J. and Gerberich, J.
   "A Note on Consistency in Questionnaire Responses"
   American Sociological Review, Vol. 11 (1946), pp. 13-5.

Curtis, A.
   "Reliability of a Report on Listening Habits"
   Journal of Applied Psychology, Vol. 23 (1939), pp. 127-30.

Davis, Harry, Douglas, Susan P., and Silk, Alvin
   "A Cross National Comparison of the Reliability of Selected
   Measurements From Consumer Surveys"
   Massachusetts Institute of Technology (1980), working paper.

Ehrenberg, A. S. C.
   "How Reliable Is Aided Recall of TV Viewing?"
   Journal of Advertising Research, Vol. 1 (June 1961), pp. 29-31.

Ferber, R.
   "The Reliability of Consumer Surveys of Financial Holdings: Demand
   Deposits"
   Journal of the American Statistical Association, Vol. 61 (December
   1966), pp. 91-103.

Ferber, Robert
   The Reliabilty of Consumer Reports of Financial Assets and Debts
   (Urbana, IL: Bureau of Economic and Business Research, University of
   Illinois, 1966).

Ferber, R.
   "The Reliability of Consumer Surveys of Financial Holdings: Time
   Deposits"
   Journal of the American Statistical Association, Vol. 60 (March
   1965), pp. 148-63.

Ferber, Robert
   "On the Reliability of Purchase Influence Studies"
   Journal of Marketing, Vol. 29 (January 1955), p. 232.

Ferber, Robert
  "Does a Panel Operation Increase the Reliabilty of Survey Data: The
  Case of Consumer Savings"
  Journal of the American Statistical Association, Vol. 50 (September
  1955), pp. 788-810.

Ferber, Robert
  "On the Reliability of Response Secured in Sample Surveys"
  Journal of the American Statistical Association, Vol. 50 (September
  1953), pp. 788-810.

Fleiss, J. L.
  "Estimating the Reliability of Interview Data"
  Psychometrika, Vol. 35 (June 1970), pp. 143-62.

Gerberich, J. B.
  "A Study of the Consistency of Informant Responses to Questions in a
  Questionnaire"
  Kent State University (1941), unpublished Master's thesis.

Green, Paul E., Rao, Vithala R., and Armani, Diana E.
  "Graphology and Marketing Research: A Pilot Experiment in Validity
  and Inter-Judge Reliability"
  Journal of Marketing, Vol. 35 (April 1971), pp. 58-62.

Hirschman, E. C., Greenberg, B., and Robertson, D. H.
  "The Intermarket Reliability of Retail Image Research: An Empirical
  Examination"
  Journal of Retailing, Vol. 54, No. 1 (1978), pp. 3-12.

Jacoby, Jacob, Chestnut, Robert, Hoyer, Wayne D., Sheluga, David A.,
  and Donahue, Michael J.
  "Psychometric Characteristics of Behavioral Process Data: Preliminary
  Findings on Validity and Reliability"
  in Hunt, H. Keith (editor)
  Advances in Consumer Research, Volume Five
  (Ann Arbor, MI: Association for Consumer Research, 1978).

Jenkins, J. G.
  "Dependability of Psychological Brand Barometers--The Problem of
  Reliability"
  Journal of Applied Psychology, Vol. 22 (1938), pp. 1-7.

Kalwani, M. U. and Silk, A. J.
  "On the Reliability and Predictive Validity of Purchase Intention
  Measures"
  Marketing Science, Vol. 1 (Summer 1982), pp. 243-86.

Lehmann, Donald R. and Britney, Kathryn
  "Determining an Appropriate Measure of Reliability for Psychographic
  Measures"
  in Greenberg, B. A. and Bellenger, D. N. (editors)
  Contemporary Marketing Thought
  (Chicago: American Marketing Association, 1977), pp. 333-6.

Lehnen, R. G.
  "Assessing Reliability in Sample Surveys"
  Public Opinion Quarterly, Vol. 35 (Winter 1971-72), pp. 578-92.

Lissitz, Robert W. and Green, Samuel B.
  "Effect of the Number of Scale Points on Reliability: A Monte Carlo
  Approach"
  Journal of Applied Psychology, Vol. 60 (February 1975), pp. 10-3.

Matell, Michael S. and Jacoby, Jacob
  "Is There an Optimal Number of Alternatives for Likert Scale Items?
  Study I: Reliability and Validity"
  Educational and Psychological Measurement, Vol. 31 (Autumn 1971), pp.
  657-74.

McCullough, James and Best, Roger
  "Conjoint Measurement: Temporal Stability and Structural Reliability"
  Journal of Marketing Research, Vol. XVI (February 1979), pp. 26-31.

Noerager, Jon P.
  "An Assessment of CAD: A Personality Instrument Developed
  Specifically for Marketing Research"
  Journal of Marketing Research, Vol. XVI (February 1979), pp. 53-9.

Parameswaran, Ravi, Greenberg, B. A., Bellenger, D. N., and Robertson,
  D. H.
  "Measuring Reliability: A Comparison of Alternative Techniques"
  Journal of Marketing Research, Vol. XVI (February 1979), pp. 18-25.

Pessemier, E. A. and Bruno, A.
  "An Empirical Investigation of the Reliability and Stability of
  Selected Activity and Opinion Measures"
  Proceedings, Second Annual Conference, Association for Consumer
  Research (1971), pp. 389-403.

Poti, S. J., Chakraborti, B., and Malaker, C. R.
    "Reliability of Data Relating Contraceptive Practices"
    in Kiser, Clyde V. (editor)
    Research in Family Planning
    (Princeton, NJ: Princeton University Press, 1962), pp. 51-65.

Silk, Alvin J.
    "A Note on the Use of Tests for the Stability of Variances in
    Reliability Studies"
    Working Paper 76-53
    European Institute for Advanced Studies in Management, Brussels
    (December 1976).

Silk, Alvin J. and Bultez, Alain
    "Product Category Variability in the Reliability of Copy Tests"
    Working Paper 76-48
    European Institute for Advanced Studies in Management
    Brussels (October 1976).

Smith, M.
    "A Note on Stability in Questionnaire Response"
    American Journal of Sociology, Vol. 38 (1933), pp. 713-20.

Symonds, Percival M.
    "On the Loss of Reliability in Ratings Due to Coarseness of the Scale"
    Journal of Experimental Psychology, Vol. 7 (December 1924), pp.
    456-61.

Tigert, Douglas J.
    "Life Style Analysis as a Basis for Media Selection"
    in Wells, W. D. (editor))
    Life Style and Psychographics
    (Chicago: American Marketing Association, 1974), pp. 171-201.

Tryon, R. C.
    "Reliability and Behavior Domain Validity: Reformation and Historical
    Critique"
    Psychological Bulletin, Vol. 54 (May 1957), pp. 229-49.

Vaillancourt, P. M.
    "Stability of Children's Survey Responses"
    Public Opinion Quarterly, Vol. 37 (Fall 1973), pp. 373-87.

Vaughn, C. L. and Reynolds, W. A.
    "Reliability of Personal Interview Data"
    Journal of Applied Psychology, Vol. 35 (1951), pp. 61-3.

Waugh, R. E.
    "Increasing the Validity and Reliability of Tourist Data"
    Journal of Marketing, Vol. 20 (January 1956), pp. 286-8.

Withey, S. B.
    "Reliability of Recall of Income"
    Public Opinion Quarterly, Vol. 18 (Summer 1954), pp. 197-204.

118.06 ---------- Unclassified (Reliability)

Joachimsthaler, Erich A., Curtis, Lane, and Michaels, Ronald E.
    "RELCON: A Program for the Estimation of Internal Consistency of
    Composites with Congeneric Measurement Properties"
    Journal of Marketing Research, Vol. XXII (May 1985), pp. 216,7.

119 ------ NOMINAL DATA, INTER-RATER, OR INTER-JUDGE RELIABILITY -----
    See also (sub)heading(s) 118.

119.01 ---------- Theory Re: Nominal Data, Inter-Rater/Judge Reliabilit

Bennett, E. M., Alpert, R., and Goldstein, A. G.
    "Communications Through Limited Response Questioning"
    Public Opinion Quarterly, Vol. 18 (1954), pp. 303-8.

Crittenden, K. S. and Hill, R. J.
    "Coding Reliability and Validity of Interview Data"
    American Sociological Review, Vol. 36 (1971), pp. 1073-80.

Dewey, M. E.
    "Coefficients of Agreement"
    British Journal of Psychiatry, Vol. 143 (1983), pp. 487-9.

Dillon, William R. and Mulani, Narendra
    "A Probabilistic Latent Class Model for Assessing Inter-Judge
    Reliability"
    Multivariate Behavioral Research, Vol. 19 (October 1984), pp. 438-58.

Fleiss, Joseph L.
    "Measuring Agreement Between Two Judges on the Presence or Absence of
    a Trait"
    Biometrics, Vol. 31 (1975), pp. 651-9.

Fleiss, Joseph L.
    "Measuring Nominal Scale Agreement Among Many Raters"
    Psychological Bulletin, Vol. 76, No. 5 (1971), pp. 378-82.

Helzer, John E., Robins, Lee N., Tarbleson, Mitchell, Woodruff, Robert
    A., Reich, Theodore, and Wish, Eric D.
    "Reliability of Psychiatric Diagnosis: A Methodological Review"
    Archives of General Psychiatry, Vol. 34 (February 1977), pp. 129-33.

Janes, Cynthia L.
    "An Extension of the Random Error Coefficient of Agreement to N by N
    Tables"
    British Journal of Psychiatry, Vol. 134 (1979), pp. 617-9.

Koran, Lorrin M.
    "Reliability of Clinical Methods, Data, and Judgments"
    New England Journal of Medicine, Vol. 293 (October 2, 1975), pp.
    695-701.

Krippendorff, K.
    "Bivariate Agreement Coefficients for Reliability of Data"
    in Borgatta, E. F. and Bohrnstedt, G. W. (editors)
    Sociological Methodology
    (San Francisco: Jossey-Bass Publishers, 1970).

Landis, J. Richard and Koch, Gary G.
    "The Measurement of Observer Agreement for Categorical Data"
    Biometrics, Vol. 33 (March 1977), pp. 159-74.

Lawlis, G. Frank and Lu, Elba
    "Judgments of Counseling Process: Reliability, Agreement, and Error"
    Psychological Bulletin, Vol. 78, No. 1 (1972), pp. 17-20.

Light, Richard J.
    "Measures of Response Agreement for Qualitative Data: Some
    Generalizations and Alternatives"
    Psychological Bulletin, Vol. 76, No. 5 (1971), pp. 365-77.

Maxwell, A. E.
    "Coefficients of Agreement Between Observers and Their Interpretation"
    British Journal of Psychiatry, Vol. 130 (1977), pp. 79-83.

Mitchell, Sandra K.
    "Interobserver Agreement, Reliability, and Generalizability of Data
    Collected in Observational Studies"
    Psychological Bulletin, Vol. 86, No. 2 (1979), pp. 376-90.

Perreault, William D., Jr. and Leigh, Laurence E.
    "Reliability of Nominal Data Based on Qualitative Judgments"
    Journal of Marketing Research, Vol. XXVI (May 1989), pp. 135-48.

119.02 ---------- Theory Re: Cohen's Kappa or K

Brennan, Robert L. and Prediger, Dal J.
    "Coefficient Kappa: Some Uses, Misuses, and Alternatives"
    Educational and Psychological Measurement, Vol. 41 (1981), pp. 687-99.

Cohen, Jacob
    "Weighted Kappa: Nominal Scale Agreement With Provision for Scaled
    Disagreement or Partial Credit"
    Psychological Bulletin, Vol. 70 (October 1968), pp. 213-20.

Cohen, Jacob
"A Coefficient of Agreement for Nominal Scales"
Educational and Psychological Measurement, Vol. 20 (1960), pp. 37-46.

Everitt, B. S.
"Moments of the Statistics Kappa and Weighted Kappa"
British Journal of Mathematical and Statistical Psychology, Vol. 21
(May 1968), pp. 97-103.

Fleiss, Joseph L., Cohen, Jacob, and Everitt, B. S.
"Large Sample Standard Errors of Kappa and Weighted Kappa"
Psychological Bulletin, Vol. 72, No. 5 (1969), pp. 323-7.

Hubert, Lawrence
"Kappa Revisited"
Psychological Bulletin, Vol. 84 (March 1977), pp. 289-97.

Kraemer, Helena C.
"Ramifications of a Population Model for K as a Coefficient of
Agreement"
Psychometrica, Vol. 44 (December 1979), pp. 461-72.

Scott, William A.
"Reliability of Content Analysis: The Case of Nominal Scale Coding"
Public Opinion Quarterly, Vol. 19 (Fall 1955), pp. 321-5.

119.03 ---------- Applications of Cohen's Kappa

Kerin, Roger A. and Cron, William L.
"Assessing Trade Show Functions and Performance: An Exploratory Study"
Journal of Marketing, Vol. 51 (July 1987), pp. 87-94.

119.04 ---------- Theory Re: Tinsley-Weiss T-Statistic

Tinsley, Howard E. A. and Weiss, David J.
"Interrater Reliability and Agreement of Subjective Judgments"
Journal of Counseling Psychology, Vol. 22 (July 1975), pp. 358-76.

119.05 ---------- Applications of Tinsley-Weiss T-Statistic

Dwyer, F. Robert and Welsh, M. Ann
"Environmental Relationships of the Internal Political Economy of
Marketing Channels"
Journal of Marketing Research, Vol. XXII (November 1985), pp. 397-414.

119.06 ---------- Unclassified Applications of Inter-Rater Reliability

Brucks, Merrie, Armstrong, Gary M., and Goldberg, Marvin E.
"Children's Use of Cognitive Defenses Against Television Advertising:
A Cognitive Response Approach"
Journal of Consumer Research, Vol. 14 (March 1988), pp. 471-82.

Cannon, Hugh M.
"A New Method for Estimating the Effect of Media Context"
Journal of Advertising Research, Vol. 22 (October/November 1982), pp.
41-8.

Garret, Dennis E.
"The Effectiveness of Marketing Policy Boycotts: Environmental
Opposition to Marketing"
Journal of Marketing, Vol. 51 (April 1987), pp. 46-57.

Green, Paul E., Rao, Vithala R., and Armani, Diana E.
"Graphology and Marketing Research: A Pilot Experiment in Validity
and Inter-Judge Reliability"
Journal of Marketing, Vol. 35 (April 1971), pp. 58-62.

Weinberger, Marc G. and Spotts, Harlan E.
"A Situational View of Information Content in TV Advertising in the
U.S. and U.K."
Journal of Marketing, Vol. 53 (January 1989), pp. 89-94.

120 -------------------- GENERALIZABILITY THEORY --------------------
        See also (sub)heading(s) 118.

120.01 ---------- Books Re: Generalizability Theory

Brennan, Robert L.
  Elements of Generalizability Theory
  (Iowa City, IA: The American College Testing Program, 1983).

Brennan, Robert L.
  Generalizability Analysis: Principles and Procedures
  ACT Technical Bulletin No. 26
  (Iowa City, IA: The American College Testing Program, 1977).

Cronbach, Lee J., Gleser, Goldine C., Nanda, Harinder, and Rajaratnam, Nageswari
  The Dependability of Behavioral Measurements: Theory of Generalizability for Scores and Profiles
  (New York: John Wiley and Sons, Inc., 1972).

120.02 ---------- Theory Re: Generalizability

Cardinet, Jean
  "Extension of Generalizability Theory and Its Applications in Educational Measurement"
  Journal of Educational Measurement, Vol. 18 (Winter 1981), pp. 183-204.

Cardinet, Jean, Tourneur, Yvan, and Allal, Linda
  "The Symmetry of Generalizability Theory: Applications to Educational Measurement"
  Journal of Educational Measurement, Vol. 13 (Summer 1976), pp. 119-35.

Conger, Anthony J.
  "A Comparison of Multi-Attribute Generalizability Strategies"
  Educational and Psychological Measurement, Vol. 41 (Spring 1981), pp. 121-9.

Cronbach, L. J., Rajaratnam, N., and Gleser, G. C.
  "Theory of Generalizability: A Liberalization of Reliability Theory"
  British Journal of Statistical Psychology, Vol. 16 (November 1963), pp. 137-63.

Gleser, Goldine C., Cronbach, L. J., and Rajaratnam, N.
  "Generalizability of Scores Influenced by Multiple Sources of Variance"
  Psychometrika, Vol. 30 (1965), pp. 395-418.

Johnson, Sandra and Bell, John F.
  "Evaluating and Predicting Survey Efficiency Using Generalizability Theory"
  Journal of Educational Measurement, Vol. 22 (Summer 1985), pp. 107-19.

Kane, Michael T.
  "A Sampling Model for Validity"
  Applied Psychological Measurement, Vol. 6 (Spring 1982), pp. 125-60.

Kane, Michael T. and Brennan, Robert L.
  "Agreement Coefficients as Indices of Dependability for Domain-Referenced Tests"
  Applied Psychological Measurement, Vol. 1 (Winter 1980), pp. 105-26.

Nussbaum, Albert
  "Multivariate Generalizability Theory in Educational Measurement: An Empirical Study"
  Applied Psychological Measurement, Vol. 8 (Spring 1984), pp. 219-30.

Peter, J. Paul
  "Reliability, Generalizability, and Consumer Research"
  in Perreault, W. D., Jr. (editor)
  Advances in Consumer Research, Volume 4
  (Atlanta, GA: Association for Consumer Research, 1977), pp. 394-400.

Rentz, Joseph O.
  "Generalizability Theory: A Comprehensive Method for Assessing and Improving the Dependability of Marketing Measures"
  Journal of Marketing Research, Vol. XXIV (February 1987), pp. 19-28.

Rentz, R. Robert
  "Rules of Thumb for Estimating Reliability Coefficients Using Generalizability Theory"
  Educational and Psychological Measurement, Vol. 40 (Autumn 1980), pp. 575-92.

Rozeboom, William W.
  "Domain Validity--Why Care?"
  Educational and Psychological Measurement, Vol. 38 (Winter 1978), pp. 81-8.

Shavelson, Richard J. and Webb, Noreen M.
    "Generalizability Theory: 1973-1980"
    British Journal of Mathematical and Statistical Psychology, Vol. 34
    (November 1981), pp. 133-66.

120.03 ---------- Applications of Generalizability Theory

Endler, N. S. and Hunt, J. Mc V.
    "Sources of Behavioral Variance as Measured by the S-R Inventory of
    Anxiousness"
    Psychological Bulletin, Vol. 65 (1966), pp. 336-46.

Endler, N. S. and Rosenstein, A. P.
    "An S-R Inventory of Anxiousness"
    Psychological Monographs, Vol. 76 (1962), pp. 1-33.

Rentz, Joseph O.
    "An Exploratory Study of the Generalizability of Selected Marketing
    Measures"
    Journal of the Academy of Marketing Science, Vol. 16 (Spring 1988),
    pp. 141-50.

Sandell, Rolf Gunnar
    "Effects of Attitudinal and Situational Factors on Reported Choice
    Behavior"
    Journal of Marketing Research, Vol. V (November 1968), pp. 405-8.

121 --------------- INTERNAL CONSISTENCY RELIABILITY ----------------
See also (sub)heading(s) 118.

121.01 ---------- Theory Re: Internal Consistency Reliability

Bentler, P. M.
"A Lower-Bound Method for the Dimension-Free Measurement of Internal Consistency"
Social Science Research, Vol. 1 (December 1972), pp. 343-57.

Burt, C.
"Test Reliability Estimated by Analysis of Variance"
British Journal of Statistical Psychology, Vol. 8 (November 1955), pp. 103-18.

Cronbach, L. J.
"Test 'Reliability': Its Meaning and Determination"
Psychometrika, Vol. 12 (March 1947), pp. 1-16.

Feldt, Leonard S.
"The Approximate Sampling Distribution of Kuder-Richardson Reliability Coefficient Twenty"
Psychometrika, Vol. 30 (September 1965), pp. 357-70.

Gilmer, J. S. and Feldt, L. S.
"Reliability Estimation for a Test with Parts of Unknown Lengths"
Psychometrika, Vol. 48 (March 1983), pp. 99-111.

Hoyt, C.
"Test Reliability Estimated by Analysis of Variance"
Psychometrika, Vol. 6 (June 1941), pp. 153-60.

Joreskog, Karl G.
"Statistical Analysis of Sets of Congeneric Tests"
Psychometrika, Vol. 36 (June 1971), pp. 109-33.

Kraemer, Helena C.
"Ramifications of a Population Model for K as a Coefficient of Reliability"
Psychometrika, Vol. 44 (December 1979), pp. 461-72.

Kuder, G. F. and Richardson, M. W.
"The Theory of the Estimation of Test Reliability"
Psychometrika, Vol. 2 (September 1937), pp. 151-60.

Tenopyr, Mary L.
"Artifactual Reliability of Forced-Choice Scales"
Journal of Applied Psychology, Vol. 73 (November 1988), pp. 749-51.

121.02 ---------- Applications of Internal Consistency Reliability

Best, Roger, Hawkins, Del I., and Albaum, Gerald
"Reliability of Measured Beliefs in Consumer Research"
in Perreault, W. D. (editor)
Advances in Consumer Research, Vol. 4
(Atlanta: Association for Consumer Research, 1977), pp. 19-23.

Davis, Harry L., Douglas, Susan P., and Silk, Alvin J.
"Measure Unreliability: A Hidden Threat to Cross-National Marketing Research"
Journal of Marketing, Vol. 45 (Spring 1981), pp. 98-109.

Joachimsthaler, Erich A. and Michaels, Ronald E.
"Alternative Internal Consistency Estimates Applied to the Job Descriptive Index"
University of Kansas (1984), unpublished manuscript.

121.03 ---------- Theory Re: Cronbach's Coefficient Alpha

Cronbach, L. J.
"Coefficient Alpha and the Internal Structure of Tests"
Psychometrika, Vol. 16 (September 1951), pp. 297-334.

Green, Samuel B., Lissitz, Robert W., and Mulaik, Stanley A.
"Limitations of Coefficient Alpha as an Index of Test Unidimensionality"
Educational and Psychological Measurement, Vol. 37 (1977), pp. 827-38.

121.04 ---------- Applications of Cronbach's Coefficient Alpha

Bearden, William O., Teel, Jesse E., and Wright, Robert R.
"Family Income Effects on Measurement of Children's Attitudes Toward Television Commercials"
Journal of Consumer Research, Vol. 6 (December 1979), pp. 308-11.

Brown, James R. and Day, Ralph L.
    "Measures of Manifest Conflict in Distribution Channels"
    Journal of Marketing Research, Vol. XVIII (August 1981), pp. 263-74.

Burke, Marian C.
    "Strategic Choice and Marketing Managers: An Examination of
    Business-Level Marketing Objectives"
    Journal of Marketing Research, Vol. XXI (November 1984), pp. 345-59.

Burnett, John J. and Oliver, Richard L.
    "Fear Appeal Effects in the Field: A Segmentation Approach"
    Journal of Marketing Research, Vol. XVI (May 1979), pp. 181-90.

Dwyer, F. Robert and Welsh, M. Ann
    "Environmental Relationships of the Internal Political Economy of
    Marketing Channels"
    Journal of Marketing Research, Vol. XXII (November 1985), pp. 397-414.

Eliashberg, Jehoshua, LaTour, Stephen A., Rangaswamy, Arvind, and
    Stern, Louis W.
    "Assessing the Predictive Accuracy of Two Utility-Based Theories in a
    Marketing Channel Negotiation Context"
    Journal of Marketing Research, Vol. XXIII (May 1986), pp. 101-10.

Eliashberg, Jehoshua and Robertson, Thomas S.
    "New Product Preannouncing Behavior: A Market Signaling Study"
    Journal of Marketing Research, Vol. XXV (August 1988), pp. 282-92.

Gaski, John F. and Nevin, John R.
    "The Differential Effects of Exercised and Unexercised Power Sources
    in a Marketing Channel"
    Journal of Marketing Research, Vol. XXII (May 1985), pp. 130-42.

Gatignon, Hubert and Robertson, Thomas S.
    "Technology Diffusion: An Empirical Test of Competitive Effects"
    Journal of Marketing, Vol. 53 (January 1989), pp. 35-49.

Ingram, Thomas N. and Bellenger, Danny N.
    "Personal and Organizational Variables: Their Relative Effect on
    Reward Valences of Industrial Salespeople"
    Journal of Marketing Research, Vol. XX (May 1983), pp. 198-205.

Jacoby, Jacob and Matell, Michael S.
    "Three-Point Likert Scales are Good Enough"
    Journal of Marketing Research, Vol. VIII (November 1971), pp. 495-500.

John, George and Martin, John
    "Effects of Organizational Structure of Marketing Planning on
    Credibility and Utilization of Plan Output"
    Journal of Marketing Research, Vol. XXI (May 1984), pp. 170-83.

Kohli, Ajay K.
    "Some Unexplored Supervisory Behaviors and Their Influence on
    Salesperson's Role Clarity, Specific Self-Esteem, Job Satisfaction,
    and Motivation"
    Journal of Marketing Research, Vol. XXII (November 1985), pp. 424-33.

Leow, Ger Ghee and Swinyard, William R.
    "Barriers to ATM Card Diffusion"
    Singapore Marketing Review, Vol. I (March 1986), pp. 39-44.

Lindquist, Jay D.
    "Measuring Children's Attitudes Toward TV Commercials: An Instrument
    Reliability Test"
    Journal of the Academy of Marketing Science, Vol. 9 (Fall 1981), pp.
    409-18.

Lumpkin, James R.
    "Shopping Orientation Segmentation of the Elderly Consumer"
    Journal of the Academy of Marketing Science, Vol. 13 (Spring 1985),
    pp. 271-89.

Moncrief, William C., III
    "Selling Activity and Sales Position Taxonomies for Industrial
    Salesforces"
    Journal of Marketing Research, Vol. XXIII (August 1986), pp. 261-70.

Riecken, Glen and Samli, A. Coskun
    "Measuring Children's Attitudes Toward Television Commercials:
    Extension and Replication"
    Journal of Consumer Research, Vol. 8 (June 1981), pp. 57-61.

Rossiter, John R.
    "Reliability of a Short Test Measuring Children's Attitudes Toward TV
    Commercials"
    Journal of Consumer Research, Vol. 3 (March 1977), pp. 179-84.

Smith, Ruth A.
    "Industrial Salesforce Job Satisfaction" (abstract)
    Journal of Marketing Research, Vol. XIX (February 1982), pp. 152,3.

Sujan, Harish
  "Smarter Versus Harder: An Exploratory Attributional Analysis of
  Salespeople's Motivation"
  Journal of Marketing Research, Vol. XXIII (February 1986), pp. 41-9.

Teas, R. Kenneth
  "An Empirical Test of Models of Salespersons' Job Expectancy and
  Instrumentality Perceptions"
  Journal of Marketing Research, Vo. XVIII (May 1981), pp. 209-26.

Teas, R. Kenneth
  "A Test of a Model of Department Store Salespeople's Job Satisfaction"
  Journal of Retailing, Vol. 57 (Spring 1981), pp. 3-25.

Tyagi, Pradeep K.
  "Perceived Organizational Climate and the Process of Salesperson
  Motivation"
  Journal of Marketing Research, Vol. XIX (May 1982), pp. 240-54.

Vigderhous, G.
  "Coefficient of Reliability Alpha" (computer abstract)
  Journal of Marketing Research, Vol. XI (May 1974), p. 194.

Williams, Kaylene C. and Spiro, Rosann L.
  "Communication Style in the Salesperson-Customer Dyad"
  Journal of Marketing Research, Vol. XXII (November 1985), pp. 434-42.

Yavas, Ugur
  "Extensions of King and Summers' Opinion Leadership Scale: A
  Reliability Study" (abstract)
  Journal of Marketing Research, Vol. XIX (February 1982), pp. 154,5.

121.05 ---------- Applications of Kuder-Richardson 20

Riecken, Glen and Yavas, Ugur
  "Internal Consistency Reliability of King and Summers' Opinion
  Leadership Scale: Further Evidence"
  Journal of Marketing Research, Vol. XX (August 1983), pp. 325-6.

121.06 ---------- Theory Re: Coefficient Beta

    See also (sub)heading(s) 122.

John, George and Roedder, Deborah L.
  "Reliability Assessments: Coefficients Alpha and Beta"
  in Bernhardt, Kenneth et al. (editors)
  The Changing Marketing Environment: New Theories and Applications
  (Chicago: American Marketing Association, 1981), pp. 354-7.

121.07 ---------- Applications of Coefficient Beta

Brown, James R., Lusch, Robert F., and Muehling, Darrel D.
  "Conflict and Power-Dependence Relations in Retailer-Supplier
  Channels"
  Journal of Retailing, Vol. 53 (Winter 1983), pp. 53-80.

Darden, William R., Hampton, Ronald, and Howell, Roy D.
  "Career Versus Organizational Commitment: Antecedents and
  Consequences of Retail Salespeople's Commitment"
  Journal of Retailing, Vol. 65 (Spring 1989), pp. 80-106.

122 ------------------- ASSESSING UNIDIMENSIONALITY -----------------
          See also (sub)heading(s) 37, 118, 121.06.

122.01 ---------- Theory Re: Assessing Unidimensionality

Anderson, James C. and Gerbing, David W.
   "Some Methods for Respecifying Measurement Models to Obtain
   Unidimensional Construct Measurement"
   Journal of Marketing Research, Vol. XIX (November 1982), pp. 453-60.

Anderson, James C., Gerbing, David W., and Hunter, John E.
   "On the Assessment of Unidimensional Measurement: Internal and
   External Consistency, and Overall Consistency Criteria"
   Journal of Marketing Research, Vol. XXIV (November 1987), pp. 432-7.

Danes, Jeffrey E. and Mann, O. Karl
   "Unidimensional Measurement and Structural Equation Models With
   Latent Variables"
   Journal of Business Research, Vol. 12 (September 1984), pp. 337-52.

Gerbing, David W. and Anderson, James C.
   "An Updated Paradigm for Scale Development Incorporating
   Unidimensionality and Its Assessment"
   Journal of Marketing Research, Vol. XXV (May 1988), pp. 186-92.

Gerbing, David W. and Anderson, James C.
   "On the Meaning of Within-Factor Correlated Measurement Errors"
   Journal of Consumer Research, Vol. 11 (June 1984), pp. 572-80.

Green, S. B., Lissitz, R., and Mulaik, S.
   "Limitations of Coefficient Alpha as an Index of Test
   Unidimensionality"
   Educational and Psychological Measurement, Vol. 37 (Winter 1977), pp.
   827-38.

Hattie, John
   "Methodology Review: Assessing Unidimensionality"
   Applied Psychological Measurement, Vol. 9 (June 1985), pp. 139-64.

Hunter, John E. and Gerbing, David W.
   "Unidimensional Measurement, Second Order Factor Analysis, and Causal
   Models"
   in Staw, B. M. and Cummings, L. L. (editors)
   Research in Organizational Behavior, Volume Four
   (Greenwich, CT: JAI Press, Inc., 1982), pp. 267-99.

John, George and Roedder, Deborah L.
   "Reliability Assessments: Coefficients Alpha and Beta"
   in Bernhardt, Kenneth et al. (editors)
   The Changing Marketing Environment: New Theories and Applications
   (Chicago: American Marketing Association, 1981), pp. 354-7.

Kenny, David A.
   Correlation and Causation
   (New York: John Wiley and Sons, Inc., 1979).

Kumar, Ajith and Dillon, William R.
   "Some Further Remarks on Measurement/Structure Interaction and the
   Unidimensionality of Constructs"
   Journal of Marketing Research, Vol. XXIV (November 1987), pp. 438-44.

Kumar, Ajith and Dillon, William R.
   "The Interaction of Measurement and Structure in Simultaneous
   Equation Models With Unobservable Variables"
   Journal of Marketing Research, Vol. .XXIV (February 1987), pp. 98-105.

McDonald, Roderick P.
   "The Dimensionality of Tests and Items"
   British Journal of Mathematical and Statistical Psychology, Vol. 34
   (May 1981), pp. 100-17.

Revelle, William
   "Hierarchical Cluster Analysis and the Internal Structure of Tests"
   Multivariate Behavioral Research, Vol. 14 (January 1979), pp. 57-74.

Spearman, Charles and Holzinger, K.
   "The Sampling Error in the Theory of Two Factors"
   British Journal of Psychology, Vol. 15 (July 1924), pp. 17-9.

Werts, C. E., Linn, R. L., and Joreskog, Karl G.
   "Intraclass Reliability Estimates: Testing Structural Assumptions"
   Educational and Psychological Measurement, Vol. 34 (Spring 1974), pp.
   25-33.

122.02 ---------- Applications of Assessing Unidimensionality

Anderson, James C.
"A Measurement Model to Assess Measure Specific Factors in Multiple-Informant Research"
Journal of Marketing Research, Vol. XXII (February 1985), pp. 86-92.

Singh, Jagdip
"Consumer Complaint Intentions and Behavior: Definitional and Taxonomical Issues"
Journal of Marketing, Vol. 52 (January 1988), pp. 93-107.

530

123 -------------------------- VALIDITY --------------------------
        See also (sub)heading(s) 124, 125, 126, 127, 128.

123.01 ---------- Books Re: Validity

Audits and Surveys Co., Inc.
    The Evaluation of the Validity of Response
    (New York: Audits and Surveys Company, Inc., 1964).

Belson, William A.
    Validity in Survey Research
    (Brookfield, VT: Gower Publishing Co.), 560 pp.

Brinberg, David and Kidder, L. H. (editors)
    Forms of Validity in Research
    (San Francisco: Jossey-Bass Publishers, 1982).

Brinberg, David and McGrath, Joseph E.
    Validity and the Research Process
    (Beverly Hills, CA: Sage Publications, Inc., 1985), 174 pp.

Carmines, Edward G. and Zeller, Richard A.
    Reliability and Validity Assessment
    (Beverly Hills, CA: Sage Publications, Inc., 1980), 68 pp.

Kirk, Jerome and Miller, Marc L.
    Reliability and Validity in Qualitative Research
    (Beverly Hills, CA: Sage Publications, Inc., 1986), 87 pp.

Osterlind, Steven J.
    Test Item Bias
    (Beverly Hills, CA: Sage Publications, Inc.).

123.02 ---------- Theory Re: Validity

Bohrnstedt, G. W.
    "Reliability and Validity Assessment in Attitude Measurement"
    in Summers, G. F. (editor)
    Attitude Measurement
    (Skokie, IL: Rand McNally, 1970), pp. 81-99.

Brinberg, David and McGrath, Joseph E.
    "A Network of Validity Concepts Within the Research Process"
    in Brinberg, David and Kidder, L. H. (editors)
    Forms of Validity in Research
    (San Francisco: Jossey-Bass Publishers, 1982), pp. 5-21.

Cattell, R. B.
    "Validity and Reliability: A Proposed More Basic Set of Concepts"
    Journal of Educational Psychology, Vol. 55 (February 1964), pp. 1-22.

Cronbach, Lee J.
    "Test Validation"
    in Thorndike, R. L. (editor)
    Educational Measurement
    (Washington, DC: American Council on Education, 1971), pp. 443-507.

Cronbach, Lee J.
    "Response Sets and Test Validity"
    Educational and Psychological Measurement, Vol. 6 (Fall 1946), pp.
    475-94.

Heeler, Roger M. and Ray, Michael L.
    "Measure Validation in Marketing"
    Journal of Marketing Research, Vol. IX (November 1972), pp. 362-71.

Heise, D. R.
    "Validity, Invalidity, and Reliability"
    in Borgatta, E. F. and Bohrnstedt, G. W. (editors)
    Sociological Methodology
    (San Francisco: Jossey-Bass, 1970), pp. 104-29.

Holbert, Neil B.
    "Point of View: On Validity in Research"
    Journal of Advertising Research, Vol. 14 (February 1974), pp. 51,2.

Ray, Michael L.
    "Introduction to the Special Section: Measurement and Marketing
    Research: Is the Flirtation going to lead to a Romance?"
    Journal of Marketing Research, Vol. XVI (February 1979), pp. 1-6.

Schmidt, F. L. and Hunter, J. E.
    "Development of a General Solution to the Problem of Validity
    Generalization"
    Journal of Applied Psychology, Vol. 62 (1977), pp. 529-40.

Tucker, L. R.
    "Maximum Validity of a Test With Equivalent Items"
    Psychometrika, Vol. 11 (March 1946), pp. 1-13.

Wilson, R. Dale, Newman, L. M., and Hastak, Manoj
   "On the Validity of Research Methods in Consumer Dealing Activities:
   An Analysis of Timing Issues"
   in Beckwith, Neil et al. (editors)
   Educators' Conference Proceedings, Series 44
   (Chicago: American Marketing Association, 1979), pp. 41-6.

123.03 ---------- Theory Re: External Validity

Berkowitz, Leonard and Donnerstein, Edward
   "External Validity is More Than Skin Deep: Some Answers to Criticism
   of Laboratory Experiments"
   American Psychologist, Vol. 37 (1982), pp. 257-75.

Calder, Bobby J., Phillips, Lynn W., and Tybout, Alice M.
   "Beyond External Validity"
   Journal of Consumer Research, Vol. 10 (June 1983), pp. 112-4.

Calder, Bobby J., Phillips, Lynn W., and Tybout, Alice M.
   "The Concept of External Validity"
   Journal of Consumer Research, Vol. 9 (December 1982), pp. 240-4.

Kruglanski, Arie
   "The Two Meanings of External Invalidity"
   Human Relations, Vol. 28 (1975), pp. 653-9.

Lynch, John G., Jr.
   "The Role of External Validity in Theoretical Research"
   Journal of Consumer Research, Vol. 10 (June 1983), pp. 109-11.

Lynch, John G., Jr.
   "On the External Validity of Experiments in Consumer Research"
   Journal of Consumer Research, Vol. 9 (December 1982), pp. 225-39.

McGrath, Joseph E. and Brinberg, David
   "External Validity and the Research Process: A Third-Party Comment on
   the Calder/Lynch Dialogue"
   Journal of Consumer Research, Vol. 10, No. 1 (1983), pp. 115-24.

Oaks, W.
   "External Validity and the Use of Real People as Subjects"
   American Psychologist, Vol. 27 (1972), pp. 959-62.

123.04 ---------- Applications of Nomological Validity

Childers, Terry L.
   "Assessment of the Psychometric Properties of an Opinion Leadership
   Scale"
   Journal of Marketing Research, Vol. XXIII (May 1986), pp. 184-8.

Comer, James M.
   "A Psychometric Assessment of a Measure of Sales Representatives'
   Power Perceptions"
   Journal of Marketing Research, Vol. XXI (May 1984), pp. 221-5.

Heide, Jan B. and John, George
   "The Role of Dependence Balancing in Safeguarding
   Transaction-Specific Assets in Conventional Channels"
   Journal of Marketing, Vol. 52 (January 1988), pp. 20-35.

John, George
   "An Empirical Investigation of Some Antecedents of Opportunism in a
   Marketing Channel"
   Journal of Marketing Research, Vol. XXI (August 1984), pp. 278-89.

Ruekert, Robert W. and Churchill, Gilbert A., Jr.
   "Reliability and Validity of Alternative Measures of Channel Member
   Satisfaction"
   Journal of Marketing Research, Vol. XXI (May 1984), pp. 226-33.

123.05 ---------- Unclassified Theory Re: Validity

Anderson, Norman H.
   "How Functional Measurement can Yield Validated Interval Scales of
   Mental Quantities"
   Journal of Applied Psychology, Vol. 61 (1976), pp. 677-92.

Baker, P. R.
   "The Validation of New Research Techniques"
   Commentary (JMRS), Vol. 7 (July 1965).

Bohrnstedt, G. W.
   "A Quick Method for Determining the Reliability and Validity of
   Multiple-Item Scales"
   American Sociological Review, Vol. 34 (August 1969), pp. 542-8.

Boruch, Robert F. and Wolins, Leroy
   "A Procedure for Estimation of Trait, Method and Error Variance
   Attributable to a Measure"
   Educational and Psychological Measurement, Vol. 30 (November 1970),
   pp. 547-74.

Campbell, D. T.
   "Factors Relevant to the Validity of Experiments in Social Settings"
   Psychological Bulletin, Vol. 54 (1957), pp. 297-312.

Cleary, T. Anne, Linn, Robert, and Walster, G. William
   "Effect of Reliability and Validity on Power of Statistical Tests"
   in Borgatta, Edgar F. and Bohrnstedt, George W. (editors)
   Sociology Methodology
   (San Francisco: Jossey-Bass, 1970), pp. 130-8.

Leone, Robert P. and Schultz, Randall L.
   "A Study of Marketing Generalizations"
   Journal of Marketing, Vol. 44 (Winter 1980), pp. 10-8.

Politz, A.
   "Science and Truth in Marketing Research"
   Harvard Business Review, Vol. 35 (January-February 1957), pp. 117-26.

Schmittlein, D. C.
   "Assessing Validity and Test-Retest Reliability for 'Pick K of N'
   Data"
   Marketing Science, Vol. 3 (Winter 1984), pp. 23-40.

Schuman, H.
   "The Random Probe: A Technique for Evaluating the Validity of Closed
   Questions"
   American Sociological Review, Vol. 31 (April 1966), pp. 218-22.

Tryon, R. C.
   "Reliability and Behavior Domain Validity: Reformation and Historical
   Critique"
   Psychological Bulletin, Vol. 54 (May 1957), pp. 229-49.

Werts, C. E., Rock, D. A., Linn, R. L., and Joreskog, K. G.
   "Validating Psychometric Assumptions Within and Between Populations"
   Educational and Psychological Measurement, Vol. 37 (1977), pp. 863-71.

Wilson, R. D., Newman, L. M., and Hastak, Manoj
   "On the Validity of Research Methods in Consumer Dealing Activity: An
   Analysis of Timing Issues"
   in Beckwith, Neil et al. (editors)
   1979 AMA Educators' Proceedings
   (Chicago: American Marketing Association, 1979), pp. 41-6.

123.06 ---------- Unclassified Validity Applications

Anderson, James C.
   The Validity of Haire's Shopping List Projective Technique"
   Journal of Marketing Research, Vol. XV (November 1978), pp. 644-9.

Andrews, Frank M. and Crandall, Rick
   "The Validity of Measures of Self-Reported Well-Being"
   Social Indicators Research, Vol. 3 (1976), pp. 1-19.

Angelmar, Reinhard, Zaltman, Gerald, and Pinson, Christian
   "An Examination of Concept Validity"
   in Venkatesan, M. (editor)
   Proceedings of the Third Annual Conference of the Association for
   Consumer Research (1972), pp. 586-93.

Arora, Raj
   "Validation of an S-O-R Model for Situation Enduring and Response
   Components of Involvement"
   Journal of Marketing Research, Vol. XIX (November 1982), pp. 505-16.

Bruno, Albert V. and Pessemier, Edgar A.
   "An Empirical Investigation of the Validity of Selected Attitude and
   Activity Measures"
   Proceedings, Third Annual Conference, Association for Consumer
   Research (1972), pp. 456-74.

Bylund, Bruce and Sanders, David
   "Validity of High Scores on Certain Self-Evaluation Questions"
   Rural Sociology, Vol. 32 (September 1957), pp. 346-51.

Cannell, Charles F. and Fowler, Floyd J.
   "A Comparison of a Self-Enumerative Procedure and a Personal
   Interview: A Validity Study"
   Public Opinion Quarterly, Vol 27 (Summer 1963), pp. 250-64.

Clemens, J.
   "Page and Advertisement Readership Studies: The Problem of Validation"
   Commentary (JMRS), Vol. 7 (July 1965).

Cronbach, Lee J. and Marlowe, David
   "A Scale of Social Desirability, Independent of Psychopathology"
   Journal of Consulting Psychology, Vol. 24 (August 1960), pp. 349-54.

Davis, E. J.
   "The Validity of Test Marketing"
   Commentary (JMRS), Vol. 7 (1965).

Ferber, R., Forsythe, J., Guthrie, H. W., and Maynes, E. S.
   "Validation of Consumer Financial Characteristics: Common Stock"
   Journal of the American Statistical Association, Vol. 64 (June 1969),
   pp. 415-32.

Ferber, Robert, Forsythe, John, Maynes, Scott E., and Guthrie, Harold
   "Validation of a National Survey of Consumer Financial
   Characteristics: Savings Accounts"
   Review of Economics and Statistics, Vol. 51 (November 1969), pp.
   436-44.

Ghiselli, Edwin E.
   "The Validity of Aptitude Tests in Personnel Selection"
   Personnel Psychology, Vol. 26 (Winter 1973), pp. 461-77.

Granbois, Donald H. and Summers, John O.
   "Primary and Secondary Validity of Consumer Purchase Probabilities"
   Journal of Consumer Research, Vol. 1 (March 1975), pp. 31-8.

Jacoby, Jacob, Chestnut, Robert, Hoyer, Wayne D., Sheluga, David A.,
   and Donahue, Michael J.
   "Psychometric Characteristics of Behavioral Process Data: Preliminary
   Findings on Validity and Reliability"
   in Hunt, H. Keith (editor)
   Advances in Consumer Research, Volume Five
   (Ann Arbor, MI: Association for Consumer Research, 1978).

Kirsch, Arthur D., Berger, Philip K., and Belford, R. J., II
   "Are Reports of Brands Bought Last Reliable and Valid?"
   Journal of Advertising Research, Vol. 2 (June 1962), pp. 34-6.

Kubany, A. J.
   "A Validation Study of the Error-Choice Technique Using Attitudes on
   National Health Insurance"
   Educational and Psychological Measurement, Vol. 13 (Summer 1953), pp.
   157-63.

Larson, Richard F. and Catton, William R., Jr.
   "Can the Mail-Back Bias Contribute to a Study's Validity?"
   American Sociological Review, Vol. 24 (April 1959), pp. 243-5.

Lastovicka, John L.
   "On the Validation of Lifestyle Traits: A Review and Illustration"
   Journal of Marketing Research, Vol. XIX (February 1982), pp. 126-38.

Levin, Irwin P., Louviere, Jordan J., Schepanski, Albert A., and
   Norman, Kent L.
   "External Validity Tests of Laboratory Studies of Information
   Integration"
   Organizational Behavior and Human Performance, Vol. 31, No. 2 (1983),
   pp. 173-93.

Matell, Michael S. and Jacoby, Jacob
   "Is There an Optimal Number of Alternatives for Likert Scale Items?
   Study I: Reliability and Validity"
   Educational and Psychological Measurement, Vol. 31 (Autumn 1971), pp.
   657-74.

Nuckols, Robert C.
   "The Validity and Comparability of Mail and Personal Interview
   Surveys"
   Journal of Marketing Research, Vol. I (February 1964), pp. 11-6.

Parry, High and Crossley, Helen
   "Validity of Responses to Survey Questions"
   Public Opinion Quarterly, Vol. 14 (Spring 1950), pp. 61-80.

Politz, A.
   "Questionnaire Validity Through the Opinion-Forming Question"
   Journal of Psychology, Vol. 36 (July 1953), pp. 11-6.

Ratchford, Brian T.
   "New Insights About the FCB Grid"
   Journal of Advertising Research, Vol. 27 (August/September 1987), pp.
   24-38.

Rothschild, Michael L. and Houston, Michael J.
   "Internal Validity, External Validty, and the Passage of Time as
   Issues in Developing Advertising Effectiveness Measures"
   in Olson, J. (editor)
   Advances in Consumer Research, Volume Seven
   (Ann Arbor, MI: Association for Consumer Research, 1980), pp. 572-6.

Scott, W. A. and Johnson, R. C.
  "Comparative Validities of Direct and Indirect Personality Tests"
  Journal of Consulting and Clinical Psychology, Vol. 38 (June 1972),
  pp. 301-18.

Stanton, Frank
  "Notes on the Validity of Mail Questionnaire Returns"
  Journal of Applied Psychology, Vol. 23 (February 1939), pp. 95-104.

Stocks, J. M. B.
  "Validating Television Advertisement Tests"
  Commentary (JMRS), Vol. 7 (July 1965).

Suchman, S., Phillips, B. S., and Streib, G. F.
  "An Analysis of the Validity of Health Questionnaires"
  Social Forces, Vol. 36 (March 1958), pp. 223-32.

Waugh, R. E.
  "Increasing the Validity and Reliability of Tourist Data"
  Journal of Marketing, Vol. 20 (January 1956), pp. 286-8.

Weiss, D. J. and Davis, R. V.
  "An Objective Validation of Factual Interview Data"
  Journal of Applied Psychology, Vol. 44 (December 1960), pp. 381-5.

Wittink, Dick R. and Montgomery, David B.
  "Predicting Validity of Trade-Off Analysis for Alternative
  Segmentation Schemes"
  in Beckwith, Neil E. (editor)
  1979 Educators' Conference Proceedings
  (Chicago: American Marketing Association, 1979), pp. 69-73.

124 -------------- MULTITRAIT-MULTIMETHOD (MTMM) MATRIX --------------
See also (sub)heading(s) 123.

124.01 ---------- Books Re: Multitrait-Multimethod (MTMM) Matrix

Sullivan, John L. and Feldman, Stanley
Multiple Indicators: An Introduction
(Beverly Hills, CA: Sage Publications, Inc., 1980), 80 pp.

124.02 ---------- Theory Re: Multitrait-Multimethod (MTMM) Matrix

Althauser, Robert P., Heberlein, Thomas A., and Scott, Robert A.
"A Causal Assessment of Validity: The Augmented
Multitrait-Multimethod Matrix"
Causal Models in the Social Sciences
(Chicago: Aldine, 1971), pp. 374-99.

Anderson, James C. and Gerbing, David W.
"Some Methods for Respecifying Measurement Models to Obtain
Unidimensional Construct Measurement"
Journal of Marketing Research, Vol. XIX (November 1982), pp. 453-60.

Campbell, Donald T. and Fiske, Donald W.
"Convergent and Discriminant Validation by the Multitrait-Multimethod
Matrix"
Psychological Bulletin, Vol. 56 (March 1959), pp. 81-105.

Campbell, Donald T. and O'Connell, Edward J.
"Methods as Diluting Trait Relations Rather Than Adding Irrelevant
Systemactic Variance"
in Brinberg, David and Kidder, L. H. (editors)
Forms of Validity in Research
(San Francisco: Jossey-Bass Publishers, 1982), pp. 93-111.

Churchill, Gilbert A., Jr.
"A Paradigm for Developing Better Measures of Marketing Constructs"
Journal of Marketing Research, Vol. XVI (February 1979), pp. 64-73.

Elbert, Norbert F. and Belohlav, James
"The Misleading Influence of Methods Variance When a
Multitrait-Multimethod Matrix Technique Is Used"
Proceedings, American Institute for Decision Sciences (1977), pp.
268-8.

Jackson, Douglas N.
"Multimethod Factor Analysis in the Evaluation of Convergent and
Discriminant Validity"
Psychological Bulletin, Vol. 72 (July 1969), pp. 30-49.

Kalleberg, A. L. and Kluegel, J. R.
"Analysis of the Multitrait-Multimethod Matrix: Some Limitations and
an Alternative"
Journal of Applied Psychology, Vol. 60 (February 1975), pp. 1-9.

Kroger, Rolf O.
"Conceptual and Empirical Independence in Test Validation: A Note on
Campbell and Fiske's 'Discriminant Validity'"
Educational and Psychological Measurement, Vol. 28 (Summer 1968), pp.
383-7.

Lincoln, James R. and Zeitz, Gerald
"Organizational Properties From Aggregate Data: Separating Individual
and Structural Effects"
American Sociological Review, Vol. 45 (June 1980), pp. 391-408.

Paisley, Matilda B., Collins, W. Andrew, and Paisley, William J.
"The Convergent-Discriminant Matrix: Multitrait-Multimethod Logic
Extended to Other Social Research Decisions"
Stanford University (1970), unpublished paper.

Ray, Michael L. and Heeler, Roger M.
"Analysis Techniques for Exploratory Use of the
Multitrait-Multimethod Matrix"
Educational and Psychological Measurement, Vol. 35 (1975), pp. 255-65.

Ray, Michael L. and Heeler, Roger M.
The Use of the Multitrait-Multimethod Matrix for Trait Development:
Cluster Analysis and Nonmetric Scaling Alternatives
Research Paper No. 10
Graduate School of Business, Stanford University (1971).

Schmitt, Neal, Coyle, Bryan W., and Saari, Bruce B.
"A Review and Critique of Analyses of Multitrait-Multimethod Matrices"
Multivariate Behavioral Research, Vol. 12 (October 1977), pp. 447-78.

Turner, Carol J.
"The Multitrait-Multimethod Matrix: 1967-1980"
Manuscript 2280
JSAS Catalog of Selected Documents in Psychology (1981).

124.03 ---------- Analytical Methods for MTMM Matrices

Cole, David A. and Maxwell, Scott E.
   "Multitrait-Multimethod Comparisons Across Populations: A
   Confirmatory Factor Analytic Approach"
   Multivariate Behavioral Research, Vol. 20 (1985), pp. 389-417.

Joreskog, Karl
   "Analyzing Psychological Data by Structural Analysis of Covariance
   Matrices"
   in Atkinson, R. C. et al. (editors)
   (San Francisco: Freeman, 1974), pp. 1-56.

Joreskog, Karl
   "Statistical Analysis of Congeneric Tests"
   Psychometrika, Vol. 36 (1971), pp. 109-33.

Joreskog, Karl and Sorbom, Dag
   LISREL: Analysis of Linear Structural Relationships by Method of
   Maximum Likelihood
   (Chicago: National Educational Resources, 1978).

Kenney, David
   "An Empirical Application of Confirmatory Factor Analysis to the
   Multitrait-Multimethod Matrix"
   Journal of Experimental Social Psychology, Vol. 12 (May 1976), pp.
   247-52.

Lomax, Richard D. and Algina, James
   "Comparison of Two Procedures for Analyzing Multitrait Multimethod
   Matrices"
   Journal of Educational Measurement, Vol. 16 (Fall 1979), pp. 177-86.

Schmidt, Neal
   "Path Analysis of Multitrait-Multimethod Matrices"
   Applied Psychological Measurement, Vol. 2 (Spring 1978), pp. 157-73.

Schmidt, Neal, Coyle, Bryan W., and Saari, Bruce B.
   "A Review and Critique of Analyses of Multitrait-Multimethod Matrices"
   Multivariate Behavioral Research, Vol. 12 (October 1977), pp. 447-78.

Werts, C., Linn, Robert, and Joreskog, Karl
   "Interclass Reliability Estimates: Testing Structural Assumptions"
   Educational and Psychological Measurement, Vol. 34 (1974), pp. 25-33.

Widaman, Keith F.
   "Hierarchically Nested Covariance Structure Models for
   Multitrait-Multimethod Data"
   Applied Psychological Measurement, Vol. 9 (March 1985), pp. 1-26.

Wothke, Werner and Browne, Michael W.
   "The Direct Product Model for the MTMM Matrix Parameterized as a
   Second Order Factor Analysis Model"
   (1988), unpublished working paper.

124.04 ---------- Applications of the Multitrait-Multimethod Matrix

Anderson, James C.
   "A Measurement Model to Assess Measure-Specific Factors in
   Multiple-Informant Research"
   Journal of Marketing Research, Vol. XXII (February 1985), pp. 86-92.

Arora, Raj
   "Validation of an S-O-R Model for Situation, Enduring, and Response
   Components of Involvement"
   Journal of Marketing Research, Vol. XIX (November 1982), pp. 505-16.

Bettman, J. R., Capon, N., and Lutz, R. J.
   "A Multimethod Approach to Validating Multi-Attribute Attitude Models"
   Proceedings, Association for Consumer Research, Fifth Annual
   Conference (1975), pp. 357-74.

Comer, James M.
   "A Psychometric Assessment of a Measure of Sales Representatives'
   Power Perceptions"
   Journal of Marketing Research, Vol. XXI (May 1984), pp. 221-5.

Cote, Joseph A. and Buckley, M. Ronald
   "Estimating Trait, Method, and Error Variance Across 70 Construct
   Validation Studies"
   Journal of Marketing Research, Vol. XXIV (August 1987), pp. 315-8.

Davis, Harry L.
   "Measurement of Husband-Wife Influence in Consumer Purchase Decisions"
   Journal of Marketing Research, Vol. VIII (August 1971), pp. 305-12.

Dillon, William R., Madden, Thomas J., and Mulani, Narendra
"Scaling Models for Categorical Variables: An Application of Latent
Structure Models"
Journal of Consumer Research, Vol. 10 (September 1983), pp. 209-24.

Faber, Ronald and Ward, Scott
Validation of Mother-Child Purchase Influence Frequency Reports by
the Multitrait-Multimethod Matrix
Report No. 75-105
(Cambridge, MA: Marketing Science Institute, 1975), 21 pp.

Foxman, Ellen R., Tansuhaj, Patriya S., and Ekstrom, Karin M.
"Family Members' Perceptions of Adolescents' Influence in Family
Decision Making"
Journal of Consumer Research, Vol. 15 (March 1989), pp. 482-91.

Futrell, Charles M.
"Measurement of Salespeople's Job Satisfaction: Convergent and
Discriminant Validity Corresponding in Sales Job Descriptive Index
Scales"
Journal of Marketing Research, Vol. XVI (November 1979), pp. 594-7.

Hicks, Jack M.
"Comparative Validation of Attitude Measures by the
Multitrait-Multimethod Matrix"
Educational and Psychological Measurement, Vol. 27 (Winter 1967), pp.
985-95.

Hopper, JoAnne Stilley, Burns, Alvin C., and Sherrell, Daniel L.
"An Assessment of the Reliability and Validity of Husband and Wife
Self-Report Purchase Decision Making Measures"
Journal of the Academy of Marketing Science, Vol. 17 (Summer 1989),
pp. 227-34.

Jaffe, Eugene D. and Nebenzahl, Israel D.
"Alternative Questionnaire Formats for Country Image Studies"
Journal of Marketing Research, Vol. XXI (November 1984), pp. 463-71.

John, George and Reve, Torger
"The Reliability and Validity of Key Informant Data From Dyadic
Relationships in Marketing Channels"
Journal of Marketing Research, Vol. XIX (November 1982), pp. 517-24.

Kavanagh, Michael J., MacKinney, Arthur C., and Wolins, Leroy
"Issues in Managerial Performance: Multitrait-Multimethod Analyses of
Ratings"
Psychological Bulletin, Vol. 75 (1971), pp. 34-49.

Lammers, H. Bruce
"A Multitrait-Multimethod Analysis of the Validity of Cognitive
Response Assessment Procedures"
in Hirschman, E. and Holbrook, M. (editors)
Advances in Consumer Research, Volume 12
(Ann Arbor, MI: Association for Consumer Research, 1985), pp. 164-8.

Lichtenstein, Donald R. and Bearden, William O.
"Measurement and Structure of Kelley's Covariance Theory"
Journal of Consumer Research, Vol. 13 (September 1986), pp. 290-6.

Madden, Thomas J., Debevec, Kathleen, and Twible, Jacquelyn L.
"Assessing the Effects of Attitude-Toward-the-Ad on Brand Attitudes:
A Multitrait-Multimethod Design"
in Houston, M. J. and Lutz, R. J. (editors)
Proceedings, Winter Educators' Conference
(Chicago: American Marketing Association, 1985), pp. 109-13.

Malhotra, Naresh K.
"Validity and Structural Reliability of Multidimensional Scaling"
Journal of Marketing Research, Vol. XXIV (May 1987), pp. 164-73.

Malhotra, Naresh K.
"A Scale to Measure Self-Concepts, Person Concepts, and Product
Concepts"
Journal of Marketing Research, Vol. XVIII (November 1981), pp. 456-64.

Menezes, Dennis and Elbert, Norbert F.
"Alternative Semantic Scaling Formats for Measuring Store Image: An
Evaluation"
Journal of Marketing Research, Vol. XVI (February 1979), pp. 80-7.

Munson, J. Michael and McIntyre, Shelby H.
"Developing Practical Procedures for the Measurement of Personal
Values in Cross-Cultural Marketing"
Journal of Marketing Research, Vol. XVI (February 1979), pp. 48-52.

Noerager, Jon P.
"An Assessment of CAD--A Personality Instrument Developed
Specifically for Marketing Research"
Journal of Marketing Research, Vol. XVI (February 1979), pp. 53-9.

Phillips, Lynn W.
  "Assessing Measurement Error in Key Informant Reports: A
  Methodological
  Note on Organizational Analysis in Marketing"
  Journal of Marketing Research, Vol. XVIII (November 1981), pp.
  395-415.

Richins, Marsha L.
  "An Analysis of Consumer Interaction Styles in the Marketplace"
  Journal of Consumer Research, Vol. 10 (June 1983), pp. 73-82.

Silk, Alvin J. and Kalwani, Manohar U.
  "Measuring Influence in Organizational Purchase Decisions"
  Journal of Marketing Research, Vol. XIX (May 1982), pp. 165-81.

Slama, Mark E. and Tashchian, Armen
  "Selected Socioeconomic and Demographic Characteristics Associated
  With Purchasing Involvement"
  Journal of Marketing, Vol. 49 (Winter 1985), pp. 72-82.

Stein, Judith A., Newcomb, Michael D., and Bentler, P. M.
  "Structure of Drug Use Behaviors and Consequences Among Young Adults"
  Journal of Applied Psychology, Vol. 73 (November 1988), pp. 595-605.

Szybillo, George J., Binstock. Sharon, and Buchanan, Lauranne
  "Measure Validation of Leisure Time Activities: Time Budgets and
  Psychographics"
  Journal of Marketing Research, Vol. XVI (February 1979), pp. 74-9.

Szybillo, George J., Sosanie, Arlene K., and Tenenbein, Aaron
  "Family Member Influence in Household Decision Making"
  Journal of Consumer Research, Vol. 6 (December 1979), pp. 312-6.

Teas, R. Kenneth, Wacker, John G., and Hughes, R. Eugene
  "A Path Analysis of Causes and Consequences of Salespeople's
  Perceptions of Role Clarity"
  Journal of Marketing Research, Vol. XVI (August 1979), pp. 355-69.

Tse, David K. and Wilton, Peter C.
  "Models of Consumer Satisfaction Formation: An Extension"
  Journal of Marketing Research, Vol. XXV (May 1988), pp. 204-12.

Westbrook, Robert A.
  "A Rating Scale for Measuring Product/Service Satisfaction"
  Journal of Marketing, Vol. 44 (Fall 1980), pp. 68-72.

Wilkes, Robert E.
  "Husband-Wife Influence in Purchase Decisions: A Confirmation and
  Extension"
  Journal of Marketing Research, Vol. XII (May 1975), pp. 224-7.

125 ---------------------- CONSTRUCT VALIDITY ----------------------
          See also (sub)heading(s) 123.

125.01 ---------- Theory Re: Construct Validity

Andrews, Frank M.
  "Construct Validity and Error Components of Survey Measures: A
  Structural Modelling Approach"
  Public Opinion Quarterly, Vol. 48 (Summer 1984), pp. 409-42.

Bechtoldt, Harold P.
  "Construct Validity: A Critique"
  American Psychologist, Vol. 14 (October 1959), pp. 619-29.

Bentler, Peter M.
  "The Interdependence of Theory, Methodology, and Empirical Data:
  Causal Modeling as an Approach to Construct Validation"
  in Kandel, D. B. (editor)
  Longitudinal Drug Research
  (New York: John Wiley and Sons, Inc., 1978), 267-302.

Campbell, Donald T.
  "Recommendations for APA Test Standards Regarding Construct, Trait,
  or Discriminant Validity"
  American Psychologist, Vol. 15 (August 1960), pp. 546-53.

Cohen, J. B.
  "Exploring Construct Validity: Or are We?"
  in Wilkie, W. D. (editor)
  Advances in Consumer Research, Volume Six
  (Ann Arbor, MI: Association for Consumer Research, 1979).

Cote, Joseph A. and Buckley, M. Ronald
  "Measurement Error and Theory Testing in Consumer Research: An
  Illustration of the Importance of Construct Validation"
  Journal of Consumer Research, Vol. 14 (March 1988), pp. 579-82.

Cote, Joseph A. and Buckley, M. Ronald
  "Estimating Trait, Method, and Error Variance Across 70 Construct
  Validation Studies"
  Journal of Marketing Research, Vol. XXIV (August 1987), pp. 315-8.

Cronbach, L. J. and Meehl, P. E.
  "Construct Validity in Psychological Tests"
  Psychological Bulletin, Vol. 52 (May 1955), pp. 281-302.

Jessor, R. and Hammond, K. R.
  "Construct Validity and the Taylor Anxiety Scale"
  Psychological Bulletin, Vol. 54 (May 1957), pp. 161-70.

Loevinger, Jane
  "Objective Tests as Instruments of Psychological Theory"
  Psychological Reports, Monograph Supplement 9 (1965), pp. 635-94.

Messick, Samuel
  "The Standard Problem: Meaning and Values in Measurement and
  Evaluation"
  American Psychologist, Vol. 30 (October 1975), pp. 955-66.

Peter, J. Paul
  "Construct Validty: A Review of Basic Issues and Marketing Practices"
  Journal of Marketing Research, Vol. XVIII (May 1981), pp. 133-45.

Psychological Bulletin
  "Technical Recommendations for Psychological Tests and Diagnostic
  Techniques"
  Psychological Bulletin Supplement (1954), pp. 201-38.

Ryan, Michael J. and O'Shaughnessy, John
  "Theory Development: The Need to Distinguish Levels of Abstraction"
  in Lamb, C. W., Jr. and Dunne, P. M. (editors)
  Theoretical Developments in Marketing
  (Chicago: American Marketing Association, 1980), pp. 47-50.

Ryan, Michael J. and Peter, J. Paul
  "Two Operational Modifications for Improving the Delineation of
  Attitudinal and Social Influences on Purchase Intentions"
  in Bernhardt, K. (editor)
  Marketing: 1776-1976 and Beyond
  (Chicago: American Marketing Association, 1976), pp. 147-50.

Schwab, Donald P.
  "Construct Validity in Organizational Behavior"
  in Staw, B. and Cummings, L. L. (editors)
  Research in Organizational Behavior
  (Greenwich, CT: JAI Press, 1980), pp. 3-43.

Tesser, Abraham and Krauss, Herbert
  "On Validating a Relationship Between Constructs"
  Educational and Psychological Measurement, Vol. 36 (Spring 1976), pp.
  111-21.

125.02 ---------- Applications of Construct Validity

Anderson, James C. and Gerbing, David W.
  "Some Methods for Respecifying Measurement Models to Obtain
  Unidimensional Construct Measurement"
  Journal of Marketing Research, Vol. XIX (November 1982), pp. 453-60.

Bagozzi, Richard P.
  "The Construct Validity of Affective, Behavioral, and Cognitive
  Components of Attitude by Analysis of Covariance Structures"
  Multivariate Behavioral Research, Vol. 13 (1978), pp. 9-31.

Bagozzi, Richard P., Tybout, Alice M., Craig, C. Samuel, and Sternthal,
  Brian
  "The Construct Validity of the Tripartite Classification of Attitudes"
  Journal of Marketing Research, Vol. XVI (February 1979), pp. 88-95.

Bettman, James R., Capon, Noel, and Lutz, Richard J.
  "Multiattribute Measurement Models and Multiattribute Attitude
  Theory: A Test of Construct Validity"
  Journal of Consumer Research, Vol. 1 (1975), pp. 1-15.

Cohen, Joel B.
  "Exploring Attitude Construct Validity"
  in Wilkie, William L. (editor)
  Advances in Consumer Research, Volume Six
  (Atlanta, GA: Association for Consumer Research, 1979), pp. 303-6.

Gerbing, David W. and Anderson, James C.
  "On the Meaning of Within-Factor Correlated Measurement Errors"
  Journal of Consumer Research, Vol. 11 (June 1984), pp. 572-80.

Hutchins, E. B. and Nonneman, A. J.
  "Construct Validty of an Environmental Assessment Technique for
  Medical Schools"
  Technical Report No. L661
  Association of American Medical Schools, Evanston, IL (1966).

Kroeber-Riel, Werner
  "Rejoinder--To Ryan"
  Journal of Consumer Research, Vol. 7 (June 1980), pp. 96-8.

Lammers, H. Bruce and Kirchner, Don F.
  "The Construct Validity of Teaching Behavior Evaluation Methods: A
  Multitrait-Multimethod Analysis"
  Journal of Marketing Education, Vol. 7 (Summer 1985), pp. 35-44.

Lehmann, Donald R. and Moore, William L.
  "Validity of Information Display Boards: An Assessment Using
  Longitudinal Data"
  Journal of Marketing Research, Vol. XVII (November 1980), pp. 450-9.

Olson, Jerry and Jacoby, Jacob
  "A Construct Validation Study of Brand Loyalty"
  Proceedings, 79th Annual Convention of the American Psychological
  Association, Vol. 6 (1971), pp. 657,8.

Patterson, C. H.
  "A Note on the Construct Validity of the Concept of Empathy"
  Personnel and Guidance Journal, Vol. 40 (May 1962), pp. 803-6.

Ryan, Michael J.
  "Psychobiology and Consumer Research: A Problem of Construct Validity"
  Journal of Consumer Research, Vol. 7 (June 1980), pp. 92-96.

Ryan, Michael J. and Becherer, Richard C.
  "A Multivariate Test of CAD Instrument Construct Validity"
  in Anderson, B. B. (editor)
  Advances in Consumer Research, Vol. 3
  (Chicago: Association for Consumer Research, 1976), pp. 149-54.

Schaninger, Charles M.
  "Perceived Risk and Personality"
  Journal of Consumer Research, Vol. 3 (September 1976), pp. 95-100.

Summers, J. O. and MacKay, D. B.
  "On the Validity and Reliability of Direct Similarity Judgments"
  Journal of Marketing Research, Vol. XIII (August 1976), pp. 289-95.

Van Raaij, W. F.
  "Cross-Cultural Research Methodology as a Case of Construct Validity"
  in Hunt, H. K. (editor)
  Advances in Consumer Research, Volume Five
  (Ann Arbor, MI: Association for Consumer Research, 1978).

Wilkes, Robert E. and Wilcox, James B.
"On the Validity and Reliability of Direct Similarity Judgments: A Comment"
Journal of Marketing Research, Vol. XIV (May 1977), pp. 261,2.

Zuckerman, Marvin and Link, Kathryn
"Construct Validity for the S.S.S."
Journal of Consulting and Clinical Psychology, Vol. 32 (1968), pp. 420-6.

126 -------------- CONVERGENT AND DISCRIMINANT VALIDITY --------------
        See also (sub)heading(s) 123.

126.01 ---------- Theory Re: Convergent and Discriminant Validity

Bagozzi, Richard P.
    "Evaluating Structural Equation Models With Unobservable Variables
    and Measurement Error: A Comment"
    Journal of Marketing Research, Vol. XVIII (August 1981), pp. 375-81.

Bagozzi, Richard P.
    "Convergent and Discriminant Validity by Analysis of Covariance
    Structures: The Case of the Affective, Behavioral, and Cognitive
    Components of Attitude"
    Proceedings, Fourth Annual Conference, Association for Consumer
    Research (1976), pp. 11-8.

Fiske, Donald W.
    "Convergent-Discriminant Validation in Measurement and Research
    Strategies"
    in Brindberg, D. and Kidder, L. (editors)
    New Directions for Methodology of Social and Behavioral Science:
    Forms of Validity in Research
    (San Francisco: Jossey-Bass Publishers, 1982), pp. 72-92.

Fornell, Claes and Denison, Daniel R.
    "Evaluating Convergent, Discriminant, and Nomological Validity via
    Confirmatory Multidimensional Scaling"
    The Graduate School of Business Administration, The University of
    Michigan (1981), working paper.

Fornell, Claes and Larcker, David F.
    "Structural Equation Models With Unobservable Variables and
    Measurement Error: Algebra and Statistics"
    Journal of Marketing Research, Vol. XVIII (August 1981), pp. 382-8.

Fornell, Claes and Larcker, David F.
    "Evaluating Structural Equation Models With Unobservable Variables
    and Measurement Error"
    Journal of Marketing Research, Vol. XVIII (February 1981), pp. 39-50.

Jackson, Douglas N.
    "Multimethod Factor Analysis in the Evaluation of Convergent and
    Discriminant Validity"
    Psychological Bulletin, Vol. 72 (July 1969), pp. 30-49.

Krause, Merton S.
    "The Implications for Convergent and Discriminant Validity Data for
    Instrument Validation"
    Psychometrika, Vol. 37 (June 1972), pp. 179-86.

Lumsden, James
    "Test Theory"
    in Rosenzweig, M. R. and Porter, L. W. (editors)
    Annual Review of Psychology
    (Palo Alto, CA: Annual Reviews, Inc., 1976).

Meehl, Paul E.
    "Theory Testing in Psychology and Physics: A Methodological Paradox"
    Philosophy of Science, Vol. 16 (June 1967), pp. 103-15.

126.02 ---------- Applications of Convergent and Discriminant Validity

Belch, George E. and Landon, E. Laird
    "Discriminant Validity of a Product-Anchored Self-Concept Measure"
    Journal of Marketing Research, Vol. XIV (May 1977), pp. 252-6.

Brown, James R. and Day, Ralph L.
    "Measures of Manifest Conflict in Distribution Channels"
    Journal of Marketing Research, Vol. XVIII (August 1981), pp. 263-74.

Evans, Martin G.
    "Convergent and Discriminant Validities Between the Cornell Job
    Descriptive Index and a Measurement of Goal Attainment"
    Journal of Applied Psychology, Vol. 53 (April 1969), pp. 102-6.

Evans, R. H.
    "The Upgraded Semantic Differential: A Further Test"
    Journal of the Market Research Society, Vol. 22 (April 1980), pp.
    143-7.

Futrell, Charles M.
    "Measurement of Salespeople's Job Satisfaction: Convergent and
    Discriminant Validity of Corresponding INDSALES and Job Descriptive
    Index Scales"
    Journal of Marketing Research, Vol. XVI (November 1979), pp. 594-7.

Gaski, John F. and Nevin, John R.
"The Differential Effects of Exercised and Unexercised Power Sources in a Marketing Channel"
Journal of Marketing Research, Vol. XXII (May 1985), pp. 130-42.

Gillet, B. and Schwab, D. P.
"Convergent and Discriminant Validities of Corresponding Job Descriptive Index and Minnesota Satisfaction Questionnaire Scales"
Journal of Applied Psychology, Vol. 60 (June 1975), pp. 313-7.

Heeler, Roger M., Okechuku, Chike, and Reid, Stan
"Attribute Importance: Contrasting Measurements"
Journal of Marketing Research, Vol. XVI (February 1979), pp. 60-3.

Lamb, Charles W., Jr. and Stem, Donald E., Jr.
"An Empirical Validation of the Randomized Response Technique"
Journal of Marketing Research, Vol. XV (November 1978), pp. 616-21.

Miniard, Paul W. and Cohen, Joel B.
"Isolating Attitudinal and Normative Influences in Behavioral Intentions Models"
Journal of Marketing Research, Vol. XVI (February 1979), pp. 102-10.

Neibecker, Bruno
"The Validity of Computer-Controlled Magnitude Scaling to Measure Emotional Impact of Stimuli"
Journal of Marketing Research, Vol. XXI (August 1984), pp. 325-31.

Noerager, Jon P.
"An Assessment of CAD: A Personality Instrument Developed Specifically for Marketing Research"
Journal of Marketing Research, Vol. XVI (February 1979), pp. 53-9.

Scott, Jerome E. and Wright, Peter
"Modeling an Organizational Buyer's Product Evaluation Strategy: Validity and Procedural Considerations"
Journal of Marketing Research, Vol. XIII (August 1976), pp. 211-24.

Steele, Howard L.
"On the Validity of Projective Questions"
Journal of Marketing Research, Vol. I (August 1964), pp. 46-9.

Summers, John O. and MacKay, David B.
"On Establishing Convergent Validity: A Reply to Wilkes and Wilcox"
Journal of Marketing Research, Vol. XIV (May 1977), pp. 263-5.

Szybillo, George J., Binstock, Sharon, and Buchanan, Lauranne
"Measure Validation of Leisure Time Activities: Time Budgets and Psychographics"
Journal of Marketing Research, Vol. XVI (February 1979), pp. 74-9.

Wilton, Peter C. and Myers, John G.
"Task, Expectancy, and Information Assessment Effects in Information Utilization Processes"
Journal of Consumer Research, Vol. 12 (March 1986), pp. 469-86.

Zinkhan, George M. and Muderrisoglu, Aydin
"Involvement, Familiarity, Cognitive Differentiation, and Advertising Recall: A Test of Convergent and Discriminant Validity"
in Hirschman, E. and Holbrook, M. (editors)
Advances in Consumer Research, Volume Twelve
(Ann Arbor, MI: Association for Consumer Research, 1985), pp. 356-61.

127 --------------- PREDICTIVE AND CONCURRENT VALIDITY ---------------
        See also (sub)heading(s) 123.

127.01 ---------- Theory Re: Predictive and Concurrent Validity

Browne, M. W.
    "Predictive Validity of a Linear Regression Equation"
    British Journal of Mathematical and Statistical Psychology, Vol. 28
    (May 1975), pp. 79-87.

Tauber, Edward M.
    "Predictive Validity in Consumer Research"
    Journal of Advertising Research, Vol. 15 (October 1975), pp. 59-64.

127.02 ---------- Applications of Predictive and Concurrent Validity

Akaah, Ishmael P. and Korgaonkar, Pradeep K.
    "An Empirical Comparison of the Predictive Validity of
    Self-Explicated, Huber-Hybrid, Traditional Conjoint, and Hybrid
    Conjoint Models"
    Journal of Marketing Research, Vol. XX (May 1983), pp. 187-97.

Anand, Punam and Stern, Louis W.
    "A Sociopsychological Explanation for Why Marketing Channel Members
    Relinquish Control"
    Journal of Marketing Research, Vol. XXII (November 1985), pp. 365-76.

Batsell, Richard R. and Lodish, Leonard M.
    "A Model and Measurement Methodology for Predicting Individual
    Consumer Choice"
    Journal of Marketing Research, Vol. XVIII (February 1981), pp. 1-12.

Bergier, Michel J.
    "Predictive Validity of Ethnic Identification Measures: An
    Illustration of the English/French Classification Dilemma in Canada"
    Journal of the Academy of Marketing Science, Vol. 14 (Summer 1986),
    pp. 37-42.

Best, Roger J.
    "Validity and Reliability of Criterion-Based Preferences"
    Journal of Marketing Research, Vol. XV (February 1978), pp. 154-60.

Blackston, Max and Van Der Zanden, Nico
    "Validity of Conjoint Analysis: Some Real Market Results"
    European Research, Vol. 8 (November 1980), pp. 243-50.

Browne, M. W.
    "Predictive Validity of a Linear Regression Equation"
    British Journal of Mathematical and Statistical Psychology, Vol. 28
    (1975), pp. 79-87.

Cattin, P.
    "A Predictive-Validity Based Procedure for Choosing Between
    Regression and Equal Weights"
    Organizational Behavior and Human Performance, Vol. 22 (August 1978),
    pp. 93-102.

Green, Paul E., Rao, Vithala R., and Armani, Diana E.
    "Graphology and Marketing Research: A Pilot Experiment in Validity
    and Inter-Judge Reliability"
    Journal of Marketing, Vol. 35 (April 1971), pp. 58-62.

Jain, Arun K., Acito, Franklin, Malhotra, Naresh, and Mahajan, Vijay
    "A Comparison of Predictive Validity of Alternative Methods for
    Estimating Parameters in Preference Models"
    School of Management, State University of New York at Buffalo (1978),
    working paper.

Joseph, Benoy and Vyas, Shailesh J.
    "Concurrent Validity of a Measure of Innovative Cognitive Style"
    Journal of the Academy of Marketing Science, Vol. 12 (Spring 1984),
    pp. 159-75.

Kalwani, M. U. and Silk, A. J.
    "On the Reliability and Predictive Validity of Purchase Intention
    Measures"
    Marketing Science, Vol. 1 (Summer 1982), pp. 243-86.

Leigh, Thomas W., MacKay, David B., and Summers, John O.
    "Reliability and Validity of Conjoint Analysis and Self-Explicated
    Weights: A Comparison"
    Journal of Marketing Research, Vol. XXI (November 1984), pp. 456-62.

Lusch, Robert F. and Ingene, Charles A.
    "The Predictive Validity of Alternative Measures of Inputs and
    Outputs in Retail Production Functions"
    in Beckwith, Neil et al. (editors)
    Proceedings, 1979 Educators' Conference
    (Chicago: American Marketing Association, 1979), pp. 330-3.

Malhotra, Naresh K.
"A Comparison of the Predictive Validity of Procedures for Analyzing Binary Data"
Journal of Business and Economic Statistics, Vol. 1 (October 1983), pp. 326-36.

Montgomery, David B. and Wittink, Dick R.
"The Predictive Validity of Conjoint Analysis for Alternative Aggregation Schemes"
Market Measurement and Analysis
(Cambridge, MA: Marketing Science Institute, 1980), pp. 298-309.

Moore, William L. and Holbrook, Morris B.
"On the Predictive Validity of Joint-Space Models in Consumer Evaluations of New Concepts"
Journal of Consumer Research, Vol. 9 (September 1982), pp. 206-10.

Myers, James H.
"More on Graphology and Marketing: An Empirical Validation of Marketing Graphology"
Journal of Marketing Research, Vol. VI (February 1969), pp. 107,8.

Neslin, Scott A.
"Linking Product Features to Perceptions: Self-Stated Versus Statistically Revealed Importance Weights"
Journal of Marketing Research, Vol. XVIII (February 1981), pp. 80-6.

Scott, Jerome E. and Wright, Peter
"Modeling an Organizational Buyer's Product Evaluation Strategy: Validity and Procedural Considerations"
Journal of Marketing Research, Vol. XIII (August 1976), pp. 211-24.

Sharma, Subhash, Durand, Richard M., and Gur-Arie, Oded
"Identification and Analysis of Moderator Variables"
Journal of Marketing Research, Vol. XVIII (August 1981), pp. 291-300.

Srinivasan, V., Jain, Arun K., and Malhotra, Naresh K.
"Improving Predictive Power of Conjoint Analysis by Constrained Parameter Estimation"
Journal of Marketing Research, Vol. XX (November 1983), pp. 433-8.

Tobolski, Francis P. and Kerr, William A.
"Predictive Value of the Empathy Test in Automobile Salesmanship"
Journal of Applied Psychology, Vol. 36 (October 1952), pp. 31-81.

Tyebjee, Tyzoon T.
"Response Latency: A New Measure for Scaling Brand Preference"
Journal of Marketing Research, Vol. XVI (February 1979), pp. 96-101.

Wittink, Dick R. and Cattin, Philippe
"Alternative Estimation Methods for Conjoint Analysis: A Monte Carlo Study"
Journal of Marketing Research, Vol. XVIII (February 1981), pp. 101-6.

Wittink, Dick R. and Montgomery, David B.
"Predictive Validity of Trade-Off Analysis for Alternative Segmentation Schemes"
in Beckwith, Neil et al. (editors)
Educators' Conference Proceedings, Series 44
(Chicago: American Marketing Association, 1979), pp. 69-73.

Zinkhan, George M. and Fornell, Claes
"A Test of Two Consumer Response Scales in Advertising"
Journal of Marketing Research, Vol. XXII (November 1985), pp. 447-52.

128 ----------------------- CROSS VALIDATION -----------------------
        See also (sub)heading(s) 123, 139.

128.01 ---------- Theory Re: Cross Validation

Coan, R. W.
    "Facts, Factors, and Artifacts: The Quest for Psychological Meaning"
    Psychological Review, Vol. 71 (March 1964), pp. 123-40.

Cudeck, Robert and Browne, Michael W.
    "Cross-Validation of Covariance Structures"
    Multivariate Behavioral Research, Vol. 18 (1983), pp. 147-67.

Efron, Bradley
    "The Jackknife, the Bootstrap, and Other Resampling Plans"
    SIAM Monograph Number 38
    (Philadelphia: Society of Industrial and Applied Mathematics, 1982).

Efron, Bradley
    "Estimating the Error Rate of a Prediction Rule: Improvement on
    Cross-Validation"
    Journal of the American Statistical Association, Vol. 78 (June 1983),
    pp. 316-31.

Efron, Bradley and Gong, Gail
    "A Leisurely Look at the Bootstrap, the Jackknife, and Cross
    Validation"
    American Statistician, Vol. 37 (February 1983), pp. 36-48.

Gollob, H. F.
    "Cross Validation Using Samples of Size One"
    American Psychological Association, Washington, DC (1967), paper
    presentation.

Herzberg, P. A.
    "The Parameters of Cross Validation"
    Psychometrika, Monograph Supplement, Vol. 34, No. 16 (1969).

Picard, Richard R. and Cook, R. Dennis
    "Cross-Validation of Regression Models"
    Journal of the American Statistical Association, Vol. 79 (September
    1984), pp. 575-83.

Wherry, R. J.
    "Comparision of Cross Validation With Statistical Inference of Betas
    and Multiple R From a Single Sample"
    Educational and Psychological Measurement, Vol. 11 (1951), pp. 23-8.

128.02 ---------- Theory Re: Simultaneous Cross Validation

Cooil, Bruce, Winer, Russell S., and Rados, David L.
    "Cross-Validation for Prediction"
    Journal of Marketing Research, Vol. XXIV (August 1987), pp. 271-9.

Crask, Melvin R. and Perreault, William D., Jr.
    "Validation of Discriminant Analysis in Marketing Research"
    Journal of Marketing Research, Vol. XIV (February 1977), pp. 60-8.

Geisser, Seymour
    "The Predictive Sample Reuse Method With Applications"
    Journal of the American Statistical Association, Vol. 70 (June 1975),
    pp. 320-8.

Lachenbruch, Peter A. and Mickey, M. Ray
    "Estimation of Error Rates in Discriminant Analysis"
    Technometrics, Vol. 10 (February 1968), pp. 1-11.

Stone, M.
    "An Asymptotic Equivalence of Choice of Model by Cross-Validation and
    Akaike's Criterion"
    Journal of the Royal Statistical Society, Series B, Vol. 39 (1977),
    pp. 44-7.

Stone, M.
    "Asymptotic For and Against Cross-Validation"
    Biometrika, Vol. 64 (April 1977), pp. 29-35.

Stone, M.
    "Cross-Validatory Choice and Assessment of Statistical Predictions"
    (with discussion)
    Journal of the Royal Statistical Society, Series B, Vol. 36 (1974),
    pp. 111-47.

128.03 ---------- Theory Re: Data Splitting or Validity Generalization

Darlington, Richard
"Multiple Regression in Psychological Research and Practice"
Psychological Bulletin, Vol. 69 (March 1968), pp. 161-82.

Dorans, Neil J. and Drasgow, Fritz
"A Note on Cross-Validating Prediction Equations"
Journal of Applied Psychology, Vol. 65 (December 1980), pp. 728,9.

McCarthy, Philip J.
"The Use of Balanced Half-Sample Replication in Cross-Validation
Studies"
Journal of the American Statistical Association, Vol. 71 (September
1976), pp. 596-604.

Mosier, Charles I.
"Problems and Designs of Cross-Validation"
Educational and Psychological Measurement, Vol. 11 (Spring 1951), pp.
5-11.

Murphy, Kevin R.
"Fooling Yourself With Cross-Validation: Single Sample Designs"
Personnel Psychology, Vol. 36 (Spring 1983), pp. 111-18.

Picard, Richard R. and Cook, R. Dennis
"Cross-Validation of Regression Models"
Journal of the American Statistical Association, Vol. 79 (September
1984), pp. 575-83.

Snee, Ronald D.
"Validation of Regression Models: Methods and Examples"
Technometrics, Vol. 19 (November 1977), pp. 415-28.

128.04 ---------- Applications of Data Splitting, Validity Generaliza'n

Darden, William R. and Howell, Roy D.
"Socialization Effects of Retail Work Experience on Shopping
Orientations"
Journal of the Academy of Marketing Science, Vol. 15 (Fall 1987), pp.
52-63.

Horst, P.
Prediction of Personal Adjustment
Bulletin 48
(New York: Social Science Research Council, 1941).

Larson, Selmer C.
"The Shrinkage of the Coefficient of Multiple Correlation"
Journal of Educational Psychology, Vol. 22 (January 1931), pp. 45-55.

Vredenburg, Harrie and Wee, Chow Hou
"The Role of Customer Service in Determining Customer Satisfaction"
Journal of the Academy of Marketing Science, Vol. 14 (Summer 1986),
pp. 17-26.

128.05 ---------- Unclassified Applications of Cross Validation

Green, Paul E. and Helsen, Kristiaan
"Cross-Validation Assessment of Alternatives to Individual-Level
Conjoint Analysis: A Case Study"
Journal of Marketing Research, Vol. XXVI (August 1989), pp. 346-50.

Peterson, Robert A. and Ross, Ivan
"How to Name New Brands"
Journal of Advertising Research, Vol. 12 (December 1972), pp. 29-34.

Tyagi, Pradeep K.
"Perceived Organizational Climate and the Process of Salesperson
Motivation"
Journal of Marketing Research, Vol. XIX (May 1982), pp. 240-54.

129 --------- COMPARATIVE STUDIES OF DATA GATHERING METHODS ----------

Abrams, Jack
    "Reducing the Risk of New Product Marketing Strategies Testing"
    Journal of Marketing Research, Vol. VI (May 1969), pp. 216-20.

Aneshensel, Carol S., Frerichs, Ralph R., Clark, Virginia A., and
    Yokopenic, Patricia A.
    "Measuring Depression in the Community: A Comparison of Telephone and
    Personal Interviews"
    Public Opinion Quarterly, Vol. 46 (1982), pp. 110-21.

Assael, Henry
    "Comparison of Brand Share Data by Three Reporting Systems"
    Journal of Marketing Research, Vol. IV (November 1967), pp. 400-1.

Baker, David and Holmes, Cliff
    "The Validity and Efficiency of Data Collection Using Screen
    Interviews Compared With Telephone Research"
    ESOMAR Congress, Montreux (1987), pp. 813-27.

Baxter, R. E.
    "Use Both Mail-Type Questionnaire and Personal Interviews in
    Readership Research"
    Printers' Ink, Vol. 203 (May 7, 1943), p. 24.

Begin, G. and Boivin, M.
    "Comparison of Data Gathered on Sensitive Questions via Direct
    Questionnaire, Randomized Response Technique, and a Projective Method"
    Psychological Reports, Vol. 47 (December 1980), pp. 743-50.

Bush, Alan J. and Hair, Joseph F., Jr.
    "An Assessment of the Mall Intercept as a Data Collection Method"
    Journal of Marketing Research, Vol. XXII (May 1985), pp. 158-67.

Bush, Alan J. and Parasuraman, A.
    "Mall Intercept Versus Telephone Interviewing Environment"
    Journal of Advertising Research, Vol. 25 (April/May 1985), pp. 36-43.

Bylund, H. B. and Baker, R. L.
    "Consumer Survey Versus Store Data for Determining Egg Consumption"
    Journal of Farm Economics, Vol. 39 (August 1957), pp. 770-7.

Cahalan, D.
    "Measuring Newspaper Readership by Telephone: Two Comparisons With
    Face-to-Face Interviews"
    Journal of Advertising Research, Vol. 1 (December 1960), pp. 1-6.

Cannell, Charles F. and Fowler, Floyd J.
    "A Comparison of a Self-Enumerative Procedure and a Personal
    Interview: A Validity Study"
    Public Opinion Quarterly, Vol. 27 (Summer 1963), pp. 250-64.

Colombotos, J.
    "Personal vs. Telephone Interviews' Effect on Responses"
    Public Health Report, Vol. 34 (September 1969), pp. 773-82.

Colombotos, John
    "The Effects of Personal vs. Telephone Interviews on Socially
    Acceptable Responses"
    Annual Meeting of the American Association for Public Opinion
    Research, Groton, CT (May 1965), paper presentation.

Coombs, L. and Freeman, R.
    "Uses of Telephone Interviews in a Longitudinal Fertility Study"
    Public Opinion Quarterly, Vol. 28 (Spring 1964), pp. 112-7.

Dunning, Bruce and Cahalan, Don
    "By-Mail vs. Field Self-Administered Questionnaires: An Armed Forces
    Survey"
    Public Opinion Quarterly, Vol. 37 (Winter 1973-74), pp. 618-24.

Ehrenberg, A. S. C.
    "A Comparison of TV Audience Measures"
    Journal of Advertising Research, Vol. 4 (December 1964), pp. 11-6.

Ellis, Albert
    "Questionnaire Versus Interview Methods in the Study of Human Love
    Relationships"
    American Sociological Review, Vol. 12 (August 1947), pp. 841-53.

Ferber, Robert and Wales, Hugh G.
    "A New Way to Measure Journal Readership"
    Journal of Advertising Research, Vol. 3 (September 1963), pp. 9-16.

Goyder, John
    "Face-to-Face Interviews and Mailed Questionnaires: The Net
    Difference in Response Rate"
    Public Opinion Quarterly, Vol. 49 (Summer 1985), pp. 234-52.

Greenberg, A. and Hanfield, H. N.
"On the Reliability of Mail Questionnaires in Product Tests"
Journal of Marketing, Vol. 21 (January 1957), pp. 342-5.

Groves, R. M.
"Actors and Questions in Telephone and Personal Interview Surveys"
Public Opinion Quarterly, Vol. 43 (1979), pp. 233-44.

Groves, R. M.
"An Experimental Comparison of National Telephone and Personal
Interview Surveys"
Survey Research Center, University of Michigan (1977), unpublished
manuscript.

Groves, Robert M. and Kahn, Robert L.
Surveys by Telephone: A National Comparison With Personal Interviews
(New York: Academic Press, Inc., 1979), 358 pp.

Hancock, John W.
"An Experimental Study of Four Methods of Measuring Unit Costs of
Obtaining Attitude Toward the Retail Store"
Journal of Applied Psychology, Vol. 24 (April 1940), pp. 213-30.

Hansell, Stephen, Sparacino, Jack, Ronchi, Don, and Strodtbeck, Fred L.
"Ego Development Responses in Written Questionnaires and Telephone
Interviews"
Journal of Personality and Social Psychology, Vol. 47 (November
1984), pp. 1118,9.

Herman, Jeanne Brett
"Mixed-Mode Data Collection: Telephone and Personal Interviewing"
Journal of Applied Psychology, Vol. 62, No. 4 (1977), pp. 399-404.

Herzog, A. Regula, Rodgers, Willard L., and Kulka, Richard A.
"Interviewing Older Adults: A Comparison of Telephone and
Face-to-Face Modalities"
Public Opinion Quarterly, Vol. 47 (Fall 1983), pp. 405-18.

Hochstim, Joseph R.
"A Critical Comparison of Three Strategies of Collecting Data From
Households"
Journal of the American Statistical Society, Vol. 62 (September
1967), pp. 976-89.

Hochstim, J. R.
"Alternatives to Personal Interviewing"
Public Opinion Quarterly, Vol. 27 (Winter 1963), pp. 629,30.

Hochstim, Joseph R.
"Comparison of Three Information Gathering Strategies in a Population
Study of Sociomedical Variables"
Proceedings, Social Statistics Section, American Statistical
Association (1962), pp. 154-9.

Hoinville, Gerald and Sykes, Wendy
"Methodological Research on Telephone Interviews"
Proceedings, The Market Research Society Conference (1984).

Hu, Michael Y. and Bruning, Edward R.
"Using Prior Experience to Explain Survey Versus Diary Recorded Usage
Data"
Journal of the Market Research Society, Vol. 30 (January 1988), pp.
59-72.

Jaffe, Eugene D., Paternak, Hanoch, and Grifel, Avi
"Response Results of Lottery Buyer Behavior Surveys: In-Home vs.
Point-of-Purchase Interviews"
Public Opinion Quarterly, Vol. 47 (Fall 1983), pp. 419-26.

Jordan, Lawrence A., Marcus, Alfred C., and Reeder, Leo G.
"Response Styles in Telephone and Household Interviewing: A Field
Experiment"
Public Opinion Quarterly, Vol. 44 (Summer 1980), pp. 210-21.

Kahn, Robert
"A Comparison of Two Methods of Collecting Data for Social Research:
The Fixed-Alternative Questionnaire and the Open-Ended Interview"
University of Michigan (1952), unpublished doctoral dissertation.

Klecka, William R. and Tuchfarber, Alfred J., Jr.
"Random Digit Dialing: A Comparison to Personal Surveys"
Public Opinion Quarterly, Vol. 42 (Spring 1978), pp. 105-14.

Klecka, William R. and Tuchfarber, Alfred J., Jr.
"Random Digit Dialing as an Efficient Method for Political Polling"
Georgia Political Science Association Journal, Vol. 2 (Spring 1974),
pp. 135-51.

Knudson, Dean O., Pope, Hallowell, and Irish, Donald P.
    "Response Differences to Questions on Sexual Standards: An
    Interview-Questionnaire Comparison"
    Public Opinion Quarterly, Vol. 31 (Summer 1967), pp. 290-7.

Kofron, J. H., Bayton, J., and Bortner, B. Z.
    "Guidelines for Choosing Between Long-Distance Telephone Interviewing"
    15th Annual Conference of The Advertising Research Foundation, New
    York (1969), paper presentation.

Krugman, H. E.
    "A Comparison of Physical and Verbal Responses to Television
    Commercials"
    Public Opinion Quarterly, Vol. 29 (Summer 1965), pp. 323-5.

Larsen, O. N.
    "The Comparative Validity of Telephone and Face-to-Face Interviews in
    the Measurement of Message Diffusion From Leaflets"
    American Sociological Review, Vol. 17 (August 1952), pp. 471-6.

Larsen, O. N. and DeFleur, M. L.
    "Validity and Reliability in Measurements of Message Diffusion"
    Research Studies of the State College of Washington, Vol. 23 (June
    1955), pp. 110-20.

Laurent, Charles K. and Pena D., I.
    An Analysis of Three Methods of Data Gathering
    (Bogota, Colombia: Instito Latinoamericano de Mercadeo Agricola 66/2,
    1966).

Levine, Daniel B. and Miller, Herman P.
    Response Variation Encountered with Different Questionnaire Forms"
    Marketing Research Report No. 163
    (U.S. Department of Agriculture, 1957).

Locander, William B., Sudman, Seymour, and Bradburn, Norman
    "An Investigation of Interview Method, Threat, and Response
    Distribution"
    Proceedings of American Statistical Association (1974).

Maynes, E. S.
    "The Anatomy of Response Errors: Consumer Saving"
    Journal of Marketing Research Vol. 2 (November 1965), pp. 368-87.

McDonagh, Edward C. and Rosenblum, A. Leon
    "A Comparison of Mailed Questionnaires and Subsequent Structured
    Interviews"
    Public Opinion Quarterly, Vol. 29 (Spring 1965), pp. 131-6.

McGinnis, R.
    "Scaling Interview Data"
    American Sociological Review, Vol. 18 (October 1953), pp. 514-21.

McIntyre, Shelby H. and Bender, Sherry D. F. G.
    "The Purchase Intercept Technique (PIT) in Comparison to Telephone
    and Mail Surveys"
    Journal of Retailing, Vol. 62 (Winter 1986), pp. 364-83.

McNeil, J.
    "Survey Measures of Changes in Household Wealth and Buying
    Expectations: A Note on Methodology"
    Proceedings of the Social Statistics Section of the American
    Statistical Association (1972), pp. 364-9.

Murray, Janet et al.
    Collection Methods in Dietary Surveys
    (Southern Cooperative Series Bulletin, Vol. 23, South Carolina
    Agricultural Experiment Station, 1952).

Newman, Joseph W. and Lockeman, Bradley D.
    "Measuring Prepurchase Information Seeking"
    Journal of Consumer Research, Vol. 2 (December 1975), pp. 216-22.

Nuckols, Robert C.
    "The Validity and Comparability of Mail and Personal Interview
    Surveys"
    Journal of Marketing Research, Vol. I (February 1964), pp. 11-6.

Oakes, R. H.
    "Differences in Responsiveness in Telephone Versus Personal
    Interviews"
    Journal of Marketing (1954), p. 169.

O'Dell, William F.
    "Personal Interviews or Mail Panels"
    Journal of Marketing, Vol. 26 (October 1962), pp. 34-9.

Parfitt, John H.
    "A Comparison of Purchase Recall With Diary Panel Records"
    Journal of Advertising Research, Vol. 7 (September 1967), pp. 16-31.

Patchen, Marvin
    "Alternative Questionnaire Approaches to Measurement of Influence in
    Organizations"
    American Journal of Sociology, Vol. 69 (July 1963), pp. 41-52.

Payne, John W. and Ragsdale, E. K. Easton
    "Verbal Protocols and Direct Observation of Supermarket Shopping
    Behavior: Some Findings and a Discussion of Methods"
    in Hunt, H. Keith (editor)
    Advances in Consumer Research, Volume Five
    (Ann Arbor, MI: Association for Consumer Research, 1978).

Payne, Stanley L.
    "Combination of Survey Methods"
    Journal of Marketing Research, Vol. I (May 1964), pp. 61,2.

Pennings, J.
    "Measures of Organizational Structure: A Methodological Note"
    American Journal of Sociology, Vol. 79 (November 1973), pp. 686-704.

Quackenbush, G. G. and Shaffer, J. D.
    Collecting Food Purchase Data by Consumer Panel
    (Michigan State University, Agricultural Experiment Station,
    Technical Bulletin 279, August 1960).

Rogers, Theresa F.
    "Interviews by Telephone and in Person: Quality of Responses and
    Field Performance"
    Public Opinion Quarterly, Vol. 40 (Spring 1976), pp. 51-65.

Russo, J. Edward
    "Eye Fixations Can Save the World: A Critical Evaluation and a
    Comparison Between Eye Fixations and Other Information Processing
    Methodologies"
    in Hunt, H. Keith (editor)
    Advances in Consumer Research, Volume Five
    (Ann Arbor, MI: Association for Consumer Research, 1978).

Sathe, V.
    "Institutional Versus Questionnaire Measures of Organizational
    Structure"
    Academy of Management Journal, Vol. 21 (June 1978), pp. 227-38.

Schmiedeskamp, J. W.
    "Reinterviews by Telephone"
    Journal of Marketing, Vol. 26 (January 1962), pp. 28-34.

Sewall, Murphy A.
    "Relative Information Contributions of Consumer Purchase Intentions
    and Management Judgment as Explanators of Sales"
    Journal of Marketing Research, Vol. XVIII (May 1981), pp. 249-53.

Shosteck, Herschel and Fairweather, William R.
    "Physician Response Rates to Mail and Personal Interview Surveys"
    Public Opinion Quarterly, Vol. 43, No. 2 (1979), pp. 206-17.

Siemiatycki, J.
    "A Comparison of Mail, Telephone and Home Interview Strategies for
    Household Health Surveys"
    American Journal of Public Health, Vol. 69 (1979), pp. 238-45.

Spencer, Nick
    "The Advantages and Disadvantages of Using Panels Instead of, or as
    Well as, Separate Surveys in Political Polling"
    Journal of the Market Research Society, Vol. 16 (October 1974), pp.
    283-6.

Stanton, John L. and Tucci, Louis A.
    "The Measurement of Consumption: A Comparison of Surveys and Diaries"
    Journal of Marketing Research, Vol. XIX (May 1982), pp. 274-7.

Stock, J. Stevens
    "Non-Sampling Errors in Sampling for Business"
    in Business Application of Statistical Sampling Methods
    Conference conducted by University of Illinois and Chicago Chapter,
    American Statistical Association (1950), pp. 117-36.

Stover, Robert V. and Stone, Walter J.
    "Hand Delivery of Self-Administered Questionnaires"
    Public Opinion Quarterly, Vol. 38 (Summer 1974), pp. 284-7.

Sudman, Seymour and Ferber, Robert
    "A Comparison of Alternative Procedures for Collecting Consumer
    Expenditure Data for Frequently Purchased Products"
    Journal of Marketing Research, Vol. XI (May 1974), pp. 128-35.

Sudman, S. and Ferber, R.
    "Some Experimentation With Recall Procedures and Diaries for Consumer
    Expenditures"
    Proceedings of the Social Statistics Section of the American
    Statistical Association (1971), pp. 247-53.

Sudman, S., Greeley, A., and Pinto, L.
    "The Effectiveness of Self-Administered Questionnaires"
    Journal of Marketing Research, Vol. II (August 1965), pp. 293-7.

Sykes, Wendy and Hoinville, Gerald
    "Methodological Research on Telephone Interviewing"
    Market Research Society Conference (March 1984), pp. 87-97.

Telser, E.
    "Data Exercises Bias in Phone vs. Personal Interview Debate"
    Marketing News, Vol. 10 (September 10, 1976), pp. 6,7.

Tigert, D. J., Barnes, J. G., and Bourgeois, J. C.
    "Research on Research: Mail Panel Versus Telephone Survey in Retail
    Image Analysis"
    The Canadian Marketer (Winter 1975), pp. 22-7.

U.S. Bureau of the Census
    Evaluation and Research Program of the U.S. Censuses of Population
    and Housing, 1960: The Employer Credit Check
    (Washington, DC: Bureau of the Census, Department of Commerce, Series
    Er60, No. 6, 1965), 14 pp.

Van Arsdol, Maurice D. and Jahn, Julius A.
    "Time and Population Sampling Applied to the Estimation of
    Expenditures of University Students"
    American Sociological Review, (December 1952), pp. 738-46.

Wadsworth, Robert N.
    "The Experience of a User of a Consumer Panel"
    Applied Statistics (November 1952), pp. 169-78.

Wheatley, J. J.
    "Self-Administered Questionnaires or Telephone Interviews"
    Journal of Marketing Research, Vol. X (February 1973), pp. 94-6.

Wind, Yoram and Lerner, David
    "On the Measurement of Purchase Data: Surveys Versus Purchase Diaries"
    Journal of Marketing Research, Vol. XVI (February 1979), pp. 39-47.

Wind, Yoram and Lerner, David
    "A Note on the Measurement of Purchase Data: Surveys vs. Purchase
    Diaries"
    Wharton School (1977), working paper.

130 ---------------- UNCLASSIFIED - DATA COLLECTION -----------------

Brighton, M.
"The Use of Optical Mark Readers in Market Research"
Journal of the Market Research Society (England), Vol. 13 (October 1971), pp. 191-200.

Cadotte, Ernest R.
"Push Button Questionnaire: A New Tool for Measuring Customer Satisfaction"
Cornell Hotel and Restaurant Administration Quarterly, Vol. 19 (February 1979), pp. 70-9.

Durrant, H. and Simmons, M.
"The Paradox of Memory in Market Research"
Journal of the Market Research Society, Vol. 10, No. 4 (1968), pp. 253-63.

Ericsson, K. Anders and Simon, Herbert A.
"Verbal Reports as Data"
Psychological Review, Vol. 87, No. 3 (1980), pp. 215-51.

Frontori, Laura, Pogliana, Antonella, and Spataro, Bruna
"Application of Play-Oneiric Tests in Basic Motivational Research and Communication Studies"
ESOMAR Congress, Rome (1984), pp. 649-68.

Gabor, Andre, Granger, Clive W. J., and Sowter, Anthony P.
"Real and Hypothetical Shop Situations in Market Research"
Journal of Marketing Research, Vol. VII (August 1970), pp. 355-9.

Gray, P. G.
"A Sample Survey With Both a Postal and an Interview Stage"
Applied Psychology, Vol. 6 (June 1957), p. 139 ff.

Harris, James R., Guffey, Hugh J. and Laumer, J. Ford, Jr.
"The Windshield Method of Questionnaire Distribution: A Viable Alternative"
Journal of the Academy of Marketing Science, Vol. 7 (Summer 1979), pp. 184-91.

Klompmaker, Jay E., Lindley, J. Daniel, and Page, Robert L.
"Using Free Papers for Customer Surveys"
Journal of Marketing, Vol. 41 (July 1977), pp. 80-2.

Levinson, H. C.
"What You Should Know About Split-Run Tests"
Printers' Ink, Vol. 241 (December 26, 1952), p. 31 ff.

Marchant, L. J.
"Survey Weighting: Avoiding the Pitfalls"
ESOMAR Seminar on Fieldwork, Sampling and Questionnaire Design, Amsterdam (1973).

Mather, Malcolm R.
"An Automated System of Collecting Point of Sale Information From Record Stores"
ESOMAR Congress, Rome (1984), pp. 213-22.

Messina, Graziella and Barbero, Franco
"Hypnosis-Derived Techniques in Market Research"
ESOMAR Congress, Rome (1984), pp. 515-29.

Nolan, J. A.
"Self Completion Questionnaires: New Uses for an Old Technique"
Market Research Society Conference, Brighton (1971).

Nosanchuk, T. A. and Marchak, M. P.
"Pretest Sensitization and Attitude Change"
Public Opinion Quarterly, Vol. 33 (Spring 1969), pp. 107-11.

Slovic, Paul
"Analyzing the Expert Judge: A Descriptive Study of a Stockbroker's Decision Processes"
Journal of Applied Psychology, Vol. 53 (August 1969), pp. 255-63.

Van Waes, D. A. et al.
"Evaluation of Research Techniques Used for Measuring the Influences of Factors Believed to be Associated With Volume of Consumer Purchases in Retail Stores"
Methods of Research in Marketing, Paper No. 1 (Ithaca, NY: Cornell University, Department of Agricultural Economics, July 1951), 42 pp.

Yinger, J. M., Ideka, K., and Laycock, F.
"Treating Matching as a Variable in a Sociological Experiment"
American Sociological Review, Vol. 32 (October 1967), pp. 801-12.

131 ----------------- ANALYTICAL METHODS - GENERAL -----------------
        See also (sub)heading(s) 209, 210, 211, 213.

131.01 ---------- Reviews of Multivariate Analytical Methods Textbooks

Hanssens, Dominique M.
  "A Comparative Review of Econometrics Books"
  Journal of Marketing Research, Vol. XIX (February 1982), pp. 156-63.

Malhotra, Naresh K.
  "Review of Multivariate Statistics Books"
  Journal of Marketing Research, Vol. XVIII (May 1981), pp. 256-62.

Rao, Vithala R.
  "Books on Quantitative Methods for Consumer Research"
  Journal of Consumer Research, Vol. 7 (September 1980), pp. 198-210.

Srivastava, Rajendra K.
  "Discrete Multivariate Analysis Books"
  Journal of Marketing Research, Vol. XVII (August 1980), pp. 395-406.

131.02 ---------- Multivariate Analytical Methods Textbooks

Aaker, David A.
  Multivariate Analysis in Marketing, Second Edition
  (Palo Alto, CA: The Scientific Press, 1981), 244 pp.

Aaker, David A.
  Multivariate Analysis in Marketing: Theory and Application
  (Belmont, CA: Wadsworth Publishing Company, 1971).

Amick, Daniel J. and Walberg, Herbert J. (editors)
  Introductory Multivariate Analysis: For Education, Psychological, and
  Social Research
  (Berkeley, CA: McCutchan Publishing Corporation, 1975).

Anderson, T. W.
  An Introduction to Multivariate Statistical Analysis, Second Edition
  (New York: John Wiley and Sons, Inc., 1984), 675 pp.

Barnett, Vic (editor)
  Interpreting Multivariate Data
  (New York: John Wiley and Sons, Inc., 1981), 374 pp.

Bennett, Spencer and Bowers, David
  An Introduction to Multivariate Techniques for Social and Behavioral
  Sciences
  (New York: Halstead Press, 1976), 156 pp.

Bernstein, Ira H., et al.
  Multivariate Analysis
  (Springer-Verlag, 1987).

Bishop, Yvonne, Feinberg, Stephen, and Holland, Paul
  Discrete Multivariate Analysis
  (Cambridge, MA: The MIT Press, 1975).

Bock, R. Darrell
  Multivariate Statistical Methods in Behavioral Research
  (New York: McGraw-Hill Book Company, 1975), 623 pp.

Bolch, Ben W. and Huang, Cliff J.
  Multivariate Statistical Methods for Business and Economics
  (Englewood Cliffs, NJ: Prentice-Hall, Inc., 1974).

Cooley, William W. and Lohnes, Paul R.
  Multivariate Data Analysis
  (New York: John Wiley and Sons, 1971).

Dillon, William R. and Goldstein, M.
  Multivariate Analysis: Methods and Applications
  (New York: John Wiley and Sons, Inc., 1984).

Eaton, Morris L.
  Multivariate Statistics: A Vector Space Approach
  (New York: John Wiley and Sons, Inc., 1983), 512 pp.

Finn, Jeremy D.
  A General Model for Multivariate Analysis
  (New York: Holt, Rinehart and Winston, Inc., 1974).

Finn, Jeremy D.
  Multivariance: Univariate and Multivariate Analysis of Variance,
  Covariance and Regression
  (Ann Arbor, MI: National Educational Resources, Inc., 1972).

Fornell, Claes (editor)
A Second Generation of Multivariate Analysis: Measurement and
Evaluation, Volume II
(New York: Praeger Publishers, 1982), 430 pp.

Fornell, Claes (editor)
A Second Generation of Multivariate Analysis: Methods, Volume I
(New York: Praeger Publishers, 1982), 392 pp.

Gifi, A.
Non-Linear Multivariate Analysis
(Leiden, The Netherlands: Department of Data Theory, University of
Leiden, 1981).

Giri, Narayan C.
Multivariate Statistical Inference
(New York: Academic Press, 1977).

Gnanadesikan, R.
Methods for Statistical Data Analysis of Multivariate Observations
(New York: John Wiley and Sons, Inc., 1977), 311 pp.

Graybill, Franklin A.
Theory and Applications of the Linear Model
(North Sechituate, MA: Duxbury Press, 1976).

Green, Paul E.
Analyzing Multivariate Data
(Hinsdale, IL: The Dryden Press, 1978), 519 pp.

Green, Paul E. (contributions by J. Douglas Carroll)
Mathematical Tools for Applied Multivariate Analysis
(New York: Academic Press, 1976), 376 pp.

Hair, J., Anderson, R. E., Tatham, R. L., and Grablowsky, B. J.
Multivariate Data Analysis, Second Edition
(Tulsa, OK: Petroleum Publishing Company, 1987), 484 pp.

Hanushek, Eric A. and Jackson, John E.
Statistical Methods for Social Scientists
(New York: Academic Press, Inc., 1977).

Harris, Richard J.
A Primer of Multivariate Statistics
(New York: Academic Press, 1975).

Hawkins, D. M.
Topics in Applied Multivariate Analysis
(New York: Cambridge University Press, 1982), 362 pp.

Horton, Raymond L.
The General Linear Model: Data Analysis in the Social and Behavioral
Sciences
(New York: McGraw-Hill Book Co., 1978), 274 pp.

Hudson, Herschel C. and Associates
Classifying Social Data
(San Francisco: Jossey-Bass Publishers, 1982), 270 pp.

Jackson, Barbara Bund
Multivariate Data Analysis: An Introduction
(Homewood, IL: Richard D. Irwin, Inc., 1983), 244 pp.

Johnson, R. A. and Wichern, D. W.
Applied Multivariate Statistical Analysis
(Englewood Cliffs, NJ: Prentice-Hall Inc., 1982).

Kabe, D. G. and Gupta, R. P. (editors)
Multivariate Statistical Inference
(New York: American Elsevier/North Holland, 1973).

Kachigan, Sam Kash
Statistical Analysis: An Interdisciplinary Introduction to Univariate
and Multivariate Methods
(New York: Radius Press, 1986), 589 pp.

Kachigan, Sam Kash
Multivariate Statistical Analysis
(New York: Radius Press, 1982), 297 pp.

Kendall, Maurice
Multivariate Analysis
(New York: Hafner Press, 1976), 210 pp.

Kendall, M. G.
A Course in Multivariate Analysis, Second Edition
(New York: Hafner Publishing Co., 1965).

Keppel, Geoffrey
    Design and Analysis: A Researcher's Handbook
    (Englewood Cliffs, NJ: Prentice-Hall, Inc., 1973), 565 pp.

Kish, L.
    Statistical Design for Research
    (New York: John Wiley and Sons, Inc., 1987).

Kramer, Clyde Y.
    A First Course in Methods of Multivariate Analysis
    (Blacksburg, VA: 1972).

Krishnaiah, Paruchuri R. (editor)
    Multivariate Analysis, IV
    (New York: American Elsevier/North Holland, 1977).

Lebart, Ludovic, Morineau, Alain, and Warwick, Kenneth M.
    Multivariate Descriptive Statistical Analysis
    (New York: John Wiley and Sons, Inc., 1984), 231 pp.

Long, J. Scott (editor)
    Common Problems/Proper Solutions
    (Newbury Park, CA: Sage Publications, Inc., 1988), 335 pp.

Mallows, Colin L. (editor)
    Design, Data and Analysis by Some Friends of Cuthbert Daniel
    (New York: John Wiley and Sons, Inc., 1987), 380 pp.

Marascuilo, Leonard A. and Levin, Joel R.
    Multivariate Statistics in the Social Sciences: A Researcher's Guide
    (Monterey, CA: Brooks/Cole, 1983).

Mardia, K. V., Kent, J. T., and Bibby, J. M.
    Multivariate Analysis
    (London, EN: Academic Press, 1979), 521 pp.

Maxwell, Albert Ernest
    Multivariate Analysis in Behavioral Research
    (New York: Halsted Press, 1977).

Morrison, Donald F.
    Multivariate Statistical Methods, Second Edition
    (New York: McGraw-Hill Book Company, 1976), 415 pp.

Namboodiri, N. Krishnan, Carter, Lewis F., and Blalock, Hubert M., Jr.
    Applied Multivariate Analysis and Experimental Designs
    (New York: McGraw-Hill, Inc., 1975), 688 pp.

Neter, John, Wasserman, William, and Kutner, Michael H.
    Applied Linear Statistical Methods: Regression, Analysis of Variance
    and Experimental Designs, Second Edition
    (Homewood, IL: Richard D. Irwin, Inc., 1985).

Norusis, Marija
    The SPSS-X Guide to Data Analysis
    (Chicago: SPSS Inc., 1986), 376 pp.

Overall, J. E. and Klett, J. C.
    Applied Multivariate Analysis
    (New York: McGraw-Hill Book Company, 1972).

Press, S. J.
    Applied Multivariate Analysis
    (New York: Holt, Rinehart and Winston, Inc., 1971).

Puri, Maden Lal and Sen, Pranab Kumar
    Nonparametric Methods in Multivariate Analysis
    (New York: John Wiley and Sons, 1971).

Rao, Calyampudi Radhakrishna
    Linear Statistical Inference and Its Applications, Second Edition
    (New York: John Wiley and Sons, Inc., 1973).

Searle, S. R.
    Linear Models
    (New York: John Wiley and Sons, 1971).

Seber, G. A. F.
    Multivariate Observations
    (New York: John Wiley and Sons, Inc., 1984), 686 pp.

Sheth, Jagdish N. (editor)
    Multivariate Methods for Market and Survey Research
    (Chicago: American Marketing Association, 1977), 398 pp.

Snell, E. J.
    Applied Statistics: A Handbook of BMDP Analyses
    (London: Chapman and Hall, 1987).

Srivastava, M. S. and Carter, Edward M.
   An Introduction to Applied Multivariate Statistics
   (New York: North Holland Publishing Company, 1983).

Srivastava, M. S. and Khatri, C. G.
   An Introduction to Multivariate Statistics
   (New York: North-Holland, 1979), 530 pp.

Stevens, James
   Applied Multivariate Statistics for the Social Sciences
   (Hillsdale, NJ: Lawrence Erlbaum Associates, Publishers, 1986).

Stopher, Peter R. and Meyburg, Arnim H.
   Surveying Sampling and Multivariate Analysis for Social Scientists
   and Engineers
   (Lexington, MA: Lexington Books, 1979), 408 pp.

Takeuchi, Kei, Yanai, Harvo, and Murherjee, Bisha Nath
   The Foundations of Multivariate Analysis
   (New York: John Wiley and Sons, Inc., 1982), 458 pp.

Tatsuoka, Maurice M.
   Multivariate Analysis: Techniques for Educational and Psychological
   Research
   (New York: John Wiley and Sons, Inc., 1971).

Thorndike, Robert M.
   Correlational Procedures for Research
   (New York, NY: Gardner Press, Inc., 1978), 340 pp.

Timm, Neil H.
   Multivariate Analysis With Applications in Education and Psychology
   (Monterey, CA: Wadsworth Publishing Co., 1975).

Toutenburg, Helge
   Prior Information in Linear Models
   (New York: John Wiley and Sons, Inc., 1982), 215 pp.

Van De Geer, John P.
   Introduction to Multivariate Analysis for the Social Sciences
   (San Francisco: W. H. Freeman, 1971).

Ward, J. H. and Jennings, E.
   Introduction to Linear Models
   (Englewood Cliffs, NJ: Prentice-Hall, Inc., 1973).

131.03 ---------- Statistical Methods Textbooks

Abraham, Bovas and Ledolter, Johannes
   Statistical Methods for Forecasting
   (New York: John Wiley and Sons, Inc., 1983), 445 pp.

Anderson, T. W.
   The Statistical Analysis of Time Series
   (New York: John Wiley and Sons, Inc., 1971).

Arnold, Steven F.
   The Theory of Linear Models and Multivariate Analysis
   (New York: John Wiley and Sons, Inc., 1981), 475 pp.

Berenson, Mark L., Levine, David M., and Goldstein, Matthew
   Intermediate Statistical Methods and Applications: A Computer Package
   Approach
   (Englewood Cliffs, NJ: Prentice-Hall, Inc., 1983), 579 pp.

Bickel, Peter J. and Doksum, Kjell A.
   Mathematical Statistics
   (Oakland, CA: Holden-Day, 1977).

Box, George E. P., Hunter, William G., and Hunter, J. Stuart
   Statistics for Experimenters: An Introduction to Design, Data
   Analysis and Model Building
   (New York: John Wiley and Sons, Inc., 1978), 186 pp.

Braverman, Jerome D. and Stewart, William C.
   Statistics for Business and Economics
   (New York: The Ronald Press Company, 1973).

Brightman, Harvey J.
   Statistics in Plain English
   (Cincinnati, OH: South-Western Publishing Company, 1986), 312 pp.

Cox, C. P.
   A Handbook of Introductory Statistical Methods
   (New York: John Wiley and Sons, Inc., 1987).

Cox, D. R. and Hinckley, D.
   Theoretical Statistics
   (London: Allen and Unwin, 1974).

Daniel, Wayne W. and Terrell, James C.
  Business Statistics, Fourth Editition
  (Boston: Houghton Mifflin Company, 1986), 878 pp.

Dietrich, Frank H., II and Shafer, Nancy J.
  Business Statistics: An Inferential Approach
  (Santa Clara, CA: Dellen Publishing Company), 810 pp.

Dowdy, Shirley and Weardon, Stanley
  Statistics for Research
  (New York: John Wiley and Sons, Inc., 1983), 537 pp.

Fisher, Ronald A.
  Statistical Methods for Research Workers, Fourteenth Edition
  (New York: Hafner Publishing Company, 1970).

Freund, John E.
  Mathematical Statistics, Second Edition
  (Englewood Cliffs, NJ: Prentice-Hall, Inc., 1971).

Glass, Gene V. and Stanley, Julian C.
  Statistical Methods in Education and Psychology
  (Englewood Cliffs, NJ: Prentice-Hall, Inc., 1970).

Greensted, C. S., Jardine, A. K. S., and MacFarlane, J. D.
  Essentials of Statistics in Marketing
  (Heinemann and Institute of Marketing and the CAM Foundation, 1978),
  257 pp.

Guilford, J. P. and Fruchter, Benjamin
  Fundamental Statistics for Psychology and Education, Fifth Edition
  (New York: McGraw-Hill Book Company, 1973).

Hampel, Frank R., Ronchetti, Elvezio M., Rousseeuw, Peter J., and
  Stahel, Werner A.
  Robust Statistics: The Approach Based on Influence Functions
  (New York: John Wiley and Sons, Inc., 1986), 502 pp.

Hanushek, E. A. and Jackson, J. E.
  Statistical Methods for Social Scientists
  (New York: Academic Press, 1977).

Hays, William L.
  Statistics for the Social Sciences, Second Edition
  (New York: Holt, Rinehart, and Winston, 1973)

Hays, William L. and Winkler, Robert L.
  Statistics: Probability, Inference, and Decision
  (New York: Holt, Rinehart, and Winston, 1971).

Hogg, R. V. and Craig, A. T.
  Introduction to Mathematical Statistics, Fourth Edition
  (New York: Macmillan, 1978).

Jessen, Raymond J.
  Statistical Survey Techniques
  (New York: John Wiley and Sons, Inc., 1978), 520 pp.

Kendall, M. G. and Stuart, A.
  The Advanced Theory of Statistics
  (New York: Hafner Publishing Company, 1973).

Kohler, Heinz
  Essentials of Statistics
  (Glenview, IL: Scott, Foresman and Company, 1988).

Kohler, Heinz
  Statistics for Business and Economics, Second Edition
  (Glenview, IL: Scott, Foresman and Company, 1988).

Madsen, Richard W. and Moeschberger, Melvin L.
  Statistical Concepts With Applications to Business and Economics,
  Second Edition
  (Englewood Cliffs, NJ: Prentice-Hall, Inc.), 776 pp.

Marascuilo, L. A.
  Statistical Methods for Behavioral Science Research
  (New York: McGraw-Hill Book Company, 1971).

Mood, Alexander M., Graybill, Franklin A., and Boes, Duane C.
  Introduction to the Theory of Statistics, Third Edition
  (New York: McGraw-Hill Book Company, 1974).

Moskowitz, Herbert and Wright, Gordon P.
  Statistics for Management and Economics
  (Columbus, OH: Charles E. Merrill Publishing Company, 1985), 786 pp.

Neter, John and Wasserman, William
  Applied Statistics
  (Boston: Allyn and Bacon, 1978).

Patchett, Isabel S.
  Statistical Methods for Managers and Administrators
  (New York: Van Nostrand Reinhold Company, 1982), 365 pp.

Pollard, William E.
  Bayesian Statistics for Evaluation Research: An Introduction
  (Beverly Hills, CA: Sage Publications, 1986), 255 pp.

Rao, C. Radhakrishna
  Linear Statistical Inference and Its Applications, Second Edition
  (New York: John Wiley and Sons, Inc., 1973).

Roberts, Harry V. and Ling, Robert E.
  Conversational Statistics With IDA
  (New York: McGraw-Hill Book Company, 1982).

Rodger, L. W.
  Statistics for Marketing
  (McGraw-Hill, 1984), 280 pp.

Rohatgi, Vijay K.
  Statistical Inference
  (New York: John Wiley and Sons, Inc., 1984), 940 pp.

Rohatgi, Vijay K.
  An Introduction to Probability Theory and Mathematical Statistics
  (New York: John Wiley and Sons, Inc., 1976).

Roscoe, J. T.
  Fundamental Research Statistics for the Behavioral Sciences
  (New York: Holt, Rinehart, and Winston, 1975).

Spurr, William A. and Bonini, Charles P.
  Statistical Analysis for Business Decisions, Revised Edition
  (Homewood, IL: Richard D. Irwin, Inc., 1973).

Stockton, John R. and Clark, Charles T.
  Introduction to Business and Economic Statistics
  (Cincinnati: South-Western, 1971), 679 pp.

Stoodley, K. D. C., Lewis, T., and Stainton, C. L. S.
  Applied Statistical Techniques
  (Chichester, EN: Ellis Horwood Limited, 1980), 310 pp.

Wonnacott, Ronald J. and Wonnacott, Thomas H.
  Statistics: Discovering Its Power
  (New York: John Wiley and Sons, Inc., 1982), 378 pp.

131.04 ---------- Books and Articles Re: Qualitative Analysis

        See also (sub)heading(s) 46.01, 79.03.

Goodman, Leo A.
  "New Methods for Analysing the Intrinsic Character of Qualitative
  Variables Using Cross-Classified Data"
  American Journal of Sociology, Vol. 93 (November 1987), pp. 529-83.

Haberman, Shelby J.
  Analysis of Qualitative Data, Volume 1, Introductory Topics
  (New York: Academic Press, 1978).

Krippendorff, Klaus
  Information Theory: Structural Models for Qualitative Data
  (Beverly Hills, CA: Sage Publications, Inc.).

Miles, Matthew B. and Huberman, A. Michael
  Qualitative Data Analysis: A Sourcebook of New Methods
  (Beverly Hills, CA: Sage Publications, Inc.), 256 pp.

131.05 ---------- Small Area Statistics

Committee on National Statistics
  Panel on Small-Area Estimates of Population and Income: Estimating
  Population and Income of Small Areas
  (Washington, DC: National Academy Press, 1980).

Platek, R., Rao, J. N. K., Sarndal, C. E., and Singh, M. P.
  Small Area Statistics: An International Symposium
  (New York: John Wiley and Sons, Inc., 1987), 278 pp.

Steinberg, J. (editor)
  Synthetic Estimates for Small Areas: Statistical Workshop Papers and
  Discussion
  NIDA Research Monograph 24, National Institute on Drug Abuse
  (Washington, DC: U.S. Government Printing Office, 1979).

131.06 ---------- Other Analytical Methods Textbooks

Bartholomew, David J.
  Mathematical Methods in Social Science
  (New York: John Wiley and Sons, Inc., 1981), 153 pp.

Cox, D. R.
  The Analysis of Binary Data
  (London: Methuen and Co. Ltd., 1970).

Daniel, Cuthbert and Wood, Fred S.
  Fitting Equations to Data, Second Edition
  (New York: John Wiley and Sons, Inc., 1980), 447 pp.

Day, R. L. and Parsons, L. J. (editors)
  Marketing Models: Quantitative Applications
  (Scranton, PA: International Textbook Co., 1971), 693 pp.

Ehrenberg, A. S. C.
  A Primer in Data Reduction
  (London and New York: John Wiley and Sons, Inc., 1982).

Ehrenberg, A. S. C.
  Data Reduction: Analyzing and Interpreting Statistical Data
  (London: John Wiley and Sons, Ltd., 1975), 391 pp.

Ferber, Robert (editor)
  Readings in the Analysis of Survey Data
  (Chicago: American Marketing Association, 1980).

Fitzroy, Peter T.
  Analytical Methods for Marketing Management
  (Maidenhead, EN: McGraw-Hill, 1976), 337 pp.

Fleiss, J. L.
  Statistical Methods for Rates and Proportions, Second Edition
  (New York: Wiley, 1981).

Fox, John and Long, J. Scott (editors)
  Modern Methods of Data Analysis
  (Newbury Park, CA: Sage Publications, 1990), 416 pp.

Hudson, Herschel C. and Associates
  Classifying Social Data
  (San Francisco: Jossey-Bass, Inc., 1982), 270 pp.

Jaech, John L.
  Statistical Analysis of Measurement Errors
  (New York: John Wiley and Sons, Inc., 1985), 293 pp.

Leamer, Edward E.
  Specification Searches: Ad Hoc Inference With Nonexperimental Data
  (New York: John Wiley and Sons, Inc., 1978), 370 pp.

Lee, Eun Sul, Forthofer, Ronald N., and Lorimer, Ronald J.
  Analyzing Complex Survey Data
  (Newbury Park, CA: Sage Publications, 1989), 80 pp.

Liebetrau, Albert M.
  Measures of Association
  (Beverly Hills, CA: Sage Publications, Inc.).

Lilien, Gary L.
  Marketing Mix Analysis With Lotus 1-2-3
  (Palo Alto, CA: The Scientific Press, 1986), 206 pp.

Marriott, F. H. C.
  The Interpretation of Multiple Observations
  (New York: Academic Press, 1974).

McNeil, Donald R.
  Interactive Data Analysis: A Practical Primer
  (New York: John Wiley and Sons, Inc., 1977), 186 pp.

Milliken, George A. and Johnson, Dallas E.
  Analysis of Messy Data, Volume 1: Designed Experiments
  (Belmont, CA: Lifetime Learning Publications, 1984), 473 pp.

Mueller, John, Schuessler, Karl, and Costner, Herbert
  Statistical Reasoning in Sociology, Third Edition
  (Boston: Houghton Mifflin, 1977).

Norusis, Marija J.
  The SPSS Guide to Data Analysis
  (Chicago: SPSS, Inc., 1986).

O'Muircheartaigh, C. A. and Payne, C. (editors)
The Analysis of Survey Data: Exploring Data Structures
(New York: John Wiley and Sons, Inc., 1977), Volume 1, 273 pp.;
Volume 2, 255 pp.

Rothenberg, T. J.
Efficient Estimation With A Priori Information
(New Haven, CT: Yale University Press, 1973).

Schussler, Karl F. (editor)
Sociological Methodology
(San Francisco: American Sociological Association, 1978).

Sonquist, John and Dunkelberg, William
Survey and Opinion Research: Procedures for Processing and Analysis
(Englewood Cliffs, NJ: Prentice-Hall, Inc., 1977), 502 pp.

Wright, Sonia R.
Quantitative Methods and Statistics: A Guide to Social Research
(Beverly Hills, CA: Sage Publications, Inc., 1979), 170 pp.

Zeisel, Hans
Say It With Figures, Sixth Edition
(New York: Harper and Row, 1985), 262 pp.

131.07 ---------- Analysis Dictionaries and Encyclopedia

        See also (sub)heading(s) 11.02.

Kruskal, William H. and Tanur, J. M.
International Encyclopedia of Statistics
(New York: The Free Press, 1978).

O'Muircheartaigh, Colin A. and Francis, David Pitt
Statistics: A Dictionary of Terms and Ideas
(Arrow Books, 1981), 295 pp.

131.08 ---------- Overviews of Analytical Methods

Alwin, Duane F. and Campbell, Richard T.
"Continuity and Change in Methods of Survey Data Analysis"
Public Opinion Quarterly, Vol. 51 (Winter 1987), pp. S139-55.

Andrews, Frank M., Klem, Laura, Davidson, Terrence N., O'Malley,
Patrick M., and Rodgers, Willard L.
A Guide for Selecting Statistical Techniques for Analyzing Social
Science Data, Second Edition
(Ann Arbor, MI: Institute for Social Research, University of
Michigan, 1981), 70 pp.

Cattell, R. B.
"Multivariate Behavioral Research and the Integrative
Challenge--Editorial"
Multivariate Behavioral Research, Vol. 1 (January 1966), pp. 4-23.

Dash, J. F. and Berenson, C.
"Techniques in Marketing Research"
Harvard Business Review, Vol. 47 (September-October 1969), pp. 14-37.

Fennessey, J.
"The General Linear Model: A New Perspective on Some Familiar Topics"
American Journal of Sociology, Vol. 74 (July 1968), pp. 1-27.

Fornell, Claes
"A Second Generation of Multivariate Analysis: Classification of
Methods and Implications for Marketing Research"
in Houston, Michael J. (editor)
Review of Marketing 1987
(Chicago: American Marketing Association, 1987), pp. 407-50.

Gatty, Ronald
"Multivariate Analysis for Marketing Research: An Evaluation"
Applied Statistics (JRSS), Vol. XV, No. 3 (1966), pp. 157-72.

Green, Paul E.
"Measurement and Data Analysis"
Journal of Marketing, Vol. 34 (January 1970), pp. 15-7.

Horst, Paul
"An Overview of the Essentials of Multivariate Analysis Methods"
in Cattell, Raymond B. (editor)
Handbook of Multivariate Experimental Psychology
(Chicago, IL: Rand McNally, 1966), pp. 129-52.

Kinnear, Thomas C. and Taylor, James R.
"Multivariate Methods in Marketing Research: A Further Attempt at
Classification"
Journal of Marketing, Vol. 35 (October 1971), pp. 56-9.

Myers, James H. and Gutman, Jonathan
   "How to Analyze Consumer Surveys"
   Journal of Advertising Research, Vol. 15 (December 1975), pp. 19-24.

Sampson, Peter
   "The Selection of Cluster Defining Variables--Comment"
   Journal of the Market Research Society, Vol. 16 (October 1974), pp.
   303,4.

Sheth, Jagdish N.
   "How to Get the Most Out of Multivariate Methods"
   European Research, Vol. 4 (November 1976), pp. 229-36.

Sheth, Jagdish N.
   "The Multivariate Revolution in Marketing Research"
   Journal of Marketing, Vol. 35 (January 1971), pp. 13-9.

Sheth, Jagdish N.
   "Multivariate Analysis in Marketing"
   Journal of Advertising Research, Vol. 10 (February 1970), pp. 29-39.

Tatsuoka, M. M. and Tiedman, D. V.
   "Statistics as an Aspect of Scientific Method in Research on Teaching"
   in Gage, N. L. (editor)
   Handbook of Research on Teaching
   (Skokie, IL: Rand McNally and Company, 1963), pp. 42-70.

Vallette-Florence, Pierre
   "A Second Generation of Multivariate Analysis: Contribution and
   Applications for Marketing Research"
   ESOMAR Congress, Montreux (1987), pp. 225-53.

Willson, E. J.
   "Computational Segmentation in the Context of Multivariate Statistics
   and Survey Analysis"
   Journal of the Market Research Society, Vol. 16 (April 1974), pp.
   108-26.

131.09 ---------- Model Selection

Daniel, Cuthbert and Wood, F. S.
   Fitting Equations to Data, Second Edition
   (New York: John Wiley and Sons, Inc., 1980).

Linhart, H. and Succhini, W.
   Model Selection
   (New York: John Wiley and Sons, Inc., 1986).

131.10 ---------- Unclassified (Analytical Methods - General)

Anderson, Harry E.
   "Regression, Discriminant Analysis, and a Standard Notation for Basic
   Statistics"
   in Cattell, R. B. (editor)
   Handbook of Multivariate Experimental Psychology
   (Chicago: Rand McNally, 1966), pp. 153-73.

Atchley, William R. and Bryant, Edwin H.
   Multivariate Statistical Methods, Among-Groups Covariation
   (New York: Halsted Press, 1975).

Ball, Geoffrey H. and Hall, David J.
   "Data Analysis in the Social Sciences: What About the Details?"
   Proceedings, Fall Joint Computer Conference (1965), pp. 533-59.

Batsell, Richard R.
   "On the Use of Hidden Surface Routines in the Analysis of Marketing
   Data"
   Journal of Marketing, Vol. 44 (Summer 1980), pp. 102-6.

Cupens, Roger
   Decomposition of Multivariate Probabilities
   (New York: Academic Press, 1975).

Faulkenberry, G. David and Mason, Robert G.
   "Matched Samples Analysis for Item Responses"
   Public Opinion Quarterly, Vol. 40 (Summer 1976), pp. 256-60.

Ferber, Robert (editor)
   Readings in the Analysis of Survey Data
   (Chicago: American Marketing Association, 1980), 249 pp.

Holmes, Cliff
   "Multivariate Analysis of Market Research Data"
   in Worcester, Robert M. (editor)
   Consumer Market Research Handbook
   (London: McGraw-Hill, 1972), pp. 312-35.

Johnson, Norman and Kotz, Samuel
  Continuous Multivariate Distributions
  (New York: John Wiley and Sons, Inc., 1972).

Johnson, Richard M.
  Using Quantitative Analysis in Marketing Research
  (Chicago: Market Facts, Inc., 1974).

Lord, F. M. and Novick, M. R.
  Statistical Theories of Mental Test Scores
  (Reading, MA: Addison-Wesley Publishing Company, 1974).

Marc, Marcel
  "Some Practical Uses of 'The Factorial Analysis of Correspondence'"
  European Research, Vol. 1 (May 1973), pp. 99-106.

Maxwell, Albert E.
  "Contour Analysis"
  Educational and Psychological Measurement, Vol. 17 (Autumn 1957), pp.
  347-60.

Mosteller, F. and Tukey, J.
  "Data Analysis Including Statistics"
  in Lindzey, G. and Aronson, E. (editors)
  The Handbook of Social Psychology, Second Edition, Volume II
  (Reading, MA: Addison-Wesley Publishing Company, 1968).

Pruzek, Robert M.
  "Methods and Problems in the Analysis of Multivariate Data"
  Review of Educational Research, Vol. 41 (1971), pp. 163-90.

Rao, Poduri S. and Sechansk, Joseph (editors)
  W. G. Cochran's Impact on Statistics
  (New York: John Wiley and Sons, Inc., 1984), 431 pp.

Rao, Vithala R.
  "Books on Quantitative Methods for Consumer Research"
  Journal of Consumer Research, Vol. 7 (September 1980), pp. 198-210.

Spilerman, S.
  "Structural Analysis and the Generation of Sociograms"
  Behavioral Science, Vol. 11 (1966), pp. 312-8.

Tukey, John W.
  "The Future of Data Analysis"
  Annals of Mathematical Statistics, Vol. 33 (March 1962), pp. 1-67.

Tyler, Fred T.
  "Some Examples of Multivariate Analysis in Educational and
  Psychological Research"
  Psychometrika, Vol. 17 (September 1952), pp. 289-96.

132 -------------- DATA EDITING, TABULATION, AND CODING --------------
        See also (sub)heading(s) 117.05, 138.

132.01 ---------- Articles, etc. Re: Data Editing, Tabulation, Coding

Adams, E. W., Fargot, R. F., and Robinson, R. E.
    "A Theory of Appropriate Statistics"
    Psychometrika, Vol. 30 (June 1965), pp. 99-127.

Benson, P. H.
    "Eliminating Consumer Biases in Survey Data by Balanced Tabulation"
    Journal of Marketing Research, Vol. I (November 1964), pp. 66-71.

Freund, R. J. and Hartley, H. O.
    "A Procedure for Automatic Data Editing"
    Journal of the American Statistical Association, Vol. 62 (June 1967),
    pp. 341-52.

Grant, Rebecca A.
    "Tips and Techniques to Simplify Survey Design, Data Entry and
    Verification"
    Working Paper Series No. 88-12
    School of BusinessAdministration, University of Western Ontario
    (April 1988).

Kroeger, A.
    "A Device for Simplifying Tabulation"
    Journal of Marketing, Vol. 18 (January 1954), pp. 285-7.

Lester, A. M.
    "The Edge Marking of Statistical Cards"
    Journal of the American Statistical Association, Vol. 44 (June 1949),
    pp. 293,4.

Little, Roderick J. A. and Smith, Philip J.
    "Editing and Imputation for Quantitative Survey Data"
    Journal of the American Statistical Association, Vol. 82 (March
    1987), pp. 58-68.

Minton, G.
    "Inspection and Correction Error in Data Processing"
    Journal of the American Statistical Association, Vol. 64 (December
    1969), pp. 1256-75.

Mrazek, G. J.
    "An Improved Hand-Tabulation Method"
    Journal of Marketing, Vol. 25 (October 1961), pp. 68-70.

Nordbotten, S.
    "Measuring the Error of Editing the Questionnaires in a Census"
    Journal of the American Statistical Association, Vol. 50 (June 1955),
    pp. 364-9.

O'Reagan, R. T.
    "Relative Costs of Computerized Error Inspection Plans"
    Journal of the American Statistical Association, Vol. 64 (December
    1969), pp. 1245-55.

Payne, S. L. and Rugg, W. D.
    "A Sampling Plan for Verifying Punching Work"
    Public Opinion Quarterly, Vol. 12 (Summer 1948), pp. 328-30.

Sidel, P. S.
    "Coding"
    in Ferber, R. (editor)
    Handbook of Marketing Research
    (New York: McGraw-Hill, 1974).

Stuart, W. J.
    "Computer Editing of Survey Data--Five Years of Experience in BLS
    Manpower Surveys"
    Journal of the American Statistical Association, Vol. 61 (June 1966),
    pp. 375-83.

Ward, D. H.
    "The Use of Edge-Punched Cards in Statistical Computation"
    Applied Statistics, Vol. 8 (June 1959), pp. 104-13.

132.02 ---------- Coding Open-Ended Responses

        See also (sub)heading(s) 34.09, 46.01, 86.05, 103.

Coke, Chris
    "Data Mechanisation and Coding Now"
    Journal of the Market Research Society, Vol. 24 (January 1982), pp.
    75,6.

Coke, C. M.
"Data Flow Mechanisation"
Market Research Society Newsletter (December 1981), p. 189.

Collins, M.
"A Coding Experiment Attached to the Industrial Tribunal's Survey"
Methodological Working Paper No. 21
(London: Social and Community Planning Research, 1979).

Collins, Martin and Kalton, Graham
"Coding Verbatim Answers to Open Questions"
Journal of the Market Research Society, Vol. 22 (October 1980), pp.
239-47.

Collins, M. and O'Brien, J.
"How Reliable Is the Coding Process"
Market Research Society Conference (1981), p. 235.

Crittenden, K. S. and Hill, R. J.
"Coding Reliability and Validity of Interview Data"
American Sociological Review, Vol. 36 (December 1971), pp. 1073-80.

Durbin, J. and Stuart, A.
"An Experimental Comparison Between Coders"
Journal of Marketing, Vol. 19 (1954), pp. 54-6.

Funkhouser, G. R. and Parker, E. B.
"Analyzing Coding Reliability: The Random-Systematic-Error
Coefficient"
Public Opinion Quarterly, Vol. 32 (Spring 1968), pp. 122-8.

Greenberg, A.
"A Method of Coding Questionnaires in Marketing Surveys"
Journal of Marketing, Vol. 14 (October 1949), pp. 456-8.

Kalton, G. and Stowell, R.
"A Study of Coder Variability"
Applied Statistics, Vol. 28, No. 3 (1979).

Kammeyer, K. C. W. and Roth, K. A.
"Coding Responses to Open-End Questions"
in Costner, H. L. (editor)
Sociological Methodology 1971
(San Francisco: Jossey-Bass, 1971), Chapter 3.

Kaufman, Carol J.
"The Application of Logical Imputation to Household Measurement"
Journal of the Market Research Society, Vol. 30 (October 1988), pp.
453-66.

McDonald, C. D. P.
"Linguistic Coding--A New Solution to an Old Problem"
Journal of the Market Research Society, Vol. 15 (July 1973), pp.
163-81.

McDonald, C. D. P. and Blythe, W. A.
"How to Handle Soft Data--A Linguistic Approach"
Thompson Awards (1971).

Mitchell, Walter G.
"Systematic Synthesis of Advertising Research Verbatims"
Journal of Advertising Research, Vol. 7 (September 1967), pp. 37-40.

Woodward, J. L. and Delott, J.
"Field Coding Versus Office Coding"
Public Opinion Quarterly, Vol. 16 (Fall 1952), pp. 432-6.

Woodward, J. L. and Franzen, R.
"A Study of Coding Reliability"
Public Opinion Quarterly, Vol. 12 (Summer 1948), pp. 253-7.

132.03 ---------- Computerized Coding of Open-Ended Responses

Frisbie, B. and Sudman, Seymour
"The Use of Computers in Coding Free Responses"
Public Opinion Quarterly, Vol. 32 (Summer 1968), pp. 216-32.

Hodges, Bob S. and Cosse, Thomas J.
"Computer Code, Edit Open-Ended Questions to Improve Survey Accuracy
and Efficiency"
Marketing News (January 21, 1983), p. 10.

Johnson, Douglas J.
"Open Ended Warfare: Cybernetic Nirvana or Information Graveyard?"
Journal of the Market Research Society, Vol. 31 (July 1989), pp.
331-61.

McDonald, Colin D. P.
  "Coding Open-Ended Answers With the Help of a Computer"
  Journal of the Market Research Society, Vol. 24 (January 1982), pp.
  9-27.

132.04 ---------- Missing Data

      See also (sub)heading(s) 22, 62.08, 117, 117.03, 133.

Bronner, Alfred E.
  "A Way to Handle Non-Response: Simulation of Missing Values"
  European Research, Vol. 11 (July 1983), pp. 86-92.

Chiu, H. Y. and Sedransk, J.
  "A Bayesian Procedure for Imputing Missing Values in Sample Surveys"
  Journal of the American Statistical Association, Vol. 81 (September
  1986), pp. 667-76.

Dodge, Yadolah
  Analysis of Experiments With Missing Data
  (New York: John Wiley and Sons, Inc., 1985), 449 pp.

Fellegi, I. P. and Holt, D.
  "A Systematic Approach to Automatic Edit and Imputation"
  Journal of the American Statistical Association, Vol. 71, No. 353
  (1976), pp. 17-35.

Gleason, Terry C. and Staelin, Richard
  "A Proposal for Handling Missing Data"
  Psychometrika, Vol. 40 (June 1975), pp. 229-52.

Griliches, Zvi, Hall, Bronwyn H., and Hausman, Jerry A.
  "Missing Data and Self-Selection in Large Panels"
  Annales de l'insee, Vols. 30-31 (April-September 1978), pp. 137-76.

Hertel, Bradley R.
  "Minimizing Error Variance Introduced by Missing Data Routines in
  Survey Analysis"
  Sociological Methods and Research, Vol. 4 (May 1976), pp. 459-74.

Kim, Jae-On and Curry, James
  "The Treatment of Missing Data in Multivariate Analysis"
  Sociological Methods and Research, Vol. 6 (November 1977), pp. 215-40.

Lansing, John and Eapen, A. T.
  "Dealing With Missing Information in Surveys"
  Journal of Marketing, Vol. 24 (October 1959), pp. 21-7.

Marini, M. M., Olsen, A. R., and Rubin, D. B.
  "Maximum-Likelihood Estimation in Panel Studies With Missing Data"
  in Schuessler, K. F. (editor)
  Sociological Methodology
  (London: Jossey-Bass Ltd., 1980), pp. 314-57.

Meulman, Jacqueline
  Homogeneity Analysis of Incomplete Data
  (Leiden, The Netherlands: DSWO Press, 1982).

Seymour, R. B.
  "Missing Data in Non-Linear Trend Analysis of Repeated Measurements
  of the Same Individuals"
  Journal of Educational Research, Vol. 54 (December 1960), pp. 141-4.

Stewart, David W.
  "Filling the Gap: A Review of the Missing Data Problem"
  in Walker, Bruce J. et al. (editors)
  An Assessment of Marketing Thought and Practice
  (Chicago: American Marketing Association, 1982), pp. 395-9.

132.05 ---------- Unclassified (Data Editing, Tabulating, and Coding)

U.S. Bureau of the Census
  Coding Performance in the 1970 Census
  (Washington, DC: U.S. Government Printing Office, 1974).

U.S. Bureau of the Census
  Evaluation and Research Program of the U.S. Censuses of Population
  and Housing, 1960: Effects of Coders
  (Washington, DC: U.S. Government Printing Office, 1972).

133 ------------------ ANALYSIS OF INCOMPLETE DATA ------------------
See also (sub)heading(s) 22, 62.08, 117, 117.03, 132.04.

133.01 ---------- Books Re: Analysis of Incomplete Data

Dodge, Yadolah
Analysis of Experiments With Missing Data
(New York: John Wiley and Sons, Inc., 1985), 449 pp.

Little, Roderick J. A. and Rubin, Donald B.
Statistical Analysis With Missing Data
(New York: John Wiley and Sons, Inc., 1987), 265 pp.

Madow, William G., Nisselson, Harold, and Olkin, Ingram
Incomplete Data in Sample Surveys, Volume 1
(New York: Academic Press, Inc., 1983).

Madow, William G., Olkin, Ingram, and Rubin, Donald B.
Incomplete Data in Sample Surveys, Volume 2
(New York: Academic Press, Inc., 1983).

133.02 ---------- General Discussions Re: Analysis of Incomplete Data

Anderson, Andy B., Basilevsky, Alexander, and Hum, Derek P. J.
"Missing Data"
in Rossi, Peter H., Wright, James D., and Anderson, Andy B. (editors)
Handbook of Survey Research
(Orlando, FL: Academic Press, Inc., 1983), pp. 415-94.

Frane, James W.
"Some Simple Procedures for Handling Missing Data in Multivariate
Analysis"
Psychometrika, Vol. 41 (September 1976), pp. 409-15.

Gleason, Terry C. and Staelin, Richard
"A Proposal for Handling Missing Data"
Psychometrika, Vol. 40 (June 1975), pp. 229-52.

Kim, Jae-On and Curry, James
"The Treatment of Missing Data in Multivariate Analysis"
Sociological Methods and Research, Vol. 6 (1977), pp. 215-60.

Timm, N. H.
"The Estimation of Variance-Covariance and Correlation Matrices From
Incomplete Data"
Psychometrika, Vol. 35, No. 4 (December 1970), pp. 417-37.

133.03 ---------- Theory Re: Expectation-Maximization (EM) Algorithm

Amemiya, Takeshi
"Regression Analysis When the Dependent Variable is Truncated"
Econometrica, Vol. 41 (November 1973), pp. 997-1016.

Boyles, Russell A.
"On the Convergence of the EM Algorithm"
Journal of the Royal Statistical Society, Vol. 45B (1983), pp. 47-50.

Carter, W. M. and Myers, R. H.
"Maximum Likelihood Estimation From Linear Combinations of Discrete
Probability Functions"
Journal of the American Statistical Association, Vol. 68 (March
1973), pp. 203-6.

Dempster, A. P., Laird, Nan M., and Rubin, Donald B.
"Maximum Likelihood From Incomplete Data via the EM Algorithm"
Journal of the Royal Statistical Society, Vol. 39B (1977), pp. 1-22.

Haberman, S. J.
"Discussion on the Paper by Professor Dempster, Professor Laird and
Dr. Rubin"
Journal of the Royal Statistical Society, Vol. 39B (1977), pp. 31,2.

Hartley, H. O.
"Maximum Likelihood Estimation From Incomplete Data"
Biometrics, Vol. 14 (June 1958), pp. 174-94.

Hartley, H. O. and Hocking, R. R.
"The Analysis of Incomplete Data"
Biometrics, Vol. 27 (December 1971), pp. 783-808.

Little, R. J. A.
"Discussion on the Paper by Professor Dempster, Professor Laird and
Dr. Rubin"
Journal of the Royal Statistical Society, Vol. 39B (1977), p. 25.

Malhotra, Naresh K.
    "Analyzing Marketing Research Data With Incomplete Information on the
    Dependent Variable"
    Journal of Marketing Research, Vol. XXIV (February 1987), pp. 74-84.

Sundberg, R.
    "An Iterative Method for Solution of the Likelihood Equations for
    Incomplete Data From Exponential Families"
    Communications in Statistics: Simulation and Computations, Vol. 5
    (1976), pp. 55-64.

Sundberg, R.
    "Maximum Likelihood Theory for Incomplete Data From an Exponential
    Family"
    Scandinavian Journal of Statistics, Vol. 1 (1974), pp. 49-58.

133.04 ---------- Bivariate and Multivariate Normal Distributions

Dahiya, R. C. and Korwar, R. M.
    "Maximum Likelihood Estimates for Bivariate Normal Distribution With
    Missing Data"
    Annals of Statistics, Vol. 8 (May 1980), pp. 687-92.

Hocking, R. R. and Marx, D. L.
    "Estimation With Incomplete Data: An Improved Computational Method
    and the Analysis of Nested Data"
    Communications in Statistics: Theory and Methods, Vol. 8A (1979), pp.
    1155-82.

133.05 ---------- Mixing Distribution

Laird, Nan
    "Nonparametric Maximum Likelihood Estimation of a Mixing Distribution"
    Journal of the American Statistical Association, Vol. 73 (December
    1978), pp. 805-11.

133.06 ---------- Regression Analysis

    See also (sub)heading(s) 159.

Little, R. J. A.
    "Maximum Likelihood Influence for Multiple Regression With Missing
    Values: A Simulation Study"
    Journal of the Royal Statistical Society, Vol. 41B (1979), pp. 76-87.

133.07 ---------- Discriminant Analysis

    See also (sub)heading(s) 177.

Little, R. J. A.
    "Consistent Regression Methods for Discriminant Analysis With
    Incomplete Data"
    Journal of the American Statistical Association, Vol. 73 (June 1978),
    pp. 319-22.

133.08 ---------- Analysis of Variance and Covariance

    See also (sub)heading(s) 179, 182.

Rubin, Donald B.
    "A Non-Iterative Algorithm for Least Squares Estimation of Missing
    Values in Any Analysis of Variance Design"
    Applied Statistics, Vol. 21 (1972), pp. 136-41.

Smith, Patricia C.
    "The Use of Analysis of Covariance to Analyze Data From Designed
    Experiments With Missing or Mixed-Up Values"
    Applied Statistics, Vol. 30 (1981), pp. 1-8.

Williams, E. R., Ratcliff, D., and Speed, T. P.
    "Estimating Missing Values in Multi-Stratum Experiments"
    Applied Statistics, Vol. 30 (1981), pp. 71,2.

133.09 ---------- Factor and Principal Components Analysis

    See also (sub)heading(s) 197.

De Ligny, C. L., Nieuwdorp, G. H. E., Brederode, W. K., Hammers, W. E.,
    and Van Houwelignen, J. C.
    "An Application of Factor Analysis With Missing Data"
    Technometrics, Vol. 23 (February 1981), pp. 91-5.

Finkbeiner, Carl
"Estimation for the Multiple Factor Model When Data are Missing"
Psychometrika, Vol. 44 (December 1979), pp. 409-20.

133.10 ---------- Binary and Multinomial Response

Chow, Winston K.
"A Look at Various Estimators in Logistic Models in the Presence of
Missing Values"
Proceedings, American Statistical Association, Business Economics
Section (1979), pp. 417-20.

Hocking, R. R. and Oxspring, H. H.
"Maximum Likelihood Estimation With Incomplete Multinomial Data"
Journal of the Royal Statistical Society, Vol. 66B (1971), pp. 65-70.

133.11 ---------- Time Series

See also (sub)heading(s) 161.

Dunsmuir, W. and Robinson, P. M.
"Parametric Estimators for Stationary Time Series With Missing
Observations"
Advanced Applied Problems, Vol. 13 (1981), pp. 129-46.

133.12 ---------- Growth Curves

Schwertman, N. C., Fridshal, D., and Magrey, J. M.
"On the Analysis of Incomplete Growth Curve Data: A Monte Carlo Study
of Two Nonparametric Procedures"
Communications in Statistics: Simulation and Computation, Vol. 10B,
Number 1 (1981), pp. 51-66.

133.13 ---------- Simultaneous Equations

Dagenais, M. G.
"Incomplete Observations and Simultaneous Equations Models"
Journal of Econometrics, Vol. 4 (August 1976), pp. 231-42.

133.14 ---------- Stochastic Models

Patel, H. I. and Khatri, C. G.
"Analysis of Incomplete Data in Experiments With Repeated
Measurements in Clinical Trials Using a Stochastic Model"
Communcations in Statistics: Theory and Methods, Vol. 10 (1981), pp.
2259-78.

133.15 ---------- Multidimensional Scaling

See also (sub)heading(s) 62.

Graef, Jed and Spence, Ian
"Using Distance Information in the Design of Large Multidimensional
Scaling Experiments"
Psychological Bulletin, Vol. 86 (January 1979), pp. 60-6.

Issac, Paul D.
"Considerations in the Selection of Stimulus Pairs for Data
Collection in Multidimension Scaling"
in Golledge, R. G. and Raynor, J. N. (editors)
Proximity and Preference: Problems in the Multidimensional Analysis
of Large Data Sets
(Minneapolis: University of Minnesota Press, 1982), pp. 80-9.

MacCallum, Robert C.
"Recovery of Structure in Incomplete Data by ALSCAL"
Psychometrika, Vol. 44 (March 1978), pp. 69-74.

Malhotra, Naresh K., Jain, Arun K., and Pinson, Christian
"The Robustness of MDS Configurations in the Case of Incomplete Data"
Journal of Marketing Research, Vol. XXV (February 1988), pp. 95-102.

Spector, Aron N. and Rivizzigno, Victoria L.
"Sampling Designs and Recovering Cognitive Representations of an
Urban Area"
in Golledge, R. G. and Raynor, J. N. (editors)
Proximity and Preference: Problems in the Multidimensional Analysis
of Large Data Sets
(Minneapolis: University of Minnesota Press, 1982), pp. 47-79.

Spence, Ian
"Monte Carlo Simulation Studies"
Applied Psychological Measurement, Vol. 7 (Fall 1983), pp. 405-26.

Spence, Ian
    "Incomplete Experimental Designs for Multidimensional Scaling"
    in Golledge, R. G. and Rayner, J. N. (editors)
    Proximity and Preference: Problems in the Multidimensional Analysis
    of Large Data Sets
    (Minneapolis: University of Minnesota Press, 1982), pp. 29-46.

Spence, Ian and Domoney, Dennis W.
    "Single Subject Incomplete Designs for Nonmetric Multidimensional
    Scaling"
    Psychometrika, Vol. 39 (December 1974), pp. 469-90.

133.16 ---------- Applications of Analysis of Incomplete Data

Malhotra, Naresh K.
    "Modeling Store Choice Based on Censored Preference Data"
    Journal of Retailing, Vol. 62 (Summer 1986), pp. 128-44.

Malhotra, Naresh K.
    "An Approach to the Measurement of Consumer Preferences Using Limited
    Information"
    Journal of Marketing Research, Vol. XXIII (February 1986), pp. 33-40.

133.17 ---------- Unclassified (Analysis of Incomplete Data)

DeSarbo, Wayne S.
    "MEMD: An APL Program for the Multivariate Estimation of Missing Data"
    Journal of Marketing Research, Vol. XV (February 1978), pp. 117,8.

DeSarbo, Wayne S., Green, Paul E., and Carroll, J. Douglas
    "An Alternating Least-Squares Procedure for Estimating Missing
    Preference Data in Product Concept Testing"
    Decision Sciences, Vol. 17 (Spring 1986), pp. 163-85.

Golany, B., Kress, M., and Phillips, F. Y.
    "Estimating Purchase Frequency Distributions With Incomplete Data"
    International Journal of Research in Marketing, Vol. 3, No. 3 (1986),
    pp. 169-79.

Winer, Russell S.
    "Attrition Bias in Econometric Models Estimated With Panel Data"
    Journal of Marketing Research, Vol. XX (May 1983), pp. 177-86.

134 --------------- OUTLIERS OR EXTREME OBSERVATIONS ----------------
    See also (sub)heading(s) 168, 179.04.

134.01 ---------- Books Re: Outliers

Barnett, Vic and Lewis, Toby
  Outliers in Statistical Data, Second Edition
  (New York: John Wiley and Sons, Inc., 1984).

Hawkins, Douglas M.
  Identification of Outliers
  (London: Chapman and Hall, 1980).

Rousseeuw, Peter J. and Leroy, Annick M.
  Robust Regression and Outlier Detection
  (New York: John Wiley and Sons, Inc., 1987).

134.02 ---------- General Discussions of Outliers

Anscombe, F. J. and Barron, Bruce A.
  "Treatment of Outliers in Samples of Size Three"
  Journal of Research of the National Bureau of Standards, B, Vol. 70,
  No. 2 (1966), pp. 141-70.

Barnett, Vic
  "The Study of Outliers: Purpose and Model"
  Applied Statistics, Vol. 27, No. 3 (1978), pp. 242-50.

Beckman, R. J. and Cook, R. Dennis
  "Outlier...s"
  Technometrics, Vol. 25 (May 1983), pp. 119-49.

Clark, Terry
  "Managing Outliers: Qualitative Issues in the Handling of Extreme
  Observations in Marketing Research"
  Marketing Research, Vol. 1 (June 1989), pp. 31-48.

Green, R. T.
  "Outlier-Prone and Outlier-Resistant Distributions"
  Journal of the American Statistical Association, Vol. 71 (1976), pp.
  502-5.

134.03 ---------- Theory Re: Identification of or Tests for Outliers

Andrews, David F. and Pregibon, Daryl
  "Finding the Outliers That Matter"
  Journal of the Royal Statistical Society, Series B, Vol. 40, No. 1
  (1978), pp. 85-93.

Bacon-Shone, J. and Fung, W. K.
  "A New Graphical Method for Detecting Single and Multiple Outliers:
  Purpose and Model"
  Applied Statistics, Vol. 36, No. 2 (1987), pp. 242-50.

Barnett, Vic
  "Principles and Methods for Handing Outliers in Data Sets"
  in Wright, Tommy (editor)
  Statistical Methods and the Improvement of Data Quality
  (Orlando, FL: Academic Press, Inc., 1983).

Barnett, Vic
  "Reduced Distance Measures and Transformations in Processing
  Multivariate Outliers"
  Australian Journal of Statistics, Vol. 25, No. 1 (1983), pp. 64-75.

Barnett, Vic
  "Some Outlier Tests for Multivariate Samples"
  South African Statistical Journal, Vol. 13 (1979), pp. 29-52.

Bendre, S. M. and Kale, B. K.
  "Masking Effect on Tests for Outliers in Normal Samples"
  Biometrika, Vol. 74 (1987), pp. 891-6.

Bendre, S. M. and Kale, B. K.
  "Masking Effect on Tests for Outliers in Exponential Samples"
  Journal of the American Statistical Association, Vol. 80 (1985), pp.
  1020-5.

Bradu, D. and Hawkins, Douglas M.
  "Location of Multiple Outliers in Two-Way Tables, Using Tetrads"
  Technometrics, Vol. 24 (1982), pp. 103-8.

Brown, B. M.
  "A Short-Cut Test for Outliers Using Residuals"
  Biometrika, Vol. 62, No. 3 (1975), pp. 623-9.

Brown, B. M.
  "Identification of the Sources of Significance in Two-Way Contingency
  Tables"
  Applied Statistics, Vol. 23 (1974), pp. 405-13.

Butler, R.
  "Outlier Discordancy Tests in the Normal Linear Model"
  Journal of the Royal Statistical Society, Series B, Vol. 45, No. 1
  (1983), pp. 120-32.

Carroll, Raymond J.
  "Robust Methods for Factorial Experiments With Outliers"
  Applied Statistics, Vol. 29, No. 3 (1980), pp. 246-51.

Chambers, R. L. and Heathcote, C. R.
  "On the Estimation of Slope and the Identification of Outliers in
  Linear Regression"
  Biometrika, Vol. 68 (1981), pp. 21-33.

Chernick, M. R., Downing, D. J., and Pike, D. H.
  "Detecting Outliers in Time Series Data"
  Journal of the American Statistical Society, Vol. 77 (1982), pp.
  743-7.

Fox, A. J.
  "Outliers in Time Series"
  Journal of the Royal Statistical Society, Series B, Vol. 43 (1972),
  pp. 350-63.

Fuchs, C. and Kenett, R.
  "A Test for Outlying Cells in the Multinomial Distribution and
  Two-Way Contingency Tables"
  Journal of the American Statistical Association, Vol. 75 (1980), pp.
  395-8.

Haberman, S. J.
  "The Analysis of Residuals in Cross-Classified Tables"
  Biometrics, Vol. 29 (1973), pp. 205-20.

Hoaglin, David C., Iglewicz, Brois, and Tukey, John W.
  "Performance of Some Resistant Rules for Outlier Labeling"
  Journal of the American Statistical Association, Vol. 81 (1986), pp.
  991-9.

Jennings, Dennis E.
  "Outliers and Residual Distributions in Logistic Regression"
  Journal of the American Statistical Association, Vol. 81 (1986), pp.
  987-90.

Kabe, D. G.
  "Testing Outliers From an Exponential Population"
  Metrika, Vol. 15 (1970), pp. 15-8.

Kotze, T. J. and Hawkins, Douglas M.
  "The Identification of Outliers in Two-Way Contingency Tables Using 2
  x 2 Subtables"
  Applied Statistics, Vol. 33, No. 2 (1984), pp. 215-23.

Marasinghe, Mervyn G.
  "A Multistage Procedure for Detecting Several Outliers in Linear
  Regression"
  Technometrics, Vol. 27, No. 4 (1985), pp. 395-9.

McMillan, R. G. and David, H. A.
  "Tests for One or Two Outliers in Normal Samples With Known Variance"
  Technometrics, Vol. 13 (1971), pp. 598-602.

Moran, M. A. and McMillan, R. G.
  "Tests for One or Two Outliers in Normal Samples With Unknown
  Variance: A Correlation"
  Technometrics, Vol. 15 (1973), pp. 637-40.

Mosteller, Frederick and Parunak, Anita
  "Identifying Extreme Cells in a Sizable Contingency Table:
  Probabilistic and Exploratory Approaches"
  in Hoaglin, David C., Mosteller, Frederick, and Tukey, John W.
  (editors)
  Exploring Data Tables, Trends, and Shapes
  (New York: John Wiley and Sons, Inc., 1985).

Muirhead, C. R.
  "Distinguishing Outlier Types in Time Series"
  Journal of the Royal Statistical Society, Series B, Vol. 48, No. 1
  (1986), pp. 39-47.

Rosner, B.
  "Percentage Points for a Generalized ESD Many-Outlier Procedure"
  Technometrics, Vol. 25 (1983), pp. 165-72.

Rosner, B.
   "On the Detection of Many Outliers"
   Technometrics, Vol. 17 (1975), pp. 221-7.

Rousseeuw, Peter J. and Van Zomeren, B. C.
   "Identification of Multivariate Outliers and Leverage Points by Means
   of Robust Covariance Matrices"
   Faculty of Mathematics and Informatics, Delft University of
   Technology, The Netherlands (1987), technical report.

Schwager, S. J. and Margolin, B.
   "Detection of Multivariate Normal Outliers"
   Annals of Statistics, Vol. 10 (1982), pp. 943-54.

Schweder, T.
   "Some 'Optimal' Methods to Detect Structural Shift or Outliers in
   Regression"
   Journal of the American Statistical Association, Vol. 71 (1976), pp.
   491-501.

Simonoff, Jeffrey S.
   "Detecting Outlying Cells in Two-Way Contingency Tables via
   Backwards-Stepping"
   Technometrics, Vol. 30, No. 3 (1988), pp. 339-45.

Sinha, Bimal Kuman
   "Detection of Multivariate Outliers in Elliptically Symmetric
   Distributions"
   Annals of Statistics, Vol. 12, No. 4 (1984), pp. 1558-65.

Tietjen, G. L. and Moore, R. H.
   "Some Grubbs-Type Statistics for the Detection of Several Outliers"
   Technometrics, Vol. 14 (1972), pp. 583-97.

134.04 ---------- Theory Re: Accommodation Techniques

Basawa, I. V., Huggins, R. M., and Staudte, R. G.
   "Robust Tests for Time Series With an Application to First-Order
   Autoregressive Processes"
   Biometrika, Vol. 72, No. 3 (1985), pp. 559-71.

Chang, Ih, Tiao, George C., and Chen, Chung
   "Estimation of Time-Series Parameters in the Presence of Outliers"
   Technometrics, Vol. 30, No. 2 (1988), pp. 193-204.

Cleveland, W. S.
   "Robust Locally Weighted Regression and Smoothing Scatter Plots"
   Journal of the American Statistical Association, Vol. 74 (1979), pp.
   829-36.

Denby, L. and Martin, R. D.
   "Robust Estimation of the First-Order Autoregressive
   Parameter"Journal of the American Statistical Association, Vol. 74
   (1979), pp. 140-6.

Emerson, John D. and Hoaglin, David C.
   "Analysis of Two-Way Tables by Medians"
   in Hoaglin, David C., Mosteller, Frederick, and Tukey, John W.
   (editors)
   Understanding Robust and Exploratory Data Analysis
   (New York: John Wiley and Sons, Inc., 1983).

Giltnan, David M., Carroll, Raymond J., and Ruppert, David
   "Some New Estimation Methods for Weighted Regression When There are
   Possible Outliers"
   Technometrics, Vol. 28, No. 3 (1986), pp. 219-30.

Gnanadesikan, R. and Kettenring, J. R.
   "Robust Estimates, Residuals and Outlier Detection With Multiresponse
   Data"
   Biometrics, Vol. 28 (1972), pp. 81-124.

Guttman, I.
   "Care and Handling of Univariate or Multivariate Outliers in
   Detecting Spuriosity--A Bayesian Approach"
   Technometrics, Vol. 15 (1973), pp. 723-38.

John, J. A.
   "Outliers in Factorial Experiments"
   Applied Statistics, Vol. 27 (1978), pp. 111-9.

Joshi, P. C.
   "Efficient Estimation of a Mean of an Exponential Distribution When
   an Outlier is Present"
   Technometrics, Vol. 14 (1972), pp. 137-44.

Kimber, A. C.
   "Trimming in Gamma Samples"
   Applied Statistics, Vol. 32 (1983), pp. 7-14.

Mahajan, Vijay, Sharma, Subhash, and Wind, Yoram
    "Parameter Estimation in Marketing Models in the Presence of
    Influential Response Data: Robust Regression and Applications"
    Journal of Marketing Research, Vol. XXI (August 1984), pp. 268-77.

Schmid, Wolfgang
    "The Multiple Outlier Problem in Time Series Analysis"
    Australian Journal of Statistics, Vol. 28, No. 3 (1986), pp. 400-13.

Tsay, Rvey S.
    "Time Series Model Specification in the Presence of Outliers"
    Journal of the American Statistical Association, Vol. 81 (1986), pp.
    583-97.

West, Mike
    "Outlier Models and Prior Distributions in Bayesian Linear Regression"
    Journal of the Royal Statistical Society, Series B, Vol. 46, No. 3
    (1984), pp. 431-9.

134.05 ---------- Theory Re: Rejection of Outliers

Anscombe, F. J.
    "Rejection of Outliers"
    Technometrics, Vol. 21 (1960), pp. 123-47.

Collett, D. and Lewis, T.
    "The Subjective Nature of Outlier Rejection Procedures"
    Applied Statistics, Vol. 25 (1976), pp. 228-36.

Dixon, W. J.
    "Rejection of Observations"
    in Sahron, A. E. and Greenberg, B. G. (editors)
    Contributions in Order Statistics
    (New York: John Wiley and Sons, Inc., 1962).

Ferguson, T. S.
    "Rules for Rejection of Outliers"
    Review de l'Institut International de Statistique, Vol. 29 (1961),
    pp. 29-43.

Ferguson, T. S.
    "On the Rejection of Outliers"
    Proceedings of the Fourth Berkeley Symposium on Mathematical
    Statistics and Probability, Volume 1 (1961), pp. 253-87.

Fieller, N. R. J.
    Some Problems Related to the Rejection of Outlying Observations
    University of Sheffield (1976), unpublished Ph.D. thesis.

Galpin, J. S. and Hawkins, Douglas M.
    "Rejection of a Single Outlier in Two- or Three-Way Layouts"
    Technometrics, Vol. 23 (1981), pp. 65-70.

King, E. P.
    "On Some Procedures for the Rejection of Suspected Data"
    Journal of the American Statistical Association, Vol. 48 (1953), pp.
    531-3.

Mirvalieu, M.
    "The Rejection of Outlying Observations in Regression Analysis"
    Theoretical Probability Ap., Vol. 23 (1978), pp. 598-602.

Pearson, E. S. and Sekar, C. Chandra
    "The Efficiency of Statistical Tools and a Criterion for the
    Rejection of Outlying Observations"
    Biometrika, Vol. 28 (1936), pp. 308-20.

Proschan, F.
    "Rejection of Outlying Observations"
    American Journal of Physics, Vol. 21 (1953), pp. 520-5.

Stefansky, W.
    "Rejecting Outliers in Factorial Designs"
    Technometrics, Vol. 14 (1972), pp. 469-79.

134.06 ---------- Masking and Swamping Effects

Atkinson, A. C.
    "Masking Unmasked"
    Biometrika, Vol. 73, No. 3 (1986), pp. 533-41.

Bendre, S. M. and Kale, B. K.
    "Masking Effect on Tests for Outliers in Normal Samples"
    Biometrika, Vol. 74 (1987), pp. 891-6.

Bendre, S. M. and Kale, B. K.
  "Masking Effect on Tests for Outliers in Exponential Samples"
  Journal of the American Statistical Association, Vol. 80 (1985), pp.
  1020-5.

134.07 ---------- Applications of Outlier Analysis

Bidwell, Clinton M., III
  "A Test of Market Efficiency: SUE/PE"
  Journal of Portfolio Management (Summer 1979), pp. 53-8.

Latane, Henry A. and Jones, Charles P.
  "Standardized Expected Earnings--1971-77"
  Journal of Finance, Vol. 34, No. 3 (1979), pp. 717-24.

Latane, Henry A. and Jones, Charles P.
  "Standardized Unexpected Earnings--A Progress Report"
  Journal of Finance, Vol. 22, No. 5 (1977), pp. 1457-65.

Sharma, Subhash and Mahajan, Vijay
  "Early Warning Indicators of Business Failure"
  Journal of Marketing, Vol. 44 (Fall 1980), pp. 80-9.

135 ---------- GRAPHICAL REPRESENTATION OF MULTIVARIATE DATA   ---------
        See also (sub)heading(s) 136, 212.

135.01 ---------- Books Re: Graphical Representation of Multi'ate Data

Cleveland, William S.
    The Elements of Graphing Data
    (Monterey, CA: Wadsworth Advanced Books and Software, 1985), 323 pp.

Tufte, Edward R.
    The Visual Display of Quantitative Information
    (Cheshire, CT: Graphics Press, 1983), 191 pp.

Wang, Peter C. C. (editor)
    Graphical Representation of Multivariate Data
    (New York: Academic Press, 1978).

Zelazny, Gene
    Say It With Charts: The Executive's Guide to Successful Presentations
    (Homewood, IL: Dow Jones-Irwin), 150 pp.

135.02 ---------- Articles etc. Re: Graphical Representation of Data

Andrews, D. F.
    "Plots of High-Dimensional Data"
    Biometrics, Vol. 28 (March 1972), pp. 125-36.

Anscombe, F. J.
    "Graphs in Statistical Analysis"
    American Statistician, Vol. 27 (February 1973), pp. 17-21.

Batsell, Richard R.
    "On the Use of Hidden Surface Routines in the Analysis of Marketing
    Data"
    Journal of Marketing, Vol. 44 (Summer 1980), pp. 102-6.

Beniger, James R. and Robyn, Dorothy L.
    "Quantitative Graphics in Statistics: A Brief History"
    American Statistician, Vol. 32 (February 1978), pp. 1-10.

Darden, William R. and Dorsch, Michael J.
    "Useful Component Analysis: Graphical Views of Marketing Data"
    Journal of the Academy of Marketing Science, Vol. 16 (Spring 1988),
    pp. 60-73.

Fienberg, Stephen E.
    "Graphical Methods in Statistics--Letter to the Editor"
    American Statistician, Vol. 34 (November 1980), p. 253.

Fienberg, Stephen E.
    "Graphical Methods in Statistics"
    American Statistician, Vol. 33 (November 1979), pp. 165-78.

Gabriel, K. R.
    "Biplot Display of Multivariate Matrices for Inspection of Data and
    Diagnosis"
    in Barnett, V. (editor)
    Interpreting Multivariate Data
    (New York: John Wiley and Sons, 1981).

Gabriel, K. R.
    "The Biplot Graphic Display of Matrices With Applications to
    Principal Components Analysis"
    Biometrika, Vol. 58, No. 3 (1971), pp. 453-67.

Kumar, V. and Rust, Roland T.
    "Market Segmentation by Inspection"
    Journal of Advertising Research, Vol. 29 (August/September 1989), pp.
    23-9.

Mahon, B. H.
    "Statistics and Decisions: The Importance of Communication and the
    Power of Graphical Presentation"
    Journal of the Royal Statistical Society, Series A, Vol. 140 (1977),
    pp. 298-310.

135.03 ---------- Theory Re: Facial Representation of Multivariate Data

Bruckner, Lawrence A.
    "On Chernoff Faces"
    in Wang, Peter C. C. (editor)
    Graphical Representation of Multivariate Data
    (New York: Academic Press, 1978), pp. 93-121.

Chernoff, Herman
"Graphical Representation as a Discipline"
in Wang, Peter C. C. (editor)
Graphical Representation of Multivariate Data
(New York: Academic Press, 1978), pp. 1-11.

Chernoff, Herman
"Using Faces to Represent Points in K-Dimensional Space Graphically"
Journal of the American Statistical Association, Vol. 68 (June 1973),
pp. 361-8.

Chernoff, Herman and Rizvi, Haseeb
"Effect on Classification of Random Permutations of Features in
Representing Multivariate Data by Faces"
Journal of the American Statistical Association, Vol. 70 (September
1975), pp. 548-54.

Huff, David L. and Black, William
"Program Faces: A Multivariate Graphical Display"
Working Paper 80-14
University of Texas, Austin (1980).

Huff, David L. and Black, William
"A Multivariate Graphical Display for Regional Analysis"
in Wang, Peter C. C. (editor)
Graphical Representation of Multivariate Data
(New York: Academic Press, 1978), pp. 199-218.

Huff, David L., Mahajan, Vijay, and Black, William C.
"Faces: A Method of Portraying Multivariate Data Graphically"
in Darden, William R. and Lusch, Robert F. (editors)
Patronage Behavior and Retail Management
(New York: North-Holland, 1983).

Huff, David L., Mahajan, Vijay, and Black, William C.
"Facial Representation of Multivariate Data"
Journal of Marketing, Vol. 45 (Fall 1981), pp. 53-9.

Jacob, Robert J. K.
"Graphical Methods in Statistics--Letter to the Editor"
American Statistician, Vol. 34 (November 1980), pp. 252,3.

135.04 ---------- Theory Re: Fourier Series

Andrews, D. F.
"Plots of Higher-Dimensional Data"
Biometrics, Vol. 28 (March 1972), pp. 125-36.

135.05 ---------- Applications of Fourier Series

Darden, William R. and Flaschner, Alan B.
"Visual Presentation of Marketing Stimuli in Hyperspace"
Journal of Marketing Research, Vol. XI (November 1974), pp. 456-61.

135.06 ---------- Theory Re: Glyphs and Metroglyphs

Anderson, Edgar
"A Semigraphical Method for the Analysis of Complex Problems"
Technometrics, Vol. 2 (August 1969), pp. 387-91.

135.07 ---------- Applications of Glyphs and Metroglyphs

Siegel, J. H., Goldwyn, R. M., and Friedman, H. P.
"Pattern and Process of the Evolution of Human Septic Shock"
Surgery, Vol. 70 (August 1971), pp. 232-45.

135.08 ---------- Evaluations, Comparisions of Graph Representations

Mezzich, Juan E. and Worthington, David R. L.
"A Comparison of Graphical Representations of Multidimensional
Psychiatric Diagnostic Data"
in Wang, Peter C. C. (editor)
Graphical Representation of Multivariate Data
(New York: Academic Press, 1978).

135.09 ---------- Other Applications of Graphical Representation

Black, William C.
"Choice-Set Definition in Patronage Modeling"
Journal of Retailing, Vol. 60 (Summer 1984), pp. 63-85.

Rust, Roland T. and Brown, Julia A. N.
"Estimation and Comparison of Market Area Densities"
Journal of Retailing, Vol. 62 (Winter 1986), pp. 410-30.

135.10 ---------- Unclassified (Graphical Representation of Mult Data)

Batsell, Richard R. and Lodish, Leonard M.
"A Model and Measurement Methodology for Predicting Individual
Consumer Choice"
The Wharton School, University of Pennsylvania (1979), working paper.

Boardman, Thomas J.
"Graphical Contributions to the Chi-Square Statistic for Two-Way
Contingency Tables"
Communications in Statistics, Vol. A6(15) (1977), pp. 1437-51.

Ehrenberg, A. S. C.
"Rudiments of Numeracy"
Journal of the Royal Statistical Society, Series A, Vol. 140 (1977),
pp. 277-97.

136 -------------------- EXPLORATORY DATA ANALYSIS -------------------
        See also (sub)heading(s) 135, 158.

136.01 ---------- Books Re: Exploratory Data Analysis

Hartwig, Frederick and Dearing, Brian E.
  Exploratory Data Analysis
  (Beverly Hills, CA: Sage Publications, Inc.).

Hoaglin, D. C., Mosteller, Frederick, and Tukey, John W.
  Understanding Robust and Exploratory Data Analysis
  (New York: John Wiley and Sons, Inc., 1983).

McNeil, D. R.
  Interactive Data Analysis: A Practical Primer
  (New York: John Wiley and Sons, 1977).

Tukey, John W.
  Exploratory Data Analysis
  (Reading, MA: Addison-Wesley, 1977).

Velleman, P. F. and Hoaglin, D. C.
  Applications, Basics, and Computing of Exploratory Data Analysis
  (Boston: Duxbury Press, 1981).

136.02 ---------- Theory Re: Exploratory Data Analysis

Alford, Geoffrey
  "Two Procedures for Exploratory Data Analysis"
  European Research, Vol. 8 (March 1980), pp. 78-85.

Alt, M. B.
  "Fact and Fiction in Survey Research: Some Philosophical
  Considerations"
  Quantitative Sociology Newsletter, Vol. 25 (1980), pp. 6-20.

Alt, Mick and Brighton, Malcolm
  "Analysing Data: Or Telling Stories?"
  Journal of the Market Research Society, Vol. 23 (October 1981), pp.
  209-19.

Armstrong, J. Scott
  "'Exploratory Analysis of Marketing Data': A Reply"
  Journal of Marketing Research, Vol. VIII (November 1971), pp. 514-7.

Armstrong, J. Scott
  "How to Avoid Exploratory Research"
  Journal of Advertising Research, Vol. 10, No. 4 (1970), pp. 27-30.

Armstrong, J. Scott and Andress, James G.
  "Exploratory Analysis of Marketing Data: Trees vs. Regression"
  Journal of Marketing Research, Vol. VII (November 1970), pp. 487-92.

Brighton, M.
  "From Astrology to Astronomy"
  The Market Research Society Annual Conference (1976).

Crocker, Douglas C.
  Comments on 'Exploratory Analysis of Marketing Data: Trees vs.
  Regression'"
  Journal of Marketing Research, Vol. III (November 1971), pp. 509-13.

De Leeuw, Jan
  Canonical Analysis of Categorical Data
  Psychological Institute, University of Leiden, The Netherlands
  (1973), unpublished doctoral dissertation.

Heiser, Willem J.
  Unfolding Analysis of Proximity Data
  Department of Data Theory, University of Leiden, Leiden, The
  Netherlands (1981).

Leamer, E. E.
  Specification Searches: Ad Hoc Inference From Nonexperimental Data
  (John Wiley and Sons, 1978).

Leinhardt, S. and Wasserman, S. S.
  "Exploratory Data Analysis: An Introduction"
  Sociological Methods (1979), pp. 311-65.

Massy, William F.
  "Principal Component Regression in Exploratory Statistical Research"
  Journal of the American Statistical Association, Vol. 60 (March
  1965), pp. 234-56.

McGill, R., Tukey, John W., and Larsen, W. A.
  "Variations of Box Plots"
  American Statistician, Vol. 32 (February 1978), pp. 12-6.

Rados, David L.
  "Two-Way Analysis of Tables in Market Research"
  Journal of the Market Research Society, Vol. 22 (October 1980), pp.
  248-62.

Selvin, H. C. and Stuart, A.
  "Data-Dredging Procedures in Survey Analysis"
  American Statistician, Vol. 20, No. 3 (1966), pp. 20-3.

136.03 ---------- Applications of Exploratory Data Analysis

Wheat, Rita and Morrision, Donald G.
  "Exploratory Data Analysis Applied to Scanner Data: How Regularly Do
  Consumers Purchase--and Does it Matter"
  ORSA/TIMS Conference, Dallas, TX (1986), paper presentation.

137 ------------------- MEASUREMENT CHARACTERISTICS -------------------
          See also (sub)heading(s) 56.

137.01 ---------- General Discussions Re: Measurement Characteristics

Carroll, John B.
   "The Nature of the Data, Or How to Choose a Correlation Coefficient"
   Psychometrika, Vol. 26 (December 1961), pp. 347-72.

Gleason, Terry C. and Staelin, Richard
   "Improving the Metric Quality of Questionnaire Data"
   Working Paper 70-70-1
   Carnegie Mellon University (1971).

Labovitz, S.
   "In Defense of Assigning Numbers to Ranks"
   American Sociological Review, Vol. 36, No. 3 (1971), pp. 520,1.

Labovitz, S.
   "The Assignment of Numbers to Rank Order Categories"
   American Sociological Review, Vol. 35 (1970), pp. 515-24.

Labovitz, S.
   "Some Observations on Measurement and Statistics"
   Social Forces, Vol. 46 (December 1967), pp. 151-60.

Lord, F. M.
   "On the Statistical Treatment of Football Numbers"
   American Psychologist, Vol. 8 (1953), pp. 750,1.

Mullet, Gary M.
   "Itemized Rating Scales: Ordinal or Interval?"
   European Research, Vol. 11 (April 1983), pp. 49-52.

Roskam, Edward E.
   "Data Theory and Mathematical Models"
   in Lingoes, J. C. et al. (editors)
   Geometric Representations of Relational Data
   (Ann Arbor, MI: Mathesis, 1979), pp. 149-235.

Somers, R. H.
   "An Approach to the Multivariate Analysis of Ordinal Data"
   American Sociological Review, Vol. 33 (December 1968), pp. 971-7.

Stevens, S. S.
   "Measurement, Statistics, and the Schemaphiric View"
   Science, Vol. 161 (1968), pp. 849-56.

Stevens, S. S.
   "Mathematics, Measurement, and Psychophysics"
   in Stevens, S. S. (editor)
   Handbook of Experimental Psychology
   (John Wiley and Sons, 1962).

Stevens, S. S.
   "The Theory of Scales of Measurement"
   Science, Vol. 103 (June 1946), pp. 677-80.

Wilson, T. P.
   "Critique of Ordinal Variables"
   Social Forces, Vol. 49 (1971), pp. 432-44.

Young, Forrest W.
   "Methods for Describing Ordinal Data With Cardinal Models"
   Journal of Mathematical Psychology, Vol. 12 (November 1975), pp.
   416-736.

137.02 ---------- Impact of Data Scale Level on Results of Analyses
          See also (sub)heading(s) 160.01, 160.04, 179.03.

Allan, G. J. Boris
   "Ordinal-Scaled Variables and Multivariate Analysis: Comment on
   Hawkes"
   American Journal of Sociology, Vol. 81 (1976), pp. 1498-1500.

Anderson, N. H.
   "Scales and Statistics: Parametric and Nonparametric"
   Psychological Bulletin, Vol. 58 (1961), pp. 305-16.

Babakus, Emin and Ferguson, Carl E., Jr.
   "On Choosing the Appropriate Measure of Association When Analyzing
   Rating Scale Data"
   Journal of the Academy of Marketing Science, Vol. 16 (Spring 1988),
   pp. 95-102.

Babakus, Emin, Ferguson, Carl E., Jr., and Joreskog, Karl G.
"The Sensitivity of Confirmatory Maximum Likelihood Factor Analysis
to Violations of Measurement Scale and Distributional Assumptions"
Journal of Marketing Research, Vol. XXIV (May 1987), pp. 222-8.

Baker, B. O., Hardyck, C. D., and Petrinovich, L. F.
"Weak Measurements vs. Strong Statistics: An Empirical Critique of S.
S. Steven's Proscription on Statistics"
Educational and Psychological Measurement, Vol. 26 (1966), pp.
291-309.

Bofinger, E.
"Maximizing the Correlation of Grouped Observations"
Journal of the American Statistical Association, Vol. 65 (December
1970), pp. 1632-8.

Bollen, Kenneth A. and Kenney, Barb H.
"Pearson's R and Coarsely Categorized Measure"
American Sociological Review (April 1981), pp. 232-39.

Boyle, R. P.
"Path Analysis and Ordinal Data"
American Journal of Sociology, Vol. 75 (January 1973), pp. 461-80.

Burke, C. J.
"Measurement Scales and Statistical Models"
in Scaling: A Sourcebook for Behavioral Scientists
(Chicago: Aldine, 1970), pp. 42-55.

Clark, M. Louise
Robustness of One Way Analysis of Variance for Ordinal Data
University of Alabama (1984), unpublished doctoral dissertation.

Cox, D. R.
"Note on Grouping"
Journal of the American Statistical Association, Vol. 52 (December
1957), pp. 543-7.

Dillon, William R. and Westin, Stuart
"Scoring Frequency Data for Discriminant Analysis: Perhaps Discrete
Procedures Can be Avoided"
Journal of Marketing Research, Vol. XIX (February 1982), pp. 44-56.

Gaito, J.
"Measurement Scales and Statistics: Resurgence of an Old
Misconception"
Psychological Bulletin, Vol. 87 (1980), pp. 564-7.

Gaito, J.
"Scale Classification and Statistics"
Psychological Review, Vol. 67 (1960), pp. 277,8.

Havlicek, Larry L. and Peterson, Nancy L.
"Effect of Violation of Assumptions Upon Significance Levels of the
Pearson r"
Psychological Bulletin (1977), pp. 373-7.

Hawkes, Ronald K.
"The Multivariate Analysis of Ordinal Measures"
American Journal of Sociology, Vol. 76 (1971), pp. 908-26.

Henkel, R. E.
"Part-Whole Correlations and the Treatment of Ordinal and
Quasi-Interval Data as Interval Data"
Pacific Sociological Review, Vol. 18 (January 1975), pp. 3-26.

Henry, Frank
"Multivariate Analysis and Ordinal Data"
American Sociological Review, Vol. 47 (1982), pp. 299-307.

Kim, Jae-On
"Multivariate Analysis of Ordinal Variables Revisited"
American Journal of Sociology, Vol. 84 (1978), pp. 448-56.

Kim, Jae-On
"Multivariate Analysis of Ordinal Variables"
American Journal of Sociology, Vol. 81 (1975), pp. 261-98.

Lawrence, Raymond J.
"How Many Categories for Respondent Classification?"
Journal of the Market Research Society, Vol. 23 (October 1981), pp.
220-38.

MacRae, A. W.
"Measurement Scales and Statistics: What can Significance Tests Tell
Us About the World?"
British Journal of Psychology, Vol. 79 (May 1988), pp. 161-71.

Mandeville, Garrett Kile
"A Monte Carlo Investigation of the Adequacy of Standard Analysis of Variance Test Procedures for Dependent Binary Variates"
University of Minnesota (1969), unpublished doctoral dissertation.

Martin, Warren S.
"Effects of Scaling on the Correlation Coefficient: Additional Considerations"
Journal of Marketing Research, Vol. XV (May 1978), pp. 304-8.

Martin, Warren S.
"The Effects of Scaling on the Correlation Coefficient: A Test of Validity"
Journal of Marketing Research, Vol. X (August 1973), pp. 316-8.

Martin, Warren S., Fruchter, Benjamin, and Mathis, William J.
"An Investigation of the Effects of the Number of Scale Intervals on Principal Components Factor Analysis"
Educational and Psychological Measurement, Vol. 34 (Autumn 1974), pp. 537-45.

Morrison, Donald G.
"Regression With Discrete Dependent Variables: The Effect on R-Square"
Journal of Marketing Research, Vol. IX (August 1972), pp. 38-40.

Morrison, Donald G.
"Upper Bounds for Correlations Between Binary Outcomes and Probabilistic Predictions"
Journal of the American Statistical Association, Vol. 67 (March 1972), pp. 68-70.

Morrison, Donald G. and Toy, Norman E.
"The Effect of Grouping Continuous Variables on Correlation Coefficients"
Marketing Science, Vol. 1 (Fall 1982), pp. 379-89.

O'Brien, R. M.
"Using Rank Category Variables to Represent Continuous Variables: Defects of Common Practice"
Social Forces, Vol. 59 (1981), pp. 1149-62.

O'Brien, R. M.
"The Use of Pearson's r With Ordinal Data"
American Sociological Review, Vol. 36 (1979), pp. 519,20.

Olsson, Ulf
"Maximum Likelihood Estimation of the Polychoric Correlation Coefficient"
Psychometrika, Vol. 44 (1979), pp. 443-59.

Olsson, U.
"On the Robustness of Factor Analysis Against Crude Classification of the Observations"
Multivariate Behavioral Research, Vol. 14 (1979), pp. 485-500.

Parasuraman, A. and Varadarajan, P. Rajan
"Robustness of Ordinal Measures of Competitive Strategy Variables Employed in Business Research: A PIMS Data-Based Analysis"
Journal of Business Research, Vol. 17 (August 1988), pp. 101-13.

Pearson, K.
"On the Measurement of the Influence of 'Broad Categories' on Correlation"
Biometrika, Vol. 9 (1913), pp. 116-39.

Peterson, Robert A. and Sharma, Subhash
"Adjusting Correlation Coefficients for the Effects of Scaling"
Proceedings of the American Statistical Association (1977).

Ploch, Donald H.
"Ordinal Measures of Association and the General Linear Model"
in Blalock, Hubert M., Jr. (editor)
Measurement in the Social Sciences
(Chicago: Aldine Publishing Company, 1974), pp. 343-68.

Reynolds, Henry
"On the Multivariate Analysis of Ordinal Measures"
American Journal of Sociology, Vol. 78 (1973), pp. 1513-6.

Smith, Robert B.
"Neighborhood Context and College Plans: An Ordinal Path Analysis"
Social Forces, Vol. 51 (1971), pp. 199-217.

Srinivasan, V. and Basu, Amiya K.
"The Metric Quality of Ordered Categorical Data"
Marketing Science, Vol. 8 (Summer 1989), pp. 205-30.

Traylor, Mark
    "Ordinal and Interval Scaling"
    Journal of the Market Research Society, Vol. 25 (October 1983), pp.
    297-303.

Wilson, T. P.
    "Reply to Somers and Smith"
    Social Forces, Vol. 53 (1974), pp. 247-51.

Wilson, T. P.
    "On Ordinal Path Analysis: Reply to Smith's Neighborhood Context and
    College Plans"
    Social Forces, Vol. 53 (1974), pp. 120-3.

138 -------------------- DATA TRANSFORMATIONS -------------------
        See also (sub)heading(s) 132.

138.01 ---------- General Discussions Re: Data Transformations

Box, George E. P. and Cox, D. R.
"An Analysis of Transformations"
Journal of the Royal Statistical Society, Series B, Vol. 26 (1964),
pp. 211-43.

Box, George E. P. and Tidwell, P. W.
"Transformations of the Independent Variables"
Technometrics, Vol. 4 (November 1962), pp. 531-550.

Deming, W. E.
Statistical Adjustment of Data
(New York: John Wiley and Sons, Inc., 1943).

Frank, Ronald E.
"Use of Transformations"
Journal of Marketing Research, Vol. III (August 1966), pp. 247-53.

Zarembka, P.
"Transformation of Variables in Econometrics"
in Zarembka, P. (editor)
Frontiers in Econometrics
(New York: Academic Press, 1974), pp. 81-104.

138.02 ---------- Theory Re: Fisher's Z Transformation of R

Fisher, Ronald A.
"On the 'Probable Error' of a Coefficient of Correlation"
Metron, Part 4 (1921), pp. 1-32.

138.03 ---------- Applications of Fisher's Z Transformation of R

Carmone, Frank J., Green, Paul E., and Jain, Arun K.
"Robustness of Conjoint Analysis: Some Monte Carlo Results"
Journal of Marketing Research, Vol. XV (May 1978), pp. 300-3.

Davis, Harry L., Hoch, Stephen J., and Ragsdale, E. K. Easton
"An Anchoring and Adjustment Model of Spousal Predictions"
Journal of Consumer Research, Vol. 13 (June 1986), pp. 25-37.

Durand, Richard M., Guffey, Hugh J., Jr., and Planchon, John M.
"An Examination of the Random Versus Nonrandom Nature of Item
Omissions"
Journal of Marketing Research, Vol. XX (August 1983), pp. 305-13.

Green, Paul E. and Maheshwari, Arun
"A Note on the Multidimensional Scaling of Conditional Proximity Data"
Journal of Marketing Research, Vol. VII (February 1970), pp. 106-10.

Malhotra, Naresh K., Jain, Arun K., and Pinson, Christian
"The Robustness of MDS Configurations in the Case of Incomplete Data"
Journal of Marketing Research, Vol. XXV (February 1988), pp. 95-102.

Miniard, Paul W., Obermiller, Carl, and Page, Thomas J., Jr.
"A Further Assessment of Measurement Influences on the
Intention-Behavior Relationship"
Journal of Marketing Research, Vol. XX (May 1983), pp. 206-12.

Park, C. Whan
"The Effect of Individual and Situation-Related Factors on
Consumer Selection of Judgmental Models"
Journal of Marketing Research, Vol. XIII (May 1976), pp. 144-51.

Rahtz, Don R. and Moore, David L.
"Product Class Involvement and Purchase Intent"
Psychology and Marketing, Vol. 6 (Summer 1989), pp. 113-27.

Szymanski, David M. and Busch, Paul S.
"Identifying the Generics-Prone Consumer: A Meta-Analysis"
Journal of Marketing Research, Vol. XXIV (November 1987), pp. 425-31.

Willett, Ronald P. and Kollat, David T.
"Customer Impulse Purchasing Behavior: Some Research Notes and a
Reply"
Journal of Marketing Research, Vol. V (August 1968), pp. 326-30.

138.04 ---------- Applications of the Arcsine Transformation

Reibstein, David J.
"The Prediction of Individual Probabilities of Brand Choice"
Journal of Consumer Research, Vol. 5 (December 1978), pp. 163-8.

Reid, Irvin D. and Preusser, David F.
    "The Impact of Alternative Consumer Education Strategies on Safety
    Knowledge and Behavior"
    Journal of the Academy of Marketing Science, Vol. 11 (Fall 1983), pp.
    382-403.

Witt, Robert E. and Bruce, Grady D.
    "Group Influence and Brand Choice Congruence"
    Journal of Marketing Research, Vol. IX (November 1972), pp. 440-3.

138.05 ---------- Applications of the Square Root Transformation

Claycamp, Henry J. and Liddy, Lucien E.
    "Prediction of New Product Performance: An Analytical Approach"
    Journal of Marketing Research, Vol. VI (November 1969), pp. 414-20.

138.06 ---------- Theory Re: Ipsative Data and Double-Centered Trans

Cattell, R. B.
    "Psychological Measurement: Normative, Ipsative, Interactive"
    Psychological Review, Vol. 51 (1944), pp. 292-303.

Clemans, W. V.
    "An Analytical and Experimental Examination of Some Properties of
    Ipsative Measures"
    University of Washington (1956), unpublished doctoral dissertation.

Cronbach, L. J. and Gleser, G. C.
    "Assessing Similarity Between Profiles"
    Psychological Bulletin, Vol. 50, No. 6 (1953).

Cunningham, W. H., Cunningham, I. C. M., and Green, R. T.
    "The Ipsative Process to Reduce Response Set Bias"
    Public Opinion Quarterly, Vol. 41 (1977), pp. 379-84.

Dillon, William R., Mulani, Narendra, and Frederick, Donald G.
    "Removing Perceptual Distortions in Product Space Analysis"
    Journal of Marketing Research, Vol. XXI (May 1984), pp. 184-93.

Gollob, H. F.
    "Confounding Sources of Variation in Factor-Analytic Techniques"
    Psychological Bulletin, Vol. 70 (1968), pp. 330-44.

Gollob, H. F.
    "A Statistical Model Which Combines Features of Factor Analytic and
    Analysis of Variance Techniques"
    Psychometrika, Vol. 33 (1968), pp. 73-115.

Gurwitz, Paul M.
    "Ipsative Rescaling: An Answer to the Response Set Problem in
    Segmentation Analysis"
    Journal of Advertising Research, Vol. 27 (June/July 1987), pp. 37-42.

Hicks, L. E.
    "Some Properties of Ipsative, Normative, and Forced-Choice Normative
    Measures"
    Psychological Bulletin, Vol. 74 (1970), pp. 167-84.

Jackson, J. J. and Alwin, D. F.
    "The Factor Analysis of Ipsative Measures"
    in Bohrnstedt, G. W. and Borgatta, E. F. (editors)
    Social Measurement: Current Issues
    (Beverly Hills, CA: Sage Publications, 1981).

Schaninger, Charles M. and Buss, W. Christian
    "Removing Response-Style Effects in Attribute-Determinance Ratings to
    Identify Market Segments"
    Journal of Business Research, Vol. 14 (June 1986), pp. 237-52.

Skinner, H. A.
    "Differentiating the Contribution of Elevation, Scatter and Shape in
    Profile Similarity"
    Educational and Psychological Measurement, Vol. 28 (1978), pp.
    297-307.

Smith, J. Walker
    "Dependence as a Research Design Strategy"
    Marketing Research, Vol. 1 (June 1989), pp. 64-6.

Tucker, L. R.
    "Factor Analysis of Double Centered Score Matrices"
    ETS Pub. No. RM-56-3
    (Princeton, NJ: Educational Testing Service, 1956).

138.07 ---------- Applications of the Double-Centered Transformation

Richins, Marsha L. and Verhage, Bronislaw J.
  "Cross-Cultural Differences in Consumer Attitudes and Their
  Implications for Complaint Management"
  International Journal of Research in Marketing, Vol. 2, No. 3 (1985),
  pp. 197-206.

138.08 ---------- Unclassified (Data Transformations)

Abelson, R. P. and Tukey, John W.
  "Efficient Conversion of Nonmetric Information Into Metric
  Information"
  Proceedings, Social Statistics Section, American Statistical
  Association (1959), pp. 226-30.

Henderson, Peter L., Brown, Sidney E., and Hind, James F.
  "On Methods: Nonquantified Adjustment of Seasonality in Time Series
  Data"
  Journal of Advertising Research, Vol. 4 (June 1964), pp. 38-44.

Johnson, Richard
  "The Minimal Transformation to Orthonormality"
  Psychometrika, Vol. 31 (March 1966), pp. 61-6.

Mullet, Gary M. and Karson, Marvin J.
  "Analysis of Purchase Intent Scales Weighted by Probability of Actual
  Purchase"
  Journal of Marketing Research, Vol. XXII (February 1985), pp. 93-6.

139 ---------------------- RESAMPLING METHODS ----------------------
          See also (sub)heading(s) 118, 128.

139.01 ---------- Books Re: Resampling Methods

Gray, Henry L. and Schucany, William R.
    The Generalized Jackknife
    (New York: Marcel Dekker, Inc., 1972).

Meehl, Paul E.
    Clinical Versus Statistical Prediction: A Theoretical Analysis and
    Review of the Literature
    (Minneapolic: University of Minnesota Press, 1954).

Wolter, K.
    Introduction to Variance Estimation
    (New York: Springer-Verlag, New York Inc., 1985).

139.02 ---------- Theory Re: Bootstrapping

Bone, Paula Fitzgerald, Sharma, Subhash, and Shimp, Terence A.
    "A Bootstrap Procedure for Evaluating Goodness-of-Fit Indices of
    Structural Equation and Confirmatory Factor Models"
    Journal of Marketing Research, Vol. XXVI (February 1989), pp. 105-11.

Dawes, Robyn M. and Corrigan, Bernard
    "Linear Models in Decision Making"
    Psychological Bulletin, Vol. 18 (1974), pp. 95-106.

Dudycha, L. W. and Naylor, J. C.
    "Characteristics of the Human Inference Process in Complex Behavior
    Situations"
    Organizational Behavior and Human Performance, Vol. 1 (1966), pp.
    110-28.

Efron, Bradley
    "Better Bootstrap Confidence Intervals"
    Journal of the American Statistical Association, Vol. 82 (March
    1987), pp. 171-85.

Efron, Bradley
    "The Jackknife, the Bootstrap, and Other Resampling Plans"
    SIAM Monograph Number 38
    (Philadelphia: Society of Industrial and Applied Mathematics, 1982).

Efron, B.
    "Bootstrap Methods: Another Look at the Jackknife"
    Annals of Statistics, Vol. 7 (1979), pp. 1-26.

Efron, Bradley and Gong, Gail
    "A Leisurely Look at the Bootstrap, the Jackknife, and Cross
    Validation"
    American Statistician, Vol. 37 (February 1983), pp. 36-48.

Einhorn, Hillel J.
    "The Use of Nonlinear, Noncompensatory Models in Decision Making"
    Psychological Bulletin, Vol. 73 (1970), pp. 221-30.

Freedman, D. A.
    "Boostrapping Regression Models"
    Annals of Statistics, Vol. 9 (December 1981), pp. 1218-28.

Green, Paul E., Carmone, Frank J., and Vankudre, Prashant
    "Bootstrapped Confidence Intervals for Conjoint Based Choice
    Simulators"
    Wharton School, University of Pennsylvania (1983), working paper.

Hope, Adery C. A.
    "A Simplified Monte Carlo Significance Test Procedure"
    Journal of the Royal Statistical Society, Vol. B30, No. 3 (1968), pp.
    582-98.

Huber, Joel
    "Bootstrapping of Data and Decisions"
    Journal of Consumer Research, Vol. 2 (December 1975), pp. 229-34.

Loh, Wei-Yin and Wu, C. F. J.
    "Comment on Better Bootstrap Confidence Intervals"
    Journal of the American Statistical Association, Vol. 82 (March
    1987), pp. 188-90.

Rao, J. N. K. and Wu, C. F. J.
    "Resampling Influence With Complex Survey Data"
    Journal of the American Statistical Association, Vol. 83 (March
    1988), pp. 231-41.

Rorer, L. G.
"A Circuitous Route to Bootstrapping"
in Haley, H. B., D'Costa, A. G., and Schafer, A. M. (editors)
Conference on Personality Measurement in Medical Education
(Washington, DC: Associations of American Medical Colleges, 1971).

Stine, Robert A.
"Bootstrap Prediction Intervals for Regression"
Journal of the American Statistical Association, Vol. 80 (December
1985), pp. 1026-31.

Wu, C. F. J.
"Jackknife, Bootstrap and Other Resampling Methods in Regression
Analysis"
Annals of Statistics, Vol. 14 (December 1986), pp. 1261-94.

Yntema, D. B. and Torgerson, W. S.
"Man-Computer Cooperation in Decisions Requiring Common Sense"
IRE Transactions of the Professional Group on Human Factors in
Electronics, HFE-2(1), (1961), pp. 20-6.

139.03 ---------- Theory Re: Jackknifing

Brillinger, David R.
"The Application of the Jackknife to the Analysis of Sample Surveys"
Journal of the Market Research Society, Vol. 8 (April 1966), pp.
74-80.

Bruno, Albert V.
"Validity in Research: An Elaboration--Comment"
Journal of Advertising Research, Vol. 15 (June 1975), pp. 39-41.

Clarkson, D. B.
"Estimating the Standard Error of Rotated Factor Loadings by
Jackknifing"
Psychometrika, Vol. 44 (September 1979), pp. 297-314.

Crask, M. R. and Perreault, W. D.
"Validation of Discriminant Analysis in Marketing Research"
Journal of Marketing Research, Vol. XIV (February 1977), pp. 60-8.

Durbin, J.
"A Note on the Application of Quenouille's Method of Bias Reduction
to the Estimation of Ratios"
Biometrika, Vol. 46 (1959), pp. 477-80.

Efron, Bradley
"The Jackknife, the Bootstrap, and Other Resampling Plans"
SIAM Monograph Number 38
(Philadelphia: Society of Industrial and Applied Mathematics, 1982).

Efron, B.
"Bootstrap Methods: Another Look at the Jackknife"
Annals of Statistics, Vol. 7 (1979), pp. 1-26.

Efron, Bradley and Gong, Gail
"A Leisurely Look at the Bootstrap, the Jackknife, and Cross
Validation"
American Statistician, Vol. 37 (February 1983), pp. 36-48.

Fenwick, Ian
"Techniques in Market Measurement: The Jackknife"
Journal of Marketing Research, Vol. XVI (August 1979), pp. 410-4.

Goldman, Arieh and Johansson, J. K.
"Determinants of Search for Lower Prices: An Empirical Assessment of
the Economics of Information Theory"
Journal of Consumer Research, Vol. 5 (December 1978), pp. 176-86.

Jones, H. L.
"Investigating the Properties of a Sample Mean by Employing Random
Subsample Means"
Journal of the American Statistical Association, Vol. 51 (March
1956), pp. 54-83.

Mantel, Nathan
"Assumption-Free Estimators Using U-Statistics and a Relationship to
the Jackknife Method"
Biometrics, Vol. 23 (September 1967), pp. 567-71.

Miller, R. G.
"The Jackknife--A Review"
Biometrika, Vol. 61 (1974), pp. 1-15.

Miller, R.
"Jackknifing Variances"
Annals of Mathematical Statistics, Vol. 39 (April 1968), pp. 567-82.

Miller, Rupert G.
"A Trustworthy Jackknife"
Annals of Mathematical Statistics, Vol. 35 (December 1964), pp.
1594-605.

Mosteller, Frederick
"The Jackknife"
Review of the International Statistical Institute, Vol. 39 (1971),
pp. 363-8.

Mosteller, Frederick and Tukey, John W.
"Data Analysis, Including Statistics"
in Lindzey, G. and Aronson, E. (editors)
The Handbook of Social Psychology, Volume Two
(Reading, MA: Addison-Wesley, 1968), pp. 80-203.

Quenouille, M. H.
"Notes on Bias in Estimation"
Biometrika, Vol. 43 (December 1956), pp. 353-60.

Quenouille, M.
"Approximate Tests of Correlation in Time Series"
Journal of the Royal Statistical Society, Vol. B11 (1949), pp. 68-84.

Schucany, W. R., Gray, H. L., and Owen, D. B.
"On Bias Reduction in Estimation"
Journal of the American Statistical Association, Vol. 66 (1971), pp.
524-33.

Sharot, T.
"The Generalized Jackknife: Finite Samples and Subsample Sizes"
Journal of the American Statistical Association, Vol. 71 (1976), pp.
451-4.

Tukey, J. W.
"Bias and Confidence in Not-Quite Large Samples" (abstract)
Annals of Mathematical Statistics, Vol. 29 (June 1958), p. 614.

Watkins, T. A.
"A Jackknife Statistic Process"
Texas Tech University (1971), Ph.D. dissertation.

Wu, C. F. J.
"Jackknife, Bootstrap and Other Resampling Methods in Regression
Analysis"
Annals of Statistics, Vol. 14 (December 1986), pp. 1261-94.

139.04 ---------- Applications of Bootstrapping

Bowman, E. H.
"Consistency and Optimality in Management Decision Making"
Management Science, Vol. 9 (1963), pp. 310-21.

Dawes, Robyn M.
"A Case Study of Graduate Admissions: Application of Three Principles
of Human Decision Making"
American Psychologist, Vol. 26 (1971), pp. 180-8.

Ebert, Ronald J. and Kruse, Thomas E.
"Bootstrapping the Security Analyst"
Journal of Applied Psychology, Vol. 63 (1978), pp. 110-9.

Goldberg, L. R.
"Man Versus Model of Man: A Rationale, Plus Some Evidence, for a
Method of Improving on Clinical Inferences"
Psychological Bulletin, Vol. 73 (1970), pp. 422-32.

Heeler, Roger M., Kearney, Michael J., and McHaffey, Bruce
"Modeling Supermarket Product Selection"
Journal of Marketing Research, Vol. X (February 1973), pp. 34-7.

Huber, Joel
"Bootstrapping of Data and Decisions"
Journal of Consumer Research, Vol. 2 (December 1975), pp. 229-34.

Kunreuther, Howard
"Extensions of Bowman's Theory of Managerial Decision Making"
Management Science, Vol. 15 (April 1969), pp. 415-39.

Lattin, James M. and McAlister, Leigh
"Using a Variety-Seeking Model to Identify Substitute and
Complementary Relationships Among Competing Products"
Journal of Marketing Research, Vol. XXII (August 1985), pp. 330-9.

Montgomery, David B.
"New Product Distribution: An Analysis of Supermarket Buyer Decisions"
(Cambridge, MA: Marketing Science Institute Research Programs, Vol.
63, 1973).

139.05 ---------- Applications of Jackknifing

Clarkson, Douglas B.
"Estimating the Standard Errors of Rotated Factor Loadings by
Jackknifing"
Psychometrika, Vol. 44 (September 1979), pp. 297-314.

Didow, Nicholas M., Jr. and Franke, George R.
"Measurement Issues in Time-Series Research: Reliability and Validity
Assessment in Modeling the Macroeconomic Effects of Advertising"
Journal of Marketing Research, Vol. XXI (February 1984), pp. 12-9.

Didow, Nicholas M., Jr., Keller, Kevin Lane, Barksdale, Hiram C., Jr.,
and Franke, George R.
"Improving Measure Quality by Alternating Least Squares Optimal
Scaling"
Journal of Marketing Research, Vol. XXII (February 1985), pp. 30-40.

Fenwick, Ian, Schellinck, D. A., and Kendall, K. W.
"Assessing the Reliability of Psychographic Analyses"
Marketing Science, Vol. 2 (Winter 1983), pp. 57-73.

Goldman, Arieh and Johansson, J. K.
"Determinants of Search for Lower Prices: An Empirical Assessment of
the Economics of Information Theory"
Journal of Consumer Research, Vol. 5 (December 1978), pp. 176-86.

Hoyer, Wayne D.
"An Examination of Consumer Decision Making for a Common Repeat
Purchase Product"
Journal of Consumer Research, Vol. 11 (December 1984), pp. 822-9.

Ireland, M. Edwin and Uselton, Gene G.
"A Distribution-Free Statistic for Management Scientists"
in Menke, W. W. and Whitehurst, C. H., Jr. (editors)
Eleventh Annual Meeting, Southeastern Chapter, The Institute of
Management Sciences (October 1976), pp. 25,6.

Johansson, Johny K., Douglas, Susan P., and Nonaka, Ikujiro
"Assessing the Impact of Country of Origin on Product Evaluations: A
New Methodological Perspective"
Journal of Marketing Research, Vol. XXII (November 1985), pp. 388-96.

Jolson, Marvin A., Anderson, Rolph E., and Leber, Nancy J.
"Profiles of Signature Goods Consumers and Avoiders"
Journal of Retailing, Vol. 57 (Winter 1981), pp. 19-38.

Jolson, Marvin A., Wiener, Joshua L., and Rosecky, Richard B.
"Correlates of Rebate Proneness"
Journal of Advertising Research, Vol. 27 (February/March 1987), pp.
33-43.

Kerin, Roger A. and Cron, William L.
"Assessing Trade Show Functions and Performance: An Exploratory Study"
Journal of Marketing, Vol. 51 (July 1987), pp. 87-94.

Malhotra, Naresh K.
"Structural Reliability and Stability of Nonmetric Conjoint Analysis"
Journal of Marketing Research, Vol. XIX (May 1982), pp. 199-207.

Midgley, David F.
"Patterns of Interpersonal Information Seeking for the Purchase of a
Symbolic Product"
Journal of Marketing Research, Vol. XX (February 1983), pp. 74-83.

Richardson, S. C.
"Assessing the Performance of a Discriminant Analysis"
Journal of the Market Research Society, Vol. 24 (January 1982), pp.
65-7.

Toussaint, Godfried T.
"Bibliography on Estimation of Misclassification"
IEEE Transactions on Information Theory, Vol. IT-20 (July 1974), pp.
472-9.

Wildt, Albert R., Lambert, Zarrel V., and Durand, Richard M.
"Applying the Jackknife Statistic in Testing and Interpreting
Canonical Weights, Loadings, and Cross-Loadings"
Journal of Marketing Research, Vol. XIX (February 1982), pp. 99-107.

140 ---------------------- MODERATOR VARIABLES ----------------------

See also (sub)heading(s) 166.

140.01 ---------- Theory Re: Moderator Variables

Abrahams, Norman M. and Alf, Edward, Jr.
"Pratfalls in Moderator Research"
Journal of Applied Psychology, Vol. 56 (June 1972), pp. 245-51.

Abrahams, Norman M. and Alf, Edward, Jr.
"Reply to Dunnette's 'Comments on Abrahams and Alf's Pitfalls in Moderator Research"
Journal of Applied Psychology, Vol. 56 (June 1972), pp. 257-61.

Arnold, Hugh J.
"Moderator Variables: A Clarification of Conceptual, Analytic, and Psychometric Issues"
Organizational Behavior and Human Performance, Vol. 29 (1982), pp. 143-74.

Cohen, Jacob
"Partialed Products are Interactions; Partialed Powers are Curve Components"
Psychological Bulletin, Vol. 85, No. 4 (1978), pp. 858-66.

Dunnette, Marvin D.
"Comments on Abrahams and Alf's 'Pratfalls in Moderator Research'"
Journal of Applied Psychology, Vol. 56 (June 1972), pp. 252-6.

Ghiselli, Edwin E.
"Comment on the Use of Moderator Variables"
Journal of Applied Psychology, Vol. 56 (June 1972), p. 270.

Gur-Arie, Oded, Durand, Richard M., and Sharma, Subhash
"Identifying Moderator Variables Using Moderated Regression Analysis"
in Franz, R. S., Hopkins, R. M., and Toma, A. G. (editors)
Proceedings, Southern Marketing Association
(Lafayette: Southern Marketing Association, 1979), pp. 189-92.

Lazarsfeld, Paul F.
"Interpretation of Statistical Relations as a Research Operation"
in Lazarsfeld, Paul F. and Rosenberg, Morris (editors)
The Language of Social Research
(Glencoe, IL: The Free Press, 1955).

Rosenberg, Morris
The Logic of Survey Analysis
(New York: Basic Books, Inc., 1968).

Saunders, David R.
"Moderator Variables in Prediction"
Educational and Psychological Measurement, Vol. 16 (Summer 1956), pp. 209-22.

Saunders, David R.
"The 'Moderator' Variable as a Useful Tool in Prediction"
in Proceedings, Invitational Conference on Testing Problems
(Princeton, NJ: Educational Testing Service, 1954).

Sharma, Subhash, Durand, Richard M., and Gur-Arie, Oded
"Identification and Analysis of Moderator Variables"
Journal of Marketing Research, Vol. XVIII (August 1981), pp. 291-300.

Velicer, Wayne F.
"The Moderator Variable Viewed as Heterogeneous Regression"
Journal of Applied Psychology, Vol. 56 (June 1972), pp. 266-9.

Zedeck, Sheldon
"Problems With the Use of 'Moderator' Variables"
Psychological Bulletin, Vol. 76 (October 1971), pp. 295-310.

Zedeck, Sheldon, Cranny, C. J., Vale, Carol A., and Smith, Patricia C.
"Comparison of 'Joint Moderators' in Three Prediction Techniques"
Journal of Applied Psychology, Vol. 55 (June 1971), pp. 234-40.

140.02 ---------- Applications of Subgroup Analysis of Mod Variables

Becherer, Richard C. and Richard, Lawrence M.
"Self-Monitoring as a Moderator Variable in Consumer Behavior"
Journal of Consumer Research, Vol. 5 (December 1978), pp. 159-63.

Bennett, Peter D. and Harrell, Gilbert D.
"The Role of Confidence in Understanding and Predicting Buyers' Attitudes and Purchase Intentions"
Journal of Consumer Research, Vol. 2 (September 1975), pp. 110-7.

Berkowitz, Eric N., Ginter, James L., and Talarzyk, W. Wayne
"An Investigation of the Effects of Specific Usage Situations on the
Prediction of Consumer Choice Behavior"
in Greenberg, Barnett A. and Bellenger, Danny N. (editors)
Contemporary Marketing Thought
(Chicago: American Marketing Association, 1977), pp. 90-4.

Bonfield, E. H.
"Attitudes, Social Influence, Personal Norms, and Intention
Interactions as Related to Brand Purchase Behavior"
Journal of Marketing Research, Vol. XI (November 1974), pp. 379-89.

Brody, Robert P. and Cunningham, Scott M.
"Personality Variables and the Consumer Decision Process"
Journal of Marketing Research, Vol. V (February 1968), pp. 50-7.

Fry, Joseph N.
"Personality Variables and Cigarette Brand Choice"
Journal of Marketing Research, Vol. VIII (August 1971), pp. 298-304.

Ghiselli, Edwin E.
"Moderating Effects and Differential Reliability and Validity"
Journal of Applied Psychology, Vol. 47 (April 1963), pp. 81-6.

Hirschman, Elizabeth C., Blumenfeld, Warren S., and Tabor, Dwight
"An Attempt to Utilize Sex as a Moderator for Profiling Bank Card
Users"
in Stolen, Justin D. and Conway, James J. (editors)
Proceedings
(Chicago: American Institute for Decision Sciences, 1977), pp. 227-9.

Hobert, Robert and Dunnette, Marvin D.
"Development of Moderator Variables to Enhance the Prediction of
Managerial Effectiveness"
Journal of Applied Psychology, Vol. 51 (February 1967), pp. 50-64.

Kohli, Ajay
"Determinants of Influence in Organizational Buying: A Contingency
Approach"
Journal of Marketing, Vol. 53 (July 1989), pp. 50-65.

Miller, Kenneth E. and Ginter, James L.
"An Investigation of Situational Variation in Brand Choice Behavior
and Attitude"
Journal of Marketing Research, Vol. VI (February 1979), pp. 111-23.

Peter, J. Paul and Ryan, Michael J.
"An Investigation of Perceived Risk at the Brand Level"
Journal of Marketing Research, Vol. XIII (May 1976), pp. 184-9.

Peters, William S. and Champoux, Joseph E.
"The Use of Moderated Regressions in Job Redesign Decisions"
Decision Sciences, Vol. 10 (January 1979), pp. 85-95.

Pettit, Kathy L., Sawa, Sonja L., and Sawa, Ghazi H.
"Frugality: A Cross-National Moderator of the Price-Quality
Relationship"
Psychology and Marketing, Vol. 2 (Winter 1985), pp. 253-65.

Sample, John and Warland, Rex H.
"Attitudes and Prediction of Behavior"
Social Forces, Vol. 51 (March 1973), pp. 292-304.

Tankersley, Clint B. and Lambert, David R.
"Social Character and the Structure of Behavioral Intention"
Journal of the Academy of Marketing Science, Vol. 6 (Winter 1978),
pp. 52-60.

Warland, Rex H. and Sample, John
"Response Certainty as a Moderator in Attitude Measurement"
Rural Sociology, Vol. 38 (Summer 1973), pp. 174-86.

141 ---------------------- HYPOTHESIS TESTING ----------------------
     See also (sub)heading(s) 139, 142, 143, 162, 167.04,
     171.08, 177.05, 184, 185.09, 198, 205.

141.01 ---------- Books Re: Hypothesis Testing

Brown, G. S.
   Probability and Scientific Inference
   (New York: Longmans, Green, 1957).

Cassel, Claes-Magnus, Sarndal, Carl-Erik, and Wretman, Jan Hakan
   Foundations of Inference in Survey Sampling
   (New York: John Wiley and Sons, Inc., 1977), 192 pp.

Caulcott, Evelyn
   Significance Tests
   (London, EN: Routledge and Kegan Paul, 1973), 145 pp.

Cohen, Jacob
   Statistical Power Analysis for the Behavioral Sciences, Revised
   Edition
   (New York: Academic Press, 1977).

Dixon, Wilfrid J. and Massey, Frank J., Jr.
   Introduction to Statistical Analysis
   (New York, NY: McGraw-Hill Book Co., 1957), 128 pp.

Edgington, Eugene S.
   Randomization Tests
   (New York: Marcel Dekker, Inc., 1980), 287 pp.

Dudewicz, Edward J.
   Introduction to Statistics and Probability
   (New York: Holt, Rinehart, and Winston, 1976).

Fisher, Ronald A.
   Statistical Methods for Research Workers, Fourteenth Edition
   (New York: Hafner Publishing Company, 1970).

Fisher, Ronald A.
   Statistical Methods and Scientific Inference, Second Edition
   (Edinburgh, Scotland: Oliver and Boyd, 1959).

Frankel, Martin R.
   Inference From Survey Samples: An Empirical Investigation
   (Ann Arbor: Institute for Social Research, The University of
   Michigan, 1971).

Guenther, William C.
   Concepts of Statistical Inference
   (New York: McGraw-Hill, 1965), 353 pp.

Hays, William L.
   Statistics for Psychologists
   (New York: Holt, Rinehart, and Winston, 1963).

Henkel, Ramon E.
   Tests of Significance
   (Beverly Hills, CA: Sage Publications, Inc., 1976), 92 pp.

Hoel, Paul
   Introduction to Mathematical Statistics
   (New York, NY: John Wiley and Sons, Inc., 1954).

Johnson, N. I. and Kotz, S.
   Discrete Distributions
   (New York: John Wiley and Sons, Inc., 1969).

Kendall, M. G. and Stuart, A.
   The Advanced Theory of Statistics, Volume One
   (London, EN: Charles Griffin, 1958).

Li, Jerome
   Introduction to Statistical Inference
   (Ann Arbor, MI: J. W. Edwards, Publisher, Inc., 1957).

Montagnon, Philip
   Foundations of Statistics--A Survey for Managers
   (Stanley Thornes, 1980), 139 pp.

Morrison, Denton E. and Henkel, Ramon E. (editors)
   The Significance Test Controversy
   (Chicago: Aldine, 1970), 333 pp.

Myers, B. L. and Enrick, N. L.
   Statistical Functions
   (Kent, OH: Kent State University Press, 1970).

Pearson, E. S. and Hartley, H. O.
    Biometrika Tables for Statisticians, Volume One
    (London: Cambridge University Press, 1958).

Pearson, K.
    Tables for Statisticians and Biometricians, Part II
    (Cambridge, England: Cambridge University Press, 1924).

Phillips, Lawrence D.
    Bayesian Statistics for Social Sciences
    (London: Thomas Nelson, 1973).

Rao, C. Radhakrishna
    Linear Statistical Inference and Its Applications
    (New York, NY: John Wiley and Sons, Inc., 1965).

Rothschild, V. and Logothetis, N.
    Probability Distributions
    (New York: John Wiley and Sons, Inc., 1986), 79 pp.

Silvey, S.
    Statistical Inference
    (London: Penguin, 1970).

Walker, H. M. and Lev, Joseph
    Statistical Inference
    (New York, NY: Henry Holt and Company, 1953).

Winer, B. J.
    Statistical Principles in Experimental Design
    (New York: McGraw-Hill Book Company, 1971).

Yule, G. U. and Kendall, M. G.
    An Introduction to the Theory of Statistics, Fourteenth Edition
    (London: Charles Griffin and Company Limited, 1950).

141.02 ---------- Theory Re: Hypothesis Testing

Alt, Mick and Brighton, Malcolm
    "Analysing Data: Or Telling Stories?"
    Journal of the Market Research Society, Vol. 23 (October 1981), pp.
    209-19.

Bakan, David
    "The Test of Significance in Psychological Research"
    Psychological Bulletin, Vol. 66 (December 1966), pp. 423-37.

Binder, A.
    "Further Considerations on Testing the Null Hypothesis and the
    Strategy and Tactics of Investigating Theoretical Models"
    Psychological Review, Vol. 70 (January 1963), pp. 107-15.

Birnbaum, A.
    "On the Foundations of Statistical Inference"
    Journal of the American Statistical Association, Vol. 57 (June 1962),
    pp. 269-306.

Box, G. E. P.
    "Nonnormality and Tests on Variances"
    Biometrika, Vol. 40 (December 1953), pp. 318-35.

Box, G. E. P.
    "A General Distribution Theory for a Class of Likelihood Criteria"
    Biometrika, Vol. 36 (December 1949), pp. 317-46.

Bradley, J. V.
    "Studies in Research Methodology VI: The Central Limit Effect for a
    Variety of Populations and Robustness of Z, T and F"
    Technical Report AMRL-TR, Wright-Patterson Air Force Base, Ohio
    (1964), pp. 64-123.

Deming, W. Edwards
    "Responsibilities in Sampling Surveys"
    in Enrick, N. L. (editor)
    Cases in Management Statistics
    (New York: Holt, Rinehart and Winston, 1962), pp. 95-100.

Dowling, G. R. and Walsh, P. K.
    "Estimating and Reporting Confidence Intervals for Market and Opinion
    Research"
    European Research, Vol. 13 (July 1985), pp. 130-3.

Edgington, E. S.
    "Randomization Tests With Statistical Control Over Concomitant
    Variables"
    Journal of Psychology, Vol. 79 (September 1971), pp. 13-9.

Edgington, E. S.
"Approximate Randomization Tests"
Journal of Psychology, Vol. 72 (July 1969), pp. 143-9.

Edgington, E. S.
"Statistical Inference From N-1 Experiments"
Journal of Psychology, Vol. 65 (March 1967), pp. 195-9.

Edgington, E. S.
"Randomization Tests"
Journal of Psychology, Vol. 57 (April 1964), pp. 455-9.

Feir-Walsh, Betty J. and Toothaker, Larry E.
"An Empirical Comparison of the ANOVA F-Test, Normal Scores Test and
Kruskal-Wallis Test Under Violations of Assumptions"
Educational and Psychological Measurement, Vol. 34 (Winter 1974), pp.
789-99.

Gardner, M.
"On the Meaning of Randomness and Some Ways to Achieve It"
Scientific American, Vol. 219 (1968), pp. 116-21.

Gitlow, Howard S.
"Joint Confidence Interval Construction for Multivariate Applications
in Marketing"
Journal of the Academy of Marketing Science, Vol. 5 (Winter-Spring
1977), pp. 37-9.

Hansen, Morris H., Madow, William G., and Tepping, Benjamin J.
"An Evaluation of Model Dependent and Probability Sampling Inferences
in Sample Surveys"
Journal of the American Statistical Association, Vol. 78 (December
1983), pp. 776-93.

Harris, C.
"Statistical Methods"
in Encyclopedia of Educational Research, Third Edition
(New York: Macmillan, 1960), pp. 397-1410.

Hope, A. C.
"A Simplified Monte Carlo Significance Test Procedure"
Journal of the Royal Statistical Society, Vol. B30 (1968), pp. 582-98.

Hotelling, H.
"The Generalization of Student's Ratio"
Annals of Mathematical Statistics, Vol. 2 (1931), p. 360.

Hsu, Tse-Chi and Feldt, Leonard S.
"The Effect of Limitations on the Number of Criterion Scores on the
Significance Level of the F-Test"
American Educational Research Journal, Vol. 6 (November 1969), pp.
515-27.

Hummel, Thomas J. and Sligo, Joseph R.
"Empirical Comparison of Univariate and Multivariate Analysis of
Variance Procedures"
Psychological Bulletin, Vol. 76 (July 1971), pp. 49-57.

Keselman, H. J., Games, Paul A., and Rogan, Joanne C.
"Type I and Type II Errors in Simultaneous and Two-Stage Multiple
Comparison Procedures"
Psychological Bulletin, Vol. 88 (September 1980), pp. 356-8.

Kish, Leslie
"Some Statistical Problems in Research Design"
American Sociological Review, Vol. 24 (June 1959), pp. 328-38.

Kurth, Rudolf
"Testing the Significance of Consumer Complaints"
Journal of Marketing Research, Vol. II (August 1965), pp. 283,4.

MacRae, A. W.
"Measurement Scales and Statistics: What can Significance Tests Tell
Us About the World?"
British Journal of Psychology, Vol. 79 (May 1988), pp. 161-71.

Meehl, Paul E.
"Theoretical Risks and Tabular Asterisks: Sir Karl, Sir Ronald, and
the Slow Progress of Soft Psychology"
Journal of Consulting and Clinical Psychology, Vol. 46 (1978), pp.
806-84.

Meehl, Paul E.
"Theory Testing in Psychology and Physics: A Methodological Paradox"
Philosophy of Science, Vol. 34 (June 1967), pp. 103-15.

Milligan, Glenn W.
"Factors That Affect Type I and Type II Error Rates in the Analysis
of Multidimensional Contingency Tables"
Psychological Bulletin, Vol. 87 (March 1980), pp. 238-44.

Myers, Buddy L. and Enrick, Norbert L.
   "Classical Error Pairs and the Bayesian Prior"
   Journal of the Academy of Marketing Science, Vol. 1 (Spring 1973),
   pp. 43-51.

Myers, B. L., Enrick, N. L., and Melcher, A. J.
   "Strategy in Research Design and Hypothesis Testing"
   Journal of the Academy of Marketing Science, Vol. 2 (Winter 1974),
   pp. 249-61.

Neher, Andrew
   "Probability Pyramiding, Research Error, and the Need for Independent
   Replication"
   Psychological Record, Vol. 17 (April 1967), pp. 257-62.

Peterson, Robert A. and Mahajan, Vijay
   "Practical Significance and Partitioning Variance in Discriminant
   Analysis"
   Decision Sciences, Vol. 7 (October 1976), pp. 649-58.

Rao, C. R.
   "Tests of Significance in Multivariate Analysis"
   Biometrika, Vol. 35 (1948), pp. 58-79.

Rosenthal, Robert
   "Interpersonal Expectations: Effects of the Experimenter's Hypothesis"
   in Rosenthal, Robert and Rosnow, Ralph L. (editors)
   Artifact in Behavioral Research
   (New York: Academic Press, 1969), pp. 181-277.

Selvin, H. C.
   "A Critique of Tests of Significance in Survey Research"
   American Sociological Review, Vol. 22 (1957), pp. 519-27.

Sprott, D. A. and Kalbfleisch, J. G.
   "Use of the Likelihood Function in Inference"
   Psychological Bulletin, Vol. 64 (July 1965), pp. 15-22.

Tukey, J. W.
   "Bias and Confidence in Not Quite Large Samples" (abstract)
   Annals of Mathematical Statistics, Vol. 29 (1958), pp. 29, 614.

Walsh, J. E.
   "Concerning the Effect of Intra-Class Correlation in Certain
   Significance Tests"
   Annals of Mathematical Statistics, Vol. 19 (1947), pp. 88-96.

Wilcox, Rand R.
   "A Review of Exact Hypothesis Testing Procedures (and Selection
   Techniques) That Control Power Regardless of the Variances"
   British Journal of Mathematical and Statistical Psychology, Vol. 37
   (May 1984), pp. 34-48.

Wolf, Gerrit and Bassler, John
   "Importance of Hypotheses: Group Comparison Analysis"
   Decision Sciences, Vol. 11 (January 1980), pp. 27-41.

Wolfowitz, J.
   "Remarks on the Theory of Testing Hypotheses"
   The New York Statistician, Vol. 18 (March 1967), pp. 1,2.

141.03 ---------- Philosophical Issues in Hypothesis Testing

Carver, R. P.
   "The Case Against Statistical Significance Testing"
   Harvard Educational Review, Vol. 48 (August 1978), pp. 278-99.

Greenwald, Anthony
   "Consequences of Prejudices Against the Null Hypothesis"
   Psychological Bulletin, Vol. 82 (January 1975), pp. 1-20.

Robinson, Harry
   "Is it Time for Marketers to Ditch Significance Tests?"
   Marketing Intelligence and Planning, Vol. 2, No. 1 (1984), pp. 62-8.

Rozeboom, W.
   "The Fallacy of the Null-Hypothesis Significance Test"
   Psychological Bulletin, Vol. 57 (September 1960), pp. 416-28.

141.04 ---------- Hyp. Testing for Other Than Simple Random Samples

      See also (sub)heading(s) 115.

Kish, Leslie
   "Confidence Intervals for Clustered Samples"
   American Sociological Review, Vol. 22 (1957), pp. 154-65.

141.05 ---------- Theory Re: Inference From Non-Random Samples

See also (sub)heading(s) 115.

Edgington, Eugene S.
"Statistical Inference and Nonrandom Samples"
Psychological Bulletin, Vol. 66 (1966), pp. 485-7.

Smith, T. M. F.
"On the Validity of Inferences From Non-Random Samples"
Journal of the Royal Statistical Society, Vol. 146, Series A General
(1983), pp. 394-403.

141.06 ---------- Theory Re: Bayesian Hypothesis Testing

Edwards, Ward, Lindman, Harold, and Savage, Leonard R.
"Bayesian Statistical Inference for Psychological Research"
Psychological Review, Vol. 70 (May 1963), pp. 193-242.

Hirschleifer, J.
"The Bayesian Approach to Statistical Decision: An Exposition"
Journal of Business, Vol. 34 (October 1961), pp. 473-5.

Iverson, Gudmund R.
Bayesian Statistical Inference
(Beverly Hills, CA: Sage Publications, Inc.).

Iverson, Gudmund R.
"Statistics According to Bayes"
in Borgatta, Edgar F. and Bohrnstedt, George W. (editors)
Sociological Methodology
(San Francisco: Jossey-Bass, 1970), pp. 185-99.

Phillips, Lawrence D.
Bayesian Statistics for Social Sciences
(London: Thomas Nelson, 1973).

Roberts, Harry V.
"Bayesian Statistics in Marketing"
Journal of Marketing, Vol. 27 (January 1963), pp. 1-4.

141.07 ---------- Applications of Bayesian Hypothesis Testing

Blattberg, Robert C.
"The Design of Advertising Experiments Using Statistical Decision
Theory"
Journal of Marketing Research, Vol. XVI (May 1979), pp. 191-202.

Ginter, James, Cooper, Martha, Obermiller, Carl, and Page, Thomas
"The Design of Advertising Experiments: An Extension"
Journal of Marketing Research, Vol. XVIII (February 1981), pp. 120-3.

Levitt, Theodore
"Industrial Purchasing Behavior: A Bayesian Reanalysis"
Journal of Business Administration, Vol. 4 (Fall 1972), pp. 79-81.

141.08 ---------- Theory Re: Strong Inference

Platt, John R.
"Strong Inference"
Science, Vol. 146 (October 16, 1964), pp. 347-53.

141.09 ---------- Applications of Strong Inference

Bettman, James R., Capon, Noel, and Lutz, Richard J.
"Cognitive Algebra in Multi-Attribute Attitude Models"
Journal of Marketing Research, Vol. XII (May 1975), pp. 151-64.

Burger, Jerry M. and Petty, Richard E.
"The Low-Ball Compliance Technique: Task or Person Commitment?"
Journal of Personality and Social Psychology, Vol. 40 (March 1981),
pp. 492-500.

Cialdini, Robert B., Cacioppo, John T., Bassett, Rodney, and Miller,
John A.
"Low-Ball Procedure for Producing Compliance Commitment Then Cost"
Journal of Personality and Social Psychology, Vol. 36 (May 1978), pp.
463-76.

141.10 ---------- Theory Re: Weak Inference

Anderson, N. H. and Shanteau, J.
"Weak Inference With Linear Models"
Psychological Bulletin, Vol. 84 (1977), pp. 1155-70.

141.11 ---------- Issues Re: Significance Levels

Alford, G.
"Estimating Confidence Limits and Sampling Tolerances in Actual
Surveys--Beyond Comfortable Formulae"
Australian Market Researcher, Vol. 6, No. 2 (1982), pp. 7-31.

Bakan, David
"The Test of Significance in Psychological Research"
Psychological Bulletin, Vol. 66 (December 1966), pp. 423-37.

Carver, Ronald P.
"The Case Against Statistical Significance Testing"
Harvard Educational Review, Vol. 48 (August 1978), pp. 278-399.

Cartwright, Dorwin
"Determinants of Scientific Progress: The Case of Research on the
Risky Shift"
American Psychologist, Vol. 28 (March 1973), pp. 222-31.

Cooper, Harris M.
"On the Significance of Effects and the Effects of Significance"
Journal of Personality and Social Psychology, Vol. 41 (1981), pp.
1013-8.

Cooper, Harris M. and Rosenthal, Robert
"Statistical Versus Traditional Procedures for Summarizing Research
Findings"
Psychological Bulletin, Vol. 87 (May 1980), pp. 442-9.

Dowling, G. R. and Walsh, P. K.
"Estimating and Reporting Confidence Intervals for Market and Opinion
Research"
European Research, Vol. 13 (July 1985), pp. 130-3.

Edgington, E. S.
"Hypothesis Testing Without Fixed Levels of Significance"
Journal of Psychology, Vol. 76 (September 1970), pp. 109-15.

Enrick, Norbert L. and Myers, Buddy L.
"A Logic System for the Choice of Risk Levels in Hypothesis Testing"
Journal of the Academy of Marketing Science, Vol. 4 (Winter-Spring
1976), pp. 396-406.

Greenwald, Anthony G.
"Does the Good Samaritan Parable Increase Helping? A Comment on
Darley and Batson's No-Effect Conclusion"
Journal of Personality and Social Psychology, Vol. 32 (October 1975),
pp. 578-83.

Greenwald, Anthony G.
"Significance, Nonsignificance, and Interpretation of an ESP
Experiment"
Journal of Experimental Social Psychology, Vol. 11 (March 1975), pp.
180-91.

Greenwald, Anthony G.
"Consequences of Prejudice Against the Null Hypothesis"
Psychological Bulletin, Vol. 82 (January 1975), pp. 1-19.

Labovitz, Sanford
"Criteria for Selecting a Significance Level: A Note on the
Sacredness of 0.05"
American Sociologist, Vol. 3 (August 1968), pp. 220-2.

Lykken, David T.
"Statistical Significance in Psychological Research"
Psychological Bulletin, Vol. 70 (September 1968), pp. 151-9.

McGuire, William J.
"The Yin and Yang of Progress in Social Psychology: Seven Koan"
Journal of Personality and Social Psychology, Vol. 26 (June 1973),
pp. 446-56.

Meyer, Donald L.
"Statistical Tests and Surveys of Power: A Critique"
American Educational Research Journal, Vol. 11 (Spring 1974), pp.
179-88.

Morrison, Denton E. and Henkel, Ramon E.
"Significance Tests Reconsidered"
American Sociologist, Vol. 4 (May 1969), pp. 131-9.

Myers, B. L. and Melcher, A. J.
    "On the Choice of Risk Levels in Managerial Decision Making"
    Management Science, Vol. 16 (October 1969), pp. B31-9.

Rosekrans, Frank M.
    "Statistical Significance and Reporting Test Results"
    Journal of Marketing Research, Vol. VI (November 1969), pp. 451-5.

Rosenthal, Robert
    "The 'File Drawer Problem' and Tolerance for Null Results"
    Psychological Bulletin, Vol. 86 (March 1979), pp. 638-41.

Rosenthal, Robert and Gaito, John
    "The Interpretation of Levels of Significance by Psychological
    Researchers"
    Journal of Psychology, Vol. 55 (1963), pp. 33-8.

Sawyer, Alan G. and Peter, J. Paul
    "The Significance of Statistical Significance Tests in Marketing
    Research"
    Journal of Marketing Research, Vol. XX (May 1983), pp. 122-33.

Selvin, Hanan C.
    "A Critique of Tests of Significance in Survey Research"
    American Sociological Review, Vol. 22 (October 1957), pp. 519-27.

Shiffler, Ronald E. and Harwood, Gordon B.
    "An Empirical Assessment of Realized Alpha-Risk When Testing
    Hypotheses"
    Educational and Psychological Measurement, Vol. 45 (Winter 1985), pp.
    811-23.

Walster, G. William and Cleary, T. Anne
    "Statistical Significance as a Decision Rule"
    in Borgatta, Edgar F. and Bohrnstedt, George W. (editors)
    Sociological Methodology
    (San Francisco: Jossey-Bass, 1970), pp. 246-54.

Winch, Robert F. and Campbell, Donald T.
    "Proof? No. Evidence? Yes. The Significance of Tests of Significance"
    American Sociologist, Vol. 4 (May 1969), pp. 140-3.

Zeisel, Hans
    "The Significance of Insignificant Differences"
    Public Opinion Quarterly, Vol. 17 (Fall 1955), pp. 319-21.

141.12 ---------- Combining Results of Independent Studies

        See also (sub)heading(s) 214.

Cooper, Harris M.
    "Statistically Combining Independent Studies: A Meta-Analysis of Sex
    Differences in Conformity Research"
    Journal of Personality and Social Psychology, Vol. 37 (1979), pp.
    131-46.

Dutka, Solomon
    "Combining Tests of Significance in Test Marketing Research
    Experiments"
    Journal of Marketing Research, Vol. XXI (February 1984), pp. 118,9.

Rosenthal, Robert
    "Combining Results of Independent Studies"
    Psychological Bulletin, Vol. 85 (December 1978), pp. 185-93.

Wallis, W. A.
    "Compounding Probabilities From Independent Significant Tests"
    Econometrica, Vol. 10 (1942), pp. 229-48.

141.13 ---------- Applications of Multivariate Tests of Mean Diff

Ahtola, Olli T.
    "The Vector Model of Preferences: An Alternative to the Fishbein
    Model"
    Journal of Marketing Research, Vol. XII (February 1975), pp. 52-9.

Bourgeois, Jacques C. and Barnes, James G.
    "Viability and Profile of the Consumerist Segment"
    Journal of Consumer Research, Vol. 5 (March 1979), pp. 217-28.

Burns, Alvin C. and Granbois, Donald H.
    "Factors Moderating the Resolution of Preference Conflict in Family
    Automobile Purchasing"
    Journal of Marketing Research, Vol. XIV (February 1977), pp. 77-86.

Etzel, Michael J. and Walker, Bruce J.
    "Advertising Strategy for Foreign Products"
    Journal of Advertising Research, Vol. 14 (June 1974), pp. 41-4.

Humphreys, Marie Adele and Kasulis, Jack J.
"Attorney Advertising"
Journal of Advertising Research, Vol. 21 (October 1981), pp. 31-7.

Lambert, Zarrel V.
"Perceptual Patterns, Information Handling, and Innovativeness"
Journal of Marketing Research, Vol. IX (November 1972), pp. 427-31.

Lambert, Zarrel V.
"Price and Choice Behavior"
Journal of Marketing Research, Vol. IX (February 1972), pp. 35-40.

Landon, E. Laird, Jr.
"Order Bias, the Ideal Rating, and the Semantic Differential"
Journal of Marketing Research, Vol. VIII (August 1971), pp. 375-8.

Robertson, Dan H. and Hackett, Donald W.
"Saleswomen: Perceptions, Problems and Prospects"
Journal of Marketing, Vol. 41 (July 1977), pp. 66-71.

Tucker, Lewis R., Jr., Dolich, Ira J., and Wilson, David
"Profiling Environmentally Responsible Consumer-Citizens"
Journal of the Academy of Marketing Science, Vol. 9 (Fall 1981), pp.
454-78.

141.14 ---------- Unclassified (Hypothesis Testing)

Barnett, H. A. R.
"The Variance of the Product of Two Independent Variables and Its
Application to an Investigation on Sample Data"
Journal of Institute Actuaries, Vol. 81 (February 1955), p. 190.

Cohen, Arthur
"Estimates of Linear Combinations of the Parameters in the Mean
Vector of a Multivariate Normal Distribution"
Annals of Mathematical Statistics, Vol. 36 (1965), pp. 78-87.

Goodman, Leo A.
"The Variance of the Product of K Random Variables"
Journal of the American Statistical Association, Vol. 57 (March
1962), pp. 54-60.

Goodman, Leo A.
"Modifications of the Dorn-Stauffer-Tibbits Method for Testing the
Significance of Comparisons on Sociological Data"
American Journal of Sociology, Vol. 66 (1961), pp. 355-63.

Goodman, Leo A.
"On the Exact Variance of Products"
Journal of the American Statistical Association, Vol. 55 (December
1960), pp. 708-13.

Mullet, Gary M. and Karson, Marvin J.
"Analysis of Purchase Intent Scales Weighted by Probability of Actual
Purchase"
Journal of Marketing Research, Vol. XXII (February 1985), pp. 93-6.

Shellard, G. D.
"Estimating the Product of Several Random Variables"
Journal of the American Statistical Association, Vol. 47 (June 1952),
pp. 216-21.

142 ------   SPECIFIC SAMPLING OR OTHER PROBABILITY DISTRIBUTIONS   ------
          See also (sub)heading(s) 107.

142.01 ---------- Books Re: Distributions

Aitchison, J. and Brown, J. A. C.
    The Lognormal Distribution: With Special Reference to Its Use in
    Economics
    (Cambridge, England: Cambridge University Press, 1957).

Benepe, O. J.
    The Sensitivity of t and F to Departures From Normality
    University of Washington (1949), Master's thesis.

Bownam, K. O. and Shenton, L. R.
    Properties of Estimators for the Gamma Distribution
    (New York: Marcel Dekker, Inc., 1987), 288 pp.

Crow, Edwin L. and Shimizu, Kunio (editors)
    Lognormal Distributions
    (New York: Marcel Dekker, Inc., 1988), 408 pp.

Hastings, N. A. J. and Peacock, J. B.
    Statistical Distributions
    (New York: John Wiley and Sons, Inc., 1974).

Johnson, Norman L. and Kotz, Samuel
    Continuous Univariate Distributions--I
    (New York: John Wiley and Sons, Inc., 1970).

Mainland, D., Hetrera, L., and Sutcliff, M.
    Statistical Tables for Use With Binomial Samples--Contingency Tests,
    Confidence Limits and Sample Size Estimates
    (New York: Department of Medical Statistics, New York University
    College of Medicine, 1956).

Rothschild, V. and Logothetis, N.
    Probability Distributions
    (New York: John Wiley and Sons, Inc., 1986), 79 pp.

Schneider, Helmut
    Truncated and Censored Samples From Normal Populations
    (New York: Marcel Dekker, Inc., 1986), 288 pp.

U.S. National Center for Health Statistics
    Distribution and Properties of Variance Estimators for Complex
    Multistage Probability Samples: An Empirical Distribution
    Vital and Health Statistics, Series 2, No. 65
    (Rochville, MD: Health Resources Administration, March 1975), 46 pp.

142.02 ---------- Articles, etc. Re: Distributions

Anscombe, F. J.
    "Sampling Theory of the Negative Binomial and Logarithmic
    Distributions"
    Biometrika, Vol. 37 (December 1950), pp. 358-82.

Bartlett, M. S.
    "A Note on Multiplying Factors for Various Chi-Squared Approximations"
    Journal of the Royal Statistical Society, Series B, Vol. 16 (1954),
    pp. 296-8.

Bearden, W. O., Sharma, S., and Teel, J. E.
    "Sample Size Effects on Chi Square and Other Statistics Used in
    Evaluating Causal Models"
    Journal of Marketing Research, Vol. XIX (November 1982), pp. 425-30.

Buchanan, Bruce and Morrison, Donald G.
    "Sampling Properties of Rate Questions With Implications for Survey
    Research"
    Marketing Science, Vol. 6 (Summer 1987), pp. 286-98.

Chu, J. T.
    "Errors in Normal Approximations to the T, Tau, and Similar Types of
    Distributions"
    Annals of Mathematical Statistics, Vol. 27 (1956), pp. 780-9.

Cochran, W. G.
    "Approximate Significance Levels of the Behrens-Fisher Test"
    Biometrics, Vol. 20 (1964), p. 191.

Diehr, G. and Hoflin, D. R.
    "Approximating the Distribution of the Sample R-Square in Best Subset
    Regression"
    Technometrics, Vol. 16 (1974), pp. 317-20.

Dunnett, C. W.
    "New Tables for Multiple Comparisons With a Control"
    Biometrics, Vol. 20 (September 1964), pp. 482-91.

Feir-Walsh, Betty J. and Toothaker, Larry E.
"An Empirical Comparison of the ANOVA F-Test, Normal Scores Test and Kruskal-Wallis Test Under Violations of Assumptions"
Educational and Psychological Measurement, Vol. 34 (Winter 1974), pp. 789-99.

Feldt, Leonard S.
"The Approximate Sampling Distribution of Kuder-Richardson Reliability Coefficient Twenty"
Psychometrika, Vol. 30 (September 1965), pp. 357-70.

Fisher, Ronald A.
"The Negative Binomial Distribution"
Annals of Eugenics, Vol. 7, Part II (1941), pp. 182-7.

Freeman, G. H. and Halton, J. H.
"Exact Probabilities for K x L Tables"
Biometrika, Vol. 38 (June 1951), pp. 141-9.

Griffiths, D. A.
"Maximum Likelihood Estimation for the Beta-Binomial Distribution and an Application to the Household Distribution of the Total Number of Cases of a Disease"
Biometrics, Vol. 29, No. 4 (1973), pp. 637-48.

Harter, H. Leon
"Tables of Range and Studentized Range"
The Annals of Mathematical Statistics, Vol. 31 (1960), p. 1123.

Heck, D. L.
"Charts of Some Upper Percentage Points of the Distribution of the Largest Characteristic Root"
Annals of Mathematical Statistics, Vol. 31 (September 1960), pp. 625-42.

Hoaglin, David C.
"Direct Approximations for Chi Squared Percentage Points"
Journal of the American Statistical Association, Vol. 72 (1977), pp. 508-15.

Holloway, L. N. and Dunn, O. J.
"The Robustness of Hotelling's T-Square"
Journal of the American Statistical Association, Vol. 62 (1967), pp. 124-36.

Hopkins, J. W. and Clay, P. P. F.
"Some Empirical Distributions of the Bivariate T-Square and Homoscedasticity Criterion M Under Unequal Variance and Leptokurtosis"
Journal of the American Statistical Association, Vol. 58 (1963), pp. 1048-53.

Ito, K. and Schull, N. J.
"On the Robustness of the T-Square Test in Multivariate Analysis of Variance When Variance-Covariance Matrices are Not Equal"
Biometrika, Vol. 51 (1964), pp. 71-82.

Mardia, K. V.
"Assessment of the Multinormality and the Robustness of Hotelling's T-Square Test"
Applied Statistics, Vol. 24 (1975), pp. 163-71.

McNemar, Quinn
"Note on the Sampling Error of the Difference Between Correlated Proportions or Percentages"
Psychometrica, Vol. 12 (June 1947), pp. 153-7.

Miller, John K.
"The Sampling Distribution and a Test for the Significance of the Bimultivariate Redundancy Statistic: A Monte Carlo Study"
Multivariate Behavioral Research, Vol. 6 (April 1975), pp. 233-44.

Patnaik, P. B.
"The Non-Central Chi-Square and F Distributions and Their Applications"
Biometrika, Vol. 37 (June 1949), pp. 202-32.

Peizer, David B. and Pratt, John W.
"A Normal Approximation for Binomial, F, Beta, and Other Common Related Tail Probabilities, I"
Journal of the American Statistical Association, Vol. 63 (1968), pp. 1416-56.

Steiger, James H., Shapiro, A., and Browne, M. W.
"On the Multivariate Asymptotic Distribution of Sequential Chi-Square Statistics"
Psychometrika, Vol. 50 (September 1985), pp. 253-63.

Swed, Freda S. and Eisenhart, C.
    "Tables for Testing Randomness of Grouping in a Sequence of
    Alternatives"
    Annals of Mathematical Statistics, Vol. 14 (March 1943), pp. 66-87.

Wallace, David L.
    "Bounds on Normal Approximations to Student's T and the Chi-Square
    Distributions"
    Annals of Mathematical Statistics, Vol. 30 (1959), pp. 1121-30.

Wilson, Edwin B. and Hilferty, Margaret M.
    "The Distribution of Chi-Square"
    Proceedings of the National Academy of Sciences, Vol. 17 (1931), pp.
    684-8.

Yao, Y.
    "An Approximate Degrees of Freedom Solution to the Multivariate
    Behrens-Fisher Problem"
    Biometrika, Vol. 52 (1965), p. 139.

143 ---------------- STATISTICAL POWER AND EFFECT SIZE ----------------

143.01 ---------- Books Re: Statistical Power and Effect Size

Cohen, Jacob
    Statistical Power Analysis for the Behavioral Sciences
    (New York: Academic Press, 1977).

Kraemer, Helena Chmura and Thiemann, Sue
    How Many Subjects? Statistical Power Analysis in Research
    (Beverly Hills, CA: Sage Publications, Inc., 1987), 120 pp.

Lipsey, Mark W.
    Design Sensitivity
    (Newbury Park, CA: Sage Publications, 1989), 224 pp.

143.02 ---------- Theory Re: Statistical Power and Effect Size

Barcikowski, Robert S.
    "Statistical Power With Group Means as the Unit of Analysis"
    Journal of Educational Statistics, Vol. 6 (1981), pp. 267-85.

Blattberg, Robert C. and Sen, Subrata K.
    "An Evaluation of the Application of Minimum Chi-Square Procedures to
    Stochastic Models of Brand Choice"
    Journal of Marketing Research, Vol. X (November 1973), pp. 421-7.

Boruch, Robert F. and Gomez, Hernando
    "Sensitivity, Bias, and Theory in Impact Evaluations"
    Professional Psychology (November 1977), pp. 411-34.

Cleary, T. Anne, Linn, Robert, and Walster, G. William
    "Effect of Reliability and Validity on Power of Statistical Tests"
    in Borgatta, Edgar F. and Bohrnstedt, George W. (editors)
    Sociology Methodology
    (San Francisco: Jossey-Bass, 1970), pp. 130-8.

Cohen, Jacob
    "Statistical Power Analysis and Research Results"
    American Educational Research Journal, Vol. 10 (Summer 1973), pp.
    225-9.

Cohen, Jacob
    "Some Statistical Issues in Psychological Research"
    in Wolman, B. B. (editor)
    Handbook of Clinical Psychology
    (New York: McGraw-Hill Book Company, 1965), pp. 95-121.

Cohen, Louis
    "Use of Paired-Comparison Analysis to Increase Statistical Power of
    Ranked Data"
    Journal of Marketing Research, Vol. IV (August 1967), pp. 309-11.

Cook, Thomas D., Gruder, Charles R., Hennigan, Karen M., and Flay,
    Brian R.
    "History of the Sleeper Effect: Some Logical Pitfalls in Accepting
    the Null Hypothesis"
    Psychological Bulletin, Vol. 86 (1978), pp. 662-79.

Cooper, Harris M.
    "On the Significance of Effects and the Effects of Significance"
    Journal of Personality and Social Psychology, Vol. 41 (1981), pp.
    1013-8.

Friedman, Herbert
    "Magnitude of Experimental Effect and a Table for Its Rapid
    Estimation"
    Psychological Bulletin, Vol. 70 (October 1968), pp. 245-51.

Glass, Gene V.
    "Summarizing Effect Sizes"
    New Directions for Methodology of Social and Behavioral Science, Vol.
    5 (1980), pp. 13-31.

Glass, Gene V. and Hakstian, A. Ralph
    "Measures of Association in Comparative Experiments: Their
    Development and Interpretation"
    American Educational Research Journal, Vol. 6 (May 1969), pp. 403-14.

Greenwald, Anthony G.
    "Consequences of Prejudice Against the Null Hypothesis"
    Psychological Bulletin, Vol. 82 (January 1975), pp. 1-19.

Latour, Stephen A.
    "Variance Explained: It Measures Neither Importance Nor Effect Size"
    Decision Sciences, Vol. 12 (January 1981), pp. 150-60.

Latour, Stephen A.
    "Effect Size Estimation: A Commentary on Wolf and Bassler"
    Decision Sciences, Vol. 12 (January 1981), pp. 136-41.

Lehmann, E. L.
  "Significance Level and Power"
  Annals of Mathematical Statistics, Vol. 29 (1958), pp. 1167-76.

Meyer, Donald L.
  "Statistical Tests and Surveys of Power: A Critique"
  American Educational Research Journal, Vol. 11 (Spring 1974), pp.
  179-88.

Overall, John E. and Dalal, Sudhin N.
  "Design of Experiments to Maximize Power Relative to Cost"
  Psychological Bulletin, Vol. 64 (November 1965), pp. 339-50.

Raudenbush, Stephen W., Becker, Betsy J., and Kalaian, Hripsime
  "Modeling Multivariate Effect Sizes"
  Psychological Bulletin, Vol. 103 (January 1988), pp. 111-20.

Rosenthal, Robert and Rubin, Donald B.
  "Comparing Effect Sizes of Independent Studies"
  Psychological Bulletin, Vol. 92 (September 1982), pp. 500-4.

Sawyer, Alan G. and Ball, A. Dwayne
  "Statistical Power and Effect Size in Marketing Research"
  Journal of Marketing Research, Vol. XVIII (August 1981), pp. 275-90.

Sechrest, Lee and Yeaton, William H.
  "Empirical Bases for Estimating Effect Size"
  in Boruch, R. F., Wortman, P. M., and Cordray, D. S. (editors)
  Reanalyzing Program Evaluation: Policies and Practices for Secondary
  Analysis of Social and Educational Programs
  (San Francisco: Jossey-Bass, 1981).

Sechrest, Lee and Yeaton, William H.
  "Estimating Magnitudes of Experimental Effects"
  Institute for Social Research, University of Michigan (1981).

Srinivasan, Y.
  "A Theoretical Comparison of the Predictive Power of the Multiple
  Regression and Equal Weighting Procedures"
  Research Paper No. 347
  Stanford University (February 1977).

Stevens, James P.
  "Power of the Multivariate Analysis of Variance Tests"
  Psychological Bulletin, Vol. 88 (November 1980), pp. 728-37.

Sutcliffe, J. P.
  "On the Relationship of Reliability to Statistical Power"
  Psychological Bulletin, Vol. 88 (September 1980), pp. 509-15.

Tversky, Amos and Kahneman, Daniel
  "Belief in the Law of Small Numbers"
  Psychological Bulletin, Vol. 76 (August 1971), pp. 105-10.

Vaughan, Graham M. and Corballis, Michael C.
  "Beyond Tests of Significance: Estimating Strengths of Effects in
  Selected ANOVA Designs"
  Psychological Bulletin, Vol. 72 (1969), pp. 204-13.

Wilcox, Rand R.
  "A Review of Exact Hypothesis Testing Procedures (and Selection
  Techniques) That Control Power Regardless of the Variances"
  British Journal of Mathematical and Statistical Psychology, Vol. 37
  (May 1984), pp. 34-48.

143.03 ---------- Measures of Effect Size

Hedges, Larry V.
  "Estimation of Effect Size for a Series of Independent Variables"
  Psychological Bulletin, Vol. 92 (March 1962), pp. 490-9.

Keren, Gideon and Lewis, Charles
  "Partial Omega Squared for ANOVA Designs"
  Educational and Psychological Measurement, Vol. 39 (Spring 1979), pp.
  119-28.

LaTour, Stephen A.
  "Variance Explained: It Measures Neither Importance Nor Effect Size"
  Decision Sciences, Vol. 12 (January 1982), pp. 150-60.

O'Grady, Kevin E.
  "Measures of Explained Variance: Cautions and Limitations"
  Psychological Bulletin, Vol. 92 (November 1982), pp. 766-77.

Rosenthal, Robert
  "Combining Results of Independent Studies"
  Psychological Bulletin, Vol. 85 (December 1978), pp. 185-93.

Rosenthal, Robert and Rubin, Donald B.
  "A Simple, General Purpose Display of Magnitude of Experimental
  Effect"
  Journal of Educational Psychology, Vol. 72, No. 2 (1982), pp. 166-9.

Sawyer, Alan G. and Page, Thomas J., Jr.
  "Incremental Goodness of Fit Indices in Structural Equation Models in
  Marketing Research"
  AMA Special Conference on Causal Modeling, Sarasota, FL (1983), paper
  presentation.

Sechrest, Lee and Yeaton, William
  "Empirical Bases for Estimating Effect Size"
  in Boruch, R. F., Wortman, P. M., and Cordray, D. S. (editors)
  Reanalyzing Program Evaluations: Policies and Practices
  (Ann Arbor, MI: University of Michigan Institute for Social Research,
  1981).

Sechrest, Lee and Yeaton, William
  "Estimating Magnitudes of Experimental Effects"
  University of Michigan Institute for Social Research (1981),
  unpublished manuscript.

143.04 ---------- Reviews of the Use of Statistical Power, Effect Size

Brewer, James K.
  "On the Power of Statistical Tests in the American Educational
  Research Journal"
  American Educational Research Journal, Vol. 9 (Summer 1972), pp.
  391-401.

Chase, Lawrence J. and Baran, Stanley J.
  "An Assessment of Quantitative Research in Mass Communication"
  Journalism Quarterly, Vol. 53 (Summer 1976), pp. 308-11.

Chase, Lawrence J. and Chase, Richard B.
  "A Statistical Power Analysis of Applied Psychological Research"
  Journal of Applied Psychology, Vol. 61(April 1976), pp. 234-7.

Chase, Lawrence J. and Tucker, Raymond K.
  "A Power-Analytic Examination of Contemporary Communication Research"
  Speech Monographs, Vol. 42 (March 1975), pp. 29-41.

Cohen, Jacob
  "The Statistical Power of Abnormal-Social Psychological Research: A
  Review"
  Journal of Abnormal and Social Psychology, Vol. 65 (1962), pp. 145-53.

Katzer, Jeffrey and Sodt, James
  "An Analysis of the Use of Statistical Theory in Communication
  Research"
  Journal of Communications, Vol. 23 (September 1973), pp. 251-65.

Kroll, Richard M. and Chase, Lawrence J.
  "Communication Disorders: A Power Analytic Assessment of Recent
  Research"
  Journal of Communication Disorders, Vol. 8 (1975), pp. 237-47.

Peterson, Robert A., Albaum, Gerald, and Beltramini, Richard F.
  "A Meta-Analysis of Effect Sizes in Consumer Behavior Experiments"
  Journal of Consumer Research, Vol. 12 (June 1985), pp. 97-103.

Sawyer, Alan G. and Ball, A. Dwayne
  "Statistical Power and Effect Size in Marketing Research"
  Journal of Marketing Research, Vol. XVIII (August 1981), pp. 275-90.

Sawyer, Alan G. and Ball, A. Dwayne
  "Statistical Power in Market Measurement and Analysis Research"
  in Leone, Robert (editor)
  Market Measurement and Analysis, Volume II
  (Austin, TX: The Institute for Management Sciences, 1980), pp. 147-67.

Sawyer, Alan G. and Peter, J. Paul
  "The Significance of Statistical Significance Tests in Marketing
  Research"
  Journal of Marketing Research, Vol. XX (May 1983), pp. 122-33.

143.05 ---------- Computer Programs for Calculating Statistical Power

Milligan, Glenn W.
  "A Computer Program for Calculating Power of the Chi-Square Test"
  Educational and Psychological Measurement, Vol. 39 (October 1979),
  pp. 681-4.

Woodward, J. A. and Overall, John E.
  "A Computer Program for Calculating Power of the F-Test"
  Educational and Psychological Measurement, Vol. 36 (Spring 1976), pp.
  165-8.

144 ------------------ POPULATION SELECTION PROCEDURES -----------------

144.01 ---------- Books Re: Population Selection Procedures

Gibbons, Jean Dickinson, Olkin, Ingram, and Sobol, Milton
    Selecting and Ordering Populations: A New Statistical Methodology
    (New York: John Wiley and Sons, Inc., 1977).

144.02 ---------- Theory Re: Population Selection Procedures

Bechhofer, R. E.
    "A Single-Sample Multiple Decision Procedure for Ranking Means of
    Normal Populations With Known Variances"
    Annals of Mathematical Statistics, Vol. 25 (March 1954), pp. 16-39.

Bechhofer, R. E., Dunnett, C. W., and Sobol, M.
    "A Two-Sample Multiple Procedure for Ranking Means of Normal
    Populations With a Common Unknown Variance"
    Biometrika, Vol. 41 (June 1954), pp. 170-6.

Gibbons, Jean Dickinson and Gur-Arie, Oded
    "Selection Procedures: A New Statistical Methodology and Its
    Applications for Marketing Research"
    Journal of Marketing Research, Vol. XVIII (November 1981), pp. 449-55.

144.03 ---------- Theory Re: Population Subset Selection Procedures

Gupta, S. S.
    "On a Decision Rule for a Problem in Ranking Means"
    Institute of Statistics, University of North Carolina (1956),
    unpublished Ph.D. thesis.

144.04 ---------- Applications of Population Selection Procedures

Becker, W. A.
    "Changes in Performance of Entries in Random Sample Tests"
    Poultry Science, Vol. 43 (May 1964), pp. 716-22.

Becker, W. A.
    "Ranking All-or-None Traits in Random Sample Tests"
    Poultry Science, Vol. 41 (September 1962), pp. 1437,8.

Becker, W. A.
    "Comparing Entries in Random Sample Tests"
    Poultry Science, Vol. 40 (November 1961), pp. 1507-14.

Chew, Victor
    Comparisions Among Treatment Means in an Analysis of Variance
    (Washington, DC: U.S. Government Printing Office, 1977), pp. 228-58.

Dalal, S. R. and Srinivasan, V.
    "Determining Sample Size for Pretesting Comparative Effectiveness of
    Advertising Copies"
    Management Science, Vol. 23 (August 1977), pp. 1284-94.

Kleijnen, J. P. C., Naylor, T. H., and Seaks, T. G.
    "The Use of Multiple Ranking Procedures to Analyze Simulations of
    Management Systems: A Tutorial"
    Management Science, Applications Series, Vol. 18 (February 1972), pp.
    B245-57.

Mamrak, Sandra A. and Amer, P. D.
    Computer Science and Technology: A Methodology for the Selection of
    Interactive Computer Services
    National Bureau of Standards Special Publication 500-44
    (Washington, DC: U.S. Government Printing Office, 1979).

Naylor, T. H., Wertz, K., and Wonnacott, T. H.
    "Some Methods for Evaluating the Effects of Economic Policies Using
    Simulation Experiments"
    Review of the International Statistical Institute, Vol. 36 (1968),
    pp. 184-200.

Naylor, T. H., Wertz, K., and Wonnacott, T. H.
    "Methods for Analyzing Data From Computer Simulations"
    Communications of the ACM, Vol. 10 (November 1967), pp. 703-10.

Soller, M. and Putter, J.
    "Probability of Correct Selection of Sires Having Highest
    Transmitting Ability"
    Journal of Dairy Science, Vol. 48 (June 1965), pp. 747,8.

Soller, M. and Putter, J.
    "On the Probability That the Best Chicken Stock Will Come Out Best in
    a Single Random Sample Test"
    Poultry Science, Vol. 43 (November 1964), pp. 1425-7.

145 ------- ALTERNATIVE MEASURES OF CORRELATION OR ASSOCIATION -------
    See also (sub)heading(s) 56, 137, 149.

145.01 ---------- Theory Re: Measures of Correlation or Association

Babakus, Emin and Ferguson, Carl E., Jr.
    "On Choosing the Appropriate Measure of Association When Analyzing
    Rating Scale Data"
    Journal of the Academy of Marketing Science, Vol. 16 (Spring 1988),
    pp. 95-102.

Bartko, John J.
    "On Various Intraclass Correlation Reliability Coefficients"
    Psychological Bulletin, Vol. 83, No. 5 (1976), pp. 762-5.

Carroll, John B.
    "The Nature of the Data, Or How to Choose a Correlation Coefficient"
    Psychometrika, Vol. 26 (December 1961), pp. 347-72.

Costner, Herbert L.
    "Criteria for Measures of Association"
    American Sociological Review, Vol. 30 (1965), pp. 341-53.

Grether, David M.
    "Correlations With Ordinal Data"
    Journal of Econometrics, Vol. 2 (1974), pp. 241-6.

Janson, S. and Vegelius, J.
    "Correlation Coefficients for More Than One Scale Type"
    Multivariate Behavioral Research, Vol. 17 (1982), pp. 274-84.

Kruskal, William H.
    "Ordinal Measures of Association"
    Journal of the American Statistical Association (1958), pp. 814-61.

Olsson, Ulf
    "Measuring Correlation in Ordered Two-Way Contingency Tables"
    Journal of Marketing Research, Vol. XVII (August 1980), pp. 391-4.

Ploch, D. H.
    "Ordinal Measures of Association and the General Linear Model"
    in Blalock, Hubert M., Jr. (editor)
    Measurement in the Social Sciences
    (Chicago: Aldine, 1974), pp. 343-68.

Wainer, Howard and Thissen, David
    "Three Steps Towards Robust Regression"
    Psychometrika, Vol. 41 (1976), pp. 9-34.

146 --------------- THEORY RE: NONPARAMETRIC STATISTICS --------------
146.01 ---------- Books Re: Nonparametric Statistics

Conover, W. J.
  Practical Nonparametric Statistics, Second Edition
  (New York: John Wiley and Sons, Inc., 1980).

Fraser, D. A. S.
  Nonparametric Methods in Statistics
  (New York: John Wiley and Sons, Inc., 1957).

Gibbons, Jean Dickinson
  Nonparametric Statistical Inference, Second Edition
  (New York: Marcel Dekker, Inc., 1985), 408 pp.

Gibbons, J. D.
  Nonparametric Methods for Quantitative Analysis
  (New York: Holt, Rinehart and Winston, 1976).

Gibbons, Jean Dickinson
  Nonparametric Statistical Inference
  (New York: McGraw-Hill Book Company, 1971).

Hettmansperger, Thomas P.
  Statistical Inference Based on Ranks
  (New York: John Wiley and Sons, Inc., 1984), 323 pp.

Hildebrand, David K., Laing, James D., and Rosenthal, Howard
  Analysis of Ordinal Data
  (Beverly Hills, CA: Sage Publications, Inc., 1977).

Hollander, M. and Wolfe, D. A.
  Nonparametric Statistical Methods
  (New York: John Wiley and Sons, Inc., 1973).

Kendall, M. G.
  Rank Correlation Methods
  (New York: Hafner Publishing Company, 1962).

Marascuilo, Leonard A. and McSweeney, Maryellen
  Nonparametric and Distribution-Free Methods for the Social Sciences
  (Belmont, CA: Wadsworth, 1977).

Noether, Gottfried E.
  Elements of Nonparametric Statistics
  (New York: John Wiley and Sons, Inc., 1967).

Puri, Maden Lal and Sen, Pranab Kumar
  Nonparametric Methods in Multivariate Analysis
  (New York: John Wiley and Sons, 1971).

Randles, Ronald H. and Wolfe, Douglas A.
  Introduction to the Theory of Nonparametric Statistics
  (New York: John Wiley and Sons, Inc., 1979), 450 pp.

Reynolds, H. T.
  Analysis of Nominal Data
  (Beverly Hills, CA: Sage Publications, Inc., 1977).

Siegel, Sidney
  Nonparametric Statistics for the Behavioral Sciences
  (New York: McGraw-Hill, 1956).

Tate, M. W. and Clelland, R. C.
  Nonparametric and Shortcut Statistics
  (Danville, IL: Interstate Printers and Publishers, Inc., 1957).

146.02 ---------- Theory Re: Kendall's Tau Beta Ordinal Correlation

Kendall, Maurice G.
  "A New Measure of Rank Correlation"
  Biometrika, Vol. 30 (June 1938), pp. 81-93.

Moran, P. A. P.
  "Partial and Multiple Rank Correlation"
  Biometrika, Vol. 38 (June 1951), pp. 26-32.

Wilson, T. P.
  "A Proportional-Reduction-in-Error Interpretation for Kendall's Tau-B"
  Social Forces, Vol. 47 (1969), pp. 340-2.

146.03 ---------- Theory Re: Kolmogorov-Smirnov Goodness of Fit Test

Kiefer, J.
  "K-Sample Analogues of the Kolmogorov-Smirnov and Cramer-V. Mises
  Tests"
  Annals of Mathematical Statistics, Vol. 30 (June 1959), pp. 420-47.

Lilliefores, Hubert W.
    "On the Kolmogorov-Smirnov Test for Normality With Mean and Variance
    Unknown"
    Journal of the American Statistical Association, Vol. 62 (June 1967),
    pp. 399-402.

Massey, Frank J., Jr.
    "The Kolmogorov-Smirnov Test for Goodness of Fit"
    Journal of the American Statistical Association, Vol. 46 (March
    1951), pp. 68-78.

Morris, John
    "Nonparametric Measures of Randomness and Goodness of Fit:
    Kolmogorov-Smirnov and Runs Tests"
    Technical Report No. 41.02
    (East Lansing, MI: Computer Institute for Social Science Research,
    Michigan State University, 1966).

146.04 ---------- Theory Re: Nonparametric Analysis of Variance

        See also (sub)heading(s) 179.

Bradley, R. A. and Terry, M. E.
    "Rank Analysis of Incomplete Block Designs: 1. The Method of Paired
    Comparisons"
    Biometrika, Vol. 39 (1952), pp. 324-45.

Gabriel, K. R. and Lachenbruch, P. A.
    "Nonparametric ANOVA in Small Samples: A Monte Carlo Study of the
    Asymptotic Approximation"
    Biometrics, Vol. 25 (September 1969), pp. 593-6.

Kruskal, William H. and Wallis, W. A.
    "Use of Ranks on One Criterion Variance Analysis"
    Journal of the American Statistical Association, Vol. 47 (December
    1952), pp. 583-621; Addendum, (1953), pp. 907-11.

Wilson, Kellog V.
    "A Distribution-Free Test of Analysis of Variance Hypotheses"
    Psychological Bulletin, Vol. 53 (January 1956), pp. 96-101.

146.05 ---------- Theory Re: Hoeffding's U-Statistic

Hoeffding, Wassily
    "A Class of Statistics With Asymptotically Normal Distribution"
    Annals of Mathematical Statistics, Vol. 19 (1948), pp. 293-325.

Lehmann, E. L.
    "Consistency and Unbiasedness of Certain Nonparametric Tests"
    Annals of Mathematical Statistics, Vol. 22 (1951), pp. 165-79.

146.06 ---------- Theory Re: Mann-Whitney U Test

Adams, David R.
    "Nonparametric Statistical Tests in Business Education Survey
    Research--The Mann-Whitney U Test"
    Delta Pi Epsilon Journal, Vol. 19 (October 1976), pp. 1-10.

Uleman, J. S.
    "The Mann-Whitney U-Test With Small Samples and Many Ties"
    Psychological Bulletin (1969).

146.07 ---------- Theory Re: Dixon-Mood Sign Test

Dixon, W. J. and Mood, A. M.
    "The Statistical Sign Test"
    Journal of the American Statistical Association, Vol. 41 (1946), pp.
    557-66.

146.08 ---------- Theory Re: Runs Tests

Morris, John
    "Nonparametric Measures of Randomness and Goodness of Fit:
    Kolmogorov-Smirnov and Runs Tests"
    Technical Report No. 41.02
    (East Lansing, MI: Computer Institute for Social Science Research,
    Michigan State University, 1966).

146.09 ---------- Theory Re: Wilcoxon Matched-Pairs, Signed-Ranks Test

Klotz, Jerome H.
"The Wilcoxon, Ties, and the Computer"
Journal of the American Statistical Association, Vol. 61 (September 1966), pp. 772-87.

146.10 ---------- Theory Re: Ridit Analysis

Bross, I. D. J.
"How to Use Ridit Analysis"
Biometrics, Vol. 14 (March 1958), pp. 18-38.

Fleiss, J. L.
Statistical Methods for Rates and Proportions, Second Edition
(New York: John Wiley and Sons, Inc., 1981).

Vigderhous, Gideon
"Analysis of Ordinal and Nominal Data--An Alternative Approach"
Journal of the Market Research Society, Vol. 18 (January 1976), pp. 17-23.

146.11 ---------- Theory Re: Testing Equality of Distribution Functions

Kruskal, William H.
"A Nonparametric Test for the Several Sample Problem"
Annals of Mathematical Statistics, Vol. 23, No. 4 (1952), pp. 525-40.

Kruskal, William H. and Wallis, W. A.
"Use of Ranks on One Criterion Variance Analysis"
Journal of the American Statistical Association, Vol. 47 (December 1952), pp. 583-621; Addendum, (1953), pp. 907-11.

McSweeney, Maryellen and Penfield, Douglas
"The Normal Scores Test for the C-Sample Problem"
British Journal of Mathematical and Statistical Psychology, Vol. 22, Part 2 (November 1969), pp. 177-92.

146.12 ---------- Theory Re: Concordance Measurement

Hollander, Myles and Sethuraman, Jayaram
"Testing for Agreement Between Two Groups of Judges"
Biometrika, Vol. 65 (1978), pp. 403-11.

Lehmann, E. L.
"Consistency and Unbiasedness of Certain Nonparametric Tests"
Annals of Mathematical Statistics, Vol. 22 (1951), pp. 165-79.

Li, Loretta and Schucany, William R.
"Some Properties of a Test for Concordance of Two Groups of Rankings"
Biometrika, Vol. 62 (1975), pp. 417-23.

Palachek, Albert D. and Kerin, Roger A.
"Alternative Approaches to the Two-Group Concordance Problem in Brand Preference Rankings"
Journal of Marketing Research, Vol. XIX (August 1982), pp. 386-9.

Quade, Dana
"Average Internal Rank Correlation"
Mathematical Centre, University of Amsterdam (1972), technical report.

Quade, Dana, Doerfler, Donald L., and Flexner, William A.
"Calculation of the Variance in a Test for Concordance of Two Group Rankings"
University of North Carolina, Chapel Hill (1977), technical report.

Ryans, Adrian B.
"Evaluating Aggregated Predictions From Models of Consumer Choice Behavior"
Journal of Marketing Research, Vol. XIII (November 1976), pp. 333-8.

Ryans, Adrian B. and Srinivasan, V.
"Improved Method for Comparing Rank-Order Preferences of Two Groups of Consumers"
Journal of Marketing Research, Vol. XVI (November 1979), pp. 583-7.

Schucany, William R. and Frawley, W. H.
"A Rank Test for Two Group Concordance"
Psychometrika, Vol. 38 (1973), pp. 249-58.

146.13 ---------- Unclassified (Theory Re: Nonparametric Statistics)

Bhapkar, V. P.
"A Nonparametric Test for the Problem of Several Samples"
Annals of Mathematical Statistics, Vol. 32 (December 1961), pp.
1108-17.

Block, Jack, Levine, Louis, and McNemar, Quinn
"Testing for the Existence of Psychometric Patterns"
Journal of Abnormal Social Psychology, Vol. 46 (July 1951), pp. 356-9.

Boyle, R. P.
"Path Analysis and Ordinal Data"
American Journal of Sociology, Vol. 75 (January 1970), pp. 461-80.

Cohen, Louis
"Use of Paired-Comparison Analysis to Increase Statistical Power of
Ranked Data"
Journal of Marketing Research, Vol. IV (August 1967), pp. 309-11.

Dalenius, Tore
"The Mode--A Neglected Statistical Parameter"
Journal of the Royal Statistical Society, Series A, Vol. 128, Part 1
(1965), pp. 110-7.

Freeman, G. H. and Halton, J. H.
"Exact Probabilities for K x L Tables"
Biometrika, Vol. 38 (June 1951), pp. 141-9.

Gregoire, T. G. and Driver, B. L.
"Analysis of Ordinal Data to Detect Population Differences"
Psychological Bulletin, Vol. 101 (January 1987), pp. 159-65.

Hawkes, R. K.
"The Multivariate Analysis of Ordinal Measures"
American Journal of Sociology, Vol. 76 (March 1971), pp. 908-26.

Horrell, James F. and Lessig, V. Parker
"A Note on a Nonparametric Test of Independence Between Two Vectors"
Journal of Marketing Research, Vol. XI (February 1974), pp. 106-8.

Kendall, M. G.
"The Treatment of Ties in Ranking Problems"
Biometrika, Vol. 33 (1945), pp. 239-51.

Kim, J. O.
"Predictive Measures of Ordinal Association"
American Journal of Sociology, Vol. 76 (March 1971), pp. 891-907.

Massey, Frank J., Jr.
"The Distribution of the Maximum Deviation Between Two Sample
Cumulative Step-Functions"
Annals of Mathematical Statistics, Vol. 22 (March 1951), pp. 125-8.

Morris, John
"Nonparametric Statistics on the Computer"
Journal of Marketing Research, Vol. VI (February 1969), pp. 86-92.

Morris, John
"T-Test Probabilities"
Communications of the Association for Computing Machinery, Vol. 11
(February 1968), p. 115.

Morris, John
"Nonparametric Statistics"
Technical Report No. 40
(East Lansing, MI: Computer Institute for Social Science Research,
Michigan State University, 1967).

Ryans, Adrian B.
"Improved Method for Comparing Rank-Order Preferences of Two Groups
of Consumers"
Journal of Marketing Research, Vol. XVI (November 1979), pp. 583-7.

Savage, I. Richard
"Nonparametric Statistics"
Journal of the American Statistical Association, Vol. 52 (September
1957), pp. 331-44.

Somers, R. H.
"An Approach to the Multivariate Analysis of Ordinal Data"
American Sociological Review, Vol. 33 (December 1968), pp. 971-7.

Tashchian, Armen and Tashchian, Roobina O.
"NPPACK: A Nonparametric Computer Package"
Journal of Marketing Research, Vol. XIX (November 1982), p. 605.

Vigderhous, Gideon
  "Analysis of Ordinal and Nominal Data--An Alternative Approach"
  Journal of the Market Research Society, Vol. 18 (January 1976), pp.
  17-23.

Wilcox, James B. and Austin, Larry M.
  "A Method for Computing the Average Spearman Rank Correlation
  Coefficient From Ordinally Structured Confusion Matrices"
  Journal of Marketing Research, Vol. XVI (August 1979), pp. 426-8.

147 ------------- NONPARAMETRIC STATISTICS APPLICATIONS -------------
147.01 ---------- Applications of Spearman's Rank Order Correlation

Berey, Lewis A. and Pollay, Richard W.
"The Influencing Role of the Child in Family Decision Making"
Journal of Marketing Research, Vol. V (February 1968), pp. 70-2.

Cannon, Hugh M.
"The 'Naive' Approach to Demographic Media Selection"
Journal of Advertising Research, Vol. 24 (April/May 1984), pp. 21-5.

Gerstner, Eitan
"Do Higher Prices Signal Higher Quality?"
Journal of Marketing Research, Vol. XXII (May 1985), pp. 209-15.

Hempel, Donald J.
"Family Buying Decisions: A Cross-Cultural Perspective"
Journal of Marketing Research, Vol. XI (August 1974), pp. 295-302.

Hoyer, Wayne D. and Cobb-Walgren, Cathy J.
"Consumer Decision Making Across Product Categories: The Influence of
Task Environment"
Psychology and Marketing, Vol. 5 (Spring 1988), pp. 45-69.

Judd, L. Lynn and Vaught, Bobby C.
"Three Differential Variables and Their Relation to Retail Strategy
and Profitability"
Journal of the Academy of Marketing Science, Vol. 16 (Fall 1988), pp.
30-7.

Lichtenstein, Donald R. and Burton, Scot
"The Relationship Between Perceived and Objective Price-Quality"
Journal of Marketing Research, Vol. XXVI (November 1989), pp. 429-43.

Lundstrom, William J. and Sciglimpaglia, Donald
"Sex Role Portrayal in Advertising"
Journal of Marketing, Vol. 41 (July 1977), pp. 72-9.

Ozanne, Urban B. and Churchill, Gilbert A., Jr.
"Five Dimensions of the Industrial Adoption Process"
Journal of Marketing Research, Vol. VIII (August 1971), pp. 322-8.

Perry, Michael and Hamm, B. Curtis
"Canonical Analysis of Relations Between Socioeconomic Risk and
Personal Influence in Purchase Decisions"
Journal of Marketing Research, Vol. VI (August 1969), pp. 351-4.

Pras, Bernard and Summers, John
"Perceived Risk and Composition Models for Multiattribute Decisions"
Journal of Marketing Research, Vol. XV (August 1978), pp. 429-379.

Traylor, Mark B.
"Product Involvement and Brand Commitment"
Journal of Advertising Research, Vol. 21 (October 1981), pp. 51-6.

Zeithaml, Valarie A. and Gilly, Mary C.
"Characteristics Affecting the Acceptance of Retailing Technologies:
A Comparison of Elderly and Nonelderly Consumers"
Journal of Retailing, Vol. 63 (Spring 1987), pp. 49-68.

147.02 ---------- Applications of Kendall's Tau Beta Ordinal Correlatio

Avlonitis, George J. and Boyle, Kevin A.
"Linkages Between Sales Management Tools and Practices: Some Evidence
From British Companies"
Journal of the Academy of Marketing Science, Vol. 17 (Spring 1989),
pp. 137-45.

Bettman, James R., John, Deborah Roedder, and Scott, Carol A.
"Covariation Assessment by Consumers"
Journal of Consumer Research, Vol. 13 (December 1986), pp. 316-26.

Friedman, Hershey H., Santeramo, Michael J., and Traina, Anthony
"Correlates of Trustworthiness for Celebrities"
Journal of the Academy of Marketing Science, Vol. 6 (Fall 1978), pp.
291-9.

Gerstner, Eitan
"Do Higher Prices Signal Higher Quality?"
Journal of Marketing Research, Vol. XXII (May 1985), pp. 209-15.

Mazursky, David and Jacoby, Jacob
"Exploring the Development of Store Images"
Journal of Retailing, Vol. 62 (Summer 1986), pp. 145-165.

O'Brien, Terrence
"Stages of Consumer Decision Making"
Journal of Marketing Research, Vol. VIII (August 1971), pp. 283-9.

Pekelman, Dov and Sen, Subrata K.
"Improving Prediction in Conjoint Measurement"
Journal of Marketing Research, Vol. XVI (May 1979), pp. 211-20.

147.03 ---------- Applications of Kolmogorov-Smirnov Goodness of Fit

Bearden, William O., Sharma, Subhash, and Teel, Jesse E., Jr.
"Sample Size Effects on Chi Square and Other Statistics Used in
Evaluating Causal Models"
Journal of Marketing Research, Vol. XIX (November 1982), pp. 425-30.

Frisbie, G. A., Jr.
"Ehrenberg's Negative Binomial Model Applied to Grocery Store Trips"
Journal of Marketing Research, Vol. XVII (August 1980), pp. 385-90.

Headen, Robert S., Klompmaker, Jay E., and Teel, Jesse E., Jr.
"Predicting Audience Exposure to Spot TV Advertising Schedules"
Journal of Marketing Research, Vol. XIV (February 1977), pp. 1-9.

147.04 ---------- Applications of Kendall's W Coeff of Concordance

Derbaix, Christian M.
"Are Consumers Unique in Terms of Cognitive and Affective Reactions
Towards the Advertising Content?"
European Journal of Marketing, Vol. 15, No. 7 (1981), pp. 12-22.

Hamm, B. Curtis and Cundiff, Edward W.
"Self-Actualization and Product Perception"
Journal of Marketing Research, Vol. VI (November 1969), pp. 470-2.

Hjorth-Andersen, Chr.
"The Concept of Quality and the Efficiency of Markets for Consumer
Products"
Journal of Consumer Research, Vol. 11 (September 1984), pp. 708-18.

147.05 ---------- Applications of Friedman's ANOVA by Ranks

Jain, Arun K., Acito, Franklin, Malhotra, Naresh K., and Mahajan, Vijay
"A Comparison of the Internal Validity of Alternative Parameter
Estimation Methods in Decompositional Multiattribute Preference
Models"
Journal of Marketing Research, Vol. XVI (August 1979), pp. 313-22.

Lusch, Robert F. and Ross, Robert H.
"The Nature of Power in a Marketing Channel"
Journal of the Academy of Marketing Science, Vol. 13 (Summer 1985),
pp. 39-56.

McClure, Peter
"Analyzing Consumer Image Data Using the Friedman Two-Way Analysis of
Variance by Ranks"
Journal of Marketing Research, Vol. VIII (August 1971), pp. 370-1.

147.06 ---------- Applications of Friedman's Repeat Measure Nonpar AOV

Losciuto, Leonard A. and Perloff, Robert
"Influence of Product Preference on Dissonance Reduction"
Journal of Marketing Research, Vol. IV (August 1967), pp. 286-90.

Stanton, John L. and Tucci, Louis A.
"The Measurement of Consumption: A Comparison of Surveys and Diaries"
Journal of Marketing Research, Vol. XIX (May 1982), pp. 274-7.

147.07 ---------- Applications of Kruskal-Wallis Ordinal AOV

Ehrenberg, A. S. C.
"On Methods: The Factor Analysis Search for Program Types"
Journal of Advertising Research, Vol. 8 (January 1968), pp. 55-63.

Jacoby, Jacob, Chestnut, Robert W., and Fisher, William A.
"A Behavioral Process Approach to Information Acquisition in
Non-Durable Purchasing"
Journal of Marketing Research, Vol. XV (November 1978), pp. 532-44.

Krisch, A. C. and Banks, S.
"Program Types Defined by Factor Analysis"
Journal of Advertising Research, Vol. 2 (September 1962), pp. 29-31.

Laczniak, Gene R., Lusch, Robert F., and Murphy, Patrick E.
"Social Marketing: Its Ethical Dimensions"
Journal of Marketing, Vol. 43 (Spring 1979), pp. 29-36.

Ozanne, Urban B. and Churchill, Gilbert A., Jr.
"Five Dimensions of the Industrial Adoption Process"
Journal of Marketing Research, Vol. VIII (August 1971), pp. 322-8.

Woodruff, Robert B.
   "Brand Information Sources, Opinion Change, and Uncertainty"
   Journal of Marketing Research, Vol. IX (November 1972), pp. 414-8.

147.08 ---------- Applications of Nonparametric Analysis of Variance

Locander, William B. and Hermann, Peter W.
   "The Effect of Self-Confidence and Anxiety on Information Seeking in
   Consumer Risk Reduction"
   Journal of Marketing Research, Vol. XVI (May 1979), pp. 268-74.

Silk, Alvin J.
   "Testing the Inverse Ad Size-Selective Exposure Hypothesis:
   Clarifying Bogart"
   Journal of Marketing Research, Vol. X (May 1973), pp. 221-3.

Smith, Stewart A.
   "Factors Influencing the Relationship Between Buying Plans and Ad
   Readership"
   Journal of Marketing Research, Vol. II (February 1965), pp. 40-4.

Swan, John E.
   "Experimental Analysis of Predecision Information Seeking"
   Journal of Marketing Research, Vol. VI (May 1969), pp. 192-7.

147.09 ---------- Applications of the Mann-Whitney U Test

Coney, Kenneth A.
   "Dogmatism and Innovation: A Replication"
   Journal of Marketing Research, Vol. IX (November 1972), pp. 453-5.

De Jonge, L. and Van Veen, W. M. Oppedijk
   "A Micro Model of Purchasing Behaviour for Consumer Durable Goods,
   Part II"
   European Research, Vol. 4 (May 1976), pp. 129-40.

Johnson, Eric J. and Russo, J. Edward
   "Product Familiarity and Learning New Information"
   Journal of Consumer Research, Vol. 11 (June 1984), pp. 542-50.

Peters, Michael P. and Venkatesan, M.
   "Exploration of Variables Inherent in Adopting an Industrial Product"
   Journal of Marketing Research, Vol. X (August 1973), pp. 312-5.

Swan, John E.
   "Experimental Analysis of Predecision Information Seeking"
   Journal of Marketing Research, Vol. VI (May 1969), pp. 192-7.

Swan, John E., Trawick, I. Fredrick, and Carroll, Maxwell G.
   "Effect of Participation in Marketing Research on Consumer Attitudes
   Toward Research and Satisfaction With a Service"
   Journal of Marketing Research, Vol. XVIII (August 1981), pp. 356-63.

Williams, Terrell, Slama, Mark, and Rogers, John
   "Behavioral Characteristics of the Recreational Shopper and
   Implications for Retail Management"
   Journal of the Academy of Marketing Science, Vol. 13 (Summer 1985),
   pp. 307-16.

Woodruff, Robert B.
   "Brand Information Sources, Opinion Change, and Uncertainty"
   Journal of Marketing Research, Vol. IX (November 1972), pp. 414-8.

147.10 ---------- Applications of the Dixon-Mood Sign Test

Dornoff, Ronald J. and Tatham, Ronald L.
   "Congruence Between Personal Image and Store Image--Reply to Martin"
   Journal of the Market Research Society, Vol. 18 (January 1976), p. 35.

Isakson, Hans R. and Maurizi, Alex R.
   "The Consumer Economics of Unit Pricing"
   Journal of Marketing Research, Vol. X (August 1973), pp. 277-85.

Martin, Warren Spencer
   "A Comment on 'Congruence Between Personal Image and Store Image'"
   Journal of the Market Research Society, Vol. 18 (January 1976), pp.
   32-4.

147.11 ---------- Applications of Wilcoxon Matched-Pairs, Signed-Ranks

Becker, Boris W. and Myers, John G.
   "Yeasaying Response Style"
   Journal of Advertising Research, Vol. 10 (December 1970), pp. 31-7.

Isakson, Hans R. and Maurizi, Alex R.
    "The Consumer Economics of Unit Pricing"
    Journal of Marketing Research, Vol. X (August 1973), pp. 277-85.

Lessig, V. Parker and Park, C. Whan
    "Predictive and Diagnostic Comparison of Two Consumer Decision Models"
    European Research, Vol. 6 (May 1978), pp. 99-104.

Maddox, R. Neil
    "Two-Factor Theory and Consumer Satisfaction: Replication and
    Extension"
    Journal of Consumer Research, Vol. 8 (June 1981), pp. 97-102.

Mazanec, Josef A. and Schweiger, Gunter C.
    "Improved Marketing Efficiency Through Multi-Product Brand Names?"
    European Research, Vol. 9 (January 1981), pp. 32-44.

McAlister, Leigh
    "Choosing Multiple Items From a Product Class"
    Journal of Consumer Research, Vol. 6 (December 1979), pp. 213-24.

Moriarty, Mark M.
    "Design Features of Forecasting Systems Involving Management
    Judgments"
    Journal of Marketing Research, Vol. XXII (November 1985), pp. 353-64.

Silk, Alvin J. and Kalwani, Manohar U.
    "Measuring Influence in Organizational Purchase Decisions"
    Journal of Marketing Research, Vol. XIX (May 1982), pp. 165-81.

147.12 ---------- Applications of Ridit Analysis

Muller, Thomas E.
    "Structural Information Factors Which Stimulate the Use of Nutrition
    Information"
    Journal of Marketing Research, Vol. XXII (May 1985), pp. 143-57.

147.13 ---------- Unclassified (Applications of Nonpar Statistics)

Binkert, Christopher C., Brunner, James A., and Simonetti, Jack L.
    "The Use of Life Style Segmentation to Determine if CATV Subscribers
    are Really Different"
    Journal of the Academy of Marketing Science, Vol. 3 (Spring 1975),
    pp. 129-36.

Hawkins, Del I. and Coney, Kenneth A.
    "Peer Group Influences on Children's Product Preferences"
    Journal of the Academy of Marketing Science, Vol. 2 (Spring 1974),
    pp. 322-31.

Martin, Claude R.
    "The Theory of Double Jeopardy"
    Journal of the Academy of Marketing Science, Vol. 1 (Fall 1973), pp.
    148-55.

Simonetti, Jack L.
    "The Impact of Market Conditions on the Organizational Structure and
    Effectiveness of Firms Operating in Italy"
    Journal of the Academy of Marketing Science, Vol. 2 (Fall 1974), pp.
    634-41.

148 ---------- CROSS CLASSIFICATION AND CHI SQUARE ANALYSIS ----------
See also (sub)heading(s) 149, 151, 152, 153.

148.01 ---------- Books Re: Cross Classification, Chi Square Analyses

Gokhale, D. V. and Kullback, Solomon
The Information in Contingency Tables
(New York: Marcel Decker, Inc., 1978), 365 pp.

Goodman, Leo A. and Kruskal, William H.
Measures of Association for Cross Classifications
(New York: Springer-Velag New York Inc., 1979), 146 pp.

Hellevik, Ottar
Introduction to Causal Analysis: Exploring Survey Data by
Crosstabulation
(Winchester, MA: Allen and Unwin, Inc., 1984), 211 pp.

Hildebrand, David K., Laing, James D., and Rosenthal, Howard
Prediction Analysis of Cross-Classifications
(New York: John Wiley and Sons, Inc., 1977), 311 pp.

Lancaster, H. O.
The Chi Squared Distribution
(New York: John Wiley and Sons, 1969).

Lesgold, Alan M.
Analysis of Contingency Tables (Act II)
(East Lansing, MI: Computer Institute for Social Science Research,
Michigan State Univesity, 1968).

Maxwell, A. E.
Analyzing Qualitative Data
(London: Matheun, 1961).

Reynolds, H. T.
The Analysis of Cross-Classifications
(New York: The Free Press, 1977), 236 pp.

Upton, Graham J. G.
The Analysis of Cross-Tabulated Data
(New York: John Wiley and Sons, Inc., 1978), 148 pp.

148.02 ---------- Theory Re: Cross Classification, Chi Square Analyses

Aitkin, M.
"A Simultaneous Test Procedure for Contingency Table Models"
Applied Statistics, Vol. 28, No. 3 (1979).

Aitkin, M.
"The Analysis of Unbalanced Cross-Classification"
Journal of the Royal Statistical Society, Series A, Vol. 141, Part 2
(1978).

Alford, Geoffrey
"Two Procedures for Exploratory Analysis"
European Research, Vol. 8 (March 1980), pp. 78-85.

Beckwith, N. E. and Morrison, D. G.
"Stochastic Interpretation of 2 x 2 Classification Tables"
Journal of the American Statistical Association, Vol. 72 (June 1977),
pp. 303-8.

Bishop, Yvonne M. M.
"Full Contingency Tables, Logits and Split Contingency Tables"
Biometrics, Vol. 25 (June 1969), pp. 383-400.

Boardman, Thomas J.
"Graphical Contributions to the Chi-Square Statistic for Two-Way
Contingency Tables"
Communications in Statistics, Vol. A6(15) (1977), pp. 1437-51.

Bresnahan, Jean L. and Shapiro, Martin M.
"A General Equation and Technique for the Exact Partitioning of
Chi-Square Contingency Tables"
Psychological Bulletin, Vol. 66 (July 1966), pp. 252-62.

Brown, J. Randall
"Error Analysis of Some Normal Approximations to the Chi-Square
Distribution"
Journal of the Academy of Marketing Science, Vol. 2 (Summer 1974),
pp. 447-54.

Castellan, N. J.
"On the Partitioning of Contingency Tables"
Psychological Bulletin, Vol. 64 (1965), pp. 330-8.

Costner, H. L.
"Criteria for Measures of Association"
American Sociological Review, Vol. 30 (June 1965), pp. 341-53.

Costner, H. L. and O'Shea, R. M.
"The Multivariate Analysis of Dichotomized Variables"
American Journal of Sociology, Vol. 70 (January 1965), pp. 455-66.

Duncan, Otis D.
"Partitioning Polyomous Variables in Multiway Contingency Analysis"
Social Science Research, Vol. 4 (September 1975), pp. 167-82.

Edwards, Allen L.
"The Use and Misuse of the Chi-Square Test--The Case of the 2 x 2
Contingency Table"
Psychological Bulletin, Vol. 43 (1950), pp. 341-6.

Fisher, R. A.
"The Conditions Under Which Chi-Square Measures the Discrepancy
Between Observation and Hypothesis"
Journal of the Royal Statistical Society, Vol. 87 (1924), pp. 442-50.

Goodman, Leo A.
"New Methods for Analysing the Intrinsic Character of Qualitative
Variables Using Cross-Classified Data"
American Journal of Sociology, Vol. 93 (November 1987), pp. 529-83.

Goodman, Leo A.
"Some Multiplicative Models for the Analysis of Cross-Classified Data"
in Cam, J. L. (editor)
Proceedings, Sixth Berkeley Symposium on Mathematical Statistics and
Probability
(Berkeley, CA: University of California Press, 1972), pp. 649-95.

Goodman, Leo A.
"A General Model for the Analysis of Surveys"
American Journal of Sociology, Vol. 77 (May 1972), pp. 1035-86.

Goodman, Leo
"Multivariate Analysis of Qualitative Data: Interactions Among
Multiple Classifications"
Journal of the American Statistical Association, Vol. 65 (March
1970), pp. 226-56.

Goodman, L. A.
"On the Multivariate Analysis of Three Dichotomous Variables"
American Journal of Sociology, Vol. 71 (November 1965), pp. 290-301.

Goodman, Leo A. and Kruskal, William H.
"Empirical Evaluation of Formal Theory"
Journal of Mathematical Sociology, Vol. III (1974), pp. 187-96.

Goodman, Leo A. and Kruskal, William H.
"More About Empirical Evaluation of Formal Theory"
Journal of Mathematical Sociology, Vol. III (1974), pp. 163-85.

Goodman, L. A. and Kruskal, W. H.
"Measures of Association for Cross Classifications, IV:
Simplification of Asymptotic Variances"
Journal of the American Statistical Association, Vol. 67 (June 1972),
pp. 415-21.

Goodman, L. and Kruskal, W.
"Measures of Association for Cross Classifications"
Journal of the American Statistical Association, Vol. 49 (1954), pp.
733-64 and Vol. 54 (1959), pp. 123-63.

Guenther, William C.
"Power and Sample Size for Approximate Chi-Square Tests"
The American Statistician, Vol. 31 (1977), pp. 83-5.

Haberman, Shelby J.
"The Analysis of Residuals in Cross-Classified Tables"
Biometrics, Vol. 29 (1973), pp. 205-20.

Hoaglin, David C.
"Direct Approximations for Chi Squared Percentage Points"
Journal of the American Statistical Association, Vol. 72 (1977), pp.
508-15.

Kimmel, H. D.
"The Relationship Between Chi Square and Size of Sample: The General
Case"
Journal of Applied Psychology, Vol. 40 (December 1956), pp. 415,6.

Lancaster, H. O. and Hamdan, M. A.
"Estimation of the Correlation Coefficient in Contingency Tables With
Possibly Nonmetrical Characters"
Psychometrika, Vol. 29 (1964), pp. 383-91.

Lee, S.
"An Example for Teaching Basic Concepts in Multidimensional Contingency Table Analysis"
American Statistician, Vol. 32 (1978), pp. 69-71.

Lewis, D. and Burke, C. J.
"The Use and Misuse of the Chi-Square Test"
Psychological Bulletin, Vol. 46, No. 6 (1949), pp. 433-89.

Margolin, B. H. and Light, R., Jr.
"An Analysis of Variance for Categorical Data II: Small Sample Comparisons With Chi-Square and Other Competitors"
Journal of the American Statistical Association, Vol. 69 (September 1974), pp. 755-64.

Martinson, E. O. and Hamdan, M. A.
"Algorithm as 87: Calculation of the Polychoric Estimate of Correlation in Contingency Tables"
Applied Statistics, Vol. 24 (1975), pp. 272-8.

Martinson, E. O. and Hamdan, M. A.
"Maximum Likelihood and Some Other Asymptotically Efficient Estimators of Correlation in Two Way Contingency Tables"
Journal of Statistical Computation and Simulation, Vol. 1 (January 1972), pp. 45-54.

Mayo, Samuel T.
"Towards Strengthening the Contingency Table as a Statistical Method"
Psychological Bulletin, Vol. 56, No. 6 (1959), pp. 461-70.

Messenger, R. and Mandell, L.
"A Modal Search Technique for Predictive Nominal Scale Multivariate Analysis"
Journal of the American Statistical Association, Vol. 67 (December 1972), pp. 768-72.

Newman, E. B. and Gerstman, L. J.
"A New Method for Analysing Printed English"
Journal of Experimental Psychology, Vol. 44 (1952), pp. 114-25.

Olsson, Ulf
"Measuring Correlation in Ordered Two-Way Contingency Tables"
Journal of Marketing Research, Vol. XVII (August 1980), pp. 391-4.

Olsson, U.
"Maximum Likelihood Estimation of the Polychoric Correlation Coefficient"
Psychometrika, Vol. 44 (1979), pp. 443-60.

Peters, Charles C.
"The Misuse of Chi-Square--A Reply to Lewis and Burke"
Psychological Bulletin, Vol. 43 (1950), pp. 331-7.

Rados, David L.
"Two-Way Analysis of Tables in Market Research"
Journal of the Market Research Society, Vol. 22 (October 1980), pp. 248-62.

Schnaars, Steven P. and Schiffman, Leon G.
"An Application of a Segmentation Design Based on a Hybrid of Canonical Correlation and Simple Crosstabulation"
Journal of the Academy of Marketing Science, Vol. 12 (Fall 1984), pp. 177-89.

Shields, W. S.
The Use of Exact Tests of the Fisher Type With Sparse Many-Category Contingency Tables
MLM Research Report 75-1
(Kingston, Ontario: Royal Military College of Canada, 1975).

Shields, William S. and Heeler, Roger M.
"Analysis of Contingency Tables With Sparse Values"
Journal of Marketing Research, Vol. XVI (August 1979), pp. 382-6.

Snee, R. D.
"Graphical Display of Two-Way Contingency Tables"
American Statistician, Vol. 28 (1974), pp. 9-12.

Sprowls, R. Clay
"Sample Sizes in Chi-Square Tests for Measuring Advertising Effectiveness"
Journal of Marketing Research, Vol. I (February 1964), pp. 60-4.

Steiger, James H., Shapiro, A., and Browne, M. W.
"On the Multivariate Asymptotic Distribution of Sequential Chi-Square Statistics"
Psychometrika, Vol. 50 (September 1985), pp. 253-63.

Tallis, G. M.
   "The Maximum Likelihood Estimation of Correlation From Contingency
   Tables"
   Biometrics, Vol. 18 (1962), pp. 342-53.

Tsai, San-Yun W. and Pohl, Norval F.
   "Chi-B: Calculating the Power of Chi Square Tests"
   Journal of Marketing Research, Vol. XV (February 1978), pp. 120,1.

Wilks, S. S.
   "The Likelihood Test of Independence in Contingency Tables"
   Annals of Mathematical Statistics, Vol. 6 (December 1935), pp. 190-6.

Winer, Russell S. and Ryan, Michael J.
   "Analyzing Cross-Classification Data: An Improved Method for
   Predicting Events"
   Journal of Marketing Research, Vol. XVI (November 1979), pp. 539-44.

Yates, F.
   "Contingency Tables Involving Small Numbers and the Chi Square Test"
   Journal of the Royal Statistical Society, Vol. 1 (1934), pp. 217-35.

Zahn, Douglas A. and Fein, Sara B.
   "Large Contingency Tables With Large Cell Frequencies: A Model Search
   Algorithm and Alternate Measures of Fit"
   Psychological Bulletin, Vol. 86 (November 1979), pp. 1189-1200.

148.03 ---------- Theory Re: Outliers in Cross Classification

Bradu, D. and Hawkins, D. M.
   "Location of Multiple Outliers in Two-Way Tables, Using Tetrads"
   Technometrics, Vol. 24 (1982), pp. 103-8.

Brown, B. M.
   "Identification of the Sources of Significance in Two-Way Contingency
   Tables"
   Applied Statistics, Vol. 23 (1974), pp. 405-13.

Fuchs, C. and Kenett, R.
   "A Test for Outlying Cells in the Multinomial Distribution and
   Two-Way Contingency Tables"
   Journal of the American Statistical Association, Vol. 75 (1980), pp.
   395-8.

Haberman, S. J.
   "The Analysis of Residuals in Cross-Classified Tables"
   Biometrics, Vol. 29 (1973), pp. 205-20.

Kotze, T. J. and Hawkins, Douglas M.
   "The Identification of Outliers in Two-Way Contingency Tables Using 2
   x 2 Subtables"
   Applied Statistics, Vol. 33, No. 2 (1984), pp. 215-23.

Mosteller, Frederick and Parunak, Anita
   "Identifying Extreme Cells in a Sizable Contingency Table:
   Probabilistic and Exploratory Approaches"
   in Hoaglin, David C., Mosteller, Frederick, and Tukey, John W.
   (editors)
   Exploring Data Tables, Trends, and Shapes
   (New York: John Wiley and Sons, Inc., 1985).

Simonoff, Jeffrey S.
   "Detecting Outlying Cells in Two-Way Contingency Tables via
   Backwards-Stepping"
   Technometrics, Vol. 30, No. 3 (1988), pp. 339-45.

148.04 ---------- Theory Re: Collapsing of Crosstabulation Tables

Goodman, Leo A.
   "Criteria for Determining Whether Certain Categories in a
   Cross-Classification Table Should be Combined, With Special Reference
   to Occupational Categories in an Occupational Mobility Table"
   American Journal of Sociology, Vol. 87 (November 1981), pp. 612-50.

Green, Paul E.
   "An AID/Logit Procedure for Analyzing Large Multiway Contingency
   Tables"
   Journal of Marketing Research, Vol. XV (February 1978), pp. 132-6.

148.05 ---------- Applications of Chi Square Crosstabulation Analysis

Akers, Fred C.
   "Negro and White Automobile-Buying Behavior: New Evidence"
   Journal of Marketing Research, Vol. V (August 1968), pp. 283-90.

Atkin, Charles K.
"Observation of Parent-Child Interaction in Supermarket
Decision-Making"
Journal of Marketing, Vol. 42 (October 1978), pp. 41-5.

Becker, Boris W. and Connor, Patrick E.
"Personal Values of the Heavy User of Mass Media"
Journal of Advertising Research, Vol. 21 (October 1981), pp. 37-43.

Belkaoui, Ahmed and Belkaoui, Janice M.
"A Comparative Analysis of the Roles Portrayed by Women in Print
Advertisements: 1958, 1970, 1972"
Journal of Marketing Research, Vol. XIII (May 1976), pp. 168-72.

Blattberg, Robert C. and Sen, Subrata K.
"An Evaluation of the Application of Minimum Chi-Square Procedures to
Stochastic Models of Brand Choice"
Journal of Marketing Research, Vol. X (November 1973), pp. 421-7.

Bourgeois, Jacques C. and Barnes, James G.
"Viability and Profile of the Consumerist Segment"
Journal of Consumer Research, Vol. 5 (March 1979), pp. 217-28.

Burton, Scot and Zinkhan, George M.
"Changes in Consumer Choice: Further Investigation of Similarity and
Attraction Effects"
Psychology and Marketing, Vol. 4 (Fall 1987), pp. 255-66.

Bush, Alan J. and Leigh, James H.
"Advertising on Cable Versus Traditional Networks"
Journal of Advertising Research, Vol. 24 (April/May 1984), pp. 33-8.

Bush, Alan, Menon, Anil, and Smart, Denise
"Media Habits of the Do-It-Yourselfers"
Journal of Advertising Research, Vol. 27 (October/November 1987), pp.
14-20.

Cunningham, Isabella C. M. and Cunningham, William H.
"Standards for Advertising Regulation"
Journal of Marketing, Vol. 41 (October 1977), pp. 92-7.

Donnelly, James H., Jr. and Etzel, Michael J.
"Degrees of Product Newness and Early Trial"
Journal of Marketing Research, Vol. X (August 1973), pp. 295-300.

Donohue, Thomas R., Meyer, Timothy P., and Henke, Lucy L.
"Black and White Children: Perceptions of TV Commercials"
Journal of Marketing, Vol. 42 (October 1978), pp. 34-40.

Hite, Robert E. and Eck, Randy
"Advertising to Children: Attitudes of Business and Consumers"
Journal of Advertising Research, Vol. 27 (October/November 1983), pp.
40-53.

Hoover, Robert J., Green, Robert T., and Saegert, Joel
"A Cross-National Study of Perceived Risk"
Journal of Marketing, Vol. 42 (July 1978), pp. 103-8.

Krugman, Dean M. and Eckrich, Donald
"Differences in Cable and Pay-Cable Audiences"
Journal of Advertising Research, Vol. 22 (August/September 1982), pp.
23-9.

Kuehn, Alfred A.
"Demonstration of the Relationship Between Psychological Factors and
Brand Choice"
Journal of Business, Vol. 36 (April 1963), pp. 237-41.

Langrehr, Frederick W.
"Consumer Images of Two Types of Competing Financial Services"
Journal of the Academy of Marketing Science, Vol. 13 (Summer 1985),
pp. 248-64.

Lynn, Jerry R.
"Newpaper Ad Impact in Nonmetropolitan Markets"
Journal of Advertising Research, Vol. 21 (August 1981), pp. 13-9.

Maronick, Thomas J. and Stiff, Ronald M.
"The Impact of a Specialty Retail Center on Downtown Shopping
Behavior"
Journal of the Academy of Marketing Science, Vol. 13 (Summer 1985),
pp. 292-306.

Murphy, Patrick E., Kangun, Norman, and Locander, William B.
"Environmentally Concerned Consumers--Racial Variations"
Journal of Marketing, Vol. 42 (October 1978), pp. 61-6.

Nevin, John R. and Churchill, Gilbert A., Jr.
"The Equal Credit Opportunity Act: An Evaluation"
Journal of Marketing, Vol. 43 (Spring 1979), pp. 95-104.

Prasad, V. Kanti
    "Communications-Effectiveness of Comparative Advertising: A
    Laboratory Analysis"
    Journal of Marketing Research, Vol. XIII (May 1976), pp. 128-37.

Punj, Girish
    "Presearch Decision Making in Consumer Durable Purchases"
    Journal of Consumer Marketing, Vol. 4 (Winter 1987), pp. 71-82.

Swan, John E., Futrell, Charles M., and Todd, John T.
    "Same Job--Different Views: Women and Men in Industrial Sales"
    Journal of Marketing, Vol. 42 (January 1978), pp. 92-8.

Trombetta, W. L., Page, Albert L., and Shah, Ramesh P.
    "A Market Segmentation Analysis of Users of a Black-Owned
    Neighborhood Shopping Center"
    Journal of the Academy of Marketing Science, Vol. 5 (Summer 1977),
    pp. 270-80.

Wall, Marjorie and Heslop, Louise A.
    "Consumer Attitudes Toward Canadian-Made Versus Imported Products"
    Journal of the Academy of Marketing Science, Vol. 14 (Summer 1986),
    pp. 27-36.

Westbrook, Robert A., Newman, Joseph W., and Taylor, James R.
    "Satisfaction/Dissatisfaction in the Purchase Decision Process"
    Journal of Marketing, Vol. 42 (October 1978), pp. 54-60.

Whitmore, William J.
    "Mail Survey Premiums and Response Bias"
    Journal of Marketing Research, Vol. XIII (February 1976), pp. 46-50.

148.06 ---------- Applications of McNemar's Test

Gensch, Dennis H.
    "Empirical Evidence Supporting the Use of Multiple Choice Models in
    Analyzing a Population"
    Journal of Marketing Research, Vol. XXIV (May 1987), pp. 197-207.

Upah, Gregory D.
    "Product Complexity Effects on Information Source Preference by
    Retail Buyers"
    Journal of Business Research, Vol. 11 (March 1983), pp. 107-26.

148.07 ---------- Applications of Cohort Analysis

McDonald, Scott Cameron
    "Procedure for the Use of Syndicated Audience Research to Develop
    Synthetic Cohorts for Historical Media Analysis"
    Journal of the Market Research Society, Vol. 28 (April 1986), pp.
    175-88.

Rentz, Joseph O., Reynolds, Fred D., and Stout, Roy G.
    "Analyzing Changing Consumption Patterns With Cohort Analysis"
    Journal of Marketing Research, Vol. XX (February 1983), pp. 12-20.

148.08 ---------- Computer Programs for Cross Classification

Creative Research Systems
    The Survey System, Version 3.1
    (Petaluma, CA: Creative Research Systems).

Lavine, Minna
    "Four Cross-Tabs Packages for IBM PCs"
    Journal of Marketing Research, Vol. XXV (November 1988), pp. 417-22.

SPSS Incorporated
    SPSS-Plus Tables, Version 2.0
    (Chicago, IL: SPSS Inc.).

Strawberry Software, Incorporated
    A-CROSS Version 1.1
    (Watertown, MA: Strawberry Software, Inc.).

Tsai, San-Yun W. and Pohl, Norval F.
    "Chi-B: Calculating the Power of Chi Square Tests"
    Journal of Marketing Research, Vol. XV (February 1978), pp. 120,1.

World Research Systems, Limited
    UNCLE 10
    (Marina del Rey, CA: World Research Systems, Ltd.).

149 -------- MEASURES OF ASSOCIATION IN CROSS CLASSIFICATIONS --------
        See also (sub)heading(s) 145.

149.01 ---------- Theory Re: Measures of Association in Cross Class

Brown, Martin B.
    "The Asymptotic Standard Errors of Some Estimates of Uncertainty in
    the Two-Way Contingency Table"
    Psychometrika, Vol. 40 (September 1975), pp. 291-6.

Brown, Martin B. and Benedetti, J. K.
    "On the Mean and Variance of the Tetrachoric Correlation Coefficient"
    Psychometrika, Vol. 42 (December 1977), pp. 347-55.

Clogg, Clifford C.
    "Some Models for the Analysis of Association in Multi-Way
    Cross-Classifications Having Ordered Classifications"
    Journal of the American Statistical Association, Vol. 77 (December
    1982), pp. 803-15.

Clogg, Clifford C.
    "Using Association Models in Sociological Research: Some Examples"
    American Journal of Sociology, Vol. 88 (July 1982), pp. 114-34.

Costner, Herbert L.
    "Criteria for Measures of Association"
    American Sociological Review, Vol. 30 (June 1965), pp. 341-51.

Feick, Lawrence F.
    "Analyzing Marketing Research Data With Association Models"
    Journal of Marketing Research, Vol. XXI (November 1984), pp. 376-86.

Goodman, Leo A.
    "Association Models and the Bivariate Normal for Contingency Tables
    With Ordered Categories"
    Biometrika, Vol. 68 (August 1981), pp. 347-55.

Goodman, Leo A.
    "Association Models and Canonical Correlation in the Analysis of
    Cross-Classifications Having Ordered Categories"
    Journal of the American Statistical Association, Vol. 76 (June 1981),
    pp. 320-34.

Goodman, Leo A.
    "Simple Models for the Analysis of Association in
    Cross-Classifications Having Ordered Categories"
    Journal of the American Statistical Association, Vol. 74 (September
    1979), pp. 537-52.

Goodman, Leo A.
    "The Analysis of Cross-Classified Data: Independence,
    Quasi-Independence, and Interactions in Contingency Tables With and
    Without Missing Entries"
    Journal of the American Statistical Association, Vol. 63 (December
    1968), pp. 1091-131.

Goodman, Leo A. and Kruskal, William H.
    "Measures of Association for Cross-Classification, II: Further
    Discussion and References"
    Journal of the American Statistical Association, Vol. 54 (March
    1959), pp. 124-63.

Goodman, Leo A. and Kruskal, William H.
    "Measures of Association for Cross Classifications"
    Journal of the American Statistical Association, Vol. 49 (December
    1954), pp. 732-74.

Hamdan, M. A.
    "The Equivalence of Tetrachoric and Maximum Likelihood Estimates of
    Rho in 2 x 2 Tables"
    Biometrika, Vol. 57 (April 1970), pp. 212-5.

Martinson, E. O. and Hamdan, M. A.
    "Calculation of the Polychoric Estimate of Correlation in Contingency
    Tables"
    Applied Statistics, Vol. 24 (1975), pp. 272-8.

Olsson, Ulf
    "Measuring Correlation in Ordered Two-Way Contingency Tables"
    Journal of Marketing Research, Vol. XVII (August 1980), pp. 391-4.

Olsson, Ulf
    "Maximum Likelihood Estimation of the Polychoric Correlation
    Coefficient"
    Psychometrika, Vol. 44 (December 1979), pp. 443-60.

Pearson, K. and Pearson, E. S.
    "On Polychoric Coefficients of Correlations"
    Biometrika, Vol. 14 (July 1922), pp. 127-56.

Yule, G. U.
  "On the Association of Attributes in Statistics"
  Philosophical Transactions Series A, Vol. 194 (1900), pp. 257-319.

149.02 ---------- Applications of Goodman and Kruskal's Gamma Coeff

Anderson, W. Thomas, Jr.
  "Identifying the Convenience-Oriented Consumer"
  Journal of Marketing Research, Vol. VIII (May 1971), pp. 179-83.

Davis, Harry L.
  "Dimensions of Marital Roles in Consumer Decision Making"
  Journal of Marketing Research, Vol. VII (May 1970), pp. 168-77.

Hisrich, Robert D., Dornoff, Ronald J., and Kernan, Jerome B.
  "Perceived Risk in Store Selection"
  Journal of Marketing Research, Vol. IX (November 1972), pp. 435-9.

Keiser, Stephen K.
  "Awareness of Brands and Slogans"
  Journal of Advertising Research, Vol. 15 (August 1975), pp. 37-43.

Montgomery, David B. and Silk, Alvin J.
  "Clusters of Consumer Interests and Opinion Leaders' Spheres of
  Influence"
  Journal of Marketing Research, Vol. VIII (August 1971), pp. 317-21.

149.03 ---------- Applications of Goodman and Kruskal's Tau

Shuchman, Abe and Perry, Michael
  "Self-Confidence and Persuasibility in Marketing: A Reappraisal"
  Journal of Marketing Research, Vol. VI (May 1969), pp. 146-54.

149.04 ---------- Applications of Yule's Q Coefficient

Silk, Alvin J.
  "Testing the Inverse Ad Size-Selective Exposure Hypothesis:
  Clarifying Bogart"
  Journal of Marketing Research, Vol. X (May 1973), pp. 221-3.

Smith, Stewart A.
  "Factors Influencing the Relationship Between Buying Plans and Ad
  Readership"
  Journal of Marketing Research, Vol. II (February 1965), pp. 40-4.

150 ------------------- LOGLINEAR MODELS (LLM) -------------------

See also (sub)heading(s) 159, 172.

150.01 ---------- Books Re: Loglinear Models

Bishop, Yvonne M., Fienberg, Stephen E., and Holland, Paul W.
Discrete Multivariate Analysis: Theory and Practice
(Cambridge, MA: MIT Press, 1975).

Fienberg, Stephen E.
The Analysis of Cross-Classified Categorical Data
(Cambridge, MA: MIT Press, 1977).

Gilbert, G. Nigel
Modelling Society: An Introduction to Loglinear Analysis for Social
Researchers
(Winchester, MA: Allen and Unwin, Inc., 1982).

Goodman, Leo A. and Magidson, Jay (editors)
Analyzing Qualitative/Categorical Data: Log-Linear Models and Latent
Structure Analysis
(Cambridge, MA: Abt Books, 1978).

Knoke, D. and Burke, P. J.
Log-Linear Models
(Beverly Hills, CA: Sage Publications, 1980).

Nerlove, Marc and Press, S. James
Univariate and Multivariate Log-Linear and Logistic Models
(Santa Monica, CA: Rand Corporation, December 1973).

150.02 ---------- Theory Re: Loglinear Models

Blattberg, Robert C. and Dolan, Robert J.
"An Assessment of the Contribution of Log Linear Models to Marketing
Research"
Journal of Marketing, Vol. 45 (Spring 1981), pp. 89-97.

Danaher, Peter J.
Estimating Multidimensional Tables From Survey Data: Predicting
Magazine Audiences
Florida State University (1987), unpublished Ph.D. dissertation.

Deming, W. Edwards and Frederick, F. Stephen
"On a Least Squares Adjustment of a Sample Frequency Table When the
Expected Marginal Totals are Known"
Annals of Mathematical Statistics, Vol. 11 (1940), pp. 427-44.

DeSarbo, Wayne S. and Hildebrand, David K.
"A Marketer's Guide to Log Linear Models for Qualitative Data
Analysis"
Journal of Marketing, Vol. 44 (Summer 1980), pp. 40-51.

Grizzle, James E., Starmer, C. Frank, and Koch, Gary G.
"Analysis of Categorical Data by Linear Models"
Biometrics, Vol. 25 (1969), pp. 489-504.

Grizzle, James E. and Williams, O. D.
"Log Linear Models and Tests of Independence for Contingency Tables"
Biometrics, Vol. 28 (1972), pp. 137-56.

Haberman, Shelby J.
"Log-Linear Models for Frequency Tables With Ordered Classifications"
Biometrics, Vol. 30 (December 1974), pp. 589-600.

Haberman, Shelby J.
"Log-Linear Models for Frequency Data: Sufficient Statistics and
Likelihood Estimations"
Annals of Statistics, Vol. 1, No. 4 (1973), pp. 617-32.

Haberman, Shelby J.
"Loglinear Fit for Contingency Tables"
Applied Statistics, Vol. 21 (1972), pp. 218-25.

Magidson, Jay, Swan, James H., and Berk, Richard A.
"Estimating Nonhierarchical and Meshed Log-Linear Models"
Sociological Methods and Research, Vol. 10 (1981), pp. 3-49.

Nelder, J. A.
"Log Linear Models for Contingency Tables: A Generalization of
Classical Least Squares"
Applied Statistics, Vol. 23 (1974), pp. 323-9.

Novak, T. P.
"Log-Linear Modelling of Multiple Brand Switching Matrices"
ORSA/TIMS Joint National Meeting, Miami (October 1986), paper
presentation.

Novak, T. P. and Koch, G. G.
  "Maximum Likelihood Fitting of Log-Linear Models to Incomplete
  Contingency Tables: An Application of Brand Switching Data"
  ORSA/TIMS Joint International Meeting, Gold Coast City, Australia
  (July 1986), paper presentation.

Read, Campbell B. and Kerin, Roger A.
  "Interpreting Three-Dimensional Contingency Tables via Log-Linear
  Models"
  Southern Methodist University (1975), unpublished paper.

150.03 ---------- Theory Re: Interactions in Loglinear Models

    See also (sub)heading(s) 153.03, 160.03.

Roy, S. N. and Kastenbaum, M. A.
  "On the Hypothesis of No 'Interaction' in Multiway Contingency Tables"
  Annals of Mathematical Statistics, Vol. 27 (1956), pp. 749-57.

150.04 ---------- Applications of Loglinear Models

Boyd, Marsha M.
  The Dirichlet Multivariate Multinomial Distribution as a Magazine
  Exposure Model
  University of Illinois at Urbana-Champaign (1985), unpublished Ph.D.
  dissertation.

Danaher, Peter J.
  "An Approximate Log-Linear Model for Predicting Magazine Readership"
  Journal of Marketing Research, Vol. XXVI (November 1989), pp. 473-9.

Danaher, Peter J.
  "A Log-Linear Model for Predicting Magazine Audiences"
  Journal of Marketing Research, Vol. XXV (November 1988), pp. 356-62.

Kelley, Craig A.
  "An Investigation of Consumer Product Warranties as Market Signals of
  Product Reliability"
  Journal of the Academy of Marketing Science, Vol. 16 (Summer 1988),
  pp. 72-8.

Mattson, Bruce and Dubinsky, Alan J.
  "Shopping Patterns: An Exploration of Some Situational Determinants"
  Psychology and Marketing, Vol. 4 (Spring 1987), pp. 47-62.

Rao, Vithala R., Wind, Yoram, and DeSarbo, Wayne S.
  "A Customized Market Response Model: Development, Estimation, and
  Empirical Testing"
  Journal of the Academy of Marketing Science, Vol. 16 (Spring 1988),
  pp. 128-40.

Ratchford, Brian T. and Stoops, Glenn T.
  "A Model and Measurement Approach for Studying Retail Productivity"
  Journal of Retailing, Vol. 64 (Fall 1988), pp. 241-63.

Schaninger, Charles M., Bourgeois, Jacques C., and Buss, W. Christian
  "French-English Canadian Subcultural Consumption Differences"
  Journal of Marketing, Vol. 49 (Spring 1985), pp. 82-92.

Shuv-Ami, Avichai and Schiffman, Leon G.
  "Time Perception in the Diffusion of Safety Hazard Information"
  Psychology and Marketing, Vol. 3 (Fall 1986), pp. 211-221.

151 ------------ MULTIVARIATE ANALYSIS OF QUALITATIVE DATA -----------
      See also (sub)heading(s) 148, 152, 153.

151.01 ---------- Books Re: Discrete Multivariate Analysis

Aickin, Mikel
    Linear Statistical Analysis of Discrete Data
    (New York: John Wiley and Sons, Inc., 1983), 358 pp.

Andersen, Erling B.
    Discrete Statistical Models With Social Science Applications
    (Amsterdam: North-Holland Publishing Company, 1980).

Bishop, Yvonne M. M., Fienberg, Stephen E., and Holland, Paul W.
    Discrete Multivariate Analysis
    (Cambridge, MA: MIT Press, 1975).

Fienberg, Stephen E.
    The Analysis of Cross-Classified Categorical Data
    (Cambridge, MA: The MIT Press, 1977), 151 pp.

Gilbert, G. N.
    Modelling Society
    (London: George Allen and Unwin, 1981).

Gokhale, D. V. and Kullback, Solomon
    The Information in Contingency Tables
    (New York: Marcel Dekker, Inc., 1978), 365 pp.

Goldstein, Matthew and Dillon, William R.
    Discrete Discriminant Analysis
    (New York: John Wiley and Sons, Inc., 1978), 186 pp.

Goodman, Leo A.
    Analyzing Qualitative/Categorical Data
    (Cambridge, MA: Abt Books, 1978), 471 pp.

Haberman, Shelby J.
    Analysis of Qualitative Data: Volume 2, New Developments
    (New York: Academic Press, 1979).

Haberman, Shelby J.
    Analysis of Qualitative Data, Volume I: Introductory Topics
    (London: Academic Press, 1978).

Haberman, Shelby J.
    The Analysis of Frequency Data
    (Chicago: University of Chicago Press, 1974).

Hildebrand, David K., Laing, James D., and Rosenthal, Howard
    Prediction Analysis of Cross-Classifications
    (New York: John Wiley and Sons, Inc., 1977), 311 pp.

Kennedy, J. J.
    Analyzing Qualitative Data
    (New York: Praeger, 1983).

Magidson, Jay (editor)
    Analyzing Qualitative/Categorical Data
    (Cambridge, MA: Abt Books, 1978).

Manski, Charles F. and McFadden, Daniel (editors)
    Structural Analysis of Discrete Data With Econometric Applications
    (Cambridge, MA: The MIT Press, 1981), 477 pp.

Reynolds, H. T.
    Analysis of Nominal Data, Second Edition
    (Beverly Hills, CA: Sage Publications, Inc.).

Reynolds, H. T.
    The Analysis of Cross Classifications
    (New York: The Free Press, 1977), 236 pp.

Srivastava, Rajendra K.
    "Discrete Multivariate Analysis Books: A Review"
    Journal of Marketing Research, Vol. XVII (August 1980), pp. 395-401.

Upton, Graham J. G.
    The Analysis of Cross-Tabulated Data
    (New York: John Wiley and Sons, Inc., 1978), 148 pp.

152 ------------ MULTIVARIATE NOMINAL SCALE ANALYSIS (MNA) -----------
       See also (sub)heading(s) 148, 151, 153.

152.01 ---------- Books Re: Multivariate Nominal Scale Analysis (MNA)

Andrews, Frank M. and Messenger, Robert C.
   Multivariate Nominal Scale Analysis
   (Ann Arbor: Survey Research Center, Institute for Social Research,
   University of Michigan, 1973), 108 pp.

152.02 ---------- Theory Re: Multivariate Nominal Scale Analysis (MNA)

Andrews, Frank M.
   Multivariate Nominal Scale Analysis: A Report on a New Analysis
   Technique and Computer Program
   (Ann Arbor, MI: Survey Research Center, University of Michigan, 1973).

Andrews, F. M., Morgan, J. N., and Messenger, R. C.
   "Comments on Reviews by Jagdish N. Sheth of MNA and THAID"
   Journal of Marketing Research, Vol. XI (November 1974), pp. 473-5.

Gitlow, Howard S.
   "Discrimination Procedures for the Analysis of Nominally Scaled Data
   Sets"
   Journal of Marketing Research, Vol. XVI (August 1979), pp. 387-93.

Messenger, R. and Mandell, L.
   "A Modal Search Technique for Predictive Nominal Scale Multivariate
   Analysis"
   Journal of the American Statistical Association, Vol. 67 (December
   1972).

O'Malley, P. M.
   "An Empirical Comparison of MNA and MDF"
   Department of Psychology, University of Michigan (1972), unpublished
   paper.

152.03 ---------- Applications of Multivariate Nominal Scale Analysis

Labay, Duncan G. and Kinnear, Thomas C.
   "Exploring the Consumer Decision Process in the Adoption of Solar
   Energy Systems"
   Journal of Consumer Research, Vol. 8 (December 1981), pp. 271-8.

153 -------------- MULTINOMIAL CLASSIFICATION ANALYSIS --------------
See also (sub)heading(s) 148, 151, 152.

153.01 ---------- Books Re: Multinomial Classification Analysis

Ball, G. H.
Classification Analysis
(Stanford, CA: SRI, 1971).

Bishop, Yvonne M., Fienberg, Stephen E., and Holland, Paul W.
Discrete Multivariate Analysis: Theory and Practice
(Cambridge, MA: The MIT Press, 1975).

Goldstein, Matthew and Dillon, William R.
Discrete Discrimination Analysis
(New York: John Wiley and Sons, Inc., 1978).

Goodman, Leo A.
Analyzing Qualitative/Categorical Data
(Cambridge, MA: Abt Books, 1978).

Haberman, Shelby J.
Analysis of Qualitative Data
(New York: Academic Press, 1978).

153.02 ---------- Theory Re: Multinomial Classification Analysis

Bartlett, M. S.
"Contingency Table Interactions"
Journal of the Royal Statistical Society, Second Supplement, Vol. B2
(1935), pp. 248-52.

Birch, M. W.
"Maximum Likelihood in Three-Way Contingency Tables"
Journal of the Royal Statistical Society, Series B (1963), pp. 220-33.

Bishop, Yvonne M. M.
"Effects of Collapsing Multi-Dimensional Contingency Tables"
Biometrics, Vol. 2 (1971), pp. 545-62.

Brown, Morton B.
"Screening Effects in Multidimensional Contingency Tables"
Applied Statistics, Vol. 25 (1976), pp. 37-46.

Cochran, William G. and Hopkins, Carl E.
"Some Classification Problems With Multivariate Qualitative Data"
Biometrics, Vol. 17 (March 1961), pp. 10-32.

Costner, Herbert L. and Wager, L. Wesley
"The Multivariate Analysis of Dichotomized Variables"
American Journal of Sociology, Vol. 70 (January 1965), pp. 455-65.

Davies, R. H. and Webford, B. P.
"A Simple Way to Analyse Multiway Tables Using Information Theory"
Journal of the Market Research Society, Vol. 11, No. 2 (1969), pp.
147-51.

Dillon, William R.
"Analyzing Large Multiway Contingency Tables: A Simple Method for
Selecting Variables"
Journal of Marketing, Vol. 43 (Fall 1979), pp. 92-102.

Dillon, William R. and Goldstein, Matthew
"On the Performance of Some Multinomial Classification Rules"
Journal of the American Statistical Association, Vol. 73 (June 1978),
pp. 305-13.

Dillon, William R., Goldstein, Matthew, and Lement, Lucy
"Analyzing Qualitative Predictors With Too Few Data: An Alternative
Approach to Handling Sparse-Cell Values"
Journal of Marketing Research, Vol. XVIII (February 1981), pp. 63-72.

Dillon, William R., Goldstein, Matthew, and Schiffman, Leon G.
"Appropriateness of Linear Discriminant and Multinomial
Classification Analysis in Marketing Research"
Journal of Marketing Research, Vol. XV (February 1978), pp. 103-12.

Dolan, Robert J.
"Market Segmentation via Alternative Discriminant Procedures"
Combined Proceedings, American Marketing Association (1975), pp.
132-6.

Fienberg, S. E. and Holland, P. W.
"On the Choice of Flattening Constants for Estimating Multinomial
Probabilities"
Journal of Multivariate Analysis, Vol. 2 (1972), pp. 127-34.

Fienberg, S. E. and Holland, P. W.
    "Methods for Eliminating Zero Counts in Contingency Tables"
    in Paul, G. P. (editor)
    Random Counts on Models and Structures
    (University Park: Pennsylvania University Press, 1970), pp. 233-60.

Forthofer, Ronald and Koch, Gary G.
    "An Analysis for Compounded Functions of Categorical Data by Linear
    Models"
    Biometrics, Vol. 29 (1973), pp. 143-57.

Gilbert, Ethel S.
    "On Discrimination Using Qualitative Variables"
    Journal of the American Statistical Association, Vol. 63 (December
    1968), pp. 116-22.

Glick, Ned
    "Sample-Based, Multinomial Classification"
    Biometrics, Vol. 29 (June 1973), pp. 241-56.

Goldstein, Matthew and Dillon, William R.
    "A Stepwise Discrete Variable Selection Procedure"
    Communications in Statistics.

Goldstein, Matthew and Wolf, Edward
    "On the Problem of Bias in Multinomial Classification"
    Biometrics, Vol. 33 (June 1977), pp. 325-31.

Goodman, Leo A.
    "A Modified Multiple Regression Approach to the Analysis of
    Dichotomous Variables"
    American Sociological Review, Vol. 37 (1972), pp. 28-46.

Goodman, Leo A.
    "The Analysis of Multidimensional Contingency Tables: Stepwise
    Procedures and Direct Estimation Methods for Building Models for
    Multiple Classifications"
    Technometrics, Vol. 13 (1971), pp. 31-62.

Goodman, Leo A.
    "The Multivariate Analysis of Qualitative Data: Interactions Among
    Multiple Classifications"
    Journal of the American Statistical Association, Vol. 65 (1970), pp.
    226-56.

Goodman, Leo A.
    "On the Multivariate Analysis of Three Dichotomous Variables"
    American Journal of Sociology, Vol. 71 (November 1965), pp. 290-301.

Green, Paul E.
    "Bayesian Classification Procedures in Analyzing Customer
    Characteristics"
    Journal of Marketing Research, Vol. I (May 1964), pp. 44-50.

Grizzle, James, Starmer, C. Frank, and Koch, Gary G.
    "Analysis of Categorical Data by Linear Models"
    Biometrics, Vol. 25 (1969), pp. 489-504.

Hills, M.
    "Discrimination and Allocation With Discrete Data"
    Journal of the Royal Statistical Society, Series 16, Vol. 16, No. 3
    (1967), pp. 237-50.

Kritzer, Herbert
    "Analyzing Contingency Tables by Weighted Least Squares: An
    Alternative to the Goodman Approach"
    Department of Political Science, Rice University, Houston, TX,
    unpublished.

Ku, H. H. and Kullback S.
    "Interaction in Multidimensional Contingency Tables: An Information
    Theoretic Approach"
    Journal of Research of the National Bureau of Standards, Vol. 72B
    (July-September 1968), pp. 159-99.

Lagarce, Raymond
    "An Analysis of Second-Order Interaction in Multidimensional
    Contingency Tables"
    Journal of Marketing Research, Vol. XI (August 1974), pp. 343-5.

Lehnen, Robert G. and Koch, Gary G.
    "A General Linear Approach to the Analysis of Non-Metric Data:
    Applications for Political Science"
    American Journal of Political Science, Vol. 18 (1974), pp. 283-313.

Lewis, B. N.
    "On the Analysis of Interaction in Multidimensional Contingency
    Tables"
    Journal of the Royal Statistical Society, Vol. A125 (1962), pp. 103-5.

Linhart, H.
"Techniques for Discriminant Analysis With Discrete Variables"
Metrika, Vol. 2 (May 1969), pp. 138-49.

Milligan, Glenn W.
"Factors That Affect Type I and Type II Error Rates in the Analysis
of Multidimensional Contingency Tables"
Psychological Bulletin, Vol. 87 (March 1980), pp. 238-44.

Moore, Dan H., II
"Evaluation of Five Discrimination Procedures for Binary Variables"
Journal of the American Statistical Association, Vol. 68 (June 1973),
pp. 399-404.

Perreault, William D. and Barksdale, Hiram C.
"A Model-Free Approach for Analysis of Complex Contingency Data in
Survey Research"
Journal of Marketing Research, Vol. XVII (November 1980), pp. 503-15.

Perreault, William D., Jr. and Gwin, John M.
"CATCLASS: A Model to Classify Consumers Based on Multivariate
Categorical Data"
Journal of Marketing Research, Vol. XV (February 1978), pp. 113-21.

Shields, William S. and Heeler, Roger M.
"Analysis of Contingency Tables With Sparse Values"
Journal of Marketing Research, Vol. XVI (August 1979), pp. 382-6.

Simpson, E. H.
"The Interpretation of Interaction in Contingency Tables"
Journal of the Royal Statistical Society, Vol. B13 (1951), pp. 238-41.

Theil, Henri
"A Multidimensional Extension of the Linear Logit Model"
International Economic Review, Vol. 10 (October 1969), pp. 251-9.

153.03 ---------- Goodman's Analysis of Interactions

    See also (sub)heading(s) 150.03, 160.03.

Goodman, Leo
"Multivariate Analysis of Qualitative Data: Interactions Among
Multiple Classifications"
Journal of the American Statistical Association, Vol. 65 (March
1970), pp. 226-56.

Prasad, V. Kanti
"Communications-Effectiveness of Comparative Advertising: A
Laboratory Analysis"
Journal of Marketing Research, Vol. XIII (May 1976), pp. 128-37.

153.04 ---------- Computer Programs for Multinomial Classification

Dillon, William R. and Goldstein, Matthew
"VARSEL: A Stepwise Discrete Variable Selection Program"
Journal of Marketing Research, Vol. XIV (August 1977), pp. 419,20.

Forthofer, Ronald and Koch, Gary G.
"A Program for the Analysis for Compounded Functions of Categorical
Data"
Computer Programs in Biomedicine, Vol. 3 (1974), pp. 237-48.

Forthofer, Ronald, Starmer, Frank, and Grizzle, James
"A Program for the Analysis of Categorical Data by Linear Models"
Journal of Biomedical Systems, Vol. 2 (1971), pp. 3-48.

Kerin, Roger, Woodward, Wayne, and Reeves, Jackie
"TRI-CHI: A Program for Interpreting Three-Dimensional Contingency
Tables via Log Linear Models"
Journal of Marketing Research, Vol. XII (February 1975), p. 82.

Kritzer, Herbert M.
"NONMET II: A Program for the Analysis of Nonmetric Data by Linear
Models"
Journal of Marketing Research, Vol. XIII (November 1976), pp. 404,5.

154 ------------ MINIMUM DISCRIMINATION INFORMATION (MDI) ------------

154.01 ---------- Books Re: Minimum Discrimination Information

Gokhale, Dattaprabhakar Y. and Kullback, Solomon
   The Information in Contingency Tables
   (New York: Marcel Dekker, Inc., 1978), 365 pp.

Kullback, Solomon
   Information Theory and Statistics
   (New York: John Wiley and Sons, Inc., 1959).

154.02 ---------- Theory Re: Minimum Discrimination Information

Brockett, Patrick L., Charnes, Abraham, and Cooper, William W.
   "M.D.I. Estimation via Unconstrained Convex Programming"
   Communications in Statistical Simulation and Computers, Vol. 139, No.
   3 (1978), pp. 223-34.

Charnes, Abraham and Cooper, William W.
   "Goal Programming and Multiple Objective Optimizations, Part I"
   European Journal of Operational Research, Vol. 1, No. 1 (1977), pp.
   39-54.

Charnes, Abraham, Cooper, William W., and Learner, David B.
   "Constrained Information Theorectic Characterizations in Consumer
   Purchase Behavior"
   Journal of the Operational Research Society, Vol. 9 (1978), pp.
   832-42.

Charnes, Abraham, Cooper, William W., Learner, David B., and Phillips,
   Fred Y.
   "An MDI Model and an Algorithm for Composite Hypothesis Testing and
   Estimation in Marketing"
   Marketing Science, Vol. 3 (Winter 1984), pp. 55-72.

Charnes, Abraham, Cooper, William W., Learner, David B., and Phillips,
   Fred Y.
   "An MDI Procedure for Vulnerability Segmentation Tests"
   Research Report CCS 376
   Center for Cybernetic Studies, University of Texas (1980).

Charnes, Abraham, Cooper, William W., Learner, David B., and Phillips,
   Fred Y.
   "The MDI Method as a Generalization of Logit, Probit and Hendry
   Models in Marketing"
   PDA-RP No. 70
   Market Research Corporation of America (1980).

Charnes, Abraham, Cooper, William W., Learner, David B., and Phillips,
   Fred Y.
   "A Theorem and Approach to Market Segmentation"
   in Leone, R. P (editor)
   Proceedings--Market Measurement and Analysis
   (TIMS College of Marketing and TIMS, 1980).

Charnes, Abraham, Cooper, William W., and Tyssedal, J.
   "Khinchin-Kullback-Leibler Estimation With Inequality Constraints"
   Research Report CCS 414
   Center for Cybernetic Studies, University of Texas (1981).

Gokhale, D. Y. and Kullback, S.
   "The Minimum Discrimination Information Approach in Analyzing
   Categorical Data"
   Communications in Statistics, Vol. A7, No. 10 (1978), pp. 987-1005.

Kumar, Ajith and Dillon, William R.
   "Constrained Discrimination via MDI Estimation: The Use of Additional
   Information in Segmentation Analysis"
   Journal of Marketing Research, Vol. XXIV (November 1987), pp. 396-403.

Philips, Fred Y.
   "A Guide to MDI Statistics for Planning and Management Model Building"
   Technical Series No. 2
   Institute for Constructive Capitalism, University of Texas at Austin
   (1980).

155 ------------ CORRESPONDENCE ANALYSIS OR DUAL SCALING ------------
          See also (sub)heading(s) 156, 157.

155.01 ---------- Books Re: Correspondence Analysis or Dual Scaling

Benzecri, J. P. et al.
  L'Analyse des Donnees, Volume II, L'Analyse des Correspondences
  (Paris: Dunod, 1973).

Benzecri, J. P. et al.
  L'Analyse des Donnees, Volume I, La Taxinomie
  (Paris: Dunod, 1973).

Bouroche, J. M. and Saporta, G.
  L'Analyse des Donnees
  (Paris: Presses Universitaires de France, 1980).

Gifi, A.
  Non-Linear Multivariate Analysis
  (Leiden, The Netherlands: Department of Data Theory, University of
  Leiden, 1981).

Greenacre, Michael J.
  Theory and Application of Correspondence Analysis
  (London: Academic Press, Inc., 1984).

Heiser, Willem J.
  Unfolding Analysis of Proximity Data
  (Leiden, The Netherlands: Department of Data Theory, University of
  Leiden, 1981).

Jambu, M. and Lebeaux, M-O.
  Cluster Analysis and Data Analysis
  (Amsterdam: North Holland Publishing Company, 1983).

Lebart, L., Morineau, A., and Tabard
  Techniques de la Description Statistique
  (Paris: Dunod, 1977).

Lebart, Ludovic, Morineau, Alain, and Warwick, Kenneth M.
  Multivariate Descriptive Statistical Analysis: Correspondence
  Analysis and Related Techniques for Large Matrices
  (New York: John Wiley and Sons, Inc., 1984).

Meulman, Jacqueline
  Homogeneity Analysis of Incomplete Data
  (Leiden, The Netherlands: DSWO Press, 1982).

Nishisato, Shizuhiko
  Analysis of Categorical Data: Dual Scaling and Its Application
  (Toronto: University of Toronto Press, 1980), 276 pp.

Nishisato, Shizuhiko and Nishisato, Ira
  An Introduction to Dual Scaling, First Edition
  (Islington, Ontario: MicroStats, 1983).

Van Rijekevorsel, Jan L. A. and De Leeuw, Jan
  Component and Correspondence Analysis
  (New York: John Wiley and Sons, Inc., 1988).

155.02 ---------- Theory Re: Correspondence Analysis or Dual Scaling

Benzecri, Jean-Paul
  "Sur le Calcul des Taux d'Inertie dans l'Analyse d'un Questionnaire"
  Cahiers de l'Analyse des Donnees, Vol. 4 (1979), pp. 377,8.

Benzecri, J. P.
  "Statistical Analysis as a Tool to Make Patterns Emerge From Data"
  in Watanabe, S. (editor)
  Methodologies of Pattern Recognition
  (New York: Academic Press, Inc., 1969), pp. 35-74.

Carroll, J. Douglas
  "Models and Methods for Multidimensional Analysis of Preferential
  Choice (or Other Dominance) Data"
  in Lantermann, E. D. and Feger, H. (editors)
  Similarity and Choice
  (Vienna: Hans Huber Publisher, 1980).

Carroll, J. Douglas
  "Generalization of Canonical Correlation Analysis to Three or More
  Sets of Variables"
  Proceedings of 76th Annual Conference of the American Psychological
  Association, Vol. 3 (1968), pp. 227,8.

Carroll, J. Douglas and Green, Paul E.
  "An INDSCAL-Based Approach to Multiple Correspondence Analysis"
  Journal of Marketing Research, Vol. XXV (May 1988), pp. 193-203.

Carroll, J. Douglas, Green, Paul E., and Schaffer, Catherine M.
   "Reply to Greenacre's Commentary on the Carroll-Green-Schaffer
   Scaling of Two-Way Correspondence Analysis Solutions"
   Journal of Marketing Research, Vol. XXVI (August 1989), pp. 366-8.

Carroll, J. Douglas, Green, Paul E., and Schaffer, Catherine M.
   "Comparing Interpoint Distances in Correspondence Analysis: A
   Clarification"
   Journal of Marketing Research, Vol. XXIV (November 1987), pp. 445-50.

Carroll, J. Douglas, Green, Paul E., and Schaffer, Catherine M.
   "Interpoint Distance Comparisons in Correspondence Analysis"
   Journal of Marketing Research, Vol. XXIII (August 1986), pp. 271-80.

Fisher, Ronald A.
   "The Precision of Discriminant Functions"
   Annals of Eugenics, London, Vol. 10 (1940), pp. 422-9.

Franke, George R.
   "Evaluating Measures Through Data Quantification: Applying Dual
   Scaling to an Advertising Copytest"
   Journal of Business Research, Vol. 13 (February 1985), pp. 61-9.

Franke, George R.
   "Dual Scaling: A Model for Interpreting and Quantifying Categorical
   Data"
   in Darden, W. et al. (editors)
   Research Methods and Causal Modeling in Marketing
   (Chicago: American Marketing Association, 1983), pp. 111-4.

Gopalan, T. K.
   "Correspondence Analysis and AHC: An Exposition of Two Data Analytic
   Techniques"
   Candian Journal of Marketing Research, Vol. 5 (1986), pp. 2-9.

Gower, J. C. and Digby, P. G. N.
   "Expressing Complex Relationships in Two Dimensions"
   in Barnett, V. (editor)
   Interpreting Multivariate Data
   (Chister, UK: John Wiley and Sons, Inc., 1981), pp. 83-118.

Green, Paul E., Schaffer, Catherine M., and Patterson, Karen M.
   "A Reduced-Space Approach to the Clustering of Categorical Data in
   Market Segmentation"
   Journal of the Market Research Society, Vol. 30 (July 1988), pp.
   267-88.

Greenacre, Michael J.
   "The Carroll-Green-Schaffer Scaling in Correspondence Analysis: A
   Theoretical and Empirical Appraisal"
   Journal of Marketing Research, Vol. XXVI (August 1989), pp. 358-65.

Greenacre, Michael J.
   "Practical Correspondence Analysis"
   in Barnett, V. (editor)
   Interpreting Multivariate Data
   (Chichester, UK: John Wiley and Sons, Inc., 1981), pp. 119-46.

Greenacre, Michael J.
   "Some Objective Methods of Graphical Display of a Data Matrix"
   Department of Statistics and Operations Research, University of South
   Africa (1978), doctoral thesis (English translation).

Greenacre, Michael J. and Hastie, Trevor
   "The Geometric Interpretation of Correspondence Analysis"
   Journal of the American Statistical Association, Vol. 82 (June 1987),
   pp. 437-47.

Hill, M. O.
   "Correspondence Analysis"
   in Kotz, S. and Johnson, N. L. (editors)
   Encyclopedia of Statistical Sciences, Volume 2
   (New York: John Wiley and Sons, Inc., 1982), pp. 204-10.

Hill, M. O.
   "Correspondence Analysis: A Neglected Multivariate Method"
   Applied Statistics, Vol. 23, No. 3 (1974), pp. 340-54.

Hirschfeld, H. O.
   "A Connection Between Correlation and Contingency"
   Proceedings of the Cambridge Philosophical Society, Vol. 31 (1935),
   pp. 520-4.

Hoffman, Donna L. and Franke, George R.
   "Correspondence Analysis: Graphical Representation of Categorical
   Data in Marketing Research"
   Journal of Marketing Research, Vol. XXIII (August 1986), pp. 213-7.

Holland, T., Levi, M., and Watson, C.
"Canonical Correlation in the Analysis of a Contingency Table"
Psychological Bulletin, Vol. 87 (1980), pp. 334-6.

Isaac, P. D. and Milligan, Glenn W.
"A Comment on the Use of Canonical Correlation in the Analysis of
Contingency Tables"
Psychological Bulletin, Vol. 93, No. 2 (1983), pp. 378-81.

Krier, M. J. and Jackson, J. E.
"Correspondence Analysis as a Tool for Survey Statisticians"
ASA Proceedings, Survey Research Methods Section, Toronto (1984), pp.
212-7.

Lebart, Ludovic
"The Significance of Eigenvalues Issued From Correspondence Analysis"
Proceedings in Computational Statistics (COMPSTAT)
(Vienna: Physica Verlag, 1976), pp. 38-45.

Nishisato, Shizuhiko
"Forced Classification Procedure of Dual Scaling: Its Mathematical
Properties"
in Bock, H. H. (editor)
Proceedings, First Conference of the International Federation of
Classification Societies
(Aachen: North-Holland, 1987).

Nishisato, Shizuhiko
"Recent Developments in Scaling and Related Areas: A Bibliographic
Review"
Japanese Journal of Behaviormetrics, Vol. 4 (1977), pp. 74-95.

Nishisato, Shizuhiko and Gaul, Wolfgang
"Marketing Data Analysis by Dual Scaling"
International Journal of Research in Marketing, Vol. 5, No. 3 (1989),
pp. 151-70.

Nishisato, Shizuhiko and Sheu, Wen-Jenn
"A Note on Dual Scaling of Successive Categories Data"
Psychometrika, Vol. 49 (December 1984), pp. 493-500.

Saporta, G.
"About Some Remarkable Properties of Generalized Canonical Analysis"
Second European Meeting of the Psychometric Society
Groningen, The Netherlands (June 1980), paper presentation.

Tenenhaus, Michel and Young, Forrest W.
"Multiple Correspondence Analysis and the Principal Components of
Qualitative Data"
Laboratory Report No. 170
The L. L. Thurstone Psychometric Laboratory, University of North
Carolina (1983).

Van Der Heijden, Peter G. M. and De Leeuw, Jan
"Correspondence Analysis Used Complementary to Loglinear Analysis"
Psychometrika, Vol. 50 (December 1985), pp. 429-48.

Vasserot, G.
"L'Analyse des Correspondances Appliquee an Marketing: Choix d'un Nom
D'Engrais"
Les Caliers de l'Analyse des Donnees, Vol. 1 (1976), pp. 319-33.

155.03 ---------- Theory Re: Multiple Correspondence Analysis

Benzecri, Jean-Paul
"Sur l'Analyse des Tableaux Binaires Associes a une Correspondance
Multiple"
Cahiers de l'Analyse des Donnees, Vol. 2 (1977), pp. 55-71.

Carroll, J. Douglas and Green, Paul E.
"An INDSCAL-Based Approach to Multiple Correspondence Analysis"
Journal of Marketing Research, Vol. XXV (May 1988), pp. 193-203.

Carroll, J. Douglas and Green, Paul E.
"A New Approach to the Multiple Correspondence Analysis of
Categorical Data"
Wharton School, University of Pennsylvania (July 1987), working paper.

Greenacre, Michael J.
"Some Limitations of Multiple Correspondence Analysis"
MULTIWAY '88: International Meeting on the Analysis of Multiway
Matrices, Rome, Italy (March 1988), paper presentation.

Greenacre, Michael J.
"Correspondence Analysis of Multivariate Categorical Data by Weighted
Least Squares"
Biometrika, Vol. 75 (September 1988), pp. 457-67.

Greenacre, Michael J.
    "Measuring Total Variation and Its Components in Multiple
    Correspondence Analysis"
    A T and T Bell Laboratories Statistical Research Report, Murray Hill,
    NJ (1987).

Tenenhaus, Michel and Young, Forrest W.
    "An Analysis and Synthesis of Multiple Correspondence Analysis,
    Optimal Scaling, Dual Scaling, Homogeneity Analysis and Other Methods
    for Quantifying Categorical Multivariate Data"
    Psychometrika, Vol. 50 (1985), pp. 91-119.

155.04 ---------- Theory Re: Matrix Decomposition Approach

Fox, Richard J.
    "Perceptual Mapping Using the Basic Structure Matrix Decomposition"
    Journal of the Academy of Marketing Science, Vol. 16 (Spring 1988),
    pp. 47-59.

Gabriel, K. R.
    "Biplot Display of Multivariate Matrices for Inspection of Data and
    Diagnosis"
    in Barnett, V. (editor)
    Interpreting Multivariate Data
    (New York: John Wiley and Sons, 1981).

Gabriel, K. R.
    "The Biplot Graphic Display of Matrices With Applications to
    Principal Components Analysis"
    Biometrika, Vol. 58, No. 3 (1971), pp. 453-67.

Good, I. J.
    "Some Applications of the Singular Decomposition of a Matrix"
    Technometrics (1964), pp. 822-31.

155.05 ---------- Applications of Correspondence Analysis, Dual Scaling

Alt, Mick and Griggs, Steve
    "A Theory of Product Success"
    Journal of the Market Research Society, Vol. 28 (July 1986), pp.
    235-67.

Franke, George R.
    "Evaluating Measures Through Data Quantification: Applying Dual
    Scaling to an Advertising Copy Test"
    Journal of Business Research, Vol. 13 (February 1985), pp. 61-9.

Green, Paul E., Rao, Vithala R., and DeSarbo, Wayne S.
    "Incoporating Group-Level Similarity Judgments in Conjoint Analysis"
    Journal of Consumer Research, Vol. 5 (December 1978), pp. 187-93.

Green, Robert T., Leonardi, Jean-Paul, Chandon, Jean-Louis, Cunningham,
    Isabella C. M., Verhage, Bronis, and Strazzieri, Alain
    "Societal Development and Family Purchasing Roles: A Cross-National
    Study"
    Journal of Consumer Research, Vol. 9 (March 1983), pp. 436-42.

Holbrook, Morris, Moore, William, and Winer, Russell S.
    "Constructing Joint Spaces From Pick-Any Data: A New Tool for
    Consumer Analysis"
    Journal of Consumer Research, Vol. 9 (June 1982), pp. 99-105.

Jarboe, Glen R.
    "A Contingency Analysis Approach to Perceptual Mapping"
    Purdue University (1981), unpublished doctoral dissertation.

Marc, Marcel
    "Some Practical Uses of 'The Factorial Analysis of Correspondence'"
    European Research, Vol. 1 (July 1973), pp. 2-8.

Meade, Nigel
    "Strategic Positioning in the UK Car Market"
    European Journal of Marketing, Vol. 21, No. 5 (1987), pp. 43-56.

Smith, J. Walker
    "Marketers' Perceptions of the Marketing Process in the Eighties"
    Journal of Advertising Research, Vol. 29 (June/July 1989), pp. RC9-16.

Weingarden, P. and Nishisato, Shizuhiko
    "Can a Method of Rank Ordering Reproduce Paired Comparisons? An
    Analysis by Dual Scaling (Correspondence Analysis)"
    Canadian Journal of Marketing Research, Vol. 5 (1986), pp. 11-8.

155.06 ----------   Computer Programs for Correspondence Analysis

Fox, Richard J.
    "Review of Correspondence Analysis PC Software Packages"
    Journal of Marketing Research, Vol. XXV (November 1988), pp. 415-7.

Greenacre, Michael J.
    "SIMCA: A Program to Perform Simple Correspondence Analysis"
    Psychometrika, Vol. 51 (March 1086), pp. 172,3.

Greenacre, Michael J.
    Correspondence Analysis: Program for the IBM PC and Compatibles,
    Version 1.1
    University of South Africa (June 1986).

Institute of Business Management
    PC-MDS, Version 4.1
    (Brigham Young University, 1987).

Lebart, L. and Morineau, A.
    "SPAD: A System of FORTRAN Programs for Correspondence Analysis"
    Journal of Marketing Research, Vol. XIX (November 1982), pp. 608,9.

Marketing Action, Incorporated
    STRATMAP, Version 5.0
    (Peoria, IL: Marketing Action, Inc., 1988).

MicroStats
    DUAL, Version 3.1
    (Islington, Ontario: MicroStats, 1986).

Research Services Company
    PASS
    (Flossmoor, IL: Research Services Co., 1987).

155.07 ----------   Unclassified (Correspondence Analysis)

Gabriel, K. R.
    "Biplot Display of Multivariate Matrices for Inspection of Data and
    Diagnosis"
    in Barnett, V. (editor)
    Interpreting Multivariate Data
    (Chichester: John Wiley and Sons, Inc., 1981), pp. 147-73.

Gabriel, K. R.
    "The Biplot Graphic Display of Matrices With Application to Principal
    Component Analysis"
    Biometrika, Vol. 58 (December 1971), pp. 453-67.

Levine, Joel H.
    "Joint-Space Analysis of 'Pick-Any' Data: Analysis of Choices From an
    Unconstrained Set of Alternatives"
    Psychometrika, Vol. 44 (March 1979), pp. 85-92.

156 -------------- EQUATIONS OF CORRESPONDENCE ANALYSIS --------------

      See also (sub)heading(s) 155.

Tenenhaus, Michel and Young, Forrest W.
   "An Analysis and Synthesis of Multiple Correspondence Analysis,
   Optimal Scaling, Dual Scaling, Homogeneity Analysis and Other Methods
   for Quantifying Categorical Multivariate Data"
   Psychometrika, Vol. 50 (March 1985), pp. 91-119.

156.01 ---------- Theory Re: Method of Reciprocal Averages

Fisher, Ronald A.
   "The Precision of Discriminant Functions"
   Annals of Eugenics, Vol. 10 (December 1940), pp. 422-9.

Hirschfeld, H. O.
   "A Connection Between Correlations and Contingency"
   Proceedings of the Cambridge Philosophical Society, Vol. 31 (October
   1935), pp. 520-4.

Horst, Paul
   "Measuring Complex Attitudes"
   Journal of Social Psychology, Vol. 6, No. 3 (1935), pp. 369-74.

Richardson, M. and Kuder, G. F.
   "Making a Rating Scale That Measures"
   Personnel Journal, Vol. 12 (June 1933), pp. 36-40.

156.02 ---------- Theory Re: Analysis of Variance Approach

Bock, R. Darrell
   "Methods and Applications of Optimal Scaling"
   Laboratory Report No. 25
   L. L. Thurstone Psychometric Laboratory
   (Chapel Hill: University of North Carolina, 1960).

De Leeuw, Jan
   Canonical Analysis of Categorical Data
   Psychological Institute, University of Leiden, The Netherlands
   (1973), unpublished doctoral dissertation.

Guttman, Louis
   "The Quantification of a Class of Attributes: A Theory and Method of
   Scale Construction"
   in The Committee on Social Adjustment (editors)
   (New York: Social Science Research Council, 1941), pp. 319-48.

Hayashi, C.
   "Multidimensional Quantifications--With The Applications to Analysis
   of Social Phenomena"
   Annals of the Institute of Statistical Mathematics, Vol. 5, No. 2
   (1954), pp. 121-43.

Hayashi, C.
   "On the Prediction of Phenomena From Qualitative Data and the
   Quantification of Qualitative Data From the Mathematico-Statistical
   Point of View"
   Annals of the Institute of Statistical Mathematics, Vol. 3, No. 2
   (1952), pp. 69-98.

Hayashi, C.
   "On the Quantification of Qualitative Data From the
   Mathematico-Statistical Point of View"
   Annals of the Institute of Statistical Mathematics, Vol. 2, No. 1
   (1950), pp. 35-47.

Nishisato, Shizuhiko
   Analysis of Categorical Data: Dual Scaling and Its Applications
   (Toronto: University of Toronto Press, 1980).

Van Rijekevorsel, Jan and De Leeuw, Jan
   "An Outline to HOMALS-1"
   Department of Data Theory, Faculty of Social Sciences, University of
   Leiden, The Netherlands (1978).

156.03 ---------- Theory Re: Principal Components Approach

Benzecri, J. P.
   "Statistical Analysis as a Tool to Make Patterns Emerge From Data"
   in Watanabe, S. (editor)
   Methodologies of Pattern Recognition
   (New York: Academic Press, Inc., 1969), pp. 35-74.

Burt, C.
   "The Factorial Analysis of Qualitative Data"
   British Journal of Psychology, Statistical Section, Vol. 3 (November
   1950), pp. 166-85.

Greenacre, Michael J.
  Theory and Application of Correspondence Analysis
  (London: Academic Press, Inc., 1984).

156.04 ---------- Theory Re: Generalized Canonical Analysis Approach

McKeon, J. J.
  "Canonical Analysis: Some Relations Between Canonical Correlation,
  Factor Analysis, Discriminant Function Analysis and Scaling Theory"
  Monograph No. 13
  Psychometrika (1966).

157 ------------------------- OPTIMAL SCALING ------------------------

See also (sub)heading(s) 155.

157.01 ---------- Theory Re: Optimal Scaling

Bock, R. Darrell
"Methods and Applications of Optimal Scaling"
Laboratory Report No. 25, L. L. Thurstone Psychometric Laboratory,
University of North Carolina, Chapel Hill.

Carroll, J. Douglas
"Categorical Conjoint Measurement"
(Murray Hill, NJ: Bell Telephone Laboratories, 1969), unpublished
paper.

Nishisato, Shizuhiko and Arri, P. S.
"Nonlinear Programming Approach to Optimal Scaling of Partially
Ordered Categories"
Psychometrika, Vol. 40 (1975), pp. 525-58.

Tanaka, Y. and Kodake, C.
"Computational Aspects of Optimal Scaling for Ordered Categories"
Behaviormetrika, Vol. 7 (1980), pp. 35-47.

Tenenhaus, Michel and Young, Forrest W.
"An Analysis and Synthesis of Multiple Correspondence Analysis,
Optimal Scaling, Dual Scaling, Homogeneity Analysis and Other Methods
for Quantifying Categorical Multivariate Data"
Psychometrika, Vol. 50 (1985), pp. 91-119.

157.02 ---------- Alternating Least Squares Optimal Scaling (ALSOS)

De Leeuw, Jan
Canonical Analysis of Categorical Data
(Leiden, The Netherlands: University of Leiden, 1973).

De Leeuw, Jan, Young, Forrest W., and Takane, Yoshio
"Additive Structure in Qualitative Data: An Alternating Least Squares
Method With Optimal Scaling Features"
Psychometrika, Vol. 41 (December 1976), pp. 471-503.

DeSarbo, Wayne S., Green, Paul E., and Carroll, J. Douglas
"An Alternating Least-Squares Procedure for Estimating Missing
Preference Data in Product-Concept Testing"
Decision Sciences, Vol. 17 (Spring 1986), pp. 163-85.

Didow, Nicholas M., Jr., Keller, Kevin Lane, Barksdale, Hiram C., Jr.,
and Franke, George R.
"Improving Measure Quality by Alternating Least Squares Optimal
Scaling"
Journal of Marketing Research, Vol. XXII (February 1985), pp. 30-40.

Kroonenberg, Pieter M. and DeLeeuw, Jan
"Principal Component Analysis of Three-Mode Data by Means of
Alternating Least Squares Algorithms"
Pshchometrika, Vol. 45 (1980), pp. 69-97.

Perreault, William D., Jr. and Young, Forrest W.
"Alternating Least Squares Optimal Scaling: Analysis of Nonmetric
Data in Marketing Research"
Journal of Marketing Research, Vol. XVII (February 1980), pp. 1-13.

Sands, R. and Young, F. W.
"Component Models for Three-Way Data: An Alternating Least Squares
Algorithm With Optimal Scaling Features"
Psychometrika, Vol. 45 (1980), pp. 39-87.

Takane, Yoshio, Young, Forrest W., and De Leeuw, Jan
"Nonmetric Individual Differences Multidimensional Scaling: An
Alternating Least Squares Method With Optimal Scaling Features"
Psychometrika, Vol. 42 (March 1977), pp. 7-67.

Young, Forrest W.
"Quantitative Analysis of Qualitative Data"
Psychometrika, Vol. 46 (December 1981), pp. 357-88.

Young, Forrest W., De Leeuw, Jan, and Takane, Yoshio
"Quantifying Qualitative Data"
in Feger H. (editor)
Similarity and Choice
(New York: Academic Press, 1979).

Young, Forrest W., Takane, Yoshio, and De Leeuw, Jan
"The Principal Components of Mixed Measurement Data: An Alternating
Least Squares Method With Optimal Scaling Features"
Psychometrika, Vol. 43 (June 1978), pp. 279-82.

157.03 ---------- Multiple Optimal Regression via Alt Least Squares

Young, Forrest W., De Leeuw, Jan, and Takane, Yoshio
  "Regression With Qualitative Variables: An Alternating Least Squares
  Method With Optimal Scaling Features"
  Psychometrika, Vol. 41 (December 1976), pp. 505-29.

157.04 ---------- Applications of Optimal Scaling

Didow, Nicholas M., Jr., Perreault, William D., Jr., and Williamson,
  Nicholas C.
  "A Cross-Sectional Optimal Scaling Analysis of the Index of Consumer
  Sentiment"
  Journal of Consumer Research, Vol. 10 (December 1983), pp. 339-47.

Holbrook, Morris
  "Comparing Multiattribute Models by Optimal Scaling"
  Journal of Consumer Research, Vol. 4 (December 1977), pp. 165-71.

157.05 ---------- OVERALS

De Leeuw, Jan and Van Der Berg, E.
  "How to Use OVERALS"
  University of Leiden, Leiden, The Netherlands (1978), unpublished
  paper.

158 ----------------------- ROBUST STATISTICS -----------------------
          See also (sub)heading(s) 136.

158.01 ---------- Books Re: Robust Statistics

Andrews, D. F. et al.
   Robust Estimates of Location: Survey and Advances
   (Princeton, NJ: Princeton University Press, 1972).

Hampel, Frank R., Rousseeuw, Peter J., Ronchetti, Elvezio M., and
   Stahel, Werner A.
   Robust Statistics
   (New York: John Wiley and Sons, Inc., 1986), 502 pp.

Hoaglin, D. C., Mosteller, F., and Tukey, J. W.
   Understanding Robust and Exploratory Data Analysis
   (New York: John Wiley and Sons, Inc., 1983).

Huber, P. J.
   Robust Statistics
   (New York: John Wiley and Sons, Inc., 1981).

Launer, R. L. and Wilkinson, G. N. (editors)
   Robustness in Statistics
   (New York: Academic Press, 1979).

158.02 ---------- Theory Re: Robust Statistics

Gross, A. M.
   "Confidence Interval Robustness With Long-Tailed Symmetrical
   Distributions"
   Journal of the American Statistical Association, Vol. 71 (1976), pp.
   409-16.

Hampel, Frank R.
   Contributions to the Theory of Robust Estimation
   University at Berkeley (1978), Ph.D. dissertation.

Hogg, R. V.
   "Statistical Robustness: One View of Its Use in Applications Today"
   American Statistician, Vol. 33 (August 1979), pp. 108-15.

Hogg, R. V.
   "An Introduction to Robust Estimation"
   in Launer, R. L. and Wilkinson, G. N. (editors)
   Robustness in Statistics
   (New York: Academic Press, 1979), pp. 1-18.

Huber, D. R.
   "Robust Statistics: A Review"
   Annals of Mathematical Statistics, Vol. 43 (1975), pp. 1041-67.

Huber, P. J.
   "Robust Estimation of a Location Parameter"
   Annals of Mathematical Statistics, Vol. 35 (1964), pp. 73-101.

Rust, Roland T. and Bornman, E. O.
   "Distribution-Free Methods of Approximating Nonlinear Marketing
   Relationships"
   Journal of Marketing Research, Vol. XIX (August 1982), pp. 372-4.

Velleman, P. F.
   "Robust Non-Linear Data Smoothers: Definitions and Recommendations"
   Economic and Social Statistics Technical Report 776-001
   Department of Economic and Social Statistics, New York State School
   of Industrial and Labor Relations, Cornell University (1976).

159 -------------------- REGRESSION ANALYSIS ----------------------
        See also (sub)heading(s) 133.06, 150, 160, 161, 162, 163,
     164, 165, 166, 167, 168, 169, 170, 174.

159.01 ---------- Books Re: Regression Analysis

Achen, Christopher H.
    Interpreting and Using Regression
    (Beverly Hills, CA: Sage Publications, Inc., 1982), 87 pp.

Bard, Y.
    Nonlinear Parameter Estimation
    (New York: Academic Press, 1974).

Belsley, David A., Kuh, Edwin, and Welsch, Roy E.
    Regression Diagnostics: Identifying Influential Data and Sources of
    Collinearity
    (New York: John Wiley and Sons, Inc., 1980), 292 pp.

Berry, William D. and Feldman, Stanley
    Multiple Regression in Practice
    Quantitative Applications in the Social Sciences, Paper No. 50
    (Beverly Hills, CA: Sage Publications, 1985), 93 pp.

Breiman, Leo, Freidman, Jerome H., Olshen, Richard A., and Stone,
    Charles J.
    Classification and Regression Trees
    (Belmont, CA: Wadsworth International, 1984).

Chatterjee, Samprit and Price, Bertram
    Regression Analysis by Example
    (New York: John Wiley and Sons, Inc., 1977), 228 pp.

Chow, Gregory C.
    Econometrics
    (New York: McGraw-Hill, Inc., 1983).

Cohen, Jacob and Cohen, Patricia
    Applied Multiple Regression/Correlation Analysis for the Behavioral
    Sciences, Second Edition
    (Hillsdale, NJ: Lawrence Erlbaum Associates, 1983).

Daniel, C. and Wood, F. S.
    Fitting Equations to Data
    (New York: John Wiey and Sons, Inc., 1980).

Dhrymes, Phoebus J.
    Introductory Econometrics
    (New York: Springer-Verlag, 1978).

Dhrymes, Phoebus J.
    Econometrics: Statistical Foundation and Applications
    (New York: Academic Press, 1975).

Dhrymes, P. J.
    Econometrics: Statistical Foundations and Applications
    (New York: Springer-Verlag, 1974), 592 pp.

Draper, N. R. and Smith, H.
    Applied Regression Analysis, Second Edition
    (New York: John Wiley and Sons, Inc., 1981), 707 pp.

Edwards, Allen L.
    An Introduction to Linear Regression and Correlation
    (San Francisco: W. H. Freeman and Company, 1976), 213 pp.

Eichhorn, Wolfgang
    Functional Equations in Economics
    (Reading, MA: Addison-Wesley Publishing Company, 1978).

Fraser, D. A.
    Inference and Linear Models
    (New York: McGraw-Hill, Inc., 1979), 297 pp.

Freund, Rudolf J. and Minton, Paul D.
    Regression Methods: A Tool for Data Analysis
    (New York: Marcel Dekker, Inc., 1979), 261 pp.

Graybill, F. A.
    Theory and Application of the Linear Model
    (North Scituate, MA: Duxbury Press, 1976).

Gunst, R. F. and Mason, R. L.
    Regression Analysis and Its Application: A Data-Oriented Approach
    (New York: Marcel Dekker, Inc., 1980), 402 pp.

Hannon, Michael T.
    Aggregation and Disaggregation in Sociology
    (Lexington, MA: D. C. Heath and Company, 1971).

Heward, James H. and Steele, Peter M.
    Business Control Through Multiple Regression Analysis
    (New York: John Wiley and Sons, Inc., 1973).

Horton, Raymond L.
    The General Linear Model: Data Analysis in the Social and Behavioral
    Sciences
    (New York: McGraw-Hill Book Company, 1978).

Intriligator, M. D.
    Econometric Models, Techniques and Applications
    (Englewood Cliffs, NJ: Prentice-Hall, 1978), 638 pp.

Johnston, J.
    Econometric Methods, Third Edition
    (New York: McGraw-Hill Book Company, 1984).

Judge, George G., Griffiths, William E., Hill, R. Carter, and Lee,
    Tsoung-Chao
    The Theory and Practice of Econometrics, Second Edition
    (New York: John Wiley and Sons, Inc., 1985), 1019 pp.

Kelejian, H. H. and Oates, W. E.
    Introduction to Econometrics
    (New York: Harper and Row, 1974).

Kerlinger, Fred N. and Pedhazur, Elazar J.
    Multiple Regression in Behavioral Research
    (New York: Holt, Rinehart and Winston, 1973).

Kleinbaum, David G. and Kupper, Lawrence L.
    Applied Regression Analysis and Other Multivariate Methods
    (North Scituate, MA: Duxbury Press, 1978), 555 pp.

Kmenta, Jan
    Elements of Econometrics
    (New York: Macmillan Publishing Co., Inc., 1971), 654 pp.

Leamer, Edward E.
    Specification Searches: Ad Hoc Inference With Nonexperimental Data
    (New York: John Wiley and Sons, Inc., 1978), 370 pp.

Lewis-Beck, Michael S.
    Applied Regression: An Introduction
    (Beverly Hills, CA: Sage Publications, Inc., 1980).

Madansky, A.
    Foundations of Econometrics
    (Amsterdam: North-Holland, 1976).

Maddala, G. S.
    Econometrics
    (New York: McGraw-Hill Book Co., 1977).

Malinvaude, E.
    Statistical Methods of Econometrics, Second Edition
    (Amsterdam: North-Holland, 1970).

Mendenhall, William and Sincich, Terry
    A Second Course in Business Statistics: Regression Analysis
    (San Francisco: Dellen Publishing Co., 1986).

Montgomery, Douglas C. and Peck Elizabeth A.
    Introduction to Linear Regression Analysis
    (New York: John Wiley and Sons, Inc., 1982), 504 pp.

Mosteller, Frederick and Tukey, John W.
    Data Analysis and Regression
    (Reading, MA: Addison-Wesley Publishing Co., 1977), 588 pp.

Myers, R. R.
    Classical and Modern Regression With Applications
    (Boston: Duxbury Press, 1986).

Neter, John and Wasserman, W.
    Applied Linear Statistical Models, Second Edition
    (Homewood, IL: Richard D. Irwin, Inc., 1985).

Newbold, Paul and Bos, Theodore
    Stochastic Parameter Regression Models
    Quantitative Applications in the Social Sciences, Paper No. 51
    (Beverly Hills, CA: Sage Publications, 1985), 79 pp.

Ostrom, Charles W., Jr.
    Time Series Analysis: Regression Techniques
    (Beverly Hills, CA: Sage Publications, Inc.).

Parsons, Leonard J. and Schultz, R. L.
    Marketing Models and Econometric Research
    (Amsterdam: North-Holland Publishing Company, 1976).

Pedhazur, Elazar J.
  Multiple Regression in Behavioral Research, Second Edition
  (New York: Holt, Rinehart and Winston, Inc., 1982).

Pindyck, R. S. and Rubinfeld, D. L.
  Econometric Models and Economic Forecasts
  (New York: McGraw-Hill Book Company, 1981).

Rao, P. and Miller, R. L.
  Applied Econometrics
  (Belmont, CA: Wadsworth, 1971).

Schroeder, Larry D., Sjoquist, David L., and Stephan, Paula E.
  Understanding Regression Analysis: An Introductory Guide
  (Beverly Hills, CA: Sage Publications, Inc., 1986), 95 pp.

Searle, S.
  Linear Models
  (New York: John Wiley and Sons, Inc., 1971).

Seber, G. A. F.
  Linear Regression Analysis
  (New York: John Wiley and Sons, Inc., 1977), 465 pp.

Stewart, Mark B. and Wallis, Kenneth F.
  Introductory Econometrics, Second Edition
  (New York: John Wiley and Sons, Inc., 1981), 337 pp.

Swamy, P. A. V. B.
  Statistical Inference in Random Coefficient Regression Models
  (New York: Springer-Verlag, 1971).

Theil, H.
  Introduction to Econometrics
  (Englewood Cliffs, NJ: Prentice-Hall, 1978).

Theil, Henri
  Principles of Econometrics
  (New York: John Wiley and Sons, 1971), 736 pp.

Toutenburg, Helge
  Prior Information in Linear Models
  (New York: John Wiley and Sons, Inc., 1982), 215 pp.

Walters, A. A.
  An Introduction to Econometrics
  (New York: W. W. Norton and Co., 1970).

Ward, J. H. and Jennings, E.
  Introduction to Linear Models
  (Englewood Cliffs, NJ: Prentice-Hall, Inc., 1973).

Weisberg, Sanford
  Applied Linear Regression
  (New York: John Wiley and Sons, Inc., 1980), 283 pp.

Wesolowsky, George O.
  Multiple Regression and Analysis of Variance
  (New York: John Wiley and Sons, Inc., 1977), 292 pp.

Wittink, Dick R.
  The Application of Regression Analysis
  (Needham Heights, MA: Allyn and Bacon, Inc, 1988), 324 pp.

Wonnacott, R. J. and Wonnacott, T. H.
  Econometrics, Second Edition
  (New York: John Wiley and Sons, Inc., 1979), 454 pp.

Wonnacott, Thomas H. and Wonnacott, Ronald J.
  Regression: A Second Course in Statistics
  (New York: John Wiley and Sons, Inc., 1981), 556 pp.

Younger, Mary Sue
  A Handbook for Linear Regression
  (North Scituate, MA: Duxbury Press, 1979), 569 pp.

Zarembka, Paul (editor)
  Frontiers in Econometrics
  (New York: Academic Press, 1974).

159.02 ---------- Theory Re: Regression Analysis

Anderson, N. H. and Shanteau, J.
  "Weak Inference With Linear Models"
  Psychological Bulletin, Vol. 84 (1977), pp. 1155-70.

Armstrong, J. Scott
  "'Exploratory Analysis of Marketing Data': A Reply"
  Journal of Marketing Research, Vol. VIII (November 1971), pp. 514-7.

Armstrong, J. Scott
"How to Avoid Exploratory Research"
Journal of Advertising Research, Vol. 10 (August 1970), pp. 27-30.

Armstrong, J. Scott and Andress, James G.
"Exploratory Analysis of Marketing Data: Trees vs. Regression"
Journal of Marketing Research, Vol. VII (November 1970), pp. 487-92.

Atkinson, A. C.
"Regresion Diagnostics, Transformations and Constructed Variables"
Journal of the Royal Statistical Society, Vol. 44 (1982), pp. 1-22.

Ball, G. H.
"Data Analysis in the Social Sciences: What About the Details?"
Proceedings of the Fall Joint Computer Conference, Las Vegas, Nevada,
1965.

Bartlett, M. S.
"Fitting a Straight Line When Both Variables are Subject to Error"
Biometrics, Vol. 5 (1949), pp. 207-12.

Bass, Frank M.
"Application of Regression Models in Marketing: Testing vs.
Forecasting"
in Sheth, Jagdish N. (editor)
Multivariate Methods for Market and Survey Research
(Chicago: American Marketing Association, 1977).

Beach, Charles M. and MacKinnon, James W.
"A Maximum Likelihood Procedure for Regression With Autocorrelated
Errors"
Econometrica, Vol. 46 (1978), pp. 51-8.

Beale, E. M. L., Kendall, M. G., and Mann, D. W.
"The Discarding of Variables in Multivariate Analysis"
Biometrika, Vol. 54 (1967), pp. 357-66.

Bellman, Richard and Roth, Robert
"Curve Fitting by Segmented Straight Lines"
Journal of the American Statistical Association, Vol. 64 (September
1969), pp. 1079-84.

Benson, P. H.
"Projecting Proportions of Consumer Response From One Sample or
Universe to Another"
Proceedings, American Psychological Association (1968), pp. 669,70.

Birnbaum, M. H.
"The Devil Rides Again: Correlation as an Index of Fit"
Psychological Bulletin, Vol. 79 (1973), pp. 239-42.

Blalock, Hubert M., Jr.
"Path Coefficients Versus Regression Coefficients"
American Journal of Sociology, Vol. 72, (1967), pp. 675,6.

Blattberg, Robert C. and Sargent, Thomas
"Regression With Non-Gaussian Disturbances: Some Sampling Results"
Graduate School of Industrial Administration, Carnegie-Mellon
University (1969), unpublished paper.

Cohen, Jacob
"Multiple Regression as a General Data-Analytic System"
Psychological Bulletin, Vol. 70 (December 1968), pp. 426-43.

Collins, Gwyn
"On Methods: Correlation and Regression"
Journal of Advertising Research, Vol. 1 (June 1961), pp. 36-40.

Cowden, Dudley J.
"The Multiple-Partial Correlation Coefficient"
Journal of the American Statistical Association, Vol. 47 (September
1952), pp. 442-56.

Crocker, Douglas C.
"Comments on 'Exploratory Analysis of Marketing Data: Trees vs.
Regression'"
Journal of Marketing Research, Vol. VIII (November 1971), pp. 509-13.

Darlington, Richard B.
"Multiple Regession in Psychological Research and Practice"
Psychological Bulletin, Vol. 69 (1968), pp. 161-82.

Dempster, A. P., Schatzoff, Martin, and Wermuth, Nancy
"A Simulation Study of Alternatives to Ordinary Least Squares"
Journal of the American Statistical Association, Vol. 72 (1977), pp.
77-91.

DuMouchel, William H. and Duncan, Greg J.
"Using Sample Survey Weights in Multiple Regression Analysis of Stratified Samples"
Journal of the American Statistical Association, Vol. 78 (September 1983), pp. 535-43.

Durbin, J.
"A Note on Regression When There is Extraneous Information About One of the Coefficients"
Journal of the American Statistical Association, Vol. 48 (September 1953), pp. 799-808.

Efron, B. and Morris, C.
"Comment to 'A Simulation Study of Alternatives to Ordinary Least Squares' by A. P. Dempster, M. Schatzoff and N. Wermuth"
Journal of the American Statistical Association, Vol. 72 (1977), pp. 91-3.

Ehrenberg, A. S. C.
"Bivariate Regression Analysis is Useless"
Applied Statistics, Vol. 12 (1963), pp. 161-79.

Einhorn, Hillel J., Kleinmuntz, Don N., and Kleinmuntz, Benjamin
"Linear Regression and Process-Tracing Models of Judgment"
Psychological Review, Vol. 86 (1979), pp. 465-85.

Ferber, Robert
"Are Correlations Any Guide to Predictive Value?"
Applied Statistics, Vol. 5 (June 1956), pp. 113-21.

Fisher, R. A.
"The Goodness of Fit and Regression Formulae, and the Distribution of Regression Coefficients"
Journal of the Royal Statistical Society, Vol. 85 (1922).

Foote, Richard J.
"A Comparison of Single and Simultaneous Equation Techniques"
Journal of Farm Economics (December 1955), pp. 975-90.

Furnival, G. M. and Wilson, R. W., Jr.
"Regression by Leaps and Bounds"
Technometrics, Vol. 16 (November 1974), pp. 499-510.

Gensch, Dennis H., Golob, Thomas F., and Recker, Wilfred W.
"Regression is Inappropriate for Analyzing Cross-Sectional Data"
1976 Educators' Proceedings
(Chicago: American Marketing Association, 1976), pp. 120-4.

Gomez-Sanchez, M.
"Econometrics: An Important Tool in Modern Marketing Research--Part II"
European Research, Vol. 4 (November 1976), pp. 250-60.

Gomez-Sanchez, M.
"Econometrics: An Important Tool in Modern Marketing Research"
European Research, Vol. 4 (September 1976), pp. 210-5.

Gordon, R. A.
"Issues in Multiple Regression"
American Journal of Sociology, Vol. 73 (March 1968), pp. 592-616.

Gunst, R. F., Webster, J. T., and Mason, Robert L.
"A Comparison of Least Squares and Latent Root Regression Estimators"
Technometrics, Vol. 18 (1976), pp. 75-83.

Gur-Arie, Oded, Durand, Richard M., and Sharma, Subhash
"Identifying Moderating Variables Using Moderated Regression Analysis"
in Franz, R. S., Hopkins, R. M., and Toma, A. G. (editors)
Proceedings, Southern Marketing Association
(Lafayette: Southern Marketing Association, 1979), pp. 189-92.

Haitovsky, Yoel
"A Note on the Maximization of R"
American Statistician, Vol. 23 (February 1969), pp. 20,1.

Hocking, R. R.
"Developments in Linear Regression Methodology: 1959-82"
Technometrics, Vol. 25 (1983), pp. 219-29.

Hocking, R. R. and Pendleton, O. J.
"The Regresson Dilemma"
Communications in Statistics--Theory and Methodology, Vol. 12 (1983), pp. 497-527.

Jennings, E.
"Fixed Effects Analysis of Variance by Regression Analysis"
Multivariate Behavioral Research, Vol. 2 (January 1967), pp. 95-108.

Joe, George W.
   "Comment on Overall and Spiegel's Least Squares Analysis of
   Experimental Data"
   Psychological Bulletin, Vol. 75 (May 1971), pp. 364-6.

Johansson, Johny K. and McAlister, Leigh
   "Using Variable Parameter Regression to Capture Individual Variations
   in Choice Models"
   National Meeting of TIMS/ORSA, Washington, DC (May 1980), paper
   presentation.

Johnson, Richard M.
   "A Simple Method for Pairwise Monotone Regression"
   Psychometrika, Vol. 40 (1975), pp. 163-8.

Keren, Gideon and Newman, Robert J.
   "Additional Consideration With Regard to Multiple Regression and
   Equal Weighting"
   Organizational Behavior and Human Performance, Vol. 22 (1978), pp.
   143-65.

Landis, Jack B.
   "On Methods: Multiple Regression Analysis--The Easy Way"
   Journal of Advertising Research, Vol. 2 (March 1962), pp. 35-42.

Marquardt, Donald W.
   "You Should Standardize the Predictor Variables in Your Regression
   Models"
   Journal of the American Statistical Association, Vol. 75 (1980), pp.
   87-91.

Massy, William F.
   "Statistical Analysis of Relations Between Variables"
   in Frank, Ronald E., Kuehn, Alfred, and Massy, William (editors)
   Quantitative Techniques in Marketing Analysis
   (Homewood, IL: Richard D. Irwin, Inc., 1962), pp. 56-95.

McGee, Victor E. and Carleton, Willard T.
   "Piecewise Regression"
   Journal of the American Statistical Association, Vol. 65 (1970), pp.
   1109-24.

Melnick, E. L. and Shoaf, F. R.
   "Multiple Regression Equals Analysis of Variance"
   Journal of Advertising Research, Vol. 17 (June 1977), pp. 27-31.

Mosteller, Frederick
   "Remarks on the Method of Paired Comparisons: The Least Squares
   Solution Assuming Equal Standard Deviations and Equal Correlations"
   Psychometrika, Vol. 16 (March 1951), pp. 3-9.

Overall, J. E. and Spiegel, D. K.
   "Concerning Least Squares Analysis of Experimental Data"
   Psychological Bulletin, Vol. 72 (1969), pp. 311-22.

Palda, Kristian S.
   "The Evaluation of Regression Results"
   Proceedings of the AMA Winter Conference (December 1963), pp. 282-7.

Ploch, Donald H.
   "Ordinal Measures of Association and the General Linear Model"
   in Blalock, Hubert M., Jr. (editor)
   Measurement in the Social Sciences
   (Chicago: Aldine Publishing Company, 1974), pp. 343-68.

Quandt, R. E.
   "Estimating the Effectiveness of Advertising: Some Pitfalls in
   Econometric Methods"
   Journal of Marketing Research, Vol. I (May 1964), pp. 51-62.

Rulon, P. J.
   "Distinctions Between Discriminant and Regression Analysis and a
   Geometric Interpretation of the Discriminant Function"
   Harvard Educational Review, Vol. 21 (June 1951), pp. 80-90.

Schutz, W. C.
   "The Little Jiffy Correlator: A Simple Technique for a Complex
   Analysis of Large Numbers of Measures on the Same Individuals"
   Educational and Psychological Measurement, Vol. 20 (Spring 1960), pp.
   111-8.

Sclove, Stanley L.
   "Improved Estimators for Coefficients in Linear Regression"
   Journal of the American Statistical Association, Vol. 63 (1968), pp.
   596-606.

Semon, T. T.
   "An Alternative Statistical 'Line of Best Fit'"
   Journal of Marketing, Vol. 24 (January 1960), pp. 73,4.

Simon, Hubert A.
"Spurious Correlation: A Causal Interpretation"
Journal of the American Statistical Association, Vol. 49 (1954), pp. 467-9.

Srinivasan, V.
"A Theoretical Comparison of the Predictive Power of the Multiple Regression and Equal Weighting Procedures"
Research Paper No. 347
Graduate School of Business, Stanford University (1977).

Stewart, J.
"Letter to the Editor"
American Statistician, Vol. 25 (April 1971), p. 40.

Swamy, P. A. V. B.
"Efficient Inferences in a Random Coefficient Regression Model"
Econometrica, Vol. 38 (March 1970), pp. 311-23.

Theil, H. and Goldberger, A. S.
"On Pure and Mixed Statistical Estimation in Economics"
International Economic Review, Vol. 2 (1961), pp. 65-8.

Tukey, J. W.
"Causation, Regression and Path Analysis"
in Kempthorne, O., Bancroft, T. A., Gowen, J. W., and Lush, J. L. (editors)
Statistics and Mathematics in Biology
(Ames, IA: Iowa State College Press, 1954), pp. 35-66.

Tukey, John W.
"One Degree of Freedom for Additivity"
Biometrics, Vol. 5 (September 1949), pp. 232-42.

Wagner, H.
"Linear Programming Techniques for Regression Analysis"
Journal of the American Statistical Association, Vol. 54 (March 1959), pp. 206-12.

Wainer, Howard
"Estimating Coefficients in Linear Models: It Don't Make No Nevermind"
Psychological Bulletin, Vol. 83 (1976), pp. 213-7.

Wampler, Roy H.
"A Report on the Accuracy of Some Widely Used Least Squares Computer Programs"
Journal of the American Statistical Association, Vol. 65 (June 1970), pp. 549-65.

Weiss, Moshe
"Letter to the Editor"
American Statistician, Vol. 24 (June 1970), p. 20.

Werts, Charles E. and Linn, Robert L.
"Causal Assumptions in Various Procedures for the Least Squares Analysis of Categorical Data"
Psychological Bulletin, Vol. 75 (June 1971), pp. 430,1.

Wherry, Robert J.
"The Wherry-Doolittle Test Selection Method"
in Stead, W. H. and Shartle, L. L. (editors)
Occupational Counseling Techniques
(New York: American Book Company, 1940), pp. 245-52.

Wildt, A. R. and McCann, J. M.
"A Regression Model for Market Segmentation Studies"
Journal of Marketing Research, Vol. XVII (August 1980), pp. 335-40.

Wirth, Edward D., Jr.
"Developing Marketing Strategy Through Multiple Regression"
Journal of Marketing Research, Vol. IV (August 1967), pp. 318,9.

Woodward, J. Arthur and Overall, John E.
"Multivariate Analysis by Multiple Regression Methods"
Psychological Bulletin, Vol. 82 (1975), pp. 21-32.

Wright, Sewall
"Path Coefficients and Path Regressions: Alternative or Complimentary Concepts"
Biometrics, Vol. 16 (1960), pp. 189-202.

Zellner, Arnold
"An Efficient Method of Estimating Seemingly Unrelated Regressions and Tests for Aggregation Bias"
Journal of the American Statistical Association, Vol. 57 (June 1962), pp. 348-68.

159.03 ---------- Theory Re: Subset Regression

Cox, D. R. and Snell, E. J.
    "The Choice of Variables in Observational Studies"
    Applied Statistics, Vol. 23 (1974), pp. 51-9.

Furnival, G. M. and Wilson, R. W.
    "Regression by Leaps and Bounds"
    Technometrics, Vol. 16 (1974), pp. 499-512.

Garside, M. J.
    "Some Computational Procedures for the Best Subset Problem"
    Applied Statistics, Vol. 20 (1971), pp. 8-15.

LaMotte, L. R.
    "The SELECT Routines: A Program for Identifying Best Subset
    Regression"
    Applied Statistics, Vol. 21 (1972), pp. 92,3.

Mallows, C. L.
    "Some Comments on Cp"
    Technometrics, Vol. 15 (1973), pp. 661-75.

Mantel, N.
    "Why Stepdown Procedures in Variable Selection"
    Technometrics, Vol. 12 (1970), pp. 621-5.

159.04 ---------- Theory Re: Constrained Regression Models

Bultez, A. V. and Naert, P. A.
    "Consistent Sum-Constrained Models"
    Journal of the American Statistical Association, Vol. 70 (September
    1975), pp. 529-35.

McGuire, T. W., Farley, J. U., Lucas, R. E. Jr., and Ring, L. W.
    "Estimation and Inference for Linear Models in Which Subsets of the
    Dependent Variable are Constrained"
    Journal of the American Statistical Association, Vol. 63 (December
    1968), pp. 1201-13.

Morrison, Donald G. and Gluck, Donald J.
    "Spurious Correlations That Result From 'Awareness vs. Usage' Type
    Regressions"
    Journal of Marketing Research, Vol. VII (August 1970), pp. 381-4.

159.05 ---------- Theory Re: Reverse Regression

Conway, D. A. and Roberts, H. V.
    "Rejoinder to Comments on 'Reverse Regression, Fairness, and
    Employment Discrimination'"
    Journal of Business and Economic Statistics, Vol. 2 (1984), pp.
    126-39.

Conway, D. A. and Roberts, H. V.
    "Reverse Regression, Fairness, and Employment Discrimination"
    Journal of Business and Economic Statistics, Vol. 1 (1983), pp. 75-85.

Goldberger, A. S.
    "Redirecting Reverse Regression"
    Journal of Business and Economic Statistics, Vol. 2 (1984), pp. 114-6.

Greene, W. H.
    "Reverse Regression: The Algebra of Discrimination"
    Journal of Business and Economic Statistics, Vol. 2 (1984), pp.
    117-20.

Michelson, S. and Blattenberger, G.
    "Reverse Regression and Employment Discrimination"
    Journal of Business and Economic Statistics, Vol. 2 (1984), pp. 121,2.

Vanhonacker, Wilfried R.
    "Measuring Market Share Rewards for Pioneering Brands: Direct Versus
    Reverse Regression"
    1985 Marketing Science Conference, Nashville (1985), paper
    presentation.

Vanhonacker, Wilfried R. and Day, Diana
    "Cross-Sectional Estimation in Marketing: Direct Versus Reverse
    Regression"
    Marketing Science, Vol. 6 (Summer 1987), pp. 254-67.

159.06 ---------- Theory Re: Clusterwise Regression
    See also (sub)heading(s) 192.

DeSarbo, Wayne S. and Cron, W. L.
    "A Maximum Likelihood Methodology for Clusterwise Linear Regression"
    Journal of Classification, Vol. 5 (1988), pp. 249-82.

DeSarbo, Wayne S., Oliver, R. L., and Rangaswamy, A.
    "A Simulated Annealing Methodology for Clusterwise Linear Regression"
    University of Michigan (1988), working paper.

Kistemaker, Cor and Wedel, Michel
    RMSCLUST User's Manual
    Report Number V88.316
    TNO-CIVO Institutes, Zeist, The Netherlands (1988), unpublished.

Spath, H.
    "Clusterwise Linear Least Absolute Deviations Regression"
    Computing, Vol. 37 (1986), 371-8.

Spath, H.
    "Algorithm 48: A Fast Algorithm for Clusterwise Linear Regression"
    Computer, Vol. 29 (1982), pp. 175-81.

Spath, H.
    "Algorithm 39: Clusterwise Linear Regression"
    Computing, Vol. 22 (1979), pp. 367-73.

Wedel, Michel and Kistemaker, Cor
    "Consumer Benefit Segmentation Using Clusterwise Linear Regression"
    International Journal of Research in Marketing, Vol. 6, No. 1 (1989),
    pp. 45-59.

159.07 ---------- Theory Re: Data Collection Design Effects

Chambers, R. L.
    "Design-Adjusted Regression With Selectivity Bias"
    Applied Statistics, Vol. 37, No. 3 (1988), pp. 323-34.

Pfeffermann, Danny
    "The Effect of Sampling Design and Response Mechanism on Multivariate
    Regression-Based Predictors"
    Journal of the American Statistical Society, Vol. 83 (September 1988).

159.08 ---------- Computer Programs for Regression Analysis

Beaton, A. E., Rubin, D. B., and Barone, J. L.
    "The Acceptability of Regression Solutions: Another Look at
    Computational Accuracy"
    Journal of the American Statistical Association, Vol. 71 (1976), pp.
    158-68.

Carroll, J. Douglas and Chang, Jih-Jie
    "How to Use PROFIT, a Computer Program for Property Fitting by
    Optimizing Non-Linear or Linear Correlations"
    (Murray Hill, NJ: Bell Telephone Laboratories, 1970).

Hui, Baldwin S. and Jagpal, Harsharanjeet S.
    "A Principal Components Regression Program for Decision Making"
    Journal of Marketing Research, Vol. XVI (November 1979), pp. 570,1.

Longley, James W.
    "An Appraisal of Least-Squares Programs for the Electronic Computer
    From the Point of View of the User"
    Journal of the American Statistical Association, Vol. 62 (September
    1967), pp. 819-41.

Mansfield, Edward R.
    "PCR: Principal Component Regression Analysis"
    Journal of Marketing Research, Vol. XV (August 1978), pp. 471,2.

Miller, Jerry L. L.
    A FORTRAN IV Program for Multiple Regression of Dichotomous Data
    (University of Arizona (CAMR 9)).

Mullet, Gary M. and Murray, Tracy W.
    "A New Method for Examining Rounding Error in Least-Squares
    Regression Computer Programs"
    Journal of the American Statistical Association, Vol. 66 (September
    1971), pp. 496-8.

Pearsall, Edward S.
    "BSR: Best Subset Regression by the Method of Branch and Bound"
    Journal of Marketing Research, Vol. XVI (November 1979), pp. 564,5.

Smith, Scott M.
    "INTEREG: An Interactive Regression Analysis With Followup Statistics"
    Journal of Marketing Research, Vol. XIX (November 1982), pp. 599,600.

Wagner, Udo
    "COLLDICO: A Program System for Performing Regression Analysis in the
    Presence of Collinearity: Diagnosis and Correction"
    Journal of Marketing Research, Vol. XVI (November 1979), p. 561.

Wampler, Roy H.
    "A Report on the Accuracy of Some Widely Used Least Squares Computer
    Programs"
    Journal of the American Statistical Association, Vol. 65 (June 1970),
    pp. 549-65.

160 ------------------ ISSUES IN REGRESSION ANALYSIS ------------------
        See also (sub)heading(s) 159, 162, 163.

160.01 ---------- R-Square Properties and Adjustments
        See also (sub)heading(s) 137.02, 160.04.

Birnbaum, Michael H.
    "The Devil Rides Again: Correlation as an Index of Fit"
    Psychological Bulletin, Vol. 79 (April 1973), pp. 239-42.

Goldberger, A. S.
    "Correlations Between Binary Outcomes and Probabilistic Prediction"
    Journal of the American Statistical Association, Vol. 68 (1973), p.
    84.

Larson, Selmer C.
    "The Shrinkage of the Coefficient of Multiple Correlation"
    Journal of Educational Psychology, Vol. 22 (January 1931), pp. 45-55.

Lawrence, Ray
    "Scale Data Points"
    Journal of the Market Research Society, Vol. 26 (April 1984), pp.
    171-3.

Montgomery, David B. and Morrison, Donald G.
    "Adjusting R-Square"
    Marketing Science Institute Technical Report
    (Cambridge, MA: 1978).

Montgomery, David B. and Morrison, Donald G.
    "A Note on Adjusting R-Square"
    Journal of Finance, Vol. 28 (1973), pp. 1009-13.

Morrison, Donald G.
    "Evaluating Market Segmentation Studies: The Properties of R-Square"
    Management Science, Vol. 19 (1973), pp. 1213-21.

Morrison, Donald G.
    "Upper Bounds for Correlations Between Binary Outcomes and
    Probabilistic Prediction"
    Journal of the American Statistical Association, Vol. 67 (1972), pp.
    65-70.

Wherry, Robert J.
    "A New Formula for Predicting the Shrinkage of the Coefficient of
    Multiple Correlations"
    Annals of Mathematical Statistics, Vol. 2 (1931), pp. 440-51.

Wildt, Albert R.
    "On Evaluating Market Segmentation Studies and the Properties of
    R-Square"
    Management Science, Vol. 22 (April 1976), pp. 904-8.

160.02 ---------- Theory Re: Multicollinearity
        See also (sub)heading(s) 170.

Althauser, R. P.
    "Multicollinearity and Non-Additive Models"
    in Blalock, H. M. (editor)
    Causal Models in the Social Sciences
    (Chicago: Aldin-Atherton, 1971).

Belsley, D. A., Kuh, E., and Welsch, R. E.
    Regression Diagnostics: Identifying Influential Data and Sources of
    Collinearity
    (New York: John Wiley and Sons, Inc., 1980).

Blalock, Hubert M., Jr.
    "Correlated Independent Variables: The Problem of Multicollinearity"
    Social Forces, Vol. 42 (December 1963), pp. 233-7.

Bradley, Ralph A. and Srivastava, Sushil S.
    "Correlation in Polynomial Regression"
    American Statistician, Vol. 33, No. 1 (1979), pp. 11-4.

Churchill, G. A.
    "A Regression Estimation Procedure for Collinear Predictors"
    Decision Sciences, Vol. 6 (1975), pp. 670-87.

Farrar, Donald E. and Glauber, Robert R.
    "Multicollinearity in Regression Analysis: The Problem Revisited"
    The Review of Economics and Statistics, Vol. 49 (February 1967), pp.
    92-107.

Gunst, R. F.
    "Toward a Balanced Assessment of Collinearity Diagnostics"
    American Statistician, Vol. 38 (1984), pp. 79-82.

Gunst, R. F. and Mason, Robert L.
"Advantages of Examining Multicollinearities in Regression Analysis"
Biometrics, Vol. 33 (1977), pp. 249-60.

Haitovsky, Yoel
"Multicollinearity in Regression Analysis: Comment"
Review of Economics and Statistics, Vol. 50 (1969), pp. 486-9.

Jagpal, Harsharanjeet S. and Hui, Baldwin S.
"The Treatment of Multicollinearity in Marketing"
Rutgers University, Graduate School of Business Administration (1979).

Krishnamurthi, Lakshman and Rangaswamy, Arvind
"The Equity Estimator for Marketing Research"
Marketing Science, Vol. 6 (Fall 1987), pp. 336-57.

Kumar, Krishna T.
"Multicollinearity in Regression Analysis"
Review of Economics and Statistics, Vol. 57 (1975), pp. 365,6.

Leamer, E. E.
"Multicollinearity: A Bayesian Interpretation"
Review of Economics and Statistics, Vol. 55 (1973), pp. 371-80.

Mansfield, E. R. and Helms, B. P.
"Detecting Multicollinearity"
American Statistician, Vol. 36, No. 3 (1982), pp. 158-60.

Mason, Robert L., Gunst, R. F., and Webster, J. T.
"Regression Analysis and Problems of Multicollinearity"
Communications in Statistics, Vol. A4 (1975), pp. 277-92.

Ofir, Chezy and Khuri, Andre
"Multicollinearity in Marketing Models: Diagnostics and Remedial
Measures"
International Journal of Research in Marketing, Vol. 3, No. 3 (1986),
pp. 181-205.

Silvey, S. D.
"Multicollinearity and Imprecise Estimation"
Journal of the Royal Statistical Society, Series B (1959), pp. 539-52.

Smith, K. W. and Sasaki, M. S.
"Decreasing Multicollinearity: A Method for Models With
Multiplicative Functions"
Sociological Methods and Research, Vol. 8, No. 1 (1979), pp. 35-56.

Snee, Ronald D. and Marquardt, Donald W.
"Collinearity Diagnostics Depend on the Domain of Prediction, the
Model, and the Data"
American Statistician, Vol. 38, No. 2 (1984), pp. 83-7.

Willan, A. W. and Watts, D. F.
"Meaningful Multicollinearity Measures"
Technometrics, Vol. 20 (1978), pp. 407-12.

Wood, Fred S.
"Effect of Centering on Collinearity and Interpretation of the
Constraint"
American Statistician, Vol. 38 (1984), pp. 88-90.

160.03 ---------- Theory Re: Interactions

See also (sub)heading(s) 150.03, 153.03, 166.

Allison, Paul D.
"Testing for Interaction in Multiple Regression"
American Journal of Sociology, Vol. 83 (1977), pp. 144-53.

Cohen, Jacob
"Partialed Products are Interactions; Partialed Powers are Curve
Components"
Psychological Bulletin, Vol. 85 (1978), pp. 858-66.

Goodman, Leo A.
"On the Exact Variance of Products"
Journal of the American Statistical Association, Vol. 55 (1960), pp.
708-13.

Green, Paul E.
"On the Analysis of Interactions in Marketing Research Data"
Journal of Marketing Research, Vol. X (November 1973), pp. 410-20.

160.04 ---------- Theory Re: Binary, Categorical, and Dummy Variables
    See also (sub)heading(s) 137.02, 160.01.

Aigner, D. J., Goldberger, A. S., and Kalton, G.
  "On the Explanatory Power of Dummy Variable Regressions"
  International Economic Review, Vol. 16 (June 1975), pp. 503-10.

Bernhardt, Kenneth L. and Kinnear, Thomas C.
  "Categorical Regression in Marketing"
  Journal of Business Research, Vol. 4 (November 1976), pp. 297-312.

Bohrnstedt, George and Carter, T. Michael
  "Robustness in Regression Analysis"
  in Costner, H. L. (editor)
  Sociological Methodology
  (San Francisco: Jossey-Bass Publishers, 1971), pp. 118-46.

Bonfield, E. H. and Karson, Marvin J.
  "Goodness of Fit Measures for Regression Models With Binary Dependent
  Variables"
  College of Commerce and Business Administration, The University of
  Alabama (1975), unpublished working paper.

Cattin, Philippe and Wittink, Dick R.
  "On the Use of Ordinary Least Squares Regression With Paired
  Comparisons and Rank Order Data"
  School of Business Administration, University of Connecticut (August
  1978), unpublished paper.

Goldberger, A. S.
  "Correlations Between Binary Outcomes and Probabilistic Prediction"
  Journal of the American Statistical Association, Vol. 68 (1973), p.
  84.

Goodman, L. A.
  "A Modified Multiple Regression Approach to the Analysis of
  Dichotomous Variables"
  American Sociological Review, Vol. 37 (February 1972), pp. 28-46.

Green, Richard D. and Doll, John P.
  "Dummy Variables and Seasonality"
  American Statistician, Vol. 28 (May 1974), pp. 60-2.

McCullagh, Peter
  "Regression Models for Ordinal Data"
  Journal of the Royal Statistical Society, Vol. 42, Series B (1980),
  pp. 109-42.

Morris, R. N.
  "Multiple Correlation and Ordinally Scaled Data"
  Social Forces, Vol. 48 (March 1970), pp. 299-311.

Morrison, Donald G.
  "Regression With Discrete Dependent Variables: The Effect on R-Square"
  Journal of Marketing Research, Vol. IX (August 1972), 338-40.

Morrison, Donald G.
  "Upper Bounds for Correlations Between Binary Outcomes and
  Probabilistic Predictions"
  Journal of the American Statistical Association, Vol. 67 (1972), pp.
  68-70.

Neter, J. and Maynes, E. S.
  "On the Appropriateness of the Correlation Coefficient, With a 0, 1
  Dependent Variable"
  Journal of the American Statistical Association, Vol. 65 (June 1970),
  pp. 501-9.

Suits, D. B.
  "Use of Dummy Variables in Regression Equations"
  Journal of the American Statistical Association, Vol. 52 (December
  1957), pp. 548-51.

Tomek, William G.
  "Using Zero-One Variables With Time Series Data in Regression
  Equations"
  Journal of Farm Economics (November 1963), pp. 814-22.

Wildt, Albert R.
  "Estimating Models of Seasonal Market Response Using Dummy Variables"
  Journal of Marketing Research, Vol. XIV (February 1977), pp. 34-41.

Zellner, Arnold and Lee, Tong Hun
  "Joint Estimation of Relationships Involving Discrete Random
  Variables"
  Econometrica, Vol. 33 (April 1965), pp. 382-94.

160.05 ---------- Theory Re: Importance of Predictor Variables
        See also (sub)heading(s) 177.07.

Amemiya, T.
    "Selection of Regressors"
    (Stanford, CA: Institute for Mathematical Studies in the Social
    Sciences, 1976), Technical Report No. 225.

Breiman, L. and Freedman, D.
    "How Many Variables Should be Entered in a Regression Equation"
    Journal of the American Statistical Association, Vol. 78 (March
    1983), pp. 131-6.

Darlington, Richard B.
    "Multiple Regression in Psychological Research and Practice"
    Psychological Bulletin, Vol. 70 (November 1968), pp. 426-43.

DeSarbo, Wayne S.
    "ORTHO: An APL Program for Computing and Contrasting Measures of
    Predictor Variable Importance in Multiple Regression"
    Journal of Marketing Research, Vol. XV (August 1978), pp. 467,8.

Gorsuch, R. L.
    "Data Analysis of Correlated Independent Variables"
    Multivariate Behavioral Research, Vol. 8 (January 1973), pp. 89-107.

Green, Paul E., Carroll, J. Douglas, and DeSarbo, Wayne S.
    "Reply to 'A Comment on a New Measure of Predictor Variable
    Importance in Multiple Regression'"
    Journal of Marketing Research, Vol. XVII (February 1980), pp. 116-8.

Green, Paul E., Carroll, J. Douglas, and DeSarbo, Wayne S.
    "A New Measure of Predictor Variable Importance in Multiple
    Regresssion"
    Journal of Marketing Research, Vol. XV (August 1978), pp. 356-60.

Hocking, R. R.
    "The Analysis and Selection of Variables in Linear Regression"
    Biometrics, Vol. 32 (March 1976), pp. 1-49.

Jackson, Barbara Bund
    "Comment on 'A New Measure of Predictor Variable Importance in
    Multiple Regression'"
    Journal of Marketing Research, Vol. XVII (February 1980), pp. 113-5.

Kennedy, W. J. and Bancroft, T. A.
    "Model Building for Prediction in Regression Based Upon Repeated
    Significance Tests"
    Annals of Mathematical Statistics, Vol. 42 (August 1971), pp. 1273-84.

Lane, D. M.
    "Testing Main Effects of Continuous Variables in Non-Additive Models"
    Multivariate Behavioral Research, Vol. 16 (1981), pp. 499-509.

Michael, W. B. and Caffrey, J. G.
    "Tables to Facilitate Computation of Partial Correlation Coefficients"
    Educational and Psychological Measurement, Vol. 16 (Summer 1956), pp.
    232-6.

Shibata, Ritei
    "An Optimal Selection of Regression Variables"
    Biometrika, Vol. 68 (April 1981), pp. 45-54.

Yi, Youjae
    "On the Evaluation of Main Effects in Multiplicative Regression
    Models"
    Journal of the Market Research Society, Vol. 31 (January 1989), pp.
    133-38.

160.06 ---------- Sample Size Determination and Effects
        See also (sub)heading(s) 114.

Milton, Sande
    "A Sample Size Formula for Multiple Regression Studies"
    Public Opinion Quarterly, Vol. 50 (Spring 1986), pp. 112-8.

161 ----------- TIME SERIES AND CROSS-SECTIONS DATA POOLING ----------
See also (sub)heading(s) 133.11, 159, 171.06.

161.01 ---------- Theory Re: Time Series, Cross-Sections Data Pooling

Balestra, P. and Nerlove, M.
"Pooling Cross-Section and Time Series Data in the Estimation of a
Dynamic Model: The Demand for Natural Gas"
Econometrica, Vol. 34 (October 1966), pp. 585-612.

Bass, Frank M. and Wittink, Dick R.
"Pooling Issues and Methods in Regression Analysis: Some Further
Reflections"
Journal of Marketing Research, Vol. XV (May 1978), pp. 277-9.

Bass, Frank M. and Wittink, Dick R.
"Pooling Issues and Methods in Regression Analysis With Examples in
Marketing Research"
Journal of Marketing Research, Vol. XII (November 1975), pp. 414-25.

Belsley, David A.
"On the Determination of Systematic Parameter Variation in the Linear
Regression Model"
Annals of Economic and Social Measurement, Vol. 2 (October 1973), pp.
487-94.

Box, G. E. P. and Jenkins, G. M.
Time Series Analysis: Forecasting and Control
(San Francisco: Holden-Day, 1976).

Box, G. E. P. and Pierce, D. A.
"Distribution of Residual Autocorrelations in Autoregressive Moving
Average Time Series Models"
Journal of the American Statistical Association, Vol. 65 (1970), pp.
1509-26.

Brobst, Robert and Gates, Roger
"Comments on Pooling Issues and Methods in Regression Analysis"
Journal of Marketing Research, Vol. XIV (November 1977), pp. 598-600.

Chetty, V. K.
"Pooling of Time Series and Cross-Section Data"
Econometrica, Vol. 36 (April 1968), pp. 279-90.

Cochrane, D. and Orcutt, G. H.
"Applications of Least Squares Regression Relationships Containing
Autocorrelated Error Terms"
Journal of the American Statistical Association, Vol. 44 (1949), pp.
32-61.

Fuller, Wayne A. and Battese, George E.
"Estimation of Linear Models With Crossed-Error Structure"
Journal of Econometrics, Vol. 2 (1974), pp. 67-78.

Goodnight, James and Wallace, T. D.
"Operational Techniques and Tables for Making Weak MSE Tests for
Restrictions in Regressions"
Econometrica, Vol. 40 (July 1972), pp. 699-709.

Gottman, John M.
Time-Series Analysis
(New York: Cambridge University Press, 1981), 400 pp.

Hoch, Irving
"Estimation of Production Function Parameters Combining Time-Series
and Cross-Section Data"
Econometrica, Vol. 30 (January 1962), pp. 34-53.

Hsiao, Cheng
"Some Estimation Methods for a Random Coefficient Model"
Institute for Mathematical Studies in the Social Sciences, Stanford
University (1977), Technical Report No. 77.

Jenkins, G. M.
Practical Experiences With Modelling and Forecasting Time Series
(St. Helier, UK: GJP Publications, 1979).

Johnson, L. W.
"Regression With Random Coefficients"
Omega, Vol. VI (1978), pp. 71-81.

Kuh, Edwin
Capital Stock Growth: A Micro-Econometric Approach
(Amsterdam: North Holland Publishing Co., 1963).

Kuh, Edwin
"The Validity of Cross-Sectionally Estimated Behavior Equations in
Time Series Applications"
Econometrica, Vol. 27 (April 1959), pp. 197-214.

Laughhunn, D. J.
    On the Predictive Value of Combining Cross-Section and Times-Series
    Data in Empirical Demand Studies
    (Urbana, IL: Bureau of Economic and Business Research, University of
    Illinois, 1969), 152 pp.

Maddala, G. S.
    "The Use of Variance Components Models in Pooling Cross Section and
    Time Series Data"
    Econometrica, Vol. 39 (March 1971), pp. 341-58.

Maddala, G. S.
    "The Use of Variance Components Models in Pooling Cross Section and
    Time Series Data"
    Econometrica, Vol. 39 (March 1971), pp. 341-58.

Maddala, G. S. and Mount, T. D.
    "Comparative Study of Alternative Estimators for Variance Components
    Models"
    Journal of the American Statistical Association, Vol. 68 (June 1973),
    pp. 324-8.

McCann, John M.
    "A Comparison of Methods of Pooling Time-Series and Cross-Section
    Data"
    in Curhan, Ronald C. (editor)
    New Marketing for Social and Economic Progress and Marketing's
    Contributions to the Firm and to Society
    (Chicago: American Marketing Association, 1974).

McCann, John M. and Reibstein, David J.
    "Forecasting the Impact of Socioeconomic and Demographic Change on
    Product Demand"
    Journal of Marketing Research, Vol. XXII (November 1985), pp. 415-23.

Nerlove, Marc
    "Further Evidences on the Estimation of Dynamic Economic Relations
    From a Time Series of Cross Sections"
    Econometrica, Vol. 39 (March 1971), pp. 359-82.

Palda, Kristian S. and Blair, Larry M.
    "A Moving Cross-Section Analysis of Demand for Toothpaste"
    Journal of Marketing Research, Vol. VII (November 1970), pp. 439-49.

Rosenberg, Barr
    "The Analysis of a Cross Section of Time Series by Stochastically
    Convergent Parameter Regression"
    Annals of Economic and Social Measurement, Vol. 2 (October 1973), pp.
    399-428.

Sayrs, Lois W.
    Pooled Time Series Analysis
    (Newbury Park, CA: Sage Publications, Inc., 1989), 80 pp.

Simon, Julian L. and Aigner, Dennis J.
    "Cross-Sectional Budget Studies, Aggregate Time-Series Studies and
    the Permanent Income Hypothesis"
    American Economic Review (1970).

Swamy, P. A. V. B.
    "Linear Models With Random Coefficients"
    in Zarembka, Paul (editor)
    Frontiers in Econometrics
    (New York: Academic Press, 1974), pp. 143-68.

Swamy, P. A. V. B.
    Statistical Inference in Random Coefficient Regression Models
    (Berlin: Springer-Verlag, 1971).

Swamy, P. A. V. B.
    "Efficient Inference in a Random Coefficient Regression Model"
    Econometrica, Vol. 38 (March 1970), pp. 311-23.

Telser, Lester G.
    "Iterative Estimation of a Set of Linear Regression Equations"
    Journal of the American Statistical Association, Vol. 59 (September
    1964), pp. 845-62.

Wallace, T. D.
    "Weaker Criteria and Tests for Linear Restrictions in Regression"
    Econometrica, Vol. 40 (July 1972), pp. 689-98.

Wittink, Dick
    "Partial Pooling: A Heuristic"
    Krannert School of Industrial Administration, Purdue University
    (1973), working paper.

161.02 ---------- Applications of Time Series and C-S Data Pooling

Gable, Myron and Mathis, Stephen A.
  "Retail Sales and the Gasoline Crisis: An Empirical Analysis"
  Journal of Retailing, Vol. 53 (Winter 1953), pp. 93-106.

Hagerty, Michael R., Carman, James M., and Russell, Gary J.
  "Estimating Elasticities With PIMS Data: Methodological Issues and
  Substantive Implications"
  Journal of Marketing Research, Vol. XXV (February 1988), pp. 1-9.

Lindberg, Bertil C.
  "International Comparison of Growth in Demand for a New Durable
  Consumer Product"
  Journal of Marketing Research, Vol. XIX (August 1982), pp. 364-71.

Moriarty, Mark
  "Feature Advertising-Price Interaction Effects in the Retail
  Environment"
  Journal of Retailing, Vol. 59 (Summer 1983), pp. 80-98.

Parsons, Leonard Jon and Abeele, Piet Vanden
  "Analysis of Sales Call Effectiveness"
  Journal of Marketing Research, Vol. XVIII (February 1981), pp. 107-13.

Schipper, Lewis
  Consumer Discretionary Behavior
  (Amsterdam: North Holland Publishing Co., 1964).

Ward, R. W. and Davis, J. E.
  "A Pooled Cross-Section Time Series Model of Coupon Promotions"
  American Journal of Agricultural Economics (August 1978), pp. 393-401.

162 ------------ STATISTICAL TESTS IN REGRESSION ANALYSIS ------------
        See also (sub)heading(s) 141, 159.

162.01 ---------- Theory Re: Statistical Tests in Regression Analysis

Ando, A. and Kaufman, G. M.
    "Evaluation of an Ad Hoc Procedure for Estimating Parameters of Some
    Linear Models"
    Review of Economics and Statistics, Vol. 48 (1966), pp. 334-40.

Andrews, D. F.
    "Significance Tests Based on Residuals"
    Biometrika, Vol. 58 (1971), pp. 139-48.

Cramer, E. M.
    "Significance Tests and Tests of Models in Multiple Regression"
    The American Statistician, Vol. 26 (October 1972), pp. 26-30.

Diehr, G. and Hoflin, D. R.
    "Approximating the Distribution of the Sample R-Square in Best Subset
    Regression"
    Technometrics, Vol. 16 (1974), pp. 317-20.

Durbin, J.
    "Testing for Serial Correlation in Least-Squares Regression When Some
    of the Regressors are Lagged Dependent Variables"
    Econometrica, Vol. 38 (May 1970), pp. 410-21.

Durbin, J. and Watson, G. S.
    "Testing for Serial Correlation in Least Squares Regression, Parts I
    and II"
    Biometrika (1950 and 1951).

Farley, John U. and Hinich, Melvin J.
    "A Test for a Shifting Slope Coefficient in a Linear Model"
    Journal of the American Statistical Association, Vol. 65 (September
    1970), pp. 1320-9.

Geary, R. C. and Leser, C. E. V.
    "Significance Tests in Multiple Regression"
    The American Statistician, Vol. 22 (February 1968), pp. 20,1.

Kenkel, James L.
    "Some Small Sample Properties of Durbin's Tests for Serial
    Correlation in Regression Models Containing Lagged Dependent
    Variables"
    Econometrica, Vol. 42 (July 1974), pp. 763-9.

McIntyre, Shelby H., Montgomery, David B., Srinivasan, V., and Weitz,
    Barton A.
    "Evaluating the Statistical Significance of Models Developed by
    Stepwise Regression"
    Journal of Marketing Research, Vol. XX (February 1983), pp. 1-11.

McIntyre, Shelby H., Montgomery, David B., Srinivasan, V., and Weitz,
    Barton A.
    Testing the Statistical Significance of Stepwise Regression Models
    Developed With a Forward Selection Procedure: A Monte Carlo Study
    Technical Report No. 46
    Graduate School of Business, Stanford University (1981).

Pearson, Egon S.
    "The Test of Significance for the Correlation Coefficient"
    Journal of the American Statistical Association, Vol. 26 (June 1931),
    pp. 128-34.

Pope, P. T. and Webster, J. T.
    "The Use of an F Statistic in Stepwise Regression Procedures"
    Technometrics, vol. 14 (1972), pp. 327-40.

Reichardt, C. S.
    "The Statistical Analysis of Data for Nonequivalent Group Designs"
    in Cook, Thomas D. and Campbell, Donald T. (editors)
    Quasi-Experimentation: Design and Analysis Issues for Field Settings
    (Chicago: Rand McNally Publishing Company, 1979).

Theil, H. and Nagar, A. L.
    "Testing the Independence of Regression Disturbances"
    Journal of the American Statistical Association, Vol. 56 (December
    1961), pp. 793-806.

Wallace, T. D.
    "Weaker Criteria and Tests for Linear Restrictions in Regression"
    Econometrica, Vol. 40 (July 1972), pp. 689-98.

Wilkinson, L.
    "Tests of Significance in Stepwise Regression"
    Psychological Bulletin, Vol. 86, No. 1 (1979), pp. 168-74.

162.02 ---------- Theory Re: Tests of Equality of Regressions

Chow, Gregory
"Tests of Equality Between Sets of Coefficients in Two Linear
Regressions"
Econometrica, Vol. 28 (1960), pp. 591-605.

Fisher, F. M.
"Tests of Equality Between Sets of Coefficients in Two Linear
Regressions: An Expository Note"
Econometrica, Vol. 38 (March 1970), pp. 361-6.

Gujarati, Damodar
"Use of Dummy Variables in Testing for Equality Between Sets of
Coefficients in Two Linear Regression: A Note"
American Statistician, Vol. 24 (February 1970), pp. 50-2.

162.03 ---------- Applications of Tests of Equality of Regressions

Bearden, William O., Headen, Robert S., Klompmaker, Jay E., and Teel,
Jesse E.
"Attentive Audience Delivery of TV Advertising Schedules"
Journal of Marketing Research, Vol. XVIII (May 1981), pp. 187-91.

Becherer, Richard C., Morgan, Fred W., and Richard, Lawrence M.
"Informal Group Influence Among
Situationally/Dispositionally-Oriented Consumers"
Journal of the Academy of Marketing Science, Vol. 10 (Summer 1982),
pp. 269-80.

Becherer, Richard C. and Richard, Lawrence M.
"Self-Monitoring as a Moderating Variable in Consumer Behavior"
Journal of Consumer Research, Vol. 5 (December 1978), pp. 159-62.

Hafstrom, Jeanne L. and Dunsing, Marilyn M.
"Socioeconomic and Social-Psychological Influences on Reasons Wives
Work"
Journal of Consumer Research, Vol. 5 (December 1978), pp. 169-75.

Headen, Robert S., Klompmaker, Jay E., and Teel, Jesse E., Jr.
"Predicting Audience Exposure to Spot TV Advertising Schedules"
Journal of Marketing Research, Vol. XIV (February 1977), pp. 1-9.

Hise, Richard T., Kelly, J. Patrick, Gable, Myron, and McDonald, James
B.
"Factors Affecting the Performance of Individual Chain Store Units:
An Empirical Analysis"
Journal of Retailing, Vol. 59 (Summer 1983), pp. 22-39.

Teas, R. Kenneth and Sibley, Stanley D.
"An Examination of the Moderating Effect of Channel Member Firm Size
on Perceptions of Preferred Channel Linkages"
Journal of the Academy of Marketing Science, Vol. 8 (Summer 1980),
pp. 277-93.

Varadarajan, P. Rajan
"Product Effort and Promotion Effort Hypotheses: An Empirical
Investigation"
Journal of the Academy of Marketing Science, Vol. 13 (Winter 1985),
pp. 47-61.

163 --------------- VALIDATION OF REGRESSION ANALYSES ---------------
        See also (sub)heading(s) 159.

163.01 ---------- Theory Re: Validation of Regression Analyses

Browne, Michael W.
    "Predictive Validity of a Linear Regression Equation"
    British Journal of Mathematical and Statistical Psychology, Vol. 28
    (1975), pp. 79-87.

Cattin, Philippe
    "Estimation of the Predictive Power of a Regression Model"
    Journal of Applied Psychology, Vol. 65 (1980), pp. 407-14.

Cattin, Philippe
    "On the Use of Formulas of the Predictive Validity of Regression in
    Consumer Research"
    Proceedings, Assocation for Consumer Research, Volume 6 (1978), pp.
    284-7.

Ferber, Robert
    "Are Correlations Any Guide to Predictive Value?"
    Applied Statistics, Vol. 5 (June 1956), pp. 113-21.

Freedman, D. A.
    "Boostrapping Regression Models"
    Annals of Statistics, Vol. 9 (December 1981), pp. 1218-28.

Morris, J. D.
    "Selecting the Best Regression Equation by Maximizing Double
    Cross-Validation Correlation"
    Behavioral Research Methods and Instrumentation, Vol. 8 (1976), p.
    389.

Picard, Richard R. and Cook, R. Dennis
    "Cross-Validation of Regression Models"
    Journal of the American Statistical Association, Vol. 79 (September
    1984), pp. 575-83.

Snee, Ronald D.
    "Validation of Regression Models: Methods and Examples"
    Technometrics, Vol. 19 (November 1977), pp. 415-28.

Stine, Robert A.
    "Bootstrap Prediction Intervals for Regression"
    Journal of the American Statistical Association, Vol. 80 (December
    1985), pp. 1026-31.

Wu, C. F. J.
    "Jackknife, Bootstrap and Other Resampling Methods in Regression
    Analysis"
    Annals of Statistics, Vol. 14 (December 1986), pp. 1261-94.

164 ---------------- REGRESSION ANALYSIS APPLICATIONS ----------------
       See also (sub)heading(s) 159.

Andreasen, Alan R. and Belk, Russell W.
    "Predictors of Attendance at the Performing Arts"
    Journal of Consumer Research, Vol. 7 (September 1980), pp. 112-20.

Axinn, Catherine N.
    "Export Performance: Do Managerial Perceptions Make a Difference?"
    International Marketing Review, Vol. 8 (Summer 1988), pp. 61-71.

Ayal, Igal
    "Industry Export Performance: Assessment and Prediction"
    Journal of Marketing, Vol. 46 (Summer 1982), pp. 54-61.

Babakus, Emin, Tat, Peter, and Cunningham, William
    "Coupon Redemption: A Motivational Perspective"
    Journal of Consumer Marketing, Vol. 5 (Spring 1988), pp. 37-43.

Bagozzi, Richard P.
    "Salesforce Performance and Satisfaction as a Function of Individual
    Difference, Interpersonal, and Situational Factors"
    Journal of Marketing Research, Vol. XV (November 1978), pp. 517-31.

Becherer, Richard C. and Richard, Lawrence M.
    "Self-Monitoring as a Moderating Variable in Consumer Behavior"
    Journal of Consumer Research, Vol. 5 (December 1979), pp. 159-62.

Bellur, Venkatakrishna V.
    "Gasoline Consumption: Can It be Curtailed?"
    Journal of the Academy of Marketing Science, Vol. 8 (Summer 1980),
    pp. 171-81.

Bhagat, Rabi S., Raju, P., and Sheth, Jagdish N.
    "Attitudinal Theories of Consumer Choice Behaviour: A Comparative
    Analysis"
    European Research, Vol. 7 (March 1979), pp. 51-62.

Box, J. M. F.
    "Extending Product Lifetime: Prospects and Opportunities"
    European Journal of Marketing, Vol. 17, No. 4 (1983), pp. 34-49.

Brooker, George
    "The Self-Actualizing Socially Conscious Consumer"
    Journal of Consumer Research, Vol. 3 (September 1976), pp. 107-12.

Bryant, W. Keith and Gerner, Jennifer L.
    "Television Use by Adults and Children: A Multivariate Analysis"
    Journal of Consumer Research, Vol. 8 (September 1981), pp. 154-61.

Cady, John F.
    "Advertising Restrictions and Retail Prices"
    Journal of Advertising Research, Vol. 16 (October 1976), pp. 27-30.

Callahan, Francis X.
    "Advertising and Profits 1969-1978"
    Journal of Advertising Research, Vol. 22 (April/May 1982), pp. 17-22.

Carnegie-Mellon University Marketing Seminar
    "Attitude Change or Attitude Formation: An Unanswered Question"
    Journal of Consumer Research, Vol. 4 (March 1978), pp. 271-6.

Cheles-Miller, Pamela
    "Reactions to Marital Roles in Commercials"
    Journal of Advertising Research, Vol. 15 (August 1975), pp. 45-9.

Churchill, Gilbert A., Jr., Ford, Neil M., and Walker, Orville, C., Jr.
    "Organizational Climate and Job Satisfaction in the Salesforce"
    Journal of Marketing Research, Vol. XIII (November 1976), pp. 323-32.

Cosmas, Stephen C. and Yannopoulos, Niki
    "Advertising Directed to Children: A Look at the Mother's Point of
    View"
    Journal of the Academy of Marketing Science, Vol. 9 (Summer 1981),
    pp. 174-90.

Crafton, Steven M. and Hoffer, George E.
    "Do Consumers Benefit From Auto Manufacturer Rebates to Dealers?"
    Journal of Consumer Research, Vol. 7 (September 1980), pp. 211-4.

Cronin, J. Joseph, Jr.
    "Determinants of Retail Profit Performance: A Consideration of Retail
    Marketing Strategies"
    Journal of the Academy of Marketing Science, Vol. 13 (Fall 1985), pp.
    40-53.

Cronin, J. Joseph, Jr.
"A Comparison of the Relative Importance of the Marketing, Financial, and Asset Management Implications of Strategic Decisions"
Journal of the Academy of Marketing Science, Vol. 13 (Spring 1985), pp. 242-58.

Crosby, Lawrence A. and Taylor, James R.
"Consumer Satisfaction With Michigan's Container Deposit Law--An Ecological Perspective"
Journal of Marketing, Vol. 46 (Winter 1982), pp. 47-60.

Derrick, Frederick W. and Lehfeld, Alane K.
"The Family Life Cycle: An Alternative Approach"
Journal of Consumer Research, Vol. 7 (September 1980), pp. 214-7.

Dhalla, Nariman K.
"Short-Term Forecasts of Advertising Expenditures"
Journal of Advertising Research, Vol. 19 (February 1979), pp. 7-14.

Dickson, Peter R. and Miniard, Paul W.
"A Further Examination of Two Laboratory Tests of the Extended Fishbein Attitude Model"
Journal of Consumer Research, Vol. 4 (March 1978), pp. 261-6.

Dresden, Mark K., Jr. and Freifelder, Leonard
"Medical Advertising Page Exposure"
Journal of Advertising Research, Vol. 15 (February 1975), pp. 43-6.

Dubinsky, Alan J. and Levy, Michael
"Influence of Organizational Fairness on Work Outcomes of Retail Salespeople"
Journal of Retailing, Vol. 65 (Summer 1989), pp. 221-52.

Duncan, Calvin P. and Olshavsky, Richard W.
"External Search: The Role of Consumer Beliefs"
Journal of Marketing Research, Vol. XIX (February 1982), pp. 32-43.

Etgar, Michael
"Effects of Administrative Control on Efficiency of Vertical Marketing Systems"
Journal of Marketing Research, Vol. XIII (February 1976), pp. 12-24.

Evans, R. H.
"Assessing Introduction Factors for a New Industrial Product"
Industrial Marketing Management, Vol. 7 (Spring 1978), pp. 128-32.

Ferber, Marianne A. and Birnbaum, Bonnie
"One Job or Two Jobs: The Implications for Young Wives"
Journal of Consumer Research, Vol. 7 (December 1980), pp. 263-71.

Frazier, Gary L. and Summers, John O.
"Perceptions of Interfirm Power and Its Use Within a Franchise Channel of Distribution"
Journal of Marketing Research, Vol. XXIII (May 1986), pp. 169-76.

Frieden, Jon B. and Downs, Phillip E.
"Testing the Social Involvement Model in an Energy Conservation Context"
Journal of the Academy of Marketing Science, Vol. 14 (Fall 1986), pp. 13-20.

Gaski, John F.
"The Impact of Environmental/Situational Forces on Industrial Channel Management"
European Journal of Marketing, Vol. 23, No. 2 (1989), pp. 15-30.

Goldman, Arieh and Johansson, J. K.
"Determinants of Search for Lower Prices: An Empirical Assessment of the Economics of Information Theory"
Journal of Consumer Research, Vol. 5 (December 1978), pp. 176-86.

Green, Paul E., Carroll, J. Douglas, and DeSarbo, Wayne S.
"Estimating Choice Probabilities in Multiattribute Decision Making"
Journal of Consumer Research, Vol. 8 (June 1981), pp. 76-84.

Hafstrom, Jeanne L. and Dunsing, Marilyn M.
"Socioeconomic and Social-Psychological Influences on Reasons Wives Work"
Journal of Consumer Research, Vol. 3 (December 1979), pp. 169-75.

Henry, Walter A.
"The Effect of Information-Processing Ability on Processing Accuracy"
Journal of Consumer Research, Vol. 7 (June 1980), pp. 42-8.

Hepburn, George C., Mayor, Thomas H., and Stafford, James E.
"Estimation of Market Area Population From Residential Electrical Utility Data"
Journal of Marketing Research, Vol. XIII (August 1976), pp. 230-6.

Heslop, Louise A., Moran, Lori, and Cousineau, Amy
  "'Consciousness' in Energy Conservation Behavior: An Exploratory
  Study"
  Journal of Consumer Research, Vol. 8 (December 1981), pp. 299-305.

Hise, Richard T. and Muczyk, Jan P.
  "The Effect of Interstate Highway on Driving Times and Regional
  Shopping Center Drawing Power"
  Journal of the Academy of Marketing Science, Vol. 5 (Winter-Spring
  1977), pp. 126-33.

Holbrook, Morris B. and Lehmann, Donald R.
  "Form Versus Content in Predicting Starch Scores"
  Journal of Advertising Research, Vol. 20 (August 1980), pp. 53-62.

Horton, Raymond L.
  "The Structure of Percieved Risk: Some Further Progress"
  Journal of the Academy of Marketing Science, Vol. 4 (Fall 1976), pp.
  694-706.

Hunt, Janet C. and Kiker, B. F.
  "The Effect of Fertility on the Time Use of Working Wives"
  Journal of Consumer Research, Vol. 7 (March 1981), pp. 380-7.

Hunt, Shelby D. and Chonko, Lawrence B.
  "Marketing and Machiavellianism"
  Journal of Marketing, Vol. 48 (Summer 1984), pp. 30-42.

John, George and Weitz, Barton A.
  "Salesforce Compensation: An Empirical Investigation of Factors
  Related to Use of Salary Versus Incentive Compensation"
  Journal of Marketing Research, Vol. XXVI (February 1989), pp. 1-14.

Johnston, Wesley J. and Bonoma, Thomas V.
  "The Buying Center: Structure and Interaction Patterns"
  Journal of Marketing, Vol. 45 (Summer 1981), pp. 143-56.

Kahn, Barbara, Moore, William L., and Glazer, Rashi
  "Experiments in Constrained Choice"
  Journal of Consumer Research, Vol. 14 (June 1987), pp. 96-113.

Lamont, Lawrence M. and Lundstrom, William J.
  "Identifying Successful Industrial Salesmen by Personality and
  Personal Characteristics"
  Journal of Marketing Research, Vol. XIV (November 1977), pp. 517-29.

Lehmann, Donald R.
  "Responses to Advertising a New Car"
  Journal of Advertising Research, Vol. 17 (August 1977), pp. 23-7.

Leuthold, Jane H.
  "Taxation and the Consumption of Household Time"
  Journal of Consumer Research, Vol. 7 (March 1981), pp. 388-94.

Levedahl, J. William
  "The Impact of Permanent and Transitory Income on Household
  Automobile Expenditure"
  Journal of Consumer Research, Vol. 7 (June 1980), pp. 55-66.

Longstreth, Molly, Coveney, Anne R., and Bowers, Jean S.
  "Conservation Characteristics Among Determinants of Residential
  Property Value"
  Journal of Consumer Research, Vol. 11 (June 1983), pp. 564-71.

Lusch, Robert F.
  "Sources of Power: Their Impact on Intrachannel Conflict"
  Journal of Marketing Research, Vol. XIII (November 1976), pp. 382-90.

Lutz, Richard J.
  "Rejoinder"
  Journal of Consumer Research, Vol. 4 (March 1978), pp. 266-71.

Lutz, Richard J.
  "An Experimental Investigation of Causal Relations Among Cognitions,
  Affect, and Behavioral Intention"
  Journal of Consumer Research, Vol. 3 (March 1977), pp. 197-208.

Marquardt, Raymond A. and Murdock, Gene W.
  "The Sales/Advertising Relationship: An Investigation of Correlations
  and Consistency in Supermarkets and Department Stores"
  Journal of Advertising Research, Vol. 24 (October/November 1984), pp.
  55-60.

McCabe, Donald L.
  "Buying Group Structure: Constriction at the Top"
  Journal of Marketing, Vol. 51 (October 1987), pp. 89-98.

Moore, Roy L. and Stephens, Lowndes F.
    "Some Communication and Demographic Determinants of Adolescent
    Consumer Learning"
    Journal of Consumer Research, Vol. 2 (September 1975), pp. 80-92.

Moore, William L. and Lehmann, Donald R.
    "Individual Differences in Search Behavior for a Nondurable"
    Journal of Consumer Research, Vol. 7 (December 1980), pp. 296-307.

Morgan, Karen J., Metzen, Edward J., and Johnson, S. R.
    "An Hedonic Index for Breakfast Cereals"
    Journal of Consumer Research, Vol. 6 (June 1979), pp. 67-75.

Moschis, George P. and Churchill, Gilbert A., Jr.
    "Consumer Socialization: A Theoretical and Empirical Analysis"
    Journal of Marketing Research, Vol. XV (November 1978), pp. 599-609.

Moschis, George P. and Moore, Roy L.
    "Decision Making Among the Young: A Socialization Perspective"
    Journal of Consumer Research, Vol. 6 (September 1979), pp. 101-12.

Park, C. Whan and Young, S. Mark
    "Consumer Response to Television Commercials: The Impact of
    Involvement and Background Music on Brand Attitude Formation"
    Journal of Marketing Research, Vol. XXIII (February 1986), pp. 11-24.

Pasold, Peter W.
    "The Effectiveness of Various Modes of Sales Behavior in Different
    Markets"
    Journal of Marketing Research, Vol. XII (May 1975), pp. 171-6.

Prasad, V. Kanti and Ring, L. Winston
    "Measuring Scales Effects of Some Marketing Mix Variables and Their
    Interactions"
    Journal of Marketing Research, Vol. XIII (November 1976), pp. 391-6.

Ratchford, Brian T.
    "The Value of Information for Selected Appliances"
    Journal of Marketing Research, Vol. XVII (February 1980), pp. 14-25.

Rentz, Joseph O., Reynolds, Fred D., and Stout, Roy G.
    "Analyzing Changing Consumption Patterns With Cohort Analysis"
    Journal of Marketing Research, Vol. XX (February 1983), pp. 12-20.

Ritchie, J. R. Brent, McDougall, Gordon H. G., and Claxton, John D.
    "Complexities of Household Energy Consumption and Conservation"
    Journal of Consumer Research, Vol. 8 (December 1981), pp. 233-42.

Robertson, Thomas S., Rossiter, John R., and Gleason, Terry C.
    "Children's Receptivity to Proprietary Medicine Advertising"
    Journal of Consumer Research, Vol. 6 (December 1979), pp. 247-55.

Robertson, Thomas S. and Wind, Yoram
    "Organizational Psychographics and Innovativeness"
    Journal of Consumer Research, Vol. 7 (June 1980), pp. 24-31.

Robinson, William T.
    "Sources of Market Pioneer Advantages: The Case of Industrial Goods
    Industries"
    Journal of Marketing Research, Vol. XXV (February 1988), pp. 87-94.

Ryan, Michael J. and Holbrook, Morris B.
    "Decision-Specific Conflict in Organizational Buyer Behavior"
    Journal of Marketing, Vol. 46 (Summer 1982), pp. 62-8.

Schlinger, Mary Jane Rawlins
    "Respondent Characteristics That Affect Copy-Test Attitude Scales"
    Journal of Advertising Research, Vol. 22 (February-March 1982), pp.
    29-35.

Schonfeld, Eugene P. and Boyd, John H.
    "The Financial Payoff in Corporate Advertising"
    Journal of Advertising Research, Vol. 22 (February/March 1982), pp.
    45-55.

Schweiger, Gunter C. and Hruschka, Harold
    "Analysis of Advertising Inquiries"
    Journal of Advertising Research, Vol. 20 (October 1980), pp. 37-9.

Sheth, Jagdish N. and Talarzyk, W. Wayne
    "Perceived Instrumentality and Value Importance as Determinents of
    Attitudes"
    Journal of Marketing Research, Vol. IX (February 1972), pp. 6-9.

Simon, Hermann
    "Dynamics of Price Elasticity and Brand Life Cycles: An Empirical
    Study"
    Journal of Marketing Research, Vol. XVI (November 1979), pp. 439-52.

Snizek, William E. and Crocker, Kenneth E.
"Professionalism and Attorney Attitudes Toward Legal Service
Advertising"
Journal of the Academy of Marketing Science, Vol. 13 (Fall 1985), pp.
101-18.

Soley, Lawrence C.
"Can Newspaper Audiences be Simulated?"
Journal of Advertising Research, Vol. 23 (October/November 1983), pp.
67-71.

Spekman, Robert E. and Stern, Louis W.
"Environmental Uncertainty and Buying Group Structure: An Empirical
Investigation"
Journal of Marketing, Vol. 43 (Spring 1979), pp. 54-64.

Staelin, Richard
"The Effects of Consumer Education on Consumer Product Safety
Behavior"
Journal of Consumer Research, Vol. 5 (June 1978), pp. 30-40.

Stephens, Lowndes F. and Moore, Roy L.
"Price Accuracy as a Consumer Skill"
Journal of Advertising Research, Vol. 15 (August 1975), pp. 27-34.

Stobaugh, Robert B. and Townsend, Phillip L.
"Price Forecasting and Strategic Planning: The Case of Petrochemicals"
Journal of Marketing Research, Vol. XII (February 1975), pp. 19-29.

Strober, Myra H. and Weinberg, Charles B.
"Working Wives and Major Family Expenditures"
Journal of Consumer Research, Vol.4 (December 1977), pp. 141-7.

Teas, R. Kenneth
"An Empirical Test of Models of Salespersons' Job Expectancy and
Instrumentality Perceptions"
Journal of Marketing Research, Vo. XVIII (May 1981), pp. 209-26.

Tellis, Gerard J. and Fornell, Claes
"The Relationship Between Advertising and Product Quality Over the
Product Life Cycle: A Contingency Theory"
Journal of Marketing Research, Vol. XXV (February 1988), pp. 64-71.

Tyagi, Pradeep K.
"The Effects of Stressful Organizational Conditions on Salesperson
Work Motivation"
Journal of the Academy of Science, Vol. 13 (Spring 1985), pp. 290-309.

Urban, Christine D.
"Correlates of Magazine Readership"
Journal of Advertising Research, Vol. 20 (August 1980), pp. 73-84.

Villani, Kathryn E. A.
"Personality/Life Style and Television Viewing Behavior"
Journal of Marketing Research, Vol. XII (November 1975), pp. 432-9.

Warshaw, Paul R.
"A New Model for Predicting Behavioral Intentions: An Alternative to
Fishbein"
Journal of Marketing Research, Vol. XVII (May 1980), pp. 153-72.

Webster, Frederick E., Jr.
"Determining the Characteristics of the Socially Conscious Consumer"
Journal of Consumer Research, Vol. 2 (December 1975), pp. 188-96.

Weitz, Barton A.
"Relationship Between Salesperson Performance and Understanding of
Customer Decision Making"
Journal of Marketing Research, Vol. XV (November 1978), pp. 501-16.

Westbrook, Robert A.
"Product/Consumption-Based Affective Responses and Postpurchase
Processes"
Journal of Marketing Research, Vol. XXIV (August 1987), pp. 258-70.

Westbrook, Robert A.
"Intrapersonal Affective Influences on Consumer Satisfaction With
Products"
Journal of Consumer Research, Vol. 7 (June 1980), pp. 49-54.

Westbrook, Robert A.
"Consumer Satisfaction as a Function of Personal Competence/Efficacy"
Journal of the Academy of Marketing Science, Vol. 8 (Fall 1980), pp.
427-37.

Wheatley, John J. and Chiu, John S. Y.
"The Effects of Price, Store Image, and Product and Respondent
Characteristics on Perceptions of Quality"
Journal of Marketing Research, Vol. XIV (May 1977), pp. 181-6.

Williams, Kaylene C. and Spiro, Rosann L.
  "Communication Style in the Salesperson-Customer Dyad"
  Journal of Marketing Research, Vol. XXII (November 1985), pp. 434-42.

Williams, Stephen C. and Longworth, John W.
  "Factors Influencing Tuna Prices in Japan and Implications for the
  Development of the Coral Sea Tuna Fishery"
  European Journal of Marketing, Vol. 23, No. 4 (1989), pp. 5-24.

Wind, Yoram and Lerner, David
  "On the Measurement of Purchase Data: Surveys Versus Purchase Diaries"
  Journal of Marketing Research, Vol. XVI (February 1979), pp. 39-47.

Winter, Frederick W.
  "Laboratory Measurement of Response to Consumer Information"
  Journal of Marketing Research, Vol. XII (November 1975), pp. 390-401.

Wittink, Dick R.
  "Exploring Territorial Differences in the Relationship Between
  Marketing Variables"
  Journal of Marketing Research, Vol. XIV (May 1977), pp. 145-54.

164.01 ---------- Applications of Linear-in-Logs Regression

Agarwal, Manoj K. and Ratchford, Brian T.
  "Estimating Demand Functions for Product Characteristics: The Case of
  Automobiles"
  Journal of Consumer Research, Vol. 7 (December 1980), pp. 249-62.

Armstrong, J. Scott
  "An Application of Econometric Models to International Marketing"
  Journal of Marketing Research, Vol. VII (May 1970), pp. 190-8.

Arora, Rajinder
  "How Promotion Elasticities Change"
  Journal of Advertising Research, Vol. 19 (June 1979), pp. 57-62.

Bettman, James R.
  "Perceived Risk and Its Components: A Model for Empirical Test"
  Journal of Marketing Research, Vol. X (May 1973), pp. 184-90.

Bird, M., Channon, C., and Ehrenberg, A. S. C.
  "Brand Image and Brand Usage"
  Journal of Marketing Research, Vol. VII (August 1970), pp. 307-14.

Bourgeois, Jacques C. and Barnes, James G.
  "Does Advertising Increase Alcohol Consumption?"
  Journal of Advertising Research, Vol. 19 (August 1979), pp. 19-29.

Carman, Roy F.
  "Improving Sales Forecasts for Appliances"
  Journal of Marketing Research, Vol. IX (May 1972), pp. 214-8.

Carroll, J. Douglas, Green, Paul E., and DeSarbo, Wayne S.
  "Optimizing the Allocation of a Fixed Resource: A Simple Model and
  Its Experimental Test"
  Journal of Marketing, Vol. 43 (January 1979), pp. 51-7.

Dalrymple, Douglas J.
  "Estimating Price and Markup Elasticities for Advertised Clothing
  Products"
  Journal of Advertising Research, Vol. 8 (December 1968), pp. 21-5.

Hagerty, Michael R., Carman, James M., and Russell, Gary J.
  "Estimating Elasticities With PIMS Data: Methodological Issues and
  Substantive Implications"
  Journal of Marketing Research, Vol. XXV (February 1988), pp. 1-9.

Headen, Robert S., Klompmaker, Jay E., and Teel, Jesse E., Jr.
  "Predicting Audience Exposure to Spot TV Advertising Schedules"
  Journal of Marketing Research, Vol. XIV (February 1977), pp. 1-9.

Heeler, Roger M. and Ray, Michael L.
  "Measure Validation in Marketing"
  Journal of Marketing Research, Vol. IX (November 1972), pp. 361-70.

Kotler, Philip
  "Marketing Mix Decisions for New Products"
  Journal of Marketing Research, Vol. I (February 1964), pp. 43-9.

Lucas, Henry C., Jr., Weinberg, Charles B., and Clowes, Kenneth W.
  "Sales Response as a Function of Territorial Potential and Sales
  Representative Workload"
  Journal of Marketing Research, Vol. XII (August 1975), pp. 298-305.

Mahajan, Vijay, Jain, Arun K., and Ratchford, Brian T.
  "Use of Binary Attributes in the Multiplicative Competitive
  Interactive Choice Model"
  Journal of Consumer Research, Vol. 5 (December 1978), pp. 210-5.

Massy, William F. and Frank, Ronald E.
    "Short Term Price and Dealing Effects in Selected Market Segments"
    Journal of Marketing Research, Vol. II (May 1965), pp. 171-85.

Menefee, John A.
    "The Demand for Consumption Time: A Longitudinal Perspective"
    Journal of Consumer Research, Vol. 8 (March 1982), pp. 391-7.

Parsons, Leonard J.
    "The Product Life Cycle and Time-Varying Advertising Elasticities"
    Journal of Marketing Research, Vol. XIV (February 1977), pp. 476-80.

Rao, Ram C. and Bass, Frank M.
    "Competition, Strategy, and Price Dynamics: A Theoretical and
    Empirical Investigation"
    Journal of Marketing Research, Vol. XXII (August 1985), pp. 283-96.

Ryans, Adrian B. and Weinberg, Charles B.
    "Territory Sales Response"
    Journal of Marketing Research, Vol. XVI (November 1979), pp. 453-65.

Sewall, Murphy A.
    "Relative Information Contributions of Consumer Purchase Intentions
    and Management Judgment as Explanators of Sales"
    Journal of Marketing Research, Vol. XVIII (May 1981), pp. 249-53.

Soley, Lawrence C.
    "Can Newspaper Audiences be Simulated?"
    Journal of Advertising Research, Vol. 23 (October/November 1983), pp.
    67-71.

Steele, Howard L.
    "On the Validity of Projective Questions"
    Journal of Marketing Research, Vol. I (August 1964), p. 469.

Wagner, Janet and Hanna, Sherman
    "The Effectiveness of Family Life Cycle Variables in Consumer
    Expenditure Research"
    Journal of Consumer Research, Vol. 10 (December 1983), pp. 281-91.

Walker, James M.
    "Voluntary Response to Energy Conservation Appeals"
    Journal of Consumer Research, Vol. 7 (June 1980), pp. 88-92.

Wittink, Dick R.
    "Advertising Increases Sensitivity to Price"
    Journal of Advertising Research, Vol. 17 (April 1977), pp. 39-42.

164.02 ---------- Applications of Generalized Least Squares (GLS)

Blattberg, Robert C. and Stivers, Samuel R.
    "A Statistical Evaluation of Transit Promotion"
    Journal of Marketing Research, Vol. VII (August 1970), pp. 293-9.

Boot, John C. G. and Teach, Richard D.
    "Consumer Distance Transitivity"
    Journal of Marketing Research, Vol. VII (November 1970), pp. 521-4.

Heeler, Roger M., Kearney, Michael J., and Mehaffey, Bruce J.
    "Modeling Supermarket Product Selection"
    Journal of Marketing Research, Vol. X (February 1973), pp. 34-7.

Sawyer, Alan G.
    "The Effects of Repetition of Refutational and Supportive Advertising
    Appeals"
    Journal of Marketing Research, Vol. X (February 1973), pp. 23-33.

164.03 ---------- Applications of Constrained Regression Models

Bass, Frank M., Cattin, Philippe, and Wittink, Dick R.
    "Firm Effects and Industry Effects in the Analysis of Market
    Structure and Profitability"
    Journal of Marketing Research, Vol. XV (February 1979), pp. 3-10.

164.04 ---------- Applications of Hierarchical Regression

Bagozzi, Richard P.
    "Expectancy-Value Attitude Models: An Analysis of Critical
    Measurement Issues"
    International Journal of Research in Marketing, Vol. 1, No. 4 (1984),
    pp. 295-310.

McQuarrie, Edward F.
    "An Alternative to Purchase Intentions: The Role of Prior Behaviour
    in Consumer Expenditure on Computers"
    Journal of the Market Research Society, Vol. 30 (October 1988), pp.
    407-37.

164.05 ---------- Applications of Seemingly Unrelated Regression
Parker, Thomas H. and Dolich, Ira J.
  "Toward Understanding Retail Bank Strategy: Seemingly Unrelated
  Regression Applied to Cross-Sectional Data"
  Journal of Retailing, Vol. 62 (Fall 1986), pp. 298-320.

165 ---------------------- NONLINEAR FUNCTIONS ----------------------
See also (sub)heading(s) 159.

165.01 ---------- Books Re: Nonlinear Functions

Bard, Y.
Nonlinear Parameter Estimation
(New York: Academic Press, 1974).

Bateman, H.
Higher Transcendental Functions, Volume II
(New York: McGraw-Hill, 1953).

Bates, Douglas M. and Watts, Donald G.
Nonlinear Regression Analysis and Its Applications
(New York: John Wiley and Sons, Inc., 1988).

Gifi, A.
Non-Linear Multivariate Analysis
(Leiden, The Netherlands: Department of Data Theory, University of Leiden, 1981).

Goldfeld, Stephen M. and Quandt, Richard E.
Nonlinear Methods in Econometrics
(Amsterdam-London: North-Holland Publishing Company, 1972).

165.02 ---------- Theory Re: Nonlinear Functions

Laroche, Michel
"A Method for Detecting Nonlinear Effects in Cross-Sectional Survey Data"
International Journal of Research in Marketing, Vol. 2, No. 1 (1985), pp. 61-72.

Rust, Roland T. and Bornman, Elizabeth O.
"Distribution-Free Methods of Approximating Nonlinear Marketing Relationships"
Journal of Marketing Research, Vol. XIX (August 1982), pp. 372-4.

165.03 ---------- Theory Re: Nonlinear Regression

Aird, Thomas J.
"Computational Solution of Global Nonlinear Least Squares Problems"
Purdue University (1973), Ph.D. dissertation.

Albaum, Gerald, Best, Roger, and Hawkins, Del I.
"The Marketing of Hamburger Buns: An Improved Model for Prediction"
Journal of the Academy of Marketing Science, Vol. 3 (Summer-Fall 1975), pp. 223-31.

Fletcher, Robert
"Generalized Inverse Methods for the Best Least Squares Solution of Systems of Non-Linear Equations"
Computer Journal, Vol. 10 (1968), pp. 392-9.

Gallant, A. R. and Goebel, J. J.
"Nonlinear Regression With Autoregressive Errors"
Journal of the American Statistical Association, Vol. 71 (December 1976), pp. 961-7.

Levenberg, Kenneth
"A Method for the Solution of Certain Nonlinear Problems in Least Squares"
Quarterly of Applied Mathematics, Vol. 2, No. 2 (1944), pp. 164-8.

Marquardt, Donald W.
"An Algorithm for the Least Squares Estimation of Nonlinear Models"
Journal of Siam, Vol. 11 (June 1963), pp. 431-41.

Meyer, R. R.
"Theoretical and Computational Aspects of Nonlinear Regression"
in Rosen, J. Ben, Mangasarian, Olvi L., and Ritter, Klaus (editors)
Nonlinear Programming
(New York: Academic Press, 1970), pp. 465-86.

Meyer, R. R. and Rothkopf, M. H.
"Comments on 'Fitting Parameters to Complex Models by Direct Search'"
Journal of Marketing Research, Vol. VIII (November 1971), pp. 518,9.

Shakun, M. F.
"Nonlinear Regression Analysis"
Industrial Quality Control, Vol. 23 (July 1966), pp. 11-3.

Shepard, R. N. and Carroll, J. D.
"Parametric Representation of Nonlinear Data Structures"
in Krishnaiah, P. R. (editor)
Multivariate Analysis
(New York: Academic Press, 1966), pp. 561-92.

Van Wormer, Theodore A. and Weiss, Doyle L.
   "'Fitting Parameters by Direct Search': A Reply"
   Journal of Marketing Research, Vol. VIII (November 1971), pp. 518,9.

Van Wormer, Theodore and Weiss, Doyle L.
   "Fitting Parameters to Complex Models by Direct Search"
   Journal of Marketing Research, Vol. VII (November 1970), pp. 503-12.

165.04 ---------- Theory Re: Piecewise or Segmented Regression

Bellman, Richard and Roth, Robert
   "Curve Fitting by Segmented Straight Lines"
   Journal of the American Statistical Association, Vol. 64 (September
   1969), pp. 1079-84.

Feder, P. I.
   "On Asymptotic Distribution Theory in Segmented Regression
   Problems--Identified Case"
   Technometrics, Vol. 16 (1975), pp. 287-99.

Hudson, D. J.
   "Fitting Segmented Curves Whose Joint Points Have to be Estimated"
   Journal of the American Statistical Association, Vol. 61 (1966), pp.
   1097-129.

McGee, Victor E. and Carleton, Willard T.
   "Piecewise Regression"
   Journal of the American Statistical Association, Vol. 65 (September
   1970), pp. 1109-24.

Poirier, Dale J.
   "Piecewise Regression Using Cubic Splines"
   Journal of the American Statistical Association, Vol. 68 (September
   1973), pp. 515-24.

Rust, Roland T.
   "Methods of Curve Fitting in Marketing Analysis"
   ORSA/TIMS Joint National Meeting (November 1980).

Sprent, P.
   "Some Hypotheses Concerning Two-Phase Regression Lines"
   Biometrics, Vol. 17 (1961), pp. 634,5.

165.05 ---------- Applications of Nonlinear Regression

Buzzell, Robert D. and Baker, Michael J.
   "Sales Effectiveness of Automobile Advertising"
   Journal of Advertising Research, Vol. 12 (June 1972), pp. 3-8.

Cox, Eli P., III
   "Family Purchase Decision Making and the Process of Adjustment"
   Journal of Marketing Research, Vol. XII (May 1975), pp. 189-95.

Hackleman, Edwin C. and Duker, Jacob M.
   "Deal Proneness and Heavy Usage: Merging Two Market Segmentation
   Criteria"
   Journal of the Academy of Marketing Science, Vol. 8 (Fall 1980), pp.
   332-44.

Horsky, Dan
   "Market Share Response to Advertising: An Example of Theory Testing"
   Journal of Marketing Research, Vol. XIV (February 1977), pp. 10-21.

Laroche, Michel and Howard, John A.
   "Nonlinear Relations in a Complex Model of Buyer Behavior"
   Journal of Consumer Research, Vol. 6 (March 1980), pp. 377-88.

Peterson, Robert A.
   "The Price-Perceived Quality Relationship: Experimental Evidence"
   Journal of Marketing Research, Vol. VII (November 1970), pp. 525-8.

Wheatley, John J., Chiu, John S. Y., and Stevens, Andrea C.
   "Demographics to Predict Consumption"
   Journal of Advertising Research, Vol. 20 (December 1980), pp. 31-8.

166 --------------- MODERATED REGRESSION ANALYSIS (MRA) --------------
       See also (sub)heading(s) 140, 159, 160.04.

166.01 ---------- Theory Re: Moderated Regression Analysis (MRA)

Anderson, Carol H.
   "Hierarchical Moderated Regression Analysis: A Useful Tool for Retail
   Management Decisions"
   Journal of Retailing, Vol. 62 (Summer 1986), pp. 186-203.

Arnold, Hugh J.
   "Testing Moderator Variable Hypotheses: A Reply to Stone and
   Hollenbeck"
   Organizational Behavior and Human Performance, Vol. 34 (1984), pp.
   214-24.

Morris, James H., Sherman, J. Daniel, and Mansfield, Edward R.
   "Failures to Detect Moderating Effects With Ordinary Least
   Squares-Moderated Multiple Regression: Some Reasons and a Remedy"
   Psychological Bulletin, Vol. 99, No. 2 (1985), pp. 282-8.

Peters, Lawrence H. and Champoux, Joseph E.
   "The Use of Moderated Regression in Job Redesign Decisions"
   Decision Sciences, Vol. 10 (1979), pp. 85-95.

Peters, Lawrence H. and Champoux, Joseph E.
   "The Role and Analysis of Moderator Variables in Organizational
   Research"
   in Mowday, R. T. and Steers, R. M. (editors)
   Research in Organizations: Issues and Controversies
   (Santa Monica, CA: Goodyear Publishing Company, 1979), pp. 239-53.

Peters, Lawrence H., O'Connor, Edward J., and Wise, Steven L.
   "The Specification and Testing of Useful Moderator Variable
   Hypotheses"
   in Bateman, T. S. and Perris, G. R. (editors)
   Method and Analysis in Organizational Research
   (Reston, VA: Reston Publishing Company, 1984), pp. 128-39.

Stone, Eugene F. and Hollenbeck, John R.
   "Some Issues With the Use of Moderated Regression"
   Organizational Behavior and Human Performance, Vol. 34 (1984), pp.
   195-213.

166.02 ---------- Applications of Moderated Regression Analysis (MRA)

Bearden, William O. and Mason, J. Barry
   "Physician and Pharmacist Perceived Risk in Generic Drugs"
   in Beckwith, Neil et al. (editors)
   Proceedings, AMA Educators' Conference
   (Chicago: American Marketing Association, 1979), pp. 577-83.

Bearden, William O. and Woodside, Arch G.
   "Consumption Occasion Influence on Consumer Brand Choice"
   Decision Sciences, Vol. 9 (April 1978), pp. 273-84.

Bearden, William O. and Woodside, Arch G.
   "Interactions of Consumption Situations and Brand Attitudes"
   Journal of Applied Psychology, Vol. 61 (December 1976), pp. 764-9.

Durand, Richard M. and Gur-Arie, Oded
   "Cognitive Differentiation: A Moderator of Behavioral Intentions"
   in Beckwith, Neil et al. (editors)
   Proceedings, AMA Educators' Conference
   (Chicago: American Marketing Association, 1979), pp. 305-8.

Horton, Raymond L.
   "Some Relationships Between Personality and Consumer Decision Making"
   Journal of Marketing Research, Vol. XVI (May 1979), pp. 233-46.

Kohli, Ajay K.
   "Effects of Supervisory Behavior: The Role of Individual Differences
   Among Salespeople"
   Journal of Marketing, Vol. 53 (October 1989), pp. 40-50.

Laroche, Michel and Howard, John A.
   "Nonlinear Relations in a Complex Model of Buyer Behavior"
   Journal of Consumer Research, Vol. 6 (March 1980), pp. 377-88.

Lichtenstein, Donald R., Burton, Scot, and O'Hara, Bradley S.
   "Marketplace Attributions and Consumer Evaluations of Discount Claims"
   Psychology and Marketing, Vol. 6 (Fall 1989), pp. 163-80.

167 -------------------- NONPARAMETRIC REGRESSION -------------------

See also (sub)heading(s) 159.

167.01 ---------- Books Re: Nonparametric Regression

Breiman, Leo, Friedman, J. H., Oshen, R. A., and Stone, Charles J.
Classification and Regression Trees
(Belmont, CA: Wadsworth Publishing Company, Inc., 1984).

Rao, B. L. S. Prakasa
Nonparametric Functional Estimation
(Orlando, FL: Academic Press, Inc., 1983).

167.02 ---------- Theory Re: Nonparametric Regression

Clarke, R. M.
"Nonparmetric Estimation of a Smooth Regression Function"
Journal of the Royal Statistical Society, Series B, Vol. 39 (1977),
pp. 107-13.

Stone, Charles J.
"Consistent Nonparmetric Regression"
Annals of Statistics, Vol. 5 (1977), pp. 595-620.

167.03 ---------- Theory Re: Flexible Regression

Rust, Roland T.
"Flexible Regression"
Journal of Marketing Research, Vol. XXV (February 1988), pp. 10-24.

Rust, Roland T. and Bornman, Elizabeth O.
"Distribution-Free Methods of Approximating Nonlinear Marketing
Relationships"
Journal of Marketing Research, Vol. XIX (August 1982), pp. 372-4.

Stone, Charles J.
"Consistent Nonparametric Regression"
Annals of Statistics, Vol. 5 (1977), pp. 595-645.

167.04 ---------- Statistical Testing in Flexible Regression

See also (sub)heading(s) 141.

Rust, Roland T. and Schmittlein, David C.
"A Bayesian Cross-Validated Likelihood Method for Comparing
Alternative Specifications of Quantitative Models"
Marketing Science, Vol. 4 (Winter 1985), pp. 20-40.

Stone, M.
"Cross-Validatory Choice and Assessment of Statistical Predictions"
Journal of the Royal Statistical Society, B, Vol. 36, No. 2 (1974),
pp. 111-47.

167.05 ---------- Computer Programs for Flexible Regression

Rust, Roland T. and Donthu, Naveen
"Users Manual for FLEX: A FORTRAN Program for Flexible Regression"
Department of Marketing Administration Working Paper, University of
Texas at Austin (1987).

167.06 ---------- Books Re: Splines

Ahlberg, J. H., Nilson, E. N., and Walsh, J. L.
The Theory of Splines and Their Application
(New York: Academic Press, 1967).

DeBoor, Carl
A Practical Guide to Splines
(New York: Springer-Verlag, 1978).

Greville, T. N. E.
Theory and Applications of Spline Functions
(New York: Academic Press, Inc., 1969).

167.07 ---------- Theory Re: Splines

Marcus, Richard D.
"How to Deal With Structural Changes in the Data"
Journal of Business Forecasting, Vol. 6 (Winter 1987/1988), pp. 14-6.

Poirier, Dale J.
"Piecewise Regression Using Cubic Splines"
Journal of the American Statistical Association, Vol. 68 (September
1973), pp. 515-24.

Silverman, B. W.
    "Some Aspects of the Spline Smoothing Approach to Non-Parametric
    Regression Curve Fitting"
    Journal of the Royal Statistical Society, Part B, Vol. 47, No. 1
    (1985), pp. 1-52.

167.08 ---------- Applications of Splines

Barth, James, Kraft, Arthur, and Kraft, John
    "Estimating the Liquidity Trap Using Spline Functions"
    Review of Economics and Statistics (May 1976), pp. 218-22.

Huff, David L. and Batsell, Richard R.
    "Delimiting the Areal Extent of a Market Area"
    Journal of Marketing Research, Vol. XIV (November 1977), pp. 581-5.

Huff, David L. and Rust, Roland T.
    "Measuring the Congruence of Market Areas"
    Journal of Marketing, Vol. 48 (Winter 1984), pp. 68-74.

Rust, Roland T.
    "Recategorizing Secondary Data"
    1981 Educators' Conference Proceedings
    (Chicago: American Marketing Association, 1981), pp. 384-6.

Schoenberg, I. J.
    "Spline Functions and the Problem of Graduation"
    Proceedings of the National Academy of Science, Vol. 52, No. 4
    (1964), pp. 947-50.

167.09 ---------- Theory Re: Kernel Estimation

Benedetti, Jaqueline K.
    "On the Nonparametric Estimation of Regression Functions"
    Journal of the Royal Statistical Society, Part B, Vol. 39, No. 2
    (1977), pp. 248-53.

Donthu, Naveen and Rust, Roland T.
    "Estimating Geographic Customer Densities Using Kernel Density
    Estimation"
    Marketing Science, Vol. 8 (Spring 1989), pp. 191-203.

Donthu, Naveen and Rust, Roland T.
    "Flexible Ideal Point Densities for Product Positioning"
    1988), unpublished working paper.

Donthu, Naveen and Rust, Roland T.
    "KPLOT: A Computer Program for Estimating and Plotting a Kernel
    Density"
    (1988), unpublished working paper.

Epanechnikov, V. A.
    "Nonparametric Estimation of a Multivariate Probability Density"
    Theory of Probability and Applications, Vol. 14 (1969), pp. 153-8.

Klonias, V. K.
    "On a Class of Nonparametric Density and Regression Estimators"
    Annals of Statistics, Vol. 12, No. 4 (1984), pp. 1263-84.

Nadaraya, E. A.
    "Remarks on Non-Parametric Estimates for Density Functions and
    Regression Curves"
    Theory of Probability and Its Applications, Vol. 15, No. 1 (1970),
    pp. 134-6.

Priestley, M. B. and Chao, M. T.
    "Non-Parametric Function Fitting"
    Journal of the Royal Statistical Society, Part B, Vol. 34, No. 3
    (1972), pp. 385-92.

Rice, John
    "Bandwidth Choice for Nonparametric Regression"
    Annals of Statistics, Vol. 12, No. 4 (1984), pp. 1215-30.

Rudemo, Mats
    "Empirical Choice of Histograms and Kernel Density Estimators"
    Scandinavian Journal of Statistics, Vol. 9, No. 2 (1982), pp. 65-78.

Watson, Geoffrey S.
    "Smooth Regression Analysis"
    Sankhya A, Vol. 26, No. 4 (1964), pp. 359-72.

Woodroofe, M.
    "On Choosing a Delta-Sequence"
    Annals of Mathematical Statistics, Vol. 41 (1970), pp. 1665-71.

167.10 ---------- Theory Re: Convolution Estimation

Clark, R. M.
    "Non-Parametric Estimation of a Smooth Regression Function"
    Journal of the Royal Statistical Society, Part B, Vol. 39, No. 1
    (1977), pp. 107-13.

Gasser, Theo and Muller, Hans-Georg
    "Kernel Estimation of Regression Functions"
    in Gasser, T. and Rosenblatt, M. (editors)
    Smoothing Techniques for Curve Estimation
    (New York: Springer-Verlag, 1979), pp. 23-66.

167.11 ---------- Theory Re: Locally Weighted Regression

Cleveland, William S.
    "Robust Locally Weighted Regression and Smoothing Scatterplots"
    Journal of the American Statistical Association (December 1979), pp.
    829-36.

Rust, Roland T. and Bornman, Elizabeth O.
    "Response Estimation for Advertising Decision Models: An Empirical
    Bayes Approach"
    in Murphy, Patrick E. et al. (editors)
    AMA Educators' Proceedings, Series 49
    (Chicago: American Marketing Association, 1984).

Rust, Roland T. and Bornman, Elizabeth O.
    "Distribution-Free Methods of Approximating Nonlinear Marketing
    Relationships"
    Journal of Marketing Research, Vol. XIX (August 1982), pp. 372-4.

167.12 ---------- Theory Re: Nonparametric Density Estimation

Cacoullos, T.
    "Estimation of a Multivariate Density"
    Annals of the Institute of Statistical Mathematics, Vol. 18 (1966),
    pp. 178-89.

Epanechnikov, V. A.
    "Nonparametric Estimation of a Multivariate Probability Density"
    Theory of Probability and Its Applications, Vol. 14, No. 1 (1969),
    pp. 153-8.

Fryer, M. J.
    "A Review of Some Nonparametric Methods of Density Estimation"
    Journal of the Institute of Mathematics Applications, Vol. 20 (1977),
    pp. 335-54.

Parzen, Emanuel
    "Nonparametric Statistical Data Modeling"
    Journal of the American Statistical Association, Vol. 74 (1979), pp.
    105-31.

Parzen, Emanuel
    "On Estimation of a Probability Density Function and Mode"
    Annals of Mathematical Statistics, Vol. 33, No. 3 (1962), pp. 1065-76.

Rao, B. L. S. Prakasa
    Nonparametric Functional Estimation
    (Orlando, FL: Academic Press, Inc., 1983).

Rosenblatt, Murray
    "Remarks on Some Nonparametric Estimates of a Density Function"
    Annals of Mathematical Statistics, Vol. 27, No. 3 (1956), pp. 1215-30.

Rudemo, Mats
    "Empirical Choice of Histograms and Kernel Density Estimators"
    Scandinavian Journal of Statistics, Vol. 9, No. 2 (1982), pp. 65-78.

Sager, Thomas W.
    "Dimensionality Reduction in Density Estimation"
    in Wegman, E. J. and DePriest, D. J. (editors)
    Statistical Image Processing and Graphics
    (New York: Marcel Dekker, 1986).

Silverman, B. W.
    Density Estimation for Statistics and Data Analysis
    (New York: Chapman and Hall, 1986).

Silverman, B. W.
    "Choosing the Window Width When Estimating a Density"
    Biometrika, Vol. 65 (1978), pp. 1-11.

Stone, Charles J.
  "An Asymptotically Optimal Window Selection Rule for Kernal Density Estimates"
  Annals of Statistics, Vol. 12, No. 4 (1984), pp. 1285-97.

Tapia, R. A. and Thompson, J. R.
  Nonparametric Probability Density Estimation
  (Baltimore: Johns Hopkins University Press, 1978).

168 ----   REGRESSION RESIDUALS, OUTLIERS, INFLUENTIAL OBSERVATIONS   ----
      See also (sub)heading(s) 134, 159, 179.04.

168.01 ---------- Books Re: Residuals, Outliers, and Influential Obs

Andrews, D. F., Bickel, F. R., Huber, P. J., Rogers, W. H., and Tukey,
     J. W.
     Robust Estimates of Location: Survey and Advances
     (Princeton, NJ: Princeton University Press, 1972).

Barnett, V. and Lewis, T.
     Outliers in Statistical Data
     (New York: John Wiley and Sons, Inc., 1978).

Belsley, David A., Kuh, Edwin, and Welsch, Roy E.
     Regression Diagnostics: Identifying Influential Data and Sources of
     Collinearity
     (New York: John Wiley and Sons, Inc., 1980).

Cook, R. D. and Weisberg, S.
     Residuals and Influence in Regression
     (New York: Chapman and Hall, 1982).

Hoaglin, D. C., Mosteller, F., and Tukey, J. W.
     Understanding Robust and Exploratory Data Analysis
     (New York: John Wiley and Sons, Inc., 1983).

Huber, P. J.
     Robust Statistics
     (New York: John Wiley and Sons, Inc., 1981).

Launer, R. L. and Wilkinson, G. N. (editors)
     Robustness in Statistics
     (New York: Academic Press, 1979).

168.02 ---------- Theory Re: Residuals, Outliers, and Influential Obs

Andrews, D. F.
     "Significance Tests Based on Residuals"
     Biometrika, Vol. 58 (1971), pp. 139-48.

Andrews, D. F. and Pregibon, D.
     "Finding the Outliers That Matter"
     Journal of the Royal Statistical Society, Series B (Methodology),
     Vol. 40, No. 1 (1978), pp. 85-93.

Anscombe, F. J.
     "Graphs in Statistical Analysis"
     American Statistician, Vol. 27 (February 1973), pp. 17-22.

Anscombe, F. J.
     "Examination of Residuals"
     Proceedings, Fourth Berkeley Symposium on Mathematical Statistics and
     Probability (1961), pp. 1-36.

Anscombe, F. J.
     "Rejection of Outliers"
     Technometrics, Vol. 2 (1960), pp. 123-47.

Anscombe, F. J. and Tukey, John W.
     "The Examination of Residuals"
     Technometrics, Vol. 5 (1963), pp. 141-60.

Beckman, R. J. and Cook, R. D.
     "Outlier....s"
     Technometrics, Vol. 25 (May 1983), pp. 119-49.

Butler, R.
     "Outlier Discordancy Tests in the Normal Linear Model"
     Journal of the Royal Statistical Society, Series B, Vol. 45, No. 1
     (1983), pp. 120-32.

Chambers, R. L. and Heathcote, C. R.
     "On the Estimation of Slope and the Identification of Outliers in
     Linear Regression"
     Biometrika, Vol. 68 (1981), pp. 21-33.

Cook, R. Dennis
     "Influential Observations in Linear Regression"
     Journal of the American Statistical Association, Vol. 74 (1979), pp.
     169-74.

Cook, R. Dennis
     "Detection of Influential Observations in Linear Regression"
     Technometrics, Vol. 19 (February 1977), pp. 15-8.

Dempster, A. P. and Gasko-Green, M.
     "New Tools for Residual Analysis"
     Annals of Statistics, Vol. 9 (1981), pp. 945-59.

Draper, Norman R. and John, J. A.
"Influential Observatins and Outliers in Regression"
Technometrics, Vol. 23 (1981), pp. 21-6.

Giltnan, David M., Carroll, Raymond J., and Ruppert, David
"Some New Estimation Methods for Weighted Regression When There are
Possible Outliers"
Technometrics, Vol. 28, No. 3 (1986), pp. 219-30.

Gnanadesikan, R. and Kettenring, J. R.
"Robust Estimates, Residuals, and Outlier Detection With
Multiresponse Data"
Biometrics, Vol. 28 (March 1972), pp. 81-124.

Hartley, H. O. and Jayatillake, K. S. E.
"Estimation for Linear Models With Unequal Variances"
Journal of the American Statistical Association, Vol. 68 (1973), pp.
189-92.

Marasinghe, Mervyn G.
"A Multistage Procedure for Detecting Several Outliers in Linear
Regression"
Technometrics, Vol. 27, No. 4 (1985), pp. 395-9.

Mirvalieu, M.
"The Rejection of Outlying Observations in Regression Analysis"
Theoretical Probability Ap., Vol. 23 (1978), pp. 598-602.

Schweder, T.
"Some 'Optimal' Methods to Detect Structural Shift or Outliers in
Regression"
Journal of the American Statistical Association, Vol. 71 (1976), pp.
491-501.

168.03 ---------- Theory Re: Robust Regression

Andrews, D. F.
"A Robust Method for Multiple Linear Regression"
Technometrics, Vol. 16 (1974), pp. 523-31.

Askin, R. G. and Montgomery, D. C.
"Augmented Robust Estimators"
Technometrics, Vol. 22 (August 1980), pp. 333-41.

Atkinson, A. C.
"Robust and Diagnostic Regression Analysis"
Communications in Statistics, Vol. All (1982), pp. 2559-72.

Cleveland, William S.
"Robust Locally Weighted Regression and Smoothing Scatterplots"
Journal of the American Statistical Association, Vol. 74 (December
1979), pp. 829-36.

Denby, L. and Martin, R. D.
"Robust Estimation of the First-Order Autoregressive Parameter"
Journal of the American Statistical Association, Vol. 74 (1979), pp.
140-6.

Dorsett, D. and Gunst, R. F.
"Bounded-Leverage Weights for Robust Regression Estimators"
Technical Report No. 171
Department of Statistics, Southern Methodist University (1976).

Gnanadesikan, R. and Kettenring, J. R.
"Robust Estimates, Residuals and Outlier Detection With Multiresponse
Data"
Biometrics, Vol. 28 (1972), pp. 81-124.

Hogg, R. V.
"Statistical Robustness: One View of Its Use in Applications Today"
The American Statistician, Vol. 33 (August 1979), pp. 108-15.

Hogg, R. V.
"An Introduction to Robust Estimation"
in Launer, R. L. and Wilkinson, G. N. (editors)
Robustness in Statistics
(New York: Academic Press, 1979), pp. 1-18.

Huber, P. J.
"Robust Regression: Asymptotics, Conjecture, and Monte Carlo"
Annals of Statistics, Vol. 1 (1973), pp. 799-821.

Huber, P. J.
"Robust Estimation of a Location Parameter"
Annals of Mathematical Statistics, Vol. 35 (1964), pp. 73-101.

Huynh, H.
"A Comparison of Four Approaches to Robust Regression"
Psychological Bulletin, Vol. 92 (1982), pp. 505-12.

Krakser, W. S. and Welsch, R. E.
   "Efficient Bounded-Influence Regression Estimation"
   Journal of the American Statistical Association, Vol. 77 (1982), pp.
   595-604.

Lenth, R. V.
   "A Computational Procedure for Robust Multiple Regression"
   Technical Report No. 53
   Department of Statistics, University of Iowa (1976).

Mahajan, Vijay, Sharma, Subhash, and Wind, Yoram
   "Parameter Estimation in Marketing Models in the Presence of
   Influential Response Data: Robust Regression and Applications"
   Journal of Marketing Research, Vol. XXI (August 1984), pp. 268-77.

Rousseeuw, Peter J. and Leroy, Annick M.
   Robust Regression and Outlier Detection
   (New York: John Wiley and Sons, Inc., 1987).

Rousseeuw, Peter J. and Van Zomeren, B. C.
   "Identification of Multivariate Outliers and Leverage Points by Means
   of Robust Covariance Matrices"
   Faculty of Mathematics and Informatics, Delft University of
   Technology, The Netherlands (1987), technical report.

Rust, Roland T. and Bornman, E. O.
   "Distribution-Free Methods of Approximating Nonlinear Marketing
   Relationships"
   Journal of Marketing Research, Vol. XIX (August 1982), pp. 372-4.

Wainer, Howard and Thissen, David
   "Three Steps Towards Robust Regression"
   Psychometrika, Vol. 41 (1976), pp. 9-34.

168.04 ---------- Computer Programs Re: Residuals, Outliers, etc.

Huang, Jen-Hung
   "DROI: A Computer Program for Detecting Remote Points, Outliers, and
   Influential Observations"
   Journal of Marketing Research, Vol. XX (November 1983), p. 444.

169 -------------------- CROSS-LAGGED CORRELATION --------------------
See also (sub)heading(s) 159, 205, 207.

169.01 ---------- Theory Re: Cross-Lagged Correlation

Campbell, Donald T. and Stanley, Julian C.
"Experimental and Quasi-Experimental Designs for Research on Teaching"
in Gage, N. L. (editor)
Handboook of Research on Teaching
(Chicago: Rand McNally, 1963), pp. 171-246.

Kenny, D. A.
"Cross Lagged Panel Correlation: A Test for Spuriousness"
Psychological Bulletin, Vol. 82 (November 1975), pp. 887-903.

Kenny, David A.
"Cross-Lagged and Synchronous Common Factors in Panel Data"
in Structural Equations in the Social Sciences
(New York: Seminar Press, 1973).

Kenny, David A. and Campbell, Donald T.
"Methodological Issues in the Analysis of Temporal Data"
in Historical Social Psychology
(Hillsdale, NJ: Lawrence Erlbaum, 1984), pp. 125-38.

Kenny, David A. and Harackiewicz, Judith M.
"Cross-Lagged Panel Correlation: Practice and Promise"
Journal of Applied Psychology, Vol. 64 (August 1979), pp. 372-9.

Pelz, Donald C.
"Comments on the Method of Cross-Lagged Correlation"
Survey Research Center, University of Michigan (1967), unpublished
paper.

Pelz, Donald C. and Andrews, Frank M.
"Detecting Causal Priorities in Panel Study Data"
American Sociological Review, Vol. 29 (December 1964), pp. 836-48.

Rickard, Stanley E., Jr.
"Using Correlations to Test Causal Hypotheses"
Northwestern University (1967), unpublished doctoral dissertation.

Rogosa, D.
"A Critique of Cross-Lagged Correlation"
Psychological Bulletin, Vol. 88 (September 1980), pp. 245-58.

Rozelle, Richard M. and Campbell, Donald T.
"More Plausible Rival Hypotheses in the Cross-Lagged Panel
Correlation Technique"
Psychological Bulletin, Vol. 71 (January 1969), pp. 74-80.

169.02 ---------- Applications of Cross-Lagged Correlation

Bass, Frank M. and Pilon, Thomas L.
"A Stochastic Brand Choice Framework for Econometric Modeling of Time
Series Market Share Behavior"
Journal of Marketing Research, Vol. XVII (November 1980), pp. 486-97.

Beatty, Sharon E. and Kahle, Lynn R.
"Alternative Hierarchies of the Attitude-Behavior Relationship: The
Impact of Brand Commitment and Habit"
Journal of the Academy of Marketing Science, Vol. 16 (Summer 1988),
pp. 1-10.

O'Brien, Terrence
"Stages of Consumer Decision Making"
Journal of Marketing, Vol. VIII (August 1971), pp. 283-9.

169.03 ---------- Computer Programs for Cross-Lagged Correlation

Kenny, David A.
"PANEL: A Computer Program for Panel Data Analysis"
Department of Psychology, University of Connecticut (1978), research
report.

170 ------------------ BIASED ESTIMATION PROCEDURES ------------------
        See also (sub)heading(s) 159, 160.02.

170.01 ---------- General Discussions of Biased Estimation Procedures

Gunst, R. F. and Mason, Robert L.
    "Biased Estimation in Regression: An Evaluation Using Mean Square
    Error"
    Journal of the American Statistical Association, Vol. 72 (1977), pp.
    616-28.

Judge, G. G. and Bock, M. E.
    "Biased Estimation"
    in Griliches, Z. and Intriligator, M. D. (editors)
    Handbook of Econometrics
    (Amsterdam: Elsevier, 1983), pp. 599-649.

170.02 ---------- Theory Re: Latent Root Regression

Gunst, R. F.
    "Similarities Among Least Squares, Principal Component, and Latent
    Root Estimators"
    1979 Conference of the American Statistical Association, Washington,
    DC, paper presentation.

Gunst, R. F., Webster, J. T., and Mason, R. L.
    "A Comparison of Least Squares and Latent Root Regression Estimators"
    Technometrics, Vol. 18 (February 1976), pp. 74-86.

Jagpal, Harsharanjeet S., Sudit, E. F., and Vinod, H. D.
    "Measuring Dynamic Marketing Mix Interactions Using Translog
    Functions"
    Journal of Business (July 1982).

Reichert, Alan K. and Moore, James S.
    "Using Latent Root Regression to Identify Nonpredictive Collinearity
    in Statistical Appraisal Models"
    American Real Estate and Urban Economics Association Journal, Vol. 14
    (1986), pp. 136-52.

Sharma, Subhash and James, William L.
    "Latent Root Regression: An Alternate Procedure for Estimating
    Parameters in the Presence of Multicollinearity"
    Journal of Marketing Research, Vol. XVIII (May 1981), pp. 154-61.

Webster, J. T., Gunst, R. F., and Mason, R. L.
    "Latent Root Regression Analysis"
    Technometrics, Vol. 16 (November 1974), pp. 513-22.

170.03 ---------- Theory Re: Ridge Regression

Cattin, Philippe
    "The Predictive Power of Ridge Regression: Some Quasi-Simulation
    Results"
    Journal of Applied Psychology, Vol. 66, No. 3 (1981), pp. 282-90.

Coniffe, D. and Stone, J.
    "A Critical View of Ridge Regression"
    The Statistician, Vol. 22 (June 1973), pp. 181-7.

Draper, N. and Van Nostrand, R. C.
    "Ridge Regression and James-Stein Estimation: Review and Comments"
    Technometrics, Vol. 21 (1979), pp. 451-66.

Erickson, G. M.
    "Using Ridge Regression to Estimate Directly Lagged Effects in
    Marketing"
    Journal of the American Statistical Association, Vol. 76 (1981), pp.
    766-73.

Farebrother, R. W.
    "The Minimum Mean Square Error Linear Estimator and Ridge Regression"
    Technometrics, Vol. 17, No. 1 (1975), pp. 127,8.

Friedman, D. J. and Montgomery, D. C.
    "Evaluation of the Predictive Performance of Biased Regression
    Estimators"
    Journal of Forecasting, Vol. 4 (1985), pp. 153-63.

Gelfand, Alan E.
    "On the Use of Ridge and Stein-Type Estimators in Prediction"
    Stanford University Technical Report (1982).

Gibbons, D. G.
    "A Simulation Study of Some Ridge Estimators"
    Journal of the American Statistical Association, Vol. 76 (1981), pp.
    131-9.

Goldstein, M. and Smith, A. F.
"Ridge Type Estimators for Regression Analysis"
Journal of the Royal Statistical Society, Series B, Vol. 36 (1974),
pp. 284-91.

Goto, Masashi and Matsubara, Yoshihiro
"Evaluation of Ordinary Ridge Regression"
Bulletin of Mathematical Statistics, Vol. 20 (1979), pp. 1-35.

Gunst, R. F.
"A Critique of Some Ridge Regression Methods: Comment"
Journal of the American Statistical Association, Vol. 75 (1980), pp.
98-100.

Gunst, R. F. and Mason, R. L.
"Biased Estimation in Regression: An Evaluation Using Mean Squared
Error"
Journal of the American Statistical Association, Vol. 72 (September
1977), pp. 616-28.

Hawkins, D. M.
"Relations Between Ridge Regression and Eigenanalysis of the
Augmented Correlation Matrix"
Technometrics, Vol. 17 (November 1975), pp. 477-80.

Hemmerle, W. J. and Brantle, T. F.
"Explicit and Constrained Generalized Ridge Regression"
Technometrics, Vol. 20 (1978), pp. 109-20.

Hoerl, Arthur E. and Kennard, Robert W.
"Ridge Regression: Iterative Estimation of the Biasing Parameter"
Communications in Statistics, Vol. A5 (1976), pp. 77-88.

Hoerl, A. E. and Kennard, R. W.
"Ridge Regression: Applications to Nonorthogonal Problems"
Technometrics, Vol. 12 (February 1970), pp. 69-82.

Hoerl, Arthur E. and Kennard, Robert W.
"Ridge Regression: Biased Estimates for Nonorthogonal Problems"
Technometrics, Vol. 12 (February 1970), pp. 55-66.

Hoerl, Arthur E., Kennard, Robert W., and Baldwin, Kent F.
"Ridge Regression: Some Simulations"
Communications in Statistics, Vol. 4 (1975), pp. 105-23.

Jagpal, Harsharanjeet S.
"Multicollinearity in Structural Equation Models With Unobservable
Variables"
Journal of Marketing Research, Vol. XIX (November 1982), pp. 431-9.

Lawless, J. F.
"Ridge and Related Estimation Procedures: Theory and Practice"
Communications in Statistics, Vol. A7 (1978), pp. 139-64.

Lawless, J. F. and Wang, P.
"A Simulation Study of Ridge and Other Regression Estimators"
Communications in Statistics, Vol. A5 (1976), pp. 307-23.

Lin, K. and Kmenta, J.
"Ridge Regression Under Alternative Loss Criteria"
Review of Economics and Statistics, Vol. 64 (1982), pp. 488-94.

Mallows, C. L.
"Some Comments on Cp"
Technometircs (August 1973), pp. 591-612.

Marquardt, D. W.
"Generalized Inverses, Ridge Regression, Biased Linear Estimation and
Non-Linear Estimation"
Technometrics, Vol. 12 (August 1970), pp. 591-612.

Marquardt, Donald W. and Snee, Ronald D.
"Ridge Regression in Practice"
American Statistician, Vol. 29 (1975), pp. 3-20.

McDonald, G. C. and Galarneau, D. I.
"A Monte Carlo Evaluation of Some Ridge-Type Estimators"
Journal of the American Statistical Association, Vol. 70 (1975), pp.
407-16.

Obenchain, R. L.
"Classical F Tests and Confidence Regions for Ridge Regression"
Technometrics, Vol. 19, No. 4 (1977), pp. 429-39.

Obenchain, R. L.
"Ridge Analysis Following a Preliminary Test of the Shrunken
Hypothesis"
Technometrics, Vol. 17 (1975), pp. 431-41.

Price, Bertram
  "Ridge Regression: Application to Nonexperimental Data"
  Psychological Bulletin, Vol. 84 (1977), pp. 759-66.

Shipchandler, Zoher and Moore, James S.
  "Examining the Effects of Regression Procedures on the Temporal
  Stability of Parameter Estimates in Marketing Models"
  Journal of the Academy of Marketing Science, Vol. 16 (Fall 1988), pp.
  79-87.

Smith, G. and Campbell, F.
  "A Critique of Some Ridge Regression Methods"
  Journal of the American Statistical Association, Vol. 75 (1980), pp.
  74-81.

Stein, Charles
  "An Approach to the Recovery of Inter-Block Information in Balanced
  Incomplete Block Designs"
  in David, F. N. (editor)
  Research Papers in Statistics
  (New York: John Wiley and Sons, Inc., 1966), pp. 351-66.

Strawderman, W. E.
  "Minimax Adaptive Generalized Ridge Regression Estimators"
  Journal of the American Statistical Association, Vol. 73 (1978), pp.
  623-8.

Theobald, C. M.
  "Generalizations of Mean Square Error Applied to Ridge Regression"
  Journal of the Royal Statistical Society, Series B, Vol. 36 (1974),
  pp. 103-6.

Thisted, R. A. and Morris, C. N.
  "Theoretical Results for Adaptive Ordinary Ridge Regression
  Estimators"
  Technical Report 94
  University of Chicago (1980).

Vinod, H. D.
  "A Survey of Ridge Regression and Related Techniques for Improvements
  Over Ordinary Least Squares"
  Review of Economics and Statistics, Vol. 60 (February 1978), pp.
  121-31.

Wichern, D. W. and Churchill, G. A.
  "A Comparison of Ridge Estimators"
  Technometrics, Vol. 20 (1978), pp. 301-11.

170.04 ---------- Applications of Ridge Regression

Bardsley, P. and Chambers, R. L.
  "Multipurpose Estimation From Unbalanced Samples"
  Applied Statistics, Vol. 33 (1984), pp. 290-9.

Kohli, Ajay K.
  "Some Unexplored Supervisory Behaviors and Their Influence on
  Salesperson's Role Clarity, Specific Self-Esteem, Job Satisfaction,
  and Motivation"
  Journal of Marketing Research, Vol. XXII (November 1985), pp. 424-33.

Mahajan, Vijay, Jain, Arun K., and Bergier, Michel
  "Parameter Estimation in Marketing Models in the Presence of
  Multicollinearity: An Application of Ridge Regression"
  Journal of Marketing Research, Vol. XIV (November 1977), pp. 586-91.

Moore, James S., Reichert, Alan K., and Cho, C. C.
  "Analyzing Temporal Stability of Appraisal Model Coefficients: An
  Application of Ridge Regression Techniques"
  American Real Estate and Urban Economics Association Journal, Vol. 12
  (1984), pp. 50-71.

Westbrook, Robert A. and Newman, Joseph W.
  "An Analysis of Shopper Dissatisfaction for Major Household
  Appliances"
  Journal of Marketing Research, Vol. XV (August 1978), pp. 456-66.

Vinod, H. D.
  "Application of the New Ridge Methods to a Study of Bell System Scale
  Economics"
  Journal of the American Statistical Association, Vol. 71 (1976), pp.
  835-41.

Vinod, H. D.
  "Ridge Estimation of a Translog Production Function"
  Proceedings, Business and Economic Statistics Section, American
  Statistical Association (1974), pp. 596-601.

170.05 ---------- Theory Re: Principal Component Regression

Greenberg, E.
"Minimum Variance Properties of Principal Component Regression"
Journal of the American Statistical Association, Vol. 70 (1975), pp.
194-7.

Gunst, R. F.
"Similarities Among Least Squares, Principal Component, and Latent
Root Estimators"
1979 Conference of the American Statistical Association, Washington,
DC, paper presentation.

Hawkins, D. M.
"On the Investigation of Alternative Regressions by Principal
Component Analysis"
Applied Statistics, Vol. 22 (1973), pp. 275-86.

Massy, W. F.
"Principal Component Regression in Exploratory Statistical Research"
Journal of the American Statistical Association, Vol. 60 (March
1965), pp. 234-56.

Silvey, S. D.
"Multicollinearity and Imprecise Estimation"
Journal of the Royal Statistical Society, Series B, Vol. 31 (1969),
pp. 539-52.

170.06 ---------- Theory Re: Equity Estimator

Krishnamurthi, Lakshman and Rangaswamy, Arvind
"The Equity Estimator for Marketing Research"
Marketing Science, Vol. 6 (Fall 1987), pp. 336-57.

Krishnamurthi, Lakshman, Rangaswamy, Arvind, and Zoltners, Andris A.
"Equity Estimator: A New Method for Sales Response Estimation in the
Presence of Multicollinearity"
Working Paper 86-019R
The Wharton School, University of Pennsylvania (1986).

170.07 ---------- Theory Re: Shrunken Estimators Regression

James, W. and Stein, C.
"Estimation With Quadratic Loss"
Proceedings, Fourth Berkeley Symposium on Mathematical Statistics and
Probability, Vol. 1 (1961), pp. 631-79.

170.08 ---------- Theory Re: Stagewise Regression

Lund, I. A.
"An Application of Stagewise and Stepwise Regression Procedures to a
Problem of Estimating Precipitation in California"
Journal of Applied Meteorology, Vol. 10 (1971), pp. 892-902.

170.09 ---------- Computer Programs for Ridge Regression

Bradley, Charles E. and McGann, Anthony F.
"RIDGEREG: A Program to Improve the Precision of Regression Estimates
for Nonorthogonal Data"
Journal of Marketing Research, Vol. XIV (August 1977), pp. 412,3.

Hui, Baldwin S. and Jagpal, Harsharanjeet S.
"RIDGE: An Integrated Ridge Regression Program"
Journal of Marketing Research, Vol. XVI (November 1979), pp. 571,2.

Jain, Arun K., Mahajan, Vijay, and Bergier, Michel
"RRIDGE: A Program for Estimating Parameters in the Presence of
Multicollinearity"
Journal of Marketing Research, Vol. XIV (November 1977), p. 561.

170.10 ---------- Computer Programs for Principal Component Regression

Hui, Baldwin S. and Jagpal, Harsharanjeet S.
"PCREG: A Principal Components Regression Program for Decision Making"
Journal of Marketing Research, Vol. XVI (November 1979), pp. 570,1.

170.11 ---------- Unclassified (Biased Estimation Procedures)

Belsley, David A.
    "Collinearity and Forecasting"
    Technical Report No. 27
    Center fo Computational Research in Economics and Management Science,
    Sloan School of Management, MIT (April 1981).

Leamer, Edward E.
    "Multicollinearity: A Bayesian Interpretation"
    Review of Economics and Statistics, Vol. 55 (1973), pp. 371-80.

Theil, Henri and Goldberger, A. S.
    "On Pure and Mixed Statistical Estimation in Economics"
    International Economic Review, Vol. 2 (1961), pp. 65-78.

Winer, B. J.
    "Statistics and Data Analysis: Trading Bias for Reduced Mean Squared
    Error"
    in Rosensweig, M. R. and Porter, L. W. (editors)
    Annual Review of Psychology
    (Palo Alto, CA: Annual Reviews Inc., 1978).

171 ----------------------- LOGIT ANALYSIS -------------------------

See also (sub)heading(s) 172, 173.

171.01 ---------- Books Re: Logit Analysis

Aldrich, John H. and Nelson, Forrest
Linear Probability, Logit, Probit Models
(Beverly Hills, CA: Sage Publications, Inc.).

Ashton, Winifred
The Logit Transformation
(London: Griffin, 1972).

Ben-Akiva, Moshe E. and Lerman, Steven R.
Discrete Choice Analysis: Theory and Applications to Travel Demand
(Cambridge, MA: MIT Press, 1985).

Bishop, Yvonne M. M., Fienberg, Stephen E., and Holland, Paul W.
Discrete Multivariate Analysis
(Cambridge, MA: MIT Press, 1975).

Cox, D. R.
The Analysis of Binary Data, Second Edition
(London: Methuen and Co., 1975).

Goodman, Leo A.
Analyzing Qualitative/Categorical Data
(Cambridge, MA: Abt Books, 1978).

Haberman, Shelby J.
Analysis of Qualitative Data
(New York: Academic Press, 1978).

Hensher, D. A. and Johnson, L. W.
Applied Discrete-Choice Modelling
(New York: John Wiley and Sons, Inc., 1981).

Knoke, David and Burke, Peter J.
Log-Linear Models
(Beverly Hills, CA: Sage Publications, Inc.).

Manski, C. F. and McFadden, Daniel (editors)
Structural Analysis of Discrete Data
(Cambridge, MA: MIT Press, 1981).

Maxwell, A. E.
Analyzing Qualitative Data
(London: Chapman and Hall, 1961).

Nerlove, Marc and Press, S. James
Univariate and Multivariate Log-Linear and Logistic Models
(Santa Monica, CA: Rand Corporation, December 1973).

171.02 ---------- Theory Re: Logit Analysis

Amemiya, Takeshi
"Qualitative Response Models: A Survey"
Journal of Economic Literature, Vol. 19 (December 1981), pp. 1483-1536.

Amemiya, Takeshi
"Qualitative Response Models"
Annals of Economic and Social Measurement, Vol. 4 (1975), pp. 363-72.

Amemiya, Takeshi and Nold, Frederick
"A Modified Logit Model"
Review of Economics and Statistics (May 1975), pp. 255-7.

Arnold, Stephen J., Roth, Victor, and Tigert, Douglas J.
"Conditional Logit Versus MDA in the Prediction of Store Choice"
in Advances in Consumer Research, Volume Eight (1980), pp. 665-70.

Berkson, J.
"Application of the Logistic Function to Bio-Assay"
Journal of the American Statistical Association, Vol. 39 (June 1944), pp. 357-65.

Birch, M. W.
"Maximum Likelihood in Three-Way Contingency Tables"
Journal of the Royal Statistical Society, Series B (1963), pp. 220-33.

Bishop, Yvonne M. M.
"Full Contingency Tables, Logits and Split Contingency Tables"
Biometrics, Vol. 25 (June 1969), pp. 383-400.

Chapman, Randall G. and Staelin, Richard
"Exploiting Rank Ordered Choice Set Data Within the Stochastic Utility Model"
Journal of Marketing Research, Vol. XIX (August 1982), pp. 288-301.

Charnes, A., Cooper, W. W., Learner, D. B., and Phillips, F. Y.
"The MDI Method as a Generalization of Logit, Probit and Hendry
Models in Marketing"
ORSA/TIMS Joint Meeting, Washington, DC (1980), presentation.

Cooper, L. G. and Nakanishi, M.
"Two Logit Models for External Analysis of Preferences"
Psychometrika, Vol. 48, No. 4 (1983), pp. 607-19.

DeSarbo, Wayne S. and Keramidas, E. M.
"A Spatial Logit Model"
Proceedings, Business and Economics Section, American Statistical
Association (1983), pp. 41-6.

Dillon, William R., Goldstein, Matthew, and Lement, Lucy
"Analyzing Qualitative Predictors With Too Few Data: An Alternative
Approach to Handling Sparse-Cell Values"
Journal of Marketing Research, Vol. XVIII (February 1981), pp. 63-72.

Doyle, P.
"The Application of Probit, Logit, and Tobit in Marketing: A Review"
Journal of Business Research, Vol. 5 (September 1977), pp. 235-48.

Duncan, Otis D.
"Partitioning Polyomous Variables in Multiway Contingency Analysis"
Social Science Research, Vol. 4 (September 1975), pp. 167-82.

Flath, David and Leonard, E. W.
"A Comparison of Two Logit Models in the Analysis of Qualitative
Marketing Data"
Journal of Marketing Research, Vol. XVI (November 1979), pp. 533-8.

Gensch, Dennis H.
"A Two-Stage Disaggregate Attribute Choice Model"
Marketing Science, Vol. 6 (Summer 1987), pp. 223-39.

Gensch, Dennis and Staelin, Richard
"The Appeal of Buying Black"
Journal of Marketing Research, Vol. IX (May 1972), pp. 141-8.

Gensch, Dennis H. and Svestka, Joseph A.
"An Exact Hierarchical Algorithm for Determining Aggregate Statistics
From Individual Choice Data"
Management Science, Vol. 25 (1979), pp. 939-52.

Goodman, Leo A.
"A General Model for the Analysis of Surveys"
American Journal of Sociology, Vol. 77 (1971), pp. 1035-86.

Goodman, Leo A.
"The Analysis of Multidimensional Contingency Tables: Stepwise
Procedures and Direct Estimation Models for Building Models for
Multiple Classifications"
Technometrics, Vol. 13 (February 1971), pp. 33-61.

Green, Paul E.
"An AID/Logit Procedure for Analyzing Large Multiway Contingency
Tables"
Journal of Marketing Research, Vol. XV (February 1978), pp. 132-6.

Green, Paul E. and Carmone, Frank J.
"Segment Congruence Analysis: A Method for Analyzing Association
Among Alternative Bases for Market Segmentation"
Journal of Consumer Research, Vol. 3 (March 1977), pp. 217-22.

Green, Paul E., Carmone, Frank J., and Wachspress, David P.
"On the Analysis of Qualitative Data in Marketing Research"
Journal of Marketing Research, Vol. XIV (February 1977), pp. 52-9.

Gumbel, E. J.
"Bivariate Logistic Distributions"
Journal of the American Statistical Association, Vol. 56 (1961), pp.
335-49.

Hausman, Jerry A.
"Specification Tests in Econometrics"
Econometrica, Vol. 46 (November 1978), pp. 1251-71.

Jennings, Dennis E.
"Outliers and Residual Distributions in Logistic Regression"
Journal of the American Statistical Association, Vol. 81 (1986), pp.
987-90.

Jones, J. Morgan and Landwehr, Jane T.
"Removing Heterogeneity Bias From Logit Model Estimation"
Marketing Science, Vol. 7 (Winter 1988), pp. 41-59.

Louviere, Jordan J.
"On the Identification of the Function Form of the Utility Expression and Its Relationship to Discrete Choice"
in Hensher, D. A. and Johnson, L. (editors)
Applied Discrete Choice Modelling
(London: Croom-Helm, 1981), pp. 385-416.

Louviere, Jordan J. and Hensher, D. A.
"Forecasting Consumer Demand for a Unique Cultural Event: An Approach Based on an Integration of Probabilistic Discrete Choice Models and Experimental Design Data"
Journal of Consumer Research (December 1983).

Louviere, Jordan J. and Woodworth, George
"Design and Analysis of Simulated Consumer Choice or Allocation Experiments: An Approach Based on Aggregate Data"
Journal of Marketing Research, Vol. XX (November 1983), pp. 350-67.

Magidson, Jay
"Some Common Pitfalls in Causal Analysis of Categorical Data"
Journal of Marketing Research, Vol. XIX (November 1982), pp. 461-71.

Malhotra, Naresh K.
"The Use of Linear Logit Models in Marketing Research"
Journal of Marketing Research, Vol. XXI (February 1984), pp. 20-31.

Malhotra, Naresh K.
"A Comparison of the Predictive Validity of Procedures for Analyzing Binary Data"
Journal of Business and Economic Statistics, Vol. 1 (October 1983), pp. 326-36.

Malhotra, Naresh K., Jain, Arun K., and Lagakos, Stephen W.
"The Information Overload Controversy: An Alternative Viewpoint"
Journal of Marketing, Vol. 46 (Spring 1982), pp. 27-37.

McFadden, Daniel
"Econometric Models of Probabilistic Choice"
in Manski, Charles F. and McFadden, Daniel (editors)
Structural Analysis of Discrete Data With Econometric Applications
(Cambridge, MA: MIT Press, 1981), pp. 198-272.

McFadden, Daniel
"Qualitative Response Models"
Econometric Society World Congress, Aix-en-France (August 1980), paper presentation.

McFadden, Daniel
"Econometric Models for Probabilistic Choice Among Products"
Journal of Business, Vol. 53 (July 1980), pp. 513-29.

McFadden, Daniel
"Quantitative Models for Analyzing Travel Behavior of Individuals: Some Recent Developments"
in Hensher, D. and Stopher, P. (editors)
Behavioral Travel Modeling
(London: Croom-Helm, 1977), pp. 279-318.

McFadden, Daniel
"Quantal Choice Analysis: A Survey"
Annals of Economic and Social Measurement, Vol. 5 (Fall 1976), pp. 363-90.

McFadden, Daniel
"On Independence, Structure, and Simultaneity in Transportation Demand Analysis"
Working Paper 7511
Institute of Transportation Studies, University of California, Berkeley (1975).

McFadden, Daniel
"Conditional Logit Analysis of Qualitative Choice Behavior"
in Zarembka, Paul (editor)
Frontiers in Econometrics
(New York: Academic Press, 1973), pp. 105-42.

McLynn, J.
"A Technical Note on a Class of Fully Competitive Choice Models"
DIM Corporation, Bethesda, MD (1973).

Montgomery, David B. and Urban, Glen L.
"Marketing Decision-Information Systems: An Emerging View"
Journal of Marketing Research, Vol. VII (May 1970), pp. 226-34.

Moore, William L. and Lehmann, Donald R.
"A Paired Comparison Nested Logit Model of Individual Preference Structures"
Journal of Marketing Research, Vol. XXVI (November 1989), pp. 420-8.

Myers, John G. and Nicosia, Francesco M.
"Some Applications of Cluster Analysis to the Study of Consumer
Typologies and Attitudinal Behavior Change"
in Arndt, Johan (editor)
Insights Into Consumer Behavior
(Boston, MA: Allyn and Bacon, Inc., 1968), pp. 127-46.

Oum, Tae Hoon
"A Warning on the Use of Linear Logit Models in Transport Mode Choice
Studies"
The Bell Journal of Economics, Vol. 10 (Spring 1979), pp. 374-88.

Perreault, William D., Jr. and Barksdale, Hiram C., Jr.
"A Model-Free Approach for Analysis of Complex Contingency Data in
Survey Research"
Journal of Marketing Research, Vol. XVII (November 1980), pp. 503-15.

Reynolds, H. T.
"Some Comments on the Causal Analysis of Surveys With Log-Linear
Models"
American Journal of Sociology, Vol. 83 (1977), pp. 127-43.

Walker, Strother H. and Duncan, David B.
"Estimation of the Probability of an Event as a Function of Several
Independent Variables"
Biometrika, Vol. 54 (1967), pp. 167-78.

Werner, J., Wendling, W., and Budde, N.
"A Comparision of Probit, Logit, and Discriminant and OLS: The
Physicians' Location Choice Problem"
Proceedings of Business and Economic Statistics Section, American
Statistical Association (1978), pp. 631-5.

Westin, Richard B.
"Predictions From Binary Choice Models"
Journal of Econometrics, Vol. 2 (May 1974), pp. 1-16.

171.03 ---------- Theory Re: Multinomial Logit Analysis (MNL)

Gensch, Dennis H. and Recker, Wilfred W.
"The Multinomial, Multiattribute Logit Choice Model"
Journal of Marketing Research, Vol. XVI (February 1979), pp. 124-32.

Hausman, Jerry A. and McFadden, Daniel
"Specification Tests for the Multinomial Logit Model"
Econometrica, Vol. 52 (1984), pp. 1219-40.

Hausman, Jerry A. and McFadden, Daniel
"Specification Tests for Multinomial Logit Model"
Department of Economics, Massachusetts Institute of Technology
(1981), working paper.

Horowitz, Joel L.
"Identification and Diagnosis of Specification Errors in the
Multinomial Logit Model"
Transportation Research, Vol. 15B (1981), pp. 345-60.

Horowitz, Joel L.
"Testing the Multinomial Logit Model Against the Multinomial Probit
Model Without Estimating the Probit Parameters"
Transportation Research, Vol. 15 (May 1981), pp. 153-62.

Horowitz, Joel L.
"The Accuracy of the Multinomial Logit Model as an Approximation to
the Multinomial Probit Model of Travel Demand"
Transportation Research, Vol. 14B (December 1980), pp. 331-42.

Horowitz, Joel L.
"A Note on the Accuracy of the Clark Approximation in the Multinomial
Logit Model"
(1979), MIT working paper.

Manrai, Ajay K. and Sinha, Prabhakant
"Elimination-by-Cutoffs"
Marketing Science, Vol. 8 (Spring 1989), pp. 133-52.

McFadden, Daniel
"The Choice Theory Approach to Market Research"
Marketing Science, Vol. 5 (Fall 1986), pp. 275-97.

Theil, Henri
"A Multinomial Extension of the Linear Logit Model"
International Economic Review, Vol. 10 (October 1969), pp. 251-9.

171.04 ---------- Theory Re: Independence From Irrelevant Alternatives

Currim, Imran S.
"Predictive Testing of Consumer Choice Models Not Subject to Independence of Irrelevant Alternatives"
Journal of Marketing Research, Vol. XIX (May 1982), pp. 208-22.

Hausman, Jerry A., Tye, W., and Train, K.
"Diagnostic Tests for the Independence From Irrelevant Alternatives Property of the Multinomial Logit Model"
Transportation Research Record (1978).

Manrai, Ajay K. and Sinha, Prabhakant
"Elimination-by-Cutoffs"
Marketing Science, Vol. 8 (Spring 1989), pp. 133-52.

McFadden, Daniel, Tye, William B., and Train, Kenneth
"An Application of Diagnostic Tests for the Independence From Irrelevant Alternatives Property of the Multinomial Logit Model"
Transportation Research Record, Vol. 637 (1977), pp. 39-46.

McFadden, Daniel, Tye, William B., and Train, Kenneth
"Diagnostic Tests for the Independence From Irrelevant Alternatives Property of the Multinomial Logit Model"
Working Paper No. 7616
Institute of Transportation Studies, University of California, Berkeley (1976).

171.05 ---------- Theory Re: Estimation Methods

Amemiya, Takeshi
"Qualitative Response Models: A Survey"
Journal of Economic Literature, Vol. 19 (December 1981), pp. 1483-1536.

Amemiya, Takeshi
"The (1/n-squared)-Order Mean Squared Errors of the Maximum Likelihood and the Minimum Logit Chi-Square Estimator"
Annals of Statistics, Vol. 8 (May 1980), pp. 488-505.

Amemiya, Takeshi
"On a Two-Step Estimation of a Multivariate Logit Model"
Journal of Econometrics, Vol. 8 (1978), pp. 13-21.

Berkson, J.
"Maximum Likelihood and Minimum Chi-Squared Estimates of the Logistic Function"
Journal of the American Statistical Association, Vol. 50 (March 1955), pp. 130-62.

Bhapkar, V. P.
"A Note on the Equivalence of Two Test Criteria for Hypotheses in Categorical Data"
Journal of the American Statistical Association, Vol. 61 (1966), pp. 228-35.

Bunch, David S.
"Maximum Likelihood Estimation of Probabilistic Choice Models"
SIAM Journal on Scientific and Statistical Computing, Vol. 8 (January 1987), pp. 56-70.

Bunch, David S. and Batsell, Richard R.
"A Monte Carlo Comparison of Estimators for the Multinomial Logit Model"
Journal of Marketing Research, Vol. XXVI (February 1989), pp. 56-68.

Bunch, David S. and Batsell, Richard R.
"A Monte Carlo Comparison of Estimators for the Multinomial Logit Model"
Graduate School of Management Technical Report GSM TR88-01
University of California, Davis (January 1988).

Chapman, R. G.
"An Approach to Estimating Logit Models of a Single Decision Maker's Choice Behavior"
in Kinner, Thomas C. (editor)
Advances in Consumer Research, Volume Eleven
(Provo, UT: Association for Consumer Research, 1984), pp. 656-61.

Cosslett, Stephen R.
"Efficient Estimation of Discrete Choice Models"
in Manski, Charles F. and McFadden, Daniel (editors)
Structural Analysis of Discrete Data With Econometric Applications
(Cambridge, MA: MIT Press, 1981), pp. 51-113.

Davis, Linda
    "Comments on a Paper by T. Amemiya on Estimation in a Dichotomous
    Logit Regression Model"
    Annals of Statistics, Vol. 12 (June 1984), pp. 778-82.

Flath, David and Leonard, E. W.
    "A Comparison of Two Logit Models in the Analysis of Qualitative
    Marketing Data"
    Journal of Marketing Research, Vol. XVI (November 1979), pp. 533-8.

Green, Paul E., Carmone, Frank J., and Wachspress, David P.
    "On the Analysis of Qualitative Data in Marketing Research"
    Journal of Marketing Research, Vol. XIV (February 1977), pp. 52-9.

Grizzle, James E., Starmer, C. Frank, and Koch, Gary G.
    "Analysis of Categorical Data by Linear Models"
    Biometrics, Vol. 25 (1969), pp. 489-504.

Guilkey, David K. and Schmidt, Peter
    "Some Small Sample Properties of Estimators and Test Statistics in
    the Multivariate Logit Model"
    Journal of Econometrics, Vol. 10 (1979), pp. 33-42.

Jones, J. Morgan and Landwehr, Jane T.
    "Removing Heterogeneity Bias From Logit Model Estimation"
    Marketing Science, Vol. 7 (Winter 1988), pp. 41-59.

Louviere, Jordan J. and Hensher, D. A.
    "On the Design and Analysis of Simulated Choice or Allocation
    Experiments in Travel Choice Modelling"
    Transportation Research Record No. 890 (1982), pp. 11-7.

Louviere, Jordan J., Woodworth, G. G., and Anderson, D. A.
    "Predicting Consumer Choice of Destination and Ticket for
    International Travel From Australia"
    South Pacific Meetings of Regional Science Association, Surfers'
    Paradise, Queensland, Australia (August 1981), paper presentation.

Manski, Charles F. and Lerman, Steven R.
    "The Estimation of Choice Probabilities From Choice Based Samples"
    Econometrica, Vol. 45 (November 1977), pp. 177-88.

Manski, Charles F. and McFadden, Daniel
    "Alternative Estimators and Sample Designs for Discrete Choice
    Analysis"
    in Manski, Charles F. and McFadden, Daniel (editors)
    Structural Analysis of Discrete Data With Econometric Applications
    (Cambridge, MA: MIT Press, 1981), pp. 2-50.

Nakanishi, Masao and Cooper, Lee G.
    "Simplified Estimation Procedures for MCI Models"
    Marketing Science, Vol. 1 (Summer 1982), pp. 314-22.

Nakanishi, Masao and Cooper, Lee G.
    "Parameter Estimation for a Multiplicative Competitive Interation
    Model-Least Squares Approach"
    Journnal ofMarketing Research, Vol. XI (August 1974), pp. 303-11.

Ortuzar, J. de D., Achondo, F. J., and Ivelic, A. M.
    "Sequential and Full Information Estimation of Hierarchical Logit
    Models: Some New Evidence"
    Eleventh Triennial Conference on Operations Research, Buenos Aires
    (1987), paper presentation.

Parks, Richard W.
    "On the Estimation of Multinomial Logit Models From Relative
    Frequency Data"
    Journal of Economics, Vol. 13 (1980), pp. 293-303.

Reibstein, D. J.
    "The Prediction of Individual Probabilities of Brand Choice"
    Journal of Consumer Research, Vol. 5 (1978), pp. 163-8.

Smith, K. C., Savin, N. E., and Robertson, J. L.
    "A Monte Carlo Comparison of Maximum Likelihood and Minimum Chi
    Square Sampling Distributions in Logit Analysis"
    Biometrics, Vol. 40 (June 1984), pp. 471-82.

Theil, Henri
    "On the Estimation of Relationships Involving Qualitative Variables"
    American Journal of Sociology, Vol. 76 (1970), pp. 103-54.

Walker, Strother H. and Duncan, David B.
    "Estimation of the Probability of an Event as a Function of Several
    Independent Variables"
    Biometrika, Vol. 54 (March 1967), pp. 167-79.

171.06 ---------- Theory Re: Pooling Logit Models
    See also (sub)heading(s) 161.

Gatignon, Hubert and Reibstein, David J.
    "Pooling Logit Models"
    Journal of Marketing Research, Vol. XXIII (August 1986), pp. 281-5.

171.07 ---------- Theory Re: Measures of Fit

Akaike, H.
    "Information Theory and an Extension of the Maximum Likelihood
    Principle"
    in Petrov, B. N. and Csaski, F. (editors)
    Second International Symposium on Information Theory
    (Budapest: Akademiai Kiado, 1973).

Hauser, John R.
    "Testing the Accuracy, Usefulness, and Significance of Probabilistic
    Choice Models: An Information Theoretic Approach"
    Operations Research, Vol. 26 (May-June 1978), pp. 406-21.

Magidson, Jay
    "Qualitative Variance, Entropy and Correlation Ratios for Nominal
    Dependent Variables"
    Social Science Research (1981).

McFadden, Daniel
    "Conditional Logit Analysis of Qualitative Choice Behavior"
    in Zarembka, P. (editor)
    Frontiers of Econometrics
    (New York: Academic Press, 1974), pp. 105-42.

171.08 ---------- Theory Re: Statistical Tests in Logit Analysis
    See also (sub)heading(s) 141.

Gensch, Dennis H.
    "Empirically Testing a Disaggregate Choice Model for Segments"
    Journal of Marketing Research, Vol. XXII (November 1985), pp. 462-7.

Hauser, J. R.
    "Testing and Accuracy, Usefulness, and Significance of Probabilistic
    Choice Models: An Information-Theoretic Approach"
    Operations Research, Vol. 26 (May-June 1978), pp. 406-21.

Malhotra, Naresh K.
    "Testing the Homogeneity of Segments for Estimating Disaggregate
    Choice Models"
    Marketing Science, Vol. 6 (Winter 1987), pp. 98,9.

Wald, A.
    "Tests of Statistical Hypotheses Concerning Several Parameters When
    the Number of Observations is Large"
    Transactions of the American Mathematical Society, Vol. 54 (1943),
    pp. 426-82.

Watson, Peter L. and Westin, Richard B.
    "Transferability of Disaggregated Mode Choice Models"
    Regional Science and Urban Economics, Vol. 5 (May 1975), pp. 227-49.

171.09 ---------- Applications of Logit Analysis

Adams, Arthur J. and Lonial, Subhash C.
    "Investigation of Giving Behavior to United Way Using Log-Linear
    Modeling and Discriminant Analysis: An Empirical Study"
    Journal of the Academy of Marketing Science, Vol. 12 (1984), pp.
    77-88.

Anderson, Erin and Coughlan, Anne T.
    "International Market Entry and Expansion via Independent or
    Integrated Channels of Distribution"
    Journal of Marketing, Vol. 51 (January 1987), pp. 71-82.

Anderson, Erin, Lodish, Leonard M., and Weitz, Barton A.
    "Resource Allocation Behavior in Conventional Channels"
    Journal of Marketing Research, Vol. XXIV (February 1987), pp. 85-97.

Arnold, Stephen J., Oum, Tae Hoon, and Tigert, Douglas J.
    "Determinant Attributes in Retail Patronage: Seasonal, Temporal,
    Regional, and International Comparisons"
    Journal of Marketing Research, Vol. XX (May 1983), pp. 149-57.

Arnold, Stephen J., Roth, Victor, and Tigert, Douglas J.
"Conditional Logit Model Versus MDA in the Prediction of Store Choice"
in Monroe, Kent B. (editor)
Advances in Consumer Research, Volume Eight
(Washington: Association for Consumer Research, 1981), pp. 665-70.

Batsell, Richard R.
"Consumer Resource Allocation Models at the Individual Level"
Journal of Consumer Research, Vol. 7 (June 1980), pp. 78-87.

Batsell, Richard R. and Lodish, Leonard M.
"A Model and Measurement Methodology for Predicting Individual
Consumer Choice"
Journal of Marketing Research, Vol. XVIII (February 1981), pp. 1-12.

Bawa, Kapil and Shoemaker, Robert W.
"Analyzing Incremental Sales From a Direct Mail Coupon Promotion"
Journal of Marketing, Vol. 53 (July 1989), pp. 66-78.

Boskin, Michael J.
"A Conditional Logit Model of Occupational Choice"
Journal of Political Economy, Vol. 82 (April 1974), pp. 389-98.

Chapman, Randall G. and Staelin, Richard
"Exploiting Rank Ordered Choice Set Data Within the Stochastic
Utility Model"
Journal of Marketing Research, Vol. XIX (August 1982), pp. 288-301.

Chapman, Randall G.
"Pricing Policy and the College Choice Process"
Research in Higher Education, Vol. 10, No. 1 (1979), pp. 37-57.

Chapman, Randall G.
"Retail Trade Area Analysis: Analytics and Statistics"
in Leone, Robert A. (editor)
Proceedings: Market Measurement and Analysis
(Providence, RI: TIMS College on Marketing and The Institute of
Management Science, 1980), pp. 40-9.

Chen, Alexander and Jensen, Helen H.
"Home Equity Use and the Life Cycle Hypothesis"
Journal of Consumer Affairs, Vol. 19 (Summer 1985), pp. 37-56.

Cooper, Lee G. and Nakanishi, Masao
"Two Logit Models for External Analysis of Preference"
Psychometrika, Vol. 48 (December 1983), pp. 607-20.

Craig, C. Samuel and McCann, John M.
"Assessing Communication Effects on Energy Conservation"
Journal of Consumer Research, Vol. 5 (September 1978), pp. 82-8.

Currim, Imran S.
"Predictive Testing of Consumer Choice Models That are Not Subject to
Independence of Irrelevant Alternatives"
Journal of Marketing Research, Vol. XIX (May 1982), pp. 208-22.

Currim, Imran S.
"Using Segmentation Approaches for Better Prediction and
Understanding From Consumer Mode Choice Models"
Journal of Marketing Research, Vol. XVIII (August 1981), pp. 301-9.

Darian, Jean C.
"In-Home Shopping: Are There Consumer Segments?"
Journal of Retailing, Vol. 63 (Summer 1987), pp. 163-86.

Dubin, Jeffrey A.
"A Nested Logit Model of Space and Water Heat System Choice"
Marketing Science, Vol. 5 (Spring 1986), pp. 112-24.

Falls, Gregory A. and Worden, Debra Drecnik
"Consumer Valuation of Protection From Creditor Remedies"
Journal of Consumer Affairs, Vol. 22 (Summer 1988), pp. 20-37.

Gaudry, M. J. I. and Wills, M. J.
"Estimating the Functional Form of Travel Demand Models"
Transportation Research, Vol. 12, No. 4 (1978), pp. 257-89.

Gautschi, David A.
"Specification of Patronage Models for Retail Center Choice"
Journal of Marketing Research, Vol. XVIII (May 1981), pp. 162-74.

Gensch, Dennis H.
"Empirical Evidence Supporting the Use of Multiple Choice Models in
Analyzing a Population"
Journal of Marketing Research, Vol. XXIV (May 1987), pp. 197-207.

Gensch, Dennis H.
"Empirically Testing a Disaggregate Choice Model for Segments"
Journal of Marketing Research, Vol. XXII (November 1985), pp. 462-7.

Gensch, Dennis H.
"Logit and Segmentation"
Working Paper 7-84
School of Business, University of Wisconsin-Milwaukee (1984).

Gensch, Dennis H.
"Targeting the Switchable Industrial Customer"
Marketing Science, Vol. 3 (Winter 1984), pp. 41-54.

Guadagni, Peter M.
"A Nested Logit Model of Product Choice and Purchase Incidence"
in Zufryden, Fred S. (editor)
Proceedings of the 1983 ORSA/TIMS Marketing Science Conference
(Los Angeles: ORSA/TIMS, 1983), pp. 90-100.

Hauser, John R. and Urban, Glen L.
"A Normative Methodology for Modeling Consumer Response to Innovation"
Operations Research, Vol. 25 (July-August 1977), pp. 579-619.

Hausman, Jerry A.
"Project Independence Report: An Appraisal of U.S. Energy Needs Up to 1985"
Bell Journal of Economics, Vol. 6 (Autumn 1975), pp. 517-51.

Henry, Michael D. and Rinne, Heikki J.
"Predicting Program Shares in New Time Slots"
Journal of Advertising Research, Vol. 24 (April/May 1984), pp. 9-17.

Huber, J.
"Accounting for Attraction Bias in Choice: An Examination of Center Seeking and Reweighting Explanations"
Thirteenth Annual Conference, Association for Consumer Research, San Francisco (October 1982), paper presentation.

Huber, Joel C., Holbrook, Morris B., and Kahn, Barbara
"Effects of Competitive Context and of Additional Information on Price Sensitivity"
Journal of Marketing Research, Vol. XXIII (August 1986), pp. 250-60.

Jain, Dipak C. and Bass, Frank M.
"Effect of Choice Set Size on Choice Probabilities: An Extended Logit Model"
International Journal of Research in Marketing, Vol. 6, No. 1 (1989), pp. 1-11.

Johnson, Eric J. and Meyer, Robert J.
"Compensatory Choice Models of Noncompensatory Processes: The Effect of Varying Context"
Journal of Consumer Research, Vol. 11 (June 1984), pp. 528-41.

Jones, J. Morgan and Zufryden, Fred S.
"An Approach for Assessing Demographic and Price Influences on Brand Purchase Behavior"
Journal of Marketing, Vol. 46 (Winter 1982), pp. 36-46.

Jones, J. Morgan and Zufryden, Fred S.
"Relating Deal Purchases and Consumer Characteristics to Repeat Purchase Probability"
Journal of the Market Research Society, Vol. 23 (April 1981), pp. 84-99.

Jones, J. M. and Zufryden, F. S.
"Adding Explanatory Variables to a Consumer Purchase Behavior Model: An Exploratory Study"
Journal of Marketing Research, Vol. XVII (August 1980), pp. 323-34.

Joskow, Paul L. and Mishkin, Frederic S.
"Electric Utility Fuel Choice Behavior in the United States"
International Economic Review, Vol. 18 (October 1977), pp. 719-36.

Kohn, Meir G., Manski, Charles F., and Mundel, David S.
"An Empirical Investigation of Factors Which Influence College-Going Behavior"
Annals of Economic and Social Measurement, Vol. 5 (Fall 1976), pp. 391-419.

Lattin, James M.
"A Model of Balanced Choice Behavior"
Marketing Science, Vol. 6 (Winter 1987), pp. 48-65.

Li, Mingche M.
"A Logit Model of Homeownership"
Econometrica, Vol. 45 (July 1977), pp. 1081-97.

Lilien, Gary L. and Wong, M. Anthony
"An Exploratory Investigation of the Structure of the Buying Center in the Metalworking Industry"
Journal of Marketing Research, Vol. XXI (February 1984), pp. 1-11.

Louviere, Jordan J. and Hensher, David A.
"Using Discrete Choice Models With Experimental Design Data to
Forecast Consumer Demand for a Unique Cultural Event"
Journal of Consumer Research, Vol. 10 (December 1983), pp. 348-61.

Louviere, Jordan J. and Woodworth, George
"Design and Analysis of Simulated Consumer Choice or Allocation
Experiments: An Approach Based on Aggregate Data"
Journal of Marketing Research, Vol. XX (November 1983), pp. 350-67.

Madden, Thomas J. and Dillon, William R.
"Causal Analysis and Latent Class Models: An Application to a
Communication Hierarchy of Effects Model"
Journal of Marketing Research, Vol. XIX (November 1982), pp. 472-90.

Magidson, Jay
"Some Common Pitfalls in Causal Analysis of Categorical Data"
Journal of Marketing Research, Vol. XIX (November 1982), pp. 461-71.

Malhotra, Naresh K.
"Stochastic Modeling of Consumer Preferences for Health Care
Institutions"
Journal of Health Care Marketing, Vol. 3 (Fall 1983).

Malhotra, Naresh K.
"Structural Reliability and Stability of Nonmetric Conjoint Analysis"
Journal of Marketing Research, Vol. XIX (May 1982), pp. 199-207.

Malhotra, Naresh K.
"Information Load and Consumer Decision Making"
Journal of Consumer Research, Vol. 8 (March 1982), pp. 419-30.

Malhotra, Naresh K.
"Multi-Stage Information Processing Behavior: An Experimental
Investigation"
Journal of the Academy of Marketing Science, Vol. 10 (Winter 1982),
pp. 54-71.

Mayer, Robert N. and Zick, Cathleen D.
"Mandating Behavioral or Technological Change: The Case of Auto
Safety"
Journal of Consumer Affairs, Vol. 20 (Summer 1986), pp. 1-18.

McFadden, Daniel
"The Measurement of Urban Travel Demand
"Journal of Public Economics, Vol. 3 (1974), pp. 303-28.

Moore, David J. and Olshavsky, Richard W.
"Brand Choice and Deep Price Discounts"
Psychology and Marketing, Vol. 6 (Fall 1989), pp. 181-96.

Perdue, Barbara C.
"The Size and Composition of the Buying Firm's Negotiation Team in
Rebuys of Component Parts"
Journal of the Academy of Marketing Science, Vol. 17 (Spring 1989),
pp. 121-8.

Qualls, William J. and Puto, Christopher P.
"Organizational Climate and Decision Framing: An Integrated Approach
to Analyzing Industrial Buying Decisions"
Journal of Marketing Research, Vol. XXVI (May 1989), pp. 179-92.

Rao, Vithala R. and McLaughlin, Edward W.
"Modeling the Decision to Add New Products by Channel Intermediaries"
Journal of Marketing, Vol. 53 (January 1989), pp. 80-8.

Silk, Alvin J. and Urban, Glen L.
"Pre-Test-Market Evaluation of New Packaged Goods: A Model and
Measurement Methodology"
Journal of Marketing Research, Vol. XV (May 1978), pp. 171-91.

Silver, Steven D.
"Interdependencies in Social and Economic Decision Making: A
Conditional Logit Model of the Joint Homeownership-Mobility Decision"
Journal of Consumer Research, Vol. 15 (September 1988), pp. 234-42.

Solgaard, Hans S.
"A Model of Audience Choice of Local TV News Program"
International Journal of Research in Marketing, Vol. 1, No. 2 (1984),
pp. 141-51.

Tversky, A.
"Elimination by Aspects: A Theory of Choice"
Psychological Review, Vol. 79 (1972), pp. 281-99.

Walters, Rockney G.
"An Empirical Investigation Into Retailer Response to Manufacturer
Trade Promotions"
Journal of Retailing, Vol. 65 (Summer 1989), pp. 253-72.

Westin, Richard B. and Watson, Peter L.
"Reported and Revealed Preferences as Determinants of Mode Choice Behavior"
Journal of Marketing Research, Vol. XII (August 1975), pp. 282-9.

White-Means, Shelley I.
"The Purchase of Medicare Supplements: A Cost Saving Mechanism in the Purchase of Physician Services"
Journal of Consumer Affairs, Vol. 22 (Winter 1988), pp. 249-63.

Zufryden, F. S.
"A Logit-Markovian Model of Consumer Purchase Behavior Based on Explanatory Variables: Empirical Evaluation and Implications for Decision Making"
Decision Sciences, Vol. 12 (1981), pp. 645-60.

171.10 ---------- Applications of Multinomial Logit Analysis

Buckley, Patrick G.
"Nested Multinomial Logit Analysis of Scanner Data for a Hierarchical Choice Model"
Journal of Business Research, Vol. 17 (September 1988).

Carpenter, Gregory S. and Lehmann, Donald R.
"A Model of Marketing Mix, Brand Switching, and Competition"
Journal of Marketing Research, Vol. XXII (August 1985), pp. 318-29.

Gatignon, Hubert and Robertson, Thomas S.
"Technology Diffusion: An Empirical Test of Competitive Effects"
Journal of Marketing, Vol. 53 (January 1989), pp. 35-49.

Guadagni, Peter M. and Little, John D. C.
"A Logit Model of Brand Choice Calibrated on Scanner Data"
Marketing Science, Vol. 2 (Summer 1983), pp. 203-38.

Gupta, Sunil
"Impact of Sales Promotions on When, What, and How Much to Buy"
Journal of Marketing Research, Vol. XXV (November 1988), pp. 342-55.

Hauser, John R.
"Testing the Accuracy, Usefulness and Significance of Probabilistic Choice Models: An Information Theoretic Approach"
Operations Research, Vol. 26 (May 1978), pp. 406-21.

Javalgi, Rajshekhar G.
"Influence of the Task Complexity on the Predictive Performance of the Nonlinear and Linear Disaggregate Models of Consumer Behavior"
Journal of Business Research, Vol. 16 (January 1988), pp. 1-16.

Krishnamurthi, Lakshman and Raj, S. P.
"A Model of Brand Choice and Purchase Quantity Price Sensitivities"
Marketing Science, Vol. 7 (Winter 1988), pp. 1-20.

Louviere, Jordan J.
"Using Discrete Choice Experiments and Multinomial Logit Choice Models to Forecast Trial in a Competitive Retail Environment: A Fast Food Restaurant Illustration"
Journal of Retailing, Vol. 60 (Winter 1984), pp. 81-107.

McFadden, Daniel
"Modelling the Choice of Residential Location"
in Karlquist, A., Lundquist, L., Snickars, F., and Weibull, J. L. (editors)
Spatial Interaction Theory and Planning Models
(Amsterdam: North-Holland Publishing Company, 1978), pp. 75-96.

Punj, Girish N. and Staelin, Richard A.
"The Choice Process for Graduate Business Schools"
Journal of Marketing Research, Vol. XV (November 1978), pp. 588-98.

White-Means, Shelley I.
"Consumer Information, Insurance, and Doctor Shopping: The Elderly Consumer's Perspective"
Journal of Consumer Affairs, Vol. 23 (Summer 1989), pp. 45-64.

171.11 ---------- Applications of Goodness of Fit in Logit Analysis

Chapman, Randall G. and Staelin, Richard
"Exploiting Rank Ordered Choice Set Data Within the Stochastic Utility Model"
Journal of Marketing Research, Vol. XIX (August 1982), pp. 288-301.

Watson, Peter L. and Westin, Richard B.
"Transferability of Disaggregate Mode Choice Models"
Regional Science and Urban Economics, Vol. 5 (1975), pp. 277-49.

171.12 ---------- Computer Programs for Logit Analysis

Ben-Akiva, Moshe
    Program for Maximum Likelihood Estimation of the Multinomial Logit
    Model
    (Cambridge, MA: Massachusetts Institute of Technology, Department of
    Civil Engineering, 1973).

Bock, R. Darrell and Yates, G.
    MULTIQUAL: A Log-Linear Analysis of Nominal or Ordinal Data by the
    Method of Maximum Likelihood
    (Chicago: National Educational Resources, Inc., 1973).

Cambridge Systematics, Inc.
    "Multinomial Logit Estimation Package: Program Documentation" Version
    2, Mod. 1
    (Cambridge, MA: Cambridge Systematics, Inc., 1974).

Crittle, F. J. and Johnson, L. W.
    Basic Logit (Blogit)--Technical Manual
    (Australian Research Board, 1980), Technical Manual ATM No. 9.

Dennis, John E., Jr., Gay, David M., and Welsch, Roy E.
    "Algorithm 573 NL2SOL--An Adaptive Nonlinear Least-Squares Algorithm
    (E4)"
    ACM Transactions on Mathematical Software, Vol. 7 (September 1981),
    pp. 369-83.

Dennis, John E., Jr., Gay, David M., and Welsch, Roy E.
    "An Adaptive Nonlinear Least Squares Algorithm"
    ACM Transactions on Mathematical Software, Vol. 7 (September 1981),
    pp. 348-68.

Dongarra, J. J., Bunch, J. R., Moler, C. B., and Stewart, G. W.
    LINPACK User's Guide
    (Philadelphia: SIAM Publications, 1979).

Gay, David M.
    "Subroutines for Unconstrained Minimization Using a
    Model/Trust-Region Approach"
    ACM Transactions on Mathematical Software, Vol. 9 (December 1983),
    pp. 503-24.

Harrell, Frank
    "The Logist Procedure"
    in Hastings, Robert P. (editor)
    The SAS Supplemental Library User's Guide, Second Edition
    (Cary, NC: SAS Institute, 1986), pp. 269-94.

Johnson, L. W. and Crittle, F. J.
    "Blogit: A Program for Estimation of Multinomial Logit Choice Models"
    Journal of Marketing Research, Vol. XVIII (November 1981), pp. 483,4.

Manski, Charles F.
    "The Conditional/Polytomous Logit Program: Instructions for Use"
    School of Urban and Public Affairs, Carnegie-Mellon University (1974).

Vigderhous, Gideon
    "Logit: An Interactive Computer Program on Logit Analysis of
    Dichotomous Response Data"
    Journal of Marketing Research, Vol. XVI (November 1979), p. 568.

172 --------------- WEIGHTED LEAST SQUARES METHODOLOGY ---------------
　　　See also (sub)heading(s) 150, 171.

172.01 ---------- Theory Re: Weighted Least Squares Methodology

Forthofer, R. N. and Lehnen, R. G.
　Public Program Analysis: A New Categorical Data Approach
　(Belmont, CA: Lifetime Learning Publications, 1981).

Grizzle, J. E., Starmer, C. F., and Koch, G. G.
　"Analysis of Categorical Data by Linear Models"
　Biometrics, Vol. 25 (1969), pp. 489-504.

Imrey, P. B., Koch, G. G., and Stokes, M. E.
　"Categorical Data Analysis: Some Reflections on the Log Linear Model
　and Logistic Regression. Part I: Historical and Methodological
　Overview"
　International Statistical Review, Vol. 49 (1981), pp. 265-83.

Koch, G. G. and Bhapkar, V. P.
　"Chi-Square Tests"
　in Encyclopedia of Statistical Science, Volume One
　(New York: John Wiley and Sons, 1982).

Landis, J. R., Stanish, W. M., Freeman, J. L., and Koch, G. G.
　"A Computer Program for the Generalized Chi-Square Analysis of
　Categorical Data Using Weighted Least Squares (GENCAT)"
　Computer Programs in Biomedicine, Vol. 6 (1976), pp. 196-231.

Novak, Thomas P. and Stangor, Charles
　"Testing Competitive Market Structures: An Application of Weighted
　Least Squares Methodology to Brand Switching Data"
　Marketing Science, Vol. 6 (Winter 1987), pp. 82-97.

173 ----------------------- PROBIT ANALYSIS -------------------------
        See also (sub)heading(s) 171.

173.01 ---------- Books Re: Probit Analysis

Aldrich, John H. and Nelson, Forrest
    Linear Probability, Logit, Probit Models
    (Beverly Hills, CA: Sage Publications, Inc.).

Daganzo, Carlos F.
    Multinomial Probit: The Theory and Its Applications to Demand
    Forecasting
    (New York: Academic Press, Inc., 1979), 222 pp.

Finney, D. J.
    Probit Analysis, Second Edition
    (Cambridge: Cambridge University Press, 1964).

173.02 ---------- Theory Re: Probit Analysis

Charnes, A., Cooper, W. W., Learner, D. B., and Phillips, F. Y.
    "The MDI Method as a Generalization of Logit, Probit and Hendry
    Models in Marketing"
    ORSA/TIMS Joint Meeting, Washington, DC (1980), presentation.

Currim, Imran S.
    "Predictive Testing of Consumer Choice Models Not Subject to
    Independence of Irrelevant Alternatives"
    Journal of Marketing Research, Vol. XIX (May 1982), pp. 208-22.

Daganzo, Carlos F., Bouthelier, F., and Sheffi, Y.
    "An Efficient Approach to Estimate and Predict Multinomial Probit
    Models"
    Transportation Research Board, 56th Meeting (1977).

Doyle, P.
    "The Application of Probit, Logit, and Tobit in Marketing: A Review"
    Journal of Business Research, Vol. 5 (September 1977), pp. 235-48.

Hartley, Michael J.
    "The Tobit and Probit Models: Maximum Likelihood Estimation by
    Ordinary Least Squares"
    State University of New York at Buffalo (1976), working paper.

Hausman, J. and Wise, D.
    "A Conditional Probit Model for Qualitative Choice: Discrete
    Decisions Recognizing Interdependence and Heterogeneous Preferences"
    Econometrica, Vol. 46, No. 2 (March 1978), pp. 403-26.

Heckman, James J.
    "Sample Selection Bias as a Specification Error"
    Econometrica, Vol. 47 (January 1979), pp. 153-62.

Horowitz, Joel
    "Testing the Multinomial Logit Model Against the Multinomial Probit
    Model Without Estimating the Probit Parameters"
    Transportation Science, Vol. 15 (May 1981), pp. 153-62.

Horowitz, J.
    "The Accuracy of the Multinomial Logit Model as an Approximation to
    the Multinomial Probit Model of Travel Demand"
    Transportation Research, Vol. 14B (December 1980), pp. 331-42.

Kamakura, Wagner A. and Srivastava, Rajendra K.
    "An Ideal-Point Probabilistic Choice Model for Heterogeneous
    Preferences"
    Marketing Science, Vol. 5 (Summer 1986), pp. 199-218.

Kamakura, Wagner A. and Srivastava, Rajendra K.
    "Predicting Choice Shares Under Conditions of Brand Interdependence"
    Journal of Marketing Research, Vol. XXI (November 1984), pp. 420-34.

Lerman, Steven R. and Manski, C. F.
    "An Estimator for the Generalized Multinomial Probit Choice Model"
    Transportation Research Board Meeting (1977), paper presentation.

McKelvey, Richard D. and Zavonia, William
    "A Statistical Model for the Analysis of Ordinal Level Dependent
    Variables"
    Journal of Mathematical Sociology, Vol. 4 (1975), pp. 103-20.

Werner, J., Wendling, W., and Budde, N.
    "A Comparision of Probit, Logit, and Discriminant and OLS: The
    Physicians' Location Choice Problem"
    Proceedings of Business and Economic Statistics Section, American
    Statistical Association (1978), pp. 631-5.

173.03 ---------- Applications of Probit Analysis

Eliashberg, Jehoshua and Robertson, Thomas S.
"New Product Preannouncing Behavior: A Market Signaling Study"
Journal of Marketing Research, Vol. XXV (August 1988), pp. 282-92.

Fast, Janet, Vosburgh, Richard E., and Frisbee, William R.
"The Effects of Consumer Education on Consumer Search"
Journal of Consumer Affairs, Vol. 23 (Summer 1989), pp. 65-90.

Feick, Lawrence F., Herrmann, Robert O., and Warland, Rex H.
"Search for Nutrition Information: A Probit Analysis of the Use of
Different Information Sources"
Journal of Consumer Affairs, Vol. 20 (Winter 1986), pp. 173-92.

Gable, Myron, Hollon, Charles J., and Dangello, Frank
"Predicting Voluntary Managerial Trainee Turnover in a Large
Retailing Organization From Information on an Employment Application
Blank"
Journal of Retailing, Vol. 60 (Winter 1984), pp. 43-63.

Hausman, J. and Wise, D.
"A Conditional Probit Model for Qualitative Choice: Discrete
Decisions Recognizing Interdependence and Heterogeneous Preferences"
Econometrica, Vol. 46 (1978), pp. 403-26.

Kau, Paul and Hill, Lowell
"A Threshold Model of Purchasing Decisions"
Journal of Marketing Research, Vol. IX (August 1972), pp. 264-70.

Rao, Vithala R. and Winter, Frederick W.
"An Application of the Multivariate Probit Model to Market
Segmentation and Product Design"
Journal of Marketing Research, Vol. XV (August 1978), pp. 361-8.

Tobin, J.
"The Application of Multivariate Probit Analysis to Economic Survey
Data"
Cowles Foundation Discussion Paper No. 1
(New Haven: Yale University Press, 1955).

Vigderhous, Gideon
"Probit Analysis of Radio Ad Awareness"
Journal of Advertising Research, Vol. 17 (April 1977), pp. 21-6.

Wilton, Peter C. and Pessemier, Edgar A.
"Forecasting the Ultimate Acceptance of an Innovation: The Effects of
Information"
Journal of Consumer Research, Vol. 8 (September 1981), pp. 162-71.

173.04 ---------- Unclassified (Probit Analysis)

Acito, Franklin
"A Monte Carlo Investigation of Conjoint Measurement Under Random
Data Conditions for Various Orthogonal Designs"
School of Business, Indiana University (1978), working paper.

Albright, R. L., Lerman, Steven R., and Manski, Charles F.
"Report on the Development of an Estimation Program for the
Multinomial Probit Model"
57th Annual Meeting of the Transportation Research Board (1978),
presentation.

Alpert, Mark I., Betak, John F., and Golden, Linda L.
"Data Gathering in Conjoint Measurement"
Graduate School of Business, The University of Texas at Austin
(1978), working paper.

Barron, F. Hutton
"Axiomatic Conjoint Measurement"
Decision Sciences, Vol. 8 (1977), pp. 48-59.

Gladhart, Peter M. and Mount, Tim D.
"Program Description for Multivariate Probit Analysis"
(Ithaca, NY: Cornell University, September 1972).

McKelvey, Richard D.
"An IBM Fortran IV Program to Perform N-Chotomous Multivariate Probit
Analysis"
Behavioral Science, Vol. 16 (March 1971), pp. 186,7.

174 ------- TOBIT (LIMITED/BOUNDED DEPENDENT VARIABLE) ANALYSIS ------
      See also (sub)heading(s) 159.

174.01 ---------- Books Re: Tobit Analysis

Maddala, G. S.
  Limited Dependent and Qualitative Variables in Econometrics
  (Cambridge, UK: Cambridge University Press, 1983).

174.02 ---------- Theory Re: Tobit Analysis

Amemiya, Takeshi
  "Tobit Models: A Survey"
  Journal of Econometrics, Vol. 24 (1984), pp. 3-61.

Amemiya, Takeshi
  "The Estimation of a Simultaneous Equation Tobit Model"
  International Economic Review, Vol. 20 (February 1979), pp. 169-81.

Amemiya, Takeshi
  "Qualitative Response Models"
  Annals of Economic and Social Measurement, Vol. 4 (Summer 1975), pp.
  363-72.

Amemiya, Takeshi
  "Multivariate Regression and Simultaneous Equation Models When the
  Dependent Variables are Truncated Normal"
  Econometrica, Vol. 42 (July 1974), pp. 999-1012.

Amemiya, Takeshi
  "Regression Analysis When the Dependent Variable is Truncated Normal"
  Econometrica, Vol. 41 (November 1973), pp. 997-1016.

Brownstein, D., Duncan, G. M., and McFadden, D.
  "QUAIL--Qualitative, Intermittant and Limited Dependent Variable
  Statistical Program"
  Working Paper Number 7402
  Urban Travel Demand Forecasting Project, Institute of Transportation
  Studies, University of California, Berkeley (1974).

Dagenais, Marcel G.
  "A Threshold Regression Model"
  Econometrica, Vol. 35 (April 1969), pp. 193-203.

Dhrymes, P.
  "Limited Dependent Variables"
  in Griliches, Z. and Intriligator, M. (editor)
  Handbook of Econometrics, Volume Three
  (Amsterdam: North Holland, 1986).

Greene, William H.
  "Estimation of Limited Dependent Variable Models by Ordinary Least
  Squares and the Method of Moments"
  Journal of Econometrics, Vol. 21 (February 1983), pp. 195-212.

Greene, William H.
  "On the Asymptotic Bias of the OLS Estimator of the TOBIT Model"
  Econometrica, Vol. 49 (March 1981), pp. 505-13.

Hartley, Michael J.
  "The Tobit and Probit Models: Maximum Likelihood Estimation by
  Ordinary Least Squares"
  State University of New York at Buffalo (1976), working paper.

Heckman, James J.
  "The Common Structure of Statistical Models of Truncation, Sample
  Selection and Limited Dependent Variables and a Simple Estimator for
  Such Models"
  Annals of Economic and Social Measurement, Vol. 5 (Fall 1976), pp.
  475-92.

Maddala, G. S.
  "Identification and Estimation Problems in Limited Dependent Variable
  Models"
  in Blinders, A. S. and Friedman, P. (editors)
  Natural Resources, Uncertainty and General Equilibrium Systems:
  Essays in Memory of Rafael Lusky
  (New York: Academic Press, Inc., 1977), pp. 219-39.

McDonald, John R. and Moffitt, Robert A.
  "The Uses of Tobit Analysis"
  Review of Economics and Statistics, Vol. 62, No. 2 (1980), pp. 318-21.

Nelson, Forrest D.
  "Censored Regression Models With Unobserved, Stochastic, Censoring
  Thresholds"
  Journal of Econometrics, Vol. 6 (November 1977), pp. 309-27.

Olsen, Randall J.
"Approximating a Truncated Normal Regression With the Methods of Moments"
Econometrica, Vol. 48 (July 1980), pp. 1099-1105.

Olsen, Randall J.
"Note on the Uniqueness of the Maximum Likelihood Estimator for the Tobit Model"
Econometrica, Vol. 46 (1978), pp. 1211-5.

Robinson, P. M.
"On the Asymptotic Properties of Estimators of Models Containing Limited Dependent Variables"
Econometrica, Vol. 50 (January 1982), pp. 27-42.

Schmee, Joseph and Hahn, Gerald J.
"A Simple Method for Regression Analysis With Censored Data"
Technometrics, Vol. 21 (November 1979), pp. 417-32.

Tobin, James
"Estimation of Relationships for Limited Dependent Variables"
Econometrica, Vol. 26 (January 1958), pp. 24-36.

Tomek, William G.
"Regression Analysis With a Limited Dependent Variable"
Journal of Farm Economics, Vol. 50 (May 1968), pp. 445-7.

174.03 ---------- Applications of Tobit Analysis

Bryant, W. Keith
"Durables and Wives' Employment Yet Again"
Journal of Consumer Research, Vol. 15 (June 1988), pp. 37-47.

Kinsey, Jean
"Determinants of Credit Card Accounts: An Application of Tobit Analysis"
Journal of Consumer Research, Vol. 8 (September 1981), pp. 172-82.

Malhotra, Naresh K.
"Modeling Store Choice Based on Censored Preference Data"
Journal of Retailing, Vol. 62 (Summer 1986), pp. 128-144.

Malhotra, Naresh K.
"An Approach to the Measurement of Consumer Preferences Using Limited Information"
Journal of Marketing Research, Vol. XXIII (February 1986), pp. 33-40.

Nelson, Julie A.
"Individual Consumption Within the Household: A Study of Expenditures on Clothing"
Journal of Consumer Affairs, Vol. 23 (Summer 1989), pp. 21-44.

Weinberg, Charles B. and Winer, Russell S.
"Working Wives and Major Family Expenditures: Replication and Extension"
Journal of Consumer Research, Vol. 10 (September 1983), pp. 259-63.

175 ------------- AUTOMATIC INTERACTION DETECTION (AID) --------------

175.01 ---------- Books Re: Automatic Interaction Dectection

Sonquist, John A.
    Multivariate Model Building: The Validation of a Search Strategy
    (Ann Arbor, MI: Survey Research Center, University of Michigan, 1970).

Sonquist, John A., Baker, Elizabeth L., and Morgan, James N.
    Searching for Structure, Revised Edition
    (Ann Arbor, MI: Survey Research Center, University of Michigan, 1973).

Sonquist, John A. and Morgan, James N.
    The Detection of Interaction Effects
    (Ann Arbor, MI: Survey Research Center, University of Michigan, 1964).

175.02 ---------- Theory Re: AID

Alford, Geoffrey
    "Two Procedures for Exploratory Analysis"
    European Research, Vol. 8 (March 1980), pp. 78-85.

Armstrong, J. Scott and Andress, James G.
    "Exploratory Analysis of Marketing Data: Trees vs. Regression"
    Journal of Marketing Research, Vol. VII (November 1970), pp. 487-92.

Bass, Frank M., Tigert, Douglas J., and Lonsdale, Ronald T.
    "Market Segmentation: Group Versus Individual Behavior"
    Journal of Marketing Research, Vol. V (August 1968), pp. 264-70.

Doyle, Peter
    "The Use of AID and Similar Search Procedures"
    Operational Research Quarterly, Vol. 24 (September 1973), pp. 465-7.

Doyle, Peter and Fenwick, Ian
    "The Pitfalls of AID Analysis"
    Journal of Marketing Research, Vol. XII (November 1975), pp. 408-13.

Green, Paul E.
    "An AID/LOGIT Procedure for Analyzing Large Multiway Contingency
    Tables"
    Journal of Marketing Research, Vol. XV (February 1978), pp. 132-6.

Kass, Gordon V.
    Significance Testing in, and Some Extensions of, Automatic
    Interaction Detection
    University of Witwatersrand, Johannesburg, South Africa (1976),
    unpublished doctoral dissertation.

Martin, Claude R. and Wright, Roger L.
    "Profit-Oriented Data Analysis for Market Segmentation: An
    Alternative to AID"
    Journal of Marketing Research, Vol. XI (August 1974), pp. 237-42.

Messenger, R. and Mandell, L.
    "A Model Search Technique for Predictive Nominal Scale Multivariate
    Analysis"
    Journal of the American Statistical Association, Vol. 67 (December
    1972), pp. 768-72.

Morgan, James N. and Sonquist, John A.
    "Problems in the Analysis of Survey Data and a Proposal"
    Journal of the American Statistical Association, Vol. 58 (September
    1963), pp. 415-34.

Parsons, Leonard J. and Ness, Thomas E.
    "Using AID and MCA to Analyze Marketing Data"
    Combined Proceedings, Spring and Fall Conference, American Marketing
    Association (1971), pp. 523-30.

Press, Laurence I., Rogers, Miles S., and Shure, Gerald H.
    "An Interactive Technique for the Analysis of Multivariate Data"
    Behavioral Science, Vol. 14 (September 1969), pp. 364-70.

Sonquist, J. A.
    "Recent Developments in Sequential Data Analysis Strategy"
    Proceedings of the Social Statistics Section of the American
    Statistical Association (1969), pp. 74-90.

Sonquist, J. A.
    "Finding Variables That Work"
    Public Opinion Quarterly, Vol. 33 (Spring 1969), pp. 83-95.

Staelin, Richard A.
    "Another Look at AID"
    Journal of Advertising Research, Vol. 11 (October 1971), pp. 23-8.

Staelin, Richard
    "A Note on Detection of Interaction"
    Public Opinion Quarterly, Vol. 34 (Fall 1970), pp. 408-11.

175.03 ---------- Applications of AID

Assael, Henry
"Segmenting Markets by Response Elasticity"
Journal of Advertising Research, Vol. 16 (April 1976), pp. 27-35.

Assael, Henry
"Segmenting Markets by Group Purchasing Behavior: An Application of the AID Technique"
Journal of Marketing Research, Vol. VII (May 1970), pp. 153-8.

Assael, Henry and Ellis, Richard B.
"A Research Design to Predict Telephone Usage Among Bell System Business Customers"
European Research, Vol. 1 (Janaury 1973), pp. 38-42, continued in European Research, Vol. 1 (March 1973), pp. 59-61.

Assael, Henry, Kofron, John H., and Burgi, Walter
"Advertising Performance as a Function of Print Ad Characteristics"
Journal of Advertising Resarch, Vol. 7 (June 1967), pp. 20-6.

Carman, James M.
"Correlates of Brand Loyalty: Some Positive Results"
Journal of Marketing Research, Vol. VII (February 1970), pp. 67-76.

Cavusgil, S. Tamer and Nevin, John R.
"Internal Determinants of Export Marketing Behavior: An Empirical Investigation"
Journal of Marketing Research, Vol. XVIII (February 1981), pp. 114-9.

Doyle, Peter
"The Application of AID and Similar Search Procedures"
Operational Research Quarterly, Vol. 24 (September 1973), pp. 465-7.

Dunkelberg, William C. and Day, George S.
"Nonresponse Bias and Callbacks in Sample Surveys"
Journal of Marketing Research, Vol. X (May 1973), pp. 160-8.

Farley, John U. and Ring, L. Winston
"'Empirical' Specification of a Buyer Behavior Model"
Journal of Marketing Research, Vol. XI (February 1974), pp. 89-96.

Gensch, Dennis H.
"Image-Measurement Segmentation"
Journal of Marketing Research, Vol. XV (August 1978), pp. 384-94.

Gensch, Dennis H. and Staelin, Richard
"The Appeal of Buying Black"
Journal of Marketing Research, Vol. IX (May 1972), pp. 141-8.

Heald, Gordon I.
"The Application of AID and Multiple Regression Techniques to the Assessment of Store Performance and Site Selection"
Operational Research Quarterly, Vol. 23 (June 1972), pp. 445-54.

Henry, Walter A.
"Cultural Values do Correlate With Consumer Behavior"
Journal of Marketing Research, Vol. XIII (May 1976), pp. 121-7.

Herrmann, R. O.
"Interaction Effects and the Analysis of Household Food Expenditures"
Journal of Farm Economics, Vol. 49 (November 1967), pp. 821-32.

Houston, Franklin S. and Davis, James L.
"'Learning' and Grade Expectations: A Study of Instructor Evaluations"
Journal of the Academy of Marketing Science, Vol. 5 (Summer 1977), pp. 195-202.

Lonial, Subhash C. and Van Auken, Stuart
"Retail Store Visitation and the Cost-Value Hypothesis: An Application of the AID Algorithm"
Journal of the Academy of Marketing Science, Vol. 6 (Summer 1978), pp. 187-94.

Martin, Claude R. and Wright, Roger L.
"Profit Orientated Data Analysis for Market Segmentation: An Alternative to AID"
Journal of Marketing Research, Vol. II (August 1974), pp. 237-42.

Newman, Joseph W. and Staelin, Richard
"Information Sources of Durable Goods"
Journal of Advertising Research, Vol. 13 (April 1973), pp. 19-29.

Newman, Joseph and Staelin, Richard
"Prepurchase Information Seeking for New Cars and Major Household Appliances"
Journal of Marketing Research, Vol. IX (August 1972), pp. 249-57.

Newman, Joseph W. and Werbel, Richard A.
  "Automobile Brand Loyalty"
  Journal of the Academy of Marketing Science, Vol. 2 (Fall 1974), pp.
  593-601.

Snowbarger, Marvin and Dunkelberg, Bill
  "A Cross-Sectional Study of Used Car Prices: 1962-64"
  Journal of Marketing Research, Vol. VII (November 1970), pp. 493-7.

Walker, Orville C., Jr. and Sauter, Richard F.
  "Consumer Preferences for Alternative Retail Credit Terms: A Concept
  Test of the Effects of Consumer Legislation"
  Journal of Marketing Research, Vol. XI (February 1974), pp. 70-8.

Wilkie, William
  "Extension and Tests of Alternative Approaches to Market Segmentation"
  Institute Paper No. 323
  Institute for Research in the Behavioral, Economic, and Management
  Sciences, Krannert Graduate School of Industrial Administration,
  Purdue University (1971).

175.04 ---------- Theory Re: Chi-Square Based AID (CHAID)

Kass, G.
  "An Exploratory Technique for Investigating Large Quantities of
  Categorical Data"
  Applied Statistics, Vol. 29 (1980), pp. 119-27.

Perreault, William D., Jr. and Barksdale, Hiram C., Jr.
  "A Model-Free Approach for Analysis of Complex Contingency Data in
  Survey Research"
  Journal of Marketing Research, Vol. XVII (November 1980), pp. 503-15.

175.05 ---------- Theory Re: Multivariate AID (MAID)

MacLachlan, Douglas L. and Johansson, Johny K.
  "Market Segmentation With Multivariate AID"
  Journal of Marketing, Vol. 45 (Winter 1981), pp. 74-84.

175.06 ---------- Computer Programs for AID Analysis

Harris, Britton, Wordley, C., and Seymour, D.
  Program Description: PENAID
  (Philadelphia, PA: Institute for Environmental Studies, University of
  Pennsylvania, 1969).

Morgan, James N. and Messenger, Robert C.
  THAID: A Sequential Analysis Program for the Analysis of Nominal
  Scale Dependent Variables
  (Ann Arbor, MI: Survey Research Center, University of Michigan, 1973).

176 ------------- MULTIPLE CLASSIFICATION ANALYSIS (MCA) -------------

176.01 ---------- Theory Re: Multiple Classification Analysis

Andrews, Frank, Morgan, James, and Sonquist, John
  Multiple Classification Analysis
  (Ann Arbor: Survey Research Center, University of Michigan, 1967).

Andrews, Frank M., Morgan, James N., Sonquist, John A., and Klem, Laura
  Multiple Classification Analysis, Second Edition
  (Ann Arbor, MI: University of Michigan, Institute for Social
  Research, 1973).

Bernhardt, Kenneth L. and Kinnear, Thomas C.
  "Categorical Regression in Marketing"
  Journal of Business Research, Vol. 4 (November 1976), pp. 297-312.

Parsons, Leonard J. and Ness, Thomas E.
  "Using AID and MCA to Analyze Marketing Data"
  Proceedings, American Marketing Association (1971), pp. 523-30.

Sonquist, John A.
  Multivariate Model Building
  (Ann Arbor: Survey Research Center, University of Michigan, 1970).

176.02 ---------- Applications of Multiple Classification Analysis

Allen, Bruce H. and Lambert, David R.
  "Searching for the Best Price: An Experimental Look at Consumer
  Search Effort"
  Journal of the Academy of Marketing Science, Vol. 6 (Fall 1978), pp.
  245-57.

Assael, Henry and Cannon, Hugh
  "Do Demographics Help in Media Selection?"
  Journal of Advertising Research, Vol. 19 (December 1979), pp. 7-11.

Cavusgil, S. Tamer and Nevin, John R.
  "Internal Determinants of Export Marketing Behavior: An Empirical
  Investigation"
  Journal of Marketing Research, Vol. XVIII (February 1981), pp. 114-9.

Henry, Walter A.
  "Cultural Values do Correlate With Consumer Behavior"
  Journal of Marketing Research, Vol. XIII (May 1976), pp. 121-7.

Hirschman, Elizabeth C.
  "Differences in Consumer Purchase Behavior by Credit Card Payment
  System"
  Journal of Consumer Research, Vol. 6 (June 1979), pp. 58-66.

Holman, Rebecca H. and Wilson, R. Dale
  "Temporal Equilibrium as a Basis for Retail Shopping Behavior"
  Journal of Retailing, Vol. 58 (Spring 1982), pp. 58-81.

Hunt, Shelby D. and Nevin, John R.
  "Power in a Channel of Distribution: Sources and Consequences"
  Journal of Marketing Research, Vol. XI (May 1974), pp. 186-93.

Myers, John G.
  "Determinants of Private Brand Attitude"
  Journal of Marketing Research, Vol. IV (February 1967), pp. 73-81.

Newman, Joseph W. and Staelin, Richard
  "Prepurchase Information Seeking for New Cars and Major Household
  Appliances"
  Journal of Marketing Research, Vol. IX (August 1972), pp. 249-57.

Newman, Joseph W. and Werbel, Richard A.
  "Automobile Brand Loyalty"
  Journal of the Academy of Marketing Science, Vol. 2 (Fall 1974), pp.
  593-601.

Newman, Joseph W. and Werbel, Richard A.
  "Multivariate Analysis of Brand Loyalty for Major Household
  Appliances"
  Journal of Marketing Research, Vol. X (November 1973), pp. 404-9.

Pessemier, Edgar A., Bemmaor, Albert C., and Hanssens, Dominique M.
  "Willingness to Supply Human Body Parts: Some Empirical Results"
  Journal of Consumer Research, Vol. 4 (December 1977), pp. 131-40.

Pessemier, Edgar A., Burger, Philip C., and Tigert, Douglas J.
  "Can New Product Buyers be Identified?"
  Journal of Marketing Research, Vol. IV (November 1967), pp. 349-54.

Peters, William H.
  "Using MCA to Segment New Car Markets"
  Journal of Marketing Research, Vol. VII (August 1970), pp. 360-3.

Snowbarger, Marvin and Dunkelberg, Bill
    "A Cross-Sectional Study of Used Car Prices: 1962-64"
    Journal of Marketing Research, Vol. VII (November 1970), pp. 493-7.

Tienda, Marta and Aborampah, Osei-Mensah
    "Energy-Related Adaptations in Low-Income Nonmetropolitan Wisconsin
    Counties"
    Journal of Consumer Research, Vol. 8 (December 1981), pp. 265-70.

177 -------------------- DISCRIMINANT ANALYSIS ---------------------

See also (sub)heading(s) 133.07, 178.

177.01 ---------- Books Re: Discriminant Analysis

Bishop, Yvonne M. M., Feinberg, Stephen E., and Holland, Paul W.
Discrete Multivariate Analysis: Theory and Practice
(Cambridge, MA: The MIT Press, 1975).

Cacoullos, T.
Discriminant Analysis and Applications
(New York: Academic Press, Inc., 1973).

Eisenbeis, Robert A. and Avery, Robert B.
Discriminant Analysis and Classification Procedures
(Lexington, MA: D. C. Heath and Company, 1972).

Goldstein, Matthew and Dillon, William R.
Discrete Discriminant Analysis
(New York: John Wiley and Sons, Inc., 1978), 186 pp.

Hodges, Joseph L., Jr.
Discriminatory Analysis
(Randolph Air Force Base, TX: Air University School of Aviation
Medicine, United States Air Force, 1955).

Johnson, Richard M.
Multiple Discriminant Analysis: Applications to Marketing Research
(Chicago: Market Facts, 1970).

Klecka, William R.
Discriminant Analysis
(Beverly Hills, CA: Sage Publications, Inc., 1980).

Lachenbruch, Peter A.
Discriminant Analysis
(New York: Hafner Press, 1975).

Tatsuoka, Maurice M.
Discriminant Analysis--The Study of Group Differences, Select Topics
in Advanced Statistics
(Champaign, IL: Institute for Personality and Ability Testing, 1970).

177.02 ---------- Theory Re: Discriminant Analysis

Bajgier, Steve M. and Hill, Arthur V.
"An Experimental Comparison of Statistical and Linear Programming
Approaches to the Discriminant Problem"
Decision Sciences, Vol. 13 (October 1982), pp. 604-18.

Bartlett, Maurice S.
"An Inverse Matrix Adjustment Arising in Discriminant Analysis"
Annals of Mathematical Statistics, Vol. 22 (March 1952), p. 167.

Bock, R. D. and Haggard, E. G.
"The Use of Multivariate Analysis of Variance in Behavior Research"
in Whitla, D. K. (editor)
Handbook of Measurement in Education, Psychology, and Sociology
(Reading, MA: Addison-Wesley, 1968).

Borgen, Fred H. and Seling, Mark J.
"Uses of Discriminant Analysis Following MANOVA"
Journal of Applied Psychology, Vol. 63 (December 1978), pp. 689-97.

Claringbold, P. J.
"Multivariate Quantal Analysis"
Journal of the Royal Statistical Society, Series B, Vol. 20, pp.
398-405.

Clunies-Ross, C. W. and Riffenburgh, R. H.
"Geometry and Linear Discrimination"
Biometrika, Vol. 47 (1960), pp. 185-9.

Cover, J. M. and Hart, P. E.
"Nearest Neighbor Pattern Classification"
IEEE Transactions on Information Theory, Vol. 13 (January 1967), pp.
21-7.

Daniels, Mark and Darcy, R.
"Notes on the Use and Interpretation of Discriminant Analysis"
American Journal of Political Science, Vol. 27 (May 1983).

Dillon, William R.
"The Performance of the Linear Discriminant Function in Nonoptimal
Situations and the Estimation of Classification Error Rates: A Review
of Recent Findings"
Journal of Marketing Research, Vol. XVI (August 1979), pp. 370-81.

Dillon, William R., Frederick, Donald G., and Tangpanichdee, Vanchai
"Decision Issues in Building Perceptual Product Spaces With
Multi-Attribute Rating Data"
Journal of Consumer Research, Vol. 12 (June 1985), pp. 47-63.

Dillon, William R., Goldstein, Matthew, and Lement, Lucy
"Analyzing Qualitative Predictors With Too Few Data: An Alternative
Approach to Handling Sparse-Cell Values"
Journal of Marketing Research, Vol. XVII (February 1980), pp. 63-72.

Dillon, William R., Goldstein, Matthew, and Schiffman, Leon G.
"Appropriateness of Linear Discriminant and Multinomial
Classification Analysis in Marketing Research"
Journal of Marketing Research, Vol. XV (February 1978), pp. 103-12.

Dillon, William R. and Westin, Stuart
"Scoring Frequency Data for Discriminant Analysis: Perhaps Discrete
Procedures Can be Avoided"
Journal of Marketing Research, Vol. XIX (February 1982), pp. 44-56.

Drevs, Robert A., Durand, Richard M., and Mattheis, T. H.
"Multiple Discriminant Analysis and Several Small Samples--To Split,
Combine, or Treat Separately"
Decision Sciences, Vol. 8 (July 1977), pp. 567-75.

Eisenbeis, Robert A.
"Pitfalls in the Application of Discriminant Analysis in Business,
Finance, and Economics"
Journal of Finance, Vol. 32 (June 1977), pp. 875-900.

Eisenbeis, Robert A. and Avery, Robert B.
"Two Aspects of Investigating Group Differences in Linear
Discriminant Analysis"
Decision Sciences, Vol. 4 (October 1973), pp. 487-93.

Fisher, Ronald A.
"The Precision of Discriminant Functions"
Annals of Eugenics, London, Vol. 10 (1940), pp. 422-9.

Fisher, R. A.
"The Use of Multiple Measurements in Taxonomic Problems"
Annals of Eugenics, Vol. 7, No. 2 (1936), pp. 179-88.

Frank, Ronald E., Massy, William F., and Morrison, Donald G.
"Bias in Multiple Discriminant Analysis"
Journal of Marketing Research, Vol. II (August 1965), pp. 250-8.

Freed, Ned and Glover, Fred
"Linear Programming and Statistical Discrimination--The LP Side"
Decision Sciences, Vol. 13 (January 1982), pp. 172-5.

Freed, Ned and Glover, Fred
"A Linear Programming Approach to the Discriminant Problem"
Decision Sciences, Vol. 12 (January 1981), pp. 68-74.

Gilbert, E. S.
"On Discrimination Using Qualitative Variables"
Journal of the American Statistical Association, Vol. 63 (1968), pp.
1399-412.

Glorfeld, Louis W. and Gaither, Norman
"On Using Linear Programming in Discriminant Problems"
Decision Sciences, Vol. 13 (January 1982), pp. 167-71.

Green, Paul E.
"Bayesian Classification Procedures in Analyzing Customer
Characteristics"
Journal of Marketing Research, Vol. I (May 1964), pp. 44-50.

Grofman, Bernard
"A Comment on Dye and MacManus' Use of Discriminant Function Analysis"
Political Methodology, Vol. 2 (1978).

Hallaq, John H.
"Adjustment for Bias in Discriminant Analysis"
Journal of the Academy of Marketing Science, Vol. 3 (Spring 1975),
pp. 172-81.

Hooley, G. J.
"Perceptual Mapping for Product Positioning: A Comparison of Two
Approaches"
European Research, Vol. 7 (January 1979), pp. 17-23,40.

Hora, Stephen C.
"A Decision Theoretic Approach to Multiple Linear Discriminant
Analysis"
Proceedings, American Institute for Decision Sciences, Boston (1973),
pp. 413-5.

Huberty, Carl J.
"Issues in the Use and Interpretation of Discriminant Analysis"
Psychological Bulletin, Vol. 95 (January 1984).

Huberty, C. J.
"Discriminant Analysis"
Review of Educational Research, Vol. 45 (Fall 1975), pp. 543-98.

Hyett, G. P. and McKenzie, J. R.
"Discrimination Tests and Repeated Paired Comparison Tests"
Journal of the Market Research Society, Vol. 18, No. 1.

Johnson, P. O.
"The Quantification of Qualitative Data by Discriminant Analysis"
Journal of the American Statistical Association, Vol. 45 (March
1950), pp. 65-76.

Johnson, Richard M.
"Market Segmentation: A Strategic Management Tool"
Journal of Marketing Research, Vol. VIII (February 1971), pp. 13-8.

Johnson, Richard M.
"Multiple Discriminant Analysis: Applications to Marketing Research"
Market Facts, Inc. (January 1970), working paper.

Kendall, Maurice G.
"Discrimination and Classification"
in Krishnaiah, P. R. (editor)
Multivariate Analysis: Proceedings of an International Symposium held
in Dayton, Ohio June 14-19, 1965
(New York: Academic Press, 1966), pp. 165-85.

King, William R.
"Structural Analysis and Descriptive Discriminant Functions"
Journal of Advertising Research, Vol. 7 (June 1967), pp. 39-43.

Klecka, William R.
"Discriminant Analysis"
Sage University Paper Series on Quantitative Applications in the
Social Sciences, 07-019
(Beverly Hills, CA: Sage Publications, 1980).

LeKluyrer, Cornelius
"The Doubtful Region in Discriminant Analysis"
Institute Paper No. 498
Krannert Graduate School of Industrial Administration, Purdue
University (March 1975).

Massy, William F.
"Bayesian Multiple Discriminant Analysis"
Working Paper No. 58
Graduate School of Business, Stanford University (July 1965).

Massy, William F.
"Discriminant Analysis of Audience Characteristics"
Journal of Advertising Research, Vol. 5 (March 1965), pp. 39-48.

Melton, Richard S.
"Some Remarks on Failure to Meet Assumptions in Discriminant Analysis"
Psychometrika, Vol. 28 (March 1963), pp. 49-53.

Michaelis, J.
"Simulation Experiments With Multiple Group Linear and Quadratic
Discriminant Analyses"
in Cacoulios, T. (editor)
Discriminant Analysis Applications
(New York: Academic Press, 1973).

Montgomery, David B.
"New Product Diffusion--An Analysis of Supermarket Buyer Decision"
Journal of Marketing Research, Vol. XII (August 1965), pp. 255-65.

Moore, Dan H., II
"Evaluation of Five Discrimination Procedures for Binary Variables"
Journal of the American Statistical Association, Vol. 68 (June 1973),
pp. 399-404.

Morrison, Donald G.
"On the Interpretation of Discriminant Analysis"
Journal of Marketing Research, Vol. VI (May 1969), pp. 156-63.

Mosteller, Frederick and Bush, Robert R.
"Selective Quantitative Techniques"
in Lindzey, Gardner (editor)
Handbook of Social Psychology, Vol. 1
(Reading, MA: Addison-Wesley, 1954).

Mosteller, F. and Tukey, J. W.
"Data Analysis, Including Statistics"
in Lindzey, G. and Aronson, E. (editors)
The Handbook of Social Psychology, Volume Two
(Reading, MA: Addison-Wesley Publishing Co., 1968), pp. 80-203.

Mosteller, Frederick and Wallace, David L.
"Inference in an Authorship Problem"
Journal of the American Statistical Association, Vol. 58 (June 1963),
pp. 275-309.

Neal, William D.
"Using Discriminant Analysis in Marketing Research: Part 2"
Marketing Research, Vol. 1 (December 1989), pp. 55-60.

Neal, William D.
"Using Discriminant Analysis in Marketing Research: Part 1"
Marketing Research, Vol. 1 (September 1989), pp. 79-81.

Paksoy, Christie H., Ferguson, Carl E., Karson, Marvin, and Martell,
Terrence
"MVBFS: A Program Using the Multivariate Behrens-Fisher Solution for
Conditional Deletion in Two-Group Discriminant Analysis Models"
Journal of Marketing Research, Vol. XIV (May 1977), p. 245.

Perreault, William D., Jr., Behrman, Douglas N., and Armstrong, G. M.
"Alternative Approaches for Interpretation of Multiple Discriminant
Analysis"
Journal of Business Research, Vol. 7 , No. 2 (1979), pp. 151-73.

Peterson, Robert A. and Mahajan, Vijay
"Practical Significance and Partitioning Variance in Discriminant
Analysis"
Decision Sciences, Vol. 7 (October 1976), pp. 649-58.

Pohl, Norval F. and Bruno, Albert V.
"The Linear Discriminant Function in Marketing Research: A Robustness
Analysis"
Proceedings, Western American Institute for Decision Sciences, Las
Vegas (March 1975), pp. 176,7.

Rao, C. R.
"Tests of Significance in Multivariate Analysis"
Biometrika, Vol. 35 (1948), pp. 58-79.

Richards, L. E.
"Detection and Incorporation of Interactive Effects in Discriminant
Analysis"
Decision Sciences, Vol. 6 (July 1975), pp. 508-12.

Richards, L. E.
"Detection of Unexplained Joint Effects Through an Analysis of
Residuals"
Decision Sciences, Vol. 4 (January 1973), pp. 40-3.

Richardson, S. C.
"Assessing the Performance of a Discriminant Analysis"
Journal of the Market Research Society, Vol. 24 (January 1982), pp.
65-7.

Rivers, Richard and Welker, Robert
"Estimating Profit Performance From Similar Profit Centers"
Journal of the Academy of Marketing Science, Vol. 9 (Spring 1981),
pp. 127-46.

Rogers, G. and Linden, J. D.
"Use of Multiple Discriminant Function Analysis in the Evaluation of
Three Multivariate Grouping Techniques"
Educational and Psychological Measurement, Vol. 33 (1973), pp.
787-802.

Rulon, P. J.
"Distinctions Between Discriminant and Regression Analysis and a
Geometric Interpretation of the Discriminant Function"
Harvard Educational Review, Vol. 21 (Spring 1951), pp. 80-90.

Sanchez, Peter M.
"The Unequal Group Size Problem in Discriminant Analysis"
Journal of the Academy of Marketing Science, Vol. 2 (Fall 1974), pp.
629-33.

Schaninger, Charles M., Lessig, V. Parker, and Panton, Don B.
"The Complementary Use of Multivariate Procedures to Investigate
Nonlinear and Interactive Relationships Between Personality and
Product Usage"
Journal of Marketing Research, Vol. XVII (February 1980), pp. 119-24.

Travers, R. M. W.
"The Use of the Discriminant Function in the Treatment of
Psychological Group Differences"
Psychometrika, Vol. 4 (1939), p. 25.

Wald, A.
"On a Statistical Problem Arising in the Classification of an
Individual into Two Groups"
Annals of Mathematical Statistics, Vol. 15 (1944).

Watson, Collin J.
"An Additional Approach for Interpretation of Multiple Discriminant
Analysis in Business Research"
Journal of Business Research, Vol. 9 (March 1981), pp. 1-12.

Werner, J., Wendling, W., and Budde, N.
"A Comparision of Probit, Logit, and Discriminant and OLS: The
Physicians' Location Choice Problem"
Proceedings of Business and Economic Statistics Section, American
Statistical Association (1978), pp. 631-5.

177.03 ---------- Distribution of the Discriminant Function

Bowker, A. H. and Sitgreaves, R.
"An Asymptotic Expansion for the Distribution of the W-Classification
Statistic"
in Solomon, H. (editor)
Studies in Item Analysis and Prediction
(Stanford: Stanford University Press, 1961), pp. 293-310.

John, S.
"Further Results on Classification by W"
Sankhya, Vol. 26 (1964), pp. 39-46.

John, S.
"The Distribution of Wald's Classification Statistic When the
Dispersion Matrix is Known"
Sankhya, Vol. 21 (1959), pp. 371-6.

Memom, A. Z. and Okamoto, M.
"Asymptotic Expansion of Distribution of Z-Statistic in Discriminant
Analysis"
Journal of Multivariate Analysis, Vol. 1 (1971), pp. 294-307.

Okamoto, M.
"An Asymptotic Expansion for the Distribution of the Linear
Discriminant Function"
Annals of Mathematical Statistics, Vol. 34 (1963), pp. 1286-301.
(correction in Annals of Mathematical Statistics, Vol. 39 (1968), pp.
1358,9)

Sitgreaves, R.
"On the Distribution of Two Random Matrices Used in Classification
Procedures"
Annals of Mathematical Statistics, Vol. 23 (1952), pp. 263-70.

Smith, C. A. B.
"Some Examples of Discrimination"
Annals of Eugenics, Vol. 13 (1947), pp. 272-82.

Teichroew, D. and Sitgreaves, R.
"Computation of an Empirical Sampling Distribution for
W-Classification Statistic"
in Solomon, H. (editor)
Studies in Item Analysis and Prediction
(Stanford: Stanford University Press, 1961), pp. 252-75.

177.04 ---------- Unequal Dispersion Matrices

Anderson, T. W. and Bahadur, R. R.
"Classification into Two Multivariate Normal Distributions With
Different Covariance Matrices"
Annals of Mathematical Statistics, Vol. 33 (1962), pp. 420-31.

Gilbert, E. S.
"The Effect of Unequal Variance-Covariance Matrices on Fisher's LDF"
Biometrics, Vol. 25 (1969), pp. 505-16.

Holloway, L. N. and Dunn, O. J.
"The Robustness of Hotelling's T-Square"
Journal of the American Statistical Association, Vol. 62 (1967), pp.
124-36.

Hopkins, J. W. and Clay, P. P. F.
"Some Empirical Distributions of the Bivariate T-Square and
Homoscedasticity Criterion M Under Unequal Variance and Leptokurtosis"
Journal of the American Statistical Association, Vol. 58 (1963), pp.
1048-53.

Ito, K. and Schull, N. J.
  "On the Robustness of the T-Square Test in Multivariate Analysis of
  Variance When Variance-Covariance Matrices are Not Equal"
  Biometrika, Vol. 51 (1964), pp. 71-82.

Mardia, K. V.
  "Assessment of the Multinormality and the Robustness of Hotelling's
  T-Square Test"
  Applied Statistics, Vol. 24 (1975), pp. 163-71.

Marks, Sidney and Dunn, Olive Jean
  "Discriminant Functions When Covariance Matrices are Unequal"
  Journal of the American Statistical Association, Vol. 69 (June 1974).

177.05 ---------- Tests of Equality of Dispersion Matrices

        See also (sub)heading(s) 141.

Box, G. E. P.
  "A General Distribution Theory for a Class of Likelihood Criteria"
  Biometrika, Vol. 36 (1949), pp. 317-46.

177.06 ---------- Effects of Multivariate Nonnormality

Andrews, D. F., Guanademkan, R., and Warner, J. L.
  "Methods for Assessing Multivariate Normality"
  in Krishniah, P. R. (editor)
  Proceedings of the International Symposium on Multivariate Analysis
  (New York: Academic Press, 1973), pp. 95-116.

Bahadur, R. R.
  "A Representation of the Joint Distribution of Responses to N
  Dichotomous Items"
  in Solomon, H. (editor)
  Studies in Item Analysis and Prediction
  (Stanford: Stanford University Press, 1961), pp. 158-68.

Chang, P. C. and Afifi, A. A.
  "Classification Based on Dichotomous and Continuous Variables"
  Journal of the American Statistical Association, Vol. 69 (1974), pp.
  336-9.

Dillon, William R. and Goldstein, Matthew
  "On the Performance of Some Multinomial Classification Rules"
  Journal of the American Statistical Association, Vol. 73 (June 1978),
  pp. 305-13.

Eisenbeis, Robert A.
  "Pitfalls in the Application of Discriminant Analysis in Business,
  Finance and Economics"
  Journal of Finance, Vol. 32 (June 1977), pp. 875-900.

Gilbert, E. S.
  "On Discrimination Using Qualitative Variables"
  Journal of the American Statistical Association, Vol. 63 (1968), pp.
  1399-412.

Hawkins, Douglas M.
  "A New Test for Multivariate Normality and Homoscedasticity"
  Technometrics, Vol. 23 (February 1981), pp. 105-10.

Hills, M.
  "Discrimination and Allocation With Discrete Data"
  Journal of the Royal Statistical Society, Vol. C16 (1967), pp. 237-50.

Krzanowski, W. J.
  "The Performance of Fisher's Linear Discriminant Function Under
  Non-Optimal Conditions"
  Technometrics, Vol. 19 (May 1977), pp. 191-200.

Krzanowski, W. J.
  "Discrimination and Classification Using Both Binary and Continuous
  Variables"
  Journal of the American Statistical Association, Vol. 70 (1975), pp.
  782-90.

Lachenbruch, P. A., Sneeringer, C., and Revo, L. T.
  "Robustness of the Linear and Quadratic Discriminant Functions to
  Certain Types of Non-Normality"
  Communications in Statistics, Vol. 1 (1973), pp. 39-56.

Linhart, H.
  "Techniques for Discriminant Analysis With Discrete Variables"
  Metrika, Vol. 2 (May 1959), pp. 138-49.

Moore, Dan H., II
"Evaluation of Five Discrimination Procedures for Binary Variables"
Journal of the American Statistical Association, Vol. 68 (June 1973),
pp. 399-404.

Zhezhel, Yu N.
"The Efficiency of a Linear Discriminant Function for Arbitrary
Distributions"
Engineering Cybernetics, Vol. 6 (1968), pp. 107-11.

177.07 ---------- Selection of Variates

See also (sub)heading(s) 160.05.

Berhman, Douglas N. and Perreault, William D.
"Isolating Predictor Variable Effects in Marketing Research
Applications of Discriminant Analysis"
Proceedings, Southern Marketing Association, New Orleans (1978), pp.
41-4.

Cattin, Philippe and Jolibert, Alain
"Measures of Relative Importance of the Predictor Variables in Linear
Discriminant Analysis: A Review"
Proceedings, American Marketing Association, Detroit (August 1983).

Cochran, W. G.
"On the Performance of the Linear Discriminant Function"
Technometrics, Vol. 6 (1964), pp. 179-90.

Karson, M. J. and Martell, T. F.
"On the Interpretation of Individual Variables in Multiple
Discriminant Analysis"
Journal of Financial and Quantitative Analysis, Vol. 15 (March 1980),
pp. 211-8.

McCabe, G. P.
"Computations for Variable Selection in Discriminant Analysis"
Technometrics, Vol. 17 (1975), pp. 103-9.

McKay, R. J.
"Simultaneous Procedures for Variable Selection in Multiple
Discriminant Analysis"
Biometrika, Vol. 64 (1977), pp. 183-90.

McKay, R. J. and Campbell, N. A.
"Variable Selection Techniques in Discriminant Analysis"
British Journal of Mathematical and Statistical Psychology, Vol. 35,
Part 1 (May 1982), pp. 1-41.

McLachlan, G. J.
"Criterion for Selecting Variables for Linear Discriminant Function"
Biometrics, Vol. 32 (September 1976), pp. 529-34.

Moran, M. A.
"The Performance of Fisher's Linear Discriminant Function With and
Without Selection of Variables"
University of Reading (1974), unpublished Ph.D. dissertation.

Urbakh, V. Yu
"Linear Discriminant Analysis: Loss of Discriminating Power When a
Variate is Omitted"
Biometrics, Vol. 27 (1971), pp. 531-4.

Watanabe, S. et al.
"Evaluation of Selection of Variables in Pattern Recognition"
in Tou, J. T. (editor)
Computer and Information Sciences, Volume Two
(New York: Academic Press, Inc., 1967).

Weiner, S. M. and Dunn, O. J.
"Elimination of Variates in Linear Discrimination Problems"
Biometrics, Vol. 22 (June 1966), pp. 268-75.

177.08 ---------- Classification Criteria and Errors

Albaum, Gerald and Baker, Kenneth
"The Sampling Problem in Validation of Multiple Discriminant Analysis"
Journal of the Market Research Society, Vol. 18 (July 1976), pp.
158-61.

Cochran, W. G. and Hopkins, C.
"Some Classification Methods With Multivariate Qualitative Data"
Biometrics, Vol. 17 (1961), pp. 10-32.

Cooley, Philip L.
"Bayesian and Cost Considerations for Optimal Classification With
Discriminant Analysis"
Journal of Risk and Insurance, Vol. 42 (June 1975), pp. 277-88.

Crask, Melvin R. and Perreault, William D., Jr.
"Validation of Discriminant Analysis in Marketing Research"
Journal of Marketing Research, Vol. XIV (February 1977), pp. 60-8.

Dasgupta
"Probability Inequalities and Error in Classification"
Technical Report No. 190
University of Minnesota, School of Statistics (1972).

DeGruijter, Dato N. M. and Hambleton, Ronald K.
"Reply" (to Van Der Linden)
Applied Psychological Measurement, Vol. 8 (Winter 1984), pp. 19,20.

DeGruijter, Dato N. M. and Hambleton, Ronald K.
"On Problems Encountered Using Decision Theory to set Cutoff Scores"
Applied Psychological Measurement, Vol. 8 (Winter 1984), pp. 1-8.

Dillon, William R.
"The Performance of the Linear Discriminant Function in Nonoptimal
Situations and the Estimation of Classification Error Rates: A Review
of Recent Findings"
Journal of Marketing Research, Vol. XVI (August 1979), pp. 370-81.

Dillon, William R. and Goldstein, Matthew
"On the Performance of Some Multinomial Classification Rules"
Journal of the American Statistical Association, Vol. 73 (June 1978),
pp. 305-13.

Dunn, O. J.
"Some Expected Values for Probabilities of Correct Classification in
Discriminant Analysis"
Technometrics, Vol. 13 (1971), pp. 345-53.

Dunn, O. J. and Varady, P. V.
"Probabilities of Correct Classification in Discriminant Analysis"
Biometrics, Vol. 22 (1966), pp. 908-24.

Fukunaga, Keinosuke and Kessell, David L.
"Nonparametric Bayes Error Estimation Using Unclassified Samples"
IEEE Transactions on Information Theory, Vol. 4 (July 1973), pp.
434-40.

Gau, George W.
"A Note on the Assessment of the Results in a Discriminant Analysis"
Decision Sciences, Vol. 9 (April 1978), pp. 341-5.

Geisser, Seymour
"Posterior Odds for Multivariate Analysis"
Journal of the Royal Statistical Society, Series B, Vol. 26 (1964),
pp. 69-76.

Glick, Ned
"Additive Estimators for Probabilities of Correct Classification"
Pattern Recognition, Vol. 10 (1978), pp. 211-22.

Glick, Ned
"Sample-Based Multinomial Classification"
Biometrics, Vol. 29 (June 1973), pp. 241-56.

Glick, Ned
"Sample-Based Classification Procedure Derived From Density Estimates"
Journal of the American Statistical Association, Vol. 67 (March
1972), pp. 116-22.

Goldstein, Matthew and Wolf, Edward
"On the Problem of Bias in Multinomial Classification"
Biometrics, Vol. 33 (June 1977), pp. 325-31.

Hills, M.
"Allocation Rules and Their Error Rates"
Journal of the Royal Statistical Society, Vol. B28 (1966), p. 1.

Hoel, P. G. and Peterson, R. P.
"A Solution to the Problem of Optimum Classification"
Annals of Mathematical Statistics, Vol. 20 (1949), pp. 433-8.

Hora, Stephen C. and Wilcox, James B.
"Estimation of Error Rates in Several-Population Discriminant
Analysis"
Journal of Marketing Research, Vol. XIX (February 1982), pp. 57-61.

Lachenbruch, P. A.
"An Almost Unbiased Method of Obtaining Confidence Intervals for the
Probability of Misclassification in Discriminant Analysis"
Biometrics, Vol. 23 (1967), pp. 639-45.

Lachenbruch, P. A.
"Discrimination Analysis When Initial Samples are Misclassified"
Technometrics, Vol. 8 (1966), pp. 657-62.

Lachenbruch, P. A. and Mickey, M. R.
    "Estimation of Error Rates in Discriminant Analysis"
    Technometrics, Vol. 10 (1968), pp. 1-11.

McCrohan, Kevin F.
    "A Cautionary Note on Intra-Group Bias in Multiple Discriminant
    Function Analysis"
    European Research, Vol. 8 (July 1980), pp. 177-80.

McLachlan, G. J.
    "Estimation of the Errors of Misclassification on the Criterion of
    Asymptotic Mean Square Error"
    Technometrics, Vol. 16 (May 1974), pp. 255,6.

Miller, R. G.
    "The Jackknife--A Review"
    Biometrika, Vol. 61 (1974), pp. 1-15.

Montgomery, David B.
    "New Product Distribution: An Analysis of Supermarket Buyer Decisions"
    Journal of Marketing Research, Vol. XII (August 1975), pp. 255-64.

Moore, David S., Whitsell, Stephen J., and Lundgrebe, David A.
    "Variance Comparisons for Unbiased Estimators of Probability of
    Correct Classification"
    IEEE Transactions on Information Theory, Vol. 22 (January 1976), pp.
    102-5.

Nath, Ravinder
    "Estimation of Misclassification Probabilities in the Linear
    Programming Approaches to the Two-Group Discriminant Problem"
    Decision Sciences, Vol. 15 (Spring 1984), pp. 248-52.

Pinches, George F.
    "Factors Influencing Classification Results From Multiple
    Discriminant Analysis"
    Journal of Business Research, Vol. 8 (December 1980), pp. 429-56.

Sedransk, N. and Okamoto, M.
    "Estimation of the Probabilities of Misclassification for a Linear
    Discriminant Function in the Univariate Normal Case"
    Annals of Institute of Statistical Mathematics, Vol. 23 (1971), pp.
    419-36.

Sitgreaves, R.
    "Some Results on the Distribution of the W-Classification Statistic"
    in Solomon, H. (editor)
    Studies in Item Analysis and Prediction
    (Stanford: Stanford University Press, 1961), pp. 241-51.

Sorum, M. J.
    "Three Probabilites of Misclassification"
    Technometrics, Vol. 14 (1972), pp. 309-16.

Sorum, M. J.
    "Estimating the Expected and the Optimal Probabilities of
    Misclassification"
    Technometrics, Vol. 14 (1972), pp. 935-43.

Sorum, M. J.
    "Estimating the Conditional Probabilities of Misclassification"
    Technometrics, Vol. 13 (1971), pp. 333-43.

Toussaint, G. T.
    "Bibliography on Estimation of Misclassification"
    IEEE Transactions on Information Theory, Vol. It-20 (July 1974), pp.
    472-9.

Van Der Linden, William J.
    "Comment" (on DeGruijter and Hambleton)
    Applied Psychological Measurement, Vol. 8 (Winter 1984), pp. 9-18.

177.09 ---------- Theory Re: Nonparametric Discriminant Analysis

Habbema, J. D. F., Hermans, J., and Van Der Brock, K.
    "A Stepwise Discrimination Program Using Density Estimation"
    in Bruckman, G. (editor)
    Compstat 1974
    (Vienna: Physica Verlag, 1974), pp. 100-10.

Hand, D. J.
    Kernel Discrimination Analysis
    (Chichester: Research Studies Press, 1982).

178 --------------- DISCRIMINANT ANALYSIS APPLICATIONS ---------------
        See also (sub)heading(s) 177.

178.01 ---------- Applications of Two-Group Discriminant Analysis

Adams, Arthur J. and Lonial, Subhash C.
    "Investigation of Giving Behavior to United Way Using Log-Linear
    Modeling and Discriminant Analysis: An Empirical Study"
    Journal of the Academy of Marketing Science, Vol. 12 (1984), pp.
    77-88.

Andrus, David M., Silver, Edward, and Johnson, Dallas E.
    "Status Brand Management and Gift Purchase: A Discriminant Analysis"
    Journal of Consumer Marketing, Vol. 3 (Winter 1986), pp. 5-13.

Badovick, Gordon J. and Beatty, Sharon E.
    "Shared Organizational Values: Measurement and Impact Upon Strategic
    Marketing Implementation"
    Journal of the Academy of Marketing Science, Vol. 15 (Spring 1987),
    pp. 19-26.

Barak, Benny and Stern, Barbara
    "Women's Age in Advertising: An Examination of Two Consumer Age
    Profiles"
    Journal of Advertising Research, Vol. 25 (December 1985/January
    1986), pp. 38-47.

Bonfield, E. H. and Robbins, John E.
    "A Method for Selecting High Payoff Marketing Strategies for
    Attracting Noncustomer Product Purchasers"
    Journal of the Academy of Marketing Science, Vol. 5 (Winter-Spring
    1977), pp. 85-93.

Bourgeois, Jacques C. and Barnes, James G.
    "Viability and Profile of the Consumerist Segment"
    Journal of Consumer Research, Vol. 5 (March 1979), pp. 217-28.

Bruning, Edward R., Kovacic, Mary L., and Oberdick, Larry E.
    "Segmentation Analysis of Domestic Airline Passenger Markets"
    Journal of the Academy of Science, Vol. 13 (Winter 1985), pp. 17-31.

Burnett, John J.
    "Psychographic and Demographic Characteristics of Blood Donors"
    Journal of Consumer Research, Vol. 8 (June 1981), pp. 62-6.

Crawford, John C., Garland, Barbara C., and Ganesh, G.
    "Identifying the Global Pro-Trade Consumer"
    International Marketing Review, Vol. 8 (Winter 1988), pp. 25-33.

Danko, William D. and MacLachlan, James M.
    "Research to Accelerate the Diffusion of a New Innovation"
    Journal of Advertising Research, Vol. 23 (June/July 1983), pp. 39-43.

Diamantopoulos, Adamantios
    "Identifying Differences Between High- and Low-Involvement Exporters"
    International Marketing Review, Vol. 8 (Summer 1988), pp. 52-60.

Etgar, Michael
    "Effects of Administrative Control on Efficiency of Vertical
    Marketing Systems"
    Journal of Marketing Research, Vol. XIII (February 1976), pp. 12-24.

Formisano, Roger A., Olshavsky, Richard W., and Tapp, Shelley
    "Choice Strategy in a Difficult Task Environment"
    Journal of Consumer Research, Vo. 8 (March 1982), pp. 474-9.

Gentry, James W.
    "Discriminant Analysis in the Credit Extension Decision"
    Credit World, Vol. 63 (November 1974), pp. 25-8.

Ghymn, Kyung-Il
    "The Relative Importance of Import Decision Variables"
    Journal of the Academy of Marketing Science, Vol. 11 (Summer 1983),
    pp. 304-12.

Goldberg, Marvin E.
    "Identifying Relevant Psychographic Segments: How Specifying Product
    Functions Can Help"
    Journal of Consumer Research, Vol. 3 (December 1976), pp. 163-9.

Gronhaug, Kjell
    "Profiling the Adopters in an Organizational Context"
    European Research, Vol. 5 (March 1977), pp. 51-55.

Gronhaug, Kjell
    "How New Car Buyers Use Advertising"
    Journal of Advertising, Vol. 15 (February 1975), pp. 49-53.

Haldeman, Virginia A., Peters, Jeanne M., and Tripple, Patricia A.
"Measuring a Consumer Energy Conservation Ethic: An Analysis of
Components"
Journal of Consumer Affairs, Vol. 21 (Summer 1987), pp. 70-85.

Handelsman, Moshe
"Varied Purchase Behaviour as a Result of Purchase History and
Perceived Brand Similarity"
Journal of the Market Research Society, Vol. 29 (July 1987), pp.
293-315.

Hirschman, Elizabeth C.
"Differences in Consumer Purchase Behavior by Credit Card Payment
System"
Journal of Consumer Research, Vol. 6 (June 1979), pp. 58-66.

Holbrook, Morris B. and Huber, Joel
"Separating Perceptual Dimensions From Affective Overtones: An
Application to Consumer Aesthetics"
Journal of Consumer Research, Vol. 5 (March 1979), pp. 272-83.

Horton, Raymond L.
"Some Relationships Between Personality and Consumer Decision Making"
Journal of Marketing Research, Vol. XVI (May 1979), pp. 233-46.

Hutton, R. Bruce and McNeil, Dennis L.
"The Value of Incentives in Stimulating Energy Conservation"
Journal of Consumer Research, Vol. 8 (December 1981), pp. 291-8.

Jolibert, Alain J. P. and Baumgartner, Gary
"Toward a Definition of the Consumerist Segment in France"
Journal of Consumer Research, Vol. 8 (June 1981), pp. 114-7.

Konopa, Leonard J. and Zallocco, Ronald L.
"A Study of Conflict Between Shopping Center Managers and Retailers
Within Regional Shopping Centers"
Journal of the Academy of Marketing Science, Vol. 9 (Summer 1981),
pp. 274-87.

Korgaonkar, Pradeep K.
"Shopping Orientations of Catalog Showroom Patrons"
Journal of Retailing, Vol. 57 (Spring 1981), pp. 78-90.

LaBarbera, Priscilla A.
"The Diffusion of Trade Association Advertising Self-Regulation"
Journal of Marketing, Vol. 47 (Winter 1983), pp. 58-67.

LaBarbera, Priscilla A. and Mazursky, David
"A Longitudinal Assessment of Consumer Satisfaction/Dissatisfaction:
The Dynamic Aspect of the Cognitive Process"
Journal of Marketing Research, Vol. XX (November 1983), pp. 393-404.

Lewis, Robert C.
"Restaurant Advertising: Appeals and Consumers' Intentions"
Journal of Advertising Research, Vol. 21 (October 1981), pp. 69-74.

McEnally, Martha R. and Hawes, Jon M.
"The Market for Generic Brand Grocery Products: A Review and
Extension"
Journal of Marketing, Vol. 48 (Winter 1984), pp. 75-83.

Michell, Paul C.
"Accord and Discord in Agency-Client Perceptions of Creativity"
Journal of Advertising Research, Vol. 24 (October/November 1984), pp.
9-24.

Montgomery, David B.
"New Product Distribution: An Analysis of Supermarket Buyer Decisions"
Journal of Marketing Research, Vol. XII (August 1975), pp. 255-64.

Nevin, John R. and Churchill, Gilbert A., Jr.
"The Equal Credit Opportunity Act: An Evaluation"
Journal of Marketing, Vol. 43 (Spring 1979), pp. 95-104.

Newman, Bruce I. and Sheth, Jagdish N.
"A Model of Primary Voter Behavior"
Journal of Consumer Research, Vol. 12 (September 1985), pp. 178-87.

O'Guinn, Thomas C. and Meyer, Timothy P.
"Segmenting the Hispanic Market: The Use of Spanish Language Radio"
Journal of Advertising Research, Vol. 23 (December 1983/January
1984), pp. 9-16.

O'Reilly, Lynn, Rucker, Margaret, Hughes, Rhonda, Gorang, Marge, and
Hand, Susan
"The Relationship of Psychological and Situational Variables to Usage
of a Second-Order Marketing System"
Journal of the Academy of Marketing Science, Vol. 12 (Summer 1984),
pp. 53-76.

Paksoy, Christie H.
"Life-Style Analysis of Major Bank Credit Card Users"
Journal of the Academy of Marketing Science, Vol. 7 (Winter-Spring
1979), pp. 40-7.

Pessemier, Edgar and Handelsman, Moshe
"Temporal Variety in Consumer Behavior"
Journal of Marketing Research, Vol. XXI (November 1984), pp. 435-44.

Pickering, J. F. and Greatorex, M.
"Evaluations of Individual Consumer Durables: Differences Between
Owners and Non-Owners and Buyers and Non-Buyers"
Journal of the Market Research Society, Vol. 22 (April 1980), pp.
97-114.

Potter, W. James, Forrest, Edward, Sapolsky, Barry S., and Ware, William
"Segmenting VCR Owners"
Journal of Advertising Research, Vol. 28 (April/May 1988), pp. 29-39.

Riordan, Edward A., Oliver, Richard L., and Donnelly, James H., Jr.
"The Unsold Prospect: Dyadic and Attitudinal Determinants"
Journal of Marketing Research, Vol. XIV (November 1977), pp. 530-7.

Ryans, Adrian B. and Deutscher, Terry
"Children and Commercial Persuasion: Some Comments"
Journal of Consumer Research, Vol. 2 (December 1975), pp. 237-9.

Saegert, Joel, Hoover, Robert J., and Hilger, Marye Tharp
"Characteristics of Mexican American Consumers"
Journal of Consumer Research, Vol. 12 (June 1985), pp. 104-9.

Sands, Saul and Moore, Peter
"Store Site Selection by Discriminant Analysis"
Journal of the Market Research Society, Vol. 23 (January 1981), pp.
40-51.

Schlegelmilch, Bodo B.
"Targeting of Fund-Raising Appeals--How to Identify Donors"
European Journal of Marketing, Vol. 22, No. 1 (1988), pp. 31-40.

Schlegelmilch, Bodo B.
"Controlling Country-Specific and Industry-Specific Influences on
Export Behaviour"
European Journal of Marketing, Vol. 20, No. 2 (1986), pp. 54-71.

Sheth, Jagdish N. and Frazier, Gary L.
"A Model of Strategy Mix Choice for Planned Social Change"
Journal of Marketing, Vol. 46 (Winter 1982), pp. 15-26.

Shuchman, Abe and Riesz, Peter C.
"Correlates of Persuasibility: The Crest Case"
Journal of Marketing Research, Vol. XII (February 1975), pp. 7-11.

Strober, Myra H. and Weinberg, Charles B.
"Strategies Used by Working and Nonworking Wives to Reduce Time
Pressures"
Journal of Consumer Research, Vol. 6 (March 1980), pp. 338-48.

Strober, Myra H. and Weinberg, Charles B.
"Working Wives and Major Family Expenditures"
Journal of Consumer Research, Vol. 4 (December 1977), pp. 141-7.

Tucker, Lewis R., Jr., Dolich, Ira J., and Wilson, David
"Profiling Environmentally Responsible Consumer-Citizens"
Journal of the Academy of Marketing Science, Vol. 9 (Fall 1981), pp.
454-78.

Webster, Frederick E., Jr.
"Determining the Characteristics of the Socially Conscious Consumer"
Journal of Consumer Research, Vol. 2 (December 1975), pp. 188-96.

Wee, Chow Hou, Loh, Choai Leng, and Kau, Ah Keng
"Shopping Behavior of Housing and Development Board Residents in
Singapore"
Singapore Marketing Review, Vol. III (1988), pp. 50-60.

Wilton, Peter C. and Pessemier, Edgar A.
"Forecasting the Ultimate Acceptance of an Innovation: The Effects of
Information"
Journal of Consumer Research, Vol. 8 (September 1981), pp. 162-71.

Yavas, Ugur
"Foreign Travel Behaviour in a Growing Vacation Market: Implications
for Tourism Marketers"
European Journal of Marketing, Vol. 21, No. 5 (1987), pp. 57-69.

Yavas, Ugur and Riecken, Glen
"Can Volunteers be Targeted?"
Journal of the Academy of Marketing Science, Vol. 13 (Spring 1985),
pp. 218-28.

Yavas, Ugur, Riecken, Glen, and Parameswaran, Ravi
"Personality, Organization-Specific Attitude, and Socioeconomic
Correlates of Charity Giving Behavior"
Journal of the Academy of Marketing Science, Vol. 9 (Winter 1981),
pp. 52-65.

178.02 ---------- Applications of N-Group Discriminant Analysis

Bahn, Kenneth D. and Granzin, Kent L.
"Benefit Segmentation in the Restaurant Industry"
Journal of the Academy of Marketing Science, Vol. 13 (Summer 1985),
pp. 226-47.

Becherer, Richard C., Richard, Lawrence M., and Wiley, James B.
"Predicting Market Behavior: Are Psychographics Really Better"
Journal of the Academy of Marketing Science, Vol. 5 (Winter-Spring
1977), pp. 75-84.

Berkowitz, E. N. and Walton, J. R.
"Contextual Influences on Consumer Price Responses: An Experimental
Analysis"
Journal of Marketing Research, Vol. XVII (August 1980), pp. 349-58.

Box, J. M. F.
"The Power of Consumer Organizations"
European Journal of Marketing, Vol. 16, No. 6 (1982), pp. 3-19.

Brooker, George
"The Self-Actualizing Socially Conscious Consumer"
Journal of Consumer Research, Vol. 3 (September 1976), pp. 107-12.

Burke, Marian C.
"Strategic Choice and Marketing Managers: An Examination of
Business-Level Marketing Objectives"
Journal of Marketing Research, Vol. XXI (November 1984), pp. 345-59.

Calantone, Roger J. and Cooper, Robert G.
"A Discriminant Model for Identifying Scenarios of Industrial New
Product Failure"
Journal of the Academy of Marketing Science, Vol. 7 (Summer 1979),
pp. 163-83.

Calantone, Roger J. and Sawyer, Alan G.
"The Stability of Benefit Segments"
Journal of Marketing Research, Vol. XV (August 1978), pp. 395-403.

Cobb, Cathy J. and Hoyer, Wayne D.
"Planned Versus Impulse Purchase Behavior"
Journal of Retailing, Vol. 62 (Winter 1986), pp. 384-409.

Curhan, Ronald C. and Kopp, Robert J.
"Obtaining Retailer Support for Trade Deals: Key Success Factors"
Journal of Advertising Research, Vol. 27 (December 1987/January
1988), pp. 51-60.

Darden, William R. and Perreault, William D., Jr.
"A Multivariate Analysis of Media Exposure and Vacation Behavior With
Life Style Covariates"
Journal of Consumer Research, Vol. 2 (September 1975), pp. 93-103.

Deshpande, Rohit, Hoyer, Wayne D., and Donthu, Naveen
"The Intensity of Ethnic Affiliation: A Study of the Sociology of
Hispanic Consumption"
Journal of Consumer Research, Vol. 13 (September 1986), pp. 214-20.

Faber, Ronald J., O'Guinn, Thomas C., and McCarty, John A.
"Ethnicity, Acculturation, and the Importance of Product Attributes"
Psychology and Marketing, Vol. 4 (Summer 1987), pp. 121-34.

Fine, Seymour H.
"Toward a Theory of Segmentation by Objectives in Social Marketing"
Journal of Consumer Research, Vol. 7 (June 1980), pp. 1-13.

Gales, K.
"Discriminant Functions of Socio-Economic Class"
Applied Statistics, Vol. 6 (June 1957), pp. 123-32.

Granzin, Kent L.
"An Investigation of the Market for Generic Products"
Journal of Retailing, Vol. 57 (Winter 1981), pp. 39-55.

Guagnano, Greg, Hawkes, Glenn R., Acredolo, Curt, and White, Nancy
"Innovation Perception and Adoption of Solar Heating Technology"
Journal of Consumer Affairs, Vol. 20 (Summer 1986), pp. 48-64.

Havlena, William J. and Holbrook, Morris B.
"The Varieties of Consumption Experience: Comparing Two Typologies of
Emotion in Consumer Behavior"
Journal of Consumer Research, Vol. 13 (December 1986), pp. 394-404.

Hite, Robert E. and Fraser, Cynthia
    "International Advertising Strategies of Multinational Corporations"
    Journal of Advertising Research, Vol. 28 (August/September 1988), pp.
    9-17.

Holbrook, M. B. and Huber, Joel
    "Separating Perceptual Dimensions From Affective Overtones by
    Chaining Factor and Discriminant Analyses: An Application to Consumer
    Aesthetics"
    Journal of Consumer Research, Vol. 5 (March 1979), pp. 272-83.

Homans, Richard and Houston, Franklin S.
    "Marketing Research for Public Health: A Demonstration of
    Differential Responses to Advertising"
    Journal of the Academy of Marketing Science, Vol. 9 (Fall 1981), pp.
    380-98.

Hooley, Graham J., Lynch, James E., and Brooksbank, Roger W.
    "Strategic Market Environments"
    Journal of Marketing Management, Vol. 4 (Winter 1988), pp. 131-47.

Huber, Joel and Holbrook, Morris B.
    "Using Attribute Ratings for Product Positioning: Some Distinctions
    Among Compositional Approaches"
    Journal of Marketing Research, Vol. XVI (November 1979), pp. 507-16.

Laulajainen, Risto
    "The Unfamiliar Tourist Destination--A Marketing Challenge"
    European Journal of Marketing, Vol. 15, No. 8 (1981), pp. 68-80.

Lucas, George H., Jr., Parasuraman, A., Davis, Robert A., and Enis, Ben
    M.
    "An Empirical Study of Salesforce Turnover"
    Journal of Marketing, Vol. 51 (July 1987), pp. 34-59.

Lumpkin, James R., Greenberg, Barnett A., and Goldstucker, Jac L.
    "Marketplace Needs of the Elderly: Determinant Attributes and Store
    Choice"
    Journal of Retailing, Vol. 61 (Summer 1985), pp. 75-105.

Madden, Thomas J., Allen, Chris T., and Twible, Jacquelyn L.
    "Attitude Toward the Ad: An Assessment of Diverse Measurement Indices
    Under Different Processing 'Sets'"
    Journal of Marketing Research, Vol. XXV (August 1988), pp. 242-52.

McConkey, C. William and Warren, William E.
    "Psychographic and Demographic Profiles of State Lottery Ticket
    Purchasers"
    Journal of Consumer Affairs, Vol. 21 (Winter 1987), pp. 314-27.

McCrohan, Kevin F. and Smith, James D.
    "Consumer Participation in the Informal Economy"
    Journal of the Academy of Marketing Science, Vol. 15 (Winter 1987),
    pp. 62-8.

Morgan, Fred W., Jr.
    "An Analysis of Experimental Buying Behavior"
    Journal of the Academy of Marketing Science, Vol. 6 (Winter-Spring
    1978), pp. 12-24.

Paoli, Jean-Mathieu
    "Designing Social Organisations for People Such as They Are"
    European Research, Vol. 7 (July 1979), pp. 175-82.

Park, C. Whan
    "The Effect of Individual and Situation-Related Factors on Consumer
    Selection of Judgmental Models"
    Journal of Marketing Research, Vol. XIII (May 1976), pp. 144-51.

Pitts, Robert E., Willenborg, John F., and Sherrell, Daniel L.
    "Consumer Adaptation to Gasoline Price Increases"
    Journal of Consumer Research, Vol. 8 (December 1981), pp. 322-30.

Richards, Elizabeth A. and Sturman, Stephen S.
    "Life-Style Segmentation in Apparel Marketing"
    Journal of Marketing, Vol. 41 (October 1977), pp. 89-91.

Richins, Marsha L.
    "Negative Word-of-Mouth by Dissatisfied Consumers: A Pilot Study"
    Journal of Marketing, Vol. 47 (Winter 1983), pp. 68-78.

Ring, Lawrence J.
    "Retail Positioning: A Multiple Discriminant Analysis Approach"
    Journal of Retailing, Vol. 55 (Spring 1979), pp. 25-36.

Robbins, John E. and Robbins, Stephanie S.
    "Museum Marketing: Identification of High, Moderate, and Low Attendee
    Segments"
    Journal of the Academy of Marketing Science, Vol. 9 (Winter 1981),
    pp. 66-76.

Robertson, Thomas S. and Rossiter, John R.
"Children and Commercial Persuasion: A Reply to Ryans and Deutscher"
Journal of Consumer Research, Vol. 3 (June 1976), pp. 58-61.

Ryans, Adrian B. and Weinberg, Charles B.
"Consumer Dynamics in Nonprofit Organizations"
Journal of Consumer Research, Vol. 5 (September 1978), pp. 89-95.

Sewall, Murphy A.
"Market Segmentation Based on Consumer Ratings of Proposed Product Designs"
Journal of Marketing Research, Vol. XV (November 1978), pp. 547-64.

Shimp, Terence and Dyer, Robert
"How the Legal Profession Views Legal Service Advertising"
Journal of Marketing, Vol. 42 (July 1978), pp. 74-81.

Spiro, Rosann L.
"Persuasion in Family Decision-Making"
Journal of Consumer Research, Vol. 9 (March 1983), pp. 393-402.

Stewart, D. B.
"Competition in the UK Automobile Market: An Empirical Study"
European Journal of Marketing, Vol. 17, No. 1 (1983), pp. 14-25.

Swartz, Teresa A. and Meyer, Luanne
"News Versus Entertainment TV Viewers"
Journal of Advertising Research, Vol. 25 (December 1985/January 1986)
pp. 9-17.

Venkatesh, Alladi
"Changing Roles of Women--A Life-Style Analysis"
Journal of Consumer Research, Vol. 7 (September 1980), pp. 189-97.

Venkatesh, Alladi and Tankersley, Clint B.
"Magazine Readership by Female Segments"
Journal of Advertising Research, Vol. 19 (August 1979), pp. 31-8.

Villani, Kathryn E. A.
"Personality/Life Style and Television Viewing Behavior"
Journal of Marketing Research, Vol. XII (November 1975), pp. 43-9.

Westbrook, Robert A. and Fornell, Claes
"Patterns of Information Source Usage Among Durable Goods Buyers"
Journal of Marketing Research, Vol. XVI (August 1979), pp. 303-12.

Yuspeh, Sonia and Fein, Gene
"Can Segments be Born Again?"
Journal of Advertising Research, Vol. 22 (June/July 1982), pp. 13-22.

179 ----------------- ANALYSIS OF VARIANCE (ANOVA) -----------------
        See also (sub)heading(s) 133.08, 146.04, 147.08, 180, 181,
        182, 183, 184, 185, 191, 211.01.

179.01 ---------- Books Re: Analysis of Variance

Ackoff, R. L.
    The Design of Social Research
    (Chicago: The University of Chicago Press, 1953).

Anderson, Virgil L. and MacLean, Robert A.
    Design of Experiments
    (New York: Marcel Dekker, Inc.).

Banks, Seymour
    Experimentation in Marketing
    (New York: McGraw-Hill Book Co., 1965).

Box, George E. P., Hunter, William G., and Hunter, J. Stuart
    Statistics for Experimenters: An Introduction to Design, Data
    Analysis, and Model Building
    (New York, NY: Wiley-Interscience, 1978), 653 pp.

Campbell, Donald T. and Stanley, Julian C.
    Experimental and Quasi-Experiental Designs in Research
    (Chicago: Rand-McNally, 1963).

Chew, Victor
    Comparisons Among Treatment Means in an Analysis of Variance
    (Washington, DC: U.S. Government Printing Office, 1977).

Cochran, W. G. and Cox, G. M.
    Experimental Designs, Second Edition
    (New York: John Wiley and Sons, Inc., 1966).

Cox, D. R.
    Planning of Experiments
    (New York: John Wiley and Sons, Inc., 1958).

Cox, Keith and Enis, Ben M.
    Experimentation for Marketing Decisions
    (New York: Intext Educational Publishers, 1973), 122 pp.

Cox, Keith K. and Enis, Ben M.
    Experimentation for Marketing Decisions
    (Scranton, PA: International Textbook, 1969).

Davies, O. L.
    The Design and Analysis of Industrial Experiments, Second Edition
    (New York: Hafner Publishing Co., 1956).

Dodge, Yadolah
    Analysis of Experiments With Missing Data
    (New York: John Wiley and Sons, Inc., 1985), 499 pp.

Edwards, Allen L.
    Experimental Design in Psychological Research
    (New York: Holt, Rinehart and Winston, Inc., 1972).

Federer, W. T.
    Experimental Design
    (New York: Macmillan, 1955).

Fisher, Sir Ronald
    Design of Experiments, Eighth Edition
    (New York, NY: Hafner Publishing Co., Inc., 1966), 265 pp.

Hicks, Charles R.
    Fundamental Concepts in the Design of Experiments
    (New York: Holt, Rinehart and Winston, 1964).

Huitson, A.
    The Analysis of Variance: A Basic Course
    (London: Griffin and Co., 1971).

Iverson, Gudmund and Norpoth, Helmut
    Analysis of Variance, Second Edition
    (Beverly Hills, CA: Sage Publications, Inc.).

Kempthorne, Oscar
    The Design and Analysis of Experiments
    (New York, NY: John Wiley and Sons, Inc., 1952).

Kirk, Roger E.
    Experimental Design, Second Edition
    (Belmont, CA: Brooks/Cole Publishing Company, 1982).

Kish, Leslie
    Statistical Design for Research
    (New York: John Wiley and Company, 1987), 250 pp.

Lee, Wayne
Experimental Design and Analysis
(San Francisco: W. H. Freeman and Company, 1975).

Lee, Wayne
Workbook for Experimental Design and Analysis
(San Francisco: W. H. Freeman and Company, 1975).

Li, C. C.
Analysis of Unbalanced Data
(New York: Cambridge University Press, 1983) 140 pp.

Lindemann, H. R.
Analysis of Variance in Complex Experimental Designs
(San Francisco: W. H. Freeman and Company, 1974).

Lindquist, E. F.
Design and Analysis of Experiments
(Boston: Houghton-Mifflin, 1956).

Matusita, K. (editor)
Recent Developments in Statistical Inference and Data Analysis
(New York: North-Holland Publishing Company, 1980), 364 pp.

Mendenhall, William
Introduction to Linear Models and the Design and Analysis of
Experiments
(Belmont, CA: Wadsworth Publishing Co., 1968).

Milliken, George and Johnson, Dallas E.
Analysis of Messy Data, Volume I: Designed Experiments
(Belmont, CA: Lifetime Learning Publications, 1984), 473 pp.

Montgomery, Douglas C.
Design and Analysis of Experiments, Second Edition
(New York: John Wiley and Sons, Inc., 1984), 538 pp.

Myers, Jerome L.
Fundamentals of Experimental Design
(Boston: Allyn and Bacon, 1980).

Neter, John, Wasserman, William, and Kutner, Michael H.
Applied Linear Statistical Models: Regression, Analysis of Variance,
and Experimental Designs
(Homewood, IL: Richard D. Irwin, Inc., 1985).

Ogawa, Junjiro
Statistical Theory in the Analysis of Experimental Designs
(New York: Marcel Dekker, Inc., 1974).

Ottestad, P.
Statistical Models and Their Experimental Applications VIII
(Riverside, NJ: Hafner, 1970), 88 pp.

Peng, K. C.
The Design and Analysis of Scientific Experiments
(Reading, Ma: Addison-Wesley Publishing Co., 1967), 252 pp.

Raghavarao, Damaraju
Constructions and Combinatorial Problems in Design of Experiments
(New York: John Wiley and Sons, 1971).

Raktoe, B. L., Hedayat, A., and Federer, W. T.
Factorial Designs
(New York: John Wiley and Sons, Inc., 1981), 209 pp.

Scheffe, H.
The Analysis of Variance
(New York: John Wiley and Sons, Inc., 1954).

Searle, R.
Linear Models
(New York: John Wiley and Sons, 1971).

Timm, Neil H.
Analysis of Variance Through Full Rank Models
(Fort Worth, TX: Society of Multivariate Experimental Psychology,
1975).

Vajda, S.
The Mathematics of Experimental Design: Incomplete Designs and Latin
Squares
Griffins Statistical Monographs and Courses, No. 23
(New York, NY: Hafner Publishing Company, 1967), 110 pp.

Venkatesan, M. and Holloway, Robert J.
An Introduction to Market Experimentation
(New York: The Free Press, 1971).

Winer, B. J.
    Statistical Principles in Experimental Design
    (New York: McGraw-Hill Book Co., 1962).

Yates, Frank
    Experimental Design
    (Darien, CO: Hafner, 1970), 296 pp.

179.02 ---------- Theory Re: Analysis of Variance

Addelman, S.
    "Orthogonal Main Effect Plans for Asymmetrical Factorial Experiments"
    Technometrics, Vol. 4 (1962), pp. 21-46.

Appelbaum, Mark I. and Cramer, Elliot M.
    "Some Problems in the Nonorthogonal Analysis of Variance"
    Psychological Bulletin, Vol. 81 (1974), pp. 335-43.

Banks, Seymour
    "On Methods: Marketing Experiments"
    Journal of Advertising Research, Vol. 3 (March 1963), pp. 34-41.

Basu, D.
    "Randomization Analysis of Experimental Data: The Fisher
    Randomization Test"
    Journal of the American Statistical Association, Vol. 75 (September
    1980), pp. 575-81.

Bechtel, G. G.
    "The Analysis of Variance and Pairwise Scaling"
    Psychometrika, Vol. 32 (1967), pp. 47-65.

Bechtel, Gordon G. and O'Connor, P. J.
    "Testing Micropreference Structures"
    Journal of Marketing Research, Vol. XVI (May 1979), pp. 247-57.

Brunk, Max and Federer, Walter
    "Experimental Designs and Probability Sampling in Marketing Research"
    Journal of the American Statistical Association, Vol. 48 (September
    1953), pp. 440-52.

Burdick, Richard K.
    "Statement of Hypotheses in the Analysis of Variance"
    Journal of Marketing Research, Vol. XX (August 1983), pp. 320-4.

Cattin, Philippe and Bliemel, Friedhelm
    "Metric vs. Nonmetric Procedures for Multiattribute Modeling: Some
    Simulation Results"
    Decision Sciences, Vol. 9 (July 1978), pp. 472-80.

Cochran, W. G. et al.
    "A Double Change-Over Design for Dairy Cattle Feeding Experiments"
    Journal of Dairy Science, Vol. 24 (November 1941), pp. 937-51.

Collins, Gwyn
    "On Methods: Analysis of Variance"
    Journal of Advertising Research, Vol. 1 (December 1961), pp. 40-6.

Dykstra, Otto, Jr.
    "Factorial Experimentation in Scheffe's Analysis of Variance for
    Paired Comparisons"
    Journal of the American Statistical Association, Vol. 53 (1958), pp.
    529-42.

Eisenhart, Churchill
    "The Assumptions Underlying the Analysis of Variance"
    Biometrics, Vol. 3 (March 1947), pp. 1-21.

Elston, R. C. and Bush, N.
    "The Hypotheses That can be Tested When There are Interactions in an
    Analysis of Variance Models"
    Biometrics, Vol. 20 (December 1964), pp. 681-98.

Feldt, Leonard S.
    "A Comparison of the Precision of Three Experimental Designs
    Employing a Concomitant Variable"
    Psychometrika, Vol. 23 (1954), pp. 335-53.

Glass, Gene V., Peckham, Percy D., and Sanders, James R.
    "Consequences of Failure to Meet Assumptions Underlying the Fixed
    Effects Analysis of Variance and Covariance"
    Review of Educational Research, Vol. 42, pp. 237-88.

Gleser, G. C., Cronbach, L. J., and Rajaratnam, N.
    "Generalizability of Scores Influenced by Multiple Sources of
    Variance"
    Psychometrika, Vol.30 (1965), pp. 395-418.

Greene, B. F. and Tukey, J. W.
"Complex Analyses of Variance: General Problems"
Psychometrika, Vol. 25 (June 1960), pp. 127-52.

Greenwald, Anthony G.
"Within-Subject Designs: To Use or Not to Use?"
Psychological Bulletin, Vol. 83 (March 1976), pp. 314-20.

Hoofnagle, William S.
"Experimental Designs in Measuring the Effectiveness of Promotion"
Journal of Marketing Research, Vol. II (May 1965), pp. 154-62.

Hummel, Thomas J. and Sligo, Joseph R.
"Empirical Comparisons of Univariate and Multivariate Analysis of
Variance Procedures"
Psychological Bulletin, Vol. 76 (July 1971), pp. 49-57.

Imhoff, J. P.
"Testing the Hypothesis of No Fixed Main-Effects in Scheffe's Mixed
Model"
Annals of Mathematical Statistics, Vol. 33 (1962), pp. 1085-95.

Jennings, E.
"Fixed Effects Analysis of Variance by Regression Analysis"
Multivariate Behavioral Research, Vol. 2 (January 1967), pp. 95-108.

Kepner, James L. and Robinson, David H.
"A Distribution-Free Rank Test for Ordered Alternatives in Randomised
Complete Block Designs"
Journal of the American Statistical Association, Vol. 79 (March
1984), pp. 212-7.

Kruskal, Joseph B.
"Analysis of Factorial Experiments by Estimating Monotone
Transformations of the Data"
Journal of the Royal Ststistical Society, Series B, Vol. 27 (1967),
pp. 251-63.

Mandel, John
"Non-Additivity in Two-Way Analysis of Variance"
Journal of the American Statistical Association, Vol. 56 (December
1961), pp. 878-88.

Melnick, E. L. and Shoaf, F. R.
"Multiple Regression Equals Analysis of Variance"
Journal of Advertising Research, Vol. 17 (June 1977), pp. 27-31.

Milligan, Glenn W. and McFillen, James M.
"Statistical Conclusion Validity in Experimental Designs Used in
Business Research"
Journal of Business Research, Vol. 12 (December 1984), pp. 437-62.

Rubin, Donald B.
"A Non-Iterative Algorithm for Least Squares Estimation of Missing
Values in Any Analysis of Variance Design"
Applied Statistics, Vol. 21 (1972), pp. 136-41.

Scheffe, H.
"The Analysis of Variance for Paired Comparisons"
Journal of the American Statistical Association, Vol. 47 (1952), pp.
381-400.

Seymour, R. B.
"Missing Data in Non-Linear Trend Analysis of Repeated Measurements
of the Same Individuals"
Journal of Educational Research, Vol. 54 (December 1960), pp. 141-4.

Speed, F. M. and Hocking, R. R.
"A Characterization of the GLM Sums of Squares"
Proceedings, Fifth Annual SAS Users' Group International Conference
(1980), pp. 215-8.

Steinhorst, R. K.
"Resolving Current Controversies in Analysis of Variance"
American Statistician, Vol. 36 (May 1982), pp. 138,9.

Uhl, K. P.
"Factorial Design--Aid to Management"
Journal of Marketing, Vol. 26 (January 1962), pp. 62-6.

Vaughan, Graham M. and Corballis, Michael C.
"Beyond Tests of Significance: Estimating Strengths of Effects in
Selected ANOVA Designs"
Psychological Bulletin, Vol. 72 (1969), pp. 204-13.

Wilkinson, G. N. and Rogers, C. E.
"Symbolic Description of Factorial Models for Analysis of Variance"
Applied Statistics, Vol. 22 (1973), pp. 392-9.

Wilks, S. S.
  "Certain Generalizations in the Analysis of Variance"
  Biometrika, Vol. 24 (November 1932), pp. 471-94.

179.03 ---------- Theory Re: Categorical or Ordinal Dependent Variables

        See also (sub)heading(s) 137.02, 185.

Clark, M. Louise
  "Robustness of One Way Analysis of Variance for Ordinal Data"
  University of Alabama (1984), unpublished doctoral dissertation.

Cochran, W. G.
  "Some Consequences When the Assumptions for the Analysis of Variance
  are Not Met"
  Biometrics, Vol. 3 (1947), pp. 22-38.

Light, R. J. and Margolin, B. H.
  "Analysis of Variance for Categorical Data"
  Journal of the American Statistical Association, Vol. 66 (September
  1971), pp. 534-44.

Lunney, Gerald H.
  "Using Analysis of Variance With a Dichotomous Variable: An Empirical
  Study"
  Journal of Educational Measurement, Vol. 7 (Winter 1970), pp. 263-9.

Mandeville, Garrett Kile
  A Monte Carlo Investigation of the Adequacy of Standard Analysis of
  Variance Test Procedures for Dependent Binary Variates
  University of Minnesota (1969), unpublished doctoral dissertation.

Margolin, B. H. and Light, R. J.
  "An Analysis of Variance for Categorical Data II: Small Sample
  Comparisons With Chi-Square and Other Competitors"
  Journal of the American Statistical Association, Vol. 69 (September
  1974), pp. 755-64.

179.04 ---------- Theory Re: Outliers in Factorial AOV

        See also (sub)heading(s) 134, 168.

Carroll, Raymond J.
  "Robust Methods for Factorial Experiments With Outliers"
  Applied Statistics, Vol. 29, No. 3 (1980), pp. 246-51.

John, J. A.
  "Outliers in Factorial Experiments"
  Applied Statistics, Vol. 27 (1978), pp. 111-9.

179.05 ---------- Theory Re: Latin Square Analysis of Variance

Banks, Seymour
  "Latin Square Experiments"
  Journal of Advertising Research, Vol. 5 (September 1965), pp. 37-46.

Bose, Raj Chandra
  "On the Application of Galois Fields to the Problem of the
  Construction of Hyper Graeco-Latin Squares"
  Sankhya, Vol. 3 (1938), pp. 328-38.

Bugelski, B. R.
  "A Note on Grant's Discussion of the Latin Square Principle in the
  Design and Analysis of Psychological Experiments"
  Psychological Bulletin, Vol. 49 (1949), pp. 49,50.

Kohli, Rajeev
  "Assessing Interaction Effects in Latin Square-Type Designs"
  International Journal of Research in Marketing, Vol. 5, No. 1 (1988),
  pp. 25-37.

Stevens, W. C.
  "The Completely Orthogonalized Latin Square"
  Annals of Eugenics, Vol. 9 (September 1938), pp. 82-93.

Youden, William J. and Hunter, J. Stuart
  "Partially Replicated Latin Squares"
  Biometrics, Vol. 11 (December 1955), pp. 399-405.

179.06 ---------- Theory Re: Nonorthogonal or Unbalanced Designs

Appelbaum, Mark I. and Cramer, Elliot M.
  "Some Problems in the Nonorthogonal Analysis of Variance"
  Psychological Bulletin, Vol. 81 (June 1974), pp. 335-43.

Burdick, D. S. and Herr, D. G.
"Counterexamples in Unbalanced Two-Way Analysis of Variance"
Communications in Statistics--Theory and Methods, Vol. A9, No. 2
(1980), pp. 231-41.

Burdick, Richard K.
"Statement of Hypotheses in the Analysis of Variance"
Journal of Marketing Research, Vol. XX (August 1983), pp. 320-4.

Herr, D. G. and Gaebelein, J.
"Nonorthogonal Two-Way Analysis of Variance"
Psychological Bulletin, Vol. 85 (January 1978), pp. 207-16.

Kutner, M. H.
"Hypothesis Testing in Linear Models (Eisenhart Model I)"
American Statistician, Vol. 28 (August 1974), pp. 98-100.

Li, Ching Chun
Analysis of Unbalanced Data: A Pre-Program Introduction
(Cambridge: Cambridge University Press, 1982), 144 pp.

Perreault, William D., Jr. and Darden, William R.
"Unequal Cell Sizes in Marketing Experiments: Use of the General
Linear Hypothesis"
Journal of Marketing Research, Vol. XII (August 1975), pp. 333-42.

Rawlings, Robert R., Jr.
"Note on Nonorthogonal Analysis of Variance"
Psychological Bulletin, Vol. 77 (May 1972), pp. 373,4.

Skillings, John H. and Mack, Gregory A.
"On the Use of a Friedman-Type Statistic in Balanced and Unbalanced
Block Designs"
Technometrics, Vol. 23 (May 1981), pp. 171-7.

Sorosky, Cindi G. and Mullet, Gary M.
"GENFRIED: A Program for Analysis of Unbalanced Block Data"
Journal of Marketing Research, Vol. XX (November 1983), 444,5.

Speed, F. M., Hocking, R. R., and Hackney, O. P.
"Methods of Analysis of Linear Models With Unbalanced Data"
Journal of the American Statistical Association, Vol. 73 (March
1978), pp. 105-12.

Steinhorst, R. K. and Everson, D. O.
"Nonorthogonal Analyses of Balance Data"
Proceedings, Fifth Annual SAS Users' Group International Conference
(1980), pp. 219-23.

Williams, John D.
"Two Way Fixed Effects Analysis of Variance With Disproportionate
Cell Frequencies"
Multivariate Behavioral Research, Vol. 7 (January 1972), pp. 67-83.

179.07 ---------- Logistic Transformation in Analysis of Variance

Bechtel, Gordon G. and O'Connor, P. J.
"Testing Micropreference Structures"
Journal of Marketing Research, Vol. XVI (May 1979), pp. 247-57.

Craig, C. Samuel and McCann, John M.
"Assessing Communication Effects on Energy Conservation"
Journal of Consumer Research, Vol. 5 (September 1978), pp. 82-8.

Domencich, Thomas and McFadden, Daniel
Urban Travel Demand: A Behavioral Analysis
(New York: North Holland Publishing Co., 1975).

Nelder, J. A. and Wedderburn, R. W. M.
"Generalized Linear Models"
Journal of the Royal Statistical Society, Series A, 135, Part 3
(1972), pp. 370-84.

179.08 ---------- Theory Re: Analysis of Means (ANOM)

Enrick, Norbert Lloyd
"Analysis of Means in Marketing Research"
Journal of the Academy of Marketing Science, Vol. 9 (Fall 1981), pp.
368-79.

180 ------------ ANALYSIS OF VARIANCE (ANOVA) APPLICATIONS -----------

See also (sub)heading(s) 179.

180.01 ---------- Applications of Factorial ANOVA Designs

Anderson, W. Thomas, Jr. and Golden, Linda L.
"Bank Promotion Strategy"
Journal of Advertising Research, Vol. 24 (April/May 1984), pp. 53-65.

Baker, Michael J. and Churchill, Gilbert A., Jr.
"The Impact of Physically Attractive Models on Advertising
Evaluations"
Journal of Marketing Research, Vol. XIV (November 1977), pp. 538-55.

Belk, Russell W.
"Situational Variables and Consumer Behavior"
Journal of Consumer Research, Vol. 2 (December 1975), pp. 157-64.

Bon, Jerome and Pras, Bernard
"Dissociation of the Roles of Buyer, Payer and Consumer"
International Journal of Research in Marketing, Vol. 1, No. 1 (1984),
pp. 7-16.

Brown, Thomas L. and Gentry, James W.
"Analysis of Risk and Risk-Reduction Strategies--A Multiple Product
Case"
Journal of the Academy of Marketing Science, Vol. 3 (Spring 1975),
pp. 148-60.

Burnkrant, Robert E. and Cousineau, Alain
"Informational and Normative Social Influence in Buyer Behavior"
Journal of Consumer Research, Vol. 2 (December 1975), pp. 206-15.

Busch, Paul and Wilson, David T.
"An Experimental Analysis of a Salesman's Expert and Referent Bases
of Social Power in the Buyer-Seller Dyad"
Journal of Marketing Research, Vol. XIII (February 1976), pp. 3-11.

Bush, Ronald F., Hair, Joseph F., Jr., and Solomon, Paul J.
"Consumers' Level of Prejudice and Response to Black Models in
Advertisements"
Journal of Marketing Research, Vol. XVI (August 1979), pp. 341-5.

Chebat, Jean-Charles and Picard, Jacques
"The Effects of Price and Message-Sidedness on Confidence in Product
and Advertisement With Personal Involvement as a Mediator Variable"
International Journal of Research in Marketing, Vol. 2, No. 2 (1985),
pp. 129-41.

Chevalier, Michel
"Increase in Sales Due to In-Store Display"
Journal of Marketing Research, Vol. XII (November 1975), pp. 426-31.

Clopton, Stephen W.
"Seller and Buying Firm Factors Affecting Industrial Buyers'
Negotiation Behavior and Outcomes"
Journal of Marketing Research, Vol. XXI (February 1984), pp. 39-53.

Craig, C. Samuel and McCann, John M.
"Item Nonresponse in Mail Surveys: Extent and Correlates"
Journal of Marketing Research, Vol. XV (May 1978), pp. 285-9.

Deighton, John
"The Interaction of Advertising and Evidence"
Journal of Consumer Research, Vol. 11 (December 1984), pp. 763-70.

Dholakia, Ruby Roy and Sternthal, Brian
"Highly Credible Sources: Persuasive Facilitators of Persuasive
Liabilities"
Journal of Consumer Research, Vol. 3 (March 1977), pp. 223-32.

Doyle, Peter and Fenwick, Ian
"Planning and Estimation in Advertising"
Journal of Marketing Research, Vol. XII (February 1975), pp. 1-6.

Droge, Cornelia and Germain, Richard
"The Impact of the Centralized Structuring of Logistics Activities on
Span of Control, Formalization and Performance"
Journal of the Academy of Marketing Science, Vol. 17 (Winter 1989),
pp. 83-9.

Eskin, Gerald J. and Baron, Penny H.
"Effects of Price and Advertising in Test-Market Experiments"
Journal of Marketing Research, Vol. XIV (November 1977), pp. 499-508.

Ford, Gary T. and Smith, Ruth Ann
"Inferential Beliefs in Consumer Evaluations: An Assessment of
Alternative Processing Strategies"
Journal of Consumer Research, Vol. 14 (December 1987), pp. 363-71.

Fritz, Nancy K.
"Claim Recall and Irritation in Television Commercials: An Advertising Effectiveness Study"
Journal of the Academy of Marketing Science, Vol. 7 (Winter-Spring 1979), pp. 1-13.

Goldberg, Marvin E., Gorn, Gerald J., and Gibson, Wendy
"TV Messages for Snack and Breakfast Foods: Do They Influence Children's Preferences?"
Journal of Consumer Research, Vol. 5 (September 1978), pp. 73-81.

Graham, John L.
"A Comparison of Japanese and American Business Negotiations"
International Journal of Research in Marketing, Vol. 1, No. 1 (1984), pp. 51-68.

Hampton, Gerald M.
"Perceived Risk in Buying Products Made Abroad by American Firms"
Journal of the Academy of Marketing Science, Vol. 5, Special Proceedings Issue (1977), pp. 45-8.

Hanna, Nessim and Wagle, John S.
"Who is Your Satisfied Customer?"
Journal of Consumer Marketing, Vol. 6 (Winter 1989), pp. 53-61.

Hermann, Peter and Locander, William B.
"The Effect of Self-Confidence and Anxiety on Risk Reduction Strategies for an Innovative Product"
Journal of the Academy of Marketing Science, Vol. 5 (Winter-Spring 1977), pp. 113-25.

Hirschman, Elizabeth C.
"People as Products: Analysis of a Complex Marketing Exchange"
Journal of Marketing, Vol. 51 (January 1987), pp. 98-108.

Hite, Robert E. and Bellizzi, Joseph A.
"Consumers' Attitudes Toward Accountants, Lawyers, and Physicians With Respect to Advertising Professional Services"
Journal of Advertising Research, Vol. 26 (June/July 1986), pp. 45-54.

Hoover, Robert J., Green, Robert T., and Saegert, Joel
"A Cross-National Study of Perceived Risk"
Journal of Marketing, Vol. 42 (July 1978), pp. 103-8.

Hornik, Jacob
"Impact of Pre-Call Request Form and Gender Interaction on Response to a Mail Survey"
Journal of Marketing Research, Vol. XIX (February 1982), pp. 144-51.

Houston, Michael J. and Rothschild, Michael L.
"Policy-Related Experiments on Information Provision: A Normative Model and Explication"
Journal of Marketing Research, Vol. XVII (November 1980), pp. 432-49.

Huppertz, John W., Arenson, Sidney J., and Evans, Richard H.
"An Application of Equity Theory to Buyer-Seller Exchange Situations"
Journal of Marketing Research, Vol. XV (May 1978), pp. 250-60.

Jaffe, Lynn J. and Berger, Paul D.
"Impact on Purchase Intent of Sex-Role Identity and Product Positioning"
Psychology and Marketing, Vol. 5 (Fall 1988), pp. 259-71.

Jolibert, Alain J. P. and Peterson, Robert A.
"Causal Attributions of Product Failure: An Exploratory Investigation"
Journal of the Academy of Marketing Science, Vol. 4 (Winter-Spring 1976), pp. 446-55.

Kisielius, Jolita and Sternthal, Brian
"Detecting and Explaining Vividness Effects in Attitudinal Judgments"
Journal of Marketing Research, Vol. XXI (February 1984), pp. 54-64.

Labrecque, David P.
"A Response Rate Experiment Using Mail Questionnaires"
Journal of Marketing, Vol. 42 (October 1978), pp. 82-3.

Lamb, Charles W., Pride, William M., and Pletcher, Barbara A.
"Should the Competing Brand be Illustrated in a Comparative Advertisement"
Journal of the Academy of Marketing Science, Vol. 6 (Summer 1978), pp. 176-86.

Lang, Larry R. and Marks, Ronald B.
"Consumer Response to Advertisements for Legal Services: An Empirical Analysis"
Journal of the Academy of Marketing Science, Vol. 8 (Fall 1980), pp. 357-73.

Locander, William B. and Spivey, W. Austin
"A Functional Approach to Attitude Measurement"
Journal of Marketing Research, Vol. XV (November 1978), pp. 576-87.

Lysonski, Steven, Singer, Alan, and Wilemon, David
"Coping With Environmental Uncertainty and Boundary Spanning in the
Product Manager's Role"
Journal of Consumer Marketing, Vol. 6 (Spring 1989), pp. 33-44.

Meyers-Levy, Joan
"Priming Effects on Product Judgments: A Hemispheric Interpretation"
Journal of Consumer Research, Vol. 16 (June 1989), pp. 76-86.

Miller, Joseph H., Jr. and Busch, Paul
"Host Selling vs. Premium TV Commercials: An Experimental Evaluation
of Their Influence on Children"
Journal of Marketing Research, Vol. XVI (August 1979), pp. 323-32.

Miller, Kenneth E. and Ginter, James L.
"An Investigation of Situational Variation in Brand Choice Behavior
and Attitude"
Journal of Marketing Research, Vol. XVI (February 1979), pp. 111-23.

Mizerski, Richard W.
"Casual Complexity: A Measure of Consumer Casual Attribution"
Journal of Marketing Research, Vol. XV (May 1978), pp. 220-8.

Mizerski, Richard W. and Settle, Robert B.
"The Influence of Social Character on Preference for Social Versus
Objective Information in Advertising"
Journal of Marketing Research, Vol. XVI (November 1979), pp. 552-8.

Monroe, Kent B.
"The Influence of Price Differences and Brand Familiarity on Brand
Preferences"
Journal of Consumer Research, Vol. 3 (June 1976), pp. 42-9.

Murphy, Patrick E., Kangun, Norman, and Locander, William B.
"Environmentally Concerned Consumers--Racial Variations"
Journal of Marketing, Vol. 42 (October 1978), pp. 61-6.

O'Guinn, Thomas C., Faber, Ronald J., and Imperia, Giovanna
"Subcultural Influences on Family Decisionmaking"
Psychology and Marketing, Vol. 3 (Winter 1986), pp. 305-17.

Park, C. Whan, Assael, Henry, and Chaiy, Seoil
"Mediating Effects of Trial and Learning on Involvement-Associated
Characteristics"
Journal of Consumer Marketing, Vol. 4 (Summer 1987), pp. 25-34.

Peterson, Robert A. and Kerin, Roger A.
"The Female Role in Advertisements: Some Experimental Evidence"
Journal of Marketing, Vol. 41 (October 1977), pp. 59-63.

Pras, Bernard and Summers, John
"Perceived Risk and Composition Models for Multiattribute Decisions"
Journal of Marketing Research, Vol. XV (August 1978), pp. 429-37.

Render, Barry and O'Connor, Thomas S.
"The Influence of Price, Store Name, and Brand Name on Perception of
Product Quality"
Journal of the Academy of Marketing Science, Vol. 4 (Fall 1976), pp.
722-30.

Rethans, Arno J., Swasy, John L., Marks, Lawrence J.
"Effects of Television Commercial Repetition, Receiver Knowledge, and
Commercial Length: A Test of the Two-Factor Model"
Journal of Marketing Research, Vol. XXIII (February 1986), pp. 50-61.

Roering, Kenneth J. and Block, Carl E.
"Population Density and Type of Purchase as Explanatory Variables in
Consumer Information Search"
Journal of the Academy of Marketing Science, Vol. 4 (Fall 1976), pp.
731-41.

Sharits, Dean and Lammers, H. Bruce
"Perceived Attributes of Models in Prime-Time and Daytime Television
Commercials: A Person Perception Approach"
Journal of Marketing Research, Vol. XX (February 1983), pp. 64-73.

Shimp, Terence A., Dyer, Robert F., and Divita, Salvatore F.
"An Experimental Test of the Harmful Effects of Premium-Oriented
Commercials on Children"
Journal of Consumer Research, Vol.3 (June 1976), pp. 1-11.

Singer, Eleanor
"The Effect of Informed Consent Procedures on Respondents' Reactions
to Surveys"
Journal of Consumer Research, Vol. 5 (June 1978), pp. 49-57.

Singer, Eleanor
"Informed Consent: Consequences for Response Rate and Response
Quality in Social Surveys"
American Sociological Review, Vol. 43 (1978), pp. 144-62.

Smith, Robert E. and Hunt, Shelby D.
"Attributional Processes and Effects in Promotional Situations"
Journal of Consumer Research, Vol. 5 (December 1979), pp. 149-58.

Steinberg, Sandon A. and Yalch, Richard F.
"When Eating Begets Buying: The Effects of Food Samples on Obese and
Nonobese Shoppers"
Journal of Consumer Research, Vol. 4 (March 1978), pp. 243-51.

Swinyard, William R.
"The Interaction Between Comparative Advertising and Copy Claim
Variation"
Journal of Marketing Research, Vol. XVIII (May 1981), pp. 175-86.

Swinyard, William R. and Coney, Kenneth A.
"Promotional Effects on a High- Versus Low-Involvement Electorate"
Journal of Consumer Research, Vol. 5 (June 1978), pp. 41-8.

Tse, David K., Lee, Kam-hon, Vertinsky, Ilan, and Wehrung, Donald A.
"Does Culture Matter? A Cross-Cultural Study of Executives' Choice,
Decisiveness, and Risk Adjustment in International Marketing"
Journal of Marketing, Vol. 52 (October 1988), pp. 81-95.

Tybout, Alice M.
"Relative Effectiveness of Three Behavioral Influence Strategies as
Supplements to Persuasion in a Marketing Context"
Journal of Marketing Research, Vol. XV (May 1978), pp. 229-42.

Varadarajan, P.
"Product Diversity and Firm Performance: An Empirical Investigation"
Journal of Marketing, Vol. 50 (July 1986), pp. 43-57.

Weijo, Richard and Lawton, Leigh
"Message Repetition, Experience and Motivation"
Psychology and Marketing, Vol. 3 (Fall 1986), pp. 165-79.

Weinberger, Marc G. and Brown, Stephen W.
"A Difference in Informational Influences: Services vs. Goods"
Journal of the Academy of Marketing Science, Vol. 5 (Fall 1977), pp.
389-402.

White, Phillip and Cundiff, Edward W.
"Assessing the Quality of Industrial Products"
Journal of Marketing, Vol. 42 (January 1978), pp. 80-6.

Williams, Robert H.
"The Motivation for Grocery Store Loyal Behavior With Marketing
Implications"
Journal of the Academy of Marketing Science, Vol. 6 (Winter-Spring
1978), pp. 61-79.

Winter, Frederick W.
"Laboratory Measurement of Response to Consumer Information"
Journal of Marketing Research, Vol. XII (November 1975), pp. 390-401.

Wright, Peter
"Consumer Choice Strategies: Simplifying vs. Optimizing"
Journal of Marketing Research, Vol. XII (February 1975), pp. 60-7.

180.02 ---------- Applications of Latin Square Analysis of Variance

        See also (sub)heading(s) 179.05.

Burgoyne, D. G. and Johnston, C. B.
"Are Shelf Space and Shelf Location Really Important?"
Business Quarterly (Summer 1968), pp. 56-60.

Cox, Keith
"The Responsiveness of Food Sales to Shelf Space Changes in
Supermarkets"
Journal of Marketing Research, Vol. I (May 1965), pp. 63-7.

Dickson, John P.
"Coordinating Images Between Media"
Journal of Advertising Research, Vol. 12 (February 1972), pp. 25-8.

Domininck, B. A., Jr.
"An Illustration of the Use of the Latin Square in Measuring the
Effectiveness of Retail Merchandising Practices"
Methods of Research in Marketing
(Ithaca, NY: Cornell University, Department of Agricultural
Economics, Paper No. 2, June 1952), p. 68.

Gatty, Ronald
    "How to Control the Duration of a Sales Test"
    Journal of Advertising Research, Vol. 5 (March 1965), pp. 18-22.

Henderson, Peter L.
    "Application of the Double Change-Over Design to Measure Carryover
    Effects of Treatments in Controlled Experiments"
    in Methods of Research in Marketing, Paper No. 3
    (Ithaca, NY: Cornell University, 1952).

Henderson, Peter, Hind, James, and Brown, Sidney
    "Sales Effects of Two Campaign Themes"
    Journal of Advertising Research, Vol. 1 (December 1961), pp. 2-11.

Hoofnagle, W. S.
    "Experimental Designs in Measuring the Effectiveness of Promotion"
    Journal of Marketing Research, Vol. II (May 1965), pp. 154-62.

Hoofnagle, William S.
    "The Effectiveness of Advertising for Farm Products"
    Journal of Advertising Research, Vol. 3 (December 1963), pp. 2-6.

Jessen, R. J.
    "A Switch-Over Experimental Design to Measure Advertising Effect"
    Journal of Advertising Research, Vol. 1 (March 1961), pp. 15-22.

Kotzan, Jeffrey A. and Evanson, Robert V.
    "Responsiveness of Drug Store Sales to Shelf Space Allocations"
    Journal of Marketing Research, Vol. VI (November 1969), pp. 465-9.

Lucas, H. L.
    "Extra-Period Latin Square Change-Over Design"
    Journal of Dairy Science, Vol. 40 (March 1957), pp. 225-39.

MacGregor, Murray
    "Uniformity Trial Experiments in Marketing Research"
    Methods of Research in Marketing, Paper No. 6, Cornell University
    (September 1958).

Mitchell, Andrew A. and Olson, Jerry C.
    "Are Product Attribute Beliefs the Only Mediator of Advertising
    Effects on Brand Attitude?"
    Journal of Marketing Research, Vol. XVIII (August 1981), pp. 318-32.

Ray, Michael L.
    "Can Order Effect in Copy Tests Indicate Long Term Advertising
    Effect?"
    Journal of Advertising Research, Vol. 9 (March 1969), pp. 45-52.

Solomon, Paul J., Bush, Ronald F., and Hair, Joseph F., Jr.
    "White and Black Consumer Sales Response to Black Models"
    Journal of Marketing Research, Vol. XIII (November 1976), pp. 431-4.

Twedt, D. W.
    "A Cash Register Test of Sales Effectiveness"
    Journal of Marketing, Vol. 26 (April 1962), pp. 41-3.

Woodside, Arch G. and Waddle, Gerald L.
    "Sales Effects of In-Store Advertising"
    Journal of Advertising Research, Vol. 15 (June 1975), pp. 29-33.

180.03 ---------- Unclassified ANOVA Applications

Ford, N. M.
    "Questionnaire Appearance and Response Rates in Mail Surveys"
    Journal of Advertising Research, Vol. 8 (September 1968), pp. 43-5.

Gross, Irwin
    "How Many Ads Does It Pay to Pretest"
    Tenth Meeting of the ARF Operations Research Discussion Group
    (New York: Advertising Research Foundation, March 10, 1964), pp. 1-18.

Kollat, David T. and Willett, Ronald P.
    "Customer Impulse Purchasing Behavior"
    Journal of Marketing Research, Vol. IV (February 1967), pp. 21-31.

Willingham, Warren W. and Jones, Marshall B.
    "On the Identification of Halo Through Analysis of Variance"
    Educational and Psychological Measurement, Vol. 18 (1958), pp. 403-7.

181 ------------------ FRACTIONAL FACTORIAL DESIGNS ------------------
        See also (sub)heading(s) 179.

181.01 ---------- Books Re: Fractional Factorial Designs

Hunter, J. Stuart
    Fractional Factorial Designs
    (Pittsburgh: Westinghouse Learning Press, 1968).

National Bureau of Standards
    Fractional Factorial Experimental Designs for Factors at Two Levels
    NBS Applied Mathematical Series, No. 48 (1957).

181.02 ---------- Theory Re: Fractional Factorial Designs

Addelman, Sidney
    "Recent Developments in the Design of Factorial Experiments"
    Journal of the American Statistical Association, Vol. 67 (March
    1972), pp. 103-11.

Addelman, Sidney
    "Techniques for Constructing Fractional Replicate Plans"
    Journal of the American Statistical Association, Vol. 58 (1963), pp.
    45-71.

Addelman, S.
    "Orthogonal Main-Effect Plans for Asymmetrical Factorial Experiments"
    Technometrics, Vol. 4 (1962), pp. 21-46.

Addelman, S.
    "Symmetric and Asymmetric Fractional Factorial Plans"
    Technometrics, Vol. 4 (February 1962), pp. 47-58.

Box, G. E. P. and Hunter, J. S.
    "The 2 Sub K-P Fractional Factorial Designs"
    Technometrics, Vol. 3 (August 1961), Part I, pp. 311-51 and Part II,
    pp. 449-58.

Connor, W. S. and Zelen, M.
    "Fractional Factorial Experiment Designs for Factors at Three Levels"
    Applied Mathematics Series
    U.S. Department of Commerce, National Bureau of Standards (1959).

Green, Paul E.
    "On the Design of Choice Experiments Involving Multifactor
    Alternatives"
    Journal of Consumer Research, Vol. 1 (September 1974), pp. 61-8.

Green, P. E.
    "On the Design of Multiattribute Choice Experiments Involving Large
    Numbers of Factors and Factor Levels"
    in Ward, S. and Wright, P. (editors)
    Advances in Consumer Research, Volume I
    (Urbana, IL: Association for Consumer Research, 1974), pp. 228-41.

Green, Paul E., Carroll, J. D., and Carmone, F. J.
    "Some New Types of Fractional Factorial Designs for Marketing
    Experiments"
    in Sheth, Jagdish N. (editor)
    Research in Marketing, Vol. 1
    (Greenwich, CT: JAI Press, 1978).

Hahn, G. J. and Shapiro, S. S.
    "A Catalog and Computer Program for the Design and Analysis of
    Symmetric and Asymmetric Fractional Factorial Experiments"
    Technical Report No. 66-C-165
    General Electric Research and Development Center, Schenectady, NY
    (1966).

Holland, Charles W. and Cravens, David W.
    "Fractional Factorial Experimental Designs in Marketing Research"
    Journal of Marketing Research, Vol. X (August 1973), pp. 270-6.

Rechtschaffner, R. L.
    "Saturated Fractions of 2N and 3N Factorial Designs"
    Technometrics, Vol. 9 (November 1967), pp. 569-76.

United States Department of Commerce, National Bureau of Standards
    "Fractional Factorial Experiment Designs for Factors at Two Levels"
    Applied Mathematics, Series 48 (April 15, 1957).

Wind, Yoram, Grashof, John F., and Goldhar, Joel D.
    "Market-Based Guidelines for Design of Industrial Products"
    Journal of Marketing, Vol. 42 (July 1978), pp. 27-37.

181.03 ---------- Applications of Fractional Factorial Designs

Bocker, Franz
  "Children's Influence on Their Mothers' Preferences: A New Approach"
  International Journal of Research in Marketing, Vol. 3, No. 1 (1986),
  pp. 39-52.

Curhan, Ronald C.
  "The Effects of Merchandising and Temporary Promotional Activities on
  the Sales of Fresh Fruits and Vegetables in Supermarkets"
  Journal of Marketing Research, Vol. XI (August 1974), pp. 286-94.

Ettenson, Richard and Wagner, Janet
  "Retail Buyers' Saleability Judgments: A Comparison of Information
  Use Across Three Levels of Experience"
  Journal of Retailing, Vol. 62 (Spring 1986), pp. 41-63.

Malhotra, Naresh K.
  "Structural Reliability and Stability of Nonmetric Conjoint Analysis"
  Journal of Marketing Research, Vol. XIX (May 1982), pp. 199-207.

182 ---------------- ANALYSIS OF COVARIANCE (ANCOVA)   ----------------
    See also (sub)heading(s) 133.08, 179.

182.01 ---------- Books Re: Analysis of Covariance

Wildt, Albert R. and Ahtola, Olli T.
  Analysis of Covariance
  (Beverly Hills, CA: Sage Publications, Inc.).

182.02 ---------- Theory Re: Analysis of Covariance

Atiqullah, M.
  "The Robustness of Covariance Analysis of a One-Way Classification"
  Biometrika, Vol. 51, Nos. 3,4 (1964), pp. 365-72.

Barrow, L. C., Jr.
  "On Methods: New Uses of Covariance Analysis"
  Journal of Advertising Research, Vol. 7 (December 1967), pp. 49-54.

Bentler, P. M. and Bonett, Douglas G.
  "Significance Tests and Goodness-of-Fit in the Analysis of Covariance
  Structures"
  Psychological Bulletin, Vol. 88 (1980), pp. 588-606.

Chamberlain, G.
  "Analysis of Covariance With Qualitative Data"
  Review of Economic Studies, Vol. 47 (1980), pp. 225-38.

Clapper, James
  Factorial Covariance Analysis Within a Decision Framework
  University of Massachusetts (1974), unpublished Ph.D. dissertation.

Cochran, William G.
  "Analysis of Covariance: Its Nature and Uses"
  Biometrics, Vol. 13 (September 1957), pp. 261-81.

Green, Paul E. and Tull, Donald S.
  "Covariance Analysis in Marketing Experimentation"
  Journal of Advertising Research, Vol. 6 (June 1966), pp. 45-53.

Henderson, Peter L., Brown, Sidney E., and Hind, James F.
  "On Methods: Nonquantified Adjustment of Seasonality in Time Series
  Data"
  Journal of Advertising Research, Vol. 4 (June 1964), pp. 38-44.

Hicks, C. R.
  "The Analysis of Covariance"
  Industrial Quality Control, Vol. 22 (December 1965), pp. 282-6.

Sorbom, Dag
  "An Alternative to the Methodology for Analysis of Covariance"
  Psychometrika, Vol. 43, No. 3 (1978), pp. 381-96.

Joreskog, K. G.
  "Analyzing Psychological Data by Structural Analysis of Covariance
  Matrices"
  in Krantz, D. H., Luce, R. D., Atkinson, R. C., and Suppes, P.
  (editors)
  Contemporary Developments in Mathematical Psychology
  (San Francisco: W. H. Freeman and Co., 1974), pp. 1-56.

Joreskog, K. G.
  "A General Method for Analysis of Covariance Structures"
  Biometrika, Vol. 57 (1970), pp. 239-51.

Smith, H. Fairfield
  "Interpretation of Adjusted Treatment Means and Regressions in
  Analysis of Covariance"
  Biometrics, Vol. 13 (September 1957), pp. 281-308.

182.03 ---------- Applications of Analysis of Covariance

Allison, Neil K.
  "A Psychometric Development of a Test for Consumer Alienation From
  the Marketplace"
  Journal of Marketing Research, Vol. XV (November 1978), pp. 565-75.

Bellizzi, Joseph and Hite, Robert E.
  "Convenience Consumption and Role Overload Convenience"
  Journal of the Academy of Marketing Science, Vol. 14 (Winter 1986),
  pp. 1-9.

Burke, Marian C. and Edell, Julie A.
  "Ad Reactions Over Time: Capturing Changes in the Real World"
  Journal of Consumer Research, Vol. 13 (June 1986), pp. 114-8.

Buyukkurt, B. Kemal
    "Integration of Serially Sampled Price Information: Modeling and Some
    Findings"
    Journal of Consumer Research, Vol. 13 (December 1986), pp. 357-73.

Celsi, Richard L. and Olson, Jerry C.
    "The Role of Involvement in Attention and Comprehension Processes"
    Journal of Consumer Research, Vol. 15 (September 1988), pp. 210-24.

Childers, Terry L. and Houston, Michael J.
    "Conditions for a Picture-Superiority Effect on Consumer Memory"
    Journal of Consumer Research, Vol. 11 (September 1984), pp. 643-54.

Craig, C. Samuel and McCann, John M.
    "Assessing Communication Effects on Energy Conservation"
    Journal of Consumer Research, Vol. 5 (September 1978), pp. 82-8.

Craig, C. Samuel, Sternthal, Brian, and Leavitt, Clark
    "Advertising Wearout: An Experimental Analysis"
    Journal of Marketing Research, Vol. XIII (November 1976), pp. 365-72.

Duker, Jacob M. and Tucker, Lewis R., Jr.
    "Womens Lib-ers Versus Independent Women: A Study of Preferences for
    Women's Roles in Advertisements"
    Journal of Marketing Research, Vol. XIV (November 1977), pp. 469-75.

Dyer, Robert F. and Kuehl, Phillip G.
    "A Longitudinal Study of Corrective Advertising"
    Journal of Marketing Research, Vol. XV (February 1978), pp. 39-48.

Dyer, Robert F. and Shimp, Terence A.
    "Reactions to Legal Advertising"
    Journal of Advertising Research, Vol. 20 (April 1980), pp. 43-51.

Edell, Julie A. and Keller, Kevin Lane
    "The Information Processing of Coordinated Media Campaigns"
    Journal of Marketing Research, Vol. XXVI (May 1989), pp. 149-63.

Edell, Julie A. and Staelin, Richard A.
    "The Information Processing of Pictures in Print Advertisements"
    Journal of Consumer Research, Vol. 10 (June 1983), pp. 45-61.

Golden, Linda L.
    "Consumer Reactions to Explicit Brand Comparisons in Advertisements"
    Journal of Marketing Research, Vol. XVI (November 1979), pp. 517-32.

Gutman, Jonathan
    "The Impact of Advertising at the Time of Consumption"
    Journal of Advertising Research, Vol. 22 (August/September 1982), pp.
    35-40.

Harmon, Robert R. and Coney, Kenneth A.
    "The Persuasive Effect of Source Credibility in Buy and Lease
    Situations"
    Journal of Marketing Research, Vol. XIX (May 1982), pp. 255-60.

Hastak, Manoj
    "Role of Unsupported Brand Evaluation Thoughts in the Persuasion
    Process"
    Psychology and Marketing, Vol. 4 (Winter 1987), pp. 323-37.

Hastak, Manoj and Olson, Jerry C.
    "Assessing the Role of Brand-Related Cognitive Responses as Mediators
    of Communication Effects on Cognitive Structure"
    Journal of Consumer Research, Vol. 15 (March 1989), pp. 444-56.

Jones, Wesley H. and Linda, Gerald
    "Multiple Criteria Effects in a Mail Survey Experiment"
    Journal of Marketing Research, Vol. XV (May 1978), pp. 280-4.

Keller, Kevin Lane
    "Memory Factors in Advertising: The Effect of Advertising Retrieval
    Cues on Brand Evaluations"
    Journal of Consumer Research, Vol. 14 (December 1987), pp. 316-33.

Kennedy, John R.
    "The Effect of Display Location on the Sales and Pilferage of
    Cigarettes"
    Journal of Marketing Research, Vol. VII (May 1970), pp. 210-5.

LaBarbera, Priscilla A.
    "Overcoming a No-Reputation Liability Through Documentation and
    Advertising Regulation"
    Journal of Marketing Research, Vol. XIX (May 1982), pp. 223-8.

Leigh, James H. and Futrell, Charles M.
    "From the Trenches to the Command Post: Perceptual and Attitudinal
    Differences Among Levels in the Marketing Management Hierarchy"
    Journal of Business Research, Vol. 13 (December 1985), pp. 511-36.

Leigh, Thomas W., Rethans, Arno J., and Whitney, Tamatha Reichenbach
"Role Portrayals of Women in Advertising: Cognitive Responses and
Advertising Effectiveness"
Journal of Advertising Research, Vol. 27 (October/November 1987), pp.
54-63.

Mitchell, Andrew A.
"The Effect of Verbal and Visual Components of Advertisements on
Brand Attitudes and Attitude Toward the Advertisement"
Journal of Consumer Research, Vol. 13 (June 1986), pp. 12-24.

Mitchell, Andrew A. and Olson, Jerry C.
"Are Product Attribute Beliefs the Only Mediator of Advertising
Effects on Brand Attitude?"
Journal of Marketing Research, Vol. XVIII (August 1981), pp. 318-32.

Paksoy, Christie, Wilkinson, J. B., and Mason, J. Barry
"Learning and Carryover Effects in Retail Experimentation"
Journal of the Market Research Society, Vol. 27 (April 1985), pp.
109-29.

Reid, Lawrence N. and Soley, Lawrence C.
"Decorative Models and the Readership of Magazine Ads"
Journal of Advertising Research, Vol. 23 (April-May 1983), pp. 27-32.

Schurr, Paul H. and Ozanne, Julie L.
"Influences on Exchange Processes: Buyers' Preconceptions of a
Seller's Trustworthiness and Bargaining Toughness"
Journal of Consumer Research, Vol. 11 (March 1985), pp. 939-53.

Sewall, Murphy A. and Sarel, Dan
"Characteristics of Radio Commercials and Their Recall Effectiveness"
Journal of Marketing, Vol. 50 (January 1986), pp. 52-60.

Sexton, Richard J. and Sexton, Terri A.
"Theoretical and Methodological Perspectives on Consumer Response to
Electricity Information"
Journal of Consumer Affairs, Vol. 21 (Winter 1987), pp. 238-57.

Shimp, Terence A., Dyer, Robert F., and Divita, Salvatore F.
"An Experimental Test of the Harmful Effects of Premium-Oriented
Commercials on Children"
Journal of Consumer Research, Vol. 3 (June 1976), pp. 1-11.

Sparkman, Richard M., Jr. and Locander, William B.
"Attribution Theory and Advertising Effectiveness"
Journal of Consumer Research, Vol. 7 (December 1980), pp. 219-24.

Spivey, W. Austin, Munson, J. Michael, and Locander, William B.
"Improving the Effectiveness of Persuasive Communications: Matching
Message With Functional Profile"
Journal of Business Research, Vol. 11 (June 1983), pp. 257-69.

Swinyard, William R. and Ray, Michael L.
"Advertising-Selling Interactions: An Attribution Theory Experiment"
Journal of Marketing Research, Vol. XIV (November 1977), pp. 509-16.

Wilkinson, J. B., Mason, J. Barry, and Paksoy, Christie H.
"Assessing the Impact of Short-Term Supermarket Strategy Variables"
Journal of Marketing Research, Vol. XIX (February 1982), pp. 72-86.

Zeithaml, Valarie A.
"The New Demographics and Market Fragmentation"
Journal of Marketing, Vol. 49 (Summer 1985), pp. 64-75.

182.04 ---------- Computer Programs for ANCOVA

Calantone, Roger J.
"IBANCOVA: A Bayesian ANCOVA Program"
Journal of Marketing Research, Vol. XX (November 1983), pp. 446,7.

183 -------------------- REPEATED MEASURES DESIGNS --------------------
            See also (sub)heading(s) 179, 191.03.

183.01 ---------- Theory Re: Repeated Measures Designs

Greenhouse, S. W. and Geisser, S.
"On Methods in the Analysis of Profile Data"
Psychometrika, Vol. 24 (1959), pp. 95-112.

LaTour, Stephen A. and Miniard, Paul W.
"The Misuse of Repeated Measures Analysis in Marketing Research"
Journal of Marketing Research, Vol. XX (February 1983), pp. 45-57.

McCall, Robert B. and Appelbaum, Mark I.
"Bias in the Analysis of Repeated-Measures Designs: Some Alternative
Approaches"
Child Development, Vol. 44 (1973), pp. 401-15.

Shaffer, Juliet Popper
"The Analysis of Variance Mixed Model With Allocated Observations:
Application to Repeated Measurement Designs"
Journal of the American Statistical Association, Vol. 76 (September
1981), pp. 607-11.

183.02 ---------- Theory Re: Multivariate Repeated Measures Designs

Bock, R. Darrell
"Multivariate Analysis of Variance of Repeated Measurements"
in Harris, C. W. (editor)
Problems in Measuring Change
(Madison, WI: The University of Wisconsin Press, 1963).

Davidson, Michael L.
"Univariate Versus Multivariate Tests in Repeated-Measures
Experiments"
Psychological Bulletin, Vol. 77 (November 1972), pp. 446-52.

Finn, Jeremy
"Multivariate Analysis of Repeated Measures Data"
Multivariage Behavioral Research, Vol. 4 (July 1969), pp. 391-410.

Lewis, Charles and Van Knippenberg, Carina
"Estimation and Model Comparisons for Repeated Measures Data"
Psychological Bulletin, Vol. 96 (July 1984), pp. 182-94.

Olsen, Chester L.
"On Choosing a Test Statistic in Multivariate Analysis of Variance"
Psychological Bulletin, Vol. 82 (July 1976), pp. 579-86.

Poor, David S.
"Analysis of Variance for Repeated Measures Designs: Two Approaches"
Psychological Bulletin, Vol. 80 (March 1973), pp. 204-9.

Ryan, Michael
"Analyzing Models With Multiple-Outcome Variables"
Decision Sciences, Vol. 4 (Fall 1978), pp. 596-611.

Stevens, James P.
"Comment on Olsen: Choosing a Test Statistic in Multivariate Analysis
of Variance"
Psychological Bulletin, Vol. 86 (March 1979), pp. 355-60.

Timm, Neil H.
"Multivariate Analysis of Variance of Repeated Measurements"
in Krishnaiah, P. R. (editor)
Handbook of Statistics, Volume 1
(New York: North-Holland, 1980), pp. 41-84.

183.03 ---------- Statistical Tests in Repeated Measures Designs

Collier, Raymond O., Jr., Baker, Frank B., Mandeville, Garrett K., and
Hayes, Thomas F.
"Estimates of Test Size for Several Test Procedures Based on
Conventional Variance Ratios in the Repeated Measures Design"
Psychometrika, Vol. 32 (September 1967), pp. 339-53.

Huynh, Huynh
"Some Approximate Tests for Repeated Measurements Designs"
Psychometrika, Vol. 43 (June 1978), pp. 161-75.

Huynh, Huynh and Feldt, Leonard S.
"Estimation of the Box Correction for Degrees of Freedom From Sample
Data in the Randomized Block and Split-Plot Designs"
Journal of Educational Statistics, Vol. 1 (1976), pp. 69-82.

Huynh, Huynh and Feldt, Leonard S.
"Conditions Under Which Mean Square Ratios in Repeated Measurements
Designs Have Exact F Distributions"
Journal of the American Statistical Association, Vol. 65 (December
1970), pp. 1582-9.

Kepner, James L. and Robinson, David H.
"A Distribution-Free Rank Test for Ordered Alternatives in Randomised
Complete Block Designs"
Journal of the American Statistical Association, Vol. 79 (March
1984), pp. 212-7.

183.04 ---------- Applications of Repeated Measures Designs

Anderson, J. C.
"The Validity of Haire's Shopping List Projective Technique"
Journal of Marketing Research, Vol. XV (November 1978), pp. 644-9.

Armstrong, Gary M., Gurol, Metin N., and Russ, Frederick A.
"Detecting and Correcting Deceptive Advertising"
Journal of Consumer Research, Vol. 6 (December 1979), pp. 237-46.

Baker, Michael J. and Churchill, Gilbert A., Jr.
"The Impact of Physically Attractive Models on Advertising
Evaluations"
Journal of Marketing Research, Vol. XIV (November 1977), pp. 538-55.

Bettman, James R., Capon, Noel, and Lutz, Richard J.
"Cognitive Algebra in Multi-Attribute Attitude Models"
Journal of Marketing Research, Vol. XII (May 1975), pp. 151-64.

Bettman, James R., Capon, Noel, and Lutz, Richard J.
"Multi-Attribute Measurement Models and Multi-Attribute Attitude
Theory: A Test of Construct Validity"
Journal of Consumer Research, Vol. 1 (March 1975), pp. 1-15.

Blaylock, Bruce K.
"Risk Perception: Evidence of an Interactive Process"
Journal of Business Research, Vol. 13 (June 1985), pp. 207-21.

Burns, Alvin C. and Granbois, Donald H.
"Factors Moderating the Resolution of Preference Conflict in Family
Automobile Purchasing"
Journal of Marketing Research, Vol. XIV (February 1977), pp. 77-86.

Bush, Ronald F., Hair, Joseph F., Jr., and Solomon, Paul J.
"Consumers' Level of Prejudice and Response to Black Models in
Advertisements"
Journal of Marketing Research, Vol. XVI (August 1979), pp. 341-5.

Charlton, P. and Ehrenberg, A. S. C.
"An Experiment in Brand Choice"
Journal of Marketing Research, Vol. XIII (May 1976), pp. 153-60.

Craig, C. Samuel, Sternthal, Brian, and Leavitt, Clark
"Advertising Wearout: An Experimental Analysis"
Journal of Marketing Research, Vol. XIII (November 1976), pp. 365-72.

Deighton, John and Schindler, Robert M.
"Can Advertising Influence Experience?"
Psychology and Marketing, Vol. 5 (Summer 1988), pp. 103-15.

Doyle, Peter and Fenwick, Ian
"Planning and Estimation in Advertising"
Journal of Marketing Research, Vol. XII (February 1975), pp. 104-6.

Duker, Jacob M. and Tucker, Lewis R., Jr.
"Women's Libbers Versus Independent Women: A Study of Preferences for
Women's Roles in Advertisements"
Journal of Marketing Research, Vol. XIV (November 1977), pp. 469-75.

Dyer, Robert F. and Kuehl, Phillip G.
"A Longitudinal Study of Corrective Advertising"
Journal of Marketing Research, Vol. XV (February 1978), pp. 39-48.

Eskin, Gerald J. and Baron, Penny H.
"Effects of Price and Advertising in Test-Market Experiments"
Journal of Marketing Research, Vol. XIV (November 1977), pp. 499-508.

Farley, John U., Katz, Jerrold P., and Lehmann, Donald R.
"Impact of Different Comparison Sets on Evaluation of a New
Subcompact Car Brand"
Journal of Consumer Research, Vol. 5 (September 1978), pp. 138-42.

Futrell, Charles M. and Jenkins, Omer C.
"Pay Secrecy Versus Pay Disclosure for Salesmen: A Longitudinal Study"
Journal of Marketing Research, Vol. XV (May 1978), pp. 214-9.

744 (183) REPEATED MEASURES DESIGNS

Futrell, Charles M. and Swan, John E.
"Anonymity and Response by Salespeople to a Mail Questionnaire"
Journal of Marketing Research, Vol. XIV (November 1977), pp. 611-6.

Golden, Linda L.
"Consumer Reactions to Explicit Brand Comparisons in Advertisements"
Journal of Marketing Research, Vol. XVI (November 1979), pp. 517-32.

Green, Robert T. and Cunningham, Isabella C. M.
"Feminine Role Perception and Family Purchasing Decisions"
Journal of Marketing Research, Vol. XII (August 1975), pp. 325-32.

Holbrook, Morris B.
"Comparing Multiattribute Attitude Models by Optimal Scaling"
Journal of Consumer Research, Vol. 4 (December 1977), pp. 165-71.

Houston, Michael J. and Jefferson, Robert W.
"The Negative Effects of Personalization on Response Patterns in Mail
Surveys"
Journal of Marketing Research, Vol. XII (February 1975), pp. 114-7.

Huber, Joel
"Predicting Preferences on Experimental Bundles of Attributes: A
Comparison of Models"
Journal of Marketing Research, Vol. XXII (Augst 1975), pp. 290-7.

Hulbert, James
"Information Processing Capacity and Attitude Measurement"
Journal of Marketing Research, Vol. XII (February 1975), pp. 104-6.

Huppertz, John W., Arenson, Sidney J., and Evans, Richard H.
"An Application of Equity Theory to Buyer-Seller Exchange Situations"
Journal of Marketing Research, Vol. XV (May 1978), pp. 250-60.

Jacoby, Jacob, Speller, Donald E., and Berning, Carol
"Brand Choice Behavior as a Function of Information Overload:
Replication and Extension"
Journal of Consumer Research, Vol. 1 (June 1974), pp. 33-42.

Jain, Arun K., Acito, Franklin, Malhotra, Naresh K., and Mahajan, Vijay
"A Comparison of the Internal Validity of Alternative parameter
Estimation Methods in Decompositional Multiattribute Preference
Models"
Journal of Marketing Research, Vol. XVI (August 1979), pp. 313-22.

Johnson, Michael D.
"Consumer Choice Strategies for Comparing Noncomparable Alternatives"
Journal of Consumer Research, Vol. 11 (December 1984), pp. 741-53.

Locander, William B. and Hermann, Peter W.
"The Effect of Self-Confidence and Anxiety on Information Seeking in
Consumer Risk Reduction"
Journal of Marketing Research, Vol. XVI (May 1979), pp. 269-74.

Marks, Lawrence J. and Kamins, Michael A.
"The Use of Product Sampling and Advertising: Effects of Sequence of
Exposure and Degree of Advertising Claim Exaggeration on Consumers'
Belief Strength, Belief Confidence, and Attitudes"
Journal of Marketing Research, Vol. XXV (August 1988), pp. 266-81.

Mazis, Michael B., Ahtola, Olli T., and Klippel, R. Eugene
"A Comparison of Four Multi-Attribute Models in the Prediction of
Consumer Attitudes"
Journal of Consumer Research, Vol. 2 (June 1975), pp. 38-52.

McNeil, Dennis L. and Wilkie, William L.
"Public Policy and Consumer Information: Impact of the New Energy
Labels"
Journal of Consumer Research, Vol. 6 (June 1979), pp. 1-11.

Menezes, Dennis and Elbert, Norbert F.
"Alternative Semantic Scaling Formats for Measuring Store Image: An
Evaluation"
Journal of Marketing Research, Vol. XVI (February 1979), pp. 80-7.

Miller, Kenneth E. and Ginter, James L.
"The Influence of Social Situational Variation in Brand Choice
Behavior and Attitude"
Journal of Marketing Research, Vol. XVI (February 1979), pp. 111-23.

Mizerski, Richard W. and Settle, Robert B.
"The Influence of Social Character on Preference for Social Versus
Objective Information in Advertising"
Journal of Marketing Research, Vol. XVI (November 1979), pp. 552-8.

Monroe, Kent B.
"The Influence of Price Differences and Brand Familiarity on Brand
Preferences"
Journal of Consumer Research, Vol. 3 (June 1976), pp. 42-9.

Morris, Michael H., Paul, Gordon W., and Rahtz, Don
"Organizational Rewards and Coalitions in the Industrial Buying Center"
International Journal of Research in Marketing, Vol. 4, No. 2 (1987), pp. 131-46.

Nakanishi, Masao and Bettman, James R.
"Attitude Models Revisited: An Individual Level Analysis"
Journal of Consumer Research, Vol. 1 (December 1974), pp. 16-21.

Parameswaran, Ravi, Greenberg, Barnett A., Bellenger, Danny N., and Robertson, Dan H.
"Measuring Reliability: A Comparison of Alternative Techniques"
Journal of Marketing Research, Vol. XVI (February 1979), pp. 18-25.

Park, C. Whan
"The Effect of Individual and Situation-Related Factors on Consumer Selection of Judgmental Models"
Journal of Marketing Research, Vol. XIII (May 1976), pp. 144-51.

Park, C. Whan and Lessig, V. Parker
"Students' and Housewives' Differences in Susceptibility to Reference Group Influence"
Journal of Consumer Research, Vol. 4 (September 1977), pp. 102-10.

Pras, Bernard and Summers, John O.
"Perceived Risk and Composition Models for Multiattribute Decisions"
Journal of Marketing Research, Vol. XV (August 1978), pp. 429-37.

Pras, Bernard and Summers, John O.
"A Comparison of Linear and Nonlinear Evaluation Process Models"
Journal of Marketing Research, Vol. XII (August 1975), pp. 276-81.

Prasad, V. Kanti
"Communication-Effectiveness of Comparative Advertising: A Laboratory Analysis"
Journal of Marketing Research, Vol. XIII (May 1976), pp. 128-37.

Scott, Jerome E. and Wright, Peter
"Modeling an Organizational Buyer's Product Evaluation Strategy: Validity and Procedural Considerations"
Journal of Marketing Research, Vol. XIII (August 1976), pp. 211-24.

Settle, Robert B. and Golden, Linda L.
"Attribution Theory and Advertiser Credibility"
Journal of Marketing Research, Vol. XI (May 1974), pp. 181-5.

Sheluga, David A., Jaccard, James, and Jacoby, Jacob
"Preference, Search, and Choice: An Integrative Approach"
Journal of Consumer Research, Vol. 6 (September 1979), pp. 166-76.

Still, Leonie V.
"Part-Time Versus Full-Time Salespeople: Individual Attributes, Organizational Commitment, and Work Attitudes"
Journal of Retailing, Vol. 59 (Summer 1983), pp. 55-79.

Swinyard, William R. and Coney, Kenneth A.
"Promotional Effects on a High- Versus Low-Involvement Electorate"
Journal of Consumer Research, Vol. 5 (June 1978), pp. 41-8.

Tollefson, John O. and Lessig, V. Parker
"Aggregation Criteria in Normative Market Segmentation Theory"
Journal of Marketing Research, Vol. XV (August 1978), pp. 346-53.

Troutman, C. Michael and Shanteau, James
"Do Consumers Evaluate Products by Adding or Averaging Attribute Information?"
Journal of Consumer Research, Vol. 3 (September 1976), pp. 101-6.

Webb, Peter H.
"Consumer Initial Processing in a Difficult Media Environment"
Journal of Consumer Research, Vol. 6 (December 1979), pp. 225-36.

Weitz, Barton A. and Wright, Peter
"Retrospective Self-Insight on Factors Considered in Product Evaluations"
Journal of Consumer Research, Vol. 6 (December 1979), pp. 280-94.

Wheatley, John J. and Chiu, John S. Y.
"The Effects of Price, Store Image, and Product and Respondent Characteristics on Perceptions of Quality"
Journal of Marketing Research, Vol. XIV (May 1977), pp. 181-6.

Winter, Frederick W.
"The Effect of Purchase Characteristics on Postdecision Product Reevaluation"
Journal of Marketing Research, Vol. XI (May 1974), pp. 164-71.

183.05 ---------- Applications of Multivariate Repeated Measures Design

Belk, Russell, Mayer, Robert, and Driscoll, Amy
    "Children's Recognition of Consumption Symbolism in Children's
    Products"
    Journal of Consumer Research, Vol. 10 (March 1984), pp. 386-97.

Hoyer, Wayne D.
    "An Examination of Consumer Decision Making for a Common Repeat
    Purchase Product"
    Journal of Consumer Research, Vol. 11 (December 1984), pp. 822-9.

Jackson, Donald W., Jr., Burdick, Richard K., and Keith, Janet E.
    "Purchasing Agents' Perceived Importance of Marketing Mix Components
    in Different Industrial Purchase Situations"
    Journal of Business Research, Vol. 13 (August 1985), pp. 361-73.

183.06 ---------- Unclassified (Repeated Measures Designs)

Box, G. E. P.
    "Some Theorems on Quadratic Forms Applied in the Study of Analysis of
    Variance Problems, II: Effects of Inequality of Variance and of
    Correlation Between Errors in the Two-Way Classification"
    Annals of Mathematical Statistics, Vol. 25 (1954), pp. 484-98.

Box, G. E. P.
    "Problems in the Analysis of Growth and Wear Curves"
    Biometrics, Vol. 6 (1950), pp. 362-89.

Pothoff, R. F. and Roy, S. N.
    "A Generalized Multivariate Analysis of Variance Model Useful
    Especially for Growth Curve Problems"
    Biometrika, Vol. 51 (1964), pp. 313-26.

184 --------------------- MULTIPLE COMPARISONS ----------------------
        See also (sub)heading(s) 141, 179.

184.01 ---------- Books Re: Multiple Comparisons

Klockars, Alan J. and Sax, Gilbert
  Multiple Comparisons
  (Beverly Hills, CA: Sage Publications, Inc., 1986).

Tukey, J. W.
  The Problem of Multiple Comparisons
  (Princeton University, 1953), 396 pp.

184.02 ---------- Theory Re: Multiple Comparisons

Carmer, S. G. and Swanson, R. M.
  "An Evaluation of Ten Pairwise Multiple Comparison Procedures by
  Monte Carlo Method"
  Journal of the American Statistical Association, Vol. 68 (March
  1973), pp. 66-74.

Ryan, Thomas A.
  "Significance Tests for Multiple Comparison of Proportions,
  Variances, and Other Statistics"
  Psychological Bulletin, Vol. 57 (July 1960), pp. 318-28.

Ryan, Thomas A.
  "Multiple Comparisons in Psychological Research"
  Psychological Bulletin, Vol. 56 (October 1959), pp. 26-47.

184.03 ---------- Post Hoc Comparisons

Payne, James L.
  "Fishing Expedition Probability: The Statistics of Post Hoc
  Hypothesizing"
  Polity, Vol. 7 (Fall 1974), pp. 130-8.

Traylor, Mark B.
  "Comment on 'An Experimental Investigation of Comparative
  Advertising: Impact of Message Appeal, Information Load, and Utility
  of Product Class'"
  Journal of Marketing Research, Vol. XVIII (May 1981), pp. 254,5.

184.04 ---------- Theory Re: Duncan's Multiple Range Test

Duncan, David B.
  "Multiple Range and Multiple F Tests"
  Biometrics, Vol. 11 (March 1955), pp. 1-42.

Duncan, D. B.
  "A Significance Test for Differences Between Ranked Treatments in an
  Analysis of Variance"
  Journal of Science, Vol. 2 (March 1955).

184.05 ---------- Theory Re: Tukey's Studentized Range Test

Keuls
  "The Use of the Studentized Range in Connection With the Analysis of
  Variance"
  Euphytica, Vol. 1 (1952), pp. 112-22.

184.06 ---------- Applications of Duncan's Multiple Range Test

Anderson, Rolph E.
  "Consumer Dissatisfaction: The Effect of Disconfirmed Expectancy on
  Perceived Product Performance"
  Journal of Marketing Research, Vol. X (February 1973), pp. 38-44.

Belk, Russell, Painter, John, and Semenik, Richard
  "Preferred Solutions to the Energy Crisis as a Function of Causal
  Attributions"
  Journal of Consumer Research, Vol. 8 (December 1981), pp. 306-12.

Calantone, Roger, Morris, Michael, and Johar, Jotindar
  "A Cross-Cultural Benefit Segmentation Analysis to Evaluate the
  Traditional Assimilation Model"
  International Journal of Research in Marketing, Vol. 2, No. 3 (1985),
  pp. 207-17.

Haley, Russell I. and Gatty, Ronald
  "The Trouble With Concept Testing"
  Journal of Marketing Research, Vol. VIII (May 1971), pp. 230-2.

Karakaya, Fahri and Stahl, Michael J.
    "Barriers to Entry and Market Entry Decisions in Consumer and
    Industrial Goods Markets"
    Journal of Marketing, Vol. 53 (April 1989), pp. 80-91.

Lessne, Greg J. and Notarantonio, Elaine M.
    "The Effect of Limits in Retail Advertisements: A Reactance Theory
    Perspective"
    Psychology and Marketing, Vol. 4 (Spring 1988), pp. 33-44.

McDaniel, Stephen W. and Kolari, James W.
    "Marketing Strategy Implications of the Miles and Snow Strategic
    Typology"
    Journal of Marketing, Vol. 51 (October 1987), pp. 19-30.

McKee, Daryl O., Varadarajan, P. Rajan, and Pride, William M.
    "Strategic Adaptability and Firm Performance: A Market-Contingent
    Perspective"
    Journal of Marketing, Vol. 53 (July 1989), pp. 21-35.

Slama, Mark E. and Tashchian, Armen
    "Selected Socioeconomic and Demographic Characteristics Associated
    With Purchasing Involvement"
    Journal of Marketing, Vol. 49 (Winter 1985), pp. 72-82.

Wang, Chih-Kang and Lamb, Charles W., Jr.
    "Foreign Environmental Factors Influencing American Consumers'
    Predispositions Toward European Products"
    Journal of the Academy of Marketing Science, Vol. 8 (Fall 1980), pp.
    345-56.

Zeithaml, Valarie A., Parasuraman, A., and Berry, Leonard L.
    "Problems and Strategies in Services Marketing"
    Journal of Marketing, Vol. 49 (Spring 1985), pp. 33-46.

184.07 ---------- Applications of Newman-Keuls Post Hoc Test

Capon, Noel and Burke, Marian
    "Individual, Product Class, and Task-Related Factors in Consumer
    Information Processing"
    Journal of Consumer Research, Vol. 7 (December 1980), pp. 314-26.

Goldberg, Marvin E., Gorn, Gerald J., and Gibson, Wendy
    "TV Messages for Snack and Breakfast Foods: Do They Influence
    Children's Preferences"
    Journal of Consumer Research, Vol. 5 (September 1978), pp. 73-81.

Jacoby, Jacob and Kyner, David B.
    "Brand Loyalty vs. Repeat Purchasing Behavior"
    Journal of Marketing Research, Vol. X (February 1973), pp. 63-9.

Mazis, Michael B.
    "Decision-Making Role and Information Processing"
    Journal of Marketing Research, Vol. IX (November 1972), pp. 447-50.

Mitchell, Andrew A. and Olson, Jerry C.
    "Are Product Attribute Beliefs the Only Mediator of Advertising
    Effects on Brand Attitude?"
    Journal of Marketing Research, Vol. XVIII (August 1981), pp. 318-32.

Mizerski, Richard W.
    "Causal Complexity: A Measure of Consumer Causal Attribution"
    Journal of Marketing Research, Vol. XV (May 1978), pp. 220-8.

Sternthal, Brian, Dholakia, Ruby, and Leavitt, Clark
    "The Persuasive Effect of Source Credibility: Tests of Cognitive
    Response"
    Journal of Consumer Research, Vol. 4 (March 1978), pp. 252-60.

Stuart, Elnora W., Shimp, Terence A., and Engle, Randall W.
    "Classical Conditioning of Consumer Attitudes: Four Experiments in an
    Advertising Context"
    Journal of Consumer Research, Vol. 14 (December 1987), pp. 334-49.

Weinberger, Marc G.
    "Products as Targets of Negative Information: Some Recent Findings"
    European Journal of Marketing, Vol. 20, No. 3/4 (1986), pp. 110-28.

184.08 ---------- Applications of Scheffe's Test for Mult Comparisons

Bellizzi, Joseph A., Krueckeberg, Harry F., Hamilton, John R., and
    Martin, Warren S.
    "Consumer Perceptions of National, Private, and Generic Brands"
    Journal of Retailing, Vol. 57 (Winter 1981), pp. 56-70.

Burnett, John J., Amason, Robert D., and Hunt, Shelby D.
"Feminism: Implications for Department Store Strategy and Salesclerk Behavior"
Journal of Retailing, Vol. 57 (Winter 1981), pp. 71-85.

Hunt, Shelby D., Wood, Van R., and Chonko, Lawrence B.
"Corporate Ethical Values and Organizational Commitment in Marketing"
Journal of Marketing Research, Vol. 53 (July 1989), pp. 79-90.

Morgansky, Michelle A.
"Cost- Versus Convenience-Oriented Consumers: Demographic, Lifestyle, and Value Perspectives"
Psychology and Marketing, Vol. 3 (Spring 1986), pp. 35-46.

Pras, Bernard and Summers, John
"Perceived Risk and Composition Models for Multiattribute Decisions"
Journal of Marketing Research, Vol. XV (August 1978), pp. 429-379.

184.09 ---------- Applications of Tukey's HSD Test

Clarke, Darral G.
"A Reply to Weinberg and Weiss"
Journal of Marketing Research, Vol. XIX (November 1982), pp. 592-4.

Earl, Ronald L. and Pride, William M.
"Do Disclosure Attempts Influence Claim Believability and Perceived Advertiser Credibility?"
Journal of the Academy of Marketing Science, Vol. 12 (Winter 1984), pp. 23-37.

Hunt, H. Keith
"Effects of Corrective Advertising"
Journal of Advertising Research, Vol. 13 (October 1973), pp. 15-22.

184.10 ---------- Applications of Tukey's Studentized Range Test

Kamins, Michael A. and Assael, Henry
"Two-sided Versus One-Sided Appeals: A Cognitive Perspective on Argumentation, Source Derogation, and the Effect of Disconfirming Trial on Belief Change"
Journal of Marketing Research, Vol. XXIV (February 1987), pp. 29-39.

184.11 ---------- Applications of the Bonferroni Procedure

Kamins, Michael A. and Marks, Lawrence J.
"An Examination Into the Effectiveness of Two-Sided Comparative Price Appeals"
Journal of the Academy of Marketing Science, Vol. 16 (Summer 1988), pp. 64-71.

185 ------ CONJOINT ANALYSIS AND MONOTONIC ANALYSIS OF VARIANCE ------
        See also (sub)heading(s) 179, 186, 187.

185.01 ---------- Books Re: Conjoint Analysis and MONANOVA

Green, Paul E. and Wind, Yoram
    Multiattribute Decisions in Marketing: A Measurement Approach
    (Hinsdale, IL: The Dryden Press, 1973).

Louviere, Jordan J.
    Analyzing Decision Making--Metric Conjoint Analysis
    (Newbury Park, CA: Sage Publications, 1988), 94 pp.

Johnson, Richard M. (editor)
    Proceedings of the Sawtooth Software Conference on Perceptual
    Mapping, Conjoint Analysis, and Computer Interviewing
    (Ketchum, ID: Sawtooth Software, Inc., 1987).

185.02 ---------- Theory Re: Conjoint Analysis and MONANOVA

Barron, F. Hutton
    "Axiomatic Conjoint Measurement"
    Decision Sciences, Vol. 8 (1977), pp. 48-59.

Bither, Stewart W. and Wright, Peter
    "Preferences Between Product Consultants: Choice vs. Preference
    Functions"
    Journal of Consumer Research, Vol. 4 (June 1971), pp. 39-47.

Blackston, Max and Van Der Zanden, Nico
    "Validity of Conjoint Analysis: Some Real Market Results"
    European Research, Vol. 8 (November 1980), pp. 243-50.

Boeker, Franz and Schweikl, Herbert
    "Better Preference Prediction With Individualized Sets of Relevant
    Attributes"
    International Journal of Research in Marketing, Vol. 5, No. 1 (1988),
    pp. 15-24.

Carmone, Frank J. and Green, Paul E.
    "Model Misspecification in Multiattribute Parameter Estimation"
    Journal of Marketing Research, Vol. XVIII (February 1981), pp. 87-93.

Carroll, J. Douglas
    "Categorical Conjoint Measurement"
    Meeting of Mathematical Psychology, Ann Arbor, MI (August 1969).

Carroll, J. D., DeSarbo, W. S., Goldberg, S., and Green, P. E.
    "A General Approach to Product Design Optimization via Conjoint
    Analysis"
    (Murray Hill, NJ: Bell Laboratories, 1980), working paper.

Cattin, Philippe and Weinberger, Marc
    "Some Validity and Reliability Issues in the Measurement of Attribute
    Utilities"
    in Olson, Jerry (editor)
    Advances in Consumer Research, Volume 7
    (Ann Arbor, MI: Association for Consumer Research, 1980), pp. 780-3.

Cattin, Philippe and Wittink, Dick R.
    "Commercial Use of Conjoint Analysis: A Survey"
    Journal of Marketing, Vol. 46 (Summer 1982), pp. 44-53.

Cattin, Philippe and Wittink, Dick R.
    "Commercial Use of Conjoint Analysis: A Survey"
    Graduate School of Business, Stanford University (1981), research
    paper.

Corstjens, Marcel L. and Gautschi, David A.
    "Conjoint Analysis: A Comparative Analysis of Specification Tests for
    the Utility Function"
    Management Science, Vol. 29 (December 1983), pp. 1393-1413.

Currim, Imran S. and Sarin, Rakesh K.
    "A Comparative Evaluation of Multiattribute Consumer Preference
    Models"
    Management Science, Vol. 30 (May 1984), pp. 543-61.

Dawes, Robyn M. and Corrigan, Bernard
    "Linear Models in Decision Making"
    Psychological Bulletin, Vol. 81 (February 1974), pp. 95-106.

DeSarbo, Wayne S. and Green, Paul E.
    "Choice-Constrained Conjoint Analysis"
    Decision Sciences, Vol. 15 (1984), pp. 297-323.

Einhorn, Hillel J.
    "The Use of Nonlinear, Noncompensatory Models in Decision Making"
    Psychological Bulletin, Vol. 73, No. 3 (1970), pp. 221-30.

Emery, D. R. and Barron, F. H.
"Axiomatic and Numerical Conjoint Measurement: An Evaluation of Diagnostic Efficacy"
Psychometrika, Vol. 44 (1979), pp. 195-210.

Emery, Douglas R., Barron, F. Hutton, and Messier, William F., Jr.
"Conjoint Measurement and the Analysis of Noisy Data: A Comment"
Journal of Accounting Research (Autumn 1982).

Fenwick, Ian
"A Problem in Quantifying Consumer Tradeoffs"
Journal of the Market Research Society, Vol. 21 (July 1979), pp. 206-10.

Green, P. E.
"On the Analysis of Interactions in Marketing Research Data"
Journal of Marketing Research, Vol. X (November 1973), pp. 410-20.

Green, Paul E. and Carmone, Frank J.
"A BIB/LOGIT Approach to Conjoint Analysis"
Wharton School, University of Pennsylvania (1977), working paper.

Green, Paul E., Carmone, Frank J., and Wind, Yoram
"Subjective Evaluation Models and Conjoint Analysis"
Behavioral Science, Vol. 17 (May 1972), pp. 288-99.

Green, Paul E., Carroll, J. Douglas, and Carmone, Frank J.
"Some New Types of Fractional Factorial Designs for Marketing Experiments"
in Sheth, J. N. (editor)
Research in Marketing, Volume I
(Greenwich, CT: JAI Press, 1978).

Green, Paul E., Carroll, J. Douglas, and DeSarbo, Wayne S.
"Hierarchical Testing in Conjoint Analysis"
Proceedings
(Association for Consumer Research, 1979), pp. 688-91.

Green, Paul E., Carroll, J. Douglas, and Goldberg, Stephen M.
"A General Approach to Product Design Optimization via Conjoint Analysis"
Journal of Marketing, Vol. 45 (Summer 1981), pp. 17-37.

Green, Paul E., Carroll, J. D., and Goldberg, S. M.
"Modeling Consumer Choice Simulators--A New Approach to the Analysis of Trade-Off Data"
University of Pennsylvania (1979), working paper.

Green, Paul E. and DeSarbo, Wayne S.
"Componential Segmentation in the Analysis of Consumer Tradeoffs"
Journal of Marketing, Vol. 43 (Fall 1979), pp. 83-91.

Green, Paul E. and DeSarbo, Wayne S.
"Additive Decomposition of Perceptions Data via Conjoint Analysis"
Journal of Consumer Research, Vol. 5 (June 1978), pp. 58-65.

Green, Paul E., DeSarbo, Wayne S., and Kedia, Pradeep K.
"Reply to: 'On the Sensitivity of Brand Choice Simulations to Attribute Importance Weights'"
Decision Sciences, Vol. 12 (1981), pp. 517-21.

Green, Paul E., DeSarbo, Wayne S., and Kedia, Pradeep K.
"On the Sensitivity of Brand Choice Simulations to Attribute Importance Weights"
Decision Sciences, Vol. 11 (1980), pp. 439-50.

Green, P. E. and Devita, M. T.
"An Interaction Model of Consumer Utility"
Journal of Consumer Research, Vol. 2 (September 1975), pp. 146-53.

Green, Paul E. and Devita, Michael T.
"A Complementarity Model of Consumer Utility for Item Collections"
Journal of Consumer Research, Vol. 1 (December 1974), pp. 56-67.

Green, Paul E. and Krieger, Abba
"Choice Rules and Sensitivity Analysis in Conjoint Simulators"
Journal of the Academy of Marketing Science, Vol. 16 (Spring 1988), pp. 114-27.

Green, Paul E., Krieger, Abba M., and Carroll, J. Douglas
"Conjoint Analysis and Multidimensional Scaling: A Complementary Approach"
Journal of Advertising Research, Vol. 27 (October/November 1987), pp. 21-7.

Green, P. E. and Rao, V. R.
"Conjoint Measurement for Quantifying Judgemental Data"
Journal of Marketing Research, Vol. VIII (August 1971), pp. 355-63.

Green, Paul E. and Rao, Vithala R.
"Nonmetric Approaches to Multivariate Analysis in Marketing"
Wharton School, University of Pennsylvania (1969), working paper.

Green, Paul E., Rao, Vithala R., and DeSarbo, Wayne S.
"Incorporating Group-Level Similarity Judgments in Conjoint Analysis"
Journal of Consumer Research, Vol. 5 (December 1978), pp. 187-93.

Green, Paul E. and Schaffer, Catherine M.
"A Simple Method for Analysing Consumer Preferences for Product Benefits"
Journal of the Market Research Society, Vol. 26 (January 1984), pp. 51-61.

Green, Paul E. and Srinivasan, V.
"Conjoint Analysis in Consumer Research: Issues and Outlook"
Journal of Consumer Research, Vol. 5 (September 1978), pp. 103-23.

Green, Paul E. and Wind, Yoram
"New Way to Measure Consumers' Judgments"
Harvard Business Review, Vol. 53 (July-August 1975), pp. 107-17.

Green, Paul E., Wind, Yoram, and Jain, Arun K.
"Benefit Bundle Analysis"
Journal of Advertising Research, Vol. 12 (April 1972), pp. 31-6.

Greene, C. Scott and Nkonge, Japhet
"Gaining a Competitive Edge Through Conjoint Analysis"
Business, Vol. 39 (April-May-June 1989).

Hagerty, Michael R.
"Improving the Predictive Power of Conjoint Analysis: The Use of Factor Analysis and Cluster Analysis"
Journal of Marketing Research, Vol. XXII (May 1985), pp. 168-84.

Hagerty, Michael R.
"Model Testing Techniques and Price-Quality Tradeoffs"
Journal of Consumer Research, Vol. 5 (December 1978), pp. 194-205.

Huber, G. P.
"Multiattribute Utility Models: A Review of Field and Field-Like Studies"
Management Science, Vol. 20 (June 1974), pp. 1393-1402.

Huber, G. P., Sahney, V., and Ford, D. L.
"A Study of Subjective Evaluation Models"
Behavioral Science, Vol. 14 (November 1969), pp. 483-9.

Huber, Joel
"Conjoint Analysis: How We Got Here and Where We Are"
in Johnson, Richard M. (editor)
Proceedings, Sawtooth Software Conference on Perceptual Mapping, Conjoint Analysis and Computer Interviewing
(Ketchum, ID: Sawtooth Software, 1987), pp. 237-52.

Johnson, Richard M.
"Beyond Conjoint Measurement: A Method of Pairwise Tradeoff Analysis"
in Anderson, B. B. (editor)
Advances in Consumer Research, Volume III
Proceedings, Association for Consumer Research (1976), pp. 353-8.

Johnson, Richard M.
"A Simple Method for Pairwise Monotone Regression"
Psychometrica, Vol. 40 (June 1975), pp. 163-8.

Johnson, Richard M.
"Trade-Off Analysis of Consumer Values"
Journal of Marketing Research, Vol. XI (May 1974), pp. 121-7.

Johnson, Richard M.
"Varieties of Conjoint Measurement"
Market Facts, Inc., Chicago (1973), working paper.

Krantz, David H.
"Conjoint Measurement: The Luce-Tukey Axiomatization and Some Extensions"
Journal of Mathematical Psychology, Vol. 1 (1964), pp. 248-77.

Krantz, David H. and Tversky, Amos
"Conjoint Measurement Analysis of Composition Rules in Psychology"
Psychological Review, Vol. 78 (1971), pp. 151-69.

Kruskal, Joseph B.
"Analysis of Factorial Experiments by Estimating Monotone Transformations of the Data"
Journal of the Royal Statistical Society, Series B, Vol. 27 (1965), pp. 251-63.

Luce, R. D. and Tukey, J. W.
"Simultaneous Conjoint Measurement: A New Type of Fundamental Measurement"
Journal of Mathematical Psychology, Vol. 1 (1964), pp. 1-27.

Madansky, Albert
"On Conjoint Analysis and Quantal Choice Models"
Journal of Business, Vol. 53 (July 1980), pp. 537-44.

Mahajan, V., Green, Paul E., and Goldberg, S. M.
"A Conjoint Model for Measuring Self- and Cross-Price/Demand Relationships"
Journal of Marketing Research, Vol. XIX (August 1982), pp. 334-42.

McClain, John O. and Rao, Vithala R.
"Tradeoffs and Conflicts in Evaluation of Health Systems Alternatives: A Methodology for Analysis"
Health Services Research, Vol. 9 (1974), pp. 35-52.

Messier, William F. and Emery, Douglas R.
"Some Cautionary Notes on the Use of Conjoint Measurment for Human Judgment Modeling"
Decision Sciences, Vol. 11 (1980), pp. 678-90.

Ohsawa, Y., Katahira, H., and Nomoto, A.
"A Critique on Conjoint Measurement by Monotone Transformation of the Data in Consumer Research"
Osaka Economic Journal, Vol. 30 (1981), pp. 243-62.

Olshavsky, Richard W. and Acito, Frank
"Conjoint Analysis and Protocol Analysis--A Simultaneous Approach"
Graduate School of Business, Indiana University (1979), working paper.

Oppedijk Van Veen, Walle M. and Beazley, David
"An Investigation of Alternative Methods of Applying the Trade-Off Model"
Journal of the Market Research Society, Vol. 19 (January 1977), pp. 2-11.

Pekelman, Dov and Sen, Subrata
"Improving Prediction in Conjoint Measurement"
Graduate School of Management, University of Rochester (1978), working paper.

Pekelman, D. and Sen, S.
"Regression Versus Interpolation in Additive Conjoint Measurement"
Proceedings, Association for Consumer Research (1976), pp. 29-34.

Pekelman, Dov and Sen, Subrata K.
"Mathematical Programming Models for the Determination of Attribute Weights"
Management Science, Vol. 20 (1974), pp. 1217-29.

Rao, Vithala R.
"Conjoint Measurement in Marketing Analysis"
in Sheth, J. N. (editor)
Multivariate Methods for Market and Survey Research
(Chicago: American Marketing Association, 1977), pp. 257-86.

Scott, J. E. and Wright, P.
"Modeling an Organizational Buyer's Product Evaluation Strategy: Validity and Procedural Considerations"
Journal of Marketing Research, Vol. XIII (August 1976), pp. 211-24.

Srinivasan, V.
"Comment on 'On Conjoint Analysis and Quantal Choice Models'"
Journal of Business, Vol. 53, No. 3, Part 2 (1980), pp. 547-50.

Teas, R. Kenneth and Perr, Andrea L.
"A Test of a Decompositional Method of Multiattribute Perceptions Measurement"
Journal of Consumer Research, Vol. 16 (December 1989), pp. 384-91.

Tversky, Amos
"A General Theory of Polynomial Conjoint Measurement"
Journal of Mathematical Psychology, Vol. 4 (1967), pp. 1-20.

Van Den Wollenberg, Arnold
"Redundancy Analysis: An Alternative for Canonical Correlation Analysis"
Psychometrika, Vol. 42 (June 1977).

Westwood, Dick, Lunn, Tony, and Beazley, David
"The Trade-Off Model and Its Extensions"
Journal of the Market Research Society, Vol. 16 (July 1974), pp. 227-41.

Wiley, James B., MacLachlan, Douglas L., and Moinpour, Reza
    "Comparison of Stated and Inferred Parameter Values in Additive
    Models: An Illustration of a Paradigm"
    in Perreault, W. D., Jr. (editor)
    Advances in Consumer Research, Volume Four
    (Atlanta: Association for Consumer Research, 1977), pp. 98-105.

Wilson, Terry C.
    "Collecting Conjoint Data Through Telephone Interviews"
    Journal of the Academy of Marketing Science, Vol. 12 (Fall 1984), pp.
    190-9.

Wilson, T. C. and Harris, B. F.
    "The Application of Additive Conjoint Analysis in Marketing Research:
    Assumptions, Advantages, and Limitations"
    Proceedings, American Marketing Association (1977), pp. 86-9.

Wind, Yoram and Myers, John G.
    "A Note on the Selection of Attributes for Conjoint Analysis"
    Wharton School (January 1977), working paper.

Wittink, Dick R. and Cattin, Philippe
    "Commercial Use of Conjoint Analysis: An Update"
    Journal of Marketing, Vol. 53 (July 1989), pp. 91-6.

Wittink, Dick R., Krishnamurthi, Lakshman, and Nutter, Julia B.
    "Comparing Derived Importance Weights Across Attributes"
    Journal of Consumer Research, Vol. 8 (March 1982), pp. 471-4.

Wittink, Dick R. and Montgomery, David B.
    "Predictive Validity of Trade-Off Analysis for Alternative
    Segmentation Schemes"
    in Beckwith, Neil E. (editor)
    1979 Educators' Conference Proceedings
    (Chicago: American Marketing Association, 1979), pp. 69-73.

Yntema, D. B. and Torgerson, Warren S.
    "Man-Computer Cooperation in Decisions Requiring Common Sense"
    IRE Transactions of the Professional Group on Human Factors in
    Electronics, HFE-2(1) (1961), pp. 20-6.

185.03 ---------- Theory Re: Hybrid Models for Conjoint Analysis

Akaah, Ishmael P.
    "Cluster Analysis Versus Q-Type Factor Analysis as a Disaggregation
    Method in Hybrid Conjoint Modeling: An Empirical Investigation"
    Journal of the Academy of Marketing Science, Vol. 16 (Summer 1988),
    pp. 11-8.

Cattin, Philippe, Hermet, Gerard, and Pioche, Alain
    "Alternative Hybrid Models for Conjoint Analysis: Some Empirical
    Results"
    Analytical Approaches to Product and Market Planning: The Second
    Conference
    (Cambridge, MA: Marketing Science Institute, October 1982), pp.
    142-52.

Green, Paul E.
    "Hybrid Models for Conjoint Analysis: An Expository Review"
    Journal of Marketing Research, Vol. XXI (May 1984), pp. 155-9.

Green, Paul E., Carroll, J. Douglas, and Wiley, James B.
    "A Cross Validation Test of Hybrid Conjoint Models"
    Proceedings, Annual Meeting of the Association for Consumer Research,
    San Francisco (1982).

Green, Paul E. and Goldberg, Stephen M.
    "A Nonmetric Version of the Hybrid Conjoint Analysis Model"
    Third ORSA/TIMS Market Measurement Conference, New York University
    (March 1981), paper presentation.

Green, Paul E. and Krieger, Abba M.
    "A Hybrid Conjoint Model for Price-Demand Estimation"
    European Journal of Operational Research, Vol. 37 (1989).

Moore, William L. and Semenik, Richard J.
    "Measuring Preferences With Hybrid Conjoint Analysis: The Impact of a
    Different Number of Attributes in the Master Design"
    Journal of Business Research, Vol. 16 (May 1988), pp. 261-74.

185.04 ---------- Theory Re: Multiple Dependent Variables

See also (sub)heading(s) 64, 189.

Carroll, J. Douglas, Green, Paul E., and Carmone, Frank J.
"CANDELINC: A New Method for Multidimensional Analysis With
Constrained Solutions"
International Congress of Psychology, Paris (July 1976), paper
presentation.

Carroll, J. Douglas, Pruzansky, S., and Kruskal, J. B.
"CANDELINC: A General Approach to Multidimensional Analysis of
Many-Way Arrays With Linear Constraints on Parameters"
Psychometrika, Vol. 45 (March 1979), pp. 3-24.

DeSarbo, Wayne S. and Carroll, J. Douglas
"Three Way Metric Unfolding"
in Keon, J. W. (editor)
Market Measurement and Analysis
(Providence, RI: TIMS College on Marketing, 1980).

DeSarbo, Wayne S., Carroll, J. Douglas, and Lehmann, Donald R.
"Three-Way Multivariate Conjoint Analysis"
Bell Laboratories, Murray Hill, NJ (1981), unpublished memorandum.

DeSarbo, Wayne S., Carroll, J. Douglas, Lehmann, Donald R., and
O'Shaughnessy, John
"Three-Way Multivariate Conjoint Analysis"
Marketing Science, Vol. 1 (Fall 1982), pp. 323-50.

185.05 ---------- Theory Re: Unacceptable Levels in Conjoint Analysis

Green, Paul E., Krieger, Abba M., and Bansal, Pradeep
"Completely Unacceptable Levels in Conjoint Analysis: A Cautionary
Note"
Journal of Marketing Research, Vol. XXV (August 1988), pp. 293-300.

Klein, Noreen M.
"Assessing Unacceptable Attribute Levels in Conjoint Analysis"
in Wallendorf, M. and Anderson, P. (editors)
Advances in Consumer Research, Volume 14
(Provo, UT: Association for Consumer Research, 1986), pp. 154-8.

185.06 ---------- Theory Re: Adaptive Conjoint Analysis (ACA)

Carmone, Frank J.
"Software Review: ACA System for Adaptive Conjoint Analysis"
Journal of Marketing Research, Vol. XXIV (August 1987), pp. 325-7.

Huber, Joel and Hansen, David
"Testing the Impact of Dimensional Complexity and Affective
Differences of Paired Concepts in Adaptive Conjoint Analysis"
in Wallendorf, Melanie and Anderson, Paul (editors)
Advances in Consumer Research, Volume Fourteen
(Provo, UT: Association for Consumer Research, 1986), pp. 159-63.

Johnson, Richard M.
"Adaptive Conjoint Analysis"
in Proceedings of the Sawtooth Software Conference on Perceptual
Mapping, Conjoint Analysis, and Computer Interviewing
(Sun Valley, ID: March 1987), pp. 253-66.

185.07 ---------- Theory Re: Aggregation Issues in Conjoint Analysis

Curry, D. and Rodgers, W.
"Aggregating Responses in Additive Conjoint Measurement"
Proceedings, Association for Consumer Research (1976), pp. 35-40.

Huber, Joel C. and Moore, William L.
"A Comparison of Alternative Ways to Aggregate Individual Conjoint
Analyses"
in Beckwith, Neil E. (editor)
1979 Educators' Conference Proceedings
(Chicago: American Marketing Association, 1979), pp. 64-8.

Jain, Arun K., Malhotra, Naresh K., and Mahajan, Vijay
"Aggregating Conjoint Data: Some Methodological Considerations and
Approaches"
in Beckwith, Neil, Houston, Michael, Middelstaedt, Robert, Monroe,
Kent B., and Ward, Scott (editors)
1979 Educators' Conference Proceedings
(Chicago: American Marketing Association, 1979), pp. 74-7.

Marr, Norman E.
"A Method for the Aggregation of the Results in a Conjoint Measurement Study"
European Research, Vol. 15 (November 1987), pp. 257-63.

Montgomery, David B. and Wittink, Dick R.
"The Predictive Validity of Conjoint Analysis for Alternative Aggregation Schemes"
Market Measurement and Analysis
(Cambridge, MA: Marketing Science Institute, 1980), pp. 298-309.

Moore, William L.
"Levels of Aggregation in Conjoint Analysis: An Empirical Comparison"
Journal of Marketing Research, Vol. XVII (November 1980), pp. 516-23.

Ogawa, Kohsuke
"An Approach to Simultaneous Estimation and Segmentation in Conjoint Analysis"
Marketing Science, Vol. 6 (Winter 1987), pp. 66-81.

Wiley, James B. and Low, James T.
"A Monte Carlo Simulation Study of Two Approaches for Aggregating Conjoint Data"
Journal of Marketing Research, Vol. XX (November 1983), pp. 405-16.

Wiley, James B. and Low, James T.
"A Generalized Logit Model to Aggregate Conjoint Data"
in Landon, Laird (editor)
Educators' Conference Proceedings
(Chicago: American Marketing Association, 1979), pp. 78-82.

185.08 ---------- Theory Re: Indexes of Fit in Conjoint Analysis

Mullet, Gary M. and Karson, Marvin J.
"Percentiles of LINMAP Conjoint Indices of Fit for Various Orthogonal Arrays: A Simulation Study"
Journal of Marketing Research, Vol. XXIII (August 1986), pp. 286-90.

185.09 ---------- Theory Re: Statistical Testing in Conjoint Analysis

See also (sub)heading(s) 141.

Eliashberg, Jehoshua and Hauser, John R.
"A Measurement Error Approach for Modelling Consumer Risk Preference"
Management Science, Vol. 31 (January 1985), pp. 1-25.

Friedman, Milton
"The Use of Ranks to Avoid the Assumption of Normality Implicit in the Analysis of Variance"
Journal of the American Statistical Association, Vol. 32 (December 1937), pp. 675-701.

Green, Paul E., Carmone, Frank J., and Vankudre, Prashant
"Bootstrapped Confidence Intervals for Conjoint Based Choice Simulators"
Wharton School, University of Pennsylvania (1983), working paper.

Kohli, Rajeev
"Assessing Attribute Significance in Conjoint Analysis: Nonparametric Tests and Empirical Evaluation"
Journal of Marketing Research, Vol. XXV (May 1988), pp. 123-33.

Kruskal, William H.
"A Nonparametric Test for the Several Sample Problem"
Annals of Mathematical Statistics, Vol. 23, No. 4 (1952), pp. 525-40.

185.10 ---------- Data Collection Issues in Conjoint Analysis

Acito, F.
"An Investigation of Some Data Collection Issues in Conjoint Measurement"
Proceedings, American Marketing Association (1977), pp. 82-5.

Alpert, Mark I., Betak, John F., and Golden, Linda L.
"Data Gathering Issues in Conjoint Measurement"
Graduate School of Business, The University of Texas at Austin (1978), working paper.

Cerro, Dan
"Conjoint Analysis by Mail"
Sawtooth Software Conference Proceedings (1988), pp. 139-44.

Chapman, Randall G. and Bolton, Ruth N.
"Attribute Presentation Order Bias and Nonstationarity in Full
Profile Conjoint Analysis Tasks"
in Lusch, Robert F. et al. (editors)
Proceedings, Educators' Conference
(Chicago: American Marketing Association, 1985), pp. 373-9.

Green, Paul E., Helsen, Kristiaan, and Shandler, Bruce
"Conjoint Internal Validity Under Alternative Profile Presentations"
Journal of Consumer Research, Vol. 15 (December 1988), pp. 392-7.

Jain, Arun K., Acito, Franklin, Malhotra, Naresh K., and Mahajan, Vijay
"Comparison of Internal Validity of Alternative Parameter Estimation
Methods in Decompositional Multi-Attribute Preference Models"
Journal of Marketing Research, Vol. XVI (August 1979), pp. 313-22.

Jain, Arun K., Malhotra, Naresh K., and Pinson, Christian
"Stability and Reliability of Part-Worth Utility in Conjoint
Analysis: A Longitudinal Investigation"
Working Paper 80/05
European Institute of Business Administration (1980).

Leigh, Thomas W., MacKay, David B., and Summers, John O.
"On Alternative Experimental Methods for Conjoint Analysis"
in Monroe, Kent (editor)
Advances in Consumer Research, Volume Eight
(Ann Arbor, MI: Association for Consumer Research, 1981), pp. 317-22.

McCullough, James M.
"Identification of Preference Through Conjoint Measurement: A
Comparison of Data Collection and Analytical Procedures"
College of Business Administration, University of Arizona (1978),
working paper.

Reibstein, David, Bateson, John E. G., and Boulding, William
"Conjoint Analysis Reliability: Empirical Findings"
Marketing Science, Vol. 7 (Summer 1988), pp. 271-86.

Segal, Madhav N.
"Reliability of Conjoint Analysis: Contrasting Data Collection
Procedures"
Journal of Marketing Research, Vol. XIX (February 1982), pp. 139-43.

Segal, Madhav N.
"Variation Among Conjoint Measurement Solutions: An Empirical
Examination of the Effect of Data Collection Differences"
University of Texas at Arlington (1979), unpublished doctoral
dissertation.

Stahl, Brent
"Conjoint Analysis by Telephone"
Sawtooth Software Conference Proceedings (1988), pp. 131-8.

185.11 ---------- Generation of Attribute Combinations

Addelman, Sidney
"Orthogonal Main-Effect Plans for Asymmetrical Factorial Experiments"
Technometrics, Vol. 4 (February 1962), pp. 21-46.

185.12 ---------- Numbers of Attributes, Attribute Levels, Profiles

Darmon, Rene Y. and Rouzies, Dominique
"Assessing Conjoint Analysis Internal Validity: The Effect of Various
Continuous Attribute Level Spacings
International Journal of Research in Marketing, Vol. 6, No. 1 (1989),
pp. 35-44.

Mullet, Gary M.
"On Conjoint Studies With Scarce Degrees of Freedom: Is There Enough
Utility to Go Around?"
Marketing Research, Vol. 1 (June 1989), pp. 24-30.

185.13 ---------- Computer Programs for Conjoint Analysis, MONANOVA

Bretton-Clark
BRIDGER, Version 1.0
(New York: Bretton-Clark, 1988).

Bretton-Clark
SIMGRAF, Version 1.0
(New York: Bretton-Clark, 1988).

Bretton-Clark
CONJOINT ANALYZER
(New York: Bretton-Clark, 1986), 53 pp.

Bretton-Clark
  CONJOINT DESIGNER
  (New York: Bretton-Clark, 1985).

Emery, Douglas R.
  "DULDST: A Numerical Conjoint Measurement Program Designed to
  Scale Data to a Dual-Distributive Model in Three Dimensions"
  Journal of Marketing Research, Vol. XIV (November 1977), pp. 558,9.

Emery, Douglas R.
  "DIST: A Numerical Conjoint Measurement Program Designed to Scale
  Data to a Distributive Model in Three Dimensions"
  Journal of Marketing Research, Vol. XIV (August 1977), pp. 413,4.

Gates, Roger
  "MULTICON: A Program for Doing Conjoint Analysis via User Selected
  Algorithm"
  Journal of Marketing Research, Vol. XIX (November 1982), pp. 604,5.

Kruskal, Joseph B. and Carmone, Frank J.
  "MONANOVA: A FORTRAN IV Program for Monotone Analysis of Variance"
  Behavioral Science, Vol. 14 (March 1969), pp. 165,6.

Kruskal, Joseph B. and Carmone, Frank J.
  "MONANOVA Four (4) Character Version: Nonmetric Analysis of Factorial
  Design"
  (Philadelphia: Marketing Science Institute, 1968).

Lambert, David R., Mathur, Kamlesh, and Reddy, N. Mohan
  "CHOISIM: A First-Choice Simulator for Conjoint Scaled Data"
  Journal of Marketing Research, Vol XXII (May 1985), pp. 219,20.

Lingoes, James C.
  The Guttman-Lingoes Nonmetric Program Series
  (Ann Arbor, MI: Mathesis Pess, 1973).

Lingoes, James C.
  "An IBM-7090 Program for Guttman-Lingoes Conjoint Measurement, I"
  Behavioral Science, Vol. 12 (November 1967), pp. 501,2.

Nehls, Lyle, Seaman, Bruce, and Montgomery, David B.
  "A PL1 Program for Trade-Off Analysis"
  (Cambridge, MA: Marketing Science Institute, 1976).

Pennell, Roger
  "Additive Representations for Two-Dimensional Tables"
  Research Bulletin Rb-7-29.
  (Princeton: Educational Testing Service, 1970).

Sawtooth Software, Incorporated
  ACA System for Adaptive Conjoint Analysis
  (Ketchum, ID: Sawtooth Software, Inc., 1986).

Sawtooth Software, Inc.
  Adaptive Conjoint Analysis System: User's Manual
  (Ketchum, ID: Sawtooth Software, Inc., 1985).

Searle, Allan D. and Srinivasan, V.
  "LINMAP (Version II): A Fortran IV Program for Analyzing Ordinal
  Preference (Dominance) Judgements via Linear Programming Techniques
  and for Conjoint Measurement"
  Journal of Marketing Research, Vol. XIV (February 1977), pp. 101-3.

Smith, Scott M.
  "CONJOINT: Conjoint Statistical Analysis"
  Journal of Marketing Research, Vol. XXII (May 1985), pp. 221,2.

Srinivasan, V. and Shocker, Allan D.
  "LINMAP (Version IV): A FORTRAN IV Program for Analyzing Ordinal
  Preference (Dominance) Judgments and for Conjoint and Tradeoff
  Analyses"
  Journal of Marketing Research, Vol. XIX (November 1982), pp. 601,2.

Srinivasan, V. and Shocker, Allan D.
  LINMAP Version IV--Users' Manual
  (Nashville, TN: Vanderbilt University, August 1981).

Tversky, Amos and Zivizn, A. A.
  "A Computer Program for Additivity Analysis"
  Behavioral Science, Vol. 11 (January 1966), pp. 78,9.

Wiley, James B. and Low, James T.
  "Market Share Analysis--A Program for Estimating Market Shares From
  Conjoint Analysis Data"
  Journal of Marketing Research, Vol. XVI (November 1979), pp. 568,9.

Young, Forrest W.
  "Polynomial Conjoint Analysis of Similarities: Definitions for a
  Specific Algorithm"
  Research Paper No. 76
  Psychometric Laboratory, University of North Carolina (1969).

185.14 ---------- Unclassified (Conjoint Analysis and/or MONANOVA)

Finkbeiner, Carl T.
  "Comparison of Conjoint Choice Simulators"
  Sawtooth Software Conference Proceedings (1988), pp. 75-103.

Johnson, Richard M.
  "Measurement of Consumer Values Using Computer Interactive Techniques"
  ORSA/TIMS Market Measurement and Analysis Conference, Stanford
  University (1979), paper presentation.

186 ------ ESTIMATION METHODS FOR CONJOINT ANALYSIS AND MONANOVA   -----
      See also (sub)heading(s) 185.

186.01 ---------- Theory Re: Estimation Methods for Conjoint Analysis

Albers, Sonke
    "Fully Nonmetric Estimation of a Continuous Nonlinear Conjoint
    Utility Function"
    International Journal of Research in Marketing, Vol. 1, No. 4 (1984),
    pp. 311-319.

Cattin, Philippe
    "On the Estimation of Continuous Utility Functions in Conjoint
    Analysis"
    in Little, J. D. and Chandon, J. L. (editors)
    Product Management and Quantitative Methods in Marketing (1982), pp.
    249-67.

Cattin, Philippe
    "Some Findings on the Estimation of Continuous Utility Functions in
    Conjoint Analysis"
    in Mitchell, Andrew (editor)
    Advances in Consumer Research, Volume Nine
    (St. Louis: Association for Consumer Research, 1981), pp. 367-72.

Cattin, Philippe and Bliemel, Friedhelm
    "Metric vs. Nonmetric Procedures for Multiattribute Modeling: Some
    Simulation Results"
    Decision Sciences, Vol. 9 (July 1978), pp. 472-80.

Cattin, Philippe, Gelfand, Alan E., and Danes, Jeffrey
    "A Simple Bayesian Procedure for Estimation in a Conjoint Model"
    Journal of Marketing Research, Vol. XX (February 1983), pp. 29-35.

Cattin, Philippe, Gelfand, Alan E., and Danes, Jeffrey
    "A Simple Bayesian Procedure for Estimation in a Conjoint Model"
    Working Paper No. 10-81
    Center for Research and Management Development, University of
    Connecticut (March, revised July 1981).

Cattin, Philippe and Punj, Girish
    "Factors Influencing the Selection of Preference Model Form for
    Continuous Utility Functions in Conjoint Analysis"
    Marketing Science, Vol. 3 (1984), pp. 73-82.

Cattin, Philippe and Wittink, Dick R.
    "A Monte Carlo Study of Metric and Non-Metric Estimation Methods for
    Multiattribute Models"
    Research Paper No. 341
    Graduate School of Business, Stanford University (1970).

Chapman, Randall G. and Staelin, Richard
    "Exploiting Rank Ordered Choice Set Data Within the Stochastic
    Utility Model"
    Journal of Marketing Research, Vol. XIX (August 1982), pp. 288-301.

Colberg, Roger T.
    "A Monte Carlo Simulation of Metric Recovery of Conjoint Measurement
    Algorithms"
    in Research Frontiers in Marketing: Dialogues and Directions, Series
    43
    (Chicago: American Marketing Association, 1978).

Corstjens, M. L. and Gautschi, D. A.
    "Conjoint Analysis: A Comparative Analysis of Specification Tests for
    the Utility Function"
    Management Science, Vol. 29 (December 1983), pp. 1393-413.

Goldberg, Stephen M.
    "An Empirical Comparison of Hybrid and Non-Hybrid Utility Estimation
    Models"
    The Wharton School, University of Pennsylvania (1980), working paper.

Green, Paul E., Carmone, Frank J., and Wind, Yoram
    "Subjective Evaluation Models and Conjoint Measurement"
    Behavioral Science, Vol. 17 (1972), pp. 288-99.

Green, Paul E., Carroll, J. Douglas, Goldberg, Stephen M., and Kedia,
    Pradeep K.
    "Product Design Optimization--A Technical Description of the POSSE
    Methodology"
    Wharton School, University of Pennsylvania (1981), working paper.

Green, Paul E., Goldberg, Stephen M., and Montemayer, Mila
    "A Hybrid Utility Estimation Model for Conjoint Analysis"
    Journal of Marketing, Vol. 45 (Winter 1981), pp. 33-41.

Green, Paul E. and Goldberg, Stephen M.
"A Nonmetric Version of the Hybrid Conjoint Analysis Model"
Third ORSA/TIMS Market Measurement Conference, New York University
(March 1981), paper presentation.

Green, Paul E., Goldberg, Stephen M., and Wiley, James B.
"A Cross-Validation of Hybrid Conjoint Models"
The Wharton School, University of Pennsylvania (1981), working paper.

Hauser, John R. and Shugan, Steven M.
"Intensity Measures of Consumer Preference"
Operations Research, Vol. 28 (March-April 1980), pp. 278-320.

Kamakura, Wagner A.
"A Least Squares Procedure fo Benefit Segmentation With Conjoint
Experiments"
Journal of Marketing Research, Vol. XXV (May 1988), pp. 157-67.

Louviere, Jordan J. and Woodworth, George
"Design and Analysis of Simulated Choice or Allocation Experiments:
An Approach Based on Aggregate Data"
Journal of Marketing Research, Vol. XX (November 1983), pp. 350-67.

Mahajan, V., Green, Paul E., and Goldberg, Stephen M.
"A Conjoint Model for Measuring Self- and Cross-Price/Demand
Relationships"
Journal of Marketing Research, Vol. XIX (August 1982), pp. 334-42.

Ogawa, Kohsuke
"An Approach to Simultaneous Estimation and Segmentation in Conjoint
Analysis"
Marketing Science, Vol. 6 (Winter 1987), pp. 66-81.

Ogawa, Kohsuke
"On Maximum Likelihood Estimator as a Conjoint Measure"
Keieishirin (Hosei Journal of Business), Vol. 18 (April 1981), pp.
37-52.

Pekelman, Dov and Sen, Subrata K.
"Measurement and Estimation of Conjoint Utility Functions"
Journal of Consumer Research, Vol. 5 (March 1979), pp. 263-71.

Pekelman, D. and Sen, S.
"Utility Function Estimation in Conjoint Measurement"
Proceedings, American Marketing Association (1975), pp. 156-61.

Srinivasan, V.
"A Strict Paired Comparison Linear Programming Approach to Non-Metric
Conjoint Analysis"
Research Paper 620
Graduate School of Business, Stanford University (September 1981).

Srinivasan, V.
"An Approach to the Modeling and Estimation of Consumer Multistage
Decision Processes"
in Shocker, Allan D. (editor)
Analytic Approaches to Product and Marketing Planning
(Cambridge, MA: Marketing Science Institute, 1979), pp. 290-4.

Srinivasan, V.
"A Model and Estimation Procedure for Multi-Stage Decision Processes"
Graduate School of Business, Stanford University (1978), working
paper.

Srinivasan, V.
"Linear Programming Computational Procedures for Ordinal Regression"
Journal of the Association for Computing Machinery, Vol. 23 (July
1976), pp. 475-87.

Srinivasan, V., Jain, Arun K., and Malhotra, Naresh K.
"Improving Predictive Power of Conjoint Analysis by Constrained
Estimation"
Journal of Marketing Research, Vol. XX (November 1983), pp. 433-8.

Srinivasan, V. and Shocker, A. D.
"Estimating the Weights for Multiple Attributes in a Composite
Criterion Using Pairwise Judgements"
Psychometrika, Vol. 38 (December 1973), pp. 473-93.

Srinivasan, V. and Shocker, Allan D.
"Linear Programming Techniques for Multi-Dimensional Analysis of
Preferences"
Psychometrika, Vol. 38 (September 1973), pp. 337-69.

Young, F. W.
"A Model for Polynomial Conjoint Analysis Algorithms"
in Shepard, R. N., Romney, A. K., and Nerlove, S. (editors)
Multidimensional Scaling: Theory and Applications in the Behavioral
Sciences, Vol. I
(New York: Academic Press, 1972).

Young, Forrest W.
"Polynomial Conjoint Analysis of Similarities: Definitions for a
Special Algorithm"
Research Paper No. 76
Psychometric Laboratory, University of North Carolina (1969).

Zellner, Arnold and Verma, Vinod K.
"A Bayesian Econometric Methodology for Estimation and Prediction in
Conjoint Analysis"
Graduate School of Business, University of Chicago (1980), working
paper.

186.02 ---------- Evaluations of Conjoint Estimation Methods

Acito, Franklin
"An Investigation of Reliability of Conjoint Measurement for Various
Orthogonal Designs"
in Franz, R. S., Hopkins, R. M., and Toma, A. (editors)
Proceedings, Southern Marketing Association 1979 Conference,
University of Southwestern Louisiana (1979), pp. 175-8.

Acito, Franklin
"A Monte Carlo Investigation of Conjoint Measurement Under Random
Data Conditions for Various Orthogonal Designs"
School of Business, Indiana University (1978), working paper.

Acito, Franklin and Jain, Arun K.
"Evaluation of Conjoint Analysis Results: A Comparison of Methods"
Journal of Marketing Research, Vol. XVII (February 1980), pp. 106-12.

Akaah, Ishmael P. and Korgaonkar, Pradeep K.
"An Empirical Comparison of the Predictive Validity of
Self-Explicated, Huber-Hybrid, Traditional Conjoint, and Hybrid
Conjoint Models"
Journal of Marketing Research, Vol. XX (May 1983), pp. 187-97.

Bateson, John E. G., Reibstein, David, and Boulding, William
"Conjoint Analysis Reliability and Validity: A Framework for Future
Research"
Review of Marketing (1987).

Carmone, Frank J., Green, Paul E., and Jain, Arun K.
"Robustness of Conjoint Analysis: Some Monte Carlo Results"
Journal of Marketing Research, Vol. XV (May 1978), pp. 300-3.

Cattin, Philippe
"A Predictive-Validity-Based Procedure for Choosing Between
Regression and Equal Weights"
Organizational Behavior and Human Performance, Vol. 22 (1978), pp.
93-102.

Cattin, Philippe and Bliemel, Friedhelm
"Metric vs. Nonmetric Procedures for Multiattribute Modeling: Some
Simulation Results"
Decision Sciences, Vol. 9 (July 1978), pp. 44-53.

Cattin, Philippe, Hermet, Gerard, and Pioche, Alain
"Alternative Hybrid Models for Conjoint Analysis: Some Empirical
Results"
Analytical Approaches to Product and Market Planning: The Second
Conference
(Cambridge, MA: Marketing Science Institute, October 1982), pp.
142-52.

Cattin, Philippe and Weinberger, Marc
"Some Validity and Reliability Issues in the Measurement of Attribute
Utilities"
in Olson, J. C. (editor)
Advances in Consumer Research, Volume Seven
(Ann Arbor, MI: Association for Consumer Research, 1980), pp. 780-3.

Cattin, Philippe and Wittink, Dick R.
"Further Beyond Conjoint Measurement: Toward Comparison of Methods"
Proceedings, Association for Consumer Research (1976), pp. 41-5.

Darmon, Rene Y.
"Internal Validity Assessment of the Conjoint Analysis Part-Worth
Model: Some Simulation Results"
Proceedings, Thirteenth International Research Seminar in Marketing
(Lalaond-les-Maures, France: IRET, 1986), pp. 202-26.

Green, Paul E., Goldberg, Stephen M., and Wiley, James B.
"A Cross Validation Test of Hybrid Conjoint Models"
Proceedings
(San Francisco, CA: Association for Consumer Research, October 1982).

Green, Paul E. and Helsen, Kristiaan
"Cross-Validation Assessment of Alternatives to Individual-Level
Conjoint Analysis: A Case Study"
Journal of Marketing Research, Vol. XXVI (August 1989), pp. 346-50.

Hagerty, Michael R.
"The Cost of Simplifying Preference Models"
Marketing Science, Vol. 5 (Fall 1986), pp. 298-319.

Huber, G. P., Daneshgar, R., and Ford, D. L.
"An Empirical Comparison of Five Utility Models for Predicting Job
Preferences"
Organizational Behavior and Human Performance, Vol. 6 (1971), pp.
267-82.

Jain, Arun K., Acito, Franklin, Malhotra, Naresh K., and Mahajan, Vijay
"A Comparison of the Internal Validity of Alternative Parameter
Estimation Methods in Decompositional Multiattribute Preference
Models"
Journal of Marketing Research, Vol. XVI (August 1979), pp. 313-22.

Karson, Marvin J. and Mullet, Gary M.
"Conjoint Utility Limits as Affected by Conjoint Design and
Estimating Program"
Marketing Research, Vol. 1 (December 1989), pp. 27-32.

Leigh, Thomas W., MacKay, David B., and Summers, John O.
"Reliability and Validity of Conjoint Analysis and Self-Explicated
Weights: A Comparison"
Journal of Marketing Research, Vol. XXI (November 1984), pp. 456-62.

Malhotra, Naresh K.
"Structural Reliability and Stability of Nonmetric Conjoint Analysis"
Journal of Marketing Research, Vol. XIX (May 1982), pp. 199-207.

McCullough, James M. and Best, Roger J.
"Conjoint Measurement: Temporal Stability and Structural Reliability"
Journal of Marketing Research, Vol. XVI (February 1979), pp. 26-31.

Oppedijk Van Veen, W. M. and Beazley, David
"An Investigation of Alternative Methods of Applying the Trade-Off
Model"
Journal of the Market Research Society, Vol. 19 (January 1977), pp.
2-11.

Reibstein, David, Bateson, John E. G., and Boulding, William
"Conjoint Analysis Reliability: Empirical Findings"
Marketing Science, Vol. 7 (Summer 1988), pp. 271-86.

Reibstein, David J., Bateson, John, and Boulding, William
"A Framework for Assessing the Reliability of Conjoint Analysis"
Working Paper 83-022
Marketing Department, The Wharton School, The University of
Pennsylvania (1983).

Segal, Madhav N.
"Alternate Form Conjoint Reliability: An Empirical Assessment"
Journal of Advertising, Vol. 13, No. 4 (1984), pp. 31-8.

Tashchian, Armen, Tashchian, Roobina O., and Slama, Mark E.
"The Impact of Individual Differences on the Validity of Conjoint
Analysis"
in Mitchell, A. (editor)
Advances in Consumer Research, Volume Nine
(Ann Arbor, MI: Association for Consumer Research, 1982), pp. 363-6.

Teas, R. Kenneth
"An Analysis of the Temporal Stability and Structural Reliability of
Metric Conjoint Analysis Procedures"
Journal of the Academy of Marketing Science, Vol. 13 (Winter 1985),
pp. 122-42.

Wittink, Dick R. and Cattin, Philippe
"Alternative Estimation Methods for Conjoint Analysis: A Monte Carlo
Study"
Journal of Marketing Research, Vol. XVIII (February 1981), pp. 101-6.

Wittink, Dick R. and Montgomery, David B.
"Predictive Validity of Tradeoff Analysis for Alternative
Segmentation Schemes"
AMA Educators' Conference Proceedings (1979), pp. 69-71.

Wittink, Dick R., Reibstein, David J., Boulding, William, Bateson, John
E. G., and Walsh, John W.
"Conjoint Reliability Approaches and Measures: A Cautionary Note"
(October 1988), working paper.

187 ----------- CONJOINT ANALYSIS AND MONANOVA APPLICATIONS ----------
          See also (sub)heading(s) 185.

Akaah, Ishmael P. and Korgaonkar, Pradeep K.
    "A Conjoint Investigation of the Relative Importance of Risk
    Relievers in Direct Marketing"
    Journal of Advertising Research, Vol. 28 (August/September 1988), pp.
    38-44.

Akaah, Ishmael P. and Yaprak, Attila
    "Identifying Target Segments for Foreign Direct Investment (FDI)
    Attraction: An Application of Conjoint Methodology"
    International Marketing Review, Vol. 8 (Autumn 1988), pp. 28-37.

Barnett, R. Parker and Srinivasan, V.
    "A Consumer Preference Approach to the Planning of Rural Primary
    Health Care Facilities"
    Operations Research (September-October 1976), pp. 991-1025.

Bennett, Peter D. and Moore, Noreen Klein
    "Consumers' Preferences for Alternative Energy Conservation Policies:
    A Trade-Off Analysis"
    Journal of Consumer Research, Vol. 8 (December 1981), pp. 313-21.

Best, R. and McCullough, J.
    "Evaluation of Food Labelling Policies Through Measurement of
    Consumer Utility"
    Proceedings, Association for Consumer Research (1977), pp. 213-9.

Bither, Stewart W. and Wright, Peter
    "Preferences Between Product Consultants: Choices vs. Preference
    Functions"
    Journal of Consumer Research, Vol. 4 (June 1977), pp. 39-47.

Boyd, Harper W., Jr., Ray, Michael L., and Strong, Edward C.
    "An Attitudinal Framework for Advertising Strategy"
    Journal of Marketing, Vol. 36 (1972), pp. 27-33.

Carroll, J. Douglas, Green, Paul E., and DeSarbo, Wayne S.
    "Optimizing the Allocation of a Fixed Resource: A Simple Model and
    Its Experimental Test"
    (Murray Hill, NJ: Bell Laboratories, 1978), working paper.

Coombs, Clyde H. and Komorita, S. S.
    "Measuring Utility of Money Through Decisions"
    American Journal of Psychology, Vol. 71 (August 1958), pp. 383-9.

Currim, I. S., Weinberg, C. B., and Wittink, D. R.
    "The Design of Subscription Programs for a Performing Arts Series"
    Journal of Consumer Research, Vol. 8 (June 1981), pp. 67-75.

Darmon, Rene Y.
    "Setting Sales Quotas With Conjoint Analysis"
    Journal of Marketing Research, Vol. XVI (February 1979), pp. 133-40.

Davidson, J. D.
    "Forecasting Traffic on STOL"
    Operations Research Quarterly, Vol. 24 (December 1973), pp. 561-9.

Etgar, Michael and Malhotra, Naresh K.
    "Determinants of Price Dependency: Personal and Perceptual Factors"
    Journal of Consumer Research, Vol. 8 (September 1981), pp. 217-22.

Falmagne, J. C.
    "Random Conjoint Measurement and Loudness Summation"
    Psychological Review, Vol. 83 (January 1976), pp. 65-79.

Fiedler, J. A.
    "Condominium Design and Pricing"
    Proceedings, Association for Consumer Research (1972), pp. 279-93.

Fletcher, Keith
    "An Analysis of Choice Criteria Using Conjoint Analysis"
    European Journal of Marketing, Vol. 22, No. 9 (1988), pp. 25-33.

Fox, Richard J. and Day, Ellen
    "Enhancing the Appeal of Service Contracts: An Empirical
    Investigation of Alternative Offerings"
    Journal of Retailing, Vol. 64 (Fall 1988), pp. 335-52.

Goldberg, Stephen M., Green, Paul E., and Wind, Yoram
    "Conjoint Analysis of Price Premiums for Hotel Amenities"
    Journal of Business, Vol. 57 (January 1984), pp. S111-32.

Green, P. E., Carmone, F. J., and Wind, Y.
    "Consumer Evaluation of Discount Cards"
    Journal of Retailing, Vol. 49 (Spring 1973), pp. 10-22.

Green, Paul E., Carroll, J. Douglas, and Goldberg, Stephen M.
"A General Approach to Product Design Optimization via Conjoint
Analysis"
Journal of Marketing, Vol. 45 (Summer 1981), pp. 17-37.

Green, Paul E. and Wind, Yoram
"New Way to Measure Consumers' Judgment"
Harvard Business Review, Vol. 53 (July-August 1975), pp. 107-17.

Green, Paul E. and Wind, Yoram
"Recent Approaches to the Modeling of Individuals' Subjective
Evaluation"
in Levine, P. (editor)
Attitude Research Bridges the Atlantic
(Chicago: American Marketing Association, 1975).

Green, Paul E., Wind, Yoram, and Jain, Arun K.
"Preference Measurement of Item Collections"
Journal of Marketing Research, Vol. IX (November 1972), pp. 371-7.

Green, Paul E., Wind, Yoram, and Jain, Arun K.
"Benefit Bundle Analysis"
Journal of Advertising Research, Vol. 12 (April 1972), pp. 31-6.

Greenhalgh, Leonard and Neslin, Scott A.
"Conjoint Analysis of Negotiator Preferences"
Journal of Conflict Resolution, Vol. 25 (June 1981), pp. 301-27.

Holbrook, Morris B.
"Integrating Compositional and Decompositional Analyses to Represent
the Intervening Role of Perceptions in Evaluative Judgments"
Journal of Marketing Research, Vol. XVIII (February 1981), pp. 13-28.

Hooley, G. J. and Lynch, J. E.
"Modelling the Student University Choice Process Through the Use of
Conjoint Measurement Techniques"
European Research, Vol. 9 (October 1981), pp. 158-70.

Hopkins, David S. P., Larreche, Jean-Claude, and Massy, William F.
"Constrained Optimization of a University Administrator's Preference
Function"
Management Science, Vol. 24 (1977), pp. 365-77.

Johnson, Richard M.
"Trade-Off Analysis of Consumer Values"
Journal of Marketing Research, Vol. XI (1974), pp. 121-7.

Krantz, D. H. and Tversky, Z. A.
"Conjoint Measurement Analysis of Composition Rules in Psychology"
Psychological Review, Vol. 78 (March 1971), pp. 151-69.

Krishnamurthi, Lakshman
"Conjoint Models of Family Decision Making"
International Journal of Research in Marketing, Vol. 5, No. 3 (1989),
pp. 185-98.

Le Claire, Kenneth A.
"Trade-Off Analysis Applied to Educational Choice Behaviour"
European Research, Vol. 8 (November 1980), pp. 251-65.

Mahajan, Vijay, Green, Paul E., and Goldberg, Stephen M.
"A Conjoint Model for Measuring Self- and Cross-Price/Demand
Relationship"
Journal of Marketing Research, Vol. XIX (August 1982), pp. 334-42.

Malhotra, Naresh K.
"Analytical Market Segmentation in Nonbusiness Situations: Marketing
the Energy Audit in the USA"
International Journal of Research in Marketing, Vol. 1, No. 2 (1984),
pp. 127-39.

McClain, John O. and Rao, Vithala R.
"Trade-Offs and Conflicts in Evaluation of Health Systems
Alternatives: A Methodology for Analysis"
Health Services Research, Vol. 9 (1974), pp. 35-52.

McCullough, J. and Mundy, W.
"Identification of Housing Market Segments Using Partial Preference
Patterns"
Proceedings, Southwestern Marketing Association (1977), p. 39.

Neslin, Scott A. and Greenhalgh, Leonard
"Nash's Theory of Cooperative Games as a Predictor of the Outcomes of
Buyer-Seller Negotiations: An Experiment in Media Purchasing"
Journal of Marketing Research, Vol. XX (November 1983), pp. 368-79.

Parker, B. R. and Srinivasan, V.
"A Consumer Preference Approach to the Planning of Rural Health Care
Facilities"
Operations Research, Vol. 24 (September-October 1976), pp. 991-1025.

Rosko, Michael D., Devita, Michael, McKenna, William F., and Walker, Lawrence R.
"Strategic Marketing Applications of Conjoint Analysis: An HMO Perspective"
Journal of Health Care Marketing, Vol. 5 (Fall 1985), pp. 27-38.

Ross, R. B.
"Measuring the Influence of Soft Variables on Travel Behaviour"
Traffic Quarterly, (July 1975), pp. 333-46.

Sands, Paul and Warwick, Kenneth
"What Product Benefits to Offer to Whom"
California Management Review, Vol. 24 (Fall 1981), pp. 69-74.

Scott, Dana
"Measurement Models and Linear Inequalities"
Journal of Mathematical Psychology, Vol. 4 (July 1964), pp. 233-48.

Scott, J. E. and Wright, Peter
"Modeling an Organizational Buyer's Product Evaluation Strategy:
Validity and Procedural Considerations"
Journal of Marketing Research, Vol. XIII (August 1976), pp. 211-24.

Sheluga, David A., Jaccard, James, and Jacoby, Jacob
"Preference, Search, and Choice: An Integrative Approach"
Journal of Consumer Research, Vol. 6 (September 1979), pp. 166-76.

Srinivasan, V., Shocker, Allan D., and Weinstein, Alan G.
"Measurement of a Composite Criterion of Managerial Success"
Organizational Behavior and Human Performance (February 1973), pp.
147-67.

Stanton, Wilbur W. and Reese, Richard M.
"Three Conjoint Segmentation Approaches to the Evaluation of
Advertising Theme Creation"
Journal of Business Research, Vol. 11 (June 1983), pp. 201-16.

Tversky, Amos
"Additivity, Utility and Subjective Probability"
Journal of Mathematical Psychology, Vol. 4 (February 1967), pp. 1-20.

Ullrich, James R. and Painter, John R.
"A Conjoint Measurement Analysis of Human Judgment"
Organizational Behavior and Human Performance, Vol. 12 (1974), pp.
50-61.

Whitmore, G. A. and Cavadias, G. S.
"Experimental Determination of Community Preferences for Water
Quality-Cost Alternatives"
Decision Sciences, Vol. 5 (1974), pp. 614-31.

Wiley, James B. and Bushnell, R.
"Market Share Estimates Based on Conjoint Analysis of Concepts"
in Wilkie, William L. (editor)
Advances in Consumer Research, Volume Six
(Miami, FL: Association for Consumer Research, 1979), pp. 582-6.

Wind, Yoram
"Preference of Relevant Others and Individual Choice Models"
Journal of Consumer Research, Vol. 3 (June 1976), pp. 50-7.

Wind, Yoram
"Recent Approaches to the Study of Organizational Buying Behvior"
in Greer, T. V. (editor)
Increasing Marketing Productivity
(Chicago: American Marketing Association, 1973).

Wind, Yoram, Grashof, John F., and Goldhar, Joel D.
"Market-Based Guidelines for Design of Industrial Products"
Journal of Marketing, Vol. 42 (July 1978), pp. 27-37.

Wind, Y. and Spitz, L. K.
"Analytical Approach to Marketing Decisions in Health-Care
Organizations"
Operations Research, Vol. 24 (September-October 1976), pp. 973-90.

Wright, Peter and Weitz, Barton
"Time Horizon Effects on Product Evaluation Strategies"
Journal of Marketing Research, Vol. XIV (November 1977), pp. 429-43.

Zicha, Michael A. and Roy, Robert A.
"Improving Share-of-Preference Models: The Inclusion of Exogenous
Marketing Variables"
Marketing Research, Vol. 1 (June 1989), pp. 49-52.

Zufryden, Fred S.
"Using Conjoint Analysis to Predict Trial and Repeat-Purchase
Patterns of New Frequently Purchased Products"
Decision Sciences, Vol. 19 (Winter 1988), pp. 55-71.

Zufryden, F. S.
  "A Conjoint Measurement-Based Approach for Optimal New Product Design
  and Market Segmentation"
  in Shocker, A. D. (editor)
  Analytic Approaches to Product and Market Planning
  (Cambridge, MA: Marketing Science Institute, 1977), pp. 100-114.

187.01 ---------- Applications of Hybrid Conjoint Analysis

Tantiwong, Duangtip and Wilton, Peter C.
  "Understanding Food Store Preferences Among the Elderly Using Hybrid
  Conjoint Measurement Models"
  Journal of Retailing, Vol. 61 (Winter 1985), pp. 35-64.

187.02 ---------- Applications of Adaptive Conjoint Analysis

Klein, Noreen M. and Yadav, Manjit S.
  "Context Effects on Effort and Accuracy in Choice: An Enquiry Into
  Adaptive Decision Making"
  Journal of Consumer Research, Vol. 15 (March 1989), pp. 411-21.

188 --------------------- FUNCTIONAL MEASUREMENT ----------------------

188.01 ---------- Books Re: Functional Measurement

Anderson, Norman H.
  Methods of Information Integration Theory
  (New York: Academic Press, Inc., 1982).

Anderson, Norman H.
  Foundations of Information Integration Theory
  (New York: Academic Press, 1981).

188.02 ---------- Theory Re: Functional Measurement

Anderson, Norman H.
  "How Functional Measurement can Yield Validated Interval Scales of
  Mental Quantities"
  Journal of Applied Psychology, Vol. 61 (1976), pp. 677-92.

Anderson, Norman H.
  "Functional Measurement and Psychophysical Judgment"
  Psychological Review, Vol. 77 (May 1970), pp. 153-70.

Bagozzi, Richard P.
  "Expectancy-Value Attitude Models: An Analysis of Critical
  Measurement Issues"
  International Journal of Research in Marketing, Vol. 1, No. 4 (1984),
  pp. 295-310.

Bettman, James R., Capon, Noel, and Lutz, Richard J.
  "Multiattribute Measurement Models and Multiattribute Theory: A Test
  of Construct Validity"
  Journal of Consumer Research, Vol. 1 (1975), pp. 1-15.

Curry, D. J., Levin, I. P., and Gray, M. J.
  "A Comparison of Additive Conjoint Measurement and Functional
  Measurement in a Study of Apartment Preferences"
  Technical Report 98
  Institute of Regional Research, University of Iowa (1978).

Lynch, John G., Jr.
  "Uniqueness Issues in the Decompositional Modeling of Multiattribute
  Overall Evaluations: An Information Integration Perspective"
  Journal of Marketing Research, Vol. XXII (February 1985), pp. 1-19.

188.03 ---------- Applications of Functional Measurement

Tantiwong, Duangtip and Wilton, Peter C.
  "Understanding Food Store Preferences Among the Elderly Using Hybrid
  Conjoint Measurement Models"
  Journal of Retailing, Vol. 61 (Winter 1985), pp. 35-64.

189 ----- MULTIPLE CRITERION/MULTIPLE PREDICTOR (MCMP) TECHNIQUES ----
   See also (sub)heading(s) 185.04, 190, 191, 204.06, 206.03.

189.01 ---------- Theory Re: External Single-Set Components Analysis

Fornell, Claes
"External Single-Set Components Analysis of Multiple
Criterion/Multiple Predictor Variables"
Multivariate Behavioral Research, Vol. 14 (1979), pp. 323-38.

Zinkhan, George M. and Locander, William B.
"ESSCA: A Multidimensional Analysis Tool for Marketing Research"
Journal of the Academy of Marketing Science, Vol. 16 (Spring 1988),
pp. 36-46.

189.02 ---------- Theory Re: Redundancy Analysis

Miller, J. K.
"The Sampling Distribution and a Test for the Significance of the
Bimultivariate Redundancy Statistic: A Monte Carlo Study"
Multivariate Behavioral Research, Vol. 10 (1975), pp. 233-44.

Van Den Wollenberg, A. L.
"Redundancy Analysis: An Alternative for Canonical Correlation
Analysis"
Psychometrika, Vol. 42 (1977), pp. 207-19.

189.03 ---------- Applications of Redundancy Analysis

Zinkhan, George M.
"An Empirical Investigation of Aided Advertising Recall"
Current Issues and Research in Advertising, Vol. 5 (1982), pp. 137-60.

190 --------------------- CANONICAL ANALYSIS ---------------------
        See also (sub)heading(s) 189, 191.

190.01 ---------- Books Re: Canonical Analysis

De Leeuw, Jan
  Canonical Analysis of Categorical Data
  (Leiden, The Netherlands: University of Leiden, 1973).

Levine, Mark S.
  Canonical Analysis and Factor Comparison
  (Beverly Hills, CA: Sage Publications, Inc., 1977).

Thompson, Bruce
  Canonical Correlation
  (Beverly Hills, CA: Sage Publications, Inc.).

190.02 ---------- Theory Re: Canonical Analysis

Akaike, H.
  "Canonical Correlation Analysis and Information Criterion"
  in Mehra and Lainiotis (editors)
  System Identification: Advances and Case Studies
  (New York: Academic Press, 1976).

Alpert, Mark I. and Peterson, Robert A.
  "On the Interpretation of Canonical Analysis"
  Journal of Marketing Research, Vol. IX (May 1972), pp. 187-92.

Bagozzi, Richard P., Fornell, Claes, and Larcker, David F.
  "Canonical Correlation Analysis as a Special Case of a Structural
  Relations Model"
  Multivariate Behavioral Research, Vol. 16 (October 1981), pp. 437-54.

Bagozzi, R. P., Fornell, C., and Larcker, D. F.
  "Canonical Correlation Analysis as a Special Case of a Structural
  Relations Model"
  Massachusetts Institute of Technology (1981), unpublished working
  paper.

Bagozzi, R. P., Johansson, J. K., and Sheth, J. N.
  "Alternatives to Canonical Correlation Analysis in Marketing
  Research: A Structural Equation Approach"
  Massachusetts Institute of Technology (1981), unpublished working
  paper.

Barcikowski, Robert S. and Stevens, James P.
  "A Monte Carlo Study of the Stability of Canonical Correlations,
  Canonical Weights and Canonical Variate-Variable Correlations"
  Multivariate Behavioral Research, Vol. 10 (July 1975), pp. 353-64.

Bartlett, M. S.
  "Multivariate Analysis"
  Journal of the Royal Statistical Society, Supplement, Vol. 9 (1947),
  pp. 176-90.

Bartlett, M. S.
  "The Statistical Significance of Canonical Correlation"
  Biometrica, Vol. 32 (1941), pp. 29-38.

Baur, Detlef
  "Canonical Analysis as an Instrument for Segmentation"
  European Research, Vol. 6 (September 1978), pp. 189-96.

Carroll, J. Douglas
  "Generalization of Canonical Correlation Analysis to Three or More
  Sets of Variables"
  Proceedings of 76th Annual Conference of the American Psychological
  Association, Vol. 3 (1968), pp. 227,8.

Cliff, Norman and Krus, David J.
  "Interpretation of Canonical Analysis: Rotated vs. Unrotated
  Solutions"
  Psychometrika, Vol. 41 (March 1976), pp. 35-42.

Coxhead, P.
  "Measuring the Relationship Between Two Sets of Variables"
  British Journal of Mathematical and Statistical Psychology, Vol. 27
  (1974), pp. 205-12.

Cramer, E. M.
  "A Generalization of Vector Correlations and Its Relation to
  Canonical Correlations"
  Multivariate Behavioral Research, Vol. 9 (1974), pp. 347-52.

Cramer, E. M. and Nicewander, W. A.
  "Some Symmetric, Invariant Measures of Multivariate Association"
  Psychometrika, Vol. 44 (March 1979), pp. 43-54.

Darlington, Richard B., Weinberg, Sharon L., and Walberg, Herbert J.
"Canonical Variate Analysis and Related Techniques"
Review of Educational Research, Vol. 43, No. 4 (1973), pp. 433-54.

De Groot, M. H. and Li, E. C. C.
"Correlations Between Similar Sets of Measurements"
Biometrics, Vol. 22 (December 1966), pp. 781-90.

De Leeuw, Jan
Canonical Analysis of Categorical Data
Psychological Institute, University of Leiden, The Netherlands
(1973), unpublished doctoral dissertation.

Etgar, Michael
"Power in Distributive Channels: A Reply"
Journal of Marketing Research, Vol. XV (August 1978), pp. 492-4.

Fornell, Claes
"Problems in the Interpretation of Canonical Analysis: The Case of
Power in Distributive Channels"
Journal of Marketing Research, Vol. XV (August 1978), p. 489.

Fornell, Claes
"Three Approaches to Canonical Analysis"
Journal of the Market Research Society, Vol. 20 (July 1978), pp.
166-81.

Fornell, Claes
"The Anatomy of Canonical Analysis"
Research Paper 1/1
Department of Business Administration, University of Lund, Sweden
(November 1976).

Fornell, Claes and Larcker, D. F.
"The Use of Canonical Correlation Analysis in Accounting Research"
Journal of Business, Finance and Accounting, Vol. 7 (1980), pp.
455-73.

Goodman, Leo A.
"Association Models and Canonical Correlation in the Analysis of
Cross-Classifications Having Ordered Categories"
Journal of the American Statistical Association, Vol. 76 (June 1981),
pp. 320-34.

Gower, J. C.
"A Q-Technique for the Calculation of Canonical Variates"
Biometrika, Vol. 53 (December 1966), pp. 588-90.

Gower, J. C.
"Some Distance Properties of Latent Root and Vector Methods Used in
Multivariate Analysis"
Biometrika, Vol. 53 (1966), pp. 325-8.

Green, Paul E., Halbert, Michael H., and Robinson, Patrick J.
"Canonical Analysis: An Exposition and Illustrative Application"
Journal of Marketing Research, Vol. III (February 1966), pp. 32-9.

Holbrook, Morris B. and Moore, William L.
"Using Canonical Correlation to Construct Product Spaces for Objects
With Known Feature Structures"
Journal of Marketing Research, Vol. XIX (February 1982), pp. 87-98.

Holland, T., Levi, M., and Watson, C.
"Canonical Correlation in the Analysis of a Contingency Table"
Psychological Bulletin, Vol. 87 (1980), pp. 334-6.

Horst, Paul
"Relations Among M Sets of Measures"
Psychometrika, Vol. 26 (June 1961), pp. 129-49.

Horton, I. F., Russell, J. S., and Moore, A. W.
"Multivariate Covariance and Canonical Analysis: A Method of
Selecting the Most Effective Discriminators in a Multivariate
Situation"
Biometrics, Vol. 24 (December 1968), pp. 845-58.

Hotelling, Harold
"Relations Between Two Sets of Variates"
Biometrika, Vol. 28 (December 1936), pp. 321-77.

Hotelling, Harold
"The Most Predictable Criterion"
Journal of Educational Psychology, Vol. 26 (February 1935), pp.
139-42.

Isaac, P. D. and Milligan, Glenn W.
"A Comment on the Use of Canonical Correlation in the Analysis of
Contingency Tables"
Psychological Bulletin, Vol. 93, No. 2 (1983), pp. 378-81.

Johansson, Johny K. and Sheth, Jagdish N.
  "Canonical Correlation and Marketing Research"
  in Sheth, Jagdish N. (editor)
  Multivariate Methods for Market and Survey Research
  (Chicago: American Marketing Association, 1977), pp. 111-31.

Kettenring, John R.
  "Canonical Analysis of Several Sets of Variables"
  Biometrika, Vol. 58 (1971), pp. 433-51.

Koons, Paul B., Jr.
  "Canonical Analysis"
  in Borko, Harold (editor)
  Computer Applications in the Behavioral Sciences
  (Englewood Cliffs, NJ: Prentice-Hall, 1962), pp. 266-79.

Krus, David J., Reynolds, Thomas, and Krus, Patricia
  "Rotation in Canonical Variate Analysis"
  Education and Psychological Measurement, Vol. 36 (1976), pp. 725-30.

Krzanowski, W. J.
  "Canonical Representation of the Location Model for Discrimination or
  Classification"
  Journal of the American Statistical Association, Vol. 71 (December
  1976), pp. 845-8.

Krzanowski, W. J.
  "Discrimination and Classification Using Both Binary and Continuous
  Variables"
  Journal of the American Statistical Association, Vol. 70 (1975), pp.
  782-90.

Lambert, Zarrel V. and Durand, Richard M.
  "Some Precautions in Using Canonical Analysis"
  Journal of Marketing Research, Vol. XII (November 1975), pp. 468-75.

Maxwell, A. E.
  "Canonical Variate Analysis When the Variables are Dichotomous"
  Educational and Psychological Measurement, Vol. 21 (1961), pp. 259-71.

McKeon, James J.
  "Canonical Analysis: Some Relations Between Canonical Correlation,
  Factor Analysis, Discriminant Function Analysis, and Scaling Theory"
  Psychometric Monographs, No. 13 (1966).

Meredith, William
  "Canonical Correlations With Fallible Data"
  Psychometrika, Vol. 29 (1964), pp. 55,6.

Miller, John K.
  "The Sampling Distribution and a Test for the Significance of the
  Bimultivariate Redundancy Statistic: A Monte Carlo Study"
  Multivariate Behavioral Research, Vol. 10 (April 1975), pp. 233-44.

Miller, John K.
  "The Development and Application of Bimultivariate Correlation: A
  Measure of Statistical Association Between Multivariate Measurement
  Sets"
  State University of New York at Buffalo (1969), unpublished doctoral
  dissertation.

Miller, John K. and Farr, David S.
  "Bimultivariate Redundancy: A Comprehensive Measure of Interbattery
  Relationship"
  Multivariate Behavioral Research, Vol. 6 (July 1971), pp. 313-24.

Moore, William L. and Holbrook, Morris B.
  "Equivalences Among Several Types of Canonical Analysis"
  Columbia University (1981), working paper.

Ragland, Robert E.
  On Some Relations Between Canonical Correlation, Multiple Regression,
  and Factor Analysis
  unpublished doctoral dissertation, University of Oklahoma (1967).

Roseboom, W. W.
  "Linear Correlations Between Sets of Variables"
  Psychometrika, Vol. 30 (March 1965), pp. 51-71.

Saporta, G.
  "About Some Remarkable Properties of Generalized Canonical Analysis"
  Second European Meeting of the Psychometric Society
  Groningen, The Netherlands (June 1980), paper presentation.

Schaninger, Charles M., Lessig, V. Parker, and Panton, Don B.
  "The Complementary Use of Multivariate Procedures to Investigate
  Nonlinear and Interactive Relationships Between Personality and
  Product Usage"
  Journal of Marketing Research, Vol. XVII (February 1980), pp. 119-24.

Schnaars, Steven P. and Schiffman, Leon G.
    "An Application of a Segmentation Design Based on a Hybrid of
    Canonical Correlation and Simple Crosstabulation"
    Journal of the Academy of Marketing Science, Vol. 12 (Fall 1984), pp.
    177-89.

Shaffer, J. P. and Gillo, M. W.
    "A Multivariate Extension of the Correlation Ratio"
    Educational and Psychological Measurement, Vol. 34 (1974), pp. 521-4.

Srikantan, K. S.
    "Canonical Association Between Nominal Measurements"
    Journal of the American Statistical Association, Vol. 65 (March
    1970), pp. 284-92.

Stewart, Douglas and Love, William
    "A General Canonical Index"
    Psychological Bulletin, Vol. 70 (September 1968), pp. 160-3.

Thorndike, Robert M.
    "Studying Canonical Analysis: Comments on Barcikowski and Stevens"
    Multivariate Behavioral Research, Vol. 11 (April 1976), pp. 249-53.

Thorndike, Robert M. and Weiss, D. J.
    "A Study of the Stabilty of Canonical Correlations and Canonical
    Components"
    Educational and Psychological Measurement, Vol. 33 (1973), pp. 123-34.

Thorndike, Robert M., and Weiss, David J.
    "Stability of Canonical Components"
    Proceedings, Vol. 5 (Part 1), pp. 107,8.

Van Den Wollenberg, A. L.
    "Redundancy Analysis--An Alternative for Canonical Correlation
    Analysis"
    Psychometrika, Vol. 42 (June 1977), pp. 207-19.

Wood, Donald A.
    "Toward the Interpretation of Canonical Dimensions"
    Multivariate Behavioral Research, Vol. 7 (October 1972), pp. 477-82.

Wood, Donald A. and Erskine, James A.
    "Analytical Strategies in Canonical Correlation: A Review and
    Application"
    Graduate School of Business, Indiana University, undated.

190.03 ---------- Statistical Tests in Canonical Analysis

Lawley, D. N.
    "Tests of Significance in Canonical Analysis"
    Biometrika, Vol. 46 (June 1959), pp. 59-66.

Mariott, F. H. C.
    "Tests of Significance in Canonical Analysis"
    Biometrika, Vol. 39 (May 1952), pp. 58-64.

Miller, John K.
    "The Sampling Distribution and a Test for the Significance of the
    Bimultivariate Redundancy Statistic: A Monte Carlo Study"
    Multivariate Research, Vol. 10 (April 1975), pp. 233-44.

Wildt, Albert R., Lambert, Zarrel V., and Durand, Richard M.
    "Applying the Jackknife Statistic in Testing and Interpreting
    Canonical Weights, Loadings, and Cross-Loadings"
    Journal of Marketing Research, Vol. XIX (February 1982), pp. 99-107.

190.04 ---------- Applications of Canonical Analysis

Alpert, Mark I.
    "Personality and the Determinants of Product Choice"
    Journal of Marketing Research, Vol. IX (February 1972), pp. 89-92.

Alpert, Mark I.
    "A Canonical Analysis of Personality and the Determinants of
    Automobile Choice"
    Combined Proceedings
    (Chicago: American Marketing Association, 1971), pp. 312-6.

Anand, Punam and Stern, Louis W.
    "A Sociopsychological Explanation for Why Marketing Channel Members
    Relinquish Control"
    Journal of Marketing Research, Vol. XXII (November 1985), pp. 365-76.

Assael, Henry
    "Segmenting Markets by Response Elasticity"
    Journal of Advertising Research, Vol. 16 (April 1976), pp. 27-35.

Avlonitis, George J.
   "Linking Different Types of Product Elimination Decisions to Their
   Performance Outcome: Project Dropstrat"
   International Journal of Research in Marketing, Vol. 4, No. 1 (1987),
   pp. 43-57.

Baumgarten, Steven A. and Ring, L. Winston
   "An Evaluation of Media Readership Constructs and Audience Profiles
   by Use of Canonical Correlation Analysis"
   Combined Proceedings, American Marketing Association (1971), pp.
   548-58.

Darden, William R. and Perreault, William D., Jr.
   "A Multivariate Analysis of Media Exposure and Vacation Behavior With
   Life Style Covariates"
   Journal of Consumer Research, Vol. 2 (September 1975), pp. 93-103.

Darden, William R. and Reynolds, Fred D.
   "Shopping Orientations and Product Usage Rates"
   Journal of Marketing Research, Vol. VIII (November 1971), pp. 505-8.

DeSarbo, Wayne S. and Hoffman, Donna L.
   "Constructing MDS Joint Spaces From Binary Choice Data: A
   Multidimensional Unfolding Threshold Model for Marketing Research"
   Journal of Marketing Research, Vol. XXIV (February 1987), pp. 40-54.

Etgar, Michael
   "Channel Environment and Channel Leadership"
   Journal of Marketing Research, Vol. XIV (February 1977), pp. 69-76.

Etgar, Michael
   "Channel Domination and Countervailing Power in Distributive Channels"
   Journal of Marketing Research Vol. XIII (August 1976), pp. 254-62.

Farley, John U. and Ring, L. Winston
   "Empirical Specification of a Buyer Behavior Model"
   Journal of Marketing Research, Vol. 11 (February 1974), pp. 89-96.

Frank, Ronald E.
   "Predicting New Product Segments"
   Journal of Advertising Research, Vol. 12 (June 1972), pp. 9-13.

Frank, Ronald E. and Strain, Charles E.
   "A Segmentation Research Design Using Consumer Panel Data"
   Journal of Marketing Research, Vol. IX (November 1972), pp. 385-90.

Futrell, Charles M., Swan, John E., and Todd, John T.
   "Job Performance Related to Management Control Systems for
   Pharmaceutical Salesman"
   Journal of Marketing Research, Vol. XIII (February 1976), pp. 25-33.

Gensch, Dennis H. and Turner, Ronald
   "Expanding the Definition of Potential Customer Using Modified
   Canonical Correlation"
   Combined Proceedings
   (Chicago: American Marketing Association, 1972), pp. 499-504.

Granzin, Kent L. and Williams, Robert H.
   "Patterns of Behavioral Characteristics as Indicants of Recreation
   Preference: A Canonical Analysis"
   Research Quarterly, Vol. 49 (May 1978), pp. 135-45.

Green, Paul E., Rao, Vithala R., and DeSarbo, Wayne S.
   "Incorporating Group-Level Similarity Judgments in Conjoint Analysis"
   Journal of Consumer Research, Vol. 5 (December 1978), pp. 187-93.

Grossbart, Sanford L. and Crosby, Lawrence A.
   "Understanding the Bases of Parental Concern and Reaction to
   Children's Food Advertising"
   Journal of Marketing, Vol. 48 (Summer 1984), pp. 79-92.

Gwin, John M.
   "Financial Institution Branching Decisions: A Macro-Heuristic"
   Journal of the Academy of Marketing Science, Vol. 13 (Spring 1985),
   pp. 259-70.

Henke, Lucy L. and Donohue, Thomas R.
   "Functional Displacement of Traditional TV Viewing by VCR Owners"
   Journal of Advertising Research, Vol. 29 (April/May 1989), pp. 18-23.

Holbrook, Morris B., Moore, William L., Dodgen, Gary N., and Havlena,
   William J.
   "Nonisomorphism, Shadow Features and Imputed Preferences"
   Marketing Science, Vol. 4 (Summer 1985), pp. 215-33.

Lessig, V. Parker
   "Relating Multivariate Measures of Store Loyalty and Store Image"
   Combined Proceedings
   (Chicago: American Marketing Association, 1972), pp. 305-9.

Lessig, V. Parker and Copley, Thomas P.
"Consumer Beliefs, Attitudes, and Brand Preferences"
Journal of the Academy of Marketing Science, Vol. 2 (Spring 1974),
pp. 357-66.

Lessig, V. Parker and Tollefson, John O.
"Prediction of Buying Behaviour From Personal Characteristics"
European Research, Vol. 1 (September 1973), pp. 184-9.

Lessig, V. and Tollefson, John O.
"Market Segmentation Through Numerical Taxonomy"
Journal of Marketing Research, Vol. VIII (November 1971), pp. 480-7.

MacKay, David B. and Olshavsky, Richard W.
"Cognitive Maps of Retail Locations: An Investigation of Some Basic
Issues"
Journal of Consumer Research, Vol. 2 (December 1975), pp. 197-205.

Neilson, Richard P. and Stanton, John
"Type of Information Sensitivity, Fatalism and Spending Behavior"
Combined Proceedings
(Chicago: American Marketing Association, 1972), pp. 400-5.

Pruden, Henry O. and Peterson, Robert A.
"Personality and Performance-Satisfaction of Industrial Salesmen"
Journal of Marketing Research, Vol. VIII (November 1971), pp. 501-4.

Richins, Marsha L.
"A Multivariate Analysis of Responses to Dissatisfaction"
Journal of the Academy of Marketing Science, Vol. 15 (Fall 1987), pp.
24-31.

Rossiter, J. R. and Robertson, T. S.
"Canonical Analysis of Developmental, Social and Experiential Factors
in Children's Comprehension of Television Advertising"
Journal of Genetic Psychology, Vol. 129 (December 1976), pp. 317-27.

Rossiter, J. R. and Robertson, T. S.
"Children's TV Commercials: Testing the Defenses"
Journal of Communication, Vol. 24 (Autumn 1974), pp. 134-144.

Schaninger, Charles M. and Buss, W. Christian
"The Relationship of Sex-Role Norms to Household Task Allocation"
Psychology and Marketing, Vol. 2 (Summer 1985), pp. 93-104.

Schaninger, Charles M. and Sciglimpaglia, Donald
"The Influence of Cognitive Personality Traits and Demographics on
Consumer Information Acquisition"
Journal of Consumer Research, Vol. 8 (September 1981), pp. 208-16.

Schul, Patrick L., Pride, William M., and Little, Taylor L.
"The Impact of Channel Leadership Behavior on Intrachannel Conflict"
Journal of Marketing, Vol. 47 (Summer 1983), pp. 21-34.

Sherman, L. and Sheth, Jagdish N.
"Cluster Analysis and Its Applications in Marketing Research"
in Sheth, J. N. (editor)
Multivariate Methods for Market and Survey Research
(Chicago: American Marketing Association, 1977).

Sheth, Jagdish N.
"Multivariate Analysis in Marketing"
Journal of Advertising Research, Vol. 10 (February 1970), pp. 29-39.

Sparks, David L. and Tucker, W. T.
"A Multivariate Analysis of Personality and Product Use"
Journal of Marketing Research, Vol. VIII (February 1971), pp. 67-70.

Srivastava, Rajendra K., Alpert, Mark I., and Shocker, Allan D.
"A Customer-Oriented Approach for Determining Market Structures"
Journal of Marketing, Vol. 48 (Spring 1984), pp. 32-45.

Stewart, David W. and Furse, David H.
"The Effects of Television Advertising Execution on Recall,
Comprehension, and Persuasion"
Psychology and Marketing, Vol. 2 (Fall 1985), pp. 135-60.

Sweeney, Timothy W., Mathews, H. Lee, and Wilson, David T.
"An Analysis of Industrial Buyers' Risk Reducing Behavior: Some
Personality Correlates"
Combined Proceedings, American Marketing Association (1972), pp.
271-81.

Westbrook, Robert A. and Fornell, Claes
"Patterns of Information Source Usage Among Durable Goods Buyers"
Journal of Marketing Research, Vol. XVI (August 1979), pp. 303-12.

Worthing, Parker M., Venkatesan, M., and Smith, Steve
    "A Modified Approach to the Exploration of Personality and Product
    Use"
    Combined Proceedings
    (Chicago: American Marketing Association, 1971), pp. 363-7.

190.05 ---------- Computer Programs for Canonical Analysis

Jain, Arun K.
    "CANCOR: Program for Canonical Correlation of Three or More Sets of
    Variables"
    Journal of Marketing Research, Vol. IX (February 1972), pp. 69,70.

Roskam, E.
    "A Program for Computing Canonical Correlations on IBM 1620"
    Educational and Psychological Measurement, Vol. 26 (Spring 1966), pp.
    193-8.

Westin, Stuart A. and Dillon, William R.
    "CANDI: A Program to Provide a Canonical Representation of Distance
    Scores"
    Journal of Marketing Research, Vol. XVI (November 1979), pp. 559,60.

191 ----------- MULTIVARIATE ANALYSIS OF VARIANCE (MANOVA) -----------
        See also (sub)heading(s) 179, 189, 190.

191.01 ---------- Books Re: Multivariate Analysis of Variance (MANOVA)

Appelbaum, Mark I.
   The MANOVA Manual: Complete Factorial Design
   Research Memorandum No. 44
   (Chapel Hill, NC: The L. L. Thurstone Psychometric Laboratory,
   University of North Carolina, 1974).

Bray, James H. and Maxwell, Scott E.
   Multivariate Analysis of Variance
   (Beverly Hills, CA: Sage Publications, Inc., 1985), 80 pp.

Finn, Jeremy D.
   A General Model for Multivariate Analysis
   (New York: Holt, Rinehart and Winston, Inc., 1974).

Roy, Samarenda Nath, Gnanadesikan, Ramanathan G., and Srivastava,
   Jagdish Narain
   Analysis and Design of Certain Quantitative Multiresponse Experiments
   (Oxford: Pergamon Press, 1971).

191.02 ---------- Theory Re: Multivariate Analysis of Variance

Bock, R. Darrell
   "Programming Univariate and Multivariate Analysis of Variance"
   Technometrics, Vol. 5 (February 1963), pp. 95-117.

Bock, R. Darrell and Haggard, Ernest A.
   "The Use of Multivariate Analysis of Variance in Behavioral Research"
   in Whitla, Dean K. (editor)
   Handbook of Measurement and Assessment in Behavioral Sciences
   (Reading, MA: Addison Wesley Publishing Company, 1968).

Borgen, Fred H. and Seling, Mark J.
   "Uses of Discriminant Analysis Following MANOVA"
   Journal of Applied Psychology, Vol. 63 (December 1978), pp. 689-97.

Box, G. E. P.
   "A General Distribution Theory for a Class of Likelihood Criteria"
   Biometrika, Vol. 36, pp. 317-46.

Darden, William R. and Reynolds, Fred D.
   "Multivariate ANOVA in Marketing: An Exposition and Case Analysis"
   Proceedings, Fourth Annual Meeting of the American Institute for
   Decision Sciences (1972), pp. 105-11.

Dillon, William R., Frederick, Donald G., and Tangpanichdee, Vanchai
   "A Note on Accounting for Sources of Variation in Perceptual Maps"
   Journal of Marketing Research, Vol. XIX (August 1982), pp. 302-11.

Hotelling, H. A.
   "A Generalized T-Test and Measure of Multivariate Dispersion"
   Proceedings of the Second Berkeley Symposium of Mathematical
   Statistics and Probability, Vol. 2 (1951), pp. 23-41.

Hotelling, H.
   "The Generalization of Student's Ratio"
   Annals of Mathematical Statistics, Vol. 2 (1931), pp. 360-78.

Kuhnel, Steffen M.
   "Testing MANOVA Designs With LISREL"
   Sociological Methods and Research, Vol. 16 (May 1988), pp. 504-23.

Olson, Chester L.
   "Comparative Robustness of Six Tests in Multivariate Analysis of
   Variance"
   Journal of the American Statistical Association, Vol. 9 (December
   1974), pp. 894-908.

Overall, John E. and Spiegel, Douglas K.
   "Concerning Least Squares Analysis of Experimental Data"
   Psychological Bulletin, Vol. 72 (November 1969), pp. 311-22.

Pothoff, R. F. and Roy, S. N.
   "A Generalized Multivariate Analysis of Variance Model Useful
   Especially for Growth Curve Problems"
   Biometrika, Vol. 51 (1964), pp. 313-26.

Spector, P. E.
   "What to do With Significant Multivariate Effects in Multivariate
   Analyses of Variance"
   Journal of Applied Psychology, Vol. 62 (April 1977), pp. 158-63.

Stevens, James P.
   "Power of the Multivariate Analysis of Variance Tests"
   Psychological Bulletin, Vol. 88 (November 1980), pp. 728-37.

Stevens, James P.
"Step-Down Analysis and Simultaneous Confidence Intervals in MANOVA"
Multivariate Behavior Research, Vol. 8 (July 1973), pp. 391-402.

Stevens, James P.
"Global Measures of Association in Multivariate Analysis of Variance"
Multivariate Behavioral Research, Vol. 7 (July 1972), pp. 373-8.

Wilks, S. S.
"Certain Generalizations in the Analysis of Variance"
Biometrika, Vol. 24 (1951), pp. 471-94.

Woodward, J. Arthur and Overall, John E.
"Multivariate Analysis by Multiple Regression Methods"
Psychological Bulletin, Vol. 82 (1975), pp. 21-32.

191.03 ---------- Theory Re: Repeated Measures MANOVA

    See also (sub)heading(s) 183.

LaTour, Stephen A. and Miniard, Paul W.
"The Misuse of Repeated Measures Analysis in Marketing Research"
Journal of Marketing Research, Vol. XX (February 1983), pp. 45-57.

O'Brien, Ralph G. and Kaiser, Mary Kister
"MANOVA Method for Analyzing Repeated Measures Designs: An Extensive Primer"
Psychological Bulletin, Vol. 97 (March 1985), pp. 316-33.

191.04 ---------- Statistical Tests in MANOVA

Mardia, K. V.
"The Effects of Nonnormality on Some Multivariate Tests and Robustness to Nonnormality in the Linear Model"
Biometrika, Vol. 58 (April 1971), pp. 105-21.

Olsen, Chester L.
"On Choosing a Test Statistic in Multivariate Analysis of Variance"
Psychological Bulletin, Vol. 82 (July 1976), pp. 579-86.

Roy, J.
"Step-Down Procedure in Multivariate Analysis"
Annals of Mathematical Statistics, Vol. 29 (December 1958), pp. 263-78.

Roy, J. and Bargman, R. E.
"Tests of Multiple Independence and the Associated Confidence Bounds"
Annals of Mathematical Statistics, Vol. 29 (June 1958), pp. 491-503.

Stevens, James
"Comment on Olsen: Choosing a Test Statistic in Multivariate Analysis of Variance"
Psychological Bulletin, Vol. 86 (March 1979), pp. 355-60.

191.05 ---------- Theory Re: Multivariate Analysis of Covariance

Appelbaum, Mark I. and Cramer, Elliot M.
"Some Problems in the Nonorthogonal Analysis of Variance"
Psychological Bulletin, Vol. 81, No. 6 (1974), pp. 335-43.

Wind, Yoram and Denny, Joseph
"Multivariate Analysis of Variance in Research on the Effectiveness of T.V. Commercials"
Journal of Marketing Research, Vol. XI (May 1974), pp. 136-42.

191.06 ---------- Applications of Multivariate Analysis of Variance

Acito, Franklin and Anderson, Ronald D.
"A Monte Carlo Comparison of Factor Analytical Methods"
Journal of Marketing Research, Vol. XVII (May 1980), pp. 228-36.

Akaah, Ishmael P. and Riordan, Edward A.
"Applicability of Marketing Knowhow in the Third World"
International Marketing Review, Vol. 8 (Spring 1988), pp. 41-55.

Armstrong, Gary M., Curol, Metin N., and Russ, Frederick A.
"Detecting and Correcting Deceptive Advertising"
Journal of Consumer Research, Vol. 6 (December 1979), pp. 237-46.

Assael, Henry and Kamins, Michael A.
"Effects of Appeal Type and Involvement on Product Disconfirmation: A Cognitive Response Approach Through Product Trial"
Journal of the Academy of Marketing Science, Vol. 17 (Summer 1989), pp. 197-207.

Barry, Thomas E., Gilly, Mary C., and Doran, Lindley E.
"Advertising to Women With Different Career Orientations"
Journal of Advertising Research, Vol. 25 (April/May 1985), pp. 26-35.

Bellizzi, Joseph A. and Hite, Robert E.
"Supervising Unethical Salesforce Behavior"
Journal of Marketing, Vol. 53 (April 1989), pp. 36-47.

Bello, Daniel C. and Williamson, Nicholas C.
"The American Export Trading Company: Designing A New International
Marketing Institution"
Journal of Marketing, Vol. 49 (Fall 1985), pp. 60-9.

Berkowitz, E. N. and Walton, J. R.
"Contextual Influences on Consumer Price Responses: An Experimental
Analysis"
Journal of Marketing Research, Vol. XVII (August 1980), pp. 349-58.

Bloch, Peter H., Ridgway, Nancy M., and Sherrell, Daniel L.
"Extending the Concept of Shopping: An Investigation of Browsing
Activity"
Journal of the Academy of Marketing Science, Vol. 17 (Winter 1989),
pp. 13-21.

Bracker, Jeffrey S. and Pearson, John N.
"The Impact of Franchising on the Financial Performance of Small
Firms"
Journal of the Academy of Science, Vol. 14 (Winter 1986), pp. 10-7.

Bruner, Gordon C., II
"Problem Recognition Styles and Search Patterns: An Empirical
Investigation"
Journal of Retailing, Vol. 62 (Fall 1986), pp. 281-97.

Burke, Marian C.
"Strategic Choice and Marketing Managers: An Examination of
Business-Level Marketing Objectives"
Journal of Marketing Research, Vol. XXI (November 1984), pp. 345-59.

Burnett, John J. and Oliver, Richard L.
"Fear Appeal Effects in the Field: A Segmentation Approach"
Journal of Marketing Research, Vol. XVI (May 1979), pp. 181-90.

Burnett, John J. and Wilkes, Robert E.
"Fear Appeals to Segments Only"
Journal of Advertising Research, Vol. 20 (October 1980), pp. 21-4.

Chiesl, Newell E. and Lamb, Steven W.
"Segmenting International Industrial Markets"
Journal of the Academy of Marketing Science, Vol. 11 (Summer 1983),
pp. 250-8.

Cort, Stanton G. and Dominguez, Luis V.
"Cross Shopping and Retail Growth"
Journal of Marketing Research, Vol. XIV (May 1977), pp. 187-92.

Crocker, Kenneth E.
"The Influence of the Amount and Type of Information on Individuals'
Perception of Legal Services"
Journal of the Academy of Marketing Science, Vol. 14 (Winter 1986),
pp. 18-27.

Cron, William L., Dubinsky, Alan J., and Michaels, Ronald E.
"The Influence of Career States on Components of Salesperson
Motivation"
Journal of Marketing, Vol. 52 (January 1988), pp. 78-92.

Darden, William R. and Perreault, William D., Jr.
"A Multivariate Analysis of Media Exposure and Vacation Behavior With
Life Style Covariates"
Journal of Consumer Research, Vol. 2 (September 1975), pp. 93-103.

Darden, William R. and Rao, C. P.
"A Linear Covariate Model of Warranty Attitudes and Behaviors"
Journal of Marketing Research, Vol. XVI (November 1979), pp. 466-77.

Della Bitta, Albert J., Monroe, Kent B., and McGinnis, John M.
"Consumer Perceptions of Comparative Price Advertisements"
Journal of Marketing Research, Vol. XVIII (November 1981), pp. 416-27.

Dickson, Peter R.
"The Impact of Enriching Case and Statistical Information on Consumer
Judgments"
Journal of Consumer Research, Vol. 8 (March 1982), pp. 398-406.

Domzal, Teresa J. and Kernan, Jerome B.
"Television Audience Segmentation According to Need Gratification"
Journal of Advertising Research, Vol 23 (October/November 1983), pp.
37-49.

Downs, Phillip E. and Haynes, Joel B.
    "Examining Retail Image Before and After a Repositioning Strategy"
    Journal of the Academy of Marketing Science, Vol. 12 (Fall 1984), pp.
    1-24.

Dwyer, F. Robert
    "Are Two Better Than One? Bargaining Behavior and Outcomes in an
    Asymmetrical Power Relationship"
    Journal of Consumer Research, Vol. 11 (September 1984), pp. 680-93.

Etgar, Michael and Goodwin, Stephen A.
    "One-Sided Versus Two-Sided Comparative Message Appeals for New Brand
    Introductions"
    Journal of Consumer Research, Vol. 8 (March 1982), pp. 460-5.

Etgar, Michael, Jain, Arun K., and Agarwal, Manoj K.
    "Salesmen-Customer Interaction: An Experimental Approach"
    Journal of the Academy of Marketing Science, Vol. 6 (Winter-Spring
    1978), pp. 1-11.

Farley, John U., Katz, Jerrold, and Lehmann, Donald R.
    "Impact of Different Comparison Sets on Evaluation of a New
    Subcompact Car Brand"
    Journal of Consumer Research, Vol. 5 (September 1978), pp. 138-42.

Festervand, Troy A., Snyder, Don R., and Tsalikis, John D.
    "Influence of Catalog vs. Store Shopping and Prior Satisfaction on
    Perceived Risk"
    Journal of the Academy of Marketing Science, Vol. 14 (Winter 1986),
    pp. 28-36.

Folkes, Valerie S.
    "Consumer Reactions to Product Failure: An Attributional Approach"
    Journal of Consumer Research, Vol. 10 (March 1984), pp. 398-409.

Ford, Gary T.
    "Adoption of Consumer Policies by States: Some Empirical Perspectives"
    Journal of Marketing Research, Vol. XV (February 1978), pp. 49-57.

Freiden, Jon B.
    "Advertising Spokesperson Effects: An Examination of Endorser Type
    and Gender on Two Audiences"
    Journal of Advertising Research, Vol. 24 (October/November 1984), pp.
    33-41.

Friedman, Hershey H. and Friedman, Linda
    "Endorser Effectiveness by Product Type"
    Journal of Advertising Research, Vol. 19 (October 1979), pp. 63-71.

Hawes, Jon M. and Lumpkin, James R.
    "Understanding the Outshopper"
    Journal of the Academy of Marketing Science, Vol. 12 (Fall 1984), pp.
    200-18.

Holmes, John H. and Crocker, Kenneth E.
    "Predispositions and the Comparative Effectiveness of Rational,
    Emotional and Discrepant Appeals for Both High Involvement and Low
    Involvement Products"
    Journal of the Academy of Marketing Science, Vol. 15 (Spring 1987),
    pp. 27-35.

Hunt, James M. and Smith, Michael F.
    "The Persuasive Impact of Two-Sided Selling Appeals for an Unknown
    Brand Name"
    Journal of the Academy of Marketing Science, Vol. 15 (Spring 1987),
    pp. 11-8.

Jackson, Donald W., Jr., Keith, Janet E., and Burdick, Richard K.
    "Purchasing Agents' Perceptions of Industrial Buying Center
    Influence: A Situational Approach"
    Journal of Marketing, Vol. 48 (Fall 1984), pp. 75-83.

Jackson, Ralph W., McDaniel, Stephen W., and Rao, C. P.
    "Food Shopping and Preparation: Psychographic Differences of Working
    Wives and Housewives"
    Journal of Consumer Research, Vol. 12 (June 1985), pp. 110-3.

Jain, Arun K. and Pinson, Christian
    "The Effect of Order of Presentation of Similarity Judgements of
    Multidimensional Scaling Results: An Empirical Examination"
    Journal of Marketing Research, Vol. XIII (November 1976), pp. 435-9.

Lambert, David R., Dornoff, Ronald J., and Kernan, Jerome B.
    "The Industrial Buyer and the Postchoice Evaluation Process"
    Journal of Marketing Research, Vol. XIV (May 1977), pp. 246-251.

Lambert, Zarrel V., Doering, Paul L., Goldstein, Eric, and McCormick,
    William C.
    "Predispositions Toward Generic Drug Acceptance"
    Journal of Consumer Research, Vol. 7 (June 1980), pp. 14-23.

Lee, Hanjoon, Acito, Frank, and Day, Ralph L.
"Evaluation and Use of Marketing Research by Decision Makers: A Behavioral Simulation"
Journal of Marketing Research, Vol. XXIV (May 1987), pp. 187-96.

Leigh, James H. and Futrell, Charles M.
"From the Trenches to the Command Post: Perceptual and Attitudinal Differences Among Levels in the Marketing Management Hierarchy"
Journal of Business Research, Vol. 13 (December 1985), pp. 511-36.

Lichtenstein, Donald R. and Bearden, William O.
"Contextual Influences on Perceptions of Merchant-Supplied Reference Prices"
Journal of Consumer Research, Vol. 16 (June 1989), pp. 55-66.

Lim, Jeen-Su and Summers, John O.
"A Non-Experimental Investigation of Demand Artifacts in a Personal Selling Experiment"
Journal of Marketing Research, Vol. XXI (August 1984), pp. 251-8.

Locander, William B. and Hermann, Peter W.
"The Effect of Self-Confidence and Anxiety on Information Seeking in Consumer Risk Reduction"
Journal of Marketing Research, Vol. XVI (May 1979), pp. 268-74.

Lumpkin, James R.
"Shopping Orientation Segmentation of the Elderly Consumer"
Journal of the Academy of Marketing Science, Vol. 13 (Spring 1985), pp. 271-89.

Lumpkin, James R. and Hawes, Jon M.
"Retailing Without Stores: An Examination of Catalog Shoppers"
Journal of Business Research, Vol. 13 (April 1985), pp. 139-51.

Marks, Lawrence J. and Kamins, Michael A.
"The Use of Product Sampling and Advertising: Effects of Sequence of Exposure and Degree of Advertising Claim Exaggeration on Consumers' Belief Strength, Belief Confidence, and Attitudes"
Journal of Marketing Research, Vol. XXV (August 1988), pp. 266-81.

Mizerski, R. W., Allison, N. K., and Calvert, S.
"A Controlled Field Study of Corrective Advertising Using Multiple Exposures and a Commercial Medium"
Journal of Marketing Research, Vol. XVII (August 1980), pp. 341-8.

Moinpour, Reza, McCullough, James M., and MacLachlan, Douglas L.
"Time Changes in Perception: A Longitudinal Application of Multidimensional Scaling"
Journal of Marketing Research, Vol. XIII (August 1976), pp. 245-53.

Mowen, John C., Keith, Janet E., Brown, Stephen W., and Jackson, Donald W., Jr.
"Utilizing Effort and Task Difficulty Information in Evaluating Salespeople"
Journal of Marketing Research, Vol. XXII (May 1985), pp. 185-91.

Park, C. Whan
"The Effect of Individual and Situation-Related Factors on Consumer Selection of Judgmental Models"
Journal of Marketing Research, Vol. XIII (May 1976), pp. 144-51.

Petroshius, Susan M. and Crocker, Kenneth E.
"An Empirical Analysis of Spokesperson Characteristics on Advertisement and Product Evaluations"
Journal of the Academy of Marketing Science, Vol. 17 (Summer 1989), pp. 217-25.

Petroshius, Susan M. and Monroe, Kent B.
"Effect of Product-Line Pricing Characteristics on Product Evaluations"
Journal of Consumer Research, Vol. 13 (March 1987), pp. 511-9.

Reynolds, Thomas J. and Jolly, James P.
"Measuring Personal Values: An Evaluation of Alternative Methods"
Journal of Marketing Research, Vol. XVII (November 1980), pp. 531-6.

Roberts, Mary Lou and Taylor, James R.
"Analyzing Proximity Judgments in an Experimental Design"
Journal of Marketing Research, Vol. XII (February 1975), pp. 68-72.

Schaninger, Charles M.
"Social Class Versus Income Revisited: An Empirical Investigation"
Journal of Marketing Research, Vol. XVIII (May 1981), pp. 192-208.

Schaninger, Charles M. and Allen, Chris T.
"Wife's Occupational Status as a Consumer Behavior Construct"
Journal of Consumer Research, Vol. 8 (September 1981), pp. 189-96.

Schaninger, Charles M., Bourgeois, Jacques C., and Buss, W. Christian
    "French-English Canadian Subcultural Consumption Differences"
    Journal of Marketing, Vol. 49 (Spring 1985), pp. 82-92.

Sirgy, M. Joseph
    "Using Self-Congruity and Ideal Congruity to Predict Purchase
    Motivation"
    Journal of Business Research, Vol. 13 (June 1985), pp. 195-206.

Stephens, Nancy and Warrens, Robert A.
    "Advertising Frequency Requirements for Older Adults"
    Journal of Advertising Research, Vol. 23 (December 1983/January
    1984), pp. 23-32.

Stern, Barbara B., Gould, Stephen J., and Barak, Benny
    "Baby Boom Singles: The Social Seekers"
    Journal of Consumer Marketing, Vol. 4 (Fall 1987), pp. 5-22.

Swan, John E., Rink, David R., Kiser, G. E., and Martin, Warren S.
    "Industrial Buyer Image of the Saleswoman"
    Journal of Marketing, Vol. 48 (Winter 1984), pp. 110-6.

Swartz, Teresa A.
    "Brand Symbols and Message Differentiation"
    Journal of Advertising Research, Vol. 23 (October/November 1983), pp.
    59-64.

Tankersley, Clint B. and Lambert, David R.
    "Social Character and the Structure of Behavioral Intention"
    Journal of the Academy of Marketing Science, Vol. 6 (Winter-Spring
    1978), pp. 52-60.

Tat, Peter, Cunningham, William A., III, and Babakus, Emin
    "Consumer Perceptions of Rebates"
    Journal of Advertising Research, Vol. 28 (August/September 1988), pp.
    45-50.

Toy, Daniel R.
    "Monitoring Communication Effects: A Cognitive Structure/Cognitive
    Response Approach"
    Journal of Consumer Research, Vol. 9 (June 1982), pp. 66-76.

Vanier, Dinoo J. and Sciglimpaglia, Donald
    "Development and Application of the Concept of User Image: The Case
    of Mass Transit Ridership"
    Journal of the Academy of Marketing Science, Vol. 9 (Fall 1981), pp.
    479-89.

Vinson, Donald E. and Lundstrom, William J.
    "The Use of Students as Experimental Subjects in Marketing Research"
    Journal of the Academy of Marketing Science, Vol. 6 (Winter-Spring
    1978), pp. 114-25.

Wilkes, Robert E.
    "Fraudulent Behavior by Consumers"
    Journal of Marketing, Vol 42 (October 1978), pp. 67-75.

Wood, Van R. and Goolsby, Jerry R.
    "Foreign Market Information Preferences of Established U.S. Exporters"
    International Marketing Review, Vol. 4 (Winter 1987), pp. 43-52.

191.07 ---------- Applications of Repeated Measures MANOVA

Dowling, G. R.
    "Product Evaluation in a Dynamic Market"
    Psychology and Marketing, Vol. 3 (Summer 1986), pp. 99-111.

Leong, Siew Meng, Busch, Paul S., and John, Deborah Roedder
    "Knowledge Bases and Salesperson Effectiveness: A Script-Theoretic
    Analysis"
    Journal of Marketing Research, Vol. XXVI (May 1989), pp. 164-78.

191.08 ---------- Applications of Multivariate Analysis of Covariance

Bearden, William O., Lichtenstein, Donald R., and Teel, Jesse E.
    "Comparison Price, Coupon, and Brand Effects on Consumer Reactions to
    Retail Newspaper Advertisement"
    Journal of Retailing, Vol. 60 (Summer 1984), pp. 11-34.

Douglas, Susan P.
    "Cross-National Comparisons and Consumer Stereotypes: A Case Study of
    Working and Non-Working Wives in the U.S. and France"
    Journal of Consumer Research, Vol. 3 (June 1976), pp. 12-20.

Dwyer, F. Robert and Welsh, M. Ann
    "Environmental Relationships of the Internal Political Economy of
    Marketing Channels"
    Journal of Marketing Research, Vol. XXII (November 1985), pp. 397-414.

Ha, Young-Won and Hoch, Stephen J.
"Ambiguity, Processing Strategy, and Advertising-Evidence Interactions"
Journal of Consumer Research, Vol. 16 (December 1989), pp. 354-60.

Lumpkin, James R. and Greenberg, Barnett A.
"Apparel-Shopping Patterns of the Elderly Consumer"
Journal of Retailing, Vol. 58 (Winter 1982), pp. 68-89.

Lumpkin, James R. and Hunt, James B.
"Mobility as an Influence on Retail Patronage Behavior of the Elderly: Testing Conventional Wisdom"
Journal of the Academy of Marketing Science, Vol. 17 (Winter 1989), pp. 1-12.

Mobley, Mary F., Bearden, William O., and Teel, Jesse E.
"An Investigation of Individual Responses to Tensile Price Claims"
Journal of Consumer Research, Vol. 15 (September 1988), pp. 273-9.

Moore, Ellen M., Bearden, William O., and Teel, Jesse E., Jr.
"Use of Labeling and Assertions of Dependency in Appeals for Consumer Support"
Journal of Consumer Research, Vol. 12 (June 1985), pp. 90-6.

Sharma, Subhash, Bearden, William O., and Teel, Jesse E.
"Differential Effects of In-Home Shopping Methods"
Journal of Retailing, Vol. 59 (Winter 1983), pp. 29-51.

Valencia, Humberto
"Hispanic Values and Subcultural Research"
Journal of the Academy of Marketing Science, Vol. 17 (Winter 1989), pp. 23-8.

Wilkes, Robert E. and Valencia, Humberto
"Shopping-Related Characteristics of Mexican-Americans and Blacks"
Psychology and Marketing, Vol. 3 (Winter 1986), pp. 247-59.

191.09 ---------- Computer Programs for MANOVA and/or MANCOVA

Cramer, Elliot M.
MANOVA: A Computer Program for Univariate and Multivariate Analysis of Variance
Research Memorandum No. 124
(Chapel Hill, NC: The L. L. Thurstone Psychometric Laboratory, University of North Carolina, 1973).

Cramer, E. M.
The Revised MANOVA Program
(Chapel Hill: University of North Carolina Psychometric Laboratory, 1967).

Finn, Jeremy D.
Multivariance: Univariate and Multivariate Analysis of Variance, Covariance and Regression--Version 5
(Ann Arbor, MI: National Education Resources, Inc., 1972).

192 ----------------------- CLUSTER ANALYSIS -----------------------
        See also (sub)heading(s) 159.06, 193, 194, 195.

192.01 ---------- Books Re: Cluster Analysis

Aldenderfer, Mark S. and Blashfield, Robert K.
    Cluster Analysis
    (Beverly Hills, CA: Sage Publications, Inc.).

Anderberg, Michael D.
    Cluster Analysis for Applications
    (New York: Academic Press, 1973).

Arabie, Phipps, Carroll, J. Douglas, and DeSarbo, Wayne S.
    Three-Way Scaling and Clustering
    (Beverly Hills, CA: Sage Publications, Inc., 1987).

Ball, G. H.
    Classification Analysis
    (Menlo Park, CA: Stanford Research Institute, 1970).

Bijnen, E. J.
    Cluster Analysis
    (Tilburg, The Netherlands: Tilburg University Press, 1973).

Duran, Benjamin S. and Odell, Patrick L.
    Cluster Analysis: A Survey
    (Berlin: Springer Verlag, 1974).

Everitt, Brian
    Cluster Analysis, Second Edition
    (New York: Halsted Press, 1980), 136 pp.

Fisher, W. D.
    Clustering and Aggregation in Economics
    (Baltimore: Johns Hopkins Press, 1969).

Hartigan, John A.
    Clustering Algorithms
    (New York: John Wiley and Sons, Inc., 1975), 351 pp.

Jambu, M. and Lebeaux, M-O.
    Cluster Analysis and Data Analysis
    (Amsterdam: North Holland Publishing Company, 1983).

Jardine, H. and Sibson, R.
    Mathematical Taxonomy
    (New York: John Wiley and Sons, Inc., 1971).

Lorr, M.
    Cluster Analysis for the Social Sciences
    (San Francisco: Jossey-Bass, 1983).

MacNaughton-Smith, P.
    Some Statistical and Other Numerical Techniques for Classifying
    Individuals
    (London: Hmso, 1965).

Romesburg, H. Charles
    Cluster Analysis for Researchers
    (Belmont, CA: Lifetime Learning Publications, 1984), 334 pp.

Sneath, Peter H. and Sokal, Robert R.
    Numerical Taxonomy: The Principles and Practice of Numerical
    Classification
    (San Francisco; W. H. Freeman and Co., 1973).

Sokal, R. R. and Sneath, P. H. A.
    Principles of Numerical Taxonomy
    (San Francisco, CA: Freeman and Company, 1963).

Spath, Helmuth
    Cluster Dissection and Analysis
    (New York: Springer-Verlag, 1985).

Spath, Helmuth
    Cluster Analysis Algorithms
    (New York: John Wiley and Sons, Inc., 1980), 226 pp.

Stephenson, W.
    The Study of Behavior
    (Chicago: University of Chicago Press, 1953).

Tryon, Robert C.
    Cluster Analysis
    (Edwards Bros., 1939).

Tryon, R. C. and Bailey, D. E.
    Cluster Analysis
    (New York: McGraw-Hill Book Co., 1970).

Van Ryzin, J. (editor)
Classification and Clustering
(New York: Academic Press, Inc., 1978), 467 pp.

192.02 ---------- Theory Re: Cluster Analysis

Aaker, David A.
"Visual Clustering Using Principal Components Analysis"
in Aaker, David A. (editor)
Multivariate Analysis in Marketing: Theory Application
(Belmont, CA: Wadsworth Publishing, 1971), pp. 321-34.

Arabie, P.
"Clustering Representations of Group Overlap"
Journal of Mathematical Sociology, Vol. 5 (1977), pp. 113-28.

Attneave, F.
"Dimensions of Similarity"
American Journal of Psychology, Vol. 63, pp. 516-56.

Bailey, D. E.
"Cluster Analysis"
in Heise, D. (editor)
Sociological Methodology
(San Francisco: Jossey-Bass, 1974).

Ball, Geoffrey H. and Friedman, Herman
"On the Status of Applications of Clustering Techniques to Behavioral
Science Data"
Proceedings of the American Statistical Association, Social
Statistics Section (1968), pp. 33-9.

Ball, G. H. and Hall, D. J.
"A Clustering Technique for Summarizing Multivariate Data"
Behavioral Science, Vol. XII (1967), pp. 153-5.

Basford, Kay E. and McLachlan, Geoffrey J.
"Cluster Analysis in a Randomized Complete Block Design"
Communication Statistics--Theory and Methods, Vol. 14 (1985), pp.
451-63.

Beale, E. M. L.
"Euclidean Cluster Analysis"
37th International Statistical Institute (1969).

Bellman, R.
"A Note on Cluster Analysis and Dynamic Programming"
Mathematical Biosciences, Vol. 18, 314 (1973), pp. 311,2.

Blashfield, Robert K.
"The Growth of Cluster Analysis: Tryon, Ward, and Johnson"
Multivariate Behavioral Research, Vol. 15 (October 1980), pp. 439-58.

Blashfield, Robert K. and Aldenderfer, M. S.
"The Literature on Cluster Analysis"
Multivariate Behavioral Research, Vol. 13 (July 1978), pp. 271-95.

Bonner, R. E.
"Some Clustering Techniques"
IBM Journal of Research and Development, Vol. 8 (January 1964), pp.
22-33.

Bottenberg, R. A. and Christal, R. E.
"An Iterative Technique for Clustering Criteria Which Retains Optimum
Predictive Efficiency"
Wright Air Development Division, Air Research and Development
Command, United States Air Force, Lacklan A. F. Base, TX (1961).

Cattell, Raymond B.
"The Three Basic Factor Analytic Research Designs--Their
Interrelations and Derivations"
Psychological Bulletin, Vol. 49 (September 1952), pp. 499-520.

Cattell, Raymond B.
"A Note on Correlation Clusters and Cluster Search Methods"
Psychometrika, Vol. 9 (September 1944), pp. 169-84.

Cattell, Raymond B. and Coulter, Malcolm A.
"Principles of Behavioral Taxonomy and the Mathematical Basis of the
Taxonomy Computer Program"
British Journal of Mathematical and Statistical Psychology, Vol. 19
(November 1966), pp. 237-69.

Claxton, John D.
"The Use of RMCA to Distinguish Clustering Artifacts From Natural
Groupings"
Journal of the Market Research Society, Vol. 17 (July 1975), pp.
198-200.

Cormack, R. M.
    "A Review of Classification"
    Journal of the Royal Statistical Society, Series A (General), Vol.
    134, Part 3 (1971), pp. 321-53.

Cox, Douglas R.
    "Note on Grouping"
    Journal of American Statistical Association, Vol. 52 (December 1957),
    pp. 543-7.

Day, George S. and Heeler, Roger M.
    "Using Cluster Analysis to Improve Marketing Experiments"
    Journal of Marketing Research, Vol. VIII (August 1971), pp. 340-7.

Doyle, P. and Hutchinson, P.
    "The Identification of Target Markets"
    Decision Sciences, Vol. 7 (1976), pp. 152-61.

Dumas, Frank M.
    "A Quick Method of Analyzing the Similarity of Profiles"
    Journal of Clinical Psychology, Vol. 2 (January 1946), pp. 362-75.

Edwards, A. W. F. and Cavalli-Sforza, L. L.
    "A Method for Cluster Analysis"
    Biometrics, Vol. 52 (June 1965), pp. 362-75.

Everitt, B. S.
    "Unresolved Problems in Cluster Analysis"
    Biometrics, Vol. 35 (1979), pp. 169-81.

Fisher, W. D.
    "On Grouping for Maximum Homogeneity"
    Journal of the American Statistical Association, Vol. 53 (December
    1958), pp. 789-98.

Fleiss, Joseph L. and Zubin, Joseph
    "On the Methods and Theory of Clustering"
    Multivariate Behavioral Research, Vol. 4 (April 1969), pp. 235-50.

Fortier, J. J. and Solomon, A.
    "Clustering Procedures"
    in Krishnaiah, P. R. (editor)
    Multivariate Analysis
    (New York: Academic Press, 1966).

Frank, Ronald E. and Green, Paul E.
    "Numerical Taxonomy in Marketing Analysis: A Review Article"
    Journal of Marketing Research, Vol. V (February 1968), pp. 83-98.

Friedman, H. P. and Rubin, J.
    "On Some Invariant Criteria for Grouping Data"
    Journal of the American Statistical Association, Vol. 62 (1967), pp.
    159-78.

Gengerelli, J. A.
    "A Method for Detecting Subgroups in a Population and Specifying
    Their Membership"
    Journal of Psychology, Vol. 55 (1953), pp. 140-8.

Golder, P. A. and Yeomans, K. A.
    "The Use of Cluster Analysis for Stratification"
    Journal of the Royal Statistical Society, Series C, Vol. 22 (1973),
    pp. 213-9.

Gower, J. C.
    "Some Distance Properties of Latent Root and Vector Methods Used in
    Multivariate Analysis"
    Biometrika, Vol. 53 (December 1966), pp. 325-38.

Gower, J. C.
    "Multivariate Analysis and Multidimensional Geometry"
    Statistician, Vol. 17, No. 1 (1966), pp. 13-28.

Green, Paul E., Frank, Ronald E., and Robinson, Patrick J.
    "Cluster Analysis in Test Market Selection"
    Management Science, Vol. 13 (1967), pp. B387-400.

Green, Paul E., Schaffer, Catherine M., and Patterson, Karen M.
    "A Reduced-Space Approach to the Clustering of Categorical Data in
    Market Segmentation"
    Journal of the Market Research Society, Vol. 30 (July 1988), pp.
    267-88.

Greenacre, Michael J.
    "Clustering the Rows and Columns of a Contingency Table"
    Report 86/3
    Department of Statistics, University of South America (August 1986).

Hansen, P. and DeLattre, M.
"Complete Link Cluster Analysis by Graph Coloring"
Journal of the American Statistical Association, Vol. 93, 362 (1978),
pp. 397-403.

Hartigan, J. A.
"Direct Clustering of a Data Matrix"
Journal of the American Statistical Association, Vol. 67 (March
1972), pp. 123-9.

Hartigan, John A.
"Representation of Similarity Matrices by Trees"
Journal of the American Statistical Association, Vol. 62 (1967), pp.
1140-58.

Heeler, R. M. and Day, G. S.
"A Supplementary Note on the Use of Cluster Analysis for
Stratification"
Applied Statistics, Vol. 24 (1975), pp. 342-4.

Heerman, E. F.
"Comments on Overall's Multivariate Methods for Profile Analysis"
Psychological Bulletin, Vol. 63 (No. 2 1965), p. 128.

Hodges, J. L., Jr.
"Discriminatory Analysis 1: Survey of Discriminatory Analysis"
USAF School of Aviation Medicine, Randolph, TX (1950).

Howard, R. N.
"Classifying a Population into Homogeneous Groups"
Proceedings of the Cambridge Conference on Operations Research
(Cambridge, EN: September 14-8, 1964).

Hubert, L. J.
"Some Applications of Graph Theory to Clustering"
Psychometrika, Vol. 39 (1974), pp. 283-309.

Hunter, John E.
"Methods of Reordering the Correlation Matrix to Facilitate Visual
Inspection and Preliminary Cluster Analysis"
Journal of Educational Measurement, Vol. 10 (Spring 1973), pp. 51-61.

Inglis, J. and Johnson, D.
"Some Observations on, and Developments in, the Analysis of
Multivariate Survey Data"
Journal of the Marketing Research Society, Vol. XII (1970), pp. 75-98.

Johnson, Richard M.
"How Can You Tell If Things are Really Clustered?"
Proceedings, New York Chapter of the American Statistical Association
(February 1972).

Johnson, S. C.
"Metric Clustering"
(Murray Hill, NJ: Bell Telephone Laboratories, Inc., 1968),
mimeographed.

Jones, F. Lancaster
"Cluster Analysis and Market Segmentation: A Note on Other
Techniques, With an Illustration From Urban Sociology"
Journal of the Market Research Society, Vol. 14, No. 2 (1972), pp.
124-6.

Joyce, T. and Channon, C.
"Classifying Market Survey Respondents"
Applied Statistics, Vol. XV (1966), pp. 191-215.

Kendall, M. G.
"Discrimination and Classification"
in Krishnaiah, P. R. (editor)
Multivariate Analysis
(New York: Academic Press, 1966), pp. 165-85.

Kernan, Jerome B.
"Choice Criteria, Decision Behavior, and Personality"
Journal of Marketing Research, Vol. V (May 1968), pp. 155-64.

Lessig, V. Parker
"Comparing Cluster Analyses With Cophenic Correlation"
Journal of Marketing Research, Vol. IX (February 1972), pp. 82-4.

Ling, R. F.
"A Probability Theory of Cluster Analysis"
Journal of the American Statistical Association, Vol. 68 (1973), pp.
159-64.

Luce, R. D.
"A Choice Theory Analysis of Similarity Judgments"
Psychometrika, Vol. 26 (September 1961), pp. 325-32.

Marriott, F. H. C.
   "Practical Problems in a Method of Cluster Analysis"
   Biometrics, Vol. 27 (1971), pp. 501-14.

McNaughton-Smith, P. et al.
   "Dissimilarity Analysis: A New Technique of Hierarchical Subdivision"
   Nature, Vol. 202 (June 1964), pp. 1033,4.

McQuitty, Louis L.
   "Typal Analysis"
   Educational and Psychological Measurement, Vol. 21 (Autumn 1961), pp.
   677-96.

McQuitty, Louis L.
   "Elementary Linkage Analysis for Isolating Orthogonal and Oblique
   Types and Typal Relevancies"
   Educational and Psychological Measurement, Vol. 17 (Summer 1957), pp.
   207-29.

McRae, D. J.
   "Clustering Multivariate Observations"
   University of North Carolina (1973), unpublished doctoral
   dissertation.

Myers, John G.
   "The Sensitivity of Dynamic Time-Path Typologies"
   Journal of Marketing Research, Vol. VIII (November 1971), pp. 472-9.

Myers, John G. and Nicosia, Francesco M.
   "Time-Path Types: From Static to Dynamic Typologies"
   Management Science, Vol. 16 (June 1970), pp. 584-96.

Myers, John G. and Nicosia, Francesco M.
   "On the Study of Consumer Typologies"
   Journal of Marketing Research, Vol. V (May 1968), pp. 182-93.

Neidell, L. A.
   "Procedures and Pitfalls In Cluster Analysis"
   Proceedings, Fall Conference, American Marketing Association (1970),
   p. 107.

Neidell, Lester A.
   "Comment: Cluster Analysis of Marketing Data"
   in Sheth, Jagdish N. (editor)
   Proceedings of the Workshop on Multivariate Methods in Marketing
   (Chicago, IL: University of Chicago, 1970).

Nunnally, Jum
   "The Analysis of Profile Data"
   Psychological Bulletin, Vol. 59 (July 1962), pp. 311-9.

Osgood, Charles E. and Suci, George J.
   "A Measure of Relation Determined by Both Mean Difference and Profile
   Information"
   Psychological Bulletin, Vol. 49 (May 1952), pp. 251-62.

Overall, J. E.
   "Note on Multivariate Methods of Profile Analysis"
   Psychological Bulletin, Vol. 61 (March 1964), pp. 195-8.

Padron, Mario
   "An Axiomatic Basis and Computational Methods for Optimal Clustering"
   Department of Industrial Engineering, The University of Florida,
   Gainsville (March 1969), Technical Report No. 18.

Parkman, John M.
   "Inter-Object Distance Versus Centroid Hierarchical Clusters in
   Euclidean Space"
   Department of Psychology, University of California, Berkeley (1967),
   mimeograph.

Peay, E. R.
   "Nonmetric Grouping: Clusters and Cliques"
   Psychometrika, Vol. 40 (1975), pp. 297-313.

Punj, Girish and Stewart, David W.
   "Cluster Analysis in Marketing Research: Review and Suggestions for
   Applications"
   Journal of Marketing Research, Vol. XX (May 1983), pp. 134-48.

Rao, C. R.
   "The Utilization of Multiple Measurements in Problems of Biological
   Classification"
   Journal of Royal Statistical Society, Section B, Vol. 10 (1948), pp.
   159-203.

Rao, M. R.
   "Cluster Analysis and Mathematical Programming"
   Journal of the American Statistical Association, Vol. 66 (1971), pp.
   662-6.

Rice, J. M.
"Statistics and Data Analysis--Art or Science?"
European Research, Vol. 8 (July 1980), pp. 165-75.

Rogers, G. and Linden, J. D.
"Use of Multiple Discriminant Function Analysis in the Evaluation of
Three Multivariate Grouping Techniques"
Educational and Psychological Measurement, Vol. 33 (1973), pp.
787-802.

Rosch, Eleanor
"Principles of Categorization"
in Rosch, Eleanor and Lloyd, Barbara J. (editors)
Cognition and Categorization
(Hillsdale, NJ: Lawrence Eribaum Association, 1978), pp. 27-48.

Roscoe, A. Marvin, Sheth, Jagdish N., and Howell, Welling
"Intertechnique Cross Validation in Cluster Analysis"
Faculty Working Paper No. 175
University of Illinois (1974).

Schaninger, Charles M., Lessig, V. Parker, and Panton, Don B.
"The Complementary Use of Multivariate Procedures to Investigate
Nonlinear and Interactive Relationships Between Personality and
Product Usage"
Journal of Marketing Research, Vol. XVII (February 1980), pp. 119-24.

Shepard, R. N.
"Representation of Structure in Similarity Data: Problems and
Prospects"
Psychometrika, Vol. 39 (1974), pp. 373-421.

Shuchman, A.
"Letter to the Editor"
Management Science, Vol. XIII (1967), pp. B688-91.

Simpson, G. G.
"Numerical Taxonomy and Biological Classification"
Science, Vol. 144 (May 1964), pp. 712,3.

Skinner, H. A.
"Dimensions and Clusters: A Hybrid Approach to Classification"
Applied Psychological Measurement, Vol. 3 (1979), pp. 327-41.

Sneath, P. H. A.
"The Application of Computer to Taxonomy"
Journal of General Microbiology, Vol. 17 (1957), pp. 201-26.

Sokal, R. R.
"Numerical Taxonomy"
Scientific American, Vol. 215 (December 1966), pp. 106-16.

Sparks, D. N.
"Euclidean Cluster Analysis"
Applied Statistics, Vol. 22 (1973), pp. 126-30.

Tryon, Robert C.
"Cluster and Factor Analysis: General Exposition"
Department of Psychology, University of California, Berkeley (1967),
mimeograph.

Tryon, Robert C.
"General Dimensions of Individual Differences: Cluster Analysis
Versus Factor Analysis"
Educational and Psychological Measurement, Vol. 18 (Autumn 1958), pp.
477-95.

Tryon, Robert C.
"Cumulative Communality Cluster Analysis"
Educational and Psychological Measurement, Vol. 18 (March 1958), pp.
3-35.

Tucker, Ledyard R.
"Cluster Analysis and the Search for Structure Underlying the
Individual Differences in Psychological Phenomena"
Conference on Cluster Analysis of Multivariate Data (1966), paper
presentation.

Webster, Harold
"A Note on Profile Similarity"
Psychological Bulletin, Vol. 49 (September 1952), pp. 538,9.

Williams, W. T., Lance, G. N., Dale, M. B., and Clifford, N. T.
"Controversy Concerning the Criteria for Taxonomic Strategies"
The Computer Journal, Vol. 14, No. 2 (1971), pp. 162-5.

Wolfe, J. H.
"Pattern Clustering by Multivariate Mixture Analysis"
Multivariate Behavioral Research, Vol. V (1970), pp. 329-50.

Yeomans, K. A. and Golder, P. A.
   "Further Observations on the Stratification of Birmingham Wards by
   Clustering: A Riposte"
   Applied Statistics, Vol. 24 (1975), pp. 345,6.

Wong, M. A.
   "A Hybrid Clustering Method for Identifying High-Density Clusters"
   Journal of the American Statistical Association, Vol. 77, No. 380
   (1982), pp. 841-7.

192.03 ---------- Theory Re: Hierarchical Cluster Analysis

Blashfield, Robert K.
   "Mixture Model Tests of Cluster Analysis: Accuracy of Four
   Agglomerative Hierarchical Methods"
   Psychological Bulletin, Vol. 83 (May 1976), pp. 377-88.

DeSarbo, Wayne S. and DeSoete, Geert
   "On the Use of Hierarchical Clustering for the Analysis of
   Nonsymmetric Proximities"
   Journal of Consumer Research, Vol. 11 (June 1984), pp. 601-10.

Hubert, Lawrence
   "Min and Max Hierarchical Clustering Using Asymmetric Similarity
   Measures"
   Psychometrika, Vol. 38 (1973), pp. 63-72.

Jardine, N. and Sibson, R.
   "The Construction of Hierarchic and Non-Hierarchic Classifications"
   Computer Journal, Vol. 11 (1968), pp. 177-84.

Johnson, Stephen C.
   "Hierarchial Clustering Schemes"
   Psychometrika, Vol. 32 (September 1967), pp. 241-54.

McQuitty, Louis L.
   "Hierachical Syndrome Analysis"
   Educational and Psychological Measurement, Vol. 20 (Summer 1960), pp.
   293-304.

Moore, William L., Pessemier, Edgar A., and Lehmann, Donald R.
   "Hierarchical Representations of Market Structures and Choice
   Processes Through Preference Trees"
   Journal of Business Research, Vol. 14 (October 1986), pp. 371-86.

Peay, E. R.
   "Hierarchical Clique Structures"
   Sociometry, Vol. 37 (1974), pp. 54-65.

Ward, Joe H.
   "Hierarchical Grouping to Optimize an Objective Function"
   Journal of the American Statistical Association (March 1963), pp.
   236-44.

192.04 ---------- Theory Re: Specific Clustering Algorithms

Bass, B. M.
   "Iterative Inverse Factor Analysis: A Rapid Method for Clustering
   Persons"
   Psychometrika, Vol. 22 (March 1957), p. 105.

Birnbaum, A. and Maxwell, A. E.
   "Classification Procedures Based on Bayes' Formula"
   Applied Statistics, Vol. 9 (November 1961), pp. 152-68.

Bottenberg, Robert A. and Christal, Raymond E.
   "An Iterative Technique for Clustering Criteria Which Retains Optimum
   Predictive Efficiency"
   Technical Note WADD-TN-61-30
   Personnel Laboratory, Wright Air Development Division, Lackland Air
   Force Base (1961).

Field, H. S. and Schoenfeldt, L. F.
   "Ward and Hook Revisited: A Two-Part Procedure for Overcoming a
   Deficiency in the Grouping of Two Persons"
   Educational and Psychological Measurement, Vol. 35 (1975), pp. 171-3.

Graves, G. W. and Whinston, A. B.
   "An Algorithm for the Quadratic Assignment Problem"
   Management Science, Vol. 13 (1970), pp. B387-400.

Hubert, L. J.
   "Monotone Invariant Clustering Procedures"
   Psychometrika, Vol. 38 (1973), pp. 47-62.

Johnson, S. C.
   "Hierarchical Clustering Schemes"
   Psychometrika, Vol. 32 (1967), pp. 241-54.

Kamen, Joseph M.
  "Quick Clustering"
  Journal of Marketing Research, Vol. VII (May 1970), pp. 199-204.

King, Benjamin K.
  "Step-Wise Clustering Procedures"
  Journal of the American Statistical Association, Vol. 62 (March
  1967), pp. 86-101.

Lance, G. N. and Williams, W. T.
  "A General Theory of Classificatory Sorting Strategies: II.
  Clustering Systems"
  Computer Journal, Vol. 10 (1967), pp. 271-7.

Lance, G. N. and Williams, W. T.
  "A General Theory of Classificatory Sorting Strategies: I.
  Hierarchical Systems"
  Computer Journal, Vol. 9 (1967), pp. 373-80.

MacQueen, J.
  "Some Methods for Classification and Analysis of Multivariate
  Observations"
  Proceedings, Fifth Berkeley Symposium on Mathematical Statistics and
  Probability, Volume I
  (Berkley, CA: University of California Press, 1967), pp. 281-97.

McQuitty, L. L.
  "A Mutual Development of Some Typological Theories and
  Pattern-Analytic Methods"
  Educational and Psychological Measurement, Vol. 17 (1967), pp. 21-46.

McQuitty, Louis L.
  "Capabilities and Improvements of Linkage Analysis As a Clustering
  Method"
  Educational and Psychological Measurement, Vol. 24 (Autumn 1964), pp.
  441-56.

Price, Leighton A.
  Hierachical Clustering Based on a Criterion of Largest Average
  Within-Cluster Similarity
  (East Lansing, MI: Computer Institute for Social Science Research,
  Michigan State University, 1969).

Sarle, Warren J.
  Cubic Clustering Criterion
  SAS Technical Report A-108
  (Cary, NC: SAS Institute, Inc., 1983).

Scott, A. J. and Symons, M. J.
  "Clustering Methods Based on Likelihood Ratio Criteria"
  Biometrics, Vol. 27 (1971), pp. 387-97.

Vinod, H.
  "Integer Programming and the Theory of Grouping"
  Journal of the American Statistical Association, Vol. 64 (1969), pp.
  507-17.

Ward, J.
  "Hierarchical Grouping to Optimize an Objective Function"
  Journal of the American Statistical Association, Vol. 58 (1963), pp.
  236-44.

192.05 ---------- Evaluations of Clustering Algorithms

Aldenderfer, M. S.
  "A Consumer Report on Cluster Analysis Software: (2) Hierarchical
  Methods"
  Department of Anthropology, Pennsylvania State University, working
  paper.

Bayne, C. K., Beauchamp, J. J., Begovich, C. L., and Kane, V. E.
  "Monte Carlo Comparisons of Selected Clustering Procedures"
  Pattern Recognition, Vol. 12 (1980), pp. 51-62.

Blashfield, R. K.
  "A Consumer Report on Cluster Analysis Software: (3) Iterative
  Partitioning Methods"
  Department of Psychology, Pennsylvania State University (1977),
  working paper.

Blashfield, R. K.
  "Mixture Model Tests of Cluster Analysis: Accuracy of Four
  Agglomerative Hierarchical Methods"
  Psychological Bulletin, Vol. 83 (1976), pp. 377-88.

Blashfield, R. K. and Morey, L. C.
  "A Comparison of Four Clustering Methods Using MMPI Monte Carlo Data"
  Applied Psychology Measurement (1980).

Cunningham, K. M. and Ogilvie, J. C.
    "Evaluation of Hierarchical Grouping Techniques: A Preliminary Study"
    Computer Journal, Vol. 15 (1972), pp. 209-13.

Edelbrock, C.
    "Comparing the Accuracy of Hierarchical Clustering Algorithms: The
    Problem of Classifying Everybody"
    Multivariate Behavioral Research, Vol. 14 (1979), pp. 367-84.

Edelbrock, C. and McLaughlin, B.
    "Hierarchical Cluster Analysis Using Intraclass Correlations: A
    Mixture Model Study"
    Multivariate Behavioral Research, Vol. 15 (1980), pp. 299-318.

Funkhouser, G. R.
    "A Note on the Reliability of Certain Clustering Algorithms"
    Journal of Marketing Research, Vol. XX (February 1983), pp. 99-102.

Gower, J. C.
    "A Comparison of Some Methods of Cluster Analysis"
    Biometrics, Vol. 23 (1967), pp. 623-37.

Helmstadter, G. C.
    "An Empirical Comparison of Methods for Estimating Profile Similarity"
    Educational and Psychological Measurement, Vol. 17 (1957), pp. 71-82.

Kuiper, F. K. and Fisher, L. A.
    "A Monte Carlo Comparison of Six Clustering Procedures"
    Biometrics, Vol. 31 (1975), pp. 777-83.

Mezzich, J. E.
    "Evaluating Clustering Methods for Psychiatric Diagnosis"
    Biological Psychiatry, Vol. 13 (1978), pp. 265-81.

Milligan, Glenn W.
    "A Monte Carlo Study of Thirty Internal Criterion Clustering
    Algorithms"
    Psychometrika, Vol. 46, No. 2 (1981), pp. 187-99.

Milligan, Glenn W.
    "A Review of Monte Carlo Tests of Cluster Analysis"
    Multivariate Behavioral Research, Vol. 16 (July 1981), pp. 379-407.

Milligan, Glenn W.
    "An Examination of the Effect of Six Types of Error Perturbation on
    Fifteen Clustering Algorithms"
    Psychometrika, Vol. 45 (1980), pp. 325-42.

Milligan, Glenn W. and Isaac, P. D.
    "The Validation of Four Ultrametric Clustering Algorithms"
    Pattern Recognition, Vol. 12 (1980), pp. 41-50.

Mojena, R.
    "Hierarchical Grouping Methods and Stopping Rules: An Evaluation"
    Computer Journal, Vol. 20 (1977), pp. 359-63.

192.06 ---------- Mapping Theory in Cluster Analysis

Oliva, Terence A. and Reidenbach, R. Eric
    "Iterative Partitioning Methods: The Use of Mapping Theory as a
    Clustering Technique"
    Journal of Marketing Research, Vol. XXII (February 1985), pp. 81-5.

Warfield, J.
    "Some Principles of Knowledge Organization"
    IEEE Transactions on Systems, Man, and Cybernetics, Vol. 9 (1979),
    pp. 317-25.

192.07 ---------- Theory Re: Overlapping Clustering

Arabie, Phipps, Carroll, J. Douglas, DeSarbo, Wayne, and Wind, Yoram
    "Overlapping Clustering: A New Method for Product Positioning"
    Journal of Marketing Research, Vol. XVIII (August 1981), pp. 310-7.

Shepard, R. and Arabie, P.
    "Additive Clustering: Representation of Similarities as Combinations
    of Discrete Overlapping Properties"
    Psychological Review, Vol. 86 (1979), pp. 87-123.

192.08 ---------- Theory Re: Fuzzy Clustering

Backer, E.
    Cluster Analysis by Optimal Decomposition of Induced Fuzzy Sets
    (Delft: University Press, 1978).

Bezdek, J. C.
"Numerical Taxonomy With Fuzzy Sets"
Journal of Mathematical Biology, Vol. 1 (1974), pp. 57-71.

Bezdek, J. C., Coray, C., Gunderson, R., and Watson, J.
"Detection and Characterization of Cluster Substructure"
SIAM Journal of Applied Mathematics, Vol. 40 (1981), pp. 339-72.

Bezdek, J. C. and Harris, J. D.
"Fuzzy Partitions and Relations: An Axiomatic Basis for Clustering"
Fuzzy Sets and Systems, Vol. 1 (1978), pp. 111-27.

Dubois, D. and Prade, H.
Fuzzy Sets and Systems: Theory and Applications
(New York: Academic Press, 1980).

Dubois, D. and Prade, H.
"New Results About Properties and Semantics of Fuzzy Set Theory
Operators"
in Wang, P. P. and Chang, S. K. (editors)
Fuzzy Sets: Theory and Applications to Policy Analysis and
Information Systems
(New York: Plenum, 1980).

Dunn, J. C.
"A Fuzzy Relative of the ISODATA Process and Its Uses in Detecting
Compact, Well Separated Clusters"
Journal of Cybernetics, Vol. 4 (1974), pp. 32-57.

Dunn, J. C.
"Some Recent Investigations of a New Fuzzy Partitioning Algorithm and
Its Application to Pattern Classification Problems"
Journal of Cybernetics, Vol. 4 (1974), pp. 1-15.

Gunderson, R. W.
"An Adaptive FCV Clustering Algorithm"
International Journal of Man-Machine Studies, Vol. 19 (1983), pp.
97-104.

Gupta, M. M., Ragade, R. K., and Yager, R. R. (editors)
Advances in Fuzzy Set Theory and Applications
(Amsterdam: North Holland, 1979).

Gustafson, D. F. and Kessel, W. C.
"Fuzzy Clustering With a Fuzzy Covariance Matrix"
in Gupta, M. M., Ragade, R. K., and Yager, R. R. (editors)
Advances in Fuzzy Set Theory and Applications
(Amsterdam: North Holland, 1979).

Kandel, A.
"Fuzzy Techniques in Pattern Recognition"
(New York: 1982).

Klement, E. P.
"Construction of Fuzzy Omega-Algebras Using Triangular Norms
"Journal of Mathematical Analysis and Applications, Vol. 86 (1982),
pp. 534-65.

Roubens, M.
"Fuzzy Clustering Algorithms and Their Cluster Validity"
European Journal of Operational Research, Vol. 10 (1982), pp. 294-301.

Roubens, M.
"Pattern Classification Problems and Fuzzy Sets"
Fuzzy Sets and Systems, Vol. 1 (1978), pp. 239-53.

Yager, R. R.
"Some Procedures for Selecting Fuzzy Set Theoretic Operators"
International Journal of General Systems, Vol. 8 (1982), pp. 115-24.

Zadeh, L. A.
"Fuzzy Sets"
Information and Control, Vol. 8 (1965), pp. 338-53.

192.09 ---------- Applications of Fuzzy Clustering

Hruschka, H.
"Market Definition and Segmentation Using Fuzzy Clustering Methods"
International Journal of Research in Marketing, Vol. 3, No. 2 (1986),
pp. 117-34.

192.10 ---------- Computer Programs for Cluster Analysis

Gott, C. D. and Mathon, W. S.
  "HIER-GRP: A Computer Program for the Hierarchical Grouping of
  Regression Equations"
  Department of the Air Force, Air Human Resources Laboratory, Lackland
  A. F. Base, TX (1961).

Howard, H. and Harris, B.
  "A Hierarchical Grouping Routine"
  University of Pennsylvania Computer Center (1966), working paper.

McClain, John O. and Rao, V. R.
  "CLUSTSIZ: A Program to Test for the Quality of Clustering of a Set
  of Objects"
  Journal of Marketing Research, Vol. XII (November 1975), pp. 456-60.

Pettit, R. G.
  "Clustering Program: Continuous Variables"
  Advanced Systems Development Division, IBM, Yorktown Heights, NY
  (1964).

Roberts, C. Richard
  "SIMDATA: A Computer Program to Produce Matrices of Similarity
  Measures for Subsequent Input to Cluster or Multidimensional Scaling
  Algorithms"
  Journal of Marketing Research, Vol. XVI (November 1979), pp. 566,7.

Rubin, J.
  "Optimal Taxonomy Program (7090-IBM-0026)"
  IBM Corporation.

Sneath, P. H. A.
  "The Application of Computers to Taxonomy"
  Journal of General Micro-Biology, Vol. 17 (August 1957), pp. 201-27.

Steinhorst, R. Kirk, Stem, Donald E., Jr., Handwerk, William C., and
  Marshall, Barbara A.
  "PRCLUSTR: Cluster Analysis of Paired Comparison Rankings"
  Journal of Marketing Research, Vol. XV (August 1978), pp. 474-6.

Tryon, R. C. and Bailey, D. E.
  "The BC Try Computer System of Cluster and Factor Analysis"
  Multivariate Behavioral Research, Vol. 1.

Wishart, D.
  "CLUSTAN IA: A FORTRAN Program for Numerical Classification"
  Computing Laboratory, St. Andrew's University, Scotland (1969).

192.11 ---------- Unclassified (Cluster Analysis)

Arabie, P. and Carroll, J. D.
  "MAPCLUS: A Mathematical Programming Approach to Fitting the ADCLUS
  Model"
  Psychometrika, Vol. 45 (1980), pp. 211-35.

Carroll, J. D. and Arabie, P.
  "INDCLUS: A Three-Way Approach to Clustering"
  Meeting of the Psychometric Society, Monterey, CA (1979), paper
  presentation.

193 ------------------ ISSUES IN CLUSTER ANALYSIS --------------------
        See also (sub)heading(s) 192.

193.01 ---------- Theory Re: Similarity, Proximity, etc. Measures

Cattell, Raymond B.
 "Rp and Other Coefficients of Pattern Similarity"
 Psychometrika, Vol. 14 (1949), pp. 279-98.

Cohen, J.
 "A Coefficient of Agreement for Nominal Scales"
 Educational and Psychological Measurement, Vol. 20 (1960), pp. 37-46.

Cronbach, Lee J. and Gleser, Goldine
 "Assessing Similarity Between Profiles"
 Psychological Bulletin, Vol. 50 (November 1953), pp. 456-73.

Friedman, H. P. and Rubin, J.
 "On Some Invariant Criteria for Grouping Data"
 Journal of the American Statistical Association, Vol. 62 (1967), pp.
 1159-69.

Green, Paul E. and Rao, Vithala R.
 "A Note on Proximity Measures and Cluster Analysis"
 Journal of Marketing Research, Vol. VI (August 1969), pp. 359-64.

Harris, C. W.
 "Characteristics of Two Measures of Profile Similarity"
 Psychometrika, Vol. 20 (1955), pp. 289-97.

Mahalanobis, P. C.
 "On the Generalized Distance in Statistics"
 Proceedings National Institute of Science, Vol. 12, India (1936), pp.
 49-58.

McIntyre, R. M. and Blashfield, R. K.
 "A Nearest-Centroid Technique for Evaluating the Minimum-Variance
 Clustering Procedure"
 Multivariate Behavior Research, Vol. 15 (1980), pp. 225-38.

Milligan, Glenn W.
 "A Monte Carlo Study of Thirty Internal Criterion Measures for
 Cluster Analysis"
 Psychometrika, Vol. 46 (June 1981), pp. 187-99.

Milligan, Glenn W. and Mahajan, Vijay
 "A Note on Procedures for Testing the Quality of a Clustering of a
 Set of Objects"
 Decision Sciences, Vol. 11 (1980), pp. 669-77.

Morrison, Donald G.
 "On Measurement Problems in Cluster Analysis"
 Management Science, Vol. 13 (August 1967), pp. B775-80.

Rand, W. M.
 "Objective Criteria for the Evaluation of Clustering Methods"
 Journal of the American Statistical Association, Vol. 66 (1971), pp.
 846-50.

193.02 ---------- Theory Re: Number of Clusters

Milligan, Glenn W. and Cooper, Martha C.
 "An Examination of Procedures for Determining the Number of Clusters
 in a Data Set"
 Psychometrika, Vol. 50 (1985).

193.03 ---------- Theory Re: Statistical Tests in Cluster Analysis

Arnold, Stephen John
 "A Test for Clusters"
 Journal of Marketing Research, Vol. XVI (November 1979), pp. 545-51.

Engelman, L. and Hartigan, J. A.
 "Percentage Points of a Test for Clusters"
 Journal of the American Statistical Association, Vol. 64 (1969), pp.
 1647,8.

Friedman, H. P. and Rubin, J.
 "On Some Invariant Criteria for Grouping Data"
 Journal of the American Statistical Association, Vol. 62 (1967), pp.
 1159-78.

Hubert, L.
 "Approximate Evaluation Techniques for the Single-Limit and
 Complete-Link Hierarchical Clustering Procedures"
 Journal of the American Statistical Association, Vol. 69, 347 (1974),
 pp. 698-704.

Hubert, L. and Levin, J. R.
   "Inference Models for Categorical Clustering"
   Psychological Bulletin, Vol. 84, No. 5 (1977), pp. 878-87.

Klastorian, T. D.
   "Assessing Cluster Analysis Results"
   Journal of Marketing Research, Vol. XX (February 1983), pp. 92-8.

Knox, G.
   "The Detection of Space-Time Interactions"
   Applied Statistics, Vol. 13 (1964), pp. 25-9.

Lee, H. L.
   "Multivariate Tests for Clusters"
   Journal of the American Statistical Association, Vol. 47, 367 (1979),
   pp. 708-14.

Ling, R. F.
   "A Probability Theory of Cluster Analysis"
   Journal of the American Statistical Association, Vol. 68, 341 (1973),
   pp. 159-64.

Mantel, N.
   "The Detection of Disease Clustering and Generalized Regression
   Approach"
   Cancer Research, Vol. 27, No. 2 (1967), pp. 209-20.

193.04 ---------- Theory Re: Comparison of Cluster Analysis Solutions

DeSarbo, Wayne S.
   "Clustering Consistency Analysis"
   Journal of the Academy of Marketing Science, Vol. 10 (Summer 1982),
   pp. 217-34.

194 ------- LATENT MIXTURE OR LATENT DISCRIMINANT (LADI) MODEL -------
   See also (sub)heading(s) 192.

194.01 ---------- Books Re: Latent Mixture or Discriminant Model

McLachlan, Geoffrey J. and Basford, Kay E.
  Mixture Models: Inference and Applications to Clustering
  (New York: Marcel Dekker, Inc., 1988).

Titterington, D. M., Smith, A. F. M., and Markov, U. E.
  Statistical Analysis of Finite Mixture Distributions
  (New York: John Wiley and Sons, Inc., 1985).

194.02 ---------- Theory Re: Latent Mixture or Discriminant Model

Aitkin, M.
  "Mixture Applications of the EM Algorithm in GLIM"
  in COMPSTAT, Proceedings in Computational Statistics
  (Vienna: Physica Verlag, 1980), pp. 537-41.

Aitkin, M., Anderson, D., and Hinde, J.
  "Statistical Modeling of Data on Teaching Styles"
  Journal of the Royal Statistical Society, Vol. A144 (1981), pp.
  419-61.

Day, Neil E.
  "Estimating the Components of a Mixture of Normal Distributions"
  Biometrika, Vol. 56 (1969), pp. 463-74.

Dillon, William R. and Mulani, Narendra
  "LADI: A Latent Discrimination Model for Analyzing Marketing Research
  Data"
  Journal of Marketing Research, Vol. XXVI (February 1989), pp. 15-29.

Wolfe, J. H.
  "Pattern Clustering by Multivariate Mixture Analysis"
  Multivariate Behavioral Research, Vol. 5, No. 3 (1970), pp. 329-50.

195 ------------------- CLUSTER ANALYSIS APPLICATIONS ------------------

See also (sub)heading(s) 192.

Aaker, David A., Stayman, Douglas M., and Vezina, Richard
  "Identifying Feelings Elicited by Advertising"
  Psychology and Marketing, Vol. 5 (Spring 1988), pp. 1-16.

Anderson, Claus and Nielsen, Simon Ortmann
  "Heavy-Medium-Light Users: Sufficient for Segmentation?"
  European Research, Vol. 9 (July 1981), pp. 91-100.

Anderson, W. Thomas, Cox, Eli P., III, and Fulcher, D. G.
  "Bank Selection Decisions and Market Segmentation"
  Journal of Marketing, Vol. 40 (1976), pp. 40-5.

Barrett, Nigel J. and Wilkinson, Ian F.
  "Export Stimulation: A Segmentation Study of the Exporting Problems
  of Australian Manufacturing Firms"
  European Journal of Marketing, Vol. 19, No. 2 (1985), pp. 53-72.

Carlson, Les and Grossbart, Sanford
  "Parental Style and Consumer Socialization of Children"
  Journal of Consumer Research, Vol. 15 (June 1988), pp. 77-94.

Burnett, John J. and Oliver, Richard L.
  "Fear Appeal Effects in the Field: A Segmentation Approach"
  Journal of Marketing Research, Vol. XVI (May 1979), pp. 181-90.

Burnett, John J. and Wilkes, Robert E.
  "Fear Appeals to Segments Only"
  Journal of Advertising Research, Vol. 20 (October 1980), pp. 21-4.

Calantone, Roger J. and Cooper, Robert G.
  "A Discriminant Model for Identifying Scenarios of Industrial New
  Product Failure"
  Journal of the Academy of Marketing Science, Vol. 7 (Summer 1979),
  pp. 163-83.

Calantone, Roger J. and Sawyer, Alan G.
  "Stability of Benefit Segments"
  Journal of Marketing Research, Vol. XV (August 1978), pp. 395-404.

Currim, Imran S.
  "Using Segmentation Approaches for Better Prediction and
  Understanding From Consumer Mode Choice Models"
  Journal of Marketing Research, Vol. XVIII (August 1981), pp. 301-9.

Dadzie, Kofi Q.
  "Demarketing Strategy in Shortage Marketing Environment"
  Journal of the Academy of Marketing Science, Vol. 17 (Spring 1989),
  pp. 157-65.

Darden, William R. and Perreault, William D., Jr.
  "A Multivariate Analysis of Media Exposure and Vacation Behavior With
  Life Style Covariates"
  Journal of Consumer Research, Vol. 2 (September 1975), pp. 93-103.

Darden, William R. and Rao, C. P.
  "A Linear Covariate Model of Warranty Attitudes and Behaviors"
  Journal of Marketing Research, Vol. XVI (November 1979), pp. 466-77.

Davis, Brian and French, Warren
  "Exploring Advertising Usage Segments Among the Aged"
  Journal of Advertising Research, Vol. 29 (February/March 1989), pp.
  22-29.

Day, Ellen, Davis, Brian, Dove, Rhonda and French, Warren
  "Reaching the Senior Citizen Market(s)"
  Journal of Advertising Research, Vol. 27 (December 1987/January
  1988), pp. 23-30.

Day, Ellen, Fox, Richard J., and Huszagh, Sandra M.
  "Segmenting the Global Market for Industrial Goods: Issues and
  Implications"
  International Marketing Review, Vol. 8 (Autumn 1988), pp. 14-27.

DeBrentani, Ulrike and Droge, Cornelia
  "The Company, Product and Market Dimensions of New Product Decision
  Scenarios"
  International Journal of Research in Marketing, Vol. 2, No. 4 (1985),
  pp. 243-53.

De Chernatony, Leslie
  "Marketers' and Consumers' Concurring Perceptions of Market Structure"
  European Journal of Marketing, Vol. 23, No. 1 (1989), pp. 7-16.

Doyle, Peter and Saunders, John
  "Market Segmentation and Positioning in Specialized Industrial
  Markets"
  Journal of Marketing, Vol. 49 (Spring 1985), pp. 24-32.

Fleishman, John A.
"Types of Political Attitude Structure: Results of a Cluster Analysis"
Public Opinion Quarterly, Vol. 50 (Fall 1986), pp. 371-86.

Ford, Gary T.
"Adoption of Consumer Policies by States: Some Empirical Perspectives"
Journal of Marketing Research, Vol. XV (February 1978), pp. 49-57.

Furse, David H., Punj, Girish N., and Stewart, David W.
"A Typology of Individual Search Strategies Among Purchasers of New
Automobiles"
Journal of Consumer Research, Vol. 10 (March 1984), pp. 417-31.

Furse, David H., Punj, Girish, and Stewart, David W.
"Individual Search Strategies in New Automobile Purchase"
in Mitchell, Andrew (editor)
Advances in Consumer Research, Volume Nine (1982), pp. 379-84.

Green, Robert T.
"Environmental Shock and Export Opportunity"
International Marketing Review, Vol. 4 (Winter 1987), pp. 30-42.

Jain, Arun K.
"A Prediction Study in Perceptual and Evaluative Mapping"
Journal of the Academy of Marketing Science, Vol. 6 (Fall 1978), pp.
300-13.

Johansson, Johny and Moinpour, Reza
"Objective and Perceived Similarity of Pacific Rim Countries"
Columbia Journal of World Business (Winter 1977), pp. 65-76.

Kiel, Geoffrey C. and Layton, Roger A.
"Dimensions of Consumer Information Seeking Behavior"
Journal of Marketing Research, Vol. XVIII (May 1981), pp. 233-9.

Landon, E. L.
"Self Concept, Ideal Self Concept, and Consumer Purchase Intentions"
Journal of Consumer Research, Vol. 1 (1974), pp. 44-51.

Lastovicka, John L., Murry, John P., Jr., Joachimsthaler, Erich A.,
Bhalla, Gaurav, and Scheurich, Jim
"A Lifestyle Typology to Model Young Male Drinking and Driving"
Journal of Consumer Research, Vol. 14 (September 1987), pp. 257-63.

Lesser, Jack A. and Hughes, Marie Adele
"The Generalizability of Psychographic Market Segments Across
Geographic Locations"
Journal of Marketing, Vol. 50 (January 1986), pp. 18-27.

Lilien, Gary L. and Wong, M. Anthony
"An Exploratory Investigation of the Structure of the Buying Center
in the Metalworking Industry"
Journal of Marketing Research, Vol. XXI (February 1984), pp. 1-11.

Locander, William B. and Spivey, W. Austin
"A Functional Approach to Attitude Measurement"
Journal of Marketing Research, Vol. XV (November 1978), pp. 576-87.

Mahajan, Vijay and Jain, Arun K.
"An Approach to Normative Segmentation"
Journal of Marketing Research, Vol. XV (August 1978), pp. 338-45.

Mills, Michael K.
"Strategic Retail Fashion Market Positioning: A Comparative Analysis"
Journal of the Academy of Marketing Science, Vol. 13 (Summer 1985),
pp. 212-25.

Moncrief, William C., III
"Selling Activity and Sales Position Taxonomies for Industrial
Salesforces"
Journal of Marketing Research, Vol. XXIII (August 1986), pp. 261-70.

Moriarty, M. and Venkatesan, M.
"Concept Evaluation and Market Segmentation"
Journal of Marketing, Vol. 42 (1978), pp. 82-6.

Moschis, George P. and Bello, Daniel C.
"Decision-Making Patterns Among International Vacationers: A
Cross-Cultural Perspective"
Psychology and Marketing, Vol. 4 (Spring 1987), pp. 75-89.

Oliver, Richard L. and DeSarbo, Wayne S.
"Response Determinants in Satisfaction Judgments"
Journal of Consumer Research, Vol. 14 (March 1988), pp. 495-507.

Rao, Vithala R. and Sabavala, Darius Jal
"Inference of Hierarchical Choice Processes From Panel Data"
Journal of Consumer Research, Vol. 8 (June 1981), pp. 85-96.

Schaninger, C. M., Lessig, V. P., and Panton, D. B.
     "The Complementary Use of Multivariate Procedures to Investigate
     Nonlinear and Interactive Relationships Between Personality and
     Product Usage"
     Journal of Marketing Research, Vol. XVII (February 1980), pp. 119-24.

Seaton, Bruce and Vogel, Ronald H.
     "An Attitudinal Evaluation of Hospitals: A Determinant Attribute and
     Market Segmentation Study"
     Journal of the Academy of Marketing Science, Vol. 6 (Winter-Spring
     1978), pp. 39-51.

Spiro, Rosann L.
     "Persuasion in Family Decision-Making"
     Journal of Consumer Research, Vol. 9 (March 1983), pp. 393-402.

Srivastava, Rajendra K., Leone, Robert P., and Shocker, Allan D.
     "Market Structure Analysis: Hierarchical Clustering of Products Based
     on Substitution-in-Use"
     Journal of Marketing, Vol. 45 (Summer 1981), pp. 38-48.

Srivastava, Rajendra K., Shocker, Allan D., and Day, George S.
     "An Exploratory Study of Usage-Situational Influences on the
     Composition of Product-Markets"
     in Hunt, H. K. (editor)
     Advances in Consumer Research
     (Ann Arbor, MI: Association for Consumer Research, 1978), pp. 32-8.

Stanley, Thomas J., Moschis, George P., and Danko, William D.
     "Financial Service Segments: The Seven Faces of the Affluent Market"
     Journal of Advertising Research, Vol. 27 (August/September 1987), pp.
     52-67.

Stayman, Douglas M., Aaker, David A., and Bruzzone, Donald E.
     "The Incidence of Commercial Types Broadcast in Prime Time: 1976-1986"
     Journal of Advertising Research, Vol. 29 (June/July 1989), pp. 26-33.

Stewart, David and Hood, Neil
     "An Empirical Examination of Customer Store Image Components in Three
     UK Retail Groups"
     European Journal of Marketing, Vol. 17, No. 4 (1983), pp. 50-62.

Stewart, David and Hood, Neil
     "A Methodology for the Evaluation of Segmentation Policy: An
     Empirical Application in the Car Industry"
     Journal of the Market Research Society, Vol. 23 (July 1981), pp.
     137-49.

Venkatraman, Meera P.
     "Opinion Leaders, Adopters, and Communicative Adopters: A Role
     Analysis"
     Psychology and Marketing, Vol. 6 (Spring 1989), pp. 51-68.

Verhage, Bronislaw J., Dahringer, Lee D., and Cundiff, Edward W.
     "Will a Global Marketing Strategy Work? An Energy Conservation
     Perspective"
     Journal of the Academy of Marketing Science, Vol. 17 (Spring 1989),
     pp. 129-36.

Wells, W. D.
     "Psychographics: A Critical Review"
     Journal of Marketing Research, Vol. XII (May 1975), pp. 196-213.

Wind, Yoram, Grashof, John F., and Goldhar, Joel D.
     "Market-Based Guidelines for Design of Industrial Products"
     Journal of Marketing, Vol. 42 (July 1978), pp. 27-37.

Yeomans, K. A. and Golder, P. A.
     "Further Observations on the Stratification of Burmingham Wards by
     Clustering: A Riposte"
     Applied Statistics, Vol. 24, No. 3 (1975), p. 345.

195.01 ---------- Applications of Hierarchical Clustering

Diamantopoulos, A. and Schlegelmilch, B. B.
     "Comparing Marketing Operations of Autonomous Subsidiaries"
     International Marketing Review, Vol. 4 (Winter 1987), pp. 53-64.

Dowling, Grahame R.
     "Strike Effects on the Structure of a Product Market"
     European Journal of Marketing, Vol. 21, No. 3 (1987), pp. 30-38.

Grover, Rajiv and Rao, Vithala R.
     "Inferring Competitive Market Structure Based on a Model of
     Interpurchase Intervals"
     International Journal of Research in Marketing, Vol. 5, No. 1 (1988),
     pp. 55-72.

Levine, David M.
  "Nonmetric Multidimensional Scaling and Hierarchical Clustering:
  Procedures for the Investigation of the Perception of Sports"
  Research Quarterly, Vol. 48 (1977), pp. 341-8.

Rao, Vithala R. and Sabavala, Darius J.
  "Inference of Hierarchical Choice Processes From Panel Data"
  Journal of Consumer Research, Vol. 8 (June 1981), pp. 85-96.

196 ------------ LATENT STRUCTURE (LATENT CLASS) ANALYSIS ------------

196.01 ---------- Books Re: Latent Structure (Latent Class) Analysis

Aigner, D. J. and Goldberger, A. S. (editors)
    Latent Variables in Socioeconomic Models
    (Amsterdam: North-Holland, 1977).

Everitt, B. S.
    An Introduction to Latent Variable Models
    (London: Chapman and Hall, 1984).

Goodman, Leo A.
    Analysing Qualitative/Categorical Data Log-Linear Models and Latent
    Structure Analysis
    (Reading, MA: Addison-Wesley, 1978).

Goodman, Leo A. and Magidson, Jay (editors)
    Analyzing Qualitative/Categorical Data: Log-Linear Models and Latent
    Structure Analysis
    (Cambridge, MA: Abt Books, 1978).

Lazarsfeld, Paul F. and Henry, Neil W.
    Latent Structure Analysis
    (Boston, MA: Houghton-Mifflin Co., 1968).

McCutcheon, Allan L.
    Latent Class Analysis
    (Beverly Hills, CA: Sage Publications, Inc., 1987), 96 pp.

Wiggins, Lee M.
    Panel Analysis: Latent Probability Model for Attitude and Behavior
    Processes
    (Amsterdam: Elsevier Science Publishing Company, Inc., 1973).

196.02 ---------- Theory Re: Latent Structure (Latent Class) Analysis

Anderson, T. W.
    "On Estimation of Parameters in Latent Structure Analysis"
    Psychometrika, Vol. 19 (1954), pp. 1-10.

Clogg, Clifford C.
    "Some Statistical Models for Analyzing Why Surveys Disagree"
    in Turner, C. F. and Martin, E. (editors)
    Surveying Subjective Phenomena, Volume Two
    (New York: Sage, 1984).

Clogg, C. C.
    "New Developments in Latent Structure Analysis"
    in Jackson, David J. and Borgetta, Edgar F. (editors)
    Factor Analysis and Measurement in Sociological Research: A
    Multi-Dimensional Perspective
    (Sage Publications, 1981).

Clogg, C. C.
    "Some Latent Structure Models for the Analysis of Likert-Type Data"
    Social Science Research, Vol. 8 (1979), pp. 287-301.

Clogg, Clifford C. and Goodman, Leo A.
    "On Scaling Models Applied to Datata From Several Groups"
    Psychometrika, Vol. 51 (1986), pp. 123-35.

Clogg, Clifford C. and Goodman, Leo A.
    "Simultaneous Latent Structure Analysis in Several Groups"
    in Tuma, N. B. (editor)
    Sociological Methodology
    (San Francisco, CA: Josey-Bass, 1985).

Clogg, Clifford C. and Goodman, Leo A.
    "Latent Structure Analysis of a Set of Multidimensional Tables"
    Journal of the American Statistical Association, Vol. 79 (December
    1984), pp. 762-71.

Clogg, Clifford C. and Munch, James M.
    "Using Simultaneous Latent Structure Models to Analyze Group
    Differences: Exploratory Analysis of Buying Style Items"
    Journal of Business Research, Vol. 12 (September 1984), pp. 319/36.

Clogg, C. C. and Sawyer, Darwin O.
    "A Comparison of Alternative Models for Analyzing the Scalability of
    Response Patterns"
    in Leinhardt, Samuel (editor)
    Sociological Methodology
    (San Francisco: Jossey-Bass Publishers, 1981), pp. 240-80.

Dayton, C. Mitchell and Macready, George B.
    "A Scaling Model With Response Errors and Intrinsically Unscalable
    Respondents"
    Psychometrika, Vol. 45 (September 1980), pp. 343-56.

Dillon, William R., Madden, Thomas J., and Mulani, Narendra
"Scaling Models for Categorical Variables: An Application of Latent
Structure Models"
Journal of Consumer Research, Vol. 10 (September 1983), pp. 209-24.

Feick, Lawrence F.
"Latent Class Models for the Analysis of Behavioral Hierarchies"
Journal of Marketing Research, Vol. XXIV (May 1987), pp. 174-86.

Feick, Lawrence F.
"Analyzing Marketing Research Data With Association Models"
Journal of Marketing Research, Vol. XXI (November 1984), pp. 376-86.

Fielding, A.
"Latent Structure Models"
in O'Muircheartaigh, C. A. and Payne, C. (editors)
The Analysis of Survey Data, Volume 1: Exploring Data Structure
(New York: John Wiley and Sons, Inc., 1977), pp. 125-57.

Formann, Anton
"Constrained Latent Class Models: Theory and Applications"
British Journal of Mathematical and Statistical Psychology, Vol. 38,
Part 1 (May 1985), pp. 87-111.

Goodman, Leo A.
"Simple Models for the Analysis of Association in
Cross-Classifications Having Ordered Categories"
Journal of the American Statistical Association, Vol. 74 (September
1979), pp. 537-52.

Goodman, Leo A.
"On the Estimation of Parameters in Latent Structure Analysis"
Psychometrika, Vol. 44 (1979), pp. 123-8.

Goodman, Leo A.
"A New Model for Scaling Response Patterns: An Application of the
Quasi-Independence Concept"
Journal of the American Statistical Association, Vol. 70 (1975), pp.
755-68.

Goodman, Leo A.
"Exploratory Latent Structure Analysis Using Both Identifiable and
Unidentifiable Models"
Biometrika, Vol. 61 (1974), pp. 215-31.

Goodman, Leo A.
"The Analysis of Systems of Qualitative Variables When Some of the
Variables are Unobservable--Part II: The Use of Modified Latent
Distance Models"
(1974), unpublished manuscript.

Goodman, Leo A.
"The Analysis of Systems of Qualitative Variables When Some of the
Variables are Unobservable--Part I: A Modified Latent Structure
Approach"
American Journal of Sociology, Vol. 79 (1974), pp. 1179-1259.

Goodman, Leo A.
"A General Model for the Analysis of Surveys"
American Journal of Sociology, Vol. 77 (1972), pp. 1035-1086.

Goodman, Leo A.
"Some Multiplicative Models for the Analysis of Cross-Classified Data"
in Cam, J. L. (editor)
Proceedings, Sixth Berkeley Symposium on Mathematical Statistics and
Probability
(Berkeley, CA: University of California Press, 1972), pp. 649-95.

Green, Bert F.
"Latent Structure Analysis and Its Relation to Factor Analysis"
Journal of the American Statistical Association, Vol. 47 (1952), pp.
71-6.

Green, Bert F.
"A General Solution for the Latent Class Model of Latent Structure
Analysis"
Psychometrika, Vol. 16 (June 1951), pp. 151-66.

Green, Paul E., Carmone, Frank J., and Wachspress, David P.
"Consumer Segmentation via Latent Class Analysis"
Journal of Consumer Research, Vol. 3 (December 1976), pp. 170-4.

Grover, Rajiv and Dillon, William R.
"A Probabilistic Model for Testing Hypothesized Hierarchical Market
Structures"
Marketing Science, Vol. 4 (Fall 1985), pp. 312-35.

Henry, N. W.
    "Latent Structure Analysis"
    in Kotz, S. and Johnson, N. L. (editors)
    Encyclopedia of Statistical Sciences
    (New York: John Wiley and Sons, 1983), pp. 497-504.

Hruschka, Harold
    "Estimation of Structural Equation Models With Qualitative Manifest
    Variables in Marketing Research by Using Latent Structure Analysis"
    Journal of Business Research, Vol. 17 (August 1988), pp. 35-41.

Kenny, David A. and Judd, Charles M.
    "Estimating the Nonlinear and Interactive Effects of Latent Variables"
    Psychological Bulletin, Vol. 96, No. 1 (1984), pp. 201-10.

Lazarsfeld, P. F.
    "Latent Structure Analysis"
    in Koch (editor)
    Psychology: A Study of a Science
    (New York: McGraw-Hill, 1959).

Lazarsfeld, Paul F.
    "The Interpretation and Computation of Some Latent Structures"
    in Stouffer, S. A. et al. (editors)
    Measurement and Prediction
    (Princeton, NJ: Princeton University Press, 1950).

Lazarsfeld, Paul F.
    "The Logical and Mathematical Foundation of Latent Structure Analysis"
    in Stouffer, S. A. et al. (editors)
    Measurement and Prediction
    (Princeton, NJ: Princeton University Press, 1950).

MacCallum, Robert
    "Specification Searches in Covariance Structure Modeling"
    Psychological Bulletin, Vol. 100, No. 1 (1986), pp. 107-20.

Madansky, Albert
    "Determinantal Methods in Latent Class Analysis"
    Psychometrika, Vol. 25 (June 1960), pp. 183-98.

Marsden, P.
    "Latent Structure Models for Relationally Defined Social Classes"
    American Journal of Sociology, Vol. 90 (1985), pp. 1002-21.

McHugh, R. B.
    "Efficient Estimation and Local Identification in Latent Class
    Analysis"
    Psychometrika, Vol. 21, No. 4 (1956), pp. 331-47.

Mooijaart, A.
    "Latent Structure Analysis for Categorical Variables"
    in Joreskog, K. G. and Wold, H. (editors)
    Systems Under Indirect Observation
    (Amsterdam: North-Holland, 1982).

Muthen, Bengt
    "A Structural Probit Model With Latent Variables"
    Journal of the American Statistical Association, Vol. 74 (December
    1979), pp. 807-11.

Myers, John G. and Nicosia, Franco M.
    "On the Dimensionality Question in Latent Structure Analysis"
    in Moyer, Reed (editor)
    Changing Marketing Systems: Consumer, Corporate and Government
    Inter-Faces
    (Chicago: American Marketing Association, 1969).

Myers, John G. and Nicosia, Francesco M.
    "New Empirical Directions in Market Segmentation: Latent Structure
    Models"
    in Moyer, Reed (editor)
    Changing Marketing Systems: Consumer, Corporate and Government
    Interfaces
    (Chicago: American Marketing Association, 1968).

Nicosia, Francesco M.
    "Latent Structure Analysis"
    in Sheth, Jagdish N. (editor)
    Multivariate Methods for Market and Survey Research
    (Chicago: American Marketing Association, 1977).

Nicosia, Francesco M. and Myers, John G.
    "Cognitive Structures, Latent Class Models, and the Leverage Index"
    American Association of Public Opinion Research National Conference,
    Santa Barbara, CA (May 1968), paper presentation.

Price, Lewis C., Dayton, C. Mitchell, and Macready, George B.
    "Discovery Algorithms for Hierarchical Relations Learning Models"
    Psychometrika, Vol. 45 (December 1980), pp. 449-65.

Proctor, C. H.
"A Probabilistic Formulation and Statistical Analysis of Guttman Scaling"
Psychometrika, Vol. 35 (March 1970), pp. 73-8.

Skene, A. M.
"Discrimination Using Latent Structure Models"
in Corsten, L. C. A. and Hermans, J. (editors)
Compstat 1978
(Vienna: Physica-Berlag, 1978).

196.03 ---------- Applications of Latent Structure (Class) Analysis

Aiken, Murray, Anderson, Dorothy, and Hinde, John
"Statistical Modelling of Data on Teaching Styles"
Journal of the Royal Statistical Society, Series A, Vol. 44, No. 4 (1981), pp. 419-61.

Clogg, Clifford C.
"Some Statistical Models for Analyzing Why Surveys Disagree"
in Turner, C. F. and Martin, E. (editors)
Surveying Subjective Phenomena, Volume Two
(New York: Russell Sage Foundation, 1985).

Colombo, Richard A. and Morrison, Donald G.
"A Brand Switching Model With Implications for Marketing Strategies"
Marketing Science, Vol. 8 (Winter 1989), pp. 89-99.

Feick, Lawrence F.
"Latent Class Models for the Analysis of Behavioral Hierarchies"
Journal of Marketing Research, Vol. XXIV (May 1987), pp. 174-86.

Grover, Rajiv
Confirmatory Analysis of Market Structures
School of Managment, University of Massachusetts, Amherst (1983),
unpublished doctoral dissertation.

Grover, Rajiv and Dillon, William R.
"A Probabilistic Model for Testing Hypothesized Hierarchical Market Structures"
Marketing Science, Vol. 4 (Fall 1985), pp. 312-35.

Grover, Rajiv and Srinivasan, V.
"A Simultaneous Approach to Market Segmentation and Market Structuring"
Journal of Marketing Research, Vol. XXIV (May 1987), pp. 139-53.

Haertel, Edward
"An Application of Latent Class Models to Assessment Data"
Applied Psychological Measurement, Vol. 8 (Summer 1984), pp. 333-46.

Haworth, Jean M. and Chell, Elizabeth
"An Application of Latent Class Analysis to the Measurement of Motivation"
Journal of the Market Research Society, Vol. 27 (April 1985), pp. 131-46.

Macready, George B.
"The Use of Latent Class Models for Assessing Prerequisite Relations and Transference Among Traits"
Psychometrika, Vol. 47 (December 1982), pp. 477-88.

Madden, Thomas J. and Dillon, William R.
"Causal Analysis and Latent Class Models: An Application to a Communication Hierarchy of Effects Model"
Journal of Marketing Research, Vol. XIX (November 1982), pp. 472-90.

Myers, John G. and Nicosia, Francesco M.
"New Empirical Directions in Market Segmentation: Latent Structure Models"
in Moyer, Reed (editor)
Changing Marketing Systems: Consumer, Corporate, and Government Interfocus
(Chicago: American Marketing Association, 1968), pp. 247-52.

Rindskopf, David
"A General Framework for Using Latent Class Analysis to Test Hierarchical and Nonhierarchical Learning Models"
Psychometrika, Vol. 48 (March 1983), pp. 85-97.

196.04 ---------- Computer Programs for Latent Structure Analysis

Clogg, Clifford
  "Unrestricted and Restricted Maximum Likelihood Latent Structure
  Analysis: A Manual for Users"
  Working Paper No. 1977-09
  Population Issues Research Office
  (Pennsylvania State University, 1977).

197 ------------ FACTOR AND PRINCIPAL COMPONENTS ANALYSIS ------------
       See also (sub)heading(s) 50, 133.09, 198, 199, 200, 201,
    202, 203.

197.01 ---------- Books Re: Factor Analysis

Burt, C.
    Factors of the Mind
    (New York: Macmillan and Company, 1941).

Burt, C. L.
    Distributions and Relations of Educational Abilities
    (London: P. S. King, 1917).

Cattell, R. B.
    The Scientific Use of Factor Analysis in the Behavioral and Life
    Sciences
    (New York: Plenum Press, 1978).

Cattell, R. B.
    Factor Analysis
    (New York: Harper and Brothers, 1952).

Comrey, Andrew L.
    A First Course in Factor Analysis
    (New York: Academic Press, 1973).

Coombs, C. H. and Kao, R. C.
    Nonmetric Factor Analysis
    (Ann Arbor: Engineering Research Institute, University of Michigan,
    1955).

Dunteman, George H.
    Principal Components Analysis
    (Newbury Park, CA: Sage Publications, Inc., 1989), 96 pp.

Ehrenberg, A. S. C. and Goodhardt, G. J.
    Factor Analysis: Limitations and Alternatives
    (Cambridge, MA: Marketing Science Institute, 1976).

Flury, Bernhard
    Common Principal Components and Related Multivariate Models
    (New York: John Wiley and Sons, Inc., 1988).

Gatty, Ronald and Heim, Ronald
    Factor Analysis Applied to Marketing Research
    (New Brunswick, NJ: Department of Agricultural Economics, Rutgers
    University, 1960).

Gorsuch, Richard L.
    Factor Analysis
    (Philadelphia: W. B. Saunders Company, 1974).

Guertin, Wilson H. and Bailey, John P., Jr.
    Introduction to Modern Factor Analysis
    (Ann Arbor, MI: Edward Bros., Inc., 1970).

Harman, H. H.
    Modern Factor Analysis, Third Edition
    (Chicago: University of Chicago Press, 1976).

Horn, J. L.
    Concepts and Methods of Correlational Analysis
    (New York: Holt, Rinehart and Winston, 1973).

Horst, Paul
    Factor Analysis of Data Matrices
    (New York: Holt, Rinehart and Winston, Inc., 1965).

Jolliffe, I. T.
    Principal Components Analysis
    (New York: Springer-Verlag, 1986), 246 pp.

Joreskog, Karl G. and Sorbom, Dag
    Advances in Factor Analysis and Structural Equation Models
    (Cambridge, MA: Abt Books, 1979), 242 pp.

Kennedy, W. J. and Gentle, J. E.
    Statistical Computing
    (New York: Marcel Dekker, 1980).

Kim, J. and Mueller, C. W.
    Factor Analysis: Statistical Methods and Practical Issues
    (Beverly Hills, CA: Sage Publications, 1978).

Kim, Jae-On and Mueller, Charles
    Introduction to Factor Analysis
    (Beverly Hills, CA: Sage Publications, Inc., 1978).

Lawley, D. N. and Maxwell, A. E.
 Factor Analysis as a Statistical Method, Second Edition
 (London: Butterworth, 1971).

Long, J. Scott
 Covariance Structure Models
 (Beverly Hills, CA: Sage Publications, Inc.).

McDonald, Ronald P.
 Factor Analysis and Related Methods
 (Hillsdale, NJ: Lawrence Erlbaum Associates, Publishers, 1985).

Mulaik, Stanley A.
 The Foundations of Factor Analysis
 (New York: McGraw-Hill Book Co., 1972).

Rummel, R. J.
 Applied Factor Analysis
 (Evanston, IL: Northwestern University Press, 1970).

Thurstone, L. L.
 Multiple Factor Analysis
 (Chicago, IL: University of Chicago Press, 1947).

197.02 ---------- Theory Re: Factor and Principal Components Analysis

Adcock, C. J.
 "Higher-Order Factor Factors"
 British Journal of Statistical Psychology, Vol. 17 (1964), pp. 153-60.

Anderson, Ronald D. and Acito, Franklin
 "On the Proper Use of Factor Analysis in Marketing Research"
 Proceedings, Mid-Western Institute for Decision Sciences
 (Chicago: Institute for Decision Sciences).

Anderson, T. W.
 "The Use of Factor Analysis in the Statistical Analysis of Multiple
 Time Series"
 Psychometrika, Vol. 21, No. 1 (1963), pp. 1-25.

Armstrong, J. Scott
 "Derivation of Theory by Means of Factor Analysis or Tom Swift and
 His Electric Factor Analysis Machine"
 American Statistician, Vol. 21 (December 1967), pp. 17-21.

Bentler, P. M.
 "A Multistructure Statistical Model Applied to Factor Analysis"
 Multivariate Behavioral Research, Vol. 11 (1976), pp. 3-25.

Bentler, Peter M. and Lee, S. Y.
 "Matrix Derivatives With Chain Rule and Rules for Simple, Hadamard,
 and Kronecker Products"
 Journal of Mathematical Psychology, Vol. 17 (1978), pp. 255-62.

Bentler, Peter M. and Lee, S. Y.
 "Some Extensions of Matrix Calculus"
 General Systems, Vol. 20 (1975), pp. 145-50.

Bock, R. D. and Bargman, R. E.
 "Analysis of Covariance Structures"
 Psychometrika, Vol. 31 (1966), pp. 507-34.

Borgers, Harrie
 "Factor Analysis: Limitations and Alternatives--Comment"
 European Research, Vol. 5 (November 1977), pp. 269-74.

Browne, Michael W.
 "Generalized Least Squares Estimators in the Analysis of Covariance
 Structures"
 South African Statistical Journal, Vol. 8 (1974), pp. 1-24.

Burt, Cyril
 "Factorial Analysis of Qualitative Data"
 British Journal of Psychology (Statistical Section), Vol. 3 (November
 1950), pp. 166-85.

Burt, Cyril L.
 "Factor Analysis by Sub-Matrices"
 Journal of Psychology, Vol. 6 (1938), pp. 339-75.

Burt, C. L.
 "Correlations Between Persons"
 British Journal of Psychology, Vol. 28 (January 1937), pp. 56-96.

Burt, Cyril L.
 "Experimental Tests of General Intelligence"
 British Journal of Psychology, Vol. 3 (1909), pp. 94-177.

Carroll, J. B.
"An Analytic Solution for Approximating Simple Structure in Factor Analysis"
Psychometrika, Vol. 18 (March 1953), pp. 23-38.

Cattell, R. B.
"The Meaning and Strategic Use of Factor Analysis"
in Cattell, R. B. (editor)
Handbook of Multivariate Experimental Psychology
(Chicago: Rand McNally and Company, 1966).

Cattell, R. B.
"Higher Order Factor Structures and Reticular-vs-Hierarchical Formulae for Their Interpretation"
in Banks, C. and Broadhurst (editors)
Studies in Psychology
(London: University of London Press, 1965), pp. 223-66.

Cattell, R. B.
"Theory of Situational, Instrument, Second-Order and Refraction Factors in Personality Structure Research"
Psychological Bulletin, Vol. 58 (March 1961), pp. 160-74.

Cattell, Raymond B.
"The Three Basic Factor-Analytic Designs--Their Interrelations and Derivatives"
Psychological Bulletin, Vol. 49 (September 1952), pp. 499-523.

Cattell, Raymond B.
"On the Disuse and Misuse of R, P, Q, and O Techniques in Clinical Psychology"
Journal of Clinical Psychology, Vol. 7 (1951), pp. 203-14.

Cattell, Raymond B.
"R, P, and Other Coefficients of Pattern Similarity"
Psychometrika, Vol. 14 (December 1949), pp. 279-98.

Cattell, Raymond B., Balcar, Karel R., Horn, J. L., and Nesselroade, J. B.
"Factor Matching Procedures: An Improvement of the S Index: With Tables"
Educational and Psychological Measurement, Vol. 29 (Winter 1969), pp. 781-92.

Cattell, R. B., Coulter, M. A., and Tsujioka, B.
"The Taxonometric Recognition of Types and Functional Emergents"
in Cattell, R. B. (editor)
Handbook of Multivariate Experimental Research
(Chicago: Rand McNally and Company, 1966), pp. 288-329.

Chang, Wei-Chien
"On Using Principal Components Before Separating a Mixture of Two Multivariate Normal Distributions"
Applied Statistics, Vol. 32, No. 3 (1983), pp. 267-75.

Clarkson, Douglas B.
"Estimating the Standard Errors of Rotated Factor Loadings by Jackknifing"
Psychometrika, Vol. 44 (September 1979), pp. 297-314.

Clemans, W. V.
An Analytic and Experimental Examination of Some Properties of Ipsative Measures
University of Washington (1956), unpublished doctoral dissertation.

Cliff, N. and Hamburger, C. D.
"The Study of Sampling Errors in Factor Analysis by Means of Artificial Experiments"
Psychological Bulletin, Vol. 68 (June 1967), pp. 430-45.

Coan, R. W.
"Facts, Factors, and Artifacts: The Quest for Psychological Measurement"
Psychological Review, Vol. 71 (March 1964), pp. 123-40.

Cohen, J.
"A Profile Similarity Coefficient Invariable Over Variable Reflection"
Psychological Bulletin, Vol. 71 (April 1969), pp. 281-4.

Cohen, J.
"Re: A Profile Similarity Coefficient Invariant Over Variable Reflection"
Proceedings, 76th Annual Convention of the American Psychological Association, Vol. 3 (1968), p. 211.

Collins, Gwyn
"On Methods: Factor Analysis"
Journal of Advertising Research, Vol. 1 (September 1961), pp. 28-32.

Collins, M. A., Ehrenberg, A. S. C., and Goodhardt, G. J.
  "Factor Analysis: A Reply to Harrie Borgers"
  European Research, Vol. 5 (November 1977), pp. 275-7.

Cormack, R. M.
  "A Review of Classification"
  Journal of the Royal Statistical Society, Series A, Vol. 134 (1971),
  pp. 321-67.

Cureton, E. E.
  "The Principal Compulsions of Factor Analysis"
  Harvard Educational Review, Vol. 9 (1939), pp. 287-95.

Dillon, William R., Frederick, Donald G., and Tangpanichdee, Vanchai
  "Decision Issues in Building Perceptual Product Spaces With
  Multi-Attribute Rating Data"
  Journal of Consumer Research, Vol. 12 (June 1985), pp. 47-63.

Dillon, William R., Mulani, Narendra, and Frederick, Donald G.
  "On the Use of Component Scores in the Presence of Group Structure"
  Journal of Consumer Research, Vol. 16 (June 1989), pp. 106-12.

Dziuban, C. D. and Shirkey, E. C.
  "When is a Correlation Matrix Appropriate for Factor Analysis"
  Psychological Bulletin, Vol. 81 (June 1974), pp. 358-61.

Eckart, Charles and Young, Gale
  "The Approximation of One Matrix by Another of Lower Rank"
  Psychometrika, Vol. 1 (September 1936), pp. 211-8.

Ehrenberg, A. S. C.
  "A Discussion on Factor Analysis"
  Statistician, Vol. 14, No. 1 (1964), pp. 47-61.

Ehrenberg, A. S. C.
  "Some Queries to Factor Analysis"
  Statistician, Vol. 13, No. 3 (1963), pp. 257-62.

Ehrenberg, A. S. C.
  "Some Questions About Factor Analysis"
  Statistician, Vol. 12, No. 3 (1962), pp. 191-208.

Ehrenberg, A. S. C. and Goodhardt, G. J.
  "Factor Analysis: Limitations and Alternatives"
  Marketing Science Institute Working Paper
  (Cambridge, A: Marketing Science Institute, 1976).

Ekeblad, Frederick A. and Stasch, Stanley F.
  "Criteria in Factor Analysis"
  Journal of Advertising Research, Vol. 7 (September 1967), pp. 48-57.

Estes, William K.
  "The Problem of Inference From Curves Based on Group Data"
  Psychological Bulletin, Vol. 53 (March 1956), pp. 134-40.

Evans, Glen T.
  "Transformation of Factor Matrices to Achieve Congruence"
  British Journal of Mathematical and Statistical Psychology, Vol. 24
  (May 1971), pp. 22-48.

Fleiss, Joseph L. and Zubin, Joseph
  "On the Methods and Theory of Clustering"
  Multivariate Behavioral Research, Vol. 4 (April 1969), pp. 235-50.

Fornell, Claes
  "Issues in the Application of Covariance Structure Analysis: A
  Comment"
  Journal of Consumer Research, Vol. 9 (March 1983), pp. 443-8.

Gabriel, K. R.
  "The Biplot Graphic Display of Matrices With Applications to
  Principal Components Analysis"
  Biometrika, Vol. 58, No. 3 (1971), pp. 453-67.

Girshick, M. A.
  "Principal Components"
  Journal of the American Statistical Association, Vol. 31 (1936), p.
  519.

Gower, J. C.
  "Some Distance Properties of Latent Root and Vector Methods Used in
  Multivariate Analysis"
  Psychometrika, Vol. 53, Nos. 3 and 4 (1966), pp. 325-38.

Green, Bert F.
  "On the Factor Score Controversy"
  Psychometrika, Vol. 41 (June 1976), pp. 263-6.

Green, B. F.
"The Orthogonal Approximation of Oblique Structure in Factor Analysis"
Psychometrika, Vol. 17 (December 1952), pp. 429-40.

Guttman, L.
"Some Necessary Conditions for Common Factor Analysis"
Psychometrika, Vol. 19 (June 1954), pp. 149-61.

Guttman, Louis
"Multiple Group Methods for Common Factor Analysis: Their Basis,
Computation, and Interpretation"
Psychometrika, Vol. 17 (1952), pp. 209-22.

Guttman, L.
"The Principal Components of Scale Analysis"
in Stouffer, S. A. et al. (editors)
Measurement and Prediction
(Princeton, NJ: Princeton University Press, 1950).

Hagglund, G.
"Factor Analysis by Instrumental Variable Methods"
Psychometrika, Vol. 47, No.2 (1982), pp. 209-22.

Harman, H. H.
"The Square Root Method and Multiple Group Methods of Factor Analysis"
Psychometrika, Vol. 19 (March 1954), pp. 39-55.

Harris, Chester W.
"On Factors and Factor Scores"
Psychometrika, Vol. 32 (December 1967), pp. 363-79.

Harris, Chester W.
"Some Rao-Guttman Relationships"
Psychometrika, Vol. 27 (September 1962), pp. 247-79.

Harris, Margaret L. and Harris, Chester W.
"A Factor Analytic Interpretation Strategy"
Educational and Psychological Measurement, Vol. 31 (1971), pp.
589-606.

Holzinger, K. J.
"A Simple Method of Factor Analysis"
Psychometrika, Vol. 9 (December 1944), pp. 257-62.

Horn, John L.
"On Subjectivity in Factor Analysis"
Educational and Psychological Measurement, Vol. 27 (1967), pp. 811-20.

Hotelling, Harold
"Analysis of Complex Statistical Variables into Principal Components"
Journal of Educational Psychology, Vol. 24 (September 1933), pp.
498-520.

Hunter, J. E. and Gerbing, David W.
"Unidimensional Measurement, Second-Order Factor Analysis and Causal
Models"
in Staw, B. M. and Cummings, L. L. (editors)
Research and Organizational Behavior, Volume IV
(Greenwich, CT: JAI Press).

Jackson, Douglas N.
"Multimethod Factor Analysis in the Evaluation of Convergent and
Discriminant Validity"
Psychological Bulletin, Vol. 72 (January 1969), pp. 30-49.

Johnson, Richard M.
"Q Analysis of Large Samples"
Journal of Marketing Research, Vol. VII (February 1970), pp. 104,5.

Jones, Marshall B.
Molar Correlation Analysis
Monograph Series No. 4
(Pensacola, FL: U.S. School of Aviation Medicine, 1960).

Joreskog, Karl G.
"Analyzing Psychological Data by Structural Analysis of Covariance
Matrices"
in Atkinson, R. C. et al. (editors)
Contemporary Developments in Mathematical Psychology, Volume II
(San Francisco: Freeman, 1974), pp. 1-56.

Joreskog, Karl G.
"Simultaneous Factor Analysis in Several Populations"
Psychometrica, Vol. 36 (December 1971), pp. 409-26.

Joreskog, Karl G.
"Statistical Analysis of Sets of Congeneric Tests"
Psychometrika, Vol. 36 (1971), pp. 109-33.

Joreskog, Karl G.
   "A General Method for Analysis of Covariance Structures"
   Biometrika, Vol. 57 (1970), pp. 239-51.

Joreskog, Karl G.
   "A General Approach to Confirmatory Maximum Likelihood Factor
   Analysis"
   Psychometrika, Vol. 34 (1969), pp. 183-202.

Joreskog, Karl G. and Sorbom, Dag
   "Recent Developments in Structural Equations Modeling"
   Journal of Marketing Research, Vol. XIX (November 1982), pp. 404-16.

Joreskog, K. G. and Van Thillo, M.
   "New Rapid Algorithms for Factor Analysis by Unweighted Least
   Squares, Generalized Least Squares and Maximum Likelihood"
   Research Bulletin, 71-5
   (Princeton, NJ: Educational Testing Service, 1971).

Jowett, G. H.
   "Factor Analysis"
   Applied Statistics, Vol. 7 (1958), pp. 114-25.

Kaiser, H. F.
   "A Second Generation Little Jiffy"
   Psychometrika, Vol. 35 (1970), p. 401.

Kaiser, Henry F.
   "Formulas for Component Scores"
   Psychometrika, Vol. 27 (March 1962), pp. 83-7.

Kaiser, H. F. and Caffrey, J.
   "Alpha Factor Analysis"
   Psychometrika, Vol. 30 (March 1965), pp. 1-14.

Karson, S. and Pool, K. B.
   "Second-Order Factors in Personality Measurement"
   Journal of Consulting Psychology, Vol. 22 (1958), pp. 299-303.

Kendall, M. G.
   "Factor Analysis as a Statistical Technique"
   Journal of the Royal Statistical Society, Vol. 121 (1950), pp. 60-73.

Kerby, Joe Kent
   "Factor Analysis: Key Tool in Consumer Behavior Research"
   Journal of the Academy of Marketing Science, Vol. 7 (Fall 1979), pp.
   374-90.

Korth, Bruce and Tucker, L. R.
   "The Distribution of Chance Congruence Coefficients From Simulated
   Data"
   Psychometrika, Vol. 40 (September 1975), pp. 361-72.

Kruskal, Joseph B. and Shepard, Roger N.
   "A Nonmetric Version of Linear Factor Analysis"
   Psychometrika, Vol. 39 (June 1974), pp. 123-57.

Lee, S. Y. and Jennrich, R. I.
   "A Study of Logarithms for Covariance Structure Analysis With
   Specific Comparisons Using Factor Analysis"
   Psychometrika, Vol. 4 (March 1979), pp. 99-113.

Levin, Joseph
   "Three-Mode Factor Analysis"
   Psychological Bulletin, Vol. 64 (December 1965), pp. 442-52.

Lingoes, J. C. and Guttman, Louis
   "Nonmetric Factor Analysis: A Rank Reducing Alternative to Linear
   Factor Analysis"
   Multivariate Behavioral Research, Vol. 2 (October 1967), pp. 485-505.

Madansky, A.
   "Instrumental Variables in Factor Analysis"
   Psychometrika, Vol. 29 (1964), pp. 105-13.

Massy, William F.
   "What is Factor Analysis?"
   Proceedings, 1964 Conference of the American Marketing Association
   (Chicago: American Marketing Association, 1969), pp. 291-307.

Massy, W. F.
   "Principal Components Regression in Exploratory Statistical Research"
   Journal of the American Statistical Association, Vol. 60 (March
   1965), pp. 234-56.

McDonald, Roderick P.
   "A Simple Comprehensive Model for the Analysis of Covariance
   Structures: Some Remarks on Applications"
   British Journal of Mathematical and Statistical Psychology, Vol. 33
   (November 1980), pp. 161-83.

McDonald, Roderick P.
"A Simple Comprehensive Model for the Analysis of Covariance Structures"
British Journal of Mathematical and Statistical Psychology, Vol. 31 (May 1978), pp. 59-72.

McDonald, R. P.
"A General Approach to Nonlinear Factor Analysis"
Psychometrika, Vol. 27 (1962), pp. 397-415.

McDonald, R. P. and Swaminathan, H.
"A Simple Matrix Calculus With Applications to Multivariate Analysis"
General Systems, Vol. 18 (1973), pp. 37-54.

Montanelli, R. G. and Humphreys, L. G.
"Latent Roots of Random Data Correlation Matrices With Squared Multiple Correlation on the Diagonal: A Monte Carlo Study"
Psychometrika, Vol. 41 (1976), pp. 341-8.

Mosier, C. I.
"Determining a Simple Structure When Loadings for Certain Tests are Known"
Psychometrika, Vol. 4 (1939), pp. 149-62.

Myers, John G. and Nicosia, Francesco M.
"On the Study of Consumer Typologies"
Journal of Marketing Research, Vol. V (May 1968), pp. 182-93.

Nunnally, J. C.
"The Analysis of Profile Data"
Psychological Bulletin, Vol. 59 (1962), pp. 311-9.

Palmer, John
"Thinking Geometrically"
European Research, Vol. 1 (September 1973), pp. 208-14.

Pawlik, K. and Cattell, R. B.
"Third-Order Factors in Objective Personality Tests"
British Journal of Psychology, Vol. LV (1964), pp. 1-18.

Ramond, Charles K.
"Factor Analysis: When to Use It"
in Shuchman, Abe (editor)
Scientific Decision Making in Business
(New York: Holt, Rinehart and Winston, Inc., 1963).

Sampson, Peter and De Almeida, Pergentino De F Mendes
"A Note on Selecting the Appropriate Factor Analytic Solution From Several Available"
European Research, Vol. 7 (September 1979), pp. 212-7.

Schmid, J. and Leiman, J. M.
"The Development of Hierarchical Factor Solutions"
Psychometrika, Vol. 22 (March 1957), pp. 53-61.

Schonemann, P. H.
"A Generalized Solution to the Orthogonal Procrustes Problem"
Psychometrika, Vol. 31 (March 1966), pp. 1-10.

Sidman, Murray
"A Note on Functional Relations Obtained From Group Data"
Psychological Bulletin, Vol. 49 (May 1952), pp. 263-9.

Spearman, C.
"General Intelligence Objectively Determined and Measured"
American Journal of Psychology, Vol. 15 (1904), pp. 201-93.

Spearman, Charles and Holzinger, K. J.
"The Sampling Error in the Theory of Two Factors"
British Journal of Psychology, Vol. 15 (July 1924), pp. 17-9.

Stephenson, William
"Some Observations on Q Technique"
Psychological Bulletin, Vol. 49 (September 1952), pp. 483-98.

Stewart, David W.
"The Application and Misapplication of Factor Analysis in Marketing Research"
Journal of Marketing Research, Vol. XVIII (February 1981), pp. 51-62.

Stinchcombe, A. L.
"A Heuristic Procedure for Interpreting Factor Analysis"
American Sociological Review, Vol. 36 (December 1971), pp. 1080-4.

Thurstone, L. L.
"Multiple Factor Analysis"
Psychological Review, Vol. 38 (1931), pp. 406-27.

Trites, David K. and Sells, Saul B.
"A Note on Alternative Methods for Estimating Factor Scores"
Journal of Applied Psychology, Vol. 39 (1955), pp. 455,6.

Tryon, Robert C.
"Cluster and Factor Analysis: General Exposition"
Department of Psychology, University of California, Berkeley (1967),
mimeograph.

Tucker, L. R.
"Note on the Minimum Number of Attributes in a Battery to Support a
Given Number of Factors in a Common Factor Analysis"
University of Illinois (1975), unpublished paper.

Tucker, L. R.
"Relations Between Multidimensional Scaling and Three-Mode Factor
Analysis"
Psychometrika, Vol. 37 (March 1972), pp. 3-27.

Tucker, Ledyard R.
"Some Mathematical Notes on Three-Mode Factor Analysis"
Psychometrika, Vol. 31 (September 1966), pp. 279-311.

Tucker, L. R.
"The Extension of Factor Analysis to Three-Dimensional Matrices"
in Frederiksen, N. and Gulliksen, H. (editors)
Contributions to Mathematical Psychology
(New York: Rinehart and Winston, 1964), pp. 109-27.

Tucker, Ledyard R.
"An Inter-Battery Method of Factor Analysis"
Psychometrika, Vol. 23 (June 1958), pp. 111-36.

Tucker, L. R.
"The Role of Correlated Factors in Factor Analysis"
Psychometrika, Vol. 5 (June 1940), pp. 141-52.

Wells, William D. and Sheth, Jagdish N.
"Factor Analysis in Marketing Research"
in Ferber, Robert (editor)
Handbook of Marketing Research
(New York: McGraw-Hill Book Company, 1974).

Wells, William D. and Sheth, Jagdish N.
"Factor Analysis in Marketing Research"
in Aaker, D. A. (editor)
Multivariate Analysis in Marketing: Theory and Applications
(Belmont, CA: Wadsworth Publishing Company, 1971).

Werts, C. E., Linn, R. L., and Joreskog, K. G.
"Interclass Reliability Estimates: Testing Structural Assumptions"
Educational and Psychological Measurement, Vol. 34 (1974), pp. 25-33.

Werts, C. E., Rock, D. A., Linn, R. L., and Joreskog, K. G.
"Validating Psychometric Assumptions Within and Between Populations"
Educational and Psychological Measurement, Vol. 37 (1977), pp. 863-71.

Wherry, Robert J.
"A New Iterative Method for Correcting Erroneous Communality
Estimates in Factor Analysis"
Psychometrika, Vol. 14 (September 1949), pp. 231-41.

Wind, Yoram, Green, Paul E., and Jain, Arun K.
"Higher Order Factor Analysis in the Classification of Psychographic
Variables"
Journal of the Market Research Society, Vol. 15 (October 1973), pp.
224-32.

Wold, H.
"Estimation of Principal Components and Related Models by Iterative
Least Squares"
in Krishnaiah, P. R. (editor)
Multivariate Analysis
(New York: Academic Press, 1966).

Wrigley, C.
"A Procedure for Objective Factor Analysis"
First Annual Meeting of the Society for Multivariate Experimental
Psychology (1960), paper presentation.

Young, Forrest W., Takane, Yoshio, and De Leeuw, Jan
"The Principal Components of Mixed Measurement Data: An Alternating
Least Squares Method With Optimal Scaling Features"
Psychometrika, Vol. 43 (June 1978), pp. 279-82.

Young, Gale and Householder, A. S.
"Matrix Approximation and Latent Roots"
American Mathematical Monthly, Vol. 45 (March 1938), pp. 165-71.

197.03 ---------- Theory Re: Multi-Mode Component Analysis

Joachimsthaler, Erich A. and Lastovicka, John L.
"4MODE1 and 4MODE2: FORTRAN IV Programs to Estimate the Four-Mode
Component Model"
Journal of Marketing Research, Vol. XXII (May 1985), pp. 222,3.

Lastovicka, John L.
"A Pilot Study of Krugman's 'Three-Exposure Theory'"
in Percy, Larry and Woodside, Arch (editors)
Advertising and Consumer Psychology
(Lexington, MA: Lexington Books/D. C. Heath and Company, 1983), pp.
333-44,85.

Lastovicka, John L.
"The Extension of Component Analysis to Four-Mode Matrices"
Psychometrika, Vol. 46 (March 1981), pp. 47-57.

Tucker, L. R.
"Some Mathematical Notes on Three-Mode Factor Analysis"
Psychometrika, Vol. 31 (September 1966), pp. 279-311.

197.04 ---------- Theory Re: Maximum Likelihood Factor Analysis

Costner, H. L. and Schoenberg, R.
"Diagnosing Indicator Ills in Multiple Indicator Models"
in Goldberger, A. S. and Duncan, O. D. (editors)
Structural Equation Models in the Social Sciences
(New York: Seminar Press, 1973), pp. 167-99.

Fuller, E. L. and Hammerle, W. J.
"Robustness of the Maximum Likelihood Estimation Procedure in Factor
Analysis"
Psychometrika, Vol. 31 (June 1966), pp. 255-66.

Gweke, John R. and Singleton, Kenneth J.
"Interpreting the Likelihood Ratio Statistic in Factor Models When
Sample Size is Small"
Journal of the American Statistical Association, Vol. 75 (March
1980), pp. 133-7.

Heeler, Roger M. and Whipple, Thomas W.
"A Monte Carlo Aid to the Evaluation of Maximum Likelihood Factor
Analysis Solutions"
British Journal of Mathematical and Statistical Psychology, Vol. 29
(May 1976), pp. 94-102.

Jackson, Douglas N. and Chan, David W.
"Maximum-Likelihood Estimation in Common Factor Analysis: A
Cautionary Note"
Psychological Bulletin, Vol. 88, No. 2 (1980), pp. 502-8.

Jennrich, R. I. and Clarkson, D. B.
"A Feasible Method for Standard Errors of Estimate in Maximum
Likelihood Factor Analysis"
Psychometrika, Vol. 45 (1980), pp. 237-47.

Joreskog, Karl G.
"Structural Analysis of Covariance and Correlational Matrices"
Psychometrika, Vol. 43 (December 1978), pp. 443-77.

Joreskog, Karl G.
"A General Method for Analysis of Covariance Structures"
Biometrika, Vol. 57, No. 2 (1970), pp. 239-51.

Joreskog, Karl G.
"Some Contributions to Maximum Likelihood Factor Analysis"
Psychometrika, Vol. 32 (December 1967), pp. 443-82.

Joreskog, Karl G. and Lawley, D. N.
"New Methods in Maximum Likelihood Factor Analysis"
British Journal of Mathematical and Statistical Psychology, Vol. 21
(May 1968), pp. 85-96.

Joreskog, K. G. and Van Thillo, M.
"New Rapid Algorithms for Factor Analysis by Unweighted Least
Squares, Generalized Least Squares and Maximum Likelihood"
Research Bulletin 71-5
(Princeton, NJ: Educational Testing Service, 1971).

Lawley, D. N.
"The Application of the Maximum Likelihood Method to Factor Analysis"
British Journal of Psychology, Vol. 33 (1943), pp. 172-5.

Lawley, D. N.
  "The Estimation of Factor Loadings by the Method of Maximum
  Likelihood"
  Proceedings of the Royal Society, Edinburgh (A), Vol. 60 (1940), pp.
  64-82.

Mitchell, Andrew A. and Olson, Jerry C.
  "Use of Restricted and Unrestricted Maximum Likelihood Factor
  Analysis to Examine Alternative Measures of Brand Loyalty"
  Proceedings, Fall Conference, American Marketing Association (1975),
  pp. 181-6.

Saris, W. E., De Pijper, W. M., and Zegwaart, P.
  "Detection of Specification Errors in Linear Structural Equation
  Models"
  in Schuessler, K. E. (editor)
  Sociological Methodology
  (San Francisco: Jossey-Bass, 1978).

Sorbom, Dag
  "Detection of Correlated Errors in Longitudinal Data"
  British Journal of Mathematical and Statistical Psychology, Vol. 28
  (1975), pp. 138-51.

Sprott, D. A.
  "Maximum Likelihood in Small Samples: Estimation in the Presence of
  Nuisance Parameters"
  Biometrika, Vol. 67 (1980), pp. 515-23.

Tucker, L. R.
  "Unrestricted Maximum Likelihood Factor Analysis Statistics"
  University of Illinois (1975), unpublished paper.

Tucker, Ledyard R. and Lewis, Charles
  "A Reliability Coefficient for Maximum Likelihood Factor Analysis"
  Psychometrika, Vol. 38 (March 1975), pp. 1-10.

Van Driel, Otto P.
  "On Various Causes of Improper Solutions in Maximum Likelihood Factor
  Analysis"
  Psychometrika, Vol. 43 (June 1978), pp. 225-43.

Young, G.
  "Maximum Likelihood Estimation and Factor Analysis"
  Psychometrika, Vol. 6 (1941), pp. 49-53.

197.05 ---------- Theory Re: Factor Analysis of Binary Data

Bartholomew, David J.
  "Factor Analysis for Categorical Data"
  Journal of the Royal Statistical Society, Vol. B42 (1980), pp.
  293-321.

Bock, R. Darrell and Lieberman, Marcus
  "Fitting a Response Model for n Dichotomously Scored Items"
  Psychometrika, Vol. 35 (June 1970), pp. 179-97.

Christoffersson, Anders
  "Factor Analysis of Dichotomized Variables"
  Psychometrika, Vol. 40 (March 1975), pp. 5-32.

Kruskal, Joseph B. and Shepard, Roger N.
  "A Nonmetric Variety of Linear Factor Analyses"
  Psychometrika, Vol. 39 (June 1974), pp. 123-57.

Muthen, Bengt
  "Factor Analysis of Dichotomous Variables: American Attitudes Toward
  Abortion"
  in Jackson and Borgatta (editors)
  Factor Analysis and Measurement in Sociological Research
  (Beverly Hills, CA: Sage Press Publications, Inc., 1981), pp. 114-36.

Muthen, Bengt
  "Contributions to Factor Analysis of Dichotomous Variables"
  Psychometrika, Vol. 43 (December 1978), pp. 551-60.

197.06 ---------- Data Issues for Factor Analysis

Armstrong, J. S. and Soelberg, P.
  "On the Interpretation of Factor Analysis"
  Psychological Bulletin, Vol. 70 (June 1968), pp. 361-4.

Bartlett, M. S.
  "A Further Note on Tests of Significance in Factor Analysis"
  British Journal of Statistical Psychology, Vol. 4 (January 1951), pp.
  1,2.

Bartlett, M. S.
   "Tests of Significance in Factor Analysis"
   British Journal of Statistical Psychology, Vol. 3 (January 1950), pp.
   77-85.

Carroll, J. B.
   "The Nature of Data, or How to Choose a Correlation Coefficient"
   Psychometrika, Vol. 26 (December 1961), pp. 347-72.

Holley, J. W.
   "A Reply to Phillip Levy: In Defense of the G Index"
   Scandinavian Journal of Psychology, Vol. 7 (1966), pp. 244-7.

Holley, J. W. and Guilford, J. P.
   "A Note on the G Index of Agreement"
   Educational and Psychological Measurement, Vol. 24 (Winter 1964), pp.
   749-53.

Jackson, J. J. and Alwin, D. F.
   "The Factor Analysis of Ipsative Measures"
   in Bohrnstedt, G. W. and Borgatta, E. F. (editors)
   Social Measurement: Current Issues
   (Beverly Hills, CA: Sage Publications, 1981).

Kaiser, H. F.
   "A Second Generation Little Jiffy"
   Psychometrika, Vol. 35 (December 1970), pp. 401-15.

Kaiser, H. F.
   "Image Analysis"
   in Harris, C. W. (editor)
   Problems in Measuring Change
   (Madison: University of Wisconsin Press, 1963).

Kaiser, H. F. and Rice, J.
   "Little Jiffy Mark IV"
   Educational and Psychological Measurement, Vol. 34 (Spring 1974), pp.
   111-7.

Olsson, Ulf
   "Maximum Likelihood Estimation of the Polychoric Correlation
   Coefficient"
   Psychometrika, Vol. 44 (December 1979), pp. 443-59.

Olsson, Ulf
   "On the Robustness of Factor Analysis Against Crude Classification of
   the Observations"
   Multivariate Behavioral Research, Vol. 14 (October 1979), pp. 485-500.

Shaycroft, M. F.
   "The Eigenvalue Myth and the Dimension Reduction Fallacy"
   American Educational Research Association Annual Meeting, Minneapolis
   (1970), paper presentation.

Tobias, S. and Carlson, J. E.
   "Brief Report: Bartlett's Test of Sphericity and Chance Findings in
   Factor Analysis"
   Multivariate Behavioral Research, Vol. 4 (October 1969), pp. 375-7.

Tucker, L. R.
   "Factor Analysis of Double Centered Score Matrices"
   ETS Pub. No. RM-56-3
   (Princeton, NJ: Educational Testing Service, 1956).

197.07 ---------- Evaluations and Comparisons of Factor Analysis Types

Acito, Franklin and Anderson, Ronald D.
   "A Monte Carlo Comparison of Factor Analytic Methods"
   Journal of Marketing Research, Vol. XVII (1980), pp. 228-36.

Block, Jack
   "The Difference Between Q and R"
   Psychological Review, Vol. 62 (1955), pp. 356-8.

Browne, M. W.
   "A Comparison of Factor Analytic Techniques"
   Psychometrika, Vol. 33 (September 1968), pp. 267-334.

Harris, M. L. and Harris, C. W.
   "A Factor Analytic Interpretation Strategy"
   Educational and Psychological Measurement, Vol. 31 (Fall 1971), pp.
   589-606.

Hubbard, Raymond and Allen, Stuart J.
   "An Empirical Comparison of Alternative Methods for Principal
   Components Extraction"
   Journal of Business Research, Vol. 15 (April 1987), pp. 173-90.

McDonald, Roderick P. and Burr, E. J.
   "A Comparison of Four Methods of Computing Factor Scores"
   Psychometrika, Vol. 32 (December 1967), pp. 381-401.

197.08 ---------- Computer Programs for Factor Analysis

Arora, Raj
   "ORTHOG: A Program for Orthogonal Least Squares Transformation of
   Factor Matrices to Congruence or to a Target Solution"
   Journal of Marketing Research, Vol. XIX (November 1982), pp. 605,6.

Arora, Raj and Vaughn, R.
   "FACSIM: A Program to Compute the Similarity Indices for Two Groups
   of Factor Solutions"
   Journal of Marketing Research, Vol. XVIII (November 1981), p. 485.

Bentler, Peter M.
   "Theory and Implementation of EQS, a Structural Equation Program"
   Department of Psychology, University of California, Los Angeles
   (1981), technical report.

Hunter, J. E. and Cohen, S. H.
   "PACKAGE: A System of Computer Routines for the Analysis of
   Correlational Data"
   Educational and Psychological Measurement, Vol. 29 (1969), pp.
   697-700.

Hunter, J. E., Gerbing, David W., Cohen, S. H., and Nicol, T. S.
   "PACKAGE 1980: A System of FORTRAN Routines for the Analysis of
   Correlational Data"
   Academic Computing Services, Baylor University, Waco, TX (1980).

International Mathematical Statistical Library
   IMSL Manual
   (Houston: International Mathematical Statistical Library, 1977).

Jennrich, R. I. and Sampson, P. F.
   "Some Problems in Making a Variance Component Algorithm Into a
   General Mixed Mode Program"
   in Gallant, A. R. and Gerig, T. M. (editors)
   Proceedings, Computer Science and Statistics: Eleventh Annual
   Symposium on the Interface
   (Raleigh, NC: The Institute of Statistics, North Carolina State
   University, 1978), pp. 56-63.

Joreskog, Karl G.
   "UMFLA: A Computer Program for Unrestricted Maximum Likelihood Factor
   Analysis"
   (Princeton, NJ: Educational Testing Service, 1966), Research
   Memorandum 66-20.

Joreskog, Karl G. and Sorbom, Dag
   LISREL IV: Analysis of Linear Structural Relationships by the Method
   of Maximum Likelihood
   (Chicago: National Educational Resources, Inc., 1978).

MacCallum, R.
   "A Comparison of Analysis Programs in SPSS, BMDP, and SAS"
   Psychometrika, Vol. 48 (June 1983), pp. 223-32.

Sorbom, Dag and Joreskog, Karl G.
   COFAMM: Confirmatory Factor Analysis With Model Modification
   (Chicago: National Educational Resources, Inc., 1976).

Stewart, David W.
   "OBVERS: A Computer Program for Obverse Factor Analysis With Rotation"
   Journal of Marketing Research, Vol. XVIII (November 1981), pp. 481,2.

Van Thillo, M. and Joreskog, K. G.
   "A General Computer Program for Simultaneous Factor Analysis in
   Several Populations"
   Research Bulletin, 70-62
   (Princeton, NJ: Educational Testing Service, 1970).

198 -------------- STATISTICAL TESTS IN FACTOR ANALYSIS --------------
        See also (sub)heading(s) 141, 197.

198.01 ---------- Theory Re: Statistical Tests in Factor Analysis

Acito, Franklin, Anderson, Ronald D., and Engledow, Jack L.
"A Simulation Study of Methods for Hypothesis Testing in Factor
Analysis"
Journal of Consumer Research, Vol. 7 (September 1980), pp. 141-50.

Ahmavaara, Yrjo
"Transformation Analysis of Factorial Data"
Annales-Academiae Scietiarum Fennicae, Vol. 88 (1954), pp. 1-150.

Bartlett, M. S.
"Tests of Significance in Factor Analysis"
British Journal of Psychology, Statistics Section, Vol. 3 (June
1950), pp. 77-85.

Bentler, Peter M. and Bonett, Douglas G.
"Significance Tests and Goodness of Fit in the Analysis of Covariance
Structures"
Psychological Bulletin, Vol. 88 (1980), pp. 588-606.

Bentler, P. M. and Bonett, D. G.
"Significance Tests and Goodness of Fit in Analysis of Covariance
Structures"
Annual Meeting, American Psychological Association (September 1980),
presentation.

Browne, Michael W.
"A Comparison of Factor Analytic Techniques"
Psychometrika, Vol. 33 (1968), pp. 267-335.

Browne, Michael W. and Kristof, Walter
"On the Oblique Rotation of a Factor Matrix to a Specified Pattern"
Psychometrika, Vol. 34 (1969), pp. 237-48.

Cliff, Norman
"Orthogonal Rotation to Congruence"
Psychometrika, Vol. 31 (1966), pp. 33-42.

Digman, John M.
"The Procrustes Class of Factor-Analytic Transformation"
Multivariate Behavioral Research, Vol. 2 (1967), pp. 89-94.

Evans, Glen T.
"Transformation of Factor Matrices to Achieve Congruence"
British Journal of Mathematical and Statistical Psychology, Vol. 24
(1971), pp. 22-48.

Geweke, John F. and Singleton, Kenneth J.
"Interpreting the Likelihood Ratio Statistic in Factor Models When
Sample Size is Small"
Journal of the American Statistical Association, Vol. 75 (March
1980), pp. 133-7.

Green, Bert F.
"The Orthogonal Approximation of an Oblique Structure in Factor
Analysis"
Psychometrika, Vol. 17 (1952), pp. 429-40.

Gruvaeus, Gunner T.
"A General Approach to Procrustes Pattern Rotation"
Psychometrika, Vol. 35 (1970), pp. 493-505.

Hakstian, A. Ralph
"A Computer Program for Generalized Oblique Procustes Factor
Transformation"
Educational and Psychological Measurement, Vol. 30 (1970), pp. 707-10.

Heeler, Roger M. and Ray, Michael L.
"Measure Validation in Marketing"
Journal of Marketing Research, Vol. IX (1972), pp. 361-70.

Hurley, John Raymond and Cattell, Raymond B.
"The Procrustes Program: Producing Direct Rotation to Test a
Hypothesized Factor Structure"
Behavioral Science, Vol. 7 (1962), pp. 258-62.

Joreskog, Karl G.
"Simultaneous Factor Analysis in Several Populations"
Psychometrika, Vol. 36 (1971), pp. 409-26.

Joreskog, Karl G.
"Testing a Simple Structure Hypothesis in Factor Analysis"
Psychometrika, Vol. 31 (June 1966), pp. 165-78.

Kalimo, Esko
     "Notes on Approximate Procrustes Rotation to Primary Pattern"
     Educational and Psychological Measurement, Vol. 31 (1971), pp. 364-9.

Long, J. Scott
     "Estimation and Hypothesis Testing in Linear Models Containing
     Measurement Error: A Review of Joreskog's Model for Analysis of
     Covariance Structures"
     Sociological Methods and Research, Vol. 5 (November 1976), pp.
     157-206.

Mosier, Charles I.
     "Determining Simple Structure When Loadings for Certain Tests are
     Known"
     Psychometrika, Vol. 4 (1939), pp. 149-62.

Rao, C. Radhakrishna
     "Estimation and Tests of Significance in Factor Analysis"
     Psychometrika, Vol. 20 (1955), pp. 93-111.

Schonemann, Peter H.
     "A Generalized Solution of the Orthogonal Procrustes Problem"
     Psychometrika, Vol. 31 (1966), pp. 1-10.

Steiger, James H., Shapiro, Alexander, and Browne, Michael W.
     "On the Multivariate Asymptotic Distribution of Sequential Chi-Square
     Statistics"
     Psychometrika, Vol. 50 (1985), pp. 253-64.

198.02 ---------- Applications of Hypothesis Testing in Factor Analysis

Ahmed, Sadrudin A. and Jackson, Douglas N.
     "Psychographics for Social Policy Decisions: Welfare Assistance"
     Journal of Consumer Research, Vol. 5 (March 1979), pp. 229-40.

Anderson, Ronald D., Engledow, Jack L., and Becker, Helmut
     "Comparisons of Advertising Attitudes Over Country, Age, and Time"
     Journal of International Business Studies, Vol. 9 (1979), pp. 27-38.

Boruch, Robert F. and Wolins, Leroy
     "A Procedure for Estimation of Trait, Method, and Error Variance
     Attributable to a Measure"
     Educational and Psychological Measurement, Vol. 30 (1970), pp. 547-74.

Heeler, Roger M., Whipple, Thomas W., and Hustad, Thomas P.
     "Maximum Likelihood Factor Analysis of Attitude Data"
     Journal of Marketing Research, Vol. XIV (1977), pp. 42-61.

Venkatesh, Alladi, Tankersley, Clint, and Chandran, Rajan
     "A Hypothesis Testing Procedure in Factor Analysis"
     in Jain, S. C. (editor)
     Research Frontiers in Marketing: Dialogues and Direction, 1978
     Educators' Proceedings
     (Chicago: American Marketing Association, 1978), pp. 87-92.

199 ------------------- FACTOR SCORE INDETERMINACY -------------------
    See also (sub)heading(s) 197.

199.01 ---------- Theory Re: Factor Score Indeterminacy

Guttman, L.
    "The Determinacy of Factor Score Matrices With Implications for Five
    Other Basic Problems of Common Factor Theory"
    British Journal of Statistical Psychology, Vol. 8 (November 1955),
    pp. 65-81.

Heerman, E. F.
    "The Algebra of Factorial Indeterminacy"
    Psychometrika, Vol. 31 (December 1965), pp. 539-43.

Heerman, E. F.
    "The Geometry of Factorial Indeterminacy"
    Psychometrika, Vol. 29 (December 1964), pp. 311-81.

Kestelman, H.
    "The Fundamental Equation of Factor Analysis"
    British Journal of Psychology, Statistical Section, Vol. 5 (March
    1951), pp. 1-6.

Ledermann, W.
    "The Orthogonal Transformation of a Factorial Matrix Into Itself"
    Psychometrika, Vol. 3 (September 1938), pp. 181-7.

Mulaik, S. A.
    "A Note on Sufficient Conditions That a Common Factor Will be
    Determinate in an Infinite Domain of Variables"
    Psychometrika, Vol. 46 (March 1981), pp. 105-7.

Mulaik, S. A.
    "The Effect of Additional Variables on Factor Indeterminacy in Models
    With a Single Common Factor"
    Psychometrika, Vol. 43 (June 1978), pp. 177-92.

Mulaik, S. A.
    "Comments on 'The Measurement of Factorial Indeterminacy'"
    Psychometrika, Vol. 41 (June 1976), pp. 249-62.

Mulaik, S. A. and McDonald, Roderick P.
    "Determinacy of Common Factors: A Nontechnical Review"
    Psychological Bulletin, Vol. 86 (March 1979), pp. 297-306.

Myer, E. P.
    "On the Relationship Between the Ratio of Number of Variables to
    Number of Factors and Factorial Indeterminacy"
    Psychometrika, Vol. 38 (September 1973), pp. 375-8.

Piaggio, N. T. H.
    "The General Factor in Spearman's Theory of Intelligence"
    Nature, Vol. 127 (January 10, 1931), pp. 56,7.

Rozeboom, W. W.
    "The Determinacy of Common Factors in Large Item Domains"
    Psychometrika, Vol. 47 (September 1982), pp. 281-95.

Schonemann, P. H.
    "Erratum"
    Psychometrika, Vol. 38 (March 1973), p. 149.

Schonemann, P. H.
    "The Minimum Average Correlation Between Equivalent Sets of
    Uncorrelated Factors"
    Psychometrika, Vol. 36 (March 1971), pp. 21-39.

Schonemann, P. H. and Wang, M. M.
    "Some New Results on Factor Indeterminacy"
    Psychometrika, Vol. 37 (March 1972), pp. 61-91.

Spearman, C.
    The Abilities of Man, Their Nature and Measurement
    (New York: Macmillan Publishing Co., Inc., 1927).

Steiger, J. H.
    "On the Empirical Equivalence of Regression Components and Common
    Factors"
    British Journal of Mathematical and Statistical Psychology, Vol. 33
    (November 1980), pp. 200-4.

Steiger, J. H.
    "Factor Indeterminacy in the 1930s and the 1970s: Some Interesting
    Parallels"
    Psychometrika, Vol. 44 (June 1979), pp. 157-67.

Steiger, J. H. and Schonemann, P. H.
    "History of Factor Indeterminacy"
    in Shye, S. (editor)
    Theory Construction and Data Analysis in the Behavioral Sciences
    (San Francisco: Jossey-Bass, 1978).

Thomson, G. H.
    "The Definition and Measurement of g (General Intelligence)"
    Journal of Educational Psychology, Vol. 26 (April 1935), pp. 241-62.

Williams, J. S.
    "A Definition for the Common Factor Analysis Model and the
    Elimination of Problems of Factor Score Indeterminacy"
    Psychometrika, Vol. 43 (September 1978), pp. 293-306.

Wilson, E. B.
    "A Review of 'The Abilities of Man, Their Nature and Measurement' by
    C. Spearman"
    Science, Vol. 67 (March 2, 1928), pp. 244-8.

199.02 ---------- Empirical Studies of Factor Score Indeterminacy

Acito, Franklin and Anderson, Ronald D.
    "A Simulation Study of Factor Score Indeterminacy"
    Journal of Marketing Research, Vol. XXIII (May 1986), pp. 111-8.

Acito, Franklin and Anderson, Ronald D.
    "A Monte Carlo Comparison of Factor Analytic Methods"
    Journal of Marketing Research, Vol. XVII (May 1980), pp. 228-36.

Horn, John L.
    "An Empirical Comparison of Methods for Estimating Factor Scores"
    Educational and Psychological Measurement, Vol. 25 (Summer 1965), pp.
    313-22.

Horn, John L. and Miller, C. W.
    "Evidence on Problems in Estimating Common Factor Scores"
    Educational and Psychological Measurement, Vol. 26 (Autumn 1966), pp.
    617-27.

McDonald, Roderick P.
    "The Indeterminacy of Components and the Definition of Common Factors"
    British Journal of Statistical Psychology, Vol. 30 (November 1977),
    pp. 165-76.

McDonald, Roderick P.
    "The Measurement of Factor Indeterminacy"
    Psychometrika, Vol. 39 (June 1974), pp. 203-22.

Velicer, W. F.
    "The Relationship Between Factor Score Estimates, Image Scores, and
    Principal Component Scores"
    Educational and Psychological Measurement, Vol. 36 (Spring 1976), pp.
    149-59.

Wackwitz, J. H. and Horn, John L.
    "On Obtaining the Best Estimate of Factor Scores Within an Ideal
    Simple Structure"
    Multivariate Behavioral Research, Vol. 6 (October 1971), pp. 389-408.

199.03 ---------- Unclassified (Factor Score Indeterminacy)

Fornell, Claes and Booknell, Fred L.
    "Two Structural Equation Models: LISREL and PLS Applied to Consumer
    Exit-Voice Theory"
    Journal of Marketing Research, Vol. XIX (November 1982), pp. 440-52.

Huber, Joel and Holbrook, Morris B.
    "Using Attribute Ratings for Product Positioning: Some Distinctions
    Among Compositional Approaches"
    Journal of Marketing Research, Vol. XVI (November 1979), pp. 507-16.

200 -------------- NUMBER OF FACTORS IN FACTOR ANALYSIS --------------
        See also (sub)heading(s) 197.

200.01 ---------- Theory Re: Number of Factors

Darden, William R. and Dorsch, Michael J.
  "Useful Component Analysis: Graphical Views of Marketing Data"
  Journal of the Academy of Marketing Science, Vol. 16 (Spring 1988),
  pp. 60-73.

Dingman, H. F., Miller, C. R., and Eyman, R. K.
  "A Comparison Between Two Analytic Rotational Solutions Where the
  Number of Factors is Indeterminate"
  Behavioral Science, Vol. 9 (January 1964), pp. 76-85.

Hakstian, A. R. and Muller, V. J.
  "Some Notes on the Number of Factors Problem"
  Multivariate Behavioral Research, Vol. 8 (October 1973), pp. 461-75.

Horn, J. L.
  "A Rationale and Test for the Number of Factors in Factor Analysis"
  Psychometrika, Vol. 30 (June 1965), pp. 179-85.

Howard, K. I. and Gordon, R. A.
  "Empirical Note on the 'Number of Factors' Problem in Factor Analysis"
  Psychological Reports, Vol. 12 (Spring 1963), pp. 247-50.

Kaiser, H. F.
  "An Index of Factor Simplicity"
  Psychometrika, Vol. 39 (1974), pp. 31-6.

Kaiser, Henry F.
  "A Note on Guttman's Lower Bounds for the Number of Common Factors"
  British Journal of Psychology, Vol. 14 (1961), pp. 1,2.

Linn, R. L.
  "A Monte Carlo Approach to the Number of Factors Problem"
  Psychometrika, Vol. 33 (March 1968), pp. 37-71.

Montanelli, R. G. and Humphreys, L. G.
  "Latent Roots of Random Data Correlation Matrices With Squared
  Multiple Correlation on the Diagonal: A Monte Carlo Study"
  Psychometrika, Vol. 41, No. 3 (1976), pp. 341-8.

Zwick, W. R. and Velicer, W. F.
  "Factors Influencing Four Rules for Determining the Number of
  Components to Retain"
  Multivariate Behavioral Research, Vol. 17 (1982), pp. 253-69.

200.02 ---------- Theory Re: Cattell's Scree Test

Cattell, R. B.
  "The Scree Test for Number of Factors"
  Multivariate Behavioral Research, Vol. 1 (April 1966), pp. 245-76.

Cattell, R. B. and Dickman, K.
  "A Dynamic Model of Physical Influences Demonstrating the Necessity
  of Oblique Simple Structure"
  Psychological Bulletin, Vol. 59 (June 1962), pp. 389-400.

Cattell, R. B. and Gorsuch, R. L.
  "The Uniqueness of Simple Structure Demonstrated by Contrasting
  'Natural Structure' and 'Random Structure' Data"
  Psychometrika, Vol. 28 (March 1963), pp. 55-67.

Cattell, R. B. and Jaspers, J.
  "A General Plasmode (No. 30-10-5-2) for Factor Analytic Exercises and
  Research"
  Multivariate Behavioral Research Monographs, Vol. 67 (1967), pp.
  1-212.

Cattell, R. B. and Sullivan, W.
  "The Scientific Nature of Factors: A Demonstration by Cups of Coffee"
  Behavioral Science, Vol. 7 (May 1962), pp. 184-93.

Cattell, R. B. and Vogelmann, S.
  "A Comprehensive Trial of the Scree and Kg Criteria for Determining
  the Number of Factors"
  Multivariate Behavioral Research, Vol. 12 (July 1977), pp. 289-325.

Tucker, L. R., Koopman, R. F., and Linn, R. L.
  "Evaluation of Factor-Analytic Research Procedures by Means of
  Simulated Correlation Matrices"
  Psychometrika, Vol. 34 (December 1969), pp. 421-59.

Woods, G. A.
  "A Computer Program for the Scree Test for Number of Factors"
  University of Hawaii (1976), manuscript.

200.03 ---------- Theory Re: Bartlett's Test

Bartlett, M. S.
  "A Further Note on Tests of Significance in Factor Analysis"
  British Journal of Statistical Psychology, Vol. 4 (January 1951), pp.
  1,2.

Bartlett, M. S.
  "Tests of Significance in Factor Analysis"
  British Journal of Statistical Psychology, Vol. 3 (January 1950), pp.
  77-85.

Gorsuch, R. L.
  "Using Bartlett's Significance Test to Determine the Number of
  Factors to Extract"
  Educational and Psychological Measurement, Vol. 33 (Summer 1973), pp.
  361-4.

Knapp, T. R. and Swoyer, V. H.
  "Some Empirical Results Concerning the Power of Bartlett's Test of
  Significance of a Correlation Matrix"
  American Educational Research Journal, Vol. 4 (Winter 1967), pp. 13-7.

200.04 ---------- Theory Re: Roots Criterion

Horn, J. L.
  "Second-Order Factors in Questionnaire Data"
  Educational and Psychological Measurement, Vol. 23 (Spring 1963), pp.
  117-34.

201 ---------- ROTATION AND COMPARISON OF FACTOR STRUCTURES ----------
    See also (sub)heading(s) 197.

201.01 ---------- General: Rotation and Comparison of Factor Structures

Dielman, T. E., Cattell, R. B., and Wagner, A.
"Evidence on the Simple Structure and Factor Invariance Achieved by
Five Rotational Methods on Four Types of Data"
Multivariate Behavioral Research, Vol. 7 (April 1972), pp. 223-31.

Dingman, H. F., Miller, C. R., and Eyman, R. K.
"A Comparison Between Two Analytic Rotational Solutions Where the
Number of Factors is Indeterminate"
Behavioral Science, Vol. 9 (January 1964), pp. 76-85.

Gorsuch, R. L.
"A Comparison of Biquartimin, Maxplane, Promax, and Varimax"
Educational and Psychological Measurement, Vol. 30 (Winter 1970), pp.
861-72.

Henderickson, A. E. and P. O. White Company
"PROMAX: A Quick Method for Rotation to Oblique Simple Structure"
British Journal of Statistical Psychology, Vol. 17, No. 1 (1964-65),
pp. 65-70.

Humphreys, Lloyd G., Ilgen, Daniel, McGrath, Diane, and Montanelli,
Richard
"Capitalization on Chance in Rotation of Factors"
Educational and Psychological Measurement, Vol. 29 (1969), pp. 259-71.

Keil, D. and Wrigley, C.
"Effects Upon Factorial Solution of Rotating Varying Numbers of
Factors"
American Psychologist, Vol. 15 (March 1960), pp. 383-9.

Levine, Mark S.
Canonical Analysis and Factor Comparison
(Beverly Hills, CA: Sage Publications, Inc.).

Meredith, W.
"Rotation to Achieve Factorial Invariance"
Psychometrika, Vol. 29 (1964), pp. 187-206.

Meredith, W.
"Notes on Factorial Invariance"
Psychometrika, Vol. 28 (1964), pp. 177-85.

Pinneau, Samuel R. and Newhouse, Albert
"Measurement of Invariance and Comparability in Factor Analysis for
Fixed Variables"
Psychometrika, Vol. 29 (September 1964), pp. 271-80.

Thompson, J. W.
"Meaningful and Unmeaningful Rotation of Factors"
Psychological Bulletin, Vol. 59 (May 1962). pp. 211-33.

Tucker, L. R.
"A Method for Synthesis of Factor Analytic Studies"
Personnel Research Section Report No. 984
(Washington, DC: Department of Army, 1951).

Wrigley, C. and Neuhaus, J.
"The Matching of Two Sets of Factors"
American Psychologist, Vol. 10 (1955), pp. 418,9.

201.02 ---------- Theory Re: Varimax Rotation Criterion

Kaiser, H. F.
"The Varimax Criterion for Analytic Rotation in Factor Analysis"
Psychometrika, Vol. 23 (September 1958), pp. 187-200.

201.03 ---------- Theory Re: Comparisons of Factor Structures

Ahmavaara, Yrjo
"Transformation Analysis of Factorial Data"
Annales Academiae Scientiarum Fennicae, Vol. 88 (1954), pp. 1-150.

Ahmavaara, Yrjo
"The Mathematical Theory of Factorial Invariance Under Selection"
Psychometrika, Vol. 19 (March 1954), pp. 27-38.

Barlow, J. A. and Burt, C.
"The Identification of Factors From Different Experiments"
British Journal of Statistical Psychology, Vol. 7 (1954), pp. 52-6.

Cattell, R. B. and Baggoley, A. R.
"The Salient Variable Similarity Index for Factor Matching"
British Journal of Statistical Psychology, Vol. 13 (May 1960), pp.
33-46.

Cavusgil, S. Tamer
"Factor Congruency Analysis: A Methodology for Cross-Cultural
Research"
Journal of the Market Research Society, Vol. 27 (April 1985), pp.
147-55.

Cliff, Norman
"Orthogonal Rotation to Congruence"
Psychometrika, Vol. 31 (March 1966), pp. 33-42.

Digman, J. M.
"The Procrustes Class of Factor-Analytic Transformation"
Multivariate Behavioral Research, Vol. 2, No. 1 (1967).

Kaiser, H. F.
"Relating Factors Between Studies Based Upon Different Individuals"
University of Illinois (1960), unpublished paper.

Korth, Bruce and Tucker, L. R.
"The Distribution of Chance Congruence Coefficients From Simulated
Data"
Psychometrika, Vol. 40 (September 1975), pp. 361-72.

Levine, M. S.
Canonical Analysis and Factor Comparison
Sage University Papers on Quantitative Applications in the Social
Sciences, 07-006
(Beverly Hills, CA and London: Sage Publications, 1977).

Schonemann, P. H.
"A Generalized Solution of the Orthogonal Procrustes Problem"
Psychometrika, Vol. 31 (March 1966), pp. 1-10.

Schonemann, P. H. and Carroll, R. M.
"Fitting One Matrix to Another Under Choice of a Central Dilation and
a Rigid Motion"
Psychometrika, Vol. 35 (June 1970), pp. 245-55.

Sorbom, Dag
"A General Method for Studying Differences in Factor Means and Factor
Structure Between Groups"
British Journal of Mathematical and Statistical Psychology, Vol. 27
(November 1974), pp. 229-39.

Tucker, L. R.
"A Method for Synthesis of Factor Analytic Studies"
Personnel Research Section Report No. 984
(Washington, DC: Department of the Army, 1951).

201.04 ---------- Applications of Comparisons of Factor Structures

Anderson, Ronald and Engledow, Jack
"A Factor Analytic Comparison of U.S. and German Information Seekers"
Journal of Consumer Research, Vol. 3 (March 1977), pp. 185-96.

Green, Paul E., Wind, Yoram, and Jain, Arun K.
"Preference Measurement of Item Collections"
Journal of Marketing Research, Vol. IX (November 1972), pp. 371-7.

Lazier, G. A., Clevenger, Theodore, Jr., and Clark, M. L.
"Stability of Factor Structure of Smith's Semantic Differential for
Theatre Concepts"
Department of Speech and Theatre Arts, University of Pittsburgh
(1964), unpublished paper.

Maddox, R. Neil
"The Structure of Consumers' Satisfaction: Cross-Product Comparisons"
Journal of the Academy of Marketing Science, Vol. 10 (Winter 1982),
pp. 37-53.

Sharpe, Louis K. and Anderson, W. Thomas, Jr.
"Concept-Scale Interaction in the Semantic Differential"
Journal of Marketing Research, Vol. IX (November 1972), pp. 432-4.

Smith, Ruth A.
"Industrial Salesforce Job Satisfaction" (abstract)
Journal of Marketing Research, Vol. XIX (February 1982), pp. 152,3.

Willson, E. J.
"Computational Segmentation in the Context of Multivariate Statistics
and Survey Analysis"
Journal of the Market Research Society, Vol. 16, No. 2 (1974), pp.
108-26.

Zinkhan, George M. and Wallendorf, Melanie
    "Service Set Similarities in Patterns of Consumer
    Satisfaction/Dissatisfaction"
    International Journal of Research in Marketing, Vol. 2, No. 3 (1985),
    pp. 227-35.

201.05 ---------- Computer Programs for Rotation and Comparison

Arora, Raj
    "ROTATE: A Program for Achieving Congruency by Rotating Factor
    Pattern Matrices of Two or More Populations"
    Journal of Marketing Research, Vol. XVIII (November 1981), pp. 484,5.

Arora, Raj and Vaughn, Ronald
    "FACSIM: A Program to Compute the Similarity Indices for Groups of
    Factor Solutions"
    Journal of Marketing Research, Vol. XVIII (November 1981), pp. 485,6.

202 ------ FACTOR OR PRINCIPAL COMPONENTS ANALYSIS APPLICATIONS ------
        See also (sub)heading(s) 197.

Aaker, David A. and Bruzzone, Donald E.
    "Viewer Perceptions of Prime-Time Television Advertising"
    Journal of Advertising Research, Vol. 21 (October 1981), pp. 15-23.

Aaker, David A. and Norris, Donald
    "Characteristics of TV Commercials Perceived as Informative"
    Journal of Advertising Research, Vol. 22 (April-May 1982), pp. 61-70.

Abougomaah, Naeim H., Schlacter, John L., and Gaidis, William
    "Elimination and Choice Phases in Evoked Set Formation"
    Journal of Consumer Marketing, Vol. 4 (Fall 1987), pp. 67-73.

Albaum, Gerald, Hawkins, Del I., and Dickson, John P.
    "Differences in Retail Store Images Within Husband-Wife Dyads"
    Journal of the Academy of Marketing Science, Vol. 7 (Summer 1979),
    pp. 144-53.

Allen, Chris T.
    "Self-Perception Based Strategies for Stimulating Energy Conservation"
    Journal of Consumer Research, Vol. 8 (March 1982), pp. 381-90.

Allison, Neil K.
    "A Psychometric Development of a Test for Consumer Alienation From
    the Marketplace"
    Journal of Marketing Research, Vol. XV (November 1978), pp. 565-75.

Anderson, Claus and Nielsen, Simon Ortmann
    "Heavy-Medium-Light Users: Sufficient for Segmentation?"
    European Research, Vol. 9 (July 1981), pp. 91-100.

Anderson, Erin, Chu, Wujin, and Weitz, Barton
    "Industrial Purchasing: An Empirical Exploration of the Buyclass
    Framework"
    Journal of Marketing, Vol. 51 (July 1987), pp. 71-86.

Anderson, Erin, Lodish, Leonard M., and Weitz, Barton A.
    "Resource Allocation Behavior in Conventional Channels"
    Journal of Marketing Research, Vol. XXIV (February 1987), pp. 85-97.

Anderson, Ronald and Engledow, Jack
    "A Factor Analytic Comparison of U.S. and German Information Seekers"
    Journal of Consumer Research, Vol. 3 (March 1977), pp. 185-96.

Anderson, R. D., Engledow, J. L., and Becker, H.
    "Evaluating the Relationships Among Attitude Toward Business, Product
    Satisfaction, Experience, and Search Effort"
    Journal of Marketing Research, Vol. XVI (August 1979), pp. 394-400.

Anderson, Ronald D., Engledow, Jack L., and Becker, Helmut
    "How Consumer Reports Subscribers See Advertising"
    Journal of Advertising Research, Vol. 18 (December 1978), pp. 29-34.

Anderson, W. Thomas and Alpert, Mark I.
    "Subject-Anticipated Versus Experimentally-Derived Measures of
    Influence: Advertising Implications"
    Journal of the Academy of Marketing Science, Vol. 3 (Spring 1975),
    pp. 119-28.

Assmus, Gert and Neslin, Scott A.
    "Optimistic and Pessimistic Estimates of Product Performance"
    Journal of Advertising Research, Vol. 23 (June/July 1983), pp. 53-8.

Avlonitis, George J.
    "The Identification of Weak Industrial Products"
    European Journal of Marketing, Vol. 20, No. 10 (1986), pp. 24-42.

Bagozzi, Richard P.
    "Convergent and Discriminant Validity by Analysis of Covariance
    Structures: The Case of the Affective, Behavioral and Cognitive
    Components of Attitude"
    in Perreault, W. D., Jr. (editor)
    Advances in Consumer Research, Volume Four
    (Association for Consumer Research, 1977).

Bagozzi, Richard P.
    "Structural Equation Models in Experimental Research"
    Journal of Marketing Research, Vol. XIV (May 1977), pp. 209-26.

Banks, Seymour
    "Cross-National Analysis of Advertising Expenditures: 1968-1979"
    Journal of Advertising Research, Vol. 26 (April/May 1986), pp. 11-24.

Batsell, Richard R.
    "Consumer Resource Allocation Models at the Individual Level"
    Journal of Consumer Research, Vol. 7 (June 1980), pp. 78-87.

Bearden, William O., Durand, Richard M., Mason, J. Barry, and Teel, Jesse E., Jr.
"Dimensions of Consumer Satisfaction/Dissatisfaction With Services: The Case of Electric Utilities"
Journal of the Academy of Marketing Science, Vol. 6 (Fall 1978), pp. 278-90.

Beatty, Sharon E. and Smith, Scott M.
"External Search Effort: An Investigation Across Several Product Categories"
Journal of Consumer Research, Vol. 14 (June 1987), pp. 83-95.

Becherer, Richard C., Richard, Lawrence M., and Wiley, James B.
"Predicting Market Behavior: Are Psychographics Really Better?"
Journal of the Academy of Marketing Science, Vol. 5 (Winter-Spring 1977), pp. 75-84.

Bhagat, Rabi S., Raju, P., and Sheth, Jagdish N.
"Attitudinal Theories of Consumer Choice Behaviour: A Comparative Analysis"
European Research, Vol. 7 (March 1979), pp. 51-62.

Binkert, Christopher C., Brunner, James A., and Simonetti, Jack L.
"The Use of Life Style Segmentation to Determine if CATV Subscribers are Really Different"
Journal of the Academy of Marketing Science, Vol. 3 (Spring 1975), pp. 129-36.

Bonfield, E. H. and Robbins, John E.
"A Method for Selecting High Payoff Marketing Strategies for Attracting Noncustomer Product Purchasers"
Journal of the Academy of Marketing Science, Vol. 5 (Winter-Spring 1977), pp. 85-93.

Brown, James R. and Day, Ralph L.
"Measures of Manifest Conflict in Distribution Channels"
Journal of Marketing Research, Vol. XVIII (August 1981), pp. 263-74.

Brown, Stephen W. and Swartz, Teresa A.
"A Gap Analysis of Professional Service Quality"
Journal of Marketing, Vol. 53 (April 1989), pp. 92-8.

Bushman, Anthony F.
"What are the Qualities of a Good Marketing Article?"
Journal of the Academy of Marketing Science, Vol. 6 (Summer 1978), pp. 151-6.

Butaney, Gul and Wortzel, Lawrence H.
"Distributor Power Versus Manufacturer Power: The Customer Role"
Journal of Marketing, Vol. 52 (January 1988), pp. 52-63.

Cagley, James W.
"A Comparison of Advertising Agency Selection Factors: Advertiser and Agency Perceptions"
Journal of Advertising Research, Vol. 26 (June/July 1986), pp. 39-44.

Calantone, Roger J. and Cooper, Robert G.
"A Discriminant Model for Identifying Scenarios of Industrial New Product Failure"
Journal of the Academy of Marketing Science, Vol. 7 (Summer 1979), pp. 163-83.

Calantone, Roger J. and Sawyer, Alan G.
"The Stability of Benefit Segments"
Journal of Marketing Research, Vol. XV (August 1978), pp. 395-403.

Calder, Bobby J. and Burnkrant, Robert E.
"Interpersonal Influence on Consumer Behavior: An Attribution Theory Approach"
Journal of Consumer Research, Vol. 4 (June 1977), pp. 29-38.

Calder, Bobby J. and Sternthal, B.
"Television Commercial Wearout: An Information Processing View"
Journal of Marketing Research, Vol. XVII (May 1980), pp. 173-86.

Capon, Noel and Farley, John U.
"The Impact of Message on Direct Mail Response"
Journal of Advertising Research, Vol. 16 (October 1976), pp. 69-75.

Cooper, Robert G.
"The Performance Impact of Product Innovation Strategies"
European Journal of Marketing, Vol. 18, No. 5 (1984), pp. 5-54.

Cort, Stanton G. and Dominguez, Luis V.
"Cross Shopping and Retail Growth"
Journal of Marketing Research, Vol. XIV (May 1977), pp. 187-92.

Cron, William L., Dubinsky, Alan J., and Michaels, Ronald E.
"The Influence of Career States on Components of Salesperson Motivation"
Journal of Marketing, Vol. 52 (January 1988), pp. 78-92.

Crosby, Lawrence A. and Taylor, James R.
"Consumer Satisfaction With Michigan's Container Deposit Law--An Ecological Perspective"
Journal of Marketing, Vol. 46 (Winter 1982), pp. 47-60.

Darden, William R. and Rao, C. P.
"A Linear Covariate Model of Warranty Attitudes and Behaviors"
Journal of Marketing Research, Vol. XVI (November 1979), pp. 466-77.

Didow, Nicholas M., Jr., Keller, Kevin Lane, Barksdale, Hiram C., Jr., and Franke, George R.
"Improving Measure Quality by Alternating Least Squares Optimal Scaling"
Journal of Marketing Research, Vol. XXII (February 1985), pp. 30-40.

Douglas, Susan P. and Urban, Christine D.
"Life-Style Analysis to Profile Women in International Markets"
Journal of Marketing, Vol. 41 (July 1977), pp. 46-54.

Eliashberg, Jehoshua and Michie, Donald A.
"Multiple Business Goals Sets as Determinants of Marketing Channel Conflict: An Empirical Study"
Journal of Marketing Research, Vol. XXI (February 1984), pp. 75-88.

Etgar, Michael
"Channel Environment and Channel Leadership"
Journal of Marketing Research, Vol. XIV (February 1977), pp. 69-76.

Ezell, Hazel F. and Motes, William H.
"Differentiating Between the Sexes: A Focus on Male-Female Grocery Shopping Attitudes and Behavior"
Journal of Consumer Marketing, Vol. 2 (Spring 1985), pp. 29-40.

Ford, Gary T.
"Adoption of Consumer Policies by States: Some Empirical Perspectives"
Journal of Marketing Research, Vol. XV (February 1978), pp. 49-57.

Frank, Ronald E. and Greenberg, Marshall G.
"Interest-Based Segments of TV Audiences"
Journal of Advertising Research, Vol. 19 (October 1979), pp. 43-52.

French, Warren A. and Fox, Richard
"Segmenting the Senior Citizen Market"
Journal of Consumer Marketing, Vol. 2 (Winter 1985), pp. 61-74.

Frisbie, Gil A., Jr.
"Demarketing Energy: Does Psychographic Research Hold the Answer?"
Journal of the Academy of Marketing Science, Vol. 8 (Summer 1980), pp. 196-211.

Fritzsche, David J. and Ferrell, O. C.
"A Delineation of Functional Areas of Competency Considered Important to Consumer Affairs Professionals"
Journal of the Academy of Marketing Science, Vol. 10 (Summer 1982), pp. 235-48.

Futrell, Charles M.
"Sales Force Job Attitudes, Design, and Behavior"
Journal of the Academy of Marketing Science, Vol. 7 (Winter-Spring 1979), pp. 101-7.

Gautschi, David A.
"Specification of Patronage Models for Retail Center Choice"
Journal of Marketing Research, Vol. XVIII (May 1981), pp. 162-74.

Gensch, Dennis H. and Golob, Thomas F.
"Testing the Consistency of Attribute Meaning in Empirical Concept Testing"
Journal of Marketing Research, Vol. XII (August 1975), pp. 348-54.

Goldman, Arieh and Johansson, J. K.
"Determinants of Search for Lower Prices: An Empirical Assessment of the Economics of Information Theory"
Journal of Consumer Research, Vol. 5 (December 1978), pp. 176-86.

Gould, Stephen J. and Stern, Barbara B.
"Gender Schema and Fashion Consciousness"
Psychology and Marketing, Vol. 6 (Summer 1989), pp. 129-45.

Hart, Susan J. and Service, Linda M.
"The Effects of Managerial Attitudes to Design on Company Performance"
Journal of Marketing Management, Vol. 4 (Winter 1988), pp. 217-29.

Hirschman, Elizabeth C.
"Communal and Associational Social Structures: Their Underlying Behavioral Components and Implications for Marketing"
Journal of the Academy of Marketing Science, Vol 7 (Summer 1979), pp. 192-213.

Holbrook, Morris B.
"Integrating Compositional and Decompositional Analyses to Represent the Intervening Role of Perceptions in Evaluative Judgments"
Journal of Marketing Research, Vol. XVIII (February 1981), pp. 13-28.

Holbrook, Morris B.
"Beyond Attitude Structure: Toward the Informational Determinants of Attitude"
Journal of Marketing Research, Vol. XV (November 1978), pp. 545-56.

Holbrook, Morris B. and Huber, Joel
"Separating Perceptual Dimensions From Affective Overtones: An Application to Consumer Aesthetics"
Journal of Consumer Research, Vol. 5 (March 1979), pp. 272-83.

Holbrook, Morris B. and Lehmann, Donald R.
"Form Versus Content in Predicting Starch Scores"
Journal of Advertising Research, Vol. 20 (August 1980), pp. 53-62.

Homans, Richard and Houston, Franklin S.
"Marketing Research for Public Health: A Demonstration of Differential Responses to Advertising"
Journal of the Academy of Marketing Science, Vol. 9 (Fall 1981), pp. 380-98.

Hornik, Jacob
"Quantitative Analysis of Visual Perception of Printed Advertisements"
Journal of Advertising Research, Vol. 20 (December 1980), pp. 41-8.

Hornik, Jacob and Schlinger, Mary Jane
"Allocation of Time to the Mass Media"
Journal of Consumer Research, Vol. 7 (March 1981), pp. 343-55.

Horton, Raymond L.
"Some Relationships Between Personality and Consumer Decision Making"
Journal of Marketing Research, Vol. XVI (May 1979), pp. 233-46.

Horton, Raymond L.
"The Structure of Perceived Risk: Some Further Progress"
Journal of the Academy of Marketing Science, Vol. 4 (Fall 1976), pp. 694-706.

Huber, Joel and Holbrook, Morris B.
"Using Attribute Ratings for Product Positioning: Some Distinctions Among Compositional Approaches"
Journal of Marketing Research, Vol. XVI (November 1979), pp, 507-16.

Hunt, Shelby D. and Burnett, John J.
"The Macromarketing/Micromarketing Dichotomy: A Taxonomical Model"
Journal of Marketing, Vol. 46 (Summer 1982), pp. 11-26.

Ingene, Charles A. and Brown, James R.
"The Structure of Gasoline Retailing"
Journal of Retailing, Vol. 63 (Winter 1987), pp. 365-392.

Jarboe, Glen R. and McDaniel, Carl D.
"A Profile of Browsers in Regional Shopping Malls"
Journal of the Academy of Marketing Science, Vol. 15 (Spring 1987), pp. 46-53.

Jones, Vernon J. and Siller, Fred H.
"Factor Analysis of Media Exposure Data Using Prior Knowledge of the Medium"
Journal of Marketing Research, Vol. XV (February 1978), pp. 137-44.

Kenney, David
"An Empirical Application of Confirmatory Factor Analysis to the Multitrait-Multimethod Matrix"
Journal of Experimental Psychology, Vol. 12 (1976), pp. 247-52.

Kiel, Geoffrey C. and Layton, Roger A.
"Dimensions of Consumer Information Seeking Behavior"
Journal of Marketing Research, Vol. XVIII (May 1981), pp. 233-9.

Kono, Ken
"Are Generics Buyers Deal-Prone? On a Relationship Between Generics Purchase and Deal-Proneness"
Journal of the Academy of Marketing Science, Vol. 13 (Winter 1985), pp. 62-74.

Lamont, Lawrence and Lundstrom, William J.
"Defining Industrial Sales Behavior: A Factor Analytic Study"
in Curham, Ronald C. (editor)
Proceedings
(Chicago: American Marketing Association, 1974), pp. 493-8.

Larreche, Jean-Claude and Montgomery, David B.
"A Framework for the Comparison of Marketing Models: A Delphi Study"
Journal of Marketing Research, Vol. XIV (November 1977), pp. 487-98.

Leigh, James H.
"An Examination of the Dimensionality of Satisfaction With Housing"
Psychology and Marketing, Vol. 4 (Winter 1987), pp. 339-54.

Locander, William B. and Spivey, W. Austin
"A Functional Approach to Attitude Measurement"
Journal of Marketing Research, Vol. XV (November 1978), pp. 576-87.

Lumpkin, James R. and Festervand, Troy A.
"Purchase Information Sources of the Elderly"
Journal of Advertising Research, Vol. 27 (December 1987/January
1988), pp. 31-43.

Lusch, Robert F.
"An Empirical Examination of the Dimensionality of Power in a Channel
of Distribution"
Journal of the Academy of Marketing Science, Vol. 5 (Fall 1977), pp.
361-8.

Lusch, Robert F.
"Sources of Power: Their Impact on Intrachannel Conflict"
Journal of Marketing Research, Vol. XIII (November 1976), pp. 382-90.

Lusch, Robert F. and Brown, James R.
"A Modified Model of Power in the Marketing Channel"
Journal of Marketing Research, Vol. XIX (August 1984), pp. 312-23.

Marton, Katherin and Boddewyn, J. J.
"Should a Corporation Keep a Low Profile?"
Journal of Advertising Research, Vol. 18 (August 1978), pp. 25-31.

McEwen, William J. and Leavitt, Clark
"A Way to Describe TV Commercials"
Journal of Advertising Research, Vol. 16 (December 1976), pp. 35-9.

Michell, Paul C. N.
"Auditing of Agency-Client Relations"
Journal of Advertising Research, Vol. 26 (December 1986/January
1987), pp. 29-41.

Michie, Donald A. and Sibley, Stanley D.
"Channel Member Satisfaction: Controversy Resolved"
Journal of the Academy of Marketing Science, Vol. 13 (Spring 1985),
pp. 188-205.

Moncrief, William C., III
"Selling Activity and Sales Position Taxonomies for Industrial
Salesforces"
Journal of Marketing Research, Vol. XXIII (August 1986), pp. 261-70.

Paksoy, Christie H.
"Life-Style Analysis of Major Bank Credit Card Users"
Journal of the Academy of Marketing Science, Vol. 7 (Winter-Spring
1979), pp. 40-7.

Paoli, Jean-Mathieu
"Designing Social Organisations for People Such as They Are"
European Research, Vol. 7 (July 1979), pp. 175-82.

Parsons, Charles K. and Hulin, Charles L.
"An Empirical Comparison of Item Response Theory and Hierarchical
Factor Analysis in Application to the Measurement of Job Satisfaction"
Journal of Applied Psychology, Vol. 67 (December 1982), pp. 826-34.

Partanen, Juha
"On National Consumption Profiles"
European Research, Vol. 7 (January 1979), pp. 27-39.

Pessemier, Edgar A., Bemmaor, Albert C., and Hanssens, Dominique M.
"Willingness to Supply Human Body Parts: Some Empirical Results"
Journal of Consumer Research, Vol. 4 (December 1977), pp. 131-40.

Piercy, Nigel
"The Role and Function of the Chief Marketing Executive and the
Marketing Department"
Journal of Marketing Management, Vol. 1 (Spring 1986), pp. 265-89.

Rao, Vithala R.
"Taxonomy of Television Programs Based on Viewing Behavior"
Journal of Marketing Research, Vol. XII (August 1975), pp. 355-8.

Reidenbach, R. Eric, Cooper, M. Bixby, and Harrison, Mary Carolyn
"A Factor Analytic Comparison of Outshopping Behavior in Larger
Retail Trade Areas"
Journal of the Academy of Marketing Science, Vol. 12 (Spring 1984),
pp. 145-58.

Riley, Stuart and Palmer, John
"Of Attitudes and Latitudes: A Repertory Grid Study of Perceptions of
Seaside Resorts"
Journal of the Market Research Society, Vol. 17 (April 1975), pp.
74-89.

Robertson, Thomas S. and Wind, Yoram
"Organizational Psychographics and Innovativeness"
Journal of Consumer Research, Vol. 7 (June 1980), pp. 24-31.

Robin, Donald P. and Reidenbach, R. Eric
"Identifying Critical Problems for Mutual Cooperation Between the
Private and Public Sectors: A Marketing Perspective"
Journal of the Academy of Marketing Science, Vol. 14 (Fall 1986), pp.
1-12.

Schlinger, Mary Jane
"A Profile of Responses to Commercials"
Journal of Advertising Research, Vol. 19 (April 1979), pp. 37-46.

Schlinger, Mary Jane and Green, Leila
"Art-Work Storyboards Versus Finished Commercials"
Journal of Advertising Research, Vol. 20 (December 1980), pp. 19-23.

Sewall, Murphy A.
"Market Segmentation Based on Consumer Ratings of Proposed Product
Designs"
Journal of Marketing Research, Vol. XV (November 1978), pp. 547-64.

Sharits, Dean and Lammers, H. Bruce
"Perceived Attributes of Models in Prime-Time and Daytime Television
Commercials: A Person Perception Approach"
Journal of Marketing Research, Vol. XX (February 1983), pp. 64-73.

Schurr, Paul H. and Calder, Bobby J.
"Psychological Effects of Restaurant Meetings on Industrial Buyers"
Journal of Marketing, Vol. 50 (January 1986), pp. 87-97.

Spekman, Robert E. and Stern, Louis W.
"Environmental Uncertainty and Buying Group Structure: An Empirical
Investigation"
Journal of Marketing, Vol. 43 (Spring 1979), pp. 54-64.

Srinivasan, V., Abeele, P. Vanden, and Butaye, I.
"The Factor Structure of Multidimensional Response to Marketing
Stimuli: A Comparison of Two Approaches"
Marketing Science, Vol. 8 (Winter 1989), pp. 78-88.

Stewart, David and Hood, Neil
"East European Competition in the UK Car Market: Some Empirical
Results"
European Journal of Marketing, Vol. 15, No. 1 (1981), pp. 10-9.

Sullivan, Daniel and Bauerschmidt, Alan
"Common Factors Underlying Incentive to Export: Studies in the
European Forestry Products Industry"
European Journal of Marketing, Vol. 22, No. 10 (1988), pp. 41-55.

Teas, R. Kenneth
"An Empirical Test of Models of Salespersons' Job Expectancy and
Instrumentality Perceptions"
Journal of Marketing Research, Vo. XVIII (May 1981), pp. 209-26.

Teel, Jesse E., Jr., Bearden, William O., and Durand, Richard M.
"Psychographic Profiles of Media Usage Segments"
Journal of the Academy of Marketing Science, Vol. 5 (Fall 1977), pp.
379-88.

Tyagi, Pradeep K.
"Perceived Organizational Climate and the Process of Salesperson
Motivation"
Journal of Marketing Research, Vol. XIX (May 1982), pp. 240-54.

Tybout, Alice M. and Hauser, John R.
"A Marketing Audit Using a Conceptual Model of Consumer Behavior:
Application and Evaluation"
Journal of Marketing, Vol. 45 (Summer 1981), pp. 82-101.

Urban, Christine D.
"Correlates of Magazine Readership"
Journal of Advertising Research, Vol. 20 (August 1980), pp. 73-84.

Vaughn, Ronald L. and Hansotia, Behram J.
  "A Multi-Attribute Approach to Understanding Shopping Behavior"
  Journal of the Academy of Marketing Science, Vol. 5 (Summer 1977),
  pp. 281-94.

Venkatesh, Alladi
  "Changing Roles of Women--A Life-Style Analysis"
  Journal of Consumer Research, Vol. 7 (September 1980), pp. 189-97.

Venkatesh, Alladi and Tankersley, Clint B.
  "Magazine Readership by Female Segments"
  Journal of Advertising Research, Vol. 19 (August 1979), pp. 31-8.

Venkatesh, Alladi and Tankersley, Clint B.
  "Criteria for the Evaluation of Product Managers--An Application of
  Multiple Group Solution"
  Journal of the Academy of Marketing Science, Vol. 6 (Fall 1978), pp.
  344-54.

Verbeke, Willem
  "Developing an Advertising Agency-Client Relationship in the
  Netherlands"
  Journal of Advertising Research, Vol. 28 (December 1988/January
  1989), pp. 19-27.

Villani, Kathryn E. A.
  "Personality/Life Style and Television Viewing Behavior"
  Journal of Marketing Research, Vol. XII (November 1975), pp. 432.

Weitzel, William, Schwarzkopf, Albert B., and Peach, E. Brian
  "The Influence of Employee Perceptions of Customer Service on Retail
  Store Sales"
  Journal of Retailing, Vol. 65 (Spring 1989), pp. 27-39.

202.01 ---------- Applications of Maximum Likelihood Factor Analysis

Heeler, Roger M., Whipple, Thomas W., and Hustad, Thomas P.
  "Maximum Likelihood Factor Analysis of Attitude Data"
  Journal of Marketing Research, Vol. XIV (February 1977), pp. 42-51.

Mitchell, A. A. and Olson, J. C.
  "The Use of Restricted and Unrestricted Maximum Likelihood Factor
  Analysis to Examine Alternative Measures of Brand Loyalty"
  Working Paper No. 29
  Pennsylvania State University (1975).

203 ------------------ CONFIRMATORY FACTOR ANALYSIS ------------------
    See also (sub)heading(s) 197, 204.

203.01 ---------- Theory Re: Confirmatory Factor Analysis

Babakus, Emin, Ferguson, Carl E., Jr., and Joreskog, Karl G.
  "The Sensitivity of Confirmatory Maximum Likelihood Factor Analysis
  to Violations of Measurement Scale and Distributional Assumptions"
  Journal of Marketing Research, Vol. XXIV (May 1987), pp. 222-8.

Bentler, Peter M.
  "Theory and Implementation of EQS, A Structural Equation Program
  (Los Angeles, CA: BMDP Statistical Software, 1985).

Bentler, Peter M.
  "Some Contributions to Efficient Statistics in Structural Models:
  Specification and Estimation of Moment Structures"
  Psychometrika, Vol. 48 (December 1983), pp. 493-517.

Bentler, Peter M.
  "Confirmatory Factor Analysis via Noniterative Estimation: A Fast,
  Inexpensive Method"
  Journal of Marketing Research, Vol. XIX (November 1982), pp. 417-24.

Burt, Ronald S.
  "Confirmatory Factor-Analysis Structures and the Theory Construction
  Process"
  Sociological Methods and Research, Vol. 2 (1973), pp. 131-87.

Cole, David A. and Maxwell, Scott E.
  "Multitrait-Multimethod Comparisons Across Populations: A
  Confirmatory Factor Analytic Approach"
  Multivariate Behavioral Research, Vol. 20 (1985), pp. 389-417.

Gerbing, David W. and Anderson, James C.
  "On the Meaning of Within-Factor Correlated Measurement Errors"
  Journal of Consumer Research, Vol. 11 (June 1984), pp. 572-80.

Gerbing, David W. and Hunter, J. E.
  "The Return to Multiple Groups: Analysis and Critique of Confirmatory
  Factor Analysis With LISREL"
  Annual Meeting of the Southwestern Psychological Association,
  Oklahoma City (April 1980), paper presentation.

Holzinger, K. J.
  "A Simple Method of Factor Analysis"
  Psychometrika, Vol. 9, No. 4 (1944), pp. 257-62.

Joreskog, Karl G.
  "Structural Analysis of Covariance and Correlation Matrices"
  Psychometrika, Vol. 43 (December 1984), pp. 443-77.

Joreskog, Karl G.
  "A General Approach to Confirmatory Maximum Likelihood Factor
  Analysis With Addendum"
  in Magidson, Jay (editor)
  Advances in Factor Analysis and Structural Equation Models
  (Cambridge, MA: Abt Books, 1979), pp. 21-43.

Joreskog, Karl G.
  "Simultaneous Factor Analysis in Several Populations"
  Psychometrika, Vol. 36 (1971), pp. 409-26.

Joreskog, Karl G.
  "Statistical Analysis of Sets of Congeneric Tests"
  Psychometrika, Vol. 36 (1971), pp. 109-33.

Joreskog, Karl G.
  "A General Approach to Confirmatory Maximum Likelihood Factor
  Analysis"
  Psychometrika, Vol. 34 (June 1969), pp. 183-202.

Joreskog, Karl G.
  "Testing a Simple Structure Hypothesis in Factor Analysis"
  Psychometrika, Vol. 31 (1966), pp. 165-78.

Long, J. Scott
  Confirmatory Factor Analysis
  (Beverly Hills, CA: Sage Publications, Inc., 1983), 88 pp.

Smith, Kent W.
  "On Estimating the Reliability of Composite Indexes Through Factor
  Analysis"
  Sociological Methods and Research, Vol. 2 (May 1974), pp 485-510.

Sorbom, Dag
  "COFAMM: Confirmatory Factor Analysis With Model Modification--Users'
  Guide"
  (Chicago: International Educational Services, 1976).

203.02 ---------- Theory Re: Goodness-of-Fit in Conf Factor Analysis

Anderson, James C. and Gerbing, David
  "The Effect of Sampling Error on Convergence, Improper Solutions, and
  Goodness-of-Fit Indices for Maximum Likelihood Confirmatory Factor
  Analysis"
  Psychometrika, Vol. 49, No. 2 (June 1984), pp. 155-73.

Anderson, James C., Gerbing, David, and Narayanan, A.
  "A Comparison of Two Alternate Residual Goodness-of-Fit Indices"
  Journal of the Market Research Society, Vol. 27 (October 1985), pp.
  283-91.

Bearden, William O. and Teel, Jesse E., Jr.
  "Sample Size Effects on Chi-Square and Other Statistics Used in
  Evaluating Causal Models"
  Journal of Marketing Research, Vol. XIX (1982), pp. 425-30.

Bentler, Peter M.
  Theory and Implementation of EQS, a Structural Equations Program
  (Los Angeles, CA: BMDP Statistical Software, 1985).

Bone, Paula Fitzgerald, Sharma, Subhash, and Shimp, Terence A.
  "A Bootstrap Procedure for Evaluating Goodness-of-Fit Indices of
  Structural Equation and Confirmatory Factor Models"
  Journal of Marketing Research, Vol. XXVI (February 1989), pp. 105-11.

Boomsma, Anne
  "The Robustness of LISREL Against Small Sample Sizes in Factor
  Analysis Models"
  in Joreskog, K. G. and Wold, H. (editors)
  Systems Under Indirect Observation: Causality, Structure, Prediction
  (Part 1)
  (Amsterdam: North-Holland, 1982), 149-73.

Sharma, Subhash and Shimp, Terence A.
  "A Note on Evaluating the Goodness-of-Fit of Confirmatory Factor
  Analysis"
  in Belk, Russell W. et al. (editors)
  AMA Educators' Conference Proceedings, Series 51
  (Chicago: American Marketing Association, 1984), pp. 360-3.

Wheaton, Blair
  "Assessment of Fit in Overidentified Models With Latent Variables"
  Sociological Methods and Research, Vol. 16 (August 1987), pp. 118-54.

203.03 ---------- Applications of Confirmatory Factor Analysis

Eliashberg, Jehoshua and Robertson, Thomas S.
  "New Product Preannouncing Behavior: A Market Signaling Study"
  Journal of Marketing Research, Vol. XXV (August 1988), pp. 282-92.

Hunt, Shelby D., Chonko, Lawrence B., and Wood, Van R.
  "Organizational Commitment and Marketing"
  Journal of Marketing, Vol. 49 (Winter 1985), pp. 112-26.

Kenny, D. A.
  "An Empirical Application of Confirmatory Factor Analysis to the
  Multitrait-Multimethod Matrix"
  Journal of Experimental Social Psychology, Vol. 12 (May 1976), pp.
  247-52.

Oliver, Richard L. and Bearden, William O.
  "Crossover Effects in the Theory of Reasoned Action: A Moderating
  Influence Attempt"
  Journal of Consumer Research, Vol. 12 (December 1985), pp. 324-40.

Oliver, Richard L. and Swan, John E.
  "Equity and Disconfirmation Perceptions as Influences on Merchant and
  Product Satisfaction"
  Journal of Consumer Research, Vol. 16 (December 1989), pp. 372-83.

Rao, Srikumar and Farley, John U.
  "Effects of Environmental Perceptions and Cognitive Complexity on
  Search and Information Processing"
  Psychology and Marketing, Vol. 4 (Winter 1987), pp. 287-302.

Venkatraman, Meera P.
  "Involvement and Risk"
  Psychology and Marketing, Vol. 6 (Fall 1989), pp. 229-47.

204 --------- CAUSAL ANALYSIS AND STRUCTURAL EQUATION MODELS ---------
       See also (sub)heading(s) 169, 203, 205, 206, 207.

204.01 ---------- Books Re: Causal Analysis

Asher, Herbert B.
  Causal Modeling, Second Edition
  (Beverly Hills, CA: Sage Publications, Inc., 1976).

Bagozzi, Richard P.
  Causal Models in Marketing
  (New York: John Wiley and Sons, Inc., 1980).

Berry, William D.
  Nonrecursive Causal Models
  (Beverly Hills, CA: Sage Publications, Inc.).

Blalock, H. M., Jr. (editor)
  Causal Models in the Social Sciences
  (Chicago: Aldine Publishing Co., 1971).

Darden, William R., Monroe, Kent B., and Dillon, William R. (editors)
  Research Methods and Causal Modeling in Marketing
  (Chicago: American Marketing Association, 1983).

Davis, James A.
  The Logic of Causal Order
  (Beverly Hills, CA: Sage Publications, Inc., 1985), 72 pp.

Fornell, Claes
  A Second Generation of Multivariate Analysis in Marketing, Volume I:
  Method
  (New York: Praeger Publishers, 1982).

Goldberger, A. S. and Duncan, O. D. (editors)
  Structural Equation Models in the Social Sciences
  (New York: Seminar Press, 1973).

Hayduk, Leslie A.
  Structural Equation Modeling With LISREL: Essentials and Advances
  (Baltimore, MD: The Johns Hopkins University Press, 1988).

Heise, D. R.
  Causal Analysis
  (New York: John Wiley and Sons, Inc., 1975).

Hellevik, Ottar
  Introduction to Causal Analysis: Exploring Survey Data by
  Crosstabulation
  (Winchester, MA: Allen and Unwin, Inc., 1984), 211 pp.

James, Lawrence R., Mulaik, S. A., and Brett, J. M.
  Causal Analysis: Assumptions, Models and Data
  (Beverly Hills, CA: Sage Publications, Inc., 1982).

Joreskog, Karl G. and Sorbom, Dag
  Analysis of Linear Structural Relationships by Maximum Likelihood
  (Chicago: Scientific Software, 1984).

Joreskog, Karl G. and Sorbom, Dag
  Advances in Factor Analysis and Structural Equation Models
  (Cambridge, MA: Abt Associates, 1979).

Joreskog, Karl G. and Wold, Herman A. (editors)
  Systems Under Indirect Observation: Causality, Structure, Prediction
  (Amsterdam: North Holland, 1981).

Kenny, D. A.
  Correlation and Causality
  (New York: John Wiley and Sons, Inc., 1979).

Long, J. Scott
  Covariance Structure Models: An Introduction to LISREL
  (Beverly Hills, CA: Sage Publications, Inc., 1983), 95 pp.

Saris, Willem and Stroukourst, Henk
  Causal Modeling in Nonexperimental Research: An Introduction to the
  LISREL Approach
  (Amsterdam, Netherlands: Sociometric Research Foundation, 1984), 335
  pp.

204.02 ---------- Theory Re: Causal Analysis

Aaker, David A. and Bagozzi, Richard P.
  "Unobservable Variables in Structural Equation Models With an
  Application in Industrial Selling"
  Journal of Marketing Research, Vol. XVI (May 1979), pp. 147-58.

Alwin, D. F. and Tessler, R. C.
  "Causal Models, Unobserved Variables, and Experimental Data"
  American Journal of Sociology, Vol. 80, No. 1 (1974), pp. 58-86.

Bagozzi, Richard P.
  "Issues in the Application of Covariance Structure Analysis: A
  Further Comment"
  Journal of Consumer Research, Vol. 9 (March 1983), pp. 449,50.

Bagozzi, Richard P.
  "Evaluating Structural Equation Models With Unobservable Variables
  and Measurement Error: A Comment"
  Journal of Marketing Research, Vol. XVIII (August 1981), pp. 375-81.

Bagozzi, Richard P.
  "Reliability Assessment by Analysis of Covariance Structures"
  in Jain, S. C. (editor)
  Research Frontiers in Marketing Dialogues and Directions
  (Chicago: American Marketing Association, 1978), pp. 71-5.

Bagozzi, Richard P.
  "Structural Equation Models in Experimental Research"
  Journal of Marketing Research, Vol. XIV (May 1977), pp. 209-26.

Bagozzi, Richard P. and Fornell, Claes
  "Theoretical Concepts, Measurements, and Meaning"
  in Fornell, C. (editor)
  A Second Generation of Multivariate Analysis, Volume II: Measurement
  and Evaluation
  (New York: Praeger, 1982).

Bagozzi, Richard P., Fornell, Claes, and Larcker, David F.
  "Canonical Correlation Analysis as a Special Case of a Structure
  Relations Model"
  Multivariate Behavior Research, Vol. 16 (1981), pp. 437-54.

Bentler, Peter M.
  "Some Contributions to Efficient Statistics for Structural Models:
  Specifications and Estimation of Moment Structures"
  Psychometrika, Vol. 48 (1983), pp. 493-517.

Bentler, Peter M.
  "Simultaneous Equations as Moment Structure Models: With an
  Introduction to Latent Variable Models"
  Journal of Econometrics, Vol. 22 (1983), pp. 13-42.

Bentler, P. M.
  "Multivariate Analysis With Latent Variables: Causal Modeling"
  in Rosenzweig, M. R. and Porter, L. W. (editors)
  Annual Review of Psychology, Volume 31
  (Palo Alto, CA: Annual Reviews, 1980), pp. 419-56.

Bentler, Peter M.
  "The Interdependence of Theory, Methodology, and Empirical Data:
  Causal Modeling as an Approach to Construct Validation"
  in Kandel, D. B. (editor)
  Longitudinal Drug Research
  (New York: John Wiley and Sons, Inc., 1978), 267-302.

Bentler, Peter M. and Weeks, D. G.
  "Linear Structural Equations With Latent Variables"
  Psychometrika, Vol. 45 (1980), pp. 289-308.

Browne, M. W.
  "Asymptotically Distribution-Free Methods for the Analysis of
  Covariance Structures"
  Journal of Mathematical and Statistical Psychology, Vol. 37 (1984),
  pp. 62-83.

Browne, Michael W.
  "Covariance Structures"
  in Hawkins, D. M. (editor)
  Topics in Applied Multivariate Analysis
  (Cambridge, UK: Cambridge University Press, 1982), pp. 72-141.

Cagli, Ugur
  "Nested Model Comparison With Structural Equation Approaches"
  Journal of Business Research, Vol. 12 (September 1984), pp. 309-18.

Cliff, Norman
  "Some Cautions Concerning the Application of Causal Modeling Methods"
  Multivariate Behavioral Research, Vol. 18 (1983), pp. 115-26.

Costner, H. L.
  "Utilizing Causal Models to Discover Flaws in Experiments"
  Sociometry, Vol. 34 (1971), pp. 398-410.

Darden, William R., Carlson, S. Michael, and Hampton, Ronald D.
  "Issues in Fitting Theoretical and Measurement Models in Marketing"
  Journal of Business Research, Vol. 12 (September 1984). pp. 273-96.

Dillon, William R.
"Investigating Causal Systems With Qualitative Variables: Goodman's
Wonderful World of Logits"
in Monroe, Kent B. (editor)
Advances in Consumer Research, Volume Eight
(Washington, DC: Association for Consumer Research, 1980), pp. 209-19.

Evrard, Yves
"Causal Modelling in Marketing: Recent Developments"
ESOMAR Congress, Rome (1984), pp. 403-20.

Fornell, Claes and Larcker, David F.
"Misapplications of Simulations in Structural Equation Models: Reply
to Acito and Anderson"
Journal of Marketing Research, Vol. XXI (February 1984), pp. 113-7.

Fornell, Claes and Larcker, David F.
"Structural Equation Models With Unobservable Variables and
Measurement Error: Algebra and Statistics"
Journal of Marketing Research, Vol. XVIII (August 1981), pp. 382-8.

Fornell, Claes and Rust, Roland T.
"Incorporating Prior Theory in Covariance Structure Analysis: A
Bayesian Approach"
University of Michigan (1986), unpublished working paper.

Joreskog, Karl G.
"Structural Analysis of Covariance and Correlation Matrices"
Psychometrika, Vol. 43, No. 4 (1978), pp. 443-77.

Joreskog, Karl G.
"Analyzing Psychological Data by Structural Analysis of Covariance
Matrices"
in Atkinson, R. C., Krantz, D. H., Luce, R. D., and Suppes, P.
(editors)
Contemporary Developments in Mathematical Psychology--Volume II
(San Francisco: W. H. Freeman, 1974), pp. 1-56.

Joreskog, Karl G.
"A General Method for Analysis of Covariance Structures"
Biometrika, Vol. 57, No. 2 (1970), pp. 239-51.

Muthen, B.
"A General Structural Equation Model With Dichotomous, Ordered
Categorical, and Continuous Latent Variable Indicators"
Psychometrika, Vol. 49 (1984), pp. 115-32.

Rindskopf, David
"Parameterizing Inequality Constraints on Unique Variances in Linear
Structural Models"
Psychometrika, Vol. 48 (1983), pp. 73-83.

Simon, H.
"Spurious Correlation: A Causal Interpretation"
in Models of Man
(New York: John Wiley and Sons, Inc., 1957), pp. 37-49.

Sorbom, Dag
"Structural Equation Models With Structured Means"
in Joreskog, Karl G. and Wold, Herman (editors)
Systems Under Indirect Observation
(Amsterdam: North-Holland Publishing Company, 1982), pp. 183-95.

Werts, Charles E., Linn, Robert L., and Joreskog, Karl G.
"Identification and Estimation in Path Analysis With Unmeasured
Variables"
American Journal of Sociology, Vol. 78 (1973), pp. 1469-84.

Werts, Charles E., Linn, Robert L., and Joreskog, Karl G.
"Estimating the Parameters of Path Models Involving Unmeasured
Variables"
in Blalock, H. M. (editor)
Causal Models in the Social Sciences
(Chicago: Aldine, 1971), pp. 400-9.

204.03 ---------- Theory Re: LISREL

Areskoug, B.
"Some Asymptotic Properties of PLS Estimators and a Simulation Study
for Comparisons Between LISREL and PLS"
in Joreskog, K. G. and Wold, H. A. (editors)
Systems Under Indirect Observation: Causality, Structure, Prediction
(Amsterdam: North Holland, 1981).

Fornell, Claes
"Issues in the Application of Covariance Structure Analysis: A
Comment"
Journal of Consumer Research, Vol. 9 (March 1983), pp. 443-8.

Fornell, Claes and Larcker, David F.
"Evaluating Structural Equation Models With Unobservable Variables
and Measurement Error"
Journal of Marketing Research, Vol. XVIII (February 1981), pp. 39-50.

Gerbing, David W. and Hunter, J. E.
"The Return to Multiple Groups: Analysis and Critique of Confirmatory
Factor Analysis With LISREL"
Annual Meeting of the Southwestern Psychological Association,
Oklahoma City (April 1980), paper presentation.

Joreskog, Karl G.
"Basic Issues in the Application of LISREL"
Data, Vol. 1 (1981), pp. 1-6.

Joreskog, Karl G.
"Structural Equation Models in the Social Sciences: Specification,
Estimation and Testing"
in Joreskog, K. G. and Sorbom, D. (editors)
Advances in Factor Analysis and Structural Equation Models
(Cambridge, MA: Abt Books, 1979), pp. 105-27.

Joreskog, Karl G.
"Structural Equation Models in the Social Sciences: Specification,
Estimation and Testing"
in Krishnaiah, P. R. (editor)
Applications of Statistics
(Amsterdam: North-Holland Publishing Company, 1977), pp. 265-87.

Joreskog, Karl G.
"A General Method for Estimating a Linear Structural Equation System"
in Goldberger, A. S. and Duncan, O. D. (editors)
Structural Equation Models in the Social Sciences
(New York: Seminar Press, 1973), pp. 85-112.

Joreskog, Karl G.
"Statistical Analysis of Sets of Congeneric Tests"
Psychometrika, Vol. 36 (June 1971), pp. 109-33.

Joreskog, Karl G.
"A General Method for Analysis of Covariance Structures"
Biometrika, Vol. 57 (1970), pp. 293-51.

Joreskog, Karl G. and Sorbom, Dag
LISREL VI: Analysis of Linear Structural Relationships by Maximum
Likelihood, Instrumental Variables and Least Square Methods
(Mooresville, IN: Scientific Software, 1986).

Joreskog, Karl G. and Sorbom, Dag
"Recent Developments in Structural Equation Modeling"
Journal of Marketing Research, Vol. XIX (November 1982), pp. 404-16.

Joreskog, Karl G. and Sorbom, Dag
LISREL V: Analysis of Linear Structural Relationships by Maximum
Likelihood and Least Square Methods
(Chicago: National Education Resources, Inc., 1981).

Joreskog, Karl G. and Sorbom, Dag
LISREL IV: Analysis of Linear Structural Relationships by the Method
of Maximum Likelihood
(Chicago: National Educational Resources, Inc., 1978).

Joreskog, Karl G. and Sorbom, Dag
"Statistical Models and Methods for Analysis of Longitudinal Data"
in Aigner, D. J. and Goldberger, A. S. (editors)
Latent Variables in Socio-Economic Models
(Amsterdam: North-Holland Publishing Company, 1977), pp. 285-325.

Rindskopf, D.
"Using Phantom and Imaginary Latent Variables to Parameterize
Constraints in Linear Structural Models"
Psychometrika, Vol. 49 (1984), pp. 37-47.

Rindskopf, D.
"Parameterizing Inequality Constraints on Unique Variances in Linear
Structural Models"
Psychometrika, Vol. 48 (1983), pp. 73-83.

Sorbom, Dag and Joreskog, Karl G.
"Recent Developments in LISREL: Automatic Starting Values"
(1982).

Teel, Jesse E., Jr., Bearden, William O., and Sharma, Subhash
"Interpreting LISREL Estimates of Explained Variance in Nonrecursive
Structural Equation Models"
Journal of Marketing Research, Vol. XXIII (May 1986), pp. 164-8.

204.04 ---------- Theory Re: Two-Step Structural Equation Modeling

Anderson, James C. and Gerbing, David W.
 "Structural Equation Modeling in Practice: A Review and Recommended
 Two-Step Approach"
 Psychological Bulletin, Vol. 103 (May 1988), pp. 411-23.

204.05 ---------- Applications of Two-Step Structural Equation Modeling

Droge, Cornelia
 "Shaping the Route to Attitude Change: Central Versus Peripheral
 Processing Through Comparative Versus Noncomparative Advertising"
 Journal of Marketing Research, Vol. XXVI (May 1989), pp. 193-204.

204.06 ---------- Theory Re: Multiple Indicator Multiple Cause (MIMC)

        See also (sub)heading(s) 189.

Costner, Herbert L. and Schoenberg, R.
 "Diagnosing Indicator Ills in Multiple Indicator Models"
 in Goldberger, A. S. and Duncan, O. D. (editors)
 Structural Equations in the Social Sciences
 (New York: Seminar Press, 1973), pp. 167-99.

Hauser, R. M. and Goldberger, Arthur S.
 "The Treatment of Unobservable Variables in Path Analysis"
 in Costner, H. L. (editor)
 Sociological Methodology 1971
 (San Francisco: Jossey-Bass, 1971), pp. 81-117.

Joreskog, Karl G. and Goldberger, Arthur S.
 "Estimation of a Model With Multiple Indicators and Multiple Causes
 of a Single Latent Variable"
 Journal of the American Statistical Association, Vol. 70 (1975), pp.
 631-9.

204.07 ---------- Theory Re: Estimation Procedures With Non-Normal Data

Boomsma, Anne
 On the Robustness of LISREL (Maximum Likelihood Estimation) Against
 Small Sample Size and Normality
 Rijksuniversiteit, Groningen (1983), unpublished doctoral
 dissertation.

Boomsma, Anne
 "The Robustness of LISREL Against Small Sample Sizes in Factor
 Analysis Models"
 in Joreskog, K. G. and Wold, H. (editors)
 Systems Under Indirect Observation: Causality, Structure, Prediction,
 Part 1
 (Amsterdam: North Holland, 1982).

Harlow, Lisa L.
 Behavior of Some Elliptical Theory Estimators With Non-Normal Data in
 Covariance Structures Framework: A Monte Carlo Study
 University of California, Los Angeles (1985), unpublished doctoral
 dissertation.

Muthen, Bengt and Kaplan, David
 "A Comparison of Some Methodologies for the Factor Analysis of
 Nonnormal Likert Variables"
 British Journal of Mathematical and Statistical Psychology, Vol. 38
 (1985), pp. 171-89.

Sharma, Subhash, Durvasula, Srinivas, and Dillon, William R.
 "Some Results on the Behavior of Alternate Covariance Structure
 Estimation Procedures in the Presence of Non-Normal Data"
 Journal of Marketing Research, Vol. XXVI (May 1989), pp. 214-21.

204.08 ---------- Theory Re: Causal Analysis of Experimental Designs

        See also (sub)heading(s) 92.

Alwin, Duane F. and Tessler, Richard C.
 "Causal Models, Unobserved Variables, and Experimental Data"
 American Journal of Sociology, Vol. 80 (July 1974), pp. 58-86.

Bagozzi, Richard P.
 "Structural Equation Models in Experimental Research"
 Journal of Marketing Research, Vol. XIV (May 1977), pp. 209-26.

Bagozzi, Richard P. and Yi, Youjae
 "On the Use of Structural Equation Models in Experimental Designs"
 Journal of Marketing Research, Vol. XXVI (August 1989), pp. 271-84.

Bray, James H. and Maxwell, Scott E.
  "Analyzing and Interpreting Significant MANOVAs"
  Review of Educational Research, Vol. 52 (Fall 1982), pp. 340-67.

Kuhnel, Steffen M.
  "Testing MANOVA Designs With LISREL"
  Sociological Methods and Research, Vol. 16 (May 1988), pp. 504-23.

204.09 ---------- Evaluations of Causal Model Estimation Methods

Babakus, Emin, Ferguson, Carl E., Jr., and Joreskog, Karl G.
  "The Sensitivity of Confirmatory Maximum Likelihood Factor Analysis
  to Violations of Measurement Scale and Distributional Assumptions"
  Journal of Marketing Research, Vol. XXV (May 1987), pp. 222-8.

Boomsma, Anne
  "Nonconvergence, Improper Solutions, and Starting Values in LISREL
  Maximum Likelihood Estimations"
  Psychometrika, Vol. 50 (June 1985), pp. 229-42.

Boomsma, Anne
  "The Robustness of LISREL Against Small Sample Sizes in Factor
  Analysis Models"
  in Joreskog, K. G. and Wold, H. (editors)
  Systems Under Indirect Observation: Causality, Structure, Prediction
  (Amsterdam: North-Holland, 1981), pp. 149-73.

Fornell, Claes and Bookstein, Fred L.
  "Two Structural Equation Models: LISREL and PLS Applied to Consumer
  Exit-Voice Theory"
  Journal of Marketing Research, Vol. XIX (November 1982), pp. 440-52.

Fornell, Claes and Bookstein, Fred L.
  "A Comparative Analysis of Two Structural Equation Models: LISREL and
  PLS Applied to Market Data"
  in Fornell, C. (editor)
  A Second Generation of Multivariate Analysis: Methods, Volume I
  (New York: Praeger, 1982).

Fornell, Claes and Bookstein, Fred L.
  "A Comparative Analysis of Two Structural Equation Models: LISREL and
  PLS Applied to Market Data"
  Graduate School of Business Administration, University of Michigan
  (1981), faculty working paper.

Tanaka, Jeff S.
  Some Results on the Estimation of Covariance Structural Models
  University of California, Los Angeles (1984), unpublished doctoral
  dissertation.

204.10 ---------- Theory Re: Causal Analysis of Categorical Data

Blythe, C. R.
  "On Simpson's Paradox and the Sure-Thing Principle"
  Journal of the American Statistical Association, Vol. 67 (1972), pp.
  364-6.

Dillon, William R.
  "Investigating Causal Systems With Qualitative Variables: Goodman's
  Wonderful World of Logits"
  in Monroe, Kent B. (editor)
  Advances in Consumer Research, Volume Eight
  (Washington, DC: Association for Consumer Research, 1980), pp. 209-19.

Green, Paul E., Carmone, Frank J., and Wachspress, D. P.
  "Consumer Segmentation via Latent Class Analysis"
  Journal of Consumer Research, Vol. 3 (1976), pp. 170-4.

Madden, Thomas J. and Dillon, William R.
  "Causal Analysis and Latent Class Models: An Application to a
  Communication Hierarchy of Effects Model"
  Journal of Marketing Research, Vol. XIX (November 1982), pp. 472-90.

Magidson, Jay
  "Some Common Pitfalls in Causal Analysis of Categorical Data"
  Journal of Marketing Research, Vol. XIX (November 1982), pp. 461-71.

Magidson, Jay
  "Qualitative Variance, Entropy and Correlation Ratios for Nominal
  Dependent Variables"
  Social Science Research, Vol. 10 (1981), pp. 177-94.

Nicosia, Francesco M.
  "Latent Structure Analysis"
  in Sheth, Jagdish N. (editor)
  Multivariate Methods for Market and Survey Research
  (Chicago: American Marketing Association, 1977).

Reynolds, H. T.
"Some Comments on the Causal Analysis of Surveys With Log-Linear
Models"
American Journal of Sociology, Vol. 83 (1977), pp. 127-43.

204.11 ---------- Theory Re: Decomposition of Effects

Alwin, D. F. and Hauser, R. M.
"The Decomposition of Effects in Path Analysis"
American Sociological Review, Vol. 40 (1975), pp. 37-47.

Graff, J. and Schmidt, P.
"A General Model for Decomposition of Effects"
in Joreskog, K. G. and Wold, H. (editors)
Systems Under Indirect Observation: Causality, Structure and
Prediction
(Amsterdam: North-Holland Publishing Co., 1982).

204.12 ---------- Theory Re: Measurement Issues in Causal Analysis

Anderson, James C. and Gerbing, David W.
"Some Methods for Respecifying Measurement Models to Obtain
Unidimensional Construct Measurement"
Journal of Marketing Research, Vol. XIX (November 1982), pp. 453-60.

Bagozzi, Richard P.
"Issues in the Application of Covariance Structure Analysis: A
Further Comment"
Journal of Consumer Research, Vol. 9 (March 1983), pp. 449,50.

Bagozzi, Richard P.
"Evaluating Structural Equation Models With Unobservable Variables
and Measurement Error: A Comment"
Journal of Marketing Research, Vol. XVIII (August 1981), pp. 375-81.

Burt, R. S.
"Interpretational Confounding of Unobserved Variables in Structural
Equation Models"
Sociological Methods and Research, Vol. 5 (August 1976), pp. 3-52.

Burt, R. S.
"Confirmatory Factor-Analysis Structures and the Theory Construction
Process"
Sociological Methods and Research, Vol. 2 (1973), pp. 131-87.

Danes, Jeffrey E.
"Unidimensional Measurement and Structural Equation Models With
Latent Variables"
Journal of Business Research, Vol. 12 (September 1984), pp. 337-52.

Gerbing, David W.
Parameter Estimation and Model Construction for Recursive Models With
Unidimensional Measurement
Department of Psychology, Michigan State University (1979),
unpublished doctoral dissertation.

Hunter, J. E.
"Methods of Reordering the Correlation Matrix to Facilitate Visual
Inspection and Preliminary Cluster Analysis"
Journal of Educational Measurement, Vol. 10, No. 1 (1973), pp. 51-61.

Kumar, Ajith and Dillon, William R.
"The Interaction of Measurement and Structure in Simultaneous
Equation Models With Unobservable Variables"
Journal of Marketing Research, Vol. XXIV (February 1987), pp. 98-105.

Smith, K. W.
"On Estimating the Reliability of Composite Indices Through Factor
Analysis"
Sociological Methods and Research, Vol. 2 (May 1974), pp. 485-510.

Spearman, C.
"Demonstration of Formulae for True Measurement of Correlation"
American Journal of Psychology, Vol. 18 (1907), pp. 161-9.

204.13 ---------- Covariance Structure--Internal Consistency

Hart, B. and Spearman, C.
"General Ability, Its Existence and Nature"
British Journal of Psychology, Vol. 5 (1913), pp. 51-84.

Spearman, C.
"Theory of Two Factors"
Psychological Review, Vol. 21 (1914), pp. 105-15.

Spearman, C.
"'General Intelligence' Objectively Determined and Measured"
American Journal of Psychology, Vol. 15 (1904), pp. 259-92.

Spearman, C. and Holzinger, K. J.
"The Sampling Error in the Theory of Two Factors"
British Journal of Psychology, Vol. 15 (1924), pp. 17-9.

204.14 ---------- Covariance Structure--External Consistency

Anderson, J. C. and Gerbing, D. W.
"Some Methods for Respecifying Measurement Models to Obtain
Unidimensional Construct Measurement"
Journal of Marketing Research, Vol. XIX (November 1982), pp. 453-60.

Fornell, Claes and Larcker, David F.
"Structural Equation Models With Unobservable Variables and
Measurement Error: Algebra and Statistics"
Journal of Marketing Research, Vol. XVIII (August 1981), pp. 382-8.

Hunter, J. E. and Gerbing, David W.
"Unidimensional Measurement, Second Order Factor Analysis and Causal
Models"
in Staw, B. M. and Cummings, L. L. (editors)
Research in Organizational Behavior, Volume IV
(Greenwich, CT: JAI Press, 1982).

Tucker, L. R.
"The Role of Correlated Factors in Factor Analysis"
Psychometrika, Vol. 5 (June 1940), pp. 141-52.

204.15 ---------- Computer Programs for Causal Analysis - PC

Bentler, Peter M.
"Theory and Implementation of EQS: A Structural Equations Program"
(Los Angeles: BMDP Statistical Software, Inc., 1985).

Joreskog, Karl G. and Sorbom, Dag
SIMPLIS User's Guide
(Mooresville, IN: Scientific Software, Inc., 1987).

Joreskog, Karl G. and Sorbom, Dag
LISREL-PC
(Mooresville, IN: Scientific Software, Inc.).

Joreskog, Karl G. and Sorbom, Dag
PRELIS
(Mooresville, IN: Scientific Software, Inc., 1986).

204.16 ---------- Computer Programs for Causal Analysis - Mainframe

Bentler, Peter M.
"Theory and Implementation of EQS, a Structural Equation Program"
Department of Psychology, University of California, Los Angeles
(1981), technical report.

Fraser, Colin
COSAN User's Guide
(New South Wales, Australia: Centre for Behavioral Studies,
University of New England Armidale, 1980).

Joreskog, Karl G. and Sorbom, Dag
LISREL VI
(Uppsala: University of Uppsala, 1984).

Joreskog, Karl G. and Sorbom, Dag
LISREL VI User's Guide
(Chicago: International Educational Services, 1983).

Joreskog, Karl G. and Sorbom, Dag
LISREL V: Analysis of Linear Structural Relationships by Maximum
Likelihood and Least Squares Methods
(Chicago: National Educational Resources, 1981).

Joreskog, Karl G. and Sorbom, Dag
LISREL V Users' Guide
(Chicago: International Educational Services, 1981).

Joreskog, Karl G. and Sorbom, Dag
LISREL: Analysis of Linear Structural Relationships by the Method of
Maximum Likelihood, Version IV, Release 2
(Chicago: National Educational Resources, Inc., 1978).

Joreskog, Karl G. and Van Thillo, Marielle
  "LISREL: A General Computer Program for Estimating a Linear
  Structural Equation System Involving Multiple Indicators of
  Unmeasured Variables"
  Research Bulletin 72-56
  (Princeton, NJ: Educational Testing Service, 1972).

204.17 ---------- Unclassified (Causal Analysis)

Bagozzi, Richard P., Fornell, Claes, and Larcker, David F.
  "Canonical Correlation Analysis as a Special Case of a Structural
  Relations Model"
  Multivariate Behavioral Research, Vol. 16 (October 1981), pp. 437-54.

Mulaik, Stanley A.
  "Comments on the Measurement of Factorial Indeterminacy"
  Psychometrika, Vol. 41 (1976), pp. 249-62.

Mulaik, Stanley A. and McDonald, Roderick P.
  "The Effect of Additional Variables on Factor Indeterminacy in Models
  With a Single Common Factor"
  Psychometrika, Vol. 43 (1978), pp. 177-92.

205 ------------------- EVALUATING CAUSAL MODELS -------------------
          See also (sub)heading(s) 141, 204.

205.01 ---------- Theory Re: Evaluating Causal Models

Acito, Franklin and Anderson, Ronald D.
    "On Simulation Methods for Investigating Structural Modeling"
    Journal of Marketing Research, Vol. XXI (February 1984), pp. 107-12.

Bagozzi, Richard P.
    "Evaluating Structural Equation Models With Unobservable Variables
    and Measurement Error: A Comment"
    Journal of Marketing Research, Vol. XVIII (August 1981), pp. 375-81.

Bagozzi, Richard P.
    "Reliability Assessment by Analysis of Covariance Structures"
    in Jain, S. C. (editor)
    Research Frontiers in Marketing: Dialogues and Directions
    (Chicago: American Marketing Association, 1978), pp. 71-5.

Bagozzi, Richard P. and Yi, Y.
    "On the Evaluation of Structural Equation Models"
    Journal of the Academy of Marketing Science, Vol. 16 (Spring 1988),
    pp. 77-94.

Balderjahn, Ingo
    "Cross-Validation of Covariance Structures in One and Multi Group
    Analysis: The Case of the Ecologically Concernced Consumers"
    Tenth Annual Meeting, German Classification Society (June 1986),
    paper presentation.

Bearden, William O., Sharma, Subhash, and Teel, Jesse E., Jr.
    "Sample Size Effects on Chi Square and Other Statistics Used in
    Evaluating Causal Models"
    Journal of Marketing Research, Vol. XIX (November 1982), pp. 425-30.

Bentler, Peter M. and Bonett, Douglas G.
    "Significance Tests and Goodness of Fit in the Analysis of Covariance
    Structures"
    Psychological Bulletin, Vol. 88, No. 3 (May 1980), pp. 588-606.

Cudeck, Robert and Browne, Michael W.
    "Cross-Validation of Covariance Structures"
    Multivariate Behavioral Research, Vol. 18 (April 1983), pp. 147-67.

Fornell, Claes
    "Issues in the Application of Covariance Structure Analysis: A
    Comment"
    Journal of Consumer Research, Vol. 9 (March 1983), pp. 443-8.

Fornell, Claes and Larcker, David F.
    "Structural Equation Models With Unobservable Variables and
    Measurement Error: Algebra and Statistics"
    Journal of Marketing Research, Vol. XVIII (August 1981), pp. 382-8.

Fornell, Claes and Larcker, David F.
    "Evaluating Structural Equation Models With Unobservable Variables
    and Measurement Error"
    Journal of Marketing Research, Vol. XVIII (February 1981), pp. 39-50.

Geweke, John F. and Singleton, Kenneth J.
    "Interpreting the Likelihood Ratio Statistic in Factor Models When
    Sample Size is Small"
    Journal of the American Statistical Association, Vol. 75 (March
    1980), pp. 133-7.

Satorra, A. and Saris, Willem E.
    "The Power of the Likelihood Ratio Test in Covariance Structure
    Analysis"
    Psychometrika, Vol. 50 (1985), pp. 83-90.

Sawyer, Alan G.
    "The Use of Incremental Goodness of Fit Indices in Structural
    Equation Model in Marketing Research"
    Journal of Business Research, Vol. 12 (September 1984), pp. 297-308.

Sprott, D. A.
    "Maximum Likelihood in Small Samples: Estimation in the Presence of
    Nuisance Parameters"
    Biometrika, Vol. 67, No. 3 (1980), pp. 515-23.

Werts, Charles E., Linn, Robert L., and Joreskog, Karl G.
    "Intraclass Reliability Estimates: Testing Structural Assumptions"
    Educational and Psychological Measurement, Vol. 34 (1974), pp. 25-33.

205.02 ---------- Theory Re: Indexes of Fit

Anderson, James C. and Gerbing, David W.
"The Effect of Sampling Error on Convergence, Improper Solutions, and Goodness-of-Fit Indices for Maximum Likelihood Confirmatory Factor Analysis"
Psychometrika, Vol. 49, No. 2 (1984), pp. 155-73.

Anderson, James C., Gerbing, David W., and Narayanan, A.
"A Comparison of Two Alternative Residual Goodness-of-Fit Indices"
Journal of the Market Research Society, Vol. 27 (October 1985), pp. 283-91.

Bearden, William O., Sharma, Subhash, and Teel, Jesse E.
"Sample Size Effects on Chi Square and Other Statistics Used in Evaluating Causal Models
"Journal of Marketing Research, Vol. XIX (November 1982), pp. 425-30.

Dillon, William R., Kumar, Ajith, and Mulani, Narendra
"Offending Estimates in Covariance Structure Analysis: Comments on the Causes of and Solutions to Heywood Cases"
Psychological Bulletin, Vol. 101 (January 1987), pp. 126-35.

Gerbing, David W. and Anderson, James C.
"Improper Solutions in the Analysis of Covariance Structures: Their Interpretability and a Comparison of Alternative Respecifications"
Psychometrika, Vol. 52 (March 1987), pp. 99-111.

Hoelter, Jon W.
"The Analysis of Covariance Structures: Goodness-of-Fit Indices"
Sociological Methods and Research, Vol. 11 (1983), pp. 325-44.

Rindskopf, David
"Parameterizing Inequality Constraints on Unique Variances in Linear Structural Models"
Psychometrika, Vol. 48 (March 1983), pp. 73-83.

Sawyer, Alan G. and Page, Thomas J., Jr.
"The Use of Incremental Goodness of Fit Indices in Structural Equation Models in Marketing Research"
Journal of Business Research, Vol. 12 (September 1984), pp. 297-308.

Sobel, Michael E. and Bohrnstedt, George W.
"Use of Null Models in Evaluating the Fit of Covariance Structure Models"
in Tuma, Nancy B. (editor)
Sociological Methodology 1985
(San Francisco: Jossey-Bass Publishers, 1985), pp. 152-78.

205.03 ---------- Theory Re: Akaike Information Criterion (AIC)

Akaike, Hirotugu
"Information Theory and an Extension of the Maximum Likelihood Principle"
in Petrov, B. N. and Csaki, F. (editors)
Second International Symposium on Information Theory
(Budapest: Akademiai Kiado, 1973), pp. 267-81.

Sakamoto, Yosiyuki, Ishiguro, Makio, and Kitagawa, Genshiro
Akaike Information Criterion Statistics
(Dordrecht, Holland: D. Reidel Publishing Company, 1986).

206 ------------------ CAUSAL ANALYSIS APPLICATIONS ------------------
          See also (sub)heading(s) 204.

Aaker, David and Bagozzi, Richard P.
    "Unobservable Variables in Structural Equation Models With an
    Application in Industrial Selling"
    Journal of Marketing Research, Vol. XVI (May 1979), pp. 147-58.

Bagozzi, Richard P.
    "Attitudes, Intentions and Behavior: A Test of Some Key Hypotheses"
    Journal of Personality and Social Psychology, Vol. 41, No. 4 (1981),
    pp. 607-27.

Bagozzi, Richard P.
    "An Examination of the Validity of Two Models of Attitude"
    Multivariate Behavioral Research, Vol. 16 (1981), pp. 323-59.

Bagozzi, Richard P.
    "The Construct Validity of Affective, Behavioral, and Cognitive
    Components of Attitude by Analysis of Covariance Structures"
    Multivariate Behavioral Research, Vol. 13 (1978), pp. 9-31.

Bagozzi, Richard P. and Burnkrant, Robert E.
    "Attitude Measurement and Behavior Change: A Reconsideration of
    Attitude Organization and Its Relationship to Behavior"
    in Wilkie, William L (editor)
    Advances in Consumer Research, Volume Six
    (Ann Arbor, MI: Association for Consumer Research, 1979).

Finn, Adam
    "Print Ad Recognition Readership Scores: An Information Processing
    Perspective"
    Journal of Marketing Research, Vol. XXV (May 1988), pp. 168-77.

Fry, Louis W., Futrell, Charles M., Parasuraman, A., and Chmielewski,
    Margaret A.
    "An Analysis of Alternative Causal Models of Salesperson Role
    Perceptions and Work-Related Attitudes"
    Journal of Marketing Research, Vol. XXIII (May 1986), pp. 153-63.

Goodman, Leo A.
    "Causal Analysis of Data From Panel Studies and Other Kinds of
    Surveys"
    American Journal of Sociology, Vol. 78 (1973), pp. 1135-91.

Lutz, Richard J.
    "An Experimental Investigation of Causal Relations Among Cognitions,
    Affect and Behavioral Intention"
    Journal of Consumer Research, Vol. 3 (1975), pp. 197-208.

206.01 ---------- Applications of LISREL

Aaker, David A., Bagozzi, Richard P., Carman, James M., and MacLachlan,
    James M.
    "On Using Response Latency to Measure Preference"
    Journal of Marketing Research, Vol. XVI (May 1980), pp. 237-44.

Achrol, Ravi S. and Stern, Louis W.
    "Environmental Determinants of Decision-Making Uncertainty in
    Marketing Channels"
    Journal of Marketing Research, Vol. XXV (February 1988), pp. 36-50.

Anderson, James C. and Narus, James A.
    "A Model of the Distributor's Perspective of Distributor-Manufacturer
    Working Relationships"
    Journal of Marketing, Vol. 48 (Fall 1984), pp. 62-74.

Anderson, Ronald D., Engledow, Jack L., and Becker, Helmut
    "Evaluating the Relationships Among Attitude Toward Business, Product
    Satisfaction, Experience, and Search Effort"
    Journal of Marketing Research, Vol. XVI (August 1979), pp. 394-400.

Arora, Raj
    "Validation of an S-O-R Model for Situation, Enduring, and Response
    Components of Involvement"
    Journal of Marketing Research, Vol. XIX (November 1982), pp. 505-16.

Arora, Raj and Cavusgil, S. Tamer
    "Image and Cost Factors in the Choice of Mental Health-Care
    Organizations: A Causal Model"
    Journal of the Academy of Marketing Science, Vol. 13 (Fall 1985), pp.
    119-29.

Bagozzi, Richard P.
    "A Field Investigation of Causal Relations Among Cognitions, Affect,
    Intentions, and Behavior"
    Journal of Marketing Research, Vol. XIX (November 1982), pp. 562-84.

Bagozzi, Richard P.
"Performance and Satisfaction in an Industrial Sales Force: An
Examination of Their Antecedents and Simultaneity"
Journal of Marketing, Vol. 44 (Spring 1980), pp. 65-77.

Bearden, William O. and Mason, J. Barry
"Determinants of Physician and Pharmacist Support of Generic Drugs"
Journal of Consumer Research, Vol. 7 (September 1980), pp. 121-30.

Bearden, William O. and Oliver, Richard L.
"The Role of Public and Private Complaining in Satisfaction With
Problem Resolution"
Journal of Consumer Affairs, Vol. 19 (Winter 1985), pp. 222-40.

Burnkrant, Robert E. and Page, Thomas J., Jr.
"An Examination of the Convergent, Discriminant, and Predictive
Validity of Fishbein's Behavioral Intention Model"
Journal of Marketing Research, Vol. XIX (November 1982), pp. 550-61.

Cadotte, Ernest R., Woodruff, Robert B., and Jenkins, Roger L.
"Expectations and Norms in Models of Consumer Satisfaction"
Journal of Marketing Research, Vol. XXIV (August 1987), pp. 305-14.

Churchill, Gilbert A., Jr. and Surprenant, Carol
"An Investigation Into the Determinants of Customer Satisfaction"
Journal of Marketing Research, Vol. XIX (November 1982), pp. 491-504.

Cronin, J. Joseph, Jr. and Morris, Michael H.
"Satisfying Customer Expectations: The Effect on Conflict and
Repurchase Intentions in Industrial Marketing Channels"
Journal of the Academy of Marketing Science, Vol. 17 (Winter 1989),
pp. 41-9.

Crosby, Lawrence A. and Stephens, Nancy
"Effects of Relationship Marketing on Satisfaction, Retention, and
Prices in the Life Insurance Industry"
Journal of Marketing Research, Vol. XXIV (November 1987), pp. 404-11.

DeBrentani, Ulrike and Droge, Cornelia
"Determinants of the New Product Screening Decision: A Structural
Model Approach"
International Journal of Research in Marketing, Vol. 5, No. 2 (1988),
pp. 91-106.

Dubinsky, Alan J., Howell, Roy D., Ingram, Thomas N., and Bellenger,
Danny N.
"Salesforce Socialization"
Journal of Marketing, Vol. 50 (October 1986), pp. 192-207.

Dwyer, F. Robert and Ho, Sejo
"Output Sector Munificence Effects on the Internal Political Economy
of Marketing Channels"
Journal of Marketing Research, Vol. XXIV (November 1987), pp. 347-58.

Fornell, Claes and Westbrook, Robert A.
"The Vicious Circle of Consumer Complaints"
Journal of Marketing, Vol. 48 (Summer 1984), pp. 68-78.

Frazier, Gary L., Gill, James D., and Kale, Sudhir H.
"Dealer Dependence Levels and Reciprocal Actions in a Channel of
Distribution in a Developing Country"
Journal of Marketing, Vol. 53 (January 1989), pp. 50-69.

Fritz, Wolfgang
"Determinants of Product Innovation Activities"
European Journal of Marketing, Vol. 23, No. 10 (1989), pp. 32-43.

Gaski, John F.
"Commentary on Howell's Observations"
Journal of Marketing Research, Vol. XXIV (February 1987), pp. 127-9.

Gaski, John F.
"Interrelations Among a Channel Entity's Power Sources: Impact of the
Exercise of Reward and Coercion on Expert, Referent, and Legitimate
Power Sources"
Journal of Marketing Research, Vol. XXIII (February 1986), pp. 62-77.

Gilly, Mary C.
"Postcomplaint Processes: From Organizational Response to Repurchase
Behavior"
Journal of Consumer Affairs, Vol. 21 (Winter 1987), pp. 293-313.

Good, Linda K., Sisler, Grovalynn F., and Gentry, James W.
"Antecedents of Turnover Intentions Among Retail Management Personnel"
Journal of Retailing, Vol. 64 (Fall 1988), pp. 295-314.

Gould, Stephen J.
"Consumer Attitudes Toward Health and Health Care: A Differential
Perspective"
Journal of Consumer Affairs, Vol. 22 (Summer 1988), pp. 96-118.

Han, C. Min
    "Country Image: Halo or Summary Construct?"
    Journal of Marketing Research, Vol. XXVI (May 1989), pp. 222-9.

Han, C. Min
    "The Role of Consumer Patriotism in the Choice of Domestic Versus
    Foreign Products"
    Journal of Advertising Research, Vol. 28 (June/July 1988), pp. 25-32.

Hauser, John R. and Urban, Glen L.
    "The Value Priority Hypothesis for Consumer Budget Plans"
    Journal of Consumer Research, Vol. 12 (March 1986), pp. 446-62.

Howell, Roy D.
    "Covariance Structure Modeling and Measurement Issues: A Note on
    'Interrelations Among a Channel Entity's Power Sources'"
    Journal of Marketing Research, Vol. XXIV (February 1987), pp. 119-26.

Jaworski, Bernard J. and McGinnis, Deborah J.
    "Marketing Jobs and Management Controls: Toward a Framework"
    Journal of Marketing Research, Vol. XXVI (November 1989), pp. 406-19.

Joachimsthaler, Erich A. and Lastovicka, John L.
    "Optimal Stimulation Level--Exploratory Behavior Models"
    Journal of Consumer Research, Vol. 11 (December 1984), pp. 830-5.

John, George and Reve, Torger
    "The Reliability and Validity of Key Informant Data From Dyadic
    Relationships in Marketing Channels"
    Journal of Marketing Research, Vol. XIX (November 1982), pp. 517-24.

Korgaonkar, P. K., Lund, Daulat, and Price, Barbara
    "A Structural Equations Approach Toward Examination of Store Attitude
    and Store Patronage Behavior"
    Journal of Retailing, Vol. 61 (Summer 1985), pp. 39-60.

Krapfel, Robert E., Jr.
    "Customer Complaint and Salesperson Response: The Effect of the
    Communication Source"
    Journal of Retailing, Vol. 64 (Summer 1988), pp. 181-98.

Leong, Siew Meng
    "The Effects of Expert and Referent Power in the Buyer-Seller Dyad: A
    Structural Equations Approach"
    Singapore Marketing Review, Vol. III (1988), pp. 28-40.

Lichtenstein, Donald R., Block, Peter H., and Black, William C.
    "Correlates of Price Acceptability"
    Journal of Consumer Research, Vol. 15 (September 1988), pp. 243-52.

Liu, Scott S. and Stout, Patricia A.
    "Effects of Message Modality and Appeal on Advertising Acceptance"
    Psychology and Marketing, Vol. 4 (Fall 1987), pp. 167-87.

Lusch, Robert F. and Laczniak, Gene R.
    "The Evolving Marketing Concept, Competitive Intensity and
    Organizational Performance"
    Journal of the Academy of Marketing Science, Vol. 15 (Fall 1987), pp.
    1-11.

MacKenzie, Scott B. and Lutz, Richard J.
    "An Empirical Examination of the Structural Antecedents of Attitude
    Toward the Ad in an Advertising Pretesting Context"
    Journal of Marketing, Vol. 53 (April 1989), pp. 48-65.

MacKenzie, Scott B. and Lutz, Richard J.
    "Testing Competing Models of Advertising Effectiveness via Structural
    Equation Models"
    Proceedings, Winter Educators' Conference
    (Chicago: American Marketing Association, 1983), pp. 70-5.

MacKenzie, Scott B., Lutz, Richard J., and Belch, George E.
    "The Role of Attitude Toward the Ad as a Mediator of Advertising
    Effectiveness: A Test of Competing Explanations"
    Journal of Marketing Research, Vol. XXIII (May 1986), pp. 130-43.

McQuiston, Daniel H.
    "Novelty, Complexity, and Importance as Causal Determinants of
    Industrial Buyer Behavior"
    Journal of Marketing, Vol. 53 (April 1989), pp. 66-79.

Michaels, Ronald E., Day, Ralph L., and Joachimsthaler, Erich A.
    "Role Stress Among Industrial Buyers: An Integrative Model"
    Journal of Marketing, Vol. 51 (April 1987), pp. 28-45.

Neibecker, Bruno
    "The Validity of Computer-Controlled Magnitude Scaling to Measure
    Emotional Impact of Stimuli"
    Journal of Marketing Research, Vol. XXI (August 1984), pp. 325-31.

Oliver, Richard L. and Bearden, William O.
"Crossover Effects in the Theory of Reasoned Action: A Moderating
Influence Attempt"
Journal of Consumer Research, Vol. 12 (December 1985), pp. 324-40.

Oliver, Richard L. and Swan, John E.
"Consumer Perceptions of Interpersonal Equity and Satisfaction in
Transactions: A Field Survey Approach"
Journal of Marketing, Vol. 53 (April 1989), pp. 21-35.

Phillips, Lynn W.
"Explaining Control Losses in Corporate Marketing Channels: An
Organizational Analysis"
Journal of Marketing Research, Vol. XIX (November 1982), pp. 525-49.

Phillips, Lynn W., Chang, Dae R., and Buzzell, Robert D.
"Product Quality, Cost Position and Business Performance: A Test of
Some Key Hypotheses"
Journal of Marketing, Vol. 47 (Spring 1983), pp. 26-43.

Punj, Girish N. and Staelin, Richard A.
"A Model of Consumer Information Search Behavior for New Automobiles"
Journal of Consumer Research, Vol.9 (March 1983), pp. 366-80.

Schul, Patrick L. and Babakus, Emin
"An Examination of the Interfirm Power-Conflict Relationship: The
Intervening Role of Channel Decision Structure"
Journal of Retailing, Vol. 64 (Winter 1988), pp. 381-404.

Shimp, Terence A. and Kavas, Alican
"The Theory of Reasoned Action Applied to Coupon Usage"
Journal of Consumer Research, Vol. 11 (December 1984), pp. 795-809.

Skinner, Steven J. and Guiltinan, Joseph P.
"Perceptions of Channel Control"
Journal of Retailing, Vol. 61 (Winter 1985), pp. 65-88.

Sujan, Harish
"Smarter Versus Harder: An Exploratory Attributional Analysis of
Salespeople's Motivation"
Journal of Marketing Research, Vol. XXIII (February 1986), pp. 41-9.

Walters, Rockney G. and MacKenzie, Scott B.
"A Structural Equations Analysis of the Impact of Price Promotions on
Store Performance"
Journal of Marketing Research, Vol XXV (February 1988), pp. 51-63.

Wilkes, Robert E., Burnett, John J., and Howell, Roy D.
"On the Meaning and Measurement of Religiosity in Consumer Research"
Journal of the Academy of Marketing Science, Vol. 14 (Spring 1986),
pp. 47-56.

206.02 ---------- Applications of Causal Analysis of Experiments

Bagozzi, Richard P.
"An Investigation of the Role of Affective and Moral Evaluations in
the Purposeful Behavior Model of Attitude"
British Journal of Social Psychology.

Bagozzi, Richard P., Yi, Youjae, and Baumgartner, Johann
"The Level of Effort Required for Behavior as a Moderator of the
Attitude-Behavior Relation"
University of Michigan (1988), unpublished working paper.

206.03 ---------- Applications of MIMC

Anderson, James C.
"A Measurement Model to Assess Measure-Specific Factors in
Multiple-Informant Research"
Journal of Marketing Research, Vol. XXII (February 1985), pp. 86-92.

Anderson, James C., Gerbing, David W., and Hunter, John E.
"On the Assessment of Unidimensional Measurement: Internal and
External Consistency, and Overall Consistency Criteria"
Journal of Marketing Research, Vol. XXIV (November 1987), pp. 432-7.

John, George and Martin, John
"Effects of Organizational Structure of Marketing Planning on
Credibility and Utilization of Plan Output"
Journal of Marketing Research, Vol. XXI (May 1984), pp. 170-83.

Schul, Patrick L., Little, Taylor E., Jr., and Pride, William M.
"Channel Climate: Its Impact on Channel Members' Satisfaction"
Journal of Retailing, Vol. 61 (Summer 1985), pp. 9-38.

Stapleton, D. D.
   "Analyzing Political Participation Data With a MIMC Model"
   in Sociological Methodology
   (San Francisco: Jossey-Bass, 1978), pp. 52-74.

206.04 ---------- Applications of the Akaike Information Criterion

Kumar, Ajith and Sashi, C. M.
   "Confirmatory Analysis of Aggregate Hierarchical Market Structures:
   Inferences From Brand-Switching Behavior"
   Journal of Marketing Research, Vol. XXVI (November 1989), pp. 444-53.

207 ------------------------ PATH ANALYSIS ------------------------
        See also (sub)heading(s) 204.

207.01 ---------- Books Re: Path Analysis

Asher, H. B.
  Causal Modeling
  (Beverly Hills, CA: Sage Publications, 1976).

Blalock, H. M., Jr.
  Causal Inferences in Nonexperimental Research
  (Chapel Hill, NC: University of North Carolina Press, 1964).

Duncan, Otis Dudley
  Introduction to Structural Equation Models
  (New York: Academic Press, 1975).

207.02 ---------- Theory Re: Path Analysis

Alwin, D. F. and Hauser, R. M.
  "The Decomposition of Effects in Path Analysis"
  American Sociological Review, Vol. 40 (February 1975), pp. 37-47.

Blalock, Hubert M., Jr.
  "Path Coefficients Versus Regression Coefficients"
  American Journal of Sociology, Vol. 72 (1967), pp. 675,6.

Blalock, H. M., Jr.
  "Causal Inference, Closed Populations, and Measures of Association"
  American Political Science Review, Vol. 61 (March 1967), pp. 130-6.

Blalock, H. M., Jr.
  "Correlated Independent Variables: The Problem of Multicollinearity"
  American Journal of Sociology, Vol. 42 (1963), pp. 233-7.

Boyle, R. P.
  "Path Analysis and Ordinal Data"
  American Journal of Sociology, Vol. 75 (January 1973), pp. 461-80.

Christopher, M. G. and Elliott, C. K.
  "Causal Path Analysis in Market Research"
  Journal of the Marketing Research Society, Vol. 12 (April 1970), pp.
  112-24.

Fox, John
  "Effect Analysis in Structural Equation Models II: Calculation of
  Specific Indirect Effects"
  Sociological Methods and Research, Vol. 14 (August 1985), pp. 81-95.

Fox, John
  "Effect Analysis in Structural Equation Models: Extensions and
  Simplified Methods of Computation"
  Sociological Methods and Research, Vol. 9 (August 1980), pp. 3-28.

Goldberger, Arthur S.
  "On Boudon's Method of Linear Causal Analysis"
  American Sociological Review, Vol. 35 (1970), pp. 97-101.

Goodman, Leo A.
  "The Analysis of Multidimensional Contingency Tables When Some
  Variables are Posterior to Others: A Modified Path Analysis Approach"
  Biometrika, Vol. 60 (1973), pp. 179-82.

Hauser, R. M. and Goldberger, A. S.
  "The Treatment of Unobservable Variables in Path Analysis"
  in Cosner, H. L. (editor)
  Sociological Methodology
  (San Francisco: Jossey-Bass, 1971), pp. 81-117.

Heise, David R.
  "Employing Nominal Variables, Induced Variables, and Block Variables
  in Path Analyses"
  Sociological Methods and Research, Vo. 1 (November 1972), pp. 147-74.

Heise, David R.
  "Problems in Path Analysis and Causal Inference"
  in Borgatta, Edgar F. (editor)
  Sociological Methodology 1969
  (San Francisco: Jossey-Bass, 1969).

James, Lawrence R.
  "The Unmeasured Variables Problem in Path Analysis"
  Journal of Applied Psychology, Vol. 65 (August 1980), pp. 415-21.

Kang, K. M. and Seneta, E.
  "Path Analysis: An Exposition"
  in Krishnaiah, P. R. (editor)
  Developments in Statistics, Volume Three, Chapter 4
  (New York: Academic Press, Inc., 1980), pp. 217-46.

Kruskal, Joseph
   "An Elegant New/Old Approach to Estimating Path Models (Structural
   Equation Models) With Unobserved Variables"
   (Murray Hill, NJ: Bell Laboratories, 1980), technical report.

Land, Kenneth C.
   "Identification, Parameter Estimation, and Hypothesis Testing in
   Recursive Sociological Models"
   in Goldberger, Arthur S. and Duncan, Otis Dudley (editors)
   Structural Equation Models in the Social Sciences
   (New York: Seminar Press, 1973), pp. 19-49.

Land, K. C.
   "On the Estimation of Path Coefficients for Unmeasured Variables From
   Correlations Among Observed Variables"
   Social Forces, Vol. 48 (June 1970), pp. 506-11.

Land, K. C.
   "Principles of Path Analysis"
   in Borgatta, E. T. (editor)
   Sociological Methodology 1969
   (San Francisco, CA: Jossey-Bass, 1969), pp. 3-37.

Lohmoller, Jan-Bernd
   "An Overview of Latent Variables Path Analysis"
   Annual Meeting of the American Educational Research Association, New
   York (March 19-23, 1982), paper presentation.

Schuessler, Karl
   "Ratio Variables and Path Models"
   in Goldberger, Arthur S. and Duncan, Otis Dudley (editors)
   Structural Equation Models in the Social Sciences
   (New York: Seminar Press, 1973), pp. 201-8.

Smith, Robert B.
   "Neighborhood Context and College Plans: An Ordinal Path Analysis"
   Social Forces, Vol. 51 (1971), pp. 199-217.

Simon, H. A.
   "Spurious Correlation: A Causal Interpretation"
   Models of Man
   (New York: John Wiley and Sons, Inc., 1957), pp. 37-49.

Somers, Robert H.
   "Analysis of Partial Rank Correlation Measures Based on the
   Product-Moment Model: Part One"
   Social Forces, Vol. 53 (1974), pp. 229-46.

Tukey, J. W.
   "Causation, Regression and Path Analysis"
   in Kempthorne. O., Bancroft, T. A., Gowen, J. W., and Lush, J. L.
   (editors)
   Statistics and Mathematics in Biology
   (Ames, IA: Iowa State College Press, 1954), pp. 35-66.

Turner, Malcolm E. and Stevens, Charles D.
   "The Regression Analysis of Causal Paths"
   Biometrics, Vol. 15 (June 1959), pp. 236-58.

Werts, C. E., Joreskog, K. G., and Linn, R. L.
   "Identification and Estimation in Path Analysis With Unmeasured
   Variables"
   American Journal of Sociology, Vol. 78 (1973), pp. 1469-84.

Werts, Charles E., Linn, Robert L., and Joreskog, Karl G.
   "Estimating the Parameters of Path Models Involving Unmeasured
   Variables"
   in Blalock, H. M. (editor)
   Causal Models in the Social Sciences
   (Chicago: Aldine, 1971), pp. 400-9.

Wilson, T. P.
   "Reply to Somers and Smith"
   Social Forces, Vol. 53 (1974), pp. 247-51.

Wilson, T. P.
   "On Ordinal Path Analysis: Reply to Smith's Neighborhood Context and
   College Plans"
   Social Forces, Vol. 53 (1974), pp. 120-3.

Wright, Sewall
   "Path Coefficients and Path Regressions: Alternatives or
   Complementary Concepts?"
   Biometrics, Vol. 16 (June 1960), pp. 189-202.

Wright, Sewall
   "The Method of Path Coefficients"
   Annals of Mathematical Statistics, Vol. 5 (1934), pp. 161-215.

Wright, S.
"Correlation and Causation"
Journal of Agricultural Research, Vol. 20 (June 1921), pp. 557-85.

Yamagishi, Toshio and Hill, Charles T.
"Adding Versus Averaging Models Revised: A Test of a Path-Analytic
Integration Model"
Journal of Personality and Social Psychology, Vol. 41 (1981), pp.
13-25.

207.03 ---------- Applications of Path Analysis

Anderson, Ronald D., Jerman, Roger E., and Constantin, James A.
"A Causal Analysis of Environment-Reward-Satisfaction Linkages for
the Sales Representative"
Journal of the Academy of Marketing Science, Vol. 7 (Summer 1979),
pp. 154-62.

Bearden, William O. and Shimp, Terence A.
"The Use of Extrinsic Cues to Facilitate Product Adoption"
Journal of Marketing Research, Vol. XIX (May 1982), pp. 229-39.

Bearden, William O. and Teel, Jesse E.
"Selected Determinants of Consumer Satisfaction and Complaint Reports"
Journal of Marketing Research, Vol. XX (February 1983), pp. 21-8.

Bearden, William O., Teel, Jesse E., Jr., and Crockett, M.
"A Path Model of Consumer Complaint Behavior"
1980 Educators' Proceedings
(Chicago: American Marketing Association, 1980), pp. 101-4.

Bedian, Arthur G. and Armenakis, Achilles A.
"A Path-Analytic Study of the Consequences of Role Conflict and
Ambiguity"
Academy of Management Journal, Vol. 24 (June 1981), pp. 417-24.

Behrman, Douglas N. and Perreault, William D., Jr.
"A Role Stress Model of the Performance and Satisfaction of
Industrial Salespersons"
Journal of Marketing, Vol. 48 (Fall 1984), pp. 9-21.

Churchill, Gilbert A., Jr. and Moschis, George P.
"Television and Interpersonal Influences on Adolescent Consumer
Learning"
Journal of Consumer Research, Vol. 6 (June 1979), pp. 23-35.

Cronin, J. Joseph, Jr. and Page, Thomas J., Jr.
"An Examination of the Relative Impact of Growth Strategies on Profit
Performance"
European Journal of Marketing, Vol. 22, No. 1 (1988), pp. 57-68.

Cronin, J. Joseph, Jr. and Skinner, Steven J.
"Marketing Outcomes, Financial Conditions, and Retail Profit
Performance"
Journal of Retailing, Vol. 60 (Winter 1984), pp. 9-22.

Crosby, Lawrence A. and Taylor, James R.
"Psychological Commitment and Its Effects on Post-Decision Evaluation
and Preference Stability Among Voters"
Journal of Consumer Research, Vol. 9 (March 1983), pp. 413-31.

Cummings, W. Theodore, Jackson, Donald W., Jr., and Ostrom, Lonnie L.
"Examining Product Managers' Job Satisfaction and Performance Using
Selected Organizational Behavior Variables"
Journal of the Academy of Markeing Science, Vol. 17 (Spring 1989),
pp. 147-56.

Deighton, John, Romer, Daniel, and McQueen, Josh
"Using Drama to Persuade"
Journal of Consumer Research, Vol. 16 (December 1989), pp. 335-43.

Deshpande, Rohit and Zaltman, Gerald
"A Comparison of Factors Affecting Research and Manager Perceptions
of Market Research Use"
Journal of Marketing Research, Vol. XXI (February 1984), pp. 32-8.

Deshpande, Rohit and Zaltman, Gerald
"Factors Affecting the Use of Market Research Information: A Path
Analysis"
Journal of Marketing Research, Vol. XIX (February 1982), pp. 14-31.

Dubinsky, Alan J. and Hartley, Steven W.
"A Path-Analytic Study of a Model of Salesperson Performance"
Journal of the Academy of Marketing Science, Vol. 14 (Spring 1986),
pp. 36-46.

Dubinsky, Alan J. and Skinner, Steven J.
"Impact of Job Characteristics on Retail Salespeople's Reactions to
Their Jobs"
Journal of Retailing, Vol. 60 (Summer 1984), pp. 35-62.

Duncan, O. D.
"Path Analysis: Sociological Examples"
American Journal of Sociology, Vol 72 (July 1966), pp. 1-16.

Folkes, Valerie S., Koletsky, Susan, and Graham, John L.
"A Field Study of Causal Inferences and Consumer Reaction: The View
From the Airport"
Journal of Consumer Research, Vol. 13 (March 1987), pp. 534-9.

Hampton, Ron, Dubinsky, Alan J., and Skinner, Steven J.
"A Model of Sales Supervisor Leadership Behavior and Retail
Salespeople's Job-Related Outcomes"
Journal of the Academy of Marketing Science, Vol. 14 (Fall 1986), pp.
33-43.

Harrell, Gilbert D., Hutt, Michael D., and Anderson, James C.
"Path Analysis of Buyer Behavior Under Conditions of Crowding"
Journal of Marketing Research, Vol. XVII (February 1980), pp. 45-51.

Hill, Ronald Paul and Ward, James C.
"Mood Manipulation in Marketing Research: An Examination of Potential
Confounding Effects"
Journal of Marketing Research, Vol. XXVI (February 1989), pp. 97-104.

Holbrook, Morris B.
"Integrating Compositional and Decompositional Analyses to Represent
the Intervening Role of Perceptions in Evaluative Judgments"
Journal of Marketing Research, Vol. XVIII (February 1981), pp. 13-28.

Holbrook, Morris
"Beyond Attitude Structure: Toward the Informational Determinants of
Attitude"
Journal of Marketing Research, Vol. XV (November 1978), pp. 546-56.

Holbrook, Morris B. and Batra, Rajeev
"Assessing the Role of Emotions as Mediators of Consumer Responses to
Advertising"
Journal of Consumer Research, Vol. 14 (December 1987), pp. 404-20.

Johansson, J. K. and Redinger, Robert
"Evaluating Advertising by Path Analysis"
Journal of Advertising Research, Vol. 19 (February 1979), pp. 29-35.

Kutschker, Michael
"The Multi-Organizational Interaction Approach to Industrial
Marketing"
Journal of Business Research, Vol. 13 (October 1985), pp. 383-403.

LaBarbera, Priscilla A. and Mazursky, David
"A Longitudinal Assessment of Consumer Satisfaction/Dissatisfaction:
The Dynamic Aspect of the Cognitive Process"
Journal of Marketing Research, Vol. XX (November 1983), pp. 393-404.

Lundstrom, William J., Kerin, Roger A., and Sciglimpaglia, Donald
"A Path Analytic Comparison of Three Causal Models Contributing to
the State of Consumer Discontent"
in Beckwith, Neil et al. (editors)
Proceedings, Educators' Conference
(Chicago: American Marketing Association, 1979), pp. 235-8.

Michaels, Ronald E., Cron, William L., Dubinsky, Alan J., and
Joachimsthaler, Erich A.
"Influence of Formalization on the Organizational Commitment and Work
Alienation of Salespeople and Industrial Buyers"
Journal of Marketing Research, Vol. XXV (November 1988), pp. 376-83.

Moore, Roy L. and Stephens, Lowndes F.
"Some Communication and Demographic Determinants of Adolescent
Consumer Learning"
Journal of Consumer Research, Vol. 2 (September 1975), pp. 80-92.

Nelson, James E., Duncan, Calvin P., and Frontczak, Nancy T.
"The Distraction Hypothesis and Radio Advertising"
Journal of Marketing, Vol. 49 (Winter 1985), pp. 60-71.

Oliver, Richard L.
"A Cognitive Model of the Antecedents and Consequences of
Satisfaction Decisions"
Journal of Marketing Research, Vol. XVII (November 1980), pp. 460-90.

Oliver, Richard L. and Berger, Philip K.
"A Path Analysis of Preventive Health Care Decision Models"
Journal of Consumer Research, Vol. 6 (September 1979), pp. 113-22.

Pavelchak, Mark A., Antil, John H., and Munch, James M.
   "The Super Bowl: An Investigation Into the Relationship Among Program
   Context, Emotional Experience, and Ad Recall"
   Journal of Consumer Research, Vol. 15 (December 1988), pp. 360-7.

Piercy, Nigel F.
   "The Power and Politics of Sales Forecasting: Uncertainty Absorption
   and the Power of the Marketing Department"
   Journal of the Academy of Marketing Science, Vol. 17 (Spring 1989),
   pp. 109-20.

Schmitt, Neal
   "Path Analysis of Multitrait-Multimethod Matrices"
   Applied Psychological Measurement, Vol. 2 (Spring 1978), pp. 157-73.

Schul, Patrick L.
   "An Investigation of Path-Goal Leadership Theory and Its Impact on
   Intrachannel Conflict and Satisfaction"
   Journal of the Academy of Marketing Science, Vol. 15 (Winter 1987),
   pp. 42-52.

Schulz, Richard M., Bigoness, William J., and Gagnon, Jean Paul
   "Research Note: Determinants of Turnover Intentions Among Retail
   Pharmacists"
   Journal of Retailing, Vol. 63 (Spring 1987), pp. 89-98.

Sims, Henry P., Jr. and Szilogyi, Andrew D.
   "Leader Structure and Subordinate Satisfaction for Two Hospital
   Administrative Levels: A Path Analysis Approach"
   Journal of Applied Psychology, Vol. 60 (April 1975), pp. 194-7.

Sirgy, M. Joseph and Samli, A. Coskun
   "A Path Analytic Model of Store Loyalty Involving Self-Concept, Store
   Image, Geographic Loyalty, and Socioeconomic Status"
   Journal of the Academy of Marketing Science, Vol. 13 (Summer 1985),
   pp. 265-91.

Solomon, Michael R. and Douglas, Susan P.
   "Diversity in Product Symbolism: The Case of Female Executive
   Clothing"
   Psychology and Marketing, Vol. 4 (Fall 1987), pp. 189-212.

Teas, R. Kenneth
   "Supervisory Behavior, Role Stress, and the Job Satisfaction of
   Industrial Salespeople"
   Journal of Marketing Research, Vol. XX (February 1983), pp. 84-91.

Teas, R. Kenneth, Wacker, John G., and Hughes, R. Eugene
   "A Path Analysis of Causes and Consequences of Salespeople's
   Perceptions of Role Clarity"
   Journal of Marketing Research, Vol. XVI (August 1979), pp. 355-69.

Tse, David K. and Wilton, Peter C.
   "Models of Consumer Satisfaction Formation: An Extension"
   Journal of Marketing Research, Vol. XXV (May 1988), pp. 204-12.

Ursic, Michael L.
   "A Model of the Consumer Decision to Seek Legal Redress"
   Journal of Consumer Affairs, Vol. 19 (Summer 1985), pp. 20-36.

Warriner, G. Keith
   "Electricity Consumption by the Elderly: Policy Implications"
   Journal of Consumer Research, Vol. 8 (December 1981), pp. 258-64.

207.04 ---------- Computer Programs for Path Analysis

Hunter, J. E. and Hunter, R. F.
   "PATHPAC: A Program for Path Analysis for Recursive Systems Using
   Either Given Path Coefficients or Using Calculated OLS Path
   Coefficients From Given Causal Influence Indicators or Using Path
   Coefficients Calculated From Given Causal Indicators by a New
   Procrustes Least Squares Method"
   (Michigan State University, 1977).

Lohmoller, Jan-Bernd
   LVPLS 1.6: Latent Variables Path Analysis With Partial Least-Squares
   Estimation"
   University of the Federal Armed Forces, Munich, Federal Republic of
   Germany (1981).

208 ----------------------- PARTIAL LEAST SQUARES ----------------------

208.01 ---------- Books Re: Partial Least Squares

Joreskog, Karl G. and Wold, Herman A. (editors)
    Systems Under Indirect Observation: Causality, Structure, Prediction
    (Amsterdam: North Holland, 1981).

Wold, Herman A. (editor)
    The Fixed Point Approach to Interdependent Systems
    (Amsterdam: North-Holland, 1981).

208.02 ---------- Theory Re: Partial Least Squares

Agren, A.
    Extensions of the Fixed-Point Method
    Department of Statistics, University of Uppsala, Sweden (1972),
    published doctoral dissertation.

Areskoug, B.
    "Some Asymptotic Properties of PLS Estimators and a Simulation Study
    for Comparisons Between LISREL and PLS"
    in Joreskog, K. G. and Wold, H. A. (editors)
    Systems Under Indirect Observation: Causality, Structure, Prediction
    (Amsterdam: North Holland, 1981).

Areskoug, B., Wold, Herman A., and Lyttkens, E.
    "Six Models With Two Blocks of Observables as Indicators for One or
    Two Latent Variables"
    Research Report No. 6
    Department of Statistics, University of Goteborg, Sweden (1975).

Barclay, Donald
    "Jackknifing in PLS"
    University of Michigan (1983), working paper.

Bergstrom, R.
    "An Investigation of the Reduced Fixed-Point Method"
    Department of Statistics, University of Uppsala, Sweden (1972),
    seminar paper.

Bodin, L.
    Recursive Fixed-Point Estimation: Theory and Application
    Department of Statistics, University of Uppsala, Sweden (1974),
    published doctoral dissertation.

Bookstein, Fred L.
    "The Geometric Meaning of Soft Modeling With Some Generalizations"
    in Joreskog, K. G. and Wold, H. A. (editors)
    Systems Under Indirect Observation: Causality, Structure, Prediction
    (Amsterdam: North Holland, 1981), pp. 2:55-74.

Bookstein, Fred L.
    "Data Analysis by Partial Least Squares"
    in Kmenta, J. and Ramsey, J. B. (editors)
    Evaluation of Econometric Models
    (New York: Academic Press, 1980), pp. 75-90.

Carroll, J. Douglas, Pruzansky, Sandra, and Kruskal, Joseph
    "CANDELINC: A General Approach to Multidimensional Analysis of
    Many-Way Arrays With Linear Constraints on Parameters"
    Psychometrika, Vol. 45 (1980), pp. 3-24.

Dupacova, Jitka and Wold, Herman A.
    "NIPALS vs. Maximum Likelihood Modelling"
    Research Report 1975:5
    Department of Statistics, University of Goteburg (1975).

Fornell, Claes and Bookstein, Fred L.
    "Two Structural Equation Models: LISREL and PLS Applied to Consumer
    Exit-Voice Theory"
    Journal of Marketing Research, Vol. XIX (November 1982), pp. 440-52.

Fornell, Claes and Bookstein, Fred L.
    "A Comparative Analysis of Two Structural Equation Models: LISREL and
    PLS Applied to Market Data"
    in Fornell, C. (editor)
    A Second Generation of Multivariate Analysis: Methods, Volume I
    (New York: Praeger, 1982).

Hui, B. S.
    "The Partial Least Squares Approach to Path Models of Indirectly
    Observed Variables With Multiple Indicators"
    University of Pennsylvania (1978), unpublished doctoral thesis.

Jagpal, Harsharanjeet S.
    "Multicollinearity in Structural Equation Models With Unobservable
    Variables"
    Journal of Marketing Research, Vol. XIX (November 1982), pp. 431-9.

Lyttkens, E.
  "The Fixed-Point Method for Estimating Interdependent Systems With
  the Underlying Model Specification"
  Journal of the Royal Statistical Society, Vol. A136 (1973), pp.
  353-94.

Lyttkens, E.
  "On the Fixed-Point Property of Wold's Iterative Estimation Method
  for Principal Components"
  in Krishnaiah, P. R. (editor)
  Multivariate Analysis
  (New York: Academic Press, 1968), pp. 335-50.

Wold, Herman
  "Systems Under Indirect Observation Using PLS"
  in Fornell, C. (editor)
  A Second Generation of Multivariate Analysis: Methods, Volume I
  (New York: Praeger, 1982).

Wold, Herman A.
  "Soft Modelling: Intermediate Between Traditional Model Building and
  Data Analysis"
  Mathematical Statistics, Vol. 6 (1980), pp. 333-46.

Wold, Herman A.
  "Model Construction and Evaluation When Theoretical Knowledge is
  Scarce--Theory and Application of Partial Least Squares"
  in Kmenta, J. and Ramsey, J. G. (editors)
  Evaluation of Econometric Models
  (New York: Academic Press, 1980), pp. 47-74.

Wold, Herman A.
  "Estimation and Evaluation of Models Where Theoretical Knowledge is
  Scarce: An Example of Partial Least Squares"
  in Ramsey, J. and Kmenta, J. (editors)
  Evaluation of Econometric Models
  (New York: Academic Press, 1979).

Wold, Herman A.
  "Path Models With Latent Variables: The NIPALS Approach"
  in Blalock, et al. (editors)
  Quantitative Sociology: International Perspectives on Mathematical
  and Statistical Model Building
  (New York: Academic Press, 1975), pp. 307-57.

Wold, Herman A.
  "Causal Flows With Latent Variables: Partings of the Ways in the
  Light of NIPALS Modeling"
  European Economic Review, Vol. 5 (1974), pp. 67-86.

Wold, Herman A.
  "A Fixed-Point Theorem With Econometric Background, I-II"
  Arkiv for Matematik, Vol. 6 (1965), pp. 209-40.

Wold, Herman A.
  "Toward a Verdict on Macroeconomic Simultaneous Equations"
  in Salviucci, P. (editor)
  Semaine d'etude sur le role de l'analyse econometrique dans la
  formulation des plans de development
  Scripta Varia 28
  (Vatican City: Pontifical Academy of Science, 1963).

208.03 ---------- Theory Re: Evaluation of Partial Least Squares Models

De Pijper, W. M. and Saris, W. E.
  "The Effect of Identification Restriction on the Test Statistic in
  Latent Variable Models"
  in Joreskog, Karl G. and Wold, Herman A. (editors)
  Systems Under Indirect Observation: Causality, Structure, Prediction
  (Amsterdam: North Holland, 1981).

Geisser, S.
  "A Predictive Approach to the Random Effect Model"
  Biometrika, Vol. 61 (1974), pp. 101-7.

Miller, John K.
  "The Sampling Distribution and a Test for Significance of the
  Bimultivariate Redundancy Statistic: A Monte Carlo Study"
  Multivariate Behavioral Research (April 1975), pp. 233-44.

Stone, M.
  "Cross-Validatory Choice and Assessment of Statistical Predictions"
  Journal of the Royal Statistical Society, Vol. B36 (1974), pp. 111-33.

208.04 ---------- Applications of Partial Least Squares

Apel, H.
  Simulation sozio-okonomischer Zusammanhange-Kritik and Modification
  von Systems Analysis
  J. W. von Goethe University, Frankfurt-am-Main, Germany (1977),
  doctoral dissertation.

Fornell, Claes and Robinson, William T.
  "Industrial Organization and Consumer Satisfaction/Dissatisfaction"
  Journal of Consumer Research, Vol. 9 (March 1983), pp. 403-12.

Fornell, Claes, Tellis, Gerard, and Zinkhan, George
  "Validity Assessment: A Structural Equation Approach Using Partial
  Least Squares"
  in Walker, B. et al. (editors)
  An Assessment of Marketing Thoughts and Practice
  (Chicago: American Marketing Association, 1982), pp. 405-9.

Jagpal, Harsharanjeet S.
  "Measuring Joint Advertising Effects in Multiproduct Firms"
  Journal of Advertising Research, Vol. 21, No. 1 (1981), pp. 65-9.

Johnson, Michael D. and Fornell, Claes
  "The Nature and Methodological Implications of the Cognitive
  Representation of Products"
  Journal of Consumer Research, Vol. 14 (September 1987), pp. 214-28.

Kowalski, B. R., Gergerlach, R. W., and Wold, Herman A.
  "Chemical Systems Under Indirect Observation"
  in Joreskog, K. G. and Wold, H. A. (editors)
  Systems Under Indirect Observation: Causality, Structure, Prediction
  (Amsterdam: North Holland, 1981).

Meissner, W. and Uhle-Fassing, M.
  "PLS--Modeling and Estimation of Politimetric Models"
  in Joreskog, K. G. and Wold, H. A. (editors)
  Systems Under Indirect Observation: Causality, Structure, Prediction
  (Amsterdam: North Holland, 1981).

Noonan, Richard
  "School Environments and School Outcomes: An Empirical Comparative
  Study Using IEA Data"
  Working Paper Series No. 26
  Institute of International Education, University of Stockholm, Sweden
  (1980).

Noonan, Richard and Wold, Herman A.
  "PLS Path Modeling With Latent Variables: Analyzing School Survey
  Data Using Partial Least Squares--Part II"
  Scandinavian Journal of Educational Research, Vol. 24 (1980), pp.
  1-24.

Noonan, Richard and Wold, Herman A.
  "NIPALS Path Modelling With Latent Variables: Analyzing School Survey
  Data Using Nonlinear Iterative Partial Least Squares"
  Scandinavian Journal of Educational Research, Vol. 21 (1977), pp.
  33-61.

Qualls, William J.
  "Household Decision Behavior: The Impact of Husbands' and Wives' Sex
  Role Orientation"
  Journal of Consumer Research, Vol. 14 (September 1987), pp. 264-79.

Wold, Herman A.
  "Factors Influencing the Outcome of Economic Sanctions: An
  Application of Soft Modelling"
  Fourth World Congress of the Econometric Society, Aix-en-Provence,
  France (1980), paper presentation.

208.05 ---------- Computer Programs for Partial Least Squares

Lohmoller, Jan-Bernd
  LVPLS 1.6: Latent Variables Path Analysis With Partial Least-Squares
  Estimation"
  University of the Federal Armed Forces, Munich, Federal Republic of
  Germany (1981).

208.06 ---------- Unclassified (Partial Least Squares)

Christensen, L. R., Jorgenson, D. W., and Lau, L. J.
  "Transcendental Logarithmic Production Frontiers"
  Review of Economics and Statistics, Vol. 55 (February 1973), pp.
  28-45.

Rothenberg, T. J.
  "Identification in Parametric Models"
  Econometrica, Vol. 39 (1971), pp. 577-91.

209 -------------- COMPARISONS OF ANALYTICAL TECHNIQUES --------------

See also (sub)heading(s) 131.

Aaker, David A. and Bagozzi, Richard P.
"Unobservable Variables in Structural Equation Models With an Application in Industrial Selling"
Journal of Marketing Research, Vol. XVI (May 1979), pp. 147-58.

Armstrong, J. S. and Andress, J. G.
"Exploratory Analysis of Marketing Data: Trees Versus Regression"
Journal of Marketing Research, Vol. VII (November 1970), pp. 487-92.

Arnold, S. J., Roth, V., and Tigert, D. J.
"Conditional Logit Versus MDA in the Prediction of Store Choice"
Advances in Consumer Research, Vol. 8 (1980), pp. 665-70.

Babakus, Emin and Ferguson, Carl E., Jr.
"On Choosing the Appropriate Measure of Association When Analyzing Rating Scale Data"
Journal of the Academy of Marketing Science, Vol. 16 (Spring 1988), pp. 95-102.

Bajgier, Steve M. and Hill, Arthur V.
"An Experimental Comparison of Statistical and Linear Programming Approaches to the Discriminant Problem"
Decision Sciences, Vol. 13 (October 1982), pp. 604-18.

Bass, Frank M., Tigert, Douglas J., and Lonsdale, Ronald T.
"Market Segmentation: Group Versus Individual Behavior"
Journal of Marketing Research, Vol. V (August 1968), pp. 264-70.

Blalock, Hubert M., Jr.
"Path Coefficients Versus Regression Coefficients"
American Journal of Sociology, Vol. 72 (1967), pp. 675,6.

Blattberg, Robert C. and Dolan, Robert J.
"An Assessment of the Contribution of Log Linear Models to Marketing Research"
Journal of Marketing, Vol. 45 (Spring 1981), pp. 89-97.

Cattin, Philippe and Bliemel, Friedhelm
"Metric vs. Nonmetric Procedures for Multiattribute Modeling: Some Simulation Results"
Decision Sciences, Vol. 9 (July 1978), pp. 472-80.

Cattin, Philippe and Wittink, Dick R.
"A Monte Carlo Study of Metric and Nonmetric Estimation Methods for Multiattribute Models"
Research Paper No. 341
Graduate School of Business, Stanford University (1976).

Costner, H. L. and O'Shea, R. M.
"The Multivariate Analysis of Dichotomized Variables"
American Journal of Sociology, Vol. 70 (January 1965), pp. 455-66.

Crocker, Douglas C.
"Comments on 'Exploratory Analysis of Marketing Data: Trees vs. Regression'"
Journal of Marketing Research, Vol. VIII (November 1971), pp. 509-13.

Currim, Imran S.
"Predictive Testing of Consumer Choice Models Not Subject to Independence of Irrelevant Alternatives"
Journal of Marketing Research, Vol. XIX (May 1982), pp. 208-22.

Darden, William R.
"Comparison of Canonical Correlation and Discriminant Analysis: A Business Research Example"
Journal of Business Administration, Vol. 6 (Fall 1974), pp. 1-15.

Dillon, William R., Goldstein, Matthew, and Lement, Lucy
"Analyzing Qualitative Predictors With Too Few Data: An Alternative Approach to Handling Sparse-Cell Values"
Journal of Marketing Research, Vol. XVIII (February 1981), pp. 63-72.

Dillon, William R., Goldstein, Matthew, and Schiffman, Leon G.
"Appropriateness of Linear Discriminant and Multinomial Classification Analysis in Marketing Research"
Journal of Marketing Research, Vol. XV (February 1978), pp. 103-12.

Englund, D., Hundt, F., and Lee, Y.
"An Empirical Comparison of Factor Analysis and Discriminant Analysis for Non-Work Trips in Evanston"
Transportation Center, Northwestern University (August 1978), technical report.

Fidler, Eduard J. and Thompson, Gerald L.
"An Experiment on Executive Decision Making"
Management Science Research Report No. 407
Graduate School of Industrial Administration, Carnegie-Mellon
University (1977).

Foote, Richard J.
"A Comparison of Single and Simultaneous Equation Techniques"
Journal of Farm Economics (December 1955), pp. 975-90.

Fornell, Claes and Bookstein, Fred L.
"Two Structural Equation Models: LISREL and PLS Applied to Consumer
Exit-Voice Theory"
Journal of Marketing Research, Vol. XIX (November 1982), pp. 440-52.

Fornell, Claes and Bookstein, Fred L.
"A Comparative Analysis of Two Structural Equation Models: LISREL and
PLS Applied to Market Data"
in Fornell, C. (editor)
A Second Generation of Multivariate Analysis: Methods, Volume I
(New York: Praeger, 1982).

Gensch, Dennis H. and Recker, Wilfred W.
"The Multinomial, Multiattribute LOGIT Choice Model"
Journal of Marketing Research, Vol. XVI (February 1979), pp. 124-32.

Gregoire, T. G. and Driver, B. L.
"Analysis of Ordinal Data to Detect Population Differences"
Psychological Bulletin, Vol. 101 (January 1987), pp. 159-65.

Gullahorn, Jeanne E.
"Multivariate Approaches in Survey Data Processing: Comparisons of
Factor, Cluster, and Guttman Analyses and of Multiple Regression and
Canonical Correlation Methods"
Society of Multivariate Experimental Psychology (1967), MBR Monograph
No. 67-1, pp. 1-73.

Gunst, R. F.
"Similarities Among Least Squares, Principal Component, and Latent
Root Estimators"
1979 Conference of the American Statistical Association, Washington,
DC, paper presentation.

Gunst, R. F., Webster, J. T., and Mason, R. L.
"A Comparison of Least Squares and Latent Root Regression Estimators"
Technometrics, Vol. 18 (February 1976), pp. 75-86.

Hauser, John R. and Koppelman, Frank S.
"Alternative Perceptual Mapping Techniques: Relative Accuracy and
Usefulness"
Journal of Marketing Research, Vol. XVI (November 1979), pp. 495-506.

Hauser, John R. and Shugan, Steven M.
"Efficient Measurement of Consumer Preference Functions: A General
Theory for Intensity of Preference"
Working Paper 602-001
Graduate School of Management, Northwestern University (1977).

Hauser, John R. and Urban, Glen L.
"A Normative Methodology for Modeling Consumer Response to Innovation"
Operations Research, Vol. 25 (1977), pp. 579-619.

Hooley, G. J.
"Perceptual Mapping for Product Positioning: A Comparison of Two
Approaches"
European Research, Vol. 7 (January 1979), pp. 17-23,40.

Huber, Joel and Holbrook, Morris B.
"Using Attribute Ratings for Product Positioning: Some Distinctions
Among Compositional Approaches"
Journal of Marketing Research, Vol. XVI (November 1979), pp, 507-16.

Hummel, Thomas J. and Sligo, Joseph R.
"Empirical Comparison of Univariate and Multivariate Analysis of
Variance Procedures"
Psychological Bulletin, Vol. 76 (July 1971), pp. 49-57.

Jacobson, Alvin L. and Lalu, N. M.
"An Empirical and Algebraic Analysis of Alternative Techniques for
Measuring Unobserved Variables"
in Blalock, Hubert M., Jr. (editor)
Measurement in the Social Sciences
(Chicago: Aldine, 1974), pp. 215-42.

Jagpal, Harsharanjeet S.
"Multicollinearity in Structural Equation Models With Unobservable
Variables"
Journal of Marketing Research, Vol. XIX (November 1982), pp. 431-9.

Jain, Arun K., Acito, Franklin, Malhotra, Naresh K., and Mahajan, Vijay
    "A Comparison of the Internal Validity of Alternative Parameter
    Estimation Methods in Decompositional Multiattribute Preference
    Models"
    Journal of Marketing Research, Vol. XVI (August 1979), pp. 313-22.

Lehmann, Donald R.
    "Some Alternatives to Linear Factor Analysis for Variable Grouping
    Applied to Buyer Behavior Variables"
    Journal of Marketing Research, Vol. XI (May 1974), pp. 206-13.

Lessig, V. Parker
    "Comparing Cluster Analyses With Cophenic Correlation"
    Journal of Marketing Research, Vol. IX (February 1972), pp. 82-4.

Louviere, Jordan J. and Woodworth, George
    "Design and Analysis of Simulated Consumer Choice or Allocation
    Experiments: An Approach Based on Aggregate Data"
    Journal of Marketing Research, Vol. XX (November 1983), pp. 350-67.

Malhotra, Naresh K.
    "A Comparision of the Predictive Validity of Procedures for Analyzing
    Binary Data"
    Journal of Business and Economic Statistics, Vol. 1 (October 1983),
    pp. 326-36.

Margolin, B. H. and Light, R. J.
    "Analysis of Variance for Categorical Data, II: Small Sample
    Comparisons With Chi-Square and Other Competitors"
    Journal of the American Statistical Association, Vol. 69 (September
    1974), pp. 755-64.

Massy, W. F.
    "Principal Components Regression in Exploratory Statistical Research"
    Journal of the American Statistical Association, Vol. 60 (March
    1965), pp. 234-56.

McCullough, James M.
    "Identification of Preference Through Conjoint Measurement: A
    Comparison of Data Collection and Analytical Procedures"
    College of Business Administration, University of Arizona (1978),
    working paper.

McKeon, James J.
    "Canonical Analysis: Some Relations Between Canonical Correlation,
    Factor Analysis, Discriminant Function Analysis, and Scaling Theory"
    Psychometric Monographs, No. 13 (1966).

Melnick, E. L. and Shoaf, F. R.
    "Multiple Regression Equals Analysis of Variance"
    Journal of Advertising Research, Vol. 17 (June 1977), pp. 27-31.

Montgomery, David B., Wittink, Dick R., and Glaze, Thomas
    "A Predictive Test of Individual Level Concept Evaluation and
    Trade-Off Analysis"
    Research Paper No. 415
    Graduate School of Business, Stanford University (1977).

Moore, William L.
    "Levels of Aggregation in Conjoint Analysis: An Empirical Comparison"
    Journal of Marketing Research, Vol. XVII (November 1980), pp. 516-23.

Neidell, Lester A. and Teach, Richard D.
    "Measuring Bank Images: A Comparison of Two Approaches"
    Journal of the Academy of Marketing Science, Vol. 2 (Spring 1974),
    pp. 374-90.

O'Malley, P. M.
    "An Empirical Comparison of MNA and MDF"
    Department of Psychology, University of Michigan (1972), unpublished
    paper.

Pekelman, Dov and Sen, Subrata K.
    "Measurement and Estimation of Conjoint Utility Functions"
    Journal of Consumer Research, Vol. 5 (March 1979), pp. 263-71.

Pekelman, D. and Sen, S.
    "Regression Versus Interpolation in Additive Conjoint Measurement"
    Proceedings, Association for Consumer Research (1976), pp. 29-34.

Perreault, William D., Jr. and Barksdale, Hiram C., Jr.
    "A Model-Free Approach for Analysis of Complex Contingency Data in
    Survey Research"
    Journal of Marketing Research, Vol. XVII (November 1980), pp. 503-15.

Platt, John R.
    "Strong Inference"
    Science, Vol. 146 (October 1964), pp. 347-53.

Ragland, Robert E.
"On Some Relations Between Canonical Correlation, Multiple
Regression, and Factor Analysis"
University of Oklahoma (1967), unpublished doctoral dissertation.

Rao, Vithala R. and Solgaard, Hans S.
"A Comparison of Qualitative Response Models of Consumer Choice"
in Bellenger, Dennis and Greenberg, Barnett (editors)
Proceedings of the 1977 AMA Educators' Conference
(Chicago: American Marketing Association, August 1977).

Rao, Vithala R. and Solgaard, Hans S.
"An Empirical Evaluation of Alternative Multiattribute Utility Models"
Graduate School of Business and Public Administration, Cornell
University (1977), working paper.

Roscoe, A. Marvin, Sheth, Jagdish N., and Howell, Welling
"Intertechnique Cross Validation in Cluster Analysis"
Working Paper No. 175
University of Illinois (1974).

Rulon, P. J.
"Distinctions Between Discriminant and Regression Analysis and a
Geometric Interpretation of the Discriminant Function"
Harvard Educational Review, Vol. 21 (June 1951), pp. 80-90.

Sampson, Peter
"The Selection of Cluster Defining Variables--Comment"
Journal of the Market Research Society, Vol. 16 (October 1974), pp.
303,4.

Saporta, G.
"About Some Remarkable Properties of Generalized Canonical Analysis"
Second European Meeting of the Psychometric Society
Groningen, The Netherlands (June 1980), paper presentation.

Schaninger, Charles M., Lessig, V. Parker, and Panton, Don B.
"The Complementary Use of Multivariate Procedures to Investigate
Nonlinear and Interactive Relationships Between Personality and
Product Usage"
Journal of Marketing Research, Vol. XVII (February 1980), pp. 119-24.

Slovic, Paul and Lichtenstein, Sarah B.
"Comparison of Bayesian and Regression Approaches to the Study of
Information Processing in Judgment"
Organizational Behavior and Human Performance, Vol. 6 (November
1971), pp. 649-744.

Srinivasan, V.
"A Theoretical Comparison of the Predictive Power of the Multiple
Regression and Equal Weighting Procedures"
Research Paper No. 347
Graduate School of Business, Stanford University (1977).

Tisdale, J. R.
"Assessing Qualitative Differences Between Sets of Data"
Journal of Psychology, Vol. 66 (July 1967), pp. 175-9.

Tryon, Robert C.
"General Dimensions of Individual Differences: Cluster Analysis
Versus Factor Analysis"
Educational and Psychological Measurement, Vol. 18 (Autumn 1958), pp.
477-95.

Tucker, L. R.
"Relations Between Multidimensional Scaling and Three-Mode Factor
Analysis"
Psychometrika, Vol. 37 (1972), pp. 3-27.

Tukey, J. W.
"Discussion Emphasizing the Connection Between Analysis of Variance
and Spectrum Analysis"
Technometrics, Vol. 3 (May 1961), pp. 191-220.

Tukey, J. W.
"Causation, Regression and Path Analysis"
in Kempthorne. O., Bancroft, T. A., Gowen, J. W., and Lush, J. L.
(editors)
Statistics and Mathematics in Biology
(Ames, IA: Iowa State College Press, 1954), pp. 35-66.

Van Den Wollenberg, A. L.
"Redundancy Analysis--An Alternative for Canonical Correlation
Analysis"
Psychometrika, Vol. 42 (June 1977), pp. 207-19.

Venkatesh, Alladi and Tankersley, Clint B.
  "Criteria for the Evaluation of Product Managers--An Application of
  Multiple Group Solution"
  Journal of the Academy of Marketing Science, Vol. 6 (Fall 1978), pp.
  344-54.

Werner, J., Wendling, W., and Budde, N.
  "A Comparision of Probit, Logit, and Discriminant and OLS: The
  Physicians' Location Choice Problem"
  Proceedings of Business and Economic Statistics Section, American
  Statistical Association (1978), pp. 631-5.

Willson, E. J.
  "Computational Segmentation in the Context of Multivariate Statistics
  and Survey Analysis"
  Journal of the Market Research Society, Vol. 16 (April 1974), pp.
  108-26.

Wright, Sewall
  "Path Coefficients and Path Regressions: Alternatives or
  Complementary Concepts?"
  Biometrics, Vol. 16 (1970), pp. 189-202.

210 -------- STATISTICAL ANALYSIS SOFTWARE - PERSONAL COMPUTER -------
       See also (sub)heading(s) 131.

210.01 ---------- Books Re: PC Statistical Analysis Software

Einstein, Gilles O. and Nocks, Elaine C.
  Learning to Use SPSS-X
  (Englewood Cliffs, NJ: Prentice-Hall, Inc., 1987).

Woodward, Wayne A., Elliott, Alan C., Gray, Henry L., and Matlock,
  Douglas C.
  Directory of Statistical Microcomputer Software
  (New York: Marcel Dekker, Inc., 1987), 752 pp.

210.02 ---------- Directories and Comprehensive Reviews

Baker, Kenneth G. and Rogers, Robert D.
  "Review and Comparison of Nine Statistical Software Packages for the
  Apple Macintosh PC"
  Journal of Marketing Research, Vol. XXIV (May 1987), pp. 241,4.

Barnett, Arnold
  "Misapplication Reviews: An Introduction"
  Interfaces, Vol. 12 (October 1982), pp. 47-9.

Bloch, Peter H.
  "Five Statistical Packages for IBM PCs: Power, But Hard Disk Not
  Required"
  Journal of Marketing Research, Vol. XXIV (August 1987), pp. 330-5.

Carpenter, James, Deloria, Dennis, and Morganstein, David
  "Statistical Software for Microcomputers: A Comparative Analysis of
  24 Packages"
  BYTE (April 1984), pp. 234-64.

Dekker, Peter and De Grefte, Ignace
  "SPSS/PC-Plus, STATGRAPHICS and the Choice of Software for
  Statistical Analysis"
  European Research, Vol. 14, No. 2 (1986), pp. 60-6.

Nijburg, Danny A.
  "Statistical Programs for the Microcomputer: An Update"
  Marketing and Research Today, Vol. 17 (May 1989), pp. 107-14.

Nijburg, Danny A. and De Grefte, Ignace
  "Microcomputer Programs for Statistical Analysis"
  European Research, Vol. 15 (May 1987), pp. 122-35.

PC Magazine
  "Statistical Analysis--Advanced"
  PC Magazine, Vol. 8, No. 5 (March 14, 1989), pp. 121-62.

PC Magazine
  "Statistical Analysis--Basic"
  PC Magazine, Vol. 8, No. 5 (March 14, 1989), pp. 169-99.

PC Magazine
  "Statistical Analysis--Econometric Modeling"
  PC Magazine, Vol. 8, No. 5 (March 14, 1989), pp. 203-20.

PC Magazine
  "Statistical Analysis--Forecasting"
  PC Magazine, Vol. 8, No. 5 (March 14, 1989), pp. 225-41.

PC Magazine
  "Scientific Graphing"
  PC Magazine, Vol. 8, No. 5 (March 14, 1989), pp. 259-86.

Woodard, Wayne A., Elliott, Alan C., and Gray, Henry L.
  Directory of Statistical Microcomputer Software
  (New York: Marcel Dekker, Inc., 1985), 472 pp.

Young, Clifford E.
  "Eight Statistics Packages for the IBM PC: From Procrustean to
  Flexible"
  Journal of Marketing Research, Vol. XXV (May 1988), pp. 219-25.

210.03 ---------- General Statistical Packages - Personal Computer

Abacus Concepts
  STATVIEW SE plus GRAPHICS
  (Berkeley, CA: Abacus Concepts).

Abacus Concepts
  STATVIEW II, Version 1.03
  (Berkeley, CA: Abacus Concepts).

Abacus Scientific Software
    SUPER STATGRAF
    (Irvine, CA: Abacus Scientific Software).

Analytical Engineering Corporation
    POWERSTAT
    (Toronto, Canada: Analytical Engineering Corporation).

Anderson-Bell Corporation
    ABstat, Version 5.10
    (Parker, CO: Anderson-Bell Corp.).

Aptech Systems
    GAUSS 1.49b
    (Seattle, WA: Aptech Systems).

BASS Institute, Incorporated
    The BASS System, Version 88.10
    (Chapel Hill, NC: BASS Institute, Inc.).

B B and A, Incorporated
    ABtab, Release 3.01
    (Canon City, CO: B B and A, Inc., 1985).

BBN Software Products Corporation
    RS/1, Version 12.1
    (Cambridge, MA: BBN Software Products Corp.).

BMDP Statistical Software
    BMDP/PC
    (Los Angeles: BMDP Statistical Software).

BMDP Statistical Software
    BMDP/PC, Version 1988
    (Los Angeles, CA: BMDP Statistical Software).

BrainPower
    StatView 1.0
    (Calabasas, CA: BrainPower).

BrainPower
    Statview 512 plus, 1.1
    (Calabasas, CA: BrainPower).

Computers for Marketing Corporation
    STATPAK: Multivariate Statistics
    (San Francisco, CA: Computers for Marketing Corporation).

Computing Resource Center
    Stata, Version 2.0
    (Los Angeles, CA: Computing Resource Center).

Conceptual Software, Incorporated
    Prodas (Professional Database Analysis System)
    (Houston, TX: Conceptual Software, Inc.).

Crunch Software Corporation
    Crunch Statistical Package, Version 3.1
    (Oakland, CA: Crunch Software Corporation).

Dubin/Rivers Research
    SST
    (Pasadena, CA: Dubin/Rivers Research).

Ecosoft, Incorporated
    Microstat II, Version 1.5
    (Indianapolis, IN: Ecosoft, Inc.).

Futures Group, The
    StatPlan III, Version 1.40
    (Glastonbury, CT: The Futures Group).

Human Systems Dynamics
    PC ANOVA, Version 1.0
    (Northridge, CA: Human Systems Dynamics).

Human Systems Dynamics
    PC Statistician, Version 1.1
    (Northridge, CA: Human Systems Dynamics).

LaPlaca, Peter J.
    MARKSTAT, Program for Basic Analysis of Marketing Research Data
    (Storrs, CT: Peter J. LaPlaca and The Futures Group, 1985), 139 pp.

Lillien, David
    MICRO-TSP, Version 5.0
    (Hightstown, NJ: McGraw-Hill, College Division).

Ming Telecomputing
  Y-STAT
  (Lincoln Center, MA: Ming Telecomputing).

Minitab, Incorporated
  Minitab Statistical Software, Version 6.1
  (State College, PA: Minitab, Inc.).

NCSS, Incorporated
  (NCSS (Number Cruncher Statistical Systems), Version 5.01
  (Kaysville, UT: NCSS, Inc.).

NH Analytical Software
  Statistix, Version 2.0
  (Roseville, MN: NH Analytical Software).

NorthWest Analytical, Incorporated
  NWA StatPak, Version 4.1
  (Portland, OR: NorthWest Analytical, Inc.).

Norusis, Marija J.
  SPSS-X Introductory Statistics Guide for Release 3
  (Chicago: SPSS Inc., 1988), 370 pp.

Odesta Corporation
  DATA DESK PROFESSIONAL, Version 2.0, Revision 5
  (Northbrook, IL: Odesta Corporation).

Penton Software, Incorporated
  Statpro, Version 2.0
  (New York: Penton Software, Inc.).

P-Stat, Incorporated
  P-Stat, Version 2.10
  (Princeton, NJ: P-Stat, Inc.).

Samna Corporation
  Decision Graphics, Version 3.1
  (Atlanta, GA: Samnda Corp.).

SAS Institute, Incorporated
  SAS (Statistical Analysis System), Version 6.03
  (Cary, NC: SAS Institute, Inc.).

Scientific Computing Associates
  SCA Statistical System
  (Lisle, IL: Scientific Computing Associates).

Scientific Programs
  Mac.Stat.Pak 1.3
  (Raleigh, NC: Scientific Programs).

Select Micro Systems
  EXSTATIX
  (Yorktown Heights, NY: Select Micro Systems).

Significant Statistics
  Sigstat
  (Provo, UT: Significant Statistics).

Softext Publishing Corporation
  SP-Stat, Version 1.02
  (New York: Softext Publishing Company).

SoftWare Tools
  Stats Tool Kit
  (Boise, ID: SoftWare Tools).

Spring Systems
  Turbo Spring-Stat, Version 2.9
  (Chicago, IL: Spring Systems).

SPSS, Incorporated
  SPSS/PC-Plus, Version 3.0
  (Chicago, IL: SPSS, Inc.).

Statistical Consultants, Incorporated
  STAN, Version II
  (Lexington, KY: Statistical Consultants, Inc., 1984).

StatSoft, Incorporated
  MACSS, Version 1.2
  (Tulsa, OK: StatSoft, Inc.).

StatSoft, Incorporated
  CSS (Complete Statistical System), Version 2.1
  (Tulsa, OK: StatSoft, Inc.).

StatSoft, Incorporated
  StatFast 2, Version 2.0
  (Tulsa, OK: Statsoft, Inc.).

Statware, Incorporated
  Stat 80 Professional Version 2.10
  (Salt Lake City, UT: Statware, Inc.).

Strategy Plus, Incorporated
  Exec-U-Stat, Version 1.4
  (Princeton, NJ: Strategy Plus, Inc.).

STSC, Incorporated
  Statgraphics, Version 3.0
  (Rockville, MD: STSC, Inc.).

Sugar Mill Software Corporation
  Stat 1, Version 3.05
  (Kailua, HI: Sugar Mill Software Corp.).

Systat, Incorporated
  FASTAT, Version 1.1
  (Evanston, IL: Systat, Inc.).

Systat, Incorporated
  Systat, Version 4.0
  (Evanston, IL: Systat, Inc.).

Tesseract Educational Systems
  MacFits 1.1
  (Houston, TX: Tesseract Educational Systems).

Walonick Associates, Incorporated
  StatPac Gold, Version 3.0
  (Minneapolis, MN: Walonick Associates, Inc.).

Winchendon Group
  ELF
  (Alexandria, VA: The Winchendon Group).

211 ------ SPECIALIZED APPLICATIONS SOFTWARE - PERSONAL COMPUTER -----
        See also (sub)heading(s) 131.

211.01 ---------- Experimental Design Software - Personal Computer
        See also (sub)heading(s) 179.

Fisk, Raymond P.
"A Review of Experimental Design Software"
Journal of Marketing Research, Vol. XXV (May 1988), pp. 225-7.

John Wiley and Sons, Incorporated
X-STAT, Version 1.1
(New York: John Wiley and Sons, Inc., 1985), 274 pp.

Joiner Associates, Incorporated
JASS, Version 2.1
(Madison, WI: Joiner Associates, Inc., 1986), 261 pp.

Stat-Ease, Incorporate
DESIGN-EASE, Version 1.1
(Minneapolis, MN: Stat-Ease, Inc., 1986), 108 pp.

Statistical Programs
EXPERIMENTAL DESIGN, Version 1.0
(Houston, TX: Statistical Programs, 1986), 23 pp.

211.02 ---------- Spreadsheet Software - Personal Computer

Abacus Scientific Software
Multifit, Version 2.0
(Irvine, CA: Abacus Scientific Software).

Abacus Scientific Software
Add a Stat, Version 2.0
(Irvine, CA: Abacus Scientific Software).

Intex Solutions, Incorporated
Forecast for 1-2-3, Version 2.1
(Needham, MA: Intex Solutions, Inc.).

Laric, Michael V. and Stiff, Ronald
Lotus 1-2-3 for Marketing and Sales
(Englewood Cliffs, NJ: Prentice-Hall, Inc.), 226 pp.

Laric, Michael V. and Stiff, Ronald
Multiplan for Marketing and Sales
(Englewood Cliffs, NJ: Prentice-Hall, Inc.), 309 pp.

Laric, Michael V. and Stiff, Ronald
Visicalc for Marketing and Sales
(Englewood Cliffs, NJ: Prentice-Hall, Inc.), 216 pp.

Lilien, Gary L.
Marketing Mix Analysis With Lotus 1-2-3
(Palo Alto, CA: The Scientific Press, 1986), 206 pp.

Walonick Associates, Incorporated
Stat-Packets
(Minneapolis, MN: Walonick Associates, Inc.).

211.03 ---------- Econometric Software - Personal Computer

Alphametrics Corporation
PowerStation, Version 1
(Bala Cynwyd, PA: Alphametrics Corp.).

Mikros, Incorporated
ESP (Econometrics Software Package)
(Lexington, MA: Mikros, Inc.).

Odin Research
OTIS, Version 1.2
(Berwyn, PA: Odin Research).

Quantitative Micro Software
Micro TSP, Version 6.0
(Irvine, CA: Quantitative Micro Software).

Scientific Software, Incorporated
Lisrel, Version 7
(Mooresville, IN: Scientific Software, Inc.).

Scientific Software, Incorporated
Prelis, Version 1
(Mooresville, IN: Scientific Software, Inc.).

Sorites Group, Incorporated
  Soritec, Version 6.3
  (Springfield, VA: Sorites Group, Inc.).

211.04 ---------- Forecasting Software - Personal Computer

Automatic Forecasting Systems, Incorporated
  AutoBox Plus, Version 2.0
  (Hatboro, PA: Automatic Forecasting Systems, Inc.).

Automatic Forecasting Systems, Incorporated
  MTS (Multiple Time Series), Version 2.0
  (Hatboro, PA: Automatic Forecasting Systems, Inc.).

Business Forecast Systems, Incorporated
  Forecast Pro, Version 1.10
  (Belmont, MA: Business Forecast Systems, Inc.).

Fleming Software
  Pro-Cast
  (Oakton, VA: Fleming Software).

Intex Solutions, Incorporated
  Forecast for 1-2-3, Version 2.1
  (Needham, MA: Intex Solutions, Inc.).

Levenbach Associates, Incorporated
  Autocast II
  (Morristown, NJ: Levenbach Associates, Inc.).

Scientific Systems, Incorporated
  Forecast Master, Version 2.0
  (Cambridge, MA: Scientific Systems, Inc.).

Smart Software, Incorporated
  SmartForecasts II, Version 2.15
  (Belmont, MA: Smart Software, Inc.).

SPSS Incorporated
  SPSS/PC-Plus TRENDS
  (Chicago: SPSS, Inc.).

TMS Systems, Incorporated
  EASYCASTER
  (Blacksburg, VA: TMS Systems, Inc.).

Walonick Associates, Incorporated
  Forecast Plus, Version 2.1
  (Minneapolis, MN: Walonick Associates, Inc.).

Wiley, James B.
  "Four Time Series Analysis Packages"
  Journal of Marketing Research, Vol. XXVI (February 1989), pp. 129-32.

211.05 ---------- File Transfer Software - Personal Computer

Conceptual Software, Incorporated
  DBMS/COPY Plus, Version 1.2
  (Houston, TX: Conceptual Software, Inc.).

Conceptual Software, Incorporated
  DBMS/COPY, Version 1.2
  (Houston, TX: Conceptual Software, Inc.).

212 -------------- GRAPHING SOFTWARE - PERSONAL COMPUTER -------------
    See also (sub)heading(s) 135.

212.01 ---------- Directories and Comprehensive Reviews

PC Magazine
  "Scientific Graphing"
  PC Magazine, Vol. 8, No. 5 (March 14, 1989), pp. 259-86.

Smith, Scott M.
  "Six Business Graphics Software Packages for Marketing Reports"
  Journal of Marketing Research, Vol. XXV (August 1988), pp. 326-8.

212.02 ---------- Programmable Graphing Software

Scientific Endeavors Corporation
  GraphiC, Version 4.1
  (Kingston, TN: Scientific Endeavors Corp.).

212.03 ---------- Two-Dimensional Graphing Software

Ashton-Tate
  Chartmaster, Version 6.2
  (Westport, CT: Ashton-Tate).

Binary Engineering Software
  Tech-Graph-Pad
  (Waltham, MA: Binary Engineering).

BV Engineering
  PCPlot, Version 3.25
  (Riverside, CA: BV Engineering).

BV Engineering
  PDP, Version 2
  (Riverside, CA: BV Engineering).

CompuVision International
  Giraph
  (New York: CompuVision International).

Golden Software, Incorporated
  Grapher
  (Golden, CO: Golden Software Inc.).

Jandel Scientific
  Signa-Plot, Version 3.1
  (Corte Madera, CA: Jandel Scientific).

Lotus Development Corporation
  Freelance Plus
  (Cambridge, MA: Lotus Development Corp.).

Market Action Research Software, Incorporated
  Mapwise Graphic Software, Version 1.0
  (Peoria, IL: Market Action Research Software, Inc., 1988).

Micrografx
  Graph Plus
  (Richardson, TX: Micrografx).

Microsoft Corporation
  Microsoft Chart, Version 3.0
  (Redmond, WA: Microsoft Corp.).

New England Software
  Graph-in-the-Box, Version 2
  (Greenwich, CT: New England Software, Inc.).

Software Clearing House, Incorporated
  GraphStation, Version 3.3
  (Cincinnati, OH: Software Clearing House, Inc.).

Software Publishing Corporation
  Harvard Graphics, Version 2.0
  (Mountain View, CA: Software Publishing Corp.).

212.04 ---------- Three-Dimensional Graphing Software

Boeing Computer Services
  Boeing Graph
  (Seattle, WA: Boeing Computer Services, Software and Education
  Products Group).

Bridge Software
  Datasurf, Version 2.0
  (Boston, MA: Bridge Software).

Design Professionals Management Systems (dpms)
    SDS, Version 2.12
    (Kirkland, WA: Design Professionals Management Systems).

Golden Software, Incorporated
    Surfer
    (Golden, CO: Golden Software, Inc.).

Three D Graphics
    Perspective Junior, Version 1.0
    (Pacific Palisades, CA: Three D Graphics).

3-D Visions
    Graftool, Version 1.1
    (Manhattan Beach, CA: 3-D Visions).

213 ------------ STATISTICAL SOFTWARE - MAINFRAME COMPUTER -----------
  . See also (sub)heading(s) 131.

213.01 ---------- General Statistical Packages - Mainframe Computer

Barr, Anthony J. et al.
  SAS User's Guide, 1979 Edition
  (Raleigh, NC: Sas Institute Inc., 1979).

Berkman, Jerry, Brownstone, David, Duncan, Gregory M., and McFadden,
  Daniel
  QUAIL 3.0 User's Manual
  (Berkeley, CA: Department of Economics, University of California,
  September 1977).

Clyde, Dean J., Cramer, Elliot M., and Sherin, Richard J.
  Multivariate Statistical Programs
  (Coral Gables, FL: University of Miami, 1966).

Coleman, Denis R.
  "Nonparametric Statistical Package"
  Graduate School of Business, Stanford University (1972), technical
  report.

Dixon, Wilfrid J.
  BMDP Statistical Software 1983
  (Berkeley, CA: University of California Press, 1983).

Finn, Jeremy
  MULTIVARIANCE VII User's Guide
  (Chicago: National Educational Resources, 1980).

Helwig, J. T.
  SAS User's Guide, 1979 Edition
  (Cary, NC: SAS Institute, 1979).

International Mathematical Statistical Library
  IMSL Manual
  (Houston, TX: International Mathematical Statistical Library, 1977).

Norusis, Marija J.
  The SPSS Guide to Data Analysis
  (Chicago, IL: SPSS Inc., 1986), 402 pp.

Reynolds, Thomas J., Lepman, Robert T., and Andrews, Robert L.
  "TOMS: A Series of APL/CRMS Programs to Facilitate the Teaching of
  Multivariate Methods and Scaling"
  Journal of Marketing Research, Vol. XIV (November 1977), pp. 559-61.

SAS Institute Inc.
  SAS Users' Guide: Statistics, Version 5 Edition
  (Cary, NC: SAS Institute, Inc., 1985).

SAS Institute Inc.
  SAS/IML User's Guide, Version 5 Edition
  (Cary, NC: SAS Institute, Inc., 1985).

SPSS Incorporated
  SPSS-X User's Guide, Second Edition
  (New York: McGraw-Hill Book Company, 1986), 988 pp.

214 ------------------------- META-ANALYSIS -----------------------
        See also (sub)heading(s) 141.12.

214.01 ---------- Books Re: Meta-Analysis

Cooper, Harris M.
    Integrating Research, Second Edition
    (Newbury Park, CA: Sage Publications, 1989), 168 pp.

Farley, John U. and Lehmann, Donald R.
    Meta-Analysis in Marketing: Generalization of Response Models
    (Lexington, MA: Lexington Books, 1986), 121 pp.

Glass, Gene V., McGaw, Barry, and Smith, Mary Lee
    Meta-Analysis in Social Research
    (Beverly Hills, CA: Sage Publications, 1981).

Hedges, Larry V. and Olkin, Ingram
    Statistical Methods for Meta-Analysis
    (Orlando, FL: Academic Press, Inc., 1985).

Hunter, John E. and Schmidt, Frank L.
    Methods of Meta-Analysis
    (Newbury Park, CA: Sage Publications, 1989), 460 pp.

Hunter, John E., Schmidt, Frank L., and Jackson, Gregg B.
    Meta-Analysis: Cumulating Research Findings Across Studies
    (Beverly Hills, CA: Sage Publications, 1982).

Rosenthal, Robert
    Meta-Analytic Procedures for Social Research
    (Newbury Park, CA: Sage Publications, 1984), 160 pp.

Wolf, Fredric M.
    Meta-Analysis: Quantitative Methods for Research Synthesis
    (Beverly Hills, CA: Sage Publications, Inc., 1986), 65 pp.

214.02 ---------- Theory Re: Meta-Analysis

Cooper, Harris M.
    "Scientific Guidelines for Conducting Integrative Research Reviews"
    Review of Educational Research, Vol. 52 (Summer 1982), pp. 291-302.

Cooper, Harris M. and Rosenthal, Robert
    "Statistical Versus Traditional Procedures for Summarizing Research
    Findings"
    Psychological Bulletin, Vol. 87 (May 1980), pp. 442-9.

Farley, John U., Lehmann, Donald R., and Ryan, Michael J.
    "Generalizing From 'Imperfect' Replication"
    Journal of Business, Vol. 54, No. 4 (1981), pp. 597-610.

Glass, Gene V.
    "Primary, Secondary, and Meta-Analysis of Research"
    Educational Researchers, Vol. 5 (1976), pp. 3-8.

Houston, Michael J., Peter, J. Paul, and Sawyer, Alan G.
    "The Role of Mea-Analysis in Consumer Behavior Research"
    in Bagozzi, R. P. and Tybout, A. M. (editors)
    Advances in Consumer Research, Volume Ten
    (Ann Arbor, MI: Association for Consumer Research, 1983), pp. 497-502.

Monroe, Kent B. and Krishnan, R.
    "A Procedure for Integrating Outcomes Across Studies"
    in Bagozzi, R. P. and Tybout, A. M. (editors)
    Advances in Consumer Research, Volume Ten
    (Ann Arbor, MI: Association for Consumer Research, 1983), pp. 503-8.

Reilly, Michael D. and Conover, Jerry N.
    "Meta-Analysis: Integrating Results From Consumer Research Studies"
    in Bagozzi, R. P. and Tybout, A. M. (editors)
    Advances in Consumer Research, Volume Ten
    (Ann Arbor, MI: Association for Consumer Research, 1983).

Rosenthal, Robert
    "Combining Results of Independent Studies"
    Psychological Bulletin, Vol. 85 (December 1978), pp. 185-93.

Ryan, Michael J. and Barclay, Donald W.
    "Integrating Results From Independent Studies"
    in Bagozzi, R. P. and Tybout, A. M. (editors)
    Advances in Consumer Research, Volume Ten
    (Ann Arbor, MI: Association for Consumer Research, 1983), pp. 492-6.

Schmidt, F. L. and Hunter, J. E.
    "Development of a General Solution to the Problem of Validity
    Generalization"
    Journal of Applied Psychology, Vol. 62 (1977), pp. 529-40.

Smith, Mary Lee
"Publication Bias and Meta-Analysis"
Evaluation in Education, Vol. 4 (1980), pp. 22-4.

Smith, Mary Lee and Glass, Gene V.
"Meta-Analysis of Psychotherapy Outcome Studies"
American Psychologist, Vol. 32 (September 1977), pp. 752-60.

214.03 ---------- Applications of Meta-Analysis

Armstrong, J. Scott and Lusk, Edward J.
"Return Postage in Mail Surveys: A Meta-Analysis"
Public Opinion Quarterly, Vol. 51 (Summer 1987), pp. 233-48.

Assmus, Gert, Farley, John U., and Lehmann, Donald R.
"How Advertising Affects Sales: Meta-Analysis of Econometric Results"
Journal of Marketing Research, Vol. XXI (February 1984), pp. 65-74.

Assmus, Gert, Farley, John U., and Lehmann, Donald R.
"How Advertising Impacts Sales: A Meta-Analysis"
Amos Tuck School of Business Administration, Dartmouth College
(1983), working paper.

Beaman, Arthur L., Cole, C. Maureen, Preston, Marilyn, Klentz, Bonnel,
and Steblay, Nancy M.
"Fifteen Years of Foot-in-the-Door Research: A Meta Analysis"
Personality and Social Psychology Bulletin, Vol. 9 (June 1983), pp.
181-96.

Churchill, Gilbert A., Jr., Ford, Neil M., Hartley, Steven W., and
Walker, Orville C., Jr.
"The Determinants of Salesperson Performance: A Meta-Analysis"
Journal of Marketing Research, Vol. XXII (May 1985), pp. 103-18.

Churchill, Gilbert A., Jr. and Peter, J. Paul
"Research Design Effects on the Reliability of Rating Scales: A
Meta-Analysis"
Journal of Marketing Research, Vol. XXI (November 1984), pp. 360-75.

Clarke, Darral G.
"A Reply to Weinberg and Weiss"
Journal of Marketing Research, Vol. XIX (November 1982), pp. 592-4.

Clarke, Darral G.
"Econometric Measurement of the Duration of Advertising Effect on
Sales"
Journal of Marketing Research, Vol. XIII (November 1976), pp. 345-57.

Cooper, Harris M.
"Statistically Combining Independent Studies: A Meta-Analysis of Sex
Differences in Conformity Research"
Journal of Personality and Social Psychology, Vol. 37 (1979), pp.
131-46.

Cooper, Harris M. and Rosenthal, Robert
"Statistical Versus Traditional Procedures for Summarizing Research
Findings"
Psychological Bulletin, Vol. 87 (May 1980), pp. 442-9.

Cronbach, Lee J. and Snow, R. E.
Aptitudes and Instructional Methods: A Handbook for Research on
Interactions
(New York: Irvington, 1977).

Dillard, James P., Hunter, John E., and Burgoon, Michael
"A Meta-Analysis of Two Sequential-Request Strategies for Gaining
Compliance: Foot-in-the-Door and Door-in-the-Face"
Annual Convention of the International Communication Association,
Dallas, TX (May 1983), paper presentation.

Farley, John U., Howard, John A., and Lehmann, Donald R.
"A Working Version of Car Buyer-Behavior Models"
Management Science, Vol. 23 (November 1976), pp. 235-47.

Farley, John U., Lehmann, Donald R., and Ryan, Michael J.
"Patterns in Parameters of Buyer Behavior Models: Generalizing From
Sparse Replication"
Marketing Science, Vol. 1, No. 2 (1982), pp. 181-204.

Farley, John U., Lehmann, Donald R., and Ryan, Michael J.
"Generalizing From Imperfect Replication"
Journal of Business, Vol. 54 (October 1981), pp. 597-610.

Fern, Edward F., Monroe, Kent B., and Avila, Ramon A.
"Effectiveness of Multiple Request Strategies: A Synthesis of
Research Results"
Journal of Marketing Research, Vol. XXIII (May 1986), pp. 144-52.

Fisher, C. D. and Gitelson, R.
  "A Meta Analysis of the Correlates of Role Conflict and Ambiguity"
  Journal of Applied Psychology, Vol. 68, No. 2 (1983), pp. 320-33.

Fox, Richard J., Crask, Melvin R., and Kim, Jonghoon
  "Mail Survey Response Rate: A Meta-Analysis of Selected Techniques
  for Inducing Response"
  Public Opinion Quarterly, Vol. 52 (Winter 1988), pp. 467-91.

Gemunden, Hans Georg
  "Perceived Risk and Information Search: A Systematic Meta-Analysis of
  the Empirical Evidence"
  International Journal of Research in Marketing, Vol. 2, No. 2 (1985),
  pp. 79-100.

Hite, Robert E. and Fraser, Cynthia
  "Meta-Analyses of Attitudes Toward Advertising by Professionals"
  Journal of Marketing, Vol. 52 (July 1988), pp. 95-105.

Hyde, Janet Shibley
  "How Large are Cognitive Gender Differences?: A Meta-Analysis Using
  Omega-Squared and d"
  American Psychologist, Vol. 36 (August 1981), pp. 892-901.

Iaffaldano, Michelle T. and Muchinsky, Paul M.
  "Job Satisfaction and Job Performance: A Meta-Analysis"
  Psychological Bulletin, Vol. 97 (March 1985), pp. 251-73.

Johnson, David W., Johnson, Roger T., and Maruyama, Geoffrey
  "Interdependence and Interpersonal Attraction Among Heterogeneous and
  Homogeneous Individuals: A Theoretical Foundation and a Meta-Analysis
  of the Research"
  Review of Educational Research, Vol. 53 (Spring 1983), pp. 5-54.

Monroe, Kent B. and Krishnan, R.
  "The Effects of Price on Subjective Product Evaluations: A Synthesis
  of Outcomes"
  in Bagozzi, R. P. and Tybout, A. M. (editors)
  Advances in Consumer Research, Volume Ten
  (Ann Arbor, MI: Association for Consumer Research, 1983).

Peter, J. Paul and Churchill, Gilbert A., Jr.
  "Relationships Among Research Design Choices and Psychometric
  Properties of Rating Scales: A Meta-Analysis"
  Journal of Marketing Research, Vol. XXIII (February 1986), pp. 1-10.

Peterson, Robert A., Albaum, Gerald, and Beltramini, Richard F.
  "A Meta-Analysis of Effect Sizes in Consumer Behavior Experiments"
  Journal of Consumer Research, Vol. 12 (June 1985), pp. 97-103.

Rao, Akshay R. and Monroe, Kent B.
  "The Effect of Price, Brand Name, and Store Name on Buyers'
  Perceptions of Product Quality: An Integrative Review"
  Journal of Marketing Research, Vol. XXVI (August 1989), pp. 351-7.

Rousseau, E. W. and Redfield, D. L.
  "Teacher Questioning"
  Evaluation in Education, An International Review Series, Vol. 4
  (1980), pp. 51,2.

Schwab, Donald P., Olian-Gottlieb, Judy D., and Heneman, Herbert G., III
  "Between-Subjects Expectancy Theory Research: A Statistical Review of
  Studies Predicting Effort and Performance"
  Psychological Bulletin, Vol. 86 (January 1979), pp. 139-47.

Sheppard, Blair H., Hartwick, Jon, and Warshaw, Paul R.
  "The Theory of Reasoned Action: A Meta-Analysis of Past Research With
  Recommendations for Modifications and Future Research"
  Journal of Consumer Research, Vol. 15 (December 1988), pp. 325-43.

Smith, Laurie P. and Koenig, Harold F.
  "Meta-Analysis on the Relationship Between Satisfaction and Manifest
  Conflict in Marketing Channels"
  in Lusch, Robert F. et al. (editors)
  1985 AMA Educators' Conference Proceedings
  (Chicago: American Marketing Association, 1985), pp. 341-7.

Stanley, Julian C. and Benbow, Camilla P.
  "Huge Sex Ratios at the Upper End"
  American Psychologist, Vol. 37 (August 1982), p. 972.

Sudman, Seymour and Bradburn, Norman M.
  Response Effects in Surveys: A Review and Synthesis
  (Chicago: Aldine, 1974).

Szymanski, David M. and Busch, Paul S.
  "Identifying the Generics-Prone Consumer: A Meta-Analysis"
  Journal of Marketing Research, Vol. XXIV (November 1987), pp. 425-31.

Tellis, Gerard J.
  "The Price Elasticity of Selective Demand: A Meta-Analysis of
  Econometric Models of Sales"
  Journal of Marketing Research, Vol. XXV (November 1988), pp. 331-4.

Tellis, Gerard J.
  "The Price Sensitivity of Competitive Demand: A Meta-Analysis of
  Sales Response Models"
  Marketing Science Institute (1988), working paper.

Weinberg, Charles B. and Weiss, Doyle L.
  "On the Econometric Measurement of the Duration of Advertising
  Effects on Sales"
  Journal of Marketing Research, Vol. XIX (November 1982), pp. 585-91.

Yu, Julie and Cooper, Harris M.
  "A Quantitative Review of Research Design Effects in Response Rates
  to Questionnaires"
  Journal of Marketing Research, Vol. XX (February 1983), pp. 319-21.

214.04 ---------- Computer Programs for Meta-Analysis

Mullen, Brian and Rosenthal, Robert
  BASIC Meta-Analysis: Procedures and Programs
  (Hillsdale, NJ: Lawrence Erlbaum Associates Inc.), 140 pp.

```
***********
*         *
*  Author *
*         *
*  Index  *
*         *
***********
```

A

Aaker, David A.   82, 82, 109, 437, 443, 454, 454, 554, 554,
    785, 798, 800, 828, 828, 837, 848, 848, 862
Abacus Concepts   867, 867
Abacus Scientific Software   868, 871, 871
Abbott, D.   367

Abbott, Pamela   255
Abdul-Ela, Abdel-Latif A.   195, 196
Abeele, Piet Vanden   99, 661, 833
Abeles, N.   479

Abelson, H. H.   25
Abelson, Robert P.   272, 272, 464, 464, 464, 469, 587
Abernathy, James R.   195, 195, 195, 195, 196, 197
Aborampah, Osei-Mensah   710

Abougomaah, Naeim H.   828
Abraham, Bovas   557
Abraham, Magid M.   46, 163
Abrahams, Norman M.   592, 592

Abrahamsen, Egil   25
Abrahamson, P.   56
Abrams, Dorothy   214
Abrams, Jack   264, 264, 426, 548

Abrams, Mark   16, 20, 166
Abramson, Paul R.   354, 354, 506
Abromson, Edward   306
Abruzzini, Pompeo   99

Absatzwirtchaft   36
Abt, Lawrence E.   381
Achabal, Dale D.   164, 166
Achen, Christopher H.   645

Achenbaum, Alvin A.   1, 125, 148
Achondo, F. J.   694
Achrol, Ravi S.   487, 496, 848
Acito, Franklin   32, 140, 384, 425, 428, 466, 467, 467, 468,
    544, 616, 703, 744, 753, 756, 757, 762, 762, 762, 763,
    778, 781, 808, 817, 819, 822, 822, 846, 864

Acito, Paul L.   167
Acker, Mary   264
Ackerman, Lee J.   257
Ackerman, Leonard   410

Ackoff, Russell L.   24, 36, 69, 69, 87, 87, 726
Acredolo, Curt   723
Adair, J.   53
Adams, Anthony J.   24

Adams, Arthur   126
Adams, Arthur J.   495, 495, 695, 720
Adams, David R.   611
Adams, E. W.   564

Adams, F. Gerard   256
Adams, J. S.   333, 350
Adams, James R.   132
Adams, William C.   388

Adcock, C. J.   808
Addelman, Sidney   412, 728, 737, 737, 737, 737, 757
Adelson, Marvin   410
Adler, Eric   94

Adler, Franz   75, 190
Adler, Kenneth P.   180, 180
Adler, Lee   17, 17, 17, 25, 25, 36, 99, 107, 151, 151, 167,
    342
Adler, Max K.   11

Adler, Patricia A.   366

K

```
*************
*           *
*  Subject  *
*           *
*  Index    *
*           *
*************
```

A

B

About the Author

John R. Dickinson received his Bachelor's, Master's, and Doctor of Business Administration degrees all at Indiana University. He has taught at Indiana and at McMaster University as well as at the University of Windsor. He is coauthor of the *Guide to International Investing* (CCH Canadian Ltd.) and *Laptop* (Business Publications, Inc.), a marketing simulation game. Other publications include over thirty articles and papers primarily investigating properties of marketing research methods.

Dr. Dickinson is president of R.O.I. Maximization, Inc., and has served as a consultant to international financial institutions, retailers, and manufacturers. He is a frequent speaker at professional seminars, conferences, and executive development programs.